M000304812

The Indo-European

Cognate Dictionary

Edited by Fiona McPherson, PhD

Wayz Press

Published 2018 by Wayz Press, Wellington, New Zealand.

Copyright © 2018 by Fiona McPherson.

All rights reserved.
No part of this publication may be reproduced, stored in a retrieval system, or transmitted in any form or by any means, electronic, mechanical, recording or otherwise, without the prior written permission of Wayz Press, a subsidiary of Capital Research Limited.

ISBN 978-1-927166-60-4

To report errors, please email errata@wayz.co.nz
For additional resources and up-to-date information about any errors, go to the Mempowered website at www.mempowered.com

Contents

German	349
Norse	358
Norwegian	364
Swedish	369
Danish	376
Icelandic	381
Welsh	387
Irish	390
Latin	394
French	413
Italian	429
Spanish	445
Portuguese	462
Romanian	477
Ancient Greek	487
Greek	496
Russian	500
Polish	506
Czech	511
Slovak	515
Macedonian	518
Lithuanian	521
Latvian	524
Albanian	527
Sanskrit	530
Hindi	535
Pashto	537
Persian	538

About this dictionary

The primary purpose of this dictionary is to help people make connections between words, and thus remember them.

Vocabulary is a sticking point for many language learners. That's because words have a certain arbitrary quality that makes them hard to memorize. There are two strategies which are very effective with this task: the keyword mnemonic, and retrieval practice. I have written about these extensively in my books *Mnemonics for Study*, and *How to learn: The 10 principles of effective revision & practice*. But you need thousands of words to have any degree of fluency, and you'll be much quicker to reach that level if you don't have to apply these strategies to all words. Which is where we come to the relative ease of learning different languages. One of the main factors determining the ease or difficulty of mastering another language is the degree to which it shares vocabulary with the language(s) you know.

By 'share', I don't mean that they necessarily have the exact same words. Rather, it has to do with cognates — words that share the same linguistic root. Some of these are glaringly obvious: Spanish importante / English important; French authentique / English authentic; German Apfel / English apple; Dutch mixen / English mix; Iceland eyland / English island. But many, many others are not so obvious.

The aim of this dictionary is to collect many of these cognates, so that we can see what words are cognate, and (because it would be a huge job — and a mammoth dictionary — to gather all cognates in all Indo-European languages), to help you learn how to recognize cognates.

You may wonder how much this will help you remember the words, if the relationship between the words is not transparently obvious. But trust me, recognizing the relationship, 'seeing' it every time you come across the word, will help you immeasurably. And because there are rules (consistent patterns rather than laws) in the way words have changed over time, accumulating these examples will help you recognize such changes when they exist in words not covered here.

But you don't have to be a language learner to enjoy this dictionary. As someone with an interest in words, I found sufficient to marvel about as I collated all this information to get me through the very many hours of tedious grunt-work required. If you find it interesting to know that infant, infantry, professor, and profane are all related through a five to six thousand year old word meaning to speak, you'll enjoy this dictionary.

Introduction

This introduction explains how the dictionary is organised, what languages are covered, and any abbreviations that are used. It also describes some of the linguistic patterns to look out for.

What languages are covered in this dictionary?

The Indo-European language 'tree' has nine living branches, and this dictionary records words from 32 languages, covering eight of these branches (the ninth branch is Armenian, consisting solely of the Armenian language; its paucity in my sources led me to exclude this). Four of these languages are technically not 'living', but because of their importance in the development of living languages, as well as (in the case of three of them) their continued use in the reading of ancient texts, they have been included. These are: Latin, Ancient Greek, Sanskrit, and Norse.

Because the dictionary is in English, and is aimed especially at English native speakers (although others will find it useful too — indeed, those learning English may find it the most useful), Germanic and Romance languages are covered far more completely than other fruitful branches. English comes from the Germanic branch, but because of the Norman invasion and the centuries under Norman French rule, has been greatly influenced by French and Latin. So in the case of the Germanic and Italic branches, descending words have been covered in much more depth.

The Celtic, Slavic, Baltic, Albanian, and Indo-Iranian languages are covered much more sparsely, the main intention being to display the breadth of the cluster, as well, of course, as providing a basis and a springboard for those wanting to learn any of those languages.

The Hellenic branch is a special case. Because Ancient Greek greatly influenced Latin, and influenced English both directly and indirectly (many of our scientific and technical terms come directly from Greek), that language is covered in more depth; however, its daughter language modern Greek is only covered lightly.

The Indo-Iranian branch is the most poorly covered, more because its languages are written in scripts I don't know, than because of any lack of words. Perhaps in a later edition I'll be able to do better.

Here is a list of the living branches of the Indo-European language tree, with the selected languages given in bold print:

Celtic: Breton, **Welsh, Irish**, Scottish Gaelic (in order of number of speakers)

Germanic:

> West Germanic: **English, Old English, Frisian, Dutch, German**

> North Germanic: **Swedish, Danish, Norwegian, Icelandic, Norse** (in order of number of speakers)

Italic: **Latin** and its descendants: **French, Italian, Spanish, Portuguese, Romanian**

Greek (Ancient, Modern)

Albanian

Balto-Slavic:

> Baltic: **Lithuanian, Latvian**

> Slavic:

>> Western: **Polish, Czech, Slovak**, Sorbian / Lusatian

>> Southern: Serbo-Croatian, **Macedonian**, Slovene, Bulgarian

>> Eastern: **Russian**, Ukrainian, Byelorussian

Armenian

Indo-Iranian:

> Iranian: **Persian**, Tajik, **Pashto**, Baluchi, Kurdish, Ossete

> Indic / Indo-Aryan: **Sanskrit, Hindi**, Punjabi, Gujarati, Marathi, Bengali, Nepali, Sinhala, Urdu, Romani

The Proto-Indo-European language

The Proto-Indo-European language (PIE) is the ultimate ancestor of all these languages, but it was spoken thousands of years in the past and we have no direct record of it. What we do have is the clear evidence in these languages, from the consistent patterns in the way their words vary, that there was such an ancestor. Following these patterns, scholars have deduced a quite extensive vocabulary — but they are still reconstructed, not 'real' words. We can never know exactly how these words were pronounced, or precisely how they were used. Conventionally, therefore, such words are written with a preceding asterisk.

Moreover, because of this uncertainty in pronunciation, the precise way in these words are written does vary. I have followed that used in my main source, which is Wiktionary. So, for those few who have some knowledge of the language, your rendering may differ slightly from that given here; for the rest of us, I imagine, the way in which these PIE words are written will look strange and rather unintelligible. If you have an interest in learning this reconstructed language, I direct you to other sources to find out how these are pronounced. For the rest of us, the words are simply tags, a way of organising the material.

Having said that, it is rather exciting to see the occasional PIE word that has been retained almost unchanged to the present day! Daughter (*d^{h}ugh$_2$tér) is an excellent example of this.

Linguistic laws

Without going into too much technical detail, it will help you spot patterns if you have some awareness of the patterns that are known to exist. This has become complicated over the years as linguists explain variations, but the initial discovery was very simple and easy to describe. So, bearing in mind that these 'rules' don't apply all the time, and there are a number of principles that describe variations to these rules, and other patterns, here are the main linguistic patterns relating to Germanic languages. These were first realised by Jacob Grimm (yes, one of the Grimm brothers, of fairy tale fame) in 1822. Grimm spotted that a p at the beginning of a word in Sanskrit, Latin, or Greek, consistently becomes f in Germanic languages. He went on to observe nine such patterns, which collectively are known as Grimm's law:

p → f

d → t

k → h

t → th

b → p

g → k

bh → b

dh → d

gh → g

Here are examples of these in action:

Latin pater is English father (p → f; t → th)

French pied is English foot (p → f; d → t)

Latin caput is Old English hafud (k → h; p → f), meaning head

Latin tres is English three (t → th)

Lithuanian dubus (from PIE *dʰewb-) is English deep (b → p)

Latin genus (race) and English kin are cognate (g → k), as is Latin ager (field) and English acre

PIE *bʰeh₂go- becomes beech in English, but that same bh sound becomes f in Latin and Greek, hence fāgus and φηγός (phēgós)

similarly, PIE *bʰréh₂tēr is brother in English, but frater in Latin and φράτηρ (phrátēr) in Greek

PIE *dʰugh₂tēr becomes daughter; PIE *dʰwer- becomes door

PIE *ǵʰer- becomes garden and garth in English, but hortus and χόρτος (khórtos) in Latin and Greek

So these are the sort of patterns you should be looking out for if you want to use this dictionary as an aid to language learning.

It's also worth noting that there's a fundamental distinction between the 'Western' and 'Eastern' branches of the Indo-European tree, that's expressed as the kentum-satem divide. This reflects the fact that most of the Western languages have a word for hundred that begins with a hard k sound, like Latin centum (in the Germanic languages, as Grimm's law describes, this k becomes h, hence our hundred). In the Eastern languages, the word for hundred begins with a soft s sound, as in the Sanskrit word satem. This distinction between a hard k and a soft s sound is thought to reflect a very early split in the Proto-Indo-European tribes, as some headed west and others east. Note how that Western-Eastern divide plays out in the branches:

Western (kentum): Celtic, Germanic, Italic, Greek, Anatolian

Eastern (satem): Balto-Slavic, Armenian, Albanian, Indo-Iranian

Bearing in mind this fundamental difference, and which branches belong to which group, will also help you spot patterns. But don't fret, if you're starting to feel intimidated! You don't need to get bogged down in the linguistic laws — the human mind is wonderfully designed for spotting patterns; it does it without any help from us. And we act all the time on patterns we subconsciously perceive, without being able to articulate them or even being aware of them. If you study the clusters with this sort of awareness, you will build up an understanding of how sounds/letters shift in different languages.

One final word about the relationships between other Indo-European language branches: I have spoken of the well-known influence of Latin, French, and Greek on English, but it is also worth noting, for those who have no knowledge of these languages, that Romanian has borrowed extensively from the Slavic languages, while Modern Greek has been influenced by Turkish and Italian. Albanian has borrowed extensively from Slavic, Greek, Latin, Italian, and Turkish. The Slavic languages are all largely mutually intelligible.

How to use this dictionary

The dictionary consists of two parts. The first contains the pages for each
Proto-Indo-European (PIE) word, showing cognates in the chosen languages
plus various descendants and derivatives. These pages are arranged
thematically:

- People
    - Kinship
    - Pronouns
    - Body
    - Bodily functions
    - Cognitive function
    - Emotion
    - Social
- Movement
    - Object motion
- Construction & Production
    - Tools
    - Dwelling
    - Mineral products
- Farming
- Flora & Fauna
    - Plants
    - Trees
    - Mammals
    - Reptiles
    - Marine animals
    - Birds
    - Insects
    - Animal products
- Environment
    - Sky

- Weather
- Terrain
- Fire
- Time
- Numbers & Wholeness
- Directions
- Basic adjectives
  - Colours

That seemed to me the most useful arrangement for browsing or studying. But of course for searching, you need an alphabetic index of all words, and that is also provided. There is a separate index for each language. Each word is cross-referenced to its Proto-Indo-European ancestor. The PIE word index links each word to its appropriate page (digital editions), or shows the appropriate page number (print edition).

The indexes are vital if you're searching, because the PIE word clusters are not simply organised thematically. Because of the greater importance of having related words next to other, you will find entries that, from the thematic perspective, don't appear to belong there. So, for example, the word meaning to separate, to divide, is found under Kinship, because the PIE word for widow derives from that word (interestingly, some of the descendants mean orphan). Similarly, the PIE word meaning stiff, surprised, is found under Mammals, because the word derives from the PIE word for hedgehog. However, I have included a brief reference to these out-of-place words in their appropriate category, to assist browsers.

Occasional instances occur of the same descendant words appearing in more than one place. This can happen because the word has multiple meanings from different roots, or because the word is a compound from two sources, or has been influenced from two or more sources. Very rarely, it may be because there is argument about the source and I have accepted both.

Because this work is not intended as an academic resource describing exactly how different words came to be, but rather a readable and accessible reference, I have glossed over some issues. So, for example, I haven't distinguished between descent and borrowing — whether a language has borrowed a word from a sister language, or had it directly from its PIE ancestor appears immaterial to me, from the point of view of the person wanting to learn the word. For the same reason (trying to simplify what is a complex enough cluster), I haven't muddied the waters by distinguishing between, say, English words that derive more directly from their PIE ancestor, and those that come via Norse, or French, when the French word is itself from Norse, or German, or Dutch. You will find what I call "derivatives" in various places, most usually after the Italic and Hellenic groups, but sometimes after others. These indicate derived words that come from a different branch. Thus, an English word that derives from Latin will be listed under Derivatives under the Italic branch, but an English word that derives from, say, Norse, will simply be listed among other English words in the Germanic branch. That is because Norse is itself a German language. If, as I mentioned, an English word derives from, say, a French word that itself derives from a Germanic language, the English word will still be listed simply among other English words in its place in the Germanic branch. This is to keep things as clean as possible, and in most cases it is obvious enough if you look at the other words that such may well have been the case. But, while interesting, it is not particularly germane to the aim, which is to show you which words are, in general, connected to each other.

Suffixes & inflexions

The reason why words within a cognate cluster can vary so much from each other comes down to three main effects:

- the consistent way in which languages change over time, as evidenced by the linguistic laws already discussed

- the way in which PIE was inflected, that is, put endings on words to show how the word was being used (e.g., as the subject, or the object) — so, for example, ekwos, meaning horse, could be expressed as ekwos, ekwe, ekwom, ekwosyo, ekwoy, ekwod, or ekwo

- the way in which daughter languages such as Latin used small words in a regular way, as suffixes. So, for example, Latin dāre spawned: addere, additiō, datum, dēdāre, ēdāre, ēditiō, ēditor, mandāre (manus +), commendāre, dēmandāre, perdāre, perditiō, perditus, praedor, praedātiō, praedātor, reddāre, trādāre, trāditiō, trāditor, vēndāre, vēnditiō, vēndōr, and more. All these regular changes, at the front and end of the word, provide potentially fruitful new paths for words to evolve. (By the way, the (manus +) signifies another convention used in this dictionary — it points to the use of another source being used in combination. Thus mandāre comes from the combination of dāre and manus.)

Common Latin suffixes include:

ab-, meaning from, away from, by, with

ad-, meaning to, used to indicate motion (advance), change (adulterate), and addition (adjunct)

ante-, meaning before, in front of

bi-, meaning twice, double

circum-, meaning around (another thing)

co-, com-, cor-, meaning with, together

de, meaning from, down, or away from

di-, dif-, dis-, meaning apart, separate

ex-, meaning out of, away from

infra-, meaning below

inter-, meaning between, among

per-, meaning through

prae-, meaning before, in front of

re-, meaning again, back

sub, meaning beneath, under

super, supra, meaning in excess, above, superior

trans, meaning across, through

ultra, meaning beyond, excessive

Additionally, PIE words varied not only in inflexions, but also more meaningfully, in terms of related words spawned by the original word. Sometimes I have separated out these words, to stand on their own (but they'll be placed next to each other), but other times they will all appear in a single cluster. The variations and descendants are listed below the root word and its meaning, before the listing of the daughter languages' descendant words. They are there simply to help you understand why some words may seem at variance with the root.

Sources

As mentioned, my principal source for these words has been Wiktionary, which has an extensive section on PIE words and their descendants. I have also used Pokorny's classic work as a check, to help me with any ambiguities and confusions. Google Translate has been useful as a check and occasional source (with due care), as well as my own collection of language dictionaries. Other sources on the Web have helped (though not enough!) with those languages written in scripts unfamiliar to me. Wiktionary also has a section on Greek and Latin roots, and their English children, which was useful; for this, I also used the Oxford English Dictionary, which, to my great pleasure, is digitally available in its full version through my public library. The creation of this dictionary, limited as it may be, would never have been possible without all of these sources available from my keyboard.

Caveat

As should be evident from my words so far, this work is not intended to be a scholarly work! I have done my best to assure a certain amount of academic rigour, rejecting items which I can't verify (and which for one reason or another warrant investigation — I haven't checked every word!). However, my intent is to provide a useful and, I hope, an interesting resource, rather than an academic one. Certainly, even apart from its potential usefulness to language learners, I found sufficient interest in the connections revealed to keep me going through what was, indeed, a great deal of tedious work! I look forward to now having it as a resource for myself, and I hope others will find it equally useful and interesting.

Abbreviations used

The abbreviations used in the dictionary are of two types: those for the various languages, that you'll see constantly, and those occasionally marking words.

Language abbreviations:

Eng: English

OE: Old English

Fris: West Frisian

Dut: Dutch

Ger: German

Nor: Norwegian Bokmål

Swe: Swedish

Dan: Danish

Ice: Icelandic

Wel: Welsh

Iri: Irish

Lat: Latin

Fr: French

Ital: Italian

Sp: Spanish

Port: Portuguese

Rom: Romanian

AnGk: Ancient Greek

Gk: Modern Greek

Rus: Russian

Pol: Polish

Cz: Czech

Slo: Slovak

Mace: Macedonian

Sans: Sanskrit

Hin: Hindi

Pash: Pashto

Pers: Persian

Word tags:

arch.: archaic

dial.: dialect

lit.: literary

obs.: obsolete

poet.: poetic

poss.: possibly

prob.: probably

reg.: regional

uncert.: uncertain

The terms "possibly", "probably", and "uncertain", all indicate levels of uncertainty about the suggested etymology. While for the most part, I have omitted uncertain words, in some cases, where I think they form a useful part of the cluster, and/or I think the plausibility is sufficiently high, I have included them.

Similarly, I have tended to omit obsolete, regional, and literary terms, but sometimes, when I think it helpful or interesting, I have included them.

People

*h₁nómṇ

name

Germanic: name (**Eng**); nama (**OE**); namme (**Fris**); naam (**Dut**); Name (**Ger**); nafn (**Norse**); navn (**Nor**); namn (**Swe**); navn (**Dan**); nafn (**Ice**)

Celtic: enw (**Wel**), ainm (**Iri**)

Italic: nōmen, agnōmen, cōgnōmen, ignōminia, ignōminiōsus, nōmenclātor, nōmenclātūra, nōminālis, nōmināre, nōminātiō, nōminātīvus, nōminātor (**Lat**);

nom, cognomen, ignominie, ignominieux, nominal, nominer, nommer, nomination (**Fr**);

nome, cognome, ignominia, ignominioso, nomenclatura, nominale, nominare, nominazione (**Ital**);

nombre, agnombre, cognome, ignominia, nomenclatura, nominal, nombrar, nominar, nominación (**Sp**);

nome, agnome, cognome, ignominia, nomenclatura, nominal, nomear, nominar, nominação (**Port**);

nume, cognomen, nominal, numără, nomina, nominaţie (**Rom**)

Derivatives: agnomen, cognomen, ignominy, ignominious, nomenclator, nomenclature, nominal, nominate, nomination, nominative, nominator, noun (**Eng**); nominal (**Ger**); номинация (nominacija) (**Rus**)

Hellenic: ὄνομᾰ (ónoma), ὀνομᾰτοποιῐ́ᾱ (onomatopoiíā), ἀνώνῠμος (anṓnumos), ἐπώνυμος (epṓnumos), σῠνώνῠμος (sunṓnumos) (**AnGk**); όνομα (ónoma), ονοματοποιία (onomatopoiía), ανώνυμος (anónymos), επώνυμος (epónymos), συνώνυμος (synónymos), σῠνώνῠμον (sunṓnumon) (**Gk**)

Derivatives: onomatopoeia, anonymous, anonym, eponymous, eponym, synonymous, synonym (**Eng**); anoniem (**Dut**); anonym, Synonymum, Synonym (**Ger**); anonym (**Nor**); anonym (**Swe**); anonym (**Dan**);

onomatopoeia, anōnymus, synōnymum (**Lat**); onomatopée, anonyme (**Fr**); anonimo (**Ital**); anónimo, sinónimo (**Sp**); anónimo, anônimo, sinónimo (**Port**); anonym (**Rom**);

анони́мный (anonímnyj) (**Rus**); anonimowy (**Pol**); anonymni, anonym (**Cz**); анонимен (anonimen) (**Mace**)

Slavic: имя (imja) (**Rus**), imię, miano (**Pol**); jméno (**Cz**); meno (**Slo**); име (ime) (**Mace**)

Albanian: emër/êmën (**Alb**)

Indo-Iranian: नामन् (nắman), नाम (nắma) (**Sans**); नाम (nām) (**Hin**); نوم (nūm) (**Pash**); نام (nâm) (**Pers**)

13

*ǵʰmṓ

person

more precisely, earthling (someone who works the earth) — from *dʰéǵʰōm

Germanic: goom, groom, bridegroom, gomeral (**Eng**); guma (**OE**); bruidegom (**Dut**); Bräutigam (**Ger**); gumi (**Norse**); gume (**Nor**); brudgum (**Swe**); brudgom (**Dan**); gumi (**Ice**) (groom meaning male servant not derived from this; its etymology is uncertain)

Celtic: dyn (**Wel**); duine (**Iri**)

Italic: homo, hūmānus, inhūmānus, hūmānitās, homunculus (**Lat**); homme, on, humain, humanité (**Fr**); hombre, humano, inhumano (**Sp**); homem, humano (**Port**); uomo, umano (**Ital**); om, uman (**Rom**)

Derivatives: human, humane, inhuman, inhumane, homunculus (**Eng**); inhuman (**Ger**)

Baltic: žmogùs (**Lith**)

*gwḗn

woman

*gʷén-eH₂-

Germanic: quean, queen (**Eng**); cwene, cwēn (**OE**); kween (**Dut**); Queen, Quän (**Ger**); kona, kvenna, kvinna, kvæn, kván (**Norse**); kone, kona, kvinna (**Nor**); kåna, kona, kvinna (**Swe**); kone, kvinde (**Dan**); kona, kvenna, kvinna, kvon (**Ice**)

Celtic: benyw, menyw (**Wel**); bean (**Iri**)

Hellenic: γυνή (gunḗ) (**AnGk**); γυναίκα (gynaíka) (**Gk**)

Derivatives: gynecology, androgynous, heterogynous, misogynist (**Eng**)

Slavic: жена (žená) (**Rus**); żona (**Pol**); žena (**Cz**); žena (**Slo**); жени (ženi) (**Mace**)

Indo-Iranian: ग्ना (gnā), जनि (jani) (**Sans**); جنی (jinëy) / نجلی (njëlëy) (**Pash**); زن (zan), زنانه (zanâne) (**Pers**)

Derivatives: zenana (**Eng**)

*mánus

person

Germanic: man, manikin, mannequin, mannish, mensk, mense (**Eng**); mann, mennisc (**OE**); man, minske (**Fris**); man, men, manneken, mannequin, mens (**Dut**); Mann, man, Mensch (**Ger**); maðr, mennskr (**Norse**); mann, menneske (**Nor**); man, människa (**Swe**); mand, menneske (**Dan**); maður, manneskja, mennskur (**Ice**)

Derivatives: mannequin (**Fr**)

Slavic: муж (muž) (**Rus**); mąż (**Pol**); muž (**Cz**); muž (**Slo**); маж (maž) (**Mace**)

Indo-Iranian: मनु (manu), मनुष्य (manuṣya), मानव (mānava) (**Sans**); मानस (mānas), मनुष्य (manuṣya), मानव (mānav) (**Hin**)

*h₂nḗr
man, power, force

Celtic: nerth, nêr (**Wel**); neart (**Iri**)

Italic: neriōsus (**Lat**)

Hellenic: ἀνήρ (anḗr), δυσ-ἄνωρ (dus-ānōr), ἀνδρός (andrós), ἀνδρόγυνος (andrógunos), Ἀλέξανδρος (Aléxandros), Ἀνδρέας (Andréas) (**AnGk**); ἄνδρας (ándras), ανδρόγυνος (andrógynos) (**Gk**)

Derivatives: androcentric, androgen, androgynous, android, andrology, androphobia, androspore, diandry, misandry, philander, polyandry, protandry, synandrous, Alexander (**Eng**); androgyne (**Fr**)

Slavic: нрав (nrav), норов (norov) (**Rus**); narów (**Pol**); mrav (**Cz**); mrav (**Slo**); нарав (narav) (**Mace**)

Baltic: nóras (**Lith**)

Albanian: njeri (**Alb**)

Indo-Iranian: नृ (nṛ́), नर (nára) (**Sans**); नर (nar) (**Hin**); نر (nër), نارینه (nâriná) (**Pash**); نر (nar), نری (nari) (**Pers**)

*wiHrós
man

Germanic: wer, wergild, werewolf, world (**Eng**); wer, werwulf, weorold, worold (**OE**); wrâld (**Fris**); weergeld, weerwold, wereld (**Dut**); Werwolf, Welt (**Ger**); verr, verǫld (**Norse**); verd, verden, varulv (**Nor**); värld, varulv (**Swe**); verden, varulv (**Dan**); ver, veröld, varúlfur (**Ice**)

Derivatives: loup-garou (**Fr**); guidrigildo (**Ital**)

Celtic: gŵr (**Wel**); fear (**Iri**)

Italic: vir, virīlis, virāgo, virtūs, triumvir (**Lat**); viril, virago, vertu (**Fr**); virile, virtù (**Ital**); viril, virtud (**Sp**); viril, virilha, virtude (**Port**); viril, vârtute, virtute (**Rom**)

Derivatives: virile, virago, virtue, triumvirate (**Eng**); viriel (**Dut**); vërtyt, virtyt (**Alb**)

Baltic: výras (**Lith**); vīrs (**Latv**)

Indo-Iranian: वीर (vīrá) (**Sans**)

*pótis

master, ruler, husband

see Movement

Kinship

*méh₂tēr
mother

Germanic: mother (**Eng**); mōdor (**OE**); moer (**Fris**); moeder (**Dut**); Mutter (**Ger**); móðir (**Norse**); mor, moder (**Nor**); mor, moder (**Swe**); mor, moder (**Dan**); móðir (**Ice**)

Celtic: modryb (**Wel**); máthair (**Iri**)

Italic: māter, māternus, māternālis, māternitās, mātricīda, mātrimōnium, matrix, mātrīcālis, mātrīcula, mātrōna, materia (**Lat**);

mére, maternel, maternité, matricide, matrice, matricule, matrone, matière (**Fr**);

madre, materno, maternità, matrimonio, matrice, madrigale, matricola, matrona, materia (**Ital**);

madre, materno, maternal, matricida, motrimonio, matriz, matrícula, madrilla, matrona, madera, materia (**Sp**);

mãe, madre, materno, matricida, matrimónio, matriz, matrícula, matrona, madeira, matéria (**Port**);

metern, matrimoniu, mătrice, matrice, materie (**Rom**)

Derivatives: mater, maternal, maternity, matricide, matrimony, matron, matrix, matriculate, madrigal, matter, material (**Eng**); matrix, matrijs (**Dut**); Materie (**Ger**); мáтрица (mátrica), матрона (matrona), материя (materija) (**Rus**)

Hellenic: μήτηρ (métēr) (**AnGk**); μητέρα (mitéra) (**Gk**)

Derivatives: haplometrosis, metrocyte, metropolis, metropolitan, Metro, pleometrosis (**Eng**)

Slavic: мать (mat') (**Rus**); matka (**Pol**); matka (**Cz**); mat' (**Slo**); мajка (majka) (**Mace**)

Baltic: mótė, moteris (**Lith**); māte (**Latv**)

Albanian: ëmë, motër (**Alb**)

Indo-Iranian: मातृ (mātṛ) (**Sans**); मां (mā), माता (mātā), मातृ (mātṛ) (lit.), मातृभाषा (mātṛbhāṣā) (**Hin**); مور (mor) (**Pash**); مادر (mâdar) (**Pers**)

*méh₂-méh₂
mama

Hellenic: μάμμη (mámmē) (**AnGk**)

Derivatives: mamma, mammal, mammary (**Eng**); mamma, mammalis (**Lat**); maman (**Fr**); mamma (**Ital**); mama (**Sp**); mama, mamã (**Port**); mamă (**Rom**)

*ph₂tḗr
father

Germanic: father (**Eng**); fæder (**OE**); faar (**Fris**); vader, va (**Dut**); Vater (**Ger**); faðir (**Norse**); far, fader (**Nor**); far, fader (**Swe**); far, fader (**Dan**); faðir (**Ice**)

Celtic: athair (**Iri**)

Italic: pater, patrare, paternus, paternālis, paternitās, patraster, patricīda, pātricius, pātrimōnium, patrōnus, perpetrare (**Lat**);

pére, paternel, paternité, parâtre, patrice, patrimoine, patron (**Fr**); padre, patrimonio, padrone, patrono (**Ital**);

padre, paterno, paternidad, padrastro, patrimonio, patrón, padrón, patrono (**Sp**);

pai, padre, paterno, paternidade, padrasto, património, patrimônio, patrão, patrono (**Port**); pater, patron (**Rom**)

Derivatives: pater, paternity, paternal, patricide, patrician, patrimony, patron, patronize, patriarch, perpetrate (**Eng**); pater, patrimonium (**Dut**); Patrimonium (**Ger**); патриций (patricij) (**Rus**)

Hellenic: πατήρ (patḗr), πατριώτης (patriṓtēs) (**AnGk**); πατέρας (patéras), πατήρ (patír), πατριώτης (patriótis) (**Gk**)

Derivatives: allopatric, allopatry, eupatrides, patriarch, patriarchy, patriot, patriotism, patrology, patronym, sympatry (**Eng**); patriot (**Dut**); Patriot (**Ger**); patriōta (**Lat**); patriote (**Fr**); patriota (**Ital**); patriota (**Sp**); patriota (**Port**)

Slavic: татко (tatko) (**Mace**)

Baltic: patinas (**Lith**)

Albanian: atë (**Alb**)

Indo-Iranian: पितृ (pitṛ̃), पिता (pitā) (**Sans**); पिता (pitā), पितृ (pitṛ) (**Hin**); پلار (plār) (**Pash**); پدر (pedar) (**Pers**)

*átta
father

Germanic: dad (uncert.) (**Eng**); heit (**Fris**); ette (**Dut**); atti (**Norse**)

Celtic: oide (**Iri**)

Italic: atta (**Lat**)

Hellenic: ἄττα (átta) (**AnGk**)

Slavic: отéц (otéc) (**Rus**); ojciec (**Pol**); otec (**Cz**); otec (**Slo**); óтец (ótec) (**Mace**)

*bʰréh₂tēr
brother

Germanic: brother (**Eng**); brōþor (**OE**); broer (**Fris**); broer, broeder (**Dut**); Bruder (**Ger**); bróðir (**Norse**); bror, broder (**Nor**); bror, broder (**Swe**); bror, broder (**Dan**); bróðir (**Ice**)

Celtic: brawd (**Wel**); bráthair (**Iri**)

Italic: frāter, confrāter, frāternus, frāternālis, frāternitās (**Lat**); frére, fraternel, fraternité (**Fr**); fratello, frate, fraternità (**Ital**); fraile, fray, fraterno, fraternidad (**Sp**); frade, freire, frei, freira, fraternidade (**Port**); frate, fraternitate (**Rom**)

Derivatives: fraternal, fraternity, friar, confrere (**Eng**)

Hellenic: φράτηρ (phrátēr) (**AnGk**)

Slavic: брат (brat) (**Rus**); brat (**Pol**); bratr (**Cz**); brat (**Slo**); брат (brat) (**Mace**)

Baltic: brolis, broterėlis (**Lith**); brālis, brātarītis (**Latv**)

Albanian: vëlla (**Alb**)

Indo-Iranian: भ्रातृ (bhrātṛ), भ्राता (bhrātā) (**Sans**); भ्रातृ (bhrātṛ) (**Hin**); ورور (wrōr) (**Pash**); برادر (birādar) (**Pers**)

*swésōr
sister

Germanic: sister (**Eng**); sweostor (**OE**); sus (**Fris**); zuster, zus (**Dut**); Schwester (**Ger**); systir (**Norse**); syster (**Nor**); syster (**Swe**); søster (**Dan**); systir (**Ice**)

Celtic: chwaer (**Wel**); siur (**Iri**)

Italic: soror, sorōritās, sōbrīnus, consōbrīnus (**Lat**); sœur, sororité, cousin (**Fr**); sorella, suora, consobrino, cugino (**Ital**); sor, sobrino (**Sp**); soror, sobrinho, consobrinho (**Port**); soră (**Rom**)

Derivatives: sororal, sororate, sororicide, sorority, cousin (**Eng**); kusin (**Swe**)

Hellenic: ἔορ (éor) (**AnGk**)

Slavic: сестра (sestrá) (**Rus**); siostra (**Pol**); sestra (**Cz**); sestra (**Slo**); сестра (sestrá) (**Mace**)

Baltic: sesuõ (**Lith**)

Albanian: vajzë (**Alb**)

Indo-Iranian: स्वसृ (svasṛ) (**Sans**); خور (xowr) (**Pash**); خواهر (xâhar), خوهر (xvahar) (**Pers**)

*dʰugh₂tḗr
daughter

Germanic: daughter (**Eng**); dohtor (**OE**); dochter (**Fris**); dochter (**Dut**); Tochter (**Ger**); dóttir (**Norse**); datter, dotter (**Nor**); dotter (**Swe**); datter (**Dan**); dóttir (**Ice**)

Hellenic: θυγάτηρ (thugátēr) (**AnGk**); θυγατέρα (thygatéra) (**Gk**)

Slavic: дочь (doč'), дóчери (dóčeri), дóчка (dóčka), дочéрний (dočérnij) (**Rus**); córka (**Pol**); dcera, dcerka (**Cz**); dcéra, dcérka (**Slo**); ќерка (ḱerka) (**Mace**)

Baltic: duktē (**Lith**)

Indo-Iranian: दुहितृ (duhitṛ) (**Sans**); धिया (dhiyā) (**Hin**); لور (lur) (**Pash**); دخت (doxt), دختر (doxtar) (**Pers**)

*snusós
daughter-in-law

Germanic: snaar, snoer (**Dut**); Schnur (**Ger**); snør, snor (**Norse**); snör (**Ice**)

Italic: nurus (**Lat**); nuora (**Ital**); nuera (**Sp**); nora (**Port**); noră (**Rom**)

Hellenic: νυός (nuós) (**AnGk**)

Slavic: снохá (snoxá) (**Rus**); snecha (**Pol**); snacha (**Cz**); снаа (snaa) (**Mace**)

Indo-Iranian: स्नुषा (snuṣā) (**Sans**)

*suh₁nús
son

Germanic: son (**Eng**); sunu (**OE**); soan (**Fris**); zoon, -zoon, -sen (**Dut**); Sohn, -sen (**Ger**); sonr, sunr (**Norse**); sønn, son, -son (**Nor**); son, -son (**Swe**); søn, -sen (**Dan**); sonur, -son (**Ice**)

Hellenic: υἱύς (huiús), υἱός (huiós) (**AnGk**); υἱός (yiós) (**Gk**)

Slavic: сын (syn) (**Rus**); syn (**Pol**); syn (**Cz**); syn (**Slo**); син (sin) (**Mace**)

Baltic: sūnus (**Lith**)

Indo-Iranian: सूनु (sūnú) (**Sans**); زوی (zoy) (**Pash**)

*h₂éwh₂os

grandfather, mother's brother

Germanic: ēam (**OE**); iem, omke (**Fris**); oom (**Dut**); Ohm, Oheim (**Ger**)

Celtic: ewythr (**Wel**); ó, ua (**Iri**)

Italic: avus, avunculus, atavus (**Lat**); ave, aïeul, oncle, atavique (**Fr**); avo, avolo (**Ital**); abuelo (**Sp**); avô (**Port**); auș, unchi (**Rom**)

Derivatives: uncle, avuncular, atavistic, atavic (**Eng**); Onkel (**Ger**); onkel (**Dan**); onkel (**Swe**)

Slavic: уй (uj) (**Rus**); wuj (**Pol**); ujo (**Slo**); вујко (vujko) (**Mace**)

Baltic: avynas (**Lith**)

*nepot-

grandson, nephew

Germanic: neve, nift (**Eng**); nefa, nift (**OE**); nift (arch.), nicht, neef (**Fris**); neef, nicht (**Dut**); Neffe, Nift, Nifte, Niftel (arch.) (**Ger**); nipt, nefi, niðr (**Norse**); nevø (**Nor**); nevø (**Dan**); nift, niður (**Ice**)

Celtic: nai (**Wel**); nia (**Iri**)

Italic: nepōs, neptis (**Lat**); neveu, nièce (**Fr**); nipote (**Ital**); nieto, nieta (**Sp**); neta, neto (**Port**); nepot, nepoată (**Rom**)

Derivatives: nepotism, nephew, niece (**Eng**)

Hellenic: ἀνεψιός (anepsiós) (**AnGk**); ανιψιός (anipsiós) (**Gk**)

Slavic: нестера (nestera) (**Rus**); nieściora (**Pol**); внук (vnuk) (**Mace**)

Baltic: nepuotis (**Lith**)

Albanian: nip (**Alb**)

Indo-Iranian: नपात् (nápāt), नप्तृ (náptṛ) (**Sans**); نوه (nave) (**Pers**)

*h₁weydʰ

to separate

*h₁widʰéwh₂ (widow)

Germanic: widow (**Eng**); widuwe (**OE**); widdo (**Fris**); weduwe, wees (**Dut**); Witwe, Waise, verwaisen (**Ger**)

Celtic: gweddw (**Wel**); feadhbh (**Iri**)

Italic: vidua, viduitās, viduus, dīvidere, dīviduus, indīviduus, dīvīsibilis, dīvīsim, dīvīsiō, dīvīsor (**Lat**); veuve, veuf, diviser, divisible, division (**Fr**); vedova, viduità, dividere, divisibile, divisione (**Ital**); viuda, viudo, viudedad, dividir, divisibile, división (**Sp**); viúva, viúvo, divisível, divisão, divisor (**Port**); văduvă, văduv, divizibil (**Rom**)

Derivatives: viduity, divide, dividual, dividuous, individual, divisible, divisim, division, divisor (**Eng**); Division (**Ger**); division (**Swe**); divisor (**Dan**); дивизия (divizija), дивизион (divizion) (**Rus**)

Hellenic: ἤθεος (éítheos) (**AnGk**)

Slavic: вдова (vdová) (**Rus**); wdowa (**Pol**); vdova (**Cz**); vdova (**Slo**); вдовица (vdovica) (**Mace**)

Baltic: vidus (**Lith**); vidus (**Latv**)

Albanian: ve (**Alb**)

Indo-Iranian: विधवा (vidhavā) (**Sans**); विद्वा (vidvā), विधवा (vidhvā) (**Hin**); بیوه (bēva) (**Pers**)

Pronouns

*egH$_2$
I

Germanic: I (**Eng**); iç (**OE**); ik (**Fris**); ik (**Dut**); ich (**Ger**); ek, jak (**Norse**); jeg (**Nor**); jag (**Swe**); jeg (**Dan**); ek, eg, ég (**Ice**)

Italic: egō (**Lat**); ego, je (**Fr**); ego, io (**Ital**); ego, yo (**Sp**); ego, eu (**Port**); eu (**Rom**)

Derivatives: ego, egotistical, egocentric, egomaniac, egoism (**Eng**)

Hellenic: ἐγώ (egố) (**AnGk**); εγώ (egó) (**Gk**)

Slavic: я (ja) (**Rus**); ja (**Pol**); já (**Cz**); ja (**Slo**); jac (jas) (**Mace**)

Baltic: àš (**Lith**); es (**Latv**)

Albanian: unë (**Alb**)

Indo-Iranian: अहम् (ahám) (**Sans**)

*H$_1$me-
me

*H$_1$meǵhi, *(H$_1$)moi

Germanic: me (**Eng**); mē, mec (**OE**); my (**Fris**); me, mij (**Dut**); mir, mich (**Ger**); mér, mik (**Norse**); meg (**Nor**); mig (**Swe**); mig (**Dan**); mér, mig (**Ice**)

Celtic: mi (**Wel**); mí (**Iri**)

Italic: mē, mēcum, mihi (**Lat**); moi, me (**Fr**); me, meco, mi (**Ital**); me, mí, conmigo (**Sp**); mim, me, comigo (**Port**); mă, mie, pe mine (**Rom**)

Hellenic: μέ (mé), ἐμέ (emé) (**AnGk**)

Slavic: меня (menjá), мне (mne) (**Rus**); mnie, mi (**Pol**); mě, mi, mně (**Cz**); ma, mňa, mne (**Slo**); мене (tebe) (**Mace**)

Baltic: mi, manè, man (**Lith**); mani, man (**Latv**)

Albanian: mua (**Alb**)

Indo-Iranian: मा (mā) (**Sans**)

*H₁meme-
of me, mine, my

*H₁mene-, * H₁mo-yo-, * H₁me-yo-my

Germanic: my, mine (**Eng**); mīn (**OE**); myn (**Fris**); mijn (**Dut**); mein (**Ger**); minn (**Norse**); mine (**Nor**); mina (**Swe**); mine (**Dan**); minn (**Ice**)

Italic: meï, meus (**Lat**); mon, ma, mes, mien, mienne (**Fr**); mio, miei (**Ital**); mía, mi (**Sp**); meu, minha, meus, minhas (**Port**); mea, meu, mei, mele (**Rom**)

Hellenic: μου (mou), ἐμεῖο (emeîo) (**AnGk**); μου (mou) (**Gk**)

Slavic: мой (moj) (**Rus**); mój (**Pol**); můj, moje (**Cz**); môj, moja (**Slo**); моj (moj) (**Mace**)

Baltic: mano (**Lith**); mans (**Latv**)

Indo-Iranian: मम (mama) (**Sans**); मेरा (merā) (**Hin**)

*wei
we

*n̥s-mé, *nos us

Germanic: we, us (**Eng**); wē, ūs (**OE**); wy, ús (**Fris**); wij, we, uns (**Dut**); wir, uns (**Ger**); vér, vit (**Norse**); vi, oss (**Nor**); vi, oss (**Swe**); vi, os (**Dan**); vér, við, okkur (**Ice**)

Celtic: ni, ny (**Wel**)

Italic: nōs, noster, nōbīscum (**Lat**); nous, notre, nôtre, nos (**Fr**); noi, noialtri, nosco, nostro (**Ital**); nos, nosotros, neustro (**Sp**); nós, conosco, nosso (**Port**); noi, nouă, nostru, noastră, noștri, noastre (**Rom**)

Hellenic: νώ (nṓ), ἡμεῖς (hēmeîs) (**AnGk**)

Slavic: мы (my), нас (nas), нам (nam), нáми (námi) (**Rus**); my, nas (**Pol**); my, nás (**Cz**); my, nás (**Slo**)

Baltic: mès, mùms, mùs (**Lith**); mēs, mums, mūs (**Latv**)

Albanian: ne (**Alb**)

Indo-Iranian: वयम् (vayam) (**Sans**); हम (ham), हमाहमी (hamāhamī) (**Hin**)

*túh₂
you

*yū (plural)

Germanic: thou, ye, you (**Eng**); þū, ġē, ēow (**OE**); do, dû, jim, jimme (**Fris**); du (dial.), gij, jij, jijlui, jullie (**Dut**); du, ihr (**Ger**); þú, ér, þér (**Norse**); du, dere (**Nor**); du, ni, I (**Swe**); du, I (**Dan**); þú, þér (**Ice**)

Celtic: ti, chwi (**Wel**); tú (**Iri**)

Italic: tū, tēcum, vōs, vobiscum, voster, votre, vôtre, vos, tuus (**Lat**); tu, vous, ton, ta, tes (**Fr**); tu, teco, voi, voialtri, vostro, tuo (**Ital**); tú, contigo, vos, vosotros, os, vuestro, tuyo (**Sp**); tu, contigo, convosco, vós, vosso (**Port**); tu, voi, vouă, vostru, voastră, voștri, voastre, tău, ta, tăi, tale (**Rom**)

Hellenic: σύ (sú), σφώ (sphó), ὑμεῖς (humeîs), σός (sós), τεός (teós) (**AnGk**); εσύ (esý) (**Gk**)

Slavic: вы (vy) (**Rus**); ty (**Pol**); ty, vy (**Cz**); ty, vy (**Slo**); ти (ti) (**Mace**)

Baltic: tù, jūs (**Lith**); tu (**Latv**)

Albanian: ti (**Alb**)

Indo-Iranian: त्वम् (tvám), युवाम् (yuvām), यूयम् (yūyám) (**Sans**); तू (tū), तुम (tum) (**Hin**); تو (tə) (**Pash**); تو (tu) (**Pers**)

*s(w)e-

separate, apart, oneself

*selbʰ-, *sewos, *swed-yo-s, *swo-lo-, *swe-dʰh₁-, *swe-dʰh₁-sḱ-, *swe-bʰuH-, *swe-tewtéh₂-

Germanic: sere (meaning set apart, separate) (arch., dial.), so, such, self (**Eng**); swā, swelc, self', seolf (**OE**);

syn, sa, sok, self (**Fris**); zich, zijn, zo, zulk, zelf, zelve (**Dut**); sich, sein, so, solch, selbst, selb, selber (**Ger**);

sik, sér, sinn, svá, slikr, sjalfr (**Norse**); seg, sin, så, slik, selv, sjøl (**Nor**); sig, sin, så, slik, själv (**Swe**); sin, så, slig, selv (**Dan**); sig, sér, sinn, svo, slikur (**Ice**)

Italic: se, sēcum, per sē, ipse, metipse, metipsimus, sē-, sed, suus, sōlus, dēsōlāre, sōlitārius, sōlitās, sōlitātim, sōlitūdo (**Lat**);

se, soi, même, son, sa, ses, seul, désoler, solitaire, solitude (**Fr**);

sé, seco, esso, stesso, adesso, medesimo, medesmo, suo, solo, desolare, solitario, solitudine (**Ital**);

se, consigo, ese, mismo, suyo, su, solo, desolar, soltero, solitario, soledumbre (**Sp**);

se, consigo, esse, mesmo, seu, sua, solo, só, solteiro, solitário, saudade, solidão, solitude (**Port**);

se, sine, îns, însă, însăși, însele, însuși, înșiși, său, sa, săi, sale, solitar (**Rom**)

Derivatives: solo, sole, desolate, solitary, solitude (**Eng**); sawl (**Wel**)

Hellenic: ἕ (hé), ἑός (heós), ἴδιος (ídios), ἰδιώτης (idiṓtēs), σφεῖς (spheîs), ὅς (hós), ἑκάς (hekás), ἕκαστος (hékastos), ἔτης (étēs), ἧλιξ (hêlix) (**AnGk**); ιδιώτης (idiótis), έκαστος (ékastos) (**Gk**)

Derivatives: idiot (**Eng**); idioot (**Dut**); Idiot (**Ger**); panécastique (**Fr**); идиóт (idiót) (**Rus**)

Slavic: -ся (-sja) / -сь (-s'), свой (svoj), себя (sebjá) (**Rus**); się, swój, siebie (**Pol**); se, svůj, sebe (**Cz**); sa, svoj, seba (**Slo**); ce (se), cвoj (svoj), ce6e (sebe) (**Mace**)

Baltic: save (**Lith**); sevi (**Latv**)

Indo-Iranian: स्व (svá), स्वतन्त्र (svatantra), स्वराज (svarāja) (**Sans**); स्वयं (svayan), ख़ुद (xud) (**Hin**); خود (xod) (**Pers**)

from which is derived *swe-dʰh₁- (see *dheH₁- to do)

*kʷis

who, what, which

kʷos, kʷei/kʷoi, *kʷid, kʷod

Germanic: who, when, why, how, where, what, which, whether, either (**Eng**); hwā, hwenne, hwȳ, hū, hwær, hwæt, hwilc, hwæþer (**OE**);

wa, wêr, wat, hokker (**Fris**); wie, hoe, waar, wat, welk, weder (arch.) (**Dut**); wer, wie, wo, was, weich, weder (**Ger**);

hverr, hví, hvé, hvar, hvat, hvilikr, hvaðarr, hvárr (**Norse**); hvem, hvor, hva, hvilken, hver (**Nor**); vem, var, vad, vilken, varken (**Swe**); hvem, hvor, hvad, hvilken, hver (**Dan**); hver, hvi, hvar, hvað, hvor, hvorki (**Ice**)

Celtic: pwy, pa (**Wel**); cé, cad (**Iri**)

Italic: quis, aliquis, quia, quīcumque, quī, cūius, quō, quoque, quot, quotiēns, quālis, quālitās, cūr, cum, quam, umquam, numquam, ubī, ubīcumque, ubīque, ūsque, ut, unde, quid, quod, uter, neuter (**Lat**);

qui, que, aucun, quiconque, quel, qualité, onc, onques, où, ubiquiste, jusque, dont, quelle (**Fr**);

chi, ca, cui, che, alcuno, quale, qualità, unqua, unque, ove (lit.), dove, ovunque, ubiquo, ubiquitario, onde (**Ital**);

quien, alguien, ca, cuyo, que, alguno, cual, cualidad, calidad, unca, nunca, ubicuo, donde, qué (**Sp**);

quem, alguém, ca, cujo, que, algum, quociente, qual, qualidade, nunca, u (arch.), ubiquo, onde (**Port**);

care, ca, cine, cui, calitate, încă, iuo (arch.), ubicuu, unde, ce (**Rom**)

Derivatives: status quo, quotient, quality, ubiquitous, neuter, neutral (**Eng**)

Hellenic: ποῖος (poîos), ποῦ (poû), πῶς (pôs), τίς (tís), πόσος (pósos), πότε (póte), ποῖ (poî), πόθεν (póthen), ὅστις (hóstis), ποδαπός (podapós), πηλίκος (pēlíkos) (**AnGk**); ποιος (poios), πού (poú), πως (pos), τι (ti), πόσος (pósos), πότε (póte) (**Gk**)

Slavic: кто (kto), никто́ (niktó), какие (kakiye), что (što), чё (čo), чо (čo), шо (šo), ничто́ (ništó), ничё (ničo)/ничо́ (ničó), кото́рый (kotóryj) (**Rus**); kto, nikt, co, nic, który (**Pol**); kdo, nikdo, co, nic, který (**Cz**); kto, nikto, čo, nič, ktorý (**Slo**); што (što), ништо (níšto) (**Mace**)

Baltic: kàs, katràs, kataràs (**Lith**); kurš, kas (**Latv**)

Indo-Iranian: किम् (kim), क (kaḥ), कि (kiḥ), कतर (katará) (**Sans**); किस (kis) (**Hin**); کﻪ (ke), چﻪ (če), چﯽ (či) (**Pers**)

*ḱi-

here, this

*ḱe-, *ḱo-, *-ḱe

Germanic: he, hither, here (**Eng**); hē, hider, hēr (**OE**); hy, hja, hijr (**Fris**); hij, hem, het, haar, hier, her (**Dut**); hier, hie (**Ger**); hit, heðra, hér (**Norse**); her (**Nor**); här (**Swe**); her (**Dan**); hér (**Ice**)

Italic: citer, cītrā, cis, -c (as in hic, illīc, tunc), -ce (as in ecce) (**Lat**)

Hellenic: σήμερον (sḗmeron), ἐκεῖνος (ekeînos), ἐκεῖ (ekeî), ἐκεῖθεν (ekeîthen) (**AnGk**); εκείνος (ekeínos), εκεί (ekeí), εκείθεν (ekeíthen) (**Gk**)

Slavic: сей (sej) (**Rus**)

Baltic: šìs (**Lith**); šis (**Latv**)

*só

this, that

Germanic: the, tho, those, this, that, there, thus (**Eng**); sē, þes, þæt, þār, þǣr, þus (**OE**); de, dy, der, dus (**Fris**); die, de, dat, het, dit, daar, der, dus, aldus (**Dut**); der, die, das, dass, dar, da (**Ger**); sá, þar, þær (**Norse**); den, det, der (**Nor**); den, det, där (**Swe**); den, det, der (**Dan**); sá, þar (**Ice**)

Probably: Germanic: then, than (**Eng**); þan, þon, þanne (**OE**); dan (**Dut**); denn, dann, dannen (**Ger**); þá, þanan (**Norse**); då (**Nor**); då (**Swe**); da (**Dan**); þá (**Ice**)

Celtic: seo (**Iri**)

Italic: sī, sic, sīve/seu, nisi, tum, tunc, tam, tamen, tandem, tantus, tantum, tot, tālis, tāliō, retaliare, iste (**Lat**);

si, ainsi, donc, tandem, tant, autant, tel (**Fr**);

se, si, cosi, dunque, tanto, tale, cotale, taglione, esto, esta, stesso, stessa (**Ital**);

si, sí, así, entonces, entonce, tamaño, tan, tandem, tanto, tal, este, esta, esto, estos, estas (**Sp**);

se, sim, assim, então, tam, tão, tandem, tanto, tal, talião, este, esta, isto, estes, estas (**Port**);

să, şi, sau, atunci, atuncea, atât, tare, atare, ăsta, asta, ăştia, astea, ăstuia, ăsteia, ăstora (**Rom**)

Derivatives: tandem, pro tanto, retaliate (**Eng**); Tandem (**Ger**); tandem (**Dut**); tandem (**Cz**)

Hellenic: ὁ (ho), ἡ (hē), τό (tó), ὡς (hōs), ὅδε (hóde), ὁδί (hodí), οὗτος (hoûtos), τηλίκος (tēlíkos), τόσος (tósos) (**AnGk**); ο (o), η (i), το (to), ούτος (oútos) (**Gk**)

Slavic: тот (tot), этот (étot) (**Rus**); ten (**Pol**); ten (**Cz**); ten (**Slo**)

Indo-Iranian: स (sá), सा (sā), तद् (tád) (**Sans**)

From ecce + iste:

Italic: cet, cette (**Fr**); questo, questa, questi, queste, costui, costei, costoro (**Ital**); aqueste, aquesta, aquesto, aquestos, aquestas (**Sp**); acest, această, aceşti, aceste, acestui, acestei, acestor (**Rom**)

*n̥-

not, un-

Germanic: un- (**Eng**); un- (**OE**); on- (**Dut**); un- (**Ger**); ú-, ó- (**Norse**); u- (**Nor**); o- (**Swe**); u- (**Dan**); ó- (**Ice**)

Celtic: an- (**Wel**); an-, éa- (**Iri**)

Italic: in-, un- (**Lat**); in- (**Fr**); in-, i-, im- (**Sp**); in-, im- (**Port**)

Derivatives: in-, ir-, il- (**Eng**)

Hellenic: ἀ- (a-), ἀν- (an-), νη- (nē-), νᾱ- (nā-), νω- (nō-) (**AnGk**); α- (a-), ά- (á-), αν- (an-), άν- (án-) (**Gk**)

Indo-Iranian: अ- (a-), अन्- (an-) (**Sans**); अ- (a-), अन- (an-) (**Hin**); نا (nâ-) (**Pers**)

Body

*krep-

body

*kérp-s, *krép-os

Germanic: riff (arch.), midriff (**Eng**); hrif, mihrif (**OE**)

Italic: corpus, corporālis, corporeus, corpulentus, corpusculum, corporātus (**Lat**); corps (**Fr**); corpo, corporeo, corpuscolo (**Ital**); cuerpo, corpóreo (**Sp**); corpo (**Port**); corp (**Rom**)

Derivatives: corporate, corporation, accorporate, corporal, corporality, bicorporal, corporeal, corporeality, corpse, corpulence, corpulent, corpuscle, corpuscular, disincorporate, extracorporeal, incorporal, incorporate, incorporation, incorporeal, corpus, corps (**Eng**); korps (**Dut**); Körper (**Ger**); corff (**Wel**); corp (**Iri**); корпус (kórpus), корпускула (korpúskula) (**Rus**); korpus (**Pol**)

Indo-Iranian: कृप् (kŕp) (**Sans**)

Head

*kapōlo

head, bowl

*kaput-

Germanic: head (**Eng**); heafod, hafola (**OE**); haed (**Fris**); hoofd (**Dut**); Haupt (**Ger**); haufuð, hǫfuð (**Norse**); hode (**Nor**); huvud (**Swe**); hoved (**Dan**); höfuð (**Ice**)

Italic: caput, capitālis, capitellum, capitium, capitō, capitulum, sinciput, -ceps, e.g. anceps, biceps, triceps (**Lat**);

capital, cheptel, chapiteau, cadeau, chevet, capitule, chapitre, chef, sinciput, biceps (**Fr**);

capo, capitale, capitello, cavezza, cavesso, capitone, cavedano, cavedine, capecchio, capitolo, bicipite (**Ital**);

cabeza, cabezo, cabo, capota, capital, cabdal, caudal, cabdillo, caudillo, cabildo, capítulo, jefe, bíceps (**Sp**);

cabo, cabedal, capital, caudal, cabeça, cabeço, capitel, cabedelo, coudel, caudilho, chefe, cabido, capítulo, ancípite, bíceps (**Port**);

cap, capăt, capital, căpeţel, biceps (**Rom**)

Derivatives: capita, capital, capitalize, decapitate, capitol, captain, capo, cattle, chattel, capitellum, capitulum, capitule, chapter, chief, chef, jefe, sinciput, syllaba anceps, biceps, bicipital (**Eng**); kapitaal, kachtel, biceps (**Dut**); Kapitel, Kapital (**Ger**); kapitel (**Nor**); kapitel (**Swe**); kapitel (**Dan**); caibidil (**Iri**); капитéль (kapitél') (**Rus**); biceps (**Pol**)

Indo-Iranian: कपुच्छल (kapúcchala), कपाल (kapāla) (**Sans**); कपाल (kapāl), कपार (kapār) (**Hin**)

*$\acute{k}erh_2$-
skull, head, top, horn

*$\acute{k}erh_2$-s-on, *$\acute{k}\r{r}h_2$e/os-, *$\acute{k}\r{r}h_2$-no-, *$\acute{k}erh_2$-wós, *$\acute{k}\r{r}h_2$-wós, *$\acute{k}erh_2$-s-ro, *krH-s-r-o/en-

Germanic: harns, hart, horn, hirn, hern (dial.), hornet (**Eng**); hærn, hærnes, heorot, horn, hirn, hyrnet (**OE**);

harsens, hoarn, hoarnbij (**Fris**); hersenen, hersens, hert, hoorn, hoorntje (**Dut**); Hirn, Hirsch, Horn, Hornisse, Hornissel (**Ger**);

hjarni, horn, hyrna (**Norse**); hjerne, hjarre, horn, hjørne (**Nor**); hjärna, hjort, horn, hörna (**Swe**); hjerne, hjort, horn, hjørne (**Dan**); hjarni, horn, hyrna (**Ice**)

Celtic: corn, carw, creyryn (**Wel**); corn, cáirrfhiadh (**Iri**)

Italic: cerebrum, cerebellum, cervus, cerva, cervārius, cervīnus, cornūs, cornū, corneus, corniculātus, cornūcōpia, cornūtus, ūnicornis, crābrō, cernuus (**Lat**);

cerveau, cervelle, cerf, corne, cor, cornu (**Fr**); cerebro, cervello, cerebellare, cervo, corno, corneo, cornuto, calabrone (**Ital**);

cerebro, cerebelo, ciervo, cervario, cuerno, córneo, cornudo (**Sp**); cérebro, cerebelo, cervo, corno, córneo, cornudo, cambrão (**Port**);

cerbă, cearbă, creier, cerebel, cerb, cerbar, corn, cornut (**Rom**)

Derivatives: cerebral, cerebellum, cerebrum, cervine, cornea, corner, cornet, -corn, tricorne, Capricorn, corniculate, cornucopia, unicorn (**Eng**); τσερβέλο (tservélo) (**Gk**)

Hellenic: κάρα (kára), κάρη (kárē), κέρας (kéras), ῥινόκερως (rhinókerōs), κρανίον (kraníon), κεράός (keraós), κεραΐς (keraḯs) (**AnGk**); κρανίο (kranío), κράνος (krános), ημικρανία (imikranía) (**Gk**)

Derivatives: cheer, keratin, rhinoceros, cranium, cranial, hemicraniectomy (**Eng**); cara, crānium (**Lat**); chère (obs./arch.), crâne (**Fr**); cranio (**Ital**); cara, cráneo (**Sp**); cara, crânio (**Port**); craniu (**Rom**)

Slavic: череп (čérep), серна (sérna), корова (koróva), шéршень (šéršen') (**Rus**); sorna, krowa, szerszeń (**Pol**); srna, kráva, sršeň (**Cz**); srna, krava, sršeň (**Slo**); черепот (čerepot), срна (srna), крава (krava), стршен (stršen) (**Mace**)

Baltic: kárvė, širšė, stìrna, širšuo (**Lith**); nicnin, stĭrna, sirsenis (**Latv**)

Albanian: krye, sorkadh (**Alb**)

Indo-Iranian: शीर्षन् (śīrṣán), शिरस् (śíras), शृङ्ग (śṛṅga), शृङ्गार (śṛṅgāra), शिर (śira) (**Sans**); سر (sar) (**Pash**); سر (sar), سرو (surū), سرنا (sornâ) (mus.) (**Pers**)

Derivatives: zurna (**Eng**); ζουρνάς (zournás) (**Gk**); зурнá (zurná) (**Rus**); зурла (zurla) (**Mace**)

*$h_2\acute{o}ws$
ear

see *h_2ew- to perceive

*$h_3\acute{o}k^ws$
eye

see *h_3ek^w- to see

*$h_3b^hr\acute{u}Hs$
eyebrow

Germanic: brow (**Eng**); brū (**OE**); Bruun (**Fris**); brauw (**Dut**); Braue (**Ger**); brún (**Norse**); brun (**Nor**); bryn (**Swe**); bryn (**Dan**); brún (**Ice**)

Celtic: bruach (**Iri**)

Hellenic: ὀφρύς (ophrús) (**AnGk**); οφρύς (ofrýs) (**Gk**)

Slavic: бровь (brov') (**Rus**); brew (**Pol**); brva (**Cz**); brva (**Slo**)

Baltic: bruvis (dial.), brùvė (**Lith**)

Indo-Iranian: भ्रू (bhrū) (**Sans**); भौंह (bhaunh) (**Hin**); وروځه (wrūja) (**Pash**); ابرو (abru) (**Pers**)

*$n\acute{e}h_2s$
nose, nostril

Germanic: nose, ness, nozzle (**Eng**); nosu (**OE**); noas (**Fris**); neus (**Dut**); Nase (**Ger**); nǫs (**Norse**); nos (**Nor**); näsa, nos (**Swe**); næse (**Dan**); nös (**Ice**)

Italic: nasus, nāsālis, nāsūtus, nāris (**Lat**); nez, naseau, narine (**Fr**); naso, nasuto, narice (**Ital**); naso, nariz, narine (**Sp**); nariz, narina (**Port**); nas, năsut, nară (**Rom**)

Derivatives: nasal, intranasa, nasalance, naris, enternarial, nares, narial, prenarial (**Eng**)

Slavic: нос (nos) (**Rus**); nos (**Pol**); nos (**Cz**); nos (**Slo**); нос (nos) (**Mace**)

Baltic: nósis (**Lith**); nāss (**Latv**)

Indo-Iranian: नासा (nāsā) (**Sans**)

*h₃éh₁os
mouth

Germanic: ōr, ōra (**OE**); óss (**Norse**); os (**Nor**); os (**Swe**); os (**Dan**); ós (**Ice**)

Italic: ōs, ōris, ōrālis, ōsculum, ōscillim, ōscillare, ōrāre, ōrātiō, ōrātor, adōrāre, perōrāre, ōrāculum (**Lat**); oraison, orateur, adorer, pérorer, oracle (**Fr**); orare, orazione, oratore, adorare, perorare, oracolo (**Ital**); orar, oración, adorar, perorar, oráculo (**Sp**); orar,oração, adorar, oráculo, orago (**Port**); ura, urare, orație, adora, oracol (**Rom**)

Derivatives: oral, oration, orifice, orison, oscillate, osculate, perorate, oracle (**Eng**); orakel (**Dut**); orakel (**Nor**); orakel (**Swe**); orakel (**Dan**); adhair (**Iri**); опáтор (orátor), оракул (orakul) (**Rus**); orákulum (**Cz**); orákulum (**Slo**); оракул (orakul) (**Mace**); orakulas (**Lith**); orākuls (**Latv**); uroj (**Alb**)

Hellenic: ἀρά (ará) (**AnGk**)

Slavic: уста (ustá) (**Rus**); usta (**Pol**); ústa (**Cz**); ústa (**Slo**); уста/усни (usta/usni) (**Mace**)

Baltic: úostas (**Lith**); osta (**Latv**)

Indo-Iranian: आस् (ās), ओष्ठ (óṣṭha), आर्यन्ति (āryanti) (**Sans**); होठ (hōṭh) (**Hin**)

*mendʰ-
to chew; jaw, mouth

Germanic: mouth (**Eng**); mūþ (**OE**); mûn (**Fris**); mond, muide, mui (**Dut**); Mund (**Ger**); muðr (**Norse**); munn (**Nor**); mun (**Swe**); mund (**Dan**); munnur, munni (**Ice**)

Celtic: mant (**Wel**)

Italic: mentum, mandere, mandibula, mandūcāre, masticāre (**Lat**); menton, mandibule, manger, mâcher, mastiquer (**Fr**); mento, mandibola, manducare, mangiare, masticare (**Ital**); mentón, mandibula, manjar, manducar, masticar (**Sp**); mandibula, manjar, manducar, mastigar (**Port**); mandibulă, mânca, mâncare, mesteca (**Rom**)

Derivatives: mentum, mandible, manducate, masticate (**Eng**)

Hellenic: μάσταξ (mástax), μᾰστῐχᾰω (mastikháō), μασάομαι (masáomai), μύσταξ (mústax) (**AnGk**)

Derivatives: moustache (**Eng**); moustache (**Fr**); mostaccio (**Ital**); mostacho (**Sp**); mustață (**Rom**)

Baltic: mute, mutīgs, mutisks (**Latv**)

Albanian: mjekë (**Alb**)

However, Latin mentum is also attributed to *men to project:

*men-
to stand out, to tower, to project

Germanic: mane (**Eng**); manu, mene (**OE**); moannen, moanjes (**Fris**); manen, maan (**Dut**); Mähne (**Ger**); mǫn, makki, men, mœnir, mœna (**Norse**); man, manke (**Nor**); man, manke (**Swe**); man, manke (**Dan**); makka, mön, men (in hálsmen) (**Ice**)

Celtic: mynydd, mwnwgl (**Wel**)

Italic: mentum, ēminēre, ēminēns, ēminentia, praeēminēre, imminēre, prōminēre, prōminēns, superēminēre, minae, minor, mināx, minitor, mōns, montānus, montāniōsus, trānsmontānus, monticellus, monticulus, montuōsus (**Lat**);

menton, éminent, éminente, éminence, imminent, mener, menace, montagne, mont, montagneux, monceau, monticule, montueux (**Fr**);

mento, eminenza, imminente, menare, minare, minace, minaccia, montagna, monte, montano, montagnoso, tramontano, monticello, moncello, montuoso (**Ital**);

mentón, eminente, eminencia, inminente, prominente, minar, menar, amenaza, menaza, minaz, montaña, monte, montano, montañoso, transmontano, montecillo, monticulo, montuoso (**Sp**);

ameaça, minaz, montanha, monte, montano, montanhoso, montijo, monticulo (**Port**);

mâna, mânare, munte, muntos, montan, muncel (**Rom**)

Derivatives: mentum, eminent, eminence, pre-eminent, imminent, prominent, promontory, supereminent, minatory, menace, minacious, monticule, Montana, mount, mountain, montane, transmontane (**Eng**); Eminenz, Monteur, montieren, Montanunion (**Ger**)

*génus
cheek, jaw, chin

Germanic: chin (**Eng**); ċinn (**OE**); kin (**Fris**); kin (**Dut**); Kinn (**Ger**); kinn (**Norse**); kinn (**Nor**); kind (**Swe**); kind (**Dan**); kinn (**Ice**)

Celtic: gên (Wel); gionach (Iri)

Italic: gena (Lat); geană (Rom)

Hellenic: γένυς (génus), γνάθος (gnáthos) (AnGk); γνάθος (gnáthos) (Gk)

Derivatives: agnathous, chilognath, compsognathus, endognathion, epignathous, exognathion, gnathic, hypognathus, mesognathion, prognathism (Eng); eurygnathus (Lat)

Baltic: žandas (Lith); zods (Latv)

Indo-Iranian: हनु (hánu) (Sans); چانه (čâne), زنخ (zanakh) (Pers)

*bʰardʰeh₂-
beard

Germanic: beard (Eng); beard (OE); burd (Fris); baard (Dut); Bart (Ger); barðr (Norse); bart (Nor)

Italic: barba, barbatus, barbula, imberbis (Lat); barbe, barbelé, imberbe (Fr); barba, barbato, barbula, imberbe (Ital); barba, barbado, imberbe (Sp); barba, barbado, imberbe (Port); barbă, bărbat, barbur (Rom)

Derivatives: barber, barbed, barbate, barbule (Eng); barf (Wel); βαρβάτος (varvátos) (Gk)

Slavic: борода (borodá), брадá (bradá) (Rus); broda (Pol); brada (Cz); brada (Slo); брада (brada), брадата (bradata) (Mace)

Baltic: barzda, barzdótas (Lith); bārda (Latv)

Indo-Iranian: بلمه (balme) (Pers)

*dn̥ǵʰwéh₂s
tongue

Germanic: tongue (Eng); tunge (OE); tonge (Fris); tong (Dut); Zunge (Ger); tunga (Norse); tunge (Nor); tunga (Swe); tunge (Dan); tunga (Ice)

Celtic: tafod (Wel); teanga (Iri)

Italic: lingua (Lat); langue (Fr); lingua (Ital); lengua (Sp); língua (Port); limbă (Rom)

Derivatives: lingua, langue, linguistic, bilingual, collingual, elinguation, language, ligula, ligular, ligule, lingual, linguiform, linguine, multilingual, prelingual, sublingual (Eng)

Slavic: язык (jazýk) (Rus); język (Pol); jazyk (Cz); jazyk (Slo); јазик (jazik) (Mace)

Baltic: liežuvis (Lith)

Albanian: giuha (**Alb**)

Indo-Iranian: जिह्वा (jihvā), जुहू (juhū) (**Sans**); जीभ (jībh), ज़बान (zabān) (**Hin**); ژبه (žǝba) (**Pash**); زبان (zabân) (**Pers**)

*ǵómbʰos
tooth, row of teeth, peg

Germanic: comb, kemb, unkempt, oakum (**Eng**); camb, cemban, ācumba (**OE**); kam, kaam, kjimme (**Fris**); kam, kemmen (**Dut**); Kamm, kämmen (**Ger**); kambr, kemba (**Norse**); kam, kjemme (**Nor**); kam, kämma, hårkam (**Swe**); kam, kjæmme, kæmme (**Dan**); kambur, kemba (**Ice**)

Perhaps: **Italic:** gemma (**Lat**); gemme (**Fr**); gemma (**Ital**); yema, gema (**Sp**); gema (**Port**); gemă (**Rom**)

Derivatives: gem (**Eng**); гемма (gemma) (**Rus**)

Hellenic: γόμφος (gómphos) (**AnGk**); γόμφος (gómfos) (**Gk**)

Derivatives: gomphus (**Lat**); gond (**Fr**); gozne, gonce (**Sp**); gonzo, gonfo- (**Port**)

Slavic: зуб (zub) (**Rus**); gęba/ząb (**Pol**); zub (**Cz**); zub (**Slo**); заб (zab) (**Mace**)

Baltic: žambas (**Lith**); zobs (**Latv**)

Albanian: dhëmb (**Alb**)

Indo-Iranian: जम्भ (jambha) (**Sans**)

*h₃dónts
tooth

Germanic: tooth, tusk (poss.) (**Eng**); tōþ, tux (poss.) (**OE**); toth, tos, tosk (**Fris**); tand (**Dut**); Zahn (**Ger**); tǫnn, toskr (**Norse**); tann, tonn (**Nor**); tand (**Swe**); tand (**Dan**); tönn (**Ice**)

Celtic: dant (**Wel**); déad (**Iri**)

Italic: dēns, dentis, dentālis, dentātus, denticulātus, denticulus (**Lat**); dent, dental (**Fr**); dente, dentale, dentato (**Ital**); diente, dental (**Sp**); dente, dental (**Port**); dinte (**Rom**)

Derivatives: dental, dentist, dentate, denticulate, denticule, denture, indent, indentation, indenture, trident, dandelion (**Eng**)

Hellenic: ὀδούς (odoús) / ὀδών (odṓns) (**AnGk**); δόντι (dónti) (**Gk**)

Derivatives: -odont, -odontia, odonto-, mastodon, odontology, orthodontics, orthodontist, periodontal, smilodon, conodont (**Eng**)

Slavic: десна (desná), десла (deslá) (dial.) (**Rus**); dziąsło (**Pol**); dáseň (**Cz**); ďasno (**Slo**)

Baltic: dantis (**Lith**)

Indo-Iranian: दत् (dát), दन् (dán), दन्त (dánta) (**Sans**); दांत (dānt), दाँत (dāt) (**Hin**); دندان (dandân) (**Pers**)

*mak-

pouch

see Tools

Limbs & Joints

*h₂er

to join, fit together

*h₂rey-, *h₂r̥h₁-sḱé-ti, *h₂r̥-h₂r̥h₁-sḱé-ti, *h₂r̥h₁-téh₂, *h₂réy-tus, *h₂ri-dʰ-mó-s, *h₂or-d-h₃onh₂-, *h₂r-éh₁(ye)-ti, *h₂ér-ti-s, *h₂r̥-tó-s, *h₂ér-tus, *h₂r̥-mó-s, *h₂r̥-mo-n-ih₂, *h₂r̥-dʰmó-s, *h₂ér-mn̥, *h₂er-dʰro-m, *h₂ér-yōs, *h₂er-eh₂-k-sneh₂

Germanic: rhyme, arm (**Eng**); rīm, earm (**OE**); earm (**Fris**); rijm, arm (**Dut**); Reim, Arm (**Ger**); rím, armr (**Norse**); rim, arm (**Swe**); arm (**Dan**); rím, armur (**Ice**)

Celtic: rhif (**Wel**); ríomh (**Iri**)

Italic: reor, ratus, ratiō, ratiōcinor, rītus, ōrdō, ōrdinālis, ōrdinārius, ordinātiō, ōrnāre, ōrdināre, arānea, arāneus, ars, artista, artifex, iners, sollers (sollus+ars), artus, arto, articulus, articulo, arma, armentum, armārium, armus, harmonia, armō, armātūra, armātus (**Lat**);

raison, ration, rite, ordo, ordre, ordinaire, orner, ordonner, araignée, rogne, art, inerte, article, orteil, arme, armoire, ars, harmonie, armer, armure, armature, armée, armé (**Fr**);

ragione, razione, rito, ordine, ornare, ordinal, ordinare, aragna, ragna, rogna, arte, inerte, articolo, ortiglio, arma, armadio, armario, armento, armare, armatura, armata, armato (**Ital**);

razón, ración, rito, orden, ornar, ordenar, ordeñar, araña, raño, arte, inerte, artejo, artículo, arma, armario, almario, armos, armar, armadura, armada, armado (**Sp**);

razão, ração, rácio, rito, ordem, ordinário, ornar, ordenar, ordenhar, aranha, ronha, arte, artelho, artículo, artigo, arma, armário, almário, armento, armar, armadura, armado (**Port**);

rațiune, rație, rit, ordin, ordine, ordona, ordonare, urdina, urdinare, râie, artă, articol, armă, armar, arm, arma, armătură, armatură, armură, armată, armat (**Rom**)

Derivatives: rate, ratio, ratiocinate, reason, ration, rite, order, ordinary, ornate, ordain, ordinate, ordination, art, inert, inertia, artifact, artifice, artifical, artisan, articulate, article, arms, ambry, almery, armoire, armomancy, armour, armoury, armature, army, armada (**Eng**);

orde, order, ordenen, ordonneren (**Dut**); Orden, Order, ordern, Ordnung, Ordo, ordinär, ordnen, ordinieren, Artikel (**Ger**); orden, ordning, ordre, ordinær, ordne (**Nor**); rit, orden, order, ordinarie, ordning, ordna (**Swe**); orden, ordning, ordre, ordinær, ordne (**Dan**); urdd, arf (**Wel**); airteagal (**Iri**);

орден (orden), ордер (order), артикул (artíkul), артикль (artikl'), арматýра (armatúra) (**Rus**); order, ordynex (**Pol**); अलमारी (almārī) (**Hin**); urdhëroj, armë (**Alb**)

Hellenic: ἀριθμός (arithmós), ἀρέσκω (aréskō), ἀραρίσκω (ararískō), ἀρετή (areté), ἀράχνη (arákhnē), ἀράχνης (arákhnēs), ἄρτι (árti), ἀμαρτή (hamarté), ἄρθρον (árthron), ἀρθρῖτις (arthrîtis), ἀρτύω (artúō), ἁρμός (harmós), ἁρμονία (harmonía), ἁρμόζω (harmózō), ἀρθμός (arthmós), ἅρμα (hárma), ἀρείων (areíōn), ἄριστος (áristos), ἀριστερός (aristerós), ἄρα (ára) (**AnGk**); αριθμός (arithmós), αρετή (aretí), αράχνη (aráchni), άρματα (ármata), άρμα (árma), αρμός (armós) (**Gk**)

Derivatives: arithmetic, logarithm, arete, arachnoid, arachnid, arachnophobia, arthropod, arthritis, harmony (**Eng**); гармония (garmonija) (**Rus**)

Slavic: ярмó (jarmó), армó (armó), ярём (jarjóm), ярémь (jarém') (**Rus**); jarzmo, jerzmo, jarmo, jirzmo, ramię (**Pol**); jařmo, jarmo, rámě (**Cz**); jarmo, járom, rameno (**Slo**); japeм (jarem), paмo (ramo) (**Mace**)

Baltic: ir (**Lith**)

Indo-Iranian: राध्नोति (rādhnoti), राध्यति (rādhyati), ऋत (r̥tá), ऋतु (r̥tú), अरम् (áram), ईर्म (irma) (**Sans**); ऋतु (r̥tu), रितु (ritu) (**Hin**); ارد (ard), رد (rad) (arch.) (**Pers**)

which may include (through *h₂reh₁-):

*Hreh₁dʰ-

to think; to arrange; to succeed, accomplish

*h₂réh₁dʰ-e-ti, *h₂réh₁dʰ-ye-ti, *h₂roh₁dʰ-éye-ti, *h₂réh₁dʰ-t, *h₂r̥h₁dʰ-néw-ti, *h₂réh₁dʰ-eh₂, *h₂r̥h₁dʰ-éh₂

Germanic: read, rede, riddle, aread (obs.) (**Eng**); rǣdan, rǣdelse, ārǣdan (**OE**); riede (**Fris**); raden, raadsel (**Dut**); raten, Rätsel, erraten (**Ger**); ráða, rœða, rǫð (**Norse**); råde, rad (**Nor**); råda, rad (**Swe**); råde, rad (**Dan**); ráða, ræða, röð (**Ice**)

Celtic: amrawdd (**Wel**)

Slavic: радéть (radét') (obs.) (**Rus**)

Indo-Iranian: राध्यति (rādhyati) (**Sans**)

*Heh₃l-
to bow, bend; elbow

Germanic: ell, elbow (**Eng**); eln, elboga (**OE**); jelne, Älbooge (**Fris**); el, elleboog, ellenboog (**Dut**); Elle, Ellbogen, Ellenbogen (**Ger**); alin, eln, ǫln, albogi, alnbogi, ǫlbogi, ǫlnbogi (**Norse**); alen, albue, olboge (**Nor**); aln, almboge, armbåge (**Swe**); alen, albue, almbue, armbue (**Dan**); alin, öln, olnbogi, olbogi (**Ice**)

Derivatives: aune (**Fr**); auna (**Ital**)

Celtic: elin, olwyn (**Wel**); uillinn (**Iri**)

Italic: ulna (**Lat**); ulna (**Ital**); ulna (**Sp**); ulna (**Port**)

Derivatives: ulna (**Eng**)

Hellenic: ὠλένη (ōlénē), ὠλήν (ōlḗn), ὠλλόν (ōllón) (**AnGk**); ωλένη (oléni) (**Gk**)

Slavic: локоть (lokot'), ланита (lanita) (**Rus**); łokieć (**Pol**); loket (**Cz**); laket' (**Slo**); лакот (lakot) (**Mace**)

Baltic: úolektis, alkūnė, elkūnė (**Lith**); olekts, elkonis (**Latv**)

Albanian: llërë (**Alb**)

Indo-Iranian: अरत्नि (aratní) (**Sans**)

*ǵónu
knee

Germanic: knee (**Eng**); cnēo (**OE**); knibbel (**Fris**); knie (**Dut**); Knie (**Ger**); kné (**Norse**); kne (**Nor**); knä (**Swe**); knæ (**Dan**); kné (**Ice**)

Celtic: glin (**Wel**); glúin (**Iri**)

Italic: genū, geniculum, genūflectere (**Lat**); genou, génuflexion (**Fr**); ginocchio, genuflettersi (**Ital**); hinojo, genuflexión (**Sp**); joelho (**Port**); genunchi (**Rom**)

Derivatives: genuflect (**Eng**)

Hellenic: γόνυ (gónu) (**AnGk**); γόνατο (gónato) (**Gk**)

Derivatives: hexagon, polygon, trigonometry, goniometer, gonion, gonitis (**Eng**)

Slavic: звено (zvenó) (**Rus**)

Albanian: gju (**Alb**)

Indo-Iranian: जानु (jānu) (**Sans**); زنگون (zengewn) (**Pash**); زانو (zânu) (**Pers**)

*h₂enk-
angle, bend

see Tools

*kenk-
knee-cup, heel

Germanic: heel, hough, hock (**Eng**); hēla, hōh, hō (**OE**); hael, häile, hajel, hägel (**Fris**); hiel, haas, haasje (**Dut**); hǽll, há, hásin (**Norse**); hel, hæl, hase (dial.) (**Nor**); häl, has (**Swe**); hæl, hase, has (**Dan**); hæll, há, hásin (**Ice**)

Baltic: kìnka, kenklė (**Lith**); cinksla (**Latv**)

Indo-Iranian: कङ्काल (kaṅkāla) (**Sans**)

but this etymology is somewhat confused with *koḱs- joint (the two might most simply be regarded as one):

*koḱs-
joint, hip

Germanic: Hachse, Hessen (**Ger**)

Italic: coxa, coxus (**Lat**); cuisse (**Fr**); coscia (**Ital**); cuja, cojo (**Sp**); coxa, coxo (**Port**); coapsă (**Rom**)

Derivatives: coxa (**Eng**); coes (**Wel**); cos (**Iri**); kofshë (**Alb**)

*(s)kel-
to bend, crook; bent, crooked; leg, heel, knee, hip

*(s)kl-eh₂-w-, *skél-os, *kōl-o-, *skel-ko-, *skelo-wero-

Germanic: slute (**Fris**); sluiten, sleutel (**Dut**); schließen, Schlüssel, schielen (**Ger**); slutte (**Nor**); sluta (**Swe**); slutte (**Dan**)

Celtic: clo (**Wel**); cló (**Iri**)

Italic: clāvis, clāvus, clāvīchordium, clāvīcula, conclāve, clāvāre, claudere, clausula, clausus, claustellum, claustrum, clausūra, conclūdere, disclūdere, disclūsus, exclūdere, exclūsiō, exclūsus, exclūsīvus, inclūdere, inclūsiō, inclūsus, interclūdere, occlūdere, praeclūdere, sēclūdere, scelus, calx, calcāneum, calcar, calceus, calceāre, discalceāre, excalceāre, excalceātus, recalcitrāre, calcāre, calcatura, conculcāre, inculcāre (**Lat**);

clé, clef, clavicorde, cheville, clavicule, conclave, clou, clouer, clore, clôturer, clos, cloître, clôture, conclure, exclure, enclore, inclure, enclos, inclus, occlure, chausse, chaussette, chausser, déchausser, récalcitrer, calquer, inculquer, scoliose (**Fr**);

chiave, clavicordo, cavicchia, cavicchio, caviglia, clavicola, conclave, chiavo, chiodo, clavo, chiavare, chiudere, chiuso, chiavistello, chiostro, chiostra, clausura, chiusura, concludere, dischiudere, dischiuso, escludere, schiudere, escluso, schiuso, includere, incluso, intercludere, occludere, precludere, calcagno, calceo, calcetto, calza, calzetta, calzino, calzone, calzare, discalzare, scalzare, ricalcitrare, calcare, conculcare, inculcare (**Ital**);

clave, llave, clavicordio, clavicula, clavija, lavija, llavija, cónclave, clavo, clavar, clausurar, cláusula, claustro, clausura, concluir, excluido, exclusivo, incluir, incluso, ocluir, calce, calcáneo, calcañar, carcañal, cálceo, calza, calceta, calcetín, calzar, descalzar, calcar, conculcar, inculcar (**Sp**);

chave, clavicula, chavelha, cravelha, cavilha, conclave, clavo, cravo, cravar, clavar, chouver, chouso, claustro, clausura, chousura, concluir, excluir, eclodir, escluso, incluir, incluso, coice, calcâneo, calcanhar, calça, calçar, descalçar, recalcitrar, calcar, calcadura, inculcar (**Port**);

cheie, claviculă, conchide, deschide, deschi, închide, închidere, închis, călcâi, încălța, încălțare, descălța, descălțare, călca, călcare, călcătură (**Rom**)

Derivatives: clavis, clavichord, clavicle, conclave, clove, cloy, cloister, close, clausula, claustrum, clausure, closure, cloture, disclude, exclude, sluice, exclusion, exclusive, enclose, include, inclusion, interclude, occlude, preclude, seclude, caltrop, calcaneum, calcaneus, calcar, excalceation, recalcitrant, calque, conculcate, inculcate (**Eng**); klooster, sluis, kous (**Dut**); Klausel, Kloster, Kelter (**Ger**); конклáв (konkláv) (**Rus**); këshyre (**Alb**); चाबी (cābī) (**Hin**)

Hellenic: κλείς (kleís), σκέλος (skélos), τρισκελίς (triskelís), κῶλον (kôlon), κυλίνδω (kulíndō), κύλινδρος (kúlindros), κῶλον (kôlon), σκώληξ (skólēx), σκολιός (skoliós), σκολίωσις (skolíōsis), σκολίωμα (skolíōma) (**AnGk**); σκέλος (skélos), σκουλήκι (skoulíki), σκολίωση (skolíosi) (**Gk**)

Derivatives: colon (the punctuation mark) (**Eng**); cōlon (**Lat**); цилúндр (cilíndr) (**Rus**); کلید (kelid) (**Pers**)

Slavic: клюкá (kljuká), ключ (ključ) (**Rus**); klucz (**Pol**); klika, klíč (**Cz**); kľuka, kľúč (**Slo**); ключ (kluč) (**Mace**)

Baltic: kliūti, kliáuti, kliūdýti (**Lith**); kļūt (**Latv**)

Indo-Iranian: सलवार (salvār) (**Hin**); شلوار (šalvâr) (**Pers**)

Derivatives: shalwar (**Eng**)

*peth₂
to fly

*péth₂-e-ti, *pí-pth₂-eti, *péth₂-r̥

Germanic: fathom (**Eng**); fæþm (outstretched arms, embrace, power, fathom) (**OE**); fiem (**Fris**); vadem, vaam (**Dut**); Faden (**Ger**); faðmr (**Norse**); favn, famn (**Nor**); famn, fagn (**Swe**); favn, farm, fadm (**Dan**); faðmur (**Ice**)

Celtic: eite, eiteog (**Iri**)

Italic: petere, appetere, appetītiō, appetītus, competere, impetere, impetus, petulāns, repetere, patēre, patēns, patera, patella, pandere, expandere, passus, passim, passer, passerīnus (**Lat**);

appétit, pétulant, pétulante, répéter, patent, patente, poêle, patelle, épandre, passer, pas, passereau (**Fr**);

pezzire, pezzente, appetito, competo, impeto, ripetere, padella, spandere, spassare, spasso, passare, passo, passero, passera (**Ital**);

pedir, apetito, competo, ímpetu, repetir, pander, paella, padilla, paila, expandir, pasar, pasa, paso, pasado, pájaro (**Sp**);

pedir, apetição, apetite, apetito, ímpeto, repetir, patela, expandir, passar, passa, passo, pássaro (**Port**);

peți, pețire, apetit, repeta, pas, pasăre (**Rom**)

Derivatives: petition, centripetal, appetite, appetition, compete, competition, competent, impetus, petulant, repeat, repetition, propitiate, paten, patency, patent, patently, impatent, patefaction, patella, patellar, patelliform, patera, patin, expand, spawn, passim, pace, pass, passerine (**Eng**);

repeteren, patent (**Dut**); Impetus, repetieren, patent, Spaß, Pass, Passus (**Ger**); repetere, patent (**Nor**); repetera, patent, passus (**Swe**); repetere, patent (**Dan**); padell (**Wel**); аппетит (appetít) (**Rus**); repetować, patent (**Pol**); patent (**Cz**)

Hellenic: πέτομαι (pétomai), πίπτω (píptō), πετάννῡμι (petánnūmi), πτῶμα (ptôma), πτῶσις (ptôsis), πτωτικός (ptōtikós), πτωτός (ptōtós), ποταμός (potamós), πέταλον (pétalon), πέτασος (pétasos) (**AnGk**); πέφτω (péfto) (**Gk**)

Derivatives: petal, anaptotic, apoptosis, peripety, proptotic, ptomaine, ptosis, symptom, hippopotamus, Mesopotamia, potamic, potamology (**Eng**)

Baltic: petỹs (**Lith**)

Indo-Iranian: पतति (pátati) (**Sans**)

from which also derives *péth₂r̥ wing:

*péth$_2$r̥

wing, feather

Germanic: feather (**Eng**); feþer (**OE**); fear (**Fris**); veder, veer (**Dut**); Feder (**Ger**); fjǫðr (**Norse**); fjær, fjør (**Nor**); fjäder (**Swe**); fjeder, fjer (**Dan**); fjöður (**Ice**)

Celtic: edn, adain (**Wel**); éan (**Iri**)

Italic: penna, pennātus (**Lat**); penne (**Fr**); penna (**Ital**); peña (**Sp**); pena (**Port**); pană (**Rom**)

Derivatives: pen (**Eng**); penn (**Nor**); penna (**Swe**); pen (**Dan**); penni (**Ice**)

Hellenic: ὑποπετρίδιος (hupopetrídios), πτερόν (pterón), πτερόω (pteróō), πτερωτός (pterōtós), πτέρυξ (ptérux) (poss.) (**AnGk**); πτέρυγα (ptéryga) (**Gk**)

Derivatives: apterous, archaeopteryx, Chiroptera, helicopter, heteropterous, homopterous, pterodactyl, pterosaur (**Eng**)

Slavic: перó (peró) (**Rus**); pióro (**Pol**); pero, péro (**Cz**); pero (**Slo**); перо (pero) (**Mace**)

Indo-Iranian: पत्र (pátra) (**Sans**); पत्र (patra) (**Hin**)

However, while penna & pinna in Latin are alternative forms of each other, some argue they have different origins, with pinna coming from *spey- sharp point:

*spey-

sharp point, stick

*spey-neh$_2$, *spey-ro-, *spid-yo-, *spid-us, *speyg-o-, *speyg-ros, *spoyg-, *(s)pīn-?

Germanic: spire, spit, spitz, spiker, spoke, spile, fin (**Eng**); spīr, spitu, spāca, finn (**OE**); spile, fin (**Fris**); spier, spit, spijker, spaak, spijl, vin (**Dut**); Spier, Spitze, Spieß, Speiche, Spell, Finne (**Ger**); spira, spikr (**Norse**); spik, spiker, finne (**Nor**); spira, spett, spik (**Swe**); spid, spiger, spile, finne (**Dan**)

Italic: pinna, spīna, spinalis, spīnōsus, spīnula, spīnus, spīca (**Lat**); épine, spinal, épineux, spinule, épi (**Fr**); spina, spinale, spinoso, spilla, spinula, spino, spiga (**Ital**); espina, espinal, espinoso, espino, espiga (**Sp**); espinha, espinal, espinhoso, espínula, espinho, espiga (**Port**); spin, spinal, spinare, spinos, spic (**Rom**)

Derivatives: spine, spinal, spinose, spinous, spinule, spinel, spiniform, spike (**Eng**); спинá (spiná) (**Rus**); spina (**Latv**); pendë, shpend, shpinë (**Alb**)

Baltic: speigleĩs (**Lith**)

Indo-Iranian: स्फय (sphyá) (**Sans**)

*pṓds
foot

Germanic: foot (**Eng**); fōt (**OE**); foet (**Fris**); voet (**Dut**); Fuß (**Ger**); fótr (**Norse**); fot (**Nor**); fot (**Swe**); fod (**Dan**); fótur (**Ice**)

Italic: pēs, bipēs, celeripēs, decempeda, pedulis, pedīculus, pedīcellus, quadrupēs (**Lat**); pied, céléripede, pédicule, pédicelle (**Fr**); piede, pedule, pedicello, decempeda (**Ital**); pie, pedul, pediculo, pedicelo (**Sp**); pé, pediculo, pedicelo (**Port**); piez, picior (**Rom**)

Derivatives: pes, biped, celeripede, pedal, pedestal, pedestrian, pedicle, pedicel, pedicure, pedigree, pedometer, quadruped, velocipede, pawn, peon, pioneer, vamp (meaning a stocking covering foot and ankle or part of the shoe covering the front of the foot, thus, to patch or refurbish) (**Eng**)

Hellenic: πούς (poús), πόδιον (pódion), ὀκτώπους (oktṓpous) (**AnGk**); πόδι (pódi), χταπόδι (chtapódi) (**Gk**)

Derivatives: tripod, podiatry, podium, pew, polyp, antipodes, octopus (**Eng**); octopus (**Dut**); ochtapas (**Iri**); podium, octopus (**Lat**); podium, puy (**Fr**); podio, poggio (**Ital**); podio, poyo, octopoda (**Sp**); pódio, poio (**Port**); podium, podiu (**Rom**); اختاپوس (oxtâpus) (**Pers**)

Slavic: пасть (past'), паду́ (padú), падёт (padjót), па́дать (pádat'), па́даю (pádaju), пеший (péšij) (**Rus**); paść, padnę, padać, pieszy (**Pol**); padat (**Cz**); padać, peši (**Slo**); паѓа (paǵa) (**Mace**)

Baltic: pėda (**Lith**); pēda (**Latv**)

Albanian: poshtë (**Alb**)

Indo-Iranian: पद् (pád), त्रिपाद (tripāda) (**Sans**); पांव (pāv), तिपाई (tipāī), पैजामा (paijāmā) (**Hin**); پښه (pẍa) (**Pash**); پای (pây), پا (pâ), پایجامه (paejamah) (**Pers**)

Derivatives: teapoy, pyjama/pajama (**Eng**)

which is derived from *ped- to walk:

*ped-
to walk, to step

*péd-ye-ti, *pi-péd-ti, *pe-pód-e, *pod-éye-ti, *ped-e-ti, *pṓd-s, *ped-óm, *ped-yós, *ped-yōs, *ped-tṃmo-, *ped-uro-

Germanic: fetter (**Eng**); feter, fatian, fetian, feċċan (**OE**); fetsje (**Fris**); veter, vatten (**Dut**); fassen (**Ger**); feta, fet, fjǫturr, fata (**Norse**); fet, fatte (**Nor**); fjät, fjätter, fatta (**Swe**); fjed, fatte (**Dan**); feta, fet, fjötur, fatta, fata (**Ice**)

Italic: oppidum, pēior, pēiōrāre, pessimus, expedīre, impedīre, peccare, peccātor, peccātum (Lat);

pire, expédier, pécher, pécheur, péché (Fr);

peggiore, peggio, peggiorare, pessimo, spedire, impedire, peccare, peccatore, peccatrice, peccato (Ital);

peor, peorar, peyorar, pésimo, expedir, impedir, pecar, pecador, pecado (Sp);

Óbidos, ópido, pior, piorar, pejorar, empiorar, péssimo, expedir, despir, impedir, pecar, pecador, pecado (Port); păcat (Rom)

Derivatives: pejorative, pessimal, pessimism, pessimist, expedite, impede, impediment (Eng); pechu, pechadur, pechod (Wel); peaca (Iri)

Hellenic: πέδον (pédon), πεδίον (pedíon), πεζός (pezós) (AnGk); πεδίο (pedío), πεζός (pezós) (Gk)

Derivatives: pedion (Eng)

Slavic: под (pod) (Rus); spód (Pol); půda (Cz); pôda (Slo)

Indo-Iranian: पद्यते (pádyate), पिब्दमान (píbdamāna), पपाद (papāda), पादयति (pādáyati), पद (pada) (Sans)

*h₃neghʰ-
nail

*h₃noghʰ-l-os, *h₃ṇghʰ-l-(e)h₂, *h₃ṇghʰ-u-, *sh₃ṇghʰ-u-

Germanic: nail (Eng); nægl (OE); neil (Fris); nagel (Dut); Nagel (Ger); nagl, negl (Norse); negl (Nor); nagel (Swe); negl (Dan); nögl, nagli (Ice)

Derivatives: нагель (nagel') (Rus)

Celtic: ewin (Wel); ionga (Iri)

Italic: ungula, ungulātus, unguis (Lat); ongle, ongulé (Fr); unghia, ungulato, unghiato (Ital); uña, ungulado (Sp); unha, ungulado (Port); unghie (Rom)

Derivatives: ungulate, ungual, ungular (Eng)

Hellenic: ὄνυξ (ónux), σαρδόνυξ (sardónux) (AnGk); νύχι (nýchi) (Gk)

Derivatives: onyx, onychite, onychomancy (divination using fingernails), onychopathy (disease of the fingernails), onychophagy (habit of biting one's nails), onychophorous (having claws), hapalonychia, mesonychid, sardonyx (Eng); sardonyx (Lat); sardonice (Ital); ónix (Port); оникс (óniks) (Rus)

Slavic: ноготь (nógot'), нога́ (nogá) (Rus); paznokieć, noga (Pol); nehet, noha (Cz); necht, noha (Slo); нокт (nokt), нога́ (nogá) (Mace)

Baltic: nagas, naga (Lith); nags (Latv)

Albanian: nyell (**Alb**)

Indo-Iranian: नख (nakhá) (**Sans**); नख (nakh), नाखुन (nāxun) (**Hin**); نک (nuk) (**Pash**); ناخن (nâxon) (**Pers**)

*méh₂-r̥

hand

Germanic: mound, mund (**Eng**); mund (**OE**); mond (**Dut**); Mund, Munt, Mündel, Vormund (**Ger**); mund (**Norse**); mund (**Ice**)

Italic: manus, āmanuēnsis, adminiculum, emancipare (+capere), manātus, manicula, mantica, manuālis, manuārius, manuātus, manubiālis, manūbrium, manūmittere, mastubor (**Lat**); main, manière (**Fr**); mano, mantice, mannaia, manubrio (**Ital**); mano, adminículo, manilla, manija, manera, manada, manubrio, manumitir (**Sp**); mão, adminículo, manilha, manícula, mangual, maneiro, maneira, manuário, manubial (**Port**); mână, amnar, mâner (**Rom**)

Derivatives: amanuensis, bimanous, emancipate, manatee, manacle, manage, manager, managerial, manageable, management, manner, manoeuvre/maneuver (+opus), manure, manicure, manual, manubial, manubrium, manumission, manumit, manuscript, masturbate (**Eng**)

manus is a popular compound, so a number of such compounds appear under other roots: mandāre, commendāre, dēmandāre, appear under *deH₃-, manifestus under *gʷʰen-, manipulus under *pleh₁- to fill, mansuescere under *swe-dʰh₁-, manūtenēre under *ten-

Hellenic: μάρη (márē) (**AnGk**)

Torso & Organs

*h₁owHdʰr̥-

udder

Germanic: udder (**Eng**); ūder (**OE**); jaar (**Fris**); uier (**Dut**); Euter (**Ger**); jūgr (**Norse**); jur (**Nor**); juver (**Swe**); yver (**Dan**); júgur (**Ice**)

Celtic: úth (**Iri**)

Italic: ūber, ūberāre, exūberāre (**Lat**); ubere, ubero (**Ital**); ubre (**Sp**); úbere, uberar (**Port**); uger (**Rom**)

Derivatives: uberous, exuberate, exuberance (**Eng**)

Hellenic: οὖθαρ (oûthar) (**AnGk**)

Slavic: вымя (výmja) (**Rus**); wymię (**Pol**); vemeno (**Cz**); vemä (**Slo**); виме (vime) (**Mace**)

Baltic: ūdroti (**Lith**)

Indo-Iranian: ऊधर् (ūdhar) (**Sans**)

*h₃enbʰ-
navel, hub

*h₃nēbʰ-o-, *h₃nobʰ-yom, *h₃nobʰ-is, *h₃nobʰ-eh₂, *h₃m̥bʰ-l-os, *h₃m̥bʰ-Vl-īkos, *h₃m̥bʰ-el-yō, *h₃nobʰ-(V?)l-ō

Germanic: navel, nave (**Eng**); nafela, nafu (**OE**); nâle (**Fris**); navel, naaf (**Dut**); Nabel, Nabe (**Ger**); nafli, nǫf (**Norse**); navle (**Nor**); nav, navel (**Swe**); navle (**Dan**); nafli (**Ice**)

Celtic: imleac (**Iri**)

Italic: umbilicus (**Lat**); nombril, ombilic (**Fr**); ombelico (**Ital**); ombligo (**Sp**); umbigo (**Port**); buric, ombilic (**Rom**)

Derivatives: umbilicus, umbilical (**Eng**)

Hellenic: ὀμφαλός (omphalós) (**AnGk**); ομφαλός (omfalós) (**Gk**)

Derivatives: omphalic, amphalectomy (**Eng**)

Baltic: naba (**Latv**)

Indo-Iranian: नाभि (nābhi), नभ्य (nábhya) (**Sans**); नाभिक (nābhik), नाभिकीय (nābhikīya) (**Hin**); ناف (nāf) (**Pers**)

*ḱḗr
heart

Germanic: heart (**Eng**); heorte (**OE**); hert (**Fris**); hart (**Dut**); Herz (**Ger**); hjarta (**Norse**); hjerte, hjarta, hjarte (**Nor**); hjärta (**Swe**); hjerte (**Dan**); hjarta (**Ice**)

Celtic: craidd (**Wel**); croí, croidhe (**Iri**)

Italic: cor, cordis, concordāre, discordāre, misericors, recordor, recordābilis (**Lat**); cœur, accorder, accorde, recorder, courage (**Fr**); cuore, accordare, accordo, ricordare, ricordabile, coraggio (**Ital**); cuerdo, acordar, acuerda, recordar, corazón, corage (**Sp**); cor, acordar, acordo, recordar (**Port**); cor, cord, acorda, acord (**Rom**)

Derivatives: accord, discord, concord, concordant, cordial, core, courage, discourage, encourage, record, misericord (**Eng**)

Hellenic: καρδιά (kardiá), κῆρ (kêr) (**AnGk**); καρδιά (kardiá) (**Gk**)

Derivatives: cardiac, cardiology (**Eng**)

Slavic: сердце (sérdce) (**Rus**); serce, środa (Wednesday - heart of the week) (**Pol**); srdce, středa (**Cz**); srdce, streda (**Slo**); срце (srce) (**Mace**)

Baltic: širdis (**Lith**); sirds (**Latv**)

Indo-Iranian: हृदय (hṛdaya), हृद् (hṛd) (**Sans**); हृदय (hṛday), हिया (hiyā), दिल (dil) (**Hin**); ژرہ (zrrə) (**Pash**); دل (del) (**Pers**)

*plewmō
lung

Italic: pulmō (**Lat**); poumon (**Fr**); pulmón (**Sp**); pulmão (**Port**); polmone (**Ital**); plămân, pulmon (**Rom**)

Derivatives: pulmonary (**Eng**)

Hellenic: πλεύμων (pleúmōn) (**AnGk**)

Slavic: płuco (**Pol**); plíce (**Cz**); pľúca (**Slo**)

Baltic: plaučiai (**Lith**); plaušas (**Latv**)

Indo-Iranian: क्लोमन् (klóman) (**Sans**)

which derives from *plew- to flow:

*plew-
to fly, flow, run

*plew-d-, *plew-k-, *plów-yos, *plowtós, *plew-t-, *plewt-yom, *pléw-e-ti, *plow-éye-ti, *pléw-mō, plow-mos, *plow-ó-s, *plu-to-s

Germanic: fleet, float, fly, fly (insect), flee, flight, flit, flow, flood (**Eng**); flēotan, flotian, flēogan, flēoge, flēon, flyht, flōwan, flōd (**OE**);

flotsje, fleane, flecht, flojen, floed (**Fris**); vlieten, vlotten, vlot, vliegen, vlieg, vlieden, vlucht, vloeien, vloed, vleugel (**Dut**); fließen, floaten, fliegen, Fliege, fliehen, Flucht, Flut, Flügel, Flotte (**Ger**);

fljóta, flytja, flota, flot, flýja, fljúga, flaumr, fleygja, fluga, flóðr, flóð, fley, floti (**Norse**); flytja, flytte, flote, flyve, fliuga, fljuge, fly, flom, flue, flod, flåte (**Nor**); flyta, flytta, flyga, fly, flygt, flygtur, flykt, flöja, fluga, flod, flotte, flotta (**Swe**); flyde, flytte, flyve, fly, flygt, flue, flod, flåde (**Dan**); fljóta, flytja, flota, flýja, fljúga, fleygja, fluga, flóa, flóð, fley, floti (**Ice**)

Derivatives: flotter, flot, flotte (**Fr**); flottare, flotta (**Ital**); flotar (**Sp**)

Italic: plaustrum, pluit, pluvius, pluvia, pluviālis, pluviōsus (**Lat**); pluie, pluvial, pluvieux, pluviôse, pleuvoir (**Fr**); pioggia, piova, pluviale, piovoso, pioggioso, piovere (**Ital**); lluvia, pluvial, lluvioso, pluvioso, llover (**Sp**); chuva, chuiva, pluvial, chuvoso, pluvioso, chover (**Port**); ploaie, ploios, ploua (**Rom**)

Derivatives: pluvial, pluvious (**Eng**)

Hellenic: πλέω (pléō), περῐ́πλους (períplous), πλοῖον (ploîon), πλύνω (plúnō), πλοῖον (ploîon), πλοῦτος (ploûtos), πλουτοκρᾰτῐ́ᾱ (ploutokratíā), πλόος (plóos) (**AnGk**); πλέω (pléo), πλοίο (ploío), πλοῦτος (ploûtos), πλουτοκρατία (ploutokratía) (**Gk**)

Derivatives: pleon, pleopod, pleuston, plutocracy (**Eng**); périple (**Fr**); плутокра́тия (plutokrátija) (**Rus**)

Slavic: плыть (plyt′), плов (plov), плот (plot) (**Rus**); pławić, płynąć, pływać, płyn, płet (**Pol**); plyn, plynout, plavat, plet′ (**Cz**); plyn, plynúť, plávať, pleť (**Slo**); плива (pliva) (**Mace**)

Baltic: plūsti, plaũtis, plaũkti, pìlti, pláuti, pláju (**Lith**); plàuši, pluts (**Latv**)

Indo-Iranian: प्लु (plu), प्लुत (pluta), प्लवते (plávate), प्लावयति (plāvayati), प्लव (plavá) (**Sans**)

but the English lung comes from a different root:

*lengʷʰ-

not heavy, agile, nimble

Germanic: lung (**Eng**); lungen (**OE**); longe, long (**Fris**); long (**Dut**); Lunge, Lungel (**Ger**); lunge (**Nor**); lunga (**Swe**); lunge (**Dan**); lunga (**Ice**)

Hellenic: ἐλαφρός (elaphrós) (**AnGk**); ελαφρός (elafrós) (**Gk**)

Albanian: lungë (uncert.) (**Alb**)

but this etymology is confused with *$h_1$lengʷʰ- light-weight (perhaps it should simply be considered as part of it):

*$h_1$lengʷʰ-

light (in weight)

*$h_1$léngʷʰ-e-ti, *h_1lŋgʷʰ-ró-s, *$h_1$lengʷʰ-to-s, *$h_1$léngʰ-u-s, *$h_1$léngʷʰ-isth$_2$-o-s, *$h_1$léngʷʰ-yōs

Germanic: light (**Eng**); lēoht (**OE**); licht (**Fris**); licht (**Dut**); leicht, lingen, gelingen (**Ger**); léttr (**Norse**); lett (**Nor**); lätt (**Swe**); let (**Dan**); léttur (**Ice**)

Celtic: ling (uncert.) (**Iri**)

Italic: levis, levitās, levāre, allevāre, ēlevāre, relevāre, sublevāre, levātus (**Lat**); liège, léger, lever, élever, relever, soulever, levé (**Fr**);

lieve, leggero, levare, allevare, elevare, rilevare, sollevare, levato, lievito (**Ital**);

leve, lieve, ligero, liviano, llevar, levantar, elevar, relevar, relvar, ralbar, solevar, sublevar, llevado, leudo (**Sp**);

leve, ligeiro, levar, levantar, elevar, relevar, relvar, sublevar, levado, lêvedo (**Port**);

uşor, lejer, lua, luare, eleva, releva, luat (**Rom**)

Derivatives: leverage, leaven, Levant, levee, lever, levitate, levity, lev, relief, bas-relief, relieve, alleviate, elevate, relevate (**Eng**)

Hellenic: ἐλαχύς (elakhús), ἐλαφρός (elaphrós), ἐλᾰχιστος (elákhistos), ἐλάσσων (elássōn) (**AnGk**); ελαφρός (elafrós) (**Gk**)

Slavic: лёгкий (ljóxkij), лёгкое (ljóxkoje), легкий (legkiy) (**Rus**); lekki (**Pol**); lehký (**Cz**); ľahký (**Slo**) лек (lek) (**Mace**)

Baltic: leñgvas, lengvùs, lengvas, lankstus, langas, lenkti (**Lith**); liêgs (**Latv**)

Albanian: lehtë (**Alb**)

Indo-Iranian: रंहति (rámhati), रंहते (rámhate), रघु (raghú), लघु (laghu), लघिष्ठ (laghiṣṭha), लघीयस् (lághīyas) (**Sans**)

*Hyékʷr̥
liver

Italic: iecur, iecorīnus (**Lat**)

Derivatives: jecorine (**Eng**)

Hellenic: ἧπαρ (hêpar), ἡπᾰτίζων (hēpatízōn) (**AnGk**); ήπαρ (ípar) (**Gk**)

Derivatives: hepato-, hepar, hepatic, hepatitis, hepatizon (**Eng**); hēpar, hēpaticus, hēpatītis, hēpatizon (**Lat**); hepático, hepatitis (**Sp**)

Slavic: џигер (džiger) (**Mace**)

Baltic: jeknos (**Lith**); aknas (**Latv**)

Indo-Iranian: यकृत् (yákṛt) (**Sans**); جگر (dzigar) (**Pash**); جگر (jegar) (**Pers**)

but the English word for liver comes from elsewhere, perhaps from *leyp fatty, sticky:

*leyp-
to stick; fat or sticky substance

Germanic: leave, beleave (obs.), liver (**Eng**); lǣfan, belīfan, lifer (**OE**); bliuwe, lever (**Fris**); blij, blijven, bleven, lever (**Dut**); bleiben, Leber (**Ger**); leifa, lifr (**Norse**); blive, bli,

48

lever (**Nor**); bliva, bli, lever (**Swe**); blive, lever (**Dan**); leifa, blífa, lifur (**Ice**)

Hellenic: λίπος (lípos) (**AnGk**); λίπος (lípos) (**Gk**)

Derivatives: lipolysis, lipoprotein, liposuction (**Eng**)

Slavic: лепи́ть (lepít'), леплю́ (lepljú) (**Rus**); lepić (**Pol**); lepit (**Cz**); lepit' (**Slo**); лепи (lepi) (**Mace**)

Baltic: lipìnti, láipioti (**Lith**); lipt, laipns (**Latv**)

Indo-Iranian: लिम्पति (limpati), लेप (lepa), लेपयति (lepayati) (**Sans**)

*splenǵʰ-
spleen

Hellenic: σπλήν (splén) (**AnGk**)

Derivatives: spleen, splenetic (**Eng**); liēn, splēn, spleneticus (**Lat**); spleen, splénétique (**Fr**); splenetico (**Ital**); esplene, esplenético (**Sp**); esplenético (**Port**); splină (**Rom**); splin (**Cz**); liesa, splïns (**Latv**)

Slavic: селезёнка (selezjónka) (**Rus**); śledziona (**Pol**); slezina (**Cz**); slezina (**Slo**); слезина (slezina) (**Mace**)

Baltic: blužnis (**Lith**)

Indo-Iranian: प्लिहन् (plihan) (**Sans**)

*negʷh-r-
kidney

Germanic: kidney (origin of kid- uncert.) (**Eng**); nēora (**OE**); nier (**Fris**); nier (**Dut**); Niere (**Ger**); nyre (**Nor**); njure (**Swe**); nyre (**Dan**); nýra (**Ice**)

Hellenic: νεφρός (nephrós) (**AnGk**); νεφρό (nefró) (**Gk**)

Derivatives: nephro-, nephrotic, nephrology, nephritis (**Eng**)

Slavic: nerka (**Pol**)

Baltic: niere (**Latv**)

*ǵʰern-
bowels

*ǵʰór-neh₂, *ǵʰer-n-yo-

Germanic: yarn (**Eng**); gearn (**OE**); jern (**Fris**); garen (**Dut**); Garn (**Ger**); garn, gǫrn (**Norse**); garn (**Nor**); garn (**Swe**); garn (**Dan**); garn, görn (**Ice**)

Italic: hernia, hīra, hariolus, haruspex (**Lat**); hernie (**Fr**); ernia, aruspice (**Ital**); hernia, hariolo, haríolo, harúspice (**Sp**); hérnia, haríolo, aríolo (**Port**); hernie (**Rom**)

Derivatives: hernia, herniated, haruspex (**Eng**); Haruspex (**Ger**)

Hellenic: χορδή (khordέ) (**AnGk**); χορδή (chordí) (**Gk**)

Derivatives: chord, cord, whipcord (**Eng**); koord, koorde (**Dut**); chorda (**Lat**); corde (**Fr**); corda (**Ital**); cuerda (**Sp**); corda (**Port**); coardă (**Rom**); хόрда (xόrda) (**Rus**)

Baltic: žarna (**Lith**); zarna (**Latv**)

Indo-Iranian: हिर (híra) (**Sans**)

*lendʰ-
loins

Germanic: lend (meaning loins) (dial.) (**Eng**); lenden (**OE**); lende, lendenen (**Dut**); Lende, Lenden (**Ger**); lend (**Norse**); länd, länder (**Swe**); lænder (**Dan**); lendar (**Ice**)

Italic: lumbus (**Lat**); lombes (**Fr**); lombo (**Ital**); lomos (**Sp**); lombo (**Port**)

Derivatives: loin, lumbar, lumbago (**Eng**); llwyn (**Wel**)

Slavic: лядвея (ljádveja) (**Rus**); lędźwia (**Pol**); ledvi, ledvina (**Cz**); l'advina (**Slo**)

Indo-Iranian: रन्ध्र (rándhra) (**Sans**); रंध्र (randhra) (**Hin**)

Internal components

*h₃ésth₁
bone

Celtic: asgwrn, ais, asen (**Wel**); easna (**Iri**)

Italic: os (**Lat**); os (**Fr**); osso (**Ital**); hueso (**Sp**); osso (**Port**); os (**Rom**)

Derivatives: ossify, ossification (**Eng**)

Hellenic: ὀστέον (ostéon) (**AnGk**); οστό (ostó) (**Gk**)

Derivatives: osteoporosis, osteopath, dysostosis, exostosis, osteoblast, osteology, periosteum, synostosis (**Eng**)

Albanian: asht, ahstë (**Alb**)

Indo-Iranian: अस्थि (ásthi) (**Sans**); अस्थि (ásthi) (**Hin**); است (ast) (rare), استخوان (ostoxân) (**Pers**)

*h₁ésh₂r̥

blood

Germanic: iron (**Eng**); īsen, īren (**OE**); izer (**Fris**); ijzer (**Dut**); Eisen, Eiser (**Ger**); ísarn, járn, jarn (**Norse**); jern, jarn (**Nor**); järn (**Swe**); jern, jærn (**Dan**); járn (**Ice**)

Celtic: haearn (**Wel**); iarann (**Iri**)

Italic: sanguis, exsanguis, sanguinārius, sanguineus, sanguināre, sanguinolentus, sanguinōsus (**Lat**);

sang, exsangue, sanguinaire, sanguin, saigner, sanguinolent (**Fr**);

sangue, esangue, sanguinario, sanguigno, sanguineo, sanguinare, sanguinolento, sanguinoso (**Ital**);

sangre, sanguinario, sangonera, sangüeño, sanguíneo, sangrar, sanguinolento, sanguinoso (**Sp**);

sangue, sanguinho, sanguineo, sangrar, sanguinoso (**Port**); sânge, sânger, sângera, sângerare, sângeros (**Rom**)

Derivatives: exsanguine, sanguinary, sanguine, sanguineous, sanguinolent, sanguinous, consanguinity (**Eng**)

Hellenic: ἔαρ (éar) (**AnGk**); ἔαρ (éar) (**Gk**)

Baltic: asinis (**Latv**)

Indo-Iranian: असृज् (asṛj) (**Sans**)

*krewh₂-

raw meat, fresh blood

*kréwh₂-s, *kréwh₂-s, *kruh₂-ró-s

Germanic: raw (**Eng**); hrēaw (**OE**); rau (**Fris**); rauw, reeuw (**Dut**); roh (**Ger**); hrár, hræ (**Norse**); rå (**Nor**); rå (**Swe**); rå (**Dan**); hrár, hræ (**Ice**)

Celtic: crau (**Wel**); cró (**Iri**)

Italic: crūdus, crūdēlis, crūdēlitās, crūditās, cruor, cruentus (**Lat**); cru, cruauté, cruel, cruelle, crudité, cruor (**Fr**); crudo, crudele, crudeltà, crudità, cruento, cruentare (**Ital**); crudo, cruel, crueldad, crúor, cruento, cruentar (**Sp**); cru, cruel, crueldade, cruor, cruento, cruentar (**Port**); crud, cruditate, crudătate, crunt, crunta, încrunta, încruntare (**Rom**)

Derivatives: crude, crudity, cruel, cruelty, cruor (**Eng**)

Hellenic: κρέας (kréas), κρούω (kroúō) (**AnGk**); κρέας (kréas) (**Gk**)

Derivatives: creosote, pancreas (**Eng**)

Slavic: кровь (krov') (**Rus**); krew (**Pol**); krev (**Cz**); krv (**Slo**); крв (krv) (**Mace**)

Baltic: kraujas (**Lith**)

Indo-Iranian: क्रव्य (kravyá) (**Sans**)

*mḗms

meat, flesh

*mḗms-ro-m

Italic: membrum, membrāna, membrānāceus, membrāneus (**Lat**); membre, membrane, membraneux (**Fr**); membro, membrana, membranaceo (**Ital**); miembro, membrana, membranáceo, membranoso (**Sp**); membro, membrana (**Port**); membru (**Rom**)

Derivatives: member (as part of body, especially genital), membrane, membranaceous, membranous (**Eng**); мембрана (membrana) (**Rus**)

Slavic: мясо (mjáso) (**Rus**); mięso (**Pol**); maso (**Cz**); mäso (**Slo**); месо (meso) (**Mace**)

Baltic: mėsa (**Lith**); miesa (**Latv**)

Albanian: mish (**Alb**)

Indo-Iranian: मांस (māṃsa), मांसम् (māṃsam), मांस् (māṃs) (**Sans**); मांस (māns) (**Hin**)

*mosgʰos

marrow, brain

Germanic: marrow (**Eng**); mearg (**OE**); moarch (**Fris**); merg (**Dut**); Mark (**Ger**); mergr (**Norse**); marg (**Nor**); märg (**Swe**); marv (**Dan**); mergur (**Ice**)

Celtic: meidd, mêr (**Wel**); meadhg, smior (**Iri**)

Slavic: мозг (mozg) (**Rus**); mózg (**Pol**); mozek (**Cz**); mozog (**Slo**); мозок (mozok) (**Mace**)

Baltic: mazgas, smēgenys (**Lith**); mezgls (**Latv**)

Indo-Iranian: मज्जन् (majján) (**Sans**); (maazghë) (**Pash**); مغز (maǧz) (**Pers**)

Bodily functions

*sweyd-
sweat, to sweat

*swéyd-e-ti, *swid-yé-ti, *swoyd-éye-ti, *swéyd-os, *swéyd-ŗ, *swid-tós, *swoyd-o-

Germanic: sweat (**Eng**); swǣtan (**OE**); swit (**Fris**); zweet (**Dut**); Schweiss, schwitzen (**Ger**); sveiti (**Norse**); svette (**Nor**); svett (**Swe**); sved (**Dan**); sveiti, sviti (**Ice**)

Celtic: chwys (**Wel**)

Italic: sūdor, sūdāre, sūdārium (**Lat**); sueur, suer, suaire (**Fr**); sudore, sudare, sudario (**Ital**); sudor, sudar, sudario (**Sp**); suor, suar, sudário (**Port**); sudoare, asuda, asudare (**Rom**)

Derivatives: exude, exudate, sudarium (**Eng**)

Hellenic: ἱδρώς (hidrṓs) (**AnGk**)

Derivatives: hidrosis, hidrotic (**Eng**)

Baltic: sviêdri (**Latv**)

Albanian: djersë (**Alb**)

Indo-Iranian: स्वेदते (svedate), स्वेदयति (svedáyati), स्वेद (svéda), स्विद्यति (svidyati) (**Sans**); (khwala) (**Pash**); خوی (xway) (arch.) (**Pers**)

*leb-
to hang loosely, lip, lick

*lh₂b-, *lh₂-né-b(ʰ)-, *lh₂b-el-os

Germanic: lip, lap, sleep (**Eng**); lippa, lapian, slǣp, slǣpan (**OE**); lippe, leppel, sliep, sliepe (**Fris**); lip, lepel, slaap, slapen (**Dut**); Lippe, Lefze, Löffel, Schlaf, schlafen (**Ger**); lepja (**Norse**); leppe (**Nor**); läpp (**Swe**); læbe, labe, leffe (**Dan**); lepja (**Ice**)

Derivatives: lippe, lévre, lamper (**Fr**)

Celtic: llefaru (**Wel**); liopa (**Iri**)

Italic: labĭum, lābrum, lambō, labāre (**Lat**); llabio, labbro, lambire, lambere (**Ital**); labio, labro, lamber, lamer (**Sp**); lábio, labro, lamber (**Port**)

Derivatives: labium, labrum, labial, labia (**Eng**)

Hellenic: λοβός (lobós) (uncert.), λάπτω (láptō), λαφύσσω (laphússō) (**AnGk**)

Slavic: лобзать (lobzát'), лопать (lópat'), слабый (slábyj) (**Rus**); słaby (**Pol**); slabý

(**Cz**); slabý (**Slo**); слаб (slab) (**Mace**)

Baltic: lūpa, lapènti, slōbti (**Lith**); lūpa (**Latv**)

Albanian: lap, lëpij (**Alb**)

Indo-Iranian: لب (lab) (**Pers**)

*swep-
to sleep

*swép-e-ti, *swop-éye-ti, *swép-no-s, *swop-no-s, *sup-no-s

Germanic: asweve, sweb, sweven (arch.) (**Eng**); swefan, swebban, swefn (**OE**); sofa, svefja, svefn (**Norse**); sove, svevn (**Nor**); sova, sömn (**Swe**); sove, søvn (**Dan**); sofa, svefja, svefn (**Ice**)

Celtic: suan (**Iri**)

Italic: sōpīre, somnus, somniātor, somnium, somniculōsus, somnifer, somniāre, somnulentus, sopor, sopōrifer (**Lat**); sommeil, somme, somnifère, songer, songe (**Fr**); sognatore, sonnifero, sonno, sonnacchioso, sognare, sogno, sopore (**Ital**); soñador, sueño, soñar, sopor (**Sp**); sonhador, sono, soniculoso, sonhar, sonho (**Port**); somn, somnifer (**Rom**)

Derivatives: somniculous, somniferous, somnolent, insomnia, somnambulist, somnifacient, somnific, somniloquy, somnial, sopor, soporific (**Eng**)

Hellenic: ὕπνος (húpnos) (**AnGk**); ύπνος (ýpnos) (**Gk**)

Derivatives: hypnosis, hypnotic, hypnagogia, hynolepsy, hypnophobia, hypnopompia, hypnotherapy, hypnotist, hypnotize (**Eng**); гипноз (gipnóz) (**Rus**)

Slavic: сон (son), спать (spat') (**Rus**); sen, spać (**Pol**); sen, spát, (**Cz**); sen, spat' (**Slo**); сон (son), спие (spie) (**Mace**)

Baltic: săpnas (**Lith**); sapnis (**Latv**) dream

Albanian: gjumë (**Alb**)

Indo-Iranian: स्वप्न (svápna), स्वपिति (svapiti) (**Sans**); स्वप्न (svapn), षुसि (ṣupti) (**Hin**); خواب (xâb) (**Pers**)

*kʷyeh₁-
to rest, rest, peace

*kʷyeh₁-, *kʷih₁-yé-ti, *kʷyeh₁-sḱe-, *kʷyéh₁-ti-s, *kʷyeh₁-to-s, *kʷih₁-l-os, *kʷih₁-l-éh₂, *kʷoyh₁-o-, *sm̥-kʷih₁-

Germanic: while (**Eng**); hwīl (**OE**); wile (**Fris**); wijl (**Dut**); Weile (**Ger**); hvila (**Norse**); hvile (**Nor**); vila (**Swe**); hvile (**Dan**); hvila (**Ice**)

Derivatives: chwila (**Pol**); chvíľa (**Slo**)

Italic: quiēscere, acquiēscere, quiēs, quiētus, requiēs, tranquillus (**Lat**); acquiescer, coi, quiet, quitte, tranquille (**Fr**); quiescenza, cheto, quieto, tranquillo (**Ital**); quedo, quieto, tranquilo (**Sp**); aquiescer, quedo, quieto, réquie, requiem, réquia, tranquilo (**Port**); încet, cet (**Rom**)

Derivatives: quiet, quiesce, quiescent, acquiesce, acquiescent, coy, quit, acquit, acquittal, inquietude, requiem, requiescat, tranquil (**Eng**); kwijt (**Dut**)

Slavic: почи́ть (počít'), поко́й (pokój) (**Rus**); pokój (**Pol**); pokoj (**Cz**); pokoj (**Slo**); покоj (pokoj), спокоj (spokoj) (**Mace**)

Indo-Iranian: شاد (šâd) (**Pers**)

*bʰewdʰ-
to be awake, be aware

*bʰéwdʰ-e-ti, *bʰu-né-dʰ-ti, *bʰe-bʰówdʰ-e, *bʰudʰ-yé-tor, *bʰudʰ-éh₁ye-ti, *bʰowdʰ-éye-ti, *bʰowdʰ-os, *bʰéwdʰ-ti-s, *bʰudʰ-o-, *bʰudʰ-tó-s, *bʰudʰ-ró-s

Germanic: bid, bede, bysen, bode (**Eng**); bēodan, bȳsen, bod (**OE**); biede (**Fris**); bieden, bod, bode (**Dut**); bieten, Bote (**Ger**); bjóða, býsn, boð, boða (**Norse**); by, byde, bisn, bud (**Nor**); bjuda, bud, båda (**Swe**); byde, bud (**Dan**); bjóða, býsn, boð, boða (**Ice**)

Celtic: rhybudd, bodd (**Wel**)

Hellenic: πεύθομαι (peúthomai), πυνθάνομαι (punthánomai), πέπυσμαι (pépusmai), πῠστῐς (pústis) (**AnGk**)

Slavic: блюсти́ (bljustí), бдеть (bdet'), бо́дрый (bódryj), бо́дрой (bódroj), бо́дер (bóder), снабди́ть (snabdit'), буди́ть (budít') (**Rus**); budzić (**Pol**); bdít, snábděti, budit, bodrý (**Cz**); bdieť, budiť, bodrý (**Slo**); бдее (bdee), бодар (bodar), снабдува (snabduva), буди (budi) (**Mace**)

Baltic: budéti, báudyti, bùsti, budrùs (**Lith**); bàudît, bust (**Latv**)

Indo-Iranian: बोधति (bódhati), बुद्ध (buddha), बोधयति (bodháyati), बुध्यते (budhyátē), बोध (bodhá), बुद्धि (buddhi) (**Sans**); بيدار (bīdār) (**Pers**)

*weǵ-
lively, awake, strong

*woǵ-, *woǵ-éye-, *weǵ-eh₁-(ye)-, *weǵ-eli-, *woǵ-ros

Germanic: wake, waker, watch (**Eng**); wacan, waccor, wæċċan (**OE**);

wekker, wacht, wachtje, wachtsje (**Fris**); wakker, wekken, wacht, wachten (**Dut**); wacker, wecken, Wacht, Wächter (**Ger**);

vakinn, vakr, vekja, vakta (**Norse**); vaken, vakt (**Nor**); vaken, vacker, väcka, vakt, vakta (**Swe**); vågen, vække, vagt (**Dan**); vakinn, vakur, vekja, vakta (**Ice**)

Derivatives: sguattero, guatare (**Ital**); вахта (vaxta) (**Rus**)

Italic: vegēre, vegetus, vegetāre, vegetābilis, vegetātiō, vigēre, vigil, vigilia, vigilāre, ēvigilāre, invigilāre, pervigilāre, vigilāns, vigilantia, vigor (**Lat**);

végétation, vigile, veille, veiller, éveiller, vigilant, vigilance, vigueur (**Fr**);

vegeto, vegetabile, vegetazione, vigile, veglia, vegliare, vegghiare, vigilare, svegliare, invigilare, vigilante, vigilanza (**Ital**);

vegetación, vigilia, velar, vigilar, desvelar, invigilar, vigilante, vigilancia, vigor (**Sp**);

végeto, vegetar, vegetação, vígil, vigília, velar, vigiar, vigilar, vigilante, vigilância (**Port**);

vigil, veghe, veghea, veghere, înveghea, priveghea, priveghere, vigilență (**Rom**)

Derivatives: vegete, vegetous, vegetable, vegetation, vigil, vigilant, invigilate, vigilance, vigor/vigour (**Eng**); vegetation (**Swe**); gŵyl (**Wel**); feighil, féile (**Iri**)

Indo-Iranian: वाज (vāja), वाजयति (vājáyati) (**Sans**)

*h₂enh₁-
to breathe

*h₂énh₁-ti, *h₂enh₁-mo-s, *h₂énh₁mn̥, *h₂enh₁-slo-s, *h₂enh₁-ǵʰ-

Germanic: ande, onde, and (dial.) (**Eng**); ande, onde, and, andian (**OE**); Omme (**Fris**); ande, adem (**Dut**); Ahnd, And, ahnden (**Ger**); anda, andi, ǫnd, angi (**Norse**); ånde (**Nor**); anda, ande, andas (**Swe**); ånde, ånd, ange (**Dan**); anda, andi (**Ice**)

Celtic: anadi, eneid (**Wel**); anam, ainmhi, anáil (**Iri**)

Italic: animus, anima, animō, animosus, anhēlus, anhēlāre, anhēlitus, hālāre (poss.), exhālāre, inhālāre (**Lat**); âme, animer, anhéler, exhaler, inhaler (**Fr**); alma, anima, animare, anelare, esalare, inalare (**Ital**); alma, ánima, animar, anhelar, aliento, exhalar, inhalar (**Sp**); alma, anima, alento, anélito, inalar (**Port**); inimă (**Rom**)

Derivatives: animal, animate, animation, anima, animism, animosity, animus, exhale, inhale (**Eng**); animieren (**Ger**)

Hellenic: ἄνεμος (ánemos) (**AnGk**); ἄνεμος (ánemos) (**Gk**)

Derivatives: anemometer, anemone (windflower) (**Eng**)

Perhaps: **Slavic**: вонь (von') (**Rus**); woń (**Pol**); vůně (**Cz**); vôňa (**Slo**)

Albanian: ëndë (**Alb**)

Indo-Iranian: अनिति (ániti), अनिल (ánila) (uncert.) (**Sans**)

*h₃meyǵʰ-
to urinate

*h₃méyǵʰ-e-ti, *h₃meyǵʰ-ye-ti, *h₃mi-ne-ǵʰ-, *h₃meyǵʰ-s-tus, *h₃moyǵʰos

Germanic: mīgan (**OE**); mige (**Fris**); mijgen, miegen, mest (prob.) (**Dut**); Mist (prob.) (**Ger**); míga (**Norse**); miga (**Swe**); mige (**Dan**); míga (**Ice**)

Italic: mēiere, mingere (**Lat**); mingere (**Ital**); mear, minger (**Sp**); mijar (**Port**)

Derivatives: micturate (**Eng**)

Hellenic: ὀμείχω (omeíkhō) (**AnGk**)

Baltic: mýžti (**Lith**); mīzt (**Latv**)

Albanian: përmjerr (**Alb**)

Indo-Iranian: मेहति (méhati), मेह (meha) (**Sans**); میزدن (mēz-), میزیدن (mēzīdan), میختن (mēxtan) (**Pers**)

*h₁ed-
to eat

*h₁édti, *h₁od-éye-, *h₁ōd-e/o-, *h₁ēd-so-, *h₂eyeri-d-to-

Germanic: eat, etch, fret, fress, ovest (**Eng**); etan, ettan, ǣs, fretan, ofett, ofet (**OE**); ite, ettjen, eattjen, ies, aas, frette, oefte (**Fris**); eten, etten, etsen, aas, vreten, fretten, ooft (**Dut**); essen, ätzen, etzen, Aas, fressen, Obst (**Ger**); eta, jotunn, etja (**Norse**); ete, eta, jotun (**Nor**); äta, jätte, as (**Swe**); æde, jætte, ætse, ås (**Dan**); eta, éta, jötunn (**Ice**)

Italic: edō, ēsse, ēst, comedere, edibilis, ēsca, esculentus (**Lat**); esche (**Fr**); esca, esculento (**Ital**); comer, comida, esca, yesca, esculento (**Sp**); comer, comida, isca (**Port**); iască (**Rom**)

Derivatives: comestible, edacity, edible, obese, escarole, esculent, esurient, inedia, inescate (**Eng**); ίσκα (íska) (**Gk**); eshkë (**Alb**)

Hellenic: ἔδω (édō), ἄριστον (áriston) (**AnGk**)

Slavic: есть (jest') (**Rus**); jeść (**Pol**); jíst (**Cz**); jesť (**Slo**); јаде (jáde) (**Mace**)

Baltic: ėdmi, ėsti (**Lith**); ēst (**Latv**)

Indo-Iranian: अत्ति (átti), आदयति (ādáyati) (**Sans**)

*peh₃-
to drink

*pí-ph₃-e-ti, *péh₃-ti-s, *ph₃-tó-s, *péh₃-tlo-m

Celtic: yfed (**Wel**); ibh, ól (**Iri**)

Italic: pōtus, pōtāre, pōtiō, bibere, pōtābilis, bibāx, bibitor, bibulus, bibitus, posca, pōculum, exbibere, imbibere (**Lat**);

potion, poison, potable, boire, bibion, buveur, imbiber (**Fr**);

pozione, bere, bevace, bibace, bevitore, bibitore, bibulo, potabile, posca, imbevere (**Ital**);

poción, ponzoña, beber, bebedor, beodo, potable, posca, embeber (**Sp**);

poção, peçonha, púcaro, beber, bebedor, bêbedo, bêbado, potável, posca, embeber (**Port**);

poţiune, bea, bere, băutor, beat, zbea, îmbiba (**Rom**)

Derivatives: potion, poison, potable, beverage, bib, beer, bibulous, posca, imbibe (**Eng**)

Hellenic: πίνω (pínō), πόσις (pósis), πῖνον (pînon), κᾰτᾰπίνω (katapínō), σῠμπόσῐον (sumpósion), ποτήρῐον (potérion) (**AnGk**); πίνω (píno), καταπίνω (katapíno), ποτήρι (potíri) (**Gk**)

Derivatives: pinocytosis, symposium (**Eng**); symposium (**Lat**)

Slavic: пить (pit'), пиво (pívo), пойть (poít') (**Rus**); pić, piwo, poić, poję (**Pol**); pít, pivo, napojit, opojit (**Cz**); piť, pivo (**Slo**); пие (píe), пиво (pivo), пои (poi (**Mace**)

Baltic: puota (**Lith**)

Albanian: pi, pije (**Alb**)

Indo-Iranian: पिबति (píbati), पात्र (pâtra) (**Sans**); पीना (pīnā) (**Hin**)

*mendʰ-
to chew

see Body: Head

*dʰeh₁(y)-
to suckle, nurse

*dʰeh₁(y)-, *dʰoh₁(y)-éye-, *dʰeh₁(y)-m̥h₁n-éh₂, *dʰeh₁(y)-to-, *dʰeh₁(y)-tu-, *dʰeh₁(y)-no-, *dʰeh₁(y)-n-os, *dʰeh₁(y)-lu-, *dʰeh₁(y)-lew-ih₂, *dʰeh₁(y)-lw-ih₂-k-, *dʰeh₁(y)-li-o-, *dʰeh₁(y)-l-éh₂-ye-ti

Germanic: doe (**Eng**); dā (**OE**); dägga, dia, di (**Swe**); dægge, då, die (**Dan**)

Celtic: dynu (**Wel**); diul, diuilim (**Iri**)

Italic: fēmina, fēmella, fēminīnus, fētus, fētāre, fēnum, fēlīx, fēlīcitās, fīlius, filia, fīliālis, fīliaster, fīliolus, affiliare, fellāre (**Lat**);

femme, femelle, féminin, foetus, faon, félicité, fils, fille, filleul, affilier (**Fr**);

femmina, femminile, femminino, feto, felice, felicità, figlio, figlia, filiale, figliastro, figliolo (**Ital**);

hembra, fémina, femenino, feto, jedar, feliz, felicidad, hijo, hija, hijastro, hijuelo, ahijar (**Sp**);

fêmea, feminino, feto, feliz, felicidade, filho, filha, filhastro, filhó, afilhar (**Port**);

famen, femelă, făt, fată, făta, fătare, ferice, fiu, fie, fiastru (**Rom**)

Derivatives: female, feminine, fetus, fawn, felicity, Fitz-, filial, fellate, affiliation (**Eng**); feminin (**Swe**); thjeshtër (**Alb**)

Hellenic: θῆλυς (thêlus), θηλή (thēlḗ), θεῖος (theîos), τίτθη (títthē), τήθη (téthē), Τηθύς (Tēthús) (**AnGk**); θηλή (thilí), θείος (theíos) (**Gk**)

Derivatives: thius (**Lat**); zio (**Ital**); tío (**Sp**); tio (**Port**)

Slavic: дойть (doíť) (dial.), дитя́ (ditjá), дитё (ditjó), де́ва (déva), деви́ца (devíca) (**Rus**); doić (arch., dial.), dziecko, dziecię, dziwka, dziewka, dziewica (**Pol**); dojit, dítě, děva, děvice (**Cz**); dojiť, dieťa, deva, devica (**Slo**); дои (doi), дете (dete), девица (devica) (**Mace**)

Baltic: dėlė (**Lith**); dēls (**Latv**)

Albanian: djathë (**Alb**)

Indo-Iranian: धयति (dhayati) (**Sans**); دايه (dâye) (**Pers**)

*ǵenH₁-
to give birth, produce

*ǵénh₁-ti, *ǵn̥h₁-yé-tor, *ǵénh₁-ye-tor, *ǵí-ǵn̥h₁-e-ti, *ǵn̥h₁-ské-ti, *ǵonh₁-éh₂, *ǵénh₁-mn̥, *ǵónh₁-o-s, *ǵénh₁-os, *ǵénh₁-ti-s, *ǵn̥h₁-tó-s, *ǵénh₁-tōr, *ǵn̥h₁-yo-, *ǵn̥h₁-i-wo-, *ǵenh₁-tl-eh₂

Germanic: kin, king, kingdom, kind (meaning type) (**Eng**); cynn, cyning, cyningdōm, cynd, -cund (**OE**);

kinne, kenne, keuning, keuningdom (**Fris**); kunne, koning, koningdom, kind (**Dut**); Künne, Kunne, König, Königtum, Kind (**Ger**);

kyn, konungr, kongr, konungdómr, kind, -kundr (**Norse**); kjønn, konge, kongedømme (**Nor**); kön, konung, kung, kungadöme (**Swe**); køn, konning, konge, kong, kongedømme (**Dan**); kyn, konungur, kóngur, konungdómur, kind (**Ice**)

Celtic: geni (**Wel**); aigne, gin, giniúint (**Iri**)

Italic: gignere, genitus, genitīvus, prīmōgenitus, primogenito, (g)nāscī, nāscēns, nātālīcius, nātālis, nātīvus, nātīvitās, nātūra, nātūrālis, nātūrālitās, germen, germānus, germānitas, germināre, genus, generālis, generāre, congener, dēgener, dēgenerāre, ingenerāre, regenerāre, generōsus, nātiō, nātus, genitor, genetrīx, genius, naevus, gēns, gentīlicius, gentīlis, gentīlitās, ingēns (**Lat**);

naître, naitre, naissance, naissant, Noël, natal, naïf, natif, nativité, nature, germe, germain, germer, genre, général, générer, congénère, dégénérer, engendrer, régénérer, généreux, nation, né, géniteur, génie, gens, gentil (**Fr**);

nascere, nascente, natalizio, natale, Natale, nativo, natività, natura, naturalità, germe, germano, germinare, germogliare, genere, generale, generare, ingenerare, nazione, nato, genitore, genitrice, genio, neo, nevo, gente, gentile, gentilità, ingente (**Ital**);

primogénito, nacer, natalicio, natal, nadal, nativo, natividad, Navidad, natura, natural, naturalidad, germen, hermandad, germán, germano, hermano, mano, germinar, género, general, generar, degenerar, engendrar, nación, nada, nato, genitor, genio, nevus, gente, gentil, ingente (**Sp**);

gentio, genitivo, primogênito, nascer, natalício, natal, Natal, natividade, natura, natural, naturalidade, germe, germanidade, irmandade, germano, irmão, mano, germinar, gênero, geral, general, gerar, degenerar, engendrar, nação, nada, nado, nato, genitor, génio, nevo, gente, gentil, gentio (**Port**);

naşte, naştere, nativ, nativitate, natură, germen, germinar, gen, general, genera, naţiune, nat, geniu, neg, nev, gintă (**Rom**)

Derivatives: genitive, primogeniture, nascent, natal, Noel, native, naïve, nativity, nature, natural, germ, germane, germinate, germination, genus, generic, genre, generate, gender, congener, congenerous, ingenerate, engender, regenerate, generous, nation, national, genitor, genius, genie, naevus, nevus, gens, genticide, gentilicial, gentilicious, gentle, gentry, gentile, gentility (**Eng**);

genereren, natie, genie (**Dut**); Genus, generieren, regenerieren, Genie, Genius (**Ger**); genus (**Swe**);

Nadolig (**Wel**); Nollaig, géineas, náisiún (**Iri**);

натура (natura), нация (nacija) (**Rus**); natura (**Pol**); gjini, gjinde (**Alb**)

Hellenic: γείνομαι (geínomai), γίγνομαι (gígnomai), γόνος (gónos), γονή (goné), γένος (génos), γένεσις (génesis), γενέτωρ (genétōr), -γνητός (-gnētós), γνωτός (gnōtós) (**AnGk**); γένος (génos) (**Gk**)

Derivatives: gonad, epigone, trigony, genesis (**Eng**); genèse (**Fr**)

Slavic: зять (zjat'), князь (knjaz') (**Rus**); zięć, ksiądz, kśǫc, kšúnc (**Pol**); zeť, kněz, kníže (**Cz**); zať, kňaz (**Slo**); зет (zet) (**Mace**)

Derivatives: cneaz (**Rom**)

Baltic: kunigas, kuningas (**Lith**); ķēniņš (**Latv**)

Indo-Iranian: जनति (jánati), जायते (jā́yate), जनिमन् (jániman), जन (jána), जनस् (jánas), जाति (jāti), जात (jātá), जनितृ (janitṛ́) (**Sans**); زادن (zâdan), زاده (zāde), زند (zand) (**Pers**)

*h₂ewg-
to grow, increase

*h₂éwg-e-ti, *h₂ug-s-, *h₂owg-éye-ti, *h₂éwg-os, *h₂ewg-os-to-s, *h₂ug-ró-s

Germanic: eke, wax (to grow), waist (**Eng**); ēacan, weaxan, wast (**OE**); waakse (**Fris**); oken, wassen (**Dut**); wachsen (**Ger**); auka, vaxa, vǫxtr (**Norse**); øke, vaksa, vokse, veksa, vekse (**Nor**); öka, växa, växt (**Swe**); øge, vokse, væsket (**Dan**); auka, vaxa, vöxtur (**Ice**)

Celtic: uchel, gwair (poss.) (**Wel**); uasal, féar (**Iri**)

Italic: augēre, adaugēre, adauctus, auctiō, auctor, auctrīx, auctōritās, augmentum, augustus, auxilium, auxiliāris, auxiliārius, exaugēre, augur, augurāre, augurium, inaugurāre (**Lat**);

auteur, autorité, août, auxiliaire, augure, augurer, heur, inaugurer (**Fr**);

autore, autrice, autorità, agosto, ausilio, ausiliare, ausiliario, augure, augurare, agurare, augurio, inaugurare (**Ital**);

auger, autor, autoridad, agosto, auxilio, auxiliar, augur, augurar, agorar, agüero, augurio, inaugurar (**Sp**);

adauto, autoridade, agosto, auxiliar, áugure, augurar, agourar, agoiro, agouro, augúrio (**Port**);

adăuga, adăugare, august, agust, gust, gustar, augur, augura, agura (**Rom**)

Derivatives: auction, augment, augmentation, authority, august, August, auxiliary, auxiliar, exaggerate, augur, augury, inaugurate, inauguration (**Eng**);

augustus (**Fris**); augustus, oogst (**Dut**); August (**Ger**); august (**Nor**); augusti (**Swe**); august (**Dan**); ágúst (**Ice**); Awst (**Wel**);

Αύγουστος (Ávgoustos) (**Gk**); аукцио́н (aukción), а́вгуст (ávgust), авгу́р (avgúr) (**Rus**); august (**Slo**); augusts (**Latv**)

Hellenic: αὐξάνω (auxánō), αὔξω (aúxō) (**AnGk**)

Derivatives: auxanography, auxanometer, auxesis, auxin, auxology, auxotrophy (**Eng**)

Baltic: áugti, aūkštas, augestis (**Lith**); augt, augsts (**Latv**)

Indo-Iranian: उक्षति (ukṣati), ओजस् (ójas), उग्र (ugrá) (**Sans**); उग्र (ugra) (**Hin**); وخشیدن (vaxšīdan) (**Pers**)

*h₂el-

to grow, nourish

*h₂él-e-ti, *h₂ol-éye-ti, *h₂el-o-mno-, *h₂el-mn̥-to-, *h₂el-mos, *h₂él-ti-s, *h₂el-tó-s, *h₂el-wó-s, *pro-h₂el-, *h₂el-dʰ-, *h₂éltrom

Germanic: world, eld, old (**Eng**); alan, worold, eald, ald, ieldu, ealdor (**OE**); wrâld, âld, jeld (**Fris**); wereld, oud, elde (**Dut**); Welt, alt, Alter (**Ger**); ala, œll, ǫld, verǫld, ellri, elztr, elli, aldr (**Norse**); ala, verden, eldre, eldst, elde, elda, alder (**Nor**); värld, äldre, äldst, âlder (**Swe**); verden, ældre, ældst, ælde, alder (**Dan**); ala, öld, veröld, eldri, elstur, elli, aldur (**Ice**) ("world" words jointly descend from this + *wiHrós)

Celtic: oil (**Iri**)

Italic: alere, alescere, alica, alimentum, alimōnia, altus, alumnus, coalere, elementum (uncert.), elementārius, abolēre, abolitiō, adolēre, adolēscere, adolēscēns, exolescere, exolētus, indolēs, obsolēscere, obsolētus, alvus, alveus, alveārium, alveolus, prōlēs, prōlētārius (**Lat**);

aliment, haut, élément, abolir, abolition, adolescent, obsolète, auge (**Fr**);

alimento, alto, alunno, abolire, abolizione, indole, obsoleto, alvino, alveo, alveolo, albiolo, prole, proletariato (**Ital**);

álaga, álica, alimento, alto, oto, alumno, elemento, abolir, abolición, índole, obsoleto, álveo, alveario, alveolo, prole, proletariado (**Sp**);

alimentar, álica, alimento, alto, aluno, elemento, abolir, abolição, índole, álveo, alvéolo, prole, proletariado (**Port**);

alac, înalt, adia, albie, albină, alveolă, albioară (**Rom**)

Derivatives: aliment, alimony, alumnus, element, elementary, abolish, abolition, adolescent, exolete, obsolesce, obsolete, alvine, alveolus, proletariat (**Eng**); adolescent (**Dut**); Element (**Ger**); element (**Swe**); ailbheolas (**Iri**); элемент (element), альвеóла (al'veóla) (**Rus**); adolescent (**Cz**); nalt (**Alb**)

Hellenic: ἀλθω (althō), ἀλθαίνω (althaínō) (**AnGk**)

*ǵʰelh₃-

to flourish; green, yellow

see Colours

*gʰreh₁-

to grow, to become green

see Colours

*h₂erHdʰ-
high; to grow

See Trees

*h₁lewdʰ-
people; to grow

see Social

*meh₂ḱ-
to raise, increase; long

See Basic adjectives

*bʰuH-
to become, grow, appear

*bʰúH-t, *bʰewH-, *bʰuH-yé-ti, *bʰowH-éye-ti, *bʰúH-tis, *bʰuH-ti-ḱo-, *bʰúH-tus, *bʰúH-mn̥, *bʰuH-eh₂, *bʰuH-tó-, *bʰuH-lo-, *bʰuH-s, *bʰúH-tlo-, *bʰuH-tlom

Germanic: be, bist (dial.), boun, bound, boon (dial.), booth (**Eng**); bēon, būan, bist (**OE**); wêze, bin (**Fris**); bouwen, zijn, wezen, bennen, ben (**Dut**); sein, bin, bist, bauen, bude (**Ger**); búa, búinn, búð (**Norse**); bo, bu, buen (**Nor**); bo (**Swe**); bo (**Dan**); búa, búð (**Ice**)

Celtic: bod (**Wel**); bí (**Iri**)

Italic: fuī, futurus, fierī, probus, improbus, probitās, probāre, approbātiō, improbāre, proba, probābilis, probābilitās, probātus, reprobāre, superbus, tribus, tribālis, tribūnal, tribūnus, tribuere, attribuere, attribūtor, contribuere, distribuere, retribuere, tribūtum, -bō (ending of future), -bam (ending of imperfect), -bundus (as in moribundus) (**Lat**);

fut, futur, probe, probité, prouver, approuver, preuve, probable, superbe, tribu, tribunal, tribun, attribuer, contribuer, distribuer, rétribuer, tribut (**Fr**);

fui, futuro, fire, probitate, probitade, probità, provare, prova, pruova, probabile, superbo, tribù, tribale, tribunale, tribuno, attribuire, contribuer, distribuire, tributo (**Ital**);

fui, futuro, probo, proba, improbo, probidad, probar, aprobar, improbar, preuba, probable, soberbio, tribu, tribunal, tribuno, atribuir, atrever, contribuir, distribuir, retribuir, treudo, tributo (**Sp**);

fui, futuro, probo, improbo, probidade, provar, aprovar, improbar, improvar, prova, provável, reprovar, soberbo, tribo, tribunal, tribuno, atribuir, atrever, contribuir, distribuir, tributo (**Port**);

fui, fi, fire (in part), proba, probă, superb, tribunal, distribui (**Rom**)

Derivatives: future, fiat, probity, probe, prove, approve, approbation, proof, probable, probability, reprove, superb, tribe, tribal, tribunal, attribute, attributor, contribute, distribute, retribution (**Eng**);

proef, distribueren (**Dut**); probieren, proben, prüfen, Probe, probat, superb (**Ger**); probat (**Dan**); promh (**Iri**);

апробáция (aprobácija), трибунáл (tribunál) (**Rus**); provë, atribuoj (**Alb**)

Hellenic: φύω (phúō), φύσις (phúsis), φυσικός (phusikós), φυτικός (phutikós), φῦμᾰ (phûma), φυή (phué), φῦλον (phûlon), φῦλή (phûlé), φύτλον (phútlon), φύω (phúō) (**AnGk**); φύση (fýsi), φυσικός (fysikós), φυσική (fysikí), φυτό (fytó), φυτεύω (fytévo), φύλο (fýlo), φυλή (fylí) (**Gk**)

Derivatives: physis, physeal, physics, -phyto-, -phyte, phylum, phyle (**Eng**); physicus, physica (**Lat**); fisico (**Ital**)

Slavic: быть (byt'), есть (jest'), есмь (jesm'), есй (jesí), бы́дло (býdlo) (**Rus**); być, jestem, jesteś, jest, bydło (**Pol**); být, jsem, jsi, je/jest, bydlo (**Cz**); byť, som, si, je (**Slo**); e (e), сум (sum), си (si) (**Mace**)

Baltic: būti, būtu, būklas, būkla, bùvintis (**Lith**); būt (**Latv**)

Albanian: bëj, bëhem (**Alb**)

Indo-Iranian: भवति (bhavati), भावयति (bhāvayati), अभूत् (abhūt), भूति (bhúti), भूमन् (bhūman) (**Sans**); है (hai) (**Hin**); بودن (budan) (**Pers**)

*H₁es-

to be

*h₁és-ti, *h₁s-ónt-ih₂, *h₁s-tós-, *h₂wes-

Germanic: is, was, were, wert, wassail, sin, sooth, soothe (**Eng**); is, wesan, synn, sōþ, sōþian (**OE**);

wêze, sûnde (**Fris**); wezen, zonde (**Dut**); sein, war, gewesen, Sünde (**Ger**);

vesa/vera, vist, synd, sannr, saðr, sannan, sǫnnun, syn, synja, ves heill (**Norse**); være, vera, vere, synd (**Nor**); vara, -vist, synd, sann, sanna (**Swe**); være, synd, sand (**Dan**); vera, vist, synd, sannur, sönnun, synja (**Ice**)

Derivatives: soin (**Fr**)

Celtic: is (**Iri**)

Italic: est, sum, ēns, entitās, essentia, intersum, possum (potis+), possibilis, potēns, armipotēns, astripotēns, bellipotēns, omnipotēns, potentia, potentialis, sōns (he who is it, i.e. guilty, criminal), insōns, interesse (inter+), praesum, praesēns, praesentia, praesentātiō, repraesentāre, repraesentātiō (**Lat**);

être, entité, essence, pouvoir, possible, puissant, omnipotent, potence, présent, présenter, présentation, représenter (**Fr**);

essere, ente, entità, essenza, interesse, potere, possibile, potente, armipotente, omnipotente, potenza, presentare, presentazione, rappresentare (**Ital**);

ser, ente, esencia, interés, poder, posible, potente, pudiente, omnipotente, potencia, sonte, insonte, presente, presentar, representar (**Sp**);

ser, ente, entidade, essência, interesse, poder, possivel, potente, omnipotente, onipotente, potência, sonte, insonte, presente, presentar, apresentar, representar (**Port**);

fi (in part), esență, putea, putere, posibil, potent, potență, putință, reprezenta (**Rom**)

Derivatives: in esse, essence, quintessence, entity, in posse, power, possible, potent, armipotent, astripotent, bellipotent, omnipotent, in potentia, potency, potential, interest, present, presence, presentation, representation (**Eng**); Essenz, Präsens, Präsentation (**Ger**); эссенция (essencija), потенция (potencija), репрезентация (reprezentacija) (**Rus**); entita (**Cz**)

Hellenic: εστι (estí), εἰμί (eimí), ἔξεστι (éxesti), ἐξουσίᾱ (exousíā), οὐσίᾱ (ousíā), πᾰρουσίᾱ (parousíā) (**AnGk**); εἰμαι (eímai), εξουσία (exousía), ουσία (ousía), παρουσία (parousía), περιουσία (periousía) (**Gk**)

Derivatives: parousie (**Fr**)

Baltic: esti, esu, esi, yra (**Lith**); esmu, esi, ir (**Latv**)

Albanian: jam, gjë (**Alb**)

Indo-Iranian: अस्ति (ásti), सत् (sat), सती (satī) (**Sans**); هست (hast) / است (ast) (**Pers**)

Derivatives: suttee (**Eng**)

*pótis

master, ruler, husband

*déms pótis (master of the house), *weyḱpotis (clan chief)

Italic: potis, possidēre (+sedēre), possessiō, possessivus, possessor, potestās (**Lat**); posseoir, posséder, possession (**Fr**); possedere, possessione, potestà, podestà (**Ital**); poseer, posesión, potestad (**Sp**); possuir, possessão, possessor, potestade, podestade (**Port**); poseda (**Rom**)

Derivatives: possess, possession, possessive, possessor, poustie (**Eng**); pushtet (**Alb**)

Hellenic: πόσις (pósis), δεσπότης (despótēs) (**AnGk**); δεσπότης (despótis) (**Gk**)

Derivatives: despot (**Eng**); despota (**Lat**)

Baltic: pats, viēšpats (**Lith**); pats (**Latv**)

Albanian: zot (**Alb**)

Indo-Iranian: पति (páti), दम्पति (dám-pati), विश्पति (víśpáti) (**Sans**); पति (pati) (**Hin**); بد (bod) (**Pers**)

*ǵerh₂-

to grow old, to mature

note connection with *gerh₂- to cry hoarsely

*ǵerh₂-, *ǵṛh₂-nó-m, *ǵerh₂-ro-, *ǵṛh₂-yéw-, *ǵ(e)rh₂-yo-, *ǵṛh₂-i-ḱo-, *ǵērh₂-s, *ǵérh₂-ont-s, *ǵérh₂-u-s, *ǵorh₂-o-

Germanic: kernel, churl, carl (**Eng**); cyrnel, ċeorl (**OE**); tsjirl, keardel, kearel (**Fris**); kerel (**Dut**); Kerl (**Ger**); karl (**Norse**); kall, kar (**Nor**); karl (**Swe**); karl (**Dan**); karl (**Ice**)

Derivatives: Charles (**Fr**); король (koról'), королица (korolíca) (**Rus**); król (**Pol**); král, Kralice (**Cz**); kráľ, králica (**Slo**); крал (kral), кралица (kralica) (**Mace**)

Hellenic: γεραρός (gerarós), γραῦς (graûs), γεραιός (geraiós), γραῖα (graîa), γῆρας (gêras), γέρας (géras), Γραικός (Graikós), γέρων (gérōn) (**AnGk**); γέροντας (gérontas) (**Gk**)

Derivatives: Greek, gringo, geronto-, erigeron, gerascophobia, periatric, gerontogracy, gerontology, gerousia, progeria (**Eng**); Grieks, Griekse (**Dut**); griechisch (**Ger**);

Graecus (**Lat**); grec, greque, grive, pie-grièche, ortie-grièche, géronto- (**Fr**); greco (**Ital**); griego, gringo (**Sp**); grego (**Port**); grec, greacă (**Rom**); grek (**Alb**)

Slavic: зрелый (zrelyj), зреть (zret') (**Rus**); zrát, zralý (**Cz**); zrelý (**Slo**)

Indo-Iranian: जरति (járati), जरत् (járat) (**Sans**)

from which is derived *ǵṛHnom corn, grain:

*ǵṛHnom

corn, grain

Germanic: corn (**Eng**); corn (**OE**); koren (**Dut**); Korn (**Ger**); korn (**Norse**); korn (**Nor**); korn (**Swe**); korn (**Dan**); korn (**Ice**)

Celtic: grawn (**Wel**); grán (**Iri**)

Italic: grānum (**Lat**); grain (**Fr**); grano (**Ital**); grano (**Sp**); grão (**Port**); grâu (**Rom**)

Derivatives: grain, grange (**Eng**)

Slavic: зерно (zernó) (**Rus**); ziarno (**Pol**); zrno (**Cz**); zrno (**Slo**); зрно (zrno) (**Mace**)

Baltic: žirnis (**Lith**); zirnis (**Latv**)

Albanian: grurë (**Alb**)

Indo-Iranian: زنی (zaṇai) ~ زری (zaṛai) (**Pash**); خرمن (xarman) (**Pers**)

*bʰleh₁-
to swell, blow up

Germanic: blow, blaze, blast, bladder (**Eng**); blōwan, blasen, blǣst (**OE**); bloeie, blieze, blaze (**Fris**); bloeien, blaaien, blazen (**Dut**); blühen, blasen, Blast (**Ger**); blása, blástr (**Norse**); blåse, blåst (**Nor**); blåsa, blåst (**Swe**); blæse, blæst (**Dan**); blása, blástur (**Ice**)

Italic: flāre, afflāre, cōnflāre, efflāre, flābrum, flāmen, flātus, īnflāre, inflatio, perflāre, sufflāre (**Lat**);

gonfler, enfler, inflation, souffler (**Fr**);

gonfiare, conflare, fiato, fiatare, enfiare, enfiagione, inflazione, soffiare (**Ital**);

hallar, flato, hinchar, inflar, hinchazón, inflación, soplar, resollar (**Sp**);

achar, aflar, flabelo, flâmine, flato, inchar, inflar, inchação, inflação, inchado, inflado, soprar, suflar (**Port**);

afla, aflare, flaur, umfla, umflare, inflație, umflăciune, suflia, suflare, suflet (**Rom**)

Derivatives: afflatus, conflate, deflate, flatus, flabellum, inflate, inflation, insufflation, soufflé, flatulence, flavor, flute (**Eng**); Souffleur (**Ger**); инфляция (infljacija) (**Rus**)

Albanian: plas (**Alb**)

Possibly:

Italic: fluere, fluēns, fluidus, affluere, affluēns, affluentia, circumfluere, cōnfluere, cōnfluentia, dēfluere, diffluere, effluere, effluvium, fluctus, fluctuāre, fluctuātiō, fluitāre, flumen, fluvius, fluviālis, fluxus, influere, īnfluentia, īnfluxus, prōfluere, refluere, superfluere, superfluus, trānsfluere (**Lat**);

fluer, affluer, affluent, confluer, diffluer, effluer, effluve, flux, fluctuer, fluctuation, fleuve, fluvial, flux, influer, influence, refluer, superflu (**Fr**);

fluire, fluente, affluire, circonfluire, confluire, defluire, effluire, effluvio, fiotto, flutto, fluttuare, fluttuazione, fluitare, fiume, fluviale, flusso, influire, profluvio, rifluire, superfluo, transfluire (**Ital**);

fluir, afluir, afluente, confluir, difluir, efluir, efluvio, fluctuar, fluctuación, fluvial, flujo, influir, refluir, superfluo (**Sp**);

fluir, fluente, afluir, afluente, afluência, circunfluir, confluir, defluir, difluir, efluir, eflúvio, flutuar, flutuação, flume, flúmen, fluxo, influir, refluir, supérfluo (**Port**);

aflui, fluctua, fluctuație, fluviu, fluvial, flux (**Rom**)

Derivatives: fluid, fluent, affluent, affluence, confluence, effluent, effluvium, fluctuate, fluctuation, flume, fluvial, flux, influx, influence, superfluous (**Eng**); флуктуация (fluktuacija), флюктуация (fljuktuacija) (**Rus**)

this may be related to *$b^h leh_1$- to cry:

*$b^h leh_1$-
to bleat, cry

Germanic: bleat, blatant (**Eng**); blǣtan (**OE**); bâlte, blêtsje, bletterje (**Fris**); blaten, bleiten (**Dut**); blähen, blaßen, blätzen, blässen (**Ger**)

Italic: flēre, flēbilis (**Lat**); feble, foible, faible (**Fr**); feble (**Sp**)

Derivatives: feeble, foible (**Eng**)

Slavic: блеять (bléjat') (**Rus**); bleti (arch.) (**Cz**); блее (blee) (**Mace**)

Baltic: bliáuti (**Lith**); blêt (**Latv**)

there is also a certain amount of conflation between *$b^h leh_1$- to swell, blow up, and *$b^h leh_3$- to bloom, to blossom:

*$b^h leh_3$-
to bloom, flower, blossom

*$b^h léh_3$-e-ti, *$b^h léh_3$-mō, *$b^h leh_3$-s-, *$b^h léh_3 tis$, *$b^h léh_3 tus$, *$b^h_{\circ} lh_3$-oto-, *$b^h olh_3$-yom

Germanic: blossom, blade, bloom, blow (to blossom, as in full-blown) (**Eng**); blōstm, blæd, blōma, blōwan (**OE**);

blom, blomme, bled (**Fris**); bloem, blad (**Dut**); Blume, Blüte, Blatt (**Ger**);

blómi, blóm, blað (**Norse**); blome, blad (**Nor**); blomma, blad (**Swe**); blomme, blad (**Dan**); blómi, blóm, blað (**Ice**)

Celtic: bláth (**Iri**)

Italic: flōs, flōris, flōrēre, flōreus, flōsculus, folium, aquifolius, exfōliāre, foliātus, foliōsus (**Lat**);

fleur, fleurir, feuille, folio, exfolier (**Fr**);

fiore, fiorire, foglia, foglio, aquifoglio, foglioso (**Ital**);

flor, florir, flósculo, hoja, folio, acebo, aquifolio, exfoliar, hojoso (**Sp**);

flor, frol, chor, florir, flósculo, folha, folho, fólio, azevinho, folhoso (**Port**);

floare, foaie, foios (**Rom**)

Derivatives: flower, flourish, floral, florid, foil, folio, exfoliate, foliate, foliage, foliose (**Eng**); plúr (**Iri**)

Hellenic: φύλλον (phúllon) (**AnGk**); φάλαινα (fálaina) (**Gk**)

Derivatives: -phyllous, chlorophyll, phyllotaxis (**Eng**)

Indo-Iranian: फुलम् (phulam) (**Sans**); بالال (balâl) (**Pers**)

*g^{w}eyh$_3$-
to live

*g^{w}éyh$_3$-e-ti, *g^{w}oyh$_3$-éye-ti, *g^{w}oyh$_3$-o-s, *g^{w}ih$_3$-wó-s, *seh$_1$mi-g^{w}ih$_3$-wó-s

Germanic: quick (**Eng**); cwic (**OE**); kwik, kwyk (**Fris**); kwik, kwiek, kek (**Dut**); quick, keck (**Ger**); kvikr, kvikna (**Norse**); kvikk, kjekk (**Nor**); kvick, kvickna (**Swe**); kvik, kvikne, kæk (**Dan**); kvikur (**Ice**)

Celtic: byw (**Wel**); beo (**Iri**)

Italic: vīvō, vīta, vītālis, vītālitās, vīvārium, vīvus, vīvāx, vīvācitās, vīvidus, vīviparus, iūgis (**Lat**); vivre, vie, vital, vivarium, vivier, vif, vivace, vivacité, vivipare (**Fr**); vivere, vita, vitale, vivo, vivace, vivacità, vivido, viviparo (**Ital**); vivir, vida, vital, vivo, vivaz, vívido, viviparo (**Sp**); viver, vida, vital, viveiro, vivo, vivaz, vívido, viviparo (**Port**); învia, via, vită, vital, viu, vivace (**Rom**)

Derivatives: revive, vital, vitality, vitamin, vivarium, vivacious, vivacity, vivid, viviparous (**Eng**); vital (**Ger**); виварий (vivarij) (**Rus**)

Hellenic: βέομαι (béomai), βείομαι (beíomai), βίος (bíos), ζάω (záō), ζωός (zōós), ζῷον (zōîon), ζῶ (zô), ζῳδϊăκός (zōidiakós), βίοτος (bíotos), βιοτή (biotḗ), ὑγιής (hugiés) (**AnGk**); βίος (víos), ζώο (zóo), ζω (zo), ζήτω (zíto) (**Gk**)

Derivatives: bio-, biology, biography, biome, biometric, biosphere, symbiosis, semiosis, azoic, zoon, zoo-, zo-, zoology, ectozoon, Mesozoic, protozoa, zoic, zoo, zooid, zoonosis, zoophagy, zodiac (**Eng**); zodiacus (**Lat**)

Slavic: живой (živój), жить (žit'), жито (žíto), живица (živíca), живот (živót) (**Rus**); żywy, żyć, żyto, żywica, żywot (**Pol**); živý, žít, žito, živice, život (**Cz**); živý, žiť, živica, život (**Slo**); жив (živ), живее (živee), живот (žívot) (**Mace**)

Baltic: gývas, gyventi, gyvatà (**Lith**); dzīvs, dzīt, dzīvot (**Latv**)

Indo-Iranian: जीवति (jīvati), जीव (jīva) (**Sans**); जीना (jīnā) (**Hin**); زیستن (zistan), جیوه (jīve), زی (zi-), زیویدن (zividan) (**Pers**)

*mer-

to die

*mér-t, *mér-ti, *mṛ-yé-tor, *mor-éye-ti, *mṛ-tós, *mṛ-wós, *mṛ-t-wós, *mér-ti-s, *mór-o-

Germanic: murth (dial.), murder, mare, nightmare (**Eng**); morþ, morþor, mare (**OE**); moard (**Fris**); moord, mare, maar, nachtmare, nachtmerrie (**Dut**); Mord, mördern, Mahr, Nachtmahr (**Ger**); morð, mara (**Norse**); mord, mara, mare (**Nor**); mord, mara (**Swe**); mord, mare (**Dan**); morð, mara (**Ice**)

Derivatives: meurtrir, cauchemar (**Fr**)

Celtic: marw (**Wel**); marbh (**Iri**)

Italic: morior, ēmorior, moribundus, mortuus, mors (**Lat**); mourir, moribond, mort, morte (**Fr**); morire, moribondo, morto, morte (**Ital**); muriri, mòriri, moribundo, muerto, muerta, muerte (**Sp**); morrer, esmorecer, moribundo, morto, morte (**Port**); muri, murire, muribund, mort, moarte (**Rom**)

Derivatives: moribund, mortal, immortal, mortician, mortuary (**Eng**); mort (**Alb**)

Hellenic: ἔμορτεν (émorten), βροτός (brotós) (poet.), ἄμβροτος (ámbrotos), ἀμβροσία (ambrosía) (**AnGk**); αμβροσία (amvrosía) (**Gk**)

Derivatives: ambrosia (**Eng**); ambrosia (**Lat**); ambroisie (**Fr**); ambrosia (**Ital**); амбро́зия (ambrózija) (**Rus**)

Slavic: мере́ть (merét'), мори́ть (morít'), мёртвый (mjórtvyj), смерть (smert'), мор (mor) (**Rus**); mrzeć, umierać, morzyć, martwy, miartwy, śmierć, mór (**Pol**); mřít, mořit, mrtvý, mertev, smrt, mor (**Cz**); mrieť, moriť, mŕtvy, mŕtvý, mŕtví, smrť, mor (**Slo**); мртов (mrtov), смрт (smrt) (**Mace**)

Baltic: mìrti, mirtis, māras (**Lith**); mirt (**Latv**)

Albanian: mërshë (**Alb**)

Indo-Iranian: अमृत (ámṛta), मरति (marati), मरते (márate), म्रियते (mriyáte), मारयति (māráyati), मार (māra), मृत (mṛtá), मर्त (márta), मृति (mṛti) (**Sans**); मरना (marnā), मृत (mṛt) (**Hin**); مردن (mordan), مرده (morde) (**Pers**)

*neḱ-

to perish, disappear

*néḱ-t, *néḱ-s-t, *néḱ-ye-ti, *ne-nóḱ-e, *noḱ-éye-ti, *neḱ-s, *neḱ-rós, *néḱ-tu-s, *néḱ-us, *néḱ-tṛh₂

Celtic: aeth, angau (**Wel**); éacht, éag (**Iri**)

Italic: nex, necare, nocēre, nocīvus, nocumentum, innocens, ēnecō, internecare, pernecare, perniciōsus, noxa, noxius (**Lat**); nuire, noyer, nocif, innocent, pernicieux

(Fr); nuocere, annegare, nocumento, nocivo, innocente (Ital); nocivo, anegar, inocente (Sp); nocivo, anegar, inocente (Port); nociv, îneca, înecare, neca, inocent (Rom)

Derivatives: innocent, innocuous, nocebo, nocive, noxious, internecine, nuisance, obnoxious, pernicious (Eng)

Hellenic: νεκρός (nekrós), νέκυς (nékus), νέκταρ (néktar) (AnGk); νεκρός (nekrós), νέκταρ (néktar) (Gk)

Derivatives: necromancy, necrophilia, necropolis, necropsis, necrotic, necrosis, necrotize, nectar, nectarine (Eng); nectar, nectareus (Lat); nectar (Fr); nettare, nettareo (Ital)

Indo-Iranian: नश् (naś), नशन्ति (naśanti), नश्यति (náśyati), ननाश (nanāśa), नाशयति (nāśáyati) (Sans)

*h₂ey-
vital force, life, age, eternity

*h₂óy-u, *h₂ey-w-es-to-, *h₂y-ew-, *h₂oy-u-s, *h₂oy-w-o-, *h₂oy-u-h₃onh₂-, *h₂y-u-h₁en-, *h₂y-(e)w-gʷih₃-

Germanic: ever, aye (Eng); ǣ, æfre (OE); ea, ieu (Fris); eeuw, echt (Dut); Ehe, je, ewig (Ger); æ, ei, ey (Norse); æ, ætíð (Ice)

Celtic: oes, oed (Wel); aois (Iri)

Italic: aevum, aetās, aeternus, aeternitās, coaevus, longaevus, longaevitās, primaevus, iūgis (Lat); éternel, éternité, longévité (Fr); evo, età, eterno, eternità, longevo, longevità (Ital); evo, edad, eterno, eternidad, longevo, longevidad (Sp); evo, idade, eterno, eternidade, longevo, longevidade (Port); ev, etate, eternitate, longevitate (Rom)

Derivatives: age, eternal, eternity, longevity, medieval, coeval, primeval (Eng); jetë (Alb)

Hellenic: αἰών (aiōn), αἰεί (aiei), ὑγιής (hugiḗs) (AnGk); αιώνας (aiónas) (Gk)

Derivatives: aeon, eon (Eng); aeon (Lat); эон (eón) (Rus)

Albanian: eshë (Alb)

Indo-Iranian: आयु (āyu) (Sans)

which includes *h₂yuh₁en- young, and *h₂eyw- law:

*h₂eyw-
justice, law

*h₂yéw-os, *h₂yew-dʰ-os, *h₂yew-es-tos, *h₂yew-es-eh₂-ye-

Italic: iūs, iūrāre, abiūrāre, abiūrātiō, adiūrāre, adiūrātiō, adiūrātor, coniūrāre, coniūrātiō, iūrāmentum, pēierāre/periurāre/perjurāre, iūstus, iūstitia, iustitiarius (**Lat**);

jurer, abjurer, conjurer, conjuration, juste, justice, justesse (**Fr**);

gius, giure, giurare, abiurare, congiurare, giuramento, giusto, giustizia, giustezza (**Ital**);

juro, jurar, abjurar, conjuración, juramento, justo, justicia, justeza (**Sp**);

juro, jurar, abjurar, abjuração, adjuração, adjurador, juramento, perjuro, perjúrio, justo, justiça, justeza (**Port**);

jura, jurare, jurământ, just, justiție (**Rom**)

Derivatives: jury, jurisprudence, abjure, abjuration, adjure, adjuration, conjure, conjuration, perjure, perjury, just, justice, justiciar, justiciary (**Eng**); juist, justitie (**Dut**); Jura, Jus, Justiz (**Ger**); юстиция (justicija) (**Rus**); gjëroj (**Alb**)

Indo-Iranian: योस् (yós) (**Sans**)

These come from Latin iūs and dīcere:

Italic: iūdex, iūdicāre, abiūdicāre, adiūdicāre, adiūdicātiō, iūdicābilis, iūdicātiō, iūdicātor, iūdicātum, iūdicātus, iūdicātōrius, iūdicātrix, iūdiciālis, iūdiciārius, praeiūdicāre, praeiūdicium (**Lat**);

juge, juger, adjuger, adjudication, judiciel, judiciaire, préjuger, préjudice (**Fr**);

giudice, giudicare, aggiudicare, aggiudicazione, giudicabile, giudicatore, iudicato, giudicato, giudicatorio, giudicatrice, giudiziale, giudiziario, pregiudicare (**Ital**);

juez, juzgar, adjudicar, adjudicación, juzgador, judicial, judiciario, perjudicar, prejuzgar, perjuicio, prejuicio (**Sp**);

juiz, julgar, abjudicar, adjudicar, adjudicação, julgador, judicial, judiciário, prejudicar, prejuízo (**Port**);

jude, judeca, judecare, adjudeca, judecător, judecată, judiciar, prejudeca, prejudiciu (**Rom**)

Derivatives: judge, judgement/judgment, judgemental, abjudge, abjudicate, adjudge, adjudicate, adjudication, injudicious, judication, judicature, judicial, judiciary, prejudge, prejudicate, prejudice, prejudicial (**Eng**); gjykatë (**Alb**)

*deyḱ-

to point out

*déyḱ-ti, *deyḱ-new-, *déyḱ-s-t, *doyḱ-éye-ti, *diḱ-eh$_2$, *déyḱ-mn̥, *diḱ-tós

Germanic: teach, toe (**Eng**); tēon, tiht, tǣċan, tā, tāhe (**OE**); tean (**Fris**); aantijgen, teen, toon (dial.) (**Dut**); ziehen, inzicht, Zehe, Zeh (**Ger**); tjá, tá (**Norse**); tå (**Nor**); te, tå (**Swe**); tå (**Dan**); tá (**Ice**)

Italic: dīcere, addīcere, addictiō, addictus, benedīcere, condīcere, condiciō, condiciōnālis, condictiō, contrādīcere, contrādictiō, contrādictor, contrādictōrius, dicāx, dictiō, dictiōnārium, dictāre, dictāmen, dictātiō, dictātor, dictātūra, dictus, dictum, dixit, ēdīcere, ēdictiō, ēdictum, indīcāre, index, indicium, interdīcere, maledīcere, maledictiō, maledictus, praedīcāre, praedictiō, valedīcere, digitus, digitālis, digitātus (**Lat**);

dire, addiction, addict, bénir, éconduire, condition, conditionnel, contredire, contradicteur, contradictoire, diction, dictionnaire, dicter, dictateur, dictature, dit, dixit, édiction, édit, indiquer, index, indice, interdire, maudire, malédiction, prédire, prédiction, doigt, digital, digitale, dé (**Fr**);

dire, addire, addetto, benedire, condizione, contraddire, contradditore, contraddittorio, dicace, dizione, dizionario, dettare, dittatore, dittatura, detto, editto, indicare, endice, indice, interdire, maledire, maledetto, predire, predizione, dito, digitale, ditale (**Ital**);

decir, adicar, adicción, adicto, bendecir, condecir, condición, contradecir, contradicción, contradictor, contradictorio, dicaz, dicción, diccionario, dictar, dictamen, dictador, dictadura, dicho, dixit, edicto, indicar, índex, índice, indicio, entredecir, interdecir, maldecir, maldición, maldito, predecir, predicción, dedo, dígito, digital, dedal (**Sp**);

dizer, adicção, adicto, benzer, bendizer, condizer, condição, contradizer, contradição, contraditor, contraditório, dicaz, dicção, dicionário, ditar, ditador, ditadura, dito, dictum, edito, índex, índice, índicio, interdizer, maldizer, maldição, maldito, predizer, predição, dedo, dígito, digital, dedal (**Port**);

zice, zicere, adicție, condiție, contradicție, dicție, dicționar, dicta, dictare, dictator, dictatură, edict, index, indice, interzice, prezice, predicție, deget, digital, degetar (**Rom**)

Derivatives: addict, addiction, benediction, condition, conditional, condiction, contradict, contradiction, contradictory, diction, dictionary, dight, dictate, dictamen, dictation, dictature, dictum, mirabile dictu, ipse dixit, edict, indicate, index, interdict, interdiction, malediction, predict, prediction, valediction, valedictorian, digit, digital, digitalis, digitate (**Eng**);

conditie, dichten, dicteren (**Dut**); benedeien, Kondition, Diktionär, dichten, Diktatur, Edikt, digital (**Ger**); dikt (**Norse**); dikt (**Nor**); kondition, dikta, diktatur, indicium (**Swe**); cynnig (**Wel**); beannaigh, mallacht (**Iri**);

έδικτο (édikto) (**Gk**); кондиция (kondícija), диктáтор (diktátor), диктатура (diktatura), эдикт (edikt), йндекс (índeks) (**Rus**); dyktator (**Pol**); bekoj, dëftoj, mallkoj (**Alb**)

Hellenic: δείκνῡμι (deíknūmi), δίκη (díkē), ἄδικος (ádikos), δῐκάζω (dikázō), δῐκᾰστής (dikastés), δῐκαιος (díkaios), δῐκαιοσύνη (dikaiosúnē), δεῖγμα (deîgma), δειγματίζω (deigmatízō) (**AnGk**); δείχνω (deíchno), δίκη (díki), άδικος (ádikos), δικάζω (dikázo), δικαστής (dikastís), δίκαιος (díkaios), δικαιοσύνη (dikaiosýni, δικαίωμα (dikaíoma), δείγμα (deígma), δειγματίζω (deigmatízo) (**Gk**)

Derivatives: dica (**Lat**)

Indo-Iranian: दिश् (diś), दिष्ट (diṣṭá), दिशति (diśáti) (**Sans**); दिशा (diśā), देश (deś) (**Hin**)

Cognitive function

*h₂ew-

to perceive, see, be aware of

*h₂ṓws, *h₂ewis

Germanic: ear (**Eng**); éare (**OE**); ear (**Fris**); oor (**Dut**); Ohr (**Ger**); eyra (**Norse**); øre (**Nor**); öra (**Swe**); øre (**Dan**); eyra (**Ice**)

Italic: auris, auricula (**Lat**); oreille (**Fr**); orecchio, auricola (**Ital**); oreja, aurícula (**Sp**); orelha, aurícula (**Port**); ureche (**Rom**)

Derivatives: aural, auricle, auricula (**Eng**)

Hellenic: οὖς (oûs), ὠτός (ōtós), ἀΐω (aḯō) (**AnGk**); αυτί (aftí) (**Gk**)

Derivatives: anotia, microtia, Myosotis, otalgia, otic, otitis, otocephaly, otolith, otology, otopathy, otophyma, otoplasty, otorrhea, otosclerosis, otoscope, ototomy, parotic, parotid, periotic, synotia (**Eng**)

Slavic: ýхо (úxo), уши (úši) (**Rus**); ucho, jawa (**Pol**); ucho (**Cz**); ucho (**Slo**); уво (uvo) (**Mace**)

Baltic: ausis (**Lith**); auss (**Latv**)

Albanian: vesh (**Alb**)

Indo-Iranian: उसि (usi), आविस् (āvís) (**Sans**); هوش (hôš), باهوش (bâhuš), مدهوش (madhuš), هوشمند (hušmand) (**Pers**)

from which derives *h₂ewis-dʰh₁- and *h₂ḱh₂owsyéti:

*h₂ewis-dʰh₁- (*h₂ew- + *dʰeh₁-)

to render hearing

Italic: audīre, audītōrium, audītōrius, audiēns, audientia, audītiō, audītor, audītus, exaudīre, oboedīre, oboediēns, subaudiō (**Lat**);

ouïr, audio, auditoire, auditorium, oyant, audience, audition, auditeur, ouïe, ouï, exaucer, obéir, obéissant (**Fr**);

udire, auditorio, udienza, audizione, uditore, udito, esaudire, ubbidire, obbedire (**Ital**);

oír, audio-, auditorio, oyente, audiencia, audición, auditor, oidor, oído, audito, obedecer, obediente (**Sp**);

ouvir, auditório, ouvinte, audiência, audição, auditor, ouvidor, ouvido, audito, obedecer, obediente **(Port)**;

auzi, auzire, auditoriu, audienţă, audiţie, auditor, auzitor, auzit **(Rom)**

Derivatives: audio, audile, audible, audiology, auditorium, auditory, audient, audience, audition, auditor, audit, obey, obedient, subaudi, subaudite **(Eng)**; Audienz **(Ger)**; audiell, audition **(Swe)**; аудито́рия (auditórija), аудиéнция (audijéncija), ауди́тор (audítor) **(Rus)**

Hellenic: αἰσθάνομαι (aisthánomai) **(AnGk)**

*h₂ḱh₂owsyéti
to be sharp-eared

*h₂eḱ- (sharp) + *h₂ows- + *-yéti

Germanic: hear, hark, harken **(Eng)**; hȳran, hēran, hīeran, hercnian, heorcnian, hyrcnian, heark, hearken **(OE)**; hearre, harkje **(Fris)**; horen **(Dut)**; hōren, horchen **(Ger)**; heyra **(Norse)**; høyra, høyre, høre **(Nor)**; höra **(Swe)**; høre **(Dan)**; heyra **(Ice)**

Hellenic: ἀκούω (akoúō) **(AnGk)**

*ḱlew-
to hear

*ḱléw-t, *ḱléw-ye-ti, *ḱlu-yé-ti, *ḱl̥-né-w-ti, *ḱe-ḱlów-e, *ḱl̥w-éh₁-ti, *ḱlow-éye-ti, *ḱléw-mn̥, *ḱléw-mn̥-to-, *ḱléw-os, *ḱlew-ēs, *ḱlow-so-s, *ḱlu-tó-s, *ḱlew-eto-, *ḱléw-tro-m, *ḱlu-n-s-, *ḱlu-s-r-, *ḱlow-steh₂, *ḱlow-ro-

Germanic: listen, loud, Lewis, Louis **(Eng)**; hlystan, hlūd, hlēoþor **(OE)**; lûd **(Fris)**; luisteren, luid, Lodewijk **(Dut)**; Leumund, laut, Ludwig, hören **(Ger)**; hljómr, hljóðr **(Norse)**; lytte **(Nor)**; lyssna **(Swe)**; lyt **(Dan)**; hlusta, hljóður **(Ice)**

Derivatives: Ludovicus (from Germanic roots for loud + battle) **(Lat)**; Louis **(Fr)**; Luigi **(Ital)**; Luis **(Sp)**; Luis **(Port)**

Celtic: clywed **(Wel)**; cluin, chuala, clú, cluas **(Iri)**

Italic: cluēre, cliēns, clientēla, inclitus **(Lat)**; client, cliente **(Fr)**; inclito **(Ital)**; cliente, inclito **(Sp)**; inclito **(Port)**

Derivatives: client **(Eng)**; Klient **(Ger)**; клиéнт (klijént) **(Rus)**

Hellenic: κλῦτε (klûte), κλείω (kleíō), κλέω (kléō), κλειτός (kleitós), κλύω (klúō), κλῠτός (klutós), κλέος (kléos), -κλῆς (-klês) in names such as Ἡρακλῆς (Hēraklês), Περικλῆς (Periklês) **(AnGk)**; κλείνω (kleíno), κλέος (kléos) **(Gk)**

Slavic: слушать (slushat'), сло́во (slóvo), слух (slux), слышать (slyšať), слу́шать (slúšať), слушаю (slúšaju), слáва (sláva) (**Rus**); słuchać, słowo, słuch, słyszeć, słuszać, słuszeć, sława (**Pol**); slouti, slyšel, slovo, sluch, slyšet, slušet, sláva (**Cz**); slovo, sluch, slyšať, slušať, sláva (**Slo**); слово (slovo), слух (sluh), слуша (sluša), слава (slava) (**Mace**)

Baltic: šlãvė, klausyti (**Lith**); sluvêt, slava, slave, klausīties (**Latv**)

Albanian: quaj (**Alb**)

Indo-Iranian: श्रु (śru), अश्रोत् (áśrot), शृणोति (śṛṇóti), शुश्राव (śuśrāva), श्रावयति (śrāváyati), श्रोमत (śrómata-), श्रुत (śrutá), श्रुति (śruti), श्रवस् (śrávas), श्रोत्र (śrótra) (**Sans**); سروب (sarub), خسرو (Xosrow) (**Pers**)

which derives from *ḱel- to incline:

*ḱel-

to incline, lean, tend towards

Germanic: hold (**Eng**); hold, unhold, unholda (**OE**); hou, houd, onhoud (**Dut**); hold, Holde, unhold, Unhold (**Ger**); hollr (**Norse**); huld (**Swe**); huld (**Dan**); hollur (**Ice**)

Italic: auscultāre, auscultātiō, auscultātor (**Lat**); ausculter, écouter (**Fr**); ascoltare, auscultare (**Ital**); escuchar, auscultar (**Sp**); escutar, auscultar, auscultador (**Port**); asculta, ascultare (**Rom**)

Derivatives: auscultate, auscultation, auscultator, scout (**Eng**)

which is probably an extension of *ḱley- to lean:

*ḱley-

to lean, slope, incline

*ḱléy-e-ti, *ḱli-néw-ti, *ḱlí-n-e-ti, *ḱli-n-yé-ti, *ḱe-ḱlóy-e, *ḱléy-o-s, *ḱléy-teh$_2$, *ḱléy-trh$_2$, *ḱley-wó-s, *ḱli-tós, *ḱlóy-dʰro-m, *ḱlóy-neh$_2$, *ḱloy-w-ó-m

Germanic: lean, ladder, low (meaning burial mound) (arch.) (**Eng**); hleonian, hlǣder, hlǣw (**OE**); lynje, leune, ljedder, leider, ljerre (**Fris**); leunen, ladder, leer (**Dut**); lehnen, ablehnen, hinauslehnen, leinen, Leiter (**Ger**); hlíð, hlaiwa (**Norse**); lina, li (**Nor**); läna, lid, li (**Swe**); læne, lid, lide, li (**Dan**); hlíð (**Ice**)

Celtic: cledd (**Wel**); clé (**Iri**)

Italic: clīnāre, acclīnāre, dēclīnāre, inclīnāre, inclīnātiō, reclīnāre, clīvus (**Lat**); incliner, inclination (**Fr**); chinare, accline, declinare, inchinare, inclinare, inclinazione (**Ital**); declinar, inclinar, inclinación (**Sp**); inclinar, inclinação (**Port**); închina, închinare, înclina, înclinare, închinăciune, înclinație (**Rom**)

Derivatives: decline, declination, incline, inclination, recline, clivus (**Eng**)

Hellenic: κλίνω (klínō), κλίννω (klínnō), κλίμα (klíma), κλῖμαξ (klîmax), κλῑμᾰκτηρῐκός (klīmaktērikós), κλίνη (klínē), κλῐ̈σῐ̈ς (klísis), κέκλιται (kéklitai), κλῆθρα (klêithra) (**AnGk**); κλίμα (klíma), κλίνη (klíni), κλίση (klísi) (**Gk**)

Derivatives: climate, climax, climacteric, clinic (**Eng**); klimaat (**Dut**); Klima (**Ger**); clima, clīmax, clīmactēricus (**Lat**); climat, climax, climatérique (**Fr**); climatérico (**Ital**); climax (**Sp**); climactérico (**Port**)

Baltic: sliet, šliñti, šleĩvas (**Lith**); šlieti (**Latv**)

Albanian: qye (**Alb**)

Indo-Iranian: श्रयति (śrayati), शिश्राय (śiśrāya), श्रित (śrita) (**Sans**); سرس (sart) (dial.) (**Pers**)

*ḱel-

to cover, conceal

*ḱél-e-ti, *ḱl̥-ye-, *ḱel-mos, *ḱel-nó-, *ḱēl-is, *ḱél-ōs, *ḱel-yo-, *ḱl̥-eh₂-

Germanic: hele, hell, helm, hall (**Eng**); helan, hell, helm, heall (**OE**); hele, hel, helm, hille (**Fris**); helen, behelen, hel, hullen, helm, hal, huls (**Dut**); hehlen, Helle, Hölle, hüllen, Helm, Halle, Hülse (**Ger**); hel, hylja, hjalmr, hǫll (**Norse**); hel, hall (**Nor**); häla, hälare, ihjäl, hölja, hjälm, hall (**Swe**); hylle, hjelm, hal (**Dan**); hylja, hjálmur, höll (**Ice**)

Derivatives: alla (**Ital**); шелом (šelom), шлем (šlem) (**Rus**); hełm (**Pol**)

Celtic: ceil, fuil (**Iri**)

Italic: cella, cellārium, cellula, color, cilium, supercilium, clam, clandestīnus, cēlāre (**Lat**);

cellier, cellule, couleur, colorer, cil, sourcil, clandestin, celer (**Fr**);

cella, cellaio, cellula, colore, colorare, ciglio, sopracciglio, clandestino, celare (**Ital**);

cela, celda, cilla, cillero, celario, cellario, célula, color, colorar, corlar, ceja, cejo, sobreceja, sobrecejo, clandestino, celar (**Sp**);

cela, celeiro, célula, cor, colorar, corar, celha, cílio, sobrancelha, supercílio (**Port**);

celar, celulă, culoare, colora, ciliu, sprânceană (**Rom**)

Derivatives: cell, cellar, cellule, color/colour, supercilious, clandestine, conceal, ceiling, occult (**Eng**); kleur (**Fris**); kelder, kleur (**Dut**); Keller (**Ger**); kjeller (**Nor**); cell, källare (**Swe**); kulør (**Dan**); kjallari (**Ice**); cell (**Wel**); κέλλα (kélla) (**AnGk**); κελί (kelí), κελάρι (kelári) (**Gk**); келья (kel'ja) (**Rus**); qilar (**Alb**)

Hellenic: καλύπτω (kalúptō), Καλυψώ (Kalupsṓ), ἀποκαλύπτω (apokalúptō), ἀποκάλυψις (apokálupsis) (**AnGk**); καλύπτω (kalýpto), κέλυφος (kélyfos), αποκαλύπτω (apokalýpto), αποκάλυψη (apokálypsi) (**Gk**)

Derivatives: apocalypse, apocalyptic, calyce, calyptra, calyx, eucalyp, eucalyptus (**Eng**); apocalypsis (**Lat**); apocalypse (**Fr**); apacailipsis (**Iri**); апокáлипсис (apokálipsis) (**Rus**)

Baltic: šálmas (**Lith**)

Indo-Iranian: शरण (śaraṇa) (**Sans**); शरण (śaraṇ) (**Hin**)

*h₃ekʷ-

to see

*h₃ókʷs, *h₃ékʷ-ti-s, *h₃ékʷ-mn̥, *h₃ekʷ-elo-s, *h₂énti-h₃kʷ-o-s, *h₁éni-h₃kʷ-o-

Germanic: eye, window (**Eng**); ēge (**OE**); each (**Fris**); oog (**Dut**); Auge (**Ger**); auga, vindauga (**Norse**); øye, vindauga, vindu (**Nor**); öga, vindöga (**Swe**); øje, vindue (**Dan**); auga, vindauga (**Ice**)

Celtic: wyneb (**Wel**); oineach (**Iri**)

Italic: oculus, inoculāre, monoculus, oculāris (**Lat**); œil, oculaire (**Fr**); occhio, inoculare, oculare (**Ital**); ojo, óculo, óculos, inocular, ocular (**Sp**); olho, óculo, óculos, inocular, ocular (**Port**); ochi (**Rom**)

Derivatives: oculus, ocular, inoculate, monocle, ullage (**Eng**); oculus (**Swe**); okulus (**Cz**)

Hellenic: ὤψ (óps), ὄσσε (ósse), ὄμμα (ómma), ὀπτικός (optikós), ὀφθαλμός (ophthalmós), ὄψις (ópsis), σύνοψις (súnopsis), ἐνωπή (enōpḗ), ὄσσομαι (óssomai), ὄψομαι (ópsomai) (**AnGk**); ὄμμα (ómma), οφθαλμός (ofthalmós) (**Gk**)

Derivatives: optic, optician, ophthalmology, exophthalmic, microphthalmia, ophthalmic, ophthalmoparesis, ophthalmoplegia, parophthalmia, xerophthalmia, synopsis (**Eng**); synopsis (**Lat**); synopsis (**Fr**); ottico (**Ital**); синóпсис (sinópsis) (**Rus**)

Slavic: окó (óko) (poet.), окнó (oknó) (**Rus**); oko, okno (**Pol**); oko, okno (**Cz**); oko, okno (**Slo**); око (oko) (**Mace**)

Baltic: akis (**Lith**); acs (**Latv**)

Albanian: sy (**Alb**)

Indo-Iranian: अक्षि (ákṣi), अनीक (ánīka) (**Sans**); आँख (ākh) (**Hin**); ابشتن (abeštan) (obs.) (**Pers**)

from which also derives *ǵʰweroh₃kʷs (see under *ǵʰwer-), *h₂énti-h₃kʷós, and *h₂eh₁tro-h₃kʷs:

*h₂énti-h₃kʷós

appearing before, having prior aspect

*h₂énti + h₃kʷós

Italic: antīquus, antīquārius, antīquitās (**Lat**); antique, antiquité (**Fr**); antico, antichità (**Ital**); antiguo, antigüedad (**Sp**); antigo, antiguidade (**Port**); antic, antichitate (**Rom**)

Derivatives: antique, antic, antiquarian, antiquary, antiquate, antiquity (**Eng**); antiek (**Dut**); antik (**Ger**); antik (**Swe**)

*h₂eh₁tro-h₃kʷs

having the appearance of fire

*h₂eh₁ter- + *h₃ekʷ-

Italic: atrōx, atrōcitās (**Lat**); atroce, atrocité (**Fr**); atroce, atrocità (**Ital**); atroz, atrocidad (**Sp**); atroz, atrocidade (**Port**); atroce, atrocitate (**Rom**)

Derivatives: atrocious, atrocity (**Eng**)

*lewk-

light, bright; to shine; to see

see Sky

*spek̂-

to see, observe

*spék̂-ye-ti, *spk̂-néw-ti, *spék̂-s-t, *spok̂-éye-ti, *spék̂-s, *spek̂-u-, *spek̂-i-, *spok̂-o-, *spok̂-éh₂, *spek̂-mm̥, *spek̂-ti-, *spk̂-tós, *spek̂-tro-, *spek̂-tlo-

Germanic: aspy, espy, spy (**Eng**); spieden, bespieden (**Dut**); spähen (**Ger**); spá, speja (**Norse**); speide (**Nor**); speja (**Swe**); spejde (**Dan**); spá, speja (**Ice**)

Derivatives: épier (**Fr**); spiare (**Ital**); espiar (**Sp**); espiar (**Port**); spiona (**Rom**)

Italic: specere, aspicere, aspectāre, aspectus, spectāre, cōnspicere, cōnspicuus, dēspicere, dēspectus, dēspectāre, dispicere, dispectus, dispectāre, exspectāre/expectāre, īnspicere, inspectum, perspicere, prōspicere, prospectus, respicere, respectāre, respectus, retrōspicere, retrōspectum, speciēs, specimen, spectrum, speculārī, speculātiō, speculum, suspicere, suspectiō, suspīciō, suspectus, -spex (e.g., auspex, haruspex), auspicium (**Lat**);

aspecter, aspect, perspectif, perspicace, perspicacité, prospectus, respecter, répit, respect, espèce, épice, specimen, spectre, spéculer, spéculation, suspicion, auspices (**Fr**);

aspettare, spettare, aspetto, dispetto, dispettare, rispettare, rispetto, specie, spettro, specolare, speculare, speculazione, specchio, specolo, aruspice (**Ital**);

aspecto, despechar, expectar, perspectivo, perspicacia, perspicaz, prospecto, respectar, respetar, respecto, respeto, especia, especie, espécimen, espectro, aspillar, especular, especulación, espejo, espéculo, harúspice (**Sp**);

aspecto, aspeto, despeitar, respeitar, respeito, espécie, espécime, espectro, especular, especulação, espelho, espéculo (**Port**);

aștepta, așteptare, deștept, deștepta (poss.), respecta, respect, specie, spectru, specula, speculație, specul (**Rom**)

Derivatives: aspect, circumspect, circumspection, conspectus, conspicuous, inconspicuous, despection, despicable, despiciency, despise, despite, disrespect, especial, expect, expectant, expectation, inspect, inspector, inspection, introspect, introspection, introspective, perspective, perspicacious, perspicuous, prospective, prospector, prospectus, prospicience, respect, respectable, respectability, respective, irrespective, respite, retrospect, retrospective, retrospection, species, special, speciality, specific, specificity, specification, conspecific, specious, spectacle, spectacular, spectant, spice, specimen, spectre/specter, spectral, spectrum, speculate, speculation, speculum, spite, suspect, suspicion, suspicious, auspice, auspicate, auspicious, inauspicious, haruspex (**Eng**);

spiegel (**Dut**); Aspekt, Spezies, Spiegel, Auspizien, Haruspex (**Ger**); speictream (**Iri**); аспéкт (aspékt), проспект (prospekt), спектр (spektr), спекуляция (spekuljácija) (**Rus**); aspekt (**Pol**)

Hellenic: σκέπτομαι (sképtomai), σκεπτϊκός (skeptikós), σκέψϊς (sképsis), σκοπεύω (skopeúō), σκοπέω (skopéō), σκοπός (skopós), σκέψατο (sképsato) (**AnGk**); σκεπτικός (skeptikós), σκοπεύω (skopévo), σκοπιά (skopiá) (**Gk**)

Derivatives: scepsis, sceptic/skeptic, sceptical, scepticism, scope, -scope, e.g., kaleidoscope, microscope, periscope, stethoscope, telescope, -scopy, e.g., endoscopy, diascopy, -scopic, e.g., microscopic, telescopic (**Eng**); scóp (**Iri**); scopus (**Lat**); scopo (**Ital**)

Indo-Iranian: पश्यति (páśyati), अस्पष्ट (áspaṣṭa), स्पाशयति (spāśayati), स्पश् (spáś), स्पष्ट (spaṣṭá), स्पशति (spaśati) (**Sans**); सिपास (sipās) (**Hin**) سپاس (sepâs)(**Pers**)

*weyd-

to see, to find, to know

*wi-né-d-ti, *wóyde, *woyd-éye-ti, *wid-eh$_1$-(ye)-, *wéyd-se-ti, *wéyd-e-ti, *wid-ró-s, *wéyd-o-, *wéyd-os, *wid-és-eh$_2$, *wéyd-tōr, *weyd-to-s, *wid-tó-s, *wéyd-tu-s, *weyd-eh$_2$-li-mo-, *weyd-oh$_2$-lo-, *n̥-weyd-h$_1$-lo-, *wid-ri-, *wid-m-h$_3$onh$_2$-, *né-wid-s, *n̥-wid-eh$_2$-

Germanic: wit, weet (arch.), wite, wise, wizard, wisdom, iwis (poet., arch.), wis (dial.), guide, guy (**Eng**); wītan, wit, wīs, wīsdōm, ġewiss, wiss (**OE**);

wite, witte, wys, wiis, wiisdom, wisse, wis (**Fris**); weten, wijten, verwijten, wijsdom, gewis, wis, ongewis (**Dut**); wissen, Wissen, verweisen, weise, weisen, gewis, wijs, Weistum, gewiss, wis, ungewiss (**Ger**);

víta, vitr, víss, vísdómr, úviss (**Norse**); vite, vis, visdom (**Nor**); veta, vita, vitter, vis, visdom, viss (**Swe**); vide, vis, uvis (**Dan**); vita, vitur, vís, vísdómur, viss, óviss (**Ice**)

Derivatives: guider (**Fr**); guidare (**Ital**); guiar (**Sp**); guiar (**Port**)

Celtic: gwybod, gweld, gwŷs (**Wel**); fios (**Iri**)

Italic: vidēre, ēvidēns, ēvidentia, invidēre, pervidēre, praevidēre, prōvidēre, prōvidentia, prōvidus, prōvīsō, revidēre, revīsiō, revisēre, vīsibilis, vīsibilitās, vīsiō, vīsō, vīsum, vīsus, -vīsor, vīsitāre, revīsitāre (**Lat**);

voir, évidence, prévoir, pourvoir, providence, revoir, réviser, visible, viser, avis, visage, voilà, revoilà, voici, visiter (**Fr**);

vedere, evidenza, prevedere, provvedere, provvidenza, rivedere, visibile, visione, viso, visivo, visitare, visita, rivisitare, rivista (**Ital**);

ver, evidencia, prever, proveer, providencia, rever, visibilidad, visión, viso, aviso, visiva, visura, visitar, visita, revisitar, revistar, revista (**Sp**);

ver, evidência, invido, prever, prover, próvido, rever, aviso, visibilidade, avejão, visão, viso, visitar, visita, revistar, revista (**Port**);

vedea, vedere, prevedea, revedea, vis, vizita, revistă (**Rom**)

Derivatives: video, evidence, evident, evidential, envy, envious, invidus, preview, previse, prevision, provide, purvey, providence, improvident, improvisation, improvise, imprudent, provision, provisional, proviso, provisory, prudence, review, revise, revision, revisal, revisionary, visible, visibility, invisible, vision, visionary, visual, advice, advise, clairvoyance, interview, invidious, supervise, survey, surveyor, surview, survise, view, vis-à-vis, visa, visage, visit, visitation, visor, vista, voilà, voyeur (**Eng**); Vision (**Ger**); evidens (**Nor**); βίντεο (vínteo) (**Gk**); vështoj (**Alb**)

Hellenic: οἶδα (oîda), ἵστωρ (hístōr), ἄ-ιστος (á-istos), εἴδω (eídō), εἶδος (eîdos), -ειδής (-eidés), εἰδάλιμος (eidálimos), εἴδωλον (eídōlon), ἀείδελος (aeídelos), ἰδέᾱ (idéā), ἱστορία (historía), ἱστορικός (historikós), ἵστωρ (hístōr), ἴδρις (ídris), ἴδμων (ídmōn), νῆις (nêis), Ἀΐδης (Aΐdēs) (**AnGk**); είδωλο (eídolo), ιδέα (idéa), ιστορία (istoría) (**Gk**)

Derivatives: -id, -oid, eidetic, eidolon, idol, idolater, idolatry, idolum, idea, idealogue, ideology, idyll, pareidolia, history, storey, story, historic, historical (**Eng**); idool, historie (**Dut**); Idee, Historie (**Ger**); historie (**Nor**); idé, historia (**Swe**); historie (**Dan**);

ystyr (**Wel**); stair, stór (**Iri**);

-īdēs, -oīdēs, īdōlum, idea, historia, historicus (**Lat**); idée, histoire, historique (**Fr**); idea, storia, storico (**Ital**); idea, historia, histórico (**Sp**); ideia, idolo, história, histórico (**Port**); istorie, istoric (**Rom**);

йдол (ídol), идéя (idéja), истóрия (istórija) (**Rus**); historia (**Pol**); historie (**Cz**); história (**Slo**); истóрија (istórija) (**Mace**); istorija (**Lith**); histori (**Alb**)

Slavic: вńдеть (vídet'), вéдать (védat') (dated/poet.), вид (vid) (**Rus**); widzieć, wiedzieć, wieść (**Pol**); vidět, vědět, vid (**Cz**); vidieť, vedieť, vid (**Slo**); вńди (vídi) (**Mace**)

Baltic: véidas, vaizdas, veizdéti (**Lith**); veĩds, viedêt (**Latv**)

Indo-Iranian: बिन्दति (vindáti), वेत्ति (vetti), अविदत् (ávidat), वेदयति (vedayati), वेत्तृ (vettr̥), वेदितृ (véditr̥), वेदस् (védas) (**Sans**); نويد (navid) (**Pers**)

*gʰed-
to find; to hold

*gʰ-né-d-, *gʰed-eh₂, *gʰed-es-eh₂

Germanic: get, beget, forget (**Eng**); ġetan, beġietan, forġietan (**OE**); ferjitte (**Fris**); vergeten (**Dut**); vergessen (**Ger**); geta (**Norse**); gjete, gjeta (**Nor**); gitta (**Swe**); gide (**Dan**); geta (**Ice**)

Italic: prehendere, apprehendere, apprehensiō, comprehendere, comprehensibilis, comprehensiō, comprehensīvus, comprehensus, dēprehendere, prehensiō, prehensus, reprehendere, reprehensibilis, reprehensiō, reprehensus, praeda, praedor, praedātiō, praedātor, hedera (**Lat**);

prendre, apprendre, appréhender, appréhension, comprendre, compréhensible, compréhension, compréhensif, compris, préhension, prison, pris, reprendre, répréhender, répréhensible, répréhension, repris, proie, prédation, prédateur, lierre (**Fr**);

prendere, apprendere, apprensione, comprendere, comprensibile, comprensione, comprensivo, compreso, imprendere, impresa, prensione, prigione, preso, riprendere, riprensibile, reprensibile, riprensione, ripreso, preda, predare, predazione, predatore, edera (**Ital**);

prender, aprender, aprehender, aprehensión, comprender, comprensible, comprensión, comprehensión, comprehensivo, deprehender, emprender, empresa, prensión, prisión, preso, reprehender, reprender, reprensible, reprehensible, reprensión, prea, preda, prear, predar, predador, hiedra, yedra (**Sp**);

prender, aprender, apreender, apreensão, compreender, compreensivel, compreensão, compreensivo, depreender, empreender, emprender, empresa, preensão, prisão, preso, repreender, repreensivel, repreensão, preia, prear, preda, predação, predador, hera (**Port**);

prinde, prindere, aprinde, aprindere, aprehenda, cuprinde, cuprindere, cuprins, deprinde, deprindere, împrinde, împrindere, prins, pradă, prăda, prădare, prădăciune, prădător, iederă (**Rom**)

Derivatives: apprehend, apprehension, comprehend, comprehension, comprehensible, incomprehensible, comprehensive, comprise, enterprise, prehension, prehensility, prison, prize, reprehend, reprehensible, reprehension, reprise, prey, prede, predation, predator, surprise (**Eng**); prooi (**Dut**); pre (**Alb**)

Hellenic: χανδάνω (khandánō) (**AnGk**)

*leys-
to trace, track

*loys-éye-, *lóys-eh$_2$, *léys-tis, *loys-tis

Germanic: lear (dial.), learn (meaning teach), list, last, learn (**Eng**); lǽran, list, lǽst, leornian (**OE**); leare, list, least (**Fris**); leren, list, leest (**Dut**); lehren, List, Leist, lernen (**Ger**); læra, list (**Norse**); lære, lest (**Nor**); lära, list, läst (**Swe**); lære, list (**Dan**); læra, list (**Ice**)

Italic: līra, dēlīrus, dēlīrium (**Lat**); délire, delirium (**Fr**); delirio (**Ital**); delirio, delírium (**Sp**); delirio (**Port**); delir (**Rom**)

Derivatives: delirious, delirium (**Eng**); delier, delirium (**Dut**); Delirium (**Ger**); delirium, dille (**Nor**); delirium (**Swe**); delirium (**Dan**); делирий (delírij) (**Rus**); delirium (**Pol**); delirium (**Cz**)

Slavic: lecha (**Pol**); lícha (**Cz**)

*ǵneh$_3$-
to recognize, know

*ǵnéh$_3$-t, ǵn̥h$_3$-ént, *ǵneh$_3$-, *ǵn̥-né-h$_3$-ti, *ǵn̥-n-h$_3$-énti, *ǵn̥h$_3$-sḱé-ti, *ǵn̥h$_3$-tó-s, *ǵneh$_3$-ti-, *ǵneh$_3$-meh$_2$, *ǵnéh$_3$-mn̥, *ǵn̥h$_3$-mén-s, *ǵnéh$_3$-mō, *ǵneh$_3$-dʰl-, *ǵneh$_3$-ri-, *ǵn̥h$_3$-ro-, *ǵn̥h$_3$-wo-

Germanic: can, con, cunning, canny, ken, couth, uncouth, kithe, know (**Eng**); cunnan, cennan, cēne, cann, cūþ, forcūþ, uncūþ, cȳþan, cnāwan (**OE**);

kunnen, kennen, kond, konden, verkonden, onkond (**Dut**); können, kennen, kühn, kund, künden (**Ger**);

kunna, kenna, kœnn, kunnr, úkunnr, kynna, kná (**Norse**); kunne, kjenne (**Nor**); kunna, känna, kön (arch.) (**Swe**); kunne, kende, køn (**Dan**); kunna, kenna, kænn, kunnur, kynna, knega (**Ice**)

Celtic: adnabod, adwaen, gwynn, gnawd (**Wel**); aithin, gnáth (**Iri**)

Italic: (g)nōscere, agnōscere, cognōscere, cognitio, incognitus, recognōscere, praecognoscere, nōvī, nōtus, nōtiō, nota, notāre, notārius, notātiō, notula, īgnōtus, nōtitia, nōtōrius, nōbilis, glōriā, glōriātiō, glōriārī, glōriōsus, gnārus, ignārus, ignōrāre, ignōtus, ignōrāntem, nārrāre, ēnārrāre, ēnārrātiō, nārrātiō, narrātīvus, nārrātor, nārrātus, gnāvus, ignāvus (**Lat**);

connaître, reconnaître, notion, note, noter, notaire, notice, noble, gloire, glorieux, ignare, ignorer, ignorant, narrer, narration, narratif (**Fr**);

noto, conoscere, riconoscere, nozione, notare, notaio, notazione, notorio, nobile, gloria, gloriare, glorioso, ignaro, ignorare, ignorante, narrare, narrativo, ignavo (**Ital**);

conocer, reconocer, noción, notar, notario, notorio, noticia, noble, gloria, gloriar, glorioso, ignaro, ignorar, añorar, ignorante, narrar, enarración, narración, narrativo (**Sp**);

noto, conhecer, reconhecer, noção, nota, notar, notário, nótula, nódoa, notícia, nobre, glória, glorioso, ignorar, ignoto, ignorante, narrar, enarração (**Port**);

cunoaşte, cunoaştere, recunoaşte, notare, nobil, glorie, ignora, ignorant (**Rom**)

Derivatives: cognosce, cognize, cognition, recognosce, recognize, reconnoiter, recognition, precognosce, precognition, notion, note, notary, notation, notice, notorious, noble, nobility, glory, gloriation, glorious, ignoramus, ignore, ignorant, narrate, enarrate, narration, narrative, narrator (**Eng**);

noteren, nobel, glorie, glorieus (**Dut**); Note, notieren, nobel, ignorieren, ignorant (**Ger**); nobel (**Swe**); nod, glóir (**Iri**);

нота (nota), нотариус (notarius), нотация (notacija) (**Rus**);

Hellenic: ἔγνων (égnōn), γνῶσις (gnôsis), γνώμη (gnṓmē), γνῶμα (gnôma), γνώμων (gnṓmōn), γιγνώσκω (gignṓskō), ἀγνώς (agnós), ἀγνωσΐᾱ (agnōsíā), ἀνᾰγΐγνώσκω (anagignóskō), γνωτός (gnōtós), γνωστός (gnōstós), γνώριμος (gnórimos) (**AnGk**); αναγιγνώσκω (anagignósko), γνώμη (gnómi), γνώριμος (gnórimos) (**Gk**)

Derivatives: gnosis, agnosia, agnostic, groma, gnomon, norm, abnormal, enormous, normal (**Eng**); normaal, normale (**Dut**); enorm, normal (**Ger**); gnosis, enorm, normal (**Nor**); enorm, normal (**Swe**); normálta (**Iri**);

anagignōscomena, grōma, nōrma, anōrmalus, ēnōrmis, nōrmālis (**Lat**); anormal, énorme (**Fr**); norma, enorme, normale (**Ital**); anormal, enorme, normal (**Sp**); groma, norma, anormal, enorme, normal (**Port**); anormal, enorm, normal (**Rom**);

норма (norma), нормальный (normál'nyj) (**Rus**); normalny (**Pol**); normální (**Cz**)

Slavic: знать (znat') (**Rus**); znać (**Pol**); znát (**Cz**); znať (**Slo**); знае (znae) (**Mace**)

Baltic: žinoti, nežinoti (**Lith**); zināt, nezināt (**Latv**)

Albanian: njoh (**Alb**)

Indo-Iranian: अज्ञात् (ajñāt), जानाति (jānāti), ज्ञात (jñātá) (**Sans**); जानना (jānnā), ज्ञात (gyāt) (**Hin**); شناختن (šenâxtan) (**Pers**)

*wer-
to heed, notice

*wer-eh₁-(ye)-ti, *wor-o-s

Germanic: ware, wary, aware, ward, lord, guard, garnish (**Eng**); wær, ġewær, weard, hlāfweard, hlāford (**OE**); gewaar (**Dut**); gewahr, Wart, Warte (**Ger**); varr, vǫrðr, varða (**Norse**); vård, vord (**Nor**); var, varsam, vård (**Swe**); var (**Dan**); var, vörður, varða (**Ice**)

Derivatives: garda (**Iri**); warda, guardare (**Lat**); garde (**Fr**); guardia, guardare (**Ital**); garda, guardar (**Sp**); guardar, guarnir (**Port**)

Italic: verēri, reverēri, reverendus, reverens, reverentia, verēcundus, verēcundia (**Lat**); révérer, révérence, véréconide, vergogne (**Fr**); riverente, riverenza, verecondo, vergogna, verecondia (**Ital**); reverente, reverencia, vergüenza (**Sp**); reverente, reverência, verecundo, vergonha, verecúndia (**Port**)

Derivatives: revere, reverend, reverent, reverence, verecund (**Eng**)

Hellenic: ὁράω (horáō), θεωρός (theōrós) (θέᾱ+), θεωρίᾱ (theōríā), θεωρητικός (theōrētikós), θεώρημα (theōrēma), ὅρασις (hórasis), ὅραμα (hórama) (**AnGk**); θεωρία (theoría), ὁραμα (órama) (**Gk**)

Derivatives: theory, theoretical, theorist, theorize, theorem (**Eng**); teoir (**Iri**); theōria (**Lat**); théorie (**Fr**); teoria (**Ital**); teoría (**Sp**); теория (teorija) (**Rus**)

*men-
mind, to think, remember

*mn̥-yé-tor, *me-món-e, *mon-éye-ti, *mn-eh$_2$-ské-ti, *mén-mn̥, *mén-os, *me-mn-os, *mén-ti-s, *mén-tro-m, *mon-(e)stro-, *mn̥(s)-dʰh$_1$-

Germanic: mind, main (dial.), minion, mint (**Eng**); mynd, gemynd, munan, myntan (**OE**);

muntsje, mintsje (**Fris**); monter, munten (**Dut**); Minne, munter, münzen (**Ger**);

minni, man, muna, munda, munr (**Norse**); munter, mun (**Nor**); minne, munter, mån (**Swe**); mon, minde, munter (**Dan**); muna, mynd, munur (**Ice**)

Celtic: cof (**Wel**); dearmad (**Iri**)

Italic: mēns, amēns, āmentia, dēmens, dēmentia, mentālis, mentiō, mentior, mendāx, mendācitās, mendācium, monēre, monitor, mōnstrum, mōnstrāre, dēmōnstrāre, dēmōnstrātiō, praemōnstrāre, mōnstruōsus, meminī, admonēre, admonitiō, praemonēre, praemonitiō, submonēre, monēta, monumentum, Minerva, memor, memoria, memoriālis, memorāre, memorābilis, memorābilia, memoriter, memorārī, rememorārī, comminīscor, commentor, commentārius, reminīscor (**Lat**);

-ment, dément, démence, mental, mention, mensonge, mentir, mendacieux, monstre, montrer, démontrer, démonstration, monstrueux, admonester, admonitio, semondre, monnaie, monument, mémoire, mémorer, mémorable, remémorer, commentaire (**Fr**);

mente, -mente, amente, amenza, demente, demenza, mentale, menzione, menzogna, mentire, mendace, mendacio, mostro, mostruoso, mostrare, dimostrare, dimostrazione, premonire, ammonire, moneta, monumento, munumento, memore, memoria, memoriale, merorare, memorabile, rammemorare, rimemorare, rimembrare (**Ital**);

mente, -mente, amente, demente, demencia, mental, mención, mentir, mendaz, muñir, monstruo, mostrar, demostrar, demostración, premostrar, amonestar, admonición, moneda, monumento, memoria, membrar, memorar, memorable, remembrar, rememorar, comentario (**Sp**);

mente, -mente, demência, mental, menção, mentir, mendace, mendaz, monir, monstro, mostrar, demonstrar, demonstração, admoestar, admonição, moeda, monumento, memória, lembrar, memorar, memorável, relembrar, remembrar, rememorar, comentário (**Port**);

demență, mental, mintal, mențiune, minciună, minți, mințire, minte, monstro, monstru, mustra, mustrare, monedă, monument, mormânt, memorie, memora (**Rom**)

Derivatives: amentia, dementia, demented, momento, mental, mentalis, mention, mendacious, mendacity, monitor, monster, monstrous, demonstrate, demonstration, premonstrate, monish, admonish, admonition, permonish, premonish, summon, submonish, submone, money, monument, memory, memorate, memorabilia, memorable, memorandum, memorial, immemorial, memoir, memoriter, rememorate, remember, remembrance, comment, commentary, commonition, commemorate, reminisce, reminiscence (**Eng**);

dement, munt, demonstreren, demonstratie (**Dut**); dement, Demenz, mental, Münze, demonstrieren, Demonstration, Monster, Kommentar (**Ger**); mynt (**Nor**); mental, mynt (**Swe**); mønt (**Dan**); mynt (**Ice**);

mynwent (**Wel**); meabhair (**Iri**);

амéнция (amḗncija), демéнция (demḗncija), монéта (monéta), монитóр (monitór), монумент (monument), демонстрúровать (demonstrírovat'), демонстрáция (demonstrácija) (**Rus**); minca (**Slo**); monedhë, moshtrë, monstër (**Alb**)

Hellenic: μένος (ménos), μαίνομαι (maínomai), μανίᾱ (maníā), μνάομαι (mnáomai), ἀμνησία (amnēsía), μνήμη (mnḗmē), μέμονα (mémona), μιμνήσκω (mimnḗskō), μανθάνω (manthánō), μάθημα (máthēma), μᾰθημᾰτῐκός (mathēmatikós), Προμηθεύς (Promētheús), αὐτόματος (autómatos), δῠσμενής (dusmenḗs), εὐμενής (eumenḗs) (**AnGk**); ἀμνησία (amnisía), μνήμη (mními) (**Gk**)

Derivatives: mania, amnesia, amnesty, anamnesis, dysmnesia, mneme, mnemonic, premonition, mathematics, automaton, automate, automatic (**Eng**); amnésie (**Fr**); мания (mánija) (**Rus**); mania (**Pol**)

Slavic: мнить (mnit'), мышлéние (myšlenije), мнение (mnenije), мысль (mysl'), мы́слить (mýslit'), мышлять (myšljat'), пáмять (pámjat') (**Rus**); mniemać, myśleć, myśl, myślać, pamięć (**Pol**); mínit, mínění, mysl, myslit, myšlet, paměť (**Cz**); mieniť, myseľ, myslieť, myšľať, pamäť (**Slo**); мисла (misla), пáмет (pámet) (**Mace**)

Baltic: mintis, mintas, minti, minéti (**Lith**); minēt (**Latv**)

Albanian: mund (**Alb**)

Indo-Iranian: मनस् (mánas), मन्यते (mányate), मन्त्र (mántra), मति (matí), मन्मन् (mánman), दुर्मनास् (durmanās), सुमनस् (sumánas) (**Sans**); दुश्मन (duśman), मंत्र (mantra) (**Hin**); دشمن (došman) (**Pers**)

Derivatives: mantra (**Eng**); mantra (**Dan**); mantra (**Fr**); mantra (**Sp**); mantra (**Port**); duşman, duşmancă (**Rom**); душма́н (dušmán), ма́нтра (mántra) (**Rus**); душман (dušman) (**Mace**)

*teng-
to think

*tong-éy, *tn̥g-yé-, *tong-tos, *tong-os

Germanic: think, bethink, thank, methinks, thought (**Eng**); þencan, beþenċan, þanc, þonc, þyncan, þōht, ġeþōht (**OE**);

tinke, tanck, tank, taensjen, tankje, tanke, dacht (in compounds) (**Fris**); denken, bedenken, dank, danken, dunken, gedachte (**Dut**); denken, bedenken, Dank, danken, dünken, Andacht (**Ger**);

þenkja, þekkja, þǫkk, þakka, þykkja, þóttr, þótti (**Norse**); tenke, tekkes, takk, takke, takka, tykkja (**Nor**); tänka, täckas, tack, tacka, tycka, tyckas (**Swe**); tænke, tak, takke, tykkes, samtykke (**Dan**); þekkja, þökk, takk, þakka, þykja, samþykkja (**Ice**)

Derivatives: dziękować (**Pol**); děkovat (**Cz**); ďakovať (**Slo**)

Italic: tongēre (**Lat**)

Albanian: ndihem (**Alb**)

*Hreh₁dʰ-
to think; to arrange; to succeed, accomplish

see Body: Limbs & Joints

*bʰeh₂-
to speak, say

*bʰéh₂-ti, *bʰ-né-h₂-ti, *bʰeh₂-meh₂, *bʰéh₂-os, *bʰoh₂-neh₂, *bʰeh₂-ni-s, *bʰéh₂-ti-s, *bʰh₂-tó-s, *bʰéh₂-tu-s, *bʰeh₂-dʰlo-, bʰh₂-new-ti

Germanic: ben, bene, bee, boon, ban, banish (**Eng**); bēn, bannan (**OE**); banne (**Fris**); bannen (**Dut**); bannen (**Ger**); bón, bœn, banna (**Norse**); bønn, banne (**Nor**); bön, banna (**Swe**); bøn, bande (**Dan**); bón, bæn, banna (**Ice**)

Derivatives: bannir (**Fr**)

Italic: fārī, effārī, effābilis, fandus, īnfandus, nefandus, fāns, īnfāns, fātum, fāma, īnfāmis, īnfāmia, fās, fastus, nefās, nefārius, nefāstus, fātus, fatērī, cōnfitērī, cōnfessiō, prōfitērī, prōfessiō, professor, fābula, fābella, fābulōsus, fābulātiō (**Lat**);

effable, enfant, fameux, infâme, infamie, faste, néfaste, confesser, confession, profession, professeur, fable, fabuleux, fabulation (**Fr**);

infante, fato, fama, infamia, infamare, fasto, nefasto, confessione, professione, professore, favola, fiaba, favella, favoloso (**Ital**);

infando, nefando, infante, hado, fama, infame, infamia, fasto, nefas, nefario, nefasto, confesar, confesión, profesión, profesor, habla, fábula, fabuloso (**Sp**);

infando, nefando, infante, fado, fama, infâmia, fasto, nefas, nefário, nefasto, confessar, confissão, profissão, professor, fábula, fala, fabela, fabuloso (**Port**);

faimă, profesiune, profesor, fabulos (**Rom**)

Derivatives: effable, ineffable, infandous, nefandous, infant, fate, fame, infamous, infamy, nefarious, nefast, confess, confession, profession, professor, fable, fabulous, confabulation (**Eng**);

faam (**Dut**); infam, Konfession (**Ger**); professor, fabel (**Swe**); fabúla, fabúlera (**Ice**);

инфант (infánt), конфéссия (konféssija), профессия (professija), профéссор (proféssor), фáбула (fábula) (**Rus**); fabuła (**Pol**); famë (**Alb**)

Hellenic: φημί (phēmí), φαμί (phamí), φήμη (phémē), φωνή (phōné), φωνέω (phōnéō), φάσις (phásis), φάτις (phátis), φατός (phatós) (**AnGk**); φήμη (fími), φωνή (foní) (**Gk**)

Derivatives: -phone, phono-, antiphon, cacophony, euphonious, homophone, microphone, megaphone, phone, phoneme, phonetic, phonics, polyphony, symphony (**Eng**)

Slavic: бáйка (bájka) (**Rus**); bajka (**Pol**); bajka (**Cz**); bájka (**Slo**); бајка (bajka) (**Mace**)

Indo-Iranian: भनति (bhánati), भाषा (bhāṣā) (**Sans**); भाषा (bhāṣā) (**Hin**)

Derivatives: bahasa (**Dut**)

*sekʷ-

to say

*sékʷ-e-ti, *sokʷ-éye-ti, *sokʷ-h₁-ye-ti, *h₁en(i)-skʷ-ih₂, *skʷ-e-tlo-m, *sokʷ-ó-s

Germanic: say, saw (meaning a saying), saga (**Eng**); seċgan, lēassagol, sagu, saga (**OE**); sizze (**Fris**); zeggen, sage (**Dut**); sagen, Sage (**Ger**);

segja, sannsǫgull, saga (**Norse**); si, soge (**Nor**); säga, saga (**Swe**); sige, sage (arch.), save (dial.) (**Dan**); segja, saga (**Ice**)

Celtic: hebu, ebe, ateb, chwedl (**Wel**); inscne, scéal, rosc (uncert.) (**Iri**)

Italic: īnsece, inquam (**Lat**)

Hellenic: ἐνέπω (enépō) / ἐννέπω (ennépō) (**AnGk**)

Slavic: сочúть (sočíť) (dial.) (**Rus**); soczyć (**Pol**); sok (**Cz**); sok (**Slo**); сочи (soči) (**Mace**)

Baltic: sakyti (**Lith**); sacīt (**Latv**)

*wekʷ-

to speak, sound out

*wékʷ-ti, *wókʷ-e-ti, *wokʷ-ye-ti, *wí-wekʷ-ti, *wé-wk-e-t, *wõkʷ-s, *wékʷ-os, *wokʷ-tlo-m, *wókʷ-to-s, *uk-tó-s, *wokʷ-smņ

Germanic: wōm, wōma, wēman (**OE**); gewagen (**Dut**); gewähnen, erwähnen (**Ger**); ómr, ómun, váttr (**Norse**)

Celtic: gwep, gwaethl (**Wel**); focal, fuaim (**Iri**)

Italic: vōx, vōcis, convīcium, vōcālis, vocāre, advocāre, advocātiō, advocātus, convocāre, ēvocāre, invocāre, prōvocāre, revocāre, vocābulum, vocābulārium, vocātiō, vocātīvus, vōciferor, vōciferātiō, vōcula (**Lat**);

voix, vocal, voyelle, avouer, avocat, convoquer, évoquer, invoquer, révoquer, vocabulaire, vocation, vocatif, vociférer, vocifération (**Fr**);

voce, vocale, vocare, avvocare, avvocato, convocare, evocare, provocare, vocabolo, vocabolario, vocazione, vocativo (**Ital**);

voz, vocal, abogar, advocar, avocar, abogado, convocar, evocar, invocar, revocar, vocablo, vocabulario, vocación, vocativo, vociferar (**Sp**);

voz, convício, vocal, vogal, advogar, advocar, advocação, advogado, convocar, provocar, vocábulo, vocabulário, vocação, vocativo (**Port**);

voce, boace, vocal, advocat, avocat, vocabulă, vocabular, vocabulariu, vocativ (**Rom**)

Derivatives: voice, vocal, vowel, vouch, advoke, avow, avouch, advocate, advocation, avocat, evoke, provoke, revoke, vocable, vocabulary, vocation, vocative, vociferous, vociferate, vociferator, vocular, vocule (**Eng**); vocaal (**Dut**); vokal, Vokal, Advokat, Vogt, Vokabel (**Ger**); vokal (**Swe**); гла́сный (glásnyj), адвока́т (advokát) (**Rus**)

Hellenic: εἶπον (eípon), ὄψ (óps), ἔπος (épos), ἐποποιία (epopoiía) (**AnGk**)

Derivatives: эпос (épos) (**Rus**)

Indo-Iranian: वक्ति (vakti), विवक्ति (vívakti), अवोचत् (avocat), वचस् (vácas), वक्त्र (vaktra), उक्त (ukta), वच् (vac), सूक्त (sūktá) (**Sans**); आवाज़ (āvāz) (**Hin**); آواز (âvâz) (**Pers**)

*werh₁-

to speak, say

*wérh₁-t, wér-ye-ti

Hellenic: εἴρω (eírō), ῥῆμα (rhêma), ῥήτωρ (rhḗtōr), ῥητορικός (rhētorikós) (**AnGk**); ῥήμα (ríma), ρητορικός (ritorikós) (**Gk**)

Derivatives: rheme, rhematic, rhetic, rhetoric (**Eng**); Rhema (**Ger**); rhētor, rhētoricus (**Lat**); rhéteur (**Fr**); rétor, rétorico (**Sp**); retor (**Pol**); ритор (ritor) (**Rus**)

Slavic: врать (vrat′) (**Rus**)

which possibly includes:

$*werd^hh_1o-$

Germanic: word (**Eng**); word (**OE**); wurd, antwird (**Fris**); woord, antwoord (**Dut**); Wort, Antwort (**Ger**); orð, andyrði (**Norse**); ord (**Nor**); ord (**Swe**); ord (**Dan**); orð, andyrði (**Ice**)

Italic: verbum, adverbium, adverbiālis, prōverbium, verbālis, verbātim, verbōsus (**Lat**); verbe, verve, adverbe, adverbial, proverbe, verbal, verbatim (**Fr**); verbo, avverbio, avverbiale, proverbio, verbale, verboso (**Ital**); verbo, adverbio, adverbial, proverbio, verbal (**Sp**); verbo, verba, advérbio, adverbial, verbal, verbatim, verboso (**Port**); verb, vorbă (poss.) (**Rom**)

Derivatives: verb, adverb, adverbial, proverb, verbal, verbatim, verbose, verbosity (**Eng**); Verb, Verbum, Adverb (**Ger**); verb (**Swe**); berf, adferf (**Wel**)

Hellenic: εἴρων (eírōn), εἰρωνεία (eirōneía) (**AnGk**)

Derivatives: irony (**Eng**); īrōnīa (**Lat**); ironia (**Ital**); ironia (**Sp**); ironia (**Port**); ирония (irónija) (**Rus**)

Baltic: var̃das (**Lith**); vārds (**Latv**)

Albanian: urtë (**Alb**)

Indo-Iranian: व्रत (vrata) (**Sans**); व्रत (vrat) (**Hin**)

*yek-

to utter

*yék-e-ti, *yék-ti-s, *yok-o-s

Germanic: jicht (**Dut**); jehen, Gicht (**Ger**); gikt (**Swe**)

Derivatives: gêne, gêner (**Fr**)

Celtic: iaith (**Wel**); icht (**Iri**)

Italic: iocus, iocor, iocōsus, ioculāris (**Lat**); jeu, jouer, jongler, jongleur (**Fr**); gioco, giuoco, giocare, giocoso (**Ital**); juego, jugar (**Sp**); jogo, jogar, jogral (**Port**); joc, juca, jucare (**Rom**)

Derivatives: joke, jocose, jocular, jocularity, juggle, jewel (poss.) (**Eng**); Jux (**Ger**); jôc (**Wel**)

*kelh₁-

to call, cry, summon

*kl̥h₁-m-, *kl̥h₁-rós, *kelh₁-o-

Germanic: hale, haul, low (as in to moo) (**Eng**); ġeholian, hlōwan (**OE**); helje (**Fris**); halen, loeien (**Dut**); holen (**Ger**); hlóa (**Norse**); hjal, hala (**Nor**); hala (**Swe**); hale (**Dan**); hjal, hjala, hlóa (**Ice**)

Derivatives: haler (**Fr**); halar (**Sp**)

Italic: clāmāre, acclāmāre, acclāmātiō, clāmor, conclāmāre, dēclāmāre, dēclāmātiō, exclāmāre, prōclāmāre, proclāmātiō, reclāmāre, rēclāmātiō, clārus, clāritās, dēclārāre, calāre, intercalāre, classis, classicus, kalendae, calendārium, concilium, conciliāre, conciliābulum, acconciliāre (**Lat**);

clamer, acclamer, clameur, conclamer, déclamer, exclamer, proclamer, proclamation, réclamer, clair, clarté, déclarer, classe, classifier, classer, classique, calendrier, calendaire, conseil, concilier, conciliabule (**Fr**);

chiamare, clamare, acclamare, clamore, conclamare, declamare, esclamare, schiamazzare, proclamare, reclamare, chiaro, clarità, dichiarare, intercalare, classe, classare, classico, classificare, classico, calendario, concilio, consiglio, consigliare, conciliabolo (**Ital**);

llamar, clamar, aclamar, aclamación, clamor, declamar, exclamar, proclamar, reclamar, claro, claridad, declarar, intercalar, clásico, calendario, concilio, consejo, concejo, conciliar, consejar, conciliábulo, aconsejar (**Sp**);

chamar, clamar, aclamar, aclamação, clamor, declamar, proclamar, reclamar, claro, claridade, declarar, intercalar, classe, classificar, classificação, classificado, classificador, clássico, calendário, concelho, concílio, conciliábulo, aconselhar (**Port**);

chema, chemare, clama, chiar, clar, claritate, declara, calendar, cărindar, consiliu (**Rom**)

Derivatives: claim, acclaim, clamour/clamor, declaim, exclaim, proclaim, proclamation, reclaim, reclamation, clear, clarity, declare, class, classify, classic, classical, calendar, nomenclature, intercalate, council, conciliate, conciliatory, conciliabule (**Eng**);

klaar, declareren, kalender (**Dut**); deklamieren, klar, deklarieren, Klasse, Kalender (**Ger**); klar, deklarere (**Nor**); klar, deklarera (**Swe**); klar, deklarere (**Dan**);

декламáция (deklamácija), прокламáция (proklamacija), рекламáция (reklamacija), календáрь (kalendár'), консúлиум (konsílium) (**Rus**); qartë, kalendar, kallënduar, kallnor, këshill (**Alb**)

Hellenic: καλέω (kaléō) (**AnGk**); καλώ (kaló) (**Gk**)

Baltic: kalba (**Lith**); kaļuot (**Latv**)

*preḱ-
to ask

*proḱ-éye-ti, *pr̥(ḱ)-sḱé-ti, *préḱ-s, *proḱ-o-

Germanic: frain (**Eng**); freġnan (**OE**); vorsen, vragen (**Dut**); Forsche, forschen, fragen (**Ger**); fregna (**Norse**); forske, frega (**Nor**); forska, fræghna (**Swe**); forske, fræghnæ (**Dan**); fregna (**Ice**)

Celtic: erchi, rheg (**Wel**)

Italic: poscere, postulāre, expostulāre, postulātūs, prex, precārius, precārī, dēprecārī, dēprecābilis, dēprecātiō, dēprecātīvus, dēprecātōrius, precātiō, precātīvus, procāre, procāx (**Lat**);

postuler, prière, prier, déprécation, déprécatif, déprécatoire (**Fr**);

postulare, precario, preghiera, plecale, pregare, deprecare, deprecabile, deprecazione, deprecativo, deprecatorio, procace (**Ital**);

postular, plegaria, precario, deprecar, deprecación, procaz (**Sp**);

prece, precário, deprecar, procace, procaz (**Port**)

Derivatives: postulate, expostulate, prayer, precarious, pray, deprecate, deprecation, deprecative, deprecatory, precation, precative (**Eng**); постулат (postulat) (**Rus**)

Slavic: просить (prosíť) (**Rus**); prosić (**Pol**); prosit (**Cz**); prosiť (**Slo**)

Baltic: prašyti (**Lith**); prasît (**Latv**)

Indo-Iranian: पृच्छति (pr̥ccháti), प्राश् (prāś) (**Sans**); पूछना (pūchnā) (**Hin**); پرسیدن (pursīdan) (**Pers**)

*seh₂g-
to seek out

see Movement

*med-
to measure; give advice, healing

see Sky

*h₃reǵ-
to straighten, right oneself; right, just

*h₃réǵ-e-ti, *h₃r̥-ne-ǵ-ti, *h₃roǵ-éye-ti, *h₃réǵ-r̥-, *h₃réǵ-s, *h₃reǵ-tó-s, *h₃réǵ-u-s,

*h₃roǵ-o-s, *h₃reǵ-dʰleh₂

Germanic: right, rank, rich, rike, rake (trail, path), drake, reckon (**Eng**); riht, ranc, reċċan, rīċe, recenian, ġerecenian (**OE**);

rjocht, räkke, ryk, rekkenje (**Fris**); recht, rank, rekken, rijk, draak, rekenen, richten, gerechten (**Dut**); recht, Recht, Gericht, rachen, rechen, rank, recken, -rich, reich, Enterich, Drache (dial.), rechnen, richten, Nachricht, Nachrichten (**Ger**);

réttr, rakkr, rekja, ríkr, riki, landreki, eikna, rétta (**Norse**); rett, rank, rekkja, rik, rike, rekne, regne, rette (**Nor**); rätt, rät, rank, räcka, rik, rike, anddrake, räkna, rätta, räta (**Swe**); ret, rank, række, rig, rige, andrik, regne, rette (**Dan**); réttur, rakkur, ríkur, reikna, rétta (**Ice**)

Derivatives: riche (**Fr**); recare, ricco (**Ital**); rico (**Sp**); rico (**Port**); рейх (rejx) (**Rus**); rzesza (**Pol**)

Celtic: rhi, rhe, rhiain, rhaith (**Wel**); rígh, éirigh, rí, ríon (**Iri**)

Italic: regere, corrigere, corrigia, correctus, correctio, corrector, dīrigere, dīrectus, ērigere, porrigere, rectus, regibilis, irregibilis, regimen, rēgula, surgere (sub+), assurgere, exsurgere, īnsurgere, resurgere, rēx, rēgnum, rēgnāre, regina, rēgālis (**Lat**);

régir, corriger, courroie, correct, correction, correcteur, diriger, droit, direct, ériger, royaume, régime, sourdre, surgir, roi, règle, règne, régner, reine, royal (**Fr**);

reggere, corregere, correggia, corretto, correzione, correttore, dirigere, diritto, dritto, diretto, ergere, erigere, porgere, retto, ritto, regime, sorgere, assorgere, assurgere, risorgere, rege, re, regola, regno, regnare, regina, reale, regale (**Ital**);

regir, corregir, correa, correcto, corrección, corrector, dirigir, derecho, directo, erguir, erigir, recto, régimen, surdir, surgir, rey, regla, reja, reino, reinar, reina, real (**Sp**);

reger, corrigir, correia, correto, correção, correcção, corretor, dirigir, direito, direto, adergar, adregar, erguer, erigir, reto, regime, surgir, surdir, exsurgir, rei, relha, regra, régua, reixa, reino, reinar, rainha, real (**Port**);

rege, curea, corecție, corecta, corija, corect, dirigui, dirija, drege, drept, direct, rug, regulă, regină, regal (**Rom**)

Derivatives: correct, correctio, correction, corrector, direct, erect, recto, rectus, regible, irregible, regimen, regime, realm, rule, surge, insurgent, insurrection, resurge, resurgent, reign, regal, royal (**Eng**);

corrigeren, correctie, dirigeren, regel, richel (**Dut**); regieren, korrigieren, dirigieren, direkt, Regel (**Ger**); regjere, korrigere (**Nor**); regera, korrigera (**Swe**); regere, regel (**Dan**); regla (**Ice**); rheol (**Wel**); díreach (**Iri**);

корректировать (korrektirovat'), коррéкция (korrékcija), коррéктор (korréktor) (**Rus**); korygować (**Pol**); korigovat (**Cz**); korrigjoj, dërgoj, drejtë (**Alb**)

Hellenic: ὀρέγω (orégō), ὄρεξῖς (órexis), ἀνορεξία (anorexía), ὀρεκτός (orektós), ὀρέγειν (oregein), ἀνόρεκτος (anórektos) (**AnGk**); ὄρεξη (órexi) (**Gk**)

Derivatives: anorectic, anorexia (**Eng**); anorexia (**Lat**); anorexie (**Fr**)

Baltic: règti, regéti (**Lith**); redzēt (**Latv**)

Indo-Iranian: राजन् (rājan), ऋञ्जते (r̥ñjate), राजयति (rājayati), राजयते (rājayate), राज्ञी (rājñī), राज् (rāj), ऋजु (r̥jú) (**Sans**); राजा (rājā), रानी (rānī) (**Hin**); رای (rāy), راست (râst) (**Pers**)

Derivatives: rani, ranee (**Eng**)

*h_2welh_1-

to rule; strong, powerful

*$h_2w̥l$-né-h_1-ti, *$h_2w̥lh_1$-eh_1-(ye)-ti, *$h_2wélh_1$-ti-s, *$h_2w̥lh_1$-etro-

Germanic: wald, Walter (**Eng**); wealdan (**OE**); geweld (**Dut**); walten, Gewalt, verwalten, verwalter (**Ger**); valda, vald (**Norse**); valda, vold (**Nor**); vålla, våld (**Swe**); valte, volde, vold (**Dan**); valda, vald (**Ice**)

Celtic: gwlad, gwaladr (**Wel**); flaith (**Iri**)

Italic: valēre, aequivalēre, aequivalēns, praevalēre, praevalēns, valē, valedīcere (+dīcere), valēns, valētūdō, valētūdinārius, validus, validitās, valor (**Lat**); valoir, équivaloir, prévaloir, vaillant, valétudinaire, valide, valeur (**Fr**); valere, equivalere, prevalere, valente, valetudinario, valido, valore (**Ital**); valer, equivaler, prevaler, valente, válido, valor (**Sp**); valer, valente, valetudinário, válido, valor (**Port**); prevala, valid, valoare (**Rom**)

Derivatives: valence, ambivalent, equivalent, equivalence, avail, prevail, prevalence, valediction, valedictorian, valiant, valent, valetudinarian, valid, validity, valor/valour, value, evaluate, evaluation (**Eng**); prevaleren (**Dut**); vlerë (**Alb**)

in part: **Italic:** pollēre, pollex, pollicaris (**Lat**); pouce, poucier (**Fr**); pollice (**Ital**); pólice, pulgar (**Sp**); pólex, pólice, polegar (**Port**); policar (**Rom**)

Derivatives: pollical, pollicate (**Eng**); pulqer (**Alb**)

Slavic: владéть (vladét') волость (vólost') (obs.), власть (vlast') (**Rus**); władać, włość (**Pol**); ovládati, vlast (**Cz**); vládat', vlast' (**Slo**); владее (vladee), власт (vlast) (**Mace**)

Baltic: veldėti, valdýti (**Lith**); vàldît (**Latv**)

*$speh_1$-

to succeed, to prosper

See Social

*$Hreh_1d^h$-

to think; to arrange; to succeed, accomplish

See Body: Limbs & Joints

*gʷerH-

to express approval, to praise

*gʷérH-e-, *gʷr̥-né-H-, *gʷr̥H-yé-, *gʷr̥H-sḱé-, *gʷérH-tis, *gʷérH-tus' *gʷorH-no-, *gʷr̥H-tós

Celtic: barnu (**Wel**); bard (**Iri**)

Derivatives: bard (**Eng**); bardus (**Lat**); barde (**Fr**); bardo (**Sp**); bardo (**Port**)

Italic: grātēs, grātus, grātificārī, grātitūdō, grātīs, grātiōsus, grātulātiō, grātuĩtus (**Lat**);

grâce, gratifier, gratis, gracieux, gré, malgré, agréer, gratuit (**Fr**);

grazia, gratis, grazioso, grado, grato, malgrado, gratuito (**Ital**);

gracia, gratis, gracioso, grado, grato, gratuito (**Sp**);

graça, gratificar, gratidão, grátis, gracioso, grado, grato, gratuito (**Port**);

graţie, gratis (**Rom**)

Derivatives: grace, gratify, gratitude, gratis, gracious, congratulate, congratulatory, congratulation, agree, agreeable, agreement, congree, disagree, disgrace, gratification, gratuitous, gratuity, gratulate, ingrate, ingratiate, ingratitude, gree, maugre (**Eng**); gratie (**Dut**)

Slavic: жрать (žrat'), жерелó (žereló), жероглó (žerogló) (dial.), гóрло (górlo), жéртва (žértva), жрéц (žréc) (**Rus**); żreć, źródło, gardło, żertwa, żerca (**Pol**); žrát, zřídlo, hrdlo, hrany (**Cz**); žrat', hrdlo, hrana (**Slo**); ждере (ždere), грло (grlo) (**Mace**)

Derivatives: jertfă (**Rom**)

Baltic: gìrti, gẽras (**Lith**); dzī̆ru (**Latv**)

Indo-Iranian: जरते (járate), गृणाति (gr̥ṇā́ti), गूर्ति (gūrtí), गूर्त (gūrtá) (**Sans**)

*keh₂n-

to sing

Germanic: hen (**Eng**); hana, henn (**OE**); hoanne, hin (**Fris**); haan, hen, hoen (uncert.) (**Dut**); Hahn, Henne, Huhn (uncert.) (**Ger**); hani, hœna (uncert.) (**Norse**); hane, høne (uncert.) (**Nor**); hane, höna (uncert.) (**Swe**); hane, høne (uncert.) (**Dan**); hani, hæna (uncert.) (**Ice**)

Derivatives: hanneton (**Fr**)

Celtic: canu (**Wel**); can (**Iri**)

Italic: canere, būcina, būcināre, būcinum, canōrus, cantāre, cantilēna, discantus, incantāre, -cen (added to names of musical instruments or parts of speech), concinere, concentus, incinere, incentīvus, luscinia (luscus+), ratiōcinārī (ratiō+), vāticinārī, carmen, carmināre, cicōnia (**Lat**);

buse, buccin, enchanter, rossignol, vaticiner, charme, cigogne (**Fr**);

buccina, canoro, cantilena, discanto, incantare, concento, usignolo, vaticinare, carme, carminare, scarmigliare, cicogna (**Ital**);

bocinar, voznar, canoro, discanto, encantar, concento, ruiseñor, vaticinar, carmen, carmenar, carminar, escarmenar, cigüeña (**Sp**);

búzio, canoro, cantilena, encantar, incentivo, rouxinol, vaticinar, vaticínio, carme, carmear, carminar, cegonha (**Port**);

buciuma, buciumare, bucium, încânta, încântare, scărmăna, scărmănare, cicogna (**Rom**)

Derivatives: buccina, canorous, accent, accentuate, cant, cantabile, cantata, cantatory, cantatrice, canticle, canticum, cantiga, cantilena, cantillate, cantillation, cantion, canto, cantor, cantus, canzona, canzone, chanson, chansonnier, chant, chanteur, chanteuse, chanticleer, concent, precentor, recant, succentor, descant, discant, discantus, enchant, enchantment, enchantress, disenchant, disenchantment, incantation, incentive, disincentive, vaticinate, vaticination, vaticinator, charm, disencharm, Carmen (**Eng**)

Hellenic: κανᾰχέω (kanakhéō), κανᾰχή (kanakhḗ), ἠικανός (ēikanós) (**AnGk**)

Indo-Iranian: कणति (kaṇati) (**Sans**); خواندن (xândan) (**Pers**)

*ǵews-

to try, to taste

*ǵéws-e-ti, *ǵows-éye-ti, *ǵu-ǵéws-ti, *ǵéws-o-s, *ǵéws-ti-s, *ǵéws-tu-s, *ǵus-tó-s

Germanic: choose, cost (manner, way) (**Eng**); ceosan, cyst, cost (**OE**); kieze, kêst (**Fris**); kiezen, kust (**Dut**); kiesen, Kust (dial.) (**Ger**); kjósa, kostr (**Norse**); kjose (**Nor**); tjusa, -kost (**Swe**); kyse, kost (**Dan**); kjósa, kostur (**Ice**)

Celtic: gwst (**Wel**); togh (**Iri**)

Italic: dēgūnō, gustāre, dēgustāre, praegustāre, gustus, gustatus (**Lat**); goût, goûter, gout, déguster, prégoûter (**Fr**); gusto, gustare, degustare, pregustare (**Ital**); gustar, gusto, degustar (**Sp**); gosto, gostar (**Port**); gust, gusta, gustare (**Rom**)

Derivatives: gusto, disgust, gustatory, degustation (**Eng**); goesting (**Dut**); gust (**Pol**)

Hellenic: γεύω (geúō), γευστός (geustós), γεῦσις (geûsis) (**AnGk**)

Derivatives: ageusia, dysgeusia (**Eng**)

Indo-Iranian: जोषति (jóṣati), जोषयासे (joṣáyāse), जुजोष (jujóṣa), जोष (jóṣa), जुष्टि (júṣṭi), जुष्ट (juṣṭá), जुषते (juṣáte) (**Sans**); دوست (dust) (**Pers**)

*per-
to try, dare, risk

*per-ih$_2$, *per-ih$_2$-ye-, *per-ih$_2$-to-, *per-ih$_2$-tlo-

Germanic: fear (**Eng**); fǽr (**OE**); gefaar (**Fris**); gevaar (**Dut**); Fahr, Gefahr (**Ger**); fare (**Nor**); fara (**Swe**); fare (**Dan**)

Italic: comperīre, experīrī, experientia, experīmentum, expertus, perītus, perītia, perīculum, perīclitor, perīculōsus (**Lat**); expérience, expert, péril, pércliter, périlleux (**Fr**); esperienza, esperto, perito, perizia, pericolo, periglio, periclitare, pericoloso (**Ital**); experiencia, experto, perito, peligro, periclitar, peligroso (**Sp**); esperiência, experto, perito, perícia, perigo, periclitar, perigoso (**Port**); experiență, pericol, periculos (**Rom**)

Derivatives: experience, experiment, peril, perilous (**Eng**); perygl (**Wel**); эксперимент (eksperiment), эксперт (ekspert) (**Rus**)

Hellenic: πεῖρα (peîra) (**AnGk**)

*dʰers-
to be bold, to dare

*dʰr̥s-néw-, *dʰe-dʰórs-e, *dʰr-n̥-s-sḱe-, *dʰérs-os-, *dʰr̥s-tós, *dʰr̥s-u-

Germanic: dare (**Eng**); durran (**OE**); durven (**Dut**); thüren, türen (**Ger**)

Hellenic: τεθαρσήκασι (tetharsékasi), θάρσος (thársos), θρᾰσύς (thrasús) (**AnGk**); θάρρος (thárros), θρασύς (thrasýs) (**Gk**)

Slavic: дерзнýть (derznú't'), дерзáть (derzát', дéрзый (dérzyj) (**Rus**); drzý (**Cz**); drzý (**Slo**); дрзне (drzne) (**Mace**)

Baltic: dr̃sti, drąsùs (**Lith**); drùošs, drùoss (**Latv**)

Indo-Iranian: धृष्णोति (dhr̥ṣṇoti), दधर्ष (dadhárṣa), धृष्ट (dhr̥ṣṭá), धृषु (dhr̥ṣu) (**Sans**)

Emotions

*sent-

to feel

*sent-ye-, *sent-n-, *sent-nos

Germanic: send, sand, sense (**Eng**); sinnan, sendan, sand (**OE**); sin (**Fris**); zinnen, zenden, zin (**Dut**); sinnen, senden, Sinn (**Ger**); sinna, senda (**Norse**); sende, senda (**Nor**); besinna, sända, sinne (**Swe**); sende (**Dan**); sinna, senda (**Ice**)

Italic: sentīre, assentīrī, cōnsentīre, cōnsēnsus, dissentīre, dissēnsus, praesentīre, sēnsibilis, sēnsōrium, sēnsus, sēnsātus, sententia, sententiōsus, sentiēns, sentimentum (**Lat**);

sentir, consentir, pressentir, sens, sentence, sentencieux, sentiment, assener, forcener, sens (**Fr**);

sentire, consentire, consenso, dissenso, senso, sensato, sentenzioso, sentimento, senno (**Ital**);

sentir, consentir, consenso, presentir, seso, sentencioso, sentimiento, sien, sentido (**Sp**);

sentir, consentir, consenso, dissentir, siso, senso, sentencioso, sentimento, sen, sentido (**Port**);

simţi, simţire, consens, sentiment, simţământ (**Rom**)

Derivatives: sense, scent, assent, consent, consensus, dissent, resent, ensorium, sensible, sensitive, sensate, sensation, sensory, sentence, sententious, sentient, sentience, sentiment (**Eng**); sensuell (**Swe**)

Baltic: sintéti (**Lith**)

*daḱru-

tear (in the eyes)

Germanic: tear (**Eng**); tēar, teagor (**OE**); trien (**Fris**); traan (**Dut**); Zähre, Tran, Träne (**Ger**); tár (**Norse**); tår (**Nor**); tår (**Swe**); tår (**Dan**); tár (**Ice**)

Celtic: deigr (**Wel**); deoir (**Iri**)

Italic: lacrĭma, lacrimāre, lacrimōsus, lacrimātiō (**Lat**); larme (**Fr**); lacrima, lacrimare, lacrimoso, lacrimazione (**Ital**); lágrima, lacrimar, lagrimar, lacrimoso, lagrimoso, lacrimación (**Sp**); lágrima, lacrimar, lacrimoso (**Port**); lacrimă, lăcrima, lăcrimare, lăcrimos (**Rom**)

Derivatives: lachrymose, lacrimation (**Eng**)

Hellenic: δάκρυ (dákru), δάκρυον (dákruon) (**AnGk**); δάκρυ (dákry) (**Gk**)

*der-
to tear, to split

*dr̥-néH-, *dr̥-nh₂-, *dér-tis, *dr̥-nos

Germanic: tear, tire (to draw, pull), retire (**Eng**); teran, torn (**OE**); tarre, toarne, teere (**Fris**); teren, toorn (**Dut**); zehren, Zorn (**Ger**); tære (**Nor**); tära (**Swe**); tære (**Dan**); tæra (**Ice**)

Derivatives: tirer, retirer (**Fr**); tirare (**Ital**); tirar (**Sp**); tirar (**Port**)

Hellenic: δέρω (dérō), δέρμα (dérma), δάρσις (dársis) (**AnGk**); δέρμα (dérma) (**Gk**)

Derivatives: dermatology, dermis, epidermis, ectoderm, hypodermic, scleroderma, taxidermy, xeroderma (**Eng**)

Slavic: драть (drat'), дерть (dert') (**Rus**); drzeć, dřít (**Pol**); drát (**Cz**); driet' (**Slo**); дере (dere) (**Mace**)

Baltic: dérti, dìrti (**Lith**)

Albanian: djerr (**Alb**)

Indo-Iranian: दृणाति (dr̥ṇā́ti), दृति (dr̥ti), दीर्यते (dīryáte) (**Sans**); دریدن (daridan) (**Pers**)

*dʰer-
to support, hold

*dʰr̥-tó, *dʰér-e-ti, *dʰí-dʰer-ti, *dʰe-dʰór-e, *dʰor-éyeti, *dʰér-mn̥, *dʰer-mos, *dʰer-o-, *dʰr̥-eh₁-nom, *dʰr̥-eh₁-tos

Germanic: darn, dern (dial.), tarnish (**Eng**); diernan (**OE**); tarnen (**Ger**) (Germanic root to do with hiding, secret)

Derivatives: ternir (**Fr**)

Celtic: drong (uncert.) (**Iri**)

Italic: firmus, firmāmentum, firmitās, firmāre, affirmāre, affirmātiō, cōnfirmāre, cōnfirmātiō, ferē, fermē, frēnum, frētus, īnfirmus, īnfirmitās (**Lat**);

ferme, firmament, fermeté, fermer, affirmer, confirmer, confirmation, frein, chanfrein, infirme (**Fr**);

fermo, firmamento, fermare, firmare, affermare, confermare, confermazione, freno, infermo, infirmo, infermità (**Ital**);

firme, firmamento, hirmar, firmar, afirmar, confirmar, confirmación, freno, enfermo, enfermedad (**Sp**);

firme, firmamento, firmar, afirmar, afirmação, confirmar, confirmação, freio, enfermo, enfermidade (**Port**);

ferm, frână, frâu (**Rom**)

Derivatives: firm, firmament, firmation, affirm, affirmation, confirm, confirmation, frenulum, refrain, chamfer, infirm, infirmity (**Eng**); Firmament, Konfirmation (**Ger**); srian (**Iri**); конфирмáция (konfirmácija) (**Rus**); konfirmácia (**Slo**); fre (**Alb**)

Baltic: deréti, darýti (**Lith**); derêt, darît (**Latv**)

Indo-Iranian: धृ (dhṛ), अधृत (adhṛta), धृथास् (dhṛthās), धरति (dhárati), धारयते (dhárate), दिधृतम् (didhṛtam), दधार (dadhāra), धारयति (dhāráyati), धारयते (dhāráyate), धर्मन् (dhárman), धर्म (dhárma) (**Sans**); धरना (dharnā) (rare), धर्म (dharma) (**Hin**); داشتن (dâštan), دار (dār) (**Pers**)

Derivatives: dharma (**Eng**)

*ḱeh₂d-

hate, strong emotion

*ḱéh₂d-o-s, *ḱéh₂d-os, *ḱéh₂d-tis, *kh₂d-os

Germanic: hate, heinous, hatel (obs.) (**Eng**); hete, hatian, hetol, hettan (**OE**); haat, haetjen, haatsje (**Fris**); haat, haten (**Dut**); Haat, Hass, hassen, hetzen (**Ger**); hatr, hata (**Norse**); hat, hate (**Nor**); hat, hata (**Swe**); had, hade (**Dan**); hatur, hata (**Ice**)

Derivatives: haine, haineux, haïr (**Fr**)

Celtic: cawdd, cas (**Wel**)

Hellenic: κῆδος (kêdos) (**AnGk**)

*h₃ed-

to hate

*h₃(o)d-, *h₃e-h₃ód-, *h₃od-éye-

Italic: ōdisse, odium, odiōsus (**Lat**); odieux (**Fr**); odiare, odio, uggia, odioso, uggioso (**Ital**); odiar, odio, odioso (**Sp**); odiar, odioso (**Port**); odios (**Rom**)

Derivatives: odium, odious (**Eng**)

Hellenic: ὠδυσάμην (ōdusámēn), ὀδύσσομαι (odússomai) (**AnGk**)

*h₃ed-
to smell, stink

*h₃e-h₃od-, *h₃éd-os, *h₃od-méh₂

Italic: olēre, redolēre, redolēns, odor, odōrāre (**Lat**); odeur (**Fr**); olire, odore, odorare (**Ital**); oler, olor, odio (**Sp**); ódio, odor (**Port**); urdoare (prob.) (**Rom**)

Derivatives: redolent, odour (**Eng**); odör (**Swe**); odér (**Cz**)

Hellenic: ὄζω (ózō), ὀδώδειν (odódein), ὀδμή (odmḗ), ὀσμή (osmḗ) (**AnGk**); οσμή (osmí) (**Gk**)

Baltic: úosti (**Lith**); ost (**Latv**)

Albanian: amëz, âmë (**Alb**)

*gʰers-
stiff, surprised

see Mammals

*ǵʰeyzd-
anger, agitation

see Social

*preyH-
to love, to please

*priH-yeti, *pri-né-H-ti, *préy-s-t, *priH-ós

Germanic: free, freedom, friend, friendly, friendship, frith (**Eng**); frēo, frēodōm, frēond, frēondlīċ, frēondsċype, frēondsċipe, friþ, friþu (**OE**);

frij, frijdoem, frije, freon, freonlik, freonskip, frede (**Fris**); vrij, vrijdom, vrijen, vriend, vriendelijk, vriendschap, vrede (**Dut**); frei, freien, Friedel, Freund, freundlich, Freundschaft, Frieden, Friede (**Ger**);

frjáls, frjá, friðill, friðla, frilla, frjándi, frændi, frýnligr, frýniligr, friðr (**Norse**); fri, fridom, frille, frende, frendelig, fred (**Nor**); fri, frälse, frälsa, fria, frilla, frände, frändlig, fred, frid (**Swe**); fri, frille, frænde, frændelig (**Dan**); frjáls, frjá, friðill, frilla, frændi, frýnilegur, friður (**Ice**)

Celtic: ffrind (**Wel**)

Italic: proprius (uncert.), prōprietās (**Lat**); propre, propriété (**Fr**); proprio, proprietà (**Ital**); propio, propiedad (**Sp**); próprio, propriedade (**Port**); propriu, proprietate (**Rom**)

Derivatives: proper, property, propriety, appropriate, proprietary (**Eng**)

Slavic: приятель (prijátel') (**Rus**); sprzyjać, przyjaciel (**Pol**); přáti, přítel (**Cz**); priať, priateľ (**Slo**); пријател (príjatel) (**Mace**)

Indo-Iranian: प्रीयते (prīyate), प्रीणाति (prīṇāti), प्रेषत् (preṣat), प्रिय (priya), प्रियायते (priyāyate) (**Sans**); प्रिय (priya) (**Hin**); آفریدن (âfaridan), فری (fari) (arch.) (**Pers**)

*lewbʰ-

to love

*lubʰ-yé-, *lowbʰ-éye-, *lubʰ-eh₁-(ye)-, *lewbʰ-os, *lubʰ-om

Germanic: lief, livelong, liever, love, lofe/loff (dial.) (**Eng**); lēof, lufu, lof (**OE**); leaf, leaflik, lof, lauwje, lauwgje, loovje (**Fris**); lief, lieflijk, lof, loven (**Dut**); lieb, lieblich, Liebe, liebling, Lob, loben (**Ger**); ljúfr, lof, lofa (**Norse**); love (**Nor**); ljuv, ljuvlig, lov, lova (**Swe**); lov, love (**Dan**); ljúfur, lof (**Ice**)

Italic: libet (**Lat**)

Derivatives: quodlibet (**Eng**)

Slavic: любóй (ljubój), любить (ljubít') (**Rus**); luby, lubić (**Pol**); libý, líbit (**Cz**); ľubý, ľúbiť (**Slo**); љуби (ljubi) (**Mace**)

Baltic: liaupsė (**Lith**)

Albanian: lyp (**Alb**)

Indo-Iranian: लुभ्यति (lúbhyati), लोभयति (lobháyati) (**Sans**)

*bʰeydʰ-

to trust

*bʰéydʰ-e-ti, *bʰe-bʰóydʰ-e, *bʰidʰ-tó-s, *bʰeydʰ-o-s, *bʰoydʰ-eh₂, *bʰoydʰ-éye-ti, *bʰoydʰ-os

Germanic: bide, abide (**Eng**); bīdan, ābīdan (**OE**); beiden, verbeiden (**Dut**); bíða, beiða (**Norse**); bie (**Nor**); bida (**Swe**); bie (**Dan**); bíða, beiða (**Ice**)

Italic: fidere, fidēlis, fidēlitās, fidēs, fīdūcia, fīdūciārius, fīdus, foedus, foedifragus, cōnfīdere, cōnfīdentia (**Lat**); fier, féal, fidèle, fidélité, foi, fédéral, fédérale, confier, confidence (**Fr**); fidare, fedele, fedeltà, fede, fido, fiducia, fiduciario, fedifrago, confidare (**Ital**); fiar, fiel, fidelidad, fe, fido, hucia, confiar, confianza (**Sp**); fiar, fiel, fé, confiar, confiança (**Port**); fidel, fidelitate, confia (**Rom**)

Derivatives: fidelity, fealty, faith, fiduciary, federal, confide, confident, confidence, infidel, perfidious (**Eng**); ffydd (**Wel**)

Hellenic: πείθω (peíthō), πέποιθᾰ (pépoitha) (**AnGk**)

Slavic: бѣдá (bědá), бедá (bedá) (**Rus**); bieda, biada (**Pol**); bída, běda (**Cz**); bieda (**Slo**); беда (beda) (**Mace**)

Baltic: bads (**Latv**)

*ǵʰer-
to yearn for

*ǵʰr̥-yé-ti, *ǵʰr̥-t-ós, *ǵʰr̥-i-t-, *ǵʰr̥-éh₂, *ǵʰér-mn̥, *ǵʰr̥-meh₂, *ǵʰer-no-

Germanic: yearn (**Eng**); georn (**OE**); jearn (**Fris**); gaarne (**Dut**); gern (**Ger**); gjarn (**Norse**); gjarn (**Ice**)

Italic: horī, hortārī, hortātiō, exhortārī, exhortātiō, dēhortārī (**Lat**); exhorter, exhortation (**Fr**); esortazione (**Ital**); exhortación (**Sp**); exortação (**Port**)

Derivatives: hortation, exhort, exhortation, dehort (**Eng**); когóрта (kogórta) (**Rus**)

Hellenic: χαίρω (khaírō), χαρτός (khartós), χάρις (kháris), χαρά (khará), χάρμα (khárma), χάρμη (khármē), χᾰ́ρῐσμᾰ (khárisma) (**AnGk**); χαίρω (chaíro), χαρά (chará), χάρισμα (chárisma) (**Gk**)

Derivatives: charisma (**Eng**); харизма (xarízma) (**Rus**)

Indo-Iranian: ह्यात् (hr̥yāt), हृत (hr̥ta) (**Sans**)

Social

*h₁lewdʰ-
people; to grow

*h₁léwdʰ-e-ti, *h₁lewdʰ-i-s, *h₁lewdʰ-er-o-s, *h₁lewdʰ-er-tos, *h₁lewdʰ-er-teh₂, *h₁léwdʰ-or-teh₂-t-s

Germanic: leod, lede, lith, leud (**Eng**); lēod, lēodan, ġelēodan (**OE**); lie, lju, ljuwe (**Fris**); lieden, luiden, lui (**Dut**); Leute (**Ger**); ljóðr, loðinn (**Norse**); lyd (**Nor**); luden (**Swe**); lyd (**Dan**); lýður, loðinn (**Ice**)

Derivatives: leude (**Fr**)

Celtic: llysiau (**Wel**); lus (**Iri**)

Italic: līber, līberālis, līberālitās, līberātiō, līberātor, līberare, libertus, libertas, lībertīnus (**Lat**); libre, libération, livraison, libérateur, livrer, libérer, liberté, libertin (**Fr**); libero, liberazione, liberatore, liberare, libertà (**Ital**); libre, liberación, liberador, librador, librar, liberar, libertad (**Sp**); livre, liberação, livração, liberador, livrador, livrar, liberar, liberdade (**Port**); liber, libertate (**Rom**)

Derivatives: libre, liberal, liberality, liberator, liberate, liberty, libertarian, libertine, deliver (**Eng**); llyfr (**Wel**)

Hellenic: ἐλεύθερος (eleútheros), ἐλευθερία (eleuthería) (**AnGk**); ελεύθερος (eléftheros), ελευθερία (elefthería) (**Gk**)

Slavic: люд (ljud), люди (ljúdi) (**Rus**); lud, ludzie (**Pol**); lid, lidé (**Cz**); ľud, ľudia (**Slo**); луѓе (luǵe) (**Mace**)

Baltic: liaudis (**Lith**); ļaudis (**Latv**)

Albanian: lind, lem (**Alb**)

Indo-Iranian: रोधति (ródhati) (**Sans**); لویدل (loyedal) (**Pash**); رستن (rostan) (**Pers**)

*tewtéh₂
tribe

Germanic: thede, theod (arch.), Theoderic, Derek, Dirk, Terry, Theobald (**Eng**); þeod, þēoden, Þēodrīc (**OE**); diet, Diederik, Dirk (**Dut**); Deutsch, Diet, Theoderich, Thibaut (**Ger**); þjóð, þjóðann (**Norse**); tjod, Tjodrik, Teovald (**Nor**); tjod (**Swe**); þjóð, Þjóðann (**Ice**)

Derivatives: Theodericus (**Lat**); Théodoric, Thierry, Thibault (**Fr**); Teodorico (**Ital**); Teodorico (**Sp**)

Celtic: tud (**Wel**); tuath (**Iri**)

Baltic: tautà (**Lith**); tàuta (**Latv**)

Albanian: tëtanë (**Alb**)

Indo-Iranian: توده (tōda) (**Pers**)

*gʰóstis
stranger, guest

Germanic: guest (**Eng**); gæst (**OE**); gast (**Fris**); gast (**Dut**); Gast (**Ger**); gestr (**Norse**); gjest (**Nor**); gäst (**Swe**); gæst (**Dan**); gestur (**Ice**)

Celtic: gwestai (**Wel**)

Italic: hostis, hospes, hospitā, hospitālis, hospitāle, hospitālia, hospitāliter, hospitālitas, hospitium, hospitāre, hospitor (**Lat**);

ost, hôte, hôpital, hospitalier, hôtel, hospitalité, hospice (**Fr**);

oste, ospite, ospedale, ospitale, ospitalità, ospizio, ospitare (**Ital**);

hueste, huésped, hospital, hostal, hospitalidad, hospicio, hospedar (**Sp**);

hoste, hóspede, hospedal, hospital, hostal, hotel, hospitalidade, hospício, hospedar (**Port**);

oaste, oaspete, ospital, spital, ospăț, ospiciu, ospăta, ospătare (**Rom**)

Derivatives: host, hostel, hotel, hostile, hospital, hospice, hospitality, inhospitable (**Eng**); Hospital, Spital, Hotel (**Ger**); σπίτι (spíti) (**AnGk**); госпиталь (gospital') (**Rus**)

Slavic: гость (gost') (**Rus**); gość (**Pol**); host (**Cz**); hosť (**Slo**); гост/гостин (gost/gostin) (**Mace**)

ghost is not related to this, but rather to a root meaning fury, anger. It exists only in the Germanic line:

*ǵʰeyzd-
anger, agitation

Germanic: ghost, ghastly (**Eng**); gāst (**OE**); geast (**Fris**); geest (**Dut**); Geist (**Ger**); gast (**Swe**)

*weyḱ-
village, settlement

*wéyḱ-s, *weyḱ-s-om, *weyḱ-os, *woyḱ-os, *weyḱ-i-, *weyḱpotis

Germanic: -wich, wick (arch., dial.) (**Eng**); wīc, wīċ (**OE**); wyk (**Fris**); wijk (**Dut**); Weich (in place names) (**Ger**)

Italic: vīcus, vīcīna, vīcīnālis, vīcīnitas, vīcīnus, vīculus, vīlla, vīllānus (**Lat**); voisine, vicinal, vicinité, voisin, villa, ville, village (**Fr**); vico, vicina, vicinale, vicinità, vicino, vicolo, villa, villano (**Ital**); vecina, vecindad, vecino, villa, villano (**Sp**); vico, vizinha, vila, vilão (**Port**); vitg, vecinătate, vecin, vilă (**Rom**)

Derivatives: vicus, vicinal, vicinity, villa, village, villein, villain (**Eng**); Weiler (**Ger**); villa (**Swe**); вилла (vílla) (**Rus**); fqinj (**Alb**)

Hellenic: οἶκος (oîkos), οἰκέω (oikéō) (**AnGk**); οίκος (oíkos) (**Gk**)

Derivatives: diocese, archdiocese, -oecious e.g. dioecious, ecesis, ecology, economy, economize, monoecy, oecology, oeconomus, oikology, oikophobia, parish (**Eng**); diœcēsis, oeconomus (**Lat**); diocèse (**Fr**)

Slavic: весь (ves'), веслина (veslina), весца (vesca) (**Rus**); wieś (**Pol**); ves (**Cz**); ves (**Slo**)

Baltic: viešas, váišinti, viešéti, viẽšpats (**Lith**); viesis (**Latv**)

Albanian: vis (**Alb**)

Indo-Iranian: विश् (víś), वेश (veśa) (**Sans**); ويس (vis) (**Pers**)

*peḱu-
wealth/cattle

Germanic: fee, feu, feoff, feud, feudatory (**Eng**); feoh (**OE**); fee (**Fris**); vee (**Dut**); Vieh, Viech (**Ger**); fé (**Norse**); fe (**Nor**); fä (**Swe**); fæ (**Dan**); fé (**Ice**)

Derivatives: fevum, feudum, feudātōrius (**Lat**); fief (**Fr**); feudo (**Ital**); feudo (**Sp**); feudo (**Port**); fief, feudă, feud (**Rom**); φέουδο (féoudo) (**Gk**)

Italic: pecū, pecus, pecuārius, pecunia, pecūlium (**Lat**); pécuniaire, pécule (**Fr**); pecora, pecoraio, pecunia (lit.), peculio, pecuniario (**Ital**); pécora, pecunia (slang), impecune, peculio, pecunio, pegullo, pecuniario (**Sp**); pécora, pegureiro, pecuária, pecúnia, peculio, pecuniário (**Port**); păcurar, peculiu, pecuniar (**Rom**)

Derivatives: peculiar, pecuniary, pecunious, impecunious, peculator (**Eng**)

Hellenic: πέκος (pékos) (**AnGk**)

Baltic: pēkus (**Lith**)

Indo-Iranian: पशु (páśu) (Sans); पशु (paśu) (Hin)

which derives from *peḱ- to fleece:

*peḱ-
to pluck, comb, shear (wool, hair)

*poḱ-s-om, *poḱ-s-mn̥, *póḱos

Germanic: fax (dial.), Fairfax, Halifax, fight (**Eng**); feax, feohtan, feht (**OE**); fjochtsje, fjuchte (**Fris**); vas, vacht, vechten (**Dut**); fechten (**Ger**); fax, fær (**Norse**); faks, fekta, fekte, får (**Nor**); fäkta, får (**Swe**); fegte, fægte, får (**Dan**); fax, fær (**Ice**)

Derivatives: фехтовать (fextovat') (**Rus**)

Italic: pectere, dēpectere, pectiō, pectitus, pexus, repectere, pecten, pectināre (**Lat**); peigne, peigner, peignoir (**Fr**); pettine, pettinare (**Ital**); peine, pendejo, peinar (**Sp**); pente, pentelho, pentear (**Port**); pieptene, pieptăna, pieptănare (**Rom**)

Derivatives: pecten (**Eng**)

Hellenic: πεκτέω (pektéō), πόκος (pókos), πέκω (pékō), κτείς (kteís), κτενίζω (ktenízō), κτένῐον (kténion) (**AnGk**); χτένα (chténa), χτενίζω (chtenízo), χτένι (chténi) (**Gk**)

Baltic: pešù, pèšti, pašýti (**Lith**)

Albanian: pilë (**Alb**)

Indo-Iranian: पक्ष्मन् (pakṣman) (**Sans**); پشم (pašm) (**Pers**)

*speh₁-
to succeed, to prosper

*spéh₁-ti, *sph₁-óy-ey, *spóh₁-e-ti, *spéh₁-s, *sph₁-rós, *swé-sph₁-t-s

Germanic: speed (**Eng**); spēd, spēdan (**OE**); spoed, spoeden (**Dut**); Sput, sputen, spuden (**Ger**)

Italic: spēs, spēcula, spērāre, spērāns, dēspērāre, prosperus, prosperare, prosperitās, sospes (**Lat**); espérer, espérance (**Fr**); sperare, speranza, sperante, prospero, prosperare (**Ital**); esperar, esperanza, prosperar (**Sp**); esperar, esperança, prosperar (**Port**); a spera, speranță (**Rom**)

Derivatives: sperate, esperance, despair, desperate, prosperous, prosperity (**Eng**); in spe (**Dut**); shpresë (**Alb**)

Slavic: спеть (spet'), спех (spex), спешить (spešíť) (**Rus**); śpiać (arch.), pośpiech, śpiech, śpieszyć (**Pol**); spět, spěch (**Cz**); spieť (**Slo**); успее (uspee) (**Mace**)

Baltic: spéti (**Lith**); spēt (**Latv**)

Indo-Iranian: स्फायते (sphāyate), स्फिर (sphirá) (**Sans**)

*wesno-

price

Italic: vēnus, vēnum, vēnālis, vēndō, vēnditiō, vēnditor, vēneō (**Lat**); vénal, vendre, vendeur (**Fr**); venale, vendere, venditore (**Ital**); venal, vender, vendedor (**Sp**); venal, vender, vendedor (**Port**); vinde, vindere, vânzător (**Rom**)

Derivatives: venal, vend, vendition, vendor (**Eng**)

Hellenic: ὦνος (ônos), ὠνέομαι (ōnéomai) (**AnGk**)

Indo-Iranian: वस्नयति (vasnayati), वस्न (vasna) (**Sans**); بها (bahâ) (**Pers**)

*kʷreyh₂-

to buy

*kʷri-né-h₂-ti, *kʷrih₂-, *kʷrih₂-tó-s

Celtic: prynu (**Wel**); crean (**Iri**)

Hellenic: ἐπριάμην (epriámēn) (**AnGk**)

Slavic: кренуть (krenut') (**Rus**)

Indo-Iranian: क्रीणाति (krīṇāti) (**Sans**); خریدن (xaridan) (**Pers**)

*kʷey-

to pay; to avenge

*kʷéy-e-ti, *kʷi-néw-ti, *kʷoy-néh₂, *kʷéy-ti-s

Hellenic: τίνω (tínō), τῖνω (tînō), τίσις (tísis), ποινή (poinḗ) (**AnGk**); ποινή (poiní) (**Gk**)

Derivatives: pain, pine, punish, punition, punitive, subpoena, penal, penalize, penalty, impune, impunity (**Eng**); pijn (**Dut**); Pein (**Ger**); pina (**Swe**); pine, pinsel (**Dan**); poen (**Wel**); poena, pūniō, pūnītiō, subpoena, poenālis, impūnis, impūnitas (**Lat**); peine, punir, punition, pénal, pénalité (**Fr**); pena, punire, punizione, impunemente (**Ital**); pena, punir, impune, impunemente, impunidad (**Sp**); pena, punir, punição, impune (**Port**)

Slavic: цена́ (cená) (**Rus**); cena (**Pol**); cena (**Cz**); cena (**Slo**); цена (cena) (**Mace**)

Baltic: káina (**Lith**); cena (**Latv**)

Indo-Iranian: चयते (cayate), अपचिति (ápa-citi) (**Sans**); کین (kin) (**Pers**)

*mey-
to change, exchange

*meyg^w-, *meyḱ, *meytH-, *moy-no-, *moy-ni-, *ḱom-moy-ni-

Germanic: mix, mash, mishmash, mis-, miss, mean, manse (**Eng**); miscian, māsc, mis-, missan, mǣne, ġemǣne (**OE**); misse, mien, gemien (**Fris**); mixen, mis-, missen, gemeen (**Dut**); mixen, mischen, Maisch, Mischmasch, miss-, mis-, missen, gemein (**Ger**); mis-, missa (**Norse**); mis-, misse, miste (**Nor**); mäsk, miss-, missa, mista (**Swe**); mask, miskmask, mis-, misse, miste (**Dan**); mis-, missa (**Ice**)

Derivatives: mélange, mélanger, més-, mé- (**Fr**)

Celtic: mysgaf, cymysgaf (**Wel**); measc (**Iri**)

Italic: migrāre, ēmigrāre, immigrāre, migrātiō, trānsmigrāre, miscēre, admiscēre, admixtus, inmiscēre, miscellus, miscellāneus, mixtiō, mixtīcius, mistūra, prōmiscuus, mūtāre, commūtāre, commūtātio, immūtāre, mūtātiō, dēmūtāre, immūtābilis, mūtābilis, mūtuor, permūtāre, permūtātiō, trānsmūtāre, trānsmūtātiō, mūtuus, mūnus, mūnia, immūnis, immūnitas, commūnis, commūnālis, commūne, commūniō, commūnicāre, commūnicātiō, mūnificens, mūnificus, mūnificentia, mūnicipium, remūnerāre (**Lat**);

émigrer, immigrer, migration, transmigrer, immiscer, mêler, mixtion, métis, promiscue, muter, muer, commuer, mutation, mutuel, permuter, transmuer, transmuter, transmutation, commun, communal, communier, communion, communauté, communiquer, communication, munificence, municipe, rémunérer, immun, immune, immunité (**Fr**);

migrare, emigrare, immigrare, trasmigrare, mescere, miscela, miscellaneo, mescolare, miscolare, mischiare, meticcio, mesticcio, mistura, mestura, promiscuo, mutare, mutabile, commutare, mutuo, permutare, trasmutare, trasmutazione, comune, comunione, comunità, comunicare, comunicazione, munifico, munificenza, municipio, immune (**Ital**);

emigrar, inmigrar, immunità, transmigrar, mecer, inmiscuirse, misceláneo, mezclar, mixtión, mestizo, mestura, mixtura, promiscuo, mudar, mutar, conmutar, demudar, inmutar, mutuo, permutar, transmutar, transmutación, común, comunal, comulgar, comunión, commūnitās, comunicar, comunicación, munificencia, municipio, remunerar, inmune, inmunidad (**Sp**);

migrar, mexer, mesclar, miscrar, mestiço, mistura, promíscuo, mudar, mutar, comutar, demudar, imutar, mútuo, mutuar, permutar, transmutar, transmutação, múnus, comum, comunal, comungar, comunicar, comunicação, munifico, munificência, município (**Port**);

migrare, meşte, mişca, mistreţ, promiscuu, muta, mutare, comuta, comun, comunal, comunica, comunicare, cumineca, cuminecare, comunicaţie, municipiu (**Rom**)

Derivatives: migrate, emigrate, immigrate, migration, migratory, transmigrate, admix, admixture, commix, commixture, immiscibility, immiscible, immix, immixture, intermix, intermixture, maslin, miscellanea, miscellany, miscellaneous, miscibility, miscible, mix, mixture, permiscible, permix, permixtion, postmix, premix, remix, meddle, mixtion, mestizo, promiscuity, promiscuous, mutation, moult, commute, commutation, immutable, mutable, permute, permutation, mutual, transmew, transmute, transmutation, common, communal, cominal, communion, community, communitas, communicate, communication, munificent, munific, munificence, municipal, municipality, remunerate, immune, immunity (**Eng**);

mutatie, communicatie (**Dut**); kommunizieren, Kommunikation (**Ger**);

миграция (migracija), коммутáция (kommutácija), пермутация (permutacija), мутация (mutacija), трансмутация (transmutacija), коммуникáция (kommunikácija), иммунитет (immunitet) (**Rus**); mutacja (**Pol**)

Hellenic: ἔμῐκτο (émikto), ἔμειξᾰ (émeixa), μίσγω (mísgō), μείγνῡμῐ (meígnūmi), μῐγνῡμῐ (mígnūmi), μῐξῐς (míxis), μεῖξῐς (meîxis) (**AnGk**); μιγνύω (mignýo) (**Gk**)

Slavic: месúть (mesíť) (**Rus**); miesić (**Pol**); mísit (**Cz**); miesiť (**Slo**); меси (mesi) (**Mace**)

Baltic: maišýti, miēši, mìšti, mìšras (**Lith**); màisît (**Latv**)

Indo-Iranian: मेथति (méthati), मिच्छमान (micchamāna), मेक्षयति (mekṣáyati), मिश्र (miśrá), मिश्रयति (miśráyati) (**Sans**); मिश्र (miśra), मिश्रण (miśraṇ) (**Hin**); آمیختن (âmixtan), آمیغ (âmeğ) (**Pers**)

*h₂eyḱ-

to possess, own

Germanic: owe, ought, own, aught, freight, fraught (**Eng**); āgan, āgen, ǽht (**OE**); eigen (**Fris**); eigen, vracht (**Dut**); eigen, eignen, Fracht (**Ger**); átt, ætt (**Norse**); eie, frakt (**Nor**); äga, ägna, ätt, frakt (**Swe**); eje, egne, æt, fragt (**Dan**); eiga, átt, ætt (**Ice**)

Derivatives: fret (**Fr**); frete (**Port**)

Indo-Iranian: ईशे (īśe), ईष्टे (īṣṭe) (**Sans**)

*h₃erbʰ-

to change allegiance, status, ownership

*h₃órbʰos, *h₃orbʰ-yo-m

Germanic: erf (reg.) (**Eng**); ierfe, yrfe, earfeþe, ierfa (**OE**); arbeid, arbeidzje (**Fris**); erf, arbeid, arbeiden, erve (arch.) (**Dut**); Erbe, Arbeit, arbeiten (**Ger**); arfr, erfi, erfiði, arfi (**Norse**); arbeid, arbeide (**Nor**); arbete, arvode, arbeta (**Swe**); arbejde, arbejde (**Dan**); erfi, arbeiði, arbeið, erfiði, arfi (**Ice**)

Italic: orbus, orbitās, orbāre (**Lat**); orbo (**Ital**); orbo, huerbo, orbedad, orbar (**Sp**); orb (**Rom**)

Derivatives: verbër (**Alb**)

Hellenic: ὀρφανός (orphanós) (**AnGk**); ορφανός (orfanós) (**Gk**)

Derivatives: orphan (**Eng**)

Slavic: раб (rab) (**Rus**); rob, rab (**Pol**); rob (**Cz**); rab (**Slo**); раб (rab), роб (rob) (**Mace**)

Indo-Iranian: अर्भ (arbha) (**Sans**)

*ker-
army

Germanic: here (meaning army, host) (obs.), harrow, harry, haricot, Walter, harborough, harbour, harbinger (**Eng**); here, heretoga, herġian, herian, herebeorg (+*bʰerǵʰ-) (**OE**); hear, hartoch (**Fris**); heer, heir, hertog, verheren, herberg (**Dut**); Heer, Herzog, heeren, Herberge (**Ger**); herr, hertogi, herja, herjan, herbergi (**Norse**); hær, hertug, herje, herberge (**Nor**); här, hertig, härja, härbärge (**Swe**); hær, hertug, hærje, hærge, herberge (**Dan**); her, hertogi, herja, herbergi (**Ice**)

Derivatives: harbwr (**Wel**); haricot, héberger, hébergeur, auberge (**Fr**); albergo (**Ital**); albergue (**Sp**); albergue (**Port**); hercogas (**Lith**); hercogs (**Latv**); керцог (gercog) (**Rus**); herzog (**Slo**)

Celtic: cordd (**Wel**); cuire (**Iri**)

Hellenic: κοίρανος (koíranos) (**AnGk**)

Baltic: kãras (**Lith**); kaȓš (**Latv**)

Indo-Iranian: کارزار (kārzār) (**Pers**)

*weyk-
to contain, envelop; yield; overcome

*wik-é-ti, *wi-né-k-ti, *wi-wéyk-ti, *wéyk-ye-ti

Germanic: wīgan, wīg (**OE**); wijgen (**Dut**); viga, vega, vig (**Norse**); väga, vig (**Swe**); vega (**Ice**)

Italic: vincere, convincere, convictiō, convictus, ēvincere, ēvictiō, pervincere, revincere, victor, victōria (**Lat**); vaincre, convaincre, évincer, victoire (**Fr**); vincere, convincere, evincere, vittoria (**Ital**); vencer, convencer, revencer, victoria (**Sp**); vencer, convencer, evencer, vitória (**Port**); învinge, învingere, convinge, evinge, previnge, victorie (**Rom**)

Derivatives: vanquish, convince, conviction, convict, evince, eviction, evict, victor, victory (**Eng**)

Slavic: век (vek), вéчный (véčnyj) (**Rus**); wiek, wieczny (**Pol**); věk, věčný (**Cz**); vek, večný (**Slo**); век (vek), вечен (večen) (**Mace**)

Baltic: veĩkti (**Lith**); vīkt (**Latv**)

Indo-Iranian: विविक्त (viviktá) (**Sans**)

*weyk-

to separate, to choose

*weyk-o, *wik-néh$_2$-ti

Germanic: witch, Wicca (**Eng**); wēoh, wēofod, wiccian, wicca (**OE**); wijreek, wije (**Fris**); wierook, wijden, wikken (**Dut**); weih- (e.g. Weihnachten, Weihrauch), weihen (**Ger**); vé, vigja (**Norse**); viga (**Swe**); vie (**Dan**); vigja (**Ice**)

Italic: victima, victimāre (**Lat**); victime (**Fr**); vittima (**Ital**); víctima, victimar (**Sp**); vítima, vitimar (**Port**); victimă, vătăma (**Rom**)

Derivatives: victim, victimize (**Eng**)

Hellenic: ἔοικα (éoika) (**AnGk**)

*welh$_1$-

to choose, to want

*welh$_1$-d-, *welh$_1$-p-, *welh$_1$-, *wélh$_1$-ye-, *wolh$_1$-éye-

Germanic: will (**Eng**); willan (**OE**); wolle (**Fris**); willen, wil (**Dut**); wollen, wählen, Wille (**Ger**); vilja, velja, vili (**Norse**); ville, velge, vilje (**Nor**); vilja, välja (**Swe**); ville, vælge, vilje (**Dan**); vilja, velja, vilji (**Ice**)

Celtic: gwell (**Wel**)

Italic: vel, velle, volēns, voluntās, voluntārius (**Lat**); vouloir, volition, volonté, volontaire, volontiers (**Fr**); volere, volente, voluntà, volontà (**Ital**); voluntad (**Sp**); vontade (**Port**); vrea, vrere (**Rom**)

Derivatives: volition, volunty, voluntary, volunteer, benevolence, malevolent, involuntary, velleity, volitient, volitive, voluptuary, voluptuous (**Eng**)

Hellenic: ἔλδομαι (éldomai), ἔλπω (élpō) (**AnGk**)

Slavic: велеть (velét'), воля (vólja) (**Rus**); wola (**Pol**); velet, vůle (**Cz**); veliť, voľa (**Slo**); воља (vólja) (**Mace**)

Baltic: vélti (**Lith**)

Indo-Iranian: वृणीते (vṛṇīté), वृणोति (vṛṇoti) (**Sans**)

*ǵews-

to try, to taste

see Cognitive function

Movement

*sed-
to sit

*sédt, *sí-sd-e-ti, *sed-ti, *séd-ye-ti, *sod-éye-ti, *sed-éh₁-ye-ti, *sed-éh₂-ye-ti, *ḱie-sd-é-ti, *sed-i-, *sed-ti-, *sed-os, *sod-o-, *sod-yom, *sed-lo-, *sed-dʰlo-, *sod-tlō-, *sed-tós, *sed-ro-, *sed-s, *ni-sd-ós

Germanic: sit, besit, set, beset, saddle (**Eng**); sittan, besittan, settan, besettan, sadul, sadol, sadel, sess (**OE**);

sitte, sette, besette, seal, sealje (**Fris**); zitten, bezitten, zetten, bezetten, zadel, zadelen (**Dut**); sitzen, setzen, besetzen, satul, Sattel, satteln (**Ger**);

sitja, setja, søðull, søðla, sess (**Norse**); sitte, sitja, sitta, besitte, sette, besette, setja, setta, sadel, sale (**Nor**); sitta, besitta, sätta, besätta, sadel, sadla (**Swe**); sidde, besidde, sætte, besætte, sadel, sadle (**Dan**); sitja, setja, söðull, söðla, sess (**Ice**)

Celtic: seddu, eistedd, sedd (**Wel**); suigh, sui (**Iri**)

Italic: sedēre, assedēre, assiduus, dēsidia, dissidentia, obsidēre, praesidēre, praesidium, praesidēns, residēre, residuus, sīdere, resīdere, subsīdere, sēdere, sēdātiō, sēdulus, sēdēs, sedēns, sedentārius, sedimentum, sessiō, solium, sella, supersedēre (**Lat**);

seoir, asseoir, assidu, obséder, présidium, praesidium, président, résider, sédiment, selle, surseoir (**Fr**);

sedere, assidere, desidia, desio, disio, ossedere, assedio, presedere, presiedere, presidio, presidente, risedere, risiedere, sedare, sede, sedimento, sessione, sella, soprassedere, soglio (**Ital**);

asear, asiduo, sentar, residir, deseo, desidia, obseder, presidir, presidio, presidente, ser (in part), sedar, sede, sedente, sedimento, sesión, silla, sobreseer (**Sp**);

sentar, residir, subsidar, desejo, desidia, presidir, presidente, rossio, residuo, ser (in part), sé, sede, sedimento, sédulo, sessão, sólio, sela, silha (**Port**);

şedea, şedere, aşeza, sesie, şa, şale (**Rom**)

Derivatives: session, sedentary, sedate, sedation, assess, assiduous, reside, subside, dissidence, obsess, possess, possession, possessor, preside, presidio, president, residual, see (as in a bishop's see), sediment, sedulous, supersede (**Eng**);

sessie (**Dut**); Präsident, Sediment (**Ger**); swydd, sail (**Wel**)

президиум (prezidium), сессия (sessija), седация (sedacija) (**Rus**); prezydent (**Pol**); shalë (**Alb**)

Hellenic: εἷσα (heîsa), ἵζω (hízō), καθίζω (kathízō), ἕζομαι (hézomai), ἕσις (hésis), ἕδος (hédos), ὁδός (hodós), ἕδρα (hédra) (**AnGk**); καθίζω (kathízo), οδός (odós) (**Gk**)

Derivatives: cathedra, chair, dodecahedron, ephedra, exedra, hexahedron, sanhedrin, tetrahedroid, hodo- (**Eng**)

Slavic: сесть (sest'), сяду (sjádu), сидеть (sidét'), садить (sadít'), сажу (sažú), садит (sádit), ход (xod), хода (xoda) (**Rus**); siąść, siedzieć, sadzić, sadzę, chód (**Pol**); sedět, chod, chůda (**Cz**); sedieť, sadiť, chod (**Slo**); од (od) (**Mace**)

Baltic: sedéti, sèstis, sodìnti (**Lith**); sēdēt, segli (**Latv**)

Indo-Iranian: सद् (sad), सीदति (sīdati), सादयति (sādáyati), सदस् (sádas) (**Sans**)

which includes *nisdós nest:

*nisdós

nest

Germanic: nest (**Eng**); nest (**OE**); nêst, nust (**Fris**); nest (**Dut**); Nest (**Ger**); näste (**Swe**)

Italic: nīdus, nīdificāre, nīdifōrmis (**Lat**); nid, niche, niais, nidiforme (**Fr**); nido, nidio, nidiforme (**Ital**); nido, nidificar (**Sp**); ninho (**Port**)

Derivatives: nidus, nide, niche, nyas, nidify, nidiform (**Eng**); nis, niche (**Dut**); nyth (**Wel**); nead (**Iri**)

Slavic: гнездо (gnezdó) (**Rus**); gniazdo (**Pol**); hnízdo (**Cz**); hniezdo (**Slo**); гнездо (gnezdo) (**Mace**)

Baltic: lizdas (**Lith**); ligzds, ligzda (**Latv**)

Indo-Iranian: नीड (nīḍá) (**Sans**)

*legh-

to lie down

*légʰ-e-ti, *légʰ-ye-ti, *logʰ-éye-ti, *lógʰ-o-s, *légʰ-os, *legʰ-ro-m, *legʰ-to-s, *légʰ-tro-m, *legʰ-yo-m, *legʰ-yeh₂, *logʰ-yo-m

Germanic: lie, lay, law, lair, offlay, allay, low (**Eng**); licgan, lecgan, læġ, leġ, leġe, lagu, leger, oflecgan, āleċġ, lāhan (**OE**);

lizze, ledsa, loch, leech (**Fris**); liggen, leggen, log, leger, afleggen, aanleggen, laag (**Dut**); liegen, legen, ablegen, anlegen, erlegen, Lager, Lug, läg (**Ger**);

liggja, leggja, lag, lǫg, legr, lóg, afleggja, lágr (**Norse**); ligge, liggje, liggja, legge, leggja, legga, log, lav (**Nor**); ligga, lägga, lag, ålägga, läger, låg (**Swe**); ligge, lægge, log, lov, lejr, lav (**Dan**); liggja, leggja, lög, lygi, lágur (**Ice**)

Derivatives: лагерь (lager') (**Rus**)

Celtic: gwely (**Wel**); luigh, lui (**Iri**)

Derivatives: Leicester (**Eng**); Liger (**Lat**); Loire (**Fr**)

Italic: lectus (**Lat**); lit, litière (**Fr**); letto, lettiga (**Ital**); lecho, lechiga (**Sp**); leito, liteira (**Port**); lectică (**Rom**)

Derivatives: litter (**Eng**)

Hellenic: λέχομαι (lékhomai), λέκτο (lékto), λόχος (lókhos), λέχος (lékhos), λέκτρον (léktron) (**AnGk**); λέκτρο (léktro) (**Gk**)

Derivatives: lochia (**Eng**)

Slavic: лечь (leč'), лежáть (ležát'), ложíться (ložít'sja), положíть (položít'), лог (log) (**Rus**); lec, leżeć, łożyć, odłóg (**Pol**); lehnout si, ležet, ložit (**Cz**); ľahnúť si, ležať, ložiť (**Slo**); лежи (leži), ложи (loži) (**Mace**)

Albanian: lag, lagtë, lagje (**Alb**)

Indo-Iranian: लेट्यति (leṭyati) (**Sans**); लेटना (leṭnā) (**Hin**)

which perhaps includes:

Italic: lēx, lēgālis, illēgālis, lēgātiō, lēgātor, lēgātus, lēgislātiō, lēgislātor, lēgitimus, ablēgāre, ablēgātiō, allēgātiō, collēga, collēgium, collēgiātus, dēlēgāre, praelēgāre, relēgāre, relēgātiō, lēgulēius (**Lat**);

loi, légal, loyal, illégal, légation, légat, législation, législateur, légitime, ablégat, alléguer, allégation, collégue, déléguer, préléguer, reléguer, relégation (**Fr**);

legge, leale, legale, illegale, legazione, legato, legislazione, legislatore, legittimo, ablegazione, allegare, collega, collegio, delegare, relegare, relegazione, leguleio (**Ital**);

ley, leal, legal, ilegal, legación, legislación, legislador, legítimo, lindo (prob.), alegar, allegación, colega, colegio, delegar, relegar, relegación (**Sp**);

lei, leal, legal, ilegal, legação, legislação, legislador, lídimo, legítimo, lindo (prob.), ablegar, ablegação, alegar, alegação, colega, delegar, relegar, relegação, leguleio, leguiejo (**Port**);

lege, leal, legal, ilegal, legitim, alega, alegaţie, delega (**Rom**)

Derivatives: legal, legislate, leal, loyal, loyalty, illegal, legality, legific, league, legacy, legatary, legatee, legatine, legation, legator, legate, legislation, legislative, legislator, legislature, legitim, legitimacy, legitimate, privilege, ablegate, ablegation, allegation, colleague, college, collegium, collegiate, delegate, delegation, relegate, relegation (**Eng**);

illegal, Kollege (**Ger**); kollega, kollegium (**Swe**); coleg (**Wel**); coláiste (**Iri**); легат (legat), коллéга (kolléga) (**Rus**); kolega (**Pol**); ligj (**Alb**)

*ḱei-

to lie down, settle; home, family; love; beloved

*ḱéy-tor, *ḱéy-wo-s, *ḱóy-mos, *ḱoy-neh₂, *ḱoy-teh₂

Germanic: home, haunt, hamlet, hangar (**Eng**); hām (**OE**); hiem (**Fris**); heem, heim, in place names: -em, -hem, -gem, hanteren, hangar (**Dut**); Heim, heimsen, hantieren (**Ger**); heimr, heim, heimta (**Norse**); hjem, heim, heimta, hemta, henta, hente, håndtere (**Nor**); hem, hämta, hantera (**Swe**); hjem, hente (**Dan**); heimur, heim, heimta (**Ice**)

Derivatives: hameau, hangar, hanter (**Fr**)

Italic: cīvis, cīvicus, cīvīlis, cīvīlitās, cīvitās, cūnae, cūnābula, incūnābula (**Lat**); civique, civil, cité, citoyen (**Fr**); civico, civile, città, cittade, cittadino, culla (**Ital**); cívico, civil, ciudad, cuna (**Sp**); cívico, civel, civil, civilizado, cividade, cidade (**Port**); civic, cetate (**Rom**)

Derivatives: civic, civil, civilian, civility, civilization, city, civitas, citizen, cunabula, incunabula (**Eng**); civil (**Dan**); ciwed, ciwdod (**Wel**); κούνια (koúnia) (**Gk**); qytet (**Alb**)

Hellenic: κεῖται (keîtai), κεῖμαι (keîmai), ἄκοιτῐς (ákoitis), κειμήλιον (keimélion), κοιμάω (koimáō), κοίτη (koítē), κώμη (kṓmē) (**AnGk**); κειμήλιο (keimílio), κοιμάμαι (koimámai), κοίτη (koíti) (**Gk**)

Derivatives: acoetis (**Lat**)

Slavic: семья (sem'ja), семейство (seméjstvo), семейный (seméjnyj) (**Rus**); семејство (semejstvo) (**Mace**)

Baltic: šeimà, šeimė, šeĩmas, kaimas, kiẽmas (**Lith**); siẽva, sàime, ciems (**Latv**)

Indo-Iranian: शये (sáye), शेते (śéte), क्षेति (kṣeti), शेव (śéva), शिव (śivá) (**Sans**)

*steh₂-

to stand

*stéh₂-t, *stí-steh₂-ti, *st-né-h₂-ti, *stéh₂-ye-ti, *ste-stóh₂-e, *sth₂-éh₁-(ye)-ti, *stoh₂-éye-ti, *steh₂-dʰlo-, *sth₂-dʰlo-m, *steh₂-gʰo-, *sth₂-e-lo-s, *stéh₂-mn̥, *steh₂-mo-, *steh₂-men-, *stoh₂-mo-, *sth₂-dʰ-mo-, *stéh₂-no-, *sth₂-(e)nt-ieh₂, *steh₂-ro-, *stéh₂-ti-s, *sth₂-tós, *stéh₂-tu-s, *sth₂-né-dʰ-, *steh₂dʰ-om, *steh₂w-, *steh₂-u-rós, *stoh₂-w-ih₂, *steh₂-weh₂

Germanic: stand, bestand, forstand, stead, stay, stud, stow, -stow, stour, shtetl (via Yiddish), stound (**Eng**); standan, bestandan, forstandan, stede, steyen, stod, stōw, stōr, stund (**OE**);

stean, stêd, stounde, stoer (**Fris**); staan, stad, stede, stee, standen, stoet, stond (**Dut**); stān, stehen, Statt, Stadt, Stute, Stunde (**Ger**);

staðr, standa, stōð, staurr, stó, stórr, stund (**Norse**); stå, stad, sted, standa, sto, stund (**Nor**); stå, stad, stånda, sto, stör, stor, stund (**Swe**); stå, stad, sted, stande, stor, stund

(**Dan**); staður, standa, stóð, stó, stór, stund (**Ice**)

Derivatives: étai (**Fr**)

Celtic: taw (**Wel**); tá, támh, sáil (**Iri**)

Italic: stāre, astāre, cōnstāre, circumstāre, circumstāntia, distāre, distāns, distantia, īnstāre, obstāre, obstāculum, obstētrīx, praestāre, restāre, superstāre, superstes, superstitiō, sistere, absistere, assistere, consistere, assistentia, dēsistere, existere, īnsistere, persistere, resistere, resistentia, subsistere, dēstināre, dēstinātiō, obstināre, stetī, stabilis, stabilīre, stabilitās, stabulum, stabulāre, stāmen, status, īnstaurāre, īnstaurātor, rēstaurāre, statiō, statūra, statuere, cōnstituere, cōnstitūtiō, dēstituere, īnstituere, īnstitutiō, īnstitūtum, prōstituere, restituere, statua, statuāria, substituere, statim (**Lat**);

circonstance, distancier, destiner, destination, étable, établar, état, été, être, ester, instaurer, restaurer, consister, désister, exister, insister, persister, résister, subsister, constater, coûter, ôter, obstacle, obstétrique, prêter, rester, superstition, stable, établir, stabilité, station, stature, statuer, consistuer, constitution, destituer, instituer, institut, restituer, statue (**Fr**);

constare, costare, circostanza, distanza, ostare, ostacolo, ostetrica, prestare, restare, resto, superstite, superstizione, interstiziale, resistere (via restitō), persistere, assistere, sussistere, desistere, insistere, consistere, esistere, resistere, destinare, stare, stabbio, stabulario, stame, stato, instaurare, ristoare, restaurare, stabile, stabilire, stabilità, stabbiare, stabulare, stagione, stazione, stazzo, stazzone, statura, costituire, costituzione, destituire, istituire, restituire, statua (**Ital**);

constar, constatar, costar, circunstancia, circunstanciar, distancia, distanciar, obstar, obstáculo, prestar, restar, resto, superstición, asistir, consistir, desistir, existir, insistir, persistir, resistir, subsistir, destinar, destinación, estar, establo, estabular, estambre, estado, estatus, instaurar, restaurar, estable, establecer, establir, estación, estatuir, constituir, constitución, destituir, instituir, prostituir, restituir, estatua (**Sp**);

constar, custar, circunstanciar, distanciar, obstar, prestar, restar, resto, superstição, destinar, estábulo, estrabo, estame, estâmina (via English), estar, estado, assistir, consistir, desistir, insistir, persistir, resistir, estável, estabelecer, estabular, estação, estatuir, constituir, constituição, destituir, instituir, instituto, prostituir, substituir, restaurar (**Port**);

consta, costa, custa, circumstanţă, distanţă, sista, insista, destina, staul, stat, sta, stare, adăsta, adăstare, superstiţie, stabil, stabili, staţie, restitui, statuie, statuă (**Rom**)

Derivatives: circumstance, consist, cost, constant, constitute, constitution, distant, distance, extant, instant, oust, obstacle, obstetrics, rest, presto, stance, stanchion, stanza, state, station, stationary, statistic, statue, statuary, staunch, stare decisis, substance, substitute, superstition, interstitial, absist, resist, resistance, persist, subsist, desist, insist, assist, assistance, exist, solstice, destine, destination, obstinate, stable, stabile, establish, stability, stamen, stamina, estate, status, stature, destitute, institute, institution, prostitute, restitute, restitution, store, instaurator, restore (**Eng**);

Status, Institution (**Ger**); station (**Swe**); ystafell (**Wel**); stad, eastát (**Iri**); σταύλος (stávlos), στώμιξ (stṓmix), σταθμός (stathmós) (**AnGk**); σταύλος (stávlos) (**Gk**); статус (státus), дистанция (distancija), конституция (konstitúcija), институт (institut), статуя (statuja) (**Rus**); kosztować (**Pol**)

Hellenic: ἵστημι (hístēmi), ἵσταμαι (hístamai), ἔστην (éstēn), ἔστηκᾰ (héstēka), στῆμᾰ (stêma), στήμων (stḗmōn), στάμνος (stámnos), στάσις (stásis), ἀνάστᾰσῐς (anástasis), ἔκστᾰσῐς (ékstasis), στᾰτός (statós), στάδιος (stádios), σταυρός (staurós), στοᾱ (stoā), στοιᾱ (stoiā), στοιή (stoié), στῳᾱ (stōiā), στῳïᾱ (stōïā) (**AnGk**); στάση (stási), ανάσταση (anástasi), έκσταση (ékstasi), σταυρός (stavrós) (**Gk**)

Derivatives: stasis, static, system, anastasis, ekstasis, ecstasy, ecstatic, stoa (**Eng**); Stasis, Ekstase (**Ger**); system (**Nor**); system (**Swe**); system (**Dan**); systēma, anastasis, ecstasis, exstasis, extasis (**Lat**); system, extase, extasié (**Fr**); sistema, estasi, estatico (**Ital**); sistema, éxtasis, extático (**Sp**); sistema, êxtase, extático (**Port**); sistem, extaz, extatic (**Rom**); экстаз (ekstáz) (**Rus**); system (**Pol**); sistemà (**Lith**); sistēma (**Latv**); sistem (**Alb**)

Slavic: стать (stat'), стоять (stojáť), стол (stol), стамой (stamój), стан (stan), старый (starŷj), стадо (stádo), ставить (stáviť) (**Rus**); stać, stół, stan, stary (uncert.), stado, stawić (**Pol**); stát, stůl, stan, starý (uncert.), stádo, stavit (**Cz**); stáť, stôl, stan, starý, stádo, staviť (**Slo**); стане (stane), стар (star), стадо (stado), стави (stavi) (**Mace**)

Baltic: stovéti, stóti, stógas, stālas, stomuõ, stuomuõ, stúomas, stónas, stóras, stovéti (**Lith**); stāt, stāmen, stātis, stāvēt (**Latv**)

Albanian: shtãj, shtãzë, shtëzë, shtat (**Alb**)

Indo-Iranian: तिष्ठति (tiṣṭhati), अस्थात् (ásthāt), तस्थौ (tastháu), स्थामन् (sthāman), स्थान (sthāna), स्थिति (sthíti), स्थित (sthitá), स्थूर (sthūrá), स्थिर (sthira) (**Sans**); स्थिति (sthiti), स्थित (sthit), स्थिर (sthir) (**Hin**); ایستادن (īstādan) (**Pers**)

*h₁ey-

to go

*h₁éy-ti, *h₁e-h₁óy-e, *h₁i-tó-s, *h₁éy-tr̥

Celtic: wyf (**Wel**)

Italic: īre, adīre, coīre, coitiō, coitus, exīre, exitus, inīre, initium, initiāre, initiātiō, itus, iter, obīre, perīre, dēperīre, praeterīre, redīre, reditus, subīre, subitō, subitus, trānseō, iānus, iānua, iānuārius (**Lat**);

aller, ir- (future tense), issu, initier, périr, dépérir, subir, subit, transir, janvier (**Fr**);

gire, ire, adire, uscire, esito, inizio, iniziare, iter, perire, deperire, subire, subito, transire, gennaio (**Ital**);

ir (in part), exir, éxito, ejido, inicio, iniciar, perecer, rédito, subir, súbito, transir, enero (**Sp**);

ir (in part), coito, êxito, inicio, iniciar, perecer, rédito, subir, súbito, estresir, janella, janeiro (**Port**);

coit, ieşi, ieşire, pieri, pierire, sui, subit, ianuarie (**Rom**)

Derivatives: coition, coitus, exit, issue, initial, initiate, initiation, itinerary, iter, obituary, perish, preterition, preterite, transit, January (**Eng**); Januar (**Ger**); coitus (**Swe**); Eanáir (**Iri**); Ιανουάριος (Ianouários), Γενάρης (Genáris) (**Gk**); инициация (iniciacija), январь (janvar') (**Rus**)

Hellenic: εἶμι (eîmi), ἰτός (itós) (**AnGk**)

Slavic: идти (idti) (**Rus**); iść (**Pol**); jít (**Cz**); ísť (**Slo**); иде (íde) (**Mace**)

Baltic: eĩti (**Lith**); iet (**Latv**)

Albanian: iki (**Alb**)

Indo-Iranian: एति (eti), यान (yāna) (**Sans**); यान (yān) (**Hin**)

*h₁weh₂-
to leave, abandon, give out

*h₁wéh₂-ye-ti, *h₁wéh₂-, *h₁uh₂-ko-, *h₁uh₂-ko-wo-, *h₁weh₂-sno-/ *h₁uh₂-sno-, *h₁weh₂-sto-, *h₁weh₂-st-en-yeh₂

Germanic: westen (obs.), want, wane (**Eng**); wēste, wēsten, wanian (**OE**); woastyn (**Fris**); woestijn (**Dut**); wüst, Wüste (**Ger**); vanta, vana (**Norse**); vanta, vana (**Ice**)

Derivatives: gâtine (**Fr**)

Celtic: fás, fásach, fásaigh (**Iri**)

Italic: vacāre, supervacāneus, vacāns, vacīvus, vacuus, vacuitās, vacuum, vānus, vānēscere, ēvānēscere, vānitās, vastus, vastāre (**Lat**);

vaquer, vacant, vacuité, vacuum, vide, vain, évanouir, vanité, vaste, gâter (**Fr**);

vacare, supervacaneo, vacuo, vacuità, vuoto, vano, vanità, vasto, guastare (**Ital**);

vagar, supervacáneo, vacio, vago, vacuo, vacuum, vano, desvanecer, evanescer, vanidad, vasto, gastar (**Sp**);

vagar, vacar, supervacâneo, vazio, vago, vácuo, vacuidade, vão, vaidade, vanidade, vasto, vastar, gastar (**Port**); vid, van, vanitate, vântă, vast (**Rom**)

Derivatives: vacate, vacation, supervacaneous, vacant, vacancy, vacuous, vacuum, vacuity, evacuate, void, vain, vaunt, vanish, vanity, vast, waste (**Eng**)

Hellenic: ἐάω (eáō) (poss.) (**AnGk**)

Baltic: vójęs (**Lith**); vâjêt (**Latv**)

Indo-Iranian: वायति (vāyati), अवासित् (avāsit), ऊन (ūná) (**Sans**)

*gʷem-
to step, come

*gʷém-t, *gʷṃskéti, *gʷṃ-yé-ti, *gʷe-gʷóm-e, *gʷémtis, *gʷém-tu-s, *gʷṃ-tó-s, *gʷṃ-dʰ-mo-

Germanic: come, become (**Eng**); cuman, bicuman (**OE**); komme, bikomme (**Fris**); komen, kommen, bekomen, bekwaam (**Dut**); kommen, bekommen, bequem (**Ger**);

koma (**Norse**); komme, koma, kome, bekomme (**Nor**); komma, bekomma, bekväm, inventarium (**Swe**); komme, bekomme (**Dan**); koma (**Ice**)

Italic: venīre, advenīre, advena, adventīcius, adventus, antevenīre, circumvenīre, contrāvenīre, convenīre, conveniēns, convenientia, conventiō, cōntiōnor, conventus, dēvenīre, ēvenīre, ēventus, intervenīre, interventio, interventor, inventiō, inventor, inventus, obvenīre, pervenīre, praevenīre, prōvenīre, prōventus, revenīre, subvenīre, supervenīre, survenir, ventiō, ventus (**Lat**);

venir, advenir, avenir, aveindre, Avent, circonvenir, contrevenir, convenir, convenant, convenance, convention, couvent, convent, devenir, événement, éventualité, intervenir, interventeur, inveniō, inventer, invention, inventeur, inventore, obvenir, parvenir, prévenir, provenir, revenir, souvenir, subvenir, vent (**Fr**);

venire, avvenire, avvento, circonvenire, convenire, convenienza, convenzione, convento, divenire, diventare, evento, eventualità, intervenire, inventàrium, invenzione, inventione, pervenire, prevenire, provenire, provento, rivenire, sovvenire, vento (**Ital**);

venir, advenir, avenir, Adviento, antevenir, circunvenir, contravenir, convenir, conveniente, conveniencia, convención, convento, devenir, eventual, eventualidad, intervenir, entrevenir, interventor, invenir, inventar, invención, inventor, prevenir, provenir, provento, revenir, subvenir, suvenir, sobrevenir, supervenir, viento, ventana (**Sp**);

vir, advir, avir, ádvena, advento, contravir, convir, conveniente, conveniência, convenção, concionar, convento, devir, evento, eventualidade, intervir, invenção, inventor, prevenir, provir, provento, revir, sobrevir, vento, venta (**Port**);

veni, venire, conveni, cuveni, convenienţă, cuviinţă, convenţie, cuvânt, deveni, eveniment, eventualitate, interveni, invenţie, inventor, inventa, reveni, vânt (**Rom**)

Derivatives: advene, advent, adventure, adventitious, avenue, circumvent, contravene, convene, convenient, convenience, convention, convent, covent, evene, event, eventual, eventually, eventuality, intervene, intervention, interventor, invent, invention, prevent, revenue, souvenir, subvene, supervene, survene, venue, venture (**Eng**);

Advent, Eventualität, Invention (**Ger**); конвéнция (konvéncija), инвéнция (invencija) (**Rus**); ewentualność (**Pol**); eventualita (**Cz**); κουβέντα (kouvénta) (**Gk**)

Hellenic: βαίνω (baínō), βάσκω (báskō), βέβηκᾰ (bébēka), βάσις (básis), ἀνᾰβᾰσῐς (anábasis), κᾰτᾰβᾰσῐς (katábasis), βατός (batós), βαθμός (bathmós) (**AnGk**); βάση (vási), ανάβαση (anávasi), κατάβαση (katávasi), βατός (vatós) (**Gk**)

Derivatives: basis, base, anabasis, katabasis (**Eng**); base (**Dut**); Basis (**Ger**); base (**Nor**); base (**Dan**); basis, anabasis (**Lat**); base, anabase, catabase (**Fr**); base (**Ital**); base (**Sp**); base (**Port**); база (baza), базис (bazis) (**Rus**); katabasis (**Pol**);

Baltic: gimti, giṁtis, giṁtas (**Lith**); dzimt, dzimts (**Latv**)

Indo-Iranian: गम् (gam), गमती (gámati), अगन् (ágan), गच्छति (gácchati), जगाम (jagāma), गति (gáti), गन्तु (gántu), गत (gatá) (**Sans**); गति (gati), गत (gat) (**Hin**); گام (gam) (**Pers**)

*ped-
to walk, to step

see Body: Limbs & Joints

*steygʰ-
to go, to climb

*stéygʰ-e-ti, *stigʰ-néw-ti, *stéygʰ-ti-s, *stóygʰ-o-s, *stoygʰ-ri-s, *stigʰ-o-s, *stigʰ-el-eh₂, *stigʰ-eh₂

Germanic: sty, stile, stair (**Eng**); stīgan, stiġel, stǣġer (**OE**); stige (**Fris**); stijgen, steeg, stegel, steiger, sticht (**Dut**); steigen, Steige, Stiegel (**Ger**); stíga, stétt, stéttr (**Norse**); stige, stætt (**Nor**); stiga (**Swe**); stige (**Dan**); stíga (**Ice**)

Celtic: staighre (**Iri**)

Possibly: **Italic:** vestīgāre, investīgāre, investīgātiō, pervestīgāre, vestīgium (**Lat**); investiguer, vestige (**Fr**); investigare, investigazione (**Ital**); investigar, investigación, vestigio (**Sp**); investigar, investigação (**Port**); vestigiu (**Rom**)

Derivatives: vestigate, investigate, pervestigate, vestige (**Eng**); vëzhgoj (**Alb**)

Hellenic: στείχω (steíkhō), στοῖχος (stoîkhos), στίχος (stíkhos), ἡμιστίχιον (hēmistíkhion), κατάστιχον (katástikhon), τετράστιχος (tetrástikhos) (**AnGk**); στίχος (stíchos) (**Gk**)

Derivatives: hemistich, tetrastich, acrostic, cadastre, distich, distichous, stich, stichic, stichomancy, stichometry, telestich (**Eng**); stichus (**Lat**); hémistiche, cadastre, tétrastiche (**Fr**); catasto (**Ital**); стих (stix) (**Rus**)

Slavic: -стичь (-stíč') e.g. постичь (postíč'), -стигнуть (-stígnut'), e.g. постигнуть (postígnut'), стезя (stezjá), стегá (stegá) (**Rus**); ścignąć, stadza (**Pol**); stihnouti, steze (**Cz**); stihnúť (**Slo**); стигне (stigne) (**Mace**)

Baltic: steĩgti (**Lith**); staĩga (**Latv**)

Albanian: shteg (**Alb**)

Indo-Iranian: स्तिघ्नोति (stighnoti) (**Sans**)

*terh₂-

to cross over, pass through; overcome

*treh₂-, *terh₂-, *tṛh₂-ṇt-s, *torh₂-éye-, *térh₂-dʰrom, *néḱ-tṛh₂

Germanic: through, thorough (**Eng**); þurh, þuruh (**OE**); door (**Dut**); durch (**Ger**)

Celtic: tra, trwy, drwy (**Wel**); thar, trá (lit.), trí, tre (**Iri**)

Italic: trāns, trānstrum (**Lat**); très, tré- (tres- before s) (**Fr**); tra- (**Ital**); tras- (**Sp**); trás, traste, trasto (**Port**)

Derivatives: trans-, transport, intransigent, transact, transaction, transcend, transient, transitory, transparent, tradition (**Eng**)

Hellenic: τέρθρον (térthron), νέκταρ (néktar) (*neḱ-+) (**AnGk**)

Indo-Iranian: तरति (tarati), तारयति (tārayati), तार (tāra), अवतार (avatāra), तिर (tirah), तिरस् (tiras), तिर्यञ्च् (tiryañc) (**Sans**); अवतार (avtār) (**Hin**); ترایيدن (tarāyīdan), تراويدن (tarāvīdan), تريوه (tarēva) (**Pers**)

Derivatives: avatar (**Eng**)

which perhaps also includes:

*térmṇ

boundary, end

Italic: terminus, terminālis, termināre (**Lat**); terme, terminer (**Fr**); termine, terminare (**Ital**); término, terminar (**Sp**); término, termo (**Port**); țărm, termen, termina (**Rom**)

Derivatives: terminus, term, terminal, terminate, termination, determine, determination, interminable (**Eng**); term, termijn (**Dut**); terfyn (**Wel**); термин (términ) (**Rus**); termin (**Pol**)

Hellenic: τέρμα (térma), τέρμων (térmōn) (**AnGk**); τέρμα (térma) (**Gk**)

Indo-Iranian: तर्मन् (tarman), सुतर्मन् (sutárman) (**Sans**)

*ḱers-

to run

see Mammals

*kek-

to jump, spring out

see Mammals

*(s)kek-
to spring, move quickly

see Mammals

*peth₂
to fly

see Body: Limbs & Joints

*plew-
to fly, flow, run

see Body: Torso & Organs

*(s)neh₂-
to swim, float

*(s)néh₂-ti, *(s)noh₂-éye-ti, *(s)néh₂-mn̥, *néh₂-u-s, *(s)n̥h₂-tós

Germanic: nōwend (**OE**); nór (**Norse**); nór (**Ice**)

Celtic: nawf, noe (**Wel**)

Italic: nō, nāns, nantis, nāvis, nāvālis, nāvicella, nāvigātiō, nāvigātor, nāvigium, nāvigāre, circumnāvigāre, naufragus, natō, natātiō, natātor, natātōrium, natātōrius, nātrīx (**Lat**);

nef, navire, naval, navale, navals, nacelle, navigation, navigateur, nager, naviguer, circumnaviguer, naufrage, natation (**Fr**);

nave, navale, navicella, navigazione, navigatore, navigio, naviglio, navigare, circumnavigare, naufragio, nuotare, natatorio, natrice (**Ital**);

nave, naval, navegación, navío, navegar, circunnavegar, nadar, nadador, nadadera, natatorio, natriz (**Sp**);

nave, nau, naval, navegação, navio, navegar, circum-navegar, náufrago, nadar, nadador (**Port**);

naie, navă, navigaţie, navigator, a naviga, circumnaviga, înota, înotare (**Rom**)

Derivatives: navy, naval, navigation, navigator, navigate, circumnavigate, natation, natatorium (**Eng**); navigere (**Nor**); navigera (**Swe**); навигация (navigacija) (**Rus**); nawigacja (**Pol**)

Hellenic: νάω (nắō), Ναϊάς (Naïás), Νηρεύς (Nēreús), νᾶμᾰ (nâma), νήϊος (nḗïos), ναῦς (naûs), ναυτικός (nautikós), ναύτης (naútēs), ναυτία (nautía), ναυσία (nausía) (**AnGk**); ναυς (nafs) (**Gk**)

Derivatives: naiad, nautical, astronaut, aeronautics, -naut, nausea (**Eng**); nauta, nauticus (**Lat**); nautique (**Fr**); nautico (**Ital**); nauta, náutico (**Sp**); náutico (**Port**)

Albanian: anije (**Alb**)

Indo-Iranian: स्ना (snā), स्नापयति (snāpáyati), स्नात (snātá), स्नाति (snāti), नाव्य (nāvyá), नौ (nau), नाव (nāva) (**Sans**); شناويدن (šenāvīdan), شنا (šenā), اشنان (ōšnān), ناو (nâv) (**Pers**)

*seh₂g-
to seek out

*séh₂g-ti, *séh₂g-ye-ti, *seh₂g-o-s, *sh₂g-eh₂, *séh₂g-ti-s

Germanic: forsake, withsake, seech, seek, socage, sake, sackless, saught, sought (**Eng**); sacan, forsacan, wiþsacan, sēċan, sōcn, sōcen, sacu, saclēas, seht, saht (**OE**);

fersaakje, sykje, saak (**Fris**); verzaken, zoeken, zaak (**Dut**); suchen, Suche, Sache (**Ger**);

sœkja, sókn, sǫk, sátt, sætt (**Norse**); forsake, søke, sokn, sak (**Nor**); försaka, söka, socken, sak (**Swe**); forsage, søge, sogn, sag (**Dan**); sókn, sök, saklaus, sátt, sætt (**Ice**)

Italic: sāgīre, praesāgīre, sāga, sagāx, sagācitās, sāgus (**Lat**); sagace, sagacité (**Fr**); presagire, saga, sagace (**Ital**); presagiar, sagaz (**Sp**); pressagiar (**Port**)

Derivatives: presage, sagacity, sagacious (**Eng**)

Hellenic: ἡγέομαι (hēgéomai), ἐξηγέομαι (exēgéomai), ἐξήγησις (exégēsis), χορηγός (khorēgós), ἡγεμών (hēgemṓn), ἡγεμονίᾱ (hēgemoníā) (**AnGk**); χορηγός (chorigós) (**Gk**)

Derivatives: exegesis, hegemon, hegemony (**Eng**); chorège (**Fr**); egemonia (**Ital**); hegemonia (**Port**); гегемо́н (gegemón), гегемо́ния (gegemónija) (**Rus**)

*ḱel-
to incline, lean, tend towards

see Cognitive function

*ḱley-
to lean, slope, incline

see Cognitive function

*lewg-
to bend, turn

*lu-né-g-ti, *lug-o-, *lug-tó-s, *lug-so-s, *lug-su-s

Germanic: lock, loquet, locket (**Eng**); loc, lūcan (**OE**); lûke (**Fris**); lok, loch, luiken (**Dut**); Loch (**Ger**); lok, lúka (**Norse**); lukke (**Nor**); lock, lucka (**Swe**); låg (**Dan**); lok, ljúka (**Ice**)

Derivatives: loquet (**Fr**); loch (**Pol**)

Celtic: ellwng, dillwng (**Wel**)

Italic: lucto, lucta, luctātiō, luctātor, ēluctārī, ēluctābilis, inēluctābilis, luxus, luxuria, luxuriosus (**Lat**); lutter, lutte, inéluctable, luxe, luxure (**Fr**); lottare, lotta, lottatore, ineluttabile, lusso (**Ital**); luchar, lucha, luchador, lujo (**Sp**); lutar, luta, lutador, luxo, luxúria, luxurioso (**Port**); lupta, luptare, luptă, luptător, lux (**Rom**)

Derivatives: luctation, ineluctable, luxury, luxurious (**Eng**); luftoj, luftë, luftëtar (**Alb**)

Hellenic: λύγος (lúgos), λυγίζω (lugízō) (**AnGk**); λυγίζω (lygízo), αλύγιστος (alýgistos), λυγαριά (lygariá), λυγιστός (lygistós) (**Gk**)

*leykʷ-
to leave

*léykʷ-t, *likʷ-e-t, *li-né-kʷ-ti,*le-lóykʷ-e, *loykʷ-éye-ti

Germanic: loan (**Eng**); lien (**Fris**); leen (**Dut**); leihen, Lehen (**Ger**); léa, ljá, lén, lán, leigja, leiga (**Norse**); len, lån (**Nor**); län, lån (**Swe**); len, lån (**Dan**); ljá, lán, leigja (**Ice**)

Celtic: lig (**Iri**)

Italic: linquere, relinquere, delinquere, dēlinquentia, dēlictum (**Lat**); délinquer, délinquant, délinquance, délit (**Fr**); delinquere, delitto (**Ital**); delinquir (**Sp**); delinquir, delinquência (**Port**)

Derivatives: relinquish, relict, delinquent, delinquency, delict (**Eng**); Delikt (**Ger**)

Hellenic: λείπω (leípō), ἔλῐπε (élipe), λιμπάνω (limpánō), λέλοιπᾰ (léloipa) (**AnGk**)

Slavic: лихóй (lixój), лишать (lišati), лишний (lišnij) (**Rus**); lichy (**Pol**); lichý (**Cz**); lichý (**Slo**)

Baltic: likti, atlaikas, laikýtiy (**Lith**); làicît (**Latv**)

Indo-Iranian: अरिचत् (áricat), रिणक्ति (riṇákti), रिरेच (riréca), रेचयति (recayati) (**Sans**); ريختن (rixtan) (**Pers**)

Object motion

*bher-

to carry

*bʰér-e-ti, *bʰor-éye-ti, *bʰr̥-yé-ti, *bʰór, *bʰor-id-eh₂, *bʰor-éh₂, *bʰēr-eh₂, *bʰer-h₁dyeh₂, *bʰér-mn̥, *bʰer-H-men-, *bʰer-no-s, *bʰor-no-m, *bʰér-ti-s, *bʰr̥-tew-no-

Germanic: bear, forbear, abear, beer (one who exists), bier, barrow, bairn, birth (**Eng**); beran, forberan, āberan, bǣr, bēr, bearwe, bearn (**OE**);

barre, bear, berje, bier, baar, barn, bern (**Fris**); baren, ontberen, beuren, gebeuren, baar, berrie, geboorte (**Dut**); entbehren, gebären, erbären, gebühren, Bahre, Geburt (**Ger**);

bera, byrja, bára, barar, barir, barn, stjúpbarn, byrð (**Norse**); bære, byrje, byrja, båre, barn (**Nor**); bära, umbära, börja, bår, bör, barn, styvbarn (**Swe**); bære, børje, båre, bør, barn (**Dan**); bera, byrja, börur, stjúpbarn (**Ice**)

Derivatives: bière, brouette, barou, birouchette (**Fr**); baroccio (**Ital**)

Celtic: beir, breith (**Iri**)

Italic: ferre, auferre, ablātiō, ablātīvus, ablātor, circumferre, circumferentia, cōnferre, collatus, dēferre, dēferēns, vās dēferēns, dēlātiō, differre, differēns, efferre, ēlātē, elātiō, -fer, īnferre, illātiō, illātīvus, inferibilis, offerre, ferculum, fertilis, fertus, interferre, intrōferre, oblātiō, oblātus, perferre, postferre, praeferre, praelātus, praeterferor, prōferre, referre, relātiō, relātīvus, sufferre, trānsferre, trānslātiō, trānslātor, trānslātus, fūr, fūrtum, fūrtīvus, fūror, forda, fōrs, fōrtuna, fōrsit, fōrtuitus (**Lat**);

ablation, circonférence, conférer, déférer, délation, différer, élation, inférer, illation, illative, offrir, oublie, oblat, préférer, prélat, proférer, référer, relation, souffrir, transférer, translation, furet, furtif, fortune (**Fr**);

ablativo, circonferenza, conferire, deferire, differire, inferire, illazione, inferibile, offrire, oblazione, oblata, oblato, preferire, prelato, proferire, riferire, relazione, soffrire, trasferire, traslazione, traslato, furetto, furo, furto, furtivo, fortuna, forse, fortuito, fortuitamente (**Ital**);

aferrar, ablación, ablativo, circunferir, circunferencia, conferir, deferir, delatar, delación, diferir, elación, inferir, ilación, ilativo, ofrecer, oblación, oblada, oblato, oblea, preferir, proferir, referir, relación, sufrir, transferir, trasladar, traslación, traslado, hurón, hurto, furtivo, furtiva, fortuna, fortuito, fortuitamente (**Sp**);

auferir, ablação, ablativo, ablator, circunferência, conferir, deferir, delação, diferir, elação, inferir, ilação, ilativo, oferecer, oblação, oblata, oblato, obrada, obreia, preferir, proferir, referir, relação, sofrer, transferir, trasladar, translação, furão, furto, fortuna, fortuito (**Port**);

ablativ, circumferință, oferi, relație, suferi, suferire, translație, fur, furt, fura, furare, furtună (**Rom**)

Derivatives: aquifer, ablation, ablative, ablator, circumference, confer, collate, conifer, defer, differ, different, difference, dilate, elated, elation, ferry, fertile, infer, illation, illative, inferible, offer, oblation, oblate, infor, Lucifer, prefer, profer, prolate, profert, refer, relate, relation, relative, suffer, transfer, translate, translation, translator, vociferous, ferret, furtive, fortune, fortuitous (**Eng**);

ouwel, prefereren, refereren, translatie, furtief, fortuin (**Dut**); Ablativ, Oblate, Relation, Translation (**Ger**); translasjon (**Nor**); oblat, translation (**Swe**); ablativ (**Dan**);

φουρτούνα (fourtoúna) (**Gk**); абляция (abljacija), облатка (oblátka), прелат (prelat), реляция (reljacija), трансляция (transljacija), фортуна (fortuna) (**Rus**); oplatka, opłatek, translacja (**Pol**); translace (**Cz**); oblátka, translácia (**Slo**); blatë, shufroj (**Alb**)

Hellenic: φέρω (phérō), μεταφέρω (metaphérō), προσφέρω (prosphérō), φορέω (phoréō), φώρ (phór), φορά (phorā), ἀνάφορα (anaphorā), δῐάφορα (diaphorā), ἐπῐφορα (epiphorā), προφορα (prophorā), προσφορα (prosphorā), φέρμα (phérma) (**AnGk**);

μεταφέρω (metaféro), μεταφορά (metaforá), φορώ (foró), φορά (forá), αναφορά (anaforá), διαφορά (diaforá), επιφορά (epiforá), προφορά (proforá), προφορικός (proforikós), προσφορά (prosforá) (**Gk**)

Derivatives: metaphor, pheromone, phosphor, phorophyte, anaphora (**Eng**); métaphore, anaphore (**Fr**)

Slavic: брать (brat'), берёжая (berjóžaja), береме́ни (bereméni), бре́мя (brémja) (**Rus**); brać, brzemię, brzemienia (**Pol**); brát, březí, břímě, břemene (**Cz**); brat', bremeno (**Slo**); бере (bere), бреме (breme) (**Mace**)

Baltic: berti, be͂rti, bernas (**Lith**); be͂rt, bērns (**Latv**)

Albanian: bie (**Alb**)

Indo-Iranian: भरति (bhárati), भारयति (bhāráyati), भर्मन् (bhárman), भरीमन् (bhárīman), भृति (bhŗtí) (**Sans**); بر (bar-), بردن (burdan) (**Pers**)

*per-

to carry forth, to fare

*por-ti, *pi-por-ti, *pér-ye-ti, *per-eh₂-yé-ti, *por-éye-ti, *pŗ-t-eh₂-yé-ti, *pér-tus, *por-teh₂, *por-tis, *pōr-is, *por-o-, *por-dʰmo-

Germanic: fare, ferry, fyrd, fure, fere, forfare (obs.), fjord, firth, ford (**Eng**); faran, fær, ferian, fyrd, fēre, forfaran, ford (**OE**); farre, fiere, furde (**Fris**); varen, veer, vaart, voeren, vervaren, voord, voorde (**Dut**); fahren, feren, Fähre, Fahrt, Fährte, Farm, führen, verfahren, Furt (**Ger**);

fara, far, ferja, ferð, farmr, fœra, fœrr, fjǫrðr (**Norse**); fare, fara, ferje, ferd, farm, føre, fjord (**Nor**); fara, färja, färd, föra, för, fjärd, fjord (**Swe**); fare, færge, fart, fært, færd, føre, før, fjord (**Dan**); fara, far, ferja, fart, ferð, farmur, færa, fær, fjörður (**Ice**)

Derivatives: fjord (**Fr**)

Celtic: rhyd (**Wel**)

Italic: portus, porta, portārius, portāre, porticus, apportāre, asportāre, asportātiō, comportāre, deportāre, exportāre, exportātiō, importāre, importūnus, importūnitās, portābilis, opportūnus, inopportūnus, opportūnitās, reportāre, supportāre, trānsportāre (**Lat**);

port, porte, portier, porche, portique, porter, apporter, comporter, déporter, exporter, exportation, importer, importunité, portable, opportun, opportunité, supporter, transporter (**Fr**);

port, porta, portiere, portico, portare, apportare, asportare, asportazione, comportare, deportare, esportare, esportazione, importare, importunità, portabile, opportuno, opportunità, sopportare, supportare, trasportare (**Ital**);

puerto, portada, puerta, portal, portero, pórtico, portar, aportar, asportar, comportar, deportar, exportar, exportación, importar, oportuno, oportunidad, reportar, soportar, transportar (**Sp**);

porto, port, porta, portão, porteiro, pórtico, portar, comportar, deportar, exportar, exportação, importar, importuno, importunidade, oportuno, oportunidade, reportar, suportar, transportar (**Port**);

purta, poartă, portar, purtare, suporta (**Rom**)

Derivatives: port, portal, porter, portico, asportation, comport, comportment, deport, disport, export, exportation, import, importunity, portable, portage, portfolio, inopportune, opportunity, purport, rapport, report, support, transport (**Eng**); poort, portaal, deporteren, exporteren, importeren (**Dut**); Pforte, Portikus, exportieren, importieren (**Ger**); port, importera (**Swe**); port (**Dan**); porth (**Wel**); port (**Iri**); πόρτα (pórta) (**Gk**); port (**Pol**); portë (**Alb**)

Hellenic: πείρω (peírō), περάω (peráō), πόρος (póros), ἄπορος (áporos), ἀπορῑ́ᾱ (aporíā), πορεύω (poreúō), εὐπορέω (euporéō), πορίζω (porízō), πορθμός (porthmós) (**AnGk**); πόρος (póros), απορία (aporía), μπορώ (boró) (**Gk**)

Derivatives: aporia (**Eng**); aporie (**Fr**)

Slavic: парить (parít') (**Rus**)

Indo-Iranian: पिपर्ति (píparti), पारयति (pāráyati), पार (pāra) (**Sans**); पार (pār) (**Hin**); پل (pol (**Pers**)

*telh₂-
to bear, undergo

*télh₂-t, *t̥l-né-h₂-ti, *te-tólh₂-e, *tolh₂-éye-, *telh₂-seh₂-(ye)-, *t̥lh₂-éh₁-(ye)-, *telh₂-mō, *t̥lh₂-tó-s

Germanic: thole (**Eng**); þolian (**OE**); dulden (**Dut**); dolen, dulden (**Ger**); þola (**Norse**);

tåle (**Nor**); tåla (**Swe**); tåle (**Dan**); þola (**Ice**)

Italic: tollere, extollere, tolerāre (**Lat**); tolérer (**Fr**); togliere, tollerare (**Ital**); toller, tullir, tolerar (**Sp**); tolher, tolerar (**Port**)

Derivatives: extol, tolerate (**Eng**)

Hellenic: ἔτλην (étlēn), τελαμών (telamṓn), τάλαντον (tálanton), ταλασίφρων (talasíphrōn), τλάντος (tlántos), τόλμα (tólma), τολμάω (tolmáō), Ἄτλας (Átlas), τλᾱτός (tlātós) (**AnGk**)

Indo-Iranian: तुलयति (tulayati), तुला (tulā) (**Sans**)

*weǵh-
to convey, to ride, to transport

*wéǵʰ-e-ti, *wéǵʰ-s-t, *woǵʰ-éye-t, *woǵʰ-lo-s, *weǵʰ-no-s, *woǵʰ-no-s, *weǵʰ-o-s, *wéǵʰ-tis, *weǵʰ-s-lom, *weǵʰ-i-tlom, *woǵʰ-o-s

Germanic: weigh, way, wain, wagon, wedge, wight, whit (**Eng**); wegan, weg, wæġn, wecgan, wiht (**OE**);

wei, wein (**Fris**); wegen, weg, wagen, wagon, wicht (**Dut**); wiegen (-wegen in derived verbs), bewegen, Bewegung, wägen, Weg, Wagen, Waggon, Wicht, Gewicht (**Ger**);

vega, vegr, vagn, véttr, vétr, vættr, vætr (**Norse**); veie, vei, veg, vogn, vette, vætte (**Nor**); väga, väg, vagn, vätte (**Swe**); veje, vej, vogn, vette, vætte (**Dan**); vega, vegur, vagn, vættur (**Ice**)

Derivatives: wagon (**Fr**); vagone (**Ital**), вагон (vagón) (**Rus**)

Celtic: gwain (**Wel**); féan (**Iri**)

Italic: vehere, vēxī (**Lat**); vit, véhicule (**Fr**); veicolo (**Ital**); vector, vehículo (**Sp**); veículo (**Port**); vehicul (**Rom**)

Derivatives: invective, inveigh, vector, vehement, vehicle (**Eng**); feithicil (**Iri**)

Hellenic: ἔχω (ékhō), ἔϝεξε (éwexe), ὀχέομαι (okhéomai) (**AnGk**)

Slavic: везти (veztí), воз (voz), возить (vozíť), весло (vesló) (**Rus**); wieźć, wóz, wozić, wiosło (**Pol**); vézt, vůz, vozit, veslo (**Cz**); viezť, voz, voziť, veslo (**Slo**); воз (voz), вози (vozi), весло (véslo) (**Mace**)

Derivatives: vâslă (**Rom**)

Baltic: vežti (**Lith**); vest (**Latv**)

Indo-Iranian: वहति (váhati), वह् (vah), वाहन (vāhana), ऊढि (ūḍhi), वहित्र (vahitra) (**Sans**); وزیدن (vazidan) / وز (vaz), بزیدن (bazidan) / بز (baz-) (**Pers**)

*H₂eǵ-
to lead, drive

*h₂éǵ-e-ti, *h₂éǵ-mn̥, *h₂éǵ-tōr, *h₂óǵ-mo-s, *h₂éǵ-ro-s, *h₂eḱs-, *h₂eǵ-dʰlo-, *h₂eǵ-ós, *h₂eǵ-treh₂, *h₂ǵ-es-, *h₂ǵ-tós

Germanic: axle (**Eng**); eax, eaxl (**OE**); as, ambacht (**Fris**); as, oksel, assel, ambacht, ambt, ambachten (**Dut**); Achse, Achsel, Armt, Amt (**Ger**); aka, ǫxl, ambátt, ambótt, embætta (**Norse**); aka (**Nor**); åka, axel, ämbete (**Swe**); age, aksel (**Dan**); aka, öxl, ambátt (**Ice**)

Celtic: amaeth (**Wel**); amhas, ambicatos (**Iri**)

Italic: agere, agmen, exāmen, exāminō, exāminātus, exāminātiō, actor, āctiō, āctrīx, āctīvus, āctus, ācta, āctitāre, āctīvitās, agitāre, agitātiō, agitātor, cōgitāre, cōgitābundus, cōgitātus, excōgitāre, peragitāre, subigitāre, axis, ālā, alar, axilla, assula, cōgere, coactus, cōactāre, cōgēns, coāgulum, coāgulō, gerere, aggerere, agger, aggestus, ēgerere, gerundium, gestiō, gestus, ingerere, suggerere, suggestiō, suggestus, ambactus, ambaxtus (**Lat**);

agir, examen, essaim, examiner, examination, acteur, action, actrice, actif, acte, activité, agiter, agitation, cogiter, cuider, cogitation, excogiter, ais, axe, aile, aisselle, attelle, atelier, cacher, cailler, coaguler, gérer, gestion, geste, ingérer, suggérer, ambacte, ambassade (**Fr**);

agire, esaminare, attore, azione, attrice, attivo, atto, attività, agitare, agitazione, cogitare, coitare, cogitabondo, cogitazione, escogitare, asse, ala, ascella, aschia, ascola, caglio, coagulo, cagliare, coagulare, quagliare, coatto, argine, gerundio, ingerire (**Ital**);

agir, examen, enjambre, examinar, examinación, actor, acción, actriz, activo, acto, acta, actitud, actividad, agitar, agitación, cogitar, cuidar, cogitación, cuidazón, cuidado, eje, ala, axila, astilla, taller, estallar, agacharse, cuajo, coágulo, coagular, cuajar, gerer, arce, arcén, gerundio, gestión, gesto, ingerir (**Sp**);

agir, exame, enxame, examinar, ator, ação, atriz, ativo, acto, ato, auto, acta, ata, atividade, agitar, agitação, agitador, cogitar, cuidar, cogitação, cuidação, cuidado, eixo, á, ala, alar, axila, acha, coatar, coágulo, coalho, gerir, gerúndio, gesto, sugerir, sugesto (**Port**);

examen, examina, actor, acțiune, act, activitate, agitare, cugeta, cugetare, ax, axă, așchie, cheag, coagul, coagula, închega, agest, gerunziu (**Rom**)

Derivatives: act, action, actor, active, activity, agent, agenda, agile, agitate, agitation, agitator, ambiguous, castigate, cogitate, cogitation, excogitate, mitigate, navigate, examine, examination, axis, aisle, ali- (as in aliethmoidal, alinasal, aliseptal, alisphenoid), alar, axilla, cogent, cogency, egest, gerund, gesture, suggest, suggestion, ambassador (**Eng**);

examen, actie, axilla, ambassade (**Dut**); agieren, Aktion, Gerundium (**Ger**); ambassade (**Nor**); agera, examen, akt (**Swe**); ambassade (**Dan**);

γερούνδιον (geroúndion) (**Gk**); актёр (aktjór), акция (ákcija), акт (akt), агитáтор (agitátor) (**Rus**); akcja (**Pol**); akce (**Cz**); kujtoj (**Alb**); بازیگر (bâzigar) (**Pers**)

Hellenic: ἄγω (ágō), ἀγωγή (agōgḗ), ἀγωγός (agōgós), δημᾰγωγός (dēmagōgós), παιδᾰγωγός (paidagōgós), ἀγών (agṓn), ἀγωνία (agōnía), ἀγωνιστής (agōnistḗs), πρωταγωνιστής (prōtagōnistḗs), ἀνᾰγω (anágō), ἐπᾰγω (epágō), ἐπαγωγή (epagogí), συνάγω (sunágō), σῠνᾰγωγή (sunagōgḗ), ἀρχισῠνᾰγωγος (arkhisunágōgos), ἄκτωρ (áktōr), ὄγμος (ógmos), ἄξων (áxōn), ἀγός (agós), ἐπακτός (epaktós) (**AnGk**);

 άγω (ágo), αγωγή (agogí), δημαγωγός (dimagogós), παιδαγωγός (paidagogós), αγών (agón), αγώνας (agónas), αγωνία (agonía), αγωνιστής (agonistís), πρωταγωνιστής (protagonistís), ανάγω (anágo), επαγωγή (epagogí), συναγωγή (synagogí) (**Gk**)

Derivatives: agoge, galactagogue, demagogue, pedagogue, pedagogy, agon, agony, agonistes, agonist, protagonist, antagonist, antagonize, epagoge, strategy, synagogue, archisynagogue, axon (**Eng**); synagoge (**Dut**); Agon, Agonie, Synagoge (**Ger**);

paedagōgus, agon, agōnia, epagōgē, synagoga, archisynagōgus, axon (**Lat**); pédagogue, agonie (**Fr**); agonia, esame, sciame (**Ital**); pedagogo (**Sp**); ágon, agonia (**Port**);

педагóг (pedagóg), агония (agonija), синагóга (sinagóga), экзамен (ekzamen) (**Rus**); axon (**Cz**); shemë (**Alb**)

Baltic: ašis (**Lith**)

Indo-Iranian: अजति (ájati), अज्मन् (ájman), अक्ष (akṣa), अज (ajá), अष्ट्रा (aṣṭrā) (**Sans**)

which may include h₂éǵros field:

*h₂éǵros
field

Germanic: acre (**Eng**); æcer (**OE**); eker, ikker (**Fris**); akker (**Dut**); Acker (**Ger**); akr (**Norse**); åker, aker (**Nor**); åker (**Swe**); ager (**Dan**); akur (**Ice**)

Italic: ager, āgrārius, agrestis, agricola, agricultor, agrīcultūra, agrīmensor, peragrāre, peregrē, peregrīnus, peregrīno, peregrīnātiō (**Lat**);

ager, aire, agraire, agricole, agriculteur, agriculture, pèlerin, pérégrin (**Fr**);

agro, agreste, agricolo, agricoltura, agrimensore, peragrare, pellegrino, peregrinare, peregrinazion (**Ital**);

agro, agrario, agrícola, agricultor, agricultura, agrimensor, peregrino, peregrinar (**Sp**);

agro, agreste, agrícola, agricultor, agricultura, agrimensor, peregrino, peregrinar (**Port**);

agru, agricultor, agricultură, agrimensor (**Rom**)

Derivatives: agrarian, agrestic, agriculture, agricultor, peregrine, pilgrim, peregrinate, peregrination (**Eng**); аграрный (agrarnyj) (**Rus**); agrární (**Cz**)

Hellenic: ἀγρός (agrós), ἄγριος (ágrios) (**AnGk**); αγρός (agrós), άγριος (ágrios) (**Gk**)

Derivatives: agronomy (**Eng**)

Indo-Iranian: अज्र (ájra), अज्र्य (ajryá) (**Sans**)

*wed^h-

to lead; to bind, secure; to pledge, guarantee

Germanic: wed, wage, gage (**Eng**); wedd, weddian, wituma (**OE**); wet, wedzje (**Fris**); wedde, wedden, weem (**Dut**); Wette, wetten, Wittum (**Ger**); veð, veðja (**Norse**); vedd (**Nor**); vad, vädja (**Swe**); vædde (**Dan**); veðja (**Ice**)

Derivatives: gage, gager (**Fr**)

Celtic: arwain, gwedd (**Wel**)

Italic: vas, praes, praedium, praediālis, praediātōrius (**Lat**); prédial (**Fr**); predio, prediale (**Ital**); predio, predial (**Sp**); prédio (**Port**)

Derivatives: praedial, predial, prediatory (**Eng**); prädial (**Ger**)

Hellenic: ἔεδνα (éedna) (**AnGk**)

Slavic: вести (vestí), водить (vodít'), вѣно (véno) (**Rus**); wieść, wodzić, wiano (**Pol**); vést, vodit, věno (**Cz**); viest, vodiť, veno (**Slo**); води (vódi) (**Mace**)

Baltic: vèsti, vādas, vadúoti (**Lith**); vest (**Latv**)

*dewk-

to pull, draw, lead

*déwk-ti, *dowk-éye-ti, *duk-s, *duk-is

Germanic: tie, tog, tug, team (**Eng**); tīeġan, toga, tēag, togian, team (**OE**); toch, team (**Fris**); teug, hertog, teugel, team, toom (**Dut**); Zug, Zog, Zügel, Team, Zaum (**Ger**); teygja, togi, tygill, taug, tog, taumr (**Norse**); tøye, tog, tug, tau, taum (**Nor**); töja, tåg, tig, tygel, team, töm (**Swe**); tøje, tog, tug, tov, tømme (**Dan**); teygja, togi, taug, toga, taumur (**Ice**)

Derivatives: cug (**Pol**)

Celtic: dwyn (**Wel**)

Italic: dūcere, abdūcere, abductiō, abductor, addūcere, adductor, aquaeductus, circumdūcere, condūcere, conductiō, conductor, conductus, dēdūcere, dēductiō, ductiō, ductus, dux, ducātus, ēdūcere, ēducātiō, indūcere, inductiō, inductus, intrōdūcere, intrōductiō, perdūcere, prōdūcere, prōductiō, prōductīvus, prōductus, redūcere, reductiō, reductus, sēdūcere, subdūcere, subductiō, trādūcere (**Lat**);

-duire, abduction, aqueduc, conduire, conduction, conducteur, conduit, déduire, déduction, douche, -duit, duc, duché, éduquer, éducation, enduire, induire, induction, enduit, induit, introduire, introduction, produire, production, productif, produit, réduire, réduction, réduit, redoute, réductible, séduire, traduire (**Fr**);

ducere, -durre, abdurre, abduzione, addurre, acquedotto, circondurre, conducibile, condurre, conduzione, condotto, dedurre, deduzione, doccione, doccia, -dotto, dotto, duce, duca, doge, dogado, dogato, ducato, educere, edurre, educare, educazione, indurre, induzione, indotto, introdurre, perdurre, produrre, produzione, produttivo, prodotto, ridurre, riduzione, ridotto, sedurre, tradurre (**Ital**);

abducir, abducción, aducir, aguaducho, acueducto, conducir, conducción, conductor, conducho, conducto, deducir, ducha, -ducido, ducto, duque, dux, ducado, educir, educar, educación, inducir, inducción, introducir, introducción, producir, producción, productivo, producto, reducir, reducción, reducto, seducir, traducir (**Sp**);

-duzir, abduzir, abdução, aduzir, aqueduto, conduzir, condução, condutor, conduto, deduzir, dedução, ducto, duto, duque, ducado, eduzir, educar, educação, induzir, indução, introduzir, introdução, produzir, produção, produtivo, produto, reduzir, redução, reduto, seduzir, traduzir (**Port**);

duce, ducere, abduce, aduce, aducere, apeduct, conduce, conducție, conductă, deduce, deducție, duș, duct, ducat, educa, educație, induce, inducție, introduce, introducție, produce, producție, productiv, reduce, arăduce, reducție, seduce, traduce (**Rom**)

Derivatives: abduce, abduct, abduction, abductor, adduce, adduct, adductor, aqueduct, conduce, conduct, conduction, conductor, conduit, deduce, deduct, deduction, ductin, duct, dux, duke, duchy, educate, education, induce, induct, induction, introduce, introduction, produce, production, productive, product, reduce, reduction, redoubt, seduce, subdue, subduct, traduce (**Eng**); -duzieren, produktiv (**Ger**); dug (**Wel**); diúc (**Iri**);

δούξ (doúx) (**AnGk**); δούκας (doúkas) (**Gk**); абдукция (abdukcija), акведук (akvedúk), кондуктор (kondúktor), дедукция (dedúkcija), индукция (indukcija), интродукция (introdukcija), продуктивный (produktívnyj), редукция (redukcija), субдукция (subdukcija) (**Rus**); akwedukt (**Pol**)

*yewg-

to yoke, harness, join

*yéwg-t, *yu-né-g-ti, *yewg-new-ti, *yowg-yo-, *yéwg-mn̥, *yéwg-o-s, *yéwg-os, *yug-ó-m, *yug-tó-s, *n̥-yug-s

Germanic: eykr (**Norse**)

Celtic: cuing (**Iri**)

Italic: iungere, abiungere, adiungere, adiunctiō, adiunctus, coniungere, disiungere, iniungere, iunctiō, sēiungere, subiungere, iūgera, iūxtā (**Lat**);

joindre, jointer, adjoindre, conjoindre, enjoindre, jouter, ajouter (**Fr**);

giungere, giuntare, aggiungere, aggiunto, congiungere, ingiungere, giunzione, raggiungere (**Ital**);

juntar, uncir, juncer, junger, justar, ayustar, conjunto (**Sp**);

junguir, jungir, juntar, adjungir, adjunção, conjungir, junção, justar, conjunto (**Port**);

ajunge, ajungere, joncţiune (**Rom**)

Derivatives: join, adjoin, adjunction, conjoin, disjoin, enjoin, junction, sejoin, subjoin, joust, juxtapose (**Eng**)

Hellenic: ζεύγνυμι (zeúgnumi), ζεῦγμα (zeûgma), ἄζυξ (ázux) (**AnGk**)

Derivatives: diazeugman, hyperzeuxis, hypozeugma, hypozeuxis, mesozeugma, prozeugma, synezeugmenon, zeugitae, zeugma (**Eng**)

Baltic: jùngti (**Lith**); jûgt (**Latv**)

Indo-Iranian: योजम् (yójam), अयुजत् (ayujat), युनक्ति (yunákti), योग्य (yógya), योगस् (yogas), युक्त (yuktá), अयुग (ayuga) (**Sans**); योग्य (yogya), युक्त (yukt) (**Hin**); جفت (ǰuft) (**Pers**)

which includes *yugóm yoke:

*yugóm
yoke

Germanic: yoke (**Eng**); ioc, geoc (**OE**); jok, jûk (**Fris**); juk (**Dut**); Joch (**Ger**); ok (**Norse**); åk (**Nor**); ok (**Swe**); åg (**Dan**); ok (**Ice**)

Celtic: iau (**Wel**)

Italic: iūgum, quadrīgae (**Lat**); joug, quadrige (**Fr**); giogo, quadriga, quadrigato (**Ital**); yugo, ubio, cuadriga (**Sp**); jugo, quadriga (**Port**); jug (**Rom**)

Derivatives: jugular, conjugal, subjugate, quadriga, quadrigal (**Eng**)

Hellenic: ζυγόν (zugón) (**AnGk**); ζυγός (zugós) (**Gk**)

Derivatives: zygon, zygote, azygous, dizygotic, heterozygote, heterozygous, monozygotic, zygoma, zygomorphic, zygomorphism, zygomycosis (**Eng**)

Slavic: иго (ígo) (**Rus**); jho (**Cz**); иго (igo) (**Mace**)

Baltic: jùngas (**Lith**); jūgs (**Latv**)

Indo-Iranian: युग (yugá) (**Sans**); युग (yug), जूआ (jūā) (**Hin**); جغ (jugh) (**Pash**); جغ (joǧ), يوغ (yuǧ) (**Pers**)

*stel-
to put, to place; to locate

*stél-ye-ti, *stel-ni-, *stol-no-s, ?*stl̥-ḱo-s, *stól-o-s, *stol-éh$_2$

Germanic: still, stall, stell (**Eng**); stille, stillan, steall, stellan (**OE**); stil, stâl, stelle (**Fris**); stil, stal, stellen (**Dut**); still, stillen, Stall, stellen, Stelle (**Ger**); stilla, stallr (**Norse**); stille, stall (**Nor**); stilla, stall, ställa (**Swe**); stille, stald (**Dan**); stilla, stallur (**Ice**)

Italic: locus, locālis, locārium, locāre, allocāre, collocāre, locātiō, loculus (**Lat**); lieu, local, loyer, louer, coucher, location (**Fr**); luogo, locale, locare, allocare, collocare, coricare, colcare, locazione (**Ital**); luego, lugar, locus, lugar, local, logar, alocar, colgar, colocar, locación (**Sp**); logo, loco, locus, lócus, lugar, local, alocar, colgar, colocar, locação, lóculo (**Port**); loc, local, culca, culcare, locație (**Rom**)

Derivatives: lieu, locus, local, locale, locality, locate, allocate, collocate, collocation, couch, accouchement, couchant, location, locative, dislocate, dislocation, locomotion, locular, loculus, milieu, relocate, relocation, translocate, translocative, unilocular (**Eng**); log (**Iri**); локация (lokacija) (**Rus**)

Hellenic: στέλλω (stéllō), στόλος (stólos), στολή (stolḗ) (**AnGk**); στέλνω (stélno), στόλος (stólos), στολή (stolí) (**Gk**)

Slavic: стлать (stlat') (**Rus**); słać (**Pol**); stláti (**Cz**); stlať (**Slo**)

Baltic: stáldas (**Lith**); stãllis (**Latv**)

*dheH₁-
to do, place, put

*dʰéh₁-t, *dʰé-dʰeh₁-ti,*dʰh₁-k-yé-ti, *dʰéh₁-ḱeh₂, *dʰh₁-m-eló-, *dʰéh₁-mn̥, *dʰóh₁-mo-s, *dʰéh₁-s, *dʰh₁-s-, *dʰéh₁-t-s, *dʰéh₁-l- *dʰéh₁-tis, *dʰóh₁-t-s, *dʰh₁-tó-s, *h₂ewis-dʰh₁-, *swe-dʰh₁-, *swe-dʰh₁-sḱ-

Germanic: do, doom, deem, fordeem, deed, misdeed, ord, orde, urdé, urdy, odd (**Eng**); dōn, dōm, dēman, fordēman, dǣd, dēd, misdǣd, ord (**OE**);

dwaan, doem, died, misdied, oerd, oarde (**Fris**); doen, doem, doemen, verdoemen, daad, misdaad, oord (**Dut**); tun, Tat, Missetat, Wohltat, Ort (**Ger**);

dómr, doema, fyrirdoema, dáð, oddr, oddi (**Norse**); dom, dømme, dåd (**Nor**); dom, döma, fördöma, dåd, misdåd, udd (**Swe**); dom, dømme, fordømme, dåd, misdåd, od (**Dan**); dómur, dæma, dáð, oddur (**Ice**)

Italic: -dere, abdere, condere, crēdere (cor+), didere, conditiō, condición, reconditus, crēdibilis, crēditor, crēdulitās, crēdulus, incrēdulus, incrēdibilis, facere, affacere, affectus, ārefacere, benefacere, benefactus, benefactor, clārificāre, cōnficere, cōnfectiō, cōnfectus, dēficere, efficere, efficiēns, effectīvus, effectus, facinus, factor, factum, factiō, fortificāre, fortificātiō, grātificārī, īnficere, iustificāre, malefaciō, olfacere, perficere, perfectus, prōficere, reficere, refectiō, sufficere, sufficientia, sacrificāre, sacrificātor, sacrificium, sānctificāre, satisfacere, scientificus, significere, simplificor, stupefacere, vērificāre, conditus, abditus, famulus, familia, familiāris, familiāritās, fētialis, fētiales, sacerdōs, sacerdōtālis, sacerdōtium, faciendus, difficilis, difficultās (**Lat**);

abscondre, condition, croire, créditeur, crédit, crédule, incrédule, incroyable, faire, bienfaire, bienfait, bienfaiteur, clarifier, confire, confection, confit, effectuer, effectif, effet, facteur, fait, façon, faction, fortifier, gratifier, infecter, malfaire, parfaire, parfait, réfection, suffire, sacrifier, sacrificateur, sacrifice, sanctifier, satisfaire, scientifique, signifier, vérifier, famille, familier, sacerdotal, sacerdoce, difficile (**Fr**);

ascondere, nascondere, condizione, credere, credibile, creditore, credito, credulo, incredulo, incredible, fare, benefare, benefatto, benefattore, confezione, confetto, effetto, fattore, fatto, fazione, fortificare, fortificazione, malfare, perfetto, rifare, sacrificare, sacrificatore, sacrifico, sacrificio, santificare, soddisfare, satisfare, significare, verificare, famulo, famiglia, familiare, sacerdote, sacerdotale, sacerdozio, faccenda, azienda, difficile (**Ital**);

condir, esconder, condición, creer, creible, acreedor, crédito, crédulo, incrédulo, increible, hacer, benefacer, bienhechor, fámulo, clarificar, confección, cohecho, efectuar, efectivo, efecto, factor, hechor, fecho, fecha, hecho, facto, facción, fortificar, infectar, perfecto, aprovecer, sacrificar, sacrificador, sacrificio, santificar, santiguar, satisfacer, científico, significar, simplificar, averiguar, verificar, familia, familiar, sacerdote, sacerdotal, sacerdocio, fachenda, faena, hacienda, facienda, difícil, dificultad (**Sp**);

esconder, absconder, recôndito, crer, crível, credível, credor, crédito, crédulo, incrédulo, incrível, fazer, afeto, arfar, fâmulo, clarificar, confecção, confeiçã, confeito, efetivo, efeito, facínora, factor, feitor, feito, facto, fato, facção, feição, perfazer, perfeito, refazer, refeição, sacrificar, sacrificador, sacrificio, sanctificar, santiguar, satisfazer, científico, significar, simplificar, averiguar, verificar, familia, familiar, sacerdote, sacerdotal, sacerdócio, faina, facienda, fazenda, difícil (**Port**);

ascunde, ascundere, condiție, crede, credere, credibil, face, facere, confecție, efect, factor, fapt, perfect, sanctifica, satisface, simplifica, verifica, familie, femeie, sacerdot, sacerdoțiu (**Rom**)

Derivatives: abscond, condition, recondite, recond, creed, credit, credo, credible, creditor, credulity, credulous, incredible, affair, affect, affection, affectation, amplify, artifact, artifice, benefactor, benefice, benefit, clarify, confection, confit, counterfeit, defeat, defect, disaffected, edifice, effect, effective, effectual, effectuate, efficacious, efficient, enfactement, facade, face, facet, facial, facile, facilitate, facility, facsimile, fact, factum, faction, factious, factitious, factor, factorial, factory, factotum, factual, fake, fashion, feasible, feat, feature, feckless, fiat, forfeit, fortify, fortification, gratify, infect, laissez-faire, malefaction, manufacture, modify, office, official, officiant, officiate, officious, olfaction, omnificent, parfait, perfect, pluperfect, prefect, prefecture, proficiency, profit, profitable, profiteer, profiterole, prolific, qualificatioun, rarefy, refectory, sacrifice, sacrificator, sanctify, satisfaction, scientific, signify, stupefy, suffice, sufficient, superficial, surface, surfeit, transfection, trifecta, unification, verify, famulus, family, familiar, familiarity, sacerdotal, hacienda, difficult, difficulty (**Eng**);

effectief, effect, feit (**Dut**); Konditor, Faktum, perfekt, Familie (**Ger**); effekt, perfekt (**Nor**); faktum (**Swe**); sagart (**Iri**);

кредитóр (kreditór), кредúт (kredít), эффект (effekt), фáктор (fáktor), факт (fakt), фортификация (fortifikacija), фамилия (famílija) (**Rus**); familje (**Alb**)

Hellenic: τίθημι (títhēmi), ἐπιτίθημι (epitíthēmi), ἐπίθετον (epítheton), ἐπεντίθημι (epentíthēmi), ἐπένθεσις (epénthesis, insertion), ἐπενθετῐκός (epenthetikós), ἔθεμεν (éthemen), ἔθηκᾰ (éthēka), θήκη (thḗkē), ἀποθήκη (apothḗkē), βῐβλῐοθήκη (bibliothḗkē), σῠνθήκη (sunthḗkē), ὑποθήκη (hupothḗkē), θεμείλια (themeília), θῆμᾰ (thêma), θημών (thēmṓn), εὐθήμων (euthḗmōn), θωμός (thōmós), θέσις (thésis), ἀντίθεσις (antíthesis), παρένθεσις (parénthesis), σῠνθεσῐς (súnthesis), ὑπόθεσις (hupóthesis), θής (thḗs), θετός (thetós), ἀντῐθετον (antítheton), θέμα (théma), θέμις (thémis), Θησεύς (Thēseús) (**AnGk**);

θήκη (thíki), αποθήκη (apothíki), βιβλιοθήκη (vivliothíki), συνθήκη (synthíki), αντίθεση (antíthesi), παρένθεση (parénthesi), υπόθεση (ypóthesi), θετός (thetós), θέμα (théma) (**Gk**)

Derivatives: epethit, epenthetic, theca, boutique, apothecary, anathema, bibliotheca, bodega, enthetic, hypothec, hypothesis, thesaurus, thesis, antithesis, parenthesis, prosthesis, synthesis, synthetic, antithet, thematic, theme, Themis, treasure (**Eng**);

apotheek, boetiek, bibliotheek, hypotheek (**Dut**); epenthetisch, Apotheke, Bibliothek, Hypothek, Thema (**Ger**); bibliotek (**Swe**); bibliotek (**Dan**);

epitheton, epithetum, thēca, apothēca, apothēcārius, bibliothēca, hypothēca, thesis, antithesis, parenthesis, hypothesis, antitheton, antithetum, thema (**Lat**); épenthétique, boutique, bibliothèque, hypothèque, antithèse, parenthèse, synthèse, thème (**Fr**); epentetico, bottega, biblioteca, ipoteca, antiteto, tema (**Ital**); apoteca, bodega, botica, biblioteca, hipoteca, tema (**Sp**); adega, bodega, botica, biblioteca, hipoteca, teima, tema (**Port**); bibliotecă, temă (**Rom**);

библиотéка (bibliotéka), синтез (síntez), гипотеза (gipóteza), тéма (téma) (**Rus**); biblioteka (**Pol**)

Slavic: деть (det'), дéлать (délat'), дéло (délo) (**Rus**); dziać, działać, dzieło, działo (**Pol**); dít, dělat, dílo, dělo (**Cz**); diať sa, dielo (**Slo**); дело (delo) (**Mace**)

Baltic: dėti (**Lith**)

Indo-Iranian: दधाति (dádhāti), अधात् (ádhāt), धामन् (dhāman), धित (dhitá), धीति (dhiti) (**Sans**)

which is also involved in $h_2$ewis-d^{h}h$_1$- (see $h_2$ew-) and *swe-d^{h}h$_1$-:

*swe-d^{h}h$_1$- (*swé (self) + *d^{h}eh$_1$-)

set as one's own

*swe-d^{h}h$_1$-sḱ-

Italic: solēre, solitus, insolitus, suescere (rare), cōnsuēscere, cōnsuētūdō, mānsuēscere, mānsuētus, mānsuētūdō (**Lat**); insolite, coutume, mâtin, mansuétude (**Fr**); solere, solito, insolito, consuetudine, costume, mansuetudine (**Ital**); soler, sólito, insólito, consuetud, costumbre, mansedumbre (**Sp**); soer, sólito, insólito, costume, manso, mansidão, mansuetude (**Port**); costum (**Rom**)

Derivatives: insolence, absolescent, consuetude, costume, custom, mansuetude, obsolete (**Eng**)

Hellenic: ἔθω (éthō), ἔθος (éthos), ἐθικός (ethikós), ἦθος (êthos), ἠθικός (ēthikós), ἠθολόγος (ēthológos), ἠθολογῐ́ᾱ (ēthologíā), ἔθνος (éthnos), ἐθνᾰ́ρχης (ethnárkhēs), ἐθνικός (ethnikós) (**AnGk**); ηθικός (ithikós), έθνος (éthnos), εθνικός (ethnikós) (**Gk**)

Derivatives: ethic, ethics, ethology, ethos, ethnarch, ethnic (**Eng**); ēthologia, ethnicus (**Lat**); éthologie, ethnie (**Fr**); etologia (**Ital**); etologia (**Sp**); etnia (**Port**); этнос (étnos) (**Rus**); स्वधा (svadhā) (**Sans**)

*keh₂p-
to seize, grab

*kh₂pyéti, *kh₂p-(e)h₁-yé-, *kh₂ptós, *kh₂p-nós, *kóh₂p-eh₂

Germanic: have, heavy, heave, haven, haaf (dial.) (**Eng**); habban, hefig, hebban, hæfen (**OE**);

hawwe, haven (**Fris**); hebben, hevig, -haftig, -achtig, haven (**Dut**); haben, hebig, Hafen, Haff (**Ger**);

hafa, hǫfigr, hǫfugr, haptr, hǫfn, haf (**Norse**); have, ha, hava, havn, hav (**Nor**); hava, ha, hamn, hav (**Swe**); have, havn, hav (**Dan**); hafa, höfugur, höfn (**Ice**)

Derivatives: havre (**Fr**)

Celtic: caeth (**Wel**); cacht, cuan (**Iri**)

Italic: capere, captus, captīvus, captūra, capsa, capsula, accipere, antecipere, auceps, capābilis, capāx, capācitās, capistrum, capessere, captāre, concipere, conceptiō, dēcipere, dēceptiō, excipere, incipere, inceptiō, inceptīvus, intercipere, nūncupō, occipere, occupāre, praeoccupāre, praeoccupātio, particeps, percipere, perceptībilis, perceptiō, perceptor, perceptus, praecipere, praeceptor, prīnceps, prīncipium, recipere, receptāculum, receptiō, reciperāre, suscipere, usucapere (**Lat**);

captif, chétif, capture, caisse, châsse, châssis, capsule, accepter, capable, capace, capacité, chevêtre, capter, acheter, concevoir, concept, conception, décevoir, inception, inceptif, occuper, préoccuper, préoccupation, occupation, percevoir, perception, précepteur, prince, princesse, principe, recevoir, réceptacle, réception (**Fr**);

capire, capere, cattivo, cattura, cassa, capsula, accettare, capace, capacità, capestro, captare, concepire, concezione, eccepire, incezzione, occupare, preoccupare, preoccupazione, occupazione, percepire, percettibile, percezione, percettore, percetto, principe, principio, ricevere, ricettacolo, ricezione (**Ital**);

caber, cativo, captivo, cautivo, captura, caja, quijada, cápsula, aceptar, capaz, capazo, capacho, capacidad, cabestro, captar, catar, acatar, concebir, concepción, decebir, decepcionar, exceptuar, incepción, ocupar, preocupar, preocupación, ocupación, percibir, percepción, principe, principio, recibir, receptáculo, recepción, receptar (**Sp**);

caber, cativo, captura, caixa, cápsula, aceitar, capaz, capacidade, cabresto, capistro, captar, catar, acatar, conceber, conceição, concepção, conceção, decepcionar, ocupar, preocupar, preocupação, ocupação, perceber, perceção, principe, principio, receber, receita, receptáculo, recepção (**Port**);

încăpea, încăpere, captiv, captură, capsă, capacitate, căpăstru, căuta, căutare, capsulă, concepe, concepție, începe, începere, apuca, apucare, ocupa, preocupa, preocupație, ocupație, pricepe, pricepere, percepe, prinț, principiu, recepe (**Rom**)

Derivatives: captive, caitiff, capture, caption, captivate, case, cash, chase, chassis, capsicum, capsule, forceps, accept, anticipate, capable, capacious, capacity, conceive, concept, conception, deceive, deception, except, inception, inceptive, incipient, intercept, nuncupate, occupy, occupate, preoccupy, preoccupate, preoccupation, occupation, participate, perceive, perceptible, perception, preceptor, prince, princess, principle, receive, recipe, receipt, recipient, receptacle, reception, susceptible, susception (**Eng**);

concipiëren, prins, prinses (**Dut**); kapieren, Kasse, Rezeption (**Ger**); kapere, kasse, prins (**Dan**); acceptera, kapsel, kapsyl (**Swe**); kassi, prins (**Ice**); cás, prionsa (**Iri**);

πρῖγκιψ (prînkips) (**AnGk**); καπίστρι (kapístri), πρίγκιπας (prígkipas) (**Gk**);

концéпция (koncércija), оккупáция (okkupácija), принц (princ), кáпсула (kápsula) (**Rus**); kasa (**Pol**); kapsa, kasa, kapacita (**Cz**);

princis (**Latv**); shqipoj, shqip, ntsep, ntseapiri, princ (**Alb**)

Hellenic: κάπτω (káptō), κώπη (kṓpē) (**AnGk**)

Slavic: чáпать (čápat'), хáпать (xápat'), хáпаю (xápaju) (**Rus**); czapić, czapać, chapać (**Pol**); čapati, čapiti, chápat (**Cz**); čapiť, chápať (**Slo**); апе (ape) (**Mace**)

Baltic: kapas, kapt (**Lith**); kàmpju, kàmpt (**Latv**)

Albanian: kap (**Alb**)

*gʰeh₁bʰ-

to seize, take

*gʰéh₁bʰ-, *gʰh̥₁bʰ-éh₁ye-, *gʰh̥₁bʰ-yé-

Celtic: gafael (**Wel**); gabh (**Iri**)

Italic: habēre, adhibēre, cohibēre, debēre, dēbitor, dēbitum, dubius, dubietās, dubiōsus, dubium, exhibēre, exhibitiō, exhibitor, habilis, dēbilis, dēbilitās, dēbilitāre, habilitās, habitāre, habitābilis, habitātiō, habitūdō, habitus, inhibēre, inhibitiō, inhibitor, prohibēre, prohibitiō, prohibitor (**Lat**);

avoir, devoir, débiteur, dette, exhiber, habile, débile, débiliter, habilité, habileté, habiter, habitante, habitation, habitude, habit, inhiber, prohiber, prohibition (**Fr**);

avere, dovere, debitore, debito, dubbio, dubbietà, dubbioso, esibire, abile, debole, debile, abilità, abitare, abitazione, abito, inibire, proibire (**Ital**);

haber, cohibir, deber, deudor, deuda, debdo, duda, exhibir, hábil, débil, debilidad, debilitar, habilidad, habitar, habitante, habitación, hábito, inhibir, prohibir, prohibición (**Sp**);

haver, dever, devedor, débito, dívida, dúbio, exibir, hábil, débil, habilidade, habitar, habitante, habitação, hábito, inibir, proibir (**Port**);

avea, avere, dator, daivet, dubios, dubiu, abil, debil, abilitate, prohibi (**Rom**)

Derivatives: aver, adhibit, endeavor, debit, debt, debenture, dubious, exhibit, exhibition, exhibitor, able, habile, Homo habilis, debile, debilitate, debility, ability, habitat, habitable, habitation, habitude, habit, inhibit, inhibition, inhibitor, prohibit, prohibition, prohibitor (**Eng**); debitor (**Nor**); aibid (**Iri**);

дебитóр (debitór), дéбет (débet), дебил (debil), габитус (gabitus) (**Rus**); inhibitor (**Cz**)

Baltic: gauti, gãvo (**Lith**)

Indo-Iranian: गभस्ति (gábhasti) (**Sans**)

*deḱ-

to take; to perceive

*déḱ-t, *déḱ-ti, *dḱ-néw-ti, *de-dóḱ-e, *dḱ-eh$_1$-(yé)-ti, *di-dḱ-sé-ti, *di-dḱ-sḱé-ti, *doḱ-éye-ti, *dḱ-tó-s, *dḱ-nó-s, *doḱ-o-, *doḱ-éh$_2$, *dóḱ-s(e)h$_2$, *dóḱ-mn̥, *déḱ-os, *déḱ-s-

Italic: decet, decus, decorāre, decor, decōrus, discere, docēre, docilis, doctor, doctōrāre, doctrīna, doctus, documentum, dīgnus, dīgnitās, dīgnō/dīgnor, indīgnus (**Lat**);

décorer, décorum, docile, docteur, doctrine, docte, document, digne, dignité, daigner, indigne (**Fr**);

decorare, decoro, docile, dottore, dottrina, dotto, documento, degno, dignità, degnità (**Ital**);

decorar, dócil, doctor, doctorar, doctrina, docto, ducho, documento, digno, digna, dino, dignidad, dignarse, indigno, indigna (**Sp**);

decorar, decoro, dócil, doutor, doutrina, docto, douto, documento, digno, dino, dignidade, dinidade, dignar (**Port**); doctor, demn, demnitate (**Rom**)

Derivatives: decorate, decoration, decorative, decorator, redecorate, decor, decorum, decorous, docile, doctor, doctrine, indoctrinate, indoctrination, document, dignity, dainty, deign (**Eng**);

doctrine (**Dut**); Doktor, Doktrin (**Ger**); doktor (**Nor**); doktor (**Swe**); doktor (**Dan**); doktor (**Ice**); dysgu (**Wel**); dínit (**Iri**);

декóр (dekór), дóктор (dóktor), доктрина (doktrina), документ (dokument) (**Rus**); doktor (**Pol**); doktor (**Cz**); doktor, denjë (**Alb**)

Hellenic: ἔδεκτο (édekto), δέχομαι (dékhomai), δέκτης (déktēs), πανδοκεῖον (pandokeîon), δέδεξο (dédexo), δεκτός (dektós), δοκός (dokós), δοχή (dokhḗ), δοκέω (dokéō), δόξᾰ (dóxa), πᾰρᾰδοξος (parádoxos), δόγμα (dógma), δογματικός (dogmatikós) (**AnGk**); δέκτης (déktis) (**Gk**)

Derivatives: paradox, dogma, dogmatic, dogmatism, dogmatist, doxology, heterodox, orthodox (**Eng**); dogma (**Dut**); dogme (**Nor**); dogm (**Swe**); dogme (**Dan**); dogma, dogmaticus, dogmatistes (**Lat**); fondic, dogme, dogmatiste (**Fr**); fondaco, dogma (**Ital**); fundago, dogma (**Sp**); alfândega, dogma (**Port**); догма (dógma) (**Rus**); dogma (**Cz**)

Indo-Iranian: दाष्टि (dáṣṭi), दाश्ति (dā́śti), दाश्नोति (dāśnóti), ददाश (dadā́śa), दीक्षते (dīkṣate), दाश् (dā́ś), दशस्यति (daśasyáti) (**Sans**)

which perhaps includes:

*deḱs-
right (side)

*deḱs-i-no-s, *deḱs-tero-s, *deḱs-i-tero-s, *deḱs-wo-s, *deḱs-i-wo-s

Germanic: Texel (**Eng**); Texel (**Dut**); zese (**Ger**)

Celtic: deau (**Wel**); deas (**Iri**)

Italic: dexter, dexteritās, ambidexter (**Lat**); dextre, dextérité (**Fr**); destro, desterità (**Ital**); diestro (**Sp**); destro (**Port**); dextru, zestre, dexteritate (**Rom**)

Derivatives: dexter, dexterity, dexetrous/dextrous, ambidexter, ambidextrous, ambidexterity, dextral, dextrin, dextrose (**Eng**)

Hellenic: δεξιτερός (dexiterós), δεξιός (dexiós) (**AnGk**); δεξιός (dexiós) (**Gk**)

Derivatives: Dexiarchia (**Eng**)

Slavic: абдешéнь (abdešén′) (**Rus**)

Baltic: dēšinas (**Lith**)

Albanian: djathtë (**Alb**)

Indo-Iranian: दक्षिण (dákṣiṇa) (**Sans**); दक्षिण (dakṣiṇ) (**Hin**)

*weyh₁-
to chase; to suppress, persecute

*wéyh₁-ti, *woyh₁-éh₂-ti, *weyh₁-neh₂, *weyh₁-u-kos, *wéyh₁-ow-, *wéyh₁-s, *wih₁-eh₂, *wih₁-elo-s, *wih₁-tós, *wóyh₁-teh₂

Germanic: wathe, regain (**Eng**); wāþ, wǣþan (**OE**); wou (**Fris**); wouw, weide, weiden (**Dut**); Weihe, Weih, Weide, weiden (**Ger**); langvé, veiði, veiða (**Norse**); langve, lomve, lomvie (**Nor**); lomvia (**Swe**); lomvie (**Dan**); langvia, langvigi, veiði, veiða (**Ice**)

Derivatives: gagner, regagner (**Fr**); guadagnare (**Ital**); guadaña (**Sp**); gadanha (**Port**)

Italic: vīs, vindex, vindicālis, vindicāre, vindicta, violāre, invītus, invītāre, via, bivium, dēvius, obviāre, obvius, pervius, impervius, praevius, quadrivium, trivium, viāticus, viāticum, viāre, viator (**Lat**);

venger, revendiquer, vindicte, violer, convier, inviter, voie, via, obvier, obvie, viatique, voyage (**Fr**);

vindice, vindicare, vendetta, violare, convitare, invitare, via, bivio, ovviare, ovvio, previo, viaggio, viaggiare, viatico (**Ital**);

vengar, vindicar, vindicta, convidar, envidar, invitar, via, obviar, obvio, previo, viaje, viático (**Sp**);

vingar, vindicar, vindicta, vindita, violar, convidar, envidar, invitar, via, obviar, óbvio, prévio, viagem (**Port**);

vindeca, vindecare, invita, învita, via, uib, voiaj (**Rom**)

Derivatives: vindical, vindicate, avenge, vindictive, violate, violence, invite, via, devious, obviate, obvious, impervious, previous, quadrivium, viatic, viaticum, voyage, aviator (**Eng**); inviteren, via, vooi (**Dut**); via (**Swe**); vijë (**Alb**)

Hellenic: ἵεμαι (híemai), ἵς (ís), ἱέρᾱξ (hiérāx) (**AnGk**)

Baltic: výti, vajóti (**Lith**); vît (**Latv**)

Indo-Iranian: वेति (véti) (**Sans**)

*gʰebʰ-
to give

Germanic: give, forgive, morning-gift, gift (**Eng**); ġiefan, forġiefan, morgenġiefu, ġift (**OE**);

jaan, ferjaan, jefte (**Fris**); geven, vergeven, morgengave, gift, gif, gave (**Dut**); geben, abgeben, vergeben, Morgengabe, Gift, Gabe, ergeben (**Ger**);

gefa, fyrirgefa, gjǫf, gipt, gæfr, gáfa (**Norse**); gi, gje, gjeva, gift, gave (**Nor**); giva, ge, gäv, gift, gåva (**Swe**); give, gæv, gift, gave (**Dan**); gefa, fyrirgefa, gjöf, gift, gæfur, gáfa (**Ice**)

*deH₃-
to give

*déh₃-t, *dé-deh₃-ti, *deh₃nis, *déh₃-no-m, *déh₃-ro-m, *déh₃-ɾ, *déh₃-ti-s, *déh₃tōr, *dh₃-tó-s

Celtic: dawn (**Wel**); dán (**Iri**)

Italic: dāre, addere, additiō, datum, dēdāre, ēdāre, ēditiō, ēditor, mandāre (manus +), commendāre, dēmandāre, perdāre, perditiō, perditus, praedor, praedātiō, praedātor, reddāre, trādere (trans+), trāditiō, trāditor, vēndāre, vēnditiō, vēndōr, dōnātiō, dōnātīvum, dōnāre, condōnāre, dōnum, dōs, dōtāre, datus (**Lat**);

addition, édition, mander, commander, demander, perdre, perdition, perte, prédation, prédateur, rendre, trahir, tradition, trahison, traitre, traître, vendre, vendeur, donation, donner, don, dot, douer, doter, date (**Fr**);

dare, addizione, dado, mandare, comandare, commendare, demandare, domandare, perdere, perdita, predare, predazione, predatore, rendere, tradire, tradizione, traditore, vendere, venditore, donazione, donare, condonare, dono, dota, dote, dotare, dato, data (**Ital**);

dar, adir, añadir, edición, editor, mandar, comandar, comendar, demandar, perder, perdición, pérdida, perta, prear, predar, predador, rendir, tradición, traición, traidor, vender, vendedor, donación, donar, condonar, don, dote, dotar, dado, dada, dato, data (**Sp**);

dar, adir, adição, edição, editor, mandar, demandar, perder, perdição, perda, prear, predar, predação, predador, render, trair, tradição, traição, traidor, vender, vendedor, doação, doar, dom, dote, dotar, dado, dada, data (**Port**);

da, dare, dar, daruri, deda, ediție, comânda, comândare, comanda, comandare, dimânda, pierde, pierdere, prăda, prădare, prădăciune, prădător, trăda, trădător, vinde, vindere, vânzător, donație, dona, dota, dat, dată (**Rom**)

Derivatives: add, addendum, addition, datum, data, edition, editor, mandate, mandamus, command, commend, demand, perdition, prede, predation, predator, render, trade, tradition, treason, traitor, vend, vendition, vendor, donate, donation, donative, condone, donor, pardon, pardonable, date (**Eng**);

Tradition (**Ger**); editor, traditie, treiteren (**Dut**); tradisjon (**Nor**); tradition (**Swe**); tradition (**Dan**); traddodiad (**Wel**); traidisiún (**Iri**);

традиция (tradícija) (**Rus**); tradycja (**Pol**); tradice (**Cz**); tradicia (**Slo**); tradicija (**Lith**); tradīcija (**Lat**); traditë, tradhtar, tradhëtar, dhuroj (**Alb**)

Hellenic: δίδωμι (dídōmi), ἔδομεν (édomen), ἔδωκᾰ (édōka), δῶρον (dôron), δόσις (dósis), δοτός (dotós), δώτωρ (dôtōr) (**AnGk**); δίδω (dído), δίνω (díno), δώρο (dóro) (**Gk**)

Derivatives: anecdote, antidote, dose, apodosis (**Eng**)

Slavic: дать (dát'), давать (davát'), передать (peredát'), предать (predát'), дань (dán'), дар (dar) (**Rus**); dać, dawać, sprzedać, dar (**Pol**); dát, dávat, daň, dar (**Cz**); dat', dávat', daň, dar (**Slo**); даде (dade), дава (dava) (**Mace**)

Baltic: duoti, duõnis (**Lith**); dot (**Latv**)

Albanian: dhashë (**Alb**)

Indo-Iranian: ददाति (dádāti), अदात् (ádāt), दान (dāna), अन्नदान (annadāna), गोदान (godāna), दिति (diti), धित (dhita), दातृ (dātṛ) (**Sans**); देना (denā), दाता (dātā) (**Hin**); دادن (dādan) (**Pers**) from which derives *dʰéh₁s god, sacred place:

*dʰéh₁s
god, deity; sacred place

*dʰh₁s-o-, *dʰeh₁s-eh₂-li-, *dʰeh₁s-yo-, *dʰeh₁s-to-, *dʰh₁s-no-

Italic: fērālis, fēriae, fēstus, fēstīvus, fēstīvālis, fēstīvitās, fēstum, fānum, fānāticus, profānus (**Lat**);

foire, férié, fête, festif, festivité, fanatique, profane (**Fr**);

ferale, feria, fiera, festa, festo, festivo, festività, fanatico, profano (**Ital**);

feria, festivo, festividad, fiesta, fanático, profano, profanar (**Sp**);

feral, feira, féria, festo, festivo, festival, festividade, festa, fanático, profano, profanar (**Port**);

ferie, festivitate (**Rom**)

Derivatives: fair, feria, festive, festival, festivity, fest, feast, fete, fiesta, fanatic, profane (**Eng**); feest, fanaticus (**Dut**); Ferien, Feier, Fest, Fete (**Ger**); ferie (**Nor**); fira, fest (**Swe**); ferie (**Dan**); festë (**Alb**)

Hellenic: θεός (theós), ἄθεος (átheos), ἀποθεόω (apotheóō), ἀποθέωσις (apothéōsis), ἔνθεος (éntheos), ἐνθουσῐᾰσμός (enthousiasmós), ἐνθουσῐᾰστής (enthousiastés), θεᾱ (theã), θεοκρᾰτῐᾱ (theokratíā), θεῖος (theîos) (**AnGk**); θεός (theós), άθεος (átheos), θεά (theá), θείος (theíos) (**Gk**)

Derivatives: theo-, apotheosis, enthusiasm, enthusiast, enthusiastic, theocracy (**Eng**); Enthusiasmus (**Ger**); atheos, entheus, enthūsiasmus, enthūsiastēs (**Lat**); théo-, enthousiasme (**Fr**); ateo, entuziasmo, teocrazia (**Ital**); ateo, entusiasmo, entusiasta (**Sp**); entusiasmo (**Port**); entuzjazm (**Pol**)

but the Germanic words for god come from a different source:

*ǵʰew-
to pour, libate

*ǵʰewd-, *ǵʰéw-ye-ti, *ǵʰi-ǵʰéw-ti, *ǵʰe-ǵʰów-e, *ǵʰu-tó-s, *ǵʰéw-tis, *ǵʰéw-mn̥, *ǵʰéw-mo-s, *ǵʰéw-tlo/eh₂, *ǵʰéw-tōr

Germanic: god, yet (dial.), yot (dial.), yote (dial.), ewte (dial.) (**Eng**); god, ġēotan (**OE**); god, jitte (**Fris**); god, gieten (**Dut**); Gott, gießen (**Ger**); goð, guð, gjóta (**Norse**); gud (**Nor**); gud, gjuta (**Swe**); gud, gyde (**Dan**); goð, guð, gjóta (**Ice**)

Italic: fūtis, fundere, adfundere, cōnfundere, cōnfūsus, cōnfūsiō, diffundere, diffūsus, diffusio, effundere, effūsus, effūsiō, fundibulum, fūsiō, īnfundere, perfundere, prōfundere, profundus, profunditās, refundere, suffundere, trānsfundere, transfūsiō, fundāmentum, fundātiō, fundātor (**Lat**);

fondre, fonderie, confondre, confus, confusion, diffuser, diffus, effusion, fusion, infondre, profond, refondre, transfusion, fondement, fondateur (**Fr**);

fondere, fonderia, confondere, confuso, confusione, diffondere, diffuso, effondere, effusione, fusione, infondere, profondere, profondo, profondità, suffondere, trasfondere, fondamenta, fondatore (**Ital**);

fundir, hundir, confundir, confuso, confusión, difundir, difuso, efundir, efusión, fundíbulo, fusión, infundir, profundo, hondo, profundidad, transfundir, fundamento, fundador (**Sp**);

fundir, confundir, confuso, confusão, difundir, difuso, efundir, efusão, fundíbulo, funil, fusão, infundir, profundo, profundidade, fundamento, fundador (**Port**);

confunda, cufunda, confuz, confuzie, efuziune, fuziune, profund, profunditate (**Rom**)

Derivatives: found (meaning to melt metal), foundry, affuse, confound, confuse, confusion, diffuse, diffusion, effuse, effusion, fusion, infusion, perfuse, perfusion, profuse, profusion, profound, profundity, refund, suffuse, suffusion, transfuse, transfusion (**Eng**); Konfusion (**Ger**); konfusjon (**Nor**); fundament (**Swe**); fundament (**Dan**); фонд (fond), трансфузия (transfuzija) (**Rus**); fundament (**Pol**); fund (**Alb**)

Hellenic: χέω (khéō), κέχῠκᾰ (kékhuka), χεῦμᾰ (kheûma), χύτλον (khútlon), χυτός (khutós) (**AnGk**)

Indo-Iranian: जुहोति (juhóti), जुहाव (juhāva), होम (hóma), होत्र (hotrá), होतृ (hótṛ), हुत (hutá) (**Sans**); ज़ोर (zor) (**Hin**); زور (zowr), ژون (žun) (**Pers**)

Derivatives: hotr (**Eng**); zor (**Rom**); ζόρι (zóri) (**Gk**)

*deh₂-
to share, divide

*deh₂-i-, *deh₂-p-, *dh₂-yé-, *deh₂-mo-

Germanic: tide (**Eng**); tīd (**OE**); tiid (**Fris**); tijd (**Dut**); Zeit (**Ger**); tíð, tíðr, tapa, tafn (**Norse**); tid, tape (**Nor**); tid, tappa (**Swe**); tid, tabe (**Dan**); tíð, tíður (**Ice**)

Italic: daps, damnum, damnāre, indemnis (**Lat**); dam, dommage, damner (**Fr**); danno, dannare (**Ital**); daño, dañar (**Sp**); dano, danar, indemne (**Port**); daună, damna, dăuna (**Rom**)

Derivatives: dapifer, damage, damn (**Eng**); dëm (**Alb**)

Hellenic: δαίομαι (daíomai), δῆμος (dêmos), δημᾰγωγός (dēmagōgós), δημοκρατέομαι (dēmokratéomai), δημοκρᾰτῐᾱ (dēmokratíā), δημοκρᾰτῐκός (dēmokratikós), ἔνδημος (éndēmos), δαίς (daís), δαῖσις (daîsis), δαιτύς (daitús), δαιτυμών (daitumṓn), δαίμων (daímōn), δαιμόνιον (daimónion), δεισιδαίμων (deisidaímōn) (**AnGk**); δῆμος (dímos), δημαγωγός (dimagogós), δημοκρατικός (dimokratikós), δεισιδαίμων (deisidaímon) (**Gk**)

Derivatives: deme, biodeme, demagogue, democracy, democratic, endemic, daimon (**Eng**); dēmos, dēmocratia, daemon, daemonium (**Lat**); démon (**Fr**); demonio (**Ital**); demonio (**Sp**); demónio (**Port**); демокра́тия (demokrátija) (**Rus**)

Albanian: ditë (**Alb**)

Indo-Iranian: दीति (dīti) (**Sans**)

*nem-

to distribute; to give, take

*ném-e-ti, *nom-éh₂, *ném-os, *ném-es-o-s, *nóm-o-s, *nom-ó-s

Germanic: nim (arch./dial.), numb, benim (obs.) (**Eng**); niman, beniman, forniman (**OE**); nimme (**Fris**); nemen, benemen, vernemen, aangenaam (**Dut**); nehmen, abnehmen, benehmen, vernehmen, angenehm (**Ger**); nema (**Norse**); förnimma (**Swe**); nemme (**Dan**); nema (**Ice**)

Italic: nemus, nemorālis, nemorōsus, numerus, numerābilis, numerālis, numerārius, numerāre, ēnumerāre, numerātiō, numerātor, numerōsitās, numerōsus, innumerābilis (**Lat**);

némoral, nombre, numéro, numéraire, nombrer, énumérer, nombreux (**Fr**);

nemorale, numero, novero, numerale, numerare, noverare, enumerare, numeratore, numerosità, numeroso (**Ital**);

número, numerario, numerar, enumerar, numerador, renumerar, numerosidad, numeroso (**Sp**);

nemoral, nemoroso, nombro, número, numerar, enumerar, numerosidade (**Port**);

numǎr, numǎra, numǎrare, numeros (**Rom**)

Derivatives: nemoral, nemorous, number, numeral, numerate, enumerate, numerator, numerous, innumerable (**Eng**); nummer (**Dut**); Nummer (**Ger**); nifer (**Wel**); номер (nómer), нумерация (numeracija) (**Rus**); numer (**Pol**); numër, numëroj (**Alb**)

Hellenic: νέμω (némō), νέμος (némos), νομή (nomḗ), νόμος (nómos), ἀνομία (anomía), ἐπίνομῖς (epinomís), οἰκονομῖᾱ (oikonomíā) (οἶκος+), νομίζω (nomízō), νόμισμα (nómisma), νομοθέτης (nomothétēs), νομοθετῐκός (nomothetikós), νομός (nomós), Νέμεσις (Némesis) (**AnGk**); νόμος (nómos), νόμισμα (nómisma), νομισματικός (nomismatikós), νομοθέτης (nomothétis), νομοθεσία (nomothesía) (**Gk**)

Derivatives: economy, oeconomus, economic, numismatic, nomothete, nomothetic, anomie, antinomy, autonomy, metronomic, nomad, nomadic, nomarch, nome, nomology, nomothetic, Numidia, nemesis (**Eng**); oekonomie (**Dut**); nummus, oeconomia, oeconomicus, Nemesis (**Lat**); nomothète (**Fr**); economia (**Ital**)

Baltic: ņemt (**Latv**)

Indo-Iranian: नमस् (námas), नमस्ते (namaste) (**Sans**); नमस्ते (namaste), नमाज़ (namāz) (**Hin**); نماز (namâz), نمسته (namaste) (**Pers**)

Derivatives: namaste (**Eng**); намáз (namáz) (**Rus**)

*krey-
to sift, separate, divide

*kreyn-, *kr̥-né-y-, *kri-n-ye-, *kri-né-h₁-, *kroyh₁-eye-, *krey-dʰrom, *kréy-mn̥, *kri-tós, *kroyn-is

Germanic: rine (**Eng**); hrīnan (**OE**); rijnen, renen, rein (**Dut**); rein (**Ger**); hrina, hreinn, hreinsa (**Norse**); rein, rense (**Nor**); ren, rensa (**Swe**); ren, rense (**Dan**); hrina, hreinn, hreinsa (**Ice**)

Celtic: crynu (**Wel**)

Italic: cernere, certus, certāre, concernere, crībrum, crībrāre, crīmen, crīminātiō, crīmināre, dēcernere, dēcrētōrius, dēcrētum, dēcrētālis, discernere, discrētiō, discrīmen, discrīmināre, excernere, excrēmentum, sēcernere, sēcrētārius, sēcrētiō, sēcrētus (**Lat**);

cerner, certain, concerner, crible, crime, incriminer, décerner, décret, décrétale, discerner, discriminer, excréter, excrément, secrétaire, ségrayer, ségrairie, sécrétion, secret (**Fr**);

cernere, cèrto, certare, concernere, cribro, cribrare, crimine, decernere, decretorio, decreto, decretale, discernere, secernere, segretario, secrezione, secreto, segreto (**Ital**);

cerner, cierto, concernir, cribo, cribar, crimen, criminar, discernir, discriminar, excretar, secretar, secretario, secreción, secreto (**Sp**);

cernir, certo, certar, crivo, crivar, discernir, discriminar, excretar, secretário, secreção, secreto, segredo (**Port**);

cerne, cert, certa, certare, ciur, crimă, discerne, secretar, secreţie, secret, săcret (**Rom**)

Derivatives: ascertain, certain, concern, concert, crime, incriminate, recrimination, decree, decretory, decretal, discern, discriminate, excrete, excern, secern, secretary, secretion, secrete, secret (**Eng**); decreet (**Dut**); Exkrement (**Ger**);

декрéт (dekrét), экскременты (ekskrementy), секретарь (sekretar'), секрет (sekrét) (**Rus**); ekskrement (**Pol**); exkrement (**Cz**); qërtoj (**Alb**)

Hellenic: κρῑ́νω (krī́nō), διακρίνω (diakrínō), κρίσις (krísis), ὑπόκρῐσῐς (hupókrisis), κριτής (krités), κρῖμα (krîma) (**AnGk**); κρίνω (kríno), διακρίνω (diakríno), κρίση (krísi), κριτής (kritís), κρίμα (kríma) (**Gk**)

Derivatives: crisis, hypocrisy (**Eng**); crisis (**Lat**); crisis (**Dut**); crisis (**Sp**)

Slavic: кроить (kroít'), край (kraj), крайна (kraína) (**Rus**); kroić, kraj, klaisa (**Pol**); krojit, kraj, krajina (**Cz**); krojiť (rare), kraj, krajina (**Slo**); крои (kroi), крај (kraj) (**Mace**)

Albanian: krahinë (**Alb**)

*bʰeyd-
to split

*bʰéyd-t ~ *bʰid-ént, *bʰi-né-d-ti ~ *bʰi-n-d-énti, *bʰoyd-o-, *bʰoyd-eh₂, *bʰidnós, *bʰidtós

Germanic: bite, boat, bait (**Eng**); bītan, bāt (**OE**); bite, boat (**Fris**); bijten, beits, beitel, boot (**Dut**); beißen, Beize, Beitel, Boot (**Ger**); bíta, bátr, beit, meina (**Norse**); bite, beita, beitel, båt (**Nor**); bita, bet, båt (**Swe**); bide, båd (**Dan**); bíta, beita, beit, bátur (**Ice**)

Derivatives: bateau (**Fr**); battello (**Ital**); bote (**Sp**); bote, batel (**Port**)

Celtic: bád (**Iri**)

Italic: fissus, fissiō, fissura, findere, bifidus, fistula (**Lat**); fesse, fission, fissurer, fendre, felle, fistule (**Fr**); fesso, fissione, fendere, fistola, fischiare (**Ital**); fiso, fisión, hender, fístula, fistra (**Sp**); fissão, fissure, fender, fístula (**Port**); fistulă (**Rom**)

Derivatives: fission, fissure, fistula, fester (**Eng**); фистула (fistula) (**Rus**)

Hellenic: φείδομαι (pheídomai) (**AnGk**)

Indo-Iranian: भेत् (bhét), भेदति (bhédati), भिन्न (bhinná), भिनत्ति (bhinatti), भिद् (bhid) (**Sans**)

*skey-

to split, to dissect

*skey-d-, *skéyd-t, *ski-né-d-ti, *skid-yé-ti, *skéyd-ye-ti, *skoyd-o-s, *skeyd-ro-s, *skéyd-ti-s, *skid-tó-s, *skey-ti, *ski-yé-ti, *skoy-eh₂, *skey-to-s, *skoyt-, *skoy-to-m

Germanic: shite, shit, shide, ski, skid, skeed, shed, shoad (reg.) (**Eng**); sċītan, sċīte, sċīd, sċādan (**OE**);

skite, skyt, skiede (**Fris**); schijten, schijt, scheiden, schedel (**Dut**); scheißen, Schiss, Scheiße, Scheit, Ski, scheiden, Schädel, Scheitel (**Ger**);

skíta, skitr, skíð (**Norse**); skite, skit, ski (**Nor**); skita, skit, ski, skid, skida, skeda (**Swe**); skide, skid, ski (**Dan**); skíta, skitur, skíð (**Ice**)

Derivatives: ski (**Fr**)

Celtic: ysgwyd (**Wel**); sciath, sciathán (**Iri**)

Italic: scindere, abscindere, abscissiō, rescindere, scissiō, scīre, cōnscīre, cōnscientia, cōnscientiōsus, nescīre, praescīre, sciēns, īnsciēns, scientia, scienter, scientificus, scīlicet, scīscere, īnscītia (**Lat**);

scinder, abscisse, scission, conscience, science, sciemment, scientifique (**Fr**);

scindere, rescindere, scissione, coscienza, nesci, scienza, scientifico (**Ital**);

escindir, abscisa, rescindir, escisión, consciencia / conciencia, ciencia, cientifico (**Sp**);

cindir, rescindir, cisão, consciência, ciente, insciente, ciência, cientifico, inscícia (**Port**);

şti, ştire, conştiinţă, neşti, neştine, nişte, niscai, ştiinţă (**Rom**)

Derivatives: abscind, abscissa, abscission, rescind, scission, scissors, conscience, conscientious, nescient, prescient, science, scientist, scienter, scientific, scilicet (sc./ scil.) (**Eng**); Gewissen (**Ger**); coinsias (**Iri**); shkencë (**Alb**)

Hellenic: σχίζω (skhízō), σχίσις (skhísis), σχιστός (skhistós) (**AnGk**)

Derivatives: schisis, schism, schismatic, schizoid, schizophrenia, diaschisis, diaschism (**Eng**)

Slavic: цедить (cedíť), чистый (čístyj), щит (ščit) (**Rus**); cedzić, czysty, szczyt (**Pol**); cedit, čistý, štít (**Cz**); cediť, čistý, štít (**Slo**); цеди (cedi), чист (čist), штит (štit) (**Mace**)

Baltic: skíesti (**Lith**); šķiêst (**Latv**)

Indo-Iranian: अच्छेदि (ácchedi), छेदि (chedi), छिनत्ति (chinátti), छित्ति (chitti), छाया (chāyā) (**Sans**)

*der-
to tear, to split

see Emotions

*h₁weydʰ
to separate

see Kinship

*h₂er
to join, fit together

see Body: Limbs & Joints

*leǵ-
to gather

*leǵ-s, *leǵ-no-, *leǵ-mṇ-, *loǵ-os

Italic: legere, allegere, allectívus, colligere, collēcta, collēctiō, collēctīvus, recolligere, dīligere, dīlēctiō, dīligēns, dīligentia, ēligere, ēlēctiō, ēlēctus, ēlegāns, ēligibilis, intellegere, intellectiō, intellēctus, intellectuālis, intellegentia, intelligibilis, lēctiō, lēctor, lēctūra, legiō, neglegere, neglectus, neglegentia, sēligere, sēlēctiō, sēlēctor, lignum, lignārius, ligneus, lignātor, lignōsus, lēx, lēgālis, illēgālis, lēgātiō, lēgātus, lēgislātiō, lēgislātor, lēgitimus, legūmen (uncert.) (**Lat**);

lire, cueillir, collecte, cueillette, collection, recueillir, diligent, diligence, élire, élit, élite, intellect, intelligence, leçon, lecteur, légion, négliger, négligence, sélection, lainier, ligneux, loi, légal, loyal, illégal, légation, légat, législation, légitime, légume (**Fr**);

leggere, cogliere, colletta, colta, collezione, colletto, colto, raccogliere, diligere, dilezione, diligente, eleggere, scegliere, eletto, elezione, intelletto, lezione, lettore, legione, negligere, negligenza, selezione, legno, legna, ligneo, legnoso, legge, leale, legale, illegale, legazione, legato, legislazione, legittimo, legume (**Ital**);

leer, coger, colegir, colecta, cosecha, colección, cogecho, cosecho, recoger, recolegir, diligente, diligencia, elegir, esleir, electo, elección, elegante, inteligir, intelecto, lección, lector, lectura, legión, negligir, negligencia, selección, leño, leña, leñero, leñador, leñoso, ley, leal, legal, ilegal, legación, legislación, legítimo, lindo (prob.), legumbre (**Sp**);

ler, colher, coligir, colecta, coleta, colheita, coleção, coleto, colheito, recolher, diligente, eleger, eleito, elegante, inteligir, intelecção, intelecto, lição, leitor, legião, negligência, seleção, lenho, lenha, lenheiro, lenhador, lenhoso, lei, leal, legal, ilegal, legislação, lídimo, legítimo, lindo (prob.), legume (**Port**);

alege, alegere, culege, culegere, colecţie, reculege, înţelege, înţelegere, înţelepciune, intelect, lecţie, lector, legiune, neglija, neglijenţă, selecţie, lemn, lemnar, lemnos, lege, leal, legal, ilegal, legumă (**Rom**)

Derivatives: legacy, legend, legendary, adlect, allective, collect, collection, collectible, collective, collector, coil, college, collegial, collegiate, colleague, cull, recollect, recollection, diligent, predilection, dilection, diligence, elect, elite, election, elective, electorate, elegant, eligible, elegibility, ineligible, illegible, legible, legibility, intellect, intellectual, intelligence, intelligent, intelligentsia, intelligible, lection, lectionary, lesson, lector, lecture, lectern, legion, legionary, neglect, negligence, negligee, negligible, select, selectance, selection, selective, legal, leal, loyal, illegal, legation, legator, legate, legislation, legislator, legitimate, legit, religion, sacrilege, legume, leguminous (**Eng**);

legioen, legio (**Dut**); kollektiv, Lektion, Legion, illegal (**Ger**); kollektiv (**Nor**); elegans, lektion, lektor, legion, legal (**Swe**); legíó (**Ice**);

llwyn (**Wel**); léigh (**Iri**);

λεγεώνα (legeóna) (**Gk**); коллékция (kollékcija), интеллект (intellekt), интеллигенция (intelligencija), лекция (lekcija), лектор (lektor), легион (legion), селекция (selekcija), легат (legat) (**Rus**); intelekt, lektor (**Pol**); lexoj, ndëgjoj, ligj (**Alb**)

Hellenic: λέγω (légō), λόγος (lógos), λογϊσμός (logismós), λογϊστϊκός (logistikós) (**AnGk**); λόγος (lógos), λογισμός (logismós), λογιστής (logistís), λογιστικός (logistikós) (**Gk**)

Derivatives: logos, logic, logistic, logistics, -logy, analogy, anthology, apology, eulogy, trilogy, etymology, tautology, terminology, biology (and many other sciences and academic subjects), dialogue, epilogue, monologue, prologue, logarithm, logogram, logophile, neologism, morphological (**Eng**); Logos (**Ger**); logistique (**Fr**); logos (**Port**); логос (logos) (**Rus**)

Albanian: mbledh, zgjedh (**Alb**)

*peh₂ǵ-
to attach

*ph₂-né-ǵ-, *ph₂ǵ-éh₂ye-ti, *ph₂ǵ-tós, *péh₂ǵ-s, *peh₂ǵ-os, *ph₂ǵ-eh₂, *peh₂ǵ-mn̥, *p(e)h₂ǵ-sleh₂, *p(e)h₂ǵ-slo-, *p(e)h₂ǵ-slo-lo-, *peh₂ǵ-sno-, *ph₂ǵ-y(e)h₂-lo-, *ph₂ǵ-sth₂- (poss.)

Possibly: **Germanic:** fast (**Eng**); fæst (**OE**); fêst (**Fris**); vast (**Dut**); fest (**Ger**); fastr (**Norse**); fast (**Nor**); fast (**Swe**); fast (**Dan**); fastur (**Ice**)

Italic: pangere, compingere, impingere, impāctus, prōpāgāre, pāx, pācātus, pācificus, pācāre, pāla, palūs, palūdōsus, palūster, pessulus, pāgina, pāgella, pāginālis, pāgus, pāgānus, pāgānismus, pāgānitās (**Lat**);

impact, propager, paix, pacifique, payer, pale, pelle, palustre, page, pays, païen, paganisme (**Fr**);

impingere, impatto, propagare, pace, pacato, pacifico, pacare, pagare, pala, palude, padule, paludoso, pagina, pagella, paese, pagano, paganità (**Ital**);

impacto, propagar, paz, pacato, pagado, pacifico, pagar, apagar, pala, paúl, palude, palustre, página, país, pagano, paganismo (**Sp**);

impacto, propagar, paz, pacifico, pagar, pá, pala, paul, palude, paludoso, palustre, pestilo, página, pagela, país, pagão, paganismo (**Port**);

împinge, împingere, pace, împăca, păca, pădure, paludă, păduros, paludos, pagină, păgân, păgânătate (**Rom**)

Derivatives: compinge, impinge, impact, propagate, pax, paxis, peace, pacific, pay, pale, page, paginal, pagan, paganism, paynim, paganity (**Eng**); paaien, pagina (**Dut**); pax (**Swe**); póg (**Iri**); поганый (poganyj) (**Rus**); paqe, pëganë, pëgërë, pagan (**Alb**)

Hellenic: ἅπαξ (hápax), πάγη (págē), πῆγμα (pêgma), πάχνη (pákhnē), πηγός (pēgós), πάγος (págos), πήγνυμι (pégnumi) (**AnGk**); πάχνη (páchni), πάγος (págos) (**Gk**)

Derivatives: pēgma (**Lat**)

Slavic: паз (paz) (**Rus**); paz (**Pol**); paz (**Cz**)

*gʷʰen-
to strike, kill

*gʷʰén-ti, *gʷʰén-ye-ti, *gʷʰn̥-sḱé-ti, *gʷʰe-gʷʰón-e, *gʷʰon-éye-ti, *gʷʰé-gʷʰn-e-t, *gʷʰén-ti-s, *gʷʰn̥-tó-s, *gʷʰón-o-s

Germanic: bane (**Eng**); bana OE); baan (**Fris**); baan (**Dut**); Bahn, U-bahn, autobahn (**Ger**); guðr, gunnr, bani, ben (**Norse**); bane, ben (**Nor**); bane (**Swe**); bane (**Dan**); gunnur, bani, ben (**Ice**)

Celtic: gwanu, gwân (**Wel**)

Object motion

Italic: -fendere, dēfendere, dēfēnsiō, offendere, infendere, īnfestus, īnfestāre, īnfestātiō, manifestus (**Lat**); offenser, défendre, infester, manifeste (**Fr**); offendere, difendere, infestare, manifesto (**Ital**); ofender, defender, enhiesto, infestar, manifiesto (**Sp**); defender, defensão (**Port**)

Derivatives: offend, defend, infest, infestation, manifest (**Eng**); Manifest (**Ger**); manifest (**Swe**); diffyn (**Wel**); afendoj (**Alb**)

Hellenic: θείνω (theínō), πέφαται (péphatai), ἔπεφνον (épephnon), φατός (phatós), φόνος (phónos) (**AnGk**); φόνος (fónos) (**Gk**)

Slavic: жать (žať), гнать (gnať), гонять (gonjať) (**Rus**); gnać, gonić (**Pol**); ždít, hnát, honit (**Cz**); honiť (**Slo**); гони (goni) (**Mace**)

Baltic: genéti, ginti, ganýti, giñti, genéti (**Lith**); dzenêt, dzīt, ganît (**Latv**)

Albanian: gjuaj (**Alb**)

Indo-Iranian: हन्ति (hanti), जघान (jaghāna), जघ्नुः (jaghnúḥ), हति (hatí), घन (ghaná) (**Sans**); हयना (hayanā) (poet.) (**Hin**)

*pleh₂k-
to hit

see Basic Adjectives

*gʷelH-
to throw, reach, pierce; to hit by throwing

*gʷelH-eti, *gʷélH-os, *gʷelH-ón-eh₂, *gʷélH-m̥n-o-, *gʷl̥H-id-yé-, *gʷl̥H-mn̥, *gʷl̥H-tós, *gʷl̥H-trom, *gʷolH-éye-, *gʷolH-mos, *gʷólH-os

Germanic: queal (dial.), quail, quell, qualm (**Eng**); cwelan, cwellan, cwealm (**OE**); kwelen, kwellen, kwalm (**Dut**); quälen, Qualm (**Ger**); kvelja (**Norse**); kvälja, kvalm (**Swe**); kvæle, kvalm, kvalme (**Dan**); kvelja (**Ice**)

Hellenic: βέλος (bélos), βελόνη (belónē), βέλεμνον (bélemnon), βαλλίζω (ballízō), βλῆμα (blêma), βλητός (blētós), βλῆτρον (blêtron), βολέω (boléō), βόλος (bólos), βάλλω (bállō), βαλλίστρα (ballístra), ὀβελίσκος (obelískos), ὀβολός (obolós), πᾰρᾰβᾰλλω (parabállō), πρόβλημᾰ (próblēma), παραβολή (parabolé), βολή (bolé), βολίς (bolís), διαβάλλω (diabállō) (**AnGk**); βέλος (vélos), βάλλω (vállo), βαλλίστρα (vallístra), παραβάλλω (paravállo), παραβολή (paravolí), πρόβλημα (próvlima), διάβολος (diávolos) (**Gk**)

Derivatives: ball, ballista, ballistic, ballistospore, obol, obolus, amphibole, bolide, bolometer, -bolic, -bolism, anabolic, catabolic, diabolic, metabolic, metabolism, metabolite, embolism, embolus, parabola, parabole, palaver, parole, parlay, parable, palabra, hyperbola, hyperbole, hyperbolic, symbol, symbolic, symbolism, symbology, tauroboly, problem, problematic, astrobleme, emblem, emblematic, belomancy, belonephobia, devil (**Eng**);

parabool, parabel, probleem, duivel (**Dut**); Parabel, Palaver, Problem, Teufel (**Ger**); problem, djevel (**Nor**); parabel, djävul (**Swe**); parabel, parabol, palaver, djævel (**Dan**); djöfull (**Ice**); problem, diafol, diawl (**Wel**); barúil, diabhal (**Iri**);

ballista, obolus, problēma, problēmaticus, diabolus (**Lat**); baliste, obole, parabole, parole, palabre, problème, problèmatique (**Fr**); balestra, balista, parabola, parola, problema, problematico, diavolo (**Ital**); ballesta, parábola, palabra, problema, problemático, diablo (**Sp**); balestra, besta, balista, parábola, palavra, problema, problemático, diabo (**Port**); balistă, parabolă, parolă, problemă, problematic, diavol (**Rom**);

парáбола (parábola), баллúста (ballísta), проблéма (probléma), дьявол (d'javol) (**Rus**); parabola, problem, diabeł (**Pol**); parabola, problém, ďábel (**Cz**); ѓавол (ǵavol) (**Mace**); problema (**Lith**); problēma (**Latv**); parabolë, përrallë, djall (**Alb**); परवलय (paravlay) (**Hin**); پول (pul) (**Pers**)

Slavic: жаль (žal'), жáло (žálo) (**Rus**)

Baltic: gélti, gélà (**Lith**)

Indo-Iranian: غوزارول (ɣwəzārawél) (**Pash**); گرزین (gerzîn) (**Pers**)

*pewǵ-
to punch; to prick, poke

*puǵ-eh₂yéti?, *pu-né-ǵ-ti, *puǵ-i-h₃onh₂-, *puǵ-, *puǵ-méh₂, *puǵ-nós, *puǵ-s, *puǵ-teh₂ts, *pu-n-ǵ-stis?

Possibly: **Germanic**: fuck, fist (**Eng**); fȳst (**OE**); fokje, fûst (**Fris**); fokken, vuist (**Dut**); Faust (**Ger**)

Italic: pungere, compungere, expungere, interpungere, punctuāre, punctuātiō, punctus, punctiō, punctum, pūgiō, pugil, pugilātor, pugnus, pugnāre, expugnāre, expugnātiō, impugnāre, oppugnāre, prōpugnāre, pugnāx, repugnāre (**Lat**);

poindre, ponctuer, point, pointe, poinçon, ponction, poing, oppugner, pugnace, répugner (**Fr**);

pungere, compungere, espungere, spuntare, interpungere, punto, punta, punzone, ponzàre, pugile, pugilatore, pugno, pugnare, espugnare, espugnazione, impugnare, oppugnare, propugnare, pugnace, ripugnare (**Ital**);

pungir, punger, puñir, expunger, expungir, punto, punta, punzón, punción, punzar, púgil, puño, puñar, expugnar, impugnar, opugnar, propugnar, pugnaz, repugnar (**Sp**);

pungir, expungir, ponto, ponta, punção, punçar, púgil, punho, expugnar, opugnar, pugnaz, repugnar (**Port**);

împunge, împungere, punge, punct, pont, pumn, repugna (**Rom**);

Derivatives: expunge, punctuate, punctuation, point, poignant, punch, puncheon, punctum, punctual, puncture, acupuncture, pungent, pugio, pugilism, pugilist, expugn, expugnation, impugn, oppugn, propugn, pugnacious, repugn, repugnant (**Eng**); punt (**Dut**); Punkt (**Ger**); punkt (**Swe**); punkt (**Dan**); ponc (**Iri**); μπουνιά (bouniá) (**Gk**); пункция (punkcija), пункт (punkt) (**Rus**); punkt, pointa (**Pol**)

Hellenic: πυγμή (pugmḗ), πύξ (púx), πύκτης (púktēs (**AnGk**)

Baltic: pušìs (**Lith**)

*men-
to stand out, to tower, to project

see Body: Head

*(s)pend-
to stretch

*(s)pénd-e-ti, *(s)pond-éye-ti, *(s)pn̥d-éh₁ye-ti, *(s)pénd-i-s, *(s)pénd-os

*(s)pénd-e-ti, *(s)pond-éye-ti, *(s)pn̥d-éh$_1$ye-ti, *(s)pénd-i-s, *(s)pénd-os

Italic: pendere, appendere, appendix, compendere, compendium, expendere, expēnsus, pēnsāre, compēnsāre, compēnsātiō, perpendere, perpendiculum, perpendiculāris, suspendere, suspēnsus, suspēnsiō, pendēre, dēpendēre, impendēre, pendēns, pendulus, prōpensiō, pondus, ponderāre, pensum (**Lat**);

appendre, appendice, compendium, peser, penser, panser, compenser, compensation, suspendre, suspension, pendre, dépendre, propension, poids, pondérer, pensum (**Fr**);

appendere, appendice, compendio, spendere, speso, spesa, pesare, pensare, compensare, compensazione, sospendere, sospensione, pendere, dipendere, pendente, pendolo, pendulo, ponderare, peso (**Ital**);

apender, apéndice, compendio, expender, expensas, pesar, pensar, compensar, compensación, recompensar, suspender, suspensión, pender, depender, propensión, peso, pienso (**Sp**);

apêndice, compêndio, expender, expensas, pesar, pensar, compensar, compensação, recompensar, suspender, suspensão, pender, depender, peso (**Port**);

apendice, păsa, păsare, compensa, compensație, prepinge, supensie, depinde, pondere, păs (**Rom**)

Derivatives: append, appendix, compendium, expend, spend, expense, compensate, compense, compensation, recompense, perpend, perpendicular, suspense, suspension, pend, depend, impend, pendant, penchant, pending, pendulum, pendulous, ponder, pensive, suspend, pound (**Eng**);

pond (**Dut**); Appendix, Kompendium, spenden, Pfund, Pensum (**Ger**); pund (**Swe**); spise (**Dan**); pendúll (**Ice**); pwys (**Wel**); aipindic (**Iri**);

πενσέω (penséo) **(Gk)**; аппéндикс (appéndiks), компенсáция (kompensácija), суспензия (suspenzija), пуд (pud) **(Rus)**; kompensacja **(Pol)**; peshoj, pezuli **(Alb)**

Slavic: пýдить (púdit'), пудúть (pudít'), пядь (pjad') **(Rus)**; pędzić, piędź **(Pol)**; puditi, píd' **(Cz)**; pudit', piad' **(Slo)**

Baltic: spęsti **(Lith)**; spiêst **(Latv)**

*ten-
to stretch, extend

*tn̥-néw-ti, *tén-t, *te-tón-e, *tn̥-é-ti, *tén-ye-ti, *ton-éye-ti, *tn̥-éh₁-(ye)-ti, *tén-onts, *tén-os, *tén-tis, *tén-tlo-, *tén-tu-s, *ton-sl-i, *tón-os, *tn̥-néh₂, *-tn̥-nó-s, *tn̥-tós

Germanic: þennan **(OE)**; dehnen **(Ger)**; þenja **(Norse)**; tänja **(Swe)**; þenja **(Ice)**

Celtic: tant **(Wel)**; téad **(Iri)**

Italic: tenēre, abstinēre, abstinēns, abstinentia, attinēre, attentus, continēre, contentus, continēns, continentia, continuus, dētinēre, dētentiō, manūtenēre (manus+), obtinēre, pertinēre, appertinēre, pertinēns, retinēre, retentiō, sustinēre, sustentāre, sustinentia, tenaculum, tenāx, tenēns, tenor, tentus, tenus, tener, tōnsillae, tendere, attendere, attentiō, contendere, contentiō, contentus, distendere, extendere, extentus, extēnsus, extēnsiō, intendere, intēnsus, intentus, intentiō, ostentāre, ostentātiō, portendere, portentus, praetendere, praetēnsus, prōtendere, tēnsus, tēnsiō **(Lat)**;

tenir, abstenir, abstinent, abstinence, attenir, attentif, contenir, content, contenance, continu, détenir, détention, maintenir, obtenir, appartenir, pertinent, retenir, rétention, rêne, soutenir, sustenter, tenaille, tenace, teneur, ténor, tendre, attendre, attention, contention, tenson, content, distendre, étendre, extension, entendre, intense, entente, intention, ostentation, prétendre, tension **(Fr)**;

tenere, astenere, astinente, astinenza, attenere, attento, contenere, contento, continenza, continuo, detenere, detenzione, mantenere, ottenere, pertenere, appartenere, pertinente, ritenere, redine, sostenere, sostentare, tenacolo, tenace, tenore, tenero, tendere, attendere, attenzione, contendere, contenzione, tenzone, contento, distendere, estendere, stendere, estenso, esteso, steso, estensione, intendere, intenso, inteso, intento, intenzione, ostentare, ostentazione, portendere, portento, pretendere, preteso, protendere, teso, tenso, tensione **(Ital)**;

tener, abstener, abstinente, abstinencia, atener, atento, contener, contento, continente, continencia, continuo, detener, detención, mantener, obtener, pertenecer, pertinente, retener, retención, rienda, sostener, sustentar, tenáculo, tenaz, tenaza, teniente, tenor, tierno, tender, atender, atención, contender, contención, contento, distender, extender, extenso, extensión, entender, intender, intenso, entesar, intento, intención, ostentar, ostentación, portento, pretender, tieso, tenso, tensión, tesón **(Sp)**;

ter, abster, abstinente, abstinência, ater, atento, conter, contente, continência, contenças, continuo, deter, detenção, manter, obter, pertencer, pertinente, reter, retenção, rédea, suster, sustentar, tenáculo, tenalha, tenaz, teor, tenor, tento, até,

155

terno, tenro, tender, atender, atenção, contender, contenção, contente, distender, estender, extenso, extensão, entender, intender, intenso, intento, intenção, ostentar, ostentação, portento, pretender, pretenso, teso, tenso, tensão, tesão (**Port**); ţine, ţinere, abstinent, abstinenţă, aţine, aţinere, atent, conteni, conţine, content, continuu, deţine, detenţiune, menţine, obţine, reţine, retenţie, susţine, tânăr, tinde, tindere, atenţie, contenţiune, content, extinde, extins, extensiune, întinde, întindere, intens, întins, intenţie, ostenta, ostentaţie, pretinde, tins, tensiune (**Rom**)

Derivatives: tenet, tenor, tenure, abstain, abstinent, abstinence, attent, attentive, contain, content, continent, continence, countenance, continuous, detain, detention, maintain, obtain, pertain, appertain, appurtenance, pertinent, rein, sustain, tenaculum, tenacious, tender, tonsils, tend, tense, attend, attention, contend, contention, content, distend, extend, extent, extense, extension, intend, intense, intent, intention, ostentate, ostentation, portend, portent, pretend, pretense, protend, tension (**Eng**); attent, continu (**Dut**); ténor (**Ice**); abstanaid (**Iri**); континéнт (kontinént), ретенция (retencija), экстенсия (ekstensija), интенция (intencija) (**Rus**)

Hellenic: τείνω (teínō), τένων (ténōn), ἀτενής (atenḗs), τάσις (tásis), τόνος (tónos), ὀξύτονος (oxútonos) (**AnGk**); τόνος (tónos), οξύτονος (oxýtonos) (**Gk**)

Derivatives: ton, tone, tune, tonus, oxytone, hypotenuse, neotony, peritoneum, tetanus, tonic, -tone, -tonia, -tonic, e.g., atonic, baritone (βαρύς+), barytone, catatonia, diatonic, dystonia, ectasia, entasis, epitasis, hemitonic, heptatonic, hypertonia, isotonic, monotonous, monotony (**Eng**); toon (**Dut**); tonus (**Lat**); ton, oxyton (**Fr**); tono, tuono (**Ital**); tono, trueno (**Sp**); tom, trom (**Port**); tun, ton (**Rom**); тóнус (tónus), тон (ton) (**Rus**)

Baltic: tìnti, tenéti, tiñklas, tānas, tandùs (**Lith**); tît, tìkls, tina (**Latv**)

Albanian: ndej, tend (**Alb**)

Indo-Iranian: तनोति (tanóti), अतन् (átan), तनस् (tánas), तति (táti), तन्ति (tantí), तन्त्र (tántra), तन्तु (tántu), तान (tāna), तत (tatá) (**Sans**); تنیدن (tanidan), تار (târ) (**Pers**)

Derivatives: tantra (**Eng**)

*sterh₃-

to spread, extend, stretch out

*str̥h₃-g-, *str̥-né-h₃-, *str̥h₃-néw-, *str̥h₃-tós, ?*str̥h₃-mn̥, *str̥h₃-mn-eh₂

Italic: strāges, strāgulus, sternere, asternere, cōnsternere, cōnsternāre, prōsternere, strāta, strātum, strātus, storea, torus, torulus (**Lat**); prosterner, estrade, store (**Fr**); sternere, prostrare, prosternare, strada, strato, stuoia, tuorlo (**Ital**); consternar, prostrar, postrar, estrada, estrado, estrato, estera, toro, tuero (**Sp**); consternar, prostrar, prosternar, estrada, estrado, estrato, estore, esteira (**Port**); aşterne, aşternere, stradă, strat (**Rom**)

Derivatives: stragulum, consternate, consternation, prostrate, prostration, street, stratum, stratify, stratus, torus, toral (**Eng**); strǣt (**OE**); strjitte (**Fris**); straat (**Dut**); Straße (**Ger**); stræti (**Norse**); strede (**Nor**); sträte, stråt (**Swe**); stræde (**Dan**); stræti (**Ice**); stryd (**Wel**); sráid (**Iri**); στράτα (stráta) (**Gk**)

Hellenic: στόρνῡμι (stórnūmi), στρωτός (strōtós), στρατός (stratós), στρᾰτηγός (stratēgós) (+ἄγω (ágō)), στρατηγία (stratēgía), στρῶμα (strôma), στρωμνή (strōmné), στέρνον (stérnon) (**AnGk**); στρατός (stratós), στρατηγός (stratigós) (**Gk**)

Derivatives: strategy, strategem, strategic, strategist, stratocracy, stratography, stratonic (**Eng**); stratēgus, stratēgia (**Lat**); stratège, stratégie (**Fr**); strategia (**Ital**); estratega (**Sp**); estratega (**Port**); стратег (strateg) (**Rus**); strategia (**Pol**)

Slavic: простереть (prosteret') (**Rus**)

Indo-Iranian: स्तृणाति (stṛnāti), स्तृणोति (stṛṇoti), स्तृत (stṛtá) (**Sans**); گستردن (gu-stardan) (**Pers**)

which includes:

*strew-

to spread, strew

*stréw-e-ti, *strow-éye-ti

Germanic: strew, straw (**Eng**); strewian, strēawian (**OE**); streauwe, struie (**Fris**); strooien, strouwen (**Dut**); streuen (**Ger**); strá (**Norse**); strø (**Nor**); strö (**Swe**); strø (**Dan**); strá (**Ice**)

Italic: struere, astruere, cōnstruere, cōnstructiō, cōnstructus, dēstruere, dēstructiō, īnstruere, īnstructiō, īnstructor, īnstrūmentum, obstruere, obstructiō, industrius (indu is a variant of in) (prob.), industria (**Lat**);

construire, construction, détruire, instruire, instruction, instructeur, obstruer, industrie (**Fr**);

costruire, costruzione, distruggere, distruzione, istruire, istruzione, istruttore, ostruzione, industria, industrioso (**Ital**);

construir, construcción, destruir, destrucción, instruir, instructor, obstruir, obstrucción, obstructivo, industria, industrioso (**Sp**);

construir, construção, destruir, instrução, obstruir, obstrução, obstrutivo, industria, industrioso (**Port**); astruca, construi, construcție, distruge (**Rom**)

Derivatives: construct, construe, construction, destroy, destruction, instruct, instruction, instructor, instrument, obstruct, obstruction, obstructive, structure, industry, industrious (**Eng**); constructie (**Dut**); konstruieren (**Ger**); konstruktion (**Dan**); ystryw (**Wel**); конструкция (konstrúkcija), деструкция (destrukcija), инструкция (instrukcija), инструктор (instrúktor), инструмент (instrument), обструкция (obstrukcija), индустрия (industríja) (**Rus**)

*trewd-
to push, thrust

*tréwd-e-ti, *trud-néh₂-ti, *trowd-eh₂yéti, *trowd-éye-ti, *trowd-o-, *trewd-tos

Germanic: threat **(Eng)**; þrēatian **(OE)**; verdrieten, droten **(Dut)**; verdrießen **(Ger)**; þrjóta, þraut, þreyta **(Norse)**; traut, traute **(Nor)**; tryta **(Swe)**; þrjóta, þraut, þreyta **(Ice)**

Celtic: cythrudd **(Wel)**

Italic: trūdere, abstrūdere, contrūdere, dētrūdere, extrūdere, intertrūdere, intrōtrūdere, intrūdere, obtrūdere/obstrūdere, prōtrūdere, retrūdere, trūsus **(Lat)**; extrudir **(Sp)**; abstruir, extrudir **(Port)**

Derivatives: abstrude, abstruse, detrude, detrusion, extrude, extrusion, extrusive, protrude, protrudent, protrusion, protrusile, intrude, intrusion, intrusive, nonintrusive, obtrude, obtrusive, inobtrusive, retrude, retruse, retrusion, retrusive **(Eng)**

Slavic: труд (trud) **(Rus)**; trud **(Pol)**; trud **(Cz)**; trud **(Slo)**; труд (trud) **(Mace)**

Baltic: triūsas **(Lith)**

Albanian: tredh, ndrydh **(Alb)**

*(s)tew-
to push, hit

*(s)tewk-, *(s)tewg-, *(s)téwg-t, *(s)tu-né-g-ti, *(s)tug-éye-ti, *stúg-s, *stug-os, *(s)tewd-, *stud-éh₁-(ye)-ti, *tu-né-d-ti, *tud-é-ti, *(s)te-(s)tówd-e, *téwd-tis, *(s)tewp-

Germanic: stock, stitch, steck, shtick, stucco, stote, stot **(Eng)**; stocc, stycce **(OE)**;

stoak, stik, stjitte **(Fris)**; stok, stuk, stik (in compounds), stoten **(Dut)**; Stock, Stück, Stuck, stoßen **(Ger)**;

stokkr, stykki **(Norse)**; stokk, stykke **(Nor)**; stock, stycke **(Swe)**; stok, stykke **(Dan)**; stokkur **(Ice)**

Derivatives: estoc, stuc **(Fr)**; stocco, stucco **(Ital)**; estuque **(Port)**

Celtic: tit **(Iri)**

Italic: studēre, studēns, studium, studiōsus, tundere, contundere, contūsiō, obtundere, pertundere, tussis, tussīre, tudiculāre, stupēre, stupefacere (+facere), stupidus, stupor, stuprum **(Lat)**;

étudier, étudiant, étude, étui, contusion, toux, tousser, toussoter, touiller, stupide, stupeur, stupre **(Fr)**;

studiare, studente, studio, ottundere, tosse, tossire, stupire, stupido, stupro **(Ital)**;

estudiar, estudiante, estudio, contusión, tos, toser, estuper, estúpido, estupro **(Sp)**;

estudar, estudante, estúdio, estudo, tosar, contusão, tosse, tossir, estúpido, estupro (**Port**);

studia, student, studiu, pătrunde, pătrundere, tuse, tuşi, tuşire (**Rom**)

Derivatives: study, student, study, studio, etude, étui, studious, contusion, obtuse, pertussis, stupefaction, stupid, stupor (**Eng**); studearje (**Fris**); studeren, student (**Dut**); studieren, Student (**Ger**); studere (**Nor**); studera, student, studium (**Swe**); studere (**Dan**); astudio (**Wel**); staidéar (**Iri**);

штудировать (študirovat'), студия (studija), контузия (kontúzija), ступор (stupor) (**Rus**); studiować, student (**Pol**); studovat, student (**Cz**); študovať (**Slo**); studijuoti (**Lith**); studēt (**Latv**); studioj (**Alb**)

Hellenic: τύκος (túkos), ἔστῠγον (éstugon), στῠγέω (stugéō), στύγος (stúgos), στύξ (stúx), τύπτω (túptō), τῠμπᾰνον (túmpanon), τύπος (túpos), στύπος (stúpos), τυπικός (tupikós) (**AnGk**); τύμπανο (týmpano), τύπος (týpos) (**Gk**)

Derivatives: tympanum, tympani, timbre, type, typical (**Eng**); type, typisch (**Dut**); Typ, typisch (**Ger**); type, typisk (**Nor**); typisk (**Swe**); typisk (**Dan**); tympanum, typus, typicus (**Lat**); timbre, type, typique (**Fr**); tipo, tipico (**Ital**); tipo, típico (**Sp**); tipo, típica (**Port**); tip, tipic (**Rom**)

Albanian: tund, shtyj (**Alb**)

Indo-Iranian: तुजन्ति (tujánti), तुञ्जन्ति (tuñjánti), तुञ्जते (tuñjáte), तुजयत् (tujáyat), नितुन्दते (nitundate), तुदति (tudáti), तुतोद (tutóda), तोपति (topati) (**Sans**)

Construction & Production

*demh₂-
to tame, domesticate

*dm̥-né-h₂-ti, *dm̥h₂-yé-ti, *domh₂-éye-ti, *domh₂-o-s, *dm̥h₂-tó-s, *domh₂-to-s, *démh₂-ti-s

Germanic: tame (**Eng**); tam, tom (**OE**); tam (**Fris**); tam, temmen (**Dut**); zahm, zähmen (**Ger**); tamr, temja (**Norse**); tam (**Nor**); tam, tämja (**Swe**); tam, tæmme (**Dan**); tamur, temja (**Ice**)

Celtic: goddef, dafad (**Wel**); damh (**Iri**)

Italic: domāre (**Lat**); domare (**Ital**); domar (**Sp**); domar (**Port**)

Hellenic: δάμνημι (dámnēmi), δμητός (dmētós), δμῆσις (dmêsis) (**AnGk**)

Derivatives: adamant, adamantine, Damian (**Eng**)

Albanian: dem (**Alb**)

Indo-Iranian: दाम्यति (dāmyati), दमायति (damāyáti), दम्य (damya) (**Sans**); دام (dām) (**Pers**)

which is presumably related to *dem- to build:

*dem-
to build, to put together

*dém-e-ti, *dóm, *dém-tis, *dem-ro-, *dm̥-n-yós

Germanic: teem, toft, timber (**Eng**); toft, timber (**OE**); tiemje, betame, betamje, timmer (**Fris**); timmer (**Dut**); ziemen, geziemen, ziemlich, Zunft, Zimmer (**Ger**); tomt, topt, tupt, tuft, timbr (**Norse**); tømmer (**Nor**); tomt, timmer (**Swe**); toft, tømmer (**Dan**); topt, tuft, timbur (**Ice**)

Celtic: devnydh, defnydd (**Wel**); damhna (**Iri**)

Italic: domus, domesticus, domāre, dominus, domina, dominātiō, dominatrix, dominium, dominārī (**Lat**);

dôme, domestique, dom, damoiseau, dame, demoiselle, domination, domaine, dominer (**Fr**);

duomo, domestico, domare, domino, don, donno, donzello, donna, dama, damigella, dominazione, dominio, dominare (**Ital**);

doméstico, amiésgado, domar, Don, don, dueño, doncel, Doña, doña, dueña, doncella, dama, dominación, dominio (**Sp**);

domicílio, doméstico, domar, Dom, dono, dona, donzela, dama, dominio, dominar (**Port**);

domiciliu, domestic, dumesnic, domn, doamnă, damă, domina (**Rom**)

Derivatives: dome, domal, domestic, domesticate, domestication, domesticity, domestique, domicile, domiciliary, major-domo, domino, don, donzel, dam, dame, madam, beldame, belladonna, madonna, damsel, demoiselle, domination, dominatrix, domain, demesne, dominion, condominium, dominate, dominant, dominance, domineer, predominant, duenna, danger, dungeon (**Eng**); dominee, dame, dominatie (**Dut**); Dom, Dame, Domina (**Ger**); dom (**Swe**)

Hellenic: δέμω (démō), δῶ (dô), δόμος (dómos) (**AnGk**)

Derivatives: apodeme, monodomy, opisthodomos, polydomy (**Eng**)

Slavic: дом (dom) (**Rus**); dom (**Pol**); dům (**Cz**); dom (**Slo**); дом (dom) (**Mace**)

Baltic: namas (**Lith**); nams (**Latv**)

Albanian: dhomë (**Alb**)

Indo-Iranian: दम् (dám), दम (dáma) (**Sans**)

*gerbʰ-
to carve

*gerbʰ-, *gr̥bʰ-, *gr̥bʰ-tó-s

Germanic: carve (**Eng**); ceorfan (**OE**); kerve (**Fris**); kerven (**Dut**); kerben (**Ger**); karve (**Nor**); karva (**Swe**); karve (**Dan**)

Hellenic: γράφω (gráphō), γράμμα (grámma), γραπτός (graptós), γραμματικός (grammatikós), γράμμή (grammḗ), γραφεύς (grapheús), γραφή (graphḗ), καταγράφω (katagráphō), σύγγράφω (sungráphō), προγράφω (prográphō), πρόγραμμα (prógramma) (**AnGk**); γράφω (gráfo), γράμμα (grámma), γραμματικός (grammatikós), γραμμή (grammí), γραφή (grafí), συγγράφω (syngráfo), γραπτός (graptós), πρόγραμμα (prógramma) (**Gk**)

Derivatives: graphic, graph, graft, epigraphy, grapheme, graphene, graphite, monograph, paragraph, photograph, telegraph, anagram, diagram, engram, epigram, grammar, hologram, pentagram, program, telegram, program, programme, programmer (**Eng**); grammatik (**Ger**); program (**Nor**); program (**Swe**); gramadeg (**Wel**);

graphicus, grammatica, programma (**Lat**); grammaire, programme, programmer (**Fr**); grammatica, programmare (**Ital**); gramática, programa (**Sp**); gramatica, programa (**Port**); program (**Rom**); program (**Pol**); program (**Cz**); program (**Slo**)

Slavic: жёреб (žéreb) (**Rus**); hřeb (**Cz**); žreb (**Slo**); ждреб (ždreb) (**Mace**)

Baltic: grĭpsta (**Latv**)

Albanian: gërvish (**Alb**)

*ǵʰer-
to scratch, scrape

Hellenic: χᾰράσσω (kharássō), χᾰρτης (khártēs), χαρτουλάριος (khartoulários), χᾰρᾰκτήρ (kharaktḗr) (**AnGk**); χάρτης (chártis), χαρακτήρας (charaktíras), χαράδρα (charádra) (**Gk**)

Derivatives: card, chart, charter, cartulary, character (**Eng**); kaart (**Dut**); Karte (**Ger**); kart (**Nor**); cairt (**Iri**);

charta, chartula, chartulārius, character (**Lat**); carte, charte, cartulaire, caractère (**Fr**); carta, cartolaio, cartulario, carattere (**Ital**); carta (**Sp**); carta, cartulário, cartorário, caractere, carácter (**Port**); carte, cartă, cărturar, cartular (**Rom**);

карта (karta), хартия (xartija), характер (xarákter) (**Rus**); karta, charakter (**Pol**); charakter (**Cz**); charakter (**Slo**); kartë (**Alb**)

Baltic: žeriù, žeřti, žarstýti (**Lith**)

*terh₁-
to rub, turn

*treh₁-, *térh₁-ye-ti, *treh₁-sḱe-ti, *torh₁-, *tórh₁-mo-s, *tórh₁-no-s, *tréh₁-mn̥, *tréh₁-tu-s, *tréh₁-ti-s, *tr̥h₁-tó-s, *térh₁-tro-m, *tr̥h₁-yō

Germanic: throw, thresh, thrash, thread (**Eng**); þrāwan, þrescan, þrǣd (**OE**); draaie, terskje, tried, trie (**Fris**); draaien, dorsen, dersen, draad (**Dut**); drehen, dreschen, Draht (**Ger**); þreskja, þráðr (**Norse**); dreie, treske, tråd (**Nor**); dreja, tröska, tråd (**Swe**); dreje, tærske, tæske, tråd (**Dan**); þreskja, þráður (**Ice**)

Derivatives: triscar (**Sp**); triscar (**Port**)

Possibly: **Germanic:** tharm (dial.) (**Eng**); þearm (**OE**); term (**Fris**); darm (**Dut**); Darm (**Ger**); þarmr (**Norse**); tarm (**Nor**); tarm (**Swe**); tarm (**Dan**); þarmur (**Ice**)

Celtic: taradr (**Wel**); tarathar (**Iri**)

Derivatives: taratrum (**Lat**); taladro (**Sp**); trado (**Port**)

Italic: terere, atterere, attrītiō, conterere, prōterere, protervus, terebra, terebrāre, trībulum, trīticum, trītūra, triō, septentriō (**Lat**); contrire, septentrion (**Fr**); protervo, terebra, tritico, settentrione (**Ital**); curtir, trillo, trilla, trigo, tritura, setentrião (**Sp**); curtir, protervo, térebra, terebrar, trilho, trilha, trigo, tritura (**Port**); septentrion (**Rom**)

Derivatives: attrition, contrite, contrition, detriment, detrimental, detrital, detrition, detritivore, detritus, retriment, tribulation, trite, triturate, triture, septentrion (**Eng**)

Hellenic: τείρω (teírō), τορεύς (toreús), τόρμος (tórmos), τόρνος (tórnos), τρῆμα (trêma), τρῆσις (trêsis), τρητός (trētós), τέρετρον (téretron), τρώγω (trṓgō), τράγος (trágos) (poss.), τέρυ (téru), τρύω (trúō), τρύχω (trúkhō), ἄτρυτος (átrutos), τετραίνω (tetraínō) (**AnGk**); τρήμα (tríma), τράγος (trágos) (**Gk**)

Derivatives: trema, monotreme, trematode (**Eng**); tréma (**Fr**)

Slavic: тере́ть (terét') (**Rus**); trzeć (**Pol**); třít (**Cz**); trieť (**Slo**); трие (trie) (**Mace**)

*(s)ker-
to cut, cut off

see Time

*lewbʰ-
to cut off

*lowbʰ-om, lub-r-ós

Germanic: lēaf (**OE**); leaf (**Fris**); loof (**Dut**); Laub, Laube (**Ger**); lauf (**Norse**); løv (**Nor**); löv (**Swe**); løv (**Dan**); lauf (**Ice**)

Italic: laubia, liber (poss.), libellus, librārius (**Lat**); loge, loger, livre, libelle, libraire (**Fr**); loggia, libro, libraio, librario (**Ital**); libro, libelo, librero (**Sp**); livro, libelo, livreiro (**Port**); librar (**Rom**)

Derivatives: lodge, lobby, libel, libellant, libellous, library, librarian, libretto (**Eng**); loge, loods, lodge, loggia, logeren (**Dut**); llyfr (**Wel**); leabhar (**Iri**)

*sek-
to cut

Germanic: saw, sax, zax (**Eng**); sagu, saga, seax (**OE**); seage, seine (**Fris**); zaag, zeis (**Dut**); Säge, Sense, Sachs (**Ger**); sǫg, sax (**Norse**); sag, saks (**Nor**); såg, sax (**Swe**); sav, saks (**Dan**); sög, sax (**Ice**)

Italic: secāre, cōnsecāre, dēsecāre, īnsecāre, īnsectus, intersecere, persecāre, prōsecāre, resecāre, sector, secūris, segmen, segmentum, serra, serrāgo, serrātus, serrāre, saxum (**Lat**); scier, disséquer (**Fr**); secare, segare, dissecare, insetto, resecare, settore, scure, segmento, serra, sasso (**Ital**); segar, disecar, insecto, rasgar, segur, sierra, serrin, serrar, sajo, saxo (**Sp**); segar, dissecar, inseto, rasgar, segure, segura, secure, serra, serragem, serrar, seixo (**Port**); diseca, insectă, piersica, secure (**Rom**)

Derivatives: secant, sect, section, dissect, insect, intersect, prosecute, resect, sector, segment, serrated (**Eng**); τσεκούρι (tsekoúri) (**Gk**); céктор (séktor), сегмент (segment) (**Rus**); sharrë, shat (**Alb**)

Slavic: céчь (séč'), секира (sekíra) (**Rus**); siec, siekiera (**Pol**); síci, síct, sekyra (**Cz**); siecť, sekať, sekera (**Slo**); секира (sekira) (**Mace**)

These may be either from *sek- (to cut) or *sek^w- (to follow):

Italic: signum, īnsignis, īnsigne, sigillum, significāre, significāns, significātiō, signāre, signātūrus, assignāre, assignātiō, cōnsignāre, dēsignāre, īnsignāre, resignāre (**Lat**);

seing (arch./ lit.), signe, insigne, sceau, signifier, signification, signer, assigner, consigner, désigner, dessiner, enseigner, résigner (**Fr**);

segno, insigne, insegna, sigillo, suggello, significare, segnare, assegnare, consegnare, designare, disegnare, disegno, insegnare (**Ital**);

seña, sino, signo, insigne, insignia, enseña, sello, sigilo, significar, signar, asignar, consignar, diseñar, diseño, enseñar, resignar (**Sp**);

senho, senha, sino, sina, signo, signa, insigne, insígnia, selo, sigilo, significar, assinar, consignar, desenhar, designar, ensinar, resenhar, resignar (**Port**);

semn, sigiliu, sugel, semna, desemna, designa, însemna, însemnare (**Rom**)

Derivatives: sign, signal, signum, segno, insignis, insignia, ensign, sigil, seal, signify, significant, sain, sign, signature, assign, assignation, consign, designate, design, resign (**Eng**); zegel (**Dut**); Siegel, segnen (**Ger**); swyn (**Wel**); séan (**Iri**); ассигнáция (assignácija) (**Rus**); shenjë, shënoj (**Alb**)

*sek^w-

to follow

*sék^w-e-tor, *sék^w-t, *sek^w-o-, *sok^w-yo-, *s_ək^w-tó-s

Germanic: seg (arch., dial.) (**Eng**); secg (**OE**); seggr (**Norse**); seggur (**Ice**)

Italic: sequī, cōnsequī, cōnsequēns, cōnsequentia, exsequī, exsequia, īnsequī, nōn sequitur, obsequī, obsequiae, obsequium, obsequiōsus, persequī, persecūtiō, prōsequī, prōsecūtor, sector, sequēns, secundus, sequāx, sequela, sequester, subsequor, subsequēns, secus, extrīnsecus, intrīnsecus, socius, sociālis, sociābilis, societās, sociō (**Lat**);

suivre, suite, séquence, conséquent, conséquence, incōnsequēns, exécuter, exsecūtiō, exécution, ensuivre, obsèques, obséquieux, persécuter, poursuivre, second, extrinsèque, intrinsèque, social, société, socio (**Fr**);

seguire, conseguire, inconseguente, eseguire, eseguizione, esecuzione, esequie, inseguire, ossequio, perseguire, perseguitare, proseguire, sequenza, secondo, sequela, susseguire, settore, socio, soccio, sociale, soccida, società (**Ital**);

seguir, conseguir, consecuente, consiguiente, consecuencia, conseguenza, ejecutar, ejecución, obsequio, obsequioso, perseguir, proseguir, secuencia, segundo, socio, socia, social, sociedad (**Sp**);

seguir, conseguir, conseqüente, consequente, conseguinte, consequência, execução, perseguir, prosseguir, sequência, segundo, sequaz, sequela, subseguir, extrínseco, intrínseco, sócio, social, sociedade (**Port**);

consecvent, consecvență, consecință, execuție, secund, soț, soață, social, societate (**Rom**)

Derivatives: sue, suant, suit, suite, segue, sequence, consequence, consequent, execute, exequies, non sequitur, obsequies, obsequious, persecute, pursue, persecution, prosecute, prosecutor, sector, second, sequela, sequester, extrinsic, intrinsic, social, sociable, society, sociate (**Eng**); executie (**Dut**); sozial (**Ger**); saig (**Wel**); экзекуция (ekzekucija), сéктор (séktor) (**Rus**); konsekwencja (**Pol**)

Hellenic: ἕπομαι (hépomai), ἑσπόμην (hespómēn) (**AnGk**)

Baltic: sèkti (**Lith**); sekt, sekot (**Latv**)

Indo-Iranian: सचते (sácate), सक्त (saktá), सचान (sacāná), सचीमहि (sacīmahi) (**Sans**); از (az) (**Pers**)

This may be related to *sekʷ- to see (which one derives from the other is uncertain):

*sekʷ-

to see, to notice

*sekʷ-e-ti, *sókʷ-o-s, *sokʷ-éh₂, *sekʷ-sḱé-ti / *sokʷ-eh₁-sḱé-ti

Germanic: see, sight (**Eng**); sēon, sīen, siht (in compounds) (**OE**); sjen, sicht (**Fris**); zien, zicht (**Dut**); sehen, Sicht, Gesicht (**Ger**); séa, sjá, sjón, sýn (**Norse**); se, syn, sjon, sikt (**Nor**); se, syn, sikt, sikte (**Swe**); se, syn, sigte (**Dan**); sjá, sjón, sýn (**Ice**)

Albanian: shoh (**Alb**)

*tetḱ-

to create, produce; to cut, hew

*tétḱ-ti, *totḱ-éye-ti, *tétḱ-ō, *tetḱ-eh₂, *tetḱ-(dʰ)lo-, *tₑtḱ-tós

Germanic: das (**Fris**); das (**Dut**); Dachs, Dechse, Dechsel (**Ger**); þǫx, þexla (**Norse**); svintoks (**Nor**); täxla (**Swe**); svintoks (**Dan**)

Derivatives: tanière (**Fr**); tasso (**Ital**); tejón (**Sp**); texugo (**Port**)

Celtic: tál (**Iri**)

165

Italic: texere, tēla, subtīlis, textilis, textō, textor, textōrius, textus, textūra (**Lat**); tisser, toile, subtil, subtile (**Fr**); tessere, tela, sottile (**Ital**); tejer, tela, sutil, subtil, textorio (**Sp**); tecer, teia, tela (**Port**); ţese, ţesere, teară, subţire (**Rom**)

Derivatives: tela, subtle, textile, texture, context, pretext, text (**Eng**); subtil (**Ger**); subtil (**Swe**); текстиль (tekstil'), текст (tekst) (**Rus**); subtelny (**Pol**); tekstils (**Latv**)

Hellenic: τίκτω (tíktō), τέχνη (tékhnē), τέκτων (téktōn), ἀρχιτέκτων (arkhitéktōn) (**AnGk**); αρχιτέκτονας (architéktonas) (**Gk**)

Derivatives: architect, polytechnic, technique, technocrat, technology, technophobia, tectonic (**Eng**); architectus (**Lat**); архитéктор (arxitéktor) (**Rus**); architekt (**Pol**)

Slavic: тесáть (tesát'), теслá (teslá) (**Rus**); ciosać, ciosła (**Pol**); tesat, tesla (**Cz**); tesať (**Slo**)

Baltic: tašýti (**Lith**); test, tèst (**Latv**)

Indo-Iranian: ताष्टि (tāṣṭi), तक्षति (tákṣati), तक्षयति (takṣayati), तक्षन् (tákṣan), तष्टा (taṣṭá) (**Sans**)

which derives from *teḱ- to sire:

*teḱ-

to sire, beget

*téḱ-t, *tḱey-, *té-tḱ-ti, *tí-tḱ-e-ti, *te-tóḱ-e, *tḱ-éy-ti, *téḱ-nom

Italic: sinō, situs, pōnere, antepōnere, appōnere, compōnere, dēpōnere, dēpositus, dispōnere, expōnere, impōnere, interpōnere, interpositiō, oppōnere, pōnēn, postis, postpōnere, praepōnere, prōpōnere, repōnere, suppōnere, superimpōnere, superpōnere, transpōnere, positus, positiō, situāre, prōpositum (**Lat**);

site, pondre, apposer, composer, depondre, déposer, disposer, exposer, imposer, interposition, opposer, ponant, proposer, supposer, superposer, poste, position, situer, situation (**Fr**);

sito, porre, apporre, comporre, deporre, diporre, deposto, diposto, disporre, esporre, sporre, opporre, ponente, preporre, proporre, riporre, supporre, sopraporre, sovrapporre, posto, spostare, posizione, situare, situazione (**Ital**);

sitio, poner, anteponer, aponer, componer, deponer, desponer, depuesto, disponer, exponer, imponer, oponer, ponente, poniente, preponer, proponer, reponer, suponer, sobreponer, superponer, puesto, posición, situar, propósito (**Sp**);

sítio, pôr, apor, compor, depor, deposto, dispor, expor, opor, poente, ponente, poste, prepor, propor, repor, supor, sobrepor, superpor, posto, posição, situar, propósito (**Port**);

pune, punere, apune, apunere, apus, compune, depune, dispune, despune, spune, spunere, expune, prepune, propune, răpune, supune, supunere, superpune, poziţie, pusăciune, situaţie (**Rom**)

Derivatives: site, situs, in situ, posit, appose, apposite, compose, deposit, deponent, dispose, expose, expound, exposition, impose, interposition, oppose, post (doorpost), postpone, prepose, preposition, prepone, propose, suppose, superimpose, superpose, transpose, posit, post, position, situation (**Eng**);

componeren, situeren, situatie (**Dut**); situieren, Situation (**Ger**); situasjon (**Nor**); post, situation (**Swe**); situationen (**Dan**); deponenssögn (**Ice**); интерпозиция (interpozicija), позйция (pozícija) (**Rus**)

Hellenic: τέκον (tékon), ἔτεκον (étekon), κτίζω (ktízō), θεόκτιτος (theóktitos), πυρίκτιτος (puríktitos), κτῖσϊς (ktísis), τέκνον (téknon), τέτοκα (tétoka) (**AnGk**); κτίσμα (ktísma), κτίστης (ktístis), χτίστης (chtístis), τέκνο (tékno) (**Gk**)

Derivatives: autoctisis (**Eng**)

Indo-Iranian: क्षेति (kṣéti), क्षियन्ति (kṣiyánti), क्षेषत् (kṣeṣat), क्षित (kṣitá), परिक्षित (parikṣita), क्षिति (kṣití), तास्थिष (tasthivas) (**Sans**)

*peyḱ-

to hew, cut out; to stitch, embroider, sting; to paint, mark, colour

*piḱ-ét, *pi-né-ḱ-ti, *péyḱ-ye-ti, *piḱ-ró-s, *piḱ-tó-s, *póyḱ-os

Germanic: fāh, fǣġan (**OE**); fech (**Ger**); fá (**Norse**); fá (**Ice**)

Italic: pingere, dēpingere, pictor, pictūra, pictus, pigmentum, auripigmentum (**Lat**); peindre, peintre, peint, pigment, piment, orpiment (**Fr**); pittare, depingere, dipingere, pittore, pittura, pinto, pigmento, pimento, orpimento (**Ital**); pintar, depenger, pintor, pintura, pinto, pigmento, pimiento (**Sp**); pintar, pintor, pintura, pigmento, pimenta (**Port**); păta, pătare, picta, pictor, pictură, pigment (**Rom**)

Derivatives: paint, depict, depiction, picture, pinto, pint, Pict, pigment, pimiento, orpiment (**Eng**); pigment (**Dut**); пигмент (pigment) (**Rus**)

Hellenic: πΐκρός (pikrós), ποικίλος (poikílos) (**AnGk**); πικρός (pikrós), ποικίλος (poikílos) (**Gk**)

Slavic: писáть (pisát′), пёстрый (pjóstryj) (**Rus**); pisać, pstry (**Pol**); psát, píši, pestrý (**Cz**); písať, pestrý (**Slo**); пишува (pišuva) (**Mace**)

Derivatives: pestriţ, pictură (**Rom**)

Baltic: piẽšti, paišaĩ, piẽšas (**Lith**)

Indo-Iranian: पिष्ट (piṣṭá), पिनष्टि (pinaṣti), पेश (péśa), पिशङ्ग (piśáṅga (**Sans**)

*werǵ-
to work, to make

*wr̥ǵyéti, *wr̥ǵtós

Germanic: work, wrought, wright (**Eng**); weorc, wyrçan, wyrhta (**OE**); wurkje, wurk (**Fris**); werken, wrochten, werk, gewrocht, wrecht (**Dut**); wirken, Werk, Gewurcht (**Ger**); yrkja, orka, virkja, verk (**Norse**); yrke, orke, virke, verk (**Nor**); yrka, orka, virka, verk (**Swe**); ørke, orke, virke, værk (**Dan**); yrkja, orka, virka, verk (**Ice**)

Celtic: gwery (**Wel**); fearg (**Iri**)

Hellenic: ἔργον (érgon), ἐνεργός (energós), ἐνέργεια (enérgeia), ἔρδω (érdō), ῥέζω (rhézō), ὀργή (orgḗ), ὀργίζω (orgízō), ὄργανον (órganon) (**AnGk**);

έργο (érgo), ενέργεια (enérgeia), άεργος (áergos), άνεργος (ánergos), εργάζομαι (ergázomai), εργαλείο (ergaleío), εργασία (ergasía), εργοδότης (ergodótis), εργατικότητα (ergatikótita), εργοστάσιο (ergostásio), οργή (orgí), όργανο (órgano) (**Gk**)

Derivatives: ergo-, allergy, argon, demiurge, dramaturgy, energy, erg, ergon, ergonomics, homorganic, liturgy, metallurgy, microorganism, organ, organic, organism, organize, orgy, surgeon, synergy, theurgy, zymurgy (**Eng**);

energīa, organum (**Lat**); énergie, orgue, organe (**Fr**); energia, organo, argano (**Ital**); energia, órgano (**Sp**); energia, órgão (**Port**); energie, organ, orgă (**Rom**); энергия (enérgija), óрган (órgan) (**Rus**); organy (**Pol**); varhany (**Cz**); ارغنون (arğanun) (**Pers**)

Slavic: вéрша (vérša) (**Rus**); wiersza (**Pol**); vrše (**Cz**); vrša, vrš (**Slo**)

Baltic: vargas, váržas (**Lith**); var̂za (**Latv**)

Albanian: argëtoj (**Alb**)

Indo-Iranian: वृज् (vr̥j), वृज्यते (vr̥jyáte), वर्ज (varja), स्ववृष्टि (svávr̥ṣṭi) (**Sans**); ورزیدن (varzidan), ورز (varz), ورزه (varza), برز (barz) (**Pers**)

*h₃ep-
to work, make; ability, force

*h₃ép-lom, *h₃ép-(i)s, *h₃ep-en-o-, *h₃ép-n-os, *h₃ép-os, *h₁su-h₃ép-os, *h₃ép-r̥

Germanic: afol, abal, æfnan, andefn (**OE**); afl, afli, efna, efni (**Norse**); avi (dial.), evne, emne (**Nor**); avel, ämna, ämne (**Swe**); avi, evne (**Dan**); afl, afli, efna, efni (**Ice**)

Italic: ops, cōpia, cōpiōsus, opulentus, officium, officiālis, opifex, operor, operāns, operārius, opus, opera, opusculum, omnis, omnisciēns, omnivorus (**Lat**);

copieux, opulent, office, officiel, opérer, œuvrer, ouvrer, ouvrier, opéraire, œuvre, opéra, opuscule, omniscient (**Fr**);

copioso, opulento, ufficio, uffizio, opificio, operare, oprare, ovrare, operaio, uopo, opera, opuscolo, ogne, ogni, omnisciente, omnivoro (**Ital**);

copioso, opulento, ofício, oficial, obrar, operar, obrero, operario, uebos, opus, ópera, huebra, obra (**Sp**);

ofício, oficial, obrar, operar, obreiro, operário, ópera, obra (**Port**); oficial, opera, op, opus, operă (**Rom**)

Derivatives: copious, opulent, official, opificer, opera, operate, cooperate, inoperable, opus, opuscule, omnibus, omniscient, omnivore (**Eng**); officieel, opera (**Dut**); offiziell (**Ger**); offisiell (**Nor**); officiell, opus (**Swe**); officiel (**Dan**); obair (**Iri**); опус (ópus), опера (ópera) (**Rus**)

Indo-Iranian: अप् (áp), अप्रस् (ápnas), अपस् (ápas), स्वपस् (svápas) (**Sans**); خوب (xub) (**Pers**)

*pleḱ-
to plait, braid

Germanic: fleohtan, fleax (**OE**); flechten (**Ger**); flétta (**Norse**)

Italic: plectere, plicāre, applicāre, complicāre, dēplicāre, displicāre, explicāre, implicāre, implicātiō, implicitus, multiplicāre, multiplicātiō, plicatilis, replicāre, supplicāre, plexus, simplex, simplicitās, duplex, multiplex, complexus (**Lat**);

plier, ployer, appliquer, compliquer, complication, déployer, éployer, expliquer, employer, impliquer, implication, multiplier, multiplication, relier, reployer, répliquer, supplier, supplication, plexus, simple, duplex, complexe (**Fr**);

piegare, applicare, complicare, complicazione, dispiegare, esplicare, spiegare, impiegare, implicare, implicazione, moltiplicare, moltiplicazione, replicare, supplicare, supplicazione, semplice, duplice (**Ital**);

llegar, plegar, pregar, allegar, aplegar, aplicar, complicar, complicación, desplegar, explicar, emplear, implicar, implicación, multiplica, multiplicación, replegar, replicar, suplicar, plexo, simple, dúplex (**Sp**);

chegar, pregar, plicar, achegar, aplicar, conchegar, aconchegar, complicar, complicação, despregar, explicar, empregar, implicar, implicação, multiplicar, multiplicação, replicar, suplicar, simples, simplice (**Port**);

pleca, plecare, apleca, aplecare, aplica, complica, complicaţie, explica, implica, implicaţie, multiplica, multiplicaţie, replica, suplica, suplicaţie, simplu (**Rom**)

Derivatives: ply, apply, appliance, applicable, application, applicator, appliqué, complicate, complication, complicity, deploy, display, explicate, explicit, employ, implicate, imply, implicit, multiply, multiplication, replicate, replica, reply, supplicate, supplication, supplicant, perplex, simple, simplicity, duplicate, duplex, triplicate, complex, plait, pleat, pliable, plight, splay (**Eng**); implizieren, simpel (**Ger**); simpel (**Swe**); импликация (implikacija) (**Rus**)

Hellenic: πλέκω (plékō), πλοκή (ploké̄) (**AnGk**); πλέκω (pléko) (**Gk**)

Derivatives: plectics, plexogenic, ploce, symplectic (**Eng**)

Slavic: плести (plestí) (**Rus**)

Baltic: pinti (**Lith**)

Albanian: plaf (**Alb**)

Indo-Iranian: प्रश्न (praśna) (**Sans**)

which is derived from *pel- to cover:

*pel-

to cover, wrap; skin, hide; cloth

*pél-n-eh$_2$, *pél-no-s, *pél-sḱo-s, *pl-ēn-(y)éh$_2$

Germanic: fell, film (**Eng**); fell, filmen (**OE**); fel, fillen (**Fris**); vel, velm (**Dut**); Fell (**Ger**); fjall, fell, feldr (**Norse**); fjell, fille (**Nor**); fjäll (**Swe**); fell, feldur (**Ice**)

Italic: pellis, pellicula, pellarius, centipelliō, versipellis (**Lat**); peau, pellicule (**Fr**); pelle, pellicola, pellaio, centopelle, pelliccia (**Ital**); piel, pelleja, película, pielero (**Sp**); pele, película, peleiro (**Port**); piele, peliculă, pielar, cimpoi (**Rom**)

Derivatives: pelt, pellicle, pellagra (**Eng**); pels (**Dut**); pels (**Nor**); päls (**Swe**); pels (**Dan**); peall (**Iri**)

Hellenic: πέλλᾱς (péllās) (**AnGk**)

Slavic: пелена (pelená), плева́ (plevá), пленá (plená) (**Rus**); pielucha (**Pol**); plena (**Cz**); пелена (pelena) (**Mace**)

Baltic: plėnė, plėnìs (**Lith**); plēne (**Latv**)

Albanian: plah (**Alb**)

*(s)teg-

to cover

*(s)teg-e-ti, *stog-éye-ti, *teg-no-, *(s)tég-os, *tog-o-, *tog-eh$_2$-, *tég-mn̥, *teg-dʰleh$_2$

Germanic: thack, thatch, deck, bedeck (**Eng**); þæc, þeċċean, þeċċan (**OE**); tek, dak, dekke, bedekke (**Fris**); dak, dekken, bedekken (**Dut**); Dach, bedecken (**Ger**); þak, þekja (**Norse**); tak, tekkja, tekkje (**Nor**); tak, täcka, betäcka (**Swe**); tag, tække (**Dan**); þak, þekja (**Ice**)

Derivatives: deque (**Port**); dach (**Pol**)

Celtic: tŷ, to (**Wel**); teach (**Iri**)

Italic: tegere, dētegere, dētēctiō, dētēctor, prōtegere, tēctum, tēgula, tegumentum, tignum, contīgnāre, contīgnātiō, toga (**Lat**); protéger, toit, tuile, tégument, toge (**Fr**); proteggere, tetto, tegola, teglia, tegghia, tegumento, toga (**Ital**); detector, proteger, techo, teja, toga (**Sp**); proteger, teto, telha, tigela, tégula (**Port**)

Derivatives: detect, detection, detective, detector, protect, protection, protective, protector, protectorate, protégé, tect, obtect, tectum, tile, tegular, tegument, tegmental, integument, contignation, tog, toga, toggery (**Eng**); tegel (**Dut**); Ziegel (**Ger**); cegła (**Pol**); dëftoj, tjegull (**Alb**)

Hellenic: στέγω (stégō), στέγος (stégos), στέγη (stégē), τέγος (tégos) (**AnGk**); στέγη (stégi) (**Gk**)

Derivatives: Stegosaurus, steganography, steganopod (**Eng**)

Baltic: stogas (**Lith**)

Indo-Iranian: स्थगति (sthagati), स्थगयति (sthagayati) (**Sans**); ठग्गी (ṭhaggī) (**Hin**)

Derivatives: thug (**Eng**)

*ḱel-

to cover, conceal

see Cognitive function

*kh₂em-

to bend, curve

*kh₂em-er-, *kh₂em-iH-no-, *kh₂em-p-

Italic: camur, campus, campester, campiō (**Lat**); cambre, cambrer, chambre, camp, champ, champêtre, champion, champignon (**Fr**); cambra, campo, Campania, campestre, campione (**Ital**); campo, campestre, campeón (**Sp**); campo, campestre, campeão (**Port**); câmp (**Rom**)

Derivatives: camp, decamp, encamp, encampment, campus, champion, Campion, campaign, champerty, camber, chamber, antechamber, chamberlain (**Eng**); camp, kamp, kampioen (**Dut**); Kampf, Kamp, Camp, Campus, Champion (**Ger**); kamp (**Swe**); kamp, champion (**Dan**); seaimpin (**Iri**); κάμπος (kámpos) (**Gk**); чемпион (čempion) (**Rus**); czempion (**Pol**); šampión (**Cz**); šampión (**Slo**); čempionas (**Lith**); čempions (**Latv**); kampion (**Alb**)

Hellenic: κμέλεθρον (kmélethron), καμάρα (kamára) (uncert.), κάμῑνος (kámīnos), καμπή (kampḗ), κάμπτω (kámptō), καμψός (kampsós), κάμπη (kámpē) (**AnGk**); καμάρα (kamára) (**Gk**)

Derivatives: cabaret, camera, camera obscura, in camera, cameral, bicameral, tricameral, unicameral, concamerate, concameration, camaraderie, comrade, viola da gamba (**Eng**); Kamera (**Ger**); kamera (**Swe**); seomra, ceamara (**Iri**); camara, camera, gamba (**Lat**); chambre, caméra (**Fr**); camera, camerlengo, gamba (**Ital**); cámara (**Sp**); câmara, câmara, cambra, câmera, camerlengo (**Port**); cămară, cameră (**Rom**)

Indo-Iranian: क्मरति (kmárati) (**Sans**); कमरबन्द (kamarband) (**Hin**); کمر (kamar), کمربند (kamarband) (**Pers**)

Derivatives: cummerbund/cummerband (**Eng**); Kummerbund (**Ger**)

*weyk-
to curve, bend; to exchange

*wi-né-k-, *wik-i-

Germanic: week (**Eng**); wice, wicu (**OE**); wike (**Fris**); week (**Dut**); Woche (**Ger**); vika (**Norse**); uke (**Nor**); vecka (**Swe**); uge (**Dan**); vika (**Ice**)

Italic: vincīre, vinctūra, vinculāre, vinculum, vīcīs, vicārius, vice versā, vicissitūdō (**Lat**); fois, vicaire, viguier, voyer, vicissitude (**Fr**); avvinghiare, vincolare, vincolo, vinco, vece, vicario, vicissitudine (**Ital**); vincular, vínculo, brinco, vez, vicario, veguer, vicisitud (**Sp**); vincular, vínculo, brinco, vez, vice, vis-, vigário, vicário (**Port**); vicar (**Rom**)

Derivatives: vincture, vinculum, vicar, vicarious, vice versa, vicissitude (**Eng**); викарий (vikarij) (**Rus**)

Hellenic: εἴκω (eíkō) (**AnGk**)

Indo-Iranian: بيختن (bīxtan (**Pers**)

*(s)kel-
to bend, crook; bent, crooked; leg, heel, knee, hip

see Body: Limbs & Joints

*lewg-
to bend, turn

see Movement

*pleh₁-
to fill

*p̥lh₁nós, *pléh₁dʰuh₁; *pelh₁u-, *pí-pleh₁, *p̥l-né-h₁-, *pleh₁-ye-, *p̥lh₁-go-, *p̥lh₁-tós, *polh₁ús, *pélh₁-u-, *pleh₁-is-on-, *ploh₁-is-, *ploh₁-isto-

Germanic: full, fill, folk, filch (**Eng**); full, fyllan, folc, fylċian (**OE**); fol, folje, folk, fel (**Fris**); vol, vullen, volk, veel (**Dut**); voll, füllen, Volk, viel, Pulk (**Ger**);

fullr, fylla, fylli, folk, fólk, fylki, fylkja, fjǫl-, flestr, fleiri (**Norse**); full, fylle, folk, fylke, flest, flere, fleire (**Nor**); full, fylla, fylle, folk, fylke, fylka, flest, flera, fler (**Swe**); fuld, fylde, folk, fylke (**Dan**); fullur, fylla, fylli, fólk, fylki, fylkja, fjöl-, fleiri (**Ice**)

Derivatives: foule (**Fr**); folla (**Ital**); полк (polk) (**Rus**); pułk (**Pol**); pulkas (**Lith**)

Celtic: llawn (**Wel**); lán (**Iri**)

Italic: plēre, plēnus, complēre, complēmentum, complētiō, complētīvus, dēplēre, explēre, implēre, implēmentum, opplēre, replēre, replētiō, supplēre, supplēmentum, duplus, simplus, simplificor, triplus, manipulus, plēbs, plēbiscītum, plēnārius, plēnitūdo, plūs, complūrēs, plūrālis, plūrifōrmis, plūrimus (**Lat**);

accomplir, complément, complétion, complet, complète, emplir, replet, suppléer, supplément, double, doubler, quadruple, triple, maniple, plèbe, plein, plénier, plénitude, plus, pluralité (**Fr**);

compiere, compire, complemento, complimento, completivo, completo, empire, replezione, repleto, supplire, sopperire, doppio, duplo, doppiare, quadruplo, triplo, manipolo, pieve, plebe, pieno, plenario, più, pluralità, riempire (**Ital**);

umplir, complemento, complimiento, cumplimiento, completivo, completo, henchir, implemento, repleto, suplir, suplemento, doble, doblo, duplo, doblar, cuádruplo, simplificar, manopla, manípulo, plebe, lleno, pleno, plenario, plenitude, pluralidad (**Sp**);

cumprir, complemento, comprimento, cumprimento, completivo, completo, encher, repleto, suprir, dobre, dobro, duplo, dobrar, dublar, quádruplo, simplificar, triplo, manopla, manápula, manípulo, plebe, cheio, pleno, plenário, plenitud, pluralidade (**Port**);

compli, cumplire, complement, compliment, complet, umple, umpiere, dublu, dubla, simplifica, plebe, plin, plus (**Rom**)

Derivatives: accomplish, complete, comply, complement, compliment, completion, completive, deplete, implement, replete, repletion, supply, supplement, double, duple, quadruple, simplify, simplification, triple, treble, maniple, pleb, plebeian, plebiscite, plenty, plenary, plenitude, plentitude, plenitudine, replenish, plus, plural, plurality (**Eng**);

dubbel (**Dut**); doppelt, Plural (**Ger**); plus (**Swe**); supplere (**Dan**); plebbi (**Ice**); plwyf (**Wel**); πληβείος (pliveíos), πληβεία (pliveía) (**Gk**)

Hellenic: πλῆτο (plêto), πολύς (polús), πίμπλημι (pímplēmi), πληθῦς (plēthūs), πλέως (pléōs), πλήρης (plérēs), πλήθω (pléthō), -πλόος (-plóos) (**AnGk**); πλήρης (plíris), πληροφορία (pliroforía) (**Gk**)

Derivatives: plethora, pleroma, plethysm, poly- (**Eng**); poly- (**Fr**)

Slavic: полный (pólnyj) (**Rus**); pełny (**Pol**); plný (**Cz**); plný (**Slo**); полн (poln) (**Mace**)

Baltic: pìlnas (**Lith**); pilns, pilēt, pildīt (**Latv**)

Albanian: plot, plotë (**Alb**)

Indo-Iranian: पिपर्ति (piparti), पृणाति (pṛnāti), पुरु (puru), प्रात् (prāt), पूर्ण (pūrṇá), पूर्णिमा (pūrṇimā) (**Sans**); पूरा (pūrā), पूर्ण (pūrṇ), पूरा (pūrā) (**Hin**); پر (porl) (**Pers**)

Perhaps:

Italic: populus, populātiō, populāris, publicus, pūblica, rēspūblica (**Lat**); peuple, population, populaire, public, république (**Fr**); popolo, popolazione, popolare, pubblico, repubblica (**Ital**); pueblo, población, popular, publico, república (**Sp**); povo, população, povoação, popular, público, república (**Port**); popor, populație, popular, public, republică (**Rom**)

Derivatives: people, pueblo, population, popular, populous, public, republic (**Eng**); republiek (**Dut**); Respublica, Republik (**Ger**); republik (**Swe**); pobl (**Wel**); pobal (**Iri**); популяция (populjacija), публика (públika), республика (respublika) (**Rus**); republika (**Slo**); публика (publika) (**Mace**); popull, pukë (**Alb**)

*ǵʰew-
to pour, libate

see Object motion

*sīw-

to sew

Germanic: sew, seam (**Eng**); sēowan, sēam (**OE**); seam (**Fris**); zoom (**Dut**); Saum (**Ger**); sýja, saumr (**Norse**); sy, søm (**Nor**); sy, söm (**Swe**); sy, søm (**Dan**); sauma, saumur (**Ice**)

Italic: suere, cōnsuere, insuere, insubulum, sūbula, sūtilis, sūtor, sūtōrius, sutura (**Lat**); coudre, ensouple, subule, suturer, suture (**Fr**); cucire, subbio, subbia, sutura (**Ital**); coser, enjulio, ensullo, subilla, sutorio, sutura (**Sp**); coser, sovela, sútil, sutura (**Port**); coase, coasere, sul (**Rom**)

Derivatives: couture, souter, sutorial, sutorian, sutorious, suture (**Eng**); Schuster (**Ger**); σούβλα (soúvla) (**Gk**)

Hellenic: ὑμήν (humḗn) (**AnGk**)

Derivatives: hymen, hymenium, hymenomycete, hymenophore, Hymenoptera (**Eng**)

Slavic: шить (šit'), шило (šilo) (**Rus**); szyć (**Pol**); šít, šídlo (**Cz**); šiť (**Slo**); шие (šíe) (**Mace**)

Baltic: siūti (**Lith**); šūt (**Latv**)

Indo-Iranian: सीव्यति (sīvyati), सूत्र (sūtra), स्यूमन् (syūman) (**Sans**); सीना (sīnā) (**Hin**)

*(s)neh₁-
to spin (thread), to sew

see Reptiles

*ser-
to bind together, thread

see Terrain

*webh-
to weave, braid

see Insects

*wes-
to clothe, wear clothes

*wés-tor, *wes-néw-, *wos-éye-ti, *wés-m̥h₁nos, *wés-mn̥, *wés-tis, *wés-tro-

Germanic: wear (**Eng**); werian (**OE**); verja (**Norse**); gangverja (**Nor**); verja (**Ice**)

Celtic: gwisg (**Wel**)

Italic: vestis, vestīre, investīre, vestīmentum, vestītus (**Lat**); vêtir, investir, vêtement (**Fr**); vestire, investire, vestimento, vestito (**Ital**); vestir, investir, envestir, embestir, vestimento, vestido (**Sp**); vestir, investir, vestem, vestido (**Port**); învește, învești, veșmânt (**Rom**)

Derivatives: vest, vestment, divest, invest, investiture, travesty (**Eng**)

Hellenic: εἷμα (heîma), εἵμαι (eímai), ἕσσαι (éssai), ἕννυμι (hénnumi), εἵματα (heímata), εἱμένος (heiménos) (**AnGk**)

Albanian: vesh (**Alb**)

Indo-Iranian: वस्ते (váste), वासयति (vāsáyati), वासयते (vāsáyate), वस्मन् (vásman), वस्त्र (vastra) (**Sans**); वस्त्र (vastra) (**Hin**); واستر (vāstar) (**Pers**)

*pekʷ-
to cook, ripen

*pokʷtós, *pékʷ-e-ti, *pékʷ-ye-ti, *pékʷ-mn̥, *pékʷ-tis, *pkʷtér, *pókʷ-o-s

Celtic: poeth (**Wel**

Italic: coquere, coctilis, coctus, coquīna, coquus (**Lat**); cuire, cuit, biscuit, cuisine, queux, cuisinier, cuisiner (**Fr**); cuocere, cotto, biscotto, cucina, cuoco, cucinario, cucinare (**Ital**); cocer, bizcocho, cochura, cocina, cocinero, coquinario, cocinar (**Sp**); cozer, cozinha, cozinheiro, cozinhar (**Port**); coace, coacere, copt, coptură (**Rom**)

Derivatives: cook, coctile, quittor, cuisine, kitchen (**Eng**); koken, keuken, kok (**Dut**); kochen, Küche, Koch (**Ger**); koke (**Nor**); koka (**Swe**); kokka (**Ice**); coginio, cegin (**Wel**); ку́хня (kúxnja), кок (kok) (**Rus**); kuq, kuzhinë (**Alb**)

Hellenic: πέσσω (péssō), πέπτω (péttō), πέπτω (péptō), πέπων (pépōn), δύσπεπτος (dúspeptos), πέμμᾰ (pémma), πέψῐς (pépsis), πέπτρια (péptria), ἀρτοκόπος (artokópos) (**AnGk**)

Derivatives: dyspepsia, pepsin, peptic, peptide, pumpkin (**Eng**)

Slavic: печь (peč'), пот (pot) (**Rus**); piec, pot (**Pol**); péci, péct, pot (**Cz**); piecť, pot (**Slo**); пече (peče), пот (pot) (**Mace**)

Baltic: kèpti (**Lith**); cept (**Latv**)

Albanian: pjek (**Alb**)

Indo-Iranian: पच् (pac), पचति (pacati), पच्यते (pácyate), पक्ति (paktí), पक्तृ (paktŕ̥) (**Sans**); पकाना (pakānā) (**Hin**); پختن (poxtan) (**Pers**)

*dʰeyǵʰ-

to knead, form, shape

*dʰéyǵʰ-ti, *dʰi-né-ǵʰ-ti, *dʰéyǵʰ-o-s, *dʰéyǵʰ-os, *dʰiǵʰ-tós, *dʰóyǵʰ-o-s, *dʰoyǵʰ-yeh$_2$

Germanic: dough, duff (dial.) (**Eng**); dāg, dāh (**OE**); daai (**Fris**); deeg (**Dut**); Teig (**Ger**); deigr, deig, digr (**Norse**); deig (**Nor**); deg, diger (**Swe**); dej, deg (**Dan**); deigur (**Ice**)

Celtic: dingid (**Iri**)

Italic: fingere, effingere, effigiēs, fictus, figūra (**Lat**); feindre, effigie, feint, fictif, figmentum, figure (**Fr**); fingere, effingere, effigie, finto, fittizio, figura (**Ital**); fingir, heñir, efigie, figura (**Sp**); fingir, finta, fita, ficto, figura (**Port**); figură (**Rom**)

Derivatives: feign, fiction, fictive, fictitious, effigy, figment, figure, configure, disfigure, figurine, transfigure (**Eng**); veinzen, fingeren, figuur (**Dut**); fingieren, Figur (**Ger**); figur (**Swe**); fingere (**Dan**); fíor (**Iri**); фигура (figura) (**Rus**); figura (**Pol**); figura (**Cz**)

Hellenic: θιγγάνω (thingánō), παράδεισος (parádeisos), τεῖχος (teîkhos) (**AnGk**); παράδεισος (parádeisos), τείχος (teíchos), τοῖχος (toîkhos), τοίχος (toíchos) (**Gk**)

Derivatives: paradise (**Eng**); paradīsus (**Lat**); parvis, paradis (**Fr**); paradiso (**Ital**); paraíso (**Sp**); paraíso (**Port**); paradis (**Rom**); Paradies (**Ger**); paradwys (**Wel**)

Slavic: де́жа́ (déžá) (**Rus**); dzieża (**Pol**); díže, díž, díža, zeď (uncert.) (**Cz**); dieža (**Slo**); зид (dzid) (uncert.) (**Mace**)

Indo-Iranian: देग्धि (degdhi), देह (deha), देही (dehī), दिग्ध (digdhá) (**Sans**); देह (deh) (**Hin**); دژ (dež), پالیز (pâlêz), پردیس (pardês) (**Pers**)

*melh₂-
to grind, to crush

see Farming

*peys-
to grind, crush

see Farming

*leyp-
to stick; fat or sticky substance

see Body: Torso & Organs

*bʰrewh₁-
to boil, brew

*bʰrewh₁-, *bʰréh₁wr̥, *bʰrowh₁-tó-, *bʰru-to-, *bʰru-tus

Germanic: brew, broth, burn, bourn, bren, brending (**Eng**); brēowan, broþ, brunna, biernan, byrnan, bærnan (**OE**);

brouwe, bearne, boarne, baarne, barne (**Fris**); brouwen, brodium, bron, born, branden (**Dut**); brauen, Brod, Born, Brunne, Brunnen, Brunn, brinnen, brennan (**Ger**);

broð, brunnr, brinna, brenna (**Norse**); brygge, bryggja, brønn, brenne (**Nor**); brygga, brunn, brinna, bränna (**Swe**); brygge, brønd, brænde (**Dan**); brugga, broð, brunnur, brenna (**Ice**)

Derivatives: brodium (**Lat**); brouet (**Fr**); brodo (**Ital**); brodio, bodrio (**Sp**); bódrio (**Port**)

Celtic: brwd (**Wel**); bruth (**Iri**)

Italic: dēfrutum, dēfritum (**Lat**)

Hellenic: φρέᾱρ (phréār), φρεῖᾱρ (phreîar) (**AnGk**); φρέαρ (fréar) (**Gk**)

Indo-Iranian: भुर्वन् (bhúrvan) (**Sans**)

*yes-
to foam, to boil

*yés-e-ti, *yós-e-ti, *yos-éye-ti, *yós-eye-ti, *yés-tu-s, *yēs-éh$_2$

Germanic: yeast (**Eng**); ġist, ġiest, ġyst (**OE**); gêst (**Fris**); gist (**Dut**); jesen, gesen, jäsen, gären, Gäscht, Gischt (**Ger**); jǫstr, œsa (**Norse**); øse (**Nor**); jäsa, jäst (**Swe**); gære (**Dan**); jöstur, æsa (**Ice**)

Celtic: ias (**Wel**)

Hellenic: ζέω (zéō), ζεστός (zestós), ζύμη (zúmē) (**AnGk**); ζύμη (zúmē) (**Gk**)

Derivatives: eczema (**Eng**)

Indo-Iranian: यसति (yásati), यासयति (yāsayati) (**Sans**); جوشیدن (jūšīdan) (**Pers**)

*h₃reyH-
to boil, churn

*h$_3$ri-né-H-ti, *h$_3$riH-yé-ti, *h$_3$riH-mó-s, *h$_3$riH-nó-s, *h$_3$riH-wó-s, *h$_3$royH-e-ti?, *h$_3$royH-ko-, *h$_3$royH-o-

Germanic: rin, run (**Eng**); rinnan, irnan, iernan (**OE**); rinne (**Fris**); rennen, geronnen (**Dut**); rinnen, rennen (**Ger**); rinna, renna (**Norse**); renne (**Nor**); rinna (**Swe**); rinde (**Dan**); renna (**Ice**)

Celtic: rian (**Iri**)

Derivatives: Rhine (**Eng**)

Italic: rīvus, dērīvāre, rīvālis, rīvālitās, rīvulus (**Lat**); ru, rivalité, ruisseau (**Fr**); rio, rivo, rivalità, rivolo, ruscello (**Ital**); río, derivar, rivalidad (**Sp**); rio, derivar, rivalidade (**Port**); râu, rivalitate (**Rom**)

Derivatives: derive, rival (**Eng**)

Slavic: ри́нуть (rínut′), ри́нуться (rínut′sja), ре́ять (réjat′), пека́ (reká), pôj (rôj) (**Rus**); rzeka, rój (**Pol**); řinout se, řeka, roj (**Cz**); rinúť sa, rieka, roj, rôj (**Slo**); рине (rine), река (reka) (**Mace**)

Baltic: raĩdît (**Latv**)

Indo-Iranian: रिणाति (riṇāti), रीयते (rīyate), रय (raya) (poss.) (**Sans**)

But it may be that the Germanic and some of the Slavic words are instead from *h$_3$er-:

*h₃er-

to move, stir; to rise, spring

*h₃ér-t, *h₃i-h₃ér-ti, *h₃ŗ-néw-ti, *h₃ér-os

Germanic: rin, run (**Eng**); rinnan, irnan, iernan (**OE**); rinne (**Fris**); rennen, geronnen (**Dut**); rinnen, rennen (**Ger**); rinna, renna (**Norse**); renne (**Nor**); rinna (**Swe**); rinde (**Dan**); renna (**Ice**)

Italic: orīrī, aborīrī, abortiō, abortīvum, abortāre, oriēns, orientālis, orīgō, orīginālis, orīginārius, oriundus, ortus (**Lat**);

abortif, orient, oriental, origine, original, originel, originaire (**Fr**);

abortivo, aborto, oriente, orientale, origine, originale, originario, oriundo (**Ital**);

aborto, oriente, oriental, origen, originario, oriundo, orto (**Sp**);

abortivo, aborto, abort, oriente, oriental, origem, originário, oriundo (**Port**);

urca, orient, oriental, origine (**Rom**)

Derivatives: aboriginal, Aborigine, abort, abortion, abortive, orient, oriental, orientation, disorient, disorientation, origin, original, originality, originary, originate, reorient, reorientation (**Eng**);

original (**Ger**); abort (**Nor**); abort, origo (**Swe**); abort (**Dan**); аборт (abórt) (**Rus**); aborts (**Latv**)

Hellenic: ὦρτο (ôrto), ὄρνῡμι (órnūmi), ὄρος (óros), ὀρίνω (orínō), ὄρμενος (órmenos) (**AnGk**); όρος (óros) (**Gk**)

Derivatives: oro-, orogenesis, orogeny, orogenic, orogenous, orography, oroheliograph, orology, orometer, oronym, oronymy, orophyte (**Eng**); oro- (**Ital**)

Slavic: ри́нуть (rínut'), ри́нуться (rínut'sja), пека́ (reká) (**Rus**); rzeka (**Pol**); řinout se, řeka (**Cz**); rinúť sa, rieka (**Slo**); рине (rine), река (reka) (**Mace**)

Indo-Iranian: आर्त (ārta), इयर्ति (íyarti), ऋणोति (ṛṇoti) (**Sans**)

Tools

*bak-

staff

Germanic: peg (**Eng**); peg (dial.) (**Dut**); pigg (**Swe**)

Celtic: bach (**Wel**); bac (**Iri**)

Italic: baculum, bacillum, imbēcillus (**Lat**); bâcle, imbécile (**Fr**); abbacchio, bacchio, bacolo, imbecille (**Ital**); báculo (**Sp**); báculo, imbecil (**Port**)

Derivatives: baculum, baculiform, imbecile (**Eng**)

Hellenic: βάκτρον (báktron), βακτηρία (baktēría) (**AnGk**)

Derivatives: bacteria (**Eng**)

Baltic: baksteléti (**Lith**); bakstit (**Latv**)

*h₂erkʷo-
bow

Germanic: arrow (**Eng**); earh, arwe (**OE**); ǫr, ǫrvar (**Norse**); ör, ǫrvar (**Ice**)

Italic: arcus, arcuātus (**Lat**); arc, arçon (**Fr**); arco, arcione, arcobaleno (**Ital**); arco, arzón, arcuado (**Sp**); arco, arção (**Port**); arc, curcubeu (**Rom**)

Derivatives: arc, arch, arcuate, arcade (**Eng**); áрка (árka) (**Rus**)

Albanian: hark (**Alb**)

*h₂erk-
to hold

*h₂érk-ti, *h₂ork-éye-ti, *h₂po-h₂ork-éye-ti, *h₂po?-h₂érk-e-ti, *h₂érk-os, *h₂erk-es-eh₂ *h₂erk-s, *h₂erk-eh₂

Germanic: fergja (**Nor**); fergja (**Ice**)

Italic: arcēre, coercēre, coercitiō, exercēre, exercitium, exercitus, porcēre, parcere, parcimōnia, arx, arcera, arca, arcārius, arcella, arcula, arcānus (**Lat**);

coercition, exercer, exercice, parcimonie, arche (**Fr**); esercire, esercizio, esercito, parco, parsimonia, arca (**Ital**); coerción, ejercer, ejercicio, ejército, parco, parsimonia, arca, arcano (**Sp**); exercício, exército, parco, parcimónia, arca, arcano (**Port**)

Derivatives: coerce, coercion, exercise, parsimony, ark, arcane (**Eng**); ǫrk (**Norse**); ark (**Nor**); áirc (**Iri**); άρκλα (árkla) (**Gk**)

Hellenic: ἄρκος (árkos), ἀρκέω (arkéō) (**AnGk**)

Albanian: arkë (**Alb**)

*seǵʰ-
to hold; to overpower

*séǵʰ-e-ti, *si-séǵʰ-ti, *soǵʰ-éye-ti, *séǵʰ-os, *si-sǵʰ-u-s, *séǵʰ-ti-s, *séǵʰ-ti-ḱo-s, *sǵʰ-éh₁?-ti-s, *sǵʰ-éh₁-mn̥, *seǵʰ-u-ro-s, *sǵʰ-h₁-do-m, *sǵʰ-h₁-ro-s, *sǵʰ-h₃-leh₂, *sóǵʰ-o-s, *séǵʰ-tōr, *seǵʰ-h₁-tleh₂

Germanic: sig (obs.) (**Eng**); sigor (**OE**); sege (**Fris**); zege (**Dut**); Sieg (**Ger**); sigr, sigra (**Norse**); seier, seire (**Nor**); seger, segra (**Swe**); sejr, sejre (**Dan**); sigur, sigra (**Ice**)

Hellenic: ἔχω (ékhō), ἐπέχω (epékhō), ἐποχή (epokhḗ), ἴσχω (ískhō), ὀχέω (okhéō), ἰσχύς (iskhús), ἕξις (héxis), ἑκτικός (hektikós), σχέσις (skhésis), σχῆμα (skhêma), ἐχυρός (ekhurós), ὀχυρός (okhurós), σχεδόν (skhedón), σχερός (skherós), σχολή (skholḗ), ὄχος (ókhos), Ἕκτωρ (Héktōr), ἐχέτλη (ekhétlē) (**AnGk**); εποχή (epochí), ισχύς (ischýs), έξη (éxi), σχήμα (schíma), σχεδόν (schedón), σχολή (scholí) (**Gk**)

Derivatives: epoch, schema, scheme, school (**Eng**); scōl (**OE**); school (**Dut**); Schema, Schule (**Ger**); skole (**Nor**); skola (**Swe**); skole (**Dan**); skóli (**Ice**); ysgol (**Wel**); scoil (**Iri**);

epocha, schēma, schola (**Lat**); époque, schéma, école (**Fr**); epoca, schema, scuola (**Ital**); época, esquema, escuela (**Sp**); época, esquema, escola (**Port**); epocă, școală (**Rom**);

cхéма (sxéma), шкóла (škóla) (**Rus**); szkoła (**Pol**); epocha, škola (**Cz**); škola (**Slo**); шкóла (škóla) (**Mace**); shkollë (**Alb**); स्कूल (skūl) (**Hin**)

Indo-Iranian: सहते (sáhate), साहयति (sāhayati), सहस् (sáhas), साढ़ (sāḍhṛ) (**Sans**)

*gʰed-
to find; to hold

See Cognitive function

*mak-
pouch

Germanic: maw (**Eng**); maga (**OE**); mage (**Fris**); maag (**Dut**); Magen (**Ger**); magi (**Norse**); mage (**Nor**); mage (**Swe**); mave (**Dan**); maga (**Ice**)

Celtic: megin (**Wel**)

Slavic: мошна (mošná) (arch.) (**Rus**)

Baltic: maišas (**Lith**); maks (**Latv**)

*h₂éḱ-mō
stone

Germanic: hammer (**Eng**); hamer (**OE**); hammer (**Fris**); hamer (**Dut**); Hammer (**Ger**); hamarr (**Norse**); hammer (**Nor**); hammare, hammar (**Swe**); hammer (**Dan**); hamar (**Ice**)

Hellenic: ἄκμων (ákmōn) (**AnGk**); ἄκμων (ákmon), ἄκμονας (ákmonas) (**Gk**)

Slavic: камень (kámen') (**Rus**); kamień (**Pol**); kámen (**Cz**); kameň (**Slo**); камен (kamen) (**Mace**)

Baltic: akmuo, ašmuo, ašmenys (**Lith**); akmens, asmens (**Latv**)

Indo-Iranian: अश्मन् (aśman) (**Sans**); آسمان (âsemân) (**Pers**)

which derives from *h₂éḱ sharp:

*h₂éḱ

sharp

*h₂eḱ-éh₁-ye-ti, *h₂eḱ-u-, *h₂eḱ-i-, *h₂eḱ-l-, *h₂oḱ-yeh₂, *h₂ḱ-eh₂, *h₂ḱ-meh₂, *h₂éḱ-mō ~ *h₂ḱ-mn-és, *h₂oḱ-et-eh₂, *h₂óḱ-ri-s, *h₂ḱ-ró-s, *h₂eḱ-stu-

Germanic: edge (**Eng**); eċġ (**OE**); igge (**Fris**); egge, eg (**Dut**); Ecke, Egge (**Ger**); egg (**Norse**); egg (**Nor**); egg, ägg (**Swe**); æg (**Dan**); egg (**Ice**)

Celtic: oged, ochr (**Wel**); achar (**Iri**)

Italic: acēre, acidus, aciditās, acus, acia, acuārius, aculeus, acuere, aciēs, occa, ocris, mediocris, mediocritās, ācer, acerbus, acerbitās, acerbāre, exacerbāre, acervus, ācrimōnia, ācritās, ācritūdō, astus, astūtus, astūtia (**Lat**);

acide, aiguille, églantier, acier, médiocrité, aigre, âcre, acerbe, exacerber, acrimonie, âcreté, astuce (**Fr**);

acido, ago, accia, aculeo, acciaio, mediocrità, acre, agro, acerbo, esacerbare, acrimonia, astuzia (**Ital**);

ácido, aguijón, acúleo, haz, acero, mediocre, mediocridad, agre, agrio, agro, acerbo, acerba, acerbidad, exacerbar, acervo, acrimonia, acritud, astucia (**Sp**);

ácido, acididade, acúleo, az, ácie, aceiro, aço, medíocre, agre, acre, acerbo, acerbidade, exacerbar, acervo, acrimônia, acridade, acritude, astuto (**Port**);

acid, ac, aţă, acar, aculeu, acru, acerb (**Rom**)

Derivatives: acid, acidity, acupuncture, aculeus, mediocre, mediocrity, acrid, acerb, acerbic, acerbity, acerbate, exacerbate, acrimony, acrimonious, acrity, acritude, astute (**Eng**); acido (**Dan**)

Hellenic: ἀκή (aké), ἀκμή (akmḗ), ὄκρις (ókris), ὀκρῖς (okrís), ἄκρος (ákros), ὀξύς (oxús), ὀξεῖᾰ (oxeîa), ὀξῠτονος (oxútonos) (**AnGk**); ακμή (akmí), ὀκρῖς (okrís), άκρος (ákros), οξύς (oxýs), οξύτονος (oxýtonos) (**Gk**)

Derivatives: acme, oxygen, oxy-, oxia, oxytone (**Eng**); acmé, oxygène, oxyton (**Fr**)

Slavic: оселок (oselók), осѣть (osét'), óстрый (óstryj) (**Rus**); osełka, jesieć (dial.), osieć (dial.), jesiótka (dial.), osiótka (dial.), ostry (**Pol**); ostrý (**Cz**); osla, ostrý (**Slo**); остар (ostar) (**Mace**)

Baltic: akéčios, ekéčios, ašrùs, aštrùs (Lith); ass, aš, ecêšas, ecêkšas, astrs (Latv)

Albanian: ath, eh, thua (Alb)

Indo-Iranian: अश्रि (áśri) (Sans); چاڑ (āčār) (Pers)

from which also derives *h₂ḱh₂owsyéti (to be sharp-eared) (see Cognitive function)

it also probably includes:

Germanic: axe (Eng); æx (OE); aks, akst (Dut); Axt (Ger); øx (Norse); øks (Nor); økse (Dan); öxi (Ice)

Italic: ascia (Lat); ascia (Ital); aja, azada, azuela (Sp); archa, enxada (Port)

Hellenic: ἀξῑ́νη (axīnē) (AnGk)

Albanian: sakice (Alb)

*gʷrh₂-n-uH-
millstone

see Basic Adjectives

*h₂enk-
angle, curve, bend

*h₂énk-ti, *h₂enk-os, *h₂énk-os, *h₂ónk-os, *h₂énk-ō, *h₂enk-ul-os, *h₂enk-ul-eh₂

this etymology is somewhat confused

Germanic: angle, ankle (Eng); angul, ongul, angel, ongel, anclēow (OE); angel, ankel (Fris); angel, enkel, enklauw (Dut); Ange (dial.), Angel, Enkel (Ger); angi, ǫ́ll, áll, ǫ́l, ál, ǫngull, ekkja (Norse); ankel (Nor); angel, ankel (Swe); ankel (Dan); öngull, ekkja (Ice)

Celtic: anghad, crafanc (Wel)

Italic: uncus, aduncus, uncīnus, uncīnātus, ungulus, angulus, angulāris, quādrangulus, triangulus, triangulum (Lat); angle, angulaire, triangle (Fr); adunco, uncino, angolo, angolare, triangolo (Ital); adunco, uncino, ángulo, angular, triángulo (Sp); adunco, ancinho, ângulo, angular, triângulo (Port); adânc, unghi, triunghi (Rom)

Derivatives: adunc, aduncity, aduncous, unciform, Uncinaria, Uncinia, uncinus, uncinate, angle, angular, quadrangle, triangle (Eng); ongl (Wel)

Hellenic: ἄγκος (ánkos), ὄγκος (ónkos), ὄγκη (ónkē), ἀγκών (ankṓn), ἀγκύλος (ankúlos), ἀγκύλη (ankúlē) (AnGk); όγκος (ógkos) (Gk)

Slavic: угол (úgol) (Rus)

Baltic: ánka (Lith); añka, ākis (Latv)

Perhaps: **Albanian:** anoj (**Alb**)

Indo-Iranian: अङ्क (aṅká), अङ्कस् (áṅkas), अचति (ácati), अञ्चति (áñcati), अङ्गुरि (aṅgúri) (**Sans**)

*keg-
hook

Germanic: hake, hook, hockey (**Eng**); haca, hōc (**OE**); heak, hoeke, hoek (**Fris**); haak, hoek (**Dut**); Haken (**Ger**); haki, hǫnk, hœkja (**Norse**); hake, huk (**Swe**); hage, huk (**Dan**); haki, hækja (**Ice**)

Derivatives: hoquet (**Fr**); гáчек (gáček) (**Rus**); hák, háček (**Cz**)

Slavic: коготь (kógot') (**Rus**)

Baltic: kengė (**Lith**)

Indo-Iranian: چنگ (čang) (**Pers**)

*spey-
sharp point, stick

see Body: Limbs & Joints

*kʷel-
wheel, circle; to turn, rotate

*kʷél-e-ti, *kʷél-ye-ti, *kʷól-o-s, *kʷé-kʷl-o-s, *kʷél-os, *kʷel-es-ye-ti, *kʷól-os, *kʷol-so-m, *kʷl̥-tó-s

Germanic: wheel (**Eng**); hwēol (**OE**); fjil, tsjil, wiele (**Fris**); wiel (**Dut**); Wiele (in compounds) (**Ger**); hjól (**Norse**); hjul (**Nor**); hjul (**Swe**); hjul (**Dan**); hjól (**Ice**)

Celtic: ymochel, dymchwel, bochel (**Wel**)

Italic: colere, -cola, colōnus, colōnia, cultūra, cultus, cultor, incola, inquilīnus, percōlere, colus (**Lat**);

cultiver, colon, colonie, culture, inquilin, percoler (**Fr**); coltivare, colono, colonia, colto, inquilino, percolare (**Ital**);

cultivar, -cola, colono, colonia, cultura, culto, incola, inquilino, cultor (**Sp**); colono, colônia, colónia, cultura, cultor, incola, inquilino, percolar (**Port**); colonie (**Rom**)

Derivatives: culture, agriculture, acculturate, colonial, colony, cult, cultivate, incult, inquiline, percolate (**Eng**); Kultur (**Ger**); колóния (kolónija), культýра (kul'túra) (**Rus**)

Hellenic: πέλω (pélō), τέλλω (téllō), πόλος (pólos), κύκλος (kúklos), τελέω (teléō), τέλεσμα (télesma), τῆλε (têle), πάλαι (pálai), πάλιν (pálin) (**AnGk**); πόλος (pólos) (**Gk**)

Derivatives: talisman, telegram, telepathy, telemetry, telegraph, telephone, telescope, television, atelophobia, teleology, telesis, toll (**Eng**); cyclus (**Dut**); syklus, sykkel (**Nor**); cykel (**Swe**); cyclus (**Lat**); cycle (**Fr**); ciclo (**Ital**); ciclo (**Sp**); ciclo (**Port**); цикл (cikl) (**Rus**)

Slavic: колеcó (kolesó) (**Rus**); koło (**Pol**); kolo (**Cz**); kolo, koleso (**Slo**); кóло (kólo) (**Mace**)

Baltic: kāklas (**Lith**); kakls (**Latv**)

Albanian: sjell (**Alb**)

Indo-Iranian: चरति (carati), चक्र (cakrá) (**Sans**); चक्र (cakra) (**Hin**); چرخ (čarx) (**Pers**)

Derivatives: chakra (**Eng**)

but many languages derive their words for wheel from *Hret- to roll:

*Hret-
to roll

*Hrét-e-ti, *Hrot-éye-ti, *Hrót-o-s, *Hrót-eh$_2$, *Hrót-h$_2$-os

Germanic: rodur (**OE**); rêd (**Fris**); rad (**Dut**); Rad (**Ger**); rǫðull (**Norse**); ratt (**Nor**); ratt (**Swe**); rat (**Dan**); rǫðull (**Ice**)

Celtic: rhedeg, rhod (**Wel**); rith, roth (**Iri**)

Italic: rota, rotātiō, rotella, rotāre, rotula, rotulare, birotus, rotundus, rotulus (**Lat**);

roue, rotation, rouelle, rouer, rôder, rôle, rotule, rond, rotonde (**Fr**);

ruota, rotazione, rotella, rotare, ruotare, rotula, baroccio, rotondo, tondo, ritondo, rocchio, rollo, rotolo (**Ital**);

rueda, rotación, rodilla, rodar, rotar, rolla, rondala, rótula, rol, redondo, rotundo, rótulo, rollo, ruejo, rundel, rol, arrollar, desarrollar (**Sp**);

roda, rotação, rodela, rodar, rotar, rolha, rótula, birrota, redondo, rotundo, rolo, rótulo (**Port**);

roată, rotaţie, rotund, rătund (**Rom**)

Derivatives: rota, rotary, rotate, rotation, rotator, rotor, rowel, control, enrol, rodeo, role, roll, rondeau, rotavirus, rotifer, rotund, rotunda, roulette, round, roundel, barouche (**Eng**); roteren, rond (**Dut**); rund, Rolle (**Ger**); ротация (rotacija) (**Rus**)

Baltic: rātas (**Lith**); rats (**Latv**)

Albanian: rrotë, rreth, rrath (**Alb**)

Indo-Iranian: रथ (ratha) (**Sans**)

*wert-

to turn, to rotate

*wért-ti, *wert-ye-, *we-wórt-e, *wort-éye-ti, *wért-tis, *wr̥t-is, *wért-mn̥

Germanic: worth, word (dial.), forworth, weird, wyrd, worthy, -ward, -wards (**Eng**); weorþan, forweorþan, wyrd, weorþ, weorþian, -weard, weardes (**OE**); wurde, woarst (poss.) (**Fris**); worden, verworden, worst (poss.), waard, -waarts (**Dut**); werden, Wurst (poss.), wert, Wert, -wärts (**Ger**); verða, urðr, verðr, verð, verða, -varðr (**Norse**); vart (past tense of bli), vorde (arch.) (**Nor**); varda, värd (**Swe**); vorde (arch.) (**Dan**); verða, urður (**Ice**)

Italic: vertere, advertere, animadvertere (animus+), āvertere, convertere, dīvertere, dīversus, ēvertere, ēversor, intervertere, invertere, obvertere, obversus, pervertere, revertī, subvertere, trānsvertere, versicolor, versiō, versāre, adversāre, adversus, conversāre, conversātiō, reversāre, subversāre, versātilis, versātus, versus, anniversārius (annus+), contrōversus, contrōversia, prōrsus, prōsa, ūniversus (unus+), versūtus, versūtia, vertebra, vertibilis, vertīgō, vertīginōsus, vortex/vertex (**Lat**);

convertir, divertir, divers, intervertir, invertir, pervertir, reverser, subvertir, version, verser, adverse, avers, versatile, vers, versus, anniversaire, controverse, prose, univers, vortex (**Fr**);

vertere, convertire, convergere, divertire, diverso, invertire, pervertire, riversare, rovesciare, versicolore, versione, versare, avverso, verso, versus, anniversario, controversia, prosa, universo, vertebra, vortice (**Ital**);

vertir, verter, advertir, convertir, divertir, diverso, divieso, intervertir, invertir, revertir, versión, versar, adverso, conversar, conversación, rebosar, revesar, versátil, aniversario, controversia, prosa, universo, vértebra, vórtice, vértice (**Sp**);

verter, advertir, converter, divertir, diverso, everter, eversor, inverter, versão, versar, vessar, adverso, conversar, conversa, conversação, reversar, revessar, versátil, versado, verso, versus, aniversário, controverso, controvérsia, prosa, universo, versuto, versúcia, vértebra, vertigem, vórtice, vórtex, vértice (**Port**);

învârti, versiune, vărsa, vărsare, conversație, revărsa, aniversar, aniversare, controversă, univers (**Rom**)

Derivatives: animadvert, avert, convert, divert, diverse, diversify, extrovert, introvert, invert, inverse, obvert, obverse, perverse, pervert, reverse, revert, subvert, transvert, transverse, version, versatile, adverse, adversity, advertise, converse, conversant, conversation, versus, anniversary, controversy, controversial, prose, universe, vertebra, vertibile, vertigo, vertiginous, vortex, vertex, vertical (**Eng**);

converteren (**Dut**); konvertieren, kontrovers, Kontroverse (**Ger**); universum (**Swe**); veirteabra (**Iri**); версия (versija) (**Rus**); kontrowersja (**Pol**); kontroverze (**Cz**); vërshoj (**Alb**)

Slavic: вороти́ть (vorotít'), вре́мя (vrémja), веретенó (veretenó), воро́та (voróta), врата́ (vratá), верте́ть (vertét') (**Rus**); wrócić, wrzemię (obs.), wrzeciono, wrota, wiercić

(Pol); vrátit, vřeteno, vrata, vrtět (Cz); vrátiť, vreteno, vráta, vrtieť (Slo); време (vreme), вретено (vreteno), врата (vrata), врти (vrti) (Mace)

Derivatives: vreme (Rom)

Baltic: versti (Lith)

Indo-Iranian: वर्त्ति (vártti), ववर्त (vavárta), वर्तयति (vartáyati), वर्त्मन् (vártman) (Sans); बाट (bāṭ) (Hin)

*welH-
to turn, to wind

Germanic: walk, waulk, well, wale, weal, wheal, welt, willow (Eng); wealcan, weallan, well, walu, wala, weliġ (OE); wylch (Fris); wortel (Dut); Walver, walzen, Wurzel (Ger); vǫlr (Norse); vol (Nor); val (dial.) (Swe); ol, vol (Dan); völur (Ice)

Derivatives: gaule (Fr)

Italic: vallum, intervallum, valva, volūmen, volūminōsus, volvere, advolvere, circumvolvere, convolvere, convolvulus, dēvolvere, dēvolūtiō, ēvolvere, ēvolūtiō, ēvolūtus, involvere, involūcrum, involūtus, revolvere, revolūtiō, volūbilis, volūbilitās, volūtāre, volūtus, voluta, vulva (Lat);

intervalle, volume, évoluer, évolution, involucre, involuté, révolution, volubile, volute, voûte (Fr);

vallo, intervallo, valva, volume, volgere, avvolgere, convolgere, convolvere, convolvolo, devolvere, evolvere, evoluzione, evoluto, involgere, involucro, involuto, involto, rivolgere, rivoluzione, volubile, voltare, volto, voluta, volta (Ital);

valla, intervalo, valva, volumen, volver, convólvulo, devolver, evolucionar, evolución, envolver, involucro, envuelto, revolver, revolución, voluble, alborotar, voltear, volcar, vuelto, voluta, bóveda, vuelta (Sp);

valo, vala, valva, volver, circunvolver, onvólvulo, devolver, evoluir, evolução, envolver, envolto, involuto, revolver, revolução, volúvel, volubilidade, voltar, voltear, volutar, volutear, abóbada (Port);

val, holba, evolua, evoluție, învoalbe, învolt, involut, revoluți, boltă, volutăe (Rom)

Derivatives: wall, intervallic, interval, valva, valve, volume, voluminous, advolution, circumvolute, circumvolve, convolute, convolution, convolve, convolvulus, devolve, devolution, evolve, evolution, involve, involucre, involucrum, involute, revolute, revolve, revolution, voluble, volubile, volubility, vault, volte, volute, vulva (Eng); weall (OE);

wal (Dut); Wall, Revolution (Ger); vall (Swe); vold (Dan); интервал (interval), эволюция (evoljucija), революция (revoljúcija) (Rus); wał, wolumen, rewolucja (Pol); vëllim (Alb)

Hellenic: ἐλύω (elúō), εἴλω (eílō), εἰλύω (eilúō), ἕλιξ (hélix), εἰλεός (eileós) (AnGk)

Derivatives: helix (**Eng**); helix (**Lat**)

Baltic: vél (**Lith**); vēl, velt (**Latv**)

Indo-Iranian: उल्ब (ulba) (**Sans**)

Possibly:

Italic: vallis (**Lat**); vallée, val, vallon (**Fr**); valle (**Ital**); valle (**Sp**); vale (**Port**); vale (**Rom**)

Derivatives: valley, vale (**Eng**); val (**Alb**)

*terh₁-
to rub, turn

See Construction & Production

Dwelling

*treb-
dwelling, settlement

Germanic: thorp, dorp, troop, tropel (**Eng**); þorp (**OE**); terp, doarp (**Fris**); dorp (**Dut**); Dorf (**Ger**); ðorp, þorp (**Norse**); torp (**Nor**); torp (**Swe**); torp (**Dan**); þorp, Þorpið (**Ice**)

Derivatives: troupe, trop, troupeau (**Fr**); truppa (**Ital**); tropa, tropel (**Sp**); tropa, tropel (**Port**)

Celtic: tref, tre (**Wel**); treabh (**Iri**)

Italic: trabs, taberna, contubernālis, contubernium, tabernāculum (**Lat**); travée, taverne, tabernacle (**Fr**); trave, taverna, tabernacolo (**Ital**); traba, taberna, tabernáculo (**Sp**); trave, taberna, taverna, contubernal, contubérnio, tabernáculo (**Port**); tavernă (**Rom**)

Derivatives: trave, tavern, tabernacle (**Eng**); tafarn (**Wel**); ταβέρνα (tavérna) (**Gk**)

Hellenic: τέρεμνον (téremnon) (**AnGk**)

Baltic: trobà (**Lith**); traba (**Latv**)

*dʰwer-
door

*dʰwốr, *dʰur-éh₂, *dʰwor-o-, *dʰwor-es-tus

Germanic: door (**Eng**); duru, dor (**OE**); doar (**Fris**); deur (**Dut**); Tür, Tor (**Ger**); dyrr

(Norse); dør (Nor); dörr (Swe); dør (Dan); dyr (Ice)

Celtic: dôr, drws (Wel); doras (Iri)

Italic: foris, forum, forēnsis (Lat); hors, dehors, for, forum, fur (Fr); fuori, foro, forense (Ital); fuera, foro (Sp); foro, fórum (Port); for (Rom)

Derivatives: forum, forensic (Eng); Forum (Ger); форум (fórum) (Rus)

Hellenic: θὔρδα (thúrda), θὐρα (thúra), θὔρᾱζε (thúrāze), θὔρεός (thureós), πᾰρᾰκλαυσῐθὔρον (paraklausíthuron) (AnGk); θὐρα (thýra), θυρεός (thyreós) (Gk)

Derivatives: thyroid, thyratron, paraklausithyron (Eng)

Slavic: дверь (dver'), двóр (dvór) (Rus); drzwi, dwór (Pol); dvůr, dveře (Cz); dvor, dvere (Slo); двер (dver), двор (dvor) (Mace)

Baltic: dùrys, dvãras (Lith); dùrvis, dvars (Latv)

Albanian: derë (Alb)

Indo-Iranian: द्वार् (dvār), द्वार (dvārah), द्वारा (dvārā), दुर (dúrah) (Sans); द्वारा (dvārā), द्वार (dvār) (Hin); ور (war) (Pash); در (dar) (Pers)

*pent-
path, road

*pént-e-ti, *pónt-h₁-s, *pónt-eh₁-s

Germanic: find, fand (Eng); findan, fandian (OE); fine (Fris); vinden, vanden (dial.) (Dut); finden, fahnden (Ger); finna, fyndr, fundr (Norse); finne, fund, faen, fanden (Nor); finna, fynd, fan (Swe); finde, fanden (Dan); finna, fundur (Ice)

Celtic: ffeindio (Wel); áit (Iri)

Italic: pōns, pontis, pontifex (Lat); pont, pontife (Fr); ponte (Ital); puente, pontifice (Sp); ponte, pontifice (Port); punte (Rom)

Derivatives: pontoon, pontiff (Eng); pont (Wel); понтифик (pontífik) (Rus)

Hellenic: πόντος (póntos), πάτος (pátos) (AnGk); πόντος (póntos), πάτος (pátos) (Gk)

Derivatives: peripatetic (Eng)

Slavic: путь (put'), пята (pjata), пятá (pjatá), пятка (pjátka) (Rus); pąć, pątnik, pięta (Pol); pouť, pata (Cz); púť, päta (Slo); пат (pat), пета (peta), петица (petica) (Mace)

Indo-Iranian: पन्था (panthāh), पथिन् (páthin) (Sans); ونده (pūnda'h) (Pash)

Derivatives: path (Eng); pæþ (OE); paad (Fris); pad (Dut); Pfad (Ger)

Mineral products

*h₂eyos
metal

Germanic: ore (**Eng**); ār (**OE**); ehern (**Ger**); eir (**Norse**); ärg (**Swe**); er, ir (**Dan**); eir (**Ice**)

Italic: aes, aēneus, aerāmen, aerūgō, aerūginōsus, aerārium (**Lat**); airain (**Fr**); rame, ruggine, rogna, rugginoso, erario (**Ital**); éneo, alambre, arambre, orín, roña, erúgine, eruginoso, roñoso (**Sp**); éneo, arame, aerugita, aeruginoso, eruginoso, erário (**Port**); aramă, rugină (**Rom**)

Derivatives: aeneous, aerugo, aerugite, æruginous, eruginous (**Eng**)

Indo-Iranian: अयस् (ayas) (**Sans**); آهن (âhan) (**Pers**)

*séh₂ls
salt

Germanic: salt, salten, silt (**Eng**); sealt, sealtan (**OE**); sâlt (**Fris**); zout, zouten, zult (**Dut**); Salz, salzen, gesalzen, Sulze, Sülze (**Ger**); salt, saltr, salta (**Norse**); salt, sylt (**Nor**); salt, salta, sylta, sylt (**Swe**); salt, salte, sylt (**Dan**); salt, saltur, salta (**Ice**)

Derivatives: silte (**Port**)

Celtic: halen, hâl (**Wel**); salann, sáile (**Iri**)

Italic: sāl, salīre (**Lat**); sel, saler, sauce (**Fr**); sale, salare, insalare, salso, salsa (**Ital**); sal, salar, salso (**Sp**); sal, salgar, salsa (**Port**); sare, săra, sărare (**Rom**)

Derivatives: saline, salinity, salary, sauce (**Eng**); saus (**Dut**); Soße (**Ger**); saus (**Nor**); sås (**Swe**); sovs (**Dan**); sos (**Rom**); σως (sos) (**Gk**); cóyc (sóus) (**Rus**); sos (**Pol**)

Hellenic: ἅλς (háls) (**AnGk**); αλάτι (aláti) (**Gk**)

Derivatives: haline, halide, halite, halochromic, halogen, halomancy, halophyte, oxohalide, thermohaline (**Eng**)

Slavic: соль (so') , сладкий (sládkij) (**Rus**); sól, słodki (**Pol**); sůl, sladký (**Cz**); soľ, sladký (**Slo**); сол (sol), сладок (sladok) (**Mace**)

Baltic: saldus, sálti (**Lith**); sāļš, salds (**Latv**)

Albanian: ngjelmët, shëllij, gjelbson (**Alb**)

Indo-Iranian: सलिल (salila) (**Sans**)

Farming

*ǵʰer-
to enclose

gʰr̥dʰ-yé-ti, ǵʰor-tós, *ǵʰor-yo, *gʰórdʰ-os, *gʰr̥dʰ-ós, *gʰerdʰ-eh₂, *gʰr̥dʰ-el-os

Germanic: yard, garden, garth, girth, kindergarten, gird, girdle (**Eng**); ġeard, gyrdan, gyrdel (**OE**);

gurdzja, gurdle (**Fris**); gaard, gaarde, gorden, gordel (**Dut**); Garten, gürten, Gürtel (**Ger**);

garðr, gjǫrð, gyrða, gyrðill (**Norse**); gard, gård, garde, gjord (**Nor**); gård, gjord, omgjorda, gördel (**Swe**); gård, gårde (dial.), gjord, gjorde (**Dan**); garður, garði, gjörð (**Ice**)

Derivatives: hangar, jardin (**Fr**); hangar (**Eng**); giardino (**Ital**); jardín (**Sp**); jardim (**Port**)

Celtic: garth (**Wel**); gort (**Iri**)

Italic: hortus, hortulānus, cohors/cors, concors, concordia (**Lat**); cohorte, cour, concorde (**Fr**); orto, coorte, corte, concordia (**Ital**); huerto, huerta, cohorte, corte, concordia (**Sp**); horto, horta, hortelão, coorte, corte (**Port**); cohortă, curte (**Rom**)

Derivatives: horticulture, antecourt, cohort, cortege, court, courteous, courtesan, courtesy, coutier, curtain, curtilage, Curtis (**Eng**); когóрта (kogórta) (**Rus**)

Hellenic: χόρτος (khórtos), χόριον (khórion) (**AnGk**)

Slavic: гóрод (górod) (**Rus**); gród (**Pol**); hrad (**Cz**); hrad (**Slo**); град (grad) (**Mace**)

Baltic: gar̃das (**Lith**); gārds (**Latv**)

Albanian: gardh (**Alb**)

Indo-Iranian: गृह (gr̥há) (**Sans**); کرت (kart) (**Pers**)

*weyk-
to contain, envelop; yield; overcome

see Social

*h₂éǵros
field

see Object motion

*H₂erH₃-
to plough

*h₂ér-ye-ti, *h₂érh₃-tro-m, *h₂erh₃wós

Germanic: ear (dial.), ard (**Eng**); erian (**OE**); erja, arðr (**Norse**); ard (**Nor**); ärja, årder (**Swe**); ærje, ard (**Dan**); erja (**Ice**)

Celtic: aredig/arddaf, arddu, aradr (**Wel**); air (**Iri**)

Italic: arāre, arabilis, arātor, aratorius, arātrum (**Lat**); arable, araire (**Fr**); arare, aratro, arabile, aratore, aratorio (**Ital**); arar, arado, aradro, arable, arador, aratorio (**Sp**); arar, arado, arável, arador (**Port**); ara, arare, arat, arabil, arător (**Rom**)

Derivatives: arable, aration, exarate (**Eng**)

Hellenic: ἀρόω (aróō), ἄροτρον (árotron) (**AnGk**); ἀροτρο (árotro) (**Gk**)

Slavic: орать (orat'), рáло (rálo), ярмó (jarmó) (**Rus**); orać, radło (**Pol**); orat, rádlo (**Cz**); orat', radlo (**Slo**); opa (ora) (**Mace**)

Baltic: árti, arklas (**Lith**); aȓt, arkls (**Latv**)

*yewg-
to yoke, harness, join

see Object motion

*yugóm
yoke

see Object motion

*H₂melǵ-
to milk

*h₂mélǵ-e-ti, *h₂molǵ-éye-ti

Germanic: milk (**Eng**); meolc (**OE**); melke, molke (**Fris**); melken, melk (**Dut**); melken, Milch (**Ger**); mjǫlk, mjólka (**Norse**); melk, mjølk, melke (**Nor**); mjölk, mjölka (**Swe**); mælk, malke (**Dan**); mjólk, mjólka, mylkur (**Ice**)

Celtic: blith (**Wel**); melg, bleacht (**Iri**)

Italic: mulgēre, ēmulgēre, mulgentia, mulsūra (**Lat**); mungere (**Ital**); mecer, muir, mulger, emulger (**Sp**); mungir (**Port**); mulge, mulgere, mulsură (**Rom**)

Derivatives: emulge, emulsion, vaccimulgence (**Eng**); emulgeren (**Dut**)

Hellenic: ἀμέλγω (amélgō) (**AnGk**); αρμέγω (armégo) (**Gk**)

Slavic: молокó (molokó) (**Rus**); mleko (**Pol**); mléko (**Cz**); mlieko, mĺzt' (**Slo**); млéко (mléko) (**Mace**)

Baltic: melžti, malkas (**Lith**); malks (**Latv**)

Albanian: mjel (**Alb**)

Indo-Iranian: मर्जति (marjati) (**Sans**); مالیدن (mālīdan) (**Pers**)

*melh₂-
to grind, to crush

*melh₂-e-ti, *ml̥-né-h₂-ti, *molh₂-e-ti, *mélh₂-ye-ti, *molh₂-mo-s,*molh₂-to-s, *melh₂-wo-m

Germanic: meal, malm, maulm, maum, mawm, maelstrom (**Eng**); melu, mealm (**OE**);

moal (**Fris**); malen, meel, malm (**Dut**); mahlen, Mehl, mühlen, Malm (dial.), malmen, zermalmen, Mahlstrom (**Ger**);

mala, mjǫl, mylja, malmr (**Norse**); male, mjøl, mel, malm (**Nor**); mala, mjöl, malm (**Swe**); male, mel, malm, malstrøm (**Dan**); mala, mjöl, málmur (**Ice**)

Celtic: malu (**Wel**); meilt (**Iri**)

Italic: molere, molīnum, molīnārius, mollis, mola, immolere, molāris, molarius (**Lat**);

moudre, moulin, meunier, meule, immoler (**Fr**);

mola, mulino, molino, mugnaio, mulinaro, molinaro, mulinaio, immolare, molare (**Ital**);

moler, molino, molinero, muela, inmolar, molar, molero (**Sp**);

moer, moinho, moleiro, imolar, molar, mó (**Port**);

moară, imola, morar (**Rom**)

Derivatives: mill, immolate, molar (**Eng**); mylen (**OE**); molen, immoleren (**Dut**); melin (**Wel**); muileann (**Iri**)

Hellenic: μύλη (múlē), μέλᾱς (mélās), μύλλω (múllō) (**AnGk**)

Derivatives: amyloid, amyloplast, amylose, amylum (**Eng**)

Slavic: молóть (molót'), мóлот (mólot), мель (mel'), мел (mel) (**Rus**); mleć, młot, miał (**Pol**); mlít, mlat, młat, měl (**Cz**); mliet', mlat (**Slo**); меле (mele), млат (mlat) (**Mace**)

Baltic: málti, smēlis (**Lith**); smēlis (**Latv**)

Indo-Iranian: मृणाति (mr̥ṇā́ti) (**Sans**)

*peys-
to grind, crush

*pi-né-s-ti, *pis-é-, ?*peys-h₂onh₂-, *pis-en-om, *pis-tós, *pis-ent-, *pis-tlo-, *póys-om, *poys-tom

Italic: pīnsere, pistor, pistrīnum, pistāre, pīnsāre, pistillum, pīlum, pīla, pīlāre, compīlāre, compīlātiō, compīlātor, oppīlāre, oppīlātiō, Pīlātus (**Lat**); pétrin, pile, piler, compiler, compilation (**Fr**); pistrino, pistare, pilo, pillo, pila, compilare, compilazione, oppilazione (**Ital**); pistar, pisar, pisto, pilo, pila, pilar, compilar, compilación (**Sp**); pistrina, pisar, pilo, pia, pilhar, compilar, compilação (**Port**); pisa, pisare, pil, piuă, împila (**Rom**)

Derivatives: pestle, pistil, pile (head of arrow; large stake), compile, compilation, oppilate, Pilate (**Eng**); pīl (**OE**); pijl (**Dut**); Pfeil (**Ger**); pil (**Swe**); компилятор (kompiljátor) (**Rus**)

Hellenic: πτίσσω (ptíssō) (**AnGk**)

Slavic: пихáть (pixát'), пшенó (pšenó), пест (pest) (**Rus**); pchać, pszono, pszenica, piasta (**Pol**); pchát, píchat, pšeno, píst, písta (**Cz**); pchať, pichať, pšeno, piest (**Slo**)

Baltic: pìsti (**Lith**); pist (**Latv**)

Indo-Iranian: पिनष्टि (pináṣṭi), पिष्ट (piṣṭá), पेश (péśa) (**Sans**)

*peh₂-
to protect, to shepherd

see Marine animals

*peḱ-
to pluck, comb, shear (wool, hair)

see Social

*kerp-
to pluck, harvest

see Time

*seH₁-

to sow (seed)

*si-sh₁-é-ti, *séh₁-ye-ti, *séH₁mņ, *sh₁-tós, *séh₁-tis, *séh₁-tus, *seh₁-tlóm

Germanic: sow, seed (**Eng**); sāwan, sǣd (**OE**); sied (**Fris**); zaaien, zaad (**Dut**); säen, Samen, Same, Saat (**Ger**); sá, sáð, sæði, sáld (**Norse**); så, sæd (**Nor**); så, säd (**Swe**); så, sæd (**Dan**); sá, sáð (**Ice**)

Celtic: hil (**Wel**); síol (**Iri**)

Italic: serere, sēmen, sēmentis, sēminālis, sēminārium, sēminārius, sēmināre, dissēmināre, satiō, satus (**Lat**);

semence, séminal, séminariste, semer, disséminer, saison (**Fr**);

seme, semente, semenza, seminarista, seminare, disseminare (**Ital**);

semen, semencera, simiente, simienza, seminarista, sembrar, diseminar, sazón (**Sp**);

semente, seminarista, semear, disseminar, azão (**Port**);

sămânță, seminarist, semăna, semănare (**Rom**)

Derivatives: semen, insemination, disseminate, sation, sative, season, seasonable, seminal, seminar, seminary, seminarian (**Eng**); seamhan (**Iri**)

Hellenic: ἧμᾰ (hêma) (**AnGk**)

Slavic: сеять (sejat') , сémя (sémja) (**Rus**); siać, siemię (**Pol**); sít, semeno (**Cz**); siat', semeno (**Slo**); cee (see), семе (seme) (**Mace**)

Baltic: sėti, sekla, semenis (**Lith**); sēt (**Latv**)

Flora & Fauna

Trees

*dóru

tree, wood

*dérw-i-s, *dérw-o-m, *dréw-o-m, *dréwh₂-no-m, *drw(h₂)-ó-s

Germanic: tree, treen (dial.), tar (**Eng**); trēow, trēowen, teru (**OE**); teer (mostly in compounds) (**Dut**); tré, tjara (**Norse**); tre (**Nor**); trä, träd, tjära (**Swe**); træ (**Dan**); tré, tjara (**Ice**)

Celtic: derwen, dâr, derw (**Wel**); dearbh, dair (**Iri**)

Hellenic: δόρυ (dóru), δρῦς (drûs) (**AnGk**); δόρυ (dóry) (**Gk**)

Derivatives: doru, dory, dryad, hamadryad (**Eng**)

Slavic: дерево (dérevo), дровá (drová) (**Rus**); drzewo, drwa (**Pol**); dřevo (**Cz**); drevo (**Slo**); дрво (drvo) (**Mace**)

Baltic: dervà, drevė (**Lith**); dreve, daȓva (**Latv**)

Albanian: dru (**Alb**)

Indo-Iranian: दारु (dãru), द्रु (drú), दर्वि (dárvi), द्रोण (dróṇa) (**Sans**); दरख़्त (daraxt) (**Hin**); لرکی (largay) (**Pash**); درخت (deraxt) (**Pers**)

which may derive from *deru- hard:

*deru-

hard, firm, strong, solid

Perhaps: **Germanic**: true, truce, troth, truth, treague, trig (**Eng**); trūwa, trēowþ (**OE**); trou (**Fris**); trouw (**Dut**); Treue (**Ger**); trú, tryggr, tryggð (**Norse**); tro, trygg, trygd (**Nor**); tro, trygg, trygd (**Swe**); tro, tryg, trygd (**Dan**); trú, tryggð (**Ice**)

Derivatives: treuga (**Lat**); trêve (**Fr**); tregua (**Ital**); tregua (**Sp**); trégua (**Port**)

Italic: dūrus, dūrāre, dūrābilis, dūrābilitās, dūracinus, dūritia, dūrēscere, indūrēscere, dūrāmen (**Lat**); dur, durer, durabilité, duracine, dureté, endurcir, duramen (**Fr**); durare, durabile, durabilità, duracina, durezza (**Ital**); duro, durar, durabilidad, durazno, dureza, endurecer (**Sp**); duro, durázio, duraz, durar, dureza, endurecer (**Port**); dur, dura (**Rom**)

196

Derivatives: dure, durable, durability, dour, durance, duration, duress, durum, endurance, obduracy, perdure, subdural, duramen (**Eng**); duren (**Dut**); dauern (**Ger**); dúr (**Iri**); δωράκινον (dōrákinon) (**AnGk**); ροδάκivο (rodákino) (**Gk**); duroj (**Alb**)

Hellenic: δροóν (droón) (**AnGk**)

*h₂erHdʰ-
high; to grow

*h₂(e)rHdʰ-wos

Celtic: ardd (**Wel**); ard (**Iri**)

Italic: arduus, arduitās, arbor, arborētum, arboreus (**Lat**); ardu, arduité, arbre (**Fr**); arduo, arduità, albero, arboreto, albereto, arboreo (**Ital**); arduo, arduidad, árbol, arboleda, arboledo, arbóreo (**Sp**); árduo, arduidade, árvore, arvoredo, arbóreo (**Port**); arbore, arbure, arbor, arboret (**Rom**)

Derivatives: arduous, arduity, arbor, arboretum, arboret, arboreous, arboreal, arborescent (**Eng**); јарбол (jarbol) (**Mace**)

Indo-Iranian: ऊर्ध्व (ūrdhvá) (**Sans**)

*gʷet-
resin, gum

Germanic: cud (**Eng**); cwidu (**OE**); Kitt (**Ger**); kváða (**Norse**); kvåde, kode, kvæde (**Nor**); kåda (**Swe**)

Celtic: bedwen, bedw (**Wel**); beith (**Iri**)

Italic: bitumen, bitūminōsus, betula (**Lat**); béton, bouleau (**Fr**); bitume, betulla (**Ital**); betún, abedul (**Sp**); betão, betume, bétula (**Port**)

Derivatives: bitumen, bituminous (**Eng**); Beton (**Ger**); битум (bítum) (**Rus**)

Indo-Iranian: जतु (jatu) (**Sans**); واللوز (žāwla) (**Pash**); ژد (žad) (**Pers**)

*wréh₂ds
root

Germanic: wort (as in bladderwort, mugwort), root, orchard (**Eng**); wyrt, rōt (**OE**); woartel, wurtel (**Fris**); wort, wortel (**Dut**); Wurz, Wurzel (**Ger**); urt, rót, jurt, virtr (**Norse**); rot, urt, vørter, vyrt, vørt (**Nor**); rot, ört, vört (**Swe**); rod, urt, vørt (**Dan**); rót, jurt, virtur (**Ice**)

Celtic: gwraidd, greddf (**Wel**); fréamh (**Iri**)

Italic: rādīx, ērādīcāre, rādīcālis, radicula, radius, rāmus, rāmōsus, rāmulus, ramulosus (**Lat**);

racine, radis, arracher, éradiquer, radical, rai, rayon, rameau, rameux, ramule (**Fr**);

radice, eradicare, radicale, radicchio, raggio, radio, ramo, ramifico, ramoso, ramulo (**Ital**);

raiz, erradicar, radical, raya, rayo, raza, radio, ramo, rama, ramifico, ramoso (**Sp**);

raiz, radical, raio, rádio, ramo, ramifico, ramoso, râmulo (**Port**);

rădăcină, ridica, radical, ridiche, rază, ram, ramură, rămuros (**Rom**)

Derivatives: radish, radix, radical, radicle, radicchio, radius, ray, eradicate, ramus, ramification, ramulose (**Eng**);

radicaal (**Dut**); radikal (**Ger**); radickal (**Nor**); radikal (**Swe**); radikal (**Dan**); radikal (**Ice**);

radikalas (**Lith**); радикал (radikal), радиус (rádius) (**Rus**); radykał (**Pol**); radikál (**Cz**); radikál (**Slo**); радикал (radikal) (**Mace**); rreze (**Alb**)

Hellenic: ρίζα (rhíza), ριζικός (rhizikós), ράδιξ (rhádix) (**AnGk**); ρίζα (ríza), ριζικός (rizikós) (**Gk**)

Derivatives: rhizome, rhizoid, ectomycorrhiza, rhizophagy, rhizomatous, rhizomorph, rhizosphere, Rhizopogon, Rhizopus (**Eng**)

Slavic: вред (vred) (**Rus**)

Albanian: rrënjë (**Alb**)

Indo-Iranian: (wulëi) (**Pash**); ريشه (rīše) (**Pers**)

*bʰeh₂go-
beech

Germanic: beech, book (**Eng**); bēce, bōc (**OE**); boeke (in compounds), boek (**Fris**); beuk, boek (**Dut**); Buche, Büche, Buch (**Ger**); bók, bok (**Norse**); bøk (**Nor**); bok (**Swe**); bøg, bog (**Dan**); beyki, bók (**Ice**)

Derivatives: bouquin (**Fr**); буква (búkva) (**Rus**); bukiew (**Pol**); bukva, bukev (**Cz**); bukev (**Slo**); буква (bukva) (**Mace**)

Italic: fāgus, fāgīnus (**Lat**); fouet, faine, faîne, fouine (**Fr**); faggio, faina (**Ital**); haya, fuina (**Sp**); faia, fuinha (**Port**); fag (**Rom**)

Derivatives: foin (**Eng**)

Hellenic: φηγός (phēgós) (**AnGk**)

Slavic: бук (buk), бузина (buziná), бас (bas), буз (buz) (**Rus**); buk, bez (**Pol**); buk, bez (**Cz**); buk, bez (**Slo**); бука (buka), боз (boz) (**Mace**)

Baltic: bukas (**Lith**)

Albanian: bung (Alb)

*bʰereǵ-
birch

Germanic: birch (Eng); birce (Eng); bjirk (Fris); berk (Dut); Birke (Ger); bjǫrk, bjarkan (Norse); bjørk, bjerk (Nor); björk (Swe); birk (Dan); birki, björk (Ice)

Italic: frāxinus, fraxineus, fraxinētum (Lat); frêne, frênaie (Fr); frassino, frassineto (Ital); fresno, fresneda (Sp); freixo, fraxíneo (Port); frasin, frăsinet (Rom)

Derivatives: φράξος (fráxos) (AnGk); φράξος (fráxos) (Gk)

Slavic: берёза (berëza), берёза (berjóza) (Rus); brzoza (Pol); bříza (Cz); breza (Slo); бреза (breza) (Mace)

Baltic: beržas (Lith); bērzs (Latv)

Indo-Iranian: भूर्ज (bhūrja) (Sans)

*h₂ébōl
apple

Germanic: apple (Eng); æppel (OE); apel (Fris); appel (Dut); Apfel (Ger); epli (Norse); eple (Nor); äpple (Swe); æble (Dan); epli (Ice)

Celtic: afal, afallen (Wel); úll, abhaill (Iri)

Slavic: яблоко (jábloko) (Rus); jabłko (Pol); jablko (Cz); jablko (Slo); јаболко (jabolko) (Mace)

Baltic: obuolỹs (Lith); ābols (Latv)

*h₂eyǵ-
oak

Germanic: oak (Eng); āc (OE); iik (Fris); eik, eek (Dut); Eiche (Ger); eik (Norse); eik (Nor); ek (Swe); eg, egetræ (Dan); eik (Ice)

Italic: aesculus (Lat); eschio (Ital); ésculo (Port)

Perhaps: Hellenic: αἰγίλωψ (aigílōps), κράταιγος (krátaigos) (AnGk)

Baltic: ąžuolas (Lith)

Albanian: enjë (Alb)

*h₃el-
alder

*h₂élis-eh₂, *h₂élis-nos

Germanic: alder (**Eng**); alor (**OE**); els (**Dut**); Erle (**Ger**); alr (**Norse**); or, older (**Nor**); al (**Swe**); el, elletræ (**Dan**); elri (**Ice**)

Derivatives: alise (**Fr**)

Italic: alnus (**Lat**); aulne (**Fr**); aino (**Ital**); alno, aliso (**Sp**); anin, arin (**Rom**)

Hellenic: ἄλιζα (áliza) (**AnGk**)

Slavic: ольха (ol'xá) (**Rus**); olcha, olsza (**Pol**); olše (**Cz**); jelša (**Slo**)

Baltic: àlksnis, èlksnis (**Lith**); ãlksnis, ẽlksnis, alksìnis (**Latv**)

Albanian: halë (**Alb**)

*h₃es-
ash

Germanic: ash (**Eng**); æsc (**OE**); esk (**Fris**); es (**Dut**); Esche (**Ger**); askr (**Norse**); ask (**Nor**); ask (**Swe**); ask (**Dan**); askur (**Ice**)

Celtic: onnen (**Wel**)

Italic: ornus (**Lat**); orne (**Fr**); orno, orniello (**Ital**); urm (**Rom**)

Hellenic: ὀξύα (oxúa) (**AnGk**)

Slavic: ясень (jasen'), осина (osina) (**Rus**); jesion, osika (**Pol**); jasan, osika (**Cz**); jaseň, osika (**Slo**)

Baltic: uosis (**Lith**); osis (**Latv**)

Albanian: ah (**Alb**)

*perkʷu-
oak

Germanic: fir, frith, firth, Perth (**Eng**); furh, fyrhþ (**OE**); vuren, vorst (**Dut**); Föhre, Forst (**Ger**); fýri, fura, fjǫrr (**Norse**); furu, fýre (**Nor**); fura, furu (**Swe**); fyr, fyrretræ (**Dan**); furu, fura (**Ice**)

Derivatives: foresta (**Lat**); forêt (**Fr**); foresta (**Ital**); foresta (**Sp**); forest (**Eng**)

Celtic: perth (**Wel**)

Italic: quercus (**Lat**); quercia (**Ital**); alcornoque (**Sp**); querco (**Port**)

Derivatives: cork (**Eng**)

Plants

*bʰars-
spike, prickle

Germanic: barley, bere (**Eng**); bærlic, bere (**OE**); barr (**Norse**); bar (**Nor**); barr (**Swe**); barr (**Ice**)

Celtic: bara (**Wel**)

Italic: far, farīna, farīnārius, farīnōsus, farrāgō, farreus (**Lat**); farine, farinier, farineux (**Fr**); farina, farragine, fraina, farinaio, farinoso (**Ital**); harina, herrén, harinoso, fárrago, rain, harinero, harnero (**Sp**); farelo, farinha, farinheiro, farinhoso, farragem, fárreo, farro (**Port**); făină, făinar, făinos (**Rom**)

Derivatives: farina, farinose, farrago, farraginous (**Eng**)

Hellenic: Φήρον (Phéron, plant deity) (**AnGk**)

Albanian: bar (**Alb**)

*bʰabʰeh₂-
bean

Germanic: bean (**Eng**); bēan (**OE**); bean (**Fris**); boon (**Dut**); Bohne (**Ger**); baun (**Norse**); bønne (**Nor**); böna (**Swe**); bønne (**Dan**); baun (**Ice**)

Italic: faba (**Lat**); fève (**Fr**); fava (**Ital**); haba (**Sp**); fava (**Port**)

Derivatives: faba bean (**Eng**); ffaen, ffa (**Wel**)

Slavic: боб (bob) (**Rus**); bób (**Pol**); bob (**Cz**); bôb (**Slo**)

*ǵr̥Hnom
corn, grain

see Bodily functions

*h₂elut-
beer

the connection between beer and alum is argued to be through bitterness

Germanic: ale (**Eng**); ealu (**OE**); aal (**Dut**); ǫl (**Norse**); øl (**Nor**); öl (**Swe**); øl (**Dan**); öl (**Ice**)

Derivatives: godaille (**Fr**)

Italic: alūmen (**Lat**); allume (**Ital**); alumbre, aluminio (**Sp**)

Derivatives: alum, aluminium (**Eng**)

Hellenic: ἀλύδοιμος (alúdoimos) (**AnGk**)

Slavic: ол (ol) (**Rus**); jełczeć, zjełczały, jełki (**Pol**)

Baltic: alùs (**Lith**); alus (**Latv**)

*wóyh₁nom

wine

Italic: vīnum, vīnētum, vīnāceus, vīndēmia, vīndēmiāre, vīnea, vīneārius, vīnōsus (**Lat**);

vin, vinasse, vendémiaire, vendange, vendanger, vigne, vineux, vinaigre (+aigre), vinaigrette (**Fr**);

vino, vigneto, vinaccia, vendemmia, vendemmiare, vigna, vinoso (**Ital**);

vino, viñedo, vinaza, vendimia, vendimiar, viña, viñero, vinoso (**Sp**);

vinho, vinhedo, vináceo, vinhaça, vindima, vindimar, vinha, vinheiro, vinhoso, vinoso (**Port**);

vin, vinaț, vie, vier, vinos (**Rom**)

Derivatives: wine, vignette, vinaceous, vintage, vine, vineal, vinosity, vinous, vinegar, vinaigrette, viniculture (**Eng**); wīn (**OE**); wyn (**Fris**); wijn (**Dut**); Wein, wimmen (**Ger**);

vín (**Norse**); vin (**Nor**); vin (**Swe**); vin (**Dan**); vín (**Ice**);

gwin (**Wel**); fíon, fíneamhain, fíniúin, fínéagar (**Iri**);

вино (výno), винегрéт (vinegrét) (**Rus**); wino (**Pol**); víno (**Cz**); vino (**Slo**); вино (vino) (**Mace**); vīns (**Latv**)

Hellenic: οἶνος (oînos) (**AnGk**); οίνος (oínos) (**Gk**)

Derivatives: oenology, oenologist, oenochoe, oenophile, oenophilia (**Eng**)

Albanian: verë, venë (**Alb**)

Indo-Iranian: وین (vīn) (prob.) (**Pers**)

*wrugʰyo-

rye

Germanic: rye (**Eng**); ryge (**OE**); rogge (**Fris**); rogge (**Dut**); Rocken, Roggen (**Ger**); rugr (**Norse**); rug (**Nor**); råg (**Swe**); rug (**Dan**); rúgur (**Ice**)

Celtic: rhyg, ryg (**Wel**)

Slavic: рожь (rož') (**Rus**); reż (**Pol**); rež (**Cz**); raž (**Slo**); 'рж ('rž) (**Mace**)

Baltic: rugys (**Lith**); rudzi (**Latv**)

*eh₃g-
berry

Germanic: acorn (**Eng**); æcern (**OE**); aker (**Fris**); aker (**Dut**); Ecker (**Ger**); akarn (**Norse**); åkorn (**Nor**); akarn (**Swe**); agern (**Dan**); akarn (**Ice**)

Celtic: aeron, eirin (**Wel**); airne (**Iri**)

Slavic: ягода (jágoda) (**Rus**); jagoda (**Pol**); jahoda (**Cz**); jahoda (**Slo**); jагода (jagoda) (**Mace**)

Baltic: úoga (**Lith**); oga (**Latv**)

*k̑alam-
reed

Germanic: halm, haulm (**Eng**); healm (**OE**); haal (**Fris**); halm (**Dut**); Halm (**Ger**); halmr (**Norse**); halm (**Nor**); halm (**Swe**); halm (**Dan**); hálmur (**Ice**)

Italic: culmus (**Lat**); culmo (**Ital**); colmo, cuelmo (**Sp**); colmo (**Port**)

Derivatives: culm (**Eng**)

Hellenic: κάλαμος (kálamos) (**AnGk**); κάλαμος (kálamos) (**Gk**)

Derivatives: calamus (**Eng**); calamus (**Lat**); calame, chaume, chalumeau (**Fr**); calamo (**Ital**); cálamo, carámbano (**Sp**); carâmb (**Rom**); kallam (**Alb**); कलम (kalama) (**Sans**); قلم (qalam) (**Pers**)

Slavic: солома (solóma) (**Rus**); słoma (**Pol**); sláma (**Cz**); slama (**Slo**); слама (slama) (**Mace**)

Baltic: salms (**Latv**)

*lino-
flax

The meaning of "line" develops because of flax products such as rope, and because linen (made from flax) is woven from threads.

Germanic: linen, line (**Eng**); līnen, līne (**OE**); linnen, line (**Fris**); linnen, lijn (**Dut**); Lein, Leinen, Leine (**Ger**); lín, lína (**Norse**); lin, rita, rite (**Nor**); lin, lina (**Swe**); linned (**Dan**);

lín, lína (**Ice**)

Celtic: llin (**Wel**); líon (**Iri**)

Italic: līnum, līnārius, līnea, līneālis, līneus, linteum, linteārius, linteolum, līneāmentum, līneāre, dēlīneāre (**Lat**);

lin, ligne, linge, linceul, linéament (**Fr**); lino, linea, lenzuolo, delineare (**Ital**); lino, linero, línea, liña, líneo, lienzo, lenzuelo, lineamento, delinear (**Sp**); linho, linheiro, linha, líneo, lenço, lençol (**Port**); in, inar, ie, linie, linţoliu (**Rom**)

Derivatives: linoleum, lino, lineal, lintearious, lineament, delineate, delineavit, linear, align, alignment, ambilineal, bilinear, collinear, curvilinear, lineage, lineate, matrilineal, multicollinearity, multilinear, nonalignment, noncollinear, nonlineal, nonlinear, quasilinear, realign, rectilinear, sesquilinear, sublineage, sublinear, supralinear, trilinear, unilinear (**Eng**); Linie (**Ger**); линия (linija) (**Rus**); linjë (**Alb**)

Hellenic: λίνov (línon) (**AnGk**)

Slavic: лён (lën) (**Rus**); len (**Pol**); len (**Cz**); l'an (**Slo**); лен (len) (**Mace**)

Baltic: linas (**Lith**); lini (**Latv**)

Albanian: li, liri/lîni (**Alb**)

Mammals

*ǵʰwer-
wild; wild animal

ǵʰwér-os

Italic: ferus, fera (**Lat**); fier (**Fr**); fiero, fiera (**Ital**); fiero, fiera (**Sp**); fera (**Port**); fiară (**Rom**)

Derivatives: fierce, feral (**Eng**)

Hellenic: θήρ (thér), θηρῖον (thēríon), φήρ (phér) (**AnGk**)

Derivatives: therio-, -there, theropod, theropsid, theriomorphic, theriolatry (**Eng**); -thērium (**Lat**); -thère (**Fr**)

Slavic: зверь (zver') (**Rus**); zwierz (**Pol**); zvěř (**Cz**); zver (**Slo**); ѕвер (dzver) (**Mace**)

Baltic: žvėris (**Lith**); zvērs (**Latv**)

Indo-Iranian: (tsaarwai) (**Pash**)

which includes *ǵʰweroh₃kʷs (*ǵʰwer- + *h₃ekʷ-):

*ǵʰweroh₃kʷs
having the appearance of a wild animal

Italic: ferōx, ferōcitās (**Lat**); féroce, férocité (**Fr**); feroce, ferocità (**Ital**); feroz, ferocidad (**Sp**); feroz (**Port**); feroce (**Rom**)

Derivatives: ferocious, ferocity (**Eng**)

*h₂r̥tḱos
bear

Celtic: arth (**Wel**)

Italic: ursus, ursa, ursīnus (**Lat**); ours, ourse (**Fr**); orso, orsa (**Ital**); oso, osa (**Sp**); usso, urso, ursa (**Port**); urs, ursă (**Rom**)

Derivatives: ursine, Ursa Major, Ursula, Ursulines (**Eng**)

Hellenic: ἄρκτος (árktos), ἀρκτικός (arktikós) (**AnGk**); άρκτος (árktos), αρκούδα (arkoúda) (**Gk**)

Derivatives: Arcturus, arctic (**Eng**); Arctūrus, arcticus (**Lat**); arktisch (**Ger**)

Baltic: irštvà (**Lith**)

Albanian: ari, arushë (**Alb**)

Indo-Iranian: ऋक्ष (ṛkṣá) (**Sans**); रीछ (rīch) (**Hin**); (yəž) (**Pash**); خرس (xirs) (**Pers**)

*wĺkʷos
wolf

Germanic: wolf (**Eng**); wulf (**OE**); wolf (**Fris**); wolf (**Dut**); Wolf (**Ger**); úlfr, ylgr (**Norse**); ulv (**Nor**); ulv, ylva (**Swe**); ulv (**Dan**); úlfur, ylgur (**Ice**)

Celtic: gweilgi (**Wel**); olc (**Iri**)

Italic: lupus, lupīnus (**Lat**); loup (**Fr**); lupo, lupino (**Ital**); lobo, lupino (**Sp**); lobo (**Port**); lup (**Rom**)

Derivatives: lupine, lupin (**Eng**)

Hellenic: λύκος (lúkos), λυκανθρωπία (lykanthropía) (**AnGk**); λύκος (lýkos), λυκάνθρωπος (lykánthropos), λυκανθρωπία (lykanthropía) (**Gk**)

Derivatives: lycanthropy (**Eng**)

Slavic: волк (volk), волкулáк (volkulák) (**Rus**); wilk, wilkołak (**Pol**); vlk, vlkodlak (**Cz**); vlk, vlkolak (**Slo**); волк (volk), вркол̂ак (vrkolak) (**Mace**)

Baltic: vĩlkas (**Lith**); vilks (**Latv**)

Albanian: ujk (**Alb**)

Indo-Iranian: वृक (vṛka) (**Sans**); वृक (vŕk) (**Hin**); ليوه (lewë) (**Pash**); گرگ (gorg), گرگان (Gorgân) (**Pers**)

*ḱwṓ
dog

Germanic: hound (**Eng**); hund (**OE**); hûn (**Fris**); hond (**Dut**); Hund (**Ger**); hundr (**Norse**); hund (**Nor**); hund (**Swe**); hund (**Dan**); hundur (**Ice**)

Celtic: ci, cwn, dyfrgi (**Wel**); cú, dobharchú (**Iri**)

Italic: canis, canīcula, canīnus (**Lat**); chien, chenille, canicule, canin (**Fr**); cane, canicola, canino (**Ital**); can, canícula, canino (**Sp**); cão, canícula, cainho, canino (**Port**); câine, caniculă, canin (**Rom**)

Derivatives: canine, canary, Canis Major, canaille (**Eng**); канйкулы (kaníkuly) (**Rus**); kanikuła (**Pol**); qen (**Alb**)

Hellenic: κύων (kúōn), kῠνάγχη (kunánkhē), kῠνικός (kunikós), kῠνόμαζον (kunómazon) (**AnGk**); κύων (kýon), κυνάγχη (kynánchi), κυνικός (kynikós) (**Gk**)

Derivatives: cynanche, cynic (**Eng**); cynanchē, cynicus, cynomazon (**Lat**)

Slavic: cýка (súka) (**Rus**); suka (**Pol**); suka (dial., arch.) (**Cz**); suka (**Slo**)

Baltic: šuo, šuñs (**Lith**); suns (**Latv**)

Albanian: shakë (**Alb**)

Indo-Iranian: श्वन् (śvā), शुनस् śvan (**Sans**); श्वान (śvān) (**Hin**); سپی (spay) (**Pash**); سگ (sag) (**Pers**)

*h₁éḱwos
horse

Perhaps from ēkʷ- water, river (because horses were considered the most precious sacrifice for the sea god), or perhaps from *h₁eḱus, meaning quick, swift.

Germanic: jór, jóreið (**Norse**); jór (**Ice**)

Celtic: cyfeb, ebol, ebran (**Wel**); each (**Iri**)

Italic: equus, equa, eques, equester, equīnus, equīsō (**Lat**); équestre (**Fr**); equino (**Ital**); yegua, ecuestre, equino (**Sp**); égua, equino (**Port**); iapă (**Rom**)

Derivatives: equine, equestrian, equison (**Eng**)

Hellenic: ἵππος (híppos), ἱππόδρομος (hippódromos), ἱπποπότᾰμος (hippopótamos), Φίλιππος (Phílippos) (**AnGk**); ίππος (íppos) (**Gk**)

Derivatives: hippocampus, hippodrome, hippopotamus, hippo-, Philip (**Eng**); hippodromos, Philippus (**Lat**); hippodrome, hippo- (**Fr**); ипподром (ippodrom), гиппопотам (gippopotám) (**Rus**)

Baltic: ašva (**Lith**)

Indo-Iranian: अश्व (áśva) (**Sans**); अश्व (aśv) (**Hin**); آس (ās) (**Pash**); اسب (asb) (**Pers**)

but the Germanic line for horse comes from *ḱers- to run:

*ḱers-
to run

*ḱr̥s-é-ti, *ḱr̥s-néh₂-ti, *ḱr̥s-kó-s, *ḱr̥s-ó-s, *ḱr̥s-tó-s

Germanic: horse, rush (**Eng**); hors, hrysċan (**OE**); hoars (**Fris**); ros (**Dut**); Ross (**Ger**); horskr, hross (**Norse**); russ, hors (dial.) (**Swe**); hors (dial.) (**Dan**); horskur, hross, hors (**Ice**)

Celtic: car (**Wel**)

Derivatives: car, chariot, career, charge, discharge (**Eng**); kar, carrosserie (**Dut**); Karren, Karre, Karosserie (**Ger**); kjerre, karosseri, karre (**Nor**); kärra, karosseri (**Swe**);

carrus, carrāria, carricāre, discarricāre, carrūca (**Lat**); car, char, charrette, carrosserie, carrière, charrière, charger, décharger, charrue (**Fr**); carro, carretta, carrozza, carrozzeria, carraia, carriera, caricare, discaricare, carruca, carroccia (**Ital**); carro, carreta, carretilla, carroza, carruaje, carrocería, carrocero, carretera, carrera, cargar, carricar, descargar, carruca (**Sp**); carro, carreta, carroça, carruagem, carroceria, carroceiro, carreteiro, carreira, carregar, descarregar (**Port**); car, încărca, încărcare, descărca, descărcare, căruță (**Rom**);

карета (kareta) (**Rus**); kareta, karoseria (**Pol**); kára (**Cz**); karro, karrarë, shkarkoj (**Alb**)

Italic: currere, currēns, accurrere, concurrere, concursus, curriculum, cursus, currus, currīlis, curūlis, cursor, cursōrius, dēcurrere, dēcurrēns, discurrere, discursus, excurrere, excursus, excursiō, incurrere, incursiō, occurrere, percurrere, praecurrere, praecursor, recurrere, succurrere, succursus (**Lat**);

courir, courre, courant, accourir, concourir, concours, curriculum, cours, curseur, discourir, discours, excursion, encourir, incursion, parcourir, précurseur, secourir, secours (**Fr**);

correre, corrente, accorrere, concorrere, concorso, curricolo, corso, cursore, corsoio, cursorio, decorrere, decorrente, discorrere, discorso, scorrere, scorso, escursione, incorrere, incursione, occorrere, percorrere, percorso, precorrere, precorso, precursore, ricorrere, soccorrere, soccorso (**Ital**);

correr, corriente, acorrer, concurrir, concurso, currículo, carrejo, corso, coso, curso, carril, cursor, decorrerse, discurrir, descorrer, discurso, escurrir, excursión, incurrir, incursión, ocurrir, percorrer, recorrer, recurrir, socorrer (**Sp**);

correr, corrente, acorrer, concorrer, concurso, currículo, corso, cosso, curso, carril, curul, cursor, decorrer, decorrente, discorrer, discurso, escorrer, excursão, incorrer, incursão, ocorrer, percorrer, recorrer, socorrer (**Port**);

cure, curent, curge, curgere, concurs, curs, cursor, cursoare, discurs, scure, scurge, excursie, încura (**Rom**)

Derivatives: courier, current, currency, concur, concourse, curriculum, course, curule, cursor, cursory, discourse, excur, excursus, excursion, incur, incursion, occur, precursor, recur, succor (**Eng**); koers (**Dut**); Kurs (**Ger**); konkurrere (**Nor**); kurs (**Swe**); курс (kurs), экскурсия (ekskursija) (**Rus**)

Hellenic: ἐπίκουρος (epíkouros) (**AnGk**)

horses also jump, and the Germanic line also follows this:

*kek-
to jump, spring out

Germanic: henchman (**Eng**); hengst, hengest (**OE**); hynst, hynder (**Fris**); hengst

(Dut); Hengst (Ger); hestr (Norse); hingst, hest (Nor); hingst, häst (Swe); hingst, hest (Dan); hestur (Ice)

Celtic: caseg (Wel)

Hellenic: κηκίω (kekio) (AnGk)

which is presumably closely related to (with a certain amount of confusion between) *(s)kek- to spring:

*(s)kek-
to spring, move quickly

Germanic: chic, shake, chicanery (Eng); sċēon, ġesċēon, sċacan (OE); schaekjen, schaakje, schaekje, skikke (Fris); geschieden, schikken, schaken (Dut); geschehen, schicken, geschickt, Geschichte, schikanieren (Ger); skikka, skaka (Norse); skje, skake, skikke (Nor); ske, skicka, skick, skaka (Swe); ske, skage (Dan); skaka, skikka (Ice)

Derivatives: chic, chicaner, chicanerie (Fr)

Celtic: ysgogi (Wel)

Slavic: скакáть (skakáť), скок (skok) (Rus); skakać (Pol); skočit (Cz); скок (skok) (Mace)

Baltic: šókti, šankùs, šankìnti (Lith); sākt (uncert.) (Latv)

but mare has a different derivation:

*marko-
horse

Germanic: marshal, mare (Eng); mearh, miere (OE); merje (Fris); merrie, maarschalk (Dut); Mähre, Marschall (Ger); marr, merr (Norse); merr (Nor); märr (Swe); mær (Dan); meri, mar (Ice)

Derivatives: maréchal (Fr); maniscalco (Ital); mariscal (Sp)

Celtic: march, marchog (Wel); marc, marcach (Iri)

*(s)táwros
wild bull, aurochs

Germanic: steer, stirk (Eng); steor, stirc (OE); stier (Dut); Stier, Sterk, Stärke, Starke (Ger); stjórr, þjórr (Norse); tyr, tjor (Nor); tjur (Swe); tyr (Dan); stjór, þjór (Ice)

Celtic: tarw (**Wel**); tarbh (**Iri**)

Derivatives: tarfr (**Norse**); tarfur (**Ice**)

Italic: taurus, tauriförmis (**Lat**); taureau, tauriforme (**Fr**); toro, tauriforme (**Ital**); toro (**Sp**); touro (**Port**); taur (**Rom**)

Derivatives: taurine, Taurus, tauriform (**Eng**)

Hellenic: ταῦρος (taûros) (**AnGk**); ταύρος (távros) (**Gk**)

Derivatives: minotaur, tauromachy (**Eng**)

Slavic: тур (tur) (**Rus**); tur (**Pol**); tur (**Cz**); tur (**Slo**)

Baltic: tauras (**Lith**); tauriņš (**Latv**)

Albanian: taroç, tauk (**Alb**)

Indo-Iranian: ستور (sotur) (**Pers**)

*gʷṓws

cattle, cow/bull

Germanic: cow, kine (**Eng**); cū, cȳ (**OE**); ko (**Fris**); koe (**Dut**); Kuh (**Ger**); kú, kýr, kó (**Norse**); ku (**Nor**); ko (**Swe**); ko (**Dan**); kýr (**Ice**)

Celtic: buwch (**Wel**); bó (**Iri**)

Italic: bōs, boārius, bovārius, bovīnus, būbalus, bubulcus, Bosporus, būcināre, būcinum (**Lat**);

bœuf, bouvier, bovin, bubale, buccin (**Fr**);

bove, bue, boaro, boario, bovaro, bovino, bufalo, bifolco, buccina (**Ital**);

buey, boyero, bovino, búbalo, búfalo, bocinar, voznar (**Sp**);

bife, boi, boieiro, bovino, búfalo, búzio (**Port**);

bou, boar, bour, buciuma, buciumare, bucium (**Rom**)

Derivatives: beef, bovine, buffalo, Bosphorus, buccina (**Eng**); buabhall (**Iri**); buall, bujk (**Alb**)

Hellenic: βοῦς (boûs), βούβαλος (boúbalos), βούτῡρον (boútūron), βουστροφηδόν (boustrophēdón), βουκόλος (boukólos), βουκολικός (boukolikós), ἑκατόμβη (hekatómbē), βουλῑμία (boulīmía) (**AnGk**); βούβαλος (noúvalos), βούτυρο (noútyro) (**Gk**)

Derivatives: butter, bucolic, hecatomb, bulimia, boustrophedron (**Eng**); butere (**OE**); bûter (**Fris**); boter (**Dut**); Butter (**Ger**); būtȳrum, būcolicus (**Lat**); beurre, bucolique (**Fr**); burro, bucolico (**Ital**); bucólico (**Sp**); bucólico (**Port**); путер (puter) (**Mace**)

Slavic: говядо (govjádo) (**Rus**); hovado (**Cz**); hovädo (**Slo**); говедо (govedo) (**Mace**)

Baltic: govs (**Latv**)

Albanian: gak, kau (**Alb**)

Indo-Iranian: गाव (gāva), गो (go) (**Sans**); गाय (gāy) (**Hin**); غوا (ghwā) (**Pash**); گاو (gāv) (**Pers**)

*uksén

ox, bull

Germanic: ox (**Eng**); oxa (**OE**); okse (**Fris**); os (**Dut**); Ochse (**Ger**); oxi, uxi (**Norse**); okse, ukse (**Nor**); oxe (**Swe**); okse (**Dan**); oxi, uxi (**Ice**)

Celtic: ych (**Wel**); oss (**Iri**)

Indo-Iranian: उक्षन् (ukṣán) (**Sans**)

*suH-

swine

Germanic: sow, swine, mereswine (porpoise, dolphin) (*mori+) (**Eng**); sū, swīn, mereswīn (**OE**); sûch, swyn (**Fris**); zeug, zwijn, meerzwijn (**Dut**); Sau, Schwein, Meerschwein, Meerschweinchen (**Ger**); sýr, svín, marsvin (**Norse**); su, sugge, svin, marsvin (**Nor**); so, sugga, svin, marsvin (**Swe**); so, svin, marsvin (**Dan**); sá, sýr, svín, marsvin (**Ice**)

Derivatives: marsouin (**Fr**)

Celtic: hwch (**Wel**); soc (**Iri**)

Italic: sūs, suīnus (**Lat**); suino (**Ital**); suíno (**Port**); sain (**Rom**)

Hellenic: ὗς (hûs), ὕαινα (húaina) (**AnGk**); ὕαινα (ýaina) (**Gk**)

Derivatives: hyena, hyenoid (**Eng**); hyena (**Dut**); Hyäne (**Ger**); hyene (**Nor**); hyena (**Swe**); hyæne (**Dan**); híena (**Ice**); hyaena (**Lat**); hyène (**Fr**); iena (**Ital**); hiena (**Sp**); hiena (**Port**); hienă (**Rom**); гиена (gijena) (**Rus**); hiena (**Pol**); hyena (**Cz**); hyena (**Slo**)

Slavic: свин (svin), свинья (svin'já) (**Rus**); świnia (**Pol**); svině (**Cz**); sviňa (**Slo**); свиња (svinja) (**Mace**)

Baltic: sivēns, suvēns (**Latv**)

Albanian: thi (**Alb**)

Indo-Iranian: सूकर (sūkara) (**Sans**); सूअर (sūar) (**Hin**); خوک (xuk), خوگ (xug) (**Pers**)

*pórḱos
piglet

Germanic: farrow, aardvark (**Eng**); fearh (**OE**); faarich (**Fris**); var, varken, aardvarken (aarde+), minivarken, spaarvarken (**Dut**); Ferkel (**Ger**); fargalt (**Swe**)

Celtic: arc, arcán (**Iri**)

Italic: porcus, porcarius, porcella, porcellus, porcīnus (**Lat**); porc, porcher, pourceau, porcin (**Fr**); porco, porca, porcaio, porcella, porcello, porcino (**Ital**); puerco, peorca, porquero, porcela, porcel, porcelo, porcino (**Sp**); porco, porca, porqueiro, porcino (**Port**); porc, poarcă, porcar, purcea, purcel, porcin (**Rom**)

Derivatives: pork, porcine (**Eng**); porchell (**Wel**)

Slavic: порося (porosjá), поросёнок (porosjónok), парсюк (parsjúk), парсýк (parsúk) (**Rus**); prosię (**Pol**); prase (**Cz**); prasa (**Slo**); прасе (prase), прасенце (prasence) (**Mace**)

Baltic: paršas (**Lith**)

*kapro
goat, buck

Germanic: haver, haversack (**Eng**); hæfer (**OE**); haver (**Dut**); Haber, Hafer, Habergeiß (dial.) (**Ger**); hafr, hafri (**Norse**); havre (**Nor**); havre (**Swe**); havre (**Dan**); hafur (**Ice**)

Derivatives: havresac (**Fr**)

Celtic: gafr, caeriwrch (**Wel**); gabhar, caora (**Iri**)

Derivatives: garron (dial.) (**Fr**); gabre (**Port**)

Italic: caper, capra, capellus, caprīnus, caprarius, capreolus (**Lat**); chèvre, chevreau, caprin, chevrier, cabrioler, cabriolet (**Fr**); cabra, capro, caprino, capraio, capriolare, cabriola (**Ital**); cabra, cabro, caprino, cabrero (**Sp**); cabra, caprino, cabreiro (**Port**); capră, caprin, căprar (**Rom**)

Derivatives: caper, caprice, caprine, cabriolet, cab, Capricorn (**Eng**)

Hellenic: κάπρος (kápros) (**AnGk**); κάπρος (kápros) (**Gk**)

Albanian: kaproll (**Alb**)

Indo-Iranian: कपृथ् (kaprtha) (**Sans**)

*bʰuHgos-
goat, ram, buck

Germanic: buck, steenbok, bouquetin, butcher (**Eng**); bucca (**OE**); bok (**Fris**); bok, reebok, steenbok (**Dut**); Bock (**Ger**); bukkr, bokkr, bokki (**Norse**); bukk, bokk (**Nor**); bock (**Swe**); buk (**Dan**); bukkur, bokkur, bokki (**Ice**)

Derivatives: bouc, bouquin, bouquetin (**Fr**)

Celtic: bwch (**Wel**); boc, búistéir (**Iri**)

Albanian: buzë (**Alb**)

Indo-Iranian: बुख (bukha) (**Sans**); وزه (wuza/buza) (**Pash**); بز (boz) (**Pers**)

*gʰaydos
young goat, kid

Germanic: goat (**Eng**); gāt (**OE**); geit (**Fris**); geit (**Dut**); Geiss, geissen (**Ger**); geit (**Norse**); geit (**Nor**); get (**Swe**); ged (**Dan**); geit (**Ice**)

Italic: haedus, haedīnus (**Lat**); ied (**Rom**)

Derivatives: haedine (**Eng**)

*h₂ówis
sheep

Germanic: ewe (**Eng**); ēowu (**OE**); ei (**Fris**); ooi (**Dut**); Aue (**Ger**); ǽr (**Norse**); ærsaud (**Nor**); ålam (**Dan**); ær (**Ice**)

Celtic: ewig (**Wel**)

Italic: ovis, ovicula, ovīnus (**Lat**); ouaille, ovin (**Fr**); ovino (**Ital**); oveja, ovino (**Sp**); ovelha, ovino (**Port**); oaie, oină (**Rom**)

Derivatives: ovine (**Eng**)

Hellenic: ὄϊς (óïs) (**AnGk**)

Slavic: овца (ovcá), овен (ovén) (**Rus**); owca (**Pol**); ovce (**Cz**); ovca (**Slo**); овца (óvca), овен (óven) (**Mace**)

Baltic: avis, ãvinas (**Lith**); avs, auns (**Latv**)

Indo-Iranian: अवि (avi) (**Sans**); عفه (afe) (**Pers**)

*h₂egʷnos
lamb

Germanic: ean, yean (**Eng**); ēanian (**OE**); antsje, eandsje, inje (**Fris**); oonen (**Dut**); öna (dial.) (**Swe**)

Celtic: oen (**Wel**); uan (**Iri**)

Italic: agnus, agnellus, agnella (**Lat**); agneau, agnelle (**Fr**); agnello, agnella (**Ital**); anho (**Port**); miel, mia (**Rom**)

Hellenic: ἀμνός (amnós), ἀμνίον (amníon) (**AnGk**)

Derivatives: amniocentesis, amniotic, amnion, amniote (**Eng**)

Slavic: ягнёнок (jagnjónok), áгнец (ágnec) (**Rus**); jagnię (**Pol**); jehně, jehnec (**Cz**); jahňa (**Slo**); járнe (jágne) (**Mace**)

Baltic: ériena (**Lith**); jērs (uncert.) (**Latv**)

*muh₂s-

mouse

Germanic: mouse (**Eng**); mūs (**OE**); mûs (**Fris**); muis (**Dut**); Maus (**Ger**); mús (**Norse**); mus (**Nor**); mus (**Swe**); mus (**Dan**); mús (**Ice**)

Italic: mūs, mūsculus, mūsculāris, mūsculōsus, mūstēla (**Lat**); muscle, moule, musculaire, musculeux (**Fr**); muscolo, muscolare (**Ital**); mur, músculo, muslo, muscular, musculoso (**Sp**); mure, muro, murganho, músculo, muscular, musculoso (**Port**); muşchi, muscular, muşchiular, musculos, muşchios, mustaila (**Rom**)

Derivatives: murine, muscle, mussel, muscular, mustelid (**Eng**); musculair (**Dut**); Muskel, Muschel, muskulär (**Ger**); muskel, muskulär (**Swe**); muskulær (**Dan**); мускул (muskul), мускулистый (muskulístyj) (**Rus**); muskul, mushk, muskulor (**Alb**)

Hellenic: μῦς (mûs) (**AnGk**)

Derivatives: musophobia (**Eng**)

Slavic: мышь (myš') (**Rus**); mysz (**Pol**); myš (**Cz**); myš (**Slo**); миш (miš) (dial.) (**Mace**)

Albanian: mi (**Alb**)

Indo-Iranian: मूष् (mūṣ), मूष (mūṣa) (**Sans**); मूस (mūs) (**Hin**); مرک (mažak), مره (maža) (**Pash**); موش (muš) (dial.), مشک (mošk) (**Pers**)

*udréh₂

otter

see Terrain

*ǵʰḗr

hedgehog

Italic: ēr, ēricius (**Lat**); hérisson (**Fr**); riccio (**Ital**); erizo, rizo (**Sp**); ouriço (**Port**); arici (**Rom**)

Derivatives: urchin (**Eng**); uriq, iriq (**Alb**)

Hellenic: χήρ (khếr), χοῖρος (khoîros), ἐχῖνος (ekhînos), ἔγχελυς (énkhelus) (**AnGk**); χοίρος (choíros), εχίνος (echínos), αχινός (achinós) (**Gk**)

Derivatives: echinoderm, echinate, echinology (**Eng**); echinus (**Lat**)

Albanian: derr (**Alb**)

from which derives *gʰers- stiff, surprised:

*gʰers-
stiff, surprised

*ǵʰérs-e-ti, *ǵʰr̥s-yé-ti, *ǵʰe-ǵʰórs-e, *ǵʰors-éye-ti, *ǵʰr̥s-éh₁-(ye)-ti, *ǵʰórs-ōs

Germanic: garstig (**Ger**); gersta (**Norse**)

Celtic: garw (**Wel**)

Italic: horrēre, hirtus, abhorrēre, abhorrēscere, horrendus, horribilis, horridus, horrificus, horripilare, horror (**Lat**); horreur, abhorrer, horrible, ordure, horrifique (**Fr**); orrore, aborrire, orrendo, orribile, orrifico, orrido (**Ital**); horror, aburrir, aborrecer, horrendo, horrible, hórrido, horripilar (**Sp**); horror, avorrir, aborrecer, hórrido, horrível (**Port**); urî, ură, borî, urdoare (uncert.) (**Rom**)

Derivatives: horror, abhor, abhorrent, horrendous, horrible, ordure, horrid, horrific (**Eng**); Horror, horrend (**Ger**); urrej, urroj (**Alb**)

Perhaps: **Slavic:** гроза́ (grozá) (**Rus**); groza (**Pol**); hrůza (**Cz**); hrôza (**Slo**); гроза (groza) (**Mace**)

Perhaps: **Baltic:** grasa, grėsti (**Lith**); grasāt (**Latv**)

Indo-Iranian: हृष् (hṛṣ), हर्षते (hárṣate), हृष्यति (hṛṣyáti), जाहृषाण (jāhṛṣāṇá), हर्षयति (harṣáyati) (**Sans**); زيږ (ziǵ) (**Pash**)

*angʷ(h)i-
eel, snake, worm, hedgehog (snake eater)

this is a somewhat confused and uncertain etymology

Germanic: ile (**Eng**); iǵil, iǵl, īl (**OE**); ychel (**Fris**); egel (**Dut**); Igel, Engerling (**Ger**); ígull (**Norse**); igle (**Nor**); igel, igelkott (**Swe**); igle (**Dan**); ígull (**Ice**)

Celtic: llys-yw-en (**Wel**)

Italic: anguilla (**Lat**); anguille (**Fr**); anguilla (**Ital**); anguila (**Sp**); enguia (**Port**); anghilă (**Rom**)

Derivatives: ngjalë (**Alb**)

Slavic: уж (už), угорь (úgor'), ёж (jož), ёжик (jóžik) (**Rus**); wąż, węgorz, jeż (**Pol**); užovka, úhoř, jež, ježek (**Cz**); jež (**Slo**); еж (еž) (**Mace**)

Baltic: angis, ungurys, ežys (**Lith**); odze, ezis (**Latv**)

Indo-Iranian: (zižgai) (**Pash**); يغنيج (yağnij) (arch.) (**Pers**)

Reptiles

*gʰelōw-
tortoise

Hellenic: χελώνη (khelónē), χέλῡς (khélūs) (**AnGk**); χελώνα (chelóna) (**Gk**)

Derivatives: chelys, chelȳdrus (**Lat**); chelonian, chelydre (**Eng**); chélydre (**Fr**)

Slavic: желвь (želv') (**Rus**); żółw (**Pol**); želva (**Cz**)

Baltic: želvė (**Lith**)

*neHtr-
snake

Germanic: adder (**Eng**); nǣddre (**OE**); njirre (**Fris**); adder (**Dut**); natara, Natter, Otter (meaning adder, viper; in compounds) (**Ger**); naðr, naðra (**Norse**); naður, naðra (**Ice**)

Celtic: neidr (**Wel**); nathair (**Iri**)

Italic: nātrīx (**Lat**); natrice (**Ital**); natriz (**Sp**)

Indo-Iranian: (nattëka) (**Pash**)

from *(s)neh$_1$- to spin (thread), to sew:

*(s)neh$_1$-
to spin (thread), to sew

*(s)néh$_1$-, *(s)néh$_1$-tr-, *(s)néh$_1$-tlo-, *snéh$_1$-w-ṛ, *snoh$_1$-t-éh$_2$

Germanic: needle, sinew, snood (**Eng**); nǣdl, seonu, snōd (**OE**); naaie, niddel, nuddel, nille, nulle (**Fris**); naiaen, naald, sneu (**Dut**); nähen, Nadel, Sehne (**Ger**); nál (**Norse**); nål, snúðr (**Nor**); nål, snod, snodd (**Swe**); nål (**Dan**); nál, snúður (**Ice**)

Celtic: nyddu (**Wel**); snáth (**Iri**)

Italic: nēre, nētus, nervus, nervōsus (**Lat**); nerf, nerveux (**Fr**); nervo, nervoso (**Ital**);

nervio, nervioso, nervoso (**Sp**); nervo, nervoso (**Port**)

Derivatives: nerve, nervous, enervate, innervate (**Eng**); nerve (**Nor**); nerfus (**Wel**); нерв (nerv) (**Rus**)

Hellenic: νέω (néō), νεῦρον (neûron), νευροειδές (neuroeidés) (**AnGk**); νεύρο (névro) (**Gk**)

Derivatives: neuron, neural, neuritis, neuroblast, neurology, neurosis, neurotic, epineurium (**Eng**); neuroīdes (**Lat**); нейрóн (nejrón) (**Rus**)

Baltic: snāte (**Latv**)

Indo-Iranian: स्नावन् (snāvan) (**Sans**)

Marine animals

*peisḱ-
fish

Germanic: fish (**Eng**); fisc (**OE**); fisk (**Fris**); vis (**Dut**); Fisch (**Ger**); fiskr (**Norse**); fisk (**Nor**); fisk (**Swe**); fisk (**Dan**); fiskur (**Ice**)

Celtic: Wysg (Usk) (**Wel**); iasc (**Iri**)

Italic: piscis, piscārius, piscīna, piscor, piscōsus (**Lat**); poisson, piscine, pêcher (**Fr**); pesce, piscina, pescare, pescoso (**Ital**); pez, peje, pesquero, piscina, pescar (**Sp**); peixe, peixeiro, piscina, pescar, piscoso (**Port**); peşte, pescar, piscină, pescos (**Rom**)

Derivatives: Pisces, piscina (basin near church's altar) (**Eng**); pysgod (**Wel**)

Slavic: пескарь (peskár') (**Rus**); piskorz (**Pol**)

Albanian: peshk (**Alb**)

which may derive from *peh₂- to feed, to protect:

*peh₂-
to protect, to shepherd

Germanic: feed, fodder, food, forage (**Eng**); fēdan, fōdor, fōda (**OE**); fiede, foer (**Fris**); voeden, voeder, voer (**Dut**); fetten, Futter (**Ger**); fœða, fóðr (**Norse**); føde, foder (**Nor**); föda, foder (**Swe**); føde, foder (**Dan**); fæða, fæði, fóður (**Ice**)

Derivatives: feurre, fouarre (**Fr**); futro (**Pol**)

Italic: pāscere, pāstus, pastiō, pastura, pārēre, appārēre, apparēns, appārēscere, appāritiō, appāritor, compārēre, trānspārēre, pābulum, pāstor, penes, penētrāre, penus, Penātes (**Lat**);

paître, repaître, repas, paisson, pâture, pasteur, pâtre, paraître, apparoir, apparaître, apparent, apparition, appariteur, comparaître, transparent, pénétrer (**Fr**);

pascere, pasto, pasciona, pastura, pastore, parere, apparire, penetrare, penetrante (**Ital**);

pacer, pasto, pación, pastura, pastor, parecer, aparir, aparecer, aparición, pábulo, penetrar, penetración, pentrante (**Sp**);

pascer, pasto, pastor, parecer, aparar, pábulo, penetrar, penetração, penetrante (**Port**);

paște, paștere, pășune, păstură, păstor, părea, părere, apărea, plaur (**Rom**)

Derivatives: pasture, pastor, appear, apparent, pablum, pabulum, penetrate (**Eng**); pastoor (**Dut**); Pastor (**Ger**); пáстырь (pástyr') (**Rus**

Hellenic: πατέομαι (patéomai), πῶμα (pôma), ποιμήν (poimḗn), Πάν (Pán), πῶυ (pôu) (**AnGk**); ποιμένας (poiménas) (**Gk**)

Derivatives: panic, pandemonium, pan- (**Eng**)

Slavic: paść (**Pol**); pást (**Cz**); pásť (**Slo**); пасат (pasat) (**Mace**)

Baltic: piemuõ (**Lith**)

Albanian: pashë (**Alb**)

Indo-Iranian: पाति (pāti), पायु (pāyú), पूषन (Pūṣan) (**Sans**); پہر (pahr), پاس (pâs), پاییدن (pāyīdan), آباد (ābād) (**Pers**)

Perhaps: **Italic**: pānis, pānārium, pānārius, pānicium, pānōsus, pāstillus (**Lat**); pain, panier, pastille, copain, compagnon (**Fr**); pane, paniere, paniccia, pastillo (**Ital**); pan, panero, panizo, panoso, pastilla (**Sp**); pão, paneiro, painço, pastilha (**Port**); pâine, pâne, paner, pâinar, pastilă (**Rom**)

Derivatives: pannier, pastille, antipasto, pastel, pastern, pastoral, repast, companion, accompany, pantry (**Eng**); पाव (pāv) (**Hin**)

*ḱonkho-
shell, mussel

Italic: congius (**Lat**); conche, conge (**Fr**); cogno, congio (**Ital**); congio (**Sp**); côngio (**Port**)

Derivatives: conch, concha, congius, cockle (**Eng**); konkylie (**Nor**); konkylie (**Dan**)

Hellenic: κόγχος (kónkhos) (**AnGk**)

Derivatives: concha, conchula, conchȳlium (**Lat**); conque, coquille (**Fr**); conca, concola, vongola, cocchiglia (**Ital**); concha, concho, conca, cuenca (**Sp**); concha, conca (**Port**)

Albanian: kungë (**Alb**)

Indo-Iranian: शङ्ख (śaṅkhá) (**Sans**)

Birds

*h₂éwis
bird

*h₂ōwy-ó-m, *h₂wéy-teh₂, *h₂wís-teh₂, *(s)h₂wy-etó-s

Celtic: hwyad (**Wel**); aoi (**Iri**)

Italic: avis, avicella, aucellus, aviārium (**Lat**); oie, oiseau (**Fr**); oca, uccello, augello (**Ital**); ave, avercilla (**Sp**); ave (**Port**)

Derivatives: avian, aviary, auspicious, auspice, aviation, aviator (**Eng**)

Hellenic: ἀετός (aetós) (**AnGk**); ἀετός (aetós), χαρταετός (chartaetós) (**Gk**)

Baltic: višta (**Lith**); vista (**Latv**)

Albanian: vito, vida, shotë (**Alb**)

Indo-Iranian: वि (ví), अवि (avi) (**Sans**)

which includes *h₂ōwyóm egg:

*h₂ōwyóm
egg

Germanic: ey, Cockney, egg (**Eng**); ǣg (**OE**); aei, aai (**Fris**); ei (**Dut**); Ei (**Ger**); egg (**Norse**); egg (**Nor**); ägg (**Swe**); æg (**Dan**); egg (**Ice**)

Celtic: ŵy (**Wel**); ubh (**Iri**)

Italic: ōvum, ōvātus (**Lat**); œuf (**Fr**); uovo (**Ital**); huevo, hueva (**Sp**); ovo, ova (**Port**); ou (**Rom**)

Derivatives: ovum, ovary, oval, ovate (**Eng**)

Hellenic: ᾠόν (ōión), ᾠοειδής (ōioeidḗs) (**AnGk**); αβγό (avgó), ωοειδής (ōoeidḗs) (**Gk**)

Slavic: яйцо (jajcó) (**Rus**); jajo, jajko, jajce (arch.) (**Pol**); vejce (**Cz**); vajce (**Slo**); jájце (jájce) (**Mace**)

Albanian: ve, vo (**Alb**)

Indo-Iranian: ھ (hā), ھگی (hagəi) (**Pash**); خایه (xâye) (slang) (**Pers**)

*gerh$_2$-

crane, to cry hoarsely

*gerh$_2$ōws, *gorh$_2$-n-

Germanic: crane, cranberry (**Eng**); cran (**OE**); kraan (**Fris**); kraan, kraanvogel (**Dut**); Kran, Kranich (**Ger**); trana, trani (uncert.) (**Norse**); kran, trane, trana (**Nor**); kran, trana (**Swe**); kran, trane (**Dan**); krani, trani (**Ice**)

Celtic: garan (**Wel**)

Italic: grūs (**Lat**); grue (**Fr**); gru (**Ital**); grulla, grúa (**Sp**); grua, grou, grulha (**Port**); grui (**Rom**)

Derivatives: Grus (**Eng**); kurrilë (**Alb**)

Hellenic: γέρανος (géranos) (**AnGk**)

Derivatives: geranium (**Eng**); geranium (**Lat**)

Slavic: журавль (žurávl') (**Rus**); żuraw (**Pol**); jeřáb (**Cz**); žeriav (**Slo**); жерав (žerav) (**Mace**)

Baltic: gérvė, garnỹs (**Lith**); dzẽrve, gaȓnis (**Latv**)

Indo-Iranian: (zaaṇëi) (**Pash**); كلنگ (kolang) (arch.) (**Pers**)

*ǵʰans-

goose

Germanic: goose (**Eng**); gōs (**OE**); goes, guos (**Fris**); gans (**Dut**); Gans (**Ger**); gás (**Norse**); gås (**Nor**); gås (**Swe**); gås (**Dan**); gæs (**Ice**)

Derivatives: ganso (**Sp**); ganso (**Port**)

Italic: ānser, ānserīnus (**Lat**); ánsar (**Sp**); anserino (**Port**)

Derivatives: anserine (**Eng**)

Hellenic: χήν (khḗn) (**AnGk**); χήνα (chína) (**Gk**)

Slavic: русь (gus') (**Rus**); gęś, gąska (**Pol**); husa (**Cz**); hus (**Slo**); руска (guska) (**Mace**)

Derivatives: gâscă (**Rom**)

Baltic: žąsis (**Lith**); zoss (**Latv**)

Albanian: gatë (**Alb**)

Indo-Iranian: हंस (haṃsa) (**Sans**); हंस (hans) (**Hin**)

*h₂eneti-
duck

Germanic: ende, drake (**Eng**); ened, ennet, annet (**OE**); ein (**Fris**); eend, draak (**Dut**); Ente, Enterich (**Ger**); ǫnd (**Norse**); and (**Nor**); and, anddrake (**Swe**); and, andrik (**Dan**); önd (**Ice**)

Italic: anas, anatīnus (**Lat**); anatra (**Ital**); ánade (**Sp**); adem (**Port**)

Derivatives: anatine (**Eng**)

Hellenic: νῆσσα (nêssa), νῆττα (nêtta), νᾶσσα (nâssa) (**AnGk**)

Slavic: утка (útka), утвá (utvá), утёнок (utjónok) (**Rus**)

Baltic: ántis (**Lith**)

Indo-Iranian: आति (āti) (**Sans**); هلۍ (helëy) (**Pash**)

*h₃érō
eagle

Germanic: erne (**Eng**); earn (**OE**); earn (**Fris**); aar, arend, adelaar (**Dut**); Aar, Adler (**Ger**); ari, ǫrn (**Norse**); ørn (**Nor**); örn (**Swe**); ørn (**Dan**); ari, örn (**Ice**)

Celtic: eryr (**Wel**); iolar (**Iri**)

Hellenic: ὄρνις (órnis), ὄρνιθος (órnithos), ὄρνῑξ (órnīx), ὄρνεον (órneon) (**AnGk**); όρνιο (órnio) (**Gk**)

Derivatives: ornithology, ornithomancy, ornithorhynchus, ornithosis (**Eng**)

Slavic: орёл (orël) (**Rus**); orzeł (**Pol**); orel (**Cz**); orol (**Slo**); орел (orel) (**Mace**)

Baltic: erelis (**Lith**); ērglis (**Latv**)

*spḗr
sparrow, bird

*spór(h₂)-w-ō, *spór(h₂)-w-o-s, *sprh₂-és-eh₂, *sprh₂-w-ó-s, *spr̥-g-

Germanic: sparrow (**Eng**); spearwa (**OE**); spreeuw (**Dut**); Sperling (**Ger**); spǫrr (**Norse**); spurv (**Nor**); sparv (**Swe**); spurv, spurre, sparre (**Dan**); spör (**Ice**)

Italic: parra (**Lat**)

Hellenic: ψάρ (psár) (**AnGk**); ψαρόνι (psaróni) (**Gk**)

*trosdos
thrush

Germanic: thrush, throstle (**Eng**); þrysce (**OE**); Drossel (**Ger**); þrǫstr (**Norse**); trost, trast (**Nor**); trast (**Swe**); trøske, drossel, trost (**Dan**); þröstur (**Ice**)

Celtic: drudwy (**Wel**); truid (**Iri**)

Italic: turdus (**Lat**); tordo (**Ital**); tordo (**Sp**); tordo (**Port**); sturz (**Rom**)

Derivatives: turdine, turdiform (**Eng**)

Hellenic: στρουθός (strouthós) (**AnGk**); στρουθίο (strouthion) (**Gk**)

Slavic: дрозд (drozd) (**Rus**); drozd (**Pol**); drozd (**Cz**); drozd (**Slo**); дрозд (drozd) (**Mace**)

Baltic: strazdas (**Lith**); strazds (**Latv**)

*nisdós
nest

see Movement

Insects

*bʰey-
bee

Germanic: bee (**Eng**); bēo (**OE**); bij (**Fris**); bij (**Dut**); Biene (**Ger**); bý (**Norse**); bie (**Nor**); bi (**Swe**); bi (**Dan**); bí, býfluga (**Ice**)

Celtic: begregyr, bydaf (**Wel**); beach, beachlann (**Iri**)

Italic: fūcus (**Lat**); fuco (**Ital**)

Hellenic: σφήξ (sphéx) (**AnGk**); σφήκα (sfíka) (**Gk**)

Derivatives: sphex (zoo.) (**Eng**)

Slavic: пчела (pčelá) (**Rus**); pszczoła (**Pol**); včela (**Cz**); včela (**Slo**); пчела (pčela) (**Mace**)

Baltic: bitė (**Lith**); bite (**Latv**)

Albanian: bletë (**Alb**)

The line which gave us the Latin *apis* is of different ancestry, possibly from Egyptian *bjt* (honey bee):

Italic: apis, apiānus, apicula, apium (**Lat**); abeille, apiculture, apiculteur, apicole (**Fr**); ape, pecchia, appio, apiolo (**Ital**); abeja, apio (**Sp**); abelha, aipo (**Port**)

Derivatives: apian, apiary, apiculture (**Eng**)

*wobs-
wasp

Germanic: wasp (**Eng**); wæps (**OE**); waps, weeps, meeps (**Fris**); wesp (**Dut**); Wespe (**Ger**); veps, kvefs (**Nor**); hveps (**Dan**); vespa (**Ice**)

Celtic: gwchi (**Wel**); foiche (**Iri**)

Italic: vespa (**Lat**); guêpe (**Fr**); vespa (**Ital**); avispa, vespa (**Sp**); vespa (**Port**); viespe (**Rom**)

Slavic: oca (osá) (**Rus**); osa (**Pol**); vosa (**Cz**); osa (**Slo**); oca (osa) (**Mace**)

Baltic: vapsvà, vapsà (**Lith**); vapsene, vespa (**Latv**)

Albanian: anza (**Alb**)

Perhaps: Indo-Iranian: کبت (gabt) (**Pers**)

from *webh- to weave, referring to the wasps' woven nests:

*webh-
to weave, braid

*wébʰ-e-ti, *wobʰ-éye-ti, *u-né-bʰ-e-ti, *ubʰ-néH-ti, *ubʰ-yéti, *wobʰ-s-éh$_2$, *wébʰ-tis, *wobʰ-yo-

Germanic: weave, web, weft (**Eng**); wefan, webb, wift (**OE**); weve, web (**Fris**); weven, web (**Dut**); weben (**Ger**); vefja, vefr, váfa (**Norse**); veve, vev (**Nor**); väva, väv (**Swe**); væve, væv (**Dan**); vefja, vefur (**Ice**)

Celtic: gwau (**Wel**)

Hellenic: ὑφαίνω (huphaínō), ὑφή (huphḗ) (**AnGk**); υφαίνω (yfaíno) (**Gk**)

Derivatives: hypha, hyphomycete, hyphopodium (**Eng**)

Baltic: vyti (**Lith**)

Albanian: venj, vej (**Alb**)

Indo-Iranian: उभ्नाति (ubhnāti), उम्भति (umbháti), उनब्द्धि (unábddhi) (**Sans**); بافتن (bâftan) (**Pers**)

223

*morwi-
ant

Germanic: mire (obs.), pismire (dial.) (**Eng**); mier (**Dut**); maurr (**Norse**); maur (**Nor**); myra (**Swe**); myre (**Dan**); maur (**Ice**)

Celtic: myrion (**Wel**)

Italic: formīca, formīcāre, formīcula (**Lat**); fourmi, fourmiller (**Fr**); formica, formicola (**Ital**); hormiga (**Sp**); formiga, formigar (**Port**); furnică, furnica, furnicare (**Rom**)

Derivatives: formaldehyde, formic acid, formicate (**Eng**)

Hellenic: μύρμηξ (múrmēx) (**AnGk**); μυρμήγκι (myrmínki) (**Gk**)

Derivatives: myrmeco-, -myrmex (**Eng**); myrmecitis, myrmecias, myrmecium (**Lat**)

Slavic: муравей (muravéj) (**Rus**); mrówka, mrowisko, mrówkojad, mrównik (**Pol**); mravenec (**Cz**); mravec (**Slo**); мравка (mravka) (**Mace**)

Albanian: morr (**Alb**)

Indo-Iranian: वम्र (vamra) (**Sans**); مورچه (murče), مور (môr) (arch.) (**Pers**)

*mus-
fly

Germanic: midge, midget (**Eng**); mycg (**OE**); mich (**Fris**); mug (**Dut**); Mücke (**Ger**); mý (**Norse**); mygg (**Nor**); mygga (**Swe**); myg (**Dan**); mý (**Ice**)

Italic: musca (**Lat**); mouche (**Fr**); mosca, moscerino (**Ital**); mosca, mosquito (**Sp**); mosca, mosquito (**Port**); muscă (**Rom**)

Derivatives: mosquito, musca (**Eng**)

Hellenic: μυῖα (muîa) (**AnGk**); μύγα (mýga) (**Gk**)

Derivatives: myiasis (**Eng**)

Slavic: муха (múxa) (**Rus**); mucha (**Pol**); moucha (**Cz**); mucha (**Slo**); мува (múva) (**Mace**)

Baltic: musė (**Lith**); muša (**Latv**)

Albanian: mizë (**Alb**)

Indo-Iranian: (mëch) (**Pash**); مگس (magas) (**Pers**)

*plou-
flea

Germanic: flea (**Eng**); flēah (**OE**); flie (**Fris**); vlo (**Dut**); Floh (**Ger**); fló (**Norse**); fló (**Ice**)

Italic: pūlex (**Lat**); puce (**Fr**); pulce (**Ital**); pulga (**Sp**); pulga (**Port**); purice (**Rom**)

Derivatives: puce (**Eng**); plws (**Wel**)

Hellenic: ψύλλα (psúlla) (**AnGk**); ψύλλος (psýllos) (**Gk**)

Slavic: блоха (bloxá) (**Rus**); pchła (**Pol**); blecha (**Cz**); blcha (**Slo**); болва (bolva) (**Mace**)

Baltic: blusa (**Lith**); blusa (**Latv**)

Albanian: plesht (**Alb**)

Indo-Iranian: प्लुषि (pluṣi) (**Sans**); ورزو (vraža) (**Pash**)

*knid-
louse, nit, louse egg

Germanic: nit (**Eng**); hnitu (**OE**); neet (**Dut**); Nisse (**Ger**); gnit (**Norse**); gnit, nit (**Ice**)

Celtic: nedd (**Wel**); sned (**Iri**)

Hellenic: κονίς (konís) (**AnGk**)

Slavic: гнида (gnída) (**Rus**); gnida (**Pol**); hnida (**Cz**); hnida (**Slo**); гнида (gnída) (**Mace**)

Baltic: gnida (**Latv**)

Albanian: thërijë/thëni (**Alb**)

*luHs-
louse

uncertain etymology

Germanic: louse (**Eng**); lūs (**OE**); lús (**Fris**); luis (**Dut**); Laus (**Ger**); lús (**Norse**); lus (**Nor**); lus (**Swe**); lus (**Dan**); lús (**Ice**)

Celtic: llau (**Wel**)

Baltic: liulė (**Lith**)

Indo-Iranian: यूका (yūkā) (**Sans**)

*wr̥mis-
worm

Germanic: worm (**Eng**); wyrm (**OE**); wjirm (**Fris**); worm, wurm (**Dut**); Wurm (**Ger**); ormr (**Norse**); orm (**Nor**); orm (**Swe**); orm (**Dan**); ormur (**Ice**)

Celtic: gwraint (**Wel**)

Italic: vermis, vermiculus, verminōsus (**Lat**); ver, vermeil, vermineux (**Fr**); verme, vermiglio, verminare, verminoso (**Ital**); verme, bermejo, verminoso (**Sp**); verme, vermelho, vermículo, vermina, verminoso (**Port**); vierme, viermănos (**Rom**)

Derivatives: vermiform, vermin, vermis, vermilion, vermiculate (**Eng**) (the meaning red developed from a colour that one can get from a scale insect)

Hellenic: ῥόμος (rhómos) (**AnGk**)

Slavic: вéрмие (vérmije) (**Rus**)

Baltic: var̃mas (**Lith**)

Albanian: rrime (**Alb**)

Animal products

*h₂ōwyóm
egg

see Birds

*glag-
milk

Italic: lac, lactarius, lacteus, lacticīnium, lactāre, lactosus, lactūca (**Lat**);

lait, lactaire, laiteron, laitier, lacté, lacter, laitue, laiteux (**Fr**);

latte, lattaio, latteo, latticino, lattare, lattuga (**Ital**);

leche, lactario, lechero, lácteo, lacticinio, lactar, lechuga, lechoso (**Sp**);

leite, lactário, leiteiro, laticínio, leituga, leitoso (**Port**);

lapte, lăptar, lăptucă, lăptos (**Rom**)

Derivatives: lactate, lactation, lactose, lactic, lettuce (**Eng**); latuw (**Dut**); llaeth (**Wel**); lacht (**Iri**); латук (latuk) (**Rus**)

Hellenic: γάλα (gála), γάλακτος (gálaktos), γαλαξίας (galaxías) (**AnGk**); γαλαξίας (galaxías) (**Gk**)

Derivatives: galactic, galactagogue, galactorrhea, polygala, galaxy (**Eng**); Galaxie (**Ger**); galaxias (**Lat**); galaxie (**Fr**); galassia (**Ital**); galaxia (**Sp**); galaxia (**Slo**)

Albanian: dhallë (**Alb**)

*h₂welh₁-
hair, wool

*h₂wĺh₁neh₂

Germanic: wool, woollen/woolen (**Eng**); wull, wullen (**OE**); wol, wolle (**Fris**); wol (**Dut**); Wolle, wollen (**Ger**); ull (**Norse**); ull (**Nor**); ull, ylle (**Swe**); uld (**Dan**); ull (**Ice**)

Celtic: gwlan (**Wel**); olann (**Iri**)

Italic: lāna, lanarius, lānōsus, lānūgō, vellus/villus, villōsus (**Lat**);

laine, lainier, laineux, villeux, velu, velouté, velours (**Fr**);

lana, lanario, lanoso, lanugine, vello, villo, velloso, villoso (**Ital**);

lana, lanero, lanoso, lanugo, vellón, vello, velloso (**Sp**);

lã, laneiro, lanoso, velo, veloso, viloso (**Port**);

lână, lânar, lânos (**Rom**)

Derivatives: lanner, lanugo, villus, villous, fluff (poss.), velvet (**Eng**)

Hellenic: λῆνος (lênos), λῶμα (lôma), λάχνη (lákhnē), λάχνος (lákhnos), λάσιος (lásios) (**AnGk**)

Slavic: волна (volná) (**Rus**); wełna (**Pol**); vlna (**Cz**); vlna (**Slo**); волна (volna) (**Mace**)

Baltic: vilna (**Lith**); vilna (**Latv**)

Indo-Iranian: ऊर्णा (ūrṇā) (**Sans**); ऊन (ūn) (**Hin**); (warrëi) (**Pash**)

*melit-
honey

Germanic: mildew, mulch (**Eng**); mildēaw, melsc (**OE**); moaldau (**Fris**); meeldauw (**Dut**); Mehltau, Meltau (**Ger**); mjöldagg (**Swe**); meldug (**Dan**); milska (**Ice**)

Celtic: mêl (**Wel**); milis, mil (**Iri**)

Italic: mel, melleus, mellifer, mellificus, mellifluus, mellītus (**Lat**); miel, mellifique, melliflue (**Fr**); miele, mellito (**Ital**); miel (**Sp**); mel (**Port**); miere (**Rom**)

Derivatives: melleous, melliferous, mellific, mellifluent, mellifluous, melliloquent, mellivorous (**Eng**)

Hellenic: μέλι (méli), μέλισσα (mélissa) (**AnGk**); μέλι (méli), μέλισσα (mélissa) (**Gk**)

Derivatives: melissophobia (**Eng**)

Albanian: mjaltë (**Alb**)

*médʰu

mead, honey

Germanic: mead **(Eng)**; meodu **(OE)**; mea **(Fris)**; mede **(Dut)**; Met **(Ger)**; mjǫðr **(Norse)**; mjød **(Nor)**; mjöd **(Swe)**; mjød **(Dan)**; mjöður **(Ice)**

Celtic: medd **(Wel)**; miodh **(Iri)**

Hellenic: μέθυ (méthu), ἀμέθῠστος (améthustos) **(AnGk)**; μέθη (méthi), μεθοκοπάω (methokopáo), μεθώ (methó), μέθυσος (méthysos), μεθύλιο (methýlio), μεθυλένιο (methylénio), μεθάνιο (methánio), μεθανόλη (methanóli) **(Gk)**

Derivatives: methylene, methane, amethyst, amethystine **(Eng)**; amethystus, amethystinus **(Lat)**; méthylène **(Fr)**; ametista **(Ital)**; amatista **(Sp)**; ametist **(Rom)**; аметист (ametíst) **(Rus)**

Slavic: мёд (mjod), мед (med), медвёдь (medvéd') **(Rus)**; miód, niedźwiedź **(Pol)**; med, medvěd **(Cz)**; med, medveď **(Slo)**; мед (med) **(Mace)**

Derivatives: mied **(Rom)**

Baltic: medus **(Lith)**; mędus **(Latv)**

Indo-Iranian: मधु (mádhu) **(Sans)**; मधु (madhu) **(Hin)**; مل (mol), می (mey) **(Pers)**

Environment

Sky

*h₂stḗr

star

Germanic: star (**Eng**); steorra (**OE**); steer, stjer (**Fris**); ster, gesternte (**Dut**); Star, Stern (**Ger**); stjarna (**Norse**); stjerne, stjerna (**Nor**); stjärna (**Swe**); stjerne (**Dan**); stjarna (**Ice**)

Celtic: sêr, seren (**Wel**)

Italic: stella, stēllāris (**Lat**); étoile, stellaire (**Fr**); stella, stellare (**Ital**); estrella, estelar, estrellar (**Sp**); estrela, estelar (**Port**); stea (**Rom**)

Derivatives: stellar, constellation, estoile (**Eng**)

Hellenic: ἀστήρ (astḗr) (**AnGk**); αστέρι (astéri) (astéri), αστέρας (astéras) (**Gk**)

Derivatives: aster, asterisk, asteroid, astral, astrology, astronaut, astronomy, monaster (**Eng**); astēr (**Lat**)

Indo-Iranian: तारा (tāra), स्तृ (stṛ́) (**Sans**); तारा (tārā) (**Hin**); ستوری (storay) (**Pash**); ستاره (setâre) (**Pers**)

which derives from *h₂eh₁s- to burn:

*h₂eh₁s-

to burn, to be dry

*h₂eHs-eh₁-(ye)-, *h₂eHs-h₂-

Probably: **Germanic:** ash (**Eng**); æsce (**OE**); jiske (**Fris**); as (**Dut**); Asche (**Ger**); aska (**Norse**); aske (**Nor**); aska (**Swe**); aske (**Dan**); aska (**Ice**)

Celtic: odyn (**Wel**); áith (**Iri**)

Italic: ārēre, ārefacere, āridus, āra, assus (**Lat**); aride (**Fr**); arido (**Ital**); árido, asar (**Sp**); arfar, assar (**Port**)

Derivatives: arid (**Eng**)

Hellenic: ἄζω (ázō), ἄσβολος (ásbolos), ἀσβόλη (asbólē) (poss.) (**AnGk**)

Slavic: ozditi (**Cz**)

Indo-Iranian: आस (ása-) (**Sans**)

*h₁ews-
to burn

*h₁éws-e-ti, *h₁us-néh₂-ti (perhaps), *h₁éwst, *h₁us-nós, *h₁us-tós

Germanic: ember (**Eng**); æmyrġe, ysle (**OE**); Ammer (dial.) (**Ger**); yrja, eimyrja, usli (**Norse**); mörja (**Swe**); emmer (poss.) (**Dan**); eimyrja (**Ice**)

Italic: ūrere, adūrere, ambūrere, būstum, combūrere, inūrere, ūrēdō, urna, usta, ustrīna, ustulāre, ustūra, ussī, ustus (**Lat**); buste, urne (**Fr**); busto, comburere, urna, ustrino, ustolare, usto (**Ital**); adurir, busto, urna (**Sp**); busto, uredo, urna, ustular (**Port**); ustura, usturare (**Rom**)

Derivatives: adure, bust, combust, urn, ustrinum (**Eng**); urne (**Nor**); busta (**Iri**); урна (úrna) (**Rus**)

Hellenic: εὔω (heúō), εὗσα (heûsa) (**AnGk**)

Baltic: usnis (**Lith**)

Albanian: (h)yll, ethe (**Alb**)

Indo-Iranian: ओषति (óṣati), उष्ण (uṣṇá), उष्ट (uṣṭa) (**Sans**)

*dʰegʷʰ-
to burn; warm, hot

*dʰégʷʰ-e-ti, *dʰogʷʰ-éye-ti, *dʰég̑ʷʰ-, *dʰg̑ʷʰ-éh₁ye-ti, *dʰg̑ʷʰ-éy-ti, *dʰegʷʰ-i-s, *dʰogʷʰ-éh₂, *dʰógʷʰ-r̥, *dʰégʷʰ-teh₂

Germanic: day, daw, dwine, dwindle (**Eng**); dæg, dagian, dwīnan (**OE**); dei, ferdwyne (**Fris**); dag, dagen, dwijnen, verdwijnen (**Dut**); Tag, tagen (**Ger**); dagr, dǫgr, daga, dvína (**Norse**); døgn, dage (**Nor**); dag, dygn, daga, dvina (**Swe**); dag, døgn, dage, tvine (**Dan**); dagur, dvina (**Ice**)

Perhaps: **Germanic**: dear, dearth (**Eng**); dēore (**OE**); djoer, djoerte (**Fris**); duur, duurte (**Dut**); teuer (**Ger**); dýrr, dýrð (**Norse**); dyr (**Nor**); dyr, dyrd (**Swe**); dyr (**Dan**); dýr, dýrð (**Ice**)

Celtic: deifio, edwino, goddaith (**Wel**); daigh, doigh (**Iri**)

Italic: fovēre, fōmentum, febris, fēbruum, februārius, sitis, sitīre, situs (**Lat**); fomenter, fièvre, février, soif (**Fr**); fomento, febbre, febbraio, sete, sito (**Ital**); fomento, fiebre, febrero, sed (**Sp**); fomento, febre, fevereiro, sede (**Port**); febră, fior, februarie, făurar, sete (**Rom**)

Derivatives: foment, fever, February (**Eng**); fefor (**OE**); februari (**Dut**); Fieber, Februar

(Ger); feber (**Dan**); Chwefror (**Wel**); fiabhras, Feabhra (**Iri**); Φεβρουάριος (Fevrouários), Φλεβάρης (Fleváris) (**Gk**); февраль (fevral') (**Rus**)

Hellenic: ἔφθῖτο (éphthito), φθίνω (phthínō), φθινύθω (phthinúthō), φθῖσῐς (phthísis), τέφρα (téphra) (**AnGk**); τέφρα (téfra) (**Gk**)

Derivatives: tephra (**Eng**)

Slavic: жечь (žeč'), дёготь (djógot') (**Rus**); żec (dated), dziegieć (**Pol**); dehet (**Cz**); decht (**Slo**); жешти (žešti) (**Mace**)

Baltic: dègti, degùtas, dēgis, dagà (**Lith**); degt, deguts (**Latv**)

Albanian: djeg, ndez (**Alb**)

Indo-Iranian: दहति (dahati), दाहयति (dāhayati), अधाक् (adhāk), क्षिधी (kṣidhī), क्षिणाति (kṣiṇāti), क्षिणोति (kṣiṇóti), क्षीयते (kṣīyáte), क्षायति (kṣāyati), क्षिति (kṣíti), क्षित (kṣitá), दग्ध (dagdhá) (**Sans**); داغ (dāġ) (**Pers**)

*dʰéh₁s
god, deity; sacred place

see Object Motion

*deyn-
day

Germanic: Lent, Lenten (**Eng**); lencten, lengten (**OE**); lente (**Dut**); Lenz (**Ger**)

Celtic: denus, dia (**Iri**)

Italic: diēs, nūndinus, perendinus, diū, diurnus, diurnālis, hodiē, hodiernus, merīdiēs, merīdiō, diēs Iovis, diēs Lunae, diēs Martis, diēs Mercuriī, diēs Veneris, diēs Saturnī, diēs Sōlis, diēs Dominica, diārium (**Lat**);

diurne, jour, journée, journal, hui, aujourd'hui, midi, jeudi, lundi, mardi, mercredi, vendredi, dimanche, séjour, séjourner (**Fr**);

dì, diurno, giorno, giornata, giornale, oggi, odierno, meridie, meriggio, meriare, meriggiare, giovedì, lunedì, martedì, mercoledì, venerdì, domenica, soggiornare (**Ital**);

día, diurno, jornada, hoy, amarizar, jueves, lunes, martes, miércoles, viernes, domingo, diario (**Sp**);

dia, diurno, jorna, diurnal, jornal, hoje, hodierno, meridio, domingo (**Port**);

zi, diurn, meriză, meriza, merizare, joi, luni, marți, miercuri, vineri, duminică (**Rom**)

Derivatives: diurnal, journal, journey, hodiern, hodiernal, a.m. (ante meridiem), p.m. (post meridiem), diary, sojourn (**Eng**); dydd Iau, dydd Llun, dydd Mawrth, dydd Mercher, dydd Gwener, dydd Sadwrn, dydd Sul (**Wel**); Dé Luain, Máirt, Dé Sathairn, Domhnach (**Iri**)

Slavic: день (den') (**Rus**); dzień (**Pol**); den (**Cz**); deň (**Slo**); ден (den) (**Mace**)

Baltic: diena (**Lith**); diena (**Latv**)

Indo-Iranian: दिन (dina) (**Sans**); दिन (din) (**Hin**)

which derives from *dyew- to be bright:

*dyew-
to be bright; sky, heaven

*dyḗws, *deynos, *deywós, *diwyós

Germanic: Tyr, Tuesday (**Eng**); Tiw, tiwesdæġ (**OE**); tiisdei (**Fris**); Týr, týsdagr, tívar (**Norse**); Ty, tirsdag (**Nor**); Tyr, tisdag (**Swe**); Tyr, Ty, Ti, tisdag, tirsdag (**Dan**); Týr (**Ice**)

Celtic: duw, dydd (**Wel**); dia (**Iri**)

Italic: deus, dea, deitās, deificāre, dīvus, dīvīnātiō, dīvīnus, dīvīnitās, dīvīnāre, diva, Iuppiter (+pater) (**Lat**); dieu, déité, déifier, devin, divin, divinité, deviner, diva (**Fr**); dio, deità, deificare, divino, divinità, divinare, indovinare, diva (**Ital**); dios, divinidad, adivinar, divinar, diva (**Sp**); deus, deidade, divindade, adivinhar, diva (**Port**); zeu, zău, zeitate, divinitate (**Rom**)

Derivatives: deity, deification, deify, divine, divination, divinity, diva, Jupiter (**Eng**); diva (**Dut**)

Hellenic: Ζεύς (Zeús) (**AnGk**); Ζευς (Zefs), Δίας (Días) (**Gk**)

Slavic: диво (divo) (**Rus**); dziw (**Pol**); div (**Cz**); div (**Slo**)

Baltic: dievas (**Lith**); dievs (**Latv**)

Indo-Iranian: द्यु (dyu), दयौ (dyáuh), द्यौष्पितृ (dyauṣ-pitṛ), देव (devá), दिव्य (divyá), द्यु (dyú), दिव (divá), द्यो (dyo) (**Sans**); देव (dev) (**Hin**); ديو (dêw) (**Pash**); ديو (div), زاوش (zāvoš) (**Pers**)

Derivatives: daeva (**Eng**)

*sóh₂wl̥
sun

Germanic: sun, Sunday, south, southern (**Eng**); sunne, sunnandæġ, sūþ, sūþerne (**OE**);

sinne, snein, súd (**Fris**); zon, zondag, zuiden, zuid (**Dut**); Sonne, Sonntag, Süden, Süd (**Ger**);

sól, sunna, sunnudagr, sunnan, suðr, suðrœnn (**Norse**); sol, søndag, sør, syd (**Nor**); sol, söndag, sunnan, söder, syd (**Swe**); sol, søndag, sønden, syd (**Dan**); sunna, sól, sunnudagur, sunnan, suður, suðrænn (**Ice**)

Celtic: haul (**Wel**); súil (**Iri**)

Italic: sōl, sōlāris, sōlārium, solstitium (**Lat**); soleil, solaire, solstice (**Fr**); sole, solare, solarium (**Ital**); sol, solar (**Sp**); sol, solar, solário (**Port**); soare, solar (**Rom**)

Derivatives: solar, solarium, insolate, solstice (**Eng**); zolder, solarium (**Dut**)

Hellenic: ἥλιος (hélios) (**AnGk**); ήλιος (élios) (ílios) (**Gk**)

Derivatives: heliotrope, perihelion, aphelion, helium, heliocentric, heliograph (**Eng**)

Slavic: солнце (sólnce) (**Rus**); słońce (**Pol**); slunce (**Cz**); slnce, slnko (**Slo**); сонце (sonce) (**Mace**)

Baltic: sáulė (**Lith**); saūle (**Latv**)

Indo-Iranian: सुर (sūra), सूर् (sūr), स्वर् (svar), सूर्य (sūrya) (**Sans**); सूरज (sūraj) (**Hin**); خور (xōr) (**Pers**)

*méh₁ns

moon, month

Germanic: moon, Monday, month (**Eng**); mōna, mōnandæg, mōnaþ (**OE**); moanne, moandei (**Fris**); maan, maandag, maand (**Dut**); Mond, Montag, Monat (**Ger**); máni, mánadagr, mánaðr (**Norse**); måne, mandag, måned (**Nor**); måne, måndag, månad (**Swe**); måne, mandag, måned (**Dan**); máni, mánudagur, mánuður (**Ice**)

Celtic: mis (**Wel**); mí (**Iri**)

Italic: mēnsis, mēnstrua, mēnstruālis, mēnstruāre, trimestris (**Lat**); mois, menstruel (**Fr**); mese, trimestre (**Ital**); mes, menstruar, menstrual (**Sp**); mês, menstruar, menstrual (**Port**);

Derivatives: menstruation, menstrual, trimester (**Eng**)

Hellenic: μήν (mén), μείς (meís), μήνη (ménē), μηνῑσκος (mēnískos) (**AnGk**); μήνας (mínas), μηνίσκος (miniskos) (**Gk**)

Derivatives: menopause, menorrhea, meniscus (**Eng**); menisco (**Port**); менйск (menísk) (**Rus**)

Slavic: месяц (mésjac) (**Rus**); miesiąc (**Pol**); měsíc (**Cz**); mesiac (**Slo**); мéсец (mésec), месечина (mesečina) (**Mace**)

Baltic: mėnuo (**Lith**); mēness, mēnesis (**Latv**)

Albanian: muaj, muej (**Alb**)

Indo-Iranian: मास (māsa), मास् (mās) (**Sans**); मास (mās), माह (māh) (**Hin**); میاشت

(myâšt) (**Pash**); ماه (mâh) (**Pers**)

which is probably from *meh₁- to measure:

*meh₁-
to measure

*mi-meh₁-, *méh₁-tis, *meh₁-lo-, *méh₁-trom, *méh₁ns (prob.), *moh₁ros

Germanic: meal (**Eng**); mǣl (as in time for eating) (**OE**); miel (**Fris**); maal, malen (**Dut**); Mahl, Mal, mal, malen (**Ger**); mál (**Norse**); mål (**Nor**); mål, måla (**Swe**); mål, male (**Dan**); mál (**Ice**)

Derivatives: malować (**Pol**)

Celtic: mawr (**Wel**); mór (**Iri**)

Italic: mētīrī, commētīrī, immēnsus, mēnsūra, mēnsūrāre, mēnsa, mēnsārius, semel (**Lat**); mesure, mesurer, moise (**Fr**); misura, misurare, mensa (**Ital**); medir, comedir, mesura, mesurar, mesa, mensa, menso, medida, metro (**Sp**); medir, mesura, mesurar, mensurar, mesa, mesário, medida (**Port**); măsură, masă (**Rom**)

Derivatives: commensurable, commensurate, immense, measure, dimension (**Eng**); mesur (**Wel**); mias (**Iri**)

Hellenic: μῆτις (mêtis), μέτρον (métron), μετρικός (metrikós) (**AnGk**); μέτρο (métro) (**Gk**)

Derivatives: metis, metron, altimeter, barometer, diameter, hexameter, isometric, meter, metre, metric, metrology, metronome, parameter, pentameter, perimeter, symmetry, telemetry, thermometer (**Eng**); Metrum (**Ger**); metrum (**Lat**); mètre (**Fr**); metro, metricus (**Ital**)

Slavic: мѐра (méra), мѐрить (mérit') (**Rus**); miara, mierzyć (**Pol**); míra, měřit, mířit (**Cz**); miera, mieriť (**Slo**); мера (mera), мери (meri) (**Mace**)

Albanian: mas (**Alb**)

Indo-Iranian: मिमीते (mímīte), असमाति (asamāti) (**Sans**)

*med-
to measure; give advice, healing

*méd-eti, *med-eh₁-(ye)-ti, *mēd-yé-ti, *méd-tus, *méd-os, *mod-ós

Germanic: mete (**Eng**); metan (**OE**); mjitte (**Fris**); meten, maat (**Dut**); messen, Maß (**Ger**); meta (**Norse**); meta (**Nor**); mäta (**Swe**); meta (**Ice**)

Italic: medeor, medicus, medicīnus, medicīnālis, medicīna, medicō, medicāmen, medicāmentum, medicātor, meditor, remedium, modus, commodus, modicus, modificō, modificātiō, modius, moderor, moderātiō, modestus, modestia, modo, modernus, modulus, modulātē, modulātiō, modulātor, multimodus, quōmodo (**Lat**);

mège, meige, médicinal, médecine, mégir, médicament, remède, mode, commode, modique, muid, modérer, modeste, moderne, moule, module, modèle, modeler, comme, comment (**Fr**);

medico, Medici, medicinale, medicina, medicare, medicatore, rimedio, modo, comodo, modificare, modio, moggio, mozzo, moderare, modesto, modestia, mo', moderno, modulo, modulare, come (**Ital**);

médico, medicinal, medicina, medicar, vedegambre, medicamento, remedio, modo, cómodo, módico, modificar, modio, moyo, moderar, modesto, modestia, moderno, molde, model, como, cómo (**Sp**);

médico, medicinal, mezinha, medicina, medicar, remédio, modo, cómodo, módico, modificar, moio, moderar, modesto, moderno, molde, módulo, como (**Port**);

medic, medicinal, medicină, remediu, mod, măi, modern, model, cum (**Rom**)

Derivatives: medic, medicinal, medicine, medicate, remedy, mode, commodious, modify, modification, modius, muid, moderate, moderation, modest, modesty, modern, mold, mould, module, modulus, modulate, modulation, modulator, model, modem, multimodal, quomodo (**Eng**);

medicus, mud (**Dut**); modus, kommod, Kommode, modern (**Ger**); medicin (**Swe**); meddyg (**Wel**);

медицина (medicina), комод (komod), модификация (modifikacija), модуль (módul') (**Rus**); medyk, medycyna (**Pol**)

Hellenic: μέδω (médō), Μέδουσᾰ (Médousa), μέδομαι (médomai), μήδομαι (médomai), μήδεα (médea) (**AnGk**)

Derivatives: Medusa (**Eng**)

*lewk-

light, bright; to shine; to see

*luktó, *lowk-éye, *lewk-éh₁-(ye)-, *léwk-s, *lewk-ós, *lewk-to-s, *léwk-so-s, *léwk-mn̥, *lewk-o-dʰro-, *lowk-s-tro-, *lówk-os, *lowk-yo-, *léwk-s-mn̥, *lowk-s-neh₂, *luk-s-nos, *luk-s-ḱós, *luk-eh₂

Germanic: light, enlight, inlight, leam, lea (**Eng**); lēoht, linlīhtan, onlīhtan, enlīhtan, īeman, lȳman, lēah (**OE**);

ljocht, inljochtsje, lāch (**Fris**); licht, lichten, inlichten, lo, loo (mostly in place names) (**Dut**); licht, Licht, leuchten, einleuchten (**Ger**);

leygr, ljótr, Ljótr, ljóss, ljómi, ljós, ljóma (**Norse**); ljos, lys (**Nor**); ljus (**Swe**); lys (**Dan**); ljótur, ljós, ljómi, ljóma (**Ice**)

Derivatives: laom (**Iri**)

Celtic: llug (**Wel**); loiscim (**Iri**)

Italic: lūx, lūcēre, luscus, lucerna, lūcidus, relūcēre, lūcifer, lūmen, lūmināre, illūmināre, lūminōsus, lūcus, lūcubrāre, ēlūcubrāre, lūcubrātiō, lustrum, lustrāre, lūna, lūnāris, lūnāticus, interlūnium, lūnula, novilūnium (**Lat**);

luire, louche, luzerne, lucide, reluire, lumière, luminaire, illuminer, allumer, lumineux, élucubrer, lustrer, lune, lunaire, lunatique, lunule (**Fr**);

luce, lucere, losco, lucido, lucifero, lume, luminare, luminaria, illuminare, alluminare, luminoso, luco, elucubrare, lustro, lustrare, luna, lunare, lunatico, interlunio, lunula, novilunio (**Ital**);

luz, lucir, lusco, lucerna, lucio, lucífero, lumbre, lumbrera, luminar, luminaria, iluminar, alumbrar, luminoso, elucubrar, lucubración, lucubrar, lustro, lustrar, luna, lunar, lunático, novilunio (**Sp**);

luz, luzir, lusco, luzerna, lucerna, lúcido, lucifero, lume, lumieira, lumeeira, luminária, luminar, iluminar, alumiar, luminoso, elucubrar, lucubração, lobrigar, lucubrar, lua, luar, lunar, lunático (**Port**);

luci, lucire, lucernă, luced, luceafăr, lume, lumină, lumânare, lumina, luminare, luminos, lucra (poss.), lună, lunatic (**Rom**)

Derivatives: lux, elucidate, lucent, lucid, Lucifer, luciferous, pellucid, translucent, lucerne, luminary, luminate, illuminate, luminous, lucubrate, lucubration, lustrum, lustre, luna, lunar, lune, lunatic, interlunation, lunule, lunula (**Eng**); lusî (**Fris**); luzerne (**Dut**); Laune (**Ger**); lune (**Dan**); люцерна (ljucerna), люмен (ljumen) (**Rus**); lucerna (**Cz**)

Hellenic: λευκός (leukós), λύχνος (lúkhnos), λύγξ (lúnx), ἀμφιλύκη (amphilúkē), λυκάβας (lukábas), λυκόφως (lukóphōs), Λυκαῖος (Lukaîos), λύκειος (lúkeios) (**AnGk**)

Derivatives: leucocyte, leukemia, Alicante (**Eng**)

Slavic: луч (luč), луна́ (luná) (**Rus**); łuczywo, łucz, łuna (**Pol**); louč, luna, lučit (**Cz**); lúč, luna, lúčiť (**Slo**); лач (lač), луна (luna) (**Mace**)

Baltic: lauka, laũkas (**Lith**); lauks (**Latv**)

Indo-Iranian: लोक (loká), रोक (roká), रोचते (rocate) (**Sans**); روز (rōz), روشن (rowšan) (**Pers**)

*bʰehₐ-
to shine

*bʰéh₂-ti, *bʰ-n̥-h₂-ye-ti, *bʰéh₂-os, *bʰóh₂-mo-s, *bʰeh₂-no-s

Germanic: beacon, buoy (**Eng**); bēacen (**OE**); biene, bjinne, beaken (**Fris**); boen, boenen, baken, baak, boei (**Dut**); bohnen, bohnern, Bake, Bauke (**Ger**); bákn (**Norse**); båk, båke (**Nor**); bona, båk (**Swe**); bone, bavn, båke (**Dan**); bákn (**Ice**)

Derivatives: bouée (**Fr**); bouy (**Sp**)

Celtic: bán (**Iri**)

Hellenic: φάντα (phánta), φαίνω (phaínō), -φᾰνής (-phanḗs), φᾰνερός (phanerós), φᾰντᾰσῐ́ᾱ (phantasíā), φᾰ́ντᾰσμᾰ (phántasma), φᾰντᾰστῐκός (phantastikós), φαινόμενον (phainómenon), ἐπιφαίνω (epiphaínō), φάος (pháos), φῶς (phôs), φωτω- (phōtō-) (**AnGk**); φαίνομαι (faínomai), φανερός (fanerós), φαντασία (fantasía), φάντασμα (fántasma), φανταστικός (fantastikós), φαινόμενο (fainómeno) (**Gk**)

Derivatives: fantasy, phantasm, phantom, fantastic, phenomenon, diaphanous, emphasis, epiphany, phanerozoic, phase, phene, phenetic, phenology, phenotype, photic, sycophant, telophase, theophany, tryptophan (**Eng**); fantoom (**Dut**); Phantom (**Ger**); fantom (**Nor**); fantom (**Swe**); fantom (**Dan**); phantasma, phaenomenon (**Lat**); fantaisie, fantôme, phantasme, phénomène (**Fr**); fantasma (**Ital**); fantasma, fenómeno (**Sp**); fantasma, abantesma, fenómeno (**Port**); fantomă (**Rom**); фантáзия (fantázija), фантóм (fantóm) (**Rus**); fantom (**Pol**)

Albanian: bëj (**Alb**)

Indo-Iranian: भाति (bhāti), भास् (bhās), भास्कर (bhāskara, भाम (bhāma), भान (bhāna) (**Sans**); بامداد (bâmdâd) (**Pers**)

*h₂ews-
dawn, east

*h₂éws-ōs, *h₂us-r-, *h₂us-ró-, *h₂ews-ro-, *h₂ews-teros, *h₂us-es-tero-, *h₂ewsḗr, *h₂wōsrih₂

Germanic: east, eastern, Easter (**Eng**); ēast, ēastre, ēostre (**OE**); east (**Fris**); oost, oosten (**Dut**); Ost, Osten, Oostern (**Ger**); austr, austan, austrœnn (**Norse**); øst, aust (**Nor**); öst, öst er, östan (**Swe**); øst (**Dan**); austur, austrænn (**Ice**)

Celtic: gwawr (**Wel**)

Italic: aurōra, aurōreus, auster, austrālis (**Lat**); aurore, austral (**Fr**); ostro, aurora, australe (**Ital**); aurora, austral (**Sp**); aurora, austral (**Port**); austru, aurora, austral (**Rom**)

Derivatives: aurora, aurorean, austral, Australia (**Eng**)

Hellenic: ἠώς (ēós), αὔρᾱ (aúrā), ἀήρ (āḗr), αὔριον (aúrion) (uncert.) (**AnGk**); αέρας (aéras), αύριο (ávrio) (**Gk**)

Derivatives: aerobic, aeroplane, aerodynamic, aerosol, aeronautics, air, aerial, aerate, aura (**Eng**); aura (**Dut**); awyr (**Wel**); aer (**Iri**); aura, āēr (**Lat**); aura, orage, air (**Fr**); aura, ora, aria (**Ital**); aura, orear, aire (**Sp**); aura, oura, oira, ar (**Port**); aură, aer (**Rom**); áypa (áura) (**Rus**); ajër (**Alb**)

Slavic: утро (útro) (**Rus**); jutro, witro (**Pol**); jitro, jutro (**Cz**); jutro (**Slo**); утро (utro) (**Mace**)

Baltic: aušrà (**Lith**); ausma, àustra (**Latv**)

Albanian: err (**Alb**)

Indo-Iranian: उषस् (uṣás), उषर् (uṣar), उस्रस् (usrás), उस्रि (usrí), उस्रा (usrá) (**Sans**); उषा (uṣā) (**Hin**)

Weather

*g^{wh}er-

warm

*g^{wh}ér-e-ti, *g^{wh}r̥-néw-ti, *g^{wh}i-g^{wh}ér-ti, *g^{wh}e-g^{wh}ór-e, *g^{wh}or-éye-ti, *g^{wh}r-éh$_1$-(ye)-ti, *g^{wh}ér-os, *g^{wh}er-mó-s, *g^{wh}or-mó-s, *g^{wh}or-nó-s, *g^{wh}r̥-nó-s

Germanic: warm (**Eng**); wearm (**OE**); waarm (**Fris**); warm, warmen (**Dut**); warm, wärmen (**Ger**); varmr, verma (**Norse**); varm (**Nor**); varm, värma (**Swe**); varm (**Dan**); varmur, verma (**Ice**)

Celtic: gwresogi (**Wel**)

Italic: formus, forceps, furnus, fornāx (**Lat**); four, fourneau, fournaise (**Fr**); forno, fornello, fornace (**Ital**); horno, hornillo, hornacho (**Sp**); forno (**Port**); furnal (**Rom**)

Derivatives: forceps, furnace (**Eng**); fornuis (**Dut**); ffwrn, ffwrnais (**Wel**); φοῦρνος (phoûrnos) (**AnGk**); φούρνος (foúrnos) (**Gk**); furrë (**Alb**)

Hellenic: θέρω (thérō), θέρομαι (théromai), θερέω (theréō), θέρος (théros), θερινός (therinós) (**AnGk**); θερινός (therinós), θερμός (thermós) (**Gk**)

Derivatives: thermal, athermancy, ectotherm, exothermic, geothermic, homeothermy, hypothermia, isotherm, thermodynamic, thermometer, thermos, thermostat (**Eng**)

Slavic: гореть (goréť), горн (gorn), горны́ (gorný), гарны́ (garný), го́рно́ (górnó), греть (gréť), грею (gréju) (**Rus**); gorzeć, gorejący, gorący, gorączka, grzać, grzeję (**Pol**); hořet, hřát, hřeji (**Cz**); horieť, grno, hriať, hreje (**Slo**); гори (gori), гре (gre) (**Mace**)

Baltic: gariù, garéti (**Lith**)

Albanian: ziej, zien, nxeh, ngroh, ngrohtë, zjarr, zjarm (**Alb**)

Indo-Iranian: घृणोति (ghr̥ṇoti), जिघर्ति (jighárti), घरयति (gharáyati), हरस् (háras), घर्म (gharmá), घृण (ghr̥ṇá) (**Sans**); घर्म (gharma) (**Hin**); گرم (garm) (**Pers**)

*ters-

dry

*térs-e-tor, *tr̥s-yé-ti, *tors-éye-ti, *tr̥s-eh$_1$(ye)-ti, *ters-o-, *tērs-os, *ters-k^{w}o-, *térs-ti-s, *térs-tu-s, *térs-us, *tr̥s-nó-, *tr̥s-tós

Germanic: thirst (**Eng**); þurst (**OE**); toarst (**Fris**); dorst, dor (**Dut**); dörren, dürr, Durst (**Ger**); þerra, þorsti, þurr (**Norse**); tørst, tørr (**Nor**); törst, torr (**Swe**); tørst, tør (**Dan**); þerra, þorsti, þurr (**Ice**)

Celtic: tir (**Wel**); tír, tirim, tearc, tart (**Iri**)

Italic: torrēre, torrefaciō, torrēns, torridus, tostus, terra, mediterrāneus, subterrāneus, terrēnus, terrestris, territōrium, territōriālis (**Lat**);

torride, torréfier, tôt, terre, terrain, terrestre, territoire, territorial (**Fr**);

tosto, terra, sotterraneo, terrestre, torrido, terreno, territorio, territoriale (**Ital**);

torrar, tórrido, ierra, terrestre, tierra, territorio, territorial (**Sp**);

torrido, terra, território, territorial (**Port**); țară, teritoriu, teritorial (**Rom**)

Derivatives: torrent, torrid, toast, terrestrial, subterranean, terrace, terracotta, terrain, territory, territorial, inter, terrene, terrenal (**Eng**);

territorium, territoriaal (**Dut**); Territorium, territorial (**Ger**); territorium (**Nor**); territorium, territoriell (**Swe**);

территория (territorija), территориальный (territorial'nyj) (**Rus**); terytorium, terytorialny (**Pol**); eritorium (**Cz**); teritórium (**Slo**); teritorija (**Lith**); teritorija (**Latv**)

Hellenic: τέρσομαι (térsomai) (**AnGk**)

Baltic: trokšti (**Lith**)

Albanian: ter (**Alb**)

Indo-Iranian: तृष्यति (tŕṣyati), वितर्षयति (vitarṣáyati), तृष्णा (tŕṣṇā), तृष्ट (tṛṣṭá) (**Sans**)

*gel-
to be cold, to freeze

*gol-, *gol-tó-s, *gōl-u-s, *gel-u-

Germanic: cold, chill, cool (**Eng**); ćeald, cald, ćele, ćiele, ćyle, cōl (**OE**); kâld, koel (**Fris**); koud, kil, koel (**Dut**); kalt, kühl, Kühle (**Ger**); kala, kaldr, kólna (**Norse**); kalen, kald (**Nor**); kala (dial.), kall (**Swe**); kold (**Dan**); kala, kaldur, kylur, kólna (**Ice**)

Italic: gelū, gelidus, gelāre, congelāre, glaciēs, glaciāre (**Lat**); gel, geler, congeler, glace, glacer (**Fr**); gelo, gelido, gelare, gelato, congelare, ghiaccio, ghiacciare (**Ital**); hielo, gélido, helar, congelar (**Sp**); gelo, gélido, gear, gelar, congelar (**Port**); ger, congela, gheață, îngheța, înghețare (**Rom**)

Derivatives: gel, gelid, jelly, congeal, gelati, gelatinous, gelatin, gelation, gelignite, gelifluction, glacier, glaciate, glacial (**Eng**)

Baltic: gelumà (**Lith**)

Indo-Iranian: शरद (śarada) (**Sans**); शरद (śarad) (**Hin**); سرد (sard) (**Pers**)

*h₁eyH-
ice, frost

*h₁eyH-kos, *h₁iH-n̥-yós, *h₁éyH-s-om

Germanic: ice (**Eng**); īs (**OE**); iis (**Fris**); ijs (**Dut**); Eis (**Ger**); iss (**Norse**); is (**Nor**); is (**Swe**); is (**Dan**); is (**Ice**)

Slavic: иней (ínej) (**Rus**); jíní (**Cz**); jínie (**Slo**)

Baltic: ýnis (**Lith**)

Indo-Iranian: يخ (yax) (**Pers**)

*yeǵ-
ice

*yeǵ-i-s, *iǵ-yeh₂, *yeǵ-ō

Germanic: icicle (**Eng**); ǵiċel (**OE**); Jäch, gicht (**Ger**); jaki, jǫkull (**Norse**); isjukel (**Nor**); jökel (**Swe**); jaki, jökull (**Ice**)

Celtic: iâ (**Wel**); oighear (**Iri**)

*sneygʷʰ-
to snow

*snéygʷʰ-e-ti, *snigʷʰ-e-ti, *sni-né-gʷʰ-ti, *snigʷʰ-yé-ti, *snígʷʰ-s, *snóygʷʰ-o-s

Germanic: snow (**Eng**); snāw, sniwan (**OE**); snije, snie (**Fris**); sneeuw, snuwen, snouwen (dial.) (**Dut**); Schnee, schneien (**Ger**); snjófa, snjáfa, snjór, snær (**Norse**); snø (**Nor**); snö (**Swe**); sne (**Dan**); snær, snjór, snjóa (**Ice**)

Celtic: nyf (**Wel**); snigh, sneachta (**Iri**)

Italic: nix, ningit/ninguit, niveus, nivōsus (**Lat**); nivôse, neige (**Fr**); neve, niveo, nevoso (**Ital**); nieve, nevoso (**Sp**); neve, nevoso (**Port**); nea, ninge, neios (**Rom**)

Derivatives: Nevada, névé, nival, nivation, niveus, subnival, subnivean (**Eng**)

Hellenic: νίφα (nipha), νίφω (níphō) (**AnGk**)

Slavic: снег (sneg) (**Rus**); śnieg (**Pol**); snih (**Cz**); sneh (**Slo**); снег (sneg) (**Mace**)

Baltic: sniegas, snigti (**Lith**); sniegs, snigt (**Latv**)

Indo-Iranian: स्नेह (snéha), स्निह्यति (snihyati) (**Sans**)

*nebʰ-
to become damp, cloudy

*nébʰ-eti, *ne-nóbʰ-e, *nébʰ-o-s, *nebʰ-e-lo-s, *n̥bʰ-ró-s, *n̥bʰ-tó-s

Germanic: nevel **(Dut)**; Nebel **(Ger)**; niflhel **(Norse)**; nifl **(Ice)**

Celtic: nef **(Wel)**; neamh **(Iri)**

Italic: nebŭlō, nebulōsus, imber, imbrifer, Neptūnus (poss.) **(Lat)**; nébuleux **(Fr)**; nebbia, nebuloso, imbrifero **(Ital)**; niebla, nebuloso **(Sp)**; névoa, nebuloso **(Port)**; negură, neguros, nebulos **(Rom)**

Derivatives: nebula, nebulous, nuance, imbriferous **(Eng)**; nebulös **(Ger)**

Hellenic: νέφος (néphos), νεφέλη (nephélē), σὔννέφει (sunnéphei), σὔννέφω (sunnéphō), σὔννένοφᾰ (sunnénopha), ἀφρός (aphrós) (uncert.) **(AnGk)**; νέφος (néfos), νεφέλη (neféli), σύννεφο (sýnnefo), αφρός (afrós) **(Gk)**

Derivatives: nephology (study of clouds), nephoscope **(Eng)**

Slavic: нёбо (njóbo) **(Rus)**; niebo **(Pol)**; nebe **(Cz)**; nebo **(Slo)**; нѐбо (nébo) **(Mace)**

Baltic: debesis **(Lith)**; debess **(Latv)**

Indo-Iranian: नभस् (nábhas), अभ्र (abhrá) **(Sans)**; आभ (ābh) **(Hin)**; نم (nam), ابر (abr) **(Pers)**

*H₂weH₁-
to blow

*h₂wéh₁-ti, *h₂wéh₁-n̥ts

Germanic: wind **(Eng)**; wind **(OE)**; wyn **(Fris)**; wind, waaien **(Dut)**; Wind, wehen **(Ger)**; vindr **(Norse)**; vind, vaie **(Nor)**; vind, vaja **(Swe)**; vind, vaje **(Dan)**; vindur **(Ice)**

Celtic: gwynt **(Wel)**; fead **(Iri)**

Italic: ventus, ventulus, ventilāre, ventilātiō, ventilātor, ventōsus, vannus **(Lat)**;

vent, ventiler, ventilation, venteux, ventouse, van **(Fr)**;

vento, ventilare, ventilazione, ventoso, ventosa, vanni **(Ital)**;

viento, ventana, ventilar, beldar, ventilación, ventoso, ventosa **(Sp)**;

vento, venta, vêntulo, ventilar, ventilação, ventoso, ventosa, abanar **(Port)**;

vânt, vântura, vântos **(Rom)**

Derivatives: ventilate, ventilation, ventilator, fan, van (a fan or device for winnowing grain) **(Eng)**; ventilator, wan **(Dut)**; βεντούζα (ventoúza) **(Gk)**; вентиляция (ventiljacija), вентилятор (ventiljátor) **(Rus)**

Hellenic: ἄημι (áēmi), ἀέντα (aénta), ἀτμός (atmós), ἄελλα (áella), αἴσθω (aísthō), ἆθλον (âthlon), ἀθλέω (athléō), ἀθλητής (athlētḗs), ἀθλητῐκός (āthlētikós), ἄθλημα (áthlēma) (**AnGk**); ατμός (atmós), αθλητής (athlitís), αθλητικός (athlitikós), άθλημα (áthlima) (**Gk**)

Derivatives: atmosphere, athlete, athletic, triathlon, decathlon, pentathlon (**Eng**); āthlēta, āthlēticus (**Lat**); атлет (atlet) (**Rus**)

Slavic: вѣять (véjat'), вѣтер (véter) (**Rus**); wiać, wiatr (**Pol**); váti, vítr (**Cz**); viať, vietor (**Slo**); ветер (veter) (**Mace**)

Baltic: vėjas (**Lith**); vētra, vējš (**Latv**)

Albanian: bundë (uncert.) (**Alb**)

Indo-Iranian: वाति (vāti), वात (vāta), वा (vā), निर्वाण (nirvāṇa) (**Sans**); वायु (vāyu), निर्वाण (nirvāṇ) (**Hin**); باد (bâd) (**Pash**); باد (bâd), وز (vaz) (**Pers**)

Derivatives: nirvana (**Eng**)

*(s)tenh$_2$-

to crash, sound, thunder, roar, moan

Germanic: thunder, Thunor, Thor, Thursday, donner, stun, stound, astonish (**Eng**); þunor, þunresdæġ, stunian (**OE**);

tonger, Tonger, tongersdei (**Fris**); donder, Donar, donderdag, steunen, stenen (**Dut**); Donar, Donner, Donnerstag, stöhnen, staunen (**Ger**);

þórr, þórsdagr, stynja (**Norse**); torden, Tor, torsdag (**Nor**); tordön, Tor, torsdag, stöna (**Swe**); torden, Thor, torsdag (**Dan**); þórsdagur, stynja (**Ice**)

Derivatives: étonner (**Fr**)

Celtic: taran (**Wel**); torann (**Iri**)

Italic: tonāre, detonāre, tonitrus (**Lat**); tonner, tonnerre, détoner (**Fr**); tuonare, detonare (**Ital**); tronar, estruendo, detonar (**Sp**); tonar, troar, estrondo, tonítruo, detonar (**Port**); tuna, tunet, detuna (**Rom**)

Derivatives: detonate, detonable (**Eng**)

Hellenic: στένει (sténei), στένω (sténō), στενάζω (stenázō), στόνος (stónos), Στέντωρ (Sténtōr) (**AnGk**)

Derivatives: stentorian (**Eng**)

Slavic: стонать (stonat'), стенать (stenat') (**Rus**); sténat (**Cz**); stenať (**Slo**); стенка (stenka) (**Mace**)

Baltic: steneti (**Lith**)

Indo-Iranian: तन्यति (tanyati) (**Sans**); (taṇā/tandar) (**Pash**); تندر (tondar) (**Pers**)

Terrain

*dʰégʰōm
earth

Italic: humus, humilis (**Lat**); humus, humble (**Fr**); umile (**Ital**); humus, humil, humilde (**Sp**); húmus, humo, húmil, húmile, humilde (**Port**); umil (**Rom**)

Derivatives: humus, humble, humiliate, exhume, exhumation, inhume, inhumation, disinhume, humate, humic, humicolous (**Eng**); Humus (**Ger**); umhal (**Iri**); гýмус (gúmus) (**Rus**)

Hellenic: χθών (khthốn), χθόνῐος (khthónios), χθαμαλός (khthamalós), χαμαί (khamaí) (**AnGk**)

Derivatives: chthonic, chthonian (**Eng**); chthonius (**Lat**); ctonio (**Ital**)

Slavic: земля (zemljá) (**Rus**); ziemia (**Pol**); země (**Cz**); zem (**Slo**); зéмja (zémja) (**Mace**)

Baltic: žemė (**Lith**); zeme (**Latv**)

Albanian: dhè (**Alb**)

Indo-Iranian: क्ष (kṣa), क्षाम् (kṣám) (**Sans**); خمکه (źmëka) (**Pash**); زمین (zamin) (**Pers**)

*h₁er-
earth

Germanic: earth, earthen (**Eng**); eorþe, eorþen (**OE**); ierde, ierden (**Fris**); aarde, aarden (**Dut**); Erde, irden (**Ger**); jǫrð (**Norse**); jord (**Nor**); jord (**Swe**); jord (**Dan**); jörð (**Ice**)

Celtic: erw (**Wel**)

Hellenic: ἔραζε (éraze) (**AnGk**)

Baltic: érdvė (uncert.) (**Lith**)

*lendʰ-
steppe, land

Germanic: land (**Eng**); land (**OE**); lân (**Fris**); land, belenden (**Dut**); Land, länden (**Ger**); land, lenda (**Norse**); land (**Nor**); landa, lända (**Swe**); land, lende (**Dan**); land, lenda (**Ice**)

Celtic: llan (**Wel**); lann (**Iri**)

Slavic: ляда (ljáda) (**Rus**); ląd (**Pol**)

Albanian: lëndinë (**Alb**)

*bʰergʰ-

to rise, high, hill, mountain

*bʰebʰórgʰe, *bʰorgʰ-éye-ti, *bʰr̥-né-gʰ-ti, *bʰérgʰ-ont-s, *bʰr̥gʰ-éh₂, *bʰérgʰ-mn̥, *bʰérgʰ-ō, *bʰérgʰ-ti-s

Germanic: borough, burgh, -bury, bur-, berg, bargh, barrow, berry (**Eng**); burh, burg, beorg, berg (**OE**); boarg (in compounds), berch (**Fris**); burg, burcht, berg (**Dut**); Burg, Berg (**Ger**); borg, berg, bjarg, bragr (**Norse**); borg, berg (**Nor**); borg, berg (**Swe**); borg, bjerg (**Dan**); borg, berg, bjarg (**Ice**)

Celtic: braint, bre, bri, bera (**Wel**); Brighid, Brid, brí (**Iri**)

Derivatives: brio (**Eng**); brio (**Fr**); brio (**Ital**); breña, brío (**Sp**); brenha, brio (**Port**)

Italic: burgus, burgensis, fortis, fortificātiō, fortificāre, fortitūdō, fortia (**Lat**); bourg, bourgeois, fort, fortifier, force (**Fr**); borgo, borghese, forte, fortficazione, fortificare, forza (**Ital**); burgés, burgués, fuerte, fortificar, fortitud, fortitúdine, fuerza (**Sp**); burgo, burguês, forte, fortitude, fortidão, força (**Port**); foarte, forta (**Rom**)

Derivatives: bourgeois, burgess, fort, forte, fortis, fortification, fortify, force (**Eng**); bourgeois (**Dut**); bourgeois (**Ger**); фортификация (fortifikacija) (**Rus**)

Hellenic: πύργος (púrgos) (**AnGk**); πύργος (pýrgos) (**Gk**)

Slavic: берег (béreg) (**Rus**); brzeg (**Pol**); břeh (**Cz**); breh (**Slo**); брег (breg) (**Mace**)

Albanian: burg, breg (**Alb**)

Indo-Iranian: बबृहाण (babṛhāṇá), बर्हयति (barháyati), बृंहति (bṛṃhati), बृहत् (bṛhát), ब्रह्मन् (bráhman) (**Sans**); بلند (boland) (**Pers**)

*kelH-

to rise, to be tall, hill

*kl̥-né-H-ti, *kelH-n-to-, *kélH-mn̥, *kélH-mn̥-eh₂, *kl̥H-ní-s, *kólH-no-s, *kolH-ō-no-s, *kolH-ō-neh₂, *kolH-weh₂, *kolH-bʰ-

Germanic: hill (**Eng**); hyll (**OE**); hel (**Fris**); hil, hul (**Dut**); hallr (**Norse**); hall (dial.) (**Nor**); hall (dial.) (**Swe**); haid (**Dan**); hallur (**Ice**)

Italic: antecellere, excellere, excellēns, excellentia, praecellere, celsus, columen, culmen, collis, collīnus, colliculus (**Lat**);

exceller, excellent, excellence, préceller, colonne, colombe, colline (**Fr**); eccellere, eccellente, eccellenza, colmo, culmine, colonna, colle, collina (**Ital**);

excelente, excelencia, cumbre, columna, cureña, collado, colina (**Sp**); exceler, excelente, excelência, cume, coluna, cole, colina (**Port**);

culme, coloană, columnă, corună, colină (**Rom**)

Derivatives: excel, excellent, excellence, precel, column, culminate, colliculus (**Eng**); col (**Dut**); kulmen (**Swe**); колóнна (kolónna) (**Rus**)

Hellenic: κολωνός (kolōnós), κολώνη (kolṓnē), κολοφών (kolophṓn) (**AnGk**); κολοφώνας (kolofónas) (**Gk**)

Derivatives: colophon (**Fr**)

Perhaps: **Slavic:** колéно (koléno) (**Rus**); kolano (**Pol**); koleno (**Cz**); koleno (**Slo**); колено (koleno) (**Mace**)

Baltic: kálnas, kalvà, kélti, kìlti, kẽlis (poss.) (**Lith**); kãlns, kalva, celis (poss.) (**Latv**)

*móri

sea

Germanic: mere, marsh, morass, mereswine (+*suH-) (**Eng**); mere, merisc, mereswīn (**OE**);

mar, mersk (**Fris**); meer, meers, moeras, meerzwijn (**Dut**); Meer, Marsch, Morast, Meerschwein, Meerschweinchen (**Ger**);

marr, marsvin (**Norse**); mar (in compounds), mersk, marsvin (**Nor**); mar (in compounds), marsvin (**Swe**); mar (in compounds), marsvin (**Dan**); mar, marsvin (**Ice**)

Derivations: mare, marais, marécage (**Fr**)

Celtic: môr (**Wel**); muir (**Iri**)

Italic: mare, marīnus, maritimus (**Lat**); mer, marin, maritime (**Fr**); mare, marino, marittimo (**Ital**); mar, marino, marítimo, marisma (**Sp**); mar, marinho, marino (**Port**); mare, marin (**Rom**)

Derivatives: maritime, marine, submarine, ultramarine, marinate, marinade (**Eng**)

Slavic: море (móre) (**Rus**); morze (**Pol**); moře (**Cz**); more (**Slo**); море (more) (**Mace**)

Baltic: marios (**Lith**); mare (**Latv**)

Albanian: përmjerr (**Alb**)

Indo-Iranian: मर्यादा (maryādā) (**Sans**)

*lókus

pond

Germanic: lay (meaning lake) (**Eng**); lagu (**OE**); lǫgr, lá (**Norse**); log (**Nor**); lag (**Swe**);

lögur, lá (**Ice**)

Celtic: llwch (**Wel**); loch (**Iri**)

Derivatives: lough (**Eng**)

Italic: lacus, lacuna, lacūnar (**Lat**); lac, lacune, lagune (**Fr**); lago, lacuna, laguna (**Ital**); lago, laguna, lacunar (**Sp**); lago, lagoa, lacuna, laguna (**Port**); lac, lacună, lagună (**Rom**)

Derivatives: lake, lacuna, lagoon, lacunar (**Eng**); лакуна (lakuna) (**Rus**)

Hellenic: λάκκος (lákkos) (**AnGk**)

Slavic: локва (lokva) (**Mace**)

*$h_2ek^weh_2$-
water

Germanic: ea (dial.), eau, yeo (reg.), eddy, eyot/ait, island, -ey, -ay (in place names), oe (poet.) (**Eng**); ēa, īgoþ, īeġland, īgland (**OE**); ie, eilân (**Fris**); a, ooibos, landouw, eiland (**Dut**); Aue, Aa, Aach (**Ger**); á, ey, eyland (**Norse**); å, øy (**Nor**); å, ö (**Swe**); å, ø, øland (**Dan**); á, ey, eyland (**Ice**)

Italic: aqua, aquārius, aquāticus, aqueus, aquilentus, aquātiō, aquātor, aquōsus, aquaeductus (**Lat**);

eau, aquarien, évier, aiguière, aquatique, gouache, aqueux, aqueduc (**Fr**);

acqua, acquaio, acquario, Acquario, Aquario, acquatico, acquazzone, guazzo, acquoso, acquedotto (**Ital**);

agua, acuario, acuático, aguador, aguaducho, acueducto (**Sp**);

água, auga, agueiro, aquário, aquático, aguoso, aquoso, aqueduto (**Port**);

apă, acvariu, apar, acvatic, apos, apeduct (**Rom**)

Derivatives: aqua, aquatic, aqueous, aquamarine, aquarium, aqueduct, gouache, akvavit, Aquarius, ewer (**Eng**); акведук (akvedúk) (**Rus**); akwedukt (**Pol**)

Possibly: **Slavic:** Ока (Oká) (**Rus**)

*wed-
water

*wod-śke-, *wódr̥, *wēd-os, *ud-rós

Germanic: wash, water, wet (**Eng**); wascan, wæter, wætan (**OE**);

waskje, wetter, wiet, wietsje (**Fris**); wassen, water (**Dut**); waschen, Wasser (**Ger**);

vaska, vatn, vátr, væta (**Norse**); vaske, vann, vatn, våt, væte (**Nor**); vaska, vatten, vattu-, våt, väta (**Swe**); vaske, vand, våd, væde (**Dan**); vaska, vatn, votur, væta (**Ice**)

Derivatives: gâcher (**Fr**); guazzare (**Ital**)

Celtic: gwer (**Wel**); uisge, uisce (**Iri**)

Derivatives: whiskey (**Eng**)

Italic: unda, inundāre, inundātiō, undāre, undulātus, undosus, redundāre, redundāns, ūter, vitrum, vitreus (**Lat**);

onde, outre, verre, vitre (**Fr**);

onda, ondare, ondoso, otre, vetro (**Ital**);

onda, inundar, inundación, ondear, ondoso, undoso, odre, vidrio (**Sp**);

onda, inundar, undar, undoso, odre, vidro (**Port**);

undă, unda, undos, vitră (**Rom**)

Derivatives: abound, abundance, inundate, surround, undine, undulate, undulant, redound, redundancy, vitreous, vitrify (**Eng**); vitrös, vitrin (**Swe**); gwydr (**Wel**)

Hellenic: ὕδωρ (húdōr), ὕδρος (húdros), ὕδρα (húdra), κλεψύδρᾱ (klepsúdrā) (**AnGk**); ὑδωρ (ýdor), κλεψύδρα (klepsýdra) (**Gk**)

Derivatives: dehydrate, hydra, Hydra, hydrate, hydrant, hydraulic, hydrogen, hydrology, hydrophobic, hydrous, clepsydra (**Eng**); hydra, Hydra, hydrus, clepsydra (**Lat**); гидра (gídra) (**Rus**)

Slavic: вода (vodá) (**Rus**); woda (**Pol**); voda (**Cz**); voda (**Slo**); вода (voda) (**Mace**)

Derivatives: vodka (**Eng**); vidër (**Alb**)

Baltic: vanduõ (**Lith**); ûdens (**Latv**)

Albanian: ujë (**Alb**)

Indo-Iranian: : उदन् (udan) (**Sans**)

from which derives *udréh$_2$ otter:

*udréh$_2$

otter

Germanic: otter (**Eng**); oter (**OE**); otter (**Fris**); otter (**Dut**); Otter (**Ger**); otr (**Norse**); oter (**Nor**); utter (**Swe**); odder (**Dan**); otur (**Ice**)

Celtic: odar (**Iri**)

Italic: lutra (**Lat**); loutre (**Fr**); lontra (**Ital**); lutria, nutria, lodra, nutra (**Sp**); lontra (**Port**); lutră (**Rom**)

Slavic: выдра (výdra) (**Rus**); wydra (**Pol**); vydra (**Cz**); vydra (**Slo**); видра (vidra) (**Mace**)

Derivatives: vidră (**Rom**); βίδρα (vidra) (**Gk**)

Baltic: ūdra, ūdras (**Lith**); ūdrs (**Latv**)

Albanian: lundra (**Alb**)

Indo-Iranian: उद्र (udrá) (**Sans**); ऊद (ūd) (**Hin**)

*lewh₃-
to wash

*léwh₃-e-ti, *lówh₃-tro-m

Germanic: lather, lye (**Eng**); lēaþor, lēaġ (**OE**); loog (**Dut**); Lauge (**Ger**); lauðr, laug (**Norse**); laug (**Nor**); lödder, lög (**Swe**); løv, lø, løj, lørdag, Løgum (**Dan**); löður (**Ice**)

Italic: lavāre, lōtium, abluere, abluēns, ablūtiō, ablūtor, dīluere, diluvium, ēluere, lavātrīna, lātrīna, perlavāre, polluere, pollūtiō (**Lat**);

laver, abluer, ablution, diluer, déluge, éluer, latrines, polluer (**Fr**);

lavare, lava, abluzione, diluire, diluvio, latrina (**Ital**);

lavar, lava, ablución, diluir, diluvio, eluir, latrina, letrina, poluir (**Sp**);

lavar, lava, abluir, ablução, abluto, diluir, latrina, perlavar, poluir (**Port**);

la, lare, latrină, spăla, spălare (**Rom**)

Derivatives: launder, laundry, lava, lavation, lavatory, lotion, abluent, ablution, alluvium, colluvium, diluent, dilute, dilution, dilutive, diluvial, diluvium, deluge, elute, eluvial, elluviation, eluvium, illuviation, illuvium, latrine, lutaceous, lutite, pollute, pollution (**Eng**);

lava, latrine (**Dut**); laben, erlaben, Latrine (**Ger**); lava (**Nor**); shpëlaj (**Alb**)

Hellenic: λούω (loúō), λουτρόν (loutrón), ἐπίλουτρον (epíloutron) (**AnGk**); λούζω (loúzo), λουτρό (loutró) (**Gk**)

Albanian: laj (**Alb**)

*poymno-
foam

Germanic: foam (**Eng**); fām (**OE**); Feim (**Ger**)

Italic: pūmex, spūma, spūmāre, spūmōsus (**Lat**); ponce, écume, spumeux (**Fr**); pomice, spuma, spumare, spumoso, spumante (**Ital**); pómez, espuma, espumar, espumoso (**Sp**); pomes, espuma, escuma, espumar, espumoso (**Port**); ponce, spumă, spuma, spumare, spumos (**Rom**)

Derivatives: pumice, pounce, spume (**Eng**); pumeks (**Pol**)

Slavic: пена (péna) (**Rus**); piana (**Pol**); pěna (**Cz**); pena (**Slo**)

Baltic: puta (**Lith**); putas (**Latv**)

Indo-Iranian: फेन (phéna) (**Sans**)

*pers-
to spray, splash

*pers-e-ti,*pe-pérs-ti, *pr̥s-ló-s, *pérs-ont-s, *pors-o-s, *pr̥s-o-s, *pérs-ti-s

Germanic: force (waterfall) (reg.) (**Eng**); fors, foss (**Norse**); foss (**Nor**); fors (**Swe**); fors, fos (**Dan**); foss (**Ice**)

Slavic: пóрох (pórox), прах (prax), перх (perx), персть (perst') (**Rus**); proch (**Pol**); prach, prsť (**Cz**); prach (**Slo**); прав (prav) (**Mace**)

Derivatives: praf (**Rom**)

Baltic: pur̃slas, pir̃kšnys, purkšti (**Lith**); pãrsla, pìrkstis (**Latv**)

Indo-Iranian: पर्षति (parṣati), पृषत् (pŕ̥ṣat) (**Sans**)

*srew-
flow, stream

sréw-e-ti, *sréw-ye-ti, *srow-mo-s, *srow-yeh$_2$, *srow-men-, *srow-o-s, *sru-tó-m, *sru-dʰ-mó-s

Germanic: stream, maelstrom (**Eng**); strēam (**OE**); stream (**Fris**); stroom (**Dut**); Strom (**Ger**); straumr (**Norse**); strøm (**Nor**); ström (**Swe**); strøm (**Dan**); straumur (**Ice**)

Celtic: ffrwd (**Wel**); sruth (**Iri**)

Italic: serum (**Lat**); sérum (**Fr**); siero (**Ital**); sero-, suero (**Sp**); soro (**Port**); zer (**Rom**)

Derivatives: serum (**Eng**); Serum (**Ger**)

Hellenic: ῥέω (rhéō), διᾰρρέω (diarrhéō), διᾰρροιᾰ (diárrhoia), καταρρέω (katarrhéō), ῥόος (rhóos), ῥεῦμα (rheûma), ῥυθμός (rhuthmós), ὁρός (horós) (**AnGk**); διαρρέω (diarréo), διάρροια (diárroia), καταρρέω (katarréo), ρεύμα (révma), ρυθμός (rythmós) (**Gk**)

Derivatives: diarrhoea, gonorrhoea, logorrhea, rheology, rheostat, rheum, rheumatic, rhythm, rhythmus (**Eng**); Rhythmus (**Ger**); rithim (**Iri**); diarrhoea, rheuma, rhythmus (**Lat**); rythme (**Fr**); diarrea, ritmo (**Ital**); diarrea, ritmo (**Sp**); diarreia, ritmo (**Port**); ритм (ritm) (**Rus**)

Slavic: струя (strujá), стрýмень (strúmen'), óстров (óstrov) (**Rus**); strumień, strumyk, ostrów, Ostrów, Ostrówek (**Pol**); strumen, ostrov (**Cz**); strumeň (dated), ostrov (**Slo**);

струja (struja), остров (ostrov) (**Mace**)

Baltic: sraujà, sraũjas, srovė, sravėti (**Lith**); strauja, stràujš, stràuja, strāve (**Latv**)

Indo-Iranian: स्रवति (srávati), स्रोतस् (srotas-) (**Sans**); رود (rōd) (**Pers**)

may be derived from *ser- to bind together, thread:

*ser-
to bind together, thread

*sér-ye-, *sér-tis, *sór-mos, *sor-wos

Germanic: sark, berserk, berserker (**Eng**); serc, searu, sierwan (**OE**); serk, särk (**Fris**); sørvi, serkr, berserkr (**Norse**); serk (**Nor**); särk, bärsärk (**Swe**); særk (**Dan**); serkur, beserkur (**Ice**)

Italic: serere, asserere, assertiō, disserere, exserere, inserere, seriēs, sermō, sors, cōnsors, cōnsortium, sortior, sortītiō (**Lat**);

assertion, insérer, série, sermon, sort, sorte, consort, consortium, sortir, sortition (**Fr**);

asserire, inserire, serie, sermone, sorte, consorte, sortire (**Ital**);

aserción, enjerir, enserir, injerir, inserir, serie, sermón, suerte, consorte, surtir (**Sp**);

asserir, enxerir, inserir, série, sermão, sorte, consorte, sortir (**Port**); soartă, soarte (**Rom**)

Derivatives: assert, assertion, assertive, dissertation, desert, desertion, exert, exertion, insert, insertion, series, serial, seriate, sermon, sorcery, sort, consort, consortium, sortition (**Eng**); серия (sérija) (**Rus**); sërë, short (**Alb**)

Hellenic: εἴρω (eírō), εἰρήνη (eirénē) (poss.), ὅρμος (hórmos) (**AnGk**); ειρήνη (eiríni), σειρά (seirá) (**Gk**)

Derivatives: eirenic, irenic, irenology (**Eng**)

Indo-Iranian: सरत् (sarat), सिरा (sirā) (**Sans**)

Fire

*dʰewh₂-
smoke, mist

Germanic: dew, dusk, dun, dye, dust, down (feathers) (**Eng**); dēaw, dox, dunn, dēag, dūst (**OE**);

dau (**Fris**); dauw, dons, duist (**Dut**); Tau, toben, Dunst, Daune, Dust (**Ger**);

dǫgg, dúnn, dust, daunn (**Norse**); dugg, dun, dust (**Nor**); dugg, dagg, dun, dust (**Swe**);

dug, dun, dyst (**Dan**); dögg, dúnn, dust, daunn (**Ice**)

Celtic: dywy (**Wel**); dúil, deathach (**Iri**)

Italic: fūmus, fūmārium, fūmāriolum, fūmāre, fūmigāre, suffīre, fimum, fūlīgō, fuscus, fuscāre, offuscāre, furvus (**Lat**);

fumée, fumer, fumiger, fuligine, offusquer (**Fr**);

fumo, fumaiolo, fumare, affumare, affumicare, fumigare, fuliggine, fosco (**Ital**);

humo, fumo, fumar, humar, ahumar, afumar, fumigar, humear, hollín, fuligo, hosco, fuscar (**Sp**);

fumo, fumar, afumar, fumegar, fumigar, fuligem, fosco, fusco (**Port**);

fum, fuma, afuma, afumare, fumega, fumegare, funingine (**Rom**)

Derivatives: fume, fumigate, fumarium (**Eng**); φουμάρω (foumáro) (**Gk**)

Hellenic: θūμός (thūmós), δūσθūμίᾱ (dusthūmíā), ἐπῑθūμίᾱ (epithūmíā), μᾰκροθūμίᾱ (makrothūmíā) (**AnGk**); θυμός (thymós), δυσθυμία (dysthymía), επιθυμία (epithymía), μακροθυμία (makrothymía) (**Gk**)

Derivatives: -thymia (e.g. hyperthymia, dysthymia, alexithymia) (**Eng**); епитимия (jepitímija), епитимья (jepitím'ja) (**Rus**)

Slavic: дым (dym) (**Rus**); dym (**Pol**); dým (**Cz**); dym (**Slo**); дим (dim) (**Mace**)

Baltic: dúlis, dujà, dūmas, dūmai (**Lith**); dūmi (**Latv**)

Indo-Iranian: धूलि (dhūli), धूम (dhūmá), धूसर (dhūsara) (**Sans**); धूल (dhūl), धूर (dhūr), धूम (dhūm), धूआँ (dhūām̐) (**Hin**); دود (dud) (**Pers**)

*h₁ngʷnis
fire

Italic: ignis, ignīre, igneus (**Lat**); igné (**Fr**); igne, igneo (**Ital**)

Derivatives: ignite, ignition, igneous (**Eng**)

Slavic: огонь (ogón') (**Rus**); ogień (**Pol**); oheň (**Cz**); oheň (**Slo**); оган (ogan) (**Mace**)

Baltic: ugnis (**Lith**); uguns (**Latv**)

Albanian: enjte (**Alb**)

Indo-Iranian: अग्नि (agní) (**Sans**); आग (āg) (**Hin**)

*h₂eydʰ-
to ignite; fire

*h₂i-n-dʰ-tór, *h₂éydʰ-e-ti, *h₂oydʰ-éye-ti, *h₂éydʰ-o-s, *h₂éydʰ-os, *h₂éydʰ-lom, *h₂éydʰteh₂t-s, *h₂éydʰ-tu-s, *h₂idʰ-tó-s

Germanic: anneal (**Eng**); ād, āl, ǣled, ǣlan, onǣlan (**OE**); eldr (**Norse**); ild (**Nor**); eld (**Swe**); ild (**Dan**); eldur (**Ice**)

Derivatives: aelwyd (**Wel**);

Celtic: Aodh (**Iri**)

Italic: aestās, aestīvus, aestuārium, aedēs, aedis, aedicula, aedificāre, aedificātiō, aedificium, aedīlis (**Lat**);

été, estival, édifier, édifice, édile (**Fr**);

estate, estivo, edicola, edificare, edificio (**Ital**);

estio, estival, estero, edificar, edificio, edil (**Sp**);

estio, estivo, esteiro, estuário, edicula, edificar, edificação, edificio, edil (**Port**);

edificiu (**Rom**)

Derivatives: aestival, aestivation/estivation, estuary, aedicula, edify, edification, edifice, aedile (**Eng**)

Hellenic: αἴθω (aíthō), αἶθος (aîthos), αἶθος (aîthos), αἰθήρ (aithér) (**AnGk**); αιθήρ (aithír), αιθέρας (aithéras) (**Gk**)

Derivatives: aether/ether, ethereal, etheric, hypaethros (**Eng**); ether (**Dut**); Äther (**Ger**); eter (**Nor**); eter (**Swe**); æter, ether (**Dan**); aether (**Lat**); éther (**Fr**); éter (**Sp**); éter (**Port**); эфир (efír) (**Rus**); eter (**Pol**); éter (**Cz**); éter (**Slo**); eteris (**Lith**); اثیر (asir) (**Pers**)

Indo-Iranian: इन्द्धे (inddhé), इद्ध (iddhá), एधते (édhate) (poss.), एध (édha), एधस् (édhas) (**Sans**)

*péh₂ur

bonfire

Germanic: fire (**Eng**); fȳr (**OE**); fjoer (**Fris**); vuur (**Dut**); Feuer (**Ger**); fúrr, fýr, fýrir, funi (**Norse**); fyr (**Nor**); fyr (**Swe**); fyr (**Dan**); fúr, funi (**Ice**)

Derivatives: fona (**Port**)

Hellenic: πῦρ (pûr), πυρά (purá), πὔρρός (purrhós) (**AnGk**); πυρ (pyr), πυρά (pyrá) (**Gk**)

Derivatives: pyromania, pyrotechnic, pyre, pyrite, pyretic, Pyrex, pyromete, pyrophore, pyro-, bureau, burel, burgeon (**Eng**); bureau (**Dut**); Büro (**Ger**); byrå (**Swe**);

pyra, burrus, burra (**Lat**); bureau, bourgeon (**Fr**); borra, burla (**Ital**); borra, burla (**Sp**); borra, burel, borla, burla, birô (**Port**); birou (**Rom**); бюро́ (bjuró) (**Rus**); biuro (**Pol**)

Slavic: пы́рей (pýrej) (**Rus**); perz, perzyna (**Pol**); pýř, pyří, pýřiti (**Cz**); pýriť sa (**Slo**); пирej (pirej) (**Mace**)

Time

*dʰǵʰ(y)es-
yesterday

*dʰǵʰyési, *dʰǵʰyesteros

Germanic: yesterday (**Eng**); geostran (**OE**); juster (**Fris**); gisteren (**Dut**); gestern (**Ger**); í gær (**Norse**); i går (**Nor**); i går (**Swe**); i går (**Dan**); í gær (**Ice**)

Celtic: ddoe (**Wel**); ané, inné (**Iri**)

Italic: herī, hesternus (**Lat**); hier (**Fr**); ieri (**Ital**); ayer, hier, yer, hesterno (**Sp**); hesterno (**Port**); ieri (**Rom**)

Hellenic: χθές (khthés) (**AnGk**); χθες (chthes) (**Gk**)

Albanian: dje (**Alb**)

Indo-Iranian: ह्यस् (hyas) (**Sans**); دیروز (diruz) (**Pers**)

*nókʷts
night

Germanic: night, nightingale (**Eng**); niht, nihtegale (**OE**); nacht, geale, geal (**Fris**); nacht, ochtend, nachtegaal (**Dut**); Nacht, Uchte (dial.), Auchte (reg.), Nachtigall (**Ger**); nátt, nǫtt, nótt, ótta (the last part of the night) (**Norse**); natt, otta, nattergal (**Nor**); natt, otte, otta, näktergal (**Swe**); nat, otte, nattergal (**Dan**); nótt, nátt, ótta, næturgali (**Ice**)

Celtic: nos, heno, trannoeth (**Wel**); anocht (**Iri**)

Italic: nox, noctēscere, nocturnus (**Lat**); nuit, nocturne (**Fr**); notte, notturno (**Ital**); noche, anochecer, nocturno (**Sp**); noite, anoitecer, noturno (**Port**); noapte, nocturn (**Rom**)

Derivatives: equinox, nocturnal (**Eng**); nüchtern (**Ger**)

Hellenic: νύξ (núx), νυκτός (nuktós), ἀκτῖς (aktîs) (**AnGk**); νυξ (nyx), νύκτα (nýkta), νύχτα (nýchta) (**Gk**)

Derivatives: nyctalgia, nyctophobia (**Eng**)

Slavic: ночь (noč') (**Rus**); noc (**Pol**); noc (**Cz**); noc (**Slo**); ноќ (noḱ) (**Mace**)

Baltic: naktis (**Lith**); nakts (**Latv**)

Albanian: natë (**Alb**)

Indo-Iranian: नक् (nák), नक्तम् (náktam), क्ति (nákti), नक्त (nákta), अक्तु (aktú) (**Sans**)

*wek(ʷ)speros
evening

Germanic: west, western (**Eng**); uest, wæst, westerne (**OE**); westen, west (**Fris**); west, westen (**Dut**); west, West, Westen (**Ger**); vestr, vestan, vestrœnn (**Norse**); vest (**Nor**); väst, väster, västan (**Swe**); vest (**Dan**); vestur (**Ice**)

Derivatives: ouest (**Fr**); oeste (**Sp**); oeste (**Port**); ovest (**Ital**); vest (**Rom**)

Italic: vesper, vespera, vespertīliō (**Lat**); vêpre (arch.) (**Fr**); vespro, vipistrello (obs.), pipistrello (**Ital**); víspera, véspero, vesperal, vespertino (**Sp**); véspera (**Port**)

Derivatives: vespers, vesperate, vespering (**Eng**); feascar (**Iri**)

Hellenic: ἕσπερος (hésperos), ἑσπέρα (hespéra), Ἑσπερίδες (hesperides) (**AnGk**)

Derivatives: Hesperides, Hesperidean (**Eng**); Hesperidēs (**Lat**)

Slavic: вечер (véčer) (**Rus**); wieczór (**Pol**); večerni (**Cz**); večerne (**Slo**); вечер (večer) (**Mace**)

Baltic: vakaras (**Lith**); vakars (**Latv**)

*yeh₁-
year, season

*yóh₁-ṛ, *yeh₁-r-o-, *yóh₁-r-eh₂

Germanic: year (**Eng**); gēar (**OE**); jjier (**Fris**); jaar (**Dut**); Jahr (**Ger**); ár (**Norse**); år (**Nor**); år (**Swe**); år (**Dan**); ári (**Ice**)

Italic: hōrnus (**Lat**)

Hellenic: ὥρα (hṓra), ὡρολογέω (hōrologéō), ὡροσκοπέω (hōroskopéō) (**AnGk**); ὥρα (óra) (**Gk**)

Derivatives: horology, horometry, horoscope, hour (**Eng**); uur (**Dut**); Uhr (**Ger**); awr (**Wel**); hōra (**Lat**); ora (**Ital**); heure (**Fr**); hora (**Sp**); hora, ora (**Port**); oară, oră (**Rom**); herë, orë (**Alb**)

Slavic: яровой (jarovój), яр (jar), ярá (jará), ярый (járyj), яровóй (jarovój), яровйк (jarovík), ярйца (jaríca), ярйна (jarína) (**Rus**); jar, jaro, jary (**Pol**); jaro (**Cz**); jaro, jar (**Slo**); japa (jara) (**Mace**)

Baltic: jorė (**Lith**)

*wet-
year, year old

*wét-os, *wet-os-to-, *wet-só-s, *wét-ru-s, *wet-us-o-s, *wet-elo-

Germanic: wether (**Eng**); weþer (**OE**); weder, weer (**Dut**); Widder, Weer (**Ger**); veðr (**Norse**); vær (**Nor**); vädur (**Swe**); væder, vædder (**Dan**); veður (**Ice**)

Italic: vetus, veterānus, vetulus, vitulus (**Lat**); vieux, vétéran, vétuste (**Fr**); vieto, vetere, veterano, vecchio, veglio, vetusto (**Ital**); viejo, veterano, vitulo, vetusto (**Sp**); velho, veterano, vitulo, vetusto (**Port**); biet, bătrân, veteran, vechi, vătui (**Rom**)

Derivatives: veteran, inveterate, vetust (lit.) (**Eng**)

Hellenic: ἔτος (étos) (**AnGk**)

Slavic: ветхий (vetxij), вётох (vétox) (**Rus**); wiotchy (**Pol**); vetchý (**Cz**); vetchý (**Slo**); ветов (vetov) (**Mace**)

Baltic: vĕtušas (**Lith**)

Albanian: vit, vjet (**Alb**)

Indo-Iranian: वत्स (vatsá) (**Sans**)

*wésr̥

spring (season)

Germanic: vár (**Norse**); vår (**Nor**); vår (**Swe**); vor (**Ice**)

Celtic: gwanwyn, gwennol (**Wel**); earrach, fáinleog (**Iri**)

Italic: vēr, vernālis (**Lat**); primevère (**Fr**); vară, vernale (**Ital**); verano (**Sp**); verão, vernal (**Port**); vară (**Rom**)

Derivatives: vernal (**Eng**); verë (**Alb**)

Hellenic: ἔαρ (éar) (**AnGk**); έαρ (éar) (**Gk**)

Slavic: весна (vesná) (**Rus**); wiosna (**Pol**); vesna (**Cz**); vesna (**Slo**)

Baltic: vāsara (**Lith**); pavasaris (**Latv**)

Indo-Iranian: वसन्त (vasanta), वसर् (vasar) (**Sans**); بهار (bahâr) (**Pers**)

*sm̥-h₂-ó-

summer

Germanic: summer (**Eng**); sumor (**OE**); simmer (**Fris**); zomer (**Dut**); Sommer (**Ger**); sumar (**Norse**); sommer (**Nor**); sommar (**Swe**); sommer (**Dan**); sumar (**Ice**)

Celtic: haf (**Wel**); samhradh (**Iri**)

Indo-Iranian: समा (sámā) (**Sans**)

*kerp-
to pluck, harvest

Germanic: harvest (**Eng**); hærfest (**OE**); hjerst (**Fris**); herfst (**Dut**); Herbst (**Ger**); haust, haustr (**Norse**); høst (**Nor**); höst (**Swe**); høst (**Dan**); haust (**Ice**)

Celtic: corrán (**Iri**)

Italic: carpēre, carpe diem, excerpere, excerptus (**Lat**); carpare, carpire (**Ital**); carpir (**Sp**); carpir (**Port**)

Derivatives: excerpt (**Eng**)

Hellenic: καρπός (karpós), χρῡσόκᾰρπος (khrūsókarpos), κρώπιον (krópion) (**AnGk**); καρπός (karpós) (**Gk**)

Derivatives: acarpous, angiocarpous, carpology, carpospore, cystocarp, endocarp, monocarpic (**Eng**); chrȳsocarpus (**Lat**)

Slavic: черпать (cherpat'), чéреп (čérep) (**Rus**); czerpać, trzop (**Pol**); střep (**Cz**); črep (**Slo**); череп (čerep) (**Mace**)

Baltic: kĩrpti (**Lith**); cìrpt (**Latv**)

Indo-Iranian: कृपाणी (kṛpāṇī), कृपाण (kṛpāṇa) (**Sans**)

which is derived from *(s)ker- to cut:

*(s)ker-
to cut, cut off

*(s)ker-t-, *kert-s-nh$_2$, *(s)k(e)r-e-b^h-, *(s)k(e)r-ey-b^h-, *(s)kr-ew-, *(s)kr-ew-p-, *sker-, *ker-ye-, *(s)kor-os, *(s)kr̥-tós, *skēr-is, *(s)kor-yo-

Germanic: sharp, shear, short, scrap, scrape, share, sherd, shard, screen, score, shirt, skirt (**Eng**); scarp, scieran, scort, scear, sċearu, sċeard, scyrte (**OE**);

skerp, skeare, skarre, skare, schird, skerte (**Fris**); scherp, scheren, schrapen, schrappen, scherm, beschermen, schare, schaar, schaarde, schort, scheur (**Dut**); scharf, scheren, schrappen, Schar, Scharte, Schirm, schirmen, Schurz (**Ger**);

skarpr, skera, skortr, skrapa, skrap, skari, skǫr, skarð, skor, skyrta (**Norse**); skarp, skjære, skård, skort, skrape (**Nor**); skarp, skära, skara, skärm, skjorta (**Swe**); skarp, skære, skort, skare, skård, skår, skrabe, skjorte (**Dan**); skarpur, skortur, skrapa, skari, skor, skarð, skær (**Ice**)

Derivatives: sciorta (**Iri**); déchirer, écharde, écran, escrimer (**Fr**); scarda, schermire (**Ital**); esquilar, esgrimir (**Sp**); esquiar, esquilar, esgrimir (**Port**); ширма (širma) (**Rus**)

Celtic: ysgar (**Wel**); scar (**Iri**)

Italic: scortum, scortea, cortex, corticeus, dēcorticāre, cēna, cēnāre, scrobis, scrībēre, āscrībēre, circumscrībēre, dēscrībēre, dēscriptiō, īnscrībēre, īnscrīptiō, praescrībēre, prōscrībēre, subscrībēre, superscrībēre, trānscrībēre, scrīptus, scrīptūra, scrūtor, scrūtinium, perscrūtor, scrūpus, scrūpulus, scrūpulōsus, curtus, curtāre, corium, coriaceus, excoriāre, carō, carnālis, carnarium, carnārius, carnifex, carnivorus, carnōsus **(Lat)**;

écorce, cortex, cène, écrire, circonscrire, décrire, description, inscrire, prescrire, proscrire, souscrire, écrit, écriture, scruter, court, écourter, cuir, coriace, cuirasse, excorier, chair, carnage, charnel, charnier, carnivore **(Fr)**;

scorza, cortice, corteccia, cena, cenare, scrivere, ascrivere, descrivere, descrizione, iscrivere, prescrivere, scritto, scrittura, scrutinio, perscrutare, scrupolo, corto, scortare, cuoio, corazza, coriaceo, escoriare, scuoiare, carne, carnale, carnaio, carnivoro, carnoso **(Ital)**;

escuerzo, corcho, corche, cortical, corteza, cortezo, cena, cenar, escribir, circunscribir, describir, descripción, inscribir, prescribir, proscribir, suscribir, transcribir, escrito, escritura, escrutar, pescudar, corto, cortar, cuero, coraza, coriáceo, escoriar, carne, carnal, carnero, carnifice, carnivoro, carnoso **(Sp)**;

córtice, cortiça, cortiço, cortíceo, ceia, cear, escrever, descrever, descrição, prescrever, escrito, escritura, escrutar, escrutínio, escrópulo, escrúpulo, curto, cortar, couro, coiro, coriáceo, couraça, escoriar, carne, carnal, carneiro, carnifice, carnivoro, carnoso **(Port)**;

scoarţă, cină, cina, cinare, scrie, scorbură, scriere, descripţie, prescrie, script, scriptură, scurt, scurta, scurtare, carne, carnal, cărnos **(Rom)**

Derivatives: cortex, cortical, decorticate, shrive, ascribe, circumscribe, conscription, describe, description, inscribe, inscription, prescribe, proscribe, subscribe, superscribe, transcribe, script, scripture, manuscript, scrutinize, scrutiny, scruple, scrupulous, curt, curtana (short sword), corium, excoriate, carnage, carnal, charnel, carnivorous, carnivore **(Eng)**;

skriuwe **(Fris)**; schrijven, schribbelen, kort **(Dut)**; schreiben, kurz **(Ger)**; skrifa **(Norse)**; skrive, kort **(Nor)**; skriva, kort **(Swe)**; skrive, kort **(Dan)**; skrifa **(Ice)**; ysgrifennu **(Wel)**; scríobh **(Iri)**; скрупул (skrupul) **(Rus)**; shkruaj, shkurtoj, kue **(Alb)**

Hellenic: σκάριφος (skáriphos), κείρω (keírō) **(AnGk)**

Slavic: копá (korá), скопá (skorá) **(Rus)**; kora, skóra **(Pol)**; kůra, skora, skura, skůra, škára **(Cz)**; kôra, skura **(Slo)**; кора (kora) **(Mace)**

Baltic: skìrti **(Lith)**

Albanian: harr **(Alb)**

Indo-Iranian: चर्मन् (cárman) **(Sans)**

*ǵʰey-
winter

*ǵʰéyōm, *ǵʰi-m-er-, *-ǵʰi-m-os

Celtic: gaeaf (**Wel**); geimhreadh (**Iri**)

Italic: hiems, hibernum, hibernus, hībernālis, hībernāre (**Lat**);

hiver, hivernal, hiberner, hiverner (**Fr**);

inverno, invernale, ibernare, invernare (**Ital**);

invierno, hibernal, hibernar, invernar (**Sp**);

inverno, hibernal, hibernar, invernar (**Port**);

iarnă, hiberna, hibernare, ierna, iernare (**Rom**)

Derivatives: hibernate, hibernal (**Eng**); mërrajë (**Alb**)

Hellenic: χιών (khiốn), χειμών (kheimốn), χεῖμα (kheîma), χειμερινός (kheimerinós), δύσχιμος (dúskhimos) (**AnGk**); χειμερινός (cheimerinós) (**Gk**)

Slavic: зима (zimá) (**Rus**); zima (**Pol**); zima (**Cz**); zima (**Slo**); зима (zíma) (**Mace**)

Baltic: žiemà (**Lith**); ziema (**Latv**)

Albanian: dimër (**Alb**)

Indo-Iranian: हिम (himá), शतहिम (śatahima) (**Sans**); हिम (him) (**Hin**); ژمی (zhëmai) (**Pash**); زمستان (zemestân) (**Pers**)

Number & Wholeness

*solh$_2$-
whole

*solh$_2$-id^{h}os, *solh$_2$-wós, *solh$_2$-wó-teh$_2$ts, *sol(h$_2$)-nós, *solh$_2$-uHt-

Italic: salvus, sollus, sollemnis (+epulum, meaning feast), sollemnitas, sollers (+ars), sollicitus (+cieo, meaning move, stir), sollicitāre, sollicitātiō, sollicitūdō, solidus, salus, salūber, salūtāre, salūtātiō, salve!, salvāre (**Lat**);

sauf, solennel, solennité, soucier, solliciter, solicitation, sollicitude, solide, solde, sol, sou, salut, salubre, saluer, salutation, sauver (**Fr**);

salvo, solenne, solennità, solerte, sollecito, sollecitare, soldo, saldo, salute, salubre, salutare, salutazione, salve, salvare (**Ital**);

salvo, solemne, solicito, solicitar, solicitud, sólido, sueldo, salud, salubre, salutación, saludar, saludación, salve, salvar (**Sp**);

solene, solerte, solicito, solicitar, solicitação, sólido, soldo, saldo, saúde, salubre, saudar, saudação, salve, salvar (**Port**);

solemn, solid, solz, salut, saluta, săruta, sărutare, salutaţie, salve, salva (**Rom**)

Derivatives: safe, salve, salvage, salvation, solemn, solemnity, solicitous, solicit, insouciant, solicitation, solid, sold, salute, salutation, salubrious, save (**Eng**); sold (**Dut**); sold (**Ger**); sold (**Dan**); sold (**Swe**); солйдный (solídnyj) (**Rus**); shëlboj (**Alb**)

Hellenic: ὅλος (hólos), ὁλότης (holótēs) (**AnGk**); όλος (ólos) (**Gk**)

Derivatives: catholic, holism, holistic, holocaust, hologram, holography, holomorphic, holonomy, holo- (**Eng**)

Albanian: gjallë (**Alb**)

Indo-Iranian: सर्व (sárva), सर्वताति (sarvátāti) (**Sans**); सब (sab), हर (har) (**Hin**); هر (har), هروانگاہ (harvānagāh) (arch.) (**Pers**)

*kóh$_2$ilus
healthy, whole

Germanic: whole, hale, hail (greet), holy, hallow, heal, health (**Eng**); hāl, hāliġ, hālgian, hǣlan, hǣlþ (**OE**);

hiel, hillich, hilligje, hielje (**Fris**); heel, heil, heilig, heiligen, helen (**Dut**); heil, heilig, heiligen, heilen (**Ger**);

heill, heilagr, helga, heila (**Norse**); hel, hellig, heile (**Nor**); hel, helig, helga, hela (**Swe**); hel, hellig, hellige, hele (**Dan**); heill, heilagur, helgur, helga, heild (**Ice**)

Slavic: цéлый (célyj) (**Rus**); cały (**Pol**); celý (**Cz**); celý (**Slo**); целиот (celiot) (**Mace**)

*sem-

together, one, same

*somHós, *sem-h₁, *sm̥-kr̥t-, *sm̥-meh₁lom, *sm̥-ḱm̥tóm, *sm̥-ǵʰéslo-, *sm̥-teros

Germanic: same, sam (dial.), some, simble (**Eng**); sama, sām-, sum, simle (**OE**);

sam, sume, sum (in compounds) (**Fris**); som- in soms, sommige, somtijds, somwijlen (**Dut**); summige (**Ger**);

samr, sumr, simul, semja (**Norse**); samme, somme, som (**Nor**); samma, somlig, sämjas (**Swe**); samme, somme (**Dan**); samur, sumur, semja (**Ice**)

Italic: sēmi-, similis, dissimilis, dissimilitūdō, dissimulātiō, dissimulāre, similāre, similāns, simul, simultās, simultāneus, assimulāre, assimulātiō, semper, sempiternus, sempiternitās, simplus, simplex, simplificor, semel, singulus, singulāris, singulāritās, mille, mīlliārium, mīlliārius (**Lat**);

semi-, similaire, dissimulation, dissimuler, sembler, ressembler, semblant, ensemble, simuler, assembler, assimiler, simple, singulier, sanglier, mille (**Fr**);

semi-, simile, dissimile, dissimulazione, somigliare, sembrare, somigliante, sembiante, insieme, simulare, assimilare, assembrare, assembiare, assomigliare, sempre, semplice, singolo, singolare, mille, miglio, migliaio, miliare (**Ital**);

semi-, símil, disimil, disimular, semejar, semejante, simular, asemblar, asemejar, asimilar, siempre, simple, simplificar, sendos, sencillo, singular, señero mil, milla, mijero, milliario, miliar (**Sp**);

semi-, símile, símil, dissimil, dissimular, semelhar, semelhante, simular, assemelhar, assimilar, sempre, sempiterno, sempiternidade, simples, simplificar, singelo, singular, senheiro, mil, miliário, milheiro (**Port**);

seamăn, semăna, semănare, simula, asemăna, asemănare, asimila, simplu, simplifica, singur, singular, mie (**Rom**)

Derivatives: semi-, simile, similar, dissimilitude, dissimulation, dissemble, dissimulate, resemble, semble, simultaneous, simulate, assimilate, assemble, simple, single, singular, singularity, million, mile, milliary (**Eng**);

simpel, singulär (**Ger**); simular, simpel (**Swe**); mil (**Wel**); singil, míle (**Iri**); ассимиля́ция (assimiljácija) (**Rus**); shëmbëllej, mijë (**Alb**)

Hellenic: εἷς (heîs), μία (mía), σῦν (sún) (uncert.), συν- (sun-) / ξύν (xún), ἡμι- (hēmi-), ὁμός (homós), ἁμόθεν (hamóthen), ἀμῆ (hamê), οὐδ-αμός (oud-amós), ἅμα (háma), ὁμαλός (homalós), ἁ- (ha-), ἅπαξ (hápax), ἑκατόν (hekatón), ἕτερος (héteros), ἑτερογενής (heterogenés) (**AnGk**); ἑνας (énas), ἑνα (éna), μία (mía), συν (syn), εκατό (ekató) (**Gk**)

Derivatives: syn-, sym-, homeopathy, homeostasis, hecato-, hetero-, heterogeneous (**Eng**)

Slavic: сам (sam), самый (sámyj), cy- (su-) (**Rus**); sam, są- (**Pol**); sám, sou- (**Cz**); sám, sú- (**Slo**); сам (sam) (**Mace**)

Baltic: sam- (**Lith**); suo- (**Lat**)

Indo-Iranian: सम् (sam), सम (sama), असामि (ásāmi), सकृत् (sakṛt), सहस्र (sahásra), एकतर (ekatara) (**Sans**); सम (sam) (**Hin**); زر (zёr) (**Pash**); هم (ham), هرگز (hargez), هزار (hezâr) (**Pers**)

*óy-nos

one

Germanic: one, an, a, any (**Eng**); ān, æniġ (**OE**); ien, ienich (**Fris**); een, enig (**Dut**); ein, einig (**Ger**); einn, einigr (**Norse**); en (**Nor**); en (**Swe**); en (**Dan**); einn, einigur (**Ice**)

With *lif- (left over): **Germanic**: eleven (**Eng**); endleofan (**OE**); alve (**Fris**); elf (**Dut**); elf (**Ger**); ellifu (**Norse**); elleve (**Nor**); elva (**Swe**); elleve (**Dan**); ellefu (**Ice**)

Celtic: un (**Wel**); aon (**Iri**)

Italic: ūnus, ūnicus, ūniō, ūnitās, ūni- (**Lat**); un, aucun, unique, union, oignon, unité, réunion (**Fr**); uno, un, alcuno, unico, unione, unità, uni- (**Ital**); uno, un, alguno, único, unión, unidad, reunión (**Sp**); um, uno, algum, único, união, unidade (**Port**); unu, un, uniune, unitate (**Rom**)

Derivatives: unique, unite, unity, union, onion, reunion, triune, unanimous, unary, unate, uni-, unicorn, uniform, unify, universal, universe, university (**Eng**); ui, ajuin, unie (**Dut**); уния (unija) (**Rus**)

Hellenic: οἷος (oîos), οἶνος (oînos), οἴνη (oínē) (**AnGk**); οίνος (oínos) (**Gk**)

Slavic: один (odín), единый (jedínyj), иной (inój), иначе (ináče), йначе (ínače) (**Rus**); jeden, jedynka, inny, indziej (in compounds), inaczej (**Pol**); jeden, jiný, jinde, jinak (**Cz**); jeden, iný, inde, inak, ináč, inakšie (**Slo**); еден (éden), инаку (ínaku) (**Mace**)

Baltic: víenas (**Lith**); viens (**Latv**)

Albanian: një (**Alb**)

Indo-Iranian: एक (éka), एव (evá), एन (ena) (**Sans**); एक (ek) (**Hin**); یک (yak), ـ (-ē) (**Pers**)

which derives from *éy / h₁e the:

*éy / h₁e

the

*yē, *yo-

Germanic: yea, yeah, yo (**Eng**); ī-, iā, ġēa, ġe (**OE**); er, ja (**Fris**); zij, ja (**Dut**); er, sie, es, ja (**Ger**); es, er, já (**Norse**); ja, jo (**Nor**); ja, jo (**Swe**); ja, jo (**Dan**); já (**Ice**)

Celtic: é, sí, ea (**Iri**)

Italic: is, ea, id, interim (inter+), inde, deinde, subinde, īdem, īdenticus, īdentitās, tamen (tam+), iam, etiam, ipse (+sum), ibī, ibīdem, ita, item (poss.), ecce (**Lat**);

en, souvent, identique, identité, jà, même (**Fr**);

mentre, ne, sovente, indentico, già, esso, essa, essi, esse, stesso, stessa, adesso, medesimo, medesmo, vi (**Ital**);

mientras, ende, dende, identidad, ya, ese, esa, eso, esos, esas, mismo, ahí (**Sp**);

mentes, ainda, idêntico, identidade, já, esse, essa, isso, esses, essas, mesmo, aí (**Port**);

îns, însă, însăşi, însele, însuşi, înşişi (**Rom**)

Derivatives: id, interim, idem, identic, identity, item (poss.) (**Eng**); id, identitet (**Dan**); id (**Cz**)

Hellenic: ὅς (hós), ὡς (hōs), οἷος (hoîos), ὅσος (hósos), ὅστις (hóstis), ἴα (ía), ἡλίκος (hēlíkos), εἰ (ei), ἐπεί (epeí), ἐπειδή (epeidé), εἶτα (eîta), εἴθε (eíthe), ἔνθα (éntha), ἔνθεν (énthen) (**AnGk**); επειδή (epeidí) (**Gk**)

Slavic: он (on) (**Rus**); on (**Pol**); on (**Cz**); on (**Slo**); тоj (toj) (**Mace**)

Baltic: jis (**Lith**)

Indo-Iranian: अयम् (ayám), यस् (yás), या (yā), यद् (yád), अतस् (átas), अत्र (átra), अथ (átʰa), अथा (átʰā), अद्धा (addʰā), अध (ádʰa), अह (áha), अधा (ádʰā), आद् (ād), इतस् (itás), इतर (ítara), इति (íti), इत्थम् (ittʰám), इत्था (ittʰā), इदा (idā), इव (iva), इह (ihá), ईम् (īm) (**Sans**); इतर (itar) (**Hin**)

*dwóH₁

two

*dwís, *d(w)is-, *dwis-eh₂, *dwis-no-

Germanic: twilight, twin, between, twain, two (**Eng**); twi-, twinn, betwēonum, twēġen, twā (**OE**); twilling, twa (**Fris**); tweeling, twee (**Dut**); Zwilling, zwei, zwo (**Ger**); tvi-, tvinnr, tveir (**Norse**); tvilling, to (**Nor**); tvilling, två (**Swe**); tvilling, tvende, to (**Dan**); tvi-, tvennur, tvenna, tveir, tvö, tvær (**Ice**)

With *lif- (left over): **Germanic:** twelve (**Eng**); twelf (**OE**); tolve, tolf (**Fris**); twaalf (**Dut**); zwölf (**Ger**); tólf (**Norse**); tolv (**Nor**); tolv (**Swe**); tolv (**Dan**); tólf (**Ice**)

Celtic: dau, dwy (**Wel**); dó, dhá (**Iri**)

Italic: bi-, du-, bis, dis-, bīnī, bīnārius, combīnāre, combīnātiō, duo (**Lat**);

de-, dé-, dés-, dis-, biner, binoter, combiner, combinaison, deux (**Fr**);

dis-, s- (though in most cases, this prefix stems from Latin ex-), binare, combinare, combinazione, due, duetto (**Ital**);

des-, dis-, binar, binare, combinar, combinación, dos (**Sp**);

des-, dis-, binar, combinar, combinação, dois, doas (**Port**);

des-, dez-, combina, combinaţie, două, doi (**Rom**)

Derivatives: dis-, binate, binary, combine, combination, deuce, doubt, dual, duet, duo, duplex, duplicity (**Eng**); Kombination (**Ger**); комбинáция (kombinácija) (**Rus**)

Hellenic: δι- (di-), δίς (dís), διά (diá), δύo (dúo) (**AnGk**); δύo (dýo), για (gia) (**Gk**)

Derivatives: dyad, diode, di- (**Eng**); di- (**Dut**); di- (**Ital**); di- (**Sp**)

Slavic: двa (dva) (**Rus**); dwa (**Pol**); dva (**Cz**); dva (**Slo**); двa (dva) (**Mace**)

Baltic: dù, dvi (**Lith**); divi (**Latv**)

Albanian: dy (**Alb**)

Indo-Iranian: द्वि (dvi-), द्वा (dvá), द्विस् (dvis) (**Sans**); दो (do) (**Hin**); وود (dwa) (**Pash**); ود (du) (**Pers**)

*tréyes
three

Germanic: three (**Eng**); þrīe (**OE**); trije (**Fris**); drie (**Dut**); drei (**Ger**); þrí-, þrír (**Norse**); tre (**Nor**); tre (**Swe**); tre (**Dan**); þrír, þrjú (**Ice**)

Celtic: tri, tair, teir (**Wel**); trí (**Iri**)

Italic: tri-, trēs, tertius, tertiō, tertiārius (**Lat**); trois, tiers (**Fr**); tre, terzo, terziare (**Ital**); tres, tercio, terciar (**Sp**); três, terço, tércio (**Port**); trei, terţ, terţiu (**Rom**)

Derivatives: tri-, triangle, triumvirate, trivia, tertiate, tertiary (**Eng**)

Hellenic: τρι- (tri-), τρεῖς (treîs), τρῐάς (triás) (**AnGk**); τρεις (treis) (**Gk**)

Derivatives: triad, trigon, tripod, triode (**Eng**); trias (**Lat**); triade (**Ital**)

Slavic: три (tri) (**Rus**); trzy (**Pol**); tři (**Cz**); tri (**Slo**); три (tri) (**Mace**)

Baltic: trỹs (**Lith**); trīs (**Latv**)

Albanian: tre, tri (**Alb**)

Indo-Iranian: त्रि- (tri-), त्रि (trí), त्रय (trayaḥ), त्रीणि (trīṇi), तिस्र (tisraḥ) (**Sans**); तीन (tīn) (**Hin**); دری (dre) (**Pash**); سه (se) (**Pers**)

*kʷetwóres
four

Germanic: four (**Eng**); fēower (**OE**); fjouwer (**Fris**); vier (**Dut**); vier (**Ger**); fjórir (**Norse**); fire (**Nor**); fyra (**Swe**); fire (**Dan**); fjórir (**Ice**)

Celtic: pedwar, pedair (**Wel**); ceithair (**Iri**)

Italic: quadr-, quattuor, quādrus, quadrāre, quadrātum, quadrātūra, quadrātus, quārtus (**Lat**); quatuor, quatre, carreau, équerre, carrer, quadrature, carré, cadrat, quart, quatorze (**Fr**); quadr-, quattro, squadra, quadro, quadrello, quadrare, quadrato, quadratura (**Ital**); cuatro, cuadro, cuadrillo, cuadrar, cuadrado, cuarto (**Sp**); quatro, quadro, quadrelo, quadrar, quadrado, quarto (**Port**); patru, pătrat, cvadrat (**Rom**)

Derivatives: quadr-, quadrangle, quadriceps, quadrilateral, quadrillion, quadruped, quadruple, quatrain, quatrefoil, square, quadrate, quadrature, quart, quarto (**Eng**); kwadraat, kwart (**Dut**); kvart (**Swe**); квадрат (kvadrat), квадратура (kvadratura) (**Rus**); kwadrat (**Pol**)

Hellenic: τετρα- (tetra-), τετράπους (tetrápous), τέσσαρες (téssares), τέτταρες (téttares) (**AnGk**); τέσσερις (tésseris) (**Gk**)

Derivatives: tetrapod, tetragon, tetrahedron, tetralogy, tetrameter, tetraphobia, tetrode, diatessaron (**Eng**)

Slavic: четыре (**Rus**); cztery (**Pol**); čtyři (**Cz**); štyri (**Slo**); четири (četiri) (**Mace**)

Baltic: keturì (**Lith**); četri (**Latv**)

Albanian: katër (**Alb**)

Indo-Iranian: चतुर्- (catur-), चतुर् (catur) (**Sans**);चार (car) (**Hin**); څلور (calor) (**Pash**); چهار (čahâr) (**Pers**)

*pénkʷe
five

Germanic: five (**Eng**); fīf (**OE**); fiif (**Fris**); vijf (**Dut**); fünf (**Ger**); fimm (**Norse**); fem (**Nor**); fem (**Swe**); fem (**Dan**); fimm (**Ice**)

Celtic: pump (**Wel**); cúig (**Iri**)

Italic: quīnque, quīnquāgintā (**Lat**); cinq, cinquante, cinquième (**Fr**); cinque, cinquanta (**Ital**); cinco, cincuenta (**Sp**); cinco, cinquenta (**Port**); cinci (**Rom**)

Derivatives: quinquefoil, quinquennial, cinque, quinary, quinate (**Eng**)

Hellenic: πέντε (pénte) (**AnGk**); πέντε (pénte) (**Gk**)

Derivatives: penta-, pentacle, pentad, pentagon, pentagram, pentalogy, pentameter, Pentateuch, pentathlete, pentathlon, pentatonic, pentomino (**Eng**); penta- (**Ital**); penta- (**Sp**)

Slavic: пять (pjat') (**Rus**); pięć (**Pol**); pět (**Cz**); päť (**Slo**); пет (pet) (**Mace**)

Baltic: penkì (**Lith**); pieci (**Latv**)

Albanian: pesë (**Alb**)

Indo-Iranian: पञ्चन् (páñcan) (**Sans**); पाँच (pāṁc) (**Hin**); پنځه (pinźë) (**Pash**); پنج (panj) (**Pers**)

Derivatives: punch (**Eng**)

*swéḱs

six

Germanic: six (**Eng**); siex (**OE**); seis (**Fris**); zes (**Dut**); sechs (**Ger**); sex (**Norse**); seks (**Nor**); sex (**Swe**); seks (**Dan**); sex (**Ice**)

Celtic: chwech (**Wel**); sé (**Iri**)

Italic: sex (**Lat**); six (**Fr**); sei (**Ital**); seis (**Sp**); seis (**Port**); şase (**Rom**)

Derivatives: sice, semester, sextain, sexennial (**Eng**)

Hellenic: ἕξ (héx) (**AnGk**); έξι (éxi) (**Gk**)

Derivatives: hexa-, hexachord, hexad, hexagon, hexahedron, hexameter, hexapod, hexatonic (**Eng**); hexa- (**Fr**); hexa- (**Lat**); esa- (**Ital**)

Slavic: шесть (šest') (**Rus**); sześć (**Pol**); šest (**Cz**); šesť (**Slo**); шест (šest) (**Mace**)

Baltic: šešì (**Lith**); seši (**Latv**)

Albanian: gjashtë (**Alb**)

Indo-Iranian: षष् (ṣáṣ), षट् (ṣaṭ), षष्टिस् (ṣaṣṭis) (**Sans**); छह (chah) (**Hin**); شش (šeš) (**Pers**)

*septḿ

seven

Germanic: seven (**Eng**); seofon (**OE**); sân (**Fris**); zeven (**Dut**); sieben (**Ger**); sjau (**Norse**); sju (**Nor**); sju (**Swe**); syv (**Dan**); sjö (**Ice**)

Celtic: saith (**Wel**); seacht (**Iri**)

Italic: septem, september, septēnārius, septimus, septimāna (**Lat**); sept, septembre, septime, semaine (**Fr**); sette, settembre, settimo, settimana (**Ital**); siete, septiembre, séptimo, sétimo, semana (**Sp**); sete, setembro, sétimo, semana (**Port**); şapte, septembrie, săptămână (**Rom**)

Derivatives: septennial, September, septenarius, septenary, septimate, septimation, septime, septimane (**Eng**); September (**Ger**); seachtain (**Iri**); Σεπτέμβριος (Septémvrios), Σεπτέμβρης (Septémvris) (**Gk**); сентябрь (sentjabr') (**Rus**)

Hellenic: ἑπτά (heptá) (**AnGk**); επτά (eptá), εφτά (eftá) (**Gk**)

Derivatives: hepta-, heptachord, heptagon, heptagram, heptahedron, heptameter, Heptateuch, heptathlon, heptatonic (**Eng**)

Slavic: семь (sem') (**Rus**); siedem (**Pol**); sedm (**Cz**); sedem (**Slo**); седум (sedum) (**Mace**)

Baltic: septynì (**Lith**); septiņi (**Latv**)

Albanian: shtatë (**Alb**)

Indo-Iranian: सप्तन् (saptán) (**Sans**); सात (sāt) (**Hin**); اووه (uwə) (**Pash**); هفت (haft) (**Pers**)

*oḱtṓw

eight

Germanic: eight (**Eng**); eahta (**OE**); acht (**Fris**); acht (**Dut**); acht (**Ger**); átta (**Norse**); åtte (**Nor**); åtta (**Swe**); otte (**Dan**); átta (**Ice**)

Celtic: wyth (**Wel**); ocht, ochtar (**Iri**)

Hellenic: ὀκτώ (oktṓ) (**AnGk**); οκτώ (októ) (**Gk**)

Derivatives: octo-, octa-, octagon, October, octopus, octogenarian, octothorpe, octoroon, octangular, octennial, octave (**Eng**); octo-, octogonaal (**Dut**); octō, octagōnon (**Lat**); huit, octagone (**Fr**); otto, ottogano (**Ital**); ocho, octágono, octógono (**Sp**); oito (**Port**); opt (**Rom**)

Slavic: восемь (vósem') (**Rus**); osiem (**Pol**); osm (**Cz**); osem (**Slo**); осум (osum) (**Mace**)

Baltic: aštuonì (**Lith**); astoņi (**Latv**)

Albanian: tetë (**Alb**)

Indo-Iranian: अष्ट (aṣṭa) (**Sans**); आठ (āṭh) (**Hin**); اته (atə) (**Pash**); هشت (hašt) (**Pers**)

*H₁néwn̥

nine

Germanic: nine (**Eng**); nigon (**OE**); njoggen (**Fris**); negen (**Dut**); neun (**Ger**); níu (**Norse**); ni (**Nor**); nio (**Swe**); ni (**Dan**); níu (**Ice**)

Celtic: naw (**Wel**); naoi (**Iri**)

Italic: novem, nōnāgintā, nōngentī, novena (**Lat**); neuf, nonante (**Fr**); nove, novanta, novecento, novena (**Ital**); nueve, noventa, novecientos, novena (**Sp**); nove, noventa, novecentos, novena (**Port**); nouă (**Rom**)

Derivatives: November, novena (**Eng**)

Hellenic: ἐννέα (ennéa), ἐνενήκοντα (enenékonta) (**AnGk**); εννέα (ennéa) (**Gk**)

Derivatives: ennead, ennea- (**Eng**)

Slavic: девять (devjat') (**Rus**); dziewięć (**Pol**); devět (**Cz**); deväť (**Slo**); девет (devet) (**Mace**)

Baltic: devynì (**Lith**); deviņi (**Latv**)

Albanian: nëntë (**Alb**)

Indo-Iranian: नवन् (návan) (**Sans**); नौ (nau) (**Hin**); نه (nə) (**Pash**); نه (noh) (**Pers**)

*dékm̥t

ten

Germanic: ten, -ty, as in twenty, thirty (**Eng**); tien, -tiġ, twēntiġ (**OE**); tsien, -tich, tweintich (**Fris**); tien, -tig, twintig (**Dut**); zehn, -zig, zwanzig (**Ger**); tíu, -tigr, tuttugu (**Norse**); ti, tyve (**Nor**); tio, -tio, tjugo, -tjog (**Swe**); ti, tyve (**Dan**); tíu, tugur, -tugu, -tiu, tuttugu (**Ice**)

Celtic: deg (**Wel**); deich (**Iri**)

Italic: decem, decānus, december, decempeda, -decim, ūndecim, duodecim, tredecim, tredecennium, quattuordecim, quīndecim, sēdecim, decima, decimō, decimus, decimalis, dēnī, dēnārius (**Lat**);

dix, doyen, décembre, onze, douze, treize, quatorze, quinze, seize, décimer, décime, dîme, décimal, dénaire, denier (**Fr**);

dieci, decano, dicembre, decempeda, undici, dodici, tredici, quattordici, quindici, sedici, decima, decimare, decimo, decimale, denario, denaro, danaro, danaio (**Ital**);

diez, decano, deán, degano, diciembre, once, doce, trece, catorce, quince, diezmar, décimo, diezmo, decimal, denario, dinero (**Sp**);

dez, decano, dezembre, onze, doze, treze, catorze, quatorze, quinze, dízima, décima, dizimar, decimar, décimo, dízimo, decimal, denário, dinheiro (**Port**);

zece, decan, decembrie, decima, zecimal, denar, dinar (**Rom**)

Derivatives: dean, doyen, December, tredecillion, tredecennial, quattuordecillion, decima, decimate, dime, decimal, denier, denar, denary, dinar, denarius (**Eng**); decaan (**Dut**); Dekan, Dezember, Dutzend (**Ger**);

Δεκέμβριος (Dekémvrios), Δεκέμβρης (Dekémvris) (**Gk**); декáн (dekán), декабрь (dekabr'), дéцима (décima) (**Rus**); dziekan (**Pol**)

Hellenic: δέκα (déka) (**AnGk**); δέκα (déka) (**Gk**)

Derivatives: deca-, decade, decad, decahedron, Decalogue, decathlon, decapod, decamer (**Eng**); deca-, decade (**Dut**); Dekade (**Ger**); dekade (**Nor**); dekad (**Swe**); dekade (**Dan**); degawd (**Wel**);

decas (**Lat**); décade (**Fr**); decade, deca (**Ital**); década (**Sp**); década (**Port**); decadă (**Rom**);

декада (dekada) (**Rus**); dekada (**Pol**); dekáda (**Cz**); dekáda (**Slo**); декада (dekada) (**Mace**); dekāde (**Latv**); dekada (**Alb**)

Slavic: дéсять (désjat') (**Rus**); dziesięć (**Pol**); deset (**Cz**); desať (**Slo**); десет (deset) (**Mace**)

Baltic: dēšimt (**Lith**); desmit (**Latv**)

Albanian: dhjetë (**Alb**)

Indo-Iranian: दश (daśa) (**Sans**); दस (das) (**Hin**); لس (ləs) (**Pash**); ده (dah) (**Pers**)

*wĩḱm̥tiH₁
twenty

(from *dwi-dḱm̥t-iH₁ two tens)

Celtic: ugain (**Wel**); fiche (**Iri**)

Italic: vīgintī, vīcēsimus (**Lat**); vingt (**Fr**); venti (**Ital**); veinte (**Sp**); vinte, vigésimo (**Port**)

Derivatives: vicenary, vicesimation, vigesimal (**Eng**)

Hellenic: εἴκοσι (eíkosi) (**AnGk**); είκοσι (eíkosi) (**Gk**)

Slavic: двáдцать (dvádcať) (**Rus**); dwadzieścia (**Pol**); dvacet (**Cz**); dvadsať (**Slo**)

Baltic: dvidešimt (**Lith**); divdesmit (**Latv**)

Albanian: njëzet (**Alb**)

Indo-Iranian: विंशति (viṃśati) (**Sans**); बीस (bīs) (**Hin**); بیست (bist) (**Pers**)

*ḱm̥tóm
hundred

Germanic: hundred (**Eng**); hundred (**OE**); hûndert (**Fris**); honderd (**Dut**); Hundert (**Ger**); hundrað (**Norse**); hundre (**Nor**); hundra (**Swe**); hundrede (**Dan**); hundrað (**Ice**)

Celtic: cant (**Wel**); céad (**Iri**)

Italic: centum, centēsimō, centēsimātiō, centi-, centipelliō, centipēs, centuria, ducentī, nōngentī, octingentī, quadringentī, quīngentī, septingentī, sescentī, trecentī, centēnārius **(Lat)**;

cent, centi-, centipède, centurie, centenaire **(Fr)**;

cento, centinaio, centi-, centopelle, centuria, duecento, novecento, ottocento, quattrocento, settecento, seicento, trecento **(Ital)**;

cien, ciento, centuria, doscientos, novecientos, ochocientos, cuatrocientos, quinientos, setecientos, seiscientos, trescientos, centenario **(Sp)**;

cem, cento, centi-, centúria, duzentos, novecentos, oitocentos, quatrocentos, quinhentos, setecentos, seiscentos, trezentos **(Port)**;

cent, sută, cimpoi, centurie **(Rom)**

Derivatives: cent, centimeter/centimetre, centipede, century, centennial, centurion, centenary, centenarial, centenarian, percentage, centesimal, centesimate, centesimation **(Eng)**;

centi-, centimeter **(Dut)**; Zenturie, Zentner **(Ger)**; centimeter **(Nor)**; centimeter **(Swe)**; centi-, centimeter **(Dan)**;

κεντηνάριον (kentēnárion) **(AnGk)**; центу́рия (centúrija) **(Rus)**; qind, njëqind **(Alb)**

Hellenic: ἑκατόν (hekatón) **(AnGk)**; εκατό (ekató) **(Gk)**

Derivatives: hecato-, hecatologue, hecatophyllous, hecatontarchy **(Eng)**

Slavic: сто (sto) **(Rus)**; sto **(Pol)**; sto **(Cz)**; sto **(Slo)**; сто (sto) **(Mace)**

Baltic: šiṁtas **(Lith)**; simts **(Latv)**

Indo-Iranian: शत (śatá), शतम् (śatam) **(Sans)**; सौ (sau) **(Hin)**; سل (səl) **(Pash)**; صد (sad) **(Pers)**

269

Directions

*per-

through, across, beyond, to go over

*peri, *pres, *pros, *pér-ur, *per-o-, *pr-eh$_2$-, *pr-ey-, *pr-i-yōs, *pr-i-is-ṃmos, *pr-i-is-ḱo-, *pr-i-is-tṇ-o-, *pr-ey-wo-, *pr-i-i-, *pr̥-, *pr̥-to-, *pr̥-tero-, *pr-is-to-, *pr-o, *pr-oH, *pr-o-tero-, *pr-oH-to-, *pr-oH-no-, *pr-o-mo-, *pr-oH-wo-, *pr-o-ḱo-, *pr-o-kʷe, *pr-o-kʷ-is-ṃmo-, *pr-o-bʰuH-, *pr-oH-tṇ-o-, *pr-u-, *pr-e-ti, *pr-o-ti, *pr-e-ti-o-, *por-so-

Germanic: far, for, fore, first, forth, forth-, further, from, fro, frame, frow (**Eng**); feor, for, fore, fyrst, forþ, furþor, fram, from, fremman, framian (**OE**);

foarst, fierder, frou (**Fris**); voor, vorst, vorder, vrouwe, vrouw (**Dut**); für, fürder, fora, vor, Fürst, Frau (**Ger**);

fyrir, fyrri, fyrst, fyrster, fram, frá, fremja, frú, freyja, Freyr (**Norse**); først, fru, frue (**Nor**); före, för, förste, första, först, förra, fram, från, främja, fru (**Swe**); først, første, frem, fra, fremme, frue, fru (**Dan**); fyrir, fyrstur, fyrst, fram, frá, fremja, frú, freyja, Freyr (**Ice**)

Derivatives: фрау (frau) (**Rus**)

Celtic: rhy (**Wel**)

Italic: per, per-, perperus, perperam, prae, praeter, prior, prīmus, prīmārius, prīmō, prīmōgenitus, prīmitīvus, prīscus, prīstinus, prīvus, prīvāre, dēprīvāre, prīvātiō, prīvātīvus, prīvātō, prīvātus, prīvilēgium, por-, prō, prō-, prōnus, prōvincia, prōvinciālis, reciprocus, procul, prope, propiō, propior, propinquus, propitius, propter, proximus, probus, improbus, reprobus, prōtinus, pretium, appretiō, pretiāre, pretiōsus, porrō (**Lat**);

par, prime, premier, primaire, primitif, primitive, priver, privation, privé, privilège, pour, Provence, prochain, proche, probe, prix, apprécier, priser (**Fr**);

per, priore, primo, primaio, primario, primiero, primogenito, privare, privazione, privata, privilegio, por, pro-, prono, proprio, prossimo, propinquo, prezzo, pregio, apprezzare, prezioso (**Ital**);

para, por, prior, primo, primario, primero, primogénito, primitivo, primitiva, privar, privación, privado, privilegio, prójimo, próximo, propíncuo, probo, proba, improbo, precio, prez, apreciar, precioso (**Sp**);

para, per, por, primo, primeiro, primário, primogênito, prisco, prístino, privar, privação, privado, pró, prono, província, provincial, próximo, propínquo, probo, improbo, preço, precioso (**Port**);

pe, prior, prim, primar, aproape, proxim, preț, prețios (**Rom**)

Derivatives: per, pellucid, perfection, permeate, pernicious, persistence, peruse, pervade, prior, priority, prime, primo, primus, premier, primary, primogenit, primogenitary, primacy, pristine, deprive, privation, private, privy, privilege, pro, pro-,

prone, procrastinate, propel, propulsion, approximate, proximity, province, provincial, reciprocal, reciprocate, proximal, propinquity, propitious, price, appraise, appreciate, precious (**Eng**);

provincie, prijs (**Dut**); per, privat, pro, Provinz, Preis (**Ger**); privilegium (**Nor**); pris (**Swe**); prif, priod (**Wel**); prióir (**Iri**);

πέρπερος (pérperos) (**AnGk**); провинция (provincija), примат (primat), привилегия (privilegija) (**Rus**); pro- (**Pol**); pro- (**Cz**)

Hellenic: περί (perí), πέρ (pér), πρέσβυς (présbus), πρεσβῠτερος (presbúteros), πεῖραρ (peîrar), πέρας (péras), πέρᾱ (pérā), πέρᾱν (pérān), πέρπερος (pérperos), πάρα (pára), παρά (pará), πάρ (pár), πάρος (páros), πρίν (prín), πρείν (preín), πρό (pró), πρωΐ (prōḯ), πρότερος (próteros), πρῶτος (prôtos), πρόμος (prómos), πρῷρα (prôîra), πρόκα (próka), πρυμνός (prumnós), προτί (protí), πρός (prós), πόρσω (pórsō), πόρρω (pórrhō) (**AnGk**); περί (perí), πέρας (péras), πέρα (péra), πέραν (péran), προς (pros) (**Gk**)

Derivatives: peri-, Pericles, pericope, perigee, perihelion, perimeter, period, periphery, periscope, presbyter, prester, priest, parable, parabola, parallel, parameter, parapagus, prologue, prostate, prow, Proterozoic, protagonist, protist, protocol, proton, protoplasm, prototype, Protozoa, prore (**Eng**); cruimhthir (**Iri**);

presbyter, prōra (**Lat**); prêtre, proue (**Fr**); prete, prora, prua (**Ital**); preste, proa (**Sp**); proa (**Port**); preot, proră, prově (**Rom**); пресви́тер (presvíter) (**Rus**)

Baltic: per, pra-, pro- (**Lith**); pāri (**Latv**)

Indo-Iranian: परि (pári), पुरस् (puras), प्रति (práti) (**Sans**)

which includes:

*p̥rh₂-k-yé-ti

Hellenic: πρᾱσσω (prā́ssō), πρᾶγμᾰ (prâgma), πρᾱγματικός (prāgmatikós), πρᾱκτικός (prāktikós), πρᾶξις (prâxis) (**AnGk**); πράγμα (prágma), πράμα (práma), πραγματικός (pragmatikós), πραγματεία (pragmateía), πρακτική (praktikí), πράξη (práxi) (**Gk**)

Derivatives: pragma, pragmatic, practic, practical, practice, practise, praxis (**Eng**); pragmatisch (**Dut**); pragmatisch, Praxis (**Ger**); praxis (**Swe**); practicus, prāxis (**Lat**); pragmatique (**Fr**); pragmatico, prassi (**Ital**); pragma, pragmático, praxis, practicar, práctica (**Sp**); pragmático, práxis, practicar (**Port**)

*terh₂-
to cross over, pass through; overcome

See Movement

*upo

under, below

*(s)up-ér, *(s)up-éri, *(s)up-ér-m̥mo-, *(s)úp-m̥mo-

Germanic: over, above, up (**Eng**); ofer, ābufan, ūp, upp, uppe (**OE**); oer, boppe, op (**Fris**); over, boven, op (**Dut**); ob, ober, oben, auf (**Ger**); of, ofr-, ofan, upp, uppi (**Norse**); ov- (**Nor**); ovan, upp, uppe (**Swe**); oven, op, oppe (**Dan**); of, ofur- (**Ice**)

Celtic: gor, gwar (**Wel**); faoi (**Iri**)

Italic: sub, subter, subterfugere, subtus, supīnus, super, superbus, superior, supernus, superāre, superus, supra-, summus, summitās, summārium (**Lat**);

sous, super, sur, superbe, supérieur, supernel, sommé, somme, summe, sommaire (**Fr**);

sotto, supino, super, superbo, superbia, superiore, superno, soprare, superare, supero, sopra, di sopra, sovra, sommo, sommità, somma, summa (**Ital**);

so, sota, soto-, supino, sobre, subterfugio, soberbio, soberbia, superior, sobrar, superar, sumo, sumidad, soma, suma (**Sp**);

sob, soto-, sota, supino, sobre, soberbo, soberba, superior, sobrar, superar, sumo, sumidade, soma, suma (**Port**);

ub, subt, supt, spre, superb, superior, supăra, supărare, asupra, deasupra, sumă (**Rom**)

Derivatives: sub, subterfuge, supine, insuperable, soprano, sovereign, summit, superb, superior, supernal, superate, supra, supercilious, superficial, superfluous, superimpose, superlative, supermarket, supernatural, supernova, superposition, superscript, supersede, supersonic, superstition, supervene, supervise, supreme, surname, surplus, surround, survive, sum, summa, consummate, consummation, summary (**Eng**);

Supinum, superb, Summe (**Ger**); σουπῖνον (soupînon) (**Gk**); сумма (summa) (**Rus**); suma (**Pol**); super, supr (**Cz**); shumë (**Alb**)

Hellenic: ὑπό (hupó), ὑπέρ (hupér) (**AnGk**)

Derivatives: hyper, hyper-, hyperbaric, hyperbola, hyperbole, Hyperion, hyperlink, hyperoxia, hyperthermia, hypertonic, hypo- (**Eng**); hyper (**Fr**); hipo- (**Sp**)

Indo-Iranian: उप (úpa), उप- (upa-), उपरि (upari), उपम (upama) (**Sans**); उप- (up-) (**Hin**)

*h₂pó

off, away, from

*h₂epo-tero-

Germanic: of, off, after (**Eng**); æf, af, of, æfter (**OE**); af, ôf, efter, after, achter (**Fris**); af, ave- in averechts, achter, van (**Dut**); ab, After, von (**Ger**); af, eptir, aptr (**Norse**); av, etter, efter, atter (**Nor**); af, av, efter, åter (**Swe**); af, efter, atter (**Dan**); af, eftir, aftur (**Ice**)

Italic: ab, ab-/a-/abs-, po-, as in pōno (**Lat**); ab- (**Fr**); ab-, as- (**Ital**); ab-, au- (**Sp**); ab-, av-, au- (**Port**); ab- (**Rom**)

Derivatives: e.g., abnormal, abrasion, absent, abstain, abstraction, aversion, avulsion, abstract (**Eng**)

Hellenic: ἀπό (apó) (**AnGk**); αππό (apó) (**Gk**)

Derivatives: aphelion, apocrine, apocryphal, apogee, apostasy, apostate (**Eng**)

Slavic: по (po) (**Rus**); po (**Pol**); po (**Cz**); po (**Slo**); по (po) (**Mace**)

Baltic: apačià (**Lith**); pa (**Latv**)

Indo-Iranian: अप (apa) (**Sans**)

*h₂ew
away from, off; again

*h₂ew-ti-

Celtic: o, hou (**Wel**)

Italic: au-, autem, aut (**Lat**); ou (**Fr**); o, od (**Ital**); o, u (**Sp**); ou (**Port**); au (**Rom**)

Hellenic: αὖ (aû), αὖτε (aûte), αὐτός (autós), αὐθέντης (authéntēs), αὐθεντικός (authentikós), αὖτις (aûtis), αὐτάρ (autár) (**AnGk**); αυτός (aftós), αφέντης (aféntis), αυθεντικός (afthentikós) (**Gk**)

Derivatives: auto, auto-, autocracy, autograph, automatic, automaton, autonomy, autarchy, autarky, autism, autistic, authentic, authenticity, effendi (**Eng**); auto, automobiel (**Dut**);

authenticus (**Lat**); auto, automobile, authentique, authenticité (**Fr**); auto, automobile, auto- (**Ital**); auto, automóvil (**Sp**); auto, automóvel (**Port**); auto (**Pol**); auto (**Slo**)

Slavic: у (u) (**Rus**); u (**Pol**); u (**Cz**); u (**Slo**)

Baltic: au (**Lith**); au (**Latv**)

Indo-Iranian: अव (ava) (**Sans**)

which possibly includes:

*h₂ew-t(i)-o-

Germanic: īeþe, ȳþan (**OE**); öde (**Ger**); auðr, eyða (**Norse**); aud, ød (**Nor**); öde, öda (**Swe**); ød (**Dan**); auður, eyða (**Ice**)

Italic: ōtium, negōtium, negōtiātiō, negōtiātor, negōtior, ōtiōsus (**Lat**); négoce, négociateur, négocier, oiseux, otiose (**Fr**); ozio, negozio, negoziatore, negoziare, ozioso

(Ital); ocio, negocio, negociación, negociador, negociar, ocioso **(Sp)**; ócio, negócio, negociador, negociar, ocioso **(Port)**; negoţ, negustor, neguţa **(Rom)**

Derivatives: negotiate, negotiation, negotiator, otiose **(Eng)**

*h₁eǵʰs

out

Celtic: a, ech- **(Wel)**; as **(Iri)**

Italic: ex, exter, externus, externālis, exterior, extrēmus, extrēmitās, extrā, extrāneus **(Lat)**; externe, extra-, étrange **(Fr)**; estero, esterno, extra-, estra-, stra-, estraneo, strano, straniero **(Ital)**; externo, exterior, extra-, extraño **(Sp)**; eis, externo, exterior, extremo, extra-, estranho **(Port)**; extra-, stră-, străin **(Rom)**

Derivatives: ex-, external, exterior, extreme, extremity, extra-, strange, extraneous **(Eng)**; ekstern **(Nor)**; estron **(Wel)**

Hellenic: ἐξ (ex), ἐκ (ek), ἐκτός (ektós) **(AnGk)**

Slavic: из (iz) **(Rus)**; z, ze **(Pol)**; z, ze **(Cz)**; z, zo **(Slo)**

Baltic: iš **(Lith)**; iz **(Latv)**

Albanian: ish **(Alb)**

*h₂ent

face, forehead, front

*h₂ént-s, *h₂énti, *h₂entíos

Germanic: and, end **(Eng)**; and, ende **(OE)**; en, in **(Fris)**; en, einde, eind **(Dut)**; und, Ende **(Ger)**; enn **(Norse)**; enn **(Nor)**; än **(Swe)**; end **(Dan)**; enn **(Ice)**

Derivatives: un **(Latv)**

Celtic: éadan **(Iri)**

Italic: ante, abante, anterior, antiae **(Lat)**; avant, ains, ainçais, antérieur **(Fr)**; ante, anti, avanti, avante, anzi, anteriore **(Ital)**; ante, antes, delante, avante **(Sp)**; ante, antes, avante, diante, anterior **(Port)**; înainte, anterior **(Rom)**

Derivatives: ante-, antebellum, antediluvian, ante meridiem (a.m.), antemortem, anterior, anticipate **(Eng)**

Hellenic: ἄντα (ánta), ἀντί (antí), ἀντίος (antíos) **(AnGk)**; αντί (antí) **(Gk)**

Derivatives: anti-, ant-, antagonist, antagonize, antibiotic, antidote, antipodes, antirrhinum **(Eng)**

Baltic: añt, antai **(Lith)**

Albanian: ende (**Alb**)

Indo-Iranian: अन्ति (anti), अन्त्य (antya) (**Sans**)

which includes:

*h₂m̥bʰi

Germanic: umb, umbe (**Eng**); ymbe (**OE**); om (**Fris**); om (**Dut**); umb, um (**Ger**); umb, um (**Norse**); om (**Nor**); om (**Swe**); om (**Dan**); um (**Ice**)

Celtic: um (**Iri**)

Italic: ambi-, ambō, ambīre (+īre), ambiēns, ambitus (**Lat**); ambi-, ambiant, ambiance (**Fr**); ambi-, ambo, ambire, ambito (**Ital**); ambos, ambo, ambir, ambiente, ámbito (**Sp**); ambi-, ambos, ambiar, ambiente, âmbito (**Port**); ambii, îmbi, îmbia (**Rom**)

Derivatives: ambi-, ambit, ambient, ambience (**Eng**); ambi-, ambient (**Ger**); ambi- (**Pol**)

Hellenic: ἀμφί (amphí) (**AnGk**)

Derivatives: amphi-, amphibian, amphibious, amphibole, amphimacer, Amphipoda, amphitheatre, amphoterism (**Eng**)

Indo-Iranian: अभि (abhí) (**Sans**)

*h₁én

in

*h₁en-d(ʰ)r-óm, *h₁éni-h₃kʷ-o-, *(h₁)ni-, *h₁(e)n-er-, *h₁(e)n-tér, *h₁énteros, *h₁en-tós, *h₁en-tr-om, *h₁ón-tr-om

Germanic: in, north, northern (**Eng**); in, norþ, norþerne (**OE**); yn, noard (**Fris**); in, noord (**Dut**); in, Nord, unter (**Ger**); i, norðan, norðr, norrœnn (**Norse**); i, nord, norrøn (**Nor**); i, nordan, norr, nord, norrön (**Swe**); i, nord, norrøn (**Dan**); i, norðan, norður, norrænn (**Ice**)

Derivatives: nord (**Fr**); nord (**Ital**); norte (**Sp**); norte (**Port**); nord (**Rom**)

Celtic: yn (**Wel**); eineach, idir, i (**Iri**)

Italic: in, inter, interesse (+esse), interim, interior, intrā, intrāre, intus, intestīnus (**Lat**); en, entre, entre-, inter-, intra-, entrer (**Fr**); in, interesse, mentre, tra, intra-, entrare, intrare, entro (**Ital**); en, entre, interés, mientras, intra-, entrar, interior, entro (**Sp**); em, interesse, entre, entrar, interior, dentro (**Port**); în, între, intra, întra, intrare, întru (**Rom**)

Derivatives: enter, inter-, interest, interim, illuminate, import, incur, intend, invite (**Eng**)

Hellenic: ἐν (en), εἰς (eis), ἐνωπή (enōpḗ), ἐντός (entós), ἔντερον (énteron), ἐντός (entós) (**AnGk**); εν (en), εις (eis), έντερο (éntero) (**Gk**)

Derivatives: emphasis, enclitic, enthusiasm (**Eng**)

Slavic: в (v), во (vo), ядрó (jadró), ядра (jádra), ятро (játro), ятрó (jatró), ятра (játra), нутрó (nutró), утрóба (utróba), внутрь (vnutr'), внутрй (vnutrí) (**Rus**); w, we, jądro, wątroba, wewnątrz (**Pol**); v, ve, jádro, játra, útroba, vnitř, uvnitř (**Cz**); v, vo, jadro, jatrá, útroba, vnútri (**Slo**); во (vo), утроба (utroba) (**Mace**)

Baltic: į/in (**Lith**); iekša (**Latv**)

Albanian: ndër (**Alb**)

Indo-Iranian: अनीक (ánīka), नि (ni), अन्तर् (antár), अन्तर (ántara), आन्त्र (āntrá) (**Sans**); اندر (andar) (arch.), در (dar), اندرون (andar) (**Pers**)

*h₁epi

on, at, near

Germanic: by, by-, be-, even, eve, evening (**Eng**); bī, bi-, be-, ǣfen, ēfen (**OE**); by, be, jûn (**Fris**); bij, be-, avond (**Dut**); bei, be-, Abend (**Ger**); aptann (**Norse**); be-, aften (**Nor**); bi, be-, afton (**Swe**); be-, aften (**Dan**); aftann (**Ice**)

Italic: ob, obs, obiectum, obsequor (+sequor), occlūdere (+claudere), offerre (+ferre), oppīlāre (+pīlāre), oppōnere, oppositiō, oppositus, apud (**Lat**);

objet, opposer, opposition (**Fr**); oggetto, opporre, opposizione (**Ital**); objeto, oponer (**Sp**); objeto, opor, apud (**Port**); obiect (**Rom**) (Descendants of compound words marked with + in the Latin can be found under those partners)

Derivatives: ob-, obdurate, obfuscate, oblique, obstinate, obstreperous, o-, occur, offend, omit, oppose, ostensible, ostentatious, object, opposite, opposition, apud (**Eng**); объект (ob"jekt), оппозиция (oppozicija) (**Rus**)

Hellenic: ἐπί (epí) (**AnGk**); επί (epí) (**Gk**)

Derivatives: ephedra, ephemeral, ephemeris, epicenter, epidemic, epilogue, epiphany, episteme, epistemic, epistemology, epitaph, epithet, epitome, epoch, eponymous (**Eng**)

Baltic: ap- (**Lith**); piedurkne (**Latv**)

Indo-Iranian: अपि (ápi) (**Sans**)

which possibly includes:

*h₁p-os-ti

Italic: post, post-, posterus, posterior, praeposterus, postīcus, pōne (**Lat**); puis, post- (**Fr**); poi, dopo (**Ital**); pues, después (**Sp**); pois, depois, após, póstero, prepóstero, postigo (**Port**); păi, apoi (**Rom**)

Derivatives: post, post-, posterior, posterity, postscript, preposterous, postical (**Eng**); post- (**Dut**)

*h₂el-
beyond, other

*h₂él-yo-s, *h₂él-tero-s, *h₂el-no-, *h₂ol-no-

Germanic: else, all **(Eng)**; elles, eall **(OE)**; al **(Fris)**; ellende, elders, al **(Dut)**; Elend, Elsass, all **(Ger)**; ella, allr **(Norse)**; eller, all, alt **(Nor)**; eller, all **(Swe)**; eller, al **(Dan)**; ella, allur **(Ice)**

Celtic: ail **(Wel)**; eile **(Iri)**

Italic: alius, aliā, inter alia, aliās, aliōrsum, alter, adulter, adulterāre, adulterīnus, adulterium, altercor, altercātiō, alterāre, ille, illīc, ultrā **(Lat)**;

ailleurs, autre, autrui, adultère, avoutre, adultérer, alterquer, altercation, le, la, les, il, elle, ils, elles, lui, leur, celle, ceux, celui, outre **(Fr)**;

altro, adulterino, altercare, altercazione, alterare, il, lo, la, i, gli, le, ecli, ella, lui, lei, loro, quello, quella, quelli, quelle, colui, colei, coloro, lì, oltre, oltra **(Ital)**;

inter alia, otro, adulterio, altercar, altercación, alterar, el, la, lo, los, las, él, ella, ello, ellos, ellas, le, les, aquel, aquella, aquello, aquellos, aquellas, allí, ultra **(Sp)**;

aliás, alhures, outro, adúltero, altercar, altercação, alterar, o, a, os, as, ele, ela, eles, elas, aquele, aquela, aquilo, aqueles, aquelas, alí, ultra **(Port)**;

alt, -l (-ul), -a (-ua), -i, -le, -lui, -ei, -lor, el, ea, ei, ele, lui, lor, îi, le, îl, o, ăl, ăla, aia, ăia, alea, ăluia, ăleia, ălora, acel, acea, acei, acele, acelui, acelei, acelor **(Rom)**

Derivatives: inter alia, et alii (et al.), alias, alibi, alien, advoutrer (obs.), adulterate, adulterine, adultery, altercate, altercation, alter, alternate, ultra **(Eng)**

Hellenic: ἄλλος (állos) **(AnGk)**

Derivatives: allegory, allogenic, allograph, allophone, parallactic, parallax **(Eng)**

Slavic: ale **(Pol)**; ale **(Cz)**; ale **(Slo)**

*h₂énteros
other, second

Germanic: other **(Eng)**; ōþer **(OE)**; oar **(Fris)**; ander, aâr **(Dut)**; ander, andere **(Ger)**; anarr **(Norse)**; annen **(Nor)**; annan, andra **(Swe)**; anden **(Dan)**; annar **(Ice)**

Baltic: añtras, añtaras **(Lith)**; ùotrs, uotars, otrs **(Latv)**

Basic adjectives

*médʰyos
middle

Germanic: mid, middle (**Eng**); mid, midd (**OE**); mid-, midden (**Fris**); mid-, midden (**Dut**); Mitte (**Ger**); miðr (**Norse**); midje (**Nor**); mid-, midja, mitten (**Swe**); midje, midten (**Dan**); miður, miðja (**Ice**)

Celtic: mi (**Iri**)

Italic: medius, mediānus, mediē, medietās, mediō, mediātor, mediocris, mediocritās, mediterrāneus, medium, medulla, merīdiēs (+diēs) (**Lat**);

mi-, médian, moyen, misaine, milieu, moitié, moyer, médiateur, médiator, médiocrité, méditerrané, médium, moelle (**Fr**);

medio, mezzo, mediano, mezzano, medietà, metà, mediare, mediatore, mezzadro, mediocrità, mediterraneo, midolla, midollo, meridie, meriggio (**Ital**);

medio, mediano, mejana, mezana, meitad, mitad, mediar, mediador, mediocre, mediocridad, mediterráneo, médium, médula, meollo (**Sp**);

médio, meio, mídia, mediano, meão, metade, mear, meado, mediar, mediador, mediocre, mediterrâneo, medula, miolo, meridio (**Port**);

mediu, miez, mezin, medie, jumătate, media, mediator, mediteran, mediteranean, măduvă, meriză (**Rom**)

Derivatives: medius, median, mean, means, mizzen, moiety, mediety, mediate, mediation, mediator, immediate, intermediary, media, mediocre, mediocrity, Mediterranean, medium, medieval, medulla, postmeridian (**Eng**); medie, medium (**Dan**); mewn (**Wel**); meán (**Iri**); медиáтор (mediátor) (**Rus**)

Hellenic: μέσος (mésos), μεσοποτάμιος (mesopotámios) (**AnGk**); μέσος (mésos), μέσο (méso) (**Gk**)

Derivatives: Mesolithic, mesozoic (**Eng**)

Slavic: межá (mežá), меж (mež) (**Rus**); miedza, między (**Pol**); mez, mezi (**Cz**); medza, medzi (**Slo**); меѓа (meǵa), меѓу (meǵu) (**Mace**)

Baltic: mēdis (**Lith**); mežs (**Latv**)

Albanian: mes (**Alb**)

Indo-Iranian: मध्य (mádhya) (**Sans**); मध्य (madhya) (**Hin**); میان (miyân) (**Pers**)

*mey-
small

*mi-néh₁-, *mi-néw-, *mi-nos-, *mi-nu-yos-

Germanic: min, minse, mince (**Eng**); min, minsian (**OE**); min, meun (**Fris**); min, minder, meun (**Dut**); Münne (**Ger**); minnr, minni (**Norse**); minske (**Nor**); mindre, minska (**Swe**); mindske (**Dan**); minni (**Ice**)

Derivatives: mincer (**Fr**)

Italic: minuere, minor, minus, minimus, minister, ministerium, ministrāre, administrāre, administrātiō, administrātor, minusculus, minūtus, minūtia, minūtal (**Lat**);

mineur, moindre, moins, minime, minimum, ministre, métier, ministère, administrer, administration, menu, mince, minute, menuise, minutie, menuaille (**Fr**);

minuire, minore, meno, minimo, ministro, mestiere, ministero, amministrare, amministrazione, minuto, minugia, minuzia, minutaglia (**Ital**);

menguar, minuir, menor, menos, mínimo, ministro, menester, ministerio, mester, administrar, administración, administrador, menudo, minuto, menucia, menuza, minucia (**Sp**);

minguar, minuir, menor, menos, mínimo, ministro, mester, ministério, mister, administrar, administração, administrador, menu, miúdo, minúcia, miúça (**Port**);

minor, ministru, administraţie, mărunt, mănunt, minut, măruntaie (**Rom**)

Derivatives: minor, minus, minimum, administer, administrate, administration, administrative, administor, maladminister, minister, ministerial, minestrone, ministrant, ministrate, ministration, ministerium, ministrative, ministry, minority, minstrel, minuscule, quasiminuscule, semiminor, menu, minute, minutia (**Eng**);

Minister, Minute (**Ger**); administrasjon, minutt (**Nor**); минúстр (minístr), администрáция (administrácija), администрáтор (administrátor) (**Rus**)

Hellenic: μείων (meíōn), μινύθω (minúthō), μόνος (mónos), μανός (manós) (**AnGk**); μόνος (mónos) (**Gk**)

Derivatives: ameiosis, ameiotic, meiobenthos, meiosis, meiotic, mono-, monachism, monad, monadic, monarchy, monastery, monastic, monatomic, monism, monk, monoid, monolith, monometer, monopod, monopoly, monopsony, monotone (**Eng**)

Slavic: мéньший (mén'šij) (**Rus**); mniejszy, mniej (**Pol**); menší, méně (**Cz**); menší, menej (**Slo**)

Baltic: menkas (**Lith**)

Indo-Iranian: मिनाति (mināti), मिनोति (minóti), मनाक् (manāk) (**Sans**)

*mrég̑ʰ-
short

*mrég̑ʰus, *mrég̑ʰ-yōs

Germanic: merry (**Eng**); myrġe, miriġe (**OE**); murk (**Ger**); myrjel (**Nor**)

Italic: brevis, brevima, brūma, breviāre, abbreviāre (**Lat**); bref, brève, brume, abréger, abrévier (**Fr**); breve, bruma, abbreviare (**Ital**); breve, bruma, abreviar (**Sp**); breve, bruma, abreviar (**Port**); brumă (**Rom**)

Derivatives: brief, breve, brevity, abbreviate, abridge (**Eng**); brief (**Dut**); Brief (**Ger**); bréf (**Norse**); brev (**Nor**); brev (**Swe**); brev (**Dan**)

Hellenic: βραχύς (brakhús), βρᾰχῐ́ων (brakhī́ōn), τρῐ́βρᾰχῠς (tríbrakhus) (**AnGk**)

Derivatives: tribrach, brachium, brachial, brachialis, brachiferous, brachialgia, brachiosaurus (**Eng**); brachial (**Ger**); braich (**Wel**); tribrachys, bracchium, bracchialis (**Lat**); tribraque, bras, brachial (**Fr**); braccio, brachiale (**Ital**); brazo, braquial, brazal (**Sp**); braço, braquial, braçal (**Port**); braț, brahial (**Rom**)

Indo-Iranian: मुह्ु (múhu, muhú), मुहुर् (múhur) (**Sans**)

*még̑h₂s
big, great

*még̑h₂-lo-s, *még̑h₂-yōs, *még̑h₂-is-to-s, *még̑h₂-is-tero-s, *m(e)g̑h₂-is-m̥mo-, *m̥g̑h₂-nós, *m̥g̑h₂-tós, *még̑h₂-mn̥-to-

Germanic: much, mickle, muckle (dial.) (**Eng**); mycel (**OE**); mekel (arch.) (**Dut**); michel (**Ger**); mikill (**Norse**); meget, mye (**Nor**); mycken, mycket (**Swe**); meget, megen (**Dan**); mikill (**Ice**)

Italic: magister, magistrālis, magistrātus, maximus, major, māiestās, māiusculus, magis, magnus, magnās, magnātus, magnificus, magnitūdō, mactus, mactāre, magmentum (**Lat**);

maestro, magister, maître, master, magistrat, maximum, majeur, maire, majesté, majuscule, mais (**Fr**);

maestro, mastro, maestrale, magistrale, massimo, maggiore, maiuscolo, maiuscola, mai, ma, magno, magnate, magnitudo, mattare (**Ital**);

maese, maeso, maestre, maestro, magister, máster, magistrado, máximo, mayor, majestad, más, mas, magno, maño, magnitud, matar (**Sp**);

mestro, maestro, magister, magistrado, máximo, major, mor, maior, majestade, maiúsculo, mais, mas, magno, manho, magnate, magnata, matar (**Port**);

maestru, magistru, măiestru, maistru, maior, mai (**Rom**)

Derivatives: maestro, magister, master, meister, mister, mistral, maximum, major, mayor, majesty, majuscule, maiuscule, magnus, magnate, magnify, magnitude, mactate (**Eng**);

master (**Fris**); maître, meester, meier (**Dut**); Magister, Master, Meister, Meier (**Ger**); mester (**Nor**); magister, mästare (**Swe**); meistari (**Ice**);

meistr (**Wel**); máistir (**Iri**);

μάγιστρος (mágistros), μάστορας (mástoras) (**Gk**);

магистр (magístr), маэстро (maéstro), мастер (máster), мэтр (mɛtr), магнат (magnat), магнитуда (magnituda) (**Rus**); maestro, magister, majster, master, mistrz (**Pol**); magistr, mistr (**Cz**); majster (**Slo**); мајстор (majstor) (**Mace**);

magistras, meistras (**Lith**); mestrs (**Latv**); mjeshtër, mjesht (**Alb**)

Hellenic: μεγᾰλος (megálos), μεγαίρω (megaírō) (poss.), μέγιστος (mégistos), μείζων (meízōn) (**AnGk**); μεγάλος (megálos), μεγαλώνω (megalóno), μέγιστος (mégistos), μείζων (meízon) (**Gk**)

Derivatives: mega, acromegaly, megalomania, megalopolis, megaphone, megafauna, megalith, mega- (**Eng**)

Indo-Iranian: महि (mahi), महा (mahā, in compounds), महत् (mahat), महात्मन् (mahātman), महाभारत (mahābhārata) (**Sans**); महा (mahā) (**Hin**); مه (meh) (arch.) (**Pers**)

*meh₂ḱ-

to raise, increase; long

*méh₂ḱ-, *méh₂ḱ-os, *méh₂ḱ-isto-, *mh₂ḱ-rós, *m̥h₂ḱ-tós, *m̥h₂ḱ-wós

Germanic: mæġer (**OE**); meager (**Fris**); mager (**Dut**); mager (**Ger**); magr (**Norse**); mager (**Nor**); mager (**Swe**); mager (**Dan**); magur (**Ice**)

Celtic: mab (**Wel**); mac (**Iri**)

Italic: macer, mactus, mactāre (**Lat**); maigre (**Fr**); magro, mattare (**Ital**); magro, matar (**Sp**); magro, matar (**Port**); macru (**Rom**)

Derivatives: meager/meagre, emaciate, macerate, mactate (**Eng**)

Hellenic: μῆκος (mêkos), μήκιστος (mḗkistos), μᾰκρός (makrós), μᾰκρηγορίᾱ (makrēgoríā), μᾰκροθῡμίᾱ (makrothūmíā), μᾰκρόουρος (makróouros) (**AnGk**); μῆκος (míkos), μακρηγορία (makrigoría), μακροθυμία (makrothymía) (**Gk**)

Derivatives: macro-, macrobiotic, macrocosm, macrophage, macron, macrochaeta, amphimacer (**Eng**); macrochaeta (+χαίτη (khaítē)), macroūrus (**Lat**)

*gʷerh₂-

heavy

*gʷréh₂us-

Celtic: bryw (**Wel**)

Italic: grāvis, gravidus, gravitās, gravāre, brūtus (**Lat**); grave, grief, gravide, gravité, grever, brut (**Fr**); grave, greve, gravido, gravità, gravare, brutto, bruto (**Ital**); grave, grávido, gravedad, gravar, bruto (**Sp**); grave, grávido, gravidade, bruto (**Port**); greu, grav, gravid, greutate (**Rom**)

Derivatives: grave, grief, gravid, gravida, gravity, gravitas, aggravate, aggrieve, degravation, gravamen, gravitate, gravitation, grieve, grievance, grievous, ingravescence, multigravida, nulligravida, primigravida, brute, brut (**Eng**); grav, gravid (**Swe**); brúid (**Iri**)

Hellenic: βαρύς (barús), βἄρεῖἄ (bareîa), βἄρῠτης (barútēs) (**AnGk**); βαρύτητα (varýtita) (**Gk**)

Derivatives: barometer, baryon, barysphere, hyperbaric, baria, abarognosis, baresthesia, bariatric, baritone, barognosis, barogram, barograph, barophobia, barycentric, hypobaric, isobar (**Eng**)

Slavic: жёрнов (žjornov) (**Rus**)

Baltic: grūts (**Latv**)

Indo-Iranian: गुरु (gurú), गुरुकुल (gurukula), गुरुत्व (gurutva) (**Sans**); गुरू (gurū), गुरुकुल (gurukul), गुरुत्व (gurutva) (**Hin**); گران (gerân) (**Pers**)

Derivatives: guru (**Eng**); Guru (**Ger**); gourou (**Fr**); gurú (**Sp**); guru (**Port**); гуру (guru) (**Rus**); guru (**Pol**); γκουρού (gkouroú) (**Gk**)

from which is derived *g^{w}rh$_2$-n-uH- millstone:

*g^{w}rh$_2$-n-uH-
millstone

Germanic: quern (**Eng**); cweorn (**OE**); kweern (**Dut**); kvern (**Norse**); kverne (**Nor**); kvarn (**Swe**); kværn (**Dan**); kvern, kvörn (**Ice**)

Celtic: breuan (**Wel**)

Slavic: жёрнов (žjornov) (**Rus**); żarnów, żarna (**Pol**); žernov, žerna (**Cz**)

Baltic: girna (**Lith**); dzirnus (**Latv**)

Indo-Iranian: ग्रावन् (grāvan) (**Sans**)

*h$_1$leng^{wh}-
light (in weight)

see Body: Torso & Organs

*leng^{wh}-
not heavy, agile, nimble

see Body: Torso & Organs

*deru-
hard

see Trees

*h₂éḱ
sharp

see Tools

*dʰewb-
deep

*dʰewb-, *dʰowb-éye-, *dʰéwb-us, *dʰub-nó-s, *dʰub-ró-s

Germanic: dope, deep, depth (**Eng**); dēop (**OE**); dope, djip, djipte (**Fris**); dopen, diep, diepte (**Dut**); taufen, tief, Taufe (**Ger**); deypa, djúpr, dýpð, dýpt (**Norse**); døpe, dyp, dybde (**Nor**); döpa, djup (**Swe**); døbe, dyb, dybde (**Dan**); djúpur, dýpt (**Ice**)

Celtic: dwfn (**Wel**); domhain (**Iri**)

Hellenic: βυθός (buthós), ἄβυσσος (ábussos) (**AnGk**); βυθός (vythós) (**Gk**)

Derivatives: abyss (**Eng**); abyssus (**Lat**); abîme, abysse (**Fr**); abisso (**Ital**); abismo (**Sp**); abismo (**Port**)

Slavic: дюбать (djúbat'), дно (dno) (**Rus**); dupa, dziupla, dno (**Pol**); ďubat, dno (**Cz**); ďubať, žďobať, ždobať, dno (**Slo**); дно (dno) (**Mace**)

Baltic: dubùs, dùgnas, daubà (**Lith**); dobs (**Latv**)

Albanian: det (**Alb**)

which may include *bʰudʰmḗn:

*bʰudʰmḗn
bottom

Germanic: bottom, bum (**Eng**); botm, bodan (**OE**); boaiem, boom (**Fris**); bodem (**Dut**); Boden (**Ger**); botn (**Norse**); bunn (**Nor**); botten (**Swe**); bund (**Dan**); botn (**Ice**)

Celtic: bonn (**Iri**)

Italic: fundus, fundāre (**Lat**); fond, fonder (**Fr**); fondo, fondare (**Ital**); fondo, fundo, hondo, fundar (**Sp**); fundo, fundar (**Port**); fund (**Rom**)

Derivatives: fund, (to) found, founder, foundation, fundament, fundamental, profound, profundity (**Eng**); fundament (**Dut**); Fundament (**Ger**); fundament (**Nor**); fundera, fundament (**Swe**); fundere, fundament (**Dan**); фонд (fond), фундамент (fundament) (**Rus**); fundament (**Pol**); fund (**Alb**)

Hellenic: πῠθμήν (puthmḗn) (**AnGk**); πυθμένας (pythménas) (**Gk**)

Indo-Iranian: बुध्न (budhná), अबुध्न (abudhná) (**Sans**); بن (bon) (**Pers**)

*h₂engʰ-

narrow, tight, to constrict

*h₂éngʰ-e-ti, *h₂éngʰ-u-s, *h₂engʰ-us-t-

Germanic: agnail, hangnail, anger, angst (**Eng**); ænge, angnægl (**OE**); ing, eangst (**Fris**); eng, angst (**Dut**); eng, Angst (**Ger**); ǫngr, angr, angist (**Norse**); angst (**Nor**); ånger, ångest (**Swe**); anger, angst (**Dan**); angur, angist (**Ice**)

Celtic: cyfyng (**Wel**); cúng (**Iri**)

Italic: angere, angor, angina, angustus, anxius, anxietās, anxiōsus (**Lat**); anguis, anxiété (**Fr**); angusto, ansietà (**Ital**); angor, angosto, ansiedad (**Sp**); angusto, ansiedade (**Port**); îngust, anxietate (**Rom**)

Derivatives: angina, anxiety, anxious (**Eng**)

Hellenic: ἄγχω (ánkhō) (**AnGk**); κυνάγχη (kynánchi) (**Gk**)

Derivatives: cynanche (**Eng**); ngushtë (**Alb**)

Slavic: узкий (úzkij), вязать (vjazát') (**Rus**); wąski, wiązać (**Pol**); úzký, vázat (**Cz**); úzky, viazať (**Slo**)

Baltic: ankštas (**Lith**)

Indo-Iranian: अंहु (aṃhu) (**Sans**)

*h₂erHdʰ-

high; to grow

see Trees

*pleth₂-

flat

*pléth₂-t, *pléth₂-eti, *ploth₂-éyeti, *pleth₂-mó, *pléth₂-os, *pléth₂-us, *plet-yo-, *pl̥th₂-enos, *pl̥th₂-ó-s

Germanic: fold (dial., poet.) (**Eng**); folde (**OE**); fold (**Norse**); fold, foll (**Nor**); fold (**Ice**)

Perhaps: Germanic: flat, flet (**Eng**); flat, flett (**OE**); flat, vlet (**Dut**); Fletz, Flötz (**Ger**); flatr, flet (**Norse**); flat, flet (**Nor**); flat (**Swe**); flad, fled (**Dan**); flatur, flet, fleti (**Ice**)

Celtic: Llydaw, llydan (**Wel**); leath, leathan (**Iri**)

Hellenic: πλᾰτᾰμών (platamṓn), πλᾶτος (plátos), Πλᾰταιᾰ (Plátaia), πλᾰτᾰνος (plátanos), πλᾰτη (plátē), πλᾰτᾱ (plátā) (**AnGk**); πλάτος (plátos), πλάτανος (plátanos), πλάτη (pláti) (**Gk**)

Slavic: плечо́ (plečó) (**Rus**); plece, plecy (**Pol**); plece (**Cz**); plece (**Slo**); плеќи (pleḱi) (**Mace**)

Baltic: plēsti, platùs (**Lith**); plašs, plats (**Latv**)

Indo-Iranian: प्रथान (prathāná), प्रथते (práthate), प्रथयति (pratháyati), प्रथिमन् (prathimán), प्रथस् (práthas), पृथिवी (pṛthivī), पृथु (pṛthú), पृथ (pṛthá) (**Sans**); पृथु (pŕthu) (**Hin**)

but the etymology is a little confused with the very similar *pleh₂k- flat:

*pleh₂k-

flat

*pleh₂-nos, *pleh₂-ro-, *pléh₂-n̥t-eh₂

Germanic: floor, flake, fluke (flatworm), field, flat, flaw (prob.) (**Eng**); flōr, flōc, flōcan, feld (**OE**); flier (**Fris**); vloer (**Dut**); Flur, Feld (**Ger**); flórr, flaga (**Norse**); flor (**Nor**); flo, flor, flaga (**Swe**); flor (dial.), flage (**Dan**); flór, flaga (**Ice**)

Celtic: llawr, lleyn, llwyn, lledu (**Wel**); lár (**Iri**)

Italic: plānus, planta, plantātiō, plantāgō, plantāre, implantāre, supplantāre, transplantāre, palam (**Lat**); plan, plante, plantain, planter (**Fr**); piano, pianta, piantaggine, piantare, impiantare (**Ital**); plan, llano, plano, planta, llantén, plantar, implantar, transplantar (**Sp**); plano, chão, porão, piano, planta, plantago, chantagem, tanchagem, tansagem, chantar, tanchar, prantar, plantar, supplantar, transplantar (**Port**); plan, plantă, plântă, împlânta, împlântare, planta, implanta (**Rom**)

Derivatives: piano, plain, explain, plan, plane, plant, plantation, plantain, implant, supplant, transplant (**Eng**); Plan, Pflanze (**Ger**); plant (**Wel**); clann (**Iri**); clan (**Eng**); clan (**Fr**); clã (**Port**)

Hellenic: πλᾰτύς (platús), πλατεῖα (plateîa), πλανάω (planáō), πλάσσω (plássō), πλάσῐς (plásis), πλάσμᾰ (plásma), πλάστης (plástēs), πλαστῐκός (plastikós), πλαστός (plastós) (**AnGk**); πλάσμα (plásma) (**Gk**)

Derivatives: place, plaza, piazza, plasma, plateau, platitude, platypus, plaice, plastic, plastron, protoplasm (**Eng**); plaats (**Dut**); Platz (**Ger**); platēa (**Lat**); place (**Fr**); piazza (**Ital**); plaza (**Sp**); praça, plateia (**Port**); piață (**Rom**)

Slavic: по́ле (póle), плоский (ploskij) (**Rus**); pole, płaski (**Pol**); pole (**Cz**); pole (**Slo**); по́ле (póle) (**Mace**)

Baltic: plonas, platus, plokščias (**Lith**); plāns, plats, plašs, plakans (**Latv**)

Indo-Iranian: प्रथस् (práthas), पृथु (pṛthú) (**Sans**)

there's also a certain amount of confusion between this one and *pleh₂k- to hit:

*pleh$_2$k-
to hit

Germanic: vloeken (**Dut**); Fluch (**Ger**); flókinn, flengja (**Norse**); flengja (**Ice**)

Italic: plangere, plāga, plēctere, plēctrum (**Lat**); plaindre, plaie, plectre (**Fr**); piangere, piaga, plaga, plettro (**Ital**); plañir, llaga, plaga, plectro (**Sp**); planger, plangente, prantear, pranto, chaga, praga, plectro (**Port**); plânge, plângere, plagă (**Rom**)

Derivatives: plangent, plague, plectrum (**Eng**)

Hellenic: πληγή (plēgḗ), πλήσσω (plḗssō) (**AnGk**)

Derivatives: apoplectic, cataplexy, hemiplegia, paraplegic (**Eng**)

Slavic: плáкать (plákat') (**Rus**); płakać (**Pol**); plakat (**Cz**); plakať (**Slo**)

Baltic: plakti (**Lith**)

Albanian: ploje (**Alb**)

Perhaps:

Italic: plaudere, applaudere, explaudere/explōdere, implaudere/implōdere (**Lat**); applaudir (**Fr**); applaudire (**Ital**); aplaudir (**Sp**); aplaudir (**Port**)

Derivatives: applaud, applause, applausive, explode, implode, plaudits, plausible (**Eng**)

*meh$_2$-
good, great; to ripen, mature; timely, opportune

*méh$_2$-yos-, *meh$_2$-nos, *meh$_2$-ni-, *meh$_2$-tis, *meh$_2$-tu-rós, *meh$_2$-tu-to-, *meh$_2$-rós, *moh$_2$-rós, *n̥-meh$_2$-u-rós

Possibly: **Germanic**: more, most (**Eng**); māra, māst (**OE**); mear, meast (**Fris**); meer, meerdere, meest (**Dut**); mehr, meist (**Ger**); meiri, mestr (**Norse**); mere (**Nor**); mera, mest (**Swe**); mere (**Dan**); meiri, meira, mestur (**Ice**)

Celtic: mwy, mad, mawr (**Wel**); maith, mór (**Iri**)

Italic: mānus, mānis, immānis, mānēs, mātūrus, immātūrus, immātūritās, mātūtīnus (**Lat**); mûr, mature, matin (**Fr**); maturo, immaturo, mattino, mattina (**Ital**); mañana, maduro, inmaduro, matutino (**Sp**); manhã, menhã, maduro, maturo, imaturo, matutino, matina (**Port**); matur, mator (**Rom**)

Derivatives: manes (spirits of dead ancestors), mature, immature, immaturity (**Eng**); Manen, Matur, Matura (**Ger**); maidin (**Iri**)

Hellenic: -μωρος (-mōros) (**AnGk**)

*new

new

*néw-os, *néweh₂ti, *néw-yos

Germanic: new (**Eng**); nīwe (**OE**); nei (**Fris**); nieuw (**Dut**); neu (**Ger**); nýr (**Norse**); ny (**Nor**); ny (**Swe**); ny (**Dan**); nýr (**Ice**)

Celtic: newydd (**Wel**); nua (**Iri**)

Italic: novus, novellus, novitās, novāre, innovāre, renovāre (**Lat**); neuf, neuve, nouveau, nouvelle, rénover (**Fr**); novo, nuovo, novità, innovare, rinnovare (**Ital**); nuevo, novillo, novilla, novedad, novar, innovar, renovar (**Sp**); novo, novilho, novidade, renovar (**Port**); nou, nuia, nuvelă, noutate, renova (**Rom**)

Derivatives: innovate, innovative, nova, novel, novelty, novity, novice, novitiate, novate, novation, renovate, renovation, supernova (**Eng**); arnoj (**Alb**)

Hellenic: νέος (néos) (**AnGk**); νέος (néos) (**Gk**)

Derivatives: neo-, neolithic, neologism, neonate, neophyte, neoteny, neon (**Eng**)

Slavic: новый (novyy) (**Rus**); nowy (**Pol**); nový (**Cz**); nový (**Slo**); нов (nov) (**Mace**)

Baltic: naujas (**Lith**); nàujš (**Latv**)

Indo-Iranian: नव (náva) (**Sans**); नया (nayā) (**Hin**); نوی (nëway) (**Pash**); نو (now) (**Pers**)

*h₂yuh₁en-

young

*h₂yuh₁en-, *h₂yowh₁en-, *h₂yuh₁n̥kós, *h₂yuh₁n̥téh₂

Germanic: young, youngling, youth (**Eng**); ġeong, ġeongling, ġeoguþ (**OE**); jong, jeugd (**Fris**); jong, jongeling, jeugd (**Dut**); jung, Jüngling, Jugend, Junge (**Ger**); ungr, unglingr (**Norse**); ung, yngling (**Nor**); ung, yngling (**Swe**); ung, yngling (**Dan**); ungur, unglingur (**Ice**)

Celtic: ieuanc, ifanc (**Wel**); óg (**Iri**)

Italic: iuvenis, iūnior, iūnīx, iuvencus, iuvenīlis, iuvenior, iuventūs (**Lat**); jeune, junior, génisse, juvénile, juveigneur (**Fr**); giovine, giovane, giuniore, giovenco, giovenile, giovanile, gioventù (**Ital**); joven, junior, juvenco, juvenil, juventud (**Sp**); jovem, júnior, juvenco, juvenil, juventude (**Port**); june, junior, junincă, junice, junc, juvenil (**Rom**)

Derivatives: junior, juvenile (**Eng**)

Slavic: юный (júnyj) (**Rus**); junak (**Pol**); jonák (**Cz**); junák (**Slo**)

Baltic: jaunas (**Lith**); jaûns (**Latv**)

Indo-Iranian: युवन् (yúvan), युवश (yuvaśá), युवता (yuvatā) (**Sans**); युवा (yuvā), जवान (javān) (**Hin**); خوان (źwân) (**Pash**); جوان (javân), جوون (javun) (**Pers**)

*sénos
old

Celtic: hen (**Wel**); sean (**Iri**)

Italic: senex, senātor, senātus, senectus, senecta, senīlis, senior (**Lat**); sénateur, sénat, sénile, seigneur, sieur, sire, monsieur, senior (**Fr**); sene, senatore, senato, senetta, signore, sere, sire (**Ital**); sene, senador, senado, senil, señor, señora, señorita, seor, senior (**Sp**); senador, senado, senhor, sênior (**Port**); senator, senat (**Rom**)

Derivatives: senior, senator, senate, senile, sire, sir, seigneur (**Eng**); senaat (**Dut**); Senat (**Ger**); senat (**Nor**); senat (**Swe**); henadur, senedd (**Wel**) seanadóir (**Iri**); сенáтор (senátor), сенáт (senát) (**Rus**); senior (**Pol**); senát (**Cz**)

Hellenic: ἕνος (hénos) (**AnGk**)

Slavic: sędziwy (**Pol**)

Baltic: sēnas (**Lith**); sens (**Latv**)

Indo-Iranian: सन (sána) (**Sans**)

*negʷ-
naked

*nogʷ-ó-s, *nogʷ-e/odʰo-, *nógʷts, *ne/ogʷ-nós, *ne/ogʷ-mós, *nogʷ-tó-s

Germanic: naken, naked (**Eng**); nacian, nacod (**OE**); neaken (**Fris**); naakt (**Dut**); nackt, nackend (**Ger**); nakinn (**Norse**); naken (**Nor**); naken (**Swe**); nøgen (**Dan**); nakinn (**Ice**)

Celtic: noeth (**Wel**); nocht (**Iri**)

Italic: nūdus, dēnūdāre, nūdāre, nūditās (**Lat**); nu, dénuder (**Fr**); nudo, denudare (**Ital**); desnudo, denudar, desnudar (**Sp**); nu, denudar, desnudar (**Port**); nud (**Rom**)

Derivatives: nude, nudity, denude, denudate (**Eng**)

Hellenic: γυμνός (gumnós), γυμνάζω (gumnázō) (**AnGk**); γυμνός (gymnós), γυμνάσιο (gymnásio) (**Gk**)

Derivatives: gymnasium, gymnastics, gymnoplast, gymnosperm (**Eng**)

Slavic: нагóй (nagój) (**Rus**); nagi (**Pol**); nahý (**Cz**); nahý (**Slo**)

Baltic: núogas (**Lith**); nuôgs (**Latv**)

Indo-Iranian: नग्न (nagná) (**Sans**); नंगा (naṅgā) (**Hin**); برهنه (barahna) (**Pers**)

*weh₁-
true

*weh₁-ros, *weh₁-reh₂

Germanic: wǣr (**OE**); wier (**Fris**); waar (**Dut**); wahr, Wahrheit (**Ger**); værr, alværð, alvara (**Norse**); alvor (**Nor**); allvar (**Swe**); alvor (**Dan**); alvara (**Ice**)

Celtic: gwir (**Wel**); fíor (**Iri**)

Italic: vērus, vērāx, vēridicus, vērificāre, verificātiō, vērisimilis, vēritās (**Lat**); voire, vrai, vérifier, vérification, vérité (**Fr**); vero, verace, verificare, verificazione, verità, vertà (**Ital**); vero, veraz, averiguar, verificar, verificación, verdad (**Sp**); vero, veraz, averiguar, verificar, verificação, verdade (**Port**); adevăr, verifica, verificație, verificațiune (**Rom**)

Derivatives: aver, veracious, verdict, veridical, verify, verisimilar, verisimilitude, verity, veritas, very (**Eng**); fraai (**Dut**); Verifikation (**Ger**); verifikation (**Swe**); верификация (verifikacija) (**Rus**); weryfikacja (**Pol**); verifikace (**Cz**); vërtetë (**Alb**)

Slavic: вѣра (véra) (**Rus**); wiara (**Pol**); víra (**Cz**); viera (**Slo**); вера (vera) (**Mace**)

Colours

*h₁rewdʰ-
red

*h₁réwdʰeti, *h₁rudʰ-éh₁-ti, *h₁rudʰ-rós, *h₁rūdʰ-yo-, *h₁rowdʰ-s-o-, *h₁rowdʰ-ós

Germanic: red, rud (**Eng**); rēad, rudian (**OE**); read (**Fris**); rood (**Dut**); rot, röten (**Ger**); rauðr, roða (**Norse**); rød (**Nor**); röd (**Swe**); rød (**Dan**); rauður (**Ice**)

Celtic: rhudd, rhwd (**Wel**); rua (**Iri**)

Italic: rubēre, rubeus, rubicundus, rubor, ruber, rubellus, rubia, rubrīca (secondary meaning came about because law titles were written in red), rubīnus, rubrīcāre, rūfus, russus (**Lat**);

rouge, rubis, rubrique, roux (**Fr**);

roggio, robbia, rosso, rubrica, rubino, rufo (**Ital**);

rubio, rúbeo, rubor, rubia, rúbrica, rubí, rubricar, rufo, rojo (**Sp**);

rúbeo, ruivo, rubro, rubor, rubrica, rubricar, roxo, russo (**Port**);

roib, roibă, roșu (**Rom**)

Derivatives: rouge, rubicund, rubella, rubious, rubric, ruby, erubescent, rubin, rufous, russet (**Eng**); rubriek (**Dut**); Rubrik, Rubin (**Ger**); rubin (**Swe**); rubin (**Dan**); rúbín (**Ice**); ρουμπίνι (roumpíni) (**Gk**); рубрика (rubrika), рубин (rubín) (**Rus**); rubin (**Pol**); rubin (**Cz**); рубин (rubin) (**Mace**)

Hellenic: ἐρεύθω (ereúthō), ἐρῠθρός (eruthrós) (**AnGk**); ερυθρός (erythrós), ρούσος (roúsos) (**Gk**)

Derivatives: erythro- (**Eng**)

Slavic: рдеть (rdet'), ру́дый (rúdyj), рудо́й (rudój), рёдрый (rjódryj) (**Rus**); rudy (**Pol**); rdíti se, rudý (**Cz**); rdieť sa, rudý (**Slo**); руд (rud) (**Mace**)

Baltic: raũdonas, rùdas (**Lith**); ruds (**Latv**)

Indo-Iranian: रुधिर (rudhirá), रोहित (róhita), लोह (lohá) (**Sans**)

*ǵʰelh₃-
to flourish; green, yellow

*ǵʰélh₃-ye-ti, *ǵʰolh₃-éh₂, *ǵʰelh₃-i-s, *ǵʰélh₃-os, *ǵʰelh₃-en-, *ǵʰ̥lh₃-o-s, *ǵʰ̥lh₃-ró-s, *ǵʰelh₃-to-s, *ǵʰolh₃-to-s, *ǵʰ̥lh₃-to-s, *ǵʰ̥lh₃-to-m, *ǵʰelh₃-wo-s

Germanic: yellow, gold (**Eng**); ġeolu, gold (**OE**); giel, goud (**Fris**); geluw, geel, goud (**Dut**); gelb, Gold (**Ger**); gulr, goll, gull (**Norse**); gul, gull (**Nor**); gul, gull, guld (**Swe**); gul, guld (**Dan**); gulur, gull (**Ice**)

Italic: holus, helvus (**Lat**)

Hellenic: χολή (kholḗ), χλωρός (khlōrós) (**AnGk**); χολή (cholí) (**Gk**)

Derivatives: chlorine, chlorophyll, pyrochlore (**Eng**)

Slavic: зелёный (zeljónyj), зо́лото (zóloto), зла́то (zláto) (arch./poet.), жёлтый (žóltyj) (**Rus**); zielony, złoto, żółty (**Pol**); zelený, zlato, žlutý (**Cz**); zelený, zlato, žltý (**Slo**); зелен (zelen), злато́ (zlató), жолт (žolt) (**Mace**)

Baltic: žélti, žãlias, žélvas (**Lith**); zèlt, zelts (**Latv**)

Albanian: dhelpërë (**Alb**)

Indo-Iranian: हरि (hari), हिरि- (hiri-) (in compounds), हिरण्य (hiraṇya) (**Sans**); زر (zar), زرد (zard) (**Pers**)

*gʰreh₁-
to grow, to become green

*gʰroh₁-(y)e-ti, *gʰroh₁-ni-s, *gʰréh₁-mn̥, *gʰreh₁-tó-s

Germanic: grow, grass, green (**Eng**); grōwan, græs, gærs, grœni, grēne (**OE**); groeie, gers, jers, grien (**Fris**); groeien, gras, geers, groen (**Dut**); Gras, grün (**Ger**); gróa, gras, grœnn, grǿnn (**Norse**); gro, gress, grønn (**Nor**); gro, gräs, grön (**Swe**); gro, græs, grøn (**Dan**); gróa, gras, grænn (**Ice**)

Italic: grāmen, grāmineus (**Lat**); gramen (**Fr**); gramigna (**Ital**); grama, gramíneo (**Sp**); grama, gramíneo (**Port**)

Derivatives: graminivorous (**Eng**)

Slavic: гринóй (grinój), грéны (grény) (**Rus**)

*pelH-

pale, gray

*polH-tós, *polH-wos

Germanic: fallow (**Eng**); fealu (**OE**); vaal (**Dut**); fahl, falb (**Ger**); fǫlr (**Norse**); falna (**Swe**); fölur (**Ice**)

Derivatives: falvus (**Lat**); fauve (**Fr**)

Celtic: llwyd (**Wel**); liath (**Iri**)

Italic: pallēre, pullus, pallidus, pallēns, pallēscere, pallor (**Lat**); pâleur, pâle (**Fr**); pallore, pallido (**Ital**); palor, pálido (**Sp**); bolor, palor, pálido (**Port**); palid, pal (**Rom**)

Derivatives: pallor, pallid, pale (**Eng**)

Hellenic: πελιτνός (pelitnós), πολιός (poliós) (**AnGk**)

Derivatives: poliomyelitis, poliosis (**Eng**); poliocephalus (**Lat**)

Slavic: полóвый (polóvyj), пелёсый (pelësyj), пелёсый (peljósyj) (**Rus**); płowy (**Pol**); plavý (**Cz**); plavý (**Slo**)

Baltic: pálvas, pelekas, pìlkas (**Lith**); pelēks (**Latv**)

Albanian: plak (**Alb**)

Indo-Iranian: पलित (palitá) (**Sans**); پیر (pir) (**Pers**)

Proto-Indo-European Roots

*angʷ(h)i-, eel, snake, worm, hedgehog, 215

*átta, father, 18

*bak-, staff, 179

*bʰabʰeh₂-, bean, 201

*bʰardʰeh₂-, beard, 33

*bʰars-, spike, prickle, 201

*bʰeh₂-, to shine, 236

*bʰeh₂-, to speak, say, 87

*bʰeh₂go-, beech, 198

*bher-, to carry, 126

*bʰereǵ-, birch, 199

*bʰergʰ-, to rise, high, hill, mountain, 243

*bʰewdʰ-, to be awake, be aware, 55

*bʰey-, bee, 222

*bʰeyd-, to split, 148

*bʰeydʰ-, to trust, 102

*bʰleh₁-, to bleat, cry, 68

*bʰleh₁-, to swell, blow up, 67

*bʰleh₃-, to bloom, flower, blossom, 68

*bʰréh₂tēr, brother, 18

*bʰrewh₁-, to boil, brew, 177

*bʰudʰmḗn, bottom, 283

*bʰuH-, to become, grow, appear, 63

*bʰuHgos-, goat, ram, buck, 212

*daḱru-, tear (in the eyes), 98

*deh₂-, to share, divide, 145

*deH₃-, to give, 142

*deḱ-, to take; to perceive, 140

*déḱm̥t, ten, 267

*deḱs-, right (side), 141

*dem-, to build, to put together, 160

*demh₂-, to tame, domesticate, 160

*der-, to tear, to split, 99

*deru-, hard, firm, strong, solid, 196

*dewk-, to pull, draw, lead, 132

*deyḱ-, to point out, 72

*deyn-, day, 231

*dʰéǵʰōm, earth, 243

*dʰegʷʰ-, to burn; warm, hot, 230

*dheH₁-, to do, place, put, 135

*dʰeh₁(y)-, to suckle, nurse, 58

*dʰéh₁s, god, deity; sacred place, 144

*dʰer-, to support, hold, 99

*dʰers-, to be bold, to dare, 97

*dʰewb-, deep, 283

*dʰewh₂-, smoke, mist, 250

*dʰeyǵʰ-, to knead, form, shape, 176

*dʰǵʰ(y)es-, yesterday, 253

*dʰugh₂tḗr, daughter, 19

*dʰwer-, door, 188

*dn̥ǵʰwéh₂s, tongue, 33

*dóru, tree, wood, 196

*dwóH₁, two, 262

*dyew-, to be bright; sky, heaven, 232

*egH₂, I, 22

*eh₃g-, berry, 203

*éy / h₁e, the, 262

*gel-, to be cold, to freeze, 239

*ǵenH₁-, to give birth, produce, 59

*ǵénus, cheek, jaw, chin, 32

*gerbʰ-, to carve, 161

*gerh₂-, crane, to cry hoarsely, 220

*ǵerh₂-, to grow old, to mature, 66

*ǵews-, to try, to taste, 96

*ǵʰans-, goose, 220

*ǵʰaydos, young goat, kid, 213

*ǵʰebʰ-, to give, 142

*ǵʰed-, to find; to hold, 82

*ǵʰeh₁bʰ-, to seize, take, 139

*ǵʰelh₃-, to flourish; green, yellow, 290

*ǵʰelōw-, tortoise, 216

*ǵʰer-, to enclose, 191

*ǵʰer-, to scratch, scrape, 162

*ǵʰer-, to yearn for, 103

*ǵʰḗr, hedgehog, 214

*ǵʰern-, bowels, 49

*gʰers-, stiff, surprised, 215

*ǵʰew-, to pour, libate, 144

*ǵʰey-, winter, 258

*ǵʰeyzd-, anger, agitation, 105

*ǵʰmṓ, person, 14

*gʰóstis, stranger, guest, 105

*gʰreh₁-, to grow, to become green, 290

*ǵʰwer-, wild; wild animal, 205

*ǵʰweroh₃kʷs, having the appearance of a wild animal, 205

*glag-, milk, 226

*ǵneh₃-, to recognize, know, 83

*ǵómbʰos, tooth, row of teeth, peg, 34

*ǵónu, knee, 37

*ǵr̥Hnom, corn, grain, 66

*gʷelH-, to throw, reach, pierce; to hit by throwing, 152

*gʷem-, to step, come, 120

*gʷén, woman, 14

*gʷerH-, to express approval, to praise, 95

*gʷerh₂-, heavy, 281

*gʷet-, resin, gum, 197

*gʷeyh₃-, to live, 69

*gʷʰen-, to strike, kill, 151

*gʷʰer-, warm, 238

*gʷóws, cattle, cow/bull, 210

*gʷr̥h₂-n-uH-, millstone, 282

*h₁ed-, to eat, 57

*h₁eǵʰs, out, 274

*h₁éḱwos, horse, 207

*h₁én, in, 275

*h₁epi, on, at, near, 276

*h₁er-, earth, 243

*H₁es-, to be, 64

*ḱonkho-, shell, mussel, *218*
*krep-, body, *28*
*krewh₂-, raw meat, fresh blood, *51*
*krey-, to sift, separate, divide, *147*
*kʷel-, wheel, circle; to turn, rotate, *184*
*kʷetwóres, four, *264*
*kʷey-, to pay; to avenge, *108*
*kʷis, who, what, which, *25*
*ḱwó, dog, *206*
*kʷreyh₂-, to buy, *108*
*kʷyeh₁-, to rest, rest, peace, *54*
*leb-, to hang loosely, lip, lick, *53*
*leǵ-, to gather, *149*
*legh-, to lie down, *114*
*lendʰ-, loins, *50*
*lendʰ-, steppe, land, *243*
*lengʷʰ-, not heavy, agile, nimble, *47*
*lewbʰ-, to cut off, *163*
*lewbʰ-, to love, *101*
*lewg-, to bend, turn, *125*
*lewh₃-, to wash, *247*
*lewk-, light, bright; to shine; to see, *235*
*leykʷ-, to leave, *125*
*leyp-, to stick; fat or sticky substance, *48*
*leys-, to trace, track, *82*
*lino-, flax, *203*
*lókus, pond, *245*
*luHs-, louse, *225*
*mak-, pouch, *181*
*mánus, person, *14*
*marko-, horse, *209*
*med-, to measure; give advice, healing, *234*
*médʰu, mead, honey, *228*
*médʰyos, middle, *278*
*méǵh₂s, big, great, *280*
*meh₁-, to measure, *234*
*méh₁ṇs, moon, month, *233*
*meh₂-, good, great; to ripen, mature; timely, *286*
*méh₂-méh₂, mama, *17*
*méh₂-ṛ, hand, *44*
*meh₂ḱ-, to raise, increase; long, *281*
*méh₂tēr, mother, *16*
*melh₂-, to grind, to crush, *193*
*melit-, honey, *227*
*mḗms, meat, flesh, *51*
*men-, mind, to think, remember, *85*
*men-, to stand out, to tower, to project, *32*
*mendʰ-, to chew; jaw, mouth, *31*
*mer-, to die, *70*
*mey-, small, *279*; to change, exchange, *109*
*móri, sea, *245*
*morwi-, ant, *224*
*mosgʰos, marrow, brain, *52*
*mréǵʰ-, short, *280*
*muh₂s-, mouse, *214*
*mus-, fly, *224*
*ṇ-, not, un-, *27*

*nebʰ-, to become damp, cloudy, *241*
*negʷ-, naked, *288*
*negʷh-r-, kidney, *49*
*néh₂s, nose, nostril, *30*
*neHtr-, snake, *216*
*neḱ-, to perish, disappear, *70*
*nem-, to distribute; to give, take, *146*
*nepot-, grandson, nephew, *20*
*new, new, *287*
*nisdós, nest, *114*
*nókʷts, night, *253*
*oḱtṓw, eight, *266*
*óy-nos, one, *261*
*ped-, to walk, to step, *42*
*peh₂-, to protect, to shepherd, *217*
*peh₂ǵ-, to attach, *150*
*péh₂ur, bonfire, *252*
*peh₃-, to drink, *58*
*peisḱ-, fish, *217*
*peḱ-, to pluck, comb, shear (wool, hair), *107*
*peḱu-, wealth/cattle, *106*
*pekʷ-, to cook, ripen, *175*
*pel-, to cover, wrap; skin, hide; cloth, *170*
*pelH-, pale, gray, *291*
*pénkʷe, five, *264*
*pent-, path, road, *189*
*per-, through, across, beyond, to go over, *270*
*per-, to carry forth, to fare, *127*
*per-, to try, dare, risk, *97*
*perkʷu-, oak, *200*
*pers-, to spray, splash, *248*
*peth₂-, to fly, *40*
*péth₂r, wing, feather, *41*
*pewǵ-, to punch; to prick, poke, *153*
*peyḱ-, to hew, cut out; to stitch, embroider, sting; to paint, mark, colour, *167*
*peys-, to grind, crush, *194*
*ph₂tḗr, father, *17*
*pleh₁-, to fill, *172*
*pleh₂k-, flat, *285*
*pleh₂k-, to hit, *286*
*pleḱ-, to plait, braid, *169*
*pleth₂-, flat, *284*
*plew-, to fly, flow, run, *46*
*plewmō, lung, *46*
*plou-, flea, *224*
*pṓds, foot, *42*
*pórḱos, piglet, *211*
*pótis, master, ruler, husband, *65*
*poymno-, foam, *248*
*preḱ-, to ask, *92*
*preyH-, to love, to please, *101*
*(s)kek-, to spring, move quickly, *209*
*(s)kel-, to bend, crook; bent, crooked; leg, heel, knee, hip, *38*
*(s)ker-, to cut, cut off, *256*
*(s)neh₁-, to spin (thread), to sew, *216*

Word Index

English

-ay, *h₂ekʷeh₂-
-bolic, -bolism, *gʷelH-
-bury, *bʰerǵʰ-
-corn, *ḱerh₂-
-ey, *h₂ekʷeh₂-
-id, *weyd-
-logy, *leǵ-
-myrmex, *morwi-
-naut, *(s)neh₂-
-odont, -odontia, *h₃dónts
-oecious, *weyḱ-
-oid, *weyd-
-phone, *bʰeh₂-
-phyllous, *bʰleh₃-
-phyte, -phyto-, *bʰuH-
-scope, -scopic, -scopy, *speḱ-
-stow, *steh₂-
-there, *ǵʰwer-
-thymia, *dʰewh₂-
-tone, -tonia, -tonic, *ten-
-ty, *déḱm̥t
-ward, -wards, *wert-
-wich, *weyḱ-
a, *óy-nos
a.m. (ante meridiem), *deyn-
aardvark, *pórḱos
abarognosis, *gʷerh₂-
abbreviate, *mréǵʰ-
abduce, abduct, abduction, abductor, *dewk-
abear, *bher-
abhor, abhorrent, *gʰers-
abide, *bʰeydʰ-
ability, *gʰeh₁bʰ-
abjudge, abjudicate, abjuration, abjure, *h₂eyw-
ablation, ablative, ablator, *bher-
able, *gʰeh₁bʰ-
ablegate, ablegation, *legh-
abluent, ablution, *lewh₃-
abnormal, *ǵneh₃-, *h₂pó
abolish, abolition, *h₂el-
aboriginal, Aborigine, abort, abortion, abortive, *h₃er-
abound, *wed-
above, *upo
abrasion, *h₂pó
abridge, *mréǵʰ-
abscind, abscissa, abscission, *skey-
abscond, *dheH₁-

absent, *h₂pó
absist, *steh₂-
absolescent, *swe-dʰh₁-
abstain, *h₂pó, *ten-
abstinence, abstinent, *ten-
abstract, abstraction, *h₂pó
abstrude, abstruse, *trewd-
abundance, *wed-
abyss, *dʰewb-
acarpous, *kerp-
accent, accentuate, *keh₂n-
accept, *keh₂p-
acclaim, *kelh₁-
accompany, *peh₂-
accomplish, *pleh₁-
accord, *ḱér
accorporate, *krep-
accouchement, *stel-
acculturate, *kʷel-
acerb, acerbate, acerbic, acerbity, acid, acidity, acme, *h₂éḱ
acorn, *eh₃g-
acquiesce, acquiescent, acquit, acquittal, *kʷyeh₁-
acre, *h₂éǵros
acrid, acrimonious, acrimony, acritude, acrity, *h₂éḱ
acromegaly, *méǵh₂s
acrostic, *steygʰ-
act, action, active, activity, actor, *H₂eǵ-
aculeus, acupuncture, *h₂éḱ
acupuncture, *pewǵ-
adamant, adamantine, *demh₂-
add, addendum, *deH₃-
adder, *neHtr-
addict, addiction, *deyḱ-
addition, *deH₃-
adduce, adduct, adductor, *dewk-
adhibit, *gʰeh₁bʰ-
adjoin, *yewg-
adjudge, adjudicate, adjudication, *h₂eyw-
adjunction, *yewg-
adjuration, adjure, *h₂eyw-
adlect, *leǵ-
administer, administor, administrate, administration, administrative, admix, admixture, *mey-
admonish, admonition, *men-
adolescent, adulterate, adulterine, adultery, *h₂el-
adunc, aduncity, aduncous, *h₂enk-
adure, *h₁ews-
advene, advent, adventitious, adventure, *gʷem-
adverb, adverbial, *wekʷ-
adverse, adversity, advertise, *wert-
advice, advise, *weyd-

advocate, advocation, advoke, *wekʷ-

advolution, *welH-

advoutrer, *h₂el-

aedicula, aedile, *h₂eydʰ-

aeneous, *h₂eyos

aeon, *h₂ey-

aerate, aerial, aerobic, aerodynamic, *h₂ews-

aeronautics, *(s)neh₂-, *h₂ews-

aeroplane, aerosol, *h₂ews-

æruginous, aerugite, aerugo, *h₂eyos

aestival, aestivation/estivation, aether/ether, *h₂eydʰ-

affair, affect, affectation, affection, *dheH₁-

affiliation, *dʰeh₁(y)-

affirm, affirmation, *dʰer-

afflatus, affluence, affluent, *bʰleh₁-

affuse, *ǵʰew-

after, *h₂pó

age, *h₂ey-

agenda, agent, *H₂eǵ-

ageusia, *ǵews-

aggravate, aggrieve, *gʷerh₂-

agile, agitate, agitation, agitator, *H₂eǵ-

agnail, *h₂enǵʰ-

agnathous, *ǵénus

agnomen, *h₁nómn̥

agnosia, agnostic, *ǵneh₃-

agoge, agon, agonist, agonistes, agony, *H₂eǵ-

agrarian, *h₂éǵros

agree, agreeable, agreement, *gʷerH-

agrestic, agricultor, agriculture, *h₂éǵros

agriculture, *kʷel-

agronomy, *h₂éǵros

air, *h₂ews-

aisle, *H₂eǵ-

akvavit, *h₂ekʷeh₂-

alar, *H₂eǵ-

alder, *h₃el-

ale, *h₂elut-

Alexander, *h₂nḗr

alexithymia, *dʰewh₂-

ali-, aliethmoidal, *H₂eǵ-

alias, alibi, *h₂el-

Alicante, *lewk-

alien, *h₂el-

align, alignment, *lino-

aliment, alimony, *h₂el-

alinasal, aliseptal, alisphenoid, *H₂eǵ-

all, *h₂el-

allay, *legh-

allective, *leǵ-

allegation, *legh-

allegory, *h₂el-

allergy, *werǵ-

alleviate, *h₁lengʷʰ-

allocate, *stel-

allogenic, allograph, *h₂el-

allopatric, allopatry, *ph₂tḗr

allophone, *h₂el-

alluvium, *lewh₃-

almery, *h₂er

alter, altercate, altercation, alternate, *h₂el-

altimeter, *meh₁-

alum, aluminium, *h₂elut-

alumnus, alveolus, alvine, *h₂el-

amanuensis, *méh₂-r̥

ambassador, *H₂eǵ-

ambi-, *h₂ent

ambidexter, ambidexterity, ambidextrous, *deks-

ambience, ambient, *h₂ent

ambiguous, *H₂eǵ-

ambilineal, *lino-

ambit, *h₂ent

ambivalent, *h₂welh₁-

ambrosia, *mer-

ambry, *h₂er

ameiosis, ameiotic, *mey-

amentia, *men-

amethyst, amethystine, *médʰu

amnesia, amnesty, *men-

amniocentesis, amnion, amniote, amniotic, *h₂egʷnos

amphalectomy, *h₃enbʰ-

amphi-, amphibian, amphibious, *h₂ent

amphibole, *gʷelH-, *h₂ent

amphimacer, *h₂ent, *meh₂ḱ-

Amphipoda, amphitheatre, amphoterism, *h₂ent

amplify, *dheH₁-

amyloid, amyloplast, amylose, amylum, *melh₂-

an, *óy-nos

anabasis, *gʷem-

anabolic, *gʷelH-

anagram, *gerbʰ-

analogy, *leǵ-

anamnesis, *men-

anaphora, *bher-

anaptotic, *peth₂

anastasis, *steh₂-

anathema, *dheH₁-

anatine, *h₂eneti-

and, *h₂enh₁-, *h₂ent

ande, *h₂enh₁-

androcentric, androgen, *h₂nḗr

androgynous, *gwén, *h₂nḗr

android, andrology, androphobia, androspore, *h₂nḗr

anecdote, *deH₃-

anemometer, anemone, *h₂enh₁-

anger, angina, *h₂enǵʰ-

angiocarpous, *kerp-

angle, angle, *h₂enk-

angst, *h₂enǵʰ-

angular, *h₂enk-

anima, *h₂enh₁-

animadvert, *wert-

animal, animate, animation, animism, animosity, animus, *h₂enh₁-

ankle, *h₂enk-
anneal, *h₂eydʰ-
anniversary, *wert-
anomie, *nem-
anonym, anonymous, *h₁nómn̥
anorectic, anorexia, *h₃reǵ-
anotia, *h₂ew-
anserine, *ǵʰans-
ant-, *h₂ent
antagonist, antagonize, *H₂eǵ-, *h₂ent
ante meridiem (a.m.), ante-, antebellum, *h₂ent
antechamber, *(s)teg-
antecourt, *ǵʰer-
antediluvian, antemortem, anterior, *h₂ent
anthology, *leǵ-
anti-, antibiotic, *h₂ent
antic, *h₂énti-h₃kʷós
anticipate, *h₂ent, *keh₂p-
antidote, *deH₃-, *h₂ent
antinomy, *nem-
antipasto, *peh₂-
antiphon, *bʰeh₂-
antipodes, *h₂ent
antipodes, *pṓds
antiquarian, antiquary, antiquate, antique, antiquity,
  *h₂énti-h₃kʷós
antirrhinum, *h₂ent
antithesis, antithet, *dheH₁-
anxiety, anxious, *h₂enǵʰ-
any, *óy-nos
aphelion, *h₂pó, *sóh₂wl̥
apian, apiary, apiculture, *bʰey-
apocalypse, apocalyptic, *ḱel-
apocrine, apocryphal, *h₂pó
apodeme, *dem-
apodosis, *deH₃-
apogee, *h₂pó
apology, *leǵ-
apoplectic, *pleh₂k-
apoptosis, *peth₂
aporia, *per-
apostasy, apostate, *h₂pó
apothecary, *dheH₁-
apotheosis, *dʰéh₁s
apparent, appear, *peh₂-
append, appendix, *pewǵ-
appertain, *ten-
appetite, appetition, *peth₂
applaud, applause, applausive, *pleh₂k-
apple, *h₂ébōl
appliance, applicable, application, applicator,
  appliqué, apply, *pleḱ-
appose, apposite, *teḱ-
appraise, appreciate, *per-
apprehend, apprehension, *weyd-
approbation, *bʰuH-
appropriate, *preyH-

approve, *bʰuH-
approximate, *per-
appurtenance, *ten-
apterous, *péth₂r̥
apud, *h₁epi
aqua, aquamarine, aquarium, Aquarius, aquatic,
  *h₂ekʷeh₂-
aqueduct, *dewk-, *h₂ekʷeh₂-
aqueous, *h₂ekʷeh₂-
aquifer, *bher-
arable, *H₂erH₃-
arachnid, arachnoid, arachnophobia, *h₂er
aration, *H₂erH₃-
arbor, arboreal, arboreous, arborescent, arboret,
  arboretum, *h₂erHdʰ-
arc, arcade, *h₂erkʷo-
arcane, *h₂erk-
arch, *h₂erkʷo-
archaeopteryx, *péth₂r̥
archdiocese, *weyḱ-
archisynagogue, *H₂eǵ-
architect, *tetḱ-
arctic, Arcturus, *h₂r̥tḱos
arcuate, *h₂erkʷo-
ard, *H₂erH₃-
arduity, arduous, *h₂erHdʰ-
aread, *Hreh₁dʰ-
arete, *h₂er
argon, *werǵ-
arid, *h₂eh₁s-
arithmetic, *h₂er
ark, *h₂erk-
arm, armada, armature, *h₂er
armipotent, *H₁es-
armoire, armomancy, armour, armoury, arms, army,
  *h₂er
arrow, *h₂erkʷo-
art, arthritis, arthropod, article, articulate, *h₂er
artifact, *dheH₁-, *h₂er
artifical, *h₂er
artifice, *dheH₁-, *h₂er
artisan, *h₂er
ascertain, *krey-
ascribe, *(s)ker-
ash, *h₂eh₁s-, *h₃es-
aspect, *speḱ-
asportation, *per-
aspy, *speḱ-
assemble, *sem-
assent, *sent-
assert, assertion, assertive, *ser-
assess, assiduous, *sed-
assign, assignation, *sek-
assimilate, *sem-
assist, assistance, *steh₂-
aster, asterisk, asteroid, *h₂stḗr
astonish, *(s)tenh₂-

astral, *$h_2$stér
astripotent, *H_1es-
astrobleme, *g^welH-
astrology, *$h_2$stér
astronaut, *(s)neh$_2$-, *$h_2$stér
astronomy, *$h_2$stér
astute, *h_2éḱ
asweve, *swep-
atavic, atavistic, *$h_2$éwh$_2$os
atelophobia, *k^wel-
athermancy, *g^{wh}er-
athlete, athletic, atmosphere, *H_2weH$_1$-
atonic, *ten-
atrocious, atrocity, *$h_2$eh$_1$tro-h$_3$k^{w}s
attend, attent, attention, attentive, *ten-
attribute, attributor, *b^huH-
attrition, *terh$_1$-
auction, *$h_2$ewg-
audible, audience, audient, audile, audio,
  audiology, audit, audition, auditor, auditorium,
  auditory, *$h_2$ewis-d^{h}h$_1$-
aught, *$h_2$eyḱ-
augment, augmentation, augur, augury, august,
  August, *$h_2$ewg-
aura, *$h_2$ews-
aural, auricle, auricula, *$h_2$ew-
aurora, aurorean, *$h_2$ews-
auscultate, auscultation, auscultator, *ḱel-
auspicate, *speḱ-
auspice, auspicious, *$h_2$éwis, *speḱ-
austral, Australia, *$h_2$ews-
autarchy, autarky, authentic, authenticity, *$h_2$ew
authority, *$h_2$ewg-
autism, autistic, auto-, auto, autocracy, *$h_2$ew
autoctisis, *teḱ-
autograph, *$h_2$ew
automate, *men-
automatic, automaton, *$h_2$ew, *men-
autonomy, *$h_2$ew, *nem-
auxanography, auxanometer, auxesis, auxiliar,
  auxiliary, auxin, auxology, auxotrophy, *$h_2$ewg-
avail, *$h_2$welh$_1$-
avatar, *terh$_2$-
avenge, *weyh$_1$-
avenue, *g^wem-
aver, *g^heh$_1$b^h-, *weh$_1$-
aversion, *$h_2$pó
avert, *wert-
avian, aviary, aviation, *$h_2$éwis
aviator, *$h_2$éwis, *weyh$_1$-
avocat, avouch, avow, *wek^w-
avulsion, *$h_2$pó
avuncular, *$h_2$éwh$_2$os
aware, *wer-
axe, *h_2éḱ
axilla, axis, axle, axon, *H_2eǵ-
aye, *$h_2$ey-

azoic, *g^weyh$_3$-
azygous, *yugóm
bacteria, baculiform, baculum, *bak-
bairn, *b^her-
bait, *b^heyd-
ball, ballista, ballistic, ballistospore, *g^welH-
ban, *b^heh$_2$-
bane, *g^{wh}en-
banish, *b^heh$_2$-
barbate, barbed, barber, barbule, *b^hard^{h}eh$_2$-
bard, *g^werH-
baresthesia, *g^werh$_2$-
bargh, *b^herǵ^h-
baria, bariatric, baritone, *g^werh$_2$-
baritone, *ten-
barley, *b^hars-
barognosis, barogram, barograph, barometer, *g^werh$_2$-
barometer, *meh$_1$-
barophobia, *g^werh$_2$-
barouche, *Hret-
barrow, *b^her-, *b^herǵ^h-
barycentric, baryon, barysphere, *g^werh$_2$-
barytone, *ten-
bas-relief, *$h_1$leng^{wh}-
base, basis, *g^wem-
be-, *$h_1$epi
be, *b^huH-
beacon, *b^heh$_2$-
bean, *b^hab^{h}eh$_2$-
bear, *b^her-
beard, *b^hard^{h}eh$_2$-
bede, *b^hewd^h-
bedeck, *(s)teg-
bee, *b^heh$_2$-, *b^hey-
beech, *b^heh$_2$go-
beef, *g^wṓws
beer, *bher-, *peh$_3$-
beget, *weyd-
beldame, *dem-
beleave, *leyp-
belladonna, *dem-
bellipotent, *H_1es-
belomancy, belonephobia, *g^welH-
ben, bene, *b^heh$_2$-
benediction, *deyḱ-
benefactor, benefice, benefit, *dheH$_1$-
benevolence, *welh$_1$-
benim, *nem-
bere, *b^hars-
berg, berry, *b^herǵ^h-
berserk, berserker, *ser-
beset, besit, *sed-
bestand, *steh$_2$-
bethink, *teng-
between, *dwóH$_1$
beverage, bib, *peh$_3$-
bibliotheca, *dheH$_1$-

catabolic, *gʷelH-

cataplexy, *pleh₂k-

catatonia, *ten-

cathedra, *sed-

catholic, *solh₂-

cattle, *kapōlo

ceiling, *ḱel-

celeripede, *pṓds

cell, cellar, cellule, *ḱel-

cent, centenarial, centenarian, centenary, centennial, centesimal, centesimate, centesmation, centimeter/ centimetre, centipede, *ḱm̥tóm

centripetal, *peth₂

centurion, century, *ḱm̥tóm

cerebellum, cerebral, cerebrum, *ḱerh₂-

certain, *krey-

cervine, *ḱerh₂-

chair, *sed-

chakra, *kʷel-

chamber, chamberlain, *(s)teg-

chamfer, *dʰer-

champerty, champion, *(s)teg-

chanson, chansonnier, chant, chanteur, chanteuse, chanticleer, *keh₂n-

chapter, *kapōlo

character, *ǵʰer-

charge, chariot, *ḱers-

charisma, *ǵʰer-

charm, *keh₂n-

charnel, *(s)ker-

chart, charter, *ǵʰer-

chase, chassis, *keh₂p-

chattel, *kapōlo

cheer, *ḱerh₂-

chef, *kapōlo

chelonian, chelydre, *gʰelōw-

chic, chicanery, *(s)kek-

chief, *kapōlo

chill, *gel-

chilognath, chin, *ǵénus

Chiroptera, *péth₂r

chlorine, *ǵʰelh₃-

chlorophyll, *bʰleh₃-, *ǵʰelh₃-

choose, *ǵews-

chord, *ǵʰern-

chthonian, chthonic, *dʰéǵʰōm

churl, *ǵerh₂-

cinque, *pénkʷe

circumference, *bʰer-

circumnavigate, *(s)neh₂-

circumscribe, *(s)ker-

circumspect, circumspection, *speḱ-

circumstance, *steh₂-

circumvent, *gʷem-

circumvolute, circumvolve, *welH-

citizen, city, civic, civil, civilian, civility, civilization, civitas, *ḱei-

claim, *kelh₁-

clairvoyance, *weyd-

clamour/clamor, *kelh₁-

clan, *pleh₂-

clandestine, *ḱel-

clarify, *dʰeH₁-

clarity, class, classic, classical, classify, *kelh₁-

claustrum, clausula, clausure, clavichord, clavicle, clavis, *(s)kel-

clear, *kelh₁-

clepsydra, *wed-

client, *ḱlew-

climacteric, climate, climax, clinic, clivus, *ḱley-

cloister, close, closure, cloture, clove, cloy, *(s)kel-

cockle, *ḱonkho-

Cockney, *h₂ōwyóm

coctile, *pekʷ-

coerce, coercion, *h₂erk-

coeval, *h₂ey-

cogency, cogent, cogitate, cogitation, *H₂eǵ-

cognition, cognize, *ǵneh₃-

cognomen, *h₁nómn̥

cognosce, *ǵneh₃-

cohort, *ǵʰer-

coil, *leǵ-

coition, coitus, *h₁ey-

cold, *gel-

collate, *bʰer-

colleague, *leǵ-, *legh-

collect, collectible, collection, collective, collector, *leǵ-

college, *leǵ-, *legh-

collegial, *leǵ-

collegiate, *leǵ-, *legh-

collegium, *legh-

colliculus, *kelH-

collinear, *lino-

collingual, *dn̥ǵʰwéh₂s

collocate, collocation, *stel-

colluvium, *lewh₃-

colon, *(s)kel-

colonial, colony, *kʷel-

color/colour, *kel-

column, *kelH-

comb, *ǵómbʰos

combination, combine, *dwóH₁

combust, *h₁ews-

comestible, *h₁ed-

cominal, *mey-

command, *deH₃-

commemorate, *men-

commend, *deH₃-

commensurable, commensurate, *meh₁-

comment, commentary, *men-

commix, commixture, *mey-

commodious, *med-

common, *mey-

commonition, *men-

courier, course, *kers-
court, courteous, courtesan, courtesy, *ǵʰer-
cousin, *swésōr
couth, *ǵneh₃-
coutier, *ǵʰer-
couture, *sīw-
covent, *gʷem-
cow, *gʷṓws
coxa, *koḱs-
coy, *kʷyeh₁-
cranberry, crane, *gerh₂-
cranial, cranium, *ḱerh₂-
credible, credit, creditor, credo, credulity, credulous,
    creed, *dheH₁-
creosote, *krewh₂-
crime, crisis, *krey-
crude, crudity, cruel, cruelty, *krewh₂-
cruor, cud, *gʷet-
cuisine, *pekʷ-
cull, *leǵ-
culm, *ḱalam-
culminate, *kelH-
cult, cultivate, culture, *kʷel-
cuman, *gʷewm-
cummerbund/cummerband, *(s)teg-
cunabula, *ḱei-
cunning, *ǵneh₃-
currency, current, curriculum, cursor, cursory, *ḱers-
curt, *(s)ker-
curtain, *ǵʰer-
curtana, *(s)ker-
curtilage, Curtis, *ǵʰer-
curule, *ḱers-
curvilinear, *lino-
custom, *swe-dʰh₁-
cynanche, *h₂enǵʰ-, *ḱwṓ
cynic, *ḱwṓ
cystocarp, *kerp-
dad, *átta
daeva, *dyew-
daimon, *deh₂-
dainty, *deḱ-
dam, *dem-
damage, *deh₂-
dame, *dem-
Damian, *demh₂-
damn, *deh₂-
damsel, *dem-
dandelion, *h₃dónts
danger, *dem-
dapifer, *deh₂-
dare, *dʰers-
darn, *dʰer-
data, date, datum, *deH₃-
daughter, *dʰugh₂tḗr
daw, day, *dʰegʷʰ-
dean, *déḱm̥t

dear, dearth, *dʰegʷʰ-
debenture, debile, debilitate, debility, debit, debt,
    *gʰeh₁bʰ-
deca-, decad, decade, decahedron, Decalogue,
    decamer, *déḱm̥t
decamp, *(s)teg-
decapitate, *kapōlo
decapod, decathlon, *déḱm̥t
decathlon, *H₂weH₁-
deceive, *keh₂p-
December, *déḱm̥t
deception, *keh₂p-
decima, decimal, decimate, *déḱm̥t
deck, *(s)teg-
declaim, declare, *kelh₁-
declination, decline, *ḱley-
decor, decorate, decoration, decorative, decorator,
    decorous, *deḱ-
decorticate, *(s)ker-
decorum, *deḱ-
decree, decretal, decretory, *krey-
deduce, deduct, deduction, *dewk-
deed, deem, *dheH₁-
deep, *dʰewb-
defeat, defect, *dheH₁-
defend, *gʷʰen-
defer, *bher-
deflate, *bʰleh₁-
degravation, *gʷerh₂-
degustation, *ǵews-
dehort, *ǵʰer-
dehydrate, *wed-
deification, deify, *dyew-
deign, *deḱ-
deity, *dyew-
delegate, delegation, *legh-
delict, *leykʷ-
delineate, delineavit, *lino-
delinquency, delinquent, *leykʷ-
delirious, delirium, *leys-
deliver, *h₁lewdʰ-
deluge, *lewh₃-
demagogue, *deh₂-, *H₂eǵ-
demand, *deH₃-
deme, *deh₂-
demented, dementia, *men-
demesne, *dem-
demiurge, *werǵ-
democracy, democratic, *deh₂-
demoiselle, *dem-
demonstrate, demonstration, *men-
denar, denarius, denary, denier, *déḱm̥t
dental, dentate, denticulate, denticule, dentist, denture,
    *h₃dónts
denudate, denude, *negʷ-
depend, *pewǵ-
depict, depiction, *peyḱ-

deplete, *pleh₁-
deploy, *pleḱ-
deponent, *teḱ-
deport, *per-
deposit, *teḱ-
deprecate, deprecation, deprecative, deprecatory,
 *preḱ-
deprive, *per-
depth, *dʰewb-
Derek, *tewtéh₂
derive, *h₃reyH-
dermatology, dermis, *der-
dern, *dʰer-
descant, *keh₂n-
describe, description, *(s)ker-
desert, desertion, *ser-
design, designate, *sek-
desist, *steh₂-
desolate, *s(w)e-
despair, *speh₁-
despection, *speḱ-
desperate, *speh₁-
despicable, despiciency, despise, despite, *speḱ-
despot, *pótis
destination, destine, destitute, *steh₂-
destroy, destruction, *strew-
detain, *ten-
detect, detection, detective, detector, *(s)teg-
detention, *ten-
determination, determine, *térmn̥
detonable, detonate, *(s)tenh₂-
detriment, detrimental, detrital, detrition, detritivore,
 detritus, *terh₁-
detrude, detrusion, *trewd-
deuce, *dwóH₁
devil, *gʷelH-
devious, *weyh₁-
devolution, devolve, *welH-
dew, *dʰewh₂-
dexetrous/dextrous, Dexiarchia, dexter, dexterity,
 dextral, dextrin, dextrose, *deḱs-
dharma, *dʰer-
di-, *dwóH₁
diabolic, *gʷelH-
diagram, *gerbʰ-
dialogue, *leǵ-
diameter, *meh₁-
diandry, *h₂nér
diaphanous, *bʰeh₂-
diarrhoea, *srew-
diary, *deyn-
diaschisis, diaschism, *skey-
diascopy, *speḱ-
diatessaron, *kʷetwóres
diatonic,dystonia, *ten-
diazeugman, *yewg-
dictamen, dictate, dictation, dictature, diction,

dictionary, dictum, *deyḱ-
differ, difference, different, *bher-
difficult, difficulty, *dheH₁-
diffuse, diffusion, *ǵʰew-
dight, digit, digital, digitalis, digitate, *deyḱ-
dignity, *deḱ-
dilate, *bher-
dilection, diligence, diligent, *leǵ-
diluent, dilute, dilution, dilutive, diluvial, diluvium, *lewh₃-
dime, *déḱm̥t
dimension, *meh₁-
dinar, *déḱm̥t
diocese, *weyḱ-
diode, *dwóH₁
dioecious, *weyḱ-
direct, *h₃reǵ-
Dirk, *tewtéh₂
dis-, *dwóH₁
disaffected, *dheH₁-
disagree, *gʷerH-
discant, discantus, *keh₂n-
discern, *krey-
discharge, *ḱers-
disclude, *(s)kel-
discord, discourage, *ḱér
discourse, *ḱers-
discriminate, *krey-
disenchant, disenchantment, disencharm, *keh₂n-
disfigure, *dʰeyǵʰ-
disgrace, *gʷerH-
disgust, *ǵews-
disincentive, *keh₂n-
disincorporate, *krep-
disinhume, *dʰéǵʰōm
disjoin, *yewg-
dislocate, dislocation, *stel-
disorient, disorientation, *h₃er-
display, *pleḱ-
disport, *per-
dispose, *teḱ-
disrespect, *speḱ-
dissect, *sek-
dissemble, *sem-
disseminate, *seH₁-
dissent, *sent-
dissertation, *ser-
dissidence, *sed-
dissimilitude, dissimulate, dissimulation, *sem-
distance, distant, *steh₂-
distend, *ten-
distich, distichous, *steygʰ-
distribute, *bʰuH-
diurnal, *deyn-
diva, *dyew-
diverse, diversify, divert, *wert-
divest, *wes-
divide, dividual, dividuous, *h₁weydʰ

divination, divine, divinity, *dyew-
divisible, divisim, division, divisor, *h₁weydʰ
dizygotic, *yugóm
do, *dheH₁-
docile, doctor, doctrine, document, *deḱ-
dodecahedron, *sed-
doe, *dʰeh₁(y)-
dogma, dogmatic, dogmatism, dogmatist, *deḱ-
domain, domal, dome, domestic, domesticate,
domestication, domesticity, domestique, domicile,
domiciliary, dominance, dominant, dominate,
domination, dominatrix, domineer, dominion,
domino, don, *dem-
donate, donation, donative, *deH₃-
donner, *(s)tenh₂-
donor, *deH₃-
donzel, *dem-
doom, *dheH₁-
door, *dʰwer-
dope, *dʰewb-
dorp, *treb-
doru, dory, *dóru
dose, *deH₃-
double, *pleh₁-
doubt, *dwóH₁
dough, *dʰeyǵʰ-
dour, *deru-
down, *dʰewh₂-
doxology, *deḱ-
doyen, *dékm̥t
drake, *h₂eneti-, *h₃reǵ-
dramaturgy, *werǵ-
dryad, *dóru
dual, *dwóH₁
dubious, *gʰeh₁bʰ-
duchy, duct, ductin, *dewk-
duenna, *dem-
duet, *dwóH₁
duff, *dʰeyǵʰ-
duke, *dewk-
dun, *dʰewh₂-
dungeon, *dem-
duo, *dwóH₁
duple, *pleh₁-
duplex, *dwóH₁, *pleḱ-
duplicate, *pleḱ-
duplicity, *dwóH₁
durability, durable, duramen, durance, duration,
dure, duress, durum, *deru-
dusk, dust, *dʰewh₂-
dux, *dewk-
dwindle, dwine, *dʰegʷʰ-
dyad, *dwóH₁
dye, *dʰewh₂-
dysgeusia, *ǵews-
dysmnesia, *men-
dysostosis, *h₃ésth₁

dyspepsia, *pekʷ-
dysthymia, *dʰewh₂-
ea, *h₂ekʷeh₂-
ean, *h₂eǵʷnos
ear, *H₂erH₃-, *h₂ew-
earth, earthen, *h₁er-
east, Easter, eastern, *h₂ews-
eat, *h₁ed-
eau, *h₂ekʷeh₂-
ecesis, *weyḱ-
echinate, echinoderm, echinology, *ǵʰér
ecology, *weyḱ-
economic, *nem-
economize, *weyḱ-
economy, *nem-, *weyḱ-
ecstasy, ecstatic, *steh₂-
ectasia, *ten-
ectoderm, *der-
ectomycorrhiza, *wréh₂ds
ectotherm, *gʷʰer-
ectozoon, *gʷeyh₃-
eczema, *yes-
edacity, *h₁ed-
eddy, *h₂ekʷeh₂-
edge, *h₂éḱ
edible, *h₁ed-
edict, *deyḱ-
edification, *h₂eydʰ-
edifice, *dheH₁-, *h₂eydʰ-
edify, *h₂eydʰ-
edition, editor, *deH₃-
educate, education, *dewk-
effable, *bʰeh₂-
effect, effective, effectual, effectuate, *dheH₁-
effendi, *h₂ew
efficacious, efficient, *dheH₁-
effigy, *dʰeyǵʰ-
effluent, effluvium, *bʰleh₁-
effuse, effusion, *ǵʰew-
egest, *H₂eǵ-
egg, *h₂ōwyóm
ego, egocentric, egoism, egomaniac, egotistical, *egH₂
eidetic, eidolon, *weyd-
eight, *oḱtṓw
eirenic, *ser-
either, *kʷis
eke, *h₂ewg-
ekstasis, *steh₂-
elated, elation, *bher-
elbow, *Heh₃l-
eld, *h₂el-
elect, election, elective, electorate, elegant, eligibility,
   *leǵ-
element, elementary, *h₂el-
elevate, *h₁lengʷʰ-
eleven, *óy-nos
eligible, *leǵ-

ferocious, ferocity, *ǵʰweroh₃kʷs
ferret, ferry, *bher-
ferry, *per-
fertile, *bher-
fest, *dʰéh₁s
fester, *bʰeyd-
festival, festive, festivity, fete, *dʰéh₁s
fetter, *ped-
fetus, *dʰeh₁(y)-
feu, feud, feudatory, *peḱu-
fever, *dʰegʷʰ-
fiat, *bʰuH-, *dheH₁-
fiction, fictitious, fictive, *dʰeyǵʰ-
fidelity, fiduciary, *bʰeydʰ-
field, *pleh₂-
fierce, *ǵʰwer-
fiesta, *dʰéh₁s
fight, *peḱ-
figment, figure, figurine, *dʰeyǵʰ-
filch, *pleh₁-
filial, *dʰeh₁(y)-
fill, *pleh₁-
film, *pel-
fin, *spey-
find, *pent-
fir, *perkʷu-
fire, *péh₂ur
firm, firmament, firmation, *dʰer-
first, firth, *per-
firth, *perkʷu-
fish, *peisḱ-
fission, fissure, *bʰeyd-
fist, *pewǵ-
fistula, *bʰeyd-
Fitz-, *dʰeh₁(y)-
five, *pénkʷe
fjord, *per-
flabellum, *bʰleh₁-
flake, *pleh₂-
flat, *pleh₂-, *pleth₂-
flatulence, flatus, flavor, *bʰleh₁-
flaw, *pleh₂-
flea, *plou-
flee, fleet, *plew-
flet, *pleth₂-
flight, flit, float, flood, *plew-
floor, *pleh₂-
floral, florid, flourish, *bʰleh₃-
flow, *plew-
flower, *bʰleh₃-
fluctuate, fluctuation, fluent, *bʰleh₁-
fluff, *h₂welh₁-
fluid, *bʰleh₁-
fluke, *pleh₂-
flume, flute, fluvial, flux, *bʰleh₁-
fly, *plew-
foam, *poymno-

fodder, *peh₂-
foible, *bʰleh₁-
foil, *bʰleh₃-
foin, *bʰeh₂go-
fold, *pleth₂-
foliage, foliate, folio, foliose, *bʰleh₃-
folk, *pleh₁-
foment, *dʰegʷʰ-
food, *peh₂-
foot, *póds
for, *per-
forage, *peh₂-
forbear, *bher-
force, *bʰerǵʰ-, *pers-
forceps, *gʷʰer-, *keh₂p-
ford, *per-
fordeem, *dheH₁-
fore, *per-
forensic, *dʰwer-
forest, *perkʷu-
forfare, *per-
forfeit, *dheH₁-
forget, *weyd-
forgive, *gʰebʰ-
formaldehyde, formic acid, formicate, *morwi-
forsake, *seh₂g-
forstand, *steh₂-
fort, forte, *bʰerǵʰ-
forth-, forth, *per-
fortification, fortify, *bʰerǵʰ-, *dheH₁-
fortis, *bʰerǵʰ-
fortuitous, fortune, *bher-
forum, *dʰwer-
forworth, *wert-
found, *bʰudʰmén, *ǵʰew-
foundation, founder, *bʰudʰmén
foundry, *ǵʰew-
four, *kʷetwóres
frain, *preḱ-
frame, *per-
fraternal, fraternity, *bʰréh₂tēr
fraught, *h₂eyḱ-
free, freedom, *preyH-
freight, *h₂eyḱ-
frenulum, *dʰer-
fress, fret, *h₁ed-
friar, *bʰréh₂tēr
friend, friendly, friendship, *preyH-
frith, *perkʷu-, *preyH-
fro, from, frow, *per-
fuck, *pewǵ-
full, *pleh₁-
fumarium, fume, fumigate, *dʰewh₂-
fund, fundament, fundamental, *bʰudʰmén
fure, *per-
furnace, *gʷʰer-
further, *per-

furtive, *bher-
fusion, *ǵʰew-
future, *bʰuH-
fyrd, *per-
gage, *wedʰ-
galactagogue, *glag-, *H₂eǵ-
galactic, galactorrhea, galaxy, *glag-
garden, *ǵʰer-
garnish, *wer-
garth, *ǵʰer-
gel, gelati, gelatin, gelatinous, gelation, gelid,
  gelifluction, gelignite, *gel-
gem, *ǵómbʰos
gender, generate, generic, generous, genesis, genie,
genitive, genitor, genius, genre, gens, genticide, gentile,
gentilicial, gentilicious, gentility, gentle, gentry, *ǵenH₁-
genuflect, *ǵónu
genus, *ǵenH₁-
geothermic, *gʷʰer-
geranium, *gerh₂-
gerascophobia, *ǵerh₂-
germ, germane, germinate, germination, *ǵenH₁-
geronto-, gerontogracy, gerontology, gerousia, *ǵerh₂-
gerund, gesture, *H₂eǵ-
get, *weyd-
ghastly, ghost, *ǵʰeyzd-
gift, *gʰebʰ-
gird, girdle, girth, *ǵʰer-
give, *gʰebʰ-
glacial, glaciate, glacier, *gel-
gloriation, glorious, glory, *ǵneh₃-
gnathic, *ǵénus
gnomon, gnosis, *ǵneh₃-
goat, *gʰaydos
god, *ǵʰew-
gold, *ǵʰelh₃-
gomeral, *ǵʰmó
gonad, *ǵenH₁-
goniometer, gonion, gonitis, *ǵónu
gonorrhoea, *srew-
goom, *ǵʰmó
goose, *ǵʰans-
gouache, *h₂ekʷeh₂-
grace, gracious, *gʷerH-
graft, *gerbʰ-
grain, *ǵr̥Hnom
graminivorous, *gʰreh₁-
grammar, *gerbʰ-
grange, *ǵr̥Hnom
graph, grapheme, graphene, graphic, graphite, *gerbʰ-
grass, *gʰreh₁-
gratification, *gʷerH-
gratify, *dʰeH₁-, *gʷerH-
gratis, gratitude, gratuitous, gratuity, gratulate, *gʷerH-
gravamen, grave, gravid, gravida, gravitas, gravitate,
  gravitation, gravity, *gʷerh₂-
gree, *gʷerH-

Greek, *ǵerh₂-
green, *gʰreh₁-
grief, grievance, grieve, grievous, *gʷerh₂-
gringo, *ǵerh₂-
groma, *ǵneh₃-
groom, *ǵʰmó
grow, *gʰreh₁-
Grus, *gerh₂-
guard, *wer-
guest, *gʰóstis
guide, *weyd-
guru, *gʷerh₂-
gustatory, gusto, *ǵews-
guy, *weyd-
gymnasium, gymnastics, gymnoplast, gymnosperm,
  *negʷ-
gynecology, *gwén
haaf, *keh₂p-
habile, habit, habitable, habitat, habitation, habitude,
  *gʰeh₁bʰ-
hacienda, *dheH₁-
haedine, *gʰaydos
hail, *kóh₂ilus
hake, *keg-
hale, *kelh₁-, *kóh₂ilus
halide, *séh₂ls
Halifax, *pek̂-
haline, halite, *séh₂ls
hall, *k̂el-
hallow, *kóh₂ilus
halm, *k̂alam-
halochromic, halogen, halomancy, halophyte, *séh₂ls
hamadryad, *dóru
hamlet, *k̂ei-
hammer, *h₂ék-mō
hangar, *ǵʰer-, *k̂ei-
hangnail, *h₂enǵʰ-
hapalonychia, *h₃negʰ-
haplometrosis, *méh₂tēr
harbinger, harborough, harbour, haricot, *ker-
hark, harken, *h₂k̂h₂owsyéti
harmony, *h₂er
harns, *k̂erh₂-
harrow, harry, *ker-
hart, *k̂erh₂-
haruspex, *ǵʰern-, *spek̂-
harvest, *kerp-
hate, hatel, *k̂eh₂d-
haul, *kelh₁-
haulm, *k̂alam-
haunt, *k̂ei-
have, haven, *keh₂p-
haver, haversack, *kapro
he, *k̂i-
head, *kapōlo
heal, health, *kóh₂ilus
hear, *h₂k̂h₂owsyéti

heart, *ḱḗr
heave, heavy, *keh₂p-
hecato-, *ḱm̥tóm, *sem-
hecatologue, *ḱm̥tóm
hecatomb, *gʷṓws
hecatontarchy, hecatophyllous, *ḱm̥tóm
heel, *kenk-
hegemon, hegemony, *seh₂g-
heinous, *ḱeh₂d-
hele, *ḱel-
helicopter, *péth₂r̥
heliocentric, heliograph, heliotrope, helium, *sóh₂wl̥
helix, *welH-
hell, helm, *ḱel-
hemicraniectomy, *ḱerh₂-
hemiplegia, *pleh₂k-
hemistich, *steygʰ-
hemitonic, *ten-
hen, *keh₂n-
henchman, *kek-
hepar, hepatic, hepatitis, hepatizon, hepato-, *Hyékʷr̥
hepta-, heptachord, heptagon, heptagram, heptahedron, heptameter, Heptateuch, heptathlon, *septm̥
heptatonic, *ten-, *septm̥
here, *ker-, *ḱi-
hern, *ḱerh₂-
hernia, herniated, *ǵʰern-
Hesperidean, Hesperides, *wek(ʷ)speros
hetero-, *sem-
heterodox, *deḱ-
heterogeneous, *sem-
heterogynous, *gwén
heteropterous, *péth₂r̥
heterozygote, heterozygous, *yugóm
hexa-, hexachord, hexad, *swéḱs
hexagon, *ǵónu, *swéḱs
hexahedron, *sed-, *swéḱs
hexameter, *meh₁-, *swéḱs
hexapod, hexatonic, *swéḱs
hibernal, hibernate, *ǵʰey-
hidrosis, hidrotic, *sweyd-
hill, *kelH-
hippo-, hippocampus, hippodrome, *h₁éḱwos
hippopotamus, *h₁éḱwos, *peth₂
hirn, *ḱerh₂-
historic, historical, history, *weyd-
hither, *ḱi-
hock, *kenk-
hockey, *keg-
hodiern, hodiernal, *deyn-
hodo-, *sed-
hold, *ḱel-
holism, holistic, holo-, holocaust, *solh₂-
hologram, *gerbʰ-, *solh₂-
holography, holomorphic, holonomy, *solh₂-
holy, *kóh₂ilus
home, *ḱei-

homeopathy, homeostasis, *sem-
homeothermy, *gʷʰer-
Homo habilis, *gʰeh₁bʰ-
homophone, *bʰeh₂-
homopterous, *péth₂r̥
homorganic, *werǵ-
homunculus, *ǵʰmṓ
hook, *keg-
horn, hornet, *ḱerh₂-
horology, horometry, horoscope, *yeh₁-
horrendous, horrible, horrid, horrific, horror, *gʰers-
horse, *ḱers-
hortation, horticulture, *ǵʰer-
hospice, hospital, hospitality, host, hostel, hostile, hotel, *gʰóstis
hotr, *ǵʰew-
hough, *kenk-
hound, *ḱwṓ
hour, *yeh₁-
how, *kʷis
human, humane, *ǵʰmṓ
humate, humble, humic, humicolous, humiliate, humus, *dʰéǵʰōm
hundred, *ḱm̥tóm
hydra, Hydra, hydrant, hydrate, hydraulic, hydrogen, hydrology, hydrophobic, hydrous, *wed-
hyena, hyenoid, *suH-
hymen, hymenium, hymenomycete, hymenophore, Hymenoptera, *sīw-
hynolepsy, *swep-
hypaethros, *h₂eydʰ-
hyper-, hyper, *upo
hyperbaric, *gʷerh₂-, *upo
hyperbola, hyperbole, gʷelH-, *upo
hyperbolic, *gʷelH-
Hyperion, hyperlink, hyperoxia, hyperthermia, *upo
hyperthymia, *dʰewh₂-
hypertonia, *ten-
hypertonic, *upo
hyperzeuxis, *yewg-
hypha, hyphomycete, hyphopodium, *webh-
hypnagogia, hypnophobia, hypnopompia, hypnosis, hypnotherapy, hypnotic, hypnotist, hypnotize, *swep-
hypo-, *upo
hypobaric, *gʷerh₂-
hypocrisy, *krey-
hypodermic, *der-
hypognathus, *ǵénus
hypotenuse, *ten-
hypothec, *dheH₁-
hypothermia, *gʷʰer-
hypothesis, *dheH₁-
hypozeugma, hypozeuxis, *yewg-
I, *egH₂
ice, *h₁eyH-
icicle, *yeǵ-
id, *éy / h₁e

idea, idealogue, *weyd-

idem, identic, identity, *éy / h₁e

ideology, *weyd-

idiot, *s(w)e-

idol, idolater, idolatry, idolum, idyll, *weyd-

igneous, ignite, ignition, *h₁ngʷnis

ignominious, ignominy, *h₁nómn̥

ignoramus, ignorant, ignore, *ǵneh₃-

il-, *n̥-

ile, *angʷ(h)i-

illation, illative, *bher-

illegal, *leǵ-, *legh-

illegible, *leǵ-

illuminate, *h₁én, *lewk-

illuviation, illuvium, *lewh₃-

imbecile, *bak-

imbibe, *peh₃-

imbriferous, *nebʰ-

immature, immaturity, *meh₂-

immediate, *médʰyos

immemorial, *men-

immense, *meh₁-

immigrate, *mey-

imminent, *men-

immiscibility, immiscible, immix, immixture, *mey-

immolate, *melh₂-

immortal, *mer-

immune, immunity, immutable, *mey-

impact, *peh₂ǵ-

impatent, *peth₂

impecunious, *peḱu-

impede, impediment, *ped-

impend, *pewǵ-

impervious, *weyh₁-

impetus, *peth₂

impinge, *peh₂ǵ-

implant, *pleh₂-

implement, *pleh₁-

implicate, implicit, *pleḱ-

implode, *pleh₂k-

imply, *pleḱ-

import, *h₁én, *per-

importunity, *per-

impose, *teḱ-

improvident, improvisation, improvise, imprudent, *weyd-

impugn, *pewǵ-

impune, impunity, *kʷey-

in camera, *(s)teg-

in esse, in posse, in potentia, *H₁es-

in situ, *teḱ-

in-, *n̥-

in, *h₁én

inaugurate, inauguration, *h₂ewg-

inauspicious, *speḱ-

incantation, incentive, *keh₂n-

inception, inceptive, incipient, *keh₂p-

inclination, incline, *ḱley-

include, inclusion, *(s)kel-

incomprehensible, *weyd-

inconspicuous, *speḱ-

incorporal, incorporate, incorporation, incorporeal, *krep-

incredible, *dheH₁-

incriminate, *krey-

inculcate, *(s)kel-

incult, *kʷel-

incunabula, *kei-

incur, *h₁én, *ḱers-

incursion, *ḱers-

indent, indentation, indenture, *h₃dónts

index, indicate, *deyḱ-

individual, *h₁weydʰ

indoctrinate, indoctrination, *deḱ-

induce, induct, induction, *dewk-

industrious, industry, *strew-

inedia, *h₁ed-

ineffable, *bʰeh₂-

ineligible, *leǵ-

ineluctable, *seh₂g-

inert, inertia, *h₂er-

inescate, *h₁ed-

infamous, infamy, infandous, infant, *bʰeh₂-

infect, *dheH₁-

infer, inferible, *bher-

infest, infestation, *gʷʰen-

infidel, *bʰeydʰ-

infirm, infirmity, *dʰer-

inflate, inflation, influence, influx, *bʰleh₁-

infor, *bher-

infusion, *ǵʰew-

ingenerate, *ǵenH₁-

ingrate, ingratiate, ingratitude, *gʷerH-

ingravescence, *gʷerh₂-

inhale, *h₂enh₁-

inhibit, inhibition, inhibitor, *gʰeh₁bʰ-

inhospitable, *gʰóstis

inhuman, inhumane, *ǵʰmṓ

inhumation, inhume, *dʰéǵʰōm

initial, initiate, initiation, *h₁ey-

injudicious, *h₂eyw-

inlight, *lewk-

innervate, *(s)neh₁-

innocent, innocuous, *nek-

innovate, innovative, *new

innumerable, *nem-

inobtrusive, *trewd-

inoculate, *h₃ekʷ-

inoperable, *h₃ep-

inopportune, *per-

inquietude, *kʷyeh₁-

inquiline, *kʷel-

inscribe, inscription, *(s)ker-

insect, *sek-

lachrymose, lacrimation, *daḱru-
lactate, lactation, lactic, lactose, *glag-
lacuna, lacunar, *lókus
ladder, *ḱley-
lagoon, *lókus
lair, *legh-
laissez-faire, *dheH₁-
lake, *lókus
land, *lendʰ-
language, langue, *dn̥ǵʰwéh₂s
lanner, lanugo, *h₂welh₁-
lap, *leb-
last, *leys-
lather, latrine, launder, laundry, lava, lavation, lavatory, *lewh₃-
law, lay, *legh-
lay, *lókus
lea, *lewk-
league, *legh-
leal, *leǵ-, *legh-
leam, *lewk-
lean, *ḱley-
lear, learn, *leys-
leave, *leyp-
leaven, *h₁lengʷʰ-
lectern, lection, lectionary, lector, lecture, *leǵ-
lede, *h₁lewdʰ-
legacy, legal, *leǵ-, *legh-
legality, legatary, *legh-
legate, *leǵ-, *legh-
legatee, legatine, *legh-
legation, legator, *leǵ-, *legh-
legend, legendary, legibility, legible, *leǵ-
legific, *legh-
legion, legionary, *leǵ-
legislate, *legh-
legislation, *leǵ-, *legh-
legislative, *legh-
legislator, *leǵ-, *legh-
legislature, *legh-
legit, *leǵ-
legitim, legitimacy, *legh-
legitimate, *leǵ-, *legh-
legume, leguminous, *leǵ-
Leicester, *legh-
lend, *lendʰ-
Lent, Lenten, *deyn-
leod, *h₁lewdʰ-
lesson, *leǵ-
lettuce, *glag-
leucocyte, *lewk-
leud, *h₁lewdʰ-
leukemia, *lewk-
lev, Levant, levee, lever, leverage, levitate, levity, *h₁lengʷʰ-
Lewis, *ḱlew-
libel, libellant, libellous, *lewbʰ-

liberal, liberality, liberate, liberator, libertarian, libertine, liberty, *h₁lewdʰ-
librarian, library, *lewbʰ-
libre, *h₁lewdʰ-
libretto, *lewbʰ-
lie, *legh-
lief, *lewbʰ-
lieu, *stel-
liever, *lewbʰ-
light, *h₁lengʷʰ-, *lewk-
ligula, ligular, ligule, *dn̥ǵʰwéh₂s
line, lineage, lineal, lineament, linear, lineate, linen, *lino-
lingua, lingual, linguiform, linguine, linguistic, *dn̥ǵʰwéh₂s
lino, linoleum, lintearious, *lino-
lip, *leb-
lipolysis, lipoprotein, liposuction, *leyp-
list, *leys-
listen, *ḱlew-
lith, *h₁lewdʰ-
litter, *legh-
liturgy, *werǵ-
livelong, *lewbʰ-
liver, *leyp-
loan, *leykʷ-
lobby, *lewbʰ-
local, locale, locality, locate, location, locative, *stel-
lochia, *legh-
lock, locket, *seh₂g-
locomotion, locular, loculus, locus, *stel-
lodge, lofe, loff, *lewbʰ-
logarithm, *h₂er-, *leǵ-
logic, logistic, logistics, logogram, logophile, *leǵ-
logorrhea, *srew-
logos, *leǵ-
loin, *lendʰ-
longevity, *h₂ey-
loquet, *seh₂g-
lord, *wer-
lotion, *lewh₃-
loud, *ḱlew-
lough, *lókus
Louis, *ḱlew-
louse, *luHs-
love, *lewbʰ-
low, *kelh₁-, *ḱley-, *legh-
loyal, *leǵ-, *legh-
loyalty, *legh-
lucent, lucerne, lucid, *lewk-
Lucifer, *bher-, *lewk-
luciferous, *lewk-
luctation, *seh₂g-
lucubrate, lucubration, *lewk-
lumbago, lumbar, *lendʰ-
luminary, luminate, luminous, luna, lunar, lunatic, lune, *lewk-

lung, *leng^{wh}-
lunula, lunule, *lewk-
lupin, lupine, *wĺk^{w}os
lustre, lustrum, *lewk-
lutaceous, lutite, *lewh$_3$-
lux, *lewk-
luxurious, luxury, *seh$_2$g-
lycanthropy, *wĺk^{w}os
lye, *lewh$_3$-
macerate, macro-, macrobiotic, macrochaeta,
   macrocosm, macron, macrophage, *meh$_2$k-
mactate, *méǵh$_2$s, *meh$_2$k̂-
madam, madonna, *dem-
madrigal, *méh$_2$tēr
maelstrom, *melh$_2$-, *srew-
maestro, magister, magnate, magnify, magnitude,
   magnus, *méǵh$_2$s
main, *men-
maintain, *ten-
maiuscule, majesty, *méǵh$_2$s
major-domo, *dem-
major, majuscule, *méǵh$_2$s
maladminister, *mey-
malediction, *deyk̂-
malefaction, *dheH$_1$-
malevolent, *welh$_1$-
malm, *melh$_2$-
mamma, mammal, mammary, *méh$_2$-méh$_2$
man, *mánus
manacle, manage, manageable, management,
   manager, managerial, manatee, *méh$_2$-ɾ
mandamus, mandate, *deH$_3$-
mandible, manducate, *mend^h-
mane, *men-
manes, *meh$_2$-
mania, *men-
manicure, *méh$_2$-ɾ
manifest, *g^{wh}en-
manikin, *mánus
maniple, *pleh$_1$-
mannequin, *mánus
manner, *méh$_2$-ɾ
mannish, *mánus
manoeuvre/maneuver, *méh$_2$-ɾ
manse, *mey-
mansuetude, *swe-d^{h}h$_1$-
mantra, *men-
manual, manubial, manubrium, *méh$_2$-ɾ
manufacture, *dheH$_1$-
manumission, manumit, manure, *méh$_2$-ɾ
manuscript, *(s)ker-, *méh$_2$-ɾ
mare, *marko-, *mer-
marinade, marinate, marine, maritime, *móri
marrow, *mosg^{h}os
marsh, *móri
marshal, *marko-
mash, maslin, *mey-

master, *méǵh$_2$s
masticate, *mend^h-
mastodon, *h$_3$dónts
masturbate, *méh$_2$-ɾ
mater, material, maternal, maternity, *méh$_2$tēr
mathematics, *men-
matricide, matriculate, *méh$_2$tēr
matrilineal, *lino-
matrimony, matrix, matron, matter, *méh$_2$tēr
mature, *meh$_2$-
maugre, *g^{w}erH-
maulm, maum, *melh$_2$-
maw, *mak-
mawm, *melh$_2$-
maximum, mayor, *méǵh$_2$s
me, *H$_1$me-
mead, *méd^{h}u
meager/meagre, *meh$_2$k-
meal, *meh$_1$-, *melh$_2$-
mean, *méd^{h}yos, *mey-
means, *méd^{h}yos
measure, *meh$_1$-
meddle, *mey-
media, median, mediate, mediation, mediator, *méd^{h}yos
medic, medicate, medicinal, medicine, *med-
mediety, *méd^{h}yos
medieval, *h$_2$ey-, *méd^{h}yos
mediocre, mediocrity, *h$_2$ék̂, *méd^{h}yos
Mediterranean, medium, medius, medulla, *méd^{h}yos
Medusa, *med-
mega-, mega, megafauna, megalith, megalomania,
   megalopolis, *méǵh$_2$s
megaphone, *b^{h}eh$_2$-, *méǵh$_2$s
meiobenthos, meiosis, meiotic, *mey-
meister, *méǵh$_2$s
melissophobia, melleous, melliferous, mellific,
   mellifluent, mellifluous, melliloquent, mellivorous, *melit-
member, membranaceous, membrane, membranous,
   *méms
memoir, memorabilia, memorable, memorandum,
   memorate, memorial, memoriter, memory, menace,
   mendacious, mendacity, *men-
meniscus, menopause, menorrhea, *méh$_1$ns
mense, mensk, *mánus
menstrual, menstruation, *méh$_1$ns
mental, mentalis, mention, mentum, *men-
mentum, *mend^h-
menu, *mey-
mere, *móri
mereswine, *suH-
merry, *mréǵ^h-
mesognathion, *ǵénus
Mesolithic, *méd^{h}yos
mesonychid, *h$_3$neg^h-
Mesopotamia, *peth$_2$
mesozeugma, *yewg-
Mesozoic, *g^{w}eyh$_3$-, *méd^{h}yos

mestizo, *mey-
metabolic, metabolism, metabolite, *gʷelH-
metallurgy, *werǵ-
metaphor, *bher-
mete, *med-
meter, *meh₁-
methane, *médʰu
methinks, *teng-
methylene, *médʰu
metis, metre, metric, *meh₁-
Metro, metrocyte, *méh₂tēr
metrology, metron, metronome, *meh₁-
metronomic, *nem-
metropolis, metropolitan, *méh₂tēr
mickle, *méǵh₂s
microorganism, *werǵ-
microphone, *bʰeh₂-
microphthalmia, *h₃ekʷ-
microscope, microscopic, *speḱ-
microtia, *h₂ew-
micturate, *h₃meyǵʰ-
mid, middle, *médʰyos
midge, midget, *mus-
midriff, *krep-
migrate, migration, migratory, *mey-
mildew, *melit-
mile, *sem-
milieu, *stel-
milk, *H₂melǵ-
mill, *melh₂-
milliary, million, *sem-
min, *mey-
minacious, minatory, *men-
mince, *mey-
mind, *men-
mine, *H₁meme-
minestrone, minimum, *mey-
minion, *men-
minister, ministerial, ministerium, ministrant,
 ministrate, ministration, ministrative, ministry,
 minor, minority, *mey-
minotaur, *(s)táwros
minse, minstrel, *mey-
mint, *men-
minus, minuscule, minute, minutia, *mey-
mirabile dictu, *deyḱ-
mire, *morwi-
mis-, *mey-
misandry, *h₂nḗr
miscellanea, miscellaneous, miscellany, miscibility,
 miscible, *mey-
misdeed, *dheH₁-
misericord, *ḱḗr
mishmash, *mey-
misogynist, *gwḗn
miss, *mey-
mister, mistral, *méǵh₂s

mitigate, *H₂eǵ-
mix, mix, mixtion, mixture, *mey-
mizzen, *médʰyos
mneme, mnemonic, *men-
mode, model, modem, moderate, moderation, modern,
 modest, modesty, modification, *med-
modify, *dheH₁-, *med-
modius, modulate, modulation, modulator, module,
 modulus, *med-
moiety, *médʰyos
molar, *melh₂-
mold, *med-
momento, *men-
monachism, monad, monadic, monarchy, *mey-
monaster, *h₂stḗr
monastery, monastic, monatomic, *mey-
Monday, *mḗh₁ns
money, monish, *men-
monism, *mey-
monitor, *men-
monk, mono-, *mey-
monocarpic, *kerp-
monocle, *h₃ekʷ-
monodomy, *dem-
monoecy, *weyḱ-
monograph, *gerbʰ-
monoid, monolith, *mey-
monologue, *leǵ-
monometer, monopod, monopoly, monopsony,
 monotone, *mey-
monotonous, monotony, *ten-
monotreme, *terh₁-
monozygotic, *yugóm
monster, monstrous, Montana, montane, *men-
month, *mḗh₁ns
monticule, monument, *men-
moon, *mḗh₁ns
morass, *móri
more, *meh₂-
moribund, *mer-
morning-gift, *gʰebʰ-
morphological, *leǵ-
mortal, mortician, mortuary, *mer-
mosquito, *mus-
most, *meh₂-
mother, *méh₂tēr
mould, *med-
moult, *mey-
mound, *méh₂-r
mount, mountain, *men-
mouse, *muh₂s-
moustache, mouth, *mendʰ-
much, muckle, *méǵh₂s
mugwort, *wréh₂ds
muid, *med-
mulch, *melit-
multicollinearity, *lino-

multigravida, *gʷerh₂-
multilinear, *lino-
multilingual, *dn̥ǵʰwéh₂s
multimodal, *med-
multiplication, multiply, *pleḱ-
mund, *méh₂-r̥
municipal, municipality, munific, munificence,
 munificent, *mey-
murder, *mer-
murine, *muh₂s-
murth, *mer-
musca, *mus-
muscle, muscular, musophobia, mussel, mustelid,
 *muh₂s-
mutable, mutation, mutual, *mey-
my, *H₁meme-
myiasis, *mus-
Myosotis, *h₂ew-
myrmeco-, *morwi-
naevus, *ǵenH₁-
naiad, *(s)neh₂-
nail, *h₃negʰ-
naïve, *ǵenH₁-
naked, naken, *negʷ-
namaste, *nem-
name, *h₁nómn̥
nares, narial, naris, *néh₂s
narrate, narration, narrative, narrator, *ǵneh₃-
nasal, nasalance, *néh₂s
nascent, natal, *ǵenH₁-
natation, natatorium, *(s)neh₂-
nation, national, native, nativity, natural, nature, *ǵenH₁-
nausea, nautical, naval, *(s)neh₂-
nave, navel, *h₃enbʰ-
navigate, *(s)neh₂-, *H₂eǵ-
navigation, navigator, navy, *(s)neh₂-
nebula, nebulous, *nebʰ-
necromancy, necrophilia, necropolis, necropsis,
 necrosis, necrotic, necrotize, nectar, nectarine, *neḱ-
needle, *(s)neh₁-
nefandous, nefarious, nefast, *bʰeh₂-
neglect, negligee, negligence, negligible, *leǵ-
negotiate, negotiation, negotiator, *h₂ew-
nemesis, nemoral, nemorous, *nem-
neo-, neolithic, *new
neologism, *leǵ-, *new
neon, neonate, neophyte, *new
neotony, *new, *ten-
nephew, *nepot-
nephology, nephoscope, *nebʰ-
nephritis, nephro-, nephrology, nephrotic, *negʷh-r-
nepotism, *nepot-
nerve, nervous, *(s)neh₁-
nescient, *skey-
ness, *néh₂s
nest, *nisdós
neural, neuritis, neuroblast, neurology, neuron,

neurosis, neurotic, *(s)neh₁-
neuter, neutral, *kʷis
Nevada, *sneygʷʰ-
neve, *nepot-
névé, *sneygʷʰ-
nevus, *ǵenH₁-
new, *new
niche, nide, nidiform, nidify, nidus, *nisdós
niece, nift, *nepot-
night, nightingale, *nókʷts
nightmare, *mer-
nim, *nem-
nine, *H₁néwn̥
nirvana, *H₂weH₁-
nit, *knid-
nival, nivation, niveus, *sneygʷʰ-
nobility, noble, *ǵneh₃-
nocebo, nocive, *neḱ-
nocturnal, *nókʷts
Noel, *ǵenH₁-
nomad, nomadic, nomarch, nome, *nem-
nomenclator, *h₁nómn̥
nomenclature, *h₁nómn̥, *kelh₁-
nominal, nominate, nomination, nominative, nominator,
 *h₁nómn̥
nomology, nomothete, nomothetic, nomothetic, *nem-
non sequitur, *sekʷ-
nonalignment, noncollinear, *lino-
nonintrusive, *trewd-
nonlineal, nonlinear, *lino-
norm, normal, *ǵneh₃-
north, northern, *h₁én
nose, *néh₂s
notary, notation, note, notice, notion, notorious, *ǵneh₃-
noun, *h₁nómn̥
nova, novate, novation, novel, novelty, *new
November, novena, *H₁néwn̥
novice, novitiate, novity, *new
noxious, *neḱ-
nozzle, *néh₂s
nuance, *nebʰ-
nude, nudity, *negʷ-
nuisance, *neḱ-
nulligravida, *gʷerh₂-
numb, number, numeral, numerate, numerator,
 numerous, Numidia, numismatic, *nem-
nuncupate, *keh₂p-
nyas, *nisdós
nyctalgia, nyctophobia, *nókʷts
o-, *h₁epi
oak, *h₂eyǵ-
oakum, *ǵómbʰos
ob-, *h₁epi
obduracy, *deru-
obdurate, *h₁epi
obedient, *h₂ewis-dʰh₁-
obese, *h₁ed-

317

obey, *h₂ewis-dʰh₁-
obfuscate, *h₁epi
obituary, *h₁ey-
object, *h₁epi
oblate, oblation, *bher-
oblique, *h₁epi
obnoxious, *neḱ-
obol, obolus, *gʷelH-
obsequies, obsequious, *sekʷ-
obsess, *sed-
obsolesce, *h₂el-
obsolete, *h₂el-, *swe-dʰh₁-
obstacle, obstetrics, *steh₂-
obstinate, *h₁epi, *steh₂-
obstreperous, *h₁epi
obstruct, obstruction, obstructive, *strew-
obtain, *ten-
obtect, *(s)teg-
obtrude, obtrusive, *trewd-
obtuse, *(s)tew-
obverse, obvert, *wert-
obviate, obvious, *weyh₁-
occlude, *(s)kel-
occult, *ḱel-
occupate, occupation, occupy, *keh₂p-
occur, *h₁epi, *ḱers-
octa-, octagon, octangular, octave, octennial, octo-,
 October, octogenarian, *oḱtṓw
octopus, *oḱtṓw, *pṓds
octoroon, octothorpe, *oḱtṓw
ocular, oculus, *h₃ekʷ-
odd, *dheH₁-
odious, odium, *h₃ed-
odonto-, odontology, *h₃dónts
odour, *h₃ed-
oe, *h₂ekʷeh₂-
oecology, *weyḱ-
oeconomus, *nem-, *weyḱ-
oenochoe, oenologist, oenology, oenophile,
 oenophilia, *wóyh₁nom
of, off, *h₂pó
offend, *gʷʰen-, *h₁epi
offer, *bher-
office, official, *dheH₁-
official, *h₃ep-
officiant, officiate, officious, *dheH₁-
offlay, *legh-
oikology, oikophobia, *weyḱ-
old, *h₂el-
olfaction, *dheH₁-
omit, *h₁epi
omnibus, *h₃ep-
omnificent, *dheH₁-
omnipotent, *H₁es-
omniscient, omnivore, *h₃ep-
omphalic, *h₃enbʰ-
onde, *h₂enh₁-

one, onion, *óy-nos
onomatopoeia, *h₁nómn̥
onychite, onychomancy, onychopathy, onychophagy,
 onychophorous, onyx, *h₃negʰ-
opera, operate, *h₃ep-
ophthalmic, ophthalmology, ophthalmoparesis,
 ophthalmoplegia, *h₃ekʷ-
opificer, *h₃ep-
opisthodomos, *dem-
oppilate, *peys-
opportunity, *per-
oppose, *h₁epi, *teḱ-
opposite, opposition, *h₁epi
oppugn, *pewǵ-
optic, optician, *h₃ekʷ-
opulent, opus, opuscule, *h₃ep-
oracle, oral, oration, *h₃éh₁os
orchard, *wréh₂ds
ord, *dheH₁-
ordain, *h₂er
orde, *dheH₁-
order, ordinary, ordinate, ordination, *h₂er
ordure, *gʰers-
ore, *h₂eyos
organ, organic, organism, organize, orgy, *werǵ-
orient, oriental, orientation, *h₃er-
orifice, *h₃éh₁os
origin, original, originality, originary, originate, *h₃er-
orison, *h₃éh₁os
ornate, *h₂er
ornithology, ornithomancy, ornithorhynchus, ornithosis,
 *h₃érō
oro-, orogenesis, orogenic, orogenous, orogeny,
 orography, oroheliograph, orology, orometer, oronym,
 oronymy, orophyte, *h₃er-
orphan, *h₃erbʰ-
orpiment, *peyḱ-
orthodontics, orthodontist, *h₃dónts
orthodox, *deḱ-
oscillate, osculate, *h₃éh₁os
ossification, ossify, *h₃ésth₁
ostensible, *h₁epi
ostentate, ostentation, *ten-
ostentatious, *h₁epi
osteoblast, osteology, osteopath, osteoporosis, *h₃ésth₁
otalgia, *h₂ew-
other, *h₂énteros
otic, otiose, *h₂ew
otitis, otocephaly, otolith, otology, otopathy, otophyma,
 otoplasty, otorrhea, otosclerosis, otoscope, ototomy,
 *h₂ew-
otter, *udréh₂
ought, *h₂eyḱ-
oust, *steh₂-
oval, ovary, ovate, *h₂ōwyóm
over, *upo
ovest, *h₁ed-

ovine, *h₂ówis
ovum, *h₂ōwyóm
owe, own, *h₂eyk̑-
ox, *uksḗn
oxia, *h₂ék̑
oxohalide, *séh₂ls
oxy-, oxygen, *h₂ék̑
oxytone, *h₂ék̑, *ten-
p.m. (post meridiem), *deyn-
pablum, pabulum, *peh₂-
pace, *péth₂
pacific, pagan, paganism, paganity, page, paginal,
 *peh₂ǵ-
pain, *kʷey-
paint, *peyk̑-
palabra, palaver, *gʷelH-
pale, *peh₂ǵ-, *pelH-
pallid, pallor, *pelH-
pan-, *peh₂-
pancreas, *krewh₂-
pandemonium, panic, pannier, pantry, *peh₂-
parable, parabola, *gʷelH-, *per-
parabole, *gʷelH-
paradise, *dʰeyǵʰ-
paradox, *dek̑-
paragraph, *gerbʰ-
paraklausithyron, *dʰwer-
parallactic, parallax, *h₂el-
parallel, *per-
parameter, *meh₁-, *per-
parapagus, *per-
paraplegic, *pleh₂k-
pardon, pardonable, *deH₃-
pareidolia, *weyd-
parenthesis, parfait, *dheH₁-
parish, *weyk̑-
parlay, parole, *gʷelH-
parophthalmia, *h₃ekʷ-
parotic, parotid, *h₂ew-
parsimony, *h₂erk-
participate, *keh₂p-
pass, passerine, passim, *peth₂
pastel, pastern, pastille, pastor, pastoral, pasture, *peh₂-
patefaction, patella, patellar, patelliform, paten,
 patency, patent, patently, *peth₂
pater, *ph₂tḗr
patera, *peth₂
paternal, paternity, *ph₂tḗr
path, *pent-
patin, *peth₂
patriarch, patriarch, patriarchy, patrician, patricide,
 patrimony, patriot, patriotism, patrology, patron,
 patronize, patronym, *ph₂tḗr
pawn, *pṓds
pax, paxis, pay, paynim, peace, *peh₂ǵ-
pecten, *pek̑-
peculator, peculiar, pecuniary, pecunious, *pek̑u-

pedagogue, pedagogy, *H₂eǵ-
pedal, pedestal, pedestrian, pedicel, pedicle, pedicure,
 pedigree, *pṓds
pedion, *ped-
pedometer, *pṓds
peg, *bak-
pejorative, *ped-
pellagra, pellicle, *pel-
pellucid, *lewk-, *per-
pelt, *pel-
pen, *péth₂r
penal, penalize, penalty, *kʷey-
penchant, pend, pendant, pending, pendulous,
 pendulum, *pewǵ-
penetrate, *peh₂-
pensive, *pewǵ-
penta-, pentacle, pentad, pentagon, *pénkʷe
pentagram, *gerbʰ-, *pénkʷe
pentalogy, *pénkʷe
pentameter, *meh₁-, *pénkʷe
Pentateuch, pentathlete, *pénkʷe
pentathlon, *H₂weH₁-, *pénkʷe
pentatonic, pentomino, *pénkʷe
peon, *pṓds
people, *pleh₁-
pepsin, peptic, peptide, *pekʷ-
per, *per-
perceive, *keh₂p-
percentage, *k̑m̥tóm
perceptible, perception, *keh₂p-
percolate, *kʷel-
perdition, *deH₃-
perdure, *deru-
peregrinate, peregrination, peregrine, *h₂éǵros
perfect, *dheH₁-
perfection, *per-
perfidious, *bʰeydʰ-
perfuse, perfusion, *ǵʰew-
peri-, *per-
periatric, *ǵerh₂-
Pericles, pericope, perigee, perihelion, *per-
perihelion, *sóh₂wl̥
peril, perilous, *per-
perimeter, *meh₁-, *per-
period, *per-
periodontal, *h₃dónts
periosteum, *h₃ésth₁
periotic, *h₂ew-
peripatetic, *pent-
peripety, *peth₂
periphery, *per-
periscope, *per-, *spek̑-
perish, *h₁ey-
peritoneum, *ten-
perjure, perjury, *h₂eyw-
permeate, *per-
permiscible, permix, permixtion, *mey-

permonish, *men-

permutation, permute, *mey-

pernicious, *neḱ-, *per-

perorate, *h₃éh₁os

perpend, perpendicular, *pewǵ-

perpetrate, *ph₂tér

perplex, *pleḱ-

persecute, persecution, *sekʷ-

persist, *steh₂-

persistence, *per-

perspective, perspicacious, perspicuous, *speḱ-

pertain, *ten-

Perth, *perkʷu-

pertinent, *ten-

pertussis, *(s)tew-

peruse, pervade, *per-

perverse, pervert, *wert-

pervestigate, *steygʰ-

pes, *pṓds

pessimal, pessimism, pessimist, *ped-

pestle, *peys-

petal, petition, petulant, *peth₂

pew, *pṓds

phanerozoic, phantasm, phantom, phase, phene,
 phenetic, phenology, phenomenon, phenotype, *bʰeh₂-

pheromone, *bher-

philander, *h₂nḗr

Philip, *h₁éḱwos

phone, phoneme, phonetic, phonics, phono-, *bʰeh₂-

phorophyte, phosphor, *bher-

photic, *bʰeh₂-

photograph, *gerbʰ-

phyle, *bʰuH-

phyllotaxis, *bʰleh₃-

phylum, physeal, physics, physis, *bʰuH-

piano, piazza, *pleh₂-

Pict, picture, pigment, *peyḱ-

Pilate, pile, *peys-

pilgrim, *h₂éǵros

pimiento, *peyḱ-

pine, *kʷey-

pinocytosis, *peh₃-

pint, pinto, *peyḱ-

pioneer, *pṓds

Pisces, piscina, *peisḱ-

pismire, *morwi-

pistil, *peys-

place, *pleh₂-

plague, *pleh₂k-

plaice, plain, *pleh₂-

plait, *pleḱ-

plan, plane, *pleh₂-

plangent, *pleh₂k-

plant, plantain, plantation, plasma, plastic, plastron,
 plateau, platitude, platypus, *pleh₂-

plaudits, plausible, *pleh₂k-

plaza, *pleh₂-

pleat, *pleḱ-

pleb, plebeian, plebiscite, *pleh₁-

plectics, *pleḱ-

plectrum, *pleh₂k-

plenary, plenitude, plenitudine, plentitude, plenty,
 *pleh₁-

pleometrosis, *méh₂tēr

pleon, pleopod, *plew-

pleroma, plethora, plethysm, *pleh₁-

pleuston, *plew-

plexogenic, pliable, plight, ploce, *pleḱ-

pluperfect, *dheH₁-

plural, plurality, plus, *pleh₁-

plutocracy, pluvial, pluvious, *plew-

ply, *pleḱ-

podiatry, podium, *pṓds

poignant, point, *pewǵ-

poison, *peh₃-

poliomyelitis, poliosis, *pelH-

pollical, pollicate, *h₂welh₁-

pollute, pollution, *lewh₃-

poly-, *pleh₁-

polyandry, *h₂nḗr

polydomy, *dem-

polygala, *glag-

polygon, *ǵónu

polyp, *pṓds

polyphony, *bʰeh₂-

polytechnic, *tetḱ-

ponder, *pewǵ-

pontiff, pontoon, *pent-

popular, population, populous, *pleh₁-

porcine, pork, *pórḱos

port, portable, portage, portal, *per-

portend, portent, *ten-

porter, portfolio, portico, *per-

posca, *peh₃-

posit, posit, position, *teḱ-

possess, possession, *pótis, *sed-

possessive, *pótis, *pótis

possessor, *sed-

possible, *H₁es-

post-, *h₁epi

post, *h₁epi, *teḱ-

posterior, posterity, postical, *h₁epi

postmeridian, *médʰyos

postmix, *mey-

postpone, *teḱ-

postscript, *h₁epi

postulate, *preḱ-

potable, *peh₃-

potamic, potamology, *peth₂

potency, potent, potential, *H₁es-

potion, *peh₃-

pounce, *poymno-

pound, *pewǵ-

poustie, *pótis

power, *H₁es-
practic, practical, practice, practise, *per-
praedial, *wedʰ-
pragma, pragmatic, praxis, *per-
pray, prayer, *preḱ-
pre-eminent, *men-
precarious, precation, precative, *preḱ-
precel, *kelH-
precentor, *keh₂n-
preceptor, *keh₂p-
precious, *per-
preclude, *(s)kel-
precognition, precognosce, *ǵneh₃-
precursor, *ḱers-
predation, predator, prede, *deH₃-, *weyd-
predial, prediatory, *wedʰ-
predict, prediction, *deyḱ-
predilection, *leǵ-
predominant, *dem-
prefect, prefecture, *dheH₁-
prefer, *bher-
prehensility, prehension, *weyd-
prejudge, prejudicate, prejudice, prejudicial, *h₂eyw-
prelingual, *dn̥ǵʰwéh₂s
premier, *per-
premix, *mey-
premonish, premonition, premonstrate, *men-
prenarial, *néh₂s
preoccupate, preoccupation, preoccupy, *keh₂p-
prepone, prepose, preposition, *teḱ-
preposterous, *h₁epi
presage, *seh₂g-
presbyter, *per-
prescient, *skey-
prescribe, *(s)ker-
presence, present, presentation, *H₁es-
preside, president, presidio, *sed-
prester, *per-
presto, *steh₂-
pretend, pretense, *ten-
preterite, preterition, *h₁ey-
pretext, *tetḱ-
prevail, prevalence, *h₂welh₁-
prevent, *gʷem-
preview, *weyd-
previous, *weyh₁-
previse, prevision, prey, *weyd-
price, priest, primacy, primary, prime, *per-
primeval, *h₂ey-
primigravida, *gʷerh₂-
primo, primogenit, primogenitary, *per-
primogeniture, *ǵenH₁-
primus, *per-
prince, princess, principle, *keh₂p-
prior, priority, *per-
prison, *weyd-
pristine, private, privation, *per-

privilege, *legh-, *per-
privy, *per-
prize, *weyd-
pro tanto, *só
pro-, pro, *per-
probability, probable, probe, probity, *bʰuH-
problem, problematic, *gʷelH-
proclaim, proclamation, *kelh₁-
procrastinate, *per-
produce, product, production, productive, *dewk-
profane, *dʰéh₁s
profer, profert, *bher-
profession, professor, *bʰeh₂-
proficiency, profit, profitable, profiteer, profiterole,
   *dheH₁-
profound, profundity, *bʰudʰmén, *ǵʰew-
profuse, profusion, *ǵʰew-
progeria, *ǵerh₂-
prognathism, *ǵénus
program, program, programme, programmer, *gerbʰ-
prohibit, prohibition, prohibitor, *gʰeh₁bʰ-
prolate, *bher-
proletariat, *h₂el-
prolific, *dheH₁-
prologue, *leǵ-, *per-
prominent, *men-
promiscuity, promiscuous, *mey-
promontory, *men-
prone, *per-
proof, *bʰuH-
propagate, *peh₂ǵ-
propel, *per-
proper, property, *preyH-
propinquity, *per-
propitiate, *peth₂
propitious, *per-
propose, *teḱ-
proprietary, propriety, *preyH-
proptotic, *peth₂
propugn, *pewǵ-
propulsion, prore, *per-
proscribe, *(s)ker-
prose, *wert-
prosecute, *sek-, *sekʷ-
prosecutor, *sekʷ-
prospective, prospector, prospectus, *speḱ-
prosperity, prosperous, *speh₁-
prospicience, *speḱ-
prostate, *per-
prosthesis, *dheH₁-
prostitute, *steh₂-
prostrate, prostration, *sterh₃-
protagonist, *H₂eǵ-, *per-
protandry, *h₂nḗr
protect, protection, protective, protector, protectorate,
   protégé, *(s)teg-
protend, *ten-

Proterozoic, protist, protocol, proton, protoplasm, *per-
protoplasm, *pleh₂-
prototype, *per-
protozoa, *gʷeyh₃-, *per-
protrude, protrudent, protrusile, protrusion, *trewd-
prove, *bʰuH-
proverb, *wekʷ-
provide, providence, *weyd-
province, provincial, *per-
provision, provisional, proviso, provisory, *weyd-
provoke, *wekʷ-
prow, proximal, proximity, *per-
prozeugma, *yewg-
prudence, *weyd-
pterodactyl, pterosaur, *péth₂r
ptomaine, ptosis, *peth₂
public, *pleh₁-
puce, *plou-
pueblo, *pleh₁-
pugilism, pugilist, pugio, pugnacious, *pewǵ-
pulmonary, *plewmō
pumice, *poymno-
pumpkin, *pekʷ-
punch, *pénkʷe, *pewǵ-
puncheon, punctual, punctuate, punctuation,
 punctum, puncture, pungent, *pewǵ-
punish, punition, punitive, *kʷey-
purport, *per-
pursue, *sekʷ-
purvey, *weyd-
pyjama, *pṓds
pyre, pyretic, Pyrex, pyrite, pyro-, *péh₂ur
pyrochlore, *ǵʰelh₃-
pyromania, pyromete, pyrophore, pyrotechnic, *péh₂ur
quadr-, *kʷetwóres
quadrangle, *h₂enk-, *kʷetwóres
quadrate, quadrature, quadriceps, *kʷetwóres
quadriga, quadrigal, *yugóm
quadrilateral, quadrillion, *kʷetwóres
quadrivium, *weyh₁-
quadruped, *kʷetwóres, *pṓds
quadruple, *kʷetwóres, *pleh₁-
quail, *gʷelH-
qualificatioun, *dheH₁-
quality, *kʷis
qualm, *gʷelH-
quart, quarto, *kʷetwóres
quasilinear, *lino-
quasiminuscule, *mey-
quatrain, quatrefoil, *kʷetwóres
quattuordecillion, *dékṃt
queal, *gʷelH-
quean, queen, *gwén
quell, *gʷelH-
quern, *gʷrh₂-n-uH-
quick, *gʷeyh₃-
quiesce, quiescent, *kʷyeh₁-

quiet, *kʷyeh₁-
quinary, quinate, quinquefoil, quinquennial, *pénkʷe
quintessence, *H₁es-
quit, *kʷyeh₁-
quittor, *pekʷ-
quodlibet, *lewbʰ-
quomodo, *med-
quotient, *kʷis
radical, radicchio, radicle, radish, radius, radix, *wréh₂ds
rake, *h₃reǵ-
ramification, ramulose, ramus, *wréh₂ds
ranee, rani, rank, *h₃reǵ-
rapport, *per-
rarefy, *dheH₁-
rate, ratio, ratiocinate, ration, *h₂er
raw, *krewh₂-
ray, *wréh₂ds
read, *Hreh₁dʰ-
realign, *lino-
realm, *h₃reǵ-
reason, *h₂er
recalcitrant, *(s)kel-
recant, *keh₂n-
receipt, receive, receptacle, reception, recipe,
 recipient, *keh₂p-
reciprocal, reciprocate, *per-
reckon, *h₃reǵ-
reclaim, reclamation, *kelh₁-
recline, *ḱley-
recognition, recognize, recognosce, *ǵneh₃-
recollect, recollection, *leǵ-
recompense, *pewǵ-
recond, recondite, *dheH₁-
reconnoiter, *ǵneh₃-
record, *ḱḗr
recrimination, *krey-
rectilinear, *lino-
recto, rectus, *h₃reǵ-
recur, *kers-
red, *h₁rewdʰ-
rede, *Hreh₁dʰ-
redecorate, *dek-
redolent, *h₃ed-
redoubt, *dewk-
redound, *wed-
reduce, reduction, *dewk-
redundancy, *wed-
refectory, *dheH₁-
refer, *bher-
refrain, *dʰer-
refund, *ǵʰew-
regain, *weyh₁-
regal, *h₃reǵ-
regenerate, *ǵenH₁-
regible, regime, regimen, reign, *h₃reǵ-
rein, *ten-
relate, relation, relative, *bher-

relegate, relegation, *legh-
relevate, *h₁lengʷʰ-
relict, *leykʷ-
relief, relieve, *h₁lengʷʰ-
religion, *leǵ-
relinquish, *leykʷ-
relocate, relocation, *stel-
remedy, *med-
remember, remembrance, rememorate, reminisce,
  reminiscence, *men-
remix, remunerate, *mey-
render, *deH₃-
renovate, renovation, *new
reorient, reorientation, *h₃er-
repast, *peh₂-
repeat, repetition, *peth₂
replenish, replete, repletion, *pleh₁-
replica, replicate, reply, *pleḱ-
report, *per-
reprehend, reprehensible, reprehension, *weyd-
representation, *H₁es-
reprise, *weyd-
reprove, *bʰuH-
republic, *pleh₁-
repugn, repugnant, *pewǵ-
requiem, requiescat, *kʷyeh₁-
rescind, *skey-
resect, *sek-
resemble, *sem-
resent, *sent-
reside, residual, *sed-
resign, *sek-
resist, resistance, *steh₂-
respect, respectability, respectable, respective,
  respite, *speḱ-
rest, restitute, restitution, restore, *steh₂-
resurge, resurgent, *h₃reǵ-
retaliate, *só
retire, *der-
retribution, *bʰuH-
retriment, *terh₁-
retrospect, retrospection, retrospective, *speḱ-
retrude, retruse, retrusion, retrusive, *trewd-
reunion, *óy-nos
revenue, *gʷem-
revere, reverence, reverend, reverent, *wer-
reverse, revert, *wert-
review, revisal, revise, revision, revisionary, *weyd-
revive, *gʷeyh₃-
revoke, *wekʷ-
revolute, revolution, revolve, *welH-
rhematic, rheme, *wekʷ-
rheology, rheostat, *srew-
rhetic, rhetoric, *wekʷ-
rheum, rheumatic, *srew-
Rhine, *h₃reyH-
rhinoceros, *ḱerh₂-

rhizoid, rhizomatous, rhizome, rhizomorph, rhizophagy,
  Rhizopogon, Rhizopus, rhizosphere, *wréh₂ds
rhyme, *h₂er
rhythm, rhythmus, *srew-
rich, *h₃reǵ-
riddle, *Hreh₁dʰ-
riff, *krep-
right, rike, *h₃reǵ-
rin, *h₃er-, *h₃reyH-
rine, *krey-
rite, *h₂er
rival, *h₃reyH-
rodeo, role, roll, rondeau, *Hret-
root, *wréh₂ds
rota, rotary, rotate, rotation, rotator, rotavirus, rotifer,
  rotor, rotund, rotunda, *Hret-
rouge, *h₁rewdʰ-
roulette, round, roundel, rowel, *Hret-
royal, *h₃reǵ-
rubella, rubicund, rubin, rubious, rubric, ruby, rud,
  rufous, *h₁rewdʰ-
rule, *h₃reǵ-
run, *h₃er-, *h₃reyH-
rush, *kers-
russet, *h₁rewdʰ-
rye, *wrugʰyo-
sacerdotal, *dheH₁-
sackless, *seh₂g-
sacrificator, sacrifice, *dheH₁-
sacrilege, *leǵ-
saddle, *sed-
safe, *solh₂-
saga, *sekʷ-
sagacious, sagacity, *seh₂g-
sain, *sek-
sake, *seh₂g-
salary, saline, salinity, salt, salten, *séh₂ls
salubrious, salutation, salute, salvage, salvation, salve,
  *solh₂-
sam, same, *sem-
sanctify, *dheH₁-
sand, *sent-
sanguinary, sanguine, sanguineous, sanguinolent,
  sanguinous, *h₁ésh₂r
sanhedrin, *sed-
sardonyx, *h₃negʰ-
sark, *ser-
sation, *seH₁-
satisfaction, *dheH₁-
sative, *seH₁-
sauce, *séh₂ls
saught, *seh₂g-
save, *solh₂-
saw, *sek-, *sekʷ-
sax, *sek-
say, *sekʷ-
scent, *sent-

somnambulist, somnial, somniculous, somnifacient,
 somniferous, somnific, somniloquy, somnolent, *swep-
sooth, soothe, *H₁es-
sopor, soporific, *swep-
soprano, *upo
sorcery, *ser-
sororal, sororate, sororicide, sorority, *swésōr
sort, sortition, *ser-
soufflé, *bʰleh₁-
sought, *seh₂g-
souter, *sīw-
south, southern, *sóh₂wl̥
souvenir, *gʷem-
sovereign, *upo
sow, *seH₁-, *suH-
sparrow, *spér
spawn, *peth₂
special, speciality, species, specific, specification,
 specificity, specimen, specious, spectacle,
 spectacular, spectant, spectral, spectre/specter,
 spectrum, spectulation, speculate, speculum, *speḱ-
speed, *speh₁-
spend, *pewǵ-
sperate, *speh₁-
sphex, *bʰey-
spice, *speḱ-
spike, spiker, spile, spinal, spine, spinel, spiniform,
 spinose, spinous, spinule, spire, spit, *spey-
spite, *speḱ-
spitz, *spey-
splay, *pleḱ-
spleen, splenetic, *splenǵʰ-
spoke, *spey-
spume, *poymno-
spy, *speḱ-
square, *kʷetwóres
stabile, stability, stable, *steh₂-
stair, *steygʰ-
stall, *stel-
stamen, stamina, stance, stanchion, stand, stanza,
 *steh₂-
star, *h₂stér
stare decisis, stasis, state, static, station, stationary,
 statistic, statuary, statue, stature, *steh₂-
status quo, *kʷis
status, staunch, stay, stead, *steh₂-
steck, *(s)tew-
steenbok, *bʰuHgos-
steer, *(s)táwros
steganography, steganopod, Stegosaurus, *(s)teg-
stell, *stel-
stellar, *h₂stér
stentorian, *(s)tenh₂-
stethoscope, *speḱ-
stich, stichic, stichomancy, stichometry, stile, *steygʰ-
still, *stel-
stirk, *(s)táwros

stitch, *(s)tew-
stoa, *steh₂-
stock, *(s)tew-
store, *steh₂-
storey, story, *weyd-
stot, stote, *(s)tew-
stound, *(s)tenh₂-, *steh₂-
stour, stow, *steh₂-
stragulum, *sterh₃-
strange, *h₁eǵʰs
strategem, strategic, strategist, *sterh₃-
strategy, *H₂eǵ-, *sterh₃-
stratify, stratocracy, stratography, stratonic, stratum,
 stratus, *sterh₃-
straw, *strew-
stream, *srew-
street, *sterh₃-
strew, structure, *strew-
stucco, *(s)tew-
stud, *steh₂-
student, studio, studious, study, study, *(s)tew-
stun, *(s)tenh₂-
stupefaction, *(s)tew-
stupefy, *dheH₁-
stupid, stupor, *(s)tew-
sty, *steygʰ-
suant, *sekʷ-
sub, *upo
subaudi, subaudite, *h₂ewis-dʰh₁-
subduct, subdue, *dewk-
subdural, *deru-
subjoin, *yewg-
subjugate, *yugóm
sublineage, sublinear, *lino-
sublingual, *dn̥ǵʰwéh₂s
submarine, *móri
submone, submonish, *men-
subnival, subnivean, *sneygʷʰ-
subpoena, *kʷey-
subscribe, *(s)ker-
subside, *sed-
subsist, substance, substitute, *steh₂-
subterfuge, *upo
subterranean, *ters-
subtle, *tetḱ-
subvene, *gʷem-
subvert, *wert-
succentor, *keh₂n-
succor, *ḱers-
such, *s(w)e-
sudarium, *sweyd-
sue, *sekʷ-
suffer, *bher-
suffice, sufficient, *dheH₁-
suffuse, suffusion, *ǵʰew-
suggest, suggestion, *H₂eǵ-
suit, suite, *sekʷ-

sum, *upo
summa, summary, *upo
summer, *sm̥-h₂-ó-
summit, *upo
summon, *men-
sun, Sunday, *sóh₂wl̥
sunu, *suh₁nús
superate, *upo
superb, *bʰuH-, *upo
supercilious, *ḱel-, *upo
supereminent, *men-
superficial, *dheH₁-, *upo
superfluous, *bʰleh₁-, *upo
superimpose, *teḱ-, *upo
superior, superlative, supermarket, supernal,
 supernatural, *upo
supernova, *new, *upo
superpose, *teḱ-
superposition, *upo
superscribe, *(s)ker-
superscript, *upo
supersede, *sed-, *upo
supersonic, *upo
superstition, *steh₂-, *upo
supervacaneous, *h₁weh₂-
supervene, *gʷem-, *upo
supervise, *upo, *weyd-
supine, *upo
supplant, *pleh₂-
supplement, *pleh₁-
supplicant, supplicate, supplication, *pleḱ-
supply, *pleh₁-
support, *per-
suppose, *teḱ-
supra, *upo
supralinear, *lino-
supreme, *upo
surface, surfeit, *dheH₁-
surge, *h₃reǵ-
surgeon, *werǵ-
surname, surplus, *upo
surprise, *weyd-
surround, *upo, *wed-
survene, *gʷem-
survey, surveyor, surview, survise, *weyd-
survive, *upo
susceptible, susception, *keh₂p-
suspect, *speḱ-
suspend, suspense, suspension, *pewǵ-
suspicion, suspicious, *speḱ-
sustain, *ten-
sutorial, sutorian, sutorious, *sīw-
suttee, *H₁es-
suture, *sīw-
sweat, *sweyd-
sweb, sweven, *swep-
swine, *suH-

sycophant, *bʰeh₂-
syllaba anceps, *kapōlo
sym-, *sem-
symbiosis, *gʷeyh₃-
symbol, symbolic, symbolism, symbology, *gʷelH-
symmetry, *meh₁-
sympatry, *ph₂tḗr
symphony, *bʰeh₂-
symplectic, *plek-
symposium, *peh₃-
symptom, *peth₂
syn-, *sem-
synagogue, *H₂eǵ-
synandrous, *h₂nḗr
synergy, *werǵ-
synezeugmenon, *yewg-
synonym, synonymous, *h₁nómn̥
synopsis, *h₃ekʷ-
synostosis, *h₃ésth₁
synotia, *h₂ew-
synthesis, synthetic, *dheH₁-
system, *steh₂-
tabernacle, *treb-
talisman, *kʷel-
tame, *demh₂-
tandem, *só
tantra, *ten-
tar, *dóru
tarnish, *dʰer-
tauriform, taurine, *(s)táwros
tauroboly, *gʷelH-
tauromachy, Taurus, *(s)táwros
tautology, *leǵ-
tavern, *treb-
taxidermy, *der-
teach, *deyḱ-
team, *dewk-
teapoy, *pṓds
tear, *daḱru-, *der-
technique, technocrat, technology, technophobia, *tetḱ-
tect, *(s)teg-
tectonic, *tetḱ-
tectum, *(s)teg-
teem, *dem-
tegmental, tegular, tegument, *(s)teg-
tela, *tetḱ-
telegram, telegraph, *gerbʰ-, *kʷel-
telemetry, *kʷel-, *meh₁-
teleology, telepathy, telephone, *kʷel-
telescope, *kʷel-, *speḱ-
telescopic, *speḱ-
telesis, *kʷel-
telestich, *steygʰ-
television, *kʷel-
telophase, *bʰeh₂-
ten, *déḱm̥t
tenacious, tenaculum, tend, tender, tenet, tenor, tense,

tension, tenure, *ten-
tephra, *dʰegʷʰ-
term, terminal, terminate, termination, *térmn̥
terminology, *leǵ-
terminus, *térmn̥
terrace, terracotta, terrain, terrenal, terrene,
 terrestrial, territorial, territory, *ters-
Terry, *tewtéh₂
tertiary, tertiate, *tréyes
tetanus, *ten-
tetrapod, tetragon, *kʷetwóres
tetrahedroid, *sed-
tetrahedron, tetralogy, tetrameter, tetraphobia,
 *kʷetwóres
tetrastich, *steygʰ-
tetrode, *kʷetwóres
Texel, *deḱs-
text, textile, texture, *tetḱ-
thack, *(s)teg-
than, *só
thank, *teng-
tharm, *terh₁-
that, *só
thatch, *(s)teg-
the, *só
theca, *dheH₁-
thede, *tewtéh₂
thematic, theme, Themis, *dheH₁-
then, *só
theo-, *dʰéh₁s
Theobald, *tewtéh₂
theocracy, *dʰéh₁s
theod, Theoderic, *tewtéh₂
theophany, *bʰeh₂-
theorem, theoretical, theorist, theorize, theory, *wer-
there, *só
therio-, theriolatry, theriomorphic, *ǵʰwer-
thermal, thermodynamic, *gʷʰer-
thermohaline, *séh₂ls
thermometer, *gʷʰer-, *meh₁-
thermos, thermostat, *gʷʰer-
theropod, theropsid, *ǵʰwer-
thesaurus, thesis, *dheH₁-
theurgy, *werǵ-
think, *teng-
thirst, *ters-
thirty, *déḱm̥t
this, tho, *só
thole, *telh₂-
Thor, *(s)tenh₂-
thorough, *terh₂-
thorp, *treb-
those, *só
thou, *túh₂
thought, *teng-
thrash, thread, *terh₁-
threat, *trewd-

three, *tréyes
thresh, *terh₁-
throstle, *trosdos
through, *terh₂-
throw, *terh₁-
thrush, *trosdos
thug, *(s)teg-
thunder, Thunor, Thursday, *(s)tenh₂-
thus, *só
thyratron, thyroid, *dʰwer-
tide, *deh₂-
tie, *dewk-
tile, *(s)teg-
timber, *dem-
timbre, *(s)tew-
tire, *der-
toast, *ters-
toe, *deyḱ-
toft, *dem-
tog, *(s)teg-, *dewk-
toga, toggery, *(s)teg-
tolerate, *telh₂-
toll, *kʷel-
ton, tone, *ten-
tongue, *dn̥ǵʰwéh₂s
tonic, tonsils, tonus, *ten-
tooth, *h₃dónts
toral, *sterh₃-
torrent, torrid, *ters-
torus, *sterh₃-
trade, *deH₃-
tradition, *deH₃-, *terh₂-
traduce, *dewk-
traitor, *deH₃-
tranquil, *kʷyeh₁-
trans-, transact, transaction, transcend, *terh₂-
transcribe, *(s)ker-
transfection, *dheH₁-
transfer, *bher-
transfigure, *dʰeyǵʰ-
transfuse, transfusion, *ǵʰew-
transient, *terh₂-
transit, *h₁ey-
transitory, *terh₂-
translate, translation, translator, *bher-
translocate, translocative, *stel-
translucent, *lewk-
transmew, transmigrate, *mey-
transmontane, *men-
transmutation, transmute, *mey-
transparent, *terh₂-
transplant, *pleh₂-
transport, *per-, *terh₂-
transpose, *teḱ-
transverse, transvert, *wert-
trave, *treb-
travesty, *wes-

treague, *deru-

treason, *deH₃-

treasure, *dheH₁-

treble, *pleh₁-

tredecennial, tredecillion, *dékm̥t

tree, treen, *dóru

trema, trematode, *terh₁-

tri-, triad, *tréyes

triangle, *h₂enk-, *tréyes

triathlon, *H₂weH₁-

tribal, tribe, *bʰuH-

tribrach, *mréǵʰ-

tribulation, *terh₁-

tribunal, *bʰuH-

tricameral, *(s)teg-

tricorne, *ḱerh₂-

trident, *h₃dónts

trifecta, *dheH₁-

trig, *deru-

trigon, *tréyes

trigonometry, *ǵónu

trigony, *ǵenH₁-

trilinear, *lino-

trilogy, *leǵ-

trimester, *méh₁n̥s

triode, *tréyes

triple, *pleh₁-

triplicate, *pleḱ-

tripod, *pṓds, *tréyes

trite, triturate, triture, *terh₁-

triumvirate, *tréyes, *wiHrós

triune, *óy-nos

trivia, *tréyes

troop, tropel, *treb-

troth, truce, true, truth, *deru-

tryptophan, *bʰeh₂-

Tuesday, *dyew-

tug, *dewk-

tune, *ten-

turdiform, turdine, *trosdos

tusk, *h₃dónts

twain, twelve, twilight, twin, two, *dwóH₁

twenty, *dékm̥t

tympani, tympanum, type, typical, *(s)tew-

Tyr, *dyew-

uberous, *h₁owHdʰr̥-

ubiquitous, *kʷis

udder, *h₁owHdʰr̥-

ullage, *h₃ekʷ-

ulna, *Heh₃l-

ultra, *h₂el-

ultramarine, *móri

umb, umbe, *h₂ent

umbilical, umbilicus, *h₃enbʰ-

un-, *n̥-

unanimous, unary, unate, *óy-nos

unciform, Uncinaria, uncinate, Uncinia, uncinus, *h₂enk-

uncle, *h₂éwh₂os

uncouth, *ǵneh₃-

undine, undulant, undulate, *wed-

ungual, ungular, ungulate, *h₃negʰ-

uni-, *óy-nos

unicameral, *(s)teg-

unicorn, *ḱerh₂-, *óy-nos

unification, *dheH₁-

uniform, unify, *óy-nos

unilinear, *lino-

unilocular, *stel-

union, unique, unite, unity, universal, *óy-nos

universe, *óy-nos, *wert-

university, *óy-nos

unkempt, *ǵómbʰos

up, *upo

urchin, *ǵʰér

urdé, urdy, *dheH₁-

urn, *h₁ews-

Ursa Major, ursine, Ursula, Ursulines, *h₂ŕ̥tḱos

us, *wei

ustrinum, *h₁ews-

vacancy, vacant, vacate, vacation, *h₁weh₂-

vaccimulgence, *H₂melǵ-

vacuity, vacuous, vacuum, vain, *h₁weh₂-

vale, *welH-

valediction, *deyḱ-, *h₂welh₁-

valedictorian, *deyḱ-, *h₂welh₁-

valence, valent, valetudinarian, valiant, valid, validity, *h₂welh₁-

valley, *welH-

valor/valour, value, *h₂welh₁-

valva, valve, *welH-

vamp, *pṓds

van, *H₂weH₁-

vanish, vanity, *h₁weh₂-

vanquish, *weyk-

vast, *h₁weh₂-

vaticinate, vaticination, vaticinator, *keh₂n-

vault, *welH-

vaunt, *h₁weh₂-

vector, *weǵh-

vegetable, vegetation, vegete, vegetous, *weǵ-

vehement, vehicle, *weǵh-

velleity, *welh₁-

velocipede, *pṓds

velvet, *h₂welh₁-

venal, *wesno-

vend, vendition, vendor, deH₃-, *wesno-

ventilate, ventilation, ventilator, *H₂weH₁-

venture, venue, *gʷem-

veracious, *weh₁-

verb, verbal, verbatim, verbose, verbosity, *wekʷ-

verdict, *weh₁-

verecund, *wer-

veridical, *weh₁-

verify, *dheH₁-, *weh₁-

wick, *weyḱ-
widow, *h₁weydʰ
wight, *weǵh-
will, *welh₁-
willow, *welH-
wind, *H₂weH₁-
window, *h₃ekʷ-
wine, *wóyh₁nom
wis, wisdom, wise, wit, *weyd-
witch, *weyḱ-
wite, *weyd-
withsake, *seh₂g-
wizard, *weyd-
wolf, *wĺkʷos
wool, *h₂welh₁-
woollen/woolen, *h₂welh₁-
word, *wekʷ-, *wert-
work, *werǵ-
world, *h₂el-, *wiHrós
worm, *wṛmis-
wort, *wréh₂ds
worth, worthy, *wert-
wright, wrought, *werǵ-
wyrd, *wert-
xeroderma, *der-
xerophthalmia, *h₃ekʷ-
yard, *ǵʰer-
yarn, *ǵʰern-
ye, *túh₂
yea, yeah, *éy / h₁e
yean, *h₂egʷnos
year, *yeh₁-
yearn, *ǵʰer-
yeast, *yes-
yellow, *ǵʰelh₃-
yeo, *h₂ekʷeh₂-
yesterday, *dʰǵʰ(y)es-
yet, *ǵʰew-
yo, *éy / h₁e
yoke, *yugóm
yot, yote, *ǵʰew-
you, *túh₂
young, youngling, youth, *h₂yuh₁en-
zax, *sek-
zenana, *gwén
zeugitae, zeugma, *yewg-
zo-, zodiac, zoic, zoo-, zoo, zooid, zoology, zoon,
zoonosis, zoophagy, *gʷeyh₃-
zurna, *ḱerh₂-
zygoma, zygomorphic, zygomorphism,
zygomycosis, zygon, zygote, *yugóm
zymurgy, *werǵ-

Old English

-cund, *ǵenH₁-
-tiǵ, *déḱm̥t
-weard, *wert-
abal, *h₃ep-
āberan, *bher-
ābīdan, *bʰeydʰ-
ābufan, *upo
āc, *h₂eyǵ-
ācumba, *ǵómbʰos
ād, *h₂eydʰ-
af, *h₂pó
afol, *h₃ep-
āgan, āgen, *h₂eyḱ-
āl, *h₂eydʰ-
alan, ald, *h₂el-
āleċǵ, *legh-
alor, *h₃el-
ān, *óy-nos
anclēow, *h₂enk-
and, *h₂enh₁-, *h₂ent
ande, *h₂enh₁-
andefn, *h₃ep-
andian, *h₂enh₁-
angel, *h₂enk-
angnæǵl, *h₂enǵʰ-
angul, *h₂enk-
annet, *h₂eneti-
ār, *h₂eyos
arwe, *h₂erkʷo-
ārǣdan, *Hreh₁dʰ-
bana, *gʷʰen-
bannan, *bʰeh₂-
bāt, *bʰeyd-
be-, *h₁epi
bēacen, *bʰeh₂-
bēan, *bʰabʰeh₂-
beard, *bʰardʰeh₂-
bearn, bearwe, *bher-
bēce, *bʰeh₂go-
beǵietan, *weyd-
belīfan, *leyp-
bēn, *bʰeh₂-
beniman, *nem-
bēo, *bʰey-
bēodan, *bʰewdʰ-
bēon, *bʰuH-
beorg, *bʰerǵʰ-
bēr, beran, *bher-
bere, *bʰars-
berg, *bʰerǵʰ-
besettan, besittan, *sed-
bestandan, *steh₂-

betwēonum, *dwóH₁
beþenċan, *teng-
bi-, bī, *h₁epi
bicuman, *gʷem-
bīdan, *bʰeydʰ-
biernan, *bʰrewh₁-
bist, *bʰuH-
bītan, *bʰeyd-
blasen, *bʰleh₁-
blōma, blōstm, *bʰleh₃-
blōwan, *bʰleh₁-, *bʰleh₃-
blæd, *bʰleh₃-
blǣst, blǣtan, *bʰleh₁-
bōc, *bʰeh₂go-
bod, *bʰewdʰ-
bodan, botm, *bʰudʰmén
brēowan, broþ, *bʰrewh₁-
brōþor, *bʰréh₂tēr
brū, *h₃bʰrúHs
brunna, *bʰrewh₁-
būan, *bʰuH-
bucca, *bʰuHgos-
burg, burh, *bʰerǵʰ-
butere, *gʷóws
byrnan, *bʰrewh₁-
bȳsen, *bʰewdʰ-
bǣr, *bher-
bǣrlic, *bʰars-
bǣrnan, *bʰrewh₁-
cald, *gel-
camb, *ǵómbʰos
cann, *ǵneh₃-
ċeald, ċele, *gel-
cemban, *ǵómbʰos
cēne, cennan, *ǵneh₃-
ceorfan, *gerbʰ-
ċeorl, *ǵerh₂-
ceosan, *ǵews-
ċiele, *gel-
ċinn, *ǵénus
cnāwan, *ǵneh₃-
cnēo, *ǵónu
cōl, *gel-
corn, *ǵr̥Hnom
cost, *ǵews-
cran, *gerh₂-
cū, *gʷóws
cuman, *gʷem-
cunnan, cūþ, *ǵneh₃-
cwealm, cwelan, cwellan, *gʷelH-
cwēn, cwene, *gʷén
cweorn, *gʷrh₂-n-uH-
cwic, *gʷeyh₃-
cwidu, *gʷet-
cȳ, *gʷóws
ċyle, *gel-
cynd, cyning, cyningdōm, cynn, *ǵenH₁-

cyrnel, *ǵerh₂-
cyst, *ǵews-
cȳþan, *ǵneh₃-
dā, *dʰeh₁(y)-
dāg, *dʰeyǵʰ-
dagian, *dʰegʷʰ-
dāh, *dʰeyǵʰ-
dēag, dēaw, *dʰewh₂-
dēd, dēman, *dheH₁-
dēop, *dʰewb-
dēore, *dʰegʷʰ-
diernan, *dʰer-
dohtor, *dʰugh₂tḗr
dōm, dōn, *dheH₁-
dor, *dʰwer-
dox, dunn, *dʰewh₂-
durran, *dʰers-
duru, *dʰwer-
dūst, *dʰewh₂-
dwīnan, *dʰegʷʰ-
dǣd, *dheH₁-
dǣg, *dʰegʷʰ-
ēa, *h₂ekʷeh₂-
ēacan, *h₂ewg-
eahta, *oḱtṓw
eald, ealdor, eall, *h₂el-
ealu, *h₂elut-
ēam, *h₂éwh₂os
ēanian, *h₂egʷnos
earfeþe, *h₃erbʰ-
earh, *h₂erkʷo-
earm, *h₂er
earn, *h₃érō
ēast, ēastre, *h₂ews-
eax, eaxl, *H₂eǵ-
eċġ, *h₂éḱ
ēfen, *h₁epi
ēge, *h₃ekʷ-
elboga, *Heh₃l-
elles, *h₂el-
eln, *Heh₃l-
embrace, *peth₂
ende, *h₂ent
endleofan, *óy-nos
ened, *h₂eneti-
enlīhtan, *lewk-
ennet, *h₂eneti-
ēostre, *h₂ews-
ēow, *túh₂
ēowu, *h₂ówis
erian, *H₂erH₃-
etan, ettan, *h₁ed-
ēare, *h₂ew-
eorþe, eorþen, *h₁er-
fāh, *peyḱ-
fām, *poymno-
fandian, *pent-

faran, *per-

fatian, *ped-

fealu, *pelH-

fearh, *pórḱos

feax, *peḱ-

feċċan, *ped-

fēdan, *peh₂-

fefor, *dʰegʷʰ-

feht, *peḱ-

feld, *pleh₂-

fell, *pel-

feoh, *peḱu-

feohtan, *peḱ-

feor, *per-

fēower, *kʷetwóres

fēre, ferian, *per-

feter, fetian, *ped-

feþer, *péth₂r

fīf, *pénkʷe

filmen, *pel-

findan, *pent-

finn, *spey-

fisc, *peisḱ-

flat, *pleth₂-

flēah, *plou-

fleax, *pleḱ-

flēogan, flēoge, *plew-

fleohtan, *pleḱ-

flēon, flēotan, *plew-

flett, *pleth₂-

flōc, flōcan, *pleh₂-

flōd, *plew-

flōr, *pleh₂-

flotian, flōwan, flyht, *plew-

fōda, fōdor, *peh₂-

folc, *pleh₁-

folde, *pleth₂-

for, *per-

forberan, *bher-

forcūþ, *ǵneh₃-

ford, *per-

fordēman, *dheH₁-

fore, forfaran, *per-

forġiefan, *gʰebʰ-

forġietan, *weyd-

forniman, *nem-

forsacan, *seh₂g-

forstandan, *steh₂-

forweorþan, *wert-

forþ, *per-

fōt, *pṓds

fram, framian, *per-

freġnan, *preḱ-

fremman, *per-

frēo, frēodōm, frēond, frēondlīċ, frēondsċipe,

frēondsċype, *preyH-

fretan, *h₁ed-

friþ, friþu, *preyH-

from, *per-

full, *pleh₁-

furh, *perkʷu-

furþor, *per-

fylċian, fyllan, *pleh₁-

fȳr, *péh₂ur

fyrd, *per-

fyrhþ, *perkʷu-

fyrst, *per-

fȳst, *pewǵ-

fæder, *ph₂tḗr

fǣġan, *peyḱ-

fær, fǣr, *per-

fæst, *peh₂ǵ-

fæþm, *peth₂

gāst, *ǵʰeyzd-

gāt, *gʰaydos

ġe, *éy / h₁e

ġē, *túh₂

ġēa, *éy / h₁e

gēar, *yeh₁-

ġeard, *ǵʰer-

gearn, *ǵʰern-

ġeholian, *kelh₁-

ġelēodan, *h₁lewdʰ-

gemynd, *men-

ġemǣne, *mey-

geoc, *yugóm

ġeoguþ, *h₂yuh₁en-

ġeolu, *ǵʰelh₃-

ġeong, ġeongling, *h₂yuh₁en-

georn, *ǵʰer-

geostran, *dʰǵʰ(y)es-

ġēotan, *ǵʰew-

ġerecenian, *h₃reǵ-

ġesċēon, *(s)kek-

ġetan, ġewiss, *weyd-

ġewær, *wer-

ġeþōht, *teng-

ġiċel, *yeǵ-

ġiefan, *gʰebʰ-

ġiest, *yes-

ġift, *gʰebʰ-

ġist, *yes-

god, *ǵʰew-

gold, *ǵʰelh₃-

gōs, *ǵʰans-

grēne, grōni, grōwan, græs, *gʰreh₁-

guma, *ǵʰmṓ

gyrdan, gyrdel, *ǵʰer-

ġyst, *yes-

gærs, *gʰreh₁-

gæst, *gʰóstis

habban, *keh₂p-

haca, *keg-

hafola, *kapōlo

hāl, hālgian, hāliġ, *kóh₂ilus
hām, *ḱei
hamer, *h₂éḱ-mō
hana, *keh₂n-
hatian, *ḱeh₂d-
hē, *ḱi-
heafod, *kapōlo
heall, *ḱel-
healm, *ḱalam-
heark, hearken, *h₂ḱh₂owsyéti
hebban, hefig, *ḱeh₂p-
hēla, *kenk-
helan, hell, helm, *ḱel-
hengest, hengst, *kek-
henn, *keh₂n-
heorcnian, *h₂ḱh₂owsyéti
heorot, *ḱerh₂-
heorte, *ḱếr
hēr, *ḱi-
hēran, hercnian, *h₂ḱh₂owsyéti
here, herebeorg, heretoga, herġian, herian, *ker-
hete, hetol, hettan, *ḱeh₂d-
hider, *ḱi-
hīeran, *h₂ḱh₂owsyéti
hirn, *ḱerh₂-
hlāford, hlāfweard, *wer-
hleonian, *ḱley-
hlēoþor, *ḱlew-
hlōwan, *kelh₁-
hlūd, hlystan, *ḱlew-
hlǣder, hlǣw, *ḱley-
hnitu, *knid-
hō, *kenk-
hōc, *keg-
hōh, *kenk-
hold, *ḱel-
horn, *ḱerh₂-
hors, *ḱers-
hrēaw, *krewh₂-
hrif, *krep-
hrīnan, *krey-
hrysċan, *ḱers-
hū, *kʷis
hund, *ḱwố
hundred, *ḱm̥tóm
hwā, hwenne, *kʷis
hwēol, *kʷel-
hwīl, *kʷyeh₁-
hwilc, hwȳ, hwær, hwæt, hwæþer, *kʷis
hyll, *kelH-
hȳran, hyrcnian, *h₂ḱh₂owsyéti
hyrnet, *ḱerh₂-
hæfen, *ḱeh₂p-
hæfer, *kapro
hǣlan, hælþ, *kóh₂ilus
hærfest, *kerp-
hærn, hærnes, *ḱerh₂-

ī-, iā, *éy / h₁e
iċ, *egH₂
īeġland, *h₂ekʷeh₂-
ieldu, *h₂el-
īeman, *lewk-
ierfa, ierfe, *h₃erbʰ-
iernan, *h₃er-, *h₃reyH-
īeþe, *h₂ew
iġil, iġl, *angʷ(h)i-
īġland, īgoþ, *h₂ekʷeh₂-
īl, *angʷ(h)i-
in, *h₁én
ioc, *yugóm
īren, *h₁ésh₂r̥
irnan, *h₃er-, *h₃reyH-
is, *H₁es-
īs, *h₁eyH-
īsen, *h₁ésh₂r̥
lagu, *legh-, *lókus
lāhan, *legh-
land, *lendʰ-
lapian, *leb-
lēaf, *lewbʰ-
lēaġ, *lewh₃-
lēah, *lewk-
lēassagol, *sekʷ-
lēaþor, *lewh₃-
lecgan, leġ, leġe, leger, *legh-
lencten, *deyn-
lenden, *lendʰ-
lengten, *deyn-
lēod, lēodan, *h₁lewdʰ-
lēof, *lewbʰ-
lēoht, *h₁lengʷʰ-, *lewk-
leornian, *leys-
liċgan, *legh-
lifer, *leyp-
līne, līnen, *lino-
linlīhtan, *lewk-
lippa, *leb-
list, *leys-
loc, *seh₂g-
lof, *lewbʰ-
lūcan, *seh₂g-
lufu, *lewbʰ-
lungen, *lengʷʰ-
lūs, *luHs-
lȳman, *lewk-
lǣfan, *leyp-
lǣġ, *legh-
lǣran, lǣst, *leys-
maga, *mak-
mann, *mánus
manu, *men-
māra, *meh₂-
mare, *mer-
māsc, *mey-

333

mãst, *meh₂-
mē, *H₁me-
mealm, *melh₂-
mearg, *mosgʰos
mearh, *marko-
mec, *H₁me-
melsc, *melit-
melu, *melh₂-
mene, *men-
mennisc, *mánus
meodu, *médʰu
meolc, *H₂melǵ-
mere, *móri
mereswīn, *suH-
merisc, *móri
metan, *med-
mid, midd, *médʰyos
miere, *marko-
mīgan, *h₃meyǵʰ-
mihrif, *ĸrep-
mildēaw, *melit-
mīn, *H₁meme-
min, minsian, *mey-
miriġe, *mréǵʰ-
mis-, miscian, *mey-
misdǣd, *dheH₁-
missan, *mey-
mōdor, *méh₂tēr
mōna, mōnandæg, mōnaþ, *méh₁ns
morgenġiefu, *gʰebʰ-
morþ, morþor, *mer-
munan, *men-
mund, *méh₂-ŗ
mūs, *muh₂s-
mūþ, *mendʰ-
mycel, *méǵh₂s
mycg, *mus-
mylen, *melh₂-
mynd, myntan, *men-
myrġe, *mréǵʰ-
mæġer, *meh₂k-
mæl, *meh₁-
mæne, *mey-
nacian, nacod, *negʷ-
nafela, nafu, *h₃enbʰ-
nama, *h₁nómņ
nefa, *nepot-
nēora, *negʷh-r-
nest, *nisdós
nift, *nepot-
nigon, *H₁néwņ
niht, nihtegale, *nókʷts
niman, *nem-
nīwe, *new
norþ, norþerne, *h₁én
nosu, *néh₂s
nōwend, *(s)neh₂-

næddre, *neHtr-
nædl, *(s)neh₁-
nægl, *h₃negʰ-
of, *h₂pó
ofer, *upo
ofet, ofett, *h₁ed-
oflecgan, *legh-
onde, *h₂enh₁-
ongel, ongul, *h₂enk-
onlīhtan, *lewk-
onǣlan, *h₂eydʰ-
ōr, *h₃éh₁os
ōra, *h₃éh₁os
ord, *dheH₁-
oter, *udréh₂
oxa, *uksén
ōþer, *h₂énteros
pīl, *peys-
power, *peth₂
pæþ, *pent-
ranc, *h₃reǵ-
rēad, *h₁rewdʰ-
reċċan, recenian, rīċe, riht, *h₃reǵ-
rīm, *h₂er-
rinnan, *h₃er-, *h₃reyH-
rodur, *Hret-
rōt, *wréh₂ds
rudian, *h₁rewdʰ-
ryge, *wrugʰyo-
rǣdan, rǣdelse, *Hreh₁dʰ-
sacan, saclēas, sacu, *seh₂g-
sadel, sadol, sadul, *sed-
saga, sagu, *sek-, *sekʷ-
saht, *seh₂g-
sãm-, sama, *sem-
sand, *sent-
sāwan, *seH₁-
sċacan, *(s)kek-
sċãdan, *skey-
scarp, scear, sċeard, sċearu, *(s)ker-
sċēon, *(s)kek-
sċīd, *skey-
scieran, *(s)ker-
sċītan, sċīte, *skey-
scōl, *seǵʰ-
scort, scyrte, *(s)ker-
sē, *só
sealt, sealtan, *séh₂ls
sēam, *sīw-
searu, *ser-
seax, *sek-
sēċan, *seh₂g-
seċg, seċgan, *sekʷ-
seht, *seh₂g-
self, *s(w)e-
sendan, *sent-
seofon, *septņ

seolf, *s(w)e-	tam, *demh₂-
sēon, *sekʷ-	tēag, *dewk-
seonu, *(s)neh₁-	teagor, *daḱru-
sēowan, *sīw-	team, *dewk-
serc, *ser-	tēar, *daḱru-
sess, settan, *sed-	tēon, *deyḱ-
sīen, *sekʷ-	teran, *der-
sierwan, *ser-	teru, *dóru
siex, *swéḱs	tīd, *deh₂-
sigor, *seǵʰ-	tīeġan, *dewk-
siht, *sekʷ-	tien, *déḱm̥t
simle, *sem-	tiht, *deyḱ-
sinnan, *sent-	timber, *dem-
sittan, *sed-	Tiw, tiwesdæġ, *dyew-
slǣp, slǣpan, *leb-	toft, *dem-
snāw, sniwan, *sneygʷʰ-	toga, togian, *dewk-
snōd, *(s)neh₁-	tom, *demh₂-
sōcen, sōcn, *seh₂g-	torn, *der-
sōþ, sōþian, *H₁es-	tōþ, *h₃dónts
spāca, *spey-	trēow, trēowen, *dóru
spearwa, *spḗr	trēowþ, trūwa, *deru-
spēd, spēdan, *speh₁-	tunge, *dn̥ǵʰwéh₂s
spīr, spitu, *spey-	tux, *h₃dónts
standan, *steh₂-	twā, twēġen, twelf, *dwóH₁
steall, *stel-	twēntiġ, *déḱm̥t
stede, *steh₂-	twi-, twinn, *dwóH₁
stellan, *stel-	tǣċan, *deyḱ-
steor, *(s)táwros	ūder, *h₁owHdʰr̥-
steorra, *h₂stḗr	uest, *wek(ʷ)speros
steyen, *steh₂-	un-, *n̥-
stīgan, stiġel, *steygʰ-	uncūþ, *ǵneh₃-
stillan, stille, *stel-	unhold, unholda, *ḱel-
stirc, *(s)táwros	ūp, upp, uppe, *upo
stocc, *(s)tew-	ūs, *wei
stod, stōr, stōw, *steh₂-	wacan, waccor, *weǵ-
strēam, *srew-	wala, walu, *welH-
strēawian, strewian, *strew-	wanian, *h₁weh₂-
strǣt, *sterh₃-	wascan, *wed-
stund, *steh₂-	wast, *h₂ewg-
stunian, *(s)tenh₂-	wāþ, *weyh₁-
stycce, *(s)tew-	wē, *wei
stǣġer, *steygʰ-	wealcan, *welH-
sū, *suH-	wealdan, *h₂welh₁-
sum, *sem-	weall, weallan, *welH-
sumor, *sm̥-h₂-ó-	weard, *wer-
sunnandæġ, sunne, *sóh₂wl̥	weardes, *wert-
sunu, *suh₁nús	wearm, *gʷʰer-
sūþ, sūþerne, *sóh₂wl̥	weaxan, *h₂ewg-
swā, *s(w)e-	webb, *webh-
swebban, swefan, swefn, *swep-	wecgan, *weǵʰ-
swelc, *s(w)e-	wedd, weddian, *wedʰ-
sweostor, *swésōr	wefan, *webh-
swīn, *suH-	weg, wegan, *weǵʰ-
swǣtan, *sweyd-	weliġ, well, *welH-
synn, *H₁es-	wēman, *wekʷ-
sǣd, *seH₁-	wēofod, wēoh, *weyk-
tā, tāhe, *deyḱ-	weorc, *werǵ-

weorold, *wiHrós

weorþ, weorþan, weorþian, *wert-

wer, *wiHrós

werian, *wes-

werwulf, *wiHrós

wesan, *H_1es-

wēste, wēsten, *$h_1$weh$_2$-

westerne, *wek(^{w})speros

weþer, *wet-

wīc, wīċ, *weyḱ-

wicca, wiccian, wice, wicu, *weyk-

widuwe, *$h_1$weyd^h

wift, *webh-

wīg, wīgan, *weyk-

wiht, *weǵh-

willan, *welh$_1$-

wīn, *wóyh$_1$nom

wind, *H_2weH$_1$-

wīs, wīsdōm, wiss, wit, wītan, *weyd-

wituma, *wed^h-

wiþsacan, *seh$_2$g-

wōm, wōma, word, *wek^w-

worold, *$h_2$el-, *wiHrós

wulf, *wĺk^{w}os

wull, wullen, *$h_2$welh$_1$-

wyrċan, *werǵ-

wyrd, *wert-

wyrhta, *werǵ-

wyrm, *wr̥mis-

wyrt, *wréh$_2$ds

wæċċan, *weǵ-

wæġn, *weǵh-

wæps, *wobs-

wǣr, *weh$_1$-

wær, *wer-

wæst, *wek(^{w})speros

wǣtan, wæter, *wed-

wǣþan, *weyh$_1$-

ymbe, *$h_2$ent

yrfe, *$h_3$erb^h-

ysle, *$h_1$ews-

ȳþan, *$h_2$ew

þan, *só

þanc, *teng-

þanne, þār, *só

þearm, *terh$_1$-

þeċċan, þeċċean, *(s)teg-

þencan, *teng-

þennan, *ten-

þeod, þēoden, Þēodrīc, *tewtéh$_2$

þes, *só

þōht, *teng-

þolian, *telh$_2$-

þon, *só

þonc, *teng-

þorp, *treb-

þrāwan, *terh$_1$-

þrēatian, *trewd-

þrescan, *terh$_1$-

þrīe, *tréyes

þrysce, *trosdos

þrǣd, *terh$_1$-

þū, *túh$_2$

þunor, þunresdæġ, *(s)tenh$_2$-

þurh, *terh$_2$-

þurst, *ters-

þuruh, *terh$_2$-

þus, *só

þyncan, *teng-

þæc, *(s)teg-

þǣr, þæt, *só

ǣ, *$h_2$ey-

æcer, *h_2éǵros

æcern, *eh$_3$g-

æf, *$h_2$pó

æfen, *$h_1$epi

æfnan, *$h_3$ep-

æfre, *$h_2$ey-

æfter, *$h_2$pó

æg, *h_2ōwyóm

æht, *$h_2$eyk-

ælan, æled, *$h_2$eyd^h-

æmyrġe, *$h_1$ews-

ænge, *$h_2$enǵ^h-

æniġ, *óy-nos

æppel, *$h_2$ébōl

æs, *$h_1$ed-

æsc, *$h_3$es-

æsce, *$h_2$eh$_1$s-

æx, *$h_2$ék

Frisian

-tich, *dékm̥t
aai, *h₂ōwyóm
aas, *h₁ed-
acht, *oktṓw
achter, *h₂pó
aei, *h₂ōwyóm
af, after, *h₂pó
aker, *eh₃g-
al, *h₂el-
Älbooge, *Heh₃l-
âld, *h₂el-
alve, *óy-nos
ambacht, *H₂eǵ-
angel, ankel, *h₂enk-
antsje, *h₂egʷnos
antwird, *wekʷ-
apel, *h₂ébōl
arbeid, arbeidzje, *h₃erbʰ-
as, *H₂eǵ-
augustus, *h₂ewg-
baan, *gʷʰen-
baar, *bher-
baarne, *bʰrewh₁-
bâlte, *bʰleh₁-
banne, *bʰeh₂-
barn, *bher-
barne, *bʰrewh₁-
barre, *bher-
be, *h₁epi
beaken, *bʰeh₂-
bean, *bʰabʰeh₂-
bear, *bher-
bearne, *bʰrewh₁-
bedekke, *(s)teg-
berch, *bʰerǵʰ-
berje, bern, *bher-
besette, *sed-
betame, betamje, *dem-
biede, *bʰewdʰ-
biene, *bʰeh₂-
bier, *bher-
bij, *bʰey-
bikomme, *gʷem-
bin, *bʰuH-
bite, *bʰeyd-
bjinne, *bʰeh₂-
bjirk, *bʰereǵ-
blaze, *bʰleh₁-
bled, *bʰleh₃-
blêtsje, bletterje, blieze, *bʰleh₁-
bliuwe, *leyp-
bloeie, *bʰleh₁-
blom, blomme, *bʰleh₃-

boaiem, *bʰudʰmḗn
boarg, *bʰerǵʰ-
boarne, *bʰrewh₁-
boat, *bʰeyd-
boek, boeke, *bʰeh₂go-
bok, *bʰuHgos-
boom, *bʰudʰmḗn
boppe, *upo
broer, *bʰréh₂tēr
brouwe, *bʰrewh₁-
Bruun, *h₃bʰrúHs
burd, *bʰardʰeh₂-
bûter, *gʷṓws
by, *h₁epi
daai, *dʰeyǵʰ-
dacht, *teng-
dak, *(s)teg-
das, *tetḱ-
dau, *dʰewh₂-
de, *só
dei, *dʰegʷʰ-
dekke, *(s)teg-
der, *só
died, *dheH₁-
djip, djipte, *dʰewb-
djoer, djoerte, *dʰegʷʰ-
do, *túh₂
doar, *dʰwer-
doarp, *treb-
dochter, *dʰugh₂tḗr
doem, *dheH₁-
dope, *dʰewb-
draaie, *terh₁-
dû, *túh₂
dus, *só
dwaan, *dheH₁-
dy, *só
ea, *h₂ey-
each, *h₃ekʷ-
eandsje, *h₂egʷnos
eangst, *h₂enǵʰ-
ear, *h₂ew-
earm, *h₂er
earn, *h₃érō
east, *h₂ews-
eattjen, *h₁ed-
efter, *h₂pó
ei, *h₂ówis
eigen, *h₂eyḱ-
eilân, *h₂ekʷeh₂-
ein, *h₂eneti-
eker, *h₂éǵros
en, *h₂ent
er, *éy / h₁e
esk, *h₃es-
ettjen, *h₁ed-
faar, *ph₂tḗr

faarich, *pórḱos
farre, *per-
fear, *péth₂r
fee, *peḱu-
fel, *pel-, *pleh₁-
ferdwyne, *dʰegʷʰ-
ferjaan, *gʰebʰ-
ferjitte, *weyd-
fersaakje, *seh₂g-
fêst, *peh₂ǵ-
fetsje, *ped-
fiede, *peh₂-
fiem, *peth₂
fierder, fiere, *per-
fiif, *pénkʷe
fillen, *pel-
fin, *spey-
fine, *pent-
fisk, *peisḱ-
fjil, *kʷel-
fjochtsje, *peḱ-
fjoer, *péh₂ur
fjouwer, *kʷetwóres
fjuchte, *peḱ-
fleane, flecht, *plew-
flie, *plou-
flier, *pleh₂-
floed, flojen, flotsje, *plew-
foarst, *per-
foer, *peh₂-
foet, *pṓds
fokje, *pewǵ-
fol, folje, folk, *pleh₁-
frede, freon, freonlik, freonskip, *preyH-
frette, *h₁ed-
frij, frijdoem, frije, *preyH-
frou, furde, *per-
fûst, *pewǵ-
gast, *gʰóstis
geal, geale, *nókʷts
geast, *ǵʰeyzd-
gefaar, *per-
geit, *gʰaydos
gemien, *mey-
gers, *gʰreh₁-
gêst, *yes-
giel, *ǵʰelh₃-
god, *ǵʰew-
goes, *ǵʰans-
goud, *ǵʰelh₃-
grien, groeie, *gʰreh₁-
guos, *ǵʰans-
gurdle, gurdzja, *ǵʰer-
haal, *ḱalam-
haat, haatsje, *ḱeh₂d-
haed, *kapõlo
hael, *kenk-

haetjen, *ḱeh₂d-
hägel, häile, hajel, *kenk-
hammer, *h₂éḱ-mō
harkje, *h₂kh₂owsyéti
harsens, *ḱerh₂-
hartoch, *ker-
haven, hawwe, *keh₂p-
heak, *keg-
hear, *ker-
hearre, *h₂kh₂owsyéti
heit, *átta
hel, *ḱel-, *ḱelH-
hele, *ḱel-
helje, *ḱelh₁-
helm, *ḱel-
hert, *ḱêr
hiel, hielje, *kóh₂ilus
hiem, *ḱei-
hijr, *ḱi-
hille, *ḱel-
hillich, hilligje, *kóh₂ilus
hin, *keh₂n-
hja, *ḱi-
hjerst, *kerp-
hoanne, *keh₂n-
hoarn, hoarnbij, *ḱerh₂-
hoars, *ḱers-
hoek, hoeke, *keg-
hokker, *kʷis
hûn, *ḱwṓ
hûndert, *ḱm̥tóm
hy, *ḱi-
hynder, hynst, *kek-
ie, *h₂ekʷeh₂-
iem, *h₂éwh₂os
ien, ienich, *óy-nos
ierde, ierden, *h₁er-
ies, *h₁ed-
ieu, *h₂ey-
igge, *h₂éḱ
iik, *h₂eyǵ-
iis, *h₁eyH-
ik, *egH₂
ikker, *h₂éǵros
in, *h₂ent
ing, *h₂enǵʰ-
inje, *h₂egʷnos
inljochtsje, *lewk-
ite, *h₁ed-
izer, *h₁ésh₂r
ja, *éy / h₁e
jaan, *gʰebʰ-
jaar, *h₁owHdʰr-
jearn, *ǵʰer-
jefte, *gʰebʰ-
jeld, *h₂el-
jelne, *Heh₃l-

jern, *ǵʰern-	lusî, *lewk-
jers, *gʰreh₁-	lynje, *ḱley-
jeugd, *h₂yuh₁en-	mage, *mak-
jim, jimme, *túh₂	man, *mánus
jiske, *h₂eh₁s-	mar, *móri
jitte, *ǵʰew-	master, *méǵh₂s
jjier, *yeh₁-	mea, *médʰu
jok, *yugóm	meager, *meh₂ḱ-
jong, *h₂yuh₁en-	mear, meast, *meh₂-
jûk, *yugóm	meeps, *wobs-
jûn, *h₁epi	melke, *H₂melǵ-
juster, *dʰǵʰ(y)es-	merje, *marko-
kaam, *ǵómbʰos	mersk, *móri
kâld, *gel-	meun, *mey-
kam, *ǵómbʰos	mich, *mus-
keardel, kearel, *ǵerh₂-	mid-, midden, *médʰyos
kenne, *ǵenH₁-	miel, *meh₁-
kerve, *gerbʰ-	mien, *mey-
kêst, *ǵews-	mige, *h₃meyǵʰ-
keuning, keuningdom, *ǵenH₁-	min, *mey-
kieze, *ǵews-	minske, *mánus
kin, *ǵénus	mintsje, *men-
kinne, *ǵenH₁-	misdied, *dheH₁-
kjimme, *ǵómbʰos	misse, *mey-
kleur, *ḱel-	mjitte, *med-
knibbel, *ǵónu	moal, *melh₂-
ko, *gʷóws	moaldau, *melit-
koel, *gel-	moandei, *méh₁n̥s
komme, *gʷem-	moanjes, *men-
kraan, *gerh₂-	moanne, *méh₁n̥s
kwik, kwyk, *gʷeyh₃-	moannen, *men-
lāch, *lewk-	moarch, *mosgʰos
lân, *lendʰ-	moard, *mer-
lauwgje, lauwje, leaf, leaf, leaflik, *lewbʰ-	moer, *méh₂tēr
leare, least, *leys-	molke, *H₂melǵ-
ledsa, leech, *legh-	mûn, *mendʰ-
leider, *ḱley-	muntsje, *men-
leppel, *leb-	mûs, *muh₂s-
leune, *ḱley-	my, *H₁me-
lever, *leyp-	myn, *H₁meme-
licht, *h₁lengʷʰ-	naaie, *(s)neh₁-
lie, *h₁lewdʰ-	nacht, *nókʷts
lien, *leykʷ-	nâle, *h₃enbʰ-
line, linnen, *lino-	namme, *h₁nómn̥
lippe, *leb-	neaken, *negʷ-
list, *leys-	neef, *nepot-
lizze, *legh-	nei, *new
ljedder, ljerre, *ḱley-	neil, *h₃negʰ-
ljocht, *lewk-	nêst, *nisdós
lju, ljuwe, *h₁lewdʰ-	nicht, *nepot-
loch, *legh-	niddel, *(s)neh₁-
lof, *lewbʰ-	nier, *negʷh-r-
long, longe, *lengʷʰ-	nift, *nepot-
loovje, *lewbʰ-	nille, *(s)neh₁-
lûd, *ḱlew-	nimme, *nem-
lûke, *seh₂g-	njirre, *neHtr-
lús, *luHs-	njoggen, *H₁néwn̥

noard, *h₁én

noas, *néh₂s

nuddel, nulle, *(s)neh₁-

nust, *nisdós

oar, *h₂énteros

oarde, *dheH₁-

oefte, *h₁ed-

oer, *upo

oerd, *dheH₁-

ôf, *h₂pó

okse, *uksḗn

om, *h₂ent

omke, *h₂éwh₂os

Omme, *h₂enh₁-

op, *upo

otter, *udréh₂

paad, *pent-

räkke, *h₃reǵ-

rau, *krewh₂-

read, *h₁rewdʰ-

rêd, *Hret-

rekkenje, *h₃reǵ-

riede, *Hreh₁dʰ-

rinne, *h₃er-, *h₃reyH-

rjocht, *h₃reǵ-

rogge, *wrugʰyo-

ryk, *h₃reǵ-

sa, *s(w)e-

saak, *seh₂g-

sâlt, *séh₂ls

sam, *sem-

sân, *septṃ

särk, *ser-

schaakje, schaekje, schaekjen, *(s)kek-

schird, *(s)ker-

seage, *sek-

seal, sealje, *sed-

seam, *sīw-

sege, *seǵʰ-

seine, *sek-

seis, *swéḱs

self, *s(w)e-

serk, *ser-

sette, *sed-

sicht, *sekʷ-

sied, *seH₁-

simmer, *sṃ-h₂-ó-

sin, *sent-

sinne, *sóh₂wḷ

sitte, *sed-

sizze, sjen, *sekʷ-

skare, skarre, skeare, skerp, skerte, *(s)ker-

skiede, *skey-

skikke, *(s)kek-

skite, *skey-

skriuwe, *(s)ker-

skyt, *skey-

sliep, sliepe, *leb-

slute, *(s)kel-

snein, *sóh₂wḷ

snie, snije, *sneygʷʰ-

soan, *suh₁nús

sok, *s(w)e-

spile, *spey-

stâl, *stel-

stean, stêd, *steh₂-

steer, *h₂stḗr

stelle, *stel-

stige, *steygʰ-

stik, *(s)tew-

stil, *stel-

stjer, *h₂stḗr

stjitte, stoak, *(s)tew-

stoer, stounde, *steh₂-

stream, *srew-

streauwe, *strew-

strjitte, *sterh₃-

struie, *strew-

studearje, *(s)tew-

sûch, *suH-

súd, *sóh₂wḷ

sum, sume, *sem-

sûnde, *H₁es-

sus, *swésōr

swit, *sweyd-

swyn, *suH-

sykje, *seh₂g-

syn, *s(w)e-

taensjen, *teng-

tam, *demh₂-

tanck, tank, tanke, tankje, *teng-

tarre, *der-

team, *dewk-

tean, *deyḱ-

teere, *der-

tek, *(s)teg-

term, *terh₁-

terp, *treb-

terskje, *terh₁-

tiemje, *dem-

tiid, *deh₂-

tiisdei, *dyew-

timmer, *dem-

tinke, *teng-

toarne, *der-

toarst, *ters-

toch, *dewk-

tolf, tolve, *dwóH₁

tonge, *dṇǵʰwéh₂s

tonger, Tonger, tongersdei, *(s)tenh₂-

tos, tosk, toth, *h₃dónts

trie, tried, *terh₁-

trien, *daḱru-

trije, *tréyes

trou, *deru-
tsien, *déḱm̥t
tsjil, *kʷel-
tsjirl, *ǵerh₂-
twa, *dwóH₁
tweintich, *déḱm̥t
twilling, *dwóH₁
ús, *wei
wa, *kʷis
waakse, *h₂ewg-
waarm, *gʷʰer-
wacht, wachtje, wachtsje, *weǵ-
waps, *wobs-
waskje, *wed-
wat, *kʷis
web, *webh-
wedzje, *wedʰ-
weeps, *wobs-
wei, wein, *weǵh-
wekker, *weǵ-
wêr, *kʷis
west, westen, *wek(ʷ)speros
wet, *wedʰ-
wetter, *wed-
weve, *webh-
wêze, *bʰuH-, *H₁es-
widdo, *h₁weydʰ
wiele, *kʷel-
wier, *weh₁-
wiet, wietsje, *wed-
wiis, wiisdom, *weyd-
wije, wijreek, wike, *weyk-
wile, *kʷyeh₁-
wis, wisse, wite, witte, *weyd-
wjirm, *wṛmis-
woarst, *wert-
woartel, *wréh₂ds
woastyn, *h₁weh₂-
wol, *h₂welh₁-
wolf, *wĺkʷos
wolle, *h₂welh₁-, *welh₁-
wou, *weyh₁-
wrâld, *h₂el-, *wiHrós
wurd, *wekʷ-
wurde, *wert-
wurk, wurkje, *werǵ-
wurtel, *wréh₂ds
wy, *wei
wyk, *weyḱ-
wylch, *welH-
wyn, *H₂weH₁-, *wóyh₁nom
wys, *weyd-
ychel, *angʷ(h)i-
yn, *h₁én

Dutch

-achtig, *keh₂p-
-em, -gem, *ḱei-
-haftig, *keh₂p-
-hem, *ḱei-
-sen, *suh₁nús
-tig, *déḱm̥t
-waarts, *wert-
-zoon, *suh₁nús
a, *h₂ekʷeh₂-
aal, *h₂elut-
aangenaam, *nem-
aanleggen, *legh-
aantijgen, *deyk-
aâr, *h₂énteros
aar, *h₃érō
aarde, aarden, *h₁er-
aardvarken, *pórḱos
aas, *h₁ed-
acht, *oḱtṓw
achter, *h₂pó
actie, *H₂eǵ-
adder, *neHtr-
adelaar, *h₃érō
adem, *h₂enh₁-
adolescent, *h₂el-
af, *h₂pó
afleggen, *legh-
ajuin, *óy-nos
aker, *eh₃g-
akker, *h₂éǵros
aks, akst, *h₂éḱ
al, *h₂el-
aldus, *só
ambacht, ambachten, ambassade, ambt, *H₂eǵ-
ande, *h₂enh₁-
ander, *h₂énteros
angel, *h₂enk-
angst, *h₂enǵʰ-
anoniem, *h₁nómn̥
antiek, *h₂énti-h₃kʷós
antwoord, *wekʷ-
apotheek, *dheH₁-
appel, *h₂ébōl
arbeid, arbeiden, *h₃erbʰ-
arend, *h₃érō
arm, *h₂er
as, *H₂eǵ-, *h₂eh₁s-
assel, *H₂eǵ-
attent, *ten-
augustus, *h₂ewg-
aura, *h₂ews-
auto, automobiel, *h₂ew-
averechts, *h₂pó

avond, *h₁epi

axilla, *H₂eǵ-

baak, *bʰeh₂-

baan, *gʷʰen-

baar, *bher-

baard, *bʰardʰeh₂-

bahasa, baken, bannen, *bʰeh₂-

baren, *bher-

base, *gʷem-

be-, *h₁epi

bedekken, *(s)teg-

bedenken, *teng-

behelen, *ḱel-

beiden, *bʰeydʰ-

beitel, beits, *bʰeyd-

bekomen, bekwaam, *gʷem-

belenden, *lendʰ-

ben, *bʰuH-

benemen, *nem-

bennen, *bʰuH-

berg, *bʰerǵʰ-

berk, *bʰereǵ-

berrie, *bher-

beschermen, *(s)ker-

bespieden, *speḱ-

beuk, *bʰeh₂go-

beuren, *bher-

bezetten, bezitten, *sed-

bibliotheek, *dheH₁-

biceps, *kapōlo

bieden, *bʰewdʰ-

bij, *bʰey-, *h₁epi

bijten, *bʰeyd-

blaaien, *bʰleh₁-

blad, *bʰleh₃-

blaten, blazen, bleiten, *bʰleh₁-

bleven, blij, blijven, *leyp-

bloeien, *bʰleh₁-

bloem, *bʰleh₃-

bod, bode, *bʰewdʰ-

bodem, *bʰudʰmén

boei, *bʰeh₂-

boek, *bʰeh₂go-

boen, boenen, *bʰeh₂-

boetiek, *dheH₁-

bok, *bʰuHgos-

boon, *bʰabʰeh₂-

boot, *bʰeyd-

born, *bʰrewh₁-

boter, *gʷóws

bourgeois, *bʰerǵʰ-

bouwen, *bʰuH-

boven, *upo

branden, *bʰrewh₁-

brauw, *h₃bʰrúHs

brief, *mréǵʰ-

brodium, *bʰrewh₁-

broeder, broer, *bʰréh₂tēr

bron, brouwen, *bʰrewh₁-

bruidegom, *ǵʰmṓ

burcht, *bʰerǵʰ-

bureau, *péh₂ur

burg, *bʰerǵʰ-

camp, *(s)teg-

carrosserie, *ḱers-

centi-, centimeter, *ḱm̥tóm

col, *kelH-

communicatie, *mey-

componeren, *teḱ-

concipiëren, *keh₂p-

conditie, *deyḱ-

constructie, *strew-

continu, *ten-

converteren, *wert-

correctie, corrigeren, *h₃reǵ-

crisis, *krey-

cyclus, *kʷel-

daad, *dheH₁-

daar, *só

dag, dagen, *dʰegʷʰ-

dak, *(s)teg-

dame, *dem-

dan, *só

dank, danken, *teng-

darm, *terh₁-

das, *tetḱ-

dat, *só

dauw, *dʰewh₂-

de, *só

deca-, decaan, decade, *déḱm̥t

declareren, *kelh₁-

decreet, *krey-

deeg, *dʰeyǵʰ-

dekken, *(s)teg-

delier, delirium, *leys-

dement, demonstratie, demonstreren, *men-

denken, *teng-

deporteren, *per-

der, *só

dersen, *terh₁-

deur, *dʰwer-

di-, *dwóH₁

dichten, dicteren, *deyḱ-

die, *só

Diederik, *tewtéh₂

diep, diepte, *dʰewb-

diet, *tewtéh₂

dirigeren, *h₃reǵ-

Dirk, *tewtéh₂

distribueren, *bʰuH-

dit, *só

diva, *dyew-

dochter, *dʰugh₂tḗr

doctrine, *deḱdoem, doemen, doen, *dheH₁-

dogma, *deḱ-

dominatie, dominee, *dem-

Donar, donder, donderdag, *(s)tenh₂-

dons, *dʰewh₂-

door, *terh₂-

dopen, *dʰewb-

dor, *ters-

dorp, *treb-

dorsen, *terh₁-

dorst, *ters-

draad, draaien, *terh₁-

draak, *h₂eneti-, *h₃reǵ-

drie, *tréyes

droten, *trewd-

du, *túh₂

dubbel, *pleh₁-

duist, *dʰewh₂-

duivel, *gʷelH-

dulden, *telh₂-

dunken, *teng-

duren, *deru-

durven, *dʰers-

dus, *só

duur, duurte, dwijnen, *dʰegʷʰ-

echt, *h₂ey-

editor, *deH₃-

eek, *h₂eyǵ-

een, *óy-nos

eend, *h₂eneti-

eeuw, *h₂ey-

effect, effectief, *dheH₁-

eg, *h₂éḱ

egel, *angʷ(h)i-

egge, *h₂éḱ

ei, *h₂ōwyóm

eigen, *h₂eyḱ-

eik, *h₂eyǵ-

eiland, *h₂ekʷeh₂-

eind, einde, *h₂ent

el, *Heh₃l-

elde, elders, *h₂el-

elf, *óy-nos

elleboog, ellenboog, *Heh₃l-

ellende, *h₂el-

els, *h₃el-

emulgeren, *H₂melǵ-

en, *h₂ent

eng, *h₂enǵʰ-

enig, *óy-nos

enkel, enklauw, *h₂enk-

erf, erve, *h₃erbʰ-

es, *h₃es-

eten, *h₁ed-

ether, *h₂eydʰ-

etsen, *h₁ed-

ette, *átta

etten, *h₁ed-

examen, *H₂eǵ-

executie, *sekʷ-

exporteren, *per-

faam, *bʰeh₂-

fanaticus, *dʰéh₁s

fantoom, *bʰeh₂-

februari, *dʰegʷʰ-

feest, *dʰéh₁s

feit, *dheH₁-

figuur, fingeren, *dʰeyǵʰ-

flat, *pleth₂-

fokken, *pewǵ-

fornuis, *gʷʰer-

fortuin, *bher-

fraai, *weh₁-

fretten, *h₁ed-

fundament, *bʰudʰmḗn

furtief, *bher-

gaard, gaarde, gaarne, *ǵʰer-

gans, *ǵʰans-

garen, *ǵʰern-

gast, *gʰóstis

gave, *gʰebʰ-

gebeuren, geboorte, *bher-

gedachte, *teng-

geel, *ǵʰelh₃-

geers, *gʰreh₁-

geest, *ǵʰeyzd-

geit, *gʰaydos

geluw, *ǵʰelh₃-

gemeen, *mey-

genereren, genie, *ǵenH₁-

gerechten, *h₃reǵ-

geronnen, *h₃er-, *h₃reyH-

geschieden, *(s)kek-

gesternte, *h₂stḗr

gevaar, *per-

geven, *gʰebʰ-

gewaar, *wer-

gewagen, *wekʷ-

geweld, *h₂welh₁-

gewis, *weyd-

gewrocht, *werǵ-

gieten, *ǵʰew-

gif, gift, *gʰebʰ-

gij, *túh₂

gist, *yes-

gisteren, *dʰǵʰ(y)es-

glorie, glorieus, *ǵneh₃-

god, *ǵʰew-

goesting, *ǵews-

gordel, gorden, *ǵʰer-

goud, *ǵʰelh₃-

gras, *gʰreh₁-

gratie, *gʷerH-

Grieks, Griekse, *ǵerh₂-

groeien, groen, *gʰreh₁-

haak, *keg-

haan, *keh₂n-

haar, *ḱi-

haas, haasje, *kenk-

haat, *ḱeh₂d-

hal, *ḱel-

halen, *kelh₁-

halm, *ḱalam-

hamer, *h₂éḱ-mō

hangar, hanteren, *ḱei-

hart, *ḱḗr

haten, *ḱeh₂d-

haven, *keh₂p-

haver, *kapro

hebben, *keh₂p-

heel, *kóh₂ilus

heer, *ker-

heil, heilig, heiligen, *kóh₂ilus

heir, *ker-

hel, helen, *ḱel-

helen, *kóh₂ilus

helm, *ḱel-

hem, *ḱi-

hen, *keh₂n-

hengst, *kek-

her, *ḱi-

herberg, *ker-

herfst, *kerp-

hersenen, hersens, hert, *ḱerh₂-

hertog, *dewk-, *ker-

het, *ḱi-, *só

hevig, *keh₂p-

hiel, *kenk-

hier, hij, *ḱi-

hil, *kelH-

historie, *weyd-

hoe, *kʷis

hoek, *keg-

hoen, *keh₂n-

hond, *ḱwṓ

honderd, *ḱm̥tóm

hoofd, *kapōlo

hoorn, hoorntje, *ḱerh₂-

horen, *h₂ḱh₂owsyéti

hou, houd, *ḱel-

hul, *kelH-

hullen, huls, *ḱel-

hyena, *suH-

hypotheek, *dheH₁-

idioot, *s(w)e-

idool, *weyd-

ijs, *h₁eyH-

ijzer, *h₁ésh₂r̥

ik, *egH₂

immoleren, *melh₂-

importeren, *per-

in spe, *speh₁-

in, *h₁én

inlichten, *lewk-

inviteren, *weyh₁-

ja, *éy / h₁e

jaar, *yeh₁-

jeugd, *h₂yuh₁en-

jicht, *yek-

jij, jijlui, *túh₂

jong, jongeling, *h₂yuh₁en-

juist, *h₂eyw-

juk, *yugóm

jullie, *túh₂

justitie, *h₂eyw-

kaart, *ǵʰer-

kachtel, *kapōlo

kalender, *kelh₁-

kam, *ǵómbʰos

kamp, kampioen, *(s)teg-

kapitaal, *kapōlo

kar, *ḱers-

kek, *gʷeyh₃-

kelder, *ḱel-

kemmen, *ǵómbʰos

kennen, *ǵneh₃-

kerel, *ǵerh₂-

kerven, *gerbʰ-

keuken, *pekʷ-

kiezen, *ǵews-

kil, *gel-

kin, *ǵénus

kind, *ǵenH₁-

klaar, *kelh₁-

kleur, *ḱel-

klimaat, *ḱley-

klooster, *(s)kel-

knie, *ǵónu

koe, *gʷṓws

koel, *gel-

koers, *ḱers-

kok, koken, *pekʷ-

komen, kommen, *gʷem-

kond, konden, *ǵneh₃-

koning, koningdom, *ǵenH₁-

koord, koorde, *ǵʰern-

koren, *ǵr̥Hnom

korps, *krep-

kort, *(s)ker-

koud, *gel-

kous, *(s)kel-

kraan, kraanvogel, *gerh₂-

kunne, *ǵenH₁-

kunnen, *ǵneh₃-

kust, *ǵews-

kwadraat, *kʷetwóres

kwalm, *gʷelH-

kwart, *kʷetwóres

kween, *gwén
kweern, *gʷrh₂-n-uH-
kwelen, kwellen, *gʷelH-
kwiek, *gʷeyh₃-
kwijt, *kʷyeh₁-
kwik, *gʷeyh₃-
laag, *legh-
ladder, *ḱley-
land, *lendʰ-
landouw, *h₂ekʷeh₂-
latrine, *lewh₃-
latuw, *glag-
lava, *lewh₃-
leen, *leykʷ-
leer, *ḱley-
leest, *leys-
leger, leggen, *legh-
legio, legioen, *leǵ-
lende, lendenen, *lendʰ-
lente, *deyn-
lepel, *leb-
leren, *leys-
leunen, *ḱley-
lever, *leyp-
licht, *lewk-, *h₁lengʷʰ-
lichten, *lewk-
lieden, *h₁lewdʰ-
lief, lieflijk, *lewbʰ-
liggen, *legh-
lijn, linnen, *lino-
lip, *leb-
list, *leys-
lo, *lewk-
loch, *seh₂g-
Lodewijk, *ḱlew-
lodge, *lewbʰ-
loeien, *kelh₁-
lof, *lewbʰ-
log, *legh-
loge, logeren, loggia, *lewbʰ-
lok, *seh₂g-
long, *lengʷʰ-
loo, *lewk-
loods, loof, *lewbʰ-
loog, *lewh₃-
loven, *lewbʰ-
lui, *h₁lewdʰ-
luid, *ḱlew-
luiden, *h₁lewdʰ-
luiken, *seh₂g-
luis, *luHs-
luisteren, *ḱlew-
luzerne, *lewk-
maag, *mak-
maal, *meh₁-
maan, *méh₁n̥s, *men-
maand, maandag, *méh₁n̥s

maar, *mer-
maarschalk, *marko-
maat, *med-
mager, *meh₂k-
maître, *méǵh₂s
malen, *meh₁-, *melh₂-
malm, *melh₂-
man, *mánus
manen, *men-
manneken, mannequin, *mánus
mare, *mer-
matrijs, matrix, *méh₂tēr
me, *H₁me-
mede, *médʰu
medicus, *med-
meel, *melh₂-
meeldauw, *melit-
meer, *meh₂-, *móri
meerdere, *meh₂-
meers, *móri
meerzwijn, *suH-
meest, *meh₂-
meester, meier, mekel, *méǵh₂s
melk, melken, *H₂melǵ-
men, mens, *mánus
merg, *mosgʰos
merrie, *marko-
mest, *h₃meyǵʰ-
meten, *med-
meun, *mey-
mid-, midden, *médʰyos
miegen, *h₃meyǵʰ-
mier, *morwi-
mij, *H₁me-
mijgen, *h₃meyǵʰ-
mijn, *H₁meme-
min, minder, *mey-
minivarken, *pórḱos
mis-, *mey-
misdaad, *dheH₁-
missen, mixen, *mey-
moeder, *méh₂tēr
moeras, *móri
molen, *melh₂-
mond, *méh₂-r̥, *mendʰ-
monter, *men-
moord, *mer-
morgengave, *gʰebʰ-
mud, *med-
mug, *mus-
mui, muide, *mendʰ-
muis, *muh₂s-
munt, munten, *men-
musculair, *muh₂s-
mutatie, *mey-
naaf, *h₃enbʰ-
naakt, *negʷ-

naald, *(s)neh₁-
naam, *h₁nómṇ
nacht, nachtegaal, *nókʷts
nachtmare, nachtmerrie, *mer-
nagel, *h₃negʰ-
naiaen, *(s)neh₁-
natie, *ǵenH₁-
navel, *h₃enbʰ-
neef, *nepot-
neet, *knid-
negen, *H₁néwṇ
nemen, *nem-
nest, *nisdós
neus, *néh₂s
nevel, *nebʰ-
niche, *nisdós
nicht, *nepot-
nier, *negʷh-r-
nieuw, *new
nis, *nisdós
nobel, *ǵneh₃-
noord, *h₁én
normaal, normale, noteren, *ǵneh₃-
nummer, *nem-
ochtend, *nókʷts
octo-, octogonaal, *oḱtṓw
octopus, *pṓds
oekonomie, *nem-
officieel, *h₃ep-
oken, *h₂ewg-
oksel, *H₂eǵ-
om, *h₂ent
on-, *ṇ-
ongewis, *weyd-
onhoud, *ḱel-
onkond, *ǵneh₃-
ontberen, *bher-
ooft, *h₁ed-
oog, *h₃ekʷ-
oogst, *h₂ewg-
ooi, *h₂ówis
ooibos, *h₂ekʷeh₁-
oom, *h₂éwh₂os
oonen, *h₂egʷnos
oor, *h₂ew-
oord, *dheH₁-
oost, oosten, *h₂ews-
op, *upo
opera, *h₃ep-
orakel, *h₃éh₁os
orde, ordenen, order, ordonneren, *h₂er
os, *uksḗn
otter, *udréh₂
oud, *h₂el-
ouwel, *bher-
over, *upo
paaien, *peh₂ǵ-

pad, *pent-
pagina, *peh₂ǵ-
parabel, parabool, *gʷelH-
pastoor, *peh₂-
patent, *peth₂
pater, patrimonium, patriot, *ph₂tḗr
peg, *bak-
pels, *pel-
pigment, *peyḱ-
pijl, *peys-
pijn, *kʷey-
plaats, *pleh₂-
pond, *pewǵ-
poort, portaal, *per-
post-, *h₁epi
pragmatisch, *per-
prefereren, *bher-
prevaleren, *h₂welh₁-
prijs, *per-
prins, prinses, *keh₂p-
probleem, *gʷelH-
proef, *bʰuH-
prooi, *weyd-
provincie, *per-
punt, *pewǵ-
raadsel, *Hreh₁dʰ-
rad, *Hret-
raden, *Hreh₁dʰ-
radicaal, *wréh₂ds
rank, *h₃reǵ-
rauw, *krewh₂-
recht, *h₃reǵ-
reebok, *bʰuHgos-
reeuw, *krewh₂-
refereren, *bher-
regel, *h₃reǵ-
rein, *krey-
rekenen, rekken, *h₃reǵ-
renen, *krey-
rennen, *h₃er-, *h₃reyH-
repeteren, *peth₂
republiek, *pleh₁-
richel, richten, rijk, *h₃reǵ-
rijm, *h₂er
rijnen, *krey-
rogge, *wrugʰyo-
rond, *Hret-
rood, *h₁rewdʰ-
ros, *ḱers-
roteren, *Hret-
rubriek, *h₁rewdʰ-
sage, *sekʷ-
saus, *séh₂ls
schaar, schaarde, *(s)ker-
schaken, *(s)kek-
schare, *(s)ker-
schedel, scheiden, *skey-

346

scheren, scherm, scherp, scheur, *(s)ker-
schijt, schijten, *skey-
schikken, *(s)kek-
school, *seǵʰ-
schort, schrapen, schrappen, schribbelen,
 schrijven, *(s)ker-
senaat, *sénos
sessie, *sed-
situatie, situeren, *teḱ-
slaap, slapen, *leb-
sleutel, sluis, sluiten, *(s)kel-
snaar, *snusós
sneeuw, *sneygʷʰ-
sneu, *(s)neh₁-
snoer, *snusós
snouwen, snuwen, *sneygʷʰ-
solarium, *sóh₂wl̥
sold, *solh₂-
sommige, soms, somtijds, somwijlen, *sem-
spaak, *spey-
spaarvarken, *pórḱos
spieden, spiegel, *speḱ-
spier, spijker, spijl, spit, *spey-
spoed, spoeden, *speh₁-
spreeuw, *spḗr
staan, stad, *steh₂-
stal, *stel-
standen, stede, stee, *steh₂-
steeg, *steygʰ-
steenbok, *bʰuHgos-
stegel, steiger, *steygʰ-
stellen, *stel-
stenen, *(s)tenh₂-
ster, *h₂stḗr
steunen, *(s)tenh₂-
sticht, *steygʰ-
stier, *(s)táwros
stijgen, *steygʰ-
stik, *(s)tew-
stil, *stel-
stoet, *steh₂-
stok, *(s)tew-
stond, *steh₂-
stoten, *(s)tew-
straat, *sterh₃-
strooien, *strew-
stroom, *srew-
strouwen, *strew-
student, studeren, stuk, *(s)tew-
synagoge, *H₂eǵ-
tam, *demh₂-
tand, *h₃dónts
tandem, *só
team, *dewk-
teen, *deyḱ-
teer, *dóru
tegel, *(s)teg-

temmen, *demh₂-
teren, *der-
term, termijn, *térmn̥
territoriaal, territorium, *ters-
teug, teugel, *dewk-
Texel, *deḱs-
tien, *déḱm̥t
tijd, *deh₂-
timmer, *dem-
tong, *dn̥ǵʰwéh₂s
toom, *dewk-
toon, *deyḱ-, *ten-
toorn, *der-
traan, *daḱru-
traditie, *deH₃-
translatie, *bʰer-
treiteren, *deH₃-
trouw, *deru-
twaalf, twee, tweeling, *dwóH₁
twintig, *déḱm̥t
type, typisch, *(s)tew-
ui, *óy-nos
uier, *h₁owHdʰr̥-
unie, *óy-nos
uns, *wei
uur, *yeh₁-
va, *ph₂tḗr
vaal, *pelH-
vaam, *peth₂
vaart, *per-
vacht, *peḱ-
vadem, *peth₂
vader, *ph₂tḗr
van, *h₂pó
vanden, *pent-
var, *pórḱos
varen, *per-
varken, *pórḱos
vas, *peḱ-
vast, *peh₂ǵ-
vatten, *ped-
vechten, *peḱ-
veder, *péth₂r̥
vee, *peḱu-
veel, *pleh₁-
veer, *per-, *péth₂r̥
veinzen, *dʰeyǵʰ-
vel, velm, *pel-
ventilator, *H₂weH₁-
verbeiden, *bʰeydʰ-
verdoemen, *dheH₁-
verdrieten, *trewd-
verdwijnen, *dʰegʷʰ-
vergeten, *weyd-
vergeven, *gʰebʰ-
verheren, *ker-
verkonden, *ǵneh₃-

vernemen, *nem-

vervaren, *per-

verwijten, *weyd-

verworden, *wert-

verzaken, *seh₂g-

veter, *ped-

via, *weyh₁-

vier, *kʷetwóres

vijf, *pénkʷe

vin, *spey-

vinden, *pent-

viriel, *wiHrós

vis, *peiśk-

vlet, *pleth₂-

vleugel, vlieden, vlieg, vliegen, vlieten, *plew-

vlo, *plou-

vloed, vloeien, *plew-

vloeken, *pleh₂k-

vloer, *pleh₂-

vlot, vlotten, vlucht, *plew-

vocaal, *wekʷ-

voeden, voeder, voer, *peh₂-

voeren, *per-

voet, *póds

vol, volk, *pleh₁-

vooi, *weyh₁-

voor, voord, voorde, vorder, *per-

vorsen, *preḱ-

vorst, *per-, *perkʷu-

vracht, *h₂eyk-

vragen, *preḱ-

vrede, *preyH-

vreten, *h₁ed-

vriend, vriendelijk, vriendschap, vrij, vrijdom,

vrijen, *preyH-

vrouw, vrouwe, *per-

vuist, *pewǵ-

vullen, *pleh₁-

vuren, *perkʷu-

vuur, *péh₂ur

waaien, *H₂weH₁-

waar, *kʷis, *weh₁-

waard, *wert-

wacht, wachten, *weǵ-

wagen, wagon, *weǵh-

wakker, *weǵ-

wal, *welH-

wan, *H₂weH₁-

warm, warmen, *gʷʰer-

wassen, *h₂ewg-, *wed-

wat, *kʷis

water, *wed-

we, *wei

web, *webh-

wedde, wedden, *wedʰ-

weder, *kʷis, *wet-

weduwe, *h₁weydʰ

week, *weyk-

weem, *wedʰ-

weer, *wet-

weergeld, weerwold, *wiHrós

wees, *h₁weydʰ

weg, wegen, *weǵh-

weide, weiden, *weyh₁-

wekken, *weǵ-

welk, *kʷis

wereld, *h₂el-, *wiHrós

werk, werken, *werǵ-

wesp, *wobs-

west, westen, *wek(ʷ)speros

weten, *weyd-

weven, *webh-

wezen, *bʰuH-, *H₁es-

wicht, *weǵh-

wie, *kʷis

wiel, *kʷel-

wierook, *weyk-

wij, *wei

wijden, wijgen, *weyk-

wijk, *weyk-

wijl, *kʷyeh₁-

wijn, *wóyh₁nom

wijsdom, wijten, *weyd-

wikken, *weyk-

wil, willen, *welh₁-

wind, *H₂weH₁-

wis, *weyd-

woestijn, *h₁weh₂-

wol, *h₂welh₁-

wolf, *wĺkʷos

woord, *wekʷ-

worden, *wert-

worm, *wr̥mis-

worst, *wert-

wort, *wréh₂ds

wortel, *welH-

wortel, *wréh₂ds

wouw, *weyh₁-

wrecht, wrochten, *werǵ-

wurm, *wr̥mis-

zaad, *seH₁-

zaag, *sek-

zaaien, *seH₁-

zaak, *seh₂g-

zadel, zadelen, *sed-

zege, *seǵʰ-

zegel, *sek-

zeggen, *sekʷ-

zeis, *sek-

zelf, zelve, *s(w)e-

zenden, *sent-

zes, *swéḱs

zetten, *sed-

zeug, *suH-

German

zeven, *septm̥
zich, *s(w)e-
zicht, zien, *sekʷ-
zij, *éy / h₁e
zijn, *bʰuH-, *s(w)e-
zin, zinnen, *sent-
zitten, *sed-
zo, *s(w)e-
zoeken, *seh₂g-
zolder, *sóh₂wl̥
zomer, *sm̥-h₂-ó-
zon, zondag, *sóh₂wl̥
zonde, *H₁es-
zoom, *sīw-
zoon, *suh₁nús
zout, zouten, *séh₂ls
zuid, zuiden, *sóh₂wl̥
zulk, *s(w)e-
zult, *séh₂ls
zus, zuster, *swésōr
zweet, *sweyd-
zwijn, *suH-

-duzieren, *dewk-
-rich, *h₃reǵ-
-sen, *suh₁nús
-wärts, *wert-
-wegen, *weǵh-
-zig, *dékm̥t
Aa, Aach, *h₂ekʷeh₂-
Aar, *h₃érō
Aas, *h₁ed-
ab, *h₂pó
Abend, *h₁epi
abgeben, *gʰebʰ-
Ablativ, *bher-
ablegen, *legh-
ablehnen, *ḱley-
abnehmen, *nem-
Achse, Achsel, *H₂eǵ-
acht, *oḱtṓw
Acker, *h₂éǵros
Adler, *h₃érō
Advent, *gʷem-
Adverb, Advokat, *wekʷ-
After, *h₂pó
agieren, Agon, Agonie, *H₂eǵ-
Ahnd, ahnden, *h₂enh₁-
Aktion, *H₂eǵ-
all, alt, Alter, *h₂el-
ambi-, ambient, *h₂ent
Ammer, *h₁ews-
Amt, *H₂eǵ-
And, *h₂enh₁-
Andacht, *teng-
ander, andere, *h₂énteros
Ange, Angel, *h₂enk-
angenehm, *nem-
Angst, *h₂enǵʰ-
animieren, *h₂enh₁-
anlegen, *legh-
anonym, *h₁nómn̥
antik, *h₂énti-h₃kʷós
Antwort, *wekʷ-
Apfel, *h₂ébōl
Apotheke, *dheH₁-
Appendix, *pewǵ-
Arbeit, arbeiten, *h₃erbʰ-
arktisch, *h₂r̥tḱos
Arm, *h₂er
Armt, *H₂eǵ-
Artikel, *h₂er
Asche, *h₂eh₁s-
Aspekt, *speḱ-
Äther, *h₂eydʰ-
ätzen, *h₁ed-

Auchte, *nókʷts
Audienz, *h₂ewis-dʰh₁-
Aue, *h₂ekʷeh₂-, *h₂ówis
auf, *upo
Auge, *h₃ekʷ-
August, *h₂ewg-
Auspizien, *speḱ-
autobahn, *gʷʰen-
Axt, *h₂éḱ
Bahn, *gʷʰen-
Bahre, *bher-
Bake, bannen, *bʰeh₂-
Bart, *bʰardʰeh₂-
Basis, *gʷem-
bauen, *bʰuH-
Bauke, *bʰeh₂-
be-, *h₁epi
bedecken, *(s)teg-
bedenken, *teng-
bei, *h₁epi
beißen, Beitel, Beize, *bʰeyd-
bekommen, *gʷem-
benedeien, *deyḱ-
benehmen, *nem-
bequem, *gʷem-
Berg, *bʰerǵʰ-
besetzen, *sed-
Beton, *gʷet-
bewegen, Bewegung, *weǵʰ-
Bibliothek, *dheH₁-
Biene, *bʰey-
bieten, *bʰewdʰ-
bin, *bʰuH-
Birke, *bʰereǵ-
bist, *bʰuH-
blähen, blasen, blaßen, blässen, Blast, *bʰleh₁-
Blatt, *bʰleh₃-
blätzen, *bʰleh₁-
bleiben, *leyp-
blühen, *bʰleh₁-
Blume, Blüte, *bʰleh₃-
Bock, *bʰuHgos-
Boden, *bʰudʰmḗn
Bohne, *bʰabʰeh₂-
bohnen, bohnern, *bʰeh₂-
Boot, *bʰeyd-
Born, *bʰrewh₁-
Bote, *bʰewdʰ-
bourgeois, *bʰerǵʰ-
brachial, *mréǵʰ-
Braue, *h₃bʰrúHs
brauen, *bʰrewh₁-
Bräutigam, *ǵʰmṓ
brennan, *bʰrewh₁-
Brief, *mréǵʰ-
brinnen, Brod, *bʰrewh₁-

Bruder, *bʰréh₂tēr
Brunn, Brunne, Brunnen, *bʰrewh₁-
Buch, Buche, Büche, *bʰeh₂go-
bude, *bʰuH-
Burg, *bʰerǵʰ-
Büro, *péh₂ur
Butter, *gʷṓws
Camp, Campus, Champion, *(s)teg-
da, *só
Dach, *(s)teg-
Dachs, *tetḱ-
Dame, *dem-
Dank, danken, *teng-
dann, dannen, dar, *só
Darm, *terh₁-
das, dass, *só
dauern, *deru-
Daune, *dʰewh₂-
Dechse, Dechsel, *tetḱ-
dehnen, *ten-
Dekade, Dekan, *déḱm̥t
deklamieren, deklarieren, *kelh₁-
Delikt, *leykʷ-
Delirium, *leys-
dement, Demenz, Demonstration, demonstrieren, *men-
denken, *teng-
denn, der, *só
Deutsch, *tewtéh₂
Dezember, *déḱm̥t
dichten, *deyḱ-
die, *só
Diet, *tewtéh₂
digital, Diktatur, Diktionär, *deyḱ-
direkt, dirigieren, *h₃reǵ-
Division, *h₁weydʰ
Doktor, Doktrin, *deḱ-
dolen, *telh₂-
Dom, Domina, *dem-
Donar, Donner, Donnerstag, *(s)tenh₂-
doppelt, *pleh₁-
Dorf, *treb-
dörren, *ters-
Drache, *h₃reǵ-
Draht, drehen, *terh₁-
drei, *tréyes
dreschen, *terh₁-
Drossel, *trosdos
du, *túh₂
dulden, *telh₂-
dünken, *teng-
Dunst, *dʰewh₂-
durch, *terh₂-
dürr, Durst, *ters-
Dust, *dʰewh₂-
Dutzend, *déḱm̥t
Ecke, *h₂éḱ
Ecker, *eh₃g-

Edikt, *deyḱ-
Egge, *h₂éḱ
Ehe, *h₂ey-
ehern, *h₂eyos
Ei, *h₂ōwyóm
Eiche, *h₂eyǵ-
eigen, eignen, *h₂eyḱ-
ein, einig, *óy-nos
einleuchten, *lewk-
Eis, *h₁eyH-
Eisen, Eiser, *h₁ésh₂r
Ekstase, *steh₂-
Element, Elend, *h₂el-
elf, *óy-nos
Ellbogen, Elle, Ellenbogen, *Heh₃l-
Elsass, *h₂el-
Eminenz, *men-
Ende, *h₂ent
eng, *h₂enǵʰ-
Engerling, *angʷ(h)i-
Enkel, *h₂enk-
enorm, *ǵneh₃-
entbehren, *bher-
Ente, *h₂eneti-
Enterich, *h₂eneti-, *h₃reǵ-
Enthusiasmus, *dʰéh₁s
epenthetisch, *dheH₁-
er, *éy / h₁e
erbären, *bher-
Erbe, *h₃erbʰ-
Erde, irden, *h₁er-
ergeben, *gʰebʰ-
erlaben, *lewh₃-
Erle, *h₃el-
erlegen, *legʰ-
erraten, *Hreh₁dʰ-
erwähnen, *wekʷ-
es, *éy / h₁e
Esche, *h₃es-
essen, *h₁ed-
Essenz, *H₁es-
etzen, *h₁ed-
Euter, *h₁owHdʰr
Eventualität, *gʷem-
ewig, *h₂ey-
Exkrement, *krey-
exportieren, *per-
Faden, *peth₂
fahl, *pelH-
fahnden, *pent-
Fahr, Fähre, fahren, Fahrt, Fährte, *per-
Faktum, *dheH₁-
falb, *pelH-
Familie, *dheH₁-
Farm, *per-
fassen, *ped-
Faust, *pewǵ-

Februar, *dʰegʷʰ-
fech, *peyḱ-
fechten, *peḱ-
Feder, *péth₂r
Feier, *dʰéh₁s
Feim, *poymno-
Feld, *pleh₂-
Fell, *pel-
feren, *per-
Ferien, *dʰéh₁s
Ferkel, *pórḱos
Fest, *dʰéh₁s
fest, *peh₂ǵ-
Fete, *dʰéh₁s
fetten, *peh₂-
Feuer, *péh₂ur
Fieber, *dʰegʷʰ-
Figur, *dʰeyǵʰ-
finden, *pent-
fingieren, *dʰeyǵʰ-
Finne, *spey-
Firmament, *dʰer-
Fisch, *peisḱ-
flechten, *pleḱ-
Fletz, *pleth₂-
Fliege, fliegen, fliehen, fließen, floaten, *plew-
Floh, *plou-
Flotte, *plew-
Flötz, *pleth₂-
Fluch, *pleh₂k-
Flucht, Flügel, *plew-
Flur, *pleh₂-
Flut, *plew-
Föhre, *perkʷu-
fora, *per-
Forsche, forschen, *preḱ-
Forst, *perkʷu-
Forum, *dʰwer-
Fracht, *h₂eyḱ-
fragen, *preḱ-
Frau, *per-
frei, freien, *preyH-
fressen, *h₁ed-
Freund, freundlich, Freundschaft, Friede, Friedel,
 Frieden, *preyH-
führen, *per-
füllen, *pleh₁-
Fundament, *bʰudʰmḗn
fünf, *pénkʷe
für, fürder, Fürst, Furt, *per-
Fuß, *pṓds
Futter, *peh₂-
Gabe, *gʰebʰ-
Galaxie, *glag-
Gans, *ǵʰans-
gären, *yes-
Garn, *ǵʰern-

garstig, *gʰers-
Garten, *ǵʰer-
Gäscht, *yes-
Gast, *gʰóstis
gebären, *bher-
geben, *gʰebʰ-
gebühren, *bher-
Geburt, *bher-
Gefahr, *per-
Geiss, geissen, *gʰaydos
Geist, *ǵʰeyzd-
gelb, *ǵʰelh₃-
gelingen, *h₁lengʷʰ-
gemein, *mey-
generieren, Genie, Genius, Genus, *ǵenH₁-
Gericht, *h₃reǵ-
gern, *ǵʰer-
Gerundium, *H₂eǵ-
gesalzen, *séh₂ls
geschehen, Geschichte, geschickt, *(s)kek-
gesen, *yes-
Gesicht, *sekʷ-
gestern, *dʰǵʰ(y)es-
gewähnen, *wekʷ-
gewahr, *wer-
Gewalt, *h₂welh₁-
gewesen, *H₁es-
Gewicht, *weǵh-
gewis, gewiss, *weyd-
Gewissen, *skey-
Gewurcht, *werǵ-
geziemen, *dem-
gicht, *yeǵ-
Gicht, *yek-
gießen, *ǵʰew-
Gift, *gʰebʰ-
Gischt, *yes-
Gold, *ǵʰelh₃-
Gott, *ǵʰew-
grammatik, *gerbʰ-
Gras, *gʰreh₁-
griechisch, *ǵerh₂-
grün, *gʰreh₁-
Gürtel, gürten, *ǵʰer-
Guru, *gʷerh₂-
Haat, *ḱeh₂d-
haben, *keh₂p-
Haber, Habergeiß, *kapro
Hachse, *koḱs-
Hafen, *keh₂p-
Hafer, *kapro
Haff, *keh₂p-
Hahn, *keh₂n-
Haken, *keg-
Halle, *ḱel-
Halm, *ḱalam-
Hammer, *h₂éḱ-mō

hantieren, *ḱei-
Haruspex, *ǵʰern-, *speḱ-
Hass, hassen, *ḱeh₂d-
Haupt, *kapōlo
hebig, *keh₂p-
Heer, heeren, *ker-
hehlen, *ḱel-
heil, heilen, heilig, heiligen, *kóh₂ilus
Heim, heimsen, *ḱei-
Helle, Helm, *ḱel-
Hengst, *kek-
Henne, *keh₂n-
Herberge, *ker-
Herbst, *kerp-
Herz, *ḱér
Herzog, *ker-
Hessen, *koḱs-
hetzen, *ḱeh₂d-
hie, hier, *ḱi-
hinauslehnen, *ḱley-
Hirn, Hirsch, *ḱerh₂-
Historie, *weyd-
hold, Holde, *ḱel-
holen, *kelh₁-
Hölle, *ḱel-
horchen, hören, *h₂ḱh₂owsyéti
hören, *ḱlew-
Horn, Hornisse, Hornissel, *ḱerh₂-
horrend, Horror, *gʰers-
Hospital, Hotel, *gʰóstis
Huhn, *keh₂n-
hüllen, Hülse, *ḱel-
Humus, *dʰéǵʰōm
Hund, *ḱwṓ
Hundert, *ḱm̥tóm
Hyäne, *suH-
Hypothek, *dheH₁-
ich, *egH₂
Idee, *weyd-
Idiot, *s(w)e-
Igel, *angʷ(h)i-
ignorant, ignorieren, *ǵneh₃-
ihr, *túh₂
illegal, *leǵ-, *legh-
Impetus, *peth₂
implizieren, *pleḱ-
importieren, *per-
in, *h₁én
infam, *bʰeh₂-
inhuman, *ǵʰmṓ
Institution, *steh₂-
Invention, *gʷem-
inzicht, *deyḱ-
ja, *éy / h₁e
Jäch, *yeǵ-
Jahr, *yeh₁-
Januar, *h₁ey-

jäsen, *yes-
je, *h₂ey-
jehen, *yek-
jesen, *yes-
Joch, *yugóm
Jugend, jung, Junge, Jüngling, *h₂yuh₁en-
Jura, Jus, Justiz, *h₂eyw-
Jux, *yek-
Kalender, *kelh₁-
kalt, *gel-
Kamera, *(s)teg-
Kamm, kämmen, *ǵómbʰos
Kamp, Kampf, *(s)teg-
kapieren, *keh₂p-
Kapital, Kapitel, *kapōlo
Karosserie, Karre, Karren, *ḱers-
Karte, *ǵʰer-
Kasse, *keh₂p-
keck, *gʷeyh₃-
Keller, *ḱel-
Kelter, *(s)kel-
kennen, *ǵneh₃-
kerben, *gerbʰ-
Kerl, *ǵerh₂-
kiesen, *ǵews-
Kind, *ǵenH₁-
Kinn, *ǵénus
Kitt, *gʷet-
klar, Klasse, *kelh₁-
Klausel, *(s)kel-
Klient, *ḱlew-
Klima, *ḱley-
Kloster, *(s)kel-
Knie, *ǵónu
Koch, kochen, *pekʷ-
Kollege, *legh-
kollektiv, *leǵ-
Kombination, *dwóH₁
kommen, *gʷem-
Kommentar, *men-
kommod, Kommode, *med-
Kommunikation, kommunizieren, *mey-
Kompendium, *pewǵ-
Kondition, *deyḱ-
Konditor, *dheH₁-
Konfession, *bʰeh₂-
Konfirmation, *dʰer-
Konfusion, *ǵʰew-
König, Königtum, *ǵenH₁-
können, *ǵneh₃-
konstruieren, *strew-
kontrovers, Kontroverse, konvertieren, *wert-
Korn, *ǵrHnom
Körper, *krep-
korrigieren, *h₃reǵ-
Kran, Kranich, *gerh₂-
Küche, *pekʷ-

Kuh, *gʷṓws
kühl, Kühle, *gel-
kühn, *ǵneh₃-
Kultur, *kʷel-
Kummerbund, *(s)teg-
kund, künden, *ǵneh₃-
Kunne, Künne, *ǵenH₁-
Kurs, *ḱers-
kurz, *(s)ker-
Kust, *ǵews-
laben, *lewh₃-
läg, Lager, *legh-
Land, länden, *lendʰ-
Latrine, *lewh₃-
Laub, Laube, *lewbʰ-
Lauge, *lewh₃-
Laune, *lewk-
Laus, *luHs-
laut, *ḱlew-
Leber, *leyp-
Lefze, *leb-
legen, *legh-
Legion, *leǵ-
Lehen, *leykʷ-
lehnen, *ḱley-
lehren, *leys-
leicht, *h₁lengʷʰ-
leihen, *leykʷ-
Lein, Leine, *lino-
leinen, *ḱley-
Leinen, *lino-
Leist, *leys-
Leiter, *ḱley-
Lektion, *leǵ-
Lende, Lenden, *lendʰ-
Lenz, *deyn-
lernen, *leys-
leuchten, *lewk-
Leumund, *ḱlew-
Leute, *h₁lewdʰ-
licht, Licht, *lewk-
lieb, Liebe, lieblich, liebling, *lewbʰ-
liegen, *legh-
lingen, *h₁lengʷʰ-
Linie, *lino-
Lippe, *leb-
List, *leys-
Lob, loben, *lewbʰ-
Loch, *seh₂g-
Löffel, *leb-
Logos, *leǵ-
Ludwig, *ḱlew-
Lug, *legh-
Lunge, Lungel, *lengʷʰ-
Magen, *mak-
mager, *meh₂ḱ-
Magister, *méǵh₂s

Mahl, *meh$_1$-

mahlen, Mahlstrom, *melh$_2$-

Mähne, *men-

Mahr, *mer-

Mähre, *marko-

Maisch, *mey-

mal, Mal, malen, *meh$_1$-

Malm, malmen, *melh$_2$-

man, *mánus

Manen, *meh$_2$-

Manifest, *g^{wh}en-

Mann, *mánus

Mark, *mosg^{h}os

Marsch, *móri

Marschall, *marko-

Maß, *med-

Master, *mégh$_2$s

Materie, *méh$_2$tēr

Matur, Matura, *meh$_2$-

Maus, *muh$_2$s-

Meer, *móri

Meerschwein, Meerschweinchen, *suH-

Mehl, *melh$_2$-

Mehltau, *melit-

mehr, *meh$_2$-

Meier, *mégh$_2$s

mein, *H$_1$meme-

meist, *meh$_2$-

Meister, *mégh$_2$s

melken, *H$_2$melg̑-

Meltau, *melit-

Mensch, *mánus

mental, *men-

messen, *med-

Met, *méd^{h}u

Metrum, *meh$_1$-

mich, *H$_1$me-

michel, *mégh$_2$s

Milch, *H$_2$melg̑-

Minister, *mey-

Minne, *men-

Minute, *mey-

mir, *H$_1$me-

mis-, mischen, Mischmasch, miss-, missen, *mey-

Missetat, *dheH$_1$-

Mist, *h$_3$meyg̑^{h}-

Mitte, *méd^{h}yos

mixen, *mey-

modern, modus, *med-

Monat, Mond, *méh$_1$n̥s

Monster, *men-

Montag, *méh$_1$n̥s

Montanunion, Monteur, montieren, *men-

Morast, *móri

Mord, mördern, *mer-

Morgengabe, *g^{h}eb^h-

Mücke, *mus-

mühlen, *melh$_2$-

Mund, *méh$_2$-r̥, *mend^h-

Mündel, *méh$_2$-r̥

Münne, *mey-

Munt, *méh$_2$-r̥

munter, Münze, münzen, *men-

murk, *mreg̑^{h}-

Muschel, Muskel, muskulär, *muh$_2$s-

Mutter, *méh$_2$tēr

Nabe, Nabel, *h$_3$enb^h-

Nachricht, Nachrichten, *h$_3$reg̑-

Nacht, *nók^{w}ts

Nachtigall, *nók^{w}ts

Nachtmahr, *mer-

nackend, nackt, *neg^w-

Nadel, *(s)neh$_1$-

Nagel, *h$_3$neg^h-

nähen, *(s)neh$_1$-

Name, *h$_1$nómn̥

Nase, *néh$_2$s

natara, Natter, *neHtr-

Nebel, nebulös, *neb^h-

Neffe, *nepot-

nehmen, *nem-

Nest, *nisdós

neu, *new

neun, *H$_1$néwn̥

Niere, *neg^{w}h-r-

Nift, Nifte, Niftel, *nepot-

Nisse, *knid-

nobel, *g̑neh$_3$-

nominal, *h$_1$nómn̥

Nord, *h$_1$én

normal, Note, notieren, *g̑neh$_3$-

nüchtern, *nók^{w}ts

Nummer, *nem-

ob, oben, ober, *upo

Oblate, *bher-

Obst, *h$_1$ed-

Ochse, *uksén

öde, *h$_2$ew

offiziell, *h$_3$ep-

Oheim, Ohm, *h$_2$éwh$_2$os

Ohr, *h$_2$ew-

Onkel, *h$_2$éwh$_2$os

Oostern, *h$_2$ews-

Orden, Order, ordern, ordinär, ordinieren, ordnen, Ordnung, Ordo, *h$_2$er

original, *h$_3$er-

Ort, *dheH$_1$-

Ost, Osten, *h$_2$ews-

Otter, *neHtr-, *udréh$_2$

Palaver, Parabel, *g^{w}elH-

Paradies, *d^{h}eyg̑^{h}-

Pass, Passus, *peth$_2$

Pastor, *peh$_2$-

patent, *peth$_2$

Patrimonium, Patriot, *ph₂tḗr
Pein, *kʷey-
Pensum, *pewǵ-
per, *per-
perfekt, *dheH₁-
Pfad, *pent-
Pfeil, *peys-
Pflanze, *pleh₂-
Pforte, *per-
Pfund, *pewǵ-
Phantom, *bʰeh₂-
Plan, Platz, *pleh₂-
Plural, *pleh₁-
Portikus, *per-
prädial, *wedʰ-
pragmatisch, *per-
Präsens, Präsentation, *H₁es-
Präsident, *sed-
Praxis, Preis, privat, pro, *per-
probat, Probe, proben, probieren, *bʰuH-
Problem, *gʷelH-
produktiv, *dewk-
Provinz, *per-
prüfen, *bʰuH-
Pulk, *pleh₁-
Punkt, *pewǵ-
quälen, Qualm, *gʷelH-
Quän, Queen, *gwḗn
quick, *gʷeyh₃-
rachen, *h₃reǵ-
Rad, *Hret-
radikal, *wréh₂ds
rank, *h₃reǵ-
raten, Rätsel, *Hreh₁dʰ-
rechen, rechnen, recht, Recht, recken, Regel, *h₃reǵ-
regenerieren, *ǵenH₁-
regieren, reich, *h₃reǵ-
Reim, *h₂er-
rein, *krey-
Relation, *bher-
rennen, *h₃er-, *h₃reyH-
repetieren, *peth₂
Republik, Respublica, *pleh₁-
Revolution, *welH-
Rezeption, *keh₂p-
Rhema, *wekʷ-
Rhythmus, *srew-
richten, *h₃reǵ-
rinnen, *h₃er-, *h₃reyH-
Rocken, Roggen, *wrugʰyo-
roh, *krewh₂-
Rolle, *Hret-
Ross, *ḱers-
rot, röten, Rubin, Rubrik, *h₁rewdʰ-
rund, *Hret-
Saat, *seH₁-
Sache, *seh₂g-

Sachs, *sek-
säen, *seH₁-
Säge, *sek-
Sage, sagen, *sekʷ-
Salz, salzen, *séh₂ls
Same, Samen, *seH₁-
Sattel, satteln, satul, *sed-
Sau, *suH-
Saum, *sīw-
Schädel, *skey-
Schar, scharf, Scharte, *(s)ker-
scheiden, Scheiße, scheißen, Scheit, Scheitel, *skey-
Schema, *seǵʰ-
scheren, *(s)ker-
schicken, *(s)kek-
schielen, *(s)kel-
schikanieren, *(s)kek-
Schirm, schirmen, *(s)ker-
Schiss, *skey-
Schlaf, schlafen, *leb-
schließen, Schlüssel, *(s)kel-
Schnee, schneien, *sneygʷʰ-
Schnur, *snusós
schrappen, schreiben, *(s)ker-
Schule, *seǵʰ-
Schurz, *(s)ker-
Schuster, *sīw-
Schwein, *suH-
Schweiss, *sweyd-
Schwester, *swésōr
schwitzen, *sweyd-
sechs, *swéḱs
Sediment, *sed-
segnen, *sek-
sehen, *sekʷ-
Sehne, *(s)neh₁-
sein, *bʰuH-, *H₁es-, *s(w)e-
selb, selber, selbst, *s(w)e-
Senat, *sénos
senden, *sent-
Sense, *sek-
September, *septṃ
Serum, *srew-
setzen, *sed-
sich, *s(w)e-
Sicht, *sekʷ-
sie, *éy / h₁e
sieben, *septṃ
Sieg, *seǵʰ-
Siegel, *sek-
simpel, *pleḱ-, *sem-
singulär, *sem-
Sinn, sinnen, *sent-
Situation, situieren, *teḱ-
sitzen, *sed-
Ski, *skey-
so, *s(w)e-

Sohn, *suh₁nús

solch, *s(w)e-

sold, *solh₂-

Sommer, *sm̥-h₂-ó-

Sonne, Sonntag, *sóh₂wl̥

Soße, *séh₂ls

Souffleur, *bʰleh₁-

sozial, *sekʷ-

spähen, *speḱ-

Spaß, *peth₂

Speiche, Spell, *spey-

spenden, *pewǵ-

Sperling, *spēr

Spezies, Spiegel, *speḱ-

Spier, Spieß, *spey-

Spital, *gʰóstis

Spitze, *spey-

spuden, Sput, sputen, *speh₁-

Stadt, *steh₂-

Stall, *stel-

stān, *steh₂-

Star, *h₂stḗr

Starke, Stärke, *(s)táwros

Stasis, Statt, Status, *steh₂-

staunen, *(s)tenh₂-

stehen, *steh₂-

Steige, steigen, *steygʰ-

Stelle, stellen, *stel-

Sterk, *(s)táwros

Stern, *h₂stḗr

Stiegel, *steygʰ-

Stier, *(s)táwros

still, stillen, *stel-

Stock, *(s)tew-

stöhnen, *(s)tenh₂-

stoßen, *(s)tew-

Straße, *sterh₃-

streuen, *strew-

Strom, *srew-

Stuck, Stück, Student, studieren, *(s)tew-

Stunde, Stute, *steh₂-

subtil, *tetḱ-

Suche, suchen, *seh₂g-

Süd, Süden, *sóh₂wl̥

Sulze, Sülze, *séh₂ls

Summe, *upo

summige, *sem-

Sünde, *H₁es-

superb, *bʰuH-, *upo

Supinum, *upo

Synagoge, *H₂eǵ-

Synonym, Synonymum, *h₁nómn̥

Tag, tagen, *dʰegʷʰ-

Tandem, *só

tarnen, *dʰer-

Tat, *dheH₁-

Tau, *dʰewh₂-

Taufe, taufen, *dʰewb-

Team, *dewk-

Teig, *dʰeyǵʰ-

territorial, Territorium, *ters-

teuer, *dʰegʷʰ-

Teufel, *gʷelH

Thema, *dheH₁-

Theoderich, Thibaut, *tewtéh₂

thüren, *dʰers-

tief, *dʰewb-

toben, *dʰewh₂-

Tochter, *dʰugh₂tḗr

Tor, *dʰwer-

Tradition, *deH₃-

Tran, Träne, *daḱru-

Translation, *bher-

Treue, *deru-

tun, *dheH₁-

Tür, *dʰwer-

türen, *dʰers-

Typ, typisch, *(s)tew-

U-bahn, *gʷʰen-

Uchte, *nókʷts

Uhr, *yeh₁-

um, umb, *h₂ent

un-, *n̥-

und, *h₂ent

ungewiss, *weyd-

unhold, Unhold, *ḱel-

uns, *wei

unter, *h₁én

Vater, *ph₂tḗr

Verb, Verbum, *wekʷ-

verdrießen, *trewd-

verfahren, *per-

vergeben, *gʰebʰ-

vergessen, *weyd-

Verifikation, *weh₁-

vernehmen, *nem-

verwaisen, *h₁weydʰ

verwalten, verwalter, *h₂welh₁-

verweisen, *weyd-

Viech, Vieh, *peḱu-

viel, *pleh₁-

vier, *kʷetwóres

Vision, *weyd-

vital, *gʷeyh₃-

Vogt, Vokabel, vokal, Vokal, *wekʷ-

Volk, voll, *pleh₁-

von, *h₂pó

vor, *per-

Vormund, *méh₂-r̥

wachsen, *h₂ewg-

Wacht, Wächter, wacker, *weǵ-

Wagen, wägen, Waggon, *weǵʰ-

wählen, *welh₁-

wahr, Wahrheit, *weh₁-

Waise, *h₁weydʰ
Wall, *welH-
walten, *h₂welh₁-
Walver, walzen, *welH-
war, *H₁es-
warm, wärmen, *gʷʰer-
Wart, Warte, *wer-
was, *kʷis
waschen, Wasser, *wed-
weben, *webh-
wecken, *weǵ-
weder, *kʷis
Weer, *wet-
Weg, *weǵh-
wehen, *H₂weH₁-
weich, *kʷis
Weich, *weyḱ-
Weide, weiden, *weyh₁-
weih-, *weyk-
Weih, Weihe, *weyh₁-
weihen, Weihnachten, Weihrauch, *weyk-
Weile, *kʷyeh₁-
Weiler, *weyḱ-
Wein, *wóyh₁nom
weise, weisen, Weistum, *weyd-
Welt, *h₂el-
Welt, *wiHrós
wer, *kʷis
werden, *wert-
Werk, *werǵ-
wert, Wert, *wert-
Werwolf, *wiHrós
Wespe, *wobs-
west, West, Westen, *wek(ʷ)speros
Wette, wetten, *wedʰ-
Wicht, *weǵh-
Widder, *wet-
wie, *kʷis
wiegen, *weǵh-
Wiele, *kʷel-
wijs, *weyd-
Wille, *welh₁-
wimmen, *wóyh₁nom
Wind, *H₂weH₁-
wir, *wei
wirken, *werǵ-
wis, wissen, Wissen, *weyd-
Wittum, *wedʰ-
Witwe, *h₁weydʰ
wo, *kʷis
Woche, *weyk-
Wohltat, *dheH₁-
Wolf, *wĺkʷos
Wolle, wollen, *h₂welh₁-
wollen, *welh₁-
Wort, *wekʷ-
Wurm, *wŕmis-

Wurst, *wert-
Wurz, *wréh₂ds
Wurzel, *welH-, *wréh₂ds
wüst, Wüste, *h₁weh₂-
zahm, zähmen, *demh₂-
Zahn, *h₃dónts
Zähre, *daḱru-
Zaum, *dewk-
Zeh, Zehe, *deyḱ-
zehn, *déḱmt
zehren, *der-
Zeit, *deh₂-
Zentner, Zenturie, *ḱmtóm
zermalmen, *melh₂-
zese, *deḱs-
Ziegel, *(s)teg-
ziehen, *deyḱ-
ziemen, ziemlich, Zimmer, *dem-
Zog, *dewk-
Zorn, *der-
Zug, Zügel, *dewk-
Zunft, *dem-
Zunge, *dn̥ǵʰwéh₂s
zwanzig, *déḱmt
zwei, Zwilling, zwo, zwölf, *dwóH₁

Norse

-kundr, *ǵenH₁-
-tigr, *dékm̥t
-varðr, *wert-
af, *h₂pó
afl, *h₃ep-
afleggja, *legh-
afli, *h₃ep-
aka, *H₂eǵ-
akarn, *eh₃g-
akr, *h₂éǵros
ala, *h₂el-
albogi, *Heh₃l-
aldr, *h₂el-
alin, *Heh₃l-
allr, *h₂el-
alnbogi, *Heh₃l-
alr, *h₃el-
alvara, alværð, *weh₁-
ambátt, ambótt, *H₂eǵ-
anarr, *h₂énteros
anda, andi, *h₂enh₁-
andyrði, *wekʷ-
angi, *h₂enh₁-, *h₂enk-
angist, *h₂enǵʰ-
angr, *h₂enǵʰ-
aptann, *h₁epi
aptr, *h₂pó
arðr, *H₂erH₃-
arfi, arfr, *h₃erbʰ-
ari, *h₃érō
armr, *h₂er
aska, *h₂eh₁s-
askr, *h₃es-
atti, *átta
auðr, *h₂ew
auga, *h₃ekʷ-
auka, *h₂ewg-
austan, *h₂ews-
austr, austrœnn, *h₂ews-
á, *h₂ekʷeh₂-
ál, áll, *h₂enk-
ár, *yeh₁-
átt, *h₂eyḱ-
átta, *oḱtṓw
bani, *gʷʰen-
banna, *bʰeh₂-
barar, *bher-
barðr, *bʰardʰeh₂-
barir, barn, *bher-
barr, *bʰars-
baun, *bʰabʰeh₂-
bákn, *bʰeh₂-
bára, *bher-

bátr, beiða, *bʰeydʰ-
beit, *bʰeyd-
ben, *gʷʰen-
bera, *bher-
berg, *bʰerǵʰ-
berserkr, *ser-
bíða, *bʰeydʰ-
bíta, *bʰeyd-
bjarg, *bʰerǵʰ-
bjarkan, bjǫrk, *bʰereǵ-
bjóða, *bʰewdʰ-
blað, *bʰleh₃-
blása, blástr, *bʰleh₁-
blóm, blómi, *bʰleh₃-
boð, boða, *bʰewdʰ-
bœn, *bʰeh₂-
bok, *bʰeh₂go-
bokki, bokkr, *bʰuHgos-
borg, *bʰerǵʰ-
botn, *bʰudʰmḗn
bók, *bʰeh₂go-
bón, *bʰeh₂-
bragr, *bʰerǵʰ-
brenna, *bʰrewh₁-
bréf, *mréǵʰ-
brinna, broð, *bʰrewh₁-
bróðir, *bʰréh₂tēr
brunnr, *bʰrewh₁-
brún, *h₃bʰrúHs
bukkr, *bʰuHgos-
búa, búð, búinn, *bʰuH-
byrð, byrja, *bher-
bý, *bʰey-
býsn, *bʰewdʰ-
daga, dagr, *dʰegʷʰ-
daunn, *dʰewh₂-
dáð, *dheH₁-
deig, deigr, *dʰeyǵʰ-
deypa, *dʰewb-
digr, *dʰeyǵʰ-
dikt, *deyḱ-
djúpr, *dʰewb-
dœma, *dheH₁-
dǫgg, *dʰewh₂-
dǫgr, *dʰegʷʰ-
dómr, *dheH₁-
dóttir, *dʰugh₂tḗr
dust, dúnn, *dʰewh₂-
dvína, *dʰegʷʰ-
dyrr, *dʰwer-
dýpð, dýpt, *dʰewb-
dýrð, dýrr, *dʰegʷʰ-
ðorp, *treb-
efna, efni, *h₃ep-
egg, *h₂éḱ, *h₂ōwyóm
ei, *h₂ey-
eik, *h₂eyǵ-

eikna, *h₃reǵ-
eimyrja, *h₁ews-
einigr, einn, *óy-nos
eir, *h₂eyos
ek, *egH₂
ekkja, *h₂enk-
eldr, *h₂eydʰ-
ella, elli, *h₂el-
ellifu, *óy-nos
ellri, *h₂el-
eln, *Heh₃l-
elztr, *h₂el-
embætta, *H₂eǵ-
enn, *h₂ent
epli, *h₂ébōl
eptir, *h₂pó
er, *éy / h₁e
erfi, erfiði, *h₃erbʰ-
erja, *H₂erH₃-
es, *éy / h₁e
eta, etja, *h₁ed-
ey, *h₂ekʷeh₂-
ey, *h₂ey-
eyða, *h₂ew
eykr, *yewg-
eyland, *h₂ekʷeh₂-
eyra, *h₂ew-
ér, *túh₂
faðir, *phₐtḗr
faðmr, *peth₂
far, fara, farmr, *per-
fastr, *peh₂ǵ-
fata, *ped-
fax, *peḱ-
fá, *peyḱ-
feldr, fell, *pel-
ferð, ferja, *per-
fet, feta, *ped-
fé, *peḱu-
fimm, *pénkʷe
finna, *pent-
fiskr, *peisḱ-
fjall, *pel-
fjǫðr, *péth₂r
fjǫl-, *pleh₁-
fjǫrðr, *per-
fjǫrr, *perkʷu-
fjǫturr, *ped-
fjórir, *kʷetwóres
flaga, *pleh₂-
flatr, *pleth₂-
flaumr, *plew-
fleiri, *pleh₁-
flengja, *pleh₂k-
flestr, *pleh₁-
flet, *pleth₂-
fley, fleygja, *plew-

flétta, *pleḱ-
fljóta, fljúga, flot, flota, floti, *plew-
fló, *plou-
flóð, flóðr, *plew-
flókinn, *pleh₂k-
flórr, *pleh₂-
fluga, flytja, flýja, *plew-
fœða, *peh₂-
fœra, fœrr, *per-
fold, *pleth₂-
folk, *pleh₁-
fǫlr, *pelH-
fors, foss, *pers-
fóðr, *peh₂-
fólk, *pleh₁-
fótr, *pṓds
fram, frá, *per-
fregna, *preḱ-
fremja, freyja, Freyr, *per-
friðill, friðla, friðr, frilla, frjá, frjáls, frjándi, *preyH-
frú, *per-
frýniligr, frýnligr, frændi, *preyH-
fullr, *pleh₁-
fundr, *pent-
funi, *péh₂ur
fura, *perkʷu-
fúrr, *péh₂ur
fylki, fylkja, fylla, fylli, *pleh₁-
fyndr, *pent-
fyrir, *per-
fyrirdœma, *dheH₁-
fyrirgefa, *gʰebʰ-
fyrri, fyrst, fyrster, *per-
fýr, *péh₂ur
fýri, *perkʷu-
fýrir, *péh₂ur
fær, *peḱ-
garðr, *ǵʰer-
garn, *ǵʰern-
gáfa, *gʰebʰ-
gás, *ǵʰans-
gefa, *gʰebʰ-
geit, *gʰaydos
gersta, *gʰers-
gestr, *gʰóstis
geta, *weyd-
gipt, *gʰebʰ-
gjarn, *ǵʰer-
gjǫf, *gʰebʰ-
gjǫrð, *ǵʰer-
gjóta, *ǵʰew-
gnit, *knid-
goð, *ǵʰew-
goll, *ǵʰelh₃-
gǫrn, *ǵʰern-
gras, grœnn, gróa, grónn, *gʰreh₁-
guð, *ǵʰew-

guðr, *gʷʰen-
gull, gulr, *ǵʰelh₃-
gumi, *ǵʰmṓ
gunnr, *gʷʰen-
gyrða, gyrðill, *ǵʰer-
gæfr, *gʰebʰ-
haf, hafa, *keh₂p-
hafr, hafri, *kapro
haki, *keg-
hallr, *kelH-
halmr, *ḱalam-
hamarr, *h₂éḱ-mō
hani, *keh₂n-
haptr, *keh₂p-
hata, hatr, *ḱeh₂d-
haufuð, *kapōlo
haust, haustr, *kerp-
há, hásin, *kenk-
heðra, *ḱi-
heila, heilagr, heill, *kóh₂ilus
heim, heimr, heimta, *ḱei-
hel, *ḱel-
helga, *kóh₂ilus
herbergi, herja, herjan, herr, hertogi, *ker-
hestr, *kek-
heyra, *h₂ḱh₂owsyéti
hér, hit, *ḱi-
hjalmr, *ḱel-
hjarni, *ḱerh₂-
hjarta, *ḱḗr
hjól, *kʷel-
hlaiwa, hlíð, *ḱley-
hljóðr, hljómr, *ḱlew-
hlóa, *kelh₁-
hœkja, *keg-
hœna, *keh₂n-
hǫfigr, hǫfn, *keh₂p-
hǫfuð, *kapōlo
hǫfugr, *keh₂p-
hǫll, hollr, *ḱel-
hǫnk, *keg-
horn, *ḱerh₂-
horskr, *ḱers-
hrár, *krewh₂-
hreinn, hreinsa, hrina, *krey-
hross, *ḱers-
hræ, *krewh₂-
hundr, *ḱwṓ
hundrað, *ḱm̥tóm
hvaðarr, hvar, hvat, hvárr, hverr, hvé, *kʷis
hvila, *kʷyeh₁-
hvilikr, hví, *kʷis
hylja, *ḱel-
hyrna, *ḱerh₂-
hæll, *kenk-
i, *h₁én
iss, *h₁eyH-

í gær, *dʰǵʰ(y)es-
ígull, *angʷ(h)i-
ísarn, *h₁ésh₂r̥
jak, *egH₂
jaki, *yeǵ-
jarn, *h₁ésh₂r̥
já, *éy / h₁e
járn, *h₁ésh₂r̥
jǫkull, *yeǵ-
jǫrð, *h₁er-
jǫstr, *yes-
jǫtunn, *h₁ed-
jór, jóreið, *h₁éḱwos
júgr, *h₁owHdʰr̥-
jurt, *wréh₂ds
kala, kaldr, *gel-
kambr, *ǵómbʰos
karl, *ǵerh₂-
kemba, *ǵómbʰos
kenna, *ǵneh₃-
kind, *ǵenH₁-
kinn, *ǵénus
kjósa, *ǵews-
kná, *ǵneh₃-
kné, *ǵónu
kœnn, *ǵneh₃-
koma, *gʷem-
kona, *gwén
kongr, konungdómr, konungr, *ǵenH₁-
korn, *ǵr̥Hnom
kostr, *ǵews-
kó, *gʷṓws
kólna, *gel-
kunna, kunnr, *ǵneh₃-
kú, *gʷṓws
kváða, *gʷet-
kván, *gwén
kvelja, *gʷelH-
kvenna, *gwén
kvern, *gʷrh₂-n-uH-
kvikna, kvikr, *gʷeyh₃-
kvinna, kvæn, *gwén
kyn, *ǵenH₁-
kynna, *ǵneh₃-
kýr, *gʷṓws
lag, *legʰ-
land, *lendʰ-
landreki, *h₃reǵ-
langvé, *weyh₁-
lauðr, *lewh₃-
lauf, *lewbʰ-
laug, *lewh₃-
lá, *lókus
lágr, *legʰ-
lán, *leykʷ-
leggja, legr, *legʰ-
leifa, *leyp-

leiga, leigja, *leykʷ-

lend, lenda, *lendʰ-

lepja, *leb-

leygr, *lewk-

léa, lén, *leykʷ-

léttr, *h₁lengʷʰ-

lifr, *leyp-

liggja, *legʰ-

list, *leys-

lín, lína, *lino-

ljá, *leykʷ-

ljóðr, *h₁lewdʰ-

ljóma, ljómi, ljós, ljóss, ljótr, Ljótr, *lewk-

ljúfr, *lewbʰ-

loðinn, *h₁lewdʰ-

lof, lofa, *lewbʰ-

lǫg, *legʰ-

lǫgr, *lókus

lok, *seh₂g-

lóg, *legʰ-

lúka, *seh₂g-

lús, *luHs-

læra, *leys-

maðr, *mánus

magi, *mak-

magr, *meh₂ḱ-

makki, *men-

mala, malmr, *melh₂-

man, *men-

mara, *mer-

marr, *marko-, *móri

marsvin, *suH-

maurr, *morwi-

mál, *meh₁-

mánadagr, mánaðr, máni, *méh₁ṇs

meina, *bʰeyd-

meiri, *meh₂-

men, *men-

mennskr, *mánus

mergr, *mosgʰos

merr, *marko-

mestr, *meh₂-

meta, *med-

mér, *H₁me-

miðr, *médʰyos

mik, *H₁me-

mikill, *méǵh₂s

minn, *H₁meme-

minni, *men-, *mey-

minnr, mis-, missa, *mey-

míga, *h₃meyǵʰ-

mjǫðr, *médʰu

mjǫl, *melh₂-

mjǫlk, mjólka, *H₂melǵ-

mœna, mœnir, mǫn, *men-

morð, *mer-

móðir, *méh₂tēr

muðr, *mendʰ-

muna, *men-

mund, *méh₂-r̥

munda, munr, *men-

mús, *muh₂s-

mylja, *melh₂-

mý, *mus-

naðr, naðra, *neHtr-

nafli, *h₃enbʰ-

nafn, *h₁nómṇ

nagl, *h₃neg-

nakinn, *negʷ-

nál, *(s)neh₁-

nátt, *nókʷts

nefi, *nepot-

negl, *h₃neg-

nema, *nem-

niðr, *nepot-

niflhel, *nebʰ-

nipt, *nepot-

níu, *H₁néwṇ

nǫf, *h₃enbʰ-

norðan, norðr, norrœnn, *h₁én

nǫs, *néh₂s

nór, *(s)neh₁-

nótt, nǫtt, *nókʷts

nýr, *new

oddi, oddr, *dheH₁-

œll, *h₂el-

œsa, *yes-

of, ofan, ofr-, *upo

ok, *yugóm

ǫl, *h₂elut-

ǫlbogi, *Heh₃l-

ǫld, *h₂el-

ǫln, ǫlnbogi, *Heh₃l-

ǫnd, *h₂eneti-, *h₂enh₁-

ǫngr, *h₂enǵʰ-

ǫngull, *h₂enk-

ǫr, *h₂erkʷo-

orð, *wekʷ-

ǫrk, *h₂erk-

orka, *werǵ-

ormr, *wr̥mis-

ǫrn, *h₃érō

ǫrvar, *h₂erkʷo-

otr, *udréh₂

oxi, *uksén

ǫxl, *H₂eǵ-

ó-, *ṇ-

ól, óll, *h₂enk-

ómr, ómun, *wekʷ-

óss, *h₃éh₁os

ótta, *nókʷts

rakkr, *h₃reǵ-

rauðr, *h₁rewdʰ-

ráða, *Hreh₁dʰ-

361

rekja, *$h_3$reǵ-
renna, *$h_3$er-, *$h_3$reyH-
rétta, réttr, riki, *$h_3$reǵ-
rinna, *$h_3$er-, *$h_3$reyH-
ríkr, *$h_3$reǵ-
rím, *$h_2$er
rǫð, *Hreh₁dʰ-
roða, *h₁rewdʰ-
rǫðull, *Hret-
rœða, *Hreh₁dʰ-
rót, *wréh₂ds
rugr, *wrugʰyo-
saðr, *H₁es-
saga, *sekʷ-
salt, salta, saltr, *séh₂ls
samr, *sem-
sannan, sannr, *H₁es-
sannsǫgull, *sekʷ-
saumr, *sīw-
sax, *sek-
sá, *seH₁-, *só
sáð, sáld, *seH₁-
sátt, *seh₂g-
seggr, segja, *sekʷ-
semja, *sem-
senda, *sent-
serkr, *ser-
sess, setja, *sed-
sex, *swéḱs
séa, *sekʷ-
sér, *s(w)e-
sigr, sigra, *seǵʰ-
sik, *s(w)e-
simul, *sem-
sinn, *s(w)e-
sinna, *sent-
sitja, *sed-
sjalfr, *s(w)e-
sjau, *septṃ
sjá, sjón, *sekʷ-
skaka, *(s)kek-
skarð, skari, skarpr, skera, *(s)ker-
skikka, *(s)kek-
skitr, skíð, skíta, *skey-
skor, skǫr, skortr, skrap, skrapa, skrifa, skyrta, *(s)ker-
slikr, *s(w)e-
snjáfa, snjófa, snjór, *sneygʷʰ-
snor, *snusós
snær, *sneygʷʰ-
snør, *snusós
sǫðla, sǫðull, *sed-
sœkja, *seh₂g-
sofa, *swep-
sǫg, *sek-
sǫk, *seh₂g-
sǫnnun, *H₁es-
sonr, *suh₁nús

sókn, *seh₂g-
sól, *sóh₂wļ
spá, speja, *speḱ-
spikr, spira, *spey-
spǫrr, *spér
staðr, *steh₂-
stallr, *stel-
standa, staurr, *steh₂-
stétt, stéttr, *steygʰ-
stilla, *stel-
stíga, *steygʰ-
stjarna, *h₂stér
stjórr, *(s)táwros
stjúpbarn, *bher-
stǫð, *steh₂-
stokkr, *(s)tew-
stó, stórr, *steh₂-
straumr, *srew-
strá, *strew-
stræti, *sterh₃-
stund, *steh₂-
stykki, *(s)tew-
stynja, *(s)tenh₂-
suðr, suðrœnn, *sóh₂wļ
sumar, *sṃ-h₂-ó-
sumr, *sem-
sunna, sunnan, sunnudagr, *sóh₂wļ
sunr, *suh₁nús
svá, *s(w)e-
svefja, svefn, *swep-
sveiti, *sweyd-
svín, *suH-
syn, synd, synja, *H₁es-
systir, *swésōr
sýja, *sīw-
sýn, *sekʷ-
sýr, *suH-
sæði, *seH₁-
sætt, *seh₂g-
sørvi, *ser-
tafn, *deh₂-
tamr, *demh₂-
tapa, *deh₂-
tarfr, *(s)táwros
taug, taumr, *dewk-
tá, *deyḱ-
tár, *daḱru-
temja, *demh₂-
teygja, *dewk-
timbr, *dem-
tíð, tíðr, *deh₂-
tíu, *déḱṃt
tívar, *dyew-
tjara, *dóru-
tjá, *deyḱ-
tog, togi, *dewk-
tomt, *dem-

tǫnn, *h₃dónts

topt, *dem-

toskr, *h₃dónts

tólf, *dwóH₁

trana, trani, *gerh₂-

tré, *dóru

trú, tryggð, tryggr, *deru-

tuft, *dem-

tunga, *dn̥ǵʰwéh₂s

tupt, *dem-

tuttugu, *dékm̥t

tveir, tvi-, tvinnr, *dwóH₁

tygill, *dewk-

Týr, týsdagr, *dyew-

ull, *h₂welh₁-

um, umb, *h₂ent

unglingr, ungr, *h₂yuh₁en-

upp, uppi, *upo

urðr, *wert-

urt, *wréh₂ds

usli, *h₁ews-

uxi, *uksḗn

ú-, *n̥-

úkunnr, *ǵneh₃-

úlfr, *wl̥kʷos

úviss, *weyd-

vagn, *weǵh-

vakinn, vakr, vakta, *weǵ-

vald, valda, *h₂welh₁-

vana, vanta, *h₁weh₂-

varða, *wer-

varmr, *gʷʰer-

varr, *wer-

vaska, vatn, *wed-

vaxa, *h₂ewg-

váfa, *webh-

vár, *wésr̥

vátr, *wed-

váttr, *wekʷ-

veð, veðja, *wedʰ-

veðr, *wet-

vefja, vefr, *webh-

vega, *weǵh-, *weyk-

vegr, *weǵh-

veiða, veiði, *weyh₁-

vekja, *weǵ-

velja, *welh₁-

verð, verða, verða, verðr, *wert-

verja, *wes-

verk, *werǵ-

verma, *gʷʰer-

verǫld, *h₂el-, *wiHrós

verr, *wiHrós

ves heill, vesa/vera, *H₁es-

vestan, vestr, vestrœnn, *wek(ʷ)speros

vé, *weyk-

vér, *wei

vétr, véttr, *weǵh-

vig, viga, vigja, vika, *weyk-

vili, vilja, *welh₁-

vindauga, *h₃ekʷ-

vindr, *H₂weH₁-

virkja, *werǵ-

virtr, *wréh₂ds

vist, *H₁es-

vit, *wei

vitr, *weyd-

vín, *wóyh₁nom

vísdómr, víss, víta, *weyd-

vǫlr, *welH-

vǫrðr, *wer-

vǫxtr, *h₂ewg-

værr, *weh₁-

væta, *wed-

vætr, vættr, *weǵh-

ylgr, *wl̥kʷos

yrja, *h₁ews-

yrkja, *werǵ-

þak, *(s)teg-

þakka, *teng-

þanan, þar, *só

þarmr, *terh₁-

þá, *só

þekja, *(s)teg-

þekkja, *teng-

þenja, *ten-

þenkja, *teng-

þerra, *ters-

þexla, *tetḱ-

þér, *túh₂

þjóð, þjóðann, *tewtéh₂

þjórr, *(s)táwros

þǫkk, *teng-

þola, *telh₂-

þorp, *treb-

þorsti, *ters-

þǫx, *tetḱ-

þórr, þórsdagr, *(s)tenh₂-

þótti, þóttr, *teng-

þraut, *trewd-

þráðr, þreskja, *terh₁-

þreyta, *trewd-

þrí-, þrír, *tréyes

þrjóta, *trewd-

þrǫstr, *trosdos

þurr, *ters-

þú, *túh₂

þykkja, *teng-

þær, *só

æ, *h₂ey-

ǽr, *h₂ówis

ætt, *h₂eyḱ-

øx, *h₂éḱ-

Norwegian

-son, *suh₁nús
abort, *h₃er-
administrasjon, *mey-
aften, *h₁epi
aka, *H₂eǵ-
aker, *h₂éǵros
ala, *h₂el-
albue, *Heh₃l-
alder, *h₂el-
alen, *Heh₃l-
all, alt, *h₂el-
alvor, *weh₁-
ambassade, *H₂eǵ-
and, *h₂eneti-
angst, *h₂enǵʰ-
ankel, *h₂enk-
annen, *h₂énteros
anonym, *h₁nómn̥
arbeid, arbeide, *h₃erbʰ-
ard, *H₂erH₃-
ark, *h₂erk-
ask, *h₃es-
aske, *h₂eh₁s-
atter, *h₂pó
aud, *h₂ew
august, *h₂ewg-
aust, *h₂ews-
av, *h₂pó
avi, *h₃ep-
bane, *gʷʰen-
banne, *bʰeh₂-
bar, *bʰars-
barn, *bher-
bart, *bʰardʰeh₂-
base, *gʷem-
be-, *h₁epi
beita, beitel, *bʰeyd-
bekomme, *gʷem-
ben, *gʷʰen-
berg, *bʰerǵʰ-
besette, besitte, *sed-
bie, *bʰey-, *bʰeydʰ-
bisn, *bʰewdʰ-
bite, *bʰeyd-
bjerk, bjørk, *bʰereǵ-
blad, *bʰleh₃-
bli, blive, *leyp-
blome, *bʰleh₃-
blåse, blåst, *bʰleh₁-
bo, *bʰuH-
bokk, *bʰuHgos-
borg, *bʰerǵʰ-
brenne, *bʰrewh₁-

brev, *mréǵʰ-
broder, bror, *bʰréh₂tēr
brun, *h₃bʰrúHs
brygge, bryggja, brønn, *bʰrewh₁-
bu, *bʰuH-
bud, *bʰewdʰ-
buen, *bʰuH-
bukk, *bʰuHgos-
bunn, *bʰudʰmḗn
by, byde, *bʰewdʰ-
byrja, byrje, bære, *bher-
bøk, *bʰeh₂go-
bønn, *bʰeh₂-
bønne, *bʰabʰeh₂-
båk, båke, *bʰeh₂-
båre, *bher-
båt, *bʰeyd-
centimeter, *ḱm̥tóm
dage, *dʰegʷʰ-
datter, *dʰugh₂tḗr
debitor, *gʰeh₁bʰ-
deig, *dʰeyǵʰ-
dekade, *déḱm̥t
deklarere, *kelh₁-
delirium, *leys-
den, der, *só
dere, *túh₂
det, *só
dikt, *deyḱ-
dille, *leys-
djevel, *gʷelH-
dogme, doktor, *deḱ-
dom, *dʰeH₁-
dotter, *dʰugh₂tḗr
dreie, *terh₁-
du, *túh₂
dugg, dun, dust, *dʰewh₂-
dybde, dyp, *dʰewb-
dyr, døgn, *dʰegʷʰ-
dømme, *dheH₁-
døpe, *dʰewb-
dør, *dʰwer-
då, *só
dåd, effekt, *dheH₁-
efter, *h₂pó
egg, *h₂éḱ, *h₂ōwyóm
eie, *h₂eyḱ-
eik, *h₂eyǵ-
ekstern, *h₁eǵʰs
elda, elde, eldre, eldst, eller, *h₂el-
elleve, *óy-nos
emne, *h₃ep-
en, *óy-nos
enn, *h₂ent
enorm, *ǵneh₃-
eple, *h₂ébōl
eta, ete, *h₁ed-

eter, $*h_2eyd^h$-
etter, $*h_2pó$
evidens, *weyd-
evne, $*h_3ep$-
fader, $*ph_2tḗr$
faen, *pent-
faks, *peḱ-
famn, $*peth_2$
fanden, *pent-
fantom, $*b^heh_2$-
far, $*ph_2tḗr$
fara, fare, fare, farm, *per-
fast, $*peh_2ǵ$-
fatte, *ped-
favn, $*peth_2$
fe, *peḱu-
fekta, fekte, *peḱ-
fem, $*pénk^we$
ferd, *per-
fergja, $*h_2erk$-
ferie, $*d^héh_1s$
ferje, *per-
fet, *ped-
fille, *pel-
finne, *pent-, *spey-
fire, $*k^wetwóres$
fisk, *peisḱ-
fjell, *pel-
fjord, *per-
fjær, fjør, $*péth_2r$
flat, $*pleth_2$-
fleire, flere, flest, $*pleh_1$-
flet, $*pleth_2$-
fliuga, fljuge, flod, flom, *plew-
flor, $*pleh_2$-
flote, flue, fly, flytja, flytte, flyve, flåte, *plew-
foder, $*peh_2$-
fold, $*pleth_2$-
folk, $*pleh_1$-
foll, $*pleth_2$-
forsake, $*seh_2g$-
forske, *preḱ-
foss, *pers-
fot, $*pṓds$
frakt, $*h_2eyḱ$-
fred, *preyH-
frega, *preḱ-
frende, frendelig, fri, fridom, frille, *preyH-
fru, frue, *per-
full, $*pleh_1$-
fund, *pent-
fundament, $*b^hud^hmḗn$
furu, $*perk^wu$-
fylke, fylle, $*pleh_1$-
fyr, $*péh_2ur$
fýre, $*perk^wu$-
føde, $*peh_2$-

føre, først, *per-
får, *peḱ-
gangverja, *wes-
gard, garde, $*ǵ^her$-
garn, $*ǵ^hern$-
gave, $*g^heb^h$-
geit, $*g^haydos$
gi, gift, gje, $*g^heb^h$-
gjest, $*g^hóstis$
gjeta, gjete, *weyd-
gjeva, $*g^heb^h$-
gjord, $*ǵ^her$-
gnosis, $*ǵneh_3$-
gress, gro, grønn, $*g^hreh_1$-
gud, $*ǵ^hew$-
gul, gull, $*ǵ^helh_3$-
gume, $*ǵ^hmṓ$
gård, $*ǵ^her$-
gås, $*ǵ^hans$-
ha, $*keh_2p$-
hala, $*kelh_1$-
hall, *ḱel-, *kelH-
halm, *ḱalam-
hammer, $*h_2éḱ$-mō
hane, $*keh_2n$-
hase, *kenk-
hat, hate, $*ḱeh_2d$-
hav, hava, have, havn, $*keh_2p$-
havre, *kapro
heile, $*kóh_2ilus$
heim, heimta, *ḱei-
hel, *ḱel-, *kenk-, $*kóh_2ilus$
hellig, $*kóh_2ilus$
hemta, henta, hente, *ḱei-
her, *ḱi-
herberge, herje, hertug, *ker-
hest, hingst, *kek-
historie, *weyd-
hjal, $*kelh_1$-
hjarre, $*ḱerh_2$-
hjarta, hjarte, *ḱḗr
hjem, *ḱei-
hjerne, $*ḱerh_2$-
hjerte, *ḱḗr
hjul, $*k^wel$-
hjørne, $*ḱerh_2$-
hode, *kapōlo
horn, $*ḱerh_2$-
hund, $*ḱwṓ$
hundre, *ḱm̥tóm
hva, hvem, hver, $*k^wis$
hvile, $*k^wyeh_1$-
hvilken, hvor, $*k^wis$
hyene, *suH-
hæl, *kenk-
hær, *ker-
høne, $*keh_2n$-

høre, *h_2ḱ$h_2$owsyéti
høst, *kerp-
høyra, høyre, *h_2ḱ$h_2$owsyéti
håndtere, *ḱei-
i går, *$d^hǵ^h$(y)es-
i, *$h_1$én
igle, *ang^w(h)i-
ild, *$h_2$eyd^h-
is, *$h_1$eyH-
isjukel, *yeǵ-
ja, *éy / h_1e
jarn, *$h_1$ésh$_2$r̥
jeg, *egH$_2$
jern, *$h_1$ésh$_2$r̥
jo, *éy / h_1e
jord, *$h_1$er-
jotun, *$h_1$ed-
jur, *$h_1$owHd^{h}r̥-
kald, kalen, *gel-
kall, *ǵerh$_2$-
kam, *ǵómb^{h}os
kapitel, *kapõlo
kar, *ǵerh$_2$-
karosseri, karre, *ḱers-
kart, *ǵ^{h}er-
karve, *gerb^h-
kinn, *ǵénus
kjekk, *g^{w}eyh$_3$-
kjeller, *ḱel-
kjemme, *ǵómb^{h}os
kjenne, *ǵneh$_3$-
kjerre, *ḱers-
kjose, *ǵews-
kjønn, *ǵenH$_1$-
klar, *kelh$_1$-
kne, *ǵónu
kode, *g^{w}et-
koke, *pek^w-
kollektiv, *leǵ-
koma, kome, komme, *g^{w}em-
kona, kone, *gwén
konfusjon, *ǵ^{h}ew-
konge, kongedømme, *ǵenH$_1$-
konkurrere, *ḱers-
konkylie, *ḱonkho-
korn, *ǵr̥Hnom
korrigere, *$h_3$reǵ-
kort, *(s)ker-
kran, *gerh$_2$-
ku, *g^{w}ṓws
kunne, *ǵneh$_3$-
kvefs, *wobs-
kverne, *g^{w}rh$_2$-n-uH-
kvikk, *g^{w}eyh$_3$-
kvinna, *gwén
kvæde, kvåde, *g^{w}et-
land, *lend^h-

langve, *weyh$_1$-
laug, *lewh$_3$-
lav, *legh-
lava, *lewh$_3$-
legga, legge, leggja, *legh-
len, *leyk^w-
leppe, *leb-
lest, *leys-
lett, *$h_1$leng^{wh}-
lever, *leyp-
li, *ḱley-
ligge, liggja, liggje, *legh-
lin, *lino-
lina, *ḱley-
ljos, *lewk-
log, *legh-, *lókus
lomve, lomvie, *weyh$_1$-
love, *lewb^h-
lukke, *seh$_2$g-
lunge, *leng^{wh}-
lus, *luHs-
lyd, *$h_1$lewd^h-
lys, *lewk-
lytte, *ḱlew-
lære, *leys-
løv, *lewb^h-
lån, *leyk^w-
mage, *mak-
mager, *meh$_2$ḱ-
male, malm, *melh$_2$-
man, *men-
mandag, *mḗh$_1$n̥s
manke, *men-
mann, *mánus
mar, *móri
mara, mare, *mer-
marg, *mosg^{h}os
marsvin, *suH-
maur, *morwi-
meg, *H$_1$me-
meget, *méǵh$_2$s
mel, *melh$_2$-
melk, melke, *H$_2$melǵ-
menneske, *mánus
mere, *meh$_2$-
merr, *marko-
mersk, *móri
mester, *méǵh$_2$s
meta, *med-
midje, *méd^{h}yos
mine, *H$_1$meme-
minske, minutt, mis-, misse, miste, *mey-
mjød, *méd^{h}u
mjøl, *melh$_2$-
mjølk, *H$_2$melǵ-
moder, mor, *méh$_2$tēr
mord, *mer-

mun, *men-	rense, *krey-
munn, *mendʰ-	repetere, *peth₂
munter, *men-	rett, rette, rik, rike, *h₃reǵ-
mus, *muh₂s-	rita, rite, *lino-
mye, *méǵh₂s	rot, *wréh₂ds
mygg, *mus-	rug, *wrugʰyo-
mynt, *men-	rød, *h₁rewdʰ-
myrjel, *mréǵʰ-	rå, *krewh₂-
mål, *meh₁-	råde, *Hreh₁dʰ-
måne, måned, *méh₁n̥s	sadel, *sed-
naken, *negʷ-	sag, *sek-
natt, nattergal, *nókʷts	sak, *seh₂g-
navigere, *(s)neh₂-	saks, *sek-
navle, *h₃enbʰ-	sale, *sed-
navn, *h₁nómn̥	salt, *séh₂ls
negl, *h₃negʰ-	samme, *sem-
nerve, *(s)neh₁-	saus, *séh₂ls
nevø, *nepot-	se, *sekʷ-
ni, *H₁néwn̥	seg, *s(w)e-
nord, *h₁én	seier, seire, *seǵʰ-
normal, *ǵneh₃-	seks, *swéḱs
norrøn, *h₁én	selv, *s(w)e-
nos, *néh₂s	senat, *sénos
ny, *new	senda, sende, *sent-
nyre, *negʷʰ-r-	serk, *ser-
nål, *(s)neh₁-	setja, setta, sette, *sed-
offisiell, *h₃ep-	si, sikt, *sekʷ-
okse, *uksḗn	sin, *s(w)e-
olboge, *Heh₃l-	sitja, sitta, sitte, *sed-
older, *h₃el-	situasjon, *teḱ-
om, *h₂ent	sjon, *sekʷ-
or, *h₃el-	sju, *septm̥
orakel, *h₃éh₁os	sjøl, *s(w)e-
ord, *wekʷ-	skake, *(s)kek-
orden, ordinær, ordne, ordning, ordre, *h₂er	skarp, *(s)ker-
orke, *werǵ-	ski, *skey-
orm, *wr̥mis-	skikke, *(s)kek-
os, *h₃éh₁os	skit, skite, *skey-
oss, *wei	skje, *(s)kek-
oter, *udréh₂	skjære, *(s)ker-
otta, *nókʷts	skole, *seǵʰ-
ov-, *upo	skort, skrape, skrive, skård, *(s)ker-
patent, *peth₂	slik, *s(w)e-
pels, *pel-	slutte, *(s)kel-
penn, *péth₂r̥	snúðr, *(s)neh₁-
perfekt, *dheH₁-	snø, *sneygʷʰ-
privilegium, *per-	soge, *sekʷ-
problem, *gʷelH-	sokn, *seh₂g-
program, *gerbʰ-	sol, *sóh₂wl̥
rad, *Hreh₁dʰ-	som, somme, *sem-
radickal, *wréh₂ds	sommer, *sm̥-h₂-ó-
rank, *h₃reǵ-	son, *suh₁nús
ratt, *Hret-	sove, *swep-
regjere, regne, *h₃reǵ-	speide, *speḱ-
rein, *krey-	spik, spiker, *spey-
rekkja, rekne, *h₃reǵ-	spurv, *spḗr
renne, *h₃er-, *h₃reyH-	stad, *steh₂-

vest, *wek(ʷ)speros
vette, *weǵh-
vev, veve, *webh-
vi, *wei
vilje, ville, *welh₁-
vin, *wóyh₁nom
vind, *H₂weH₁-
vindauga, vindu, *h₃ekʷ-
virke, *werǵ-
vis, visdom, vite, *weyd-
vogn, *weǵh-
vokse, *h₂ewg-
vol, *welH-
vold, *h₂welh₁-
vord, *wer-
vorde, *wert-
vyrt, *wréh₂ds
vær, *wet-
være, *H₁es-
væte, *wed-
vætte, *weǵh-
vørt, vørter, *wréh₂ds
vår, *wésr̥
vård, *wer-
våt, *wed-
yngling, *h₂yuh₁en-
yrke, *werǵ-
ærsaud, *h₂ówis
ød, *h₂ew
øke, *h₂ewg-
øks, *h₂éḱ
øl, *h₂elut-
øre, *h₂ew-
ørn, *h₃érō
øse, *yes-
øst, *h₂ews-
øy, *h₂ekʷeh₂-
øye, *h₃ekʷ-
å, *h₂ekʷeh₂-
åk, *yugóm
åker, *h₂éǵros
åkorn, *eh₃g-
ånde, *h₂enh₁-
år, *yeh₁-
åtte, *oḱtṓw

Swedish

-kost, *ǵews-
-son, *suh₁nús
-tio, -tjog, *déḱm̥t
-vist, *H₁es-
abort, *h₃er-
acceptera, *keh₂p-
af, *h₂pó
afton, *h₁epi
agera, *H₂eǵ-
akarn, *eh₃g-
akt, *H₂eǵ-
al, *h₃el-
all, *h₂el-
allvar, *weh₁-
almboge, aln, *Heh₃l-
and, *h₂eneti-
anda, andas, *h₂enh₁-
anddrake, *h₂eneti-, *h₃reǵ-
ande, *h₂enh₁-
andra, *h₂énteros
angel, ankel, *h₂enk-
annan, *h₂énteros
anonym, *h₁nómn̥
antik, *h₂énti-h₃kʷós
arbeta, arbete, *h₃erbʰ-
arm, *h₂er
armbåge, *Heh₃l-
arvode, *h₃erbʰ-
as, *h₁ed-
ask, *h₃es-
aska, *h₂eh₁s-
audiell, audition, *h₂ewis-dʰh₁-
augusti, *h₂ewg-
av, *h₂pó
avel, *h₃ep-
axel, *H₂eǵ-
bane, *gʷʰen-
banna, *bʰeh₂-
barn, *bher-
barr, *bʰars-
be-, *h₁epi
bekomma, bekväm, *gʷem-
berg, *bʰerǵʰ-
besinna, *sent-
besitta, besätta, *sed-
bet, *bʰeyd-
betäcka, *(s)teg-
bi, *bʰey-, *h₁epi
bibliotek, *dheH₁-
bida, *bʰeydʰ-
bita, *bʰeyd-
bjuda, *bʰewdʰ-

björk, *bʰereǵ-
blad, *bʰleh₃-
bli, bliva, *leyp-
blomma, *bʰleh₃-
blåsa, blåst, *bʰleh₁-
bo, *bʰuH-
bock, *bʰuHgos-
bok, *bʰeh₂go-
bona, *bʰeh₂-
borg, *bʰerǵʰ-
botten, *bʰudʰmḗn
brev, *mréǵʰ-
brinna, *bʰrewh₁-
broder, bror, *bʰréh₂tēr
brudgum, *ǵʰmṓ
brunn, brygga, *bʰrewh₁-
bryn, *h₃bʰrúHs
bränna, *bʰrewh₁-
bud, *bʰewdʰ-
byrå, *péh₂ur
båda, *bʰewdʰ-
båk, *bʰeh₂-
bår, *bher-
båt, *bʰeyd-
bära, *bher-
bärsärk, *ser-
bön, *bʰeh₂-
böna, *bʰabʰeh₂-
bör, börja, *bher-
cell, *ḱel-
centimeter, *ḱm̥tóm
coitus, *h₁ey-
cykel, *kʷel-
dag, daga, *dʰegʷʰ-
dagg, *dʰewh₂-
deg, *dʰeyǵʰ-
dekad, *déḱm̥t
deklarera, *kelh₁-
delirium, *leys-
den, det, *só
di, dia, *dʰeh₁(y)-
diger, *dʰeyǵʰ-
dikta, diktatur, *deyḱ-
division, *h₁weydʰ
djup, *dʰewb-
djävul, *gʷelH-
dogm, doktor, *deḱ-
dom, *dem-, *dheH₁-
dotter, *dʰugh₂tḗr
dreja, *terh₁-
du, *túh₂
dugg, dun, dust, *dʰewh₂-
dvina, dygn, dyr, dyrd, *dʰegʷʰ-
då, *só
dåd, *dheH₁-
dägga, *dʰeh₁(y)-

där, *só
döma, *dheH₁-
döpa, *dʰewb-
dörr, *dʰwer-
efter, *h₂pó
egg, *h₂éḱ
ek, *h₂eyǵ-
eld, *h₂eydʰ-
elegans, *leǵ-
element, eller, *h₂el-
elva, en, *óy-nos
enorm, *ǵneh₃-
eter, *h₂eydʰ-
examen, *H₂eǵ-
fabel, *bʰeh₂-
fader, *ph₂tḗr
fagn, *peth₂
faktum, *dheH₁-
falna, *pelH-
famn, *peth₂
fan, *pent-
fantom, *bʰeh₂-
far, *ph₂tḗr
fara, *per-, *per-
fargalt, *pórḱos
fast, *peh₂ǵ-
fatta, *ped-
fem, *pénkʷe
feminin, *dʰeh₁(y)-
fest, *dʰéh₁s
figur, *dʰeyǵʰ-
finna, *pent-
fira, *dʰéh₁s
fisk, *peisḱ-
fjord, *per-
fjäder, *péth₂r̥
fjäll, *pel-
fjärd, *per-
fjät, fjätter, *ped-
flaga, *pleh₂-
flat, *pleth₂-
fler, flera, flest, *pleh₁-
flo, *pleh₂-
flod, *plew-
flor, *pleh₂-
flotta, flotte, fluga, fly, flyga, flygt, flygtur, flykt, flyta,
   flytta, flöja, *plew-
foder, *peh₂-
folk, *pleh₁-
fors, *pers-
forska, *preḱ-
fot, *pṓds
frakt, *h₂eyḱ-
fram, *per-
fred, fri, fria, frid, frilla, *preyH-
fru, från, *per-
fræghna, *preḱ-

frälsa, frälse, *preyH-
främja, *per-
frände, frändlig, *preyH-
full, *pleh₁-
fundament, *bʰudʰmḗn, *ǵʰew-
fundera, *bʰudʰmḗn
fura, furu, *perkʷu-
fylka, fylke, fylla, fylle, *pleh₁-
fynd, *pent-
fyr, *péh₂ur
fyra, *kʷetwóres
får, *peḱ-
fä, *peḱu-
fäkta, *peḱ-
färd, färja, *per-
föda, *peh₂-
för, för, föra, *per-
fördöma, *dheH₁-
före, *per-
förnimma, *nem-
förra, *per-
försaka, *seh₂g-
först, första, förste, *per-
garn, *ǵʰern-
gast, *ǵʰeyzd-
ge, *gʰebʰ-
genus, *ǵenH₁-
get, *gʰaydos
gift, *gʰebʰ-
gikt, *yek-
gitta, *weyd-
giva, *gʰebʰ-
gjord, *ǵʰer-
gjuta, *ǵʰew-
grav, gravid, *gʷerh₂-
gro, gräs, grön, *gʰreh₁-
gud, *ǵʰew-
gul, guld, gull, *ǵʰelh₃-
gård, *ǵʰer-
gås, *ǵʰans-
gåva, *gʰebʰ-
gäst, *gʰóstis
gäv, *gʰebʰ-
gördel, *ǵʰer-
ha, *keh₂p-
hake, *keg-
hala, *kelh₁-
hall, *ḱel-, *kelH-
halm, *ḱalam-
hammar, hammare, *h₂éḱ-mō
hamn, *keh₂p-
hane, *keh₂n-
hantera, *ḱei-
has, *kenk-
hat, hata, *ḱeh₂d-
hav, hava, *keh₂p-
havre, *kapro

hel, hela, helga, helig, *kóh₂ilus
hem, *ḱei-
hertig, *ker-
hingst, *kek-
historia, *weyd-
hjort, *ḱerh₂-
hjul, *kʷel-
hjälm, *ḱel-
hjärna, *ḱerh₂-
hjärta, *ḱḗr
horn, *ḱerh₂-
hors, *ḱers-
huk, *keg-
huld, *ḱel-
hund, *ḱwṓ
hundra, *ḱm̥tóm
huvud, *kapōlo
hyena, *suH-
hårkam, *ǵómbʰos
häl, *kenk-
häla, hälare, *ḱel-
hämta, *ḱei-
här, *ker-, *ḱi-
härbärge, härja, *ker-
häst, *kek-
hölja, *ḱel-
höna, *keh₂n-
höra, *h₂ḱh₂owsyéti
hörna, *ḱerh₂-
höst, *kerp-
i går, *dʰǵʰ(y)es-
i, *h₁én
I, *túh₂
idé, *weyd-
igel, igelkott, *angʷ(h)i-
ihjäl, *ḱel-
importera, *per-
indicium, *deyḱ-
inventarium, *gʷem-
is, *h₁eyH-
ja, *éy / h₁e
jag, *egH₂
jo, *éy / h₁e
jord, *h₁er-
juver, *h₁owHdʰr̥-
järn, *h₁ésh₂r̥
jäsa, jäst, *yes-
jätte, *h₁ed-
jökel, *yeǵ-
kala, kall, *gel-
kam, *ǵómbʰos
kamera, kamp, *(s)teg-
kapitel, *kapōlo
kapsel, kapsyl, *keh₂p-
karl, *ǵerh₂-
karosseri, *ḱers-
karva, *gerbʰ-

kind, *ǵénus
klar, *kelh₁-
knä, *ǵónu
ko, *gʷóws
koka, *pekʷ-
kollega, kollegium, *legh-
komma, *gʷem-
kona, *gwén
kondition, *deyk-
konung, *ǵenH₁-
korn, *ǵr̥Hnom
korrigera, *h₃reǵ-
kort, *(s)ker-
kran, *gerh₂-
kulmen, *kelH-
kung, kungadöme, *ǵenH₁-
kunna, *ǵneh₃-
kurs, *ḱers-
kusin, *swésōr
kvalm, *gʷelH-
kvarn, *gʷrh₂-n-uH-
kvart, *kʷetwóres
kvick, kvickna, *gʷeyh₃-
kvinna, *gwén
kvälja, *gʷelH-
kåda, *gʷet-
kåna, *gwén
källare, *ḱel-
kämma, *ǵómbʰos
känna, *ǵneh₃-
kärra, *ḱers-
kön, *ǵenH₁-, *ǵneh₃-
lag, *legh-, *lókus
landa, *lendʰ-
legal, legion, lektion, lektor, *leǵ-
lever, *leyp-
li, lid, *ḱley-
ligga, *legh-
lin, lina, *lino-
list, *leys-
ljus, *lewk-
ljuv, ljuvlig, *lewbʰ-
lock, *seh₂g-
lomvia, *weyh₁-
lov, lova, *lewbʰ-
lucka, *seh₂g-
luden, *h₁lewdʰ-
lunga, *lengʷʰ-
lus, *luHs-
lyssna, *ḱlew-
låg, *legh-
lån, *leykʷ-
läger, lägga, *legh-
län, *leykʷ-
läna, *ḱley-
länd, lända, länder, *lendʰ-
läpp, *leb-

lära, läst, *leys-
lätt, *h₁lengʷʰ-
lödder, lög, *lewh₃-
löv, *lewbʰ-
mage, *mak-
mager, *meh₂k-
magister, *méǵh₂s
mala, malm, *melh₂-
man, *mánus, *men-
manifest, *gʷʰen-
manke, *men-
mar, *móri
mara, *mer-
marsvin, *suH-
medicin, *med-
mental, *men-
mera, mest, *meh₂-
mid-, midja, *médʰyos
mig, *H₁me-
miga, *h₃meyǵʰ-
mina, *H₁meme-
mindre, *mey-
minne, *men-
minska, *mey-
misdåd, *dheH₁-
miss-, missa, mista, *mey-
mitten, *médʰyos
mjöd, *médʰu
mjöl, *melh₂-
mjöldagg, *melit-
mjölk, mjölka, *H₂melǵ-
moder, mor, *méh₂tēr
mord, *mer-
mun, *mendʰ-
munter, *men-
mus, muskel, muskulär, *muh₂s-
mycken, mycket, *méǵh₂s
mygga, *mus-
mynt, *men-
myra, *morwi-
mål, måla, *meh₁-
mån, *men-
månad, måndag, måne, *méh₁n̥s
människa, *mánus
märg, *mosgʰos
märr, *marko-
mäsk, *mey-
mästare, *méǵh₂s
mäta, *med-
mörja, *h₁ews-
nagel, *h₃negʰ-
naken, *negʷ-
namn, *h₁nómn̥
natt, *nókʷts
nav, navel, *h₃enbʰ-
navigera, *(s)neh₂-
ni, *túh₂

nio, *H₁néwn̥
njure, *negʷh-r-
nobel, *ǵneh₃-
nord, nordan, *h₁én
normal, *ǵneh₃-
norr, norrön, *h₁én
nos, *néh₂s
ny, *new
nål, *(s)neh₁-
näktergal, *nókʷts
näsa, *néh₂s
näste, *nisdós
o-, *n̥-
oblat, *bher-
oculus, *h₃ekʷ-
odör, *h₃ed-
officiell, *h₃ep-
ok, *yugóm
om, *h₂ent
omgjorda, *ǵʰer-
onkel, *h₂éwh₂os
opus, *h₃ep-
orakel, *h₃éh₁os
ord, *wekʷ-
orden, order, ordinarie, ordna, ordning, *h₂er
origo, *h₃er-
orka, *werǵ-
orm, *wr̥mis-
os, *h₃éh₁os
oss, *wei
otta, otte, *nókʷts
ovan, *upo
oxe, *uksḗn
parabel, *gʷelH-
passus, patent, *peth₂
pax, *peh₂ǵ-
penna, *péth₂r̥
pigg, *bak-
pil, *peys-
pina, *kʷey-
plus, *pleh₁-
port, *per-
post, *teḱ-
praxis, pris, *per-
professor, *bʰeh₂-
program, *gerbʰ-
pund, punkt, *pewǵ-
päls, *pel-
rad, *Hreh₁dʰ-
radikal, *wréh₂ds
rank, *h₃reǵ-
ratt, *Hret-
regera, *h₃reǵ-
ren, rensa, *krey-
repetera, *peth₂
republik, *pleh₁-
rik, rike, *h₃reǵ-

rim, *h₂er
rinna, *h₃er-, *h₃reyH-
rit, *h₂er
rot, *wréh₂ds
rubin, *h₁rewdʰ-
russ, *ḱers-
rå, *krewh₂-
råda, *Hreh₁dʰ-
råg, *wrugʰyo-
räcka, räkna, rät, räta, rätt, rätta, *h₃reǵ-
röd, *h₁rewdʰ-
sadel, sadla, *sed-
saga, *sekʷ-
sak, *seh₂g-
salt, salta, *séh₂ls
samma, *sem-
sann, sanna, *H₁es-
sax, *sek-
se, *sekʷ-
seger, segra, *seǵʰ-
senat, *sénos
sensuell, *sent-
sex, *swéḱs
sig, *s(w)e
sikt, sikte, *sekʷ-
simpel, *pleḱ-, *sem-
simular, *sem-
sin, *s(w)e
sinne, *sent-
sitta, *sed-
situation, *teḱ-
sju, *septm̥
själv, *s(w)e
skaka, *(s)kek-
skara, skarp, *(s)ker-
ske, *(s)kek-
skeda, ski, *skey-
skick, skicka, *(s)kek-
skid, skida, skit, skita, *skey-
skjorta, *(s)ker-
skola, *seǵʰ-
skriva, skära, skärm, *(s)ker-
slik, *s(w)e
sluta, *(s)kel-
snod, snodd, *(s)neh₁-
snö, *sneygʷʰ-
so, *suH-
socken, *seh₂g-
sol, *sóh₂wl̥
sold, *solh₂-
somlig, *sem-
sommar, *sm̥-h₂-ó-
son, *suh₁nús
sova, *swep-
sparv, *spér
speja, *speḱ-
spett, spik, spira, *spey-

stad, *steh₂-

stall, *stel-

station, *steh₂-

stiga, *steygʰ-

stilla, *stel-

stjärna, *h₂stḗr

sto, *steh₂-

stock, *(s)tew-

stor, *steh₂-

stråt, sträte, *sterh₃-

strö, *strewt-

ström, *srew-

student, studera, studium, *(s)tew-

stund, *steh₂-

stycke, *(s)tew-

styvbarn, *bher-

stå, stånda, *steh₂-

ställa, *stel-

stöna, *(s)tenh₂-

stör, *steh₂-

subtil, *tetḱ-

sugga, *suH-

sunnan, *sóh₂wl̥

svett, *sweyd-

svin, *suH-

sy, *sīw-

syd, *sóh₂wl̥

sylt, sylta, *séh₂ls

syn, *sekʷ-

synd, *H₁es-

system, *steh₂-

syster, *swésōr

så, *s(w)e-, *seH₁-

såg, *sek-

sås, *séh₂ls

säd, *seH₁-

säga, *sekʷ-

sämjas, *sem-

sända, *sent-

särk, *ser-

sätta, *sed-

söder, *sóh₂wl̥

söka, *seh₂g-

söm, *sīw-

sömn, *swep-

söndag, *sóh₂wl̥

tack, tacka, *teng-

tak, *(s)teg-

tam, *demh₂-

tand, *h₃dónts

tappa, *deh₂-

tarm, *terh₁-

te, *deyḱ-

team, *dewk-

territoriell, territorium, *ters-

tid, *deh₂-

tig, *dewk-

timmer, *dem-

tio, *déḱm̥t

tisdag, *dyew-

tjod, *tewtéh₂

tjugo, *déḱm̥t

tjur, *(s)táwros

tjusa, *ǵews-

tjära, *dóru

tolv, *dwóH₁

tomt, *dem-

Tor, tordön, *(s)tenh₂-

torp, *treb-

torr, *ters-

torsdag, *(s)tenh₂-

tradition, *deH₃-

trana, *gerh₂-

translation, *bher-

trast, *trosdos

tre, *tréyes

tro, trygd, trygg, *deru-

tryta, *trewd-

tråd, *terh₁-

trä, träd, *dóru

tröska, *terh₁-

tunga, *dn̥ǵʰwéh₂s

tvilling, två, *dwóH₁

tycka, tyckas, *teng-

tygel, *dewk-

typisk, *(s)tew-

Tyr, *dyew-

tå, *deyḱ-

tåg, *dewk-

tåla, *telh₂-

tår, *daḱru-

täcka, *(s)teg-

täckas, *teng-

tämja, *demh₂-

tänja, *ten-

tänka, *teng-

tära, *der-

täxla, *tetḱ-

töja, töm, *dewk-

törst, *ters-

udd, *dheH₁-

ull, *h₂welh₁-

ulv, *wl̥kʷos

umbära, *bher-

ung, *h₂yuh₁en-

universum, *wert-

upp, uppe, *upo

utter, *udréh₂

vacker, *weǵ-

vad, *kʷis, *wedʰ-

vagn, *weǵh-

vaja, *H₂weH₁-

vaken, vakt, vakta, *weǵ-

val, vall, *welH-

var, *kʷis, *wer-
vara, *H₁es-
varda, *wert-
varken, *kʷis
varm, *gʷʰer-
varsam, *wer-
varulv, *wiHrós
vaska, vatten, vattu-, *wed-
vecka, *weyk-
vegetation, *weǵ-
vem, *kʷis
verb, *wekʷ-
verifikation, *weh₁-
verk, *werǵ-
veta, *weyd-
vi, *wei
via, *weyh₁-
vig, viga, *weyk-
vila, *kʷyeh₁-
vilja, *welh₁-
vilken, *kʷis
villa, *weyḱ-
vin, *wóyh₁nom
vind, *H₂weH₁-
vindöga, *h₃ekʷ-
virka, *werǵ-
vis, visdom, viss, vita, *weyd-
vitrin, vitrös, *wed-
vitter, *weyd-
vokal, *wekʷ-
våld, vålla, *h₂welh₁-
vår, *wésr̥
vård, *wer-
våt, *wed-
väcka, *weǵ-
vädja, *wedʰ-
vädur, *wet-
väg, väga, *weǵh-
väga, *weyk-
välja, *welh₁-
värd, *wert-
värld, *h₂el-, *wiHrós
värma, *gʷʰer-
väst, västan, väster, *wek(ʷ)speros
väta, *wed-
vätte, *weǵh-
väv, väva, *webh-
växa, växt, *h₂ewg-
vört, *wréh₂ds
ylle, *h₂welh₁-
ylva, *wḷkʷos
yngling, *h₂yuh₁en-
yrka, *werǵ-
å, *h₂ekʷeh₂-
åka, *H₂eǵ-
åker, *h₂éǵros
ålder, *h₂el-

ålägga, *legh-
ånger, ångest, *h₂enǵʰ-
år, *yeh₁-
årder, *H₂erH₃-
åter, *h₂pó
åtta, *oḱtōw
äga, *h₂eyḱ-
ägg, *h₂éḱ, *h₂ōwyóm
ägna, *h₂eyḱ-
äldre, äldst, *h₂el-
ämbete, *H₂eǵ-
ämna, ämne, *h₃ep-
än, *h₂ent
äpple, *h₂ébōl
ärg, *h₂eyos
ärja, *H₂erH₃-
äta, *h₁ed-
ätt, *h₂eyḱ-
ö, *h₂ekʷeh₂-
öda, öde, *h₂ew
öga, *h₃ekʷ-
öka, *h₂ewg-
öl, *h₂elut-
öna, *h₂egʷnos
öra, *h₂ew-
örn, *h₃érō
ört, *wréh₂ds
öst er, öst, östan, *h₂ews-

Danish

-sen, *suh₁nús
ablativ, *bher-
abort, *h₃er-
acido, *h₂ék
af, *h₂pó
aften, *h₁epi
age, *H₂eǵ-
ager, *h₂éǵros
agern, *eh₃g-
aksel, *H₂eǵ-
al, *h₂el-
albue, *Heh₃l-
alder, *h₂el-
alen, almbue, *Heh₃l-
alvor, *weh₁-
ambassade, *H₂eǵ-
and, *h₂eneti-
anden, *h₂énteros
andrik, *h₂eneti-, *h₃reǵ-
ange, *h₂enh₁-
anger, angst, *h₂enǵʰ-
ankel, *h₂enk-
anonym, *h₁nómn̥
arbejde, arbejde, *h₃erbʰ-
ard, *H₂erH₃-
arm, *h₂er
armbue, *Heh₃l-
ask, *h₃es-
aske, *h₂eh₁s-
atter, *h₂pó
august, *h₂ewg-
avi, *h₃ep-
bande, *bʰeh₂-
bane, *gʷʰen-
barn, *bher-
base, *gʷem-
bavn, *bʰeh₂-
be-, *h₁epi
bekomme, *gʷem-
besidde, besætte, *sed-
bi, *bʰey-
bibliotek, *dheH₁-
bide, bie, *bʰeydʰ-
birk, *bʰereǵ-
bjerg, *bʰerǵʰ-
blad, *bʰleh₃-
blive, *leyp-
blomme, *bʰleh₃-
blæse, blæst, *bʰleh₁-
bo, *bʰuH-
bog, *bʰeh₂go-
bone, *bʰeh₂-
borg, *bʰerǵʰ-

brev, *mréǵʰ-
broder, bror, *bʰréh₂tēr
brudgom, *ǵʰmṓ
brygge, *bʰrewh₁-
bryn, *h₃bʰrúHs
brænde, brønd, *bʰrewh₁-
bud, *bʰewdʰ-
buk, *bʰuHgos-
bund, *bʰudʰmḗn
byde, *bʰewdʰ-
bære, *bher-
bøg, *bʰeh₂go-
bøn, *bʰeh₂-
bønne, *bʰabʰeh₂-
bør, børje, *bher-
båd, *bʰeyd-
båke, *bʰeh₂-
båre, *bher-
centi-, centimeter, *ḱm̥tóm
champion, *(s)teg-
civil, *ḱei-
da, *só
dag, dage, *dʰegʷʰ-
datter, *dʰugh₂tḗr
deg, dej, *dʰeyǵʰ-
dekade, *déḱm̥t
deklarere, *kelh₁-
delirium, *leys-
den, der, det, *só
die, *dʰeh₁(y)-
divisor, *h₁weydʰ
djævel, *gʷelH-
dogme, doktor, *deḱ-
dom, *dheH₁-
dreje, *terh₁-
drossel, *trosdos
du, *túh₂
dug, dun, *dʰewh₂-
dyb, dybde, *dʰewb-
dyr, *dʰegʷʰ-
dyst, *dʰewh₂-
dægge, *dʰeh₁(y)-
døbe, *dʰewb-
døgn, *dʰegʷʰ-
dømme, *dheH₁-
dør, *dʰwer-
då, *dʰeh₁(y)-
dåd, *dheH₁-
efter, *h₂pó
eg, egetræ, *h₂eyǵ-
egne, eje, *h₂eyḱ-
el, *h₃el-
eller, *h₂el-
elletræ, *h₃el-
elleve, *óy-nos
emmer, *h₁ews-
en, *óy-nos

end, *h₂ent
er, *h₂eyos
ether, *h₂eydʰ-
evne, *h₃ep-
fader, *ph₂tḗr
fadm, *peth₂
fanden, *pent-
fantom, *bʰeh₂-
far, *ph₂tḗr
fare, *per-, *per-
farm, *peth₂
fart, *per-
fast, *peh₂ǵ-
fatte, *ped-
favn, *peth₂
feber, *dʰegʷʰ-
fegte, *peḱ-
fem, *pénkʷe
ferie, *dʰéh₁s
finde, *pent-
fingere, *dʰeyǵʰ-
finne, *spey-
fire, *kʷetwóres
fisk, *peisḱ-
fjed, *ped-
fjeder, fjer, *péth₂r
fjord, *per-
flad, *pleth₂-
flage, *pleh₂-
fled, *pleth₂-
flod, *plew-
flor, *pleh₂-
flue, fly, flyde, flygt, flytte, flyve, flåde, *plew-
fod, *pṓds
foder, *peh₂-
folk, *pleh₁-
fordømme, *dheH₁-
fors, *pers-
forsage, *seh₂g-
forske, *preḱ-
fos, *pers-
fra, *per-
fragt, *h₂eyḱ-
frem, fremme, *per-
fri, frille, *preyH-
fru, frue, *per-
fræghnæ, *preḱ-
frænde, frændelig, *preyH-
fuld, *pleh₁-
fundament, *bʰudʰmḗn
fundament, *ǵʰew-
fundere, *bʰudʰmḗn
fylde, fylke, *pleh₁-
fyr, *péh₂ur, *perkʷu-
fyrretræ, *perkʷu-
fæ, *peḱu-
fægte, *peḱ-

færd, færge, fært, *per-
føde, *peh₂-
før, føre, først, første, *per-
får, *peḱ-
garn, *ǵʰern-
gave, *gʰebʰ-
ged, *gʰaydos
gide, *weyd-
gift, give, *gʰebʰ-
gjord, gjorde, *ǵʰer-
gro, græs, grøn, *gʰreh₁-
gud, *ǵʰew-
gul, guld, *ǵʰelh₃-
gyde, *ǵʰew-
gære, *yes-
gæst, *gʰóstis
gæv, *gʰebʰ-
gård, gårde, *ǵʰer-
gås, *ǵʰans-
had, hade, *ḱeh₂d-
hage, *keg-
haid, *kelH-
hal, *ḱel-
hale, *kelh₁-
halm, *ḱalam-
hammer, *h₂éḱ-mō
hane, *keh₂n-
has, hase, *kenk-
hav, have, havn, *keh₂p-
havre, *kapro
hel, hele, hellig, hellige, *kóh₂ilus
hente, *ḱei-
her, *ḱi-
herberge, hertug, *ker-
hest, hingst, *kek-
historie, *weyd-
hjelm, *ḱel-
hjem, *ḱei-
hjerne, *ḱerh₂-
hjerte, *ḱḗr
hjort, *ḱerh₂-
hjul, *kʷel-
hjørne, horn, *ḱerh₂-
hors, *ḱers-
hoved, *kapōlo
huk, *keg-
huld, *ḱel-
hund, *ḱwṓ
hundrede, *ḱm̥tóm
hvad, hvem, *kʷis
hveps, *wobs-
hver, *kʷis
hvile, *kʷyeh₁-
hvilken, hvor, *kʷis
hylle, *ḱel-
hyæne, *suH-
hæl, *kenk-

377

hær, hærge, hærje, *ker-

høne, *keh₂n-

høre, *h₂ḱh₂owsyéti

høst, *kerp-

i går, *dʰǵʰ(y)es-

i, *h₁én

I, *túh₂

id, identitet, *éy / h₁e

igle, *angʷ(h)i-

ild, *h₂eydʰ-

ir, *h₂eyos

is, *h₁eyH-

ja, *éy / h₁e

jeg, *egH₂

jern, *h₁ésh₂r̥

jo, *éy / h₁e

jord, *h₁er-

jærn, *h₁ésh₂r̥

jætte, *h₁ed-

kam, *ǵómbʰos

kamp, *(s)teg-

kapere, *keh₂p-

kapitel, *kapōlo

karl, *ǵerh₂-

karve, *gerbʰ-

kasse, *keh₂p-

kende, *ǵneh₃-

kind, *ǵénus

kjæmme, *ǵómbʰos

klar, *kelh₁-

knæ, *ǵónu

ko, *gʷṓws

kold, *gel-

komme, *gʷem-

kone, *gwḗn

kong, konge, kongedømme, *ǵenH₁-

konkylie, *ḱonkho-

konning, *ǵenH₁-

konstruktion, *strew-

korn, *ǵr̥Hnom

kort, *(s)ker-

kost, *ǵews-

kran, *gerh₂-

kulør, *ḱel-

kunne, *ǵneh₃-

kvalm, kvalme, *gʷelH-

kvik, kvikne, *gʷeyh₃-

kvinde, *gwḗn

kvæle, *gʷelH-

kværn, *gʷrh₂-n-uH-

kyse, *ǵews-

kæk, *gʷeyh₃-

kæmme, *ǵómbʰos

køn, *ǵenH₁-, *ǵneh₃-

labe, *leb-

land, *lendʰ-

lav, *legh-

leffe, *leb-

lejr, *legh-

len, *leykʷ-

lende, *lendʰ-

let, *h₁lengʷʰ-

lever, *leyp-

li, lid, lide, *ḱley-

ligge, *legh-

linned, *lino-

list, *leys-

log, *legh-

lomvie, *weyh₁-

lov, *legh-, *lewbʰ-

love, *lewbʰ-

lune, *lewk-

lunge, *lengʷʰ-

lus, *luHs-

lyd, *h₁lewdʰ-

lys, *lewk-

lyt, *ḱlew-

læbe, *leb-

lægge, *legh-

lænder, *lendʰ-

læne, *ḱley-

lære, *leys-

lø, Løgum, løj, lørdag, *lewh₃-

løv, *lewbʰ-, *lewh₃-

låg, *seh₂g-

lån, *leykʷ-

mager, *meh₂ḱ-

male, *meh₁-, *melh₂-

malke, *H₂melǵ-

malm, malstrøm, *melh₂-

man, *men-

mand, *mánus

mandag, *mḗh₁n̥s

manke, mantra, *men-

mar, *móri

mare, *mer-

marsvin, *suH-

marv, *mosgʰos

mask, *mey-

mave, *mak-

medie, medium, *médʰyos

megen, meget, *méǵh₂s

mel, *melh₂-

meldug, *melit-

menneske, *mánus

mere, *meh₂-

midje, midten, *médʰyos

mig, *H₁me-

mige, *h₃meyǵʰ-

minde, *men-

mindske, *mey-

mine, *H₁meme-

mis-, *mey-

misdåd, *dheH₁-

miskmask, misse, miste, *mey-

mjød, *médʰu

moder, *méh₂tēr

mon, *men-

mor, *méh₂tēr

mord, *mer-

mund, *mendʰ-

munter, *men-

mus, muskulær, *muh₂s-

myg, *mus-

myre, *morwi-

mælk, *H₂melǵ-

mær, *marko-

mønt, *men-

mål, *meh₁-

måne, måned, *méh₁ns

nat, nattergal, *nókʷts

navle, *h₃enbʰ-

navn, *h₁nómṇ

negl, *h₃negʰ-

nemme, *nem-

nevø, *nepot-

ni, *H₁néwṇ

nord, norrøn, *h₁én

ny, *new

nyre, *negʷh-r-

næse, *néh₂s

nøgen, *negʷ-

nål, *(s)neh₁-

od, *dheH₁-

odder, *udréh₂

officiel, *h₃ep-

okse, *uksḗn

ol, *welH-

om, *h₂ent

onkel, *h₂éwh₂os

op, oppe, *upo

orakel, *h₃éh₁os

ord, *wekʷ-

orden, ordinær, ordne, ordning, ordre, *h₂er

orke, *werǵ-

orm, *wṛmis-

os, *h₃éh₁os, *wei

otte, *nókʷts, *oḱtṓw

oven, *upo

palaver, parabel, parabol, *gʷelH-

patent, *peth₂

pels, *pel-

pen, *péth₂r

pine, pinsel, *kʷey-

port, *per-

prins, *keh₂p-

probat, *bʰuH-

punkt, *pewǵ-

rad, *Hreh₁dʰ-

radikal, *wréh₂ds

rank, *h₃reǵ-

rat, *Hret-

regel, regere, regne, *h₃reǵ-

ren, rense, *krey-

repetere, *peth₂

ret, rette, rig, rige, *h₃reǵ-

rinde, *h₃er-, *h₃reyH-

rod, *wréh₂ds

rubin, *h₁rewdʰ-

rug, *wrugʰyo-

række, *h₃reǵ-

rød, *h₁rewdʰ-

rå, *krewh₂-

råde, *Hreh₁dʰ-

sadel, sadle, *sed-

sag, *seh₂g-

sage, *sekʷ-

saks, *sek-

salt, salte, *séh₂ls

samme, *sem-

samtykke, *teng-

sand, *H₁es-

sav, *sek-

save, se, *sekʷ-

sejr, sejre, *seǵʰ-

seks, *swéḱs

selv, *s(w)e-

sende, *sent-

sidde, *sed-

sige, sigte, *sekʷ-

sin, *s(w)e-

situationen, *teḱ-

skage, *(s)kek-

skare, skarp, *(s)ker-

ske, *(s)kek-

skid, ski, skide, *skey-

skjorte, *(s)ker-

skole, *seǵʰ-

skort, skrabe, skrive, skære, skår, skård, *(s)ker-

slig, *s(w)e-

slutte, *(s)kel-

sne, *sneygʷʰ-

so, *suH-

sogn, *seh₂g-

sol, *sóh₂wl̥

sold, *solh₂-

somme, *sem-

sommer, *sm̥-h₂-ó-

sove, *swep-

sovs, *séh₂ls

sparre, *spḗr

spejde, *speḱ-

spid, spiger, spile, *spey-

spise, *pewǵ-

spurre, spurv, *spḗr

stad, *steh₂-

stald, *stel-

stande, sted, *steh₂-

stige, *steyg^h-
stille, *stel-
stjerne, *h₂stḗr
stok, *(s)tew-
stor, *steh₂-
stræde, *sterh₃-
strø, *strew-
strøm, *srew-
studere, *(s)tew-
stund, *steh₂-
stykke, *(s)tew-
stå, *steh₂-
supplere, *pleh₁-
sved, *sweyd-
svin, *suH-
svintoks, *tetḱ-
sy, *sīw-
syd, *sóh₂wḷ
sylt, *séh₂ls
syn, *sekʷ-
synd, *H₁es-
system, *steh₂-
syv, *septm̥
sæd, *seH₁-
særk, *ser-
sætte, *sed-
søge, *seh₂g-
søm, *sīw-
søn, *suh₁nús
søndag, sønden, *sóh₂wḷ
søster, *swésōr
søvn, *swep-
så, *s(w)e-, *seH₁-
tabe, *deh₂-
tag, *(s)teg-
tak, takke, *teng-
tam, *demh₂-
tand, *h₃dónts
tarm, *terh₁-
Thor, *(s)tenh₂-
ti, *déḱm̥t
Ti, *dyew-
tid, *deh₂-
tirsdag, tisdag, *dyew-
to, *dwóH₁
toft, *dem-
tog, *dewk-
tolv, *dwóH₁
torden, *(s)tenh₂-
torp, *treb-
torsdag, *(s)tenh₂-
tov, *dewk-
tradition, *deH₃-
trane, *gerh₂-
tre, *tréyes
tro, *deru-
trost, *trosdos

tryg, trygd, *deru-
træ, *dóru
trøske, *trosdos
tråd, *terh₁-
tug, *dewk-
tunge, *dn̥ǵʰwéh₂s
tvende, tvilling, *dwóH₁
tvine, *dʰegʷʰ-
Ty, *dyew-
tykkes, *teng-
typisk, *(s)tew-
tyr, *(s)táwros
Tyr, *dyew-
tyve, *déḱm̥t
tække, *(s)teg-
tæmme, *demh₂-
tænke, *teng-
tære, *der-
tærske, tæske, *terh₁-
tøje, tømme, *dewk-
tømmer, *dem-
tør, tørst, *ters-
tå, *deyḱ-
tåle, *telh₂-
tår, *daḱru-
u-, *n̥-
uge, *weyk-
uld, *h₂welh₁-
ulv, *wḷkʷos
ung, *h₂yuh₁en-
urt, *wréh₂ds
uvis, *weyd-
vagt, *weǵ-
vaje, *H₂weH₁-
valte, *h₂welh₁-
vand, *wed-
var, *wer-
varm, *gʷʰer-
varulv, *wiHrós
vaske, *wed-
vej, veje, *weǵh-
verden, *h₂el-, *wiHrós
vest, *wek(ʷ)speros
vette, *weǵh-
vi, *wei
vide, *weyd-
vie, *weyk-
vilje, ville, *welh₁-
vin, *wóyh₁nom
vind, *H₂weH₁-
vindue, *h₃ekʷ-
virke, *werǵ-
vis, *weyd-
vogn, *weǵh-
vokse, *h₂ewg-
vol, *welH-
vold, *h₂welh₁-, *welH-

volde, *h₂welh₁-
vorde, *wert-
vædde, *wedʰ-
vædder, *wet-
væde, *wed-
væder, *wet-
vække, *weǵ-
vækst, *h₂ewg-
vælge, *welh₁-
være, *H₁es-
værk, *werǵ-
vætte, *weǵh-
væv, væve, *webh-
vørt, *wréh₂ds
våd, *wed-
vågen, *weǵ-
yngling, *h₂yuh₁en-
yver, *h₁owHdʰr̥-
æble, *h₂ébōl
æde, *h₁ed-
æg, *h₂ék, *h₂ōwyóm
ælde, ældre, ældst, *h₂el-
ærje, *H₂erH₃-
æt, *h₂eyḱ-
æter, *h₂eydʰ-
ætse, *h₁ed-
ø, *h₂ekʷeh₂-
ød, *h₂ew
øge, *h₂ewg-
øje, *h₃ekʷ-
økse, *h₂ék
øl, *h₂elut-
øland, *h₂ekʷeh₂-
øre, *h₂ew-
ørke, *werǵ-
ørn, *h₃érō
øst, *h₂ews-
å, *h₂ekʷeh₂-
åg, *yugóm
ålam, *h₂ówis
ånd, ånde, *h₂enh₁-
år, *yeh₁-
ås, *h₁ed-

Icelandic

-son, *suh₁nús
-tiu, -tugu, *déḱm̥t
af, *h₂pó
afl, afli, *h₃ep-
aftann, *h₁epi
aftur, *h₂pó
aka, *H₂eǵ-
akarn, *eh₃g-
akur, *h₂éǵros
ala, aldur, *h₂el-
alin, *Heh₃l-
allur, *h₂el-
alvara, *weh₁-
ambátt, *H₂eǵ-
anda, andi, *h₂enh₁-
andyrði, *wekʷ-
angist, angur, *h₂enǵʰ-
annar, *h₂énteros
arbeið, arbeiði, arfi, *h₃erbʰ-
ari, *h₃érō
armur, *h₂er
aska, *h₂eh₁s-
askur, *h₃es-
auður, *h₂ew
auga, *h₃ekʷ-
auka, *h₂ewg-
austrænn, austur, *h₂ews-
á, *h₂ekʷeh₂-
ágúst, *h₂ewg-
ári, *yeh₁-
átt, *h₂eyḱ-
átta, *oktṓw
bani, *gʷʰen-
banna, *bʰeh₂-
barr, *bʰars-
baun, *bʰabʰeh₂-
bákn, *bʰeh₂-
bátur, *bʰeyd-
beiða, *bʰeydʰ-
beit, beita, *bʰeyd-
ben, *gʷʰen-
bera, *bher-
berg, *bʰerǵʰ-
beserkur, *ser-
beyki, *bʰeh₂go-
birki, *bʰereǵ-
bí, *bʰey-
bíða, *bʰeydʰ-
bíta, *bʰeyd-
bjarg, *bʰerǵʰ-
bjóða, *bʰewdʰ-
björk, *bʰereǵ-
blað, *bʰleh₃-

blása, blástur, *bʰleh₁-
blífa, *leyp-
blóm, blómi, *bʰleh₃-
boð, boða, *bʰewdʰ-
bokki, bokkur, *bʰuHgos-
borg, *bʰerǵʰ-
botn, *bʰudʰmén
bók, *bʰeh₂go-
bón, *bʰeh₂-
brenna, broð, *bʰrewh₁-
bróðir, *bʰréh₂tēr
brugga, brunnur, *bʰrewh₁-
brún, *h₃bʰrúHs
bukkur, *bʰuHgos-
búa, búð, *bʰuH-
byrja, *bher-
býfluga, *bʰey-
býsn, *bʰewdʰ-
bæn, *bʰeh₂-
börur, *bher-
dagur, *dʰegʷʰ-
daunn, *dʰewh₂-
dáð, *dheH₁-
deigur, *dʰeyǵʰ-
deponenssögn, *teḱ-
djúpur, *dʰewb-
djöfull, *gʷelH-
doktor, *deḱ-
dómur, *dheH₁-
dóttir, *dʰugh₂tḗr
dust, dúnn, *dʰewh₂-
dvina, *dʰegʷʰ-
dyr, *dʰwer-
dýpt, *dʰewb-
dýr, dýrð, *dʰegʷʰ-
dæma, *dheH₁-
dögg, *dʰewh₂-
efna, efni, *h₃ep-
eftir, *h₂pó
eg, *egH₂
egg, *h₂éḱ, *h₂ōwyóm
eiga, *h₂eyḱ-
eik, *h₂eyǵ-
eimyrja, *h₁ews-
einigur, einn, *óy-nos
eir, *h₂eyos
ek, *egH₂
ekkja, *h₂enk-
eldri, *h₂el-
eldur, *h₂eydʰ-
ella, *h₂el-
ellefu, *óy-nos
elli, *h₂el-
elri, *h₃el-
elstur, *h₂el-
enn, *h₂ent
epli, *h₂ébōl

erfi, erfiði, *h₃erbʰ-
erja, *H₂erH₃-
eta, *h₁ed-
ey, *h₂ekʷeh₂-
eyða, *h₂ew
eyland, *h₂ekʷeh₂-
eyra, *h₂ew-
ég, *egH₂
éta, *h₁ed-
fabúla, fabúlera, *bʰeh₂-
faðir, *ph₂tḗr
faðmur, *peth₂
far, fara, farmur, fart, *per-
fastur, *peh₂ǵ-
fata, fatta, *ped-
fax, *peḱ-
fá, *peyḱ-
feldur, fell, *pel-
ferð, *per-
fergja, *h₂erk-
ferja, *per-
fet, feta, *ped-
fé, *peḱu-
fimm, *pénkʷe
finna, *pent-
fiskur, *peisḱ-
fjórir, *kʷetwóres
fjöður, *péth₂r
fjöl-, *pleh₁-
fjörður, *per-
fjötur, *ped-
flaga, *pleh₂-
flatur, *pleth₂-
fleiri, *pleh₁-
flengja, *pleh₂k-
flet, fleti, *pleth₂-
fley, fleygja, fljóta, fljúga, flota, floti, *plew-
fló, *plou-
flóa, flóð, *plew-
flór, *pleh₂-
fluga, flytja, flýja, *plew-
fold, *pleth₂-
foss, *pers-
fóður, *peh₂-
fólk, *pleh₁-
fótur, *pṓds
fram, frá, *per-
fregna, *preḱ-
fremja, freyja, Freyr, *per-
friðill, friður, frilla, frjá, frjáls, *preyH-
frú, *per-
frýnilegur, frændi, *preyH-
fullur, *pleh₁-
fundur, *pent-
funi, *péh₂ur
fura, furu, *perkʷu-
fúr, *péh₂ur

fylki, fylkja, fylla, fylli, *pleh$_1$-

fyrir, *per-

fyrirgefa, *g^{h}eb^h-

fyrst, fyrstur, *per-

fæða, fæði, *peh$_2$-

fær, *peḱ-, *per-

færa, *per-

fölur, *pelH-

garði, garður, *ǵ^{h}er-

garn, *ǵ^{h}ern-

gáfa, gefa, *g^{h}eb^h-

geit, *g^{h}aydos

gestur, *g^{h}óstis

geta, *weyd-

gift, *g^{h}eb^h-

gjarn, *ǵ^{h}er-

gjóta, *ǵ^{h}ew

gjöf, *g^{h}eb^h-

gjörð, *ǵ^{h}er-

gnit, *knid-

goð, *ǵ^{h}ew

gras, gróa, grænn, *g^{h}reh$_1$-

guð, *ǵ^{h}ew

gull, gulur, *ǵ^{h}elh$_3$-

gumi, *ǵ^{h}mṓ

gunnur, *g^{wh}en-

gæfur, *g^{h}eb^h-

gæs, *ǵ^{h}ans-

görn, *ǵ^{h}ern-

hafa, *keh$_2$p-

hafur, *kapro

haki, *keg-

hallur, *kelH-

hamar, *h$_2$éḱ-mō

hani, *keh$_2$n-

hata, hatur, *ḱeh$_2$d-

haust, *kerp-

há, *kenk-

hálmur, *ḱalam-

hálsmen, *men-

hásin, *kenk-

heilagur, heild, heill, *kóh$_2$ilus

heim, heimta, heimur, *ḱei-

helga, helgur, *kóh$_2$ilus

her, herbergi, herja, hertogi, *ker-

hestur, *kek-

heyra, *h$_2$ḱh$_2$owsyéti

hér, *ḱi-

híena, *suH-

hjal, hjala, *kelh$_1$-

hjarni, *ḱerh$_2$-

hjarta, *ḱḗr

hjálmur, *ḱel-

hjól, *k^{w}el-

hlíð, *ḱley-

hljóður, *ḱlew-

hlóa, *kelh$_1$-

hlusta, *ḱlew-

hollur, *ḱel-

horn, *ḱerh$_2$-

hors, horskur, *ḱers-

hrár, *krewh$_2$-

hreinn, hreinsa, hrina, *krey-

hross, *ḱers-

hræ, *krewh$_2$-

hundrað, *ḱm̥tóm

hundur, *ḱwṓ

hvað, hvar, hver, hvi, *k^{w}is

hvila, *k^{w}yeh$_1$-

hvor, hvorki, *k^{w}is

hylja, *ḱel-

hyrna, *ḱerh$_2$-

hækja, *keg-

hæll, *kenk-

hæna, *keh$_2$n-

höfn, *keh$_2$p-

höfuð, *kapōlo

höfugur, *keh$_2$p-

höll, *ḱel-

i, *h$_1$én

is, *h$_1$eyH-

í gær, *d^{h}ǵ^h(y)es-

ígull, *ang^w(h)i-

jaki, *yeǵ-

já, *éy / h$_1$e

járn, *h$_1$ésh$_2$r̥

jór, *h$_1$éḱwos

jörð, *h$_1$er-

jurt, *wréh$_2$ds

júgur, *h$_1$owHd^{h}r̥-

jökull, *yeǵ-

jöstur, *yes-

jötunn, *h$_1$ed-

kala, kaldur, *gel-

kambur, *ǵómb^{h}os

karl, *ǵerh$_2$-

kassi, *keh$_2$p-

kemba, *ǵómb^{h}os

kenna, *ǵneh$_3$-

kind, *ǵenH$_1$-

kinn, *ǵénus

kjallari, *ḱel-

kjósa, *ǵews-

knega, *ǵneh$_3$-

kné, *ǵónu

kokka, *pek^w-

koma, *g^{w}em-

kona, *g^{w}én

konungdómur, konungur, *ǵenH$_1$-

korn, *ǵr̥Hnom

kostur, *ǵews-

kólna, *gel-

kóngur, *ǵenH$_1$-

krani, *gerh$_2$-

kunna, kunnur, *ǵneh₃-
kvelja, *gʷelH-
kvenna, *gwén
kvern, *gʷrh₂-n-uH-
kvikur, *gʷeyh₃-
kvinna, kvon, *gwén
kvörn, *gʷrh₂-n-uH-
kylur, *gel-
kyn, *ǵenH₁-
kynna, *ǵneh₃-
kýr, *gʷṓws
kænn, *ǵneh₃-
land, *lendʰ-
langvia, langvigi, *weyh₁-
lauf, *lewbʰ-
lá, *lókus
lágur, *legh-
lán, *leykʷ-
leggja, *legh-
legíó, *leǵ-
leifa, *leyp-
leigja, *leykʷ-
lenda, lendar, *lendʰ-
lepja, *leb-
léttur, *h₁lengʷʰ-
lifur, *leyp-
liggja, *legh-
list, *leys-
lín, lína, *lino-
ljá, *leykʷ-
ljóma, ljómi, ljós, ljótur, *lewk-
ljúfur, *lewbʰ-
ljúka, *seh₂g-
loðinn, *h₁lewdʰ-
lof, *lewbʰ-
lok, *seh₂g-
lunga, *lengʷʰ-
lús, *luHs-
lygi, *legh-
lýður, *h₁lewdʰ-
læra, *leys-
löður, *lewh₃-
lög, *legh-
lögur, *lókus
maður, *mánus
maga, *mak-
magur, *meh₂ḱ-
makka, *men-
mala, *melh₂-
manneskja, *mánus
mar, *marko-, *móri
mara, *mer-
marsvin, *suH-
maur, *morwi-
mál, *meh₁-
málmur, *melh₂-
máni, mánudagur, mánuður, *mḗh₁n̥s

meira, meiri, *meh₂-
meistari, *méǵh₂s
mennskur, *mánus
mergur, *mosgʰos
meri, *marko-
mestur, *meh₂-
meta, *med-
mér, *H₁me-
miðja, miður, *médʰyos
mig, *H₁me-
mikill, *méǵh₂s
milska, *melit-
minn, *H₁meme-
minni, mis-, missa, *mey-
míga, *h₃meyǵʰ-
mjólk, mjólka, *H₂melǵ-
mjöður, *médʰu
mjöl, *melh₂-
morð, *mer-
móðir, *méh₂tēr
muna, *men-
mund, *méh₂-r̥
munni, munnur, *mendʰ-
munur, *men-
mús, *muh₂s-
mylkur, *H₂melǵ-
mynd, mynt, *men-
mý, *mus-
mön, *men-
naðra, naður, *neHtr-
nafli, *h₃enbʰ-
nafn, *h₁nómn̥
nagli, *h₃negʰ-
nakinn, *negʷ-
nál, *(s)neh₁-
nátt, *nókʷts
nema, *nem-
niður, *nepot-
nifl, *nebʰ-
nift, *nepot-
nit, *knid-
níu, *H₁néwn̥
norðan, norður, norrænn, *h₁én
nór, *(s)neh₂-
nótt, *nókʷts
nýr, *new
nýra, *negʷh-r-
næturgali, *nókʷts
nögl, *h₃negʰ-
nös, *néh₂s
oddur, *dheH₁-
of, ofur-, *upo
ok, *yugóm
okkur, *wei
olbogi, olnbogi, *Heh₃l-
orð, *wekʷ-
orka, *werǵ-

ormur, *wr̥mis-
ǫrvar, *h₂erkʷo-
otur, *udréh₂
oxi, *uksḗn
ó-, *n̥-
ós, *h₃éh₁os
ótta, *nókʷts
óviss, *weyd-
pendúll, *pewǵ-
penni, *péth₂r
plebbi, *pleh₁-
prins, *keh₂p-
radikal, *wréh₂ds
rakkur, *h₃reǵ-
rauður, *h₁rewdʰ-
ráða, *Hreh₁dʰ-
regla, reikna, *h₃reǵ-
renna, *h₃er-, *h₃reyH-
rétta, réttur, ríkur, *h₃reǵ-
rím, *h₂er
rǫðull, *Hret-
rót, *wréh₂ds
rúbín, *h₁rewdʰ-
rúgur, *wrugʰyo-
ræða, röð, *Hreh₁dʰ-
saga, *sekʷ-
saklaus, *seh₂g-
salt, salta, saltur, *séh₂ls
samur, *sem-
samþykkja, *teng-
sannur, *H₁es-
sauma, saumur, *sīw-
sax, *sek-
sá, *seH₁-, *só, *suH-
sáð, *seH₁-
sátt, *seh₂g-
seggur, segja, *sekʷ-
semja, *sem-
senda, *sent-
serkur, *ser-
sess, setja, *sed-
sex, *swéḱs
sér, sig, *s(w)e-
sigra, sigur, *seǵʰ-
sinn, *s(w)e-
sinna, *sent-
sitja, *sed-
sjá, sjón, *sekʷ-
sjö, *septm̥
skaka, *(s)kek-
skarð, skari, skarpur, *(s)ker-
skikka, *(s)kek-
skitur, skíð, skíta, *skey-
skor, skortur, *(s)ker-
skóli, *seǵʰ-
skrapa, skrifa, skær, *(s)ker-
slikur, *s(w)e-
snjóa, snjór, *sneygʷʰ-
snúður, *(s)neh₁-
snær, *sneygʷʰ-
snör, *snusós
sofa, *swep-
sonur, *suh₁nús
sókn, *seh₂g-
sól, *sóh₂wl̥
spá, speja, *speḱ-
spör, *spḗr
staður, *steh₂-
stallur, *stel-
standa, *steh₂-
stilla, *stel-
stíga, *steygʰ-
stjarna, *h₂stḗr
stjór, *(s)táwros
stjúpbarn, *bher-
stokkur, *(s)tew-
stó, stóð, stór, *steh₂-
straumur, *srew-
strá, *strew-
stræti, *sterh₃-
stund, *steh₂-
stynja, *(s)tenh₂-
suðrænn, suður, *sóh₂wl̥
sumar, *sm̥-h₂-ó-
sumur, *sem-
sunna, sunnan, sunnudagur, *sóh₂wl̥
svefja, svefn, *swep-
sveiti, sviti, *sweyd-
svín, *suH-
svo, *s(w)e-
synd, synja, *H₁es-
systir, *swésōr
sýn, *sekʷ-
sýr, *suH-
sætt, *seh₂g-
söðla, söðull, *sed-
sög, *sek-
sök, *seh₂g-
sönnun, *H₁es-
takk, *teng-
tamur, *demh₂-
tarfur, *(s)táwros
taug, taumur, *dewk-
tá, *deyḱ-
tár, *daḱru-
temja, *demh₂-
teygja, *dewk-
ténor, *ten-
timbur, *dem-
tíð, tíður, *deh₂-
tíu, *déḱm̥t
tjara, *dóru
toga, togi, *dewk-
topt, *dem-

385

tólf, *dwóH₁
trani, *gerh₂-
tré, *dóru
trú, tryggð, *deru-
tuft, *dem-
tugur, *dékm̥t
tunga, *dn̥ǵʰwéh₂s
tuttugu, *dékm̥t
tveir, tvenna, tvennur, tvi-, tvær, tvö, *dwóH₁
Týr, *dyew-
tæra, *der-
tönn, *h₃dónts
ull, *h₂welh₁-
um, *h₂ent
unglingur, ungur, *h₂yuh₁en-
urður, *wert-
uxi, *uksén
úlfur, *wĺkʷos
vagn, *weǵh-
vakinn, vakta, vakur, *weǵ-
vald, valda, *h₂welh₁-
vana, vanta, *h₁weh₂-
var, varða, *wer-
varmur, *gʷʰer-
varúlfur, *wiHrós
vaska, vatn, *wed-
vaxa, *h₂ewg-
veðja, *wedʰ-
veður, *wet-
vefja, vefur, *webh-
vega, *weǵh-, *weyk-
vegur, *weǵh-
veiða, veiði, *weyh₁-
vekja, *weǵ-
velja, *welh₁-
ver, *wiHrós
vera, *H₁es-
verða, *wert-
verja, *wes-
verk, *werǵ-
verma, *gʷʰer-
veröld, *h₂el-, *wiHrós
vespa, *wobs-
vestur, *wek(ʷ)speros
vér, við, *wei
vigja, vika, *weyk-
vilja, vilji, *welh₁-
vindauga, *h₃ekʷ-
vindur, *H₂weH₁-
virka, *werǵ-
virtur, *wréh₂ds
viss, *weyd-
vist, *H₁es-
vita, vitur, *weyd-
vín, *wóyh₁nom
vís, vísdómur, *weyd-
vor, *wésr̥

votur, væta, *wed-
vættur, *weǵh-
völur, *welH-
vörður, *wer-
vöxtur, *h₂ewg-
ylgur, *wĺkʷos
yrkja, *werǵ-
þak, *(s)teg-
þakka, *teng-
þar, *só
þarmur, *terh₁-
þá, *só
þekja, *(s)teg-
þekkja, *teng-
þenja, *ten-
þerra, *ters-
þér, *túh₂
þjóð, Þjóðann, *tewtéh₂
þjór, *(s)táwros
þola, *telh₂-
þorp, Þorpið, *treb-
þorsti, *ters-
þórsdagur, *(s)tenh₂-
þraut, *trewd-
þráður, þreskja, *terh₁-
þreyta, *trewd-
þrír, *tréyes
þrjóta, *trewd-
þrjú, *tréyes
þröstur, *trosdos
þurr, *ters-
þú, *túh₂
þykja, þökk, *teng-
æ, *h₂ey-
ær, *h₂ówis
æsa, *yes-
ætíð, *h₂ey-
ætt, *h₂eyḱ-
öl, *h₂elut-
öld, *h₂el-
öln, *Heh₃l-
önd, *h₂eneti-
öngull, *h₂enk-
ör, *h₂erkʷo-
örn, *h₃érō
öxi, *h₂éḱ
öxl, *H₂eǵ-

Welsh

a, *h₁eǵʰs
adain, *péth₂r
adferf, *wekʷ-
adnabod, adwaen, *ǵneh₃-
aelwyd, *h₂eydʰ-
aeron, *eh₃g-
aeth, *neḱ-
afal, afallen, *h₂ébōl
ail, *h₂el-
ais, *h₃ésth₁
amaeth, *H₂eǵ-
amrawdd, *Hreh₁dʰ-
an-, *ṇ-
anadi, *h₂enh₁-
angau, *neḱ-
anghad, *h₂enk-
aradr, *H₂erH₃-
ardd, *h₂erHdʰ-
arddu, aredig/arddaf, *H₂erH₃-
arf, *h₂er
arth, *h₂ŕtḱos
arwain, *wedʰ-
asen, asgwrn, *h₃ésth₁
astudio, *(s)tew-
ateb, *sekʷ-
awr, *yeh₁-
Awst, *h₂ewg-
awyr, *h₂ews-
bach, *bak-
bara, *bʰars-
barf, *bʰardʰeh₂-
barnu, *gʷerH-
bedw, bedwen, *gʷet-
begregyr, *bʰey-
benyw, *gwén
bera, *bʰerǵʰ-
berf, *wekʷ-
blith, *H₂melǵ-
bochel, *kʷel-
bod, *bʰuH-
bodd, *bʰewdʰ-
braich, *mréǵʰ-
braint, *bʰerǵʰ-
brawd, *bʰréh₂tēr
bre, *bʰerǵʰ-
breuan, *gʷrh₂-n-uH-
bri, *bʰerǵʰ-
brwd, *bʰrewh₁-
bryw, *gʷerh₂-
buwch, *gʷṓws
bwch, *bʰuHgos-
bydaf, *bʰey-
byw, *gʷeyh₃-

caeriwrch, *kapro
caeth, *keh₂p-
cant, *ḱṃtóm
canu, *keh₂n-
car, *ḱers-
carw, *ḱerh₂-
cas, *keh₂d-
caseg, *kek-
cawdd, *ḱeh₂d-
cegin, *pekʷ-
cell, *ḱel-
chwaer, *swésōr
chwech, *swéḱs
chwedl, *sekʷ-
Chwefror, *dʰegʷʰ-
chwi, *túh₂
chwys, *sweyd-
ci, *ḱwṓ
ciwdod, ciwed, *ḱei-
cledd, *ḱley-
clo, *(s)kel-
clywed, *ḱlew-
coes, *koḱs-
cof, *men-
coginio, *pekʷ-
coleg, *legh-
cordd, *ker-
corff, *krep-
corn, *ḱerh₂-
crafanc, *h₂enk-
craidd, *ḱḗr
crau, *krewh₂-
creyryn, *ḱerh₂-
crynu, *krey-
cwn, *ḱwṓ
cyfeb, *h₁éḱwos
cyfyng, *h₂enǵʰ-
cymysgaf, *mey-
cynnig, *deyḱ-
cythrudd, *trewd-
dafad, *demh₂-
dant, *h₃dónts
dâr, *dóru
dau, *dwóH₁
dawn, *deH₃-
ddoe, *dʰǵʰ(y)es-
deau, *deḱs-
defnydd, *dem-
deg, degawd, *déḱṃt
deifio, *dʰegʷʰ-
deigr, *daḱru-
derw, derwen, *dóru
devnydh, *dem-
diafol, diawl, *gʷelH-
diffyn, *gʷʰen-
dillwng, *seh₂g-
dôr, *dʰwer-

387

drudwy, *trosdos
drws, *dʰwer-
drwy, *terh₂-
dug, *dewk-
duw, *dyew-
dwfn, *dʰewb-
dwy, *dwóH₁
dwyn, *dewk-
dydd Gwener, dydd Iau, dydd Llun, dydd Mawrth,
 dydd Mercher, dydd Sadwrn, dydd Sul, *deyn-
dydd, *dyew-
dyfrgi, *ḱwṓ
dymchwel, *kʷel-
dyn, *ǵʰmṓ
dynu, *dʰeh₁(y)-
dysgu, *deḱ-
dywy, *dʰewh₂-
ebe, *sekʷ-
ebol, ebran, *h₁éḱwos
ech-, *h₁eǵʰs
edn, *péth₂r̥
edwino, *dʰegʷʰ-
eirin, *eh₃g-
eistedd, *sed-
elin, *Heh₃l-
ellwng, *seh₂g-
eneid, *h₂enh₁-
enw, *h₁nómn̥
erchi, *preḱ-
erw, *h₁er-
eryr, *h₃érō
estron, *h₁eǵʰs
ewig, *h₂ówis
ewin, *h₃negʰ-
ewythr, *h₂éwh₂os
ffa, ffaen, *bʰabʰeh₂-
ffeindio, *pent-
ffrind, *preyH-
ffrwd, *srew-
ffwrn, ffwrnais, *gʷʰer-
ffydd, *bʰeydʰ-
gaeaf, *ǵʰey-
gafael, *gʰeh₁bʰ-
gafr, *kapro
garan, *gerh₂-
garth, *ǵʰer-
garw, *gʰers-
gên, *ǵénus
geni, *ǵenH₁-
glin, *ǵónu
gnawd, *ǵneh₃-
goddaith, *dʰegʷʰ-
goddef, *demh₂-
gor, *upo
gramadeg, *gerbʰ-
grawn, *ǵr̥Hnom
greddf, *wréh₂ds

gwaethl, *wekʷ-
gwain, *weǵʰ-
gwair, *h₂ewg-
gwaladr, *h₂welh₁-
gwân , gwanu, *gʷʰen-
gwanwyn, *wésr̥
gwar, *upo
gwau, *webh-
gwawr, *h₂ews-
gwchi, *wobs-
gwedd, *wedʰ-
gweddw, *h₁weydʰ
gweilgi, *wl̥kʷos
gweld, *weyd-
gwell, *welh₁-
gwely, *legh-
gwennol, *wésr̥
gwep, *wekʷ-
gwer, *wed-
gwery, *werǵ-
gwestai, *gʰóstis
gwian, *h₂welh₁-
gwin, *wóyh₁nom
gwir, *weh₁-
gwisg, *wes-
gwlad, *h₂welh₁-
gŵr, *wiHrós
gwraidd, *wréh₂ds
gwraint, *wr̥mis-
gwresogi, *gʷʰer-
gwst, *ǵews-
gwybod, *weyd-
gwydr, *wed-
gŵyl, *weǵ-
gwynn, *ǵneh₃-
gwynt, *H₂weH₁-
gwŷs, *weyd-
haearn, *h₁ésh₂r̥
haf, *sm̥-h₂-ó-
hâl, halen, *séh₂ls
harbwr, *ker-
haul, *sóh₂wl̥
hebu, *sekʷ-
hen, henadur, *sénos
heno, *nókʷts
hil, *seH₁-
hou, *h₂ew
hwch, *suH-
hwyad, *h₂éwis
iâ, *yeǵ-
iaith, *yek-
ias, *yes-
iau, *yugóm
ieuanc, ifanc, *h₂yuh₁en-
jôc, *yek-
llaeth, *glag-
llan, *lendʰ-

llau, *luHs-
llawn, *pleh₁-
llawr, lledu, *pleh₂-
llefaru, *leb-
lleyn, *pleh₂-
llin, *lino-
llug, *lewk-
llwch, *lókus
llwyd, *pelH-
llwyn, *leǵ-
llwyn, *lendʰ-, *pleh₂-
llydan, Llydaw, *pleth₂-
llyfr, *h₁lewdʰ-, *lewbʰ-
llys-yw-en, *angʷ(h)i-
llysiau, *h₁lewdʰ-
mab, *meh₂ḱ-
mad, *meh₂-
malu, *melh₂-
mant, *mendʰ-
march, marchog, *marko-
marw, *mer-
mawr, *meh₁-, *meh₂-
medd, *médʰu
meddyg, *med-
megin, *mak-
meidd, *mosgʰos
meistr, *méǵh₂s
mêl, *melit-
melin, *melh₂-
menyw, *gwḗn
mêr, *mosgʰos
mesur, *meh₁-
mewn, *médʰyos
mi, *H₁me-
mil, *sem-
mis, *mḗh₁ns
modryb, *méh₂tēr
môr, *móri
mwnwgl, *men-
mwy, *meh₂-
mynwent, mynydd, *men-
myrion, *morwi-
mysgaf, *mey-
Nadolig, *ǵenH₁-
nai, *nepot-
naw, *H₁néwn̥
nawf, *(s)neh₂-
nedd, *knid-
nef, *nebʰ-
neidr, *neHtr-
nêr, *h₂nḗr
nerfus, *(s)neh₁-
nerth, *h₂nḗr
newydd, *new
ni, *wei
nifer, *nem-
noe, *(s)neh₂-

noeth, *negʷ-
nos, *nókʷts
ny, *wei
nyddu, *(s)neh₁-
nyf, *sneygʷʰ-
nyth, *nisdós
o, *h₂ew
ochr, *h₂éḱ
odyn, *h₂eh₁s-
oed, *h₂ey-
oen, *h₂egʷnos
oes, *h₂ey-
oged, *h₂éḱ
olwyn, *Heh₃l-
ongl, *h₂enk-
onnen, *h₃es-
pa, *kʷis
padell, *peth₂
paradwys, *dʰeyǵʰ-
pechadur, pechod, pechu, *ped-
pedair, pedwar, *kʷetwóres
perth, *perkʷu-
perygl, *per-
plant, *pleh₂-
plws, *plou-
plwyf, pobl, *pleh₁-
poen, *kʷey-
pont, *pent-
porchell, *pórḱos
porth, prif, priod, *per-
problem, *gʷelH-
prynu, *kʷreyh₂-
pump, *pénkʷe
pwy, *kʷis
pwys, *pewǵ-
pysgod, *peisḱ-
rhaith, rhe, *h₃reǵ-
rhedeg, *Hret-
rheg, *preḱ-
rheol, rhi, rhiain, *h₃reǵ-
rhif, *h₂er-
rhod, *Hret-
rhudd, rhwd, *h₁rewdʰ-
rhy, *per-
rhybudd, *bʰewdʰ-
rhyd, *per-
rhyg, ryg, *wrugʰyo-
saig, *sekʷ-
sail, *sed-
saith, *septm̥
sawl, *s(w)e-
sedd, seddu, *sed-
senedd, *sénos
sêr, seren, *h₂stḗr
stryd, *sterh₃-
swydd, *sed-
swyn, *sek-

tafarn, *treb-
tafod, *dn̥ǵʰwéh₂s
tair, *tréyes
tant, *ten-
taradr, *terh₁-
taran, *(s)tenh₂-
tarw, *(s)táwros
taw, *steh₂-
teir, *tréyes
terfyn, *térmn̥
ti, *túh₂
tir, *ters-
to, *(s)teg-
tra, *terh₂-
traddodiad, *deH₃-
trannoeth, *nókʷts
tre, tref, *treb-
tri, *tréyes
trwy, *terh₂-
tud, *tewtéh₂
tŷ, *(s)teg-
uchel, *h₂ewg-
ugain, *wīkm̥tiH₁
un, *óy-nos
urdd, *h₂er
ŵy, *h₂ōwyóm
wyf, *h₁ey-
wyneb, *h₃ekʷ-
Wysg (Usk), *peisk-
wyth, *oḱtṓw
ych, *uksḗn
yfed, *peh₃-
ymochel, *kʷel-
yn, *h₁én
ysgar, *(s)ker-
ysgogi, *(s)kek-
ysgol, *seǵʰ-
ysgrifennu, *(s)ker-
ysgwyd, *skey-
ystafell, *steh₂-
ystryw, *strew-
ystyr, *weyd-

Irish

abhaill, *h₂ébōl
abstanaid, *ten-
achar, *h₂éḱ
adhair, *h₃éh₁os
aer, *h₂ews-
aibid, *gʰeh₁bʰ-
aigne, *ǵenH₁-
ailbheolas, *h₂el-
ainm, *h₁nómn̥
ainmhi, *h₂enh₁-
aipindic, *pewǵ-
air, *H₂erH₃-
áirc, *h₂erk-
airne, *eh₃g-
airteagal, *h₂er
áit, *pent-
áith, *h₂eh₁s-
aithin, *ǵneh₃-
ambicatos, amhas, *H₂eǵ-
an-, *n̥-
anáil, anam, *h₂enh₁-
ané, *dʰǵʰ(y)es-
anocht, *nókʷts
Aodh, *h₂eydʰ-
aoi, *h₂éwis
aois, *h₂ey-
aon, *óy-nos
apacailipsis, *ḱel-
arc, arcán, *pórḱos
ard, *h₂erHdʰ-
as, *h₁eǵʰs
athair, *ph₂tér
bac, *bak-
bád, *bʰeyd-
bán, *bʰeh₂-
bard, *gʷerH-
barúil, *gʷelH-
beach, beachlann, *bʰey-
bean, *gwḗn
beannaigh, *deyḱ-
beir, *bher-
beith, *gʷet-
beo, *gʷeyh₃-
bí, *bʰuH-
bláth, *bʰleh₃-
bleacht, *H₂melǵ-
bó, *gʷốws
boc, *bʰuHgos-
bonn, *bʰudʰmḗn
bráthair, *bʰréh₂tēr
breith, *bher-
brí, Brid, Brighid, *bʰerǵʰ-
bruach, *h₃bʰrúHs

brúid, *g^werh_2-	dínit, *$deḱ$-
bruth, *b^hrewh_1-	díreach, *$h_3reǵ$-
buabhall, *$g^wṓws$	diúc, *$dewk$-
búistéir, *b^huHgos-	diuilim, diul, *$d^heh_1(y)$-
busta, *h_1ews-	dó, *$dwóH_1$
cacht, *keh_2p-	dobharchú, *$ḱwṓ$
cad, *k^wis	doigh, *d^heg^{wh}-
caibidil, *$kapōlo$	domhain, *d^hewb-
cáirrfhiadh, *$ḱerh_2$-	Domhnach, *$deyn$-
cairt, *$ǵ^her$-	doras, *d^hwer-
can, *keh_2n-	drong, *d^her-
caora, *$kapro$	dúil, *d^hewh_2-
cás, *keh_2p-	duine, *$ǵ^hmṓ$
cé, *k^wis	dúr, *$deru$-
céad, *$ḱm̥tóm$	é, *$éy$ / h_1e
ceamara, *$(s)teg$-	éa-, *$ṇ$-
ceil, *$ḱel$-	ea, *$éy$ / h_1e
ceithair, *$k^wetwóres$	each, *$h_1éḱwos$
chuala, *$ḱlew$-	éacht, *$neḱ$-
clann, *$pleh_2$-	éadan, *h_2ent
clé, *$ḱley$-	éag, *$neḱ$-
cló, *$(s)kel$-	éan, *$péth_2r̥$
clú, cluas, cluin, *$ḱlew$-	Eanáir, *h_1ey-
coinsias, *$skey$-	earrach, *$wésr̥$
coláiste, *$legh$-	easna, *$h_3ésth_1$
corn, *$ḱerh_2$-	eastát, *$steh_2$-
corp, *$krep$-	eile, *h_2el-
corrán, *$kerp$-	eineach, *$h_1én$
cos, *$koḱs$-	éirigh, *$h_3reǵ$-
crean, *k^wreyh_2-	eite, eiteog, *$peth_2$
cró, *$krewh_2$-	fáinleog, *$wésr̥$
croí, croidhe, *$ḱḗr$	faoi, *upo
cruimhthir, *per-	fás, fásach, fásaigh, *h_1weh_2-
cú, *$ḱwṓ$	Feabhra, *d^heg^{wh}-
cuan, *keh_2p-	fead, *H_2weH_1-
cúig, *$pénk^we$	feadhbh, *h_1weyd^h
cuing, *$yewg$-	féan, *$weǵ^h$-
cuire, *ker-	féar, *h_2ewg-
cúng, *$h_2enǵ^h$-	fear, *$wiHrós$
daigh, *d^heg^{wh}-	fearg, *$werǵ$-
dair, *$dóru$	feascar, *$wek^{(w)}speros$
damh, *$demh_2$-	feighil, féile, *$weǵ$-
damhna, *dem-	feithicil, *$weǵ^h$-
dán, *deH_3-	fiabhras, *d^heg^{wh}-
Dé Luain, Dé Sathairn, *$deyn$-	fiche, *$wīḱm̥tiH_1$
déad, *$h_3dónts$	fínéagar, fíneamhain, fíniúin, fíon, *$wóyh_1nom$
dearbh, *$dóru$	fíor, *$d^heyǵ^h$-
dearmad, *men-	fíor, *weh_1-
deas, *$deḱs$-	fios, *$weyd$-
deathach, *d^hewh_2-	flaith, *h_2welh_1-
deich, *$déḱm̥t$	focal, *wek^w-
denus, *$deyn$-	foiche, *$wobs$-
deoir, *$daḱru$-	fréamh, *$wréh_2ds$
dhá, *$dwóH_1$	fuaim, *wek^w-
dia, *$deyn$-, *$dyew$-	fuil, *$ḱel$-
diabhal, *g^welH-	gabh, *$g^heh_1b^h$-
dingid, *$d^heyǵ^h$-	gabhar, *$kapro$

garda, *wer-
geimhreadh, *ǵʰey-
géineas, gin, giniúint, *ǵenH₁-
gionach, *ǵénus
glóir, *ǵneh₃-
glúin, *ǵónu
gnáth, *ǵneh₃-
gort, *ǵʰer-
grán, *ǵr̥Hnom
i, *h₁én
iarann, *h₁ésh₂r̥
iasc, *peisḱ-
ibh, *peh₃-
icht, *yek-
idir, *h₁én
imleac, *h₃enbʰ-
inné, *dʰǵʰ(y)es-
inscne, *sekʷ-
iolar, *h₃érō
ionga, *h₃negʰ-
is, *H₁es-
lacht, *glag-
lán, *pleh₁-
lann, *lendʰ-
laom, *lewk-
lár, *pleh₂-
leabhar, *lewbʰ-
leath, leathan, *pleth₂-
léigh, *leǵ-
liath, *pelH-
lig, *leykʷ-
ling, *h₁lengʷʰ-
líon, *lino-
liopa, *leb-
loch, *lókus
log, *stel-
loiscim, *lewk-
lui, luigh, *legh-
lus, *h₁lewdʰ-
mac, *meh₂ḱ-
maidin, *meh₂-
Máirt, *deyn-
máistir, *méǵh₂s
maith, *meh₂-
mallacht, *deyk-
marbh, *mer-
marc, marcach, *marko-
máthair, *méh₂tēr
meabhair, *men-
meadhg, *mosgʰos
meán, *médʰyos
measc, *mey-
meilt, *melh₂-
melg, *H₂melǵ-
mí, *H₁me-
mi, *médʰyos
mí, *méh₁n̥s

mias, *meh₁-
mil, *melit-
míle, *sem-
milis, *melit-
miodh, *médʰu
mór, *meh₁-
mór, *meh₂-
muileann, *melh₂-
muir, *móri
náisiún, *ǵenH₁-
naoi, *H₁néwn̥
nathair, *neHtr-
nead, *nisdós
neamh, *nebʰ-
neart, *h₂nḗr
nia, *nepot-
nocht, *negʷ-
nod, *ǵneh₃-
Nollaig, *ǵenH₁-
normálta, *ǵneh₃-
nua, *new
ó, *h₂éwh₂os
obair, *h₃ep-
ocht, *oḱtṓw
ochtapas, *pṓds
ochtar, *oḱtṓw
odar, *udréh₂
óg, *h₂yuh₁en-
oide, *átta
oighear, *yeǵ-
oil, *h₂el-
oineach, *h₃ekʷ-
ól, *peh₃-
olann, *h₂welh₁-
olc, *wl̥kʷos
oss, *uksḗn
peaca, *ped-
peall, *pel-
plúr, *bʰleh₃-
pobal, *pleh₁-
póg, *peh₂ǵ-
ponc, *pewǵ-
port, prióir, *per-
prionsa, *keh₂p-
promh, *bʰuH-
rí, *h₃reǵ-
rian, *h₃reyH-
rígh, *h₃reǵ-
ríomh, *h₂er-
ríon, *h₃reǵ-
rith, *Hret-
rithim, *srew-
rosc, *sekʷ-
roth, *Hret-
rua, rúibín, *h₁rewdʰ-
sagart, *dheH₁-
sáil, *steh₂-

sáile, salann, *séh₂ls
samhradh, *sm̥-h₂-ó-
scar, *(s)ker-
scéal, *sekʷ-
sciath, sciathán, *skey-
sciorta, *(s)ker-
scoil, *seǵʰ-
scóp, *speḱ-
scríobh, *(s)ker-
sé, *swéḱs
seacht, seachtain, *septm̥
seaimpin, *(s)teg-
seamhan, *seH₁-
séan, *sek-
sean, seanadóir, *sénos
seo, *só
seomra, *(s)teg-
sí, *éy / h₁e
singil, *sem-
síol, *seH₁-
siur, *swésōr
smior, *mosgʰos
snáth, *(s)neh₁-
sneachta, *sneygʷʰ-
sned, *knid-
snigh, *sneygʷʰ-
soc, *suH-
speictream, *speḱ-
sráid, *sterh₃-
srian, *dʰer-
sruth, *srew-
stad, *steh₂-
staidéar, *(s)tew-
staighre, *steygʰ-
stair, stór, *weyd-
suan, *swep-
sui, suigh, *sed-
súil, *sóh₂wl̥
tá, *steh₂-
tál, *tetḱ-
támh, *steh₂-
tarathar, *terh₁-
tarbh, *(s)táwros
tart, *ters-
teach, *(s)teg-
téad, *ten-
teanga, *dn̥ǵʰwéh₂s
tearc, *ters-
teoir, *wer-
thar, *terh₂-
tír, tirim, *ters-
tit, *(s)tew-
togh, *ǵews-
torann, *(s)tenh₂-
trá, *terh₂-
traidisiún, *deH₃-
tre, *terh₂-

treabh, *treb-
trí, *terh₂-, *tréyes
truid, *trosdos
tú, *túh₂
tuath, *tewtéh₂
ua, *h₂éwh₂os
uan, *h₂egʷnos
uasal, *h₂ewg-
ubh, *h₂ōwyóm
uillinn, *Heh₃l-
uisce, uisge, *wed-
úll, *h₂ébōl
um, *h₂ent
umhal, *dʰéǵʰōm
úth, *h₁owHdʰr̥-
veirteabra, *wert-

Latin

-bam, -bō, -bundus, *bʰuH-
-c, -ce, *ḱi-
-cen, *keh₂n-
-ceps, *kapōlo
-cola, *kʷel-
-decim, *déḱm̥t
-fer, *bher-
-īdēs, -oīdēs, *weyd-
-spex, *speḱ-
-thērium, *ǵʰwer-
-vīsor, *weyd-
(g)nāscī, *ǵenH₁-
(g)nōscere, *ǵneh₃-
ab-/a-/abs-, ab, *h₂pó
abante, *h₂ent
abbreviāre, *mréǵʰ-
abdere, abditus, *dheH₁-
abdūcere, abductiō, abductor, *dewk-
abhorrēre, abhorrēscere, *gʰers-
abiūdicāre, *h₂eyw-
abiungere, *yewg-
abiūrāre, abiūrātiō, *h₂eyw-
ablātiō, ablātīvus, ablātor, *bher-
ablēgāre, ablēgātiō, *legh-
abluēns, abluere, ablūtiō, ablūtor, *lewh₃-
abolēre, abolitiō, *h₂el-
aborīrī, abortāre, abortiō, abortīvum, *h₃er-
abscindere, abscissiō, *skey-
absistere, *steh₂-
abstinēns, abstinentia, abstinēre, *ten-
abstrūdere, *trewd-
abyssus, *dʰewb-
accipere, *keh₂p-
acclāmāre, acclāmātiō, *kelh₁-
acclīnāre, *ḱley-
acconciliāre, *kelh₁-
accurrere, *ḱers-
ācer, acerbāre, acerbitās, acerbus, acēre, acervus, acia, aciditās, acidus, aciēs, *h₂éḱ
acoetis, *ḱei-
acquiēscere, *kʷyeh₁-
ācrimōnia, ācritās, ācritūdō, *h₂éḱ
ācta, āctiō, āctitāre, āctīvitās, āctīvus, actor, āctrīx, āctus, *H₂éǵ-
acuārius, acuere, aculeus, acus, *h₂éḱ
adauctus, adaugēre, *h₂ewg-
addere, *deH₃-
addīcere, addictiō, addictus, *deyḱ-
additiō, *deH₃-
addūcere, adductor, *dewk-
adfundere, *ǵʰew-
adhibēre, *gʰeh₁bʰ-
adīre, *h₁ey-

adiūdicāre, adiūdicātiō, *h₂eyw-
adiunctiō, adiunctus, adiungere, *yewg-
adiūrāre, adiūrātiō, adiūrātor, *h₂eyw-
adminiculum, *méh₂-r̥
administrāre, administrātiō, administrātor, admiscēre, admixtus, *mey-
admonēre, admonitiō, *men-
adolēre, adolēscēns, adolēscere, *h₂el-
adōrāre, *h₃éh₁os
adulter, adulterāre, adulterīnus, adulterium, *h₂el-
aduncus, *h₂enk-
adūrere, *h₁ews-
advena, advenīre, adventīcius, adventus, *gʷem-
adverbiālis, adverbium, *wekʷ-
adversāre, adversus, advertere, *wert-
advocāre, advocātiō, advocātus, *wekʷ-
advolvere, *welH-
aedēs, aedicula, aedificāre, aedificātiō, aedificium, aedīlis, aedis, *h₂eydʰ-
aēneus, *h₂eyos
aeon, *h₂ey-
aequivalēns, aequivalēre, *h₂welh₁-
āēr, *h₂ews-
aerāmen, aerārium, aerūginōsus, aerūgō, aes, *h₂eyos
aesculus, *h₂eyǵ-
aestās, aestīvus, aestuārium, *h₂eydʰ-
aetās, aeternitās, aeternus, *h₂ey-
aether, *h₂eydʰ-
aevum, *h₂ey-
affacere, affectus, *dheH₁-
affiliare, *dʰeh₁(y)-
affirmāre, affirmātiō, *dʰer-
afflāre, affluēns, affluentia, affluere, *bʰleh₁-
ager, *h₂éǵros
agere, agger, aggerere, aggestus, agitāre, agitātiō, agitātor, agmen, *H₂éǵ-
agnella, agnellus, *h₂egʷnos
agnōmen, *h₁nómn̥
agnōscere, *ǵneh₃-
agnus, *h₂egʷnos
agon, agōnia, *H₂éǵ-
āgrārius, agrestis, agricola, agricultor, agrīcultūra, agrīmensor, *h₂éǵros
ālā, alar, *H₂eǵ-
alere, alescere, aliā, aliās, alica, alimentum, alimōnia, aliōrsum, *h₂el-
aliquis, *kʷis
alius, *h₂el-
allectīvus, *leǵ-
allēgātiō, *legh-
allegere, *leǵ-
allevāre, *h₁lengʷʰ-
allocāre, *stel-
alnus, *h₃el-
alter, alterāre, altercātiō, altercor, altus, *h₂el-
alūmen, *h₂elut-
alumnus, alveārium, alveolus, alveus, alvus, *h₂el-

āmanuēnsis, *méh₂-r̥
ambactus, ambaxtus, *H₂eǵ-
ambi-, *h₂ent
ambidexter, *deḱs-
ambiēns, ambīre, ambitus, ambō, *h₂ent
ambrosia, *mer-
ambūrere, *h₁ews-
amēns, *men-
āmentia, *men-
amethystinus, amethystus, *médʰu
anabasis, *gʷem-
anagignōscomena, *ǵneh₃-
anas, *h₂eneti-
anastasis, *steh₂-
anatīnus, *h₂eneti-
anceps, *kapōlo
angere, angina, angor, *h₂enǵʰ-
anguilla, *angʷ(h)i-
angulāris, angulus, *h₂enk-
angustus, *h₂enǵʰ-
anhēlāre, anhēlitus, anhēlus, anima, *h₂enh₁-
animadvertere, *wert-
animō, animosus, animus, *h₂enh₁-
anniversārius, *wert-
anōnymus, *h₁nómn̥
anorexia, *h₃reǵ-
anōrmalus, *ǵneh₃-
ānser, ānserīnus, *ǵʰans-
ante, *h₂ent
antecellere, *kelH-
antecipere, *keh₂p-
antepōnere, *teḱ-
anterior, *h₂ent
antevenīre, *gʷem-
antiae, *h₂ent
antīquārius, antīquitās, antīquus, *h₂énti-h₃kʷós
antithesis, antitheton, antithetum, *dheH₁-
anxietās, anxiōsus, anxius, *h₂enǵʰ-
apiānus, apicula, apis, apium, *bʰey-
apocalypsis, *ḱel-
apothēca, apothēcārius, *dheH₁-
apparēns, appārēre, appārēscere, appāritiō,
  appāritor, *peh₂-
appendere, appendix, *pewǵ-
appertinēre, *ten-
appetere, appetītiō, appetītus, *peth₂
applaudere, *pleh₂k-
applicāre, *pleḱ-
appōnere, *teḱ-
apportāre, *per-
apprehendere, apprehensiō, *weyd-
appretiō, *per-
approbātiō, *bʰuH-
apud, *h₁epi
aqua, *h₂ekʷeh₂-
aquaeductus, *dewk-, *h₂ekʷeh₂-
aquārius, aquāticus, aquātiō, aquātor, aqueus,
  *h₂ekʷeh₂-

aquifolius, *bʰleh₃-
aquilentus, aquōsus, *h₂ekʷeh₂-
āra, *h₂eh₁s-
arabilis, *H₂erH₃-
arānea, arāneus, *h₂er
arāre, arātor, aratorius, arātrum, *H₂erH₃-
arbor, arborētum, arboreus, *h₂erHdʰ-
arca, arcānus, arcārius, arcella, arcera, arcēre, *h₂erk-
archisynagōgus, *H₂eǵ-
architectus, *tetḱ-
arcticus, Arctūrus, *h₂r̥tḱos
arcuātus, *h₂erkʷo-
arcula, *h₂erk-
arcus, *h₂erkʷo-
arduitās, *h₂erHdʰ-
arduus, *h₂erHdʰ-
ārefacere, *dheH₁-, *h₂eh₁s-
ārēre, āridus, *h₂eh₁s-
arma, armārium, armātūra, armātus, armentum, *h₂er
armipotēns, *H₁es-
armō, armus, ars, articulo, articulus, artifex, artista,
  arto, artus, *h₂er
arx, *h₂erk-
ascia, *h₂éḱ
āscrībēre, *(s)ker-
aspectāre, aspectus, aspicere, *speḱ-
asportāre, asportātiō, *per-
assedēre, *sed-
assentīrī, *sent-
asserere, assertiō, *ser-
assiduus, *sed-
assignāre, assignātiō, *sek-
assimulāre, assimulātiō, *sem-
assistentia, assistere, *steh₂-
assula, *H₂eǵ-
assurgere, *h₃reǵ-
assus, *h₂eh₁s-
astāre, *steh₂-
astēr, *h₂stḗr
asternere, *sterh₃-
astripotēns, *H₁es-
astruere, *strew-
astus, astūtia, astūtus, *h₂éḱ
atavus, *h₂éwh₂os
atheos, *dʰéh₁s
āthlēta, āthlēticus, *H₂weH₁-
atrōcitās, atrōx, *h₂eh₁tro-h₃kʷs
atta, *átta
attendere, attentiō, attentus, *ten-
atterere, *terh₁-
attinēre, *ten-
attribuere, attribūtor, *bʰuH-
attrītiō, *terh₁-
au-, *h₂ew
aucellus, *h₂éwis
auceps, *keh₂p-
auctiō, auctor, auctōritās, auctrīx, *h₂ewg-

audiēns, audientia, audīre, audītiō, audītor,
auditōrium, audītōrius, audītus, *h₂ewis-dʰh₁-
auferre, *bher-
augēre, augmentum, augur, augurāre, augurium,
　augustus, *h₂ewg-
aura, *h₂ews-
auricula, *h₂ew-
auripigmentum, *peyḱ-
auris, *h₂ew-
aurōra, aurōreus, *h₂ews-
auscultāre, auscultātiō, auscultātor, *ḱel-
auspex, auspicium, *speḱ-
auster, austrālis, *h₂ews-
aut, autem, authenticus, *h₂ew
auxiliāris, auxiliārius, auxilium, *h₂ewg-
āvertere, *wert-
aviārium, avicella, avis, *h₂éwis
avunculus, avus, *h₂éwh₂os
axilla, axis, axon, *H₂eǵ-
bacillum, baculum, *bak-
ballista, *gʷelH-
barba, barbatus, barbula, *bʰardʰeh₂-
bardus, *gʷerH-
basis, *gʷem-
bellipotēns, *H₁es-
benedīcere, *deyḱ-
benefacere, benefactor, benefactus, *dheH₁-
betula, *gʷet-
bi-, *dwóH₁
bibāx, bibere, bibitor, bibitus, *peh₃-
bibliothēca, *dheH₁-
bibulus, *peh₃-
biceps, *kapōlo
bifidus, *bʰeyd-
bīnārius, bīnī, *dwóH₁
bipēs, *pṓds
birotus, *Hret-
bis, *dwóH₁
bitumen, bitūminōsus, *gʷet-
bivium, *weyh₁-
boārius, bōs, Bosporus, bovārius, bovīnus, *gʷṓws
bracchialis, bracchium, breviāre, brevima, brevis,
　*mréǵʰ-
brodium, *bʰrewh₁-
brūma, *mréǵʰ-
brūtus, *gʷerh₂-
būbalus, bubulcus, *gʷṓws
būcina, *keh₂n-
būcināre, būcinum, *gʷṓws, *keh₂n-
būcolicus, *gʷṓws
burgensis, burgus, *bʰerǵʰ-
burra, burrus, *péh₂ur
būstum, *h₁ews-
būtȳrum, *gʷṓws
calamus, *ḱalam-
calāre, *kelh₁-
calcāneum, calcar, calcāre, calcatura, calceāre,

calceus, *(s)kel-
calendārium, *kelh₁-
calx, *(s)kel-
camara, camera, campester, campiō, campus, camur,
　*(s)teg-
canere, *keh₂n-
canīcula, canīnus, canis, *ḱwṓ
canōrus, cantāre, cantilēna, *keh₂n-
capābilis, capācitās, capāx, *keh₂p-
capellus, caper, *kapro
capere, capessere, capistrum, *keh₂p-
capitālis, capitellum, capitium, capitō, capitulum,
　*kapōlo
capra, caprarius, capreolus, caprīnus, *kapro
capsa, capsula, captāre, captīvus, captūra, captus,
　*keh₂p-
caput, *kapōlo
cara, *ḱerh₂-
carmen, *keh₂n-
carmināre, *keh₂n-
carnālis, carnarium, carnārius, carnifex, carnivorus,
　carnōsus, carō, *(s)ker-
carpe diem, carpēre, *kerp-
carrāria, carricāre, carrūca, carrus, *ḱers-
cēlāre, *ḱel-
celeripēs, *pṓds
cella, cellārium, cellula, *ḱel-
celsus, *kelH-
cēna, cēnāre, *(s)ker-
centēnārius, centēsimātiō, centēsimō, centi-, *ḱm̥tóm
centipelliō, *ḱm̥tóm, *pel-
centipēs, centum, centuria, *ḱm̥tóm
cerebellum, cerebrum, *ḱerh₂-
cernere, *krey-
cernuus, *ḱerh₂-
certāre, certus, *krey-
cerva, cervārius, cervīnus, cervus, *ḱerh₂-
character, charta, chartula, chartulārius, *ǵʰer-
chelȳdrus, chelys, *gʰelōw-
chorda, *ǵʰern-
chrȳsocarpus, *kerp-
chthonius, *dʰéǵʰōm
cicōnia, *keh₂n-
cilium, *ḱel-
circumdūcere, *dewk-
circumferentia, circumferre, *bher-
circumfluere, *bʰleh₁-
circumnāvigāre, *(s)neh₂-
circumscrībēre, *(s)ker-
circumstāntia, circumstāre, *steh₂-
circumvenīre, *gʷem-
circumvolvere, *welH-
cis, citer, cītrā, *ḱi-
cīvicus, cīvīlis, cīvīlitās, cīvis, cīvitās, *ḱei-
clam, *ḱel-
clāmāre, clāmor, *kelh₁-
clandestīnus, *ḱel-

clārificāre, *dheH₁-

clāritās, clārus, classicus, classis, *kelh₁-

claudere, claustellum, claustrum, clausula,
 clausūra, clausus, clāvāre, clāvīchordium,
 clāvīcula, clāvis, clāvus, *(s)kel-

clepsydra, *wed-

cliēns, clientēla, *ḱlew

clima, clīmactēricus, clīmax, clīnāre, clīvus, *ḱley-

cluēre, *ḱlew-

cōactāre, coactus, *H₂eǵ-

coaevus, *h₂ey-

coāgulō, coāgulum, *H₂eǵ-

coalere, *h₂el-

coctilis, coctus, *pekʷ-

coercēre, coercitiō, *h₂erk-

cōgēns, cōgere, cōgitābundus, cōgitāre, cōgitātus,
 *H₂eǵ-

cognitio, *ǵneh₃-

cōgnōmen, *h₁nómn̥

cognōscere, *ǵneh₃-

cohibēre, *gʰeh₁bʰ-

cohors/cors, *ǵʰer-

coīre, coitiō, coitus, *h₁ey-

colere, *kʷel-

collatus, *bher-

collēcta, collēctiō, collēctīvus, *leǵ-

collēga, collēgiātus, collēgium, *legh-

colliculus, *kelH-

colligere, *leǵ-

collīnus, collis, *kelH-

collocāre, *stel-

cōlon, *(s)kel-

colōnia, colōnus, *kʷel-

color, *ḱel-

columen, *kelH-

colus, *kʷel-

combīnāre, combīnātiō, *dwóH₁

combūrere, *h₁ews-

comedere, *h₁ed-

commendāre, *deH₃-

commentārius, commentor, *men-

commētīrī, *meh₁-

comminīscor, *men-

commodus, *med-

commūnālis, commūne, commūnicāre, commūnicātiō,
 commūniō, commūnis, commūtāre, commūtātiō, *mey-

compārēre, *peh₂-

compendere, compendium, compēnsāre,
 compēnsātiō, *pewǵ-

comperīre, *per-

competere, *peth₂

compīlāre, compīlātiō, compīlātor, *peys-

compingere, *peh₂ǵ-

complēmentum, complēre, complētiō, complētīvus,
 *pleh₁-

complexus, complicāre, *pleḱ-

complūrēs, *pleh₁-

compōnere, *teḱ-

comportāre, *per-

comprehendere, comprehensibilis, comprehensiō,
 comprehensīvus, comprehensus, *weyd-

compungere, *pewǵ-

concentus, *keh₂n-

conceptiō, *keh₂p-

concernere, *krey-

concha, conchula, conchȳlium, *ḱonkho-

conciliābulum, conciliāre, concilium, *kelh₁-

concinere, *keh₂n-

concipere, *keh₂p-

conclāmāre, *kelh₁-

conclāve, conclūdere, *(s)kel-

concordāre, *ḱér

concordia, concors, *ǵʰer-

conculcāre, *(s)kel-

concurrere, concursus, *ḱers-

condere, *dheH₁-

condīcere, condiciō, *deyḱ-

condición, *dheH₁-

condiciōnālis, condictiō, *deyḱ-

conditiō, conditus, *dheH₁-

condōnāre, *deH₃-

condūcere, conductiō, conductor, conductus, *dewk-

cōnfectiō, cōnfectus, *dheH₁-

cōnferre, *bher-

cōnfessiō, *bʰeh₂-

cōnficere, *dheH₁-

cōnfidentia, cōnfidere, *bʰeydʰ-

cōnfirmāre, cōnfirmātiō, *dʰer-

cōnfitērī, *bʰeh₂-

cōnflāre, cōnfluentia, cōnfluere, *bʰleh₁-

confrāter, *bʰréh₂tēr

cōnfundere, cōnfusiō, cōnfūsus, *ǵʰew-

congelāre, *gel-

congener, *ǵenH₁-

congius, *ḱonkho-

coniungere, *yewg-

coniūrāre, coniūrātiō, *h₂eyw-

cōnscientia, cōnscientiōsus, cōnscīre, *skey-

cōnsecāre, *sek-

cōnsēnsus, cōnsentīre, *sent-

cōnsequēns, cōnsequentia, cōnsequī, *sekʷ-

cōnsignāre, *sek-

consistere, *steh₂-

consōbrīnus, *swésōr

cōnsors, cōnsortium, *ser-

cōnspicere, cōnspicuus, *speḱ-

cōnstāre, *steh₂-

cōnsternāre, cōnsternere, *sterh₃-

cōnstituere, cōnstitūtiō, *steh₂-

cōnstructiō, cōnstructus, cōnstruere, *strew-

cōnsuere, *sīw-

cōnsuēscere, cōnsuētūdō, *swe-dʰh₁-

contendere, contentiō, contentus, contentus, *ten-

conterere, *terh₁-

contīgnāre, contīgnātiō, *(s)teg-
continēns, continentia, continēre, continuus, *ten-
cōntiōnor, *gʷem-
contrādīcere, contrādictiō, contrādictor,
  contrādictōrius, *deyḱ-
contrăvenīre, *gʷem-
contribuere, *bʰuH-
contrŏversia, contrŏversus, *wert-
contrūdere, *trewd-
contubernālis, contubernium, *treb-
contundere, contūsiō, *(s)tew-
conveniēns, convenientia, convenīre, conventiō,
  conventus, *gʷem-
conversāre, conversātiō, convertere, *wert-
convīcium, *wekʷ-
convictiō, convictus, convincere, *weyk-
convocāre, *wekʷ-
convolvere, convolvulus, *welH-
cōpia, cōpiōsus, *h₃ep-
coquere, coquīna, coquus, *pekʷ-
cor, cordis, coriaceus, corium, *(s)ker-
corneus, corniculātus, cornū, cornūcōpia, cornūs,
  cornūtus, *ḱerh₂-
corporālis, corporātus, corporeus, corpulentus,
  corpus, corpusculum, *krep-
correctio, corrector, correctus, corrigere, corrigia,
  *h₃reǵ-
cortex, corticeus, *(s)ker-
coxa, coxus, *koḱs-
crābrō, crānium, *ḱerh₂-
crēdere, crēdibilis, crēditor, crēdulitās, crēdulus,
  *dheH₁-
crībrāre, crībrum, crīmen, crīmināre, crīminātiō,
  crisis, *krey-
crūdēlis, crūdēlitās, crūditās, crūdus, cruentus,
  cruor, *krewh₂-
cūius, *kʷis
culmen, *kelH-
culmus, *ḱalam-
cultor, cultūra, cultus, *kʷel-
cum, *kʷis
cūnābula, cūnae, *ḱei-
cūr, *kʷis
currēns, currere, curriculum, currīlis, currus, cursor,
  cursōrius, cursus, *ḱers-
curtāre, curtus, *(s)ker-
curūlis, *ḱers-
cyclus, *kʷel-
cynanchē, cynicus, cynomazon, *ḱwó
daemon, daemonium, damnāre, damnum, daps, *deh₂-
dāre, datum, datus, *deH₃-
dea, *dyew-
debēre, dēbilis, dēbilitāre, dēbilitās, dēbitor, dēbitum,
  *gʰeh₁bʰ-
decānus, decas, decem, december, decempeda,
  *déḱm̥t
decempeda, *pṓds

dēceptiō, *keh₂p-
dēcernere, *krey-
decet, *deḱ-
decima, decimalis, decimō, decimus, *déḱm̥t
dēcipere, *keh₂p-
dēclāmāre, dēclāmātiō, dēclārāre, *kelh₁-
dēclīnāre, *ḱley-
decor, decorāre, *deḱ-
dēcorticāre, *(s)ker-
decōrus, *deḱ-
dēcrētālis, dēcrētōrius, dēcrētum, *krey-
dēcurrēns, dēcurrere, *ḱers-
decus, *deḱ-
dēdāre, *deH₃-
dēdūcere, dēductiō, *dewk-
dēfendere, dēfēnsiō, *gʷʰen-
dēferēns, dēferre, *bher-
dēficere, *dheH₁-
dēfluere, *bʰleh₁-
dēfritum, dēfrutum, *bʰrewh₁-
dēgener, dēgenerāre, *ǵenH₁-
dēgūnō, dēgustāre, *ǵews-
dēhortārī, *ǵʰer-
deificāre, *dyew-
deinde, *éy / h₁e
deitās, *dyew-
dēlātiō, *bher-
dēlēgāre, *legh-
dēlictum, *leykʷ-
dēlīneāre, *lino-
dēlinquentia, delinquere, *leykʷ-
dēlīrium, dēlīrus, *leys-
dēmandāre, *deH₃-
dēmens, dēmentia, *men-
dēmocratia, *deh₂-
dēmōnstrāre, dēmōnstrātiō, *men-
dēmos, *deh₂-
dēmūtāre, *mey-
dēnārius, dēnī, *déḱm̥t
dēns, dentālis, dentātus, denticulātus, denticulus,
  dentis, *h₃dónts
dēnūdāre, *negʷ-
dēpectere, *peḱ-
dēpendēre, *pewǵ-
dēperīre, *h₁ey-
dēpingere, *peyḱ-
dēplēre, *pleh₁-
dēplicāre, *pleḱ-
dēpōnere, *tek-
deportāre, *per-
dēpositus, *tek-
dēprecābilis, dēprecārī, dēprecātiō, dēprecātīvus,
  dēprecātōrius, *preḱ-
dēprehendere, *weyd-
dēprīvāre, *per-
dērīvāre, *h₃reyH-
dēscrībēre, dēscriptiō, *(s)ker-

dēsecāre, *sek-
dēsidia, *sed-
dēsignāre, *sek-
dēsistere, *steh₂-
dēsōlāre, *s(w)e-
dēspectāre, dēspectus, *speḱ-
dēspērāre, *speh₁-
dēspicere, *speḱ-
despota, *pótis
dēstināre, dēstinātiō, dēstituere, *steh₂-
dēstructiō, dēstruere, *strew-
dētēctiō, dētēctor, dētegere, *(s)teg-
dētentiō, dētinēre, *ten-
detonāre, *(s)tenh₂-
dētrūdere, *trewd-
deus, *dyew-
dēvenīre, *gʷem-
dēvius, *weyh₁-
dēvolūtiō, dēvolvere, *welH-
dexter, dexteritās, *deḱs-
diabolus, *gʷelH-
diārium, *deyn-
diarrhoea, *srew-
dica, dicāx, dīcere, dictāmen, dictāre, dictātiō, dictātor,
  dictātūra, dictiō, dictiōnārium, dictum, dictus, *deyḱ-
didere, *dheH₁-
diēs Dominica, diēs Iovis, diēs Lunae, diēs Martis,
  diēs Mercuriī, diēs Saturnī, diēs Sōlis, diēs Veneris,
  diēs, *deyn-
differēns, differre, *bher-
difficilis, difficultās, *dheH₁-
diffluere, *bʰleh₁-
diffundere, diffusio, diffūsus, *ǵʰew-
digitālis, digitātus, digitus, *deyḱ-
dīgnitās, dīgnō/dīgnor, dīgnus, *deḱ-
dīlēctiō, dīligēns, dīligentia, dīligere, *leǵ-
dīluere, diluvium, *lewh₃-
diœcēsis, *weyḱ-
dīrectus, dīrigere, *h₃reǵ-
dis-, *dwóH₁
discalceāre, *(s)kel-
discantus, *keh₂n-
discarricāre, *ḱers-
discere, *deḱ-
discernere, *krey-
disclūdere, disclūsus, *(s)kel-
discordāre, *ḱḗr
discrētiō, discrīmen, discrīmināre, *krey-
discurrere, discursus, *ḱers-
disiungere, *yewg-
dispectāre, dispectus, dispicere, *speḱ-
displicāre, *pleḱ-
dispōnere, *teḱ-
dissēmināre, *seH₁-
dissēnsus, dissentīre, *sent-
disserere, *ser-
dissidentia, *sed-

dissimilis, dissimilitūdō, dissimulāre, dissimulātiō, *sem-
distāns, distantia, distāre, *steh₂-
distendere, *ten-
distribuere, *bʰuH-
diū, diurnālis, diurnus, *deyn-
diva, *dyew-
dīversus, dīvertere, *wert-
dīvidere, dīviduus, *h₁weydʰ
dīvīnāre, dīvīnātiō, dīvīnitās, dīvīnus, *dyew-
dīvīsibilis, dīvīsim, dīvīsiō, dīvīsor, *h₁weydʰ
dīvus, *dyew-
dixit, *deyḱ-
docēre, docilis, doctor, doctōrāre, doctrīna, doctus,
  documentum, dogma, dogmaticus, dogmatistes, *deḱ-
domāre, *dem-, *demh₂-
domesticus, domina, dominārī, dominātiō, dominatrix,
  dominium, dominus, domus, *dem-
dōnāre, dōnātiō, dōnātīvum, dōnum, dōs, dōtāre, *deH₃-
du-, *dwóH₁
dubietās, dubiōsus, dubium, dubius, *gʰeh₁bʰ-
ducātus, *dewk-
ducentī, *ḱm̥tóm
dūcere, ductiō, ductus, *dewk-
duo, *dwóH₁
duodecim, *déḱm̥t
duplex, *pleḱ-
duplus, *pleh₁-
dūrābilis, dūrābilitās, dūracinus, dūrāmen, dūrāre,
  dūrēscere, dūritia, dūrus, *deru-
dux, *dewk-
ea, *éy / h₁e
ecce, *éy / h₁e, *ḱi-
echinus, *ǵʰér
ecstasis, *steh₂-
ēdāre, *deH₃-
edibilis, *h₁ed-
ēdīcere, ēdictiō, ēdictum, *deyḱ-
ēditiō, ēditor, *deH₃-
edō, *h₁ed-
ēducātiō, ēdūcere, *dewk-
effābilis, effārī, *bʰeh₂-
effectīvus, effectus, *dheH₁-
efferre, *bher-
efficere, efficiēns, *dheH₁-
effigiēs, effingere, *dʰeyǵʰ-
efflāre, effluere, effluvium, *bʰleh₁-
effundere, effūsiō, effūsus, *ǵʰew-
ēgerere, *H₂eǵ-
egō, *egH₂
ēlātē, ēlātiō, *bher-
ēlēctiō, ēlēctus, ēlegāns, *leǵ-
elementārius, elementum, *h₂el-
ēlevāre, *h₁lengʷʰ-
ēligere, ēligibilis, *leǵ-
ēluctābilis, ēluctārī, *seh₂g-
ēlūcubrāre, *lewk-
ēluere, *lewh₃-

emancipare, *méh₂-r̥

ēmigrāre, *mey-

ēminēns, ēminentia, ēminēre, *men-

ēmorior, *mer-

ēmulgēre, *H₂melǵ-

ēnārrāre, ēnārrātiō, *ǵneh₃-

ēnecō, *neḱ-

energīa, *werǵ-

ēnōrmis, *ǵneh₃-

ēns, *H₁es-

entheus, enthūsiasmus, enthūsiastēs, *dʰéh₁s

entitās, *H₁es-

ēnumerāre, *nem-

epagōgē, *H₂eǵ-

epitheton, epithetum, *dheH₁-

epocha, *seǵʰ-

equa, eques, equester, equīnus, equīsō, equus,
   *h₁éḱwos

ēr, *ǵʰḗr

ērādīcāre, *wréh₂ds

ēricius, *ǵʰḗr

ērigere, *h₃reǵ-

ēsca, esculentus, ēsse, *h₁ed-

essentia, *H₁es-

ēst, *h₁ed-

est, *H₁es-

ethnicus, ēthologia, *swe-dʰh₁-

etiam, *éy / h₁e

eurygnathus, *ǵénus

ēvānēscere, *h₁weh₂-

ēvenīre, ēventus, *gʷem-

ēversor, ēvertere, *wert-

ēvictiō, *weyk-

ēvidēns, ēvidentia, *weyd-

ēvigilāre, *weǵ-

ēvincere, *weyk-

ēvocāre, *wekʷ-

ēvolūtiō, ēvolūtus, ēvolvere, *welH-

ex, *h₁eǵʰs

exacerbāre, *h₂éḱ

exāmen, exāminātiō, exāminātus, exāminō, *H₂eǵ-

exaudīre, *h₂ewis-dʰh₁-

exaugēre, *h₂ewg-

exbibere, *peh₃-

excalceāre, excalceātus, *(s)kel-

excellēns, excellentia, excellere, *kelH-

excernere, *krey-

excerpere, excerptus, *kerp-

excipere, *keh₂p-

exclāmāre, *kelh₁-

exclūdere, exclūsiō, exclūsīvus, exclūsus, *(s)kel-

excōgitāre, *H₂eǵ-

excoriāre, *(s)ker-

excrēmentum, *krey-

excurrere, excursiō, excursus, *ḱers-

exercēre, exercitium, exercitus, *h₂erk-

exfōliāre, *bʰleh₃-

exhālāre, *h₂enh₁-

exhibēre, exhibitiō, exhibitor, *gʰeh₁bʰ-

exhortārī, exhortātiō, *ǵʰer-

exīre, *h₁ey-

existere, *steh₂-

exitus, *h₁ey-

exolescere, exolētus, *h₂el-

expandere, *peth₂

expedīre, *ped-

expendere, expēnsus, *pewǵ-

experientia, experīmentum, experīrī, expertus, *per-

explaudere/explōdere, *pleh₂k-

explēre, *pleh₁-

explicāre, *pleḱ-

expōnere, *tek-

exportāre, exportātiō, *per-

expostulāre, *prek-

expugnāre, expugnātiō, expungere, *pewǵ-

exsanguis, *h₁ésh₂r̥

exsequī, exsequia, *sekʷ-

exserere, *ser-

exspectāre/expectāre, *speḱ-

exstasis, *steh₂-

exsurgere, *h₃reǵ-

extasis, *steh₂-

extendere, extēnsiō, extēnsus, extentus, *ten-

exter, exterior, externālis, externus, *h₁eǵʰs

extollere, *telh₂-

extrā, extrāneus, extrēmitās, extrēmus, *h₁eǵʰs

extrīnsecus, *sekʷ-

extrūdere, *trewd-

exūberāre, *h₁owHdʰr̥-

faba, *bʰabʰeh₂-

fābella, fābula, fābulātiō, fābulōsus, *bʰeh₂-

facere, faciendus, facinus, factiō, factor, factum, *dheH₁-

fāgīnus, fāgus, *bʰeh₂go-

falvus, *pelH-

fāma, *bʰeh₂-

familia, familiāris, familiāritās, famulus, *dheH₁-

fānāticus, *dʰéh₁s

fandus, fāns, *bʰeh₂-

fānum, *dʰéh₁s

far, *bʰars-

fārī, *bʰeh₂-

farīna, farīnārius, farīnōsus, farrāgō, farreus, *bʰars-

fās, fastus, fatērī, fātum, fātus, *bʰeh₂-

febris, februārius, fēbruum, *dʰegʷʰ-

fēlīcitās, fēlīx, fellāre, fēmella, fēmina, fēminīnus,
   fēnum, *dʰeh₁(y)-

fera, *ǵʰwer-

fērālis, *dʰéh₁s

ferculum, *bher-

ferē, *dʰer-

fēriae, *dʰéh₁s

fermē, *dʰer-

ferōcitās, ferōx, *ǵʰweroh₃kʷs

ferre, fertilis, fertus, *bherferus, *ǵʰwer-

fēstīvālis, fēstīvitās, fēstīvus, fēstum, fēstus, *dʰéh₁s

fētāre, *dʰeh₁(y)-

fētiales, fētialis, *dheH₁-

fētus, *dʰeh₁(y)-

feudātōrius, feudum, fevum, *peḱu-

fictus, *dʰeyǵʰ-

fidēlis, fidēlitās, fīdere, fidēs, fīdūcia, fīdūciārius,

  fīdus, *bʰeydʰ-

fierī, *bʰuH-

figūra, *dʰeyǵʰ-

filia, fīliālis, fīliaster, fīliolus, fīlius, *dʰeh₁(y)-

fimum, *dʰewh₂-

findere, *bʰeyd-

fingere, *dʰeyǵʰ-

firmāmentum, firmāre, firmitās, firmus, *dʰer-

fissiō, fissura, fissus, fistula, *bʰeyd-

flābrum, flāmen, flāre, flātus, flēbilis, flēre, *bʰleh₁-

flōrēre, flōreus, flōris, flōs, flōsculus, *bʰleh₃-

fluctuāre, fluctuātiō, fluctus, fluēns, fluere, fluidus,

  fluitāre, flumen, fluviālis, fluvius, fluxus, *bʰleh₁-

foedifragus, foedus, *bʰeydʰ-

foliātus, foliōsus, folium, *bʰleh₃-

fōmentum, *dʰegʷʰ-

forceps, *gʷʰer-

forda, *bher-

forēnsis, *dʰwer-

foresta, *perkʷu-

foris, *dʰwer-

formīca, formīcāre, formīcula, *morwi-

formus, fornāx, *gʷʰer-

fōrs, fōrsit, *bher-

fortia, *bʰerǵʰ-

fortificāre, *bʰerǵʰ-, *dheH₁-

fortificātiō, *bʰerǵʰ-, *dheH₁-

fortis, fortitūdō, *bʰerǵʰ-

fōrtuitus, fōrtuna, *bher-

forum, *dʰwer-

fovēre, *dʰegʷʰ-

frāter, frāternālis, frāternitās, frāternus, *bʰréh₂tēr

fraxinētum, fraxineus, frāxinus, *bʰereǵ-

frēnum, frētus, *dʰer-

fūcus, *bʰey-

fuī, *bʰuH-

fūlīgō, fūmāre, fūmāriolum, fūmārium, fūmigāre,

  fūmus, *dʰewh₂-

fundāmentum, *ǵʰew-

fundāre, *bʰudʰmén

fundātiō, fundātor, fundere, fundibulum, *ǵʰew-

fundus, *bʰudʰmén

fūr, *bher-

furnus, *gʷʰer-

fūror, fūrtīvus, fūrtum, *bher-

furvus, fuscāre, fuscus, *dʰewh₂-

fūsiō, fūtis, *ǵʰew-

futurus, *bʰuH-

galaxias, *glag-

gamba, *(s)teg-

gelāre, gelidus, gelū, *gel-

gemma, *ǵómbʰos

gena, *ǵénus

generālis, generāre, generōsus, genetrīx, *ǵenH₁-

geniculum, *ǵónu

genitīvus, genitor, genitus, genius, gēns, gentīlicius,

  gentīlis, gentīlitās, *ǵenH₁-

genū, genūflectere, *ǵónu

genus, *ǵenH₁-

geranium, *gerh₂-

gerere, *H₂eǵ-

germānitas, germānus, germen, germināre, *ǵenH₁-

gerundium, gestiō, gestus, *H₂eǵ-

gignere, *ǵenH₁-

glaciāre, glaciēs, *gel-

glōriā, glōriārī, glōriātiō, glōriōsus, gnārus, gnāvus,

  *ǵneh₃-

gomphus, *ǵómbʰos

Graecus, *ǵerh₂-

grāmen, grāmineus, *gʰreh₁-

grammatica, *gerbʰ-

grānum, *ǵr̥Hnom

graphicus, *gerbʰ-

grātēs, *gʷerH-

grātificārī, *dheH₁-, *gʷerH-

grātiōsus, grātīs, grātitūdō, grātuītus, grātulātiō, grātus,

  *gʷerH-

gravāre, gravidus, grāvis, gravitās, *gʷerh₂-

grōma, *ǵneh₃-

grūs, *gerh₂-

guardare, *wer-

gustāre, gustatus, gustus, *ǵews-

habēre, habilis, habilitās, habitābilis, habitāre,

  habitātiō, habitūdō, habitus, *gʰeh₁bʰ-

haedīnus, haedus, *gʰaydos

hālāre, *h₂enh₁-

hariolus, *ǵʰern-

harmonia, *h₂er

haruspex, *ǵʰern-, *speḱ-

hedera, *weyd-

helix, *welH-

helvus, *ǵʰelh₃-

hēpar, hēpaticus, hēpatītis, hēpatizon, *Hyékʷr̥

herī, *dʰǵʰ(y)es-

hernia, *ǵʰern-

Hesperidēs, *wek(ʷ)speros

hesternus, *dʰǵʰ(y)es-

hexa-, *swéḱs

hībernālis, hībernāre, hibernum, hibernus, *ǵʰey-

hic, *ḱi-

hiems, *ǵʰey-

hippodromos, *h₁éḱwos

hīra, *ǵʰern-

hirtus, *gʰers-

historia, historicus, *weyd-

hodiē, hodiernus, *deynholus, *ǵʰelh₃-

homo, homunculus, *ǵʰmṓ

hōra, *yeh₁-

horī, *ǵʰer-

hōrnus, *yeh₁-

horrendus, horrēre, horribilis, horridus, horrificus,
　horripilare, horror, *gʰers-

hortārī, hortātiō, hortulānus, hortus, *ǵʰer-

hospes, hospitā, hospitāle, hospitālia, hospitālis,
　hospitālitas, hospitāliter, hospitāre, hospitium,
　hospitor, hostis, *gʰóstis

hūmānitās, hūmānus, *ǵʰmṓ

humilis, humus, *dʰéǵʰōm

hyaena, *suH-

hydra, Hydra, hydrus, *wed-

hypothēca, hypothesis, *dheH₁-

iam, *éy / h₁e

iānua, iānuārius, iānus, *h₁ey-

ibī, ibīdem, id, *éy / h₁e

idea, *weyd-

īdem, īdenticus, īdentitās, *éy / h₁e

īdōlum, *weyd-

iecorīnus, iecur, *Hyékʷr̥

ignārus, ignāvus, *ǵneh₃-

igneus, ignīre, ignis, *h₁n̥gʷnis

ignōminia, ignōminiōsus, *h₁nómn̥

ignōrāntem, ignōrāre, ignōtus, īgnōtus, *ǵneh₃-

illātiō, illātīvus, *bher-

ille, *h₂el-

illēgālis, *leǵ-

illēgālis, *legh-

illīc, *h₂el-, *ḱi-

illūmināre, *lewk-

imbēcillus, *bak-

imber, *nebʰ-

imberbis, *bʰardʰeh₂-

imbibere, *peh₃-

imbrifer, *nebʰ-

immānis, immātūritās, immātūrus, *meh₂-

immēnsus, *meh₁-

immigrāre, *mey-

imminēre, *men-

immolere, *melh₂-

immūnis, immūnitas, immūtābilis, immūtāre, *mey-

impāctus, *peh₂ǵ-

impedīre, *ped-

impendēre, *pewǵ-

impervius, *weyh₁-

impetere, impetus, *peth₂

impingere, *peh₂ǵ-

implantāre, *pleh₂-

implaudere/implōdere, *pleh₂k-

implēmentum, implēre, *pleh₁-

implicāre, implicātiō, implicitus, *pleḱ-

impōnere, *teḱ-

importāre, importūnitās, importūnus, *per-

improbāre *bʰuH-

improbus, *bʰuH-, *per-

impugnāre, *pewǵ-

impūnis, impūnitas, *kʷey-

in-, *n̥-

in, *h₁én

inaugurāre, *h₂ewg-

incantāre, incentīvus, *keh₂n-

inceptiō, inceptīvus, *keh₂p-

incinere, *keh₂n-

incipere, *keh₂p-

inclīnāre, inclīnātiō, *ḱley-

inclitus, *ḱlew-

inclūdere, inclūsiō, inclūsus, *(s)kel-

incognitus, *ǵneh₃-

incola, *kʷel-

incrēdibilis, incrēdulus, *dheH₁-

inculcāre, *(s)kel-

incūnābula, *ḱei-

incurrere, incursiō, *ḱers-

inde, *éy / h₁e

indemnis, *deh₂-

index, indīcāre, indicium, *deyḱ-

indīgnus, *deḱ-

indīviduus, *h₁weydʰ-

indolēs, *h₂el-

indūcere, inductiō, inductus, *dewk-

indūrēscere, *deru-

industria, industrius, *strew-

inēluctābilis, *seh₂g-

iners, *h₂er

īnfāmia, īnfāmis, īnfandus, īnfāns, *bʰeh₂-

infendere, *gʷʰen-

inferibilis, īnferre, *bher-

īnfestāre, īnfestātiō, īnfestus, *gʷʰen-

īnficere, *dheH₁-

īnfirmitās, īnfirmus, *dʰer-

īnflāre, inflatio, īnfluentia, influere, īnfluxus, *bʰleh₁-

īnfundere, *ǵʰew-

ingenerāre, ingēns, *ǵenH₁-

ingerere, *H₂eǵ-

inhālāre, *h₂enh₁-

inhibēre, inhibitiō, inhibitor, *gʰeh₁bʰ-

inhūmānus, *ǵʰmṓ

inīre, initiāre, initiātiō, initium, *h₁ey-

iniungere, *yewg-

inmiscēre, *mey-

innocens, *neḱ-

innovāre, *new

innumerābilis, *nem-

inoculāre, *h₃ekʷ-

inopportūnus, *per-

inquam, *sekʷ-

inquilīnus, *kʷel-

īnsciēns, īnscītia, *skey-

īnscrībēre, īnscrīptiō, *(s)ker-

īnsecāre, *sek-

īnsece, *sekʷ-

īnsectus, *sek-
īnsequī, *sekʷ-
inserere, *ser-
īnsignāre, īnsigne, īnsignis, *sek-
īnsistere, *steh₂-
insolitus, *swe-dʰh₁-
insōns, *H₁es-
inspectum, īnspicere, *speḱ-
īnstāre, īnstaurāre, īnstaurātor, īnstituere, īnstitutiō,
   īnstitūtum, *steh₂-
īnstructiō, īnstructor, īnstruere, īnstrūmentum, *strew-
insubulum, insuere, *sīw-
īnsurgere, *h₃reǵ-
intellectiō, intellectuālis, intellēctus, intellegentia,
   intellegere, intelligibilis, *leǵ-
intendere, intēnsus, intentiō, intentus, *ten-
inter alia, *h₂el-
inter, *h₁én
intercalāre, *kelh₁-
intercipere, *keh₂p-
interclūdere, *(s)kel-
interdīcere, *deyḱ-
interesse, *h₁én, *H₁es-
interferre, *bher-
interim, *éy / h₁e, *h₁én
interior, *h₁én
interlūnium, *lewk-
internecare, *neḱ-
interpōnere, interpositiō, *teḱ-
interpungere, *pewǵ-
intersecare, *sek-
intersum, *H₁es-
intertrūdere, *trewd-
intervallum, *welH-
intervenīre, interventio, interventor, *gʷem-
intervertere, *wert-
intestīnus, intrā, intrāre, *h₁én
intrīnsecus, *sekʷ-
intrōdūcere, intrōductiō, *dewk-
intrōferre, *bher-
intrōtrūdere, intrūdere, *trewd-
intus, *h₁én
inundāre, inundātiō, *wed-
inūrere, *h₁ews-
inventiō, inventor, inventus, *gʷem-
invertere, *wert-
investīgāre, investīgātiō, *steygʰ-
investīre, *wes-
invidēre, *weyd-
invigilāre, *weǵ-
invītāre, invītus, *weyh₁-
invocāre, *wekʷ-
involūcrum, involūtus, involvere, *welH-
iocor, iocōsus, ioculāris, iocus, *yek-
ipse, *éy / h₁e, *s(w)e-
īre, *h₁ey-
īrōnīa, *wekʷ-

irregibilis, *h₃reǵ-
is, *éy / h₁e
iste, *só
ita, item, *éy / h₁e
iter, itus, *h₁ey-
iūdex, iūdicābilis, iūdicāre, iūdicātiō, iūdicātor,
   iūdicātōrius, iūdicātrix, iūdicātum, iūdicātus, iūdiciālis,
   iūdiciārius, *h₂eyw-
iūgera, *yewg-
iūgis, *gʷeyh₃-, *h₂ey-
iūgum, *yugóm
iunctiō, iungere, *yewg-
iūnior, iūnīx, *h₂yuh₁en-
Iuppiter, *dyew-
iūrāmentum, iūrāre, iūs, *h₂eyw-
iustificāre, *dheH₁-
iūstitia, iustitiarius, iūstus, *h₂eyw-
iuvencus, iuvenīlis, iuvenior, iuvenis, iuventūs,
   *h₂yuh₁en-
iūxtā, *yewg-
kalendae, *kelh₁-
labāre, labïum, lābrum, *leb-
lac, *glag-
lacrĭma, lacrimāre, lacrimātiō, lacrimōsus, *daḱru-
lactāre, lactarius, lacteus, lacticīnium, lactosus,
   lactūca, *glag-
lacuna, lacūnar, lacus, *lókus
lambō, *leb-
lāna, lanarius, lānōsus, lānūgō, *h₂welh₁-
lātrīna, *lewh₃-
laubia, *lewbʰ-
lavāre, lavātrīna, *lewh₃-
lēctiō, lēctor, lēctūra, *leǵ-
lectus, *legh-
lēgālis, lēgātiō, *leǵ-, *legh-
lēgātor, *legh-
lēgātus, *leǵ-, *legh-
legere, legiō, lēgislātiō, *leǵ-
lēgislātiō, *legh-
lēgislātor, *leǵ-
lēgislātor, *legh-
lēgitimus, *leǵ-, *legh-
lēgulēius, *legh-
legūmen, *leǵ-
levāre, levātus, levis, levitās, *h₁lengʷʰ-
lēx, *leǵ-, *legh-
libellus, *lewbʰ-
līber, *h₁lewdʰ-
liber, *lewbʰ-
līberālis, līberālitās, līberare, līberātiō, līberātor, libertas,
   lībertīnus, libertus, *h₁lewdʰ-
libet, librārius, *lewbʰ-
liēn, *splenǵʰ-
Liger, *legh-
lignārius, lignātor, ligneus, lignōsus, lignum, *leǵ-
līnārius, līnea, līneālis, līneāmentum, līneāre, līneus,
   *lino-

lingua, *dn̥ǵʰwéh₂s
linquere, *leykʷ-
linteārius, linteolum, linteum, līnum, *lino-
līra, *leys-
locālis, locāre, locārium, locātiō, loculus, locus, *stel-
longaevitās, longaevus, *h₂ey-
lōtium, *lewh₃-
lūcēre, lucerna, lūcidus, lūcifer, *lewk-
lucta, luctātiō, luctātor, lucto, *seh₂g-
lūcubrāre, lūcubrātiō, lūcus, *lewk-
Ludovicus, *ḱlew-
lumbus, *lendʰ-
lūmen, lūmināre, lūminōsus, lūna, lūnāris, lūnāticus,
    lūnula, *lewk-
lupīnus, lupus, *wl̥kʷos
luscinia, *keh₂n-
luscus, lustrāre, lustrum, *lewk-
lutra, *udréh₂
lūx, *lewk-
luxuria, luxuriosus, luxus, *seh₂g-
macer, macrochaeta, macroūrus, *meh₂ḱ-
mactāre, *méǵh₂s, *meh₂ḱ-
mactus, *méǵh₂s, *meh₂ḱ-
magis, magister, magistrālis, magistrātus, magmentum,
    magnās, magnātus, magnificus, magnitūdō, magnus,
    māiestās, māiusculus, major, *méǵh₂s
maledīcere, maledictiō, maledictus, *deyḱ-
malefaciō, *dheH₁-
mamma, mammalis, *méh₂-méh₂
manātus, *méh₂-r̥
mandāre, *deH₃-
mandere, mandibula, mandūcāre, *mendʰ-
mānēs, *meh₂-
manicula, *méh₂-r̥
manifestus, *gʷʰen-
manipulus, *pleh₁-
mānis, *meh₂-
mānsuēscere, mānsuētūdō, mānsuētus, *swe-dʰh₁-
mantica, manuālis, manuārius, manuātus,
    manubiālis, manūbrium, manūmittere, *méh₂-r̥
mānus, *meh₂-
manus, *méh₂-r̥
manūtenēre, *ten-
mare, marīnus, maritimus, *móri
masticāre, *mendʰ-
mastubor, *méh₂-r̥
māter, materia, māternālis, māternitās, māternus,
    mātrīcālis, mātricīda, mātrīcula, mātrimōnium,
    matrix, mātrōna, *méh₂tēr
mātūrus, mātūtīnus, *meh₂-
maximus, *méǵh₂s
mē, mēcum, *H₁me-
medeor, *med-
mediānus, mediātor, *médʰyos
medicāmen, medicāmentum, medicātor, medicīna,
    medicīnālis, medicīnus, medicō, medicus, *med-
mediē, medietās, mediō, *médʰyos

mediocris, *h₂éḱ
mediocris, *médʰyos
mediocritās, *h₂éḱ, *médʰyos
mediterrāneus, *médʰyos, *ters-
meditor, *med-
medium, medius, medulla, *médʰyos
meī, *H₁meme-
mēiere, *h₃meyǵʰ-
mel, melleus, mellifer, mellificus, mellifluus, mellītus,
    *melit-
membrāna, membrānāceus, membrāneus, membrum,
    *méms
meminī, memor, memorābilia, memorābilis, memorāre,
    memorārī, memoria, memoriālis, memoriter,
    mendācitās, mendācium, mendāx, mēns, *men-
mēnsa, mēnsārius, *meh₁-
mēnsis, mēnstrua, mēnstruālis, mēnstruāre, *méh₁n̥s
mēnsūra, mēnsūrāre, *meh₁-
mentālis, mentiō, mentior, mentum, *men-
mentum, *mendʰ-
merīdiēs, *deyn-, *médʰyos
merīdiō, *deyn-
metipse, metipsimus, *s(w)e-
mētīrī, metrum, *meh₁-
meus, *H₁meme-
migrāre, migrātiō, *mey-
mihi, *H₁me-
mille, mīlliārium, mīlliārius, *sem-
minae, mināx, Minerva, *men-
mingere, *h₃meyǵʰ-
minimus, minister, ministerium, ministrāre, *mey-
minitor, minor, *men-
minor, minuere, minus, minusculus, minūtal, minūtia,
    minūtus, miscellāneus, miscellus, miscēre, *mey-
misericors, *ḱér
mistūra, mixtīcius, mixtiō, *mey-
moderātiō, modernus, moderor, modestia, modestus,
    modicus, modificātiō, modificō, modius, modo,
    modulātē, modulātiō, modulātor, modulus, modus,
    *med-
mola, molāris, molarius, molere, molīnārius, molīnum,
    mollis, *melh₂-
monēre, monēta, monitor, *men-
monoculus, *h₃ekʷ-
mōns, mōnstrāre, mōnstrum, mōnstruōsus,
    montāniōsus, montānus, monticellus, monticulus,
    montuōsus, monumentum, *men-
moribundus, *bʰuH-, *mer-
morior, mors, mortuus, *mer-
mulgentia, mulgēre, mulsūra, *H₂melǵ-
multimodus, *med-
multiplex, multiplicāre, multiplicātiō, *pleḱ-
mūnia, mūnicipium, mūnificens, mūnificentia,
    mūnificus, mūnus, *mey-
mūs, *muh₂s-
musca, *mus-
mūsculāris, mūsculōsus, mūsculus, mūstēla, *muh₂s-

mūtābilis, mūtāre, mūtātiō, mūtuor, mūtuus, *mey-
myrmecias, myrmecitis, myrmecium, *morwi-
naevus, *ǵenH₁-
nāns, nantis, *(s)neh₂-
nāris, *néh₂s
nārrāre, nārrātiō, narrātīvus, nārrātor, nārrātus, *ǵneh₃-
nāsālis, *néh₂s
nāscēns, *ǵenH₁-
nasus, nāsūtus, *néh₂s
nātālīcius, nātālis, *ǵenH₁-
natātiō, natātor, natātōrium, natātōrius, *(s)neh₂-
nātiō, nātīvitās, nātīvus, *ǵenH₁-
natō, *(s)neh₂-
nātrīx, *(s)neh₂-, *neHtr-
nātūra, nātūrālis, nātūrālitās, nātus, *ǵenH₁-
naufragus, nauta, nauticus, nāvālis, nāvicella, nāvigāre,
nāvigātiō, nāvigātor, nāvigium, nāvis, *(s)neh₂-
nebūlō, nebulōsus, *nebʰ-
necare, nectar, nectareus, *neḱ-
nefandus, nefārius, nefās, nefāstus, *bʰeh₂-
neglectus, neglegentia, neglegere, *leǵ-
negōtiātiō, negōtiātor, negōtior, negōtium, *h₂ew
Nemesis, nemorālis, nemorōsus, nemus, *nem-
nepōs, neptis, *nepot-
Neptūnus, *nebʰ-
nēre, *(s)neh₁-
neriōsus, *h₂nḗr
nervōsus, nervus, *(s)neh₁-
nescīre, *skey-
nētus, neuroīdes, *(s)neh₁-
neuter, *kʷis
nex, *neḱ-
nīdificāre, nīdifōrmis, nīdus, *nisdós
ningit/ninguit, *sneygʷʰ-
nisi, *só
niveus, nivōsus, nix, *sneygʷʰ-
nō, *(s)neh₂-
nōbilis, *ǵneh₃-
nōbīscum, *wei
nocēre, nocīvus, *neḱ-
noctēscere, nocturnus, *nókʷts
nocumentum, *neḱ-
nōmen, nōmenclātor, nōmenclātūra, nōminālis,
nōmināre, nōminātiō, nōminātīvus, nōminātor, *h₁nómn̥
nōn sequitur, *sekʷ-
nōnāgintā, nōngentī, *H₁néwn̥
nōngentī, *ḱm̥tóm
nōrma, nōrmālis, *ǵneh₃-
nōs, noster, *wei
nota, notāre, notārius, notātiō, nōtiō, nōtitia,
nōtōrius, notula, nōtus, *ǵneh₃-
novāre, novellus, *new
novem, novena, *H₁néwn̥
nōvī, *ǵneh₃-
novilūnium , *lewk-
novitās, novus, *new
nox, *nókʷts

noxa, noxius, *neḱ-
nūdāre, nūditās, nūdus, *negʷ-
numerābilis, numerālis, numerāre, numerārius,
numerātiō, numerātor, numerōsitās, numerōsus,
numerus, nummus, *nem-
numquam, *kʷis
nūncupō, *keh₂p-
nūndinus, *deyn-
nurus, *snusós
ob, obiectum, *h₁epi
obīre, *h₁ey-
oblātiō, oblātus, *bher-
oboediēns, oboedīre, *h₂ewis-dʰh₁-
obolus, *gʷelH-
obs, *h₁epi
obsequī, obsequiae, obsequiōsus, obsequium, *sekʷ-
obsequor, *h₁epi
obsidēre, *sed-
obsolēscere, obsolētus, *h₂el-
obstāculum, obstāre, obstētrīx, obstināre, *steh₂-
obstructiō, obstruere, *strew-
obtinēre, *ten-
obtrūdere/obstrūdere, *trewd-
obtundere, *(s)tew-
obvenīre, *gʷem-
obversus, obvertere, *wert-
obviāre, obvius, *weyh₁-
occa, *h₂éḱ
occipere, *keh₂p-
occlūdere, *(s)kel-, *h₁epi
occupāre, *keh₂p-
occurrere, *ḱers-
ocris, *h₂éḱ
octagōnon, *oḱtṓw
octingentī, *ḱm̥tóm
octō, *oḱtṓw
octopus, *póds
oculāris, oculus, *h₃ekʷ-
odiōsus, ōdisse, odium, odor, odōrāre, *h₃ed-
oeconomia, oeconomicus, *nem-
oeconomus, *weyḱ-
offendere, *gʷʰen-
offerre, *bher-, *h₁epi
officiālis, officium, *h₃ep-
offuscāre, *dʰewh₂-
olēre, *h₃ed-
olfacere, *dheH₁-
omnipotēns, *H₁es-
omnis, omnisciēns, omnivorus, *h₃ep-
onomatopoeia, *h₁nómn̥
opera, operāns, operārius, operor, opifex, *h₃ep-
oppidum, *ped-
oppīlāre, *h₁epi, *peys-
oppīlātiō, *peys-
opplēre, *pleh₁-
oppōnere, *h₁epi, *teḱ-
opportūnitās, opportūnus, *per-

pīla, pīlāre, Pīlātus, pīlum, *peys-
pingere, *peyḱ-
pinna, *spey-
pīnsāre, pīnsere, *peys-
piscārius, piscīna, piscis, piscor, piscōsus, *peisḱ-
pistāre, pistillum, pistor, pistrīnum, *peys-
plāga, plangere, *pleh₂k-
planta, plantāgō, plantāre, plantātiō, plānus, platēa,
   *pleh₂-
plaudere, *pleh₂k-
plaustrum, *plew-
plēbiscītum, plēbs, *pleh₁-
plēctere, *pleh₂k-
plectere, *pleḱ-
plēctrum, *pleh₂k-
plēnārius, plēnitūdo, plēnus, plēre, *pleh₁-
plexus, plicāre, plicatilis, *pleḱ-
pluit, *plew-
plūrālis, plūrifōrmis, plūrimus, plūs, *pleh₁-
pluvia, pluviālis, pluviōsus, pluvius, *plew-
po-, *h₂pó
pōculum, *peh₃-
podium, *póds
poena, poenālis, *kʷey-
poliocephalus, *pelH-
pollēre, pollex, pollicaris, *h₂welh₁-
polluere, pollūtiō, *lewh₃-
ponderāre, pondus, *pewǵ-
pōne, *h₁epi
pōnēn, pōnere, *teḱ-
pōno, *h₂pó
pōns, pontifex, pontis, *pent-
populāris, populātiō, populus, *pleh₁-
por-, *per-
porcarius, porcella, porcellus, *pórḱos
porcēre, *h₂erk-
porcīnus, porcus, *pórḱos
porrigere, *h₃reǵ-
porrō, porta, portābilis, portāre, portārius, *per-
portendere, portentus, *ten-
porticus, portus, *per-
posca, *peh₃-
poscere, *preḱ-
positiō, positus, *teḱ-
possessiō, possessivus, possessor, *pótis
possibilis, *H₁es-
possidēre, *pótis
possum, *H₁es-
post-, post, posterior, posterus, *h₁epi
postferre, *bher-
postīcus, *h₁epi
postis, postpōnere, *teḱ-
postulāre, postulātūs, *preḱ-
pōtābilis, pōtāre, *peh₃-
potēns, potentia, potentialis, *H₁es-
potestās, *pótis
pōtiō, *peh₃-

potis, *pótis
pōtus, *peh₃-
practicus, prae, *per-
praecellere, *kelH-
praeceptor, praecipere, *keh₂p-
praeclūdere, *(s)kel-
praecognoscere, *ǵneh₃-
praecurrere, praecursor, *kers-
praeda, *weyd-
praedātiō, praedātor, *deH₃-, *weyd-
praediālis, praediātōrius, *wedʰ-
praedīcāre, praedictiō, *deyḱ-
praedium, *wedʰ-
praedor, *deH₃-, *weyd-
praeēminēre, *men-
praeferre, *bher-
praegustāre, *ǵews-
praeiūdicāre, praeiūdicium, *h₂eyw-
praelātus, *bher-
praelēgāre, *legh-
praemonēre, praemonitiō, praemōnstrāre, *men-
praeoccupāre, praeoccupātio, *keh₂p-
praepōnere, *teḱ-
praeposterus, *h₁epi
praes, *wedʰ-
praesāgīre, *seh₂g-
praescīre, *skey-
praescrībēre, *(s)ker-
praesēns, praesentātiō, praesentia, *H₁es-
praesentīre, *sent-
praesidēns, praesidēre, praesidium, *sed-
praestāre, *steh₂-
praesum, *H₁es-
praetendere, praetēnsus, *ten-
praeter, *per-
praeterferor, *bher-
praeterīre, *h₁ey-
praevalēns, praevalēre, *h₂welh₁-
praevenīre, *gʷem-
praevidēre, *weyd-
praevius, *weyh₁-
prāxis, *per-
precārī, precārius, precātiō, precātīvus, *preḱ-
prehendere, prehensiō, prehensus, *weyd-
presbyter, pretiāre, pretiōsus, pretium, *per-
prex, *preḱ-
primaevus, *h₂ey-
prīmārius, prīmitīvus, prīmō, *per-
primogenito, *ǵenH₁-
prīmōgenitus, *ǵenH₁-, *per-
prīmus, *per-
prīnceps, prīncipium, *keh₂p-
prior, prīscus, prīstinus, prīvāre, prīvātiō, prīvātīvus,
   prīvātō, prīvātus, prīvilēgium, prīvus, prō-, prō, *per-
proba, probābilis, probābilitās, probāre, probātus,
   probitās, *bʰuH-
problēma, problēmaticus, *gʷelH-

probus, *bʰuH-, *per-
procāre, procāx, *preḱ-
prōclāmāre, proclāmātiō, *kelh₁-
procul, *per-
prōdūcere, prōductiō, prōductīvus, prōductus, *dewk-
profānus, *dʰéh₁s
prōferre, *bher-
prōfessiō, professor, *bʰeh₂-
prōficere, *dheH₁-
prōfitērī, *bʰeh₂-
prōfluere, *bʰleh₁-
prōfundere, profunditās, profundus, *ǵʰew-
programma, *gerbʰ-
prohibēre, prohibitiō, prohibitor, *gʰeh₁bʰ-
prōlēs, prōlētārius, *h₂el-
prōminēns, prōminēre, *men-
prōmiscuus, *mey-
prōnus, *per-
prōpāgāre, *peh₂ǵ-
prope, *per-
prōpensiō, *pewǵ-
propinquus, propiō, propior, propitius, *per-
prōpōnere, prōpositum, *tek-
prōprietās, proprius, *preyH-
propter, *per-
prōpugnāre, *pewǵ-
prōra, *per-
prōrsus, prōsa, *wert-
prōscrībēre, *(s)ker-
prōsecāre, *sek-
prōsecūtor, prōsequī, *sekʷ-
prospectus, *speḱ-
prosperare, prosperitās, prosperus, *speh₁-
prōspicere, *speḱ-
prōsternere, *sterh₃-
prōstituere, *steh₂-
prōtegere, *(s)teg-
prōtendere, *ten-
prōterere, protervus, *terh₁-
prōtinus, *per-
prōtrūdere, *trewd-
prōvenīre, prōventus, *gʷem-
prōverbium, *wekʷ-
prōvidentia, prōvidēre, prōvidus, *weyd-
prōvincia, prōvinciālis, *per-
prōvīsō, *weyd-
prōvocāre, *wekʷ-
proximus, *per-
pūblica, publicus, *pleh₁-
pugil, pugilātor, pūgiō, pugnāre, pugnāx, pugnus, *pewǵ-
pūlex, *plou-
pullus, *pelH-
pulmō, *plewmō
pūmex, *poymno-
punctiō, punctuāre, punctuātiō, punctum, punctus, pungere, *pewǵ-

pūniō, pūnītiō, *kʷey-
pyra, *péh₂ur
quadr-, *kʷetwóres
quādrangulus, *h₂enk-
quadrāre, quadrātum, quadrātūra, quadrātus, *kʷetwóres
quadrīgae, *yugóm
quadringentī, *ḱm̥tóm
quadrivium, *weyh₁-
quadrupēs, *póds
quādrus, *kʷetwóres
quālis, quālitās, quam, *kʷis
quārtus, quattuor, *kʷetwóres
quattuordecim, *dékm̥t
quercus, *perkʷu-
quī, quia, quīcumque, quid, *kʷis
quiēs, quiēscere, quiētus, *kʷyeh₁-
quīndecim, *dékm̥t
quīngentī, *ḱm̥tóm
quīnquāgintā, quīnque, *pénkʷe
quis, quō, quod, *kʷis
quōmodo, *med-
quoque, quot, quotiēns, *kʷis
rādīcālis, radicula, radius, rādīx, rāmōsus, ramulosus, rāmulus, rāmus, *wréh₂ds
ratiō, *h₂er
ratiōcinārī, *keh₂n-
ratiōcinor, ratus, *h₂er
recalcitrāre, *(s)kel-
receptāculum, receptiō, reciperāre, recipere, *keh₂p-
reciprocus, *per-
reclāmāre, rēclāmātiō, *kelh₁-
reclīnāre, *ḱley-
recognōscere, *ǵneh₃-
recolligere, *leǵ-
reconditus, *dheH₁-
recordābilis, recordor, *ḱér
rectus, *h₃reǵ-
recurrere, *ḱers-
reddāre, *deh₃-
redīre, reditus, *h₁ey-
redolēns, redolēre, *h₃ed-
redūcere, reductiō, reductus, *dewk-
redundāns, redundāre, *wed-
refectiō, *dheH₁-
referre, *bher-
reficere, *dheH₁-
refluere, *bʰleh₁-
refundere, *ǵʰew-
rēgālis, *h₃reǵ-
regenerāre, *ǵenH₁-
regere, regibilis, regimen, regina, rēgnāre, rēgnum, rēgula, *h₃reǵ-
relātiō, relātīvus, *bher-
relēgāre, relēgātiō, *legh-
relevāre, *h₁lengʷʰ-
relinquere, *leykʷ-

relūcēre, *lewk-
remedium, *med-
rememorārī, reminīscor, *men-
remūnerāre, *mey-
renovāre, *new
reor, *h₂er
repectere, *peḱ-
repetere, *peth₂
replēre, replētiō, *pleh₁-
replicāre, *pleḱ-
repōnere, *teḱ-
reportāre, *per-
repraesentāre, repraesentātiō, *H₁es-
reprehendere, reprehensibilis, reprehensiō,
  reprehensus, *weyd-
reprobāre, *bʰuH-
reprobus, *per-
repugnāre, *pewǵ-
requiēs, *kʷyeh₁-
rescindere, *skey-
resecāre, *sek-
residēre, resīdere, residuus, *sed-
resignāre, *sek-
resistentia, resistere, *steh₂-
respectāre, respectus, respicere, *speḱ-
rēspūblica, *pleh₁-
restāre, rēstaurāre, restituere, *steh₂-
resurgere, *h₃reǵ-
retaliare, *só
retentiō, retinēre, *ten-
retribuere, *bʰuH-
retrōspectum, retrōspicere, *speḱ-
retrūdere, *trewd-
revenīre, *gʷem-
reverendus, reverens, reverentia, reverērī, *wer-
reversāre, revertī, *wert-
revidēre, *weyd-
revincere, *weyk-
revisēre, revīsiō, revīsitāre, *weyd-
revocāre, *wekʷ-
revolūtiō, revolvere, *welH-
rēx, *h₃reǵ-
rhētor, rhētoricus, *wekʷ-
rheuma, rhythmus, *srew-
rītus, *h₂er
rīvālis, rīvālitās, rīvulus, rīvus, *h₃reyH-
rota, rotāre, rotātiō, rotella, rotula, rotulare,
  rotulus, rotundus, *Hret-
rubellus, ruber, rubēre, rubeus, rubia, rubicundus,
  rubīnus, rubor, rubrīca, rubrīcāre, rūfus, russus,
  *h₁rewdʰ-
sacerdōs, sacerdōtālis, sacerdōtium, sacrificāre,
  sacrificātor, sacrificium, *dheH₁-
sāga, sagācitās, sagāx, sāgīre, sāgus, *seh₂g-
sāl, salīre, *séh₂ls
salūber, salus, salūtāre, salūtātiō, salvāre, salve!,
  salvus, *solh₂-

sānctificāre, *dheH₁-
sanguināre, sanguinārius, sanguineus,
  sanguinolentus, sanguinōsus, sanguis, *h₁ésh₂r
sardonyx, *h₃negʰ-
satiō, *seH₁-
satisfacere, *dheH₁-
satus, *seH₁-
saxum, *sek-
scelus, *(s)kel-
schēma, schola, *seǵʰ-
sciēns, scienter, scientia, *skey-
scientificus, *dheH₁-, *skey-
scīlicet, scindere, scīre, scīscere, scissiō, *skey-
scopus, *speḱ-
scortea, scortum, scrībēre, scrīptūra, scrīptus, scrobis,
  scrūpulōsus, scrūpulus, scrūpus, scrūtinium, scrūtor,
  *(s)ker-
sē-, se, *s(w)e-
secāre, *sek-
sēcernere, *krey-
sēclūdere, *(s)kel-
sēcrētārius, sēcrētiō, sēcrētus, *krey-
sector, *sek-, *sekʷ-
sēcum, *s(w)e-
secundus, *sekʷ-
secūris, *sek-
secus, *sekʷ-
sed, *s(w)e-
sēdātiō, *sed-
sēdecim, *déḱm̥t
sedēns, sedentārius, sedēre, sedere, sēdēs,
  sedimentum, *sed-
sēdūcere, *dewk-
sēdulus, *sed-
segmen, segmentum, *sek-
sēiungere, *yewg-
sēlēctiō, sēlēctor, sēligere, *leǵ-
sella, *sed-
semel, *meh₁-, *sem-
sēmen, sēmentis, *seH₁-
sēmi-, *sem-
sēminālis, sēmināre, sēminārium, sēminārius, *seH₁-
semper, sempiternitās, sempiternus, *sem-
senātor, senātus, senecta, senectus, senex, senīlis,
  senior, *sénos
sēnsātus, sēnsibilis, sēnsōrium, sēnsus, sententia,
  sententiōsus, sentiēns, sentimentum, sentīre, *sent-
septem, september, septēnārius, *septm̥
septentriō, *terh₁-
septimāna, septimus, *septm̥
septingentī, *ḱm̥tóm
sequāx, sequela, sequēns, sequester, sequī, *sekʷ-
serere, *seH₁-
serere, seriēs, sermō, *ser-
serra, serrāgo, serrāre, serrātus, *sek-
serum, *srew-
sescentī, *ḱm̥tóm

sessiō, *sed-

sex, *swéḱs

sī, sic, *só

sīdere, *sed-

sigillum, signāre, signātūrus, significāns, significāre, significātiō, *sek-

significere, *dheH₁-

signum, *sek-

similāns, similāre, similis, *sem-

simplex, *pleḱ-, *sem-

simplicitās, *pleḱ-

simplificor, *dheH₁-

simplīficor, *pleh₁-, *sem-

simplus, *pleh₁-, *sem-

simul, simultāneus, simultās, *sem-

sinciput, *kapōlo

singulāris, singulāritās, singulus, *sem-

sinō, *teḱ-

sistere, *steh₂-

sitīre, sitis, *dʰegʷʰ-

situāre, *teḱ-

situs, *dʰegʷʰ-, *teḱ-

sīve/seu, *só

sōbrīnus, *swésōr

sociābilis, sociālis, societās, sociō, socius, *sekʷ-

sōl, sōlāris, sōlārium, *sóh₂wl̥

solēre, *swe-dʰh₁-

solidus, *solh₂-

sōlitārius, sōlitās, sōlitātim, sōlitūdō, *s(w)e-

solitus, *swe-dʰh₁-

solium, *sed-

sollemnis, sollemnitas, *solh₂-

sollers, *h₂er, *solh₂-

sollicitāre, sollicitātiō, sollicitūdō, sollicitus, sollus, *solh₂-

solstitium, *sóh₂wl̥

sōlus, *s(w)e-

somniāre, somniātor, somniculōsus, somnifer, somnium, somnulentus, somnus, *swep-

sōns, *H₁es-

sōpīre, sopor, sopōrifer, *swep-

soror, sorōritās, *swésōr

sors, sortior, sortītiō, *ser-

sospes, *speh₁-

specere, speciēs, specimen, spectāre, spectrum, *speḱ-

spēcula, *speh₁-

speculārī, speculātiō, speculum, *speḱ-

spērāns, spērāre, spēs, *speh₁-

spīca, spīna, spinalis, spīnōsus, spīnula, spīnus, *spey-

splēn, spleneticus, *splenǵʰ-

spūma, spūmāre, spūmōsus, *poymno-

stabilīre, stabilis, stabilitās, stabulāre, stabulum, stāmen, stāre, statim, statiō, statua, statuāria, statuere, statūra, status, *steh₂-

stella, stēllāris, *h₂stér

sternere, *sterh₃-

stetī, *steh₂-

stichus, *steygʰ-

storea, strāges, strāgulus, strāta, stratēgia, stratēgus, strātum, strātus, *sterh₃-

struere, *strew-

studēns, studēre, studiōsus, studium, *(s)tew-

stupefacere, *dheH₁-, *(s)tew-

stupēre, stupidus, stupor, stuprum, *(s)tew-

sub, *upo

subaudiō, *h₂ewis-dʰh₁-

subdūcere, subductiō, *dewk-

subigitāre, *H₂eǵ-

subinde, *éy / h₁e

subīre, subitō, subitus, *h₁ey-

subiungere, *yewg-

sublevāre, *h₁lengʷʰ-

submonēre, *men-

subpoena, *kʷey-

subscrībēre, *(s)ker-

subsequēns, subsequor, *sekʷ-

subsīdere, *sed-

subsistere, substituere, *steh₂-

subter, subterfugere, *upo

subterrāneus, *ters-

subtīlis, *tetḱ-

subtus, *upo

sūbula, *sīw-

subvenīre, *gʷem-

subversāre, subvertere, *wert-

succurrere, succursus, *ḱers-

sūdāre, sūdārium, sūdor, *sweyd-

suere, *sīw-

suescere, *swe-dʰh₁-

sufferre, *bher-

sufficere, sufficientia, *dheH₁-

suffīre, *dʰewh₂-

sufflāre, *bʰleh₁-

suffundere, *ǵʰew-

suggerere, suggestiō, suggestus, *H₂eǵ-

suīnus, *suH-

sum, *H₁es-

summārium, summitās, summus, *upo

suo-, *sem-

super, superāre, *upo

superbus, *bʰuH-, *upo

supercilium, *ḱel-

superēminēre, *men-

superfluere, superfluus, *bʰleh₁-

superimpōnere, *teḱ-

superior, supernus, *upo

superpōnere, *teḱ-

superscrībēre, *(s)ker-

supersedēre, *sed-

superstāre, superstes, superstitiō, *steh₂-

superus, *upo

supervacāneus, *h₁weh₂-

supervenīre, *gʷem-

supīnus, *upo

supplantāre, *pleh₂-
supplēmentum, *pleh₁-
supplēre, *pleh₁-
supplicāre, *plek-
suppōnere, *teḱ-
supportāre, *per-
supra-, *upo
surgere, *h₃reǵ-
survenir, *gʷem-
sūs, *suH-
suscipere, *keh₂p-
suspectiō, suspectus, *speḱ-
suspendere, suspēnsiō, suspēnsus, *pewǵ-
suspicere, suspīciō, *speḱ-
sustentāre, sustinentia, sustinēre, *ten-
sūtilis, sūtor, sūtōrius, sutura, *sīw-
suus, *s(w)e-
symposium, *peh₃-
synagoga, *H₂eǵ-
synōnymum, *h₁nómn̥
synopsis, *h₃ekʷ-
systēma, *steh₂-
taberna, tabernāculum, *treb-
tāliō, tālis, tam, *só
tamen, *éy / h₁e, *só
tandem, tantum, tantus, *só
taratrum, *terh₁-
taurifōrmis, taurus, *(s)táwros
tēctum, *(s)teg-
tēcum, *túh₂
tegere, tēgula, tegumentum, *(s)teg-
tēla, *tetḱ-
tenaculum, tenāx, tendere, tenēns, tener, tenēre,
 tenor, tēnsiō, tēnsus, tentus, tenus, *ten-
terebra, terebrāre, terere, *terh₁-
terminālis, termināre, terminus, *térmn̥
terra, terrēnus, terrestris, territōriālis, territōrium, *ters-
tertiārius, tertiō, tertius, *tréyes
texere, textilis, textō, textor, textōrius, textūra,
 textus, *tetḱ-
thēca, thema, *dheH₁-
Theodericus, *tewtéh₂
theōria, *wer-
thesis, *dheH₁-
thius, *dʰeh₁(y)-
tignum, toga, *(s)teg-
tolerāre, tollere, *telh₂-
tonāre, *(s)tenh₂-
tongēre, *teng-
tonitrus, *(s)tenh₂-
tōnsillae, tonus, *ten-
torrefaciō, torrēns, torrēre, torridus, *ters-
torulus, torus, *sterh₃-
tostus, *ters-
tot, *só
trabs, *treb-
trādere, tradīcija, trādiriō, trāditor, *deH₃-

trādūcere, *dewk-
tranquillus, *kʷyeh₁-
trāns, *terh₂-
trānscrībēre, *(s)ker-
trānseō, *h₁ey-
trānsferre, *bher-
trānsfluere, *bʰleh₁-
trānsfundere, transfūsiō, *ǵʰew-
trānslātiō, trānslātor, trānslātus, *bher-
trānsmigrāre, *mey-
trānsmontānus, *men-
trānsmūtāre, trānsmūtātiō, *mey-
trānspārēre, *peh₂-
transplantāre, *pleh₂-
transpōnere, *teḱ-
trānsportāre, *per-
trānstrum, *terh₂-
trānsvertere, *wert-
trecentī, *ḱm̥tóm
tredecennium, tredecim, *déḱm̥t
trēs, *tréyes
treuga, *deru-
tri-, *tréyes
triangulum, triangulus, *h₂enk-
trias, *tréyes
tribālis, *bʰuH-
tribrachys, *mréǵʰ-
tribuere, *bʰuH-
trībulum, *terh₁-
tribūnal, tribūnus, tribus, tribūtum, *bʰuH-
triceps, *kapōlo
trimestris, *méh₁n̥s
triō, *terh₁-
triplus, *pleh₁-
trīticum, trītūra, *terh₁-
triumvir, *wiHrós
trivium, *weyh₁-
trūdere, trūsus, *trewd-
tū, *túh₂
tudiculāre, *(s)tew-
tum, *só
tunc, *ḱi-, *só
tundere, *(s)tew-
turdus, *trosdos
tussīre, tussis, *(s)tew-
tuus, *túh₂
tympanum, typicus, typus, *(s)tew-
ūber, ūberāre, *h₁owHdʰr̥-
ubī, ubīcumque, ubīque, *kʷis
ulna, *Heh₃l-
ultrā, *h₂el-
umbilicus, *h₃enbʰ-
umquam, *kʷis
un-, *n̥-
uncīnātus, *h₂enk-
uncīnus, *h₂enk-
uncus, *h₂enk-

unda, *wed-
undāre, *wed-
unde, *kʷis
ūndecim, *dékm̥t
undosus, undulātus, *wed-
unguis, ungula, ungulātus, *h₃negʰ-
ungulus, *h₂enk-
ūni-, *óy-nos
ūnicornis, *ḱerh₂-
ūnicus, ūniō, ūnitās, *óy-nos
ūniversus, *wert-
ūnus, *óy-nos
ūrēdō, ūrere, urna, *h₁ews-
ursa, ursīnus, ursus, *h₂ŕ̥tḱos
ūsque, *kʷis
ussī, usta, ustrīna, ustulāre, ustūra, ustus, *h₁ews-
usucapere, *keh₂p-
ut, uter, *kʷis
ūter, *wed-
vacāns, vacāre, vacīvus, vacuitās, vacuum,
  vacuus, *h₁weh₂-
valē, *h₂welh₁-
valedīcere, *deyḱ-, *h₂welh₁-
valēns, valēre, valētūdinārius, valētūdō, validitās,
  validus, *h₂welh₁-
vallis, vallum, *welH-
valor, *h₂welh₁-
valva, *welH-
vānēscere, vānitās, *h₁weh₂-
vannus, *H₂weH₁-
vānus, *h₁weh₂-
vās dēferēns, *bher-
vas, *wedʰ-
vastāre, vastus, *h₁weh₂-
vāticinārī, *keh₂n-
vegēre, vegetābilis, vegetāre, vegetātiō, vegetus,
  *weǵ-
vehere, *weǵʰ-
vel, velle, *welh₁-
vellus/villus, *h₂welh₁-
vēnālis, *wesno-
vēndāre, vēnditiō, *deH₃-
vēnditiō, vēnditor, vēndō, *wesno-
vēndōr, *deH₃-
vēneō, *wesno-
venīre, *gʷem-
ventilāre, ventilātiō, ventilātor, *H₂weH₁-
ventiō, *gʷem-
ventōsus, ventulus, *H₂weH₁-
ventus, *gʷem-, *H₂weH₁-
vēnum, vēnus, *wesno-
vēr, *wésr̥
vērāx, *weh₁-
verbālis, verbātim, verbōsus, verbum, *wekʷ-
verēcundia, verēcundus, verēri, *wer-
vēridicus, *weh₁-
vērificāre, *dheH₁-, *weh₁-

verificātiō, vērisimilis, vēritās, *weh₁-
vermiculus, verminōsus, vermis, *wr̥mis-
vernālis, *wésr̥
versāre, versātilis, versātus, versicolor, versiō, *wert-
versipellis, *pel-
versus, versūtia, versūtus, vertebra, vertere, vertibilis,
  vertīginōsus, vertīgō, *wert-
vērus, *weh₁-
vespa, *wobs-
vesper, vespera, vespertīliō, *wek(ʷ)speros
vestīgāre, vestīgium, *steygʰ-
vestīmentum, vestīre, vestis, vestītus, *wes-
veterānus, vetulus, vetus, *wet-
vēxī, *weǵh-
via, viāre, viāticum, viāticus, viator, *weyh₁-
vicārius, vice versā, *weyk-
vīcēsimus, *wīkm̥tiH₁
vīcīna, vīcīnālis, vīcīnitas, vīcīnus, *weyḱ-
vīcīs, vicissitūdō, victima, victimāre, victor, victōria,
  *weyk-
vīculus, vīcus, *weyḱ-
vidēre, *weyd-
vidua, viduitās, viduus, *h₁weydʰ
vigēre, vigil, vigilāns, vigilantia, vigilāre, vigilia, *weǵ-
vīgintī, *wīkm̥tiH₁
vigor, *weǵ-
vīlla, vīllānus, *weyḱ-
villōsus, *h₂welh₁-
vīnāceus, *wóyh₁nom
vincere, vincīre, vinctūra, vinculāre, vinculum, *weyk-
vīndēmia, vīndēmiāre, *wóyh₁nom
vindex, vindicālis, vindicāre, vindicta, *weyh₁-
vīnea, vīneārius, vīnētum, vīnōsus, vīnum, *wóyh₁nom
violāre, *weyh₁-
vir, virāgo, virīlis, virtūs, *wiHrós
vīs, *weyh₁-
vīsibilis, vīsibilitās, vīsiō, vīsitāre, vīsō, vīsum, vīsus,
  *weyd-
vīta, vītālis, vītālitās, *gʷeyh₃-
vitreus, vitrum, *wed-
vitulus, *wet-
vīvācitās, vīvārium, vīvāx, vīvidus, vīviparus, vīvō,
  vīvus, *gʷeyh₃-
vobiscum, *túh₂
vocābulārium, vocābulum, vocālis, vocāre, vocātiō,
  vocātīvus, vōciferātiō, vōciferor, vōcis, vōcula, *wekʷ-
volēns, *welh₁-
volūbilis, volūbilitās, volūmen, volūminōsus, *welH-
voluntārius, voluntās, *welh₁-
voluta, volūtāre, volūtus, volvere, *welH-
vortex/vertex, *wert-
vos, vōs, voster, votre, vôtre, *túh₂
vōx, *wekʷ-
vulva, *welH-
warda, *wer-
zodiacus, *gʷeyh₃-

French

-duire, -duit, *dewk-
-ment, *men-
-thère, *ǵʰwer-
ab-, *h₂pó
abduction, *dewk-
abeille, *bʰey-
abhorrer, *gʰers-
abîme, *dʰewb-
abjurer, *h₂eyw-
ablation, *bher-
ablégat, *legh-
abluer, ablution, *lewh₃-
abolir, abolition, *h₂el-
abortif, *h₃er-
abréger, abrévier, *mréǵʰ-
abscisse, *skey-
abscondre, *dheH₁-
abstenir, abstinence, abstinent, *ten-
abysse, *dʰewb-
accepter, *keh₂p-
acclamer, *kelh₁-
accomplir, *pleh₁-
accorde, accorder, *ḱér
accourir, *ḱers-
acerbe, *h₂éḱ
acheter, *keh₂p-
acide, acier, acmé, *h₂éḱ
acquiescer, *kʷyeh₁-
âcre, âcreté, acrimonie, *h₂éḱ
acte, acteur, actif, action, activité, actrice, *H₂eǵ-
addict, addiction, *deyḱ-
addition, *deH₃-
adjoindre, *yewg-
adjudication, adjuger, *h₂eyw-
administration, administrer, *mey-
admonester, admonitio, *men-
adolescent, *h₂el-
adorer, *h₃éh₁os
adultère, adultérer, *h₂el-
advenir, *gʷem-
adverbe, adverbial, *wekʷ-
adverse, *wert-
affilier, *dʰeh₁(y)-
affirmer, *dʰer-
affluent, affluer, *bʰleh₁-
ager, *h₂éǵros
agir, agitation, agiter, *H₂eǵ-
agneau, agnelle, *h₂egʷnos
agonie, *H₂eǵ-
agraire, *h₂éǵros
agréer, *gʷerH-
agricole, agriculteur, agriculture, *h₂éǵros
aïeul, *h₂éwh₂os

aigre, *h₂éḱ
aiguière, *h₂ekʷeh₂-
aiguille, *H₂éḱ
aile, *H₂eǵ-
ailleurs, *h₂el-
ainçais, ains, *h₂ent
ainsi, *só
air, *h₂ews-
airain, *h₂eyos
aire, *h₂éǵros
ais, aisselle, *H₂eǵ-
ajouter, *yewg-
aliment, *h₂el-
alise, *h₃el-
allégation, alléguer, *legh-
aller, *h₁ey-
allumer, *lewk-
altercation, alterquer, *h₂el-
ambacte, ambassade, *H₂eǵ-
ambi-, ambiance, ambiant, *h₂ent
ambroisie, *mer-
âme, *h₂enh₁-
amnésie, *men-
anabase, *gʷem-
anaphore, *bher-
androgyne, *h₂nḗr
angle, *h₂enk-
anguille, *angʷ(h)i-
anguis, *h₂enǵʰ-
angulaire, *h₂enk-
anhéler, animer, *h₂enh₁-
anniversaire, *wert-
anonyme, *h₁nómn̥
anorexie, *h₃reǵ-
anormal, *ǵneh₃-
antérieur, *h₂ent
antique, antiquité, *h₂énti-h₃kʷós
antithèse, *dheH₁-
anxiété, *h₂enǵʰ-
août, *h₂ewg-
apicole, apiculteur, apiculture, *bʰey-
apocalypse, *ḱel-
aporie, *per-
apparaître, apparent, appariteur, apparition, apparoir, *peh₂-
appartenir, *ten-
appendice, appendre, *pewǵ-
appétit, *peth₂
applaudir, *pleh₂k-
appliquer, *pleḱ-
apporter, *per-
apposer, *teḱ-
apprécier, *per-
appréhender, appréhension, apprendre, *weyd-
approuver, *bʰuH-
aquarien, aquatique, *h₂ekʷeh₂-
aqueduc, *dewk-, *h₂ekʷeh₂-

aqueux, $*h_2ek^weh_2$-

arable, $*H_2erH_3$-

araignée, $*h_2er$

araire, $*H_2erH_3$-

arbre, $*h_2erHd^h$-

arc, $*h_2erk^wo$-

arche, $*h_2erk$-

arçon, $*h_2erk^wo$-

ardu, arduité, $*h_2erHd^h$-

aride, $*h_2eh_1s$-

armature, arme, armé, armée, armer, armoire,

  armure, $*h_2er$

arracher, $*wréh_2ds$

ars, art, article, $*h_2er$

aspect, aspecter, $*spek$-

assembler, $*sem$-

assener, $*sent$-

asseoir, $*sed$-

assertion, $*ser$-

assidu, $*sed$-

assigner, $*sek$-

assimiler, $*sem$-

astuce, $*h_2ék$

atavique, $*h_2éwh_2os$

atelier, $*H_2eǵ$-

atroce, atrocité, $*h_2eh_1tro$-h_3k^ws

attelle, $*H_2eǵ$-

attendre, attention, attenir, attentif, $*ten$-

attribuer, $*b^huH$-

auberge, $*ker$-

aucun, $*k^wis$, $*óy$-nos

audience, audio, auditeur, audition, auditoire,

  auditorium, $*h_2ewis$-d^hh_1-

auge, $*h_2el$-

augure, augurer, $*h_2ewg$-

aujourd'hui, $*deyn$-

aulne, $*h_3el$-

aune, $*Heh_3l$-

aura, aurore, $*h_2ews$-

ausculter, $*ḱel$-

auspices, $*spek$-

austral, $*h_2ews$-

autant, $*só$

auteur, $*h_2ewg$-

authenticité, authentique, auto, automobile, $*h_2ew$

autorité, $*h_2ewg$-

autre, autrui, $*h_2el$-

auxiliaire, $*h_2ewg$-

avant, $*h_2ent$

ave, $*h_2éwh_2os$

aveindre, avenir, Avent, $*g^wem$-

avers, $*wert$-

avis, $*weyd$-

avocat, $*wek^w$-

avoir, $*g^heh_1b^h$-

avouer, $*wek^w$-

avoutre, $*h_2el$-

axe, $*H_2eǵ$-

bâcle, $*bak$-

baliste, $*g^welH$-

bannir, $*b^heh_2$-

barbe, barbelé, $*b^hard^heh_2$-

barde, $*g^werH$-

barou, $*bher$-

base, $*g^wem$-

bateau, $*b^heyd$-

bénir, $*deyḱ$-

béton, $*g^wet$-

beurre, $*g^wóws$

bibion, $*peh_3$-

bibliothèque, $*dheH_1$-

biceps, $*kapõlo$

bienfaire, bienfait, bienfaiteur, $*dheH_1$-

bière, $*bher$-

biner, binoter, $*dwóH_1$

birouchette, $*bher$-

biscuit, $*pek^w$-

bœuf, $*g^wóws$

boire, $*peh_3$-

bouc, $*b^huHgos$-

bouée, $*b^heh_2$-

bouleau, $*g^wet$-

bouquetin, $*b^huHgos$-

bouquin, $*b^heh_2go$-

bouquin, $*b^huHgos$-

bourg, bourgeois, $*b^herǵ^h$-

bourgeon, $*péh_2ur$

boutique, $*dheH_1$-

bouvier, bovin, $*g^wóws$

brachial, bras, bref, brève, $*mréǵ^h$-

brio, $*b^herǵ^h$-

brouet, $*b^hrewh_1$-

brouette, $*bher$-

brume, $*mréǵ^h$-

brut, $*g^werh_2$-

bubale, $*g^wóws$

buccin, $*g^wóws$, $*keh_2n$-

bucolique, $*g^wóws$

bureau, $*péh_2ur$

buse, $*keh_2n$-

buste, $*h_1ews$-

buveur, $*peh_3$-

cabrioler, cabriolet, $*kapro$

cacher, $*H_2eǵ$-

cadastre, $*steyg^h$-

cadeau, $*kapõlo$

cadrat, $*k^wetwóres$

cailler, $*H_2eǵ$-

caisse, $*keh_2p$-

calame, $*ḱalam$-

calendaire, calendrier, $*kelh_1$-

calquer, $*(s)kel$-

cambre, cambrer, caméra, camp, $*(s)teg$-

canicule, canin, $*ḱwó$

capable, capace, capacité, *keh₂p-

capital, capitule, *kapõlo

caprin, *kapro

capsule, capter, captif, capture, *keh₂p-

car, *ḱers-

caractère, *ǵʰer-

carnage, carnivore, *(s)ker-

carré, carreau, carrer, *kʷetwóres

carrière, carrosserie, *ḱers-

carte, cartulaire, *ǵʰer-

catabase, *gʷem-

cauchemar, *mer-

celer, *ḱel-

céléripede, *póds

celle, *h₂el-

cellier, cellule, *ḱel-

celui, *h₂el-

cène, *(s)ker-

cent, centenaire, centi-, centipède, centurie, *ḱm̥tóm

cerf, *ḱerh₂-

cerner, certain, *krey-

cerveau, cervelle, *ḱerh₂-

cet, cette, *só

ceux, *h₂el-

chair, *(s)ker-

chalumeau, *ḱalam-

chambre, chambre, champ, champêtre,
 champignon, champion, *(s)teg-

chanfrein, *dʰer-

chapiteau, chapitre, *kapõlo

char, charger, *ḱers-

Charles, *ǵerh₂-

charme, *keh₂n-

charnel, charnier, *(s)ker-

charrette, charrière, charrue, *ḱers-

charte, *ǵʰer-

châsse, châssis, *keh₂p-

chaume, *ḱalam-

chausse, chausser, chaussette, *(s)kel-

chef, *kapõlo

chélydre, *gʰelõw-

chenille, *ḱwó

cheptel, *kapõlo

chère, *ḱerh₂-

chétif, *keh₂p-

chevet, *kapõlo

chevêtre, *keh₂p-

cheville, *(s)kel-

chèvre, chevreau, chevrier, *kapro

chic, chicaner, chicanerie, *(s)kek-

chien, *ḱwó

chorège, *seh₂g-

cigogne, *keh₂n-

cil, *ḱel-

cinq, cinquante, cinquième, *pénkʷe

circonférence, *bher-

circonscrire, *(s)ker-

circonstance, *steh₂-

circonvenir, *gʷem-

circumnaviguer, *(s)neh₂-

cité, citoyen, civil, civique, *ḱei-

clair, clamer, clameur, *kelh₁-

clan, *pleh₂-

clandestin, *ḱel-

clarifier, *dheH₁-

clarté, classe, classer, classifier, classique, *kelh₁-

clavicorde, *(s)kel-

clavicule, clé, clef, *(s)kel-

client, cliente, *ḱlew-

climat, climatérique, climax, *ḱley-

cloître, clore, clos, clôture, clôturer, clou, clouer, *(s)kel-

coaguler, *H₂eǵ-

coercition, *h₂erk-

cœur, *ḱér

cogitation, cogiter, *H₂eǵ-

cognomen, *h₁nómn̥

cohorte, *ǵʰer-

coi, *kʷyeh₁-

collecte, collection, *leǵ-

collégue, *legh-

colline, colombe, *kelH-

colon, colonie, *kʷel-

colonne, colophon, *kelH-

colorer, *ḱel-

combinaison, combiner, *dwóH₁

commander, *deH₃-

comme, comment, *med-

commentaire, *men-

commode, *med-

commuer, commun, communal, communauté,
 communication, communier, communion,
 communiquer, *mey-

compagnon, comparaître, *peh₂-

compendium, compensation, compenser, *pewǵ-

compilation, compiler, *peys-

complément, complet, complète, complétion, *pleh₁-

complexe, complication, compliquer, *pleḱ-

comporter, *per-

composer, *tek-

compréhensible, compréhensif, compréhension,
 comprendre, compris, *weyd-

concept, conception, *keh₂p-

concerner, *krey-

concevoir, *keh₂p-

conche, *ḱonkho-

conciliabule, concilier, conclamer, *kelh₁-

conclave, conclure, *(s)kel-

concorde, *ǵʰer-

concourir, concours, *ḱers-

condition, *deyḱ-, *dheH₁-

conditionnel, *deyḱ-

conducteur, conduction, conduire, conduit, *dewk-

confection, *dheH₁-

conférer, *bher-

confesser, confession, *bʰeh₂-
confidence, confier, *bʰeydʰ-
confire, *dheH₁-
confirmation, confirmer, *dʰer-
confit, *dheH₁-
confluer, *bʰleh₁-
confondre, confus, confusion, *ǵʰew-
conge, *ḱonkho-
congeler, *gel-
congénère, *ǵenH₁-
conjoindre, *yewg-
conjuration, conjurer, *h₂eyw-
connaître, *ǵneh₃-
conque, *ḱonkho-
conscience, *skey-
conseil, *kelh₁-
consentir, *sent-
conséquence, conséquent, *sekʷ-
consigner, *sek-
consister, consistuer, *steh₂-
consort, consortium, *ser-
constater, constitution, *steh₂-
construction, construire, *strew-
contenance, contenir, content, content, contention,
 continu, *ten-
contradicteur, contradictoire, contredire, *deyḱ-
contrevenir, *gʷem-
contribuer, *bʰuH-
contrire, *terh₁-
controverse, *wert-
contusion, *(s)tew-
convaincre, *weyk-
convenance, convenant, convenir, convent,
 convention, *gʷem-
convertir, *wert-
convier, *weyh₁-
convoquer, *wekʷ-
copain, *peh₂-
copieux, *h₃ep-
coquille, *ḱonkho-
cor, *ḱerh₂-
corde, *ǵʰern-
coriace, *(s)ker-
corne, cornu, *ḱerh₂-
corps, *krep-
correct, correcteur, correction, corriger, *h₃reǵ-
cortex, *(s)ker-
coucher, *stel-
coudre, *sīw-
couleur, *ḱel-
cour, *ǵʰer-
courage, *ḱḗr
courant, courir, courre, *ḱers-
courroie, *h₃reǵ-
cours, *ḱers-
court, *(s)ker-
cousin, *swésōr

coûter, *steh₂-
coutume, *swe-dʰh₁-
couvent, *gʷem-
crâne, *ḱerh₂-
crédit, créditeur, crédule, *dheH₁-
crible, crime, *krey-
croire, *dheH₁-
cru, cruauté, crudité, cruel, cruelle, cruor, *krewh₂-
cueillette, cueillir, *leǵ-
cuider, *H₂eǵ-
cuir, cuirasse, *(s)ker-
cuire, cuisine, cuisiner, cuisinier, *pekʷ-
cuisse, *koks-
cuit, *pekʷ-
cultiver, culture, *kʷel-
curriculum, curseur, *ḱers-
cycle, *kʷel-
daigner, *deḱ-
dam, *deh₂-
dame, *dem-
damner, *deh₂-
damoiseau, *dem-
date, *deH₃-
de-, *dwóH₁
dé, *dwóH₁, *deyḱ-
débile, débiliter, débiteur, *gʰeh₁bʰ-
décade, décembre, *déḱm̥t
décerner, *krey-
décevoir, *keh₂p-
décharger, *ḱers-
déchausser, *(s)kel-
déchirer, *(s)ker-
décimal, décime, décimer, *déḱm̥t
déclamer, déclarer, *kelh₁-
décorer, décorum, *deḱ-
décret, décrétale, *krey-
décrire, *(s)ker-
déduction, déduire, *dewk-
défendre, *gʷʰen-
déférer, *bher-
dégénérer, *ǵenH₁-
déguster, *ǵews-
dehors, *dʰwer-
déifier, déité, *dyew-
délation, *bher-
déléguer, *legh-
délinquance, délinquant, délinquer, *leykʷ-
délire, delirium, *leys-
délit, *leykʷ-
déluge, *lewh₃-
demander, *deH₃-
démence, dément, *men-
demoiselle, *dem-
démon, *deh₂-
démonstration, démontrer, *men-
dénaire, denier, *déḱm̥t
dent, dental, *h₃dónts

dénuder, *neg^w-

dépendre, *pewǵ-

dépérir, *h₁ey-

déployer, *pleḱ-

depondre, *teḱ-

déporter, *per-

déposer, *teḱ-

déprécatif, déprécation, déprécatoire, *preḱ-

dés-, *dwóH₁

description, *(s)ker-

désigner, *sek-

désister, *steh₂-

désoler, *s(w)e-

dessiner, *sek-

destination, destiner, destituer, *steh₂-

détenir, détention, *ten-

détoner, *(s)tenh₂-

détruire, *strew-

dette, *gʰeh₁bʰ-

deux, *dwóH₁

devenir, *gʷem-

devin, deviner, *dyew-

devoir, *gʰeh₁bʰ-

dextérité, dextre, *deḱs-

dictateur, dictature, dicter, diction, dictionnaire, *deyḱ-

dieu, *dyew-

différer, *bher-

difficile, *dheH₁-

diffluer, *bʰleh₁-

diffus, diffuser, *ǵʰew-

digital, digitale, *deyḱ-

digne, dignité, *deḱ-

diligence, diligent, *leǵ-

diluer, *lewh₃-

dimanche, *deyn-

dîme, *déḱm̥t

diocèse, *weyḱ-

dire, *deyḱ-

direct, diriger, *h₃reǵ-

dis-, *dwóH₁

discerner, *krey-

discourir, discours, *ḱers-

discriminer, *krey-

disposer, *teḱ-

disséminer, *seH₁-

disséquer, *sek-

dissimulation, dissimuler, *sem-

distancier, *steh₂-

distendre, *ten-

distribuer, *bʰuH-

dit, *deyḱ-

diurne, *deyn-

diva, *dyew-

divers, divertir, *wert-

divin, divinité, *dyew-

diviser, divisible, division, *h₁weydʰ-

dix, *déḱm̥t

dixit, *deyḱ-

docile, docte, docteur, doctrine, document, dogmatiste, dogme, *deḱ-

doigt, *deyḱ-

dom, domaine, dôme, domestique, domination, dominer, *dem-

dommage, *deh₂-

don, donation, *deH₃-

donc, *só

donner, *deH₃-

dont, *kʷis

dot, doter, *deH₃-

double, doubler, *pleh₁-

douche, *dewk-

douer, *deH₃-

douze, doyen, *déḱm̥t

droit, *h₃reǵ-

duc, duché, *dewk-

duplex, *pleḱ-

dur, durabilité, duracine, duramen, durer, dureté, *deru-

eau, *h₂ekʷeh₂-

écharde, *(s)ker-

école, *seǵʰ-

éconduire, *deyḱ-

écorce, écourter, *(s)ker-

écouter, *ḱel-

écran, écrire, écrit, écriture, *(s)ker-

écume, *poymno-

édiction, *deyḱ-

édifice, édifier, édile, *h₂eydʰ-

édit, *deyḱ-

édition, *deH₃-

éducation, éduquer, *dewk-

effable, *bʰeh₂-

effectif, effectuer, effet, *dheH₁-

effigie, *dʰeyǵʰ-

effluer, effluve, *bʰleh₁-

effusion, *ǵʰew-

églantier, *h₂éḱ

ego, *egH₂

élation, *bher-

élément, *h₂el-

élever, *h₁lengʷʰ-

élire, élit, élite, *leǵ-

elle, elles, *h₂el-

élucubrer, *lewk-

éluer, *lewh₃-

émigrer, *mey-

éminence, éminent, éminente, *men-

emplir, *pleh₁-

employer, *pleḱ-

en, *éy / h₁e, *h₁én

enchanter, *keh₂n-

enclore, enclos, *(s)kel-

encourir, *ḱers-

enduire, enduit, *dewk-

endurcir, *deru-

énergie, *werǵ-
enfant, *bʰeh₂-
enfler, *bʰleh₁-
engendrer, *ǵenH₁-
enjoindre, *yewg-
énorme, *ǵneh₃-
enseigner, *sek-
ensemble, *sem-
ensouple, *sīw-
ensuivre, *sekʷ-
entendre, entente, *ten-
enthousiasme, *dʰéh₁s
entité, *H₁es-
entre-, entre, entrer, *h₁én
énumérer, *nem-
épandre, *peth₂
épenthétique, *dheH₁-
épi, *spey-
épice, épier, *speḱ-
épine, épineux, *spey-
éployer, *pleḱ-
époque, *seǵʰ-
équerre, *kʷetwóres
équestre, *h₁éḱwos
équivaloir, *h₂welh₁-
éradiquer, *wréh₂ds
ériger, *h₃reǵ-
esche, *h₁ed-
escrimer, *(s)ker-
espèce, *speḱ-
espérance, espérer, *speh₁-
essaim, *H₂eǵ-
essence, *H₁es-
ester, *steh₂-
estival, *h₂eydʰ-
estoc, *(s)tew-
estrade, *sterh₃-
établar, étable, établir, étai, état, *steh₂-
été, *h₂eydʰ-, *steh₂-
étendre, *ten-
éternel, éternité, *h₂ey-
éther, *h₂eydʰ-
ethnie, éthologie, *swe-dʰh₁-
étoile, *h₂stḗr
étonner, *(s)tenh₂-
étrange, *h₁eǵʰs
être, *H₁es-, *steh₂-
étude, étudiant, étudier, étui, *(s)tew-
évanouir, *h₁weh₂-
éveiller, *weǵ-
événement, éventualité, *gʷem-
évidence, *weyd-
évier, *h₂ekʷeh₂-
évincer, *weyk-
évoluer, évolution, *welH-
évoquer, *wekʷ-
exacerber, *h₂éḱ

examen, examination, examiner, *H₂eǵ-
exaucer, *h₂ewis-dʰh₁-
excellence, excellent, exceller, *kelH-
exclamer, *kelh₁-
exclure, *(s)kel-
excogiter, *H₂eǵ-
excorier, *(s)ker-
excrément, excréter, *krey-
excursion, *ḱers-
exécuter, exécution, *sekʷ-
exercer, exercice, *h₂erk-
exfolier, *bʰleh₃-
exhaler, *h₂enh₁-
exhiber, *gʰeh₁bʰ-
exhortation, exhorter, *ǵʰer-
exister, *steh₂-
expédier, *ped-
expérience, expert, *per-
expliquer, *pleḱ-
exportation, exporter, *per-
exposer, *teḱ-
exsangue, *h₁ésh₂r
exsecūtiō, *sekʷ-
extase, extasié, *steh₂-
extension, *ten-
externe, extra-, *h₁eǵʰs
extrinsèque, *sekʷ-
fable, fabulation, fabuleux, *bʰeh₂-
façon, facteur, faction, *dheH₁-
faible, *bʰleh₁-
faine, faîne, *bʰeh₂go-
faire, fait, *dheH₁-
fameux, *bʰeh₂-
familier, famille, *dheH₁-
fanatique, *dʰéh₁s
fantaisie, fantôme, *bʰeh₂-
faon, *dʰeh₁(y)-
farine, farineux, farinier, *bʰars-
faste, *bʰeh₂-
fauve, *pelH-
féal, *bʰeydʰ-
feble, *bʰleh₁-
fédéral, fédérale, *bʰeydʰ-
feindre, feint, *dʰeyǵʰ-
félicité, *dʰeh₁(y)-
felle, *bʰeyd-
femelle, féminin, femme, *dʰeh₁(y)-
fendre, *bʰeyd-
férié, *dʰéh₁s
ferme, fermer, fermeté, *dʰer-
féroce, férocité, *ǵʰweroh₃kʷs
fesse, *bʰeyd-
festif, festivité, fête, *dʰéh₁s
feuille, *bʰleh₃-
feurre, *peh₂-
fève, *bʰabʰeh₂-
février, *dʰegwʰ-

hiberner, *ǵʰey-
hier, *dʰǵʰ(y)es-
hippo-, hippodrome, *h₁ékwos
histoire, historique, *weyd-
hiver, hivernal, hiverner, *ǵʰey-
homme, *ǵʰmṓ
hôpital, *gʰóstis
hoquet, *keg-
horreur, horrible, horrifique, *gʰers-
hors, *dʰwer-
hospice, hospitalier, hospitalité, hôte, hôtel, *gʰóstis
hui, *deyn-
huit, *oktṓw
humain, humanité, *ǵʰmṓ
humble, humus, *dʰéǵʰōm
hyène, *suH-
hyper, *upo
hypothèque, *dheH₁-
idée, *weyd-
identique, identité, *éy / h₁e
ignare, *ǵneh₃-
igné, *h₁ngʷnis
ignominie, ignominieux, *h₁nómṇ
ignorant, ignorer, *ǵneh₃-
il, *h₂el-
illation, illative, *bher-
illégal, *leǵ-, *legh-
illuminer, *lewk-
ils, *h₂el-
imbécile, *bak-
imberbe, *bʰardʰeh₂-
imbiber, *peh₃-
immigrer, *mey-
imminent, *men-
immiscer, *mey-
immoler, *melh₂-
immun, immune, immunité, *mey-
impact, *peh₂ǵ-
implication, impliquer, *plek-
importer, importunité, *per-
imposer, *teḱ-
in-, *ṇ-
inaugurer, *h₂ewg-
inceptif, inception, *keh₂p-
inclination, incliner, *ḱley-
inclure, inclus, *(s)kel-
incōnsequēns, *sekʷ-
incrédule, *dheH₁-
incriminer, *krey-
incroyable, *dheH₁-
inculquer, *(s)kel-
incursion, *ḱers-
index, indice, *deyḱ-
indigne, *deḱ-
indiquer, *deyḱ-
induction, induire, induit, *dewk-
industrie, *strew-

inéluctable, *seh₂g-
inerte, *h₂er-
infâme, infamie, *bʰeh₂-
infecter, *dheH₁-
inférer, *bher-
infester, *gʷʰen-
infirme, *dʰer-
inflation, influence, influer, *bʰleh₁-
infondre, *ǵʰew-
ingérer, *H₂eǵ-
inhaler, *h₂enh₁-
inhiber, *gʰeh₁bʰ-
initier, *h₁ey-
innocent, *neḱ-
inquilin, *kʷel-
inscrire, *(s)ker-
insérer, *ser-
insigne, *sek-
insister, *steh₂-
insolite, *swe-dʰh₁-
instaurer, instituer, institut, *steh₂-
instructeur, instruction, instruire, *strew-
intellect, intelligence, *leǵ-
intense, intention, *ten-
inter-, *h₁én
interdire, *deyḱ-
interposition, *teḱ-
intervalle, *welH-
intervenir, interventeur, *gʷem-
intervertir, *wert-
intra-, *h₁én
intrinsèque, *sekʷ-
introduction, introduire, *dewk-
inveniō, inventer, inventeur, invention, inventore, *gʷem-
invertir, *wert-
investiguer, *steygʰ-
investir, *wes-
inviter, *weyh₁-
involucre, involuté, *welH-
invoquer, *wekʷ-
ir-, issu, *h₁ey-
jà, *éy / h₁e
janvier, *h₁ey-
jardin, *ǵʰer-
je, *egH₂
jeu, *yek-
jeudi, *deyn-
jeune, *h₂yuh₁en-
joindre, jointer, *yewg-
jongler, jongleur, jouer, *yek-
joug, *yugóm
jour, journal, journée, *deyn-
jouter, *yewg-
judiciaire, judiciel, juge, juger, *h₂eyw-
junior, *h₂yuh₁en-
jurer, *h₂eyw-
jusque, *kʷis

juste, justesse, justice, *h₂eyw-
juveigneur, juvénile, *h₂yuh₁en-
la, *h₂el-
lac, *lókus
lactaire, lacté, lacter, *glag-
lacune, lagune, *lókus
laine, laineux, *h₂welh₁-
lainier, *h₂welh₁-, *leǵ-
lait, laiteron, laiteux, laitier, laitue, *glag-
lamper, *leb-
langue, *dn̥ǵʰwéh₂s
larme, *daḱru-
latrines, laver, *lewh₃-
le, *h₂el-
leçon, lecteur, légal, *leǵ-
légal, *legh-
légat, légation, *leǵ-, *legh-
léger, *h₁lengʷʰ-
légion, *leǵ-
législateur, *legh-
législation, légitime, *leǵ-, *legh-
légume, *leǵ-
les, *h₂el-
leude, *h₁lewdʰ-
leur, *h₂el-
levé, lever, *h₁lengʷʰ-
lévre, *leb-
libelle, *lewbʰ-
libérateur, libération, libérer, liberté, libertin, *h₁lewdʰ-
libraire, *lewbʰ-
libre, liège, *h₁lengʷʰ-
lierre, *weyd-
lieu, *stel-
ligne, *lino-
ligneux, *leǵ-
lin, linceul, linéament, linge, *lino-
lippe, *leb-
lire, *leǵ-
lit, litière, *legh-
livraison, *h₁lewd-
livre, *lewbʰ-
livrer, *h₁lewd-
local, location, *stel-
loge, loger, *lewbʰ-
logistique, loi, *leǵ-
loi, Loire, *legh-
lombes, *lendʰ-
longévité, *h₂ey-
loquet, *seh₂g-
louche, *lewk-
louer, *stel-
Louis, *ḱlew-
loup-garou, *wiHrós
loup, *wĺkʷos
loutre, *udréh₂
loyal, *leǵ-
loyal, *legh-

loyer, *stel-
lucide, *lewk-
lui, *h₂el-
luire, lumière, luminaire, lumineux, lunaire, lunatique, *lewk-
lundi, *deyn-
lune, lunule, lustrer, *lewk-
lutte, lutter, luxe, luxure, *seh₂g-
luzerne, *lewk-
ma, *H₁meme-
mâcher, *mendʰ-
maestro, magister, magistrat, *méǵh₂s
maigre, *meh₂ḱ-
main, *méh₂-r̥
maintenir, *ten-
maire, mais, maître, majesté, majeur, majuscule, *méǵh₂s
malédiction, *deyḱ-
malfaire, *dheH₁-
malgré, *gʷerH-
maman, *méh₂-méh₂
mander, *deH₃-
mandibule, manger, *mendʰ-
manière, *méh₂-r̥
manifeste, *gʷʰen-
maniple, *pleh₁-
mannequin, *mánus
mansuétude, *swe-dʰh₁-
mantra, *men-
marais, *móri
mardi, *deyn-
mare, marécage, *móri
maréchal, *marko-
marin, maritime, *móri
marsouin, *suH-
master, *méǵh₂s
mastiquer, *mendʰ-
maternel, maternité, matière, *méh₂tēr
matin, *meh₂-
mâtin, *swe-dʰh₁-
matrice, matricide, matricule, matrone, *méh₂tēr
mature, *meh₂-
maudire, *deyḱ-
maximum, *méǵh₂s
mé-, *mey-
me, *H₁me-
médecine, *med-
médian, médiateur, médiator, *médʰyos
médicament, médicinal, *med-
médiocrité, *h₂éḱ
médiocrité, méditerrané, médium, *médʰyos
mège, mégir, meige, *med-
mélange, mélanger, mêler, *mey-
mellifique, melliflue, *melit-
membrane, membraneux, membre, *mḗms
même, *éy / h₁e, *s(w)e-
mémoire, mémorable, mémorer, menace, mendacieux,

mener, mensonge, *men-

menstruel, *mḗh₂n̥s

mental, mention, mentir, menton, *men-

menton, *mendʰ-

menu, menuaille, menuise, *mey-

mer, *móri

mercredi, *deyn-

mére, *méh₂tēr

més-, *mey-

mes, *H₁meme-

mesure, mesurer, *meh₁-

métaphore, *bher-

méthylène, *médʰu

métier, métis, *mey-

mètre, *meh₁-

meule, meunier, *melh₂-

meurtrir, *mer-

mi-, *médʰyos

midi, *deyn-

miel, *melit-

mien, mienne, *H₁meme-

migration, *mey-

milieu, *médʰyos

mille, *sem-

mince, mincer, mineur, minime, minimum,
  ministère, ministre, minute, minutie, *mey-

misaine, *médʰyos

mixtion, *mey-

mode, modèle, modeler, modérer, moderne,
  modeste, modique, module, *med-

moelle, *médʰyos

moi, *H₁me-

moindre, moins, *mey-

mois, *mḗh₁n̥s

moise, *meh₁-

moitié, *médʰyos

mon, *H₁meme-

monceau, monnaie, *men-

monsieur, *sénos

monstre, monstrueux, mont, montagne, montagneux,
  monticule, montrer, montueux, monument, *men-

moribond, mort, morte, *mer-

mouche, *mus-

moudre, *melh₂-

moule, *med-, *muh₂s-

moulin, *melh₂-

mourir, *mer-

moustache, *mendʰ-

moyen, moyer, *médʰyos

muer, *mey-

muid, *med-

multiplication, multiplier, *pleḱ-

municipe, munificence, *mey-

mûr, *meh₂-

muscle, musculaire, musculeux, *muh₂s-

mutation, muter, mutuel, *mey-

nacelle, nager, *(s)neh₂-

naïf, naissance, naissant, naitre, naître, *ǵenH₁-

narine, *néh₂s

narratif, narration, narrer, *ǵneh₃-

naseau, *néh₂s

natal, *ǵenH₁-

natation, *(s)neh₂-

natif, nation, nativité, nature, *ǵenH₁-

naufrage, nautique, naval, navale, navals, navigateur,
  navigation, naviguer, navire, *(s)neh₂-

né, *ǵenH₁-

nébuleux, *nebʰ-

nectar, *neḱ-

nef, *(s)neh₂-

néfaste, *bʰeh₂-

négligence, négliger, *leǵ-

négoce, négociateur, négocier, *h₂ew

neige, *sneygʷʰ-

némoral, *nem-

nerf, nerveux, *(s)neh₁-

neuf, *H₁néwn̥, *new

neuve, *new

neveu, *nepot-

nez, *néh₂s

niais, niche, nid, nidiforme, *nisdós

nièce, *nepot-

nivôse, *sneygʷʰ-

noble, *ǵneh₃-

nocif, *neḱ-

nocturne, *nókʷts

Noël, *ǵenH₁-

nom, *h₁nómn̥

nombre, nombrer, nombreux, *nem-

nombril, *h₃enbʰ-

nominal, nomination, nominer, nommer, *h₁nómn̥

nomothète, *nem-

nonante, *H₁néwn̥

nord, *h₁én

nos, *wei

notaire, note, noter, notice, notion, *ǵneh₃-

notre, nôtre, nous, *wei

nouveau, nouvelle, *new

noyer, *neḱ-

nu, *negʷ-

nuire, *neḱ-

nuit, *nókʷts

numéraire, numéro, *nem-

obéir, obéissant, *h₂ewis-dʰh₁-

objet, *h₁epi

oblat, *bher-

obole, *gʷelH-

obséder, *sed-

obsèques, obséquieux, *sekʷ-

obsolète, *h₂el-

obstacle, obstétrique, *steh₂-

obstruer, *strew-

obtenir, *ten-

obvenir, *gʷem-

obvie, obvier, *weyh$_1$-
occlure, *(s)kel-
occupation, occuper, *keh$_2$p-
octagone, *oḱtṓw
oculaire, *h$_3$ekʷ-
odeur, odieux, *h$_3$ed-
œil, *h$_3$ekʷ-
œuf, *h$_2$ōwyóm
œuvre, œuvrer, *h$_3$ep-
offenser, *gʷʰen-
office, officiel, *h$_3$ep-
offrir, *bher-
offusquer, *dʰewh$_2$-
oie, *h$_2$éwis
oignon, *óy-nos
oiseau, *h$_2$éwis
oiseux, *h$_2$ew
ombilic, *h$_3$enbʰ-
omnipotent, *H$_1$es-
omniscient, *h$_3$ep-
on, *ǵʰmṓ
onc, *kʷis
oncle, *h$_2$éwh$_2$os
onde, *wed-
ongle, ongulé, *h$_3$negʰ-
onomatopée, *h$_1$nómn̥
onques, *kʷis
onze, *déḱm̥t
opéra, opéraire, opérer, *h$_3$ep-
opportun, opportunité, *per-
opposer, *h$_1$epi, *teḱ-
opposition, *h$_1$epi
oppugner, *pewǵ-
opulent, opuscule, *h$_3$ep-
oracle, *h$_3$éh$_1$os
orage, *h$_2$ews-
oraison, orateur, *h$_3$éh$_1$os
ordinaire, ordo, ordonner, ordre, *h$_2$er
ordure, *gʰers-
oreille, *h$_2$ew-
organe, orgue, *werǵ-
orient, oriental, originaire, original, origine,
  originel, *h$_3$er-
orne, *h$_3$es-
orner, *h$_2$er
orpiment, *peyḱ-
orteil, *h$_2$er
ortie-grièche, *ǵerh$_2$-
os, *h$_3$ésth$_1$
ost, *gʰóstis
ostentation, *ten-
ôter, *steh$_2$-
otiose, ou, *h$_2$ew
où, *kʷis
ouaille, *h$_2$ówis
oublie, *bher-
ouest, *wek(ʷ)speros

ouï, ouïe, ouïr, *h$_2$ewis-dʰh$_1$-
ours, ourse, *h$_2$r̥tḱos
outre, *h$_2$el-, *wed-
ouvrer, ouvrier, *h$_3$ep-
ovin, *h$_2$ówis
oxygène, oxyton, *h$_2$éḱ
oxyton, *ten-
oyant, *h$_2$ewis-dʰh$_1$-
pacifique, paganisme, page, païen, *peh$_2$ǵ-
pain, paisson, paître, *peh$_2$-
paix, *peh$_2$ǵ-
palabre, *gʷelH-
pale, *peh$_2$ǵ-
pâle, pâleur, *pelH-
palustre, *peh$_2$ǵ-
panécastique, *s(w)e-
panier, *peh$_2$-
panser, *pewǵ-
par, *per-
parabole, *gʷelH-
paradis, *dʰeyǵʰ-
paraître, *peh$_2$-
parâtre, *ph$_2$tḗr
parcimonie, *h$_2$erk-
parcourir, *ḱers-
parenthèse, parfaire, parfait, *dheH$_1$-
parole, *gʷelH-
parousie, *H$_1$es-
parvenir, *gʷem-
parvis, *dʰeyǵʰ-
pas, passer, passereau, *peth$_2$
pasteur, pastille, *peh$_2$-
patelle, patent, patente, *peth$_2$
paternel, paternité, *ph$_2$tḗr
pâtre, *peh$_2$-
patrice, patrimoine, patriote, patron, *ph$_2$tḗr
pâture, *peh$_2$-
payer, pays, *peh$_2$ǵ-
peau, *pel-
péché, pécher, *ped-
pêcher, *peisk-
pécheur, *ped-
pécule, pécuniaire, *peḱu-
pédagogue, *H$_2$eǵ-
pédicelle, pédicule, *pṓds
peigne, peigner, peignoir, *peḱ-
peindre, *peyḱ-
peine, *kʷey-
peint, peintre, *peyḱ-
pèlerin, *h$_2$éǵros
pelle, *peh$_2$ǵ-
pellicule, *pel-
pénal, pénalité, *kʷey-
pendre, *pewǵ-
pénétrer, *peh$_2$-
penne, *péth$_2$r
penser, pensum, *pewǵ-

423

perception, percevoir, *keh₂p-
percoler, *kʷel-
perdition, perdre, *deH₃-
pére, *ph₂tḗr
pérégrin, *h₂éǵros
péricliter, *per-
péril, *per-
périlleux, *per-
périple, *plew-
périr, *h₁ey-
permuter, *mey-
pernicieux, *neḱ-
pérorer, *h₃éh₁os
persécuter, *sekʷ-
persister, *steh₂-
perspectif, perspicace, perspicacité, *speḱ-
perte, *deH₃-
pertinent, *ten-
pervertir, *wert-
peser, *pewǵ-
pétrin, *peys-
pétulant, pétulante, *peth₂
peuple, *pleh₁-
phantasme, phénomène, *bʰeh₂-
pie-grièche, *ǵerh₂-
pied, *pṓds
pigment, *peyḱ-
pile, piler, *peys-
piment, *peyḱ-
pire, *ped-
piscine, *peisḱ-
place, *pleh₂-
plaie, plaindre, *pleh₂k-
plan, plantain, plante, planter, *pleh₂-
plèbe, *pleh₁-
plectre, *pleh₂k-
plein, plénier, plénitude, *pleh₁-
pleuvoir, *plew-
plexus, plier, ployer, *pleḱ-
pluie, *plew-
pluralité, plus, *pleh₁-
pluvial, pluvieux, pluviôse, *plew-
podium, *pṓds
poêle, *peth₂
poids, poinçon, poindre, poing, point, pointe, *pewǵ-
poison, *peh₃-
poisson, *peisḱ-
polluer, *lewh₃-
poly-, *pleh₁-
ponant, *teḱ-
ponce, *poymno-
ponction, ponctuer, pondérer, *pewǵ-
pondre, *teḱ-
pont, pontife, *pent-
populaire, population, *pleh₁-
porc, *pórḱos
porche, *per-

porcher, porcin, *pórḱos
port, portable, porte, porter, portier, portique, *per-
position, *teḱ-
posséder, posseoir, possession, *pótis
possible, *H₁es-
post-, *h₁epi
poste, *teḱ-
postuler, *preḱ-
potable, *peh₃-
potence, *H₁es-
potion, *peh₃-
pouce, poucier, *h₂welh₁-
poumon, *plewmõ
pour, *per-
pourceau, *pórḱos
poursuivre, *sekʷ-
pourvoir, *weyd-
pouvoir, *H₁es-
praesidium, *sed-
pragmatique, *per-
préceller, *kelH-
précepteur, *keh₂p-
précurseur, *ḱers-
prédateur, prédation, *deH₃-, *weyd-
prédial, *wedʰ-
prédiction, prédire, *deyḱ-
préférer, *bher-
prégoûter, *ǵews-
préhension, *weyd-
préjudice, préjuger, *h₂eyw-
prélat, *bher-
préléguer, *legh-
premier, *per-
prendre, *weyd-
préoccupation, préoccuper, *keh₂p-
prescrire, *(s)ker-
présent, présentation, présenter, *H₁es-
président, présidium, *sed-
pressentir, *sent-
prétendre, *ten-
prêter, *steh₂-, *per-
preuve, *bʰuH-
prévaloir, *h₂welh₁-
prévenir, *gʷem-
prévoir, *weyd-
prier, prière, *preḱ-
primaire, prime, *per-
primevère, *wésr̥
primitif, primitive, *per-
prince, princesse, principe, *keh₂p-
pris, *weyd-
priser, *per-
prison, *weyd-
privation, privé, priver, privilège, prix, *per-
probable, *bʰuH-
probe, *bʰuH-, *per-
probité, *bʰuH-

problèmatique, problème, *gʷelH-
prochain, proche, *per-
proclamation, proclamer, *kelh₁-
productif, production, produire, produit, *dewk-
profane, *dʰéh₁s
proférer, *bher-
professeur, profession, *bʰeh₂-
profond, *ǵʰew-
programme, programmer, *gerbʰ-
prohiber, prohibition, *gʰeh₁bʰ-
proie, *weyd-
promiscue, *mey-
propager, *peh₂ǵ-
propension, *pewǵ-
proposer, *teḱ-
propre, propriété, *preyH-
proscrire, *(s)ker-
prose, *wert-
prospectus, *speḱ-
prosterner, *sterh₃-
protéger, *(s)teg-
proue, *per-
prouver, *bʰuH-
Provence, *per-
provenir, *gʷem-
proverbe, *wekʷ-
providence, *weyd-
public, *pleh₁-
puce, *plou-
pugnace, *pewǵ-
puis, *h₁epi
puissant, *H₁es-
punir, punition, *kʷey-
puy, *póds
quadrature, *kʷetwóres
quadrige, *yugóm
quadruple, *pleh₁-
qualité, *kʷis
quart, *kʷetwóres
quatorze, *déḱm̥t, *kʷetwóres
quatre, quatuor, *kʷetwóres
que, quel, quelle, *kʷis
queux, *pekʷ-
qui, quiconque, *kʷis
quiet, *kʷyeh₁-
quinze, *déḱm̥t
quitte, *kʷyeh₁-
racine, radical, radis, rai, *wréh₂ds
raison, *h₂er
rameau, rameux, ramule, *wréh₂ds
ration, *h₂er
rayon, *wréh₂ds
récalcitrer, *(s)kel-
réceptacle, réception, recevoir, *keh₂p-
réclamer, *kelh₁-
reconnaître, *ǵneh₃-
recorder, *ḱér

recueillir, *leǵ-
redoute, réductible, réduction, réduire, réduit, *dewk-
réfection, *dheH₁-
référer, *bher-
refluer, *bʰleh₁-
refondre, *ǵʰew-
regagner, *weyh₁-
régénérer, *ǵenH₁-
régime, régir, règle, règne, régner, reine, *h₃reǵ-
relation, *bher-
relégation, reléguer, *legh-
relever, *h₁lengʷʰ-
relier, *plek-
reluire, *lewk-
remède, *med-
remémorer, *men-
rémunérer, *mey-
rendre, *deH₃-
rêne, *ten-
rénover, *new
repaître, repas, *peh₂-
répéter, *peth₂
répit, *speḱ
replet, *pleh₁-
répliquer, reployer, *pleḱ-
répréhender, répréhensible, répréhension, reprendre, *weyd-
représenter, *H₁es-
repris, *weyd-
république, *pleh₁-
répugner, *pewǵ-
résider, *sed-
résigner, *sek-
résister, *steh₂-
respect, respecter, *speḱ-
ressembler, *sem-
restaurer, rester, restituer, *steh₂-
retenir, rétention, *ten-
retirer, *der-
rétribuer, *bʰuH-
réunion, *óy-nos
revendiquer, *weyh₁-
revenir, *gʷem-
révérence, révérer, *wer-
reverser, *wert-
réviser, revoilà, revoir, *weyd-
révolution, *welH-
révoquer, rhéteur, *wekʷ-
riche, *h₃reǵ-
rite, *h₂er
rivalité, *h₃reyH-
rôder, *Hret-
rogne, *h₂er
roi, *h₃reǵ-
rôle, rond, *Hret-
rossignol, *keh₂n-
rotation, rotonde, rotule, roue, rouelle, rouer, *Hret-

rouge, roux, *h₁rewdʰ-
royal, royaume, *h₃reǵ-
ru, *h₃reyH-
rubis, rubrique, *h₁rewdʰ-
ruisseau, *h₃reyH-
rythme, *srew-
sa, *s(w)e-
sacerdoce, sacerdotal, sacrificateur, sacrifice,
  sacrifier, *dheH₁-
sagace, sagacité, *seh₂g-
saigner, *h₁ésh₂r
saison, *seH₁-
saler, *séh₂ls
salubre, saluer, salut, salutation, *solh₂-
sanctifier, *dheH₁-
sang, *h₁ésh₂r
sanglier, *sem-
sanguin, sanguinaire, sanguinolent, *h₁ésh₂r
satisfaire, *dheH₁-
sauce, *séh₂ls
sauf, sauver, *solh₂-
sceau, *sek-
schéma, *seǵʰ-
sciemment, science, *skey-
scientifique, *dheH₁-, *skey-
scier, *sek-
scinder, scission, *skey-
scoliose, *(s)kel-
scruter, *(s)ker-
se, *s(w)e-
second, *sekʷ-
secourir, secours, *ḱers-
secret, secrétaire, sécrétion, *krey-
sédiment, *sed-
séduire, *dewk-
ségrairie, ségrayer, *krey-
seigneur, *sénos
seing, *sek-
seize, *déḱm̥t
séjour, séjourner, *deyn-
sel, *séh₂ls
sélection, *leǵ-
selle, *sed-
semaine, *septm̥
semblant, sembler, *sem-
semence, semer, *seH₁-
semi-, *sem-
séminal, séminariste, *seH₁-
semondre, *men-
sénat, sénateur, sénile, senior, *sénos
sens, sens, sentence, sentencieux, sentiment,
  sentir, *sent-
seoir, *sed-
sept, septembre, *septm̥
septentrion, *terh₁-
septime, *septm̥
séquence, *sekʷ-

série, sermon, *ser-
sérum, *srew-
ses, seul, *s(w)e-
si, *só
sieur, *sénos
signe, signer, signification, *sek-
signifier, *dheH₁-, *sek-
similaire, *sem-
simple, *pleḱ-, *sem-
simuler, *sem-
sinciput, *kapōlo
singulier, *sem-
sire, *sénos
site, situation, situer, *teḱ-
six, *swéḱs
ski, *skey-
social, société, socio, *sekʷ-
sœur, *swésōr
soi, *s(w)e-
soif, *dʰegʷʰ-
soin, *H₁es-
sol, *solh₂-
solaire, *sóh₂wl̥
solde, *solh₂-
soleil, *sóh₂wl̥
solennel, solennité, solicitation, solide, *solh₂-
solitaire, solitude, *s(w)e-
solliciter, sollicitude, *solh₂-
solstice, *sóh₂wl̥
sommaire, *upo
somme, *swep-, *upo
sommé, *upo
sommeil, somnifère, *swep-
son, *s(w)e-
songe, songer, *swep-
sororité, *swésōr
sort, sorte, sortir, sortition, *ser-
sou, soucier, *solh₂-
souffler, *bʰleh₁-
souffrir, *bher-
soulever, *h₁lengʷʰ-
sourcil, *ḱel-
sourdre, *h₃reǵ-
sous, *upo
souscrire, *(s)ker-
soutenir, *ten-
souvenir, *gʷem-
souvent, *éy / h₁e
specimen, spectre, spéculation, spéculer, *speḱ-
spinal, spinule, *spey-
spleen, splénétique, *splenǵʰ-
spumeux, *poymno-
stabilité, stable, station, statue, statuer, stature, *steh₂-
stellaire, *h₂stér
store, stratège, stratégie, *sterh₃-
stuc, stupeur, stupide, stupre, *(s)tew-
suaire, *sweyd-

venir, vent, *gʷem-

vent, venteux, ventilation, ventiler, ventouse,
*H₂weH₁-

vêpre, *wek⁽ʷ⁾speros

ver, *wr̥mis-

verbal, verbatim, verbe, *wekʷ-

vérécondie, vergogne, *wer-

vérification, *weh₁-

vérifier, *dheH₁-, *weh₁-

vérité, *weh₁-

vermeil, vermineux, *wr̥mis-

verre, *wed-

vers, versatile, verser, version, versus, *wert-

vertu, *wiHrós

verve, *wekʷ-

vestige, *steygʰ-

vêtement, *wes-

vétéran, *wet-

vêtir, *wes-

vétuste, *wet-

veuf, veuve, *h₁weydʰ

via, viatique, *weyh₁-

vicaire, *weyk-

vicinal, vicinité, *weyḱ-

vicissitude, victime, victoire, *weyk-

vide, *h₁weh₂-

vie, *gʷeyh₃-

vieux, *wet-

vif, *gʷeyh₃-

vigilance, vigilant, vigile, *weǵ-

vigne, *wóyh₁nom

vigueur, *weǵ-

viguier, *weyk-

villa, village, ville, *weyḱ-

villeux, *h₂welh₁-

vin, vinaigre, vinaigrette, vinasse, *wóyh₁nom

vindicte, *weyh₁-

vineux, *wóyh₁nom

vingt, *wīḱm̥tiH₁

violer, *weyh₁-

virago, viril, *wiHrós

visage, viser, visible, visiter, *weyd-

vit, *weǵh-

vital, *gʷeyh₃-

vitre, *wed-

vivace, vivacité, vivarium, vivier, vivipare, vivre,
*gʷeyh₃-

vocabulaire, vocal, vocatif, vocation, vocifération,
vociférer, *wekʷ-

voici, *weyd-

voie, *weyh₁-

voilà, voir, *weyd-

voire, *weh₁-

voisin, voisine, *weyḱ-

voix, *wekʷ-

volition, volontaire, volonté, volontiers, *welh₁-

volubile, volume, volute, *welH-

vortex, *wert-

vouloir, *welh₁-

vous, *túh₂

voûte, *welH-

voyage, *weyh₁-

voyelle, *wekʷ-

voyer, *weyk-

vrai, *weh₁-

wagon, *weǵh-

Italian

-dotto, -durre, *dewk-
-mente, *men-
ab-, *h₂pó
abbacchio, *bak-
abbreviare, *mréǵʰ-
abdurre, abduzione, *dewk-
abile, abilità, *gʰeh₁bʰ-
abisso, *dʰewb-
abitare, abitazione, abito, *gʰeh₁bʰ-
abiurare, *h₂eyw-
ablativo, *bher-
ablegazione, *legh-
abluzione, *lewh₃-
abolire, abolizione, *h₂el-
aborrire, *gʰers-
abortivo, aborto, *h₃er-
accettare, *keh₂p-
accia, acciaio, *h₂éḱ
acclamare, *kelh₁-
accline, *ḱley-
accordare, accordo, *ḱér
accorrere, *kers-
acerbo, acido, *h₂éḱ
acqua, acquaio, acquario, Acquario, acquatico,
  acquazzone, *h₂ekʷeh₂-
acquedotto, *dewk-, *h₂ekʷeh₂-
  acquoso, *h₂ekʷeh₂-
acre, acrimonia, aculeo, *h₂éḱ
addetto, addire, *deyḱ-
addizione, *deH₃-
addurre, *dewk-
adesso, *éy / h₁e, *s(w)e-
adire, *h₁ey-
adorare, *h₃éh₁os
adulterino, *h₂el-
adunco, *h₂enk-
affermare, *dʰer-
affluire, *bʰleh₁-
affumare, affumicare, *dʰewh₂-
aggiudicare, aggiudicazione, *h₂eyw-
aggiungere, aggiunto, *yewg-
agire, agitare, agitazione, *H₂eǵ-
agnella, agnello, *h₂egʷnos
ago, *h₂éḱ
agonia, *H₂eǵ-
agosto, *h₂ewg-
agreste, agricolo, agricoltura, agrimensore, agro,
  *h₂éǵros
agro, *h₂éḱ
agurare, *h₂ewg-
aino, *h₃el-
ala, *H₂eǵ-
albereto, *h₂erHdʰ-

albergo, *ker-
albero, *h₂erHdʰ-
albiolo, *h₂el-
alcuno, *kʷis, *óy-nos
alimento, *h₂el-
alla, *ḱel-
allegare, *legh-
allevare, *h₁lengʷʰ-
allocare, *stel-
allume, *h₂elut-
alluminare, *lewk-
alma, *h₂enh₁-
alterare, altercare, altercazione, alto, altro, alunno,
  alveo, alveolo, alvino, *h₂el-
ambi-, ambire, ambito, ambo, *h₂ent
ambrosia, *mer-
amente, amenza, *men-
ametista, *médʰu
amministrare, amministrazione, *mey-
ammonire, *men-
anatra, *h₂eneti-
anelare, *h₂enh₁-
angolare, angolo, *h₂enk-
anguilla, *angʷ(h)i-
angusto, *h₂enǵʰ-
anima, animare, *h₂enh₁-
annegare, *neḱ-
anniversario, *wert-
anonimo, *h₁nómņ
ansietà, *h₂enǵʰ-
ante, anteriore, anti, *h₂ent
antichità, antico, *h₂énti-h₃kʷós
antiteto, *dheH₁-
anzi, *h₂ent
ape, apiolo, *bʰey-
apparire, *peh₂-
appartenere, *ten-
appendere, appendice, *pewǵ-
appetito, *peth₂
appio, *bʰey-
applaudire, *pleh₂k-
applicare, *pleḱ-
apporre, *teḱ-
apportare, *per-
apprendere, apprensione, *weyd-
apprezzare, *per-
Aquario, *h₂ekʷeh₂-
aquifoglio, *bʰleh₃-
arabile, *H₂erH₃-
aragna, *h₂er
arare, aratore, aratorio, aratro, *H₂erH₃-
arboreo, arboreto, *h₂erHdʰ-
arca, *h₂erk-
arcione, arco, arcobaleno, *h₂erkʷo-
arduità, arduo, *h₂erHdʰ-
argano, *werǵ-
argine, *H₂eǵ-

aria, *h₂ews-
arido, *h₂eh₁s-
arma, armadio, armare, armario, armata, armato, armatura, armento, *h₂er
armipotente, *H₁es-
arte, articolo, *h₂er
aruspice, *ǵʰern-
aruspice, *speḱ-
as-, *h₂pó
ascella, aschia, *H₂eǵ-
ascia, *h₂éḱ
ascola, *H₂eǵ-
ascoltare, *ḱel-
ascondere, *dheH₁-
ascrivere, *(s)ker-
aspettare, aspetto, *speḱ-
asportare, asportazione, *per-
asse, *H₂eǵ-
assedio, *sed-
assegnare, *sek-
assembiare, assembrare, *sem-
asserire, *ser-
assidere, *sed-
assimilare, *sem-
assistere, *steh₂-
assomigliare, *sem-
assorgere, assurgere, *h₃reǵ-
astenere, astinente, astinenza, *ten-
astuzia, *h₂éḱ
ateo, *dʰéh₁s
atroce, atrocità, *h₂eh₁tro-h₃kʷs
attendere, attenere, attento, attenzione, *ten-
attività, attivo, atto, attore, *H₂eǵ-
attribuire, *bʰuH-
attrice, *H₂eǵ-
auditorio, audizione, *h₂ewis-dʰh₁-
augello, *h₂éwis
augurare, augure, augurio, *h₂ewg-
auna, *Heh₃l-
aura, *h₂ews-
auricola, *h₂ew-
aurora, *h₂ews-
auscultare, *ḱel-
ausiliare, ausiliario, ausilio, *h₂ewg-
australe, *h₂ews-
auto-, auto, automobile, *h₂ew
autore, autorità, autrice, *h₂ewg-
avante, avanti, *h₂ent
avere, *gʰeh₁bʰ-
avo, avolo, *h₂éwh₂os
avvenire, avvento, *gʷem-
avverbiale, avverbio, *wekʷ-
avverso, *wert-
avvinghiare, *weyk-
avvocare, avvocato, *wekʷ-
avvolgere, *welH-
azienda, *dheH₁-

azione, *H₂eǵ-
bacchio, bacolo, *bak-
balestra, balista, *gʷelH-
barba, barbato, barbula, *bʰardʰeh₂-
baroccio, *bher-, *Hret-
base, *gʷem-
battello, *bʰeyd-
benedire, *deyḱ-
benefare, benefatto, benefattore, *dheH₁-
bere, *peh₃-
betulla, *gʷet-
bevace, bevitore, bibace, bibitore, *peh₃-
biblioteca, *dheH₁-
bibulo, *peh₃-
bicipite, *kapōlo
bifolco, *gʷṓws
binare, *dwóH₁
biscotto, *pekʷ-
bitume, *gʷet-
bivio, *weyh₁-
boario, boaro, *gʷṓws
borghese, borgo, *bʰergʰ-
borra, *péh₂ur
bottega, *dheH₁-
bovaro, bove, bovino, *gʷṓws
braccio, brachiale, breve, *mréǵʰ-
brio, *bʰergʰ-
brodo, *bʰrewh₁-
bruma, *mréǵʰ-
bruto, brutto, *gʷerh₂-
buccina, *gʷṓws, *keh₂n-
bucolico, bue, bufalo, *gʷṓws
burla, *péh₂ur
burro, *gʷṓws
busto, *h₁ews-
ca, *kʷis
cabra, cabriola, *kapro
cagliare, caglio, *H₂eǵ-
calabrone, *ḱerh₂-
calamo, *ḱalam-
calcagno, calcare, calceo, calcetto, *(s)kel-
calendario, *kelh₁-
calza, calzare, calzetta, calzino, calzone, *(s)kel-
cambra, camera, camerlengo, Campania, campestre, campione, campo, *(s)teg-
cane, canicola, canino, *ḱwó
canoro, cantilena, *keh₂n-
capace, capacità, *keh₂p-
capecchio, *kapōlo
capere, capestro, capire, *keh₂p-
capitale, capitello, capitolo, capitone, capo, *kapōlo
capraio, caprino, capriolare, capro, *kapro
capsula, captare, *keh₂p-
carattere, *ǵʰer-
caricare, *ḱers-
carme, carminare, *keh₂n-
carnaio, carnale, carne, carnivoro, carnoso, *(s)ker-

carpare, carpire, *kerp-
carraia, carretta, carriera, carro, carroccia,
 carrozza, carrozzeria, carruca, *ḱers-
carta, cartolaio, cartulario, *ǵʰer-
cassa, *keh₂p-
catasto, *steygʰ-
cattivo, cattura, *keh₂p-
cavedano, cavedine, cavesso, cavezza, *kapōlo
cavicchia, cavicchio, caviglia, *(s)kel-
celare, cella, cellaio, cellula, *ḱel-
cena, cenare, *(s)ker-
centi-, centinaio, cento, centopelle, *ḱm̥tóm
centopelle, *pel-
centuria, *ḱm̥tóm
cerebellare, cerebro, *ḱerh₂-
cernere, certare, cèrto, *krey-
cervello, cervo, *ḱerh₂-
che, *kʷis
cheto, *kʷyeh₁-
chi, *kʷis
chiamare, chiaro, *kelh₁-
chiavare, chiave, chiavistello, chiavo, *(s)kel-
chinare, *ḱley-
chiodo, chiostra, chiostro, chiudere, chiuso,
 chiusura, *(s)kel-
ciclo, *kʷel-
cicogna, *keh₂n-
ciglio, *ḱel-
cinquanta, cinque, *pénkʷe
circondurre, *dewk-
circonferenza, *bher-
circonfluire, *bʰleh₁-
circonvenire, *gʷem-
circostanza, *steh₂-
circumnavigare, *(s)neh₂-
città, cittade, cittadino, civico, civile, *ḱei-
clamare, clamore, *kelh₁-
clandestino, *ḱel-
clarità, classare, classe, classico, classico,
 classificare, *kelh₁-
clausura, clavicola, clavicordo, clavo, *(s)kel-
climatérico, *ḱley-
coagulare, coagulo, coatto, *H₂eǵ-
cocchiglia, *ḱonkho-
cogitabondo, cogitare, cogitazione, *H₂eǵ-
cogliere, *leǵ-
cogno, *ḱonkho-
cognome, *h₁nómn̥
coitare, *H₂eǵ-
colcare, *stel-
colei, *h₂el-
colle, *kelH-
collega, collegio, *legh-
colletta, colletto, collezione, *leǵ-
collina, *kelH-
collocare, *stel-
colmo, *kelH-

colonia, *kʷel-
colonna, *kelH-
colono, *kʷel-
colorare, colore, *ḱel-
coloro, *h₂el-
colta, *leǵ-
coltivare, colto, *kʷel-
colto, *leǵ-
colui, *h₂el-
comandare, *deH₃-
combinare, combinazione, *dwóH₁
comburere, *h₁ews-
come, *med-
commendare, *deH₃-
commutare, *mey-
comodo, *med-
compendio, compensare, compensazione, *pewǵ-
competo, *peth₂
compiere, *pleh₁-
compilare, compilazione, *peys-
compire, complemento, completivo, completo, *pleh₁-
complicare, complicazione, *pleḱ-
complimento, *pleh₁-
comporre, *teḱ-
comportare, *per-
comprendere, comprensibile, comprensione,
 comprensivo, compreso, *weyd-
compungere, *pewǵ-
comune, comunicare, comunicazione, comunione,
 comunità, *mey-
conca, *ḱonkho-
concento, *keh₂n-
concepire, *keh₂p-
concernere, *krey-
concezione, *keh₂p-
conciliabolo, concilio, conclamare, *kelh₁-
conclave, concludere, *(s)kel-
concola, *ḱonkho-
concordia, *ǵʰer-
concorrere, concorso, *ḱers-
conculcare, *(s)kel-
condizione, *deyḱ-, *dheH₁-
condonare, *deH₃-
condotto, conducibile, condurre, conduzione, *dewk-
conferire, *bher-
confermare, confermazione, *dʰer-
confessione, *bʰeh₂-
confetto, confezione, *dheH₁-
confidare, *bʰeydʰ-
conflare, confluire, *bʰleh₁-
confondere, confusione, confuso, *ǵʰew-
congelare, *gel-
congio, *ḱonkho-
congiungere, *yewg-
congiurare, *h₂eyw-
conoscere, *ǵneh₃-
consegnare, *sek-

conseguire, *sekʷ-
consenso, consentire, *sent-
consigliare, consiglio, *kelh₁-
consistere, *steh₂-
consobrino, *swésōr
consorte, *ser-
constare, *steh₂-
consuetudine, *swe-dʰh₁-
contendere, contenere, contento, contento,
 contenzione, continenza, continuo, *ten-
contraddire, contradditore, contraddittorio, *deyk̑-
contribuer, *bʰuH-
controversia, *wert-
convenienza, convenire, convento, convenzione,
 *gʷem-
convergere, convertire, *wert-
convincere, *weyk-
convitare, *weyh₁-
convocare, *wekʷ-
convolgere, convolvere, convolvolo, *welH-
coorte, *ǵʰer-
copioso, *h₃ep-
coraggio, *k̑ḗr
corazza, *(s)ker-
corda, *ǵʰern-
coriaceo, *(s)ker-
coricare, *stel-
corneo, corno, cornuto, *k̑erh₂-
corpo, corporeo, corpuscolo, *krep-
corregere, correggia, *h₃reǵ-
corrente, correre, *k̑ers-
corretto, correttore, correzione, *h₃reǵ-
corso, corsoio, *k̑ers-
corte, *ǵʰer-
corteccia, cortice, corto, *(s)ker-
coscia, *kok̑s-
coscienza, *skey-
cosi, *só
costare, *steh₂-
costei, *só
costituire, costituzione, *steh₂-
costoro, *só
costruire, costruzione, *strew-
costui, *só
costume, *swe-dʰh₁-
cotale, *só
cotto, *pekʷ-
cranio, *k̑erh₂-
credere, credibile, credito, creditore, credulo, *dheH₁-
cribrare, cribro, crimine, *krey-
crudele, crudeltà, crudità, crudo, cruentare,
 cruento, *krewh₂-
ctonio, *dʰéǵʰōm
cucina, cucinare, cucinario, *pekʷ-
cucire, *sīw-
cugino, *swésōr
cui, *kʷis

culla, *k̑ei-
culmine, *kelH-
culmo, *k̑alam-
cuocere, cuoco, *pekʷ-
cuoio, *(s)ker-
cuore, *k̑ḗr
curricolo, cursore, cursorio, *k̑ers-
dado, *deH₃-
dama, damigella, *dem-
danaio, danaro, *dékm̥t
dannare, danno, *deh₂-
dare, data, dato, *deH₃-
debile, debito, debitore, debole, *gʰeh₁bʰ-
deca, decade, decano, decempeda, *dékm̥t
decempeda, *pṓds
decernere, *krey-
decima, decimale, decimare, decimo, *dékm̥t
declamare, *kelh₁-
declinare, *k̑ley-
decorare, decoro, *dek-
decorrente, decorrere, *k̑ers-
decretale, decreto, decretorio, *krey-
dedurre, deduzione, *dewk-
deferire, *bher-
defluire, *bʰleh₁-
degnità, degno, *dek-
degustare, *ǵews-
deificare, deità, *dyew-
delegare, *legh-
delineare, *lino-
delinquere, *leykʷ-
delirio, *leys-
delitto, *leykʷ-
demandare, *deH₃-
demente, demenza, *men-
demonio, *deh₂-
denario, denaro, *dékm̥t
dentale, dentato, dente, *h₃dónts
denudare, *negʷ-
deperire, *h₁ey-
depingere, *peyk-
deporre, *tek-
deportare, *per-
deposto, *tek-
deprecabile, deprecare, deprecativo, deprecatorio,
 deprecazione, *prek-
descrivere, descrizione, *(s)ker-
desidia, *sed-
designare, *sek-
desio, *sed-
desistere, *steh₂-
desolare, *s(w)e-
desterità, *dek̑s-
destinare, destituire, *steh₂-
destro, *dek̑s-
detenere, detenzione, *ten-
detonare, *(s)tenh₂-

dettare, detto, *deyḱ-
devolvere, *welH-
di sopra, *upo
di-, *dwóH₁
dì, *deyn-
diarrea, *srew-
diavolo, *gʷelH-
dicace, *deyḱ-
dicembre, *déḱm̥t
dichiarare, *kelh₁-
dieci, *déḱm̥t
difendere, *gʷʰen-
differire, *bher-
difficile, *dheH₁-
diffondere, diffuso, *ǵʰew-
digitale, *deyḱ-
dignità, *deḱ-
dilezione, diligente, diligere, *leǵ-
diluire, diluvio, *lewh₃-
dimostrare, dimostrazione, *men-
dio, *dyew-
dipendere, *pewǵ-
dipingere, *peyḱ-
diporre, diposto, *teḱ-
dire, *deyḱ-
diretto, dirigere, diritto, *h₃reǵ-
dis-, *dwóH₁
discalzare, *(s)kel-
discanto, *keh₂n-
discaricare, *ḱers-
discernere, *krey-
dischiudere, dischiuso, *(s)kel-
discorrere, discorso, *ḱers-
disegnare, disegno, *sek-
disio, *sed-
dispettare, dispetto, *speḱ-
dispiegare, *pleḱ-
disporre, *teḱ-
dissecare, *sek-
disseminare, *seH₁-
dissenso, *sent-
dissimile, dissimulazione, *sem-
distanza, *steh₂-
distendere, *ten-
distribuire, *bʰuH-
distruggere, distruzione, *strew-
ditale, dito, dittatore, dittatura, *deyḱ-
diurno, *deyn-
diva, *dyew-
divenire, diventare, *gʷem-
diverso, divertire, *wert-
dividere, *h₁weydʰ
divinare, divinità, divino, *dyew-
divisibile, divisione, *h₁weydʰ
dizionario, dizione, *deyḱ-
doccia, doccione, *dewk-
docile, documento, *deḱ-

dodici, *déḱm̥t
dogado, dogato, doge, *dewk-
dogma, *deḱ-
domandare, *deH₃-
domare, *dem-, *demh₂-
domenica, *deyn-
domestico, dominare, dominazione, dominio, domino,
don, *dem-
donare, donazione, *deH₃-
donna, donno, *dem-
dono, *deH₃-
donzello, *dem-
dopo, *h₁epi
doppiare, doppio, *pleh₁-
dota, dotare, dote, *deH₃-
dotto, *deḱ-
dotto, *dewk-
dottore, dottrina, *deḱ-
dove, *kʷis
dovere, *gʰeh₁bʰ-
dritto, *h₃reǵ-
dubbietà, dubbio, dubbioso, *gʰeh₁bʰ-
duca, ducato, duce, ducere, *dewk-
due, *dwóH₁
duecento, *ḱm̥tóm
duetto, *dwóH₁
dunque, *só
duomo, *dem-
duplice, *pleḱ-
duplo, *pleh₁-
durabile, durabilità, duracina, durare, durezza, *deru-
eccellente, eccellenza, eccellere, *kelH-
eccepire, *keh₂p-
ecli, *h₂el-
economia, *nem-
edera, *weyd-
edicola, edificare, edificio, *h₂eydʰ-
editto, *deyḱ-
educare, educazione, educere, edurre, *dewk-
effetto, *dheH₁-
effigie, effingere, *dʰeyǵʰ-
effluire, effluvio, *bʰleh₁-
effondere, effusione, *ǵʰew-
egemonia, *seh₂g-
ego, *egH₂
eleggere, eletto, *leǵ-
elevare, *h₁lengʷʰ-
elezione, *leǵ-
ella, *h₂el-
elucubrare, *lewk-
emigrare, *mey-
eminenza, *men-
empire, *pleh₁-
endice, *deyḱ-
energia, *werǵ-
enfiagione, enfiare, *bʰleh₁-
enorme, *ǵneh₃-

ente, entità, *H_1es-
entrare, entro, *$h_1$én
entuziasmo, *d^héh$_1$s
enumerare, *nem-
epentetico, *dheH$_1$-
epoca, *seǵ^h-
equino, *h_1éḱwos
equivalere, *$h_2$welh$_1$-
eradicare, *wréh$_2$ds
erario, *$h_2$eyos
ergere, erigere, *$h_3$reǵ-
ernia, *ǵ^{h}ern-
esa-, *swéḱs
esacerbare, *h_2éḱ
esalare, *$h_2$enh$_1$-
esame, esaminare, *H$_2$eǵ-
esangue, *$h_1$ésh$_2$r
esaudire, *$h_2$ewis-d^{h}h$_1$-
esca, *$h_1$ed-
eschio, *$h_2$eyǵ-
esclamare, *kelh$_1$-
escludere, escluso, *(s)kel-
escogitare, *H$_2$eǵ-
escoriare, *(s)ker-
esculento, *$h_1$ed-
escursione, *ḱers-
esecuzione, eseguire, eseguizione, esequie, *sek^w-
esercire, esercito, esercizio, *$h_2$erk-
esibire, *g^{h}eh$_1$b^h-
esistere, *steh$_2$-
esito, *$h_1$ey-
esortazione, *ǵ^{h}er-
esperienza, esperto, *per-
esplicare, *pleḱ-
esporre, *teḱ-
esportare, esportazione, *per-
espugnare, espugnazione, espungere, *pewǵ-
essa, esse, *éy / h$_1$e
essenza, essere, *H_1es-
essi, esso, *éy / h$_1$e
esso, *s(w)e-
esta, *só
estasi, *steh$_2$-
estate, *$h_2$eyd^h-
estatico, *steh$_2$-
estendere, estensione, estenso, *ten-
esterno, estero, *h_1eǵ^{h}s
esteso, *ten-
estivo, *$h_2$eyd^h-
esto, *só
estra-, estraneo, *h_1eǵ^{h}s
età, eternità, eterno, *$h_2$ey-
etologia, *swe-d^{h}h$_1$-
evento, eventualità, *g^{w}em-
evidenza, *weyd-
evincere, *weyk-
evo, *$h_2$ey-

evocare, *wek^w-
evoluto, evoluzione, evolvere, *welH-
extra-, *h_1eǵ^{h}s
faccenda, *dheH$_1$-
faggio, faina, *b^{h}eh$_2$go-
fama, *b^{h}eh$_2$-
famiglia, familiare, famulo, *dheH$_1$-
fanatico, *d^{h}éh$_1$s
fantasma, *b^{h}eh$_2$-
fare, *dheH$_1$-
farina, farinaio, farinoso, farragine, *b^{h}ars-
fasto, fato, *b^{h}eh$_2$-
fatto, fattore, *dheH$_1$-
fava, *b^{h}ab^{h}eh$_2$-
favella, favola, favoloso, *b^{h}eh$_2$-
fazione, *dheH$_1$-
febbraio, febbre, *d^{h}eg^{wh}-
fede, fedele, fedeltà, fedifrago, *b^{h}eyd^h-
felice, felicità, femmina, femminile, femminino,
　　*d^{h}eh$_1$(y)-
fendere, *b^{h}eyd-
ferale, feria, *d^{h}éh$_1$s
fermare, fermo, *d^{h}er-
feroce, ferocità, *ǵ^{h}weroh$_3$k^{w}s
fesso, *b^{h}eyd-
festa, festività, festivo, festo, *d^{h}éh$_1$s
feto, *d^{h}eh$_1$(y)-
feudo, *peku-
fiaba, *b^{h}eh$_2$-
fiatare, fiato, *b^{h}leh$_1$-
fidare, fido, fiducia, fiduciario, *b^{h}eyd^h-
fiera, *d^{h}éh$_1$s, *ǵ^{h}wer-
fiero, *ǵ^{h}wer-
figlia, figliastro, figlio, figliolo, *d^{h}eh$_1$(y)-
figura, *d^{h}eyǵ^h-
filiale, *d^{h}eh$_1$(y)-
fingere, finto, *d^{h}eyǵ^h-
fiore, fiorire, *b^{h}leh$_3$-
fiotto, *b^{h}leh$_1$-
fire, *b^{h}uH-
firmamento, firmare, *d^{h}er-
fischiare, *b^{h}eyd-
fisico, *b^{h}uH-
fissione, fistola, *b^{h}eyd-
fittizio, *d^{h}eyǵ^h-
fiume, *b^{h}leh$_1$-
flotta, flottare, *plew-
fluente, fluire, fluitare, flusso, flutto, fluttuare,
　　fluttuazione, fluviale, *b^{h}leh$_1$-
foglia, foglio, foglioso, *b^{h}leh$_3$-
folla, *pleh$_1$-
fomento, *d^{h}eg^{wh}-
fondaco, *deḱ-
fondamenta, *ǵ^{h}ew-
fondare, *b^{h}ud^{h}mḗn
fondatore, fondere, fonderia, *ǵ^{h}ew-
fondo, *b^{h}ud^{h}mḗn

forense, *dʰwer-

foresta, *perkʷu-

formica, formicola, *morwi-

fornace, fornello, forno, *gʷʰer-

foro, *dʰwer-

forse, *bher-

forte, *bʰerǵʰ-

fortificare, fortificazione, *bʰerǵʰ-, *dheH₁-

fortuitamente, fortuito, fortuna, *bher-

forza, *bʰerǵʰ-

fosco, *dʰewh₂-

fraina, *bʰars-

frassineto, frassino, *bʰereǵ-

frate, fratello, fraternità, *bʰréh₂tēr

freno, *dʰer-

fuco, *bʰey-

fui, *bʰuH-

fuliggine, fumaiolo, fumare, fumigare, fumo, *dʰewh₂-

fuori, *dʰwer-

furetto, furo, furtivo, furto, *bher-

fusione, *ǵʰew-

futuro, *bʰuH-

galassia, *glag-

gamba, *(s)teg-

gelare, gelato, gelido, gelo, *gel-

gemma, *ǵómbʰos

generale, generare, genere, genio, genitore,

  genitrice, *ǵenH₁-

gennaio, *h₁ey-

gente, gentile, gentilità, *ǵenH₁-

genuflettersi, *ǵónu

germano, germe, germinare, germogliare, *ǵenH₁-

gerundio, *H₂eǵ-

ghiacciare, ghiaccio, *gel-

già, *éy / h₁e

giardino, *ǵʰer-

ginocchio, *ǵónu

giocare, gioco, giocoso, *yek-

giogo, *yugóm

giornale, giornata, giorno, *deyn-

giovane, giovanile, *h₂yuh₁en-

giovedì, *deyn-

giovenco, giovenile, gioventù, giovine, *h₂yuh₁en-

gire, *h₁ey-

giudicabile, giudicare, giudicato, giudicatore,

  giudicatorio, giudicatrice, giudice, giudiziale,

  giudiziario, *h₂eyw-

giungere, *yewg-

giuniore, *h₂yuh₁en-

giuntare, giunzione, *yewg-

giuoco, *yek-

giuramento, giurare, giure, gius, giustezza,

  giustizia, giusto, *h₂eyw-

gli, *h₂el-

gloria, gloriare, glorioso, *ǵneh₃-

gonfiare, *bʰleh₁-

grado, *gʷerH-

gramigna, *gʰreh₁-

grammatica, *gerbʰ-

grano, *ǵrHnom

gratis, grato, gratuito, *gʷerH-

gravare, grave, gravido, gravità, *gʷerh₂-

grazia, grazioso, *gʷerH-

greco, *ǵerh₂-

greve, *gʷerh₂-

gru, *gerh₂-

guadagnare, *weyh₁-

guardare, guardia, *wer-

guastare, *h₁weh₂-

guatare, *weǵ-

guazzare, *wed-

guazzo, *h₂ekʷeh₂-

guidare, *weyd-

guidrigildo, *wiHrós

gustare, gusto, *ǵews-

i, *h₂el-

ibernare, *ǵʰey-

idea, *weyd-

iena, *suH-

ieri, *dʰǵʰ(y)es-

ignaro, ignavo, *ǵneh₃-

igne, igneo, *h₁ngʷnis

ignominia, ignominioso, *h₁nómņ

ignorante, ignorare, *ǵneh₃-

il, *h₂el-

illazione, *bher-

illegale, *leǵ-, *legh-

illuminare, *lewk-

imbecille, *bak-

imberbe, *bʰardʰeh₂-

imbevere, *peh₃-

imbrifero, *nebʰ-

immaturo, *meh₂-

immigrare, *mey-

imminente, *men-

immolare, *melh₂-

immune, *mey-

impatto, *peh₂ǵ-

impedire, *ped-

impeto, *peth₂

impiantare, *pleh₂-

impiegare, *plek-

impingere, *peh₂ǵ-

implicare, implicazione, *plek-

importare, importunità, *per-

imprendere, impresa, *weyd-

impugnare, *pewǵ-

impunemente, *kʷey-

in, *h₁én

inalare, *h₂enh₁-

inaugurare, *h₂ewg-

incantare, *keh₂n-

incezzione, *keh₂p-

inchinare, inclinare, inclinazione, *ḱley-

435

inclito, *ḱlew-
includere, incluso, *(s)kel-
inconseguente, *sekʷ-
incorrere, *ḱers-
incredibile, incredulo, *dheH₁-
inculcare, *(s)kel-
incursione, *ḱers-
indentico, *éy / h₁e
indicare, indice, *deyḱ-
indole, *h₂el-
indotto, *dewk-
indovinare, *dyew-
indurre, *dewk-
industria, industrioso, *strew-
induzione, *dewk-
ineluttabile, *seh₂g-
inerte, *h₂er-
infamare, infamia, infante, *bʰeh₂-
inferibile, inferire, *bher-
infermità, infermo, *dʰer-
infestare, *gʷʰen-
infirmo, *dʰer-
inflazione, influire, *bʰleh₁-
infondere, *ǵʰew-
ingenerare, ingente, *ǵenH₁-
ingerire, *H₂eǵ-
ingiungere, *yewg-
inibire, *gʰeh₁bʰ-
iniziare, inizio, *h₁ey-
innocente, *neḱ-
innovare, *new
inoculare, *h₃ekʷ-
inquilino, *kʷel-
insalare, *séh₂ls
insegna, insegnare, *sek-
inseguire, *sekʷ-
inserire, *ser-
insetto, *sek-
insieme, *sem-
insigne, *sek-
insistere, *steh₂-
insolito, *swe-dʰh₁-
instaurare, *steh₂-
intelletto, *leǵ-
intendere, intenso, intento, intenzione, *ten-
intercalare, *kelh₁-
intercludere, *(s)kel-
interdire, *deyḱ-
interesse, *h₁én, *H₁es-
interlunio, *lewk-
interpungere, *pewǵ-
interstiziale, *steh₂-
intervallo, *welH-
intervenire, *gʷem-
inteso, *ten-
intra-, intrare, *h₁én
introdurre, *dewk-

inventārium, inventione, invenzione, *gʷem-
invernale, invernare, inverno, *ǵʰey-
invertire, *wert-
investigare, investigazione, *steygʰ-
investire, *wes-
invigilare, *weǵ-
invitare, *weyh₁-
involgere, involto, involucro, involuto, *welH-
io, *egH₂
ipoteca, *dheH₁-
ire, *h₁ey-
ironia, *wekʷ-
iscrivere, *(s)ker-
istituire, *steh₂-
istruire, istruttore, istruzione, *strew-
iter, *h₁ey-
iudicato, *h₂eyw-
la, *h₂el-
labbro, *leb-
lacrima, lacrimare, lacrimazione, lacrimoso, *daḱru-
lacuna, lago, laguna, *lókus
lambere, lambire, *leb-
lana, lanario, lanoso, lanugine, *h₂welh₁-
latrina, *lewh₃-
lattaio, lattare, latte, latteo, latticino, lattuga, *glag-
lava, lavare, *lewh₃-
le, *h₂el-
leale, legale, legato, legazione, legge, *leǵ-, *legh-
leggere, *leǵ-
leggero, *h₁lengʷʰ-
legione, *leǵ-
legislatore, *legh-
legislazione, legittimo, *leǵ-, *legh-
legna, legno, legnoso, *leǵ-
leguleio, *legh-
legume, *leǵ-
lei, *h₂el-
lenzuolo, *lino-
lettiga, letto, *legh-
lettore, *leǵ-
levare, levato, *h₁lengʷʰ-
lezione, *leǵ-
lì, *h₂el-
liberare, liberatore, liberazione, libero, libertà, *h₁lewdʰ-
libraio, librario, libro, *lewbʰ-
lieve, lievito, *h₁lengʷʰ-
ligneo, *leǵ-
linea, *lino-
lingua, *dn̥ǵʰwéh₂s
lino, *lino-
llabio, *leb-
lo, *h₂el-
locale, locare, locazione, *stel-
loggia, *lewbʰ-
lombo, *lendʰ-
longevità, longevo, *h₂ey-
lontra, *udréh₂

loro, *h₂el-
losco, *lewk-
lotta, lottare, lottatore, *seh₂g-
luce, lucere, lucido, lucifero, luco, *lewk-
lui, *h₂el-
Luigi, *ḱlew-
lume, luminare, luminaria, luminoso, luna, lunare,
  lunatico, *lewk-
lunedi, *deyn-
lunula, *lewk-
luogo, *stel-
lupino, lupo, *wĺkʷos
lusso, *seh₂g-
lustrare, lustro, *lewk-
ma, *méǵh₂s
madre, madrigale, *méh₂tēr
maestrale, maestro, maggiore, magistrale,
  magnate, magnitudo, magno, *méǵh₂s
magro, *meh₂ḱ-
mai, maiuscola, maiuscolo, *méǵh₂s
maledetto, maledire, *deyḱ-
malfare, *dheH₁-
malgrado, *gʷerH-
mamma, *méh₂-méh₂
mandare, *deH₃-
mandibola, manducare, mangiare, *mendʰ-
manifesto, *gʷʰen-
manipolo, *pleh₁-
maniscalco, *marko-
mannaia, mano, *méh₂-ɾ
mansuetudine, *swe-dʰh₁-
mantenere, *ten-
mantice, manubrio, *méh₂-ɾ
mare, marino, marittimo, *móri
martedi, *deyn-
massimo, *méǵh₂s
masticare, *mendʰ-
mastro, *méǵh₂s
materia, maternità, materno, matrice, matricola,
  matrimonio, matrona, *méh₂tēr
mattare, *méǵh₂s, *meh₂ḱ-
mattina, mattino, maturo, *meh₂-
me, meco, *H₁me-
medesimo, medesmo, *éy / h₁e, *s(w)e-
mediano, mediare, mediatore, *médʰyos
medicare, medicatore, Medici, medicina,
  medicinale, medico, *med-
medietà, medio, *médʰyos
mediocrità, *h₂éḱ, *médʰyos
mediterraneo, *médʰyos
mellito, *melit-
membrana, membranaceo, membro, *méms
memorabile, memore, memoria, memoriale,
menare, mendace, mendacio, *men-
meno, *mey-
mensa, *meh₁-
mentale, mente, mentire, mento, *men-

mento, *mendʰ-
mentre, *éy / h₁e, *h₁én
menzione, menzogna, *men-
mercoledì, meriare, meridie, *deyn-
meridie, *médʰyos
meriggiare, *deyn-
meriggio, *deyn-, *médʰyos
merorare, *men-
mescere, mescolare, *mey-
mese, *méh₁n̥s
mesticcio, mestiere, mestura, *mey-
metà, *médʰyos
meticcio, *mey-
metricus, metro, *meh₁-
mezzadro, mezzano, mezzo, *médʰyos
mi, *H₁me-
midolla, midollo, *médʰyos
miei, *H₁meme-
miele, *melit-
migliaio, miglio, *sem-
migrare, *mey-
miliare, mille, *sem-
minaccia, minace, minare, *men-
mingere, *h₃meyǵʰ-
minimo, ministero, ministro, minore, minugia, minuire,
  minutaglia, minuto, minuzia, *mey-
mio, *H₁meme-
miscela, miscellaneo, mischiare, miscolare, mistura,
  *mey-
misura, misurare, *meh₁-
mo', moderare, moderno, modestia, modesto,
  modificare, modio, modo, modulare, modulo, moggio,
  *med-
mola, molare, molinaro, molino, *melh₂-
moltiplicare, moltiplicazione, *pleḱ-
moncello, moneta, montagna, montagnoso, montano,
  monte, monticello, montuoso, *men-
monumento, moribondo, morire, morte, morto, *mer-
mosca, moscerino, *mus-
mostaccio, *mendʰ-
mostrare, mostro, mostruoso, *men-
mozzo, *med-
mugnaio, mulinaio, mulinaro, mulino, *melh₂-
mungere, *H₂melǵ-
municipio, munificenza, munifico, *mey-
munumento, *men-
muscolare, muscolo, *muh₂s-
mutabile, mutare, mutuo, *mey-
narice, *néh₂s
narrare, narrativo, *ǵneh₃-
nascente, nascere, *ǵenH₁-
nascondere, *dheH₁-
naso, nasuto, *néh₂s
natale, Natale, natalizio, *ǵenH₁-
natatorio, *(s)neh₂-
natività, nativo, nato, *ǵenH₁-
natrice, *(s)neh₂-, *neHtr-

natura, naturalità, *ǵenH₁-

naufragio, nautico, navale, nave, navicella, navigare,

 navigatore, navigazione, navigio, naviglio, *(s)neh₂-

nazione, *ǵenH₁-

ne, *éy / h₁e

nebbia, nebuloso, *nebʰ-

nefasto, *bʰeh₂-

negligenza, negligere, *leǵ-

negoziare, negoziatore, negozio, *h₂ew

nemorale, *nem-

neo, *ǵenH₁-

nervo, nervoso, *(s)neh₁-

nesci, *skey-

nettare, nettareo, *neḱ-

neve, *sneygʷʰ-

nevo, *ǵenH₁-

nevoso, *sneygʷʰ-

nidiforme, nidio, nido, *nisdós

nipote, *nepot-

niveo, *sneygʷʰ-

nobile, *ǵneh₃-

nocivo, nocumento, *neḱ-

noi, noialtri, *wei

nome, nomenclatura, nominale, nominare,

 nominazione, *h₁nómn̥

nord, *h₁én

norma, normale, *ǵneh₃-

nosco, nostro, *wei

notaio, notare, notazione, noto, notorio, *ǵneh₃-

notte, notturno, *nókʷts

novanta, nove, novecento, *H₁néwn̥

novecento, *ḱm̥tóm

novena, *H₁néwn̥

noverare, novero, *nem-

novilunio, *lewk-

novità, novo, *new

nozione, *ǵneh₃-

nudo, *negʷ-

numerale, numerare, numeratore, numero,

 numerosità, numeroso, *nem-

nuocere, *neḱ-

nuora, *snusós

nuotare, *(s)neh₂-

nuovo, *new

o, *h₂ew

obbedire, *h₂ewis-dʰh₁-

oblata, oblato, oblazione, *bher-

obsoleto, *h₂el-

oca, *h₂éwis

occhio, *h₃ekʷ-

occludere, *(s)kel-

occorrere, *ḱers-

occupare, occupazione, *keh₂p-

oculare, *h₃ekʷ-

od, *h₂ew

odiare, *h₃ed-

odierno, *deyn-

odio, odioso, odorare, odore, *h₃ed-

offendere, *gʷʰen-

offrire, *bher-

oggetto, *h₁epi

oggi, *deyn-

ogne, ogni, *h₃ep-

olire, *h₃ed-

oltra, oltre, *h₂el-

ombelico, *h₃enbʰ-

omnipotente, *H₁es-

omnisciente, omnivoro, *h₃ep-

onda, ondare, *wed-

onde, *kʷis

ondoso, *wed-

opera, operaio, operare, opificio, *h₃ep-

oppilazione, *peys-

opporre, *h₁epi, *teḱ-

opportunità, opportuno, *per-

opposizione, *h₁epi

oppugnare, *pewǵ-

oprare, opulento, opuscolo, *h₃ep-

ora, *h₂ews-, *yeh₁-

oracolo, orare, oratore, orazione, *h₃éh₁os

orbo, *h₃erbʰ-

ordinal, ordinare, ordine, *h₂er

orecchio, *h₂ew-

organo, *werǵ-

orientale, oriente, originale, originario, origine, oriundo,

 *h₃er-

ornare, *h₂er

orniello, orno, *h₃es-

oro-, *h₃er-

orpimento, *peyḱ-

orrendo, orribile, orrido, orrifico, orrore, *gʰers-

orsa, orso, *h₂ŕ̥tḱos

ortiglio, *h₂er

orto, *ǵʰer-

ospedale, ospitale, ospitalità, ospitare, ospite, ospizio,

 *gʰóstis

ossedere, *sed-

ossequio, *sekʷ-

osso, *h₃ésth₁

ostacolo, ostare, *steh₂-

oste, *gʰóstis

ostentare, ostentazione, *ten-

ostetrica, *steh₂-

ostro, *h₂ews-

ostruzione, *strew-

otre, *wed-

ottenere, *ten-

ottico, *h₃ekʷ-

otto, *oḱtṓw

ottocento, *ḱm̥tóm

ottogano, *oḱtṓw

ottundere, *(s)tew-

ove, *kʷis

ovest, *wek(ʷ)speros

ovino, *h₂ówis
ovrare, *h₃ep-
ovunque, *kʷis
ovviare, ovvio, *weyh₁-
ozio, ozioso, *h₂ew
pacare, pacato, pace, pacifico, *peh₂ǵ-
padella, *peth₂
padre, padrone, *ph₂tḗr
padule, paese, paganità, pagano, pagare, pagella,
  pagina, pala, *peh₂ǵ-
pallido, pallore, *pelH-
palude, paludoso, *peh₂ǵ-
pane, paniccia, paniere, *peh₂-
parabola, *gʷelH-
paradiso, *dʰeyǵʰ-
parco, *h₂erk-
parere, *peh₂-
parola, *gʷelH-
parsimonia, *h₂erk-
pascere, pasciona, *peh₂-
passare, passera, passero, passo, *peth₂
pastillo, pasto, pastore, pastura, *peh₂-
patrimonio, patriota, patrono, *ph₂tḗr
peccare, peccato, peccatore, peccatrice, *ped-
pecchia, *bʰey-
pecora, pecoraio, peculio, pecunia, pecuniario, *peḱu-
pedicello, pedule, *pṓds
peggio, peggiorare, peggiore, *ped-
pellaio, pelle, *pel-
pellegrino, *h₂éǵros
pelliccia, pellicola, *pel-
pena, *kʷey-
pendente, pendere, pendolo, pendulo, *pewǵ-
penetrante, penetrare, *peh₂-
penna, *péth₂r
pensare, *pewǵ-
penta-, *pénkʷe
per, *per-
peragrare, *h₂éǵros
percepire, percettibile, percetto, percettore,
  percezione, *keh₂p-
percolare, *kʷel-
percorrere, percorso, *ḱers-
perdere, perdita, *deH₃-
perdurre, *dewk-
peregrinare, peregrinazion, *h₂éǵros
perfetto, *dheH₁-
periclitare, pericolo, pericoloso, periglio, *per-
perire, *h₁ey-
perito, perizia, *per-
permutare, *mey-
perorare, *h₃éh₁os
perscrutare, *(s)ker-
perseguire, perseguitare, *sekʷ-
persistere, *steh₂-
pertenere, pertinente, *ten-
pervenire, *gʷem-

pervertire, *wert-
pesare, *pewǵ-
pescare, pesce, pescoso, *peisḱ-
peso, *pewǵ-
pessimo, *ped-
pettinare, pettine, *peḱ-
pezzente, pezzire, *peth₂
piaga, piangere, *pleh₂k-
piano, pianta, piantaggine, piantare, piazza, *pleh₂-
piede, *pṓds
piegare, *pleḱ-
pieno, pieve, *pleh₁-
pigmento, *peyḱ-
pila, pillo, pilo, *peys-
pimento, pinto, *peyḱ-
pioggia, pioggioso, piova, piovere, piovoso, *plew-
pipistrello, *wek(ʷ)speros
piscina, *peisḱ-
pistare, pistrino, *peys-
pittare, pittore, pittura, *peyḱ-
più, *pleh₁-
plaga, *pleh₂k-
plebe, *pleh₁-
plecale, *preḱ-
plenario, *pleh₁-
plettro, *pleh₂k-
pluralità, *pleh₁-
pluviale, *plew-
podestà, *pótis
podio, poggio, *pṓds
poi, *h₁epi
pollice, *h₂welh₁-
polmone, *plewmō
pomice, *poymno-
ponderare, *pewǵ-
ponente, *teḱ-
ponte, *pent-
ponzàre, *pewǵ-
popolare, popolazione, popolo, *pleh₁-
por, *per-
porca, porcaio, porcella, porcello, porcino, porco,
  *pórḱos
porgere, *h₃reǵ-
porre, *teḱ-
port, porta, portabile, portare, *per-
portendere, portento, *ten-
portico, portiere, *per-
posca, *peh₃-
posizione, *teḱ-
possedere, possessione, *pótis
possibile, *H₁es-
posto, *teḱ-
postulare, *preḱ-
potabile, *peh₃-
potente, potenza, potere, *H₁es-
potestà, *pótis
pozione, *peh₃-

pragmatico, prassi, *per-
precario, *preḱ-
precludere, *(s)kel-
precorrere, precorso, precursore, *ḱers-
preda, *weyd-
predare, predatore, predazione, *deH₃-, *weyd-
prediale, predio, *wedʰ-
predire, predizione, *deyk-
preferire, *bher-
pregare, preghiera, *preḱ-
pregio, *per-
pregiudicare, *h₂eyw-
pregustare, *ǵews-
prelato, *bher-
premonire, *men-
prendere, prensione, *weyd-
preoccupare, preoccupazione, *keh₂p-
preporre, *teḱ-
presagire, *seh₂g-
prescrivere, *(s)ker-
presedere, *sed-
presentare, presentazione, *H₁es-
presidente, presidio, presiedere, *sed-
preso, *weyd-
prestare, *steh₂-
prete, *per-
pretendere, preteso, *ten-
prevalere, *h₂welh₁-
prevedere, *weyd-
prevenire, *gʷem-
previo, *weyh₁-
prezioso, prezzo, *per-
prigione, *weyd-
primaio, primario, primiero, primo, primogenito, *per-
principe, principio, *keh₂p-
priore, privare, privata, privazione, privilegio, pro-, *per-
probabile, probità, probitade, probitate, *bʰuH-
problema, problematico, *gʷelH-
procace, *preḱ-
proclamare, *kelh₁-
prodotto, produrre, produttivo, produzione, *dewk-
profano, *dʰéh₁s
proferire, *bher-
professione, professore, *bʰeh₂-
profluvio, *bʰleh₁-
profondere, profondità, profondo, *ǵʰew-
programmare, *gerbʰ-
proibire, *gʰeh₁bʰ-
prole, proletariato, *h₂el-
promiscuo, *mey-
prono, *per-
propagare, *peh₂ǵ-
propinquo, *per-
proporre, *teḱ-
proprietà, *preyH-
proprio, *per-, *preyH-
propugnare, *pewǵ-

prora, *per-
prosa, *wert-
proseguire, *sekʷ-
prosperare, prospero, *speh₁-
prossimo, *per-
prosternare, prostrare, *sterh₃-
proteggere, *(s)teg-
protendere, *ten-
protervo, *terh₁-
prova, provare, *bʰuH-
provenire, provento, *gʷem-
proverbio, provocare, *wekʷ-
provvedere, provvidenza, *weyd-
prua, *per-
pruova, *bʰuH-
pubblico, *pleh₁-
pugilatore, pugile, pugnace, pugnare, pugno, *pewǵ-
pulce, *plou-
pungere, *pewǵ-
punire, punizione, *kʷey-
punta, punto, punzone, *pewǵ-
quadr-, quadrare, quadrato, quadratura, quadrello, *kʷetwóres
quadriga, quadrigato, *yugóm
quadro, *kʷetwóres
quadruplo, *pleh₁-
quagliare, *H₂eǵ-
quale, qualità, *kʷis
quattordici, *déḱm̥t
quattro, *kʷetwóres
quattrocento, *ḱm̥tóm
quella, quelle, quelli, quello, *h₂el-
quercia, *perkʷu-
questa, queste, questi, questo, *só
quiescenza, quieto, *kʷyeh₁-
quindici, *déḱm̥t
raccogliere, *leǵ-
radicale, radicchio, radice, radio, raggio, *wréh₂ds
raggiungere, *yewg-
ragione, ragna, *h₂er
rame, *h₂eyos
ramifico, *wréh₂ds
rammemorare, *men-
ramo, ramoso, ramulo, *wréh₂ds
rappresentare, *H₁es-
razione, *h₂er
re, reale, recare, *h₃reǵ-
reclamare, *kelh₁-
redine, *ten-
regale, rege, reggere, regime, regina, regnare, regno, regola, *h₃reǵ-
relazione, *bher-
relegare, relegazione, *legh-
rendere, *deH₃-
repleto, replezione, *pleh₁-
replicare, *pleḱ-
reprensibile, *weyd-

repubblica, *pleh₁-
rescindere, *skey-
resecare, *sek-
resistere, resistere, restare, restaurare, restituire,
  resto, *steh₂-
retto, *h₃reǵ-
ricalcitrare, *(s)kel-
riccio, *ǵʰér
ricco, *h₃reǵ-
ricettacolo, ricevere, ricezione, *keh₂p-
riconoscere, *ǵneh₃-
ricordabile, ricordare, *ḱér
ricorrere, *ḱers-
ridotto, ridurre, riduzione, *dewk-
riempire, *pleh₁-
rifare, *dheH₁-
riferire, *bher-
rifluire, *bʰleh₁-
rilevare, *h₁lengʷʰ-
rimedio, *med-
rimembrare, rimemorare, *men-
rinnovare, *new
rio, *h₃reyH-
ripetere, *peth₂
riporre, *teḱ-
riprendere, riprensibile, riprensione, ripreso, *weyd-
ripugnare, *pewǵ-
risedere, risiedere, *sed-
risorgere, *h₃reǵ-
rispettare, rispetto, *speḱ-
ristoare, *steh₂-
ritenere, *ten-
ritmo, *srew-
rito, *h₂er
ritondo, *Hret-
ritto, *h₃reǵ-
rivalità, *h₃reyH-
rivedere, *weyd-
rivenire, *gʷem-
riverente, riverenza, *wer-
riversare, *wert-
rivisitare, rivista, *weyd-
rivo, *h₃reyH-
rivolgere, *welH-
rivolo, *h₃reyH-
rivoluzione, *welH-
robbia, *h₁rewdʰ-
rocchio, *Hret-
roggio, *h₁rewdʰ-
rogna, *h₂er, *h₂eyos
rollo, *Hret-
rosso, *h₁rewdʰ-
rotare, rotazione, rotella, rotolo, rotondo, rotula, *Hret-
rovesciare, *wert-
rubino, rubrica, rufo, *h₁rewdʰ-
ruggine, rugginoso, *h₂eyos
ruota, ruotare, *Hret-

ruscello, *h₃reyH-
s-, *dwóH₁
sacerdotale, sacerdote, sacerdozio, sacrificare,
  sacrificatore, sacrificio, sacrifico, *dheH₁-
saga, sagace, *seh₂g-
salare, *séh₂ls
saldo, *solh₂-
sale, salsa, salso, *séh₂ls
salubre, salutare, salutazione, salute, salvare, salve,
  salvo, *solh₂-
sangue, sanguigno, sanguinare, sanguinario,
  sanguineo, sanguinolento, sanguinoso, *h₁ésh₂r
santificare, *dheH₁-
sardonice, *h₃negʰ-
sasso, *sek-
satisfare, *dheH₁-
scalzare, *(s)kel-
scarda, *(s)ker-
scarmigliare, *keh₂n-
scegliere, *leǵ-
schema, *seǵʰ-
schermire, *(s)ker-
schiamazzare, *kelh₁-
schiudere, *(s)kel-
schiuso, *(s)kel-
sciame, *H₂eǵ-
scientifico, scienza, scindere, scissione, *skey-
scopo, *speḱ-
scorrere, scorso, *ḱers-
scortare, scorza, scritto, scrittura, scrivere, scrupolo,
  scrutinio, scuoiare, *(s)ker-
scuola, *seǵʰ-
scure, *sek-
sé, *s(w)e-
se, *só
secare, *sek-
secernere, *krey-
seco, *s(w)e-
secondo, *sekʷ-
secreto, secrezione, *krey-
sedare, sede, sedere, *sed-
sedici, *déḱmt
sedimento, *sed-
sedurre, *dewk-
segare, segmento, segnare, segno, *sek-
segretario, segreto, *krey-
seguire, *sekʷ-
sei, *swéḱs
seicento, *ḱmtóm
selezione, *leǵ-
sella, *sed-
sembiante, sembrare, *sem-
seme, semente, semenza, *seH₁-
semi-, *sem-
seminare, seminarista, *seH₁-
semplice, *pleḱ-, *sem-
sempre, *sem-

senato, senatore, sene, senetta, *sénos
senno, sensato, senso, sentenzioso, sentimento,
 sentire, *sent-
sequela, sequenza, *sekʷ-
sere, *sénos
serie, sermone, *ser-
serra, *sek-
sessione, *sed-
sete, *dʰegʷʰ-
sette, *septm̥
settecento, *ḱm̥tóm
settembre, *septm̥
settentrione, *terh₁-
settimana, settimo, *septm̥
settore, *sek-, *sekʷ-
sguattero, *weǵ-
si, *só
siero, *srew-
sigillo, *sek-
significare, *dheH₁-, *sek-
signore, *sénos
simile, simulare, singolare, singolo, *sem-
sire, *sénos
sistema, *steh₂-
sito, *dʰegʷʰ-, *teḱ-
situare, situazione, *teḱ-
soccida, soccio, *sekʷ-
soccorrere, soccorso, *ḱers-
sociale, società, socio, *sekʷ-
soddisfare, *dheH₁-
soffiare, *bʰleh₁-
soffrire, *bher-
soggiornare, *deyn-
soglio, *sed-
sognare, sognatore, sogno, *swep-
solare, solarium, *sóh₂wl̥
soldo, *solh₂-
sole, *sóh₂wl̥
solenne, solennità, *solh₂-
solere, *swe-dʰh₁-
solerte, *solh₂-
solitario, *s(w)e-
solito, *swe-dʰh₁-
solitudine, *s(w)e-
sollecitare, sollecito, *solh₂-
sollevare, *h₁lengʷʰ-
solo, *s(w)e-
somigliante, somigliare, *sem-
somma, sommità, sommo, *upo
sonnacchioso, sonnifero, sonno, sopore, *swep-
sopperire, *pleh₁-
sopportare, *per-
sopra, *upo
sopracciglio, *ḱel-
sopraporre, *teḱ-
soprare, *upo
soprassedere, *sed-

sorella, *swésōr
sorgere, *h₃reǵ-
sorte, sortire, *ser-
sospendere, sospensione, *pewǵ-
sostenere, sostentare, *ten-
sotterraneo, *ters-
sottile, *tetḱ-
sotto, *upo
sovente, *éy / h₁e
sovra, *upo
sovrapporre, *teḱ-
sovvenire, *gʷem-
spandere, spassare, spasso, *peth₂
specchio, specie, specolare, specolo, speculare,
 speculazione, *speḱ-
spedire, *ped-
spendere, *pewǵ-
sperante, speranza, sperare, *speh₁-
spesa, speso, *pewǵ-
spettare, spettro, spiare, *speḱ-
spiegare, *plek-
spiga, spilla, spina, spinale, spino, spinoso, spinula,
 *spey-
splenetico, *splenǵʰ-
sporre, spostare, *teḱ-
spuma, spumante, spumare, spumoso, *poymno-
spuntare, *pewǵ-
squadra, *kʷetwóres
stabbiare, stabbio, stabile, stabilire, stabilità, stabulare,
 stabulario, stagione, stame, stare, stato, statua,
 statura, stazione, stazzo, stazzone, *steh₂-
stella, stellare, *h₂stḗr
stendere, *ten-
sternere, *sterh₃-
steso, *ten-
stessa, *éy / h₁e, *só
stesso, *éy / h₁e, *s(w)e-, *só
stocco, *(s)tew-
storia, storico, *weyd-
stra-, *h₁eǵʰs
strada, *sterh₃-
straniero, strano, *h₁eǵʰs
strategia, strato, *sterh₃-
stucco, studente, studiare, studio, *(s)tew-
stuoia, *sterh₃-
stupido, stupire, stupro, *(s)tew-
subbia, subbio, *sīw-
subire, subito, *h₁ey-
sudare, sudario, sudore, *sweyd-
suffondere, *ǵʰew-
suggello, *sek-
suino, *suH-
summa, *upo
suo, *s(w)e-
suora, *swésōr
super, superare, superbia, *upo
superbo, *bʰuH-, *upo

superfluo, *bʰleh₁-
superiore, superno, supero, *upo
superstite, superstizione, *steh₂-
supervacaneo, *h₁weh₂-
supino, *upo
supplicare, supplicazione, *plek-
supplire, *pleh₁-
supporre, *tek-
supportare, *per-
susseguire, *sekʷ-
sussistere, *steh₂-
sutura, *sīw-
svegliare, *weǵ-
tabernacolo, *treb-
taglione, tale, tanto, *só
tasso, *tetḱ-
tauriforme, *(s)táwros
taverna, *treb-
teco, *túh₂
tegghia, teglia, tegola, tegumento, *(s)teg-
tela, *tetḱ-
tema, *dheH₁-
tenace, tenacolo, tendere, tenere, tenero, tenore,
 tensione, tenso, tenzone, *ten-
teocrazia, *dʰéh₁s
Teodorico, *tewtéh₂
teoria, *wer-
terebra, *terh₁-
terminare, termine, *térmņ
terra, terreno, terrestre, territoriale, territorio, *ters-
terziare, terzo, *tréyes
teso, *ten-
tessere, *tetḱ-
tetto, *(s)teg-
tipico, tipo, *(s)tew-
tirare, *der-
toga, *(s)teg-
togliere, tollerare, *telh₂-
tondo, *Hret-
tono, *ten-
tordo, *trosdos
toro, *(s)táwros
torrido, *ters-
tosse, tossire, *(s)tew-
tosto, *ters-
tra-, *terh₂-
tra, *h₁én
tradire, traditore, tradizione, *deH₃-
tradurre, *dewk-
tramontano, *men-
tranquillo, *kʷyeh₁-
transfluire, *bʰleh₁-
transire, *h₁ey-
trasferire, *bher-
trasfondere, *ǵʰew-
traslato, traslazione, *bher-
trasmigrare, trasmutare, trasmutazione, *mey-

trasportare, *per-
trave, *treb-
tre, *tréyes
trecento, *ḱm̥tóm
tredici, *déḱm̥t
tregua, *deru-
triade, *tréyes
triangolo, *h₂enk-
tribale, tribù, tribunale, tribuno, tributo, *bʰuH-
trimestre, *méh₁ns
triplo, *pleh₁-
tritico, *terh₁-
truppa, *treb-
tu, tuo, *túh₂
tuonare, *(s)tenh₂-
tuono, *ten-
tuorlo, *sterh₃-
ubbidire, *h₂ewis-dʰh₁-
ubere, ubero, *h₁owHdʰr̥-
ubiquitario, ubiquo, *kʷis
uccello, *h₂éwis
udienza, udire, udito, uditore, *h₂ewis-dʰh₁-
ufficio, uffizio, *h₃ep-
uggia, uggioso, *h₃ed-
ulna, *Heh₃l-
umano, *ǵʰmṓ
umile, *dʰéǵʰōm
un, *óy-nos
uncino, *h₂enk-
undici, *déḱm̥t
unghia, unghiato, ungulato, *h₃negʰ-
uni-, unico, unione, unità, *óy-nos
universo, *wert-
uno, *óy-nos
unqua, unque, *kʷis
uomo, *ǵʰmṓ
uopo, *h₃ep-
uovo, *h₂ōwyóm
urna, *h₁ews-
uscire, *h₁ey-
usignolo, *keh₂n-
usto, ustolare, ustrino, *h₁ews-
vacare, vacuità, vacuo, *h₁weh₂-
vagone, *weǵʰ-
valente, valere, valetudinario, valido, *h₂welh₁-
valle, vallo, *welH-
valore, *h₂welh₁-
valva, *welH-
vanità, *h₁weh₂-
vanni, *H₂weH₁-
vano, *h₁weh₂-
vară, *wésr̥
vasto, *h₁weh₂-
vaticinare, *keh₂n-
vecchio, *wet-
vece, *weyk-
vedere, *weyd-

vedova, *h₁weydʰ
vegetabile, vegetazione, vegeto, vegghiare,
 veglia, vegliare, *weǵ-
veglio, *wet-
veicolo, *weǵh-
vello, velloso, *h₂welh₁-
venale, *wesno-
vendemmia, vendemmiare, *wóyh₁nom
vendere, *deH₃-, *wesno-
vendetta, *weyh₁-
venditore, *deH₃-, *wesno-
venerdi, *deyn-
venire, *gʷem-
venti, *wīḱm̥tiH₁
ventilare, ventilazione, *H₂weH₁-
vento, *gʷem-, *H₂weH₁-
ventosa, ventoso, *H₂weH₁-
verace, *weh₁-
verbale, verbo, verboso, *wekʷ-
verecondia, verecondo, vergogna, *wer-
verificare, *dheH₁-, *weh₁-
verificazione, verità, *weh₁-
verme, vermiglio, verminare, verminoso, *wr̥mis-
vernale, *wésr̥
vero, *weh₁-
versare, versicolore, versione, verso, versus, *wert-
vertà, *weh₁-
vertebra, vertere, *wert-
vertù, *wiHrós
vespa, *wobs-
vespro, *wek(ʷ)speros
vestimento, vestire, vestito, *wes-
veterano, vetere, *wet-
vetro, *wed-
vetusto, *wet-
vi, *éy / h₁e
via, *weyh₁-
viaggiare, viaggio, viatico, *weyh₁-
vicario, *weyk-
vicina, vicinale, vicinità, vicino, *weyḱ-
vicissitudine, *weyk-
vico, vicolo, *weyḱ-
viduità, *h₁weydʰ
vieto, *wet-
vigilante, vigilanza, vigilare, vigile, *weǵ-
vigna, vigneto, *wóyh₁nom
villa, villano, *weyḱ-
villo, villoso, *h₂welh₁-
vinaccia, *wóyh₁nom
vincere, vinco, vincolare, vincolo, *weyk-
vindicare, vindice, *weyh₁-
vino, vinoso, *wóyh₁nom
violare, *weyh₁-
vipistrello, *wek(ʷ)speros
virile, virtù, *wiHrós
visibile, visione, visita, visitare, visivo, viso, *weyd-
vita, vitale, *gʷeyh₃-

vittima, vittoria, *weyk-
vivace, vivacità, vivere, vivido, viviparo, vivo, *gʷeyh₃-
vocabolario, vocabolo, vocale, vocare, vocativo,
 vocazione, voce, *wekʷ-
voi, voialtri, *túh₂
volente, volere, volgere, volontà, volta, voltare, volto,
 volubile, volume, voluntà, voluta, *welH-
vongola, *ḱonkho-
vortice, *wert-
vostro, *túh₂
vuoto, *h₁weh₂-
zio, *dʰeh₁(y)-

Spanish

-ducido, *dewk-
-mente, *men-
ab-, *h₂pó
abducción, abducir, *dewk-
abedul, *gʷet-
abeja, *bʰey-
abismo, *dʰewb-
abjurar, *h₂eyw-
ablación, ablativo, *bher-
ablución, *lewh₃-
abogado, abogar, *wekʷ-
abolición, abolir, *h₂el-
aborrecer, *gʰers-
aborto, *h₃er-
abreviar, *mrégʰ-
abscisa, *skey-
abstener, abstinencia, abstinente, *ten-
abuelo, *h₂éwh₂os
aburrir, *gʰers-
acatar, *keh₂p-
acción, *H₂eǵ-
acebo, *bʰleh₃-
aceptar, *keh₂p-
acerba, acerbidad, acerbo, acero, acervo, ácido, *h₂éḱ
aclamación, aclamar, aconsejar, *kelh₁-
acordar, *ḱér
acorrer, *ḱers-
acreedor, *dheH₁-
acrimonia, acritud, *h₂éḱ
acta, actitud, actividad, activo, acto, actor, actriz, *H₂eǵ-
acuario, acuático, *h₂ekʷeh₂-
acueducto, *dewk-, *h₂ekʷeh₂-
acuerda, *ḱér
acúleo, *h₂éḱ
adicar, adicción, adicto, *deyḱ-
adir, *deH₃-
adivinar, *dyew-
adjudicación, adjudicar, *h₂eyw-
adminículo, *méh₂-r̥
administración, administrador, administrar, *mey-
admonición, *men-
adorar, *h₃éh₁os
aducir, *dewk-
adulterio, *h₂el-
adunco, *h₂enk-
adurir, *h₁ews-
advenir, *gʷem-
adverbial, adverbio, *wekʷ-
adverso, advertir, *wert-
Adviento, *gʷem-
advocar, *wekʷ-
aferrar, *bher-
afirmar, *dʰer-

afluente, afluir, *bʰleh₁-
afumar, *dʰewh₂-
agacharse, agir, agitación, agitar, *H₂eǵ-
agnombre, *h₁nómn̥
agorar, agosto, *h₂ewg-
agrario, *h₂éǵros
agre, *h₂éḱ
agrícola, agricultor, agricultura, agrimensor, *h₂éǵros
agrio, *h₂éḱ
agro, *h₂éǵros, *h₂éḱ
agua, aguador, *h₂ekʷeh₂-
aguaducho, *dewk-, *h₂ekʷeh₂-
agüero, *h₂ewg-
aguijón, *h₂éḱ
ahí, *éy / h₁e
ahijar, *dʰeh₁(y)-
ahumar, *dʰewh₂-
aire, *h₂ews-
aja, *h₂éḱ
ala, *H₂eǵ-
álaga, *h₂el-
alambre, *h₂eyos
albergue, *ker-
alborotar, *welH-
alcornoque, *perkʷu-
alegar, *legh-
alguien, alguno, *kʷis
alguno, *óy-nos
álica, *h₂el-
aliento, *h₂enh₁-
alimento, *h₂el-
aliso, *h₃el-
allegación, *legh-
allegar, *pleḱ-
allí, *h₂el-
alma, *h₂enh₁-
almario, *h₂er
alno, *h₃el-
alocar, *stel-
alterar, altercación, altercar, alto, *h₂el-
alumbrar, *lewk-
alumbre, aluminio, *h₂elut-
alumno, alveario, álveo, alveolo, *h₂el-
amarizar, *deyn-
amatista, *médʰu
ambiente, ambir, ámbito, ambo, ambos, *h₂ent
amenaza, amente, *men-
amiésgado, *dem-
amonestar, *men-
ánade, *h₂eneti-
anegar, *neḱ-
angor, angosto, *h₂engʰ-
anguila, *angʷ(h)i-
angular, ángulo, *h₂enk-
anhelar, ánima, animar, *h₂enh₁-
aniversario, *wert-
anochecer, *nókʷts

anónimo, *h₁nómṇ
anormal, *ǵneh₃-
ánsar, *ǵʰans-
ansiedad, *h₂enǵʰ-
ante, *h₂ent
anteponer, *teḱ
antes, *h₂ent
antevenir, *gʷem-
antigüedad, antiguo, *h₂énti-h₃kʷós
añadir, *deH₃-
añorar, *ǵneh₃-
apagar, *peh₂ǵ-
aparecer, aparición, aparir, *peh₂-
apender, apéndice, *pewǵ-
apetito, *peth₂
apio, *bʰey-
aplaudir, *pleh₂k-
aplegar, aplicar, *pleḱ-
aponer, *teḱ-
aportar, *per-
apoteca, *dheH₁-
apreciar, *per-
aprehender, aprehensión, aprender, *weyd-
aprobar, *bʰuH-
aprovecer, *dheH₁-
aquel, aquella, aquellas, aquello, aquellos, *h₂el-
aquesta, aquestas, aqueste, aquesto, aquestos, *só
aquifolio, *bʰleh₃-
arable, arado, arador, aradro, *H₂erH₃-
arambre, *h₂eyos
araña, *h₂er
arar, aratorio, *H₂erH₃-
árbol, arboleda, arboledo, arbóreo, *h₂erHdʰ-
arca, arcano, *h₂erk-
arce, arcén, *H₂eǵ-
arco, arcuado, *h₂erkʷo-
arduidad, arduo, *h₂erHdʰ-
árido, *h₂eh₁s-
arma, armada, armado, armadura, armar,
 armario, armos, *h₂er
arrollar, *Hret-
arte, artejo, artículo, *h₂er
arzón, *h₂erkʷo-
asar, *h₂eh₁s-
asear, *sed-
asemblar, asemejar, *sem-
aserción, *ser-
así, *só
asiduo, *sed-
asignar, *sek-
asimilar, *sem-
asistir, *steh₂-
aspecto, aspillar, *speḱ-
asportar, *per-
astilla, *H₂eǵ-
astucia, *h₂éḱ

atención, atender, atener, atento, *ten-
ateo, *dʰéh₁s
atrever, atribuir, *bʰuH-
atrocidad, atroz, *h₂eh₁tro-h₃kʷs
au-, *h₂pó
audición, audiencia, audio-, audito, auditor, auditorio,
 *h₂ewis-dʰh₁-
auger, augur, augurar, augurio, *h₂ewg-
aura, *h₂ews-
aurícula, *h₂ew-
aurora, *h₂ews-
auscultar, *ḱel-
austral, *h₂ews-
auto, automóvil, *h₂ew
autor, autoridad, auxiliar, auxilio, *h₂ewg-
avante, *h₂ent
ave, *h₂éwis
avenir, *gʷem-
avercilla, *h₂éwis
averiguar, *dheH₁-, *weh₁-
aviso, *weyd-
avispa, *wobs-
avocar, *wekʷ-
axila, *H₂eǵ-
ayer, *dʰǵʰ(y)es-
ayustar, *yewg-
azada, azuela, *h₂éḱ
báculo, *bak-
ballesta, *gʷelH-
barba, barbado, *bʰardʰeh₂-
bardo, *gʷerH-
base, *gʷem-
bebedor, beber, *peh₃-
beldar, *H₂weH₁-
bendecir, *deyḱ-
benefacer, *dheH₁-
beodo, *peh₃-
bermejo, *wṛmis-
betún, *gʷet-
biblioteca, *dheH₁-
bíceps, *kapōlo
bienhechor, *dheH₁-
binar, binare, *dwóH₁
bizcocho, *pekʷ-
bocinar, *gʷōws, *keh₂n-
bodega, *dheH₁-
bodrio, *bʰrewh₁-
borra, *péh₂ur
bote, *bʰeyd-
botica, *dheH₁-
bouy, *bʰeh₂-
bóveda, *welH-
bovino, boyero, *gʷōws
braquial, brazal, brazo, *mréǵʰ-
breña, *bʰerǵʰ-
breve, *mréǵʰ-
brinco, *weyk-

brío, *bʰerǵʰ-
brodio, *bʰrewh₁-
bruma, *mréǵʰ-
bruto, *gʷerh₂-
búbalo, bucólico, buey, búfalo, *gʷṓws
burgés, burgués, *bʰerǵʰ-
burla, *péh₂ur
busto, *h₁ews-
ca, *kʷis
cabdal, cabdillo, *kapōlo
caber, cabestro, *keh₂p-
cabeza, cabezo, cabildo, cabo, *kapōlo
cabra, cabrero, cabro, *kapro
caja, *keh₂p-
cálamo, *ḱalam-
calcáneo, calcañar, calcar, calce, cálceo,
 calceta, calcetín, *(s)kel-
calendario, *kelh₁-
calidad, *kʷis
calza, calzar, *(s)kel-
cámara, campeón, campestre, campo, *(s)teg-
can, canícula, canino, *ḱwṓ
canoro, *keh₂n-
capacho, capacidad, capaz, capazo, *keh₂p-
capital, capítulo, capota, *kapōlo
caprino, *kapro
cápsula, captar, captivo, captura, *keh₂p-
cara, *ḱerh₂-
carámbano, *ḱalam-
carcañal, *(s)kel-
cargar, *ḱers-
carmen, carmenar, carminar, *keh₂n-
carnal, carne, carnero, carnifice, carnivoro,
 carnoso, *(s)ker-
carpir, *kerp-
carrejo, carrera, carreta, carretera, carretilla,
 carricar, carril, carro, carrocería, carrocero,
 carroza, carruaje, carruca, *ḱers-
carta, *ǵʰer-
catar, cativo, *keh₂p-
catorce, *déḱm̥t
caudal, caudillo, *kapōlo
cautivo, *keh₂p-
ceja, cejo, cela, celar, celario, celda, cellario,
 célula, *ḱel-
cena, cenar, *(s)ker-
centenario, centuria, *ḱm̥tóm
cerebelo, cerebro, *ḱerh₂-
cerner, *krey-
cervario, *ḱerh₂-
ciclo, *kʷel-
cien, *ḱm̥tóm
ciencia, *skey-
científico, *dheH₁-, *skey-
ciento, *ḱm̥tóm
cierto, *krey-
ciervo, *ḱerh₂-

cigüeña, *keh₂n-
cilla, cillero, *ḱel-
cinco, cincuenta, *pénkʷe
circunferencia, circunferir, *bher-
circunnavegar, *(s)neh₂-
circunscribir, *(s)ker-
circunstancia, circunstanciar, *steh₂-
circunvenir, *gʷem-
ciudad, cívico, civil, *ḱei-
clamar, clamor, *kelh₁-
clandestino, *ḱel-
claridad, *kelh₁-
clarificar, *dheH₁-
claro, clásico, *kelh₁-
claustro, cláusula, clausura, clausurar, clavar, clave,
 clavicordio, clavicula, clavija, clavo, *(s)kel-
cliente, *ḱlew-
climax, *ḱley-
coagular, coágulo, *H₂eǵ-
cocer, cochura, cocina, cocinar, cocinero, *pekʷ-
coerción, *h₂erk-
cogecho, coger, *leǵ-
cogitación, cogitar, *H₂eǵ-
cognome, *h₁nómn̥
cohecho, *dheH₁-
cohibir, *gʰeh₁bʰ-
cohorte, *ǵʰer-
cojo, *koḱs-
colección, colecta, *leǵ-
colega, colegio, *legh-
colegir, *leǵ-
colgar, *stel-
colina, collado, *kelH-
colmo, *ḱalam-
colocar, *stel-
colonia, colono, *kʷel-
color, colorar, *ḱel-
columna, *kelH-
comandar, *deh₃-
combinación, combinar, *dwóH₁
comedir, *meh₁-
comendar, *deh₃-
comentario, *men-
comer, comida, *h₁ed-
commūnitās, *mey-
como, cómo, cómodo, *med-
compendio, compensación, compensar, *pewǵ-
competo, *peth₂
compilación, compilar, *peys-
complemento, completivo, completo, *pleh₁-
complicación, complicar, *pleḱ-
complimiento, *pleh₁-
componer, *teḱ-
comportar, *per-
comprehensión, comprehensivo, comprender,
 comprensible, comprensión, *weyd-
comulgar, común, comunal, comunicación, comunicar,

comunión, *mey-
conca, *ḱonkho-
concebir, *keh₂p-
concejo, *kelh₁-
concento, *keh₂n-
concepción, *keh₂p-
concernir, *krey-
concha, concho, *ḱonkho-
conciliábulo, conciliar, concilio, *kelh₁-
cónclave, concluir, *(s)kel-
concordia, *ǵʰer-
conculcar, *(s)kel-
concurrir, concurso, *ḱers-
condecir, condición, *deyḱ-
condición, condir, *dheH₁-
condonar, *deH₃-
conducción, conducho, conducir, conducto,
 conductor, *dewk-
confección, *dheH₁-
conferir, *bher-
confesar, confesión, *bʰeh₂-
confianza, confiar, *bʰeydʰ-
confirmación, confirmar, *dʰer-
confluir, *bʰleh₁-
confundir, confusión, confuso, *ǵʰew-
congelar, *gel-
congio, *ḱonkho-
conjunto, *yewg-
conjuración, *h₂eyw-
conmigo, *H₁me-
conmutar, *mey-
conocer, *ǵneh₃-
consciencia / conciencia, *skey-
consecuencia, consecuente, conseguenza,
 conseguir, *sekʷ-
consejar, consejo, *kelh₁-
consenso, consentir, *sent-
consignar, *sek-
consigo, *s(w)e-
consiguiente, *sekʷ-
consistir, *steh₂-
consorte, *ser-
constar, constatar, *steh₂-
consternar, *sterh₃-
constitución, constituir, *steh₂-
construcción, construir, *strew-
consuetud, *swe-dʰh₁-
contención, contender, contener, contento,
 contento, *ten-
contigo, *túh₂
continencia, continente, continuo, *ten-
contradecir, contradicción, contradictor,
 contradictorio, *deyḱ-
contravenir, *gʷem-
contribuir, *bʰuH-
controversia, *wert-
contusión, *(s)tew-

convencer, *weyk-
convención, conveniencia, conveniente, convenir,
 convento, *gʷem-
conversación, conversar, convertir, *wert-
convidar, *weyh₁-
convocar, *wekʷ-
convólvulo, *welH-
copioso, *h₃ep-
coquinario, *pekʷ-
corage, *ḱḗr
coraza, *(s)ker-
corazón, *ḱḗr
corche, corcho, coriáceo, *(s)ker-
corlar, *kel-
córneo, cornudo, *ḱerh₂-
corpóreo, *krep-
correa, corrección, correcto, corrector, corregir, *h₃reǵ-
correr, corriente, corso, *ḱers-
cortar, *(s)ker-
corte, *ǵʰer-
corteza, cortezo, cortical, corto, *(s)ker-
cosecha, cosecho, *leǵ-
coser, *sīw-
coso, *ḱers-
costar, *steh₂-
costumbre, *swe-dʰh₁-
cráneo, *ḱerh₂-
crédito, crédulo, creer, creible, *dheH₁-
cribar, cribo, crimen, criminar, crisis, *krey-
crudo, cruel, crueldad, cruentar, cruento, crúor,
 *krewh₂-
cuadrado, cuadrar, *kʷetwóres
cuadriga, *yugóm
cuadrillo, cuadro, *kʷetwóres
cuádruplo, *pleh₁-
cuajar, cuajo, *H₂eǵ-
cual, cualidad, *kʷis
cuarto, cuatro, *kʷetwóres
cuatrocientos, *ḱm̥tóm
cuelmo, *ḱalam-
cuenca, *ḱonkho-
cuerda, *ǵʰern-
cuerdo, *ḱḗr
cuerno, *ḱerh₂-
cuero, *(s)ker-
cuerpo, *krep-
cuidado, cuidar, cuidazón, *H₂eǵ-
cuja, *koḱs-
cultivar,-cola, culto, cultor, cultura, *kʷel-
cumbre, *kelH-
cumplimiento, *pleh₁-
cuna, *ḱei-
cureña, *kelH-
currículo, curso, cursor, *ḱers-
curtir, *terh₁-
cuyo, *kʷis
dada, dado, *deH₃-

dama, *dem-

dañar, daño, *deh₂-

dar, data, dato, *deH₃-

deán, *déḱm̥t

debdo, deber deudor, débil, debilidad,
 debilitar, *gʰeh₁bʰ-

década, decano, *déḱm̥t

decebir, decepcionar, *keh₂p-

decimal, décimo, *déḱm̥t

decir, *deyḱ-

declamar, declarar, *kelh₁-

declinar, *ḱley-

decorar, *deḱ-

decorrerse, *ḱers-

dedal, dedo, *deyḱ-

deducir, *dewk-

defender, *gʷʰen-

deferir, *bher-

degano, *déḱm̥t

degenerar, *ǵenH₁-

degustar, *ǵews-

delación, *bher-

delante, *h₂ent

delatar, *bher-

delegar, *legh-

delinear, *lino-

delinquir, *leykʷ-

delirio, delírium, *leys-

demandar, *deH₃-

demencia, demente, *men-

demonio, *deh₂-

demostración, demostrar, *men-

demudar, *mey-

denario, *déḱm̥t

dende, *éy / h₁e

dental, *h₃dónts

denudar, *negʷ-

depender, *pewǵ-

depenger, *peyḱ-

deponer, *teḱ-

deportar, *per-

deprecación, deprecar, *preḱ-

deprehender, *weyd-

depuesto, *teḱ-

derecho, *h₃reǵ-

derivar, *h₃reyH-

des-, *dwóH₁

desarrollar, *Hret-

descalzar, *(s)kel-

descargar, descorrer, *ḱers-

describir, descripción, *(s)ker-

deseo, desidia, *sed-

desistir, *steh₂-

desnudar, desnudo, *negʷ-

desolar, *s(w)e-

despechar, *speḱ-

desplegar, *pleḱ-

desponer, *teḱ-

después, *h₁epi

destinación, destinar, destituir, *steh₂-

destrucción, destruir, *strew-

desvanecer, *h₁weh₂-

desvelar, *weǵ-

detector, *(s)teg-

detención, detener, *ten-

detonar, *(s)tenh₂-

deuda, *gʰeh₁bʰ-

devenir, *gʷem-

devolver, *welH-

di-, *dwóH₁

día, *deyn-

diablo, *gʷelH-

diario, *deyn-

diarrea, *srew-

dicaz, dicción, diccionario, dicho, *deyḱ-

diciembre, *déḱm̥t

dictador, dictadura, dictamen, dictar, *deyḱ-

diente, *h₃dónts

diestro, *deks-

diez, diezmar, diezmo, *déḱm̥t

diferir, *bher-

difícil, dificultad, *dheH₁-

difluir, *bʰleh₁-

difundir, difuso, *ǵʰew-

digital, dígito, *deyḱ-

digna, dignarse, dignidad, digno, *deḱ-

diligencia, diligente, *leǵ-

diluir, diluvio, *lewh₃-

dinero, *déḱm̥t

dino, *deḱ-

dios, *dyew-

directo, dirigir, *h₃reǵ-

dis-, *dwóH₁

discanto, *keh₂n-

discernir, discriminar, *krey-

discurrir, discurso, *ḱers-

disecar, *sek-

diseminar, *seH₁-

diseñar, diseño, *sek-

disimil, disimular, *sem-

disponer, *teḱ-

distancia, distanciar, *steh₂-

distender, *ten-

distribuir, *bʰuH-

diurno, *deyn-

diva, *dyew-

diverso, divertir, *wert-

dividir, *h₁weydʰ

divieso, *wert-

divinar, divinidad, *dyew-

divisibile, división, *h₁weydʰ

dixit, *deyḱ-

doblar, doble, doblo, *pleh₁-

doce, *déḱm̥t

dócil, docto, doctor, doctorar, doctrina, documento, dogma, *deḱ-

domar, *dem-, *demh$_2$-

doméstico, dominación, *dem-

domingo, *deyn-

dominio, *dem-

don, *deH$_3$-, *dem-

Don, *dem-

donación, donar, *deH$_3$-

doncel, doncella, *dem-

donde, *kʷis

doña, Doña, *dem-

dos, *dwóH$_1$

doscientos, *ḱm̥tóm

dotar, dote, *deH$_3$-

ducado, ducha, *dewk-

ducho, *deḱ-

ducto, *dewk-

duda, *gʰeh$_1$bʰ-

dueña, dueño, *dem-

dúplex, *pleḱ-

duplo, *pleh$_1$-

duque, *dewk-

durabilidad, durar, durazno, dureza, duro, *deru-

dux, *dewk-

ecuestre, *h$_1$éḱwos

edad, *h$_2$ey-

edición, *deH$_3$-

edicto, *deyḱ-

edificar, edificio, edil, *h$_2$eydʰ-

editor, *deH$_3$-

educación, educar, educir, *dewk-

efectivo, efecto, efectuar, *dheH$_1$-

efigie, *dʰeyǵʰ-

efluir, efluvio, *bʰleh$_1$-

efundir, efusión, *ǵʰew-

ego, *egH$_2$

eje, *H$_2$eǵ-

ejecución, ejecutar, *sekʷ-

ejercer, ejercicio, ejército, *h$_2$erk-

ejido, *h$_1$ey-

el, él, *h$_2$el-

elación, *bher-

elección, electo, elegante, elegir, *leǵ-

elemento, *h$_2$el-

elevar, *h$_1$lengʷʰ-

ella, ellas, ello, ellos, *h$_2$el-

elucubrar, *lewk-

eluir, *lewh$_3$-

embeber, *peh$_3$-

embestir, *wes-

emigrar, *mey-

eminencia, eminente, *men-

emplear, *pleḱ-

emprender, empresa, *weyd-

emulger, *H$_2$melǵ-

en, *h$_1$én

enarración, *ǵneh$_3$-

encantar, *keh$_2$n-

ende, *éy / h$_1$e

endurecer, *deru-

éneo, *h$_2$eyos

energia, *werǵ-

enero, *h$_1$ey-

enfermedad, enfermo, *dʰer-

engendrar, *ǵenH$_1$-

enhiesto, *gʷʰen-

enjambre, *H$_2$eǵ-

enjerir, *ser-

enjulio, *sīw-

enorme, *ǵneh$_3$-

enseña, enseñar, *sek-

enserir, *ser-

ensullo, *sīw-

ente, *H$_1$es-

entender, entesar, *ten-

entonce, entonces, *só

entrar, entre, *h$_1$én

entredecir, *deyḱ-

entrevenir, *gʷem-

entro, *h$_1$én

entusiasmo, entusiasta, *dʰéh$_1$s

enumerar, *nem-

envestir, *wes-

envidar, *weyh$_1$-

envolver, envuelto, *welH-

época, *seǵʰ-

equino, *h$_1$éḱwos

equivaler, *h$_2$welh$_1$-

erguir, erigir, *h$_3$reǵ-

erizo, *ǵʰér

erradicar, *wréh$_2$ds

erúgine, eruginoso, *h$_2$eyos

esa, esas, *éy / h$_1$e

esca, *h$_1$ed-

escarmenar, *keh$_2$n-

escindir, escisión, *skey-

esconder, *dheH$_1$-

escoriar, escribir, escrito, escritura, escrutar, *(s)ker-

escuchar, *ḱel-

escuela, *seǵʰ-

escuerzo, *(s)ker-

esculento, *h$_1$ed-

escurrir, *kers-

ese, *éy / h$_1$e, *s(w)e-

esencia, *H$_1$es-

esgrimir, *(s)ker-

esleir, *leǵ-

eso, esos, *éy / h$_1$e

especia, especie, espécimen, espectro, especulación, especular, espéculo, espejo, *speḱ-

esperanza, esperar, *speh$_1$-

espiar, *speḱ-

espiga, espina, espinal, espino, espinoso, *speyesplene, esplenético, *splenǵʰ-

espuma, espumar, espumoso, *poymno-

esquema, *seǵʰ-

esquilar, *(s)ker-

esta, *só

estable, establecer, establir, establo, estabular, estación, estado, *steh₂-

estallar, *H₂eǵ-

estambre, estar, *steh₂-

estas, *só

estatua, estatuir, estatus, *steh₂-

este, *só

estelar, *h₂stér

estera, *sterh₃-

estero, estio, estival, *h₂eydʰ-

esto, estos, *só

estrada, estrado, estratega, estrato, *sterh₃-

estrella, estrellar, *h₂stér

estruendo, *(s)tenh₂-

estudiante, estudiar, estudio, estuper, estúpido, estupro, *(s)tew-

éter, *h₂eydʰ-

eternidad, eterno, *h₂ey-

etologia, *swe-dʰh₁-

evanescer, *h₁weh₂-

eventual, eventualidad, *gʷem-

evidencia, *weyd-

evo, *h₂ey-

evocar, *wekʷ-

evolución, evolucionar, *welH-

exacerbar, *h₂éḱ

examen, examinación, examinar, *H₂eǵ-

excelencia, excelente, *kelH-

exceptuar, *keh₂p-

exclamar, *kelh₁-

excluido, exclusivo, *(s)kel-

excretar, *krey-

excursión, *ḱers-

exfoliar, *bʰleh₃-

exhalar, *h₂enh₁-

exhibir, *gʰeh₁bʰ-

exhortación, *ǵʰer-

exir, *h₁ey-

existir, *steh₂-

éxito, *h₁ey-

expandir, *peth₂

expectar, *speḱ-

expedir, *ped-

expender, expensas, *pewǵ-

experiencia, experto, *per-

explicar, *pleḱ-

exponer, *teḱ-

exportación, exportar, *per-

expugnar, expunger, expungir, *pewǵ-

éxtasis, extático, *steh₂-

extender, extensión, extenso, *ten-

exterior, externo, extra-, extraño, *h₁eǵʰs

extrudir, *trewd-

fábula, fabuloso, *bʰeh₂-

facción, *dheH₁-

fachenda, facienda, facto, factor, faena, *dheH₁-

fama, *bʰeh₂-

familia, familiar, fámulo, *dheH₁-

fanático, *dʰéh₁s

fantasma, *bʰeh₂-

fárrago, *bʰars-

fasto, *bʰeh₂-

fe, *bʰeydʰ-

feble, *bʰleh₁-

febrero, *dʰegʷʰ-

fecha, fecho, *dheH₁-

felicidad, feliz, femenino, fémina, *dʰeh₁(y)-

fenómeno, *bʰeh₂-

feria, *dʰéh₁s

ferocidad, feroz, *ǵʰweroh₃kʷs

festividad, festivo, *dʰéh₁s

feto, *dʰeh₁(y)-

feudo, *peḱu-

fiar, fidelidad, fido, *bʰeydʰ-

fiebre, *dʰegʷʰ-

fiel, *bʰeydʰ-

fiera, fiero, *ǵʰwer-

fiesta, *dʰéh₁s

figura, fingir, *dʰeyǵʰ-

firmamento, firmar, firme, *dʰer-

fisión, fiso, fistra, fístula, *bʰeyd-

flato, *bʰleh₁-

flor, florir, flósculo, *bʰleh₃-

flotar, *plew-

fluctuación, fluctuar, fluir, flujo, fluvial, *bʰleh₁-

folio, *bʰleh₃-

fomento, *dʰegʷʰ-

fondo, *bʰudʰmén

foresta, *perkʷu-

foro, *dʰwer-

fortificar, *bʰerǵʰ-, *dheH₁-

fortitud, fortitúdine, *bʰerǵʰ-

fortuitamente, fortuito, fortuna, *bher-

fraile, fraternidad, fraterno, fray, *bʰréh₂tēr

freno, *dʰer-

fresneda, fresno, *bʰereǵ-

fuera, *dʰwer-

fuerte, fuerza, *bʰerǵʰ-

fui, *bʰuH-

fuina, *bʰeh₂go-

fuligo, fumar, fumigar, fumo, *dʰewh₂-

fundador, *ǵʰew-

fundago, *deḱ-

fundamento, *ǵʰew-

fundar, *bʰudʰmén

fundíbulo, fundir, *ǵʰew-

fundo, *bʰudʰmén

furtiva, furtivo, *bher-

fuscar, *dʰewh₂-

fusión, *ǵʰew-
futuro, *bʰuH-
galaxia, *glag-
ganso, *ǵʰans-
garda, *wer-
gastar, *h₁weh₂-
gélido, *gel-
gema, *ǵómbʰos
general, generar, género, genio, genitor, gente,
  gentil, *ǵenH₁-
genuflexión, *ǵónu
gerer, *H₂eǵ-
germán, germano, germen, germinar, *ǵenH₁-
gerundio, gestión, gesto, *H₂eǵ-
gloria, gloriar, glorioso, *ǵneh₃-
gonce, gozne, *ǵómbʰos
gracia, gracioso, grado, *gʷerH-
grama, *gʰreh₁-
gramática, *gerbʰ-
gramíneo, *gʰreh₁-
grano, *ǵr̥Hnom
gratis, grato, gratuito, *gʷerH-
gravar, grave, gravedad, grávido, *gʷerh₂-
griego, gringo, *ǵerh₂-
grúa, grulla, *gerh₂-
guadaña, *weyh₁-
guardar, *wer-
guiar, *weyd-
gurú, *gʷerh₂-
gustar, gusto, *ǵews-
haba, *bʰabʰeh₂-
haber, hábil, habilidad, habitación, habitante,
  habitar, hábito, *gʰeh₁bʰ-
habla, *bʰeh₂-
hacer, hacienda, *dheH₁-
hado, *bʰeh₂-
halar, *kelh₁-
hallar, *bʰleh₁-
harina, harinero, harinoso, *bʰars-
hariolo, haríolo, *ǵʰern-
harnero, *bʰars-
harúspice, *ǵʰern-, *speḱ-
haya, *bʰeh₂go-
haz, *h₂éḱ
hecho, hechor, *dheH₁-
helar, *gel-
hembra, *dʰeh₁(y)-
henchir, *pleh₁-
hender, *bʰeyd-
heñir, *dʰeyǵʰ-
hepático, hepatitis, *Hyékʷr̥
hermandad, hermano, *ǵenH₁-
hernia, *ǵʰern-
herrén, *bʰars-
hesterno, *dʰǵʰ(y)es-
hibernal, hibernar, *ǵʰey-
hiedra, *weyd-

hielo, *gel-
hiena, *suH-
hier, *dʰǵʰ(y)es-
hija, hijastro, hijo, hijuelo, *dʰeh₁(y)-
hinchar, hinchazón, *bʰleh₁-
hinojo, *ǵónu
hipo-, *upo
hipoteca, *dheH₁-
hirmar, *dʰer-
historia, histórico, *weyd-
hoja, hojoso, *bʰleh₃-
hollín, *dʰewh₂-
hombre, *ǵʰmṓ
hondo, *bʰudʰmḗn, *ǵʰew-
hora, *yeh₁-
hormiga, *morwi-
hornacho, hornillo, horno, *gʷʰer-
horrendo, horrible, hórrido, horripilar, horror, *gʰers-
hosco, *dʰewh₂-
hospedar, hospicio, hospital, hospitalidad, hostal,
  *gʰóstis
hoy, *deyn-
hucia, *bʰeydʰ-
huebra, *h₃ep-
huerbo, *h₃erbʰ-
huerta, huerto, *ǵʰer-
hueso, *h₃ésth₁
huésped, hueste, *gʰóstis
hueva, huevo, *h₂ōwyóm
humano, *ǵʰmṓ
humar, humear, *dʰewh₂-
humil, humilde, *dʰéǵʰōm
humo, *dʰewh₂-
humus, *dʰéǵʰōm
hundir, *ǵʰew-
hurón, hurto, *bher-
i-, *n̥-
idea, *weyd-
identidad, *éy / h₁e
ierra, *ters-
ignaro, *ǵneh₃-
ignominia, *h₁nómn̥
ignorante, ignorar, *ǵneh₃-
ilación, ilativo, *bher-
ilegal, *leǵ-, *legʰ-
iluminar, *lewk-
im-, *n̥-
imberbe, *bʰardʰeh₂-
immunità, *mey-
impacto, *peh₂ǵ-
impecune, *peḱu-
impedir, *ped-
ímpetu, *peth₂
implantar, *pleh₂-
implemento, *pleh₁-
implicación, implicar, *pleḱ-
imponer, *teḱ-

importar, *per-

improbar, improbo, *bʰuH-

improbo, *per-

impugnar, *pewǵ-

impune, impunemente, impunidad, *kʷey-

in-, *n̥-

inaugurar, *h₂ewg-

incepción, *keh₂p-

inclinación, inclinar, *ḱley-

inclito, *ḱlew-

incluir, incluso, *(s)kel-

incola, *kʷel-

incrédulo, increible, *dheH₁-

inculcar, *(s)kel-

incurrir, incursión, *ḱers-

índex, indicar, índice, indicio, *deyḱ-

indigna, indigno, *deḱ-

índole, *h₂el-

inducción, inducir, *dewk-

industria, industrioso, *strew-

inerte, *h₂er-

infame, infamia, infando, infante, *bʰeh₂-

infectar, *dheH₁-

inferir, *bher-

infestar, *gʷʰen-

inflación, inflar, influir, *bʰleh₁-

infundir, *ǵʰew-

ingente, *ǵenH₁-

ingerir, *H₂eǵ-

inhalar, *h₂enh₁-

inhibir, *gʰeh₁bʰ-

inhumano, *ǵʰmó

iniciar, inicio, *h₁ey-

injerir, *ser-

inmaduro, *meh₂-

inmigrar, *mey-

inminente, *men-

inmiscuirse, *mey-

inmolar, *melh₂-

inmune, inmunidad, inmutar, *mey-

innovar, *new

inocente, *neḱ-

inocular, *h₃ekʷ-

inquilino, *kʷel-

inscribir, *(s)ker-

insecto, *sek-

inserir, *ser-

insigne, insignia, *sek-

insistir, *steh₂-

insólito, *swe-dʰh₁-

insonte, *H₁es-

instaurar, instituir, *steh₂-

instructor, instruir, *strew-

intelecto, inteligir, *leǵ-

intención, intender, intenso, intento, *ten-

inter alia, *h₂el-

intercalar, *kelh₁-

interdecir, *deyḱ-

interés, *h₁én

interés, *H₁es-

interior, *h₁én

intervalo, *welH-

intervenir, interventor, *gʷem-

intervertir, *wert-

intra-, *h₁én

introducción, introducir, *dewk-

inundación, inundar, *wed-

invención, invenir, inventar, inventor, *gʷem-

invernar, *ǵʰey-

invertir, *wert-

investigación, investigar, *steygʰ-

investir, *wes-

invierno, *ǵʰey-

invigilar, *weǵ-

invitar, *weyh₁-

invocar, *wekʷ-

involucro, *welH-

ir, *h₁ey-

ironia, *wekʷ-

jardín, *ǵʰer-

jedar, *dʰeh₁(y)-

jefe, *kapõlo

jornada, *deyn-

joven, *h₂yuh₁en-

judicial, judiciario, *h₂eyw-

juego, *yek-

jueves, *deyn-

juez, *h₂eyw-

jugar, *yek-

juncer, junger, *yewg-

junior, *h₂yuh₁en-

juntar, *yewg-

juramento, jurar, juro, *h₂eyw-

justar, *yewg-

justeza, justicia, justo, *h₂eyw-

juvenco, juvenil, juventud, *h₂yuh₁en-

juzgador, juzgar, *h₂eyw-

la, *h₂el-

labio, labro, *leb-

lacrimación, lacrimar, lacrimoso, *daḱru-

lactar, lactario, lácteo, lacticinio, *glag-

lacunar, lago, *lókus

lágrima, lagrimar, lagrimoso, *daḱru-

laguna, *lókus

lamber, lamer, *leb-

lana, lanero, lanoso, lanugo, *h₂welh₁-

las, *h₂el-

latrina, lava, lavar, *lewh₃-

lavija, *(s)kel-

le, *h₂el-

leal, *leǵ-, *legh-

lección, *leǵ-

leche, lechero, *glag-

lechiga, lecho, *legh-

453

lechoso, lechuga, *glag-

lector, lectura, leer, legación, *leǵ-

legación, *legh-

legal, *leǵ-, *legh-

legión, *leǵ-

legislación, *leǵ-, *legh-

legislador, *legh-

legítimo, *leǵ-, *legh-

legumbre, *leǵ-

lengua, *dn̥ǵʰwéh₂s

lenzuelo, *lino-

leña, leñador, leñero, leño, leñoso, *leǵ-

les, *h₂el-

letrina, *lewh₃-

leudo, levantar, leve, *h₁lengʷʰ-

ley, *leǵ-, *legh-

libelo, *lewbʰ-

liberación, liberador, liberar, libertad, librador,
 librar, libre, *h₁lewdʰ-

librero, libro, *lewbʰ-

lienzo, *lino-

lieve, ligero, *h₁lengʷʰ-

lindo, *leǵ-, *legh-

línea, lineamento, líneo, linero, lino, liña, *lino-

liviano, *h₁lengʷʰ-

llaga, *pleh₂k-

llamar, *kelh₁-

llano, llantén, *pleh₂-

llave, llavija, *(s)kel-

llegar, *pleǵ-

lleno, *pleh₁-

llevado, llevar, *h₁lengʷʰ-

llover, lluvia, lluvioso, *plew-

lo, *h₂el-

lobo, *wl̥kʷos

locación, local, locus, *stel-

lodra, *udréh₂

logar, *stel-

lomos, *lendʰ-

longevidad, longevo, *h₂ey-

los, *h₂el-

lucerna, *lewk-

lucha, luchador, luchar, *seh₂g-

lucífero, lucio, lucir, lucubración, lucubrar, *lewk-

luego, lugar, lugar, *stel-

Luis, *ḱlew-

lujo, *seh₂g-

lumbre, lumbrera, luminar, luminaria, luminoso,
 luna, lunar, lunático, *lewk-

lunes, *deyn-

lupino, *wl̥kʷos

lusco, lustrar, lustro, *lewk-

lutria, *udréh₂

luz, *lewk-

madera, madre, madrilla, *méh₂tēr

maduro, *meh₂-

maese, maeso, maestre, maestro, magister,

magistrado, magnitud, magno, *méǵh₂s

magro, *meh₂ḱ-

majestad, *méǵh₂s

maldecir, maldición, maldito, *deyḱ-

mama, *méh₂-méh₂

manada, *méh₂-r̥

mandar, *deH₃-

mandibula, manducar, *mendʰ-

manera, *méh₂-r̥

manifiesto, *gʷʰen-

manija, manilla, *méh₂-r̥

manípulo, *pleh₁-

manjar, *mendʰ-

mano, *ǵenH₁-, *méh₂-r̥

manopla, *pleh₁-

mansedumbre, *swe-dʰh₁-

mantener, *ten-

mantra, *men-

manubrio, manumitir, *méh₂-r̥

mañana, *meh₂-

maño, *méǵh₂s

mar, marino, *móri

mariscal, *marko-

marisma, marítimo, *móri

martes, *deyn-

mas, más, máster, *méǵh₂s

masticar, *mendʰ-

matar, *méǵh₂s, *meh₂ḱ-

materia, maternal, materno, matricida, matrícula,
 matriz, matrona, *méh₂tēr

matutino, *meh₂-

máximo, mayor, *méǵh₂s

me, *H₁me-

mear, *h₃meyǵʰ-

mecer, *H₂melǵ-, *mey-

mediador, mediano, mediar, *médʰyos

medicamento, medicar, medicina, medicinal, médico,
 *med-

medida, *meh₁-

medio, *médʰyos

mediocre, mediocridad, *h₂éḱ, *médʰyos

medir, *meh₁-

mediterráneo, médium, médula, meitad, mejana,
 *médʰyos

membrana, membranáceo, membranoso, *mḗms

membrar, memorable, memorar, memoria, menar,
 menaza, mención, mendaz, *men-

menester, menguar, menor, menos, *mey-

mensa, menso, *meh₁-

menstrual, menstruar, *mḗh₁n̥s

mental, mente, mentir, *men-

mentón, *men-, *mendʰ-

menucia, menudo, menuza, *mey-

meollo, *médʰyos

mes, *mḗh₁n̥s

mesa, *meh₁-

mester, mestizo, mestura, *mey-

mesura, mesurar, metro, *meh$_1$-
mezana, *méd^{h}yos
mezclar, *mey-
mí, *H$_1$me-, *H$_1$meme-
mía, *H$_1$meme-
miel, *melit-
miembro, *mḗms
mientras, *éy / h$_1$e, *h$_1$én
miércoles, *deyn-
mijero, miliar, milla, milliario, *sem-
minar, minaz, *men-
minger, *h$_3$meyǵ^h-
mínimo, ministerio, ministro, minucia, minuir,
  minuto, misceláneo, *mey-
mismo, *éy / h$_1$e, *s(w)e-
mitad, *méd^{h}yos
mixtión, mixtura, *mey-
model, moderar, moderno, modestia, modesto,
  módico, modificar, modio, modo, *med-
molar, *melh$_2$-
molde, *med-
moler, molero, molinero, molino, *melh$_2$-
moneda, monstruo, montano, montaña,
  montañoso, monte, montecillo, monticulo,
  montuoso, monumento, *men-
moribundo, mòriri, *mer-
mosca, mosquito, *mus-
mostacho, *mend^h-
mostrar, *men-
motrimonio, *méh$_2$tēr
moyo, *med-
mudar, *mey-
muela, *melh$_2$-
muerta, muerte, muerto, *mer-
muir, mulger, *H$_2$melǵ-
multiplica, multiplicación, *pleḱ-
municipio, munificencia, *mey-
muñir, *men-
mur, *muh$_2$s-
muriri, *mer-
muscular, músculo, musculoso, muslo, *muh$_2$s-
mutar, mutuo, *mey-
nacer, nación, nada, *ǵenH$_1$-
nadadera, nadador, *(s)neh$_2$-
nadal, *ǵenH$_1$-
nadar, *(s)neh$_2$-
narine, nariz, *néh$_2$s
narración, narrar, narrativo, *ǵneh$_3$-
naso, *néh$_2$s
natal, natalicio, *ǵenH$_1$-
natatorio, *(s)neh$_2$-
natividad, nativo, nato, *ǵenH$_1$-
natriz, *(s)neh$_2$-, *neHtr-
natura, natural, naturalidad, *ǵenH$_1$-
nauta, náutico, naval, nave, navegación,
  navegar, *(s)neh$_2$-
Navidad, *ǵenH$_1$-

navío, *(s)neh$_2$-
nebuloso, *neb^h-
nefando, nefario, nefas, nefasto, *b^{h}eh$_2$-
negligencia, negligir, *leǵ-
negociación, negociador, negociar, negocio, *h$_2$ew
nervio, nervioso, nervoso, *(s)neh$_1$-
neustro, *wei
nevoso, *sneyg^{wh}-
nevus, *ǵenH$_1$-
nidificar, nido, *nisdós
niebla, *neb^h-
nieta, nieto, *nepot-
nieve, *sneyg^{wh}-
noble, *ǵneh$_3$-
noche, *nók^{w}ts
noción, *ǵneh$_3$-
nocivo, *neḱ-
nocturno, *nók^{w}ts
nombrar, nombre, nomenclatura, nominación, nominal,
  nominar, *h$_1$nómn̩
normal, *ǵneh$_3$-
norte, *h$_1$én
nos, nosotros, *wei
notar, notario, noticia, notorio, *ǵneh$_3$-
novar, *new
novecientos, *H$_1$néwn̩, *ḱm̩tóm
novedad, *new
novena, noventa, *H$_1$néwn̩
novilla, novillo, *new
novilunio, *lewk-
nuera, *snusós
nueve, *H$_1$néwn̩
nuevo, *new
numerador, numerar, numerario, número,
  numerosidad, numeroso, *nem-
nunca, *k^{w}is
nutra, nutria, *udréh$_2$
o, *h$_2$ew
obedecer, obediente, *h$_2$ewis-d^{h}h$_1$-
objeto, *h$_1$epi
oblación, oblada, oblato, oblea, *bher-
obra, obrar, obrero, *h$_3$ep-
obseder, *sed-
obsequio, obsequioso, *sek^w-
obsoleto, *h$_2$el-
obstáculo, obstar, *steh$_2$-
obstrucción, obstructivo, obstruir, *strew-
obtener, *ten-
obviar, obvio, *weyh$_1$-
ocho, *oḱtṓw
ochocientos, *ḱm̩tóm
ocio, ocioso, *h$_2$ew
ocluir, *(s)kel-
octágono, octógono, *oḱtṓw
octopoda, *pṓds
ocular, óculo, óculos, *h$_3$ek^w-
ocupación, ocupar, *keh$_2$p-

ocurrir, *ḱers-
odiar, odio, odio, odioso, *h₃ed-
odre, *wed-
oeste, *wek(ʷ)speros
ofender, *gʷʰen-
oficial, oficio, *h₃ep-
ofrecer, *bher-
oído, oidor, oír, ojo, *h₃ekʷ-
oler, olor, *h₃ed-
ombligo, *h₃enbʰ-
omnipotente, *H₁es-
once, *déḱm̥t
onda, ondear, ondoso, *wed-
ópera, operar, operario, *h₃ep-
oponer, *h₁epi, *teḱ-
oportunidad, oportuno, *per-
opugnar, *pewǵ-
opulento, opus, *h₃ep-
oración, oráculo, orar, *h₃éh₁os
orbar, orbedad, orbo, *h₃erbʰ-
orden, ordenar, ordeñar, *h₂er
orear, *h₂ews-
oreja, *h₂ew-
órgano, *werǵ-
oriental, oriente, origen, originario, *h₃er-
orín, *h₂eyos
oriundo, *h₃er-
ornar, *h₂er
orto, *h₃er-
os, *túh₂
osa, oso, *h₂ŕ̥tkos
ostentación, ostentar, *ten-
oto, otro, *h₂el-
oveja, ovino, *h₂ówis
oyente, *h₂ewis-dʰh₁-
pábulo, *peh₂-
pacato, *peh₂ǵ-
pacer, *peh₂-
pacifico, *peh₂ǵ-
pación, *peh₂-
padilla, *peth₂
padrastro, padre, padrón, *ph₂tér
paella, *peth₂
pagado, paganismo, pagano, pagar, página, *peh₂ǵ-
paila, *peth₂
país, *peh₂ǵ-
pájaro, *peth₂
pala, *peh₂ǵ-
palabra, *gʷelH-
pálido, palor, *pelH-
palude, palustre, *peh₂ǵ-
pan, *peh₂-
pander, *peth₂
panero, panizo, panoso, *peh₂-
para, *per-
parábola, *gʷelH-
paraíso, *dʰeyǵʰ-

parco, *h₂erk-
parecer, *peh₂-
parsimonia, *h₂erk-
pasa, pasado, pasar, paso, *peth₂
pastilla, pasto, pastor, pastura, *peh₂-
paternidad, paterno, patrimonio, patriota, patrón,
   patrono, *ph₂tér
paúl, paz, *peh₂ǵ-
pecado, pecador, pecar, *ped-
pécora, peculio, pecunia, pecuniario, pecunio, *peḱu-
pedagogo, *H₂eǵ-
pedicelo, pediculo, *póds
pedir, *peth₂
pedul, *póds
pegullo, *peḱu-
peinar, peine, *peḱ-
peje, *peisḱ-
película, *pel-
peligro, peligroso, *per-
pelleja, *pel-
pena, *kʷey-
pendejo, *peḱ-
pender, *pewǵ-
penetración, penetrar, *peh₂-
pensar, *pewǵ-
penta-, *pénkʷe
pentrante, *peh₂-
peña, *péth₂r
peor, peorar, *ped-
peorca, *pórḱos
percepción, percibir, *keh₂p-
percorrer, *ḱers-
perder, perdición, pérdida, *deH₃-
perecer, *h₁ey-
peregrinar, peregrino, *h₂éǵros
perfecto, *dheH₁-
periclitar, perito, *per-
perjudicar, perjuicio, *h₂eyw-
permutar, *mey-
perorar, *h₃éh₁os
perseguir, *sekʷ-
persistir, *steh₂-
perspectivo, perspicacia, perspicaz, *speḱ-
perta, *deH₃-
pertenecer, pertinente, *ten-
pesar, *pewǵ-
pescar, *peisḱ-
pescudar, *(s)ker-
pésimo, *ped-
peso, *pewǵ-
pesquero, *peisḱ-
peyorar, *ped-
pez, *peisḱ-
pie, *póds
piel, pielero, *pel-
pienso, *pewǵ-
pigmento, *peyḱ-

pila, pilar, pilo, *peys-

pimiento, pintar, pinto, pintor, pintura, *peyḱ-

pisar, *peys-

piscina, *peisḱ-

pistar, pisto, *peys-

plaga, *pleh₂k-

plan, plano, planta, plantar, *pleh₂-

plañir, *pleh₂k-

plaza, *pleh₂-

plebe, *pleh₁-

plectro, *pleh₂k-

plegar, plegaria, *preḱ-

plenario, plenitude, pleno, *pleh₁-

plexo, *pleḱ-

pluralidad, *pleh₁-

pluvial, pluvioso, *plew-

población, *pleh₁-

poción, *peh₃-

poder, *H₁es-

podio, *pṓds

pólice, *h₂welh₁-

poluir, *lewh₃-

pómez, *poymno-

ponente, poner, poniente, *teḱ-

pontifice, *pent-

ponzoña, *peh₃-

popular, *pleh₁-

por, *per-

porcel, porcela, porcelo, porcino, porquero, *pórḱos

portada, portal, portar, *per-

portento, *ten-

portero, pórtico, *per-

posca, *peh₃-

poseer, posesión, *pótis

posible, *H₁es-

posición, *teḱ-

postrar, *sterh₃-

postular, *preḱ-

potable, *peh₃-

potencia, potente, *H₁es-

potestad, *pótis

poyo, *pṓds

práctica, practicar, pragma, pragmático, praxis, *per-

prea, *weyd-

prear, *deH₃-, *weyd-

precario, *preḱ-

precio, precioso, *per-

preda, *weyd-

predador, predar, *deH₃-, *weyd-

predecir, *deyḱ-

predial, *wedʰ-

predicción, *deyḱ-

predio, *wedʰ-

preferir, *bher-

pregar, *pleḱ-

prejuicio, prejuzgar, *h₂eyw-

premostrar, *men-

prender, prensión, *weyd-

preocupación, preocupar, *keh₂p-

preponer, *teḱ-

presagiar, *seh₂g-

prescribir, *(s)ker-

presentar, presente, *H₁es-

presentir, *sent-

presidente, presidio, presidir, *sed-

preso, *weyd-

prestar, *steh₂-

preste, *per-

pretender, *ten-

preuba, *bʰuH-

prevaler, *h₂welh₁-

prevenir, *gʷem-

prever, *weyd-

previo, *weyh₁-

prez, primario, primero, primitiva, primitivo, primo, *per-

primogénito, *ǵenH₁-, *per-

principe, principio, *keh₂p-

prior, *per-

prisión, *weyd-

privación, privado, privar, privilegio, proa, *per-

proba, *bʰuH-, *per-

probable, probar, probidad, *bʰuH-

problema, problemático, *gʷelH-

probo, *bʰuH-, *per-

procaz, *preḱ-

proclamar, *kelh₁-

producción, producir, productivo, producto, *dewk-

profanar, profano, *dʰéh₁s

proferir, *bher-

profesión, profesor, *bʰeh₂-

profundidad, profundo, *ǵʰew-

programa, *gerbʰ-

prohibición, prohibir, *gʰeh₁bʰ-

prójimo, *per-

prole, proletariado, *h₂el-

prominente, *men-

promiscuo, *mey-

propagar, *peh₂ǵ-

propensión, *pewǵ-

propiedad, *preyH-

propíncuo, *per-

propio, *preyH-

proponer, propósito, *teḱ-

propugnar, *pewǵ-

prosa, *wert-

proscribir, *(s)ker-

proseguir, *sekʷ-

prospecto, *speḱ-

prosperar, *speh₁-

prostituir, *steh₂-

prostrar, *sterh₃-

proteger, *(s)teg-

proveer, *weyd-

provenir, provento, *gʷem-

proverbio, *wekʷ-
providencia, *weyd-
próximo, *per-
publico, *pleh₁-
pudiente, *H₁es-
pueblo, *pleh₁-
puente, *pent-
puerco, *pórḱos
puerta, puerto, *per-
pues, *h₁epi
puesto, *teḱ-
púgil, pugnaz, *pewǵ-
pulga, *plou-
pulgar, *h₂welh₁-
pulmón, *plewmō
punción, punger, pungir, *pewǵ-
punir, *kʷey-
punta, punto, punzar, punzón, puñar, puñir,
 puño, *pewǵ-
que, qué, *kʷis
quedo, *kʷyeh₁-
quien, *kʷis
quieto, *kʷyeh₁-
quijada, *keh₂p-
quince, *déḱm̥t
quinientos, *ḱm̥tóm
ración, *h₂er
radical, radio, *wréh₂ds
rain, *bʰars-
raiz, *wréh₂ds
ralbar, *h₁lengʷʰ-
rama, ramifico, ramo, ramoso, *wréh₂ds
raño, *h₂er
rasgar, *sek-
raya, rayo, raza, *wréh₂ds
razón, *h₂er
real, *h₃reǵ-
rebosar, *wert-
recepción, receptáculo, receptar, recibir, *keh₂p-
reclamar, *kelh₁-
recoger, recolegir, *leǵ-
recompensar, *pewǵ-
reconocer, *ǵneh₃-
recordar, *ḱér-
recorrer, *ḱers-
recto, *h₃reǵ-
recurrir, *ḱers-
rédito, *h₁ey-
redondo, *Hret-
reducción, reducir, reducto, *dewk-
referir, *bher-
refluir, *bʰleh₁-
régimen, regir, regla, reina, reinar, reino, reja, *h₃reǵ-
relación, *bher-
relegación, relegar, *legh-
relevar, relvar, *h₁lengʷʰ-
remedio, *med-

remembrar, rememorar, *men-
remunerar, *mey-
rendir, *deH₃-
renovar, *new
renumerar, *nem-
repetir, *peth₂
replegar, *pleḱ-
repleto, *pleh₁-
replicar, *pleḱ-
reponer, *teḱ-
reportar, *per-
reprehender, reprehensible, reprender, reprensible,
 reprensión, *weyd-
representar, *H₁es-
república, *pleh₁-
repugnar, *pewǵ-
rescindir, *skey-
residir, *sed-
resignar, *sek-
resistir, *steh₂-
resollar, *bʰleh₁-
respectar, respecto, respetar, respeto, *speḱ-
restar, restaurar, restituir, resto, *steh₂-
retención, retener, *ten-
rétor, rétorico, *wekʷ-
retribuir, *bʰuH-
reunión, *óy-nos
revencer, *weyk-
revenir, *gʷem-
rever, *weyd-
reverencia, reverente, *wer-
revertir, revesar, *wert-
revisitar, revista, revistar, *weyd-
revocar, *wekʷ-
revolución, revolver, *welH-
rey, rico, *h₃reǵ-
rienda, *ten-
río, *h₃reyH-
ritmo, *srew-
rito, *h₂er
rivalidad, *h₃reyH-
rizo, *ǵʰér-
rodar, rodilla, *Hret-
rojo, *h₁rewdʰ-
rol, rol, rolla, rollo, rondala, *Hret-
roña, roñoso, *h₂eyos
rotación, rotar, rótula, rótulo, rotundo, *Hret-
rúbeo, rubí, rubia, rubio, rubor, rúbrica, rubricar,
 *h₁rewdʰ-
rueda, ruejo, *Hret-
rufo, *h₁rewdʰ-
ruiseñor, *keh₂n-
rundel, *Hret-
sacerdocio, sacerdotal, sacerdote, sacrificador,
 sacrificar, sacrificio, *dheH₁-
sagaz, *seh₂g-
sajo, *sek-

sal, salar, salso, *séh₂ls

salubre, salud, saludación, saludar, salutación,
 salvar, salve, salvo, *solh₂-

sangonera, sangrar, sangre, sangüeño, sanguinario,
 sanguíneo, sanguinolento, sanguinoso, *h₁ésh₂r

santificar, santiguar, satisfacer, *dheH₁-

saxo, *sek-

sazón, *seH₁-

se, *s(w)e-

secreción, secretar, secretario, secreto, *krey-

secuencia, *sekʷ-

sed, *dʰegʷʰ-

sedar, sede, sedente, sedimento, *sed-

seducir, *dewk-

segar, *sek-

seguir, segundo, *sekʷ-

segur, *sek-

seis, *swéḱs

seiscientos, *ḱm̥tóm

selección, *leǵ-

sello, *sek-

semana, *septm̥

sembrar, *seH₁-

semejante, semejar, *sem-

semen, semencera, *seH₁-

semi-, *sem-

seminarista, *seH₁-

senado, senador, *sénos

sencillo, sendos, *sem-

sene, senil, senior, *sénos

sentar, *sed-

sentencioso, sentido, sentimiento, sentir, *sent-

seña, *sek-

señero mil, *sem-

señor, señora, señorita, seor, *sénos

septiembre, séptimo, *septm̥

ser, *H₁es-, *sed-

serie, sermón, *ser-

sero-, *srew-

serrar, serrin, *sek-

sesión, *sed-

seso, *sent-

setecientos, *ḱm̥tóm

setentrião, *terh₁-

sétimo, *septm̥

si, sí, *só

siempre, *sem-

sien, *sent-

sierra, *sek-

siete, *septm̥

sigilo, signar, *sek-

significar, *dheH₁-, *sek-

signo, *sek-

silla, *sed-

simiente, simienza, *seH₁-

símil, *sem-

simple, *pleḱ-, *sem-

simplificar, *dheH₁-, *pleh₁-, *sem-

simular, singular, *sem-

sino, *sek-

sinónimo, *h₁nómn̥

sistema, *steh₂-

sitio, situar, *teḱ-

so, soberbia, *upo

soberbio, *bʰuH-, *upo

sobrar, sobre, *upo

sobreceja, sobrecejo, *ḱel-

sobreponer, *teḱ-

sobreseer, *sed-

sobrevenir, *gʷem-

sobrino, *swésōr

socia, social, sociedad, socio, *sekʷ-

socorrer, *ḱers-

sol, solar, *sóh₂wl̥

soledumbre, *s(w)e-

solemne, *solh₂-

soler, *swe-dʰh₁-

solevar, *h₁lengʷʰ-

solicitar, solicito, solicitud, sólido, *solh₂-

solitario, *s(w)e-

sólito, *swe-dʰh₁-

solo, soltero, *s(w)e-

soma, *upo

sonte, *H₁es-

soñador, soñar, *swep-

soplar, *bʰleh₁-

sopor, *swep-

soportar, *per-

sor, *swésōr

sostener, *ten-

sota, soto-, *upo

su, *s(w)e-

subilla, *sīw-

subir, súbito, *h₁ey-

sublevar, *h₁lengʷʰ-

subsistir, *steh₂-

subterfugio, *upo

subtil, *tetḱ-

subvenir, *gʷem-

sudar, sudario, sudor, *sweyd-

sueldo, *solh₂-

sueño, *swep-

suero, *srew-

suerte, *ser-

sufrir, *bher-

suma, sumidad, sumo, superar, *upo

superfluo, *bʰleh₁-

superior, *upo

superponer, *teḱ-

superstición, *steh₂-

supervacáneo, *h₁weh₂-

supervenir, *gʷem-

supino, *upo

suplemento, *pleh₁-

suplicar, *plek̑-
suplir, *pleh₁-
suponer, *tek̑-
surdir, surgir, *h₃reǵ-
surtir, *ser-
suscribir, *(s)ker-
suspender, suspensión, *pewǵ-
sustentar, *ten-
sutil, *tetk̑-
sutorio, sutura, *sīw-
suvenir, *gʷem-
suyo, *s(w)e-
taberna, tabernáculo, *treb-
tal, *só
taladro, *terh₁-
taller, *H₂eǵ-
tamaño, tan, tandem, tanto, *só
techo, teja, *(s)teg-
tejer, tejón, tela, *tetk̑-
tema, *dheH₁-
tenáculo, tenaz, tenaza, tender, tener, teniente,
 tenor, tensión, tenso, *ten-
Teodorico, *tewtéh₂
teoría, *wer-
terciar, tercio, *tréyes
terminar, término, *térmn̥
terrestre, territorial, territorio, *ters-
tesón, *ten-
textorio, *tetk̑-
tierno, *ten-
tierra, *ters-
tieso, *ten-
tío, *dʰeh₁(y)-
típico, tipo, *(s)tew-
tirar, *der-
toga, *(s)teg-
tolerar, toller, *telh₂-
tono, *ten-
tordo, *trosdos
toro, *(s)táwros, *sterh₃-
torrar, tórrido, *ters-
tos, toser, *(s)tew-
traba, *treb-
tradición, *deH₃-
traducir, *dewk-
traición, traidor, *deH₃-
tranquilo, *kʷyeh₁-
transcribir, *(s)ker-
transferir, *bher-
transfundir, *ǵʰew-
transir, *h₁ey-
transmigrar, *mey-
transmontano, *men-
transmutación, transmutar, *mey-
transplantar, *pleh₂-
transportar, *per-
tras-, *terh₂-

traslación, trasladar, traslado, *bher-
trece, *dék̑m̥t
tregua, *deru-
tres, *tréyes
trescientos, *k̑m̥tóm
treudo, *bʰuH-
triángulo, *h₂enk-
tribu, tribunal, tribuno, tributo, *bʰuH-
trigo, trilla, trillo, triscar, tritura, *terh₁-
tronar, *(s)tenh₂-
tropa, tropel, *treb-
trueno, *ten-
tú, *túh₂
tuero, *sterh₃-
tullir, *telh₂-
tuyo, *túh₂
u, *h₂ew
ubicuo, *kʷis
ubio, *yugóm
ubre, *h₁owHdʰr̥-
uebos, *h₃ep-
ulna, *Heh₃l-
ultra, *h₂el-
umplir, *pleh₁-
un, *óy-nos
unca, *kʷis
uncino, *h₂enk-
uncir, *yewg-
undoso, *wed-
ungulado, *h₃negʰ-
único, unidad, unión, *óy-nos
universo, *wert-
uno, *óy-nos
uña, *h₃negʰ-
urna, *h₁ews-
vacio, vacuo, vacuum, vagar, vago, *h₁weh₂-
valente, valer, válido, *h₂welh₁-
valla, valle, *welH-
valor, *h₂welh₁-
valva, *welH-
vanidad, vano, vasto, *h₁weh₂-
vaticinar, *keh₂n-
vecina, vecindad, vecino, *weyk̑-
vector, *weǵʰ-
vedegambre, *med-
vegetación, *weǵ-
veguer, *weyk-
vehículo, *weǵʰ-
veinte, *wīk̑m̥tiH₁
velar, *weǵ-
vello, vellón, velloso, *h₂welh₁-
venal, *wesno-
vencer, *weyk-
vendedor, vender, *deH₃-, *wesno-
vendimia, vendimiar, *wóyh₁nom
vengar, *weyh₁-
venir, *gʷem-

ventana, *gʷem-, *H₂weH₁-

ventilación, ventilar, ventosa, ventoso, *H₂weH₁-

ver, *weyd-

verano, *wésr̥

veraz, *weh₁-

verbal, verbo, *wekʷ-

verdad, *weh₁-

vergüenza, *wer-

verificación, *weh₁-

verificar, *dheH₁-, *weh₁-

verme, verminoso, *wr̥mis-

vero, *weh₁-

versar, versátil, versión, vértebra, verter, vértice,
 vertir, *wert-

vespa, *wobs-

vesperal, véspero, vespertino, *wek(ʷ)speros

vestido, *wes-

vestigio, *steygʰ-

vestimento, vestir, *wes-

veterano, vetusto, *wet-

vez, *weyk-

via, viaje, viático, *weyh₁-

vicario, vicisitud, víctima, victimar, victoria, *weyk-

vida, *gʷeyh₃-

vidrio, *wed-

viejo, *wet-

viento, *gʷem-, *H₂weH₁-

viernes, *deyn-

vigilancia, vigilante, vigilar, vigilia, vigor, *weǵ-

villa, villano, *weyḱ-

vinaza, *wóyh₁nom

vincular, vínculo, *weyk-

vindicar, vindicta, *weyh₁-

vino, vinoso, viña, viñedo, viñero, *wóyh₁nom

viril, virtud, *wiHrós

visibilidad, visión, visita, visitar, visiva, viso, *weyd-

víspera, *wek(ʷ)speros

visura, *weyd-

vital, *gʷeyh₃-

vitulo, *wet-

viuda, viudedad, *viudo, *h₁weydʰ

vivaz, vívido, viviparo, vivir, vivo, *gʷeyh₃-

vocablo, vocabulario, vocación, vocal, vocativo,
 vociferar, *wekʷ-

volcar, voltear, voluble, volumen, voluntad, *welh₁-

voluta, volver, *welH-

vórtice, *wert-

vos, vosotros, *túh₂

voz, *wekʷ-

voznar, *gʷṓws, *keh₂n-

vuelta, vuelto, *welH-

vuestro, *túh₂

ya, *éy / h₁e

yedra, *weyd-

yegua, *h₁éḱwos

yema, *ǵómbʰos

yer, *dʰǵʰ(y)es-

yesca, *h₁ed-

yo, *egH₂

yugo, *yugóm

Portuguese

-duzir, *dewk-
-mente, *men-
á, *H₂eǵ-
a, *h₂el-
ab-, *h₂pó
abanar, *H₂weH₁-
abantesma, *bʰeh₂-
abdução, abduzir, *dewk-
abelha, *bʰey-
abismo, *dʰewb-
abjudicar, abjuração, abjurar, *h₂eyw-
ablação, ablativo, ablator, *bher-
ablegação, ablegar, *legh-
ablução, abluir, abluto, *lewh₃-
abóbada, *welH-
abolição, abolir, *h₂el-
aborrecer, *gʰers-
abort, abortivo, aborto, *h₃er-
abreviar, *mréǵʰ-
absconder, *dheH₁-
abster, abstinência, abstinente, *ten-
abstruir, *trewd-
ação, *H₂eǵ-
acatar, *keh₂p-
aceiro, *h₂ék
aceitar, *keh₂p-
acerbidade, acerbo, acervo, *h₂ék
acha, *H₂eǵ-
achar, *bʰleh₁-
achegar, *pleḱ-
acididade, ácido, ácie, *h₂ék
aclamação, aclamar, *kelh₁-
aço, *h₂ék
aconchegar, *pleḱ-
aconselhar, *kelh₁-
acordar, acordo, *ḱér
acorrer, *ḱers-
acre, acridade, acrimônia, acritude, *h₂ék
acta, acto, *H₂eǵ-
acúleo, *h₂ék
adauto, *h₂ewg-
adega, *dheH₁-
adem, *h₂eneti-
adergar, *h₃reǵ-
adição, *deH₃-
adicção, adicto, *deyḱ-
adir, *deH₃-
adivinhar, *dyew-
adjudicação, adjudicar, *h₂eyw-
adjunção, adjungir, *yewg-
adjuração, adjurador, *h₂eyw-
adminículo, *méh₂-r̥

administração, administrador, administrar, *mey-
admoestar, admonição, *men-
adorar, *h₃éh₁os
adregar, *h₃reǵ-
adúltero, *h₂el-
adunco, *h₂enk-
aduzir, *dewk-
ádvena, advento, *gʷem-
adverbial, advérbio, *wekʷ-
adverso, advertir, *wert-
advir, *gʷem-
advocação, advocar, advogado, advogar, *wekʷ-
aeruginoso, aerugita, *h₂eyos
afeto, *dheH₁-
afilhar, *dʰeh₁(y)-
afirmação, afirmar, *dʰer-
aflar, afluência, afluente, afluir, *bʰleh₁-
afumar, *dʰewh₂-
agir, agitação, agitador, agitar, *H₂eǵ-
agnome, *h₁nómn̥
agoiro, *h₂ewg-
ágon, agonia, *H₂eǵ-
agosto, agourar, agouro, *h₂ewg-
agre, *h₂ék
agreste, agrícola, agricultor, agricultura, agrimensor,
  agro, *h₂éǵros
água, agueiro, aguoso, *h₂ekʷeh₂-
aí, ainda, *éy / h₁e
aipo, *bʰey-
ala, alar, *H₂eǵ-
albergue, *ker-
alegação, alegar, *legh-
alento, *h₂enh₁-
alfândega, *deḱ-
alguém, algum, *kʷis
algum, *óy-nos
alhures, alí, aliás, álica, alimentar, alimento, *h₂el-
alma, *h₂enh₁-
almário, *h₂er
alocar, *stel-
alterar, altercação, altercar, alto, *h₂el-
alumiar, *lewk-
aluno, álveo, alvéolo, *h₂el-
ambi-, ambiar, ambiente, âmbito, ambos, *h₂ent
ameaça, *men-
ancinho, *h₂enk-
ancípite, *kapōlo
anegar, *neḱ-
anélito, *h₂enh₁-
angular, ângulo, *h₂enk-
angusto, *h₂enǵʰ-
anho, *h₂egʷnos
anima, *h₂enh₁-
aniversário, *wert-
anoitecer, *nókʷts
anónimo, anônimo, *h₁nómn̥
anormal, *ǵneh₃-

anserino, *ǵʰans-
ansiedade, *h₂enǵʰ-
ante, anterior, antes, *h₂ent
antigo, antiguidade, *h₂énti-h₃kʷós
aparar, *peh₂-
apêndice, *pewǵ-
apetição, apetite, apetito, *peth₂
aplaudir, *pleh₂k-
aplicar, *pleḱ-
apor, *teḱ-
após, *h₁epi
apreender, apreensão, aprender, *weyd-
apresentar, *H₁es-
aprovar, *bʰuH-
apud, *h₁epi
aquário, aquático, *h₂ekʷeh₂-
aqueduto, *dewk-, *h₂ekʷeh₂-
aquela, aquelas, aquele, aqueles, *h₂el-
aquiescer, *kʷyeh₁-
aquilo, *h₂el-
aquoso, *h₂ekʷeh₂-
ar, *h₂ews-
arado, arador, *H₂erH₃-
arame, *h₂eyos
aranha, *h₂er
arar, arável, *H₂erH₃-
arbóreo, *h₂erHdʰ-
arca, arcano, *h₂erk-
arção, *h₂erkʷo-
archa, *h₂éḱ
arco, *h₂erkʷo-
arduidade, árduo, *h₂erHdʰ-
arfar, *dheH₁-, *h₂eh₁s-
aríolo, *ǵʰern-
arma, armado, armadura, armar, armário,
  armento, arte, artelho, artículo, artigo, *h₂er
árvore, arvoredo, *h₂erHdʰ-
as, *h₂el-
aspecto, aspeto, *speḱ-
assar, *h₂eh₁s-
assemelhar, *sem-
asserir, *ser-
assim, *só
assimilar, *sem-
assinar, *seḱ-
assistir, *steh₂-
astuto, *h₂éḱ
ata, *H₂eǵ-
até, atenção, atender, atento, ater, *ten-
atividade, ativo, ato, ator, *H₂eǵ-
atrever, atribuir, *bʰuH-
atriz, *H₂eǵ-
atrocidade, atroz, *h₂eh₁tro-h₃kʷs
au-, *h₂pó
audição, audiência, audito, auditor, auditório,
  *h₂ewis-dʰh₁-
auferir, *bher-

auga, *h₂ekʷeh₂-
augurar, áugure, augúrio, *h₂ewg-
aura, *h₂ews-
aurícula, *h₂ew-
aurora, *h₂ews-
auscultador, auscultar, *ḱel-
austral, *h₂ews-
auto, *H₂eǵ-, *h₂ew
automóvel, *h₂ew
autoridade, auxiliar, *h₂ewg-
av-, *h₂pó
avante, *h₂ent
ave, *h₂éwis
avejão, *weyd-
averiguar, *dheH₁-, *weh₁-
avir, *gʷem-
aviso, *weyd-
avô, *h₂éwh₂os
avorrir, *gʰers-
axila, *H₂eǵ-
az, *h₂éḱ
azão, *seH₁-
azevinho, *bʰleh₃-
báculo, *bak-
balestra, balista, *gʷelH-
barba, barbado, *bʰardʰeh₂-
bardo, *gʷerH-
base, *gʷem-
batel, *bʰeyd-
bêbado, bêbedo, bebedor, beber, *peh₃-
bendizer, benzer, *deyḱ-
besta, *gʷelH-
betão, bétula, betume, *gʷet-
biblioteca, *dheH₁-
bíceps, *kapōlo
bife, *gʷốws
binar, *dwóH₁
birô, *péh₂ur
birrota, *Hret-
bodega, *dheH₁-
bódrio, *bʰrewh₁-
boi, boieiro, *gʷốws
bolor, *pelH-
borla, borra, *péh₂ur
bote, *bʰeyd-
botica, *dheH₁-
bovino, *gʷốws
braçal, braço, braquial, *mréǵʰ-
brenha, *bʰerǵʰ-
breve, *mréǵʰ-
brinco, *weyk-
brio, *bʰerǵʰ-
bruma, *mréǵʰ-
bruto, *gʷerh₂-
bucólico, búfalo, *gʷốws
burel, *péh₂ur
burgo, burguês, *bʰerǵʰ-

burla, *péh₂ur
busto, *h₁ews-
búzio, *gʷṓws, *keh₂n-
ca, *kʷis
cabeça, cabeço, cabedal, cabedelo, *kapōlo
caber, *keh₂p-
cabido, cabo, *kapōlo
cabra, cabreiro, *kapro
cabresto, *keh₂p-
cainho, *ḱwṓ
caixa, *keh₂p-
calça, calcadura, calcâneo, calcanhar, calcar,
 calçar, *(s)kel-
calendário, *kelh₁-
câmara, câmara, cambra, *(s)teg-
cambrão, *ḱerh₂-
câmera, camerlengo, campeão, campestre,
 campo, *(s)teg-
canícula, canino, *ḱwṓ
canoro, cantilena, *keh₂n-
cão, *ḱwṓ
capacidade, capaz, capistro, *keh₂p-
capital, capitel, capítulo, *kapōlo
caprino, *kapro
cápsula, captar, captura, *keh₂p-
cara, *ḱerh₂-
carácter, caractere, *ǵʰer-
carme, carmear, carminar, *keh₂n-
carnal, carne, carneiro, carnifice, carnivoro,
 carnoso, *(s)ker-
carpir, *kerp-
carregar, carreira, carreta, carreteiro, carril, carro,
 carroça, carroceiro, carroceria, carruagem, *ḱers-
carta, cartorário, cartulário, *ǵʰer-
catar, cativo, *keh₂p-
catorze, *déḱm̥t
caudal, caudilho, *kapōlo
cavilha, *(s)kel-
cear, *(s)ker-
cegonha, *keh₂n-
ceia, *(s)ker-
cela, celeiro, celha, célula, *ḱel-
cem, centi-, cento, centúria, *ḱm̥tóm
cerebelo, cérebro, *ḱerh₂-
cernir, certar, certo, *krey-
cervo, *ḱerh₂-
chaga, *pleh₂k-
chamar, *kelh₁-
chantagem, chantar, *pleh₂-
chão, *pleh₂-
chave, chavelha, *(s)kel-
chefe, *kapōlo
chegar, *pleḱ-
cheio, *pleh₁-
chor, *bʰleh₃-
chouso, chousura, chouver, *(s)kel-
chover, chuiva, chuva, chuvoso, *plew-

ciclo, *kʷel-
cidade, *ḱei-
ciência, ciente, *skey-
científico, *dheH₁-, *skey-
cílio, *ḱel-
cinco, *pénkʷe
cindir, *skey-
cinquenta, *pénkʷe
circum-navegar, *(s)neh₂-
circunferência, *bher-
circunfluir, *bʰleh₁-
circunstanciar, *steh₂-
circunvolver, *welH-
cisão, *skey-
civel, cívico, cividade, civil, civilizado, *ḱei-
clã, *pleh₂-
clamar, clamor, claridade, *kelh₁-
clarificar, *dheH₁-
claro, classe, clássico, classificação, classificado,
 classificador, classificar, *kelh₁-
claustro, clausura, clavar, clavicula, clavo, *(s)kel-
climactérico, *ḱley-
coágulo, coalho, coatar, cogitação, cogitar, *H₂eǵ-
cognome, *h₁nómn̥
coice, *(s)kel-
coiro, *(s)ker-
coito, *h₁ey-
cole, *kelH-
coleção, colecta, *leǵ-
colega, *legh-
coleta, coleto, *leǵ-
colgar, *stel-
colheita, colheito, colher, coligir, *leǵ-
colina, *kelH-
colmo, *ḱalam-
colocar, *stel-
colónia, colônia, colono, *kʷel-
colorar, *ḱel-
coluna, *kelH-
combinação, combinar, *dwóH₁
comentário, *men-
comer, comida, *h₁ed-
comigo, *H₁me-
como, cómodo, *med-
compêndio, compensação, compensar, *pewǵ-
compilação, compilar, *peys-
complemento, completivo, completo, *pleh₁-
complicação, complicar, *pleḱ-
compor, *tek-
comportar, *per-
compreender, compreensão, compreensivel,
 compreensivo, *weyd-
comprimento, *pleh₁-
comum, comunal, comungar, comunicação,
 comunicar, comutar, *mey-
conca, *ḱonkho-
conceber, conceção, conceição, *keh₂p-

concelho, *kelh₁-
concepção, *keh₂p-
concha, *k̑onkho-
conchegar, *plek̑-
conciliábulo, concílio, *kelh₁-
concionar, *gʷem-
conclave, concluir, *(s)kel-
concorrer, concurso, *k̑ers-
condição, condizer, *deyk̑-
condução, conduto, condutor, conduzir, *dewk-
confecção, confeiçã, confeito, *dheH₁-
conferir, *bher-
confessar, *bʰeh₂-
confiança, confiar, *bʰeydʰ-
confirmação, confirmar, *dʰer-
confissão, *bʰeh₂-
confluir, *bʰleh₁-
confundir, confusão, confuso, *ǵʰew-
congelar, *gel-
côngio, *k̑onkho-
conhecer, *ǵneh₃-
conjungir, conjunto, *yewg-
conosco, *wei
consciência, *skey-
conseguinte, conseguir, *sekʷ-
consenso, consentir, *sent-
consequência, consequente, conseqüente, *sekʷ-
consignar, *sek-
consigo, *s(w)e-
consistir, *steh₂-
consobrinho, *swésōr
consorte, *ser-
constar, *steh₂-
consternar, *sterh₃-
constituição, constituir, *steh₂-
construção, construir, *strew-
contenção, contenças, contender, contente,
  contente, conter, *ten-
contigo, *túh₂
continência, continuo, *ten-
contradição, contraditor, contraditório, contradizer,
  *deyk̑-
contravir, *gʷem-
contribuir, *bʰuH-
controvérsia, controverso, *wert-
contubernal, contubérnio, *treb-
contusão, *(s)tew-
convenção, *gʷem-
convencer, *weyk-
conveniência, conveniente, convento, *gʷem-
conversa, conversação, conversar, converter, *wert-
convício, *wekʷ-
convidar, *weyh₁-
convir, *gʷem-
convocar, *wekʷ-
convosco, *túh₂
coorte, *ǵʰer-

cor, *k̑el-, *k̑ér
corar, *k̑el-
corda, *ǵʰern-
coriáceo, *(s)ker-
córneo, corno, cornudo, *k̑erh₂-
corpo, *krep-
correção, correcção, correia, *h₃reǵ-
corrente, correr, *k̑ers-
correto, corretor, corrigir, *h₃reǵ-
corso, *k̑ers-
cortar, *(s)ker-
corte, *ǵʰer-
cortiça, córtice, cortíceo, cortiço, *(s)ker-
coser, *sīw-
cosso, *k̑ers-
costume, *swe-dʰh₁-
coudel, *kapōlo
couraça, couro, *(s)ker-
coxa, coxo, *kok̑s-
cozer, cozinha, cozinhar, cozinheiro, *pekʷ-
crânio, *k̑erh₂-
cravar, cravelha, cravo, *(s)kel-
crédito, credível, credor, crédulo, crer, *dheH₁-
crivar, *krey-
crível, *dheH₁-
crivo, *krey-
cru, cruel, crueldade, cruentar, cruento, cruor, *krewh₂-
cuidação, cuidado, cuidar, *H₂eǵ-
cujo, *kʷis-
cultor, cultura, *kʷel-
cume, *kelH-
cumprimento, cumprir, *pleh₁-
currículo, curso, cursor, *k̑ers-
curtir, *terh₁-
curto, *(s)ker-
curul, *k̑ers-
custar, *steh₂-
dada, dado, *deH₃-
dama, *dem-
danar, dano, *deh₂-
dar, data, *deH₃-
débil, débito, *ǵʰeh₁bʰ-
década, decano, *dék̑m̥t
decepcionar, *keh₂p-
décima, decimal, decimar, décimo, *dék̑m̥t
declamar, declarar, *kelh₁-
decorar, decoro, *dek-
decorrente, decorrer, *k̑ers-
dedal, dedo, *deyk̑-
dedução, deduzir, *dewk-
defender, defensão, *gʷʰen-
deferir, *bher-
defluir, *bʰleh₁-
degenerar, *ǵenH₁-
deidade, *dyew-
delação, *bher-
delegar, *legh-

delinquência, delinquir, *leykʷ-
delirio, *leys-
demandar, *deH₃-
demência, *men-
demónio, *deh₂-
demonstração, demonstrar, *men-
demudar, *mey-
denário, *déḱm̥t
dental, dente, *h₃dónts
dentro, *h₁én
denudar, *negʷ-
depender, *pewǵ-
depois, *h₁epi
depor, *teḱ-
deportar, *per-
deposto, *teḱ-
deprecar, *preḱ-
depreender, *weyd-
deque, *(s)teg-
derivar, *h₃reyH-
des-, *dwóH₁
descalçar, *(s)kel-
descarregar, *ḱers-
descrever, descrição, *(s)ker-
desejo, *sed-
desenhar, *sek-
desidia, *sed-
designar, *sek-
desistir, *steh₂-
desnudar, *negʷ-
despeitar, *speḱ-
despir, *ped-
despregar, *pleḱ-
destinar, destituir, *steh₂-
destro, *deḱs-
destruir, *strew-
detenção, deter, *ten-
detonar, *(s)tenh₂-
deus, *dyew-
devedor, dever, *gʰeh₁bʰ-
devir, *gʷem-
devolver, *welH-
dez, dezembre, *déḱm̥t
dia, *deyn-
diabo, *gʷelH-
diante, *h₂ent
diarreia, *srew-
dicaz, dicção, dicionário, dictum, *deyḱ-
diferir, *bher-
difícil, *dheH₁-
difluir, *bʰleh₁-
difundir, difuso, *ǵʰew-
digital, dígito, *deyḱ-
dignar, dignidade, digno, *deḱ-
diligente, *leǵ-
diluir, *lewh₃-
dinheiro, *déḱm̥t

dinidade, dino, *deḱ-
direito, direto, dirigir, *h₃reǵ-
dis-, *dwóH₁
discernir, *krey-
discorrer, *ḱers-
discriminar, *krey-
discurso, *ḱers-
dispor, *teḱ-
dissecar, *sek-
disseminar, *seH₁-
dissentir, *sent-
dissimil, dissimular, *sem-
distanciar, *steh₂-
distender, *ten-
distribuir, *bʰuH-
ditador, ditadura, ditar, dito, *deyḱ-
diurnal, diurno, *deyn-
diva, *dyew-
diverso, divertir, *wert-
dívida, *gʰeh₁bʰ-
divindade, *dyew-
divisão, divisível, divisor, *h₁weydʰ-
dizer, *deyḱ-
dízima, dizimar, dízimo, *déḱm̥t
doação, doar, *deH₃-
doas, *dwóH₁
dobrar, dobre, dobro, *pleh₁-
dócil, docto, documento, dogma, *deḱ-
dois, *dwóH₁
dom, *deH₃-
Dom, *dem-
domar, *dem-, *demh₂-
doméstico, domicílio, dominar, *dem-
domingo, *deyn-
dominio, dona, dono, donzela, *dem-
dotar, dote, *deH₃-
douto, doutor, doutrina, *deḱ-
doze, *déḱm̥t
dúbio, *gʰeh₁bʰ-
dublar, *pleh₁-
ducado, ducto, *dewk-
duplo, *pleh₁-
duque, *dewk-
durar, duraz, durázio, dureza, duro, *deru-
duto, *dewk-
duzentos, *ḱm̥tóm
eclodir, *(s)kel-
edição, *deH₃-
edicula, edificação, edificar, edificio, edil, *h₂eydʰ-
edito, *deyḱ-
editor, *deH₃-
educação, educar, eduzir, *dewk-
efeito, efetivo, *dheH₁-
efluir, eflúvio, *bʰleh₁-
efundir, efusão, *ǵʰew-
ego, *egH₂
égua, *h₁éḱwos

eis, *h_1eǵʰs
eixo, *H_2eǵ-
ela, *$h_2$el-
elação, *bher-
elas, ele, *$h_2$el-
elegante, eleger, eleito, *leǵ-
elemento, eles, *$h_2$el-
elevar, *$h_1$lengʷʰ-
elucubrar, *lewk-
em, *$h_1$én
embeber, *peh_3-
empiorar, *ped-
empreender, *weyd-
empregar, *plek-
emprender, empresa, *weyd-
enarração, *ǵneh_3-
encantar, *keh_2n-
encher, *pleh_1-
endurecer, *deru-
éneo, *$h_2$eyos
energia, *werǵ-
enfermidade, enfermo, *dʰer-
engendrar, *ǵenH_1-
enguia, *angʷ(h)i-
enorme, *ǵneh_3-
ensinar, *sek-
então, *só
ente, *H_1es-
entender, *ten-
entidade, *H_1es-
entrar, entre, *$h_1$én
entusiasmo, *dʰéh_1s
enumerar, *nem-
envidar, *weyh_1-
envolto, envolver, *welH-
enxada, *$h_2$ék
enxame, *H_2eǵ-
enxerir, *ser-
época, *seǵʰ-
equino, *$h_1$ékwos
erário, *$h_2$eyos
erguer, erigir, *$h_3$reǵ-
eruginoso, *$h_2$eyos
escluso, *(s)kel-
escola, *seǵʰ-
esconder, *dheH_1-
escoriar, *(s)ker-
escorrer, *ḱers-
escrever, escrito, escritura, escrópulo, escrúpulo,
  escrutar, escrutínio, *(s)ker-
ésculo, *$h_2$eyǵ-
escuma, *poymno-
escutar, *ḱel-
esgrimir, *(s)ker-
esmorecer, *mer-
espécie, espécime, espectro, especulação,
  especular, espéculo, espelho, *speḱ-

esperança, esperar, *speh_1-
esperiência, *per-
espiar, *speḱ-
espiga, espinal, espinha, espinho, espinhoso,
  espínula, *spey-
esplenético, *splenǵʰ-
espuma, espumar, espumoso, *poymno-
esquema, *seǵʰ-
esquiar, esquilar, *(s)ker-
essa, essas, *éy / h_1e
esse, *éy / h_1e, *s(w)e-
essência, *H_1es-
esses, *éy / h_1e
esta, *só
estabelecer, estabular, estábulo, estação, estado,
  estame, estâmina, estar, *steh_2-
estas, *só
estatuir, estável, *steh_2-
este, *só
esteira, *sterh_3-
esteiro, *$h_2$eydʰ-
estelar, *$h_2$stḗr
estender, *ten-
estes, *só
estio, estivo, *$h_2$eydʰ-
estore, *sterh_3-
estrabo, *steh_2-
estrada, estrado, *sterh_3-
estranho, *h_1eǵʰs
estratega, estrato, *sterh_3-
estrela, *$h_2$stḗr
estresir, *$h_1$ey-
estrondo, *(s)tenh_2-
estuário, *$h_2$eydʰ-
estudante, estudar, estúdio, estudo, estúpido, estupro,
  estuque, *(s)tew-
éter, *$h_2$eydʰ-
eternidade, eterno, *$h_2$ey-
etnia, *swe-dʰh_1-
eu, *egH_2
evencer, *weyk-
evento, eventualidade, *gʷem-
eversor, everter, *wert-
evidência, *weyd-
evo, *$h_2$ey-
evolução, evoluir, *welH-
exacerbar, *$h_2$ék
exame, examinar, *H_2eǵ-
excelência, excelente, *kelH-
exceler, *kelH-
excluir, *(s)kel-
excretar, *krey-
excursão, *ḱers-
execução, *sekʷ-
exercício, exército, *$h_2$erk-
exibir, *gʰeh_1bʰ-
êxito, *$h_1$ey-

exortação, *ǵʰer-

expandir, *petʰ₂

expedir, *ped-

expender, expensas, *pewǵ-

experto, *per-

explicar, *pleḱ-

expor, *teḱ-

exportação, exportar, *per-

expugnar, expungir, *pewǵ-

exsurgir, *h₃reǵ-

êxtase, extático, *steh₂-

extensão, extenso, *ten-

exterior, externo, extra-, extremo, *h₁eǵʰs

extrínseco, *sekʷ-

extrudir, *trewd-

fabela, fábula, fabuloso, *bʰeh₂-

facção, facienda, facínora, facto, factor, *dheH₁-

fado, *bʰeh₂-

faia, *bʰeh₂go-

faina, *dheH₁-

fala, fama, *bʰeh₂-

familia, familiar, fâmulo, *dheH₁-

fanático, *dʰéh₁s

fantasma, *bʰeh₂-

farelo, farinha, farinheiro, farinhoso, farragem,

　fárreo, farro, *bʰars-

fasto, *bʰeh₂-

fato, *dheH₁-

fava, *bʰabʰeh₂-

fazenda, fazer, *dheH₁-

fé, *bʰeydʰ-

febre, *dʰegʷʰ-

feição, *dheH₁-

feira, *dʰéh₁s

feito, feitor, *dheH₁-

felicidade, feliz, fêmea, feminino, *dʰeh₁(y)-

fender, bʰeyd-

fenómeno, *bʰeh₂-

fera, *ǵʰwer-

feral, féria, *dʰéh₁s

feroz, *ǵʰweroh₃kʷs

festa, festival, festividade, festivo, festo, *dʰéh₁s

feto, *dʰeh₁(y)-

feudo, *peḱu-

fevereiro, *dʰegʷʰ-

fiar, *bʰeydʰ-

ficto, *dʰeyǵʰ-

fiel, *bʰeydʰ-

figura, *dʰeyǵʰ-

filha, filhastro, filho, filhó, *dʰeh₁(y)-

fingir, finta, *dʰeyǵʰ-

firmamento, firmar, firme, *dʰer-

fissão, fissure, fístula, *bʰeyd-

fita, *dʰeyǵʰ-

flabelo, flâmine, flato, *bʰleh₁-

flor, florir, flósculo, *bʰleh₃-

fluente, fluir, flume, flúmen, flutuação, flutuar,

fluxo, *bʰleh₁-

folha, folho, folhoso, fólio, *bʰleh₃-

fomento, *dʰegʷʰ-

fona, *péh₂ur

força, *bʰerǵʰ-

formiga, formigar, *morwi-

forno, *gʷʰer-

foro, *dʰwer-

forte, fortidão, fortitude, *bʰerǵʰ-

fortuito, fortuna, *bher-

fórum, *dʰwer-

fosco, *dʰewh₂-

frade, fraternidade, *bʰréh₂tēr

fraxíneo, *bʰereǵ-

frei, *bʰréh₂tēr

freio, *dʰer-

freira, freire, *bʰréh₂tēr

freixo, *bʰereǵ-

frete, *h₂eyḱ-

frol, *bʰleh₃-

fui, *bʰuH-

fuinha, *bʰeh₂go-

fuligem, fumar, fumegar, fumigar, fumo, *dʰewh₂-

fundador, fundamento, *ǵʰew-

fundar, *bʰudʰmén

fundíbulo, fundir, *ǵʰew-

fundo, *bʰudʰmén

funil, *ǵʰew-

furão, furto, *bher-

fusão, *ǵʰew-

fusco, *dʰewh₂-

futuro, *bʰuH-

gabre, *kapro

gadanha, *weyh₁-

ganso, *ǵʰans-

gastar, *h₁weh₂-

gear, gelar, gélido, gelo, *gel-

gema, *ǵómbʰos

general, gênero, génio, genitivo, genitor, gente, gentil,

　gentio, gentio, geral, gerar, *ǵenH₁-

gerir, *H₂eǵ-

germanidade, germano, germe, germinar, *ǵenH₁-

gerúndio, gesto, *H₂eǵ-

glória, glorioso, *ǵneh₃-

gonfo-, gonzo, *ǵómbʰos

gostar, gosto, *ǵews-

graça, gracioso, grado, *gʷerH-

grama, *gʰreh₁-

gramatica, *gerbʰ-

gramíneo, *gʰreh₁-

grão, *ǵrHnom

gratidão, gratificar, grátis, grato, gratuito, *gʷerH-

grave, gravidade, grávido, *gʷerh₂-

grego, *ǵerh₂-

groma, *ǵneh₃-

grou, grua, grulha, *gerh₂-

guardar, guarnir, *wer-

guiar, *weyd-
guru, *gʷerh₂-
hábil, habilidade, habitação, habitante, habitar,
 hábito, *gʰeh₁bʰ-
haríolo, *ǵʰern-
haver, *gʰeh₁bʰ-
hegemonia, *seh₂g-
hera, *weyd-
hérnia, *ǵʰern-
hesterno, *dʰǵʰ(y)es-
hibernal, hibernar, *ǵʰey-
hiena, *suH-
hipoteca, *dheH₁-
história, histórico, *weyd-
hodierno, hoje, *deyn-
homem, *ǵʰmó
hora, *yeh₁-
hórrido, horrível, horror, *gʰers-
horta, hortelão, horto, *ǵʰer-
hospedal, hospedar, hóspede, hospício, hospital,
 hospitalidade, hostal, hoste, hotel, *gʰóstis
humano, *ǵʰmó
húmil, humilde, húmile, humo, húmus, *dʰéǵʰōm
idade, *h₂ey-
ideia, *weyd-
idêntico, identidade, *éy / h₁e
ídolo, *weyd-
ignominia, *h₁nómṇ
ignorante, ignorar, ignoto, *ǵneh₃-
ilação, ilativo, *bher-
ilegal, *leǵ-, *legh-
iluminar, *lewk-
im-, *ṇ-
imaturo, *meh₂-
imbecil, *bak-
imberbe, *bʰardʰeh₂-
imolar, *melh₂-
impacto, *peh₂ǵ-
impedir, *ped-
ímpeto, *peth₂
implicação, implicar, *pleḱ-
importar, importunidade, importuno, *per-
improbar, *bʰuH-
improbo, *bʰuH-, *per-
improvar, *bʰuH-
impune, *kʷey-
imutar, *mey-
in-, *ṇ-
inalar, *h₂enh₁-
incentivo, *keh₂n-
inchação, inchado, inchar, *bʰleh₁-
inclinação, inclinar, *ḱley-
inclito, *ḱlew-
incluir, incluso, *(s)kel-
incola, *kʷel-
incorrer, *ḱers-
incrédulo, incrível, *dheH₁-

inculcar, *(s)kel-
incursão, *ḱers-
indemne, *deh₂-
índex, índice, indício, *deyḱ-
índole, *h₂el-
indução, *dewk-
industria, industrioso, *strew-
induzir, *dewk-
infâmia, infando, infante, *bʰeh₂-
inferir, *bher-
inflação, inflado, inflar, influir, *bʰleh₁-
infundir, *ǵʰew-
inibir, *gʰeh₁bʰ-
iniciar, inicio, *h₁ey-
inocente, *neḱ-
inocular, *h₃ekʷ-
inquilino, *kʷel-
inscícia, insciente, *skey-
inserir, *ser-
inseto, insigne, insígnia, *sek-
insistir, *steh₂-
insólito, *swe-dʰh₁-
insonte, *H₁es-
instituir, instituto, *steh₂-
instrução, *strew-
intelecção, intelecto, inteligir, *leǵ-
intenção, intender, intenso, intento, *ten-
intercalar, *kelh₁-
interdizer, *deyḱ-
interesse, *h₁én, *H₁es-
interior, *h₁én
intervir, *gʷem-
intrínseco, *sekʷ-
introdução, introduzir, *dewk-
inundar, *wed-
invenção, inventor, *gʷem-
invernar, inverno, *ǵʰey-
inverter, *wert-
investigação, investigar, *steygʰ-
investir, *wes-
invido, *weyd-
invitar, *weyh₁-
involuto, *welH-
ir, *h₁ey-
irmandade, irmão, *ǵenH₁-
ironia, *wekʷ-
isca, *h₁ed-
isso, *éy / h₁e
isto, *só
já, *éy / h₁e
janeiro, janella, *h₁ey-
jardim, *ǵʰer-
joelho, *ǵónu
jogar, jogo, jogral, *yek-
jorna, jornal, *deyn-
jovem, *h₂yuh₁en-
judicial, judiciário, *h₂eyw-

jugo, *yugóm
juiz, julgador, julgar, *h₂eyw-
junção, jungir, junguir, *yewg-
júnior, *h₂yuh₁en-
juntar, *yewg-
juramento, jurar, juro, *h₂eyw-
justar, *yewg-
justeza, justiça, justo, *h₂eyw-
juvenco, juvenil, juventude, *h₂yuh₁en-
lã, *h₂welh₁-
lábio, labro, *leb-
lacrimar, lacrimoso, *daḱru-
lactário, *glag-
lacuna, lago, lagoa, *lókus
lágrima, *daḱru-
laguna, *lókus
lamber, *leb-
laneiro, lanoso, *h₂welh₁-
laticínio, *glag-
latrina, lava, lavar, *lewh₃-
leal, *leǵ-, *legh-
legação, *legh-
legal, *leǵ-, *legh-
legião, *leǵ-
legislação, *leǵ-, *legh-
legislador, *legh-
legítimo, *leǵ-, *legh-
leguiejo, leguleio, *legh-
legume, *leǵ-
lei, *leǵ-, *legh-
leite, leiteiro, *glag-
leito, *legh-
leitor, *leǵ-
leitoso, leituga, *glag-
lembrar, *men-
lenço, lençol, *lino-
lenha, lenhador, lenheiro, lenho, lenhoso, ler, *leǵ-
levado, levantar, levar, leve, lêvedo, *h₁lengʷʰ-
libelo, *lewbʰ-
liberação, liberador, liberar, liberdade, *h₁lewdʰ-
lição, *leǵ-
lídimo, *leǵ-, *legh-
ligeiro, *h₁lengʷʰ-
lindo, *leǵ-, *legh-
líneo, *lino-
língua, *dn̩ǵʰwéh₂s
linha, linheiro, linho, *lino-
liteira, *legh-
livração, livrador, livrar, livre, *h₁lewdʰ-
livreiro, livro, *lewbʰ-
lobo, *wĺkʷos
lobrigar, *lewk-
locação, local, loco, lóculo, locus, lócus, logo, *stel-
logos, *leǵ-
lombo, *lendʰ-
longevidade, longevo, *h₂ey-
lontra, *udréh₂

lua, luar, lucerna, lúcido, lucifero, lucubração, lucubrar,
  *lewk-
lugar, *stel-
Luis, *ḱlew-
lume, lumeeira, lumieira, luminar, luminária, luminoso,
  lunar, lunático, lusco, *lewk-
luta, lutador, lutar, luxo, luxúria, luxurioso, *seh₂g-
luz, luzerna, luzir, *lewk-
madeira, madre, *méh₂tēr
maduro, *meh₂-
mãe, *méh₂tēr
maestro, magister, magistrado, magnata, magnate,
  magno, *méǵh₂s
magro, *meh₂ḱ-
maior, mais, maiúsculo, majestade, major, *méǵh₂s
maldição, maldito, maldizer, *deyḱ-
mama, mamã, *méh₂-méh₂
manápula, *pleh₁-
mandar, *deH₃-
mandibula, manducar, *mendʰ-
maneira, maneiro, mangual, *méh₂-r̥
manhã, *meh₂-
manho, *méǵh₂s
manícula, manilha, *méh₂-r̥
manípulo, *pleh₁-
manjar, *mendʰ-
mano, *ǵenH₁-
manopla, *pleh₁-
mansidão, manso, mansuetude, *swe-dʰh₁-
manter, *ten-
mantra, *men-
manuário, manubial, mão, *méh₂-r̥
mar, marinho, marino, *móri
mas, *méǵh₂s
mastigar, *mendʰ-
matar, *méǵh₂s, *meh₂ḱ-
matéria, materno, *méh₂tēr
matina, *meh₂-
matricida, matrícula, matrimónio, matriz, matrona,
  *méh₂tēr
maturo, matutino, *meh₂-
máximo, *méǵh₂s
me, *H₁me-
meado, meão, mear, mediador, mediano, mediar,
  *médʰyos
medicar, medicina, medicinal, médico, *med-
medida, *meh₁-
médio, *médʰyos
medíocre, *h₂ék, *médʰyos
medir, *meh₁-
mediterrâneo, medula, meio, *médʰyos
mel, *melit-
membrana, membro, *méms
memorar, memorável, memória, menção, mendace,
  mendaz, *men-
menhã, *meh₂-
menisco, *méh₁n̩s

menor, menos, *mey-

menstrual, menstruar, *méh₁ns

mensurar, *meh₁-

mental, mente, *men-

mentes, *éy / h₁e

mentir, *men-

menu, *mey-

meridio, *deyn-, *médʰyos

mês, *méh₁ns

mesa, mesário, *meh₁-

mesclar, *mey-

mesmo, *éy / h₁e

mesmo, *s(w)e-

mester, mestiço, *mey-

mestro, *méǵh₂s

mesura, mesurar, *meh₁-

metade, *médʰyos

meu, meus, *H₁meme-

mexer, *mey-

mezinha, *med-

mídia, *médʰyos

migrar, *mey-

mijar, *h₃meyǵʰ-

mil, milheiro, miliário, *sem-

mim, *H₁me-

minaz, *men-

minguar, *mey-

minha, minhas, *H₁meme-

mínimo, ministério, ministro, minúcia, minuir, *mey-

miolo, *médʰyos

miscrar, mister, mistura, miúça, miúdo, *mey-

mó, *melh₂-

moderar, moderno, modesto, módico, modificar, modo, módulo, *med-

moeda, *men-

moer, moinho, *melh₂-

moio, *med-

molar, *melh₂-

molde, *med-

moleiro, *melh₂-

monir, monstro, montanha, montanhoso, montano, monte, monticulo, montijo, monumento, *men-

mor, *méǵh₂s

moribundo, morrer, morte, morto, *mer-

mosca, mosquito, *mus-

mostrar, *men-

mudar, *mey-

multiplicação, multiplicar, *pleḱ-

mungir, *H₂melǵ-

município, munificência, munifico, múnus, *mey-

mure, murganho, muro, muscular, músculo, musculoso, *muh₂s-

mutar, mutuar, mútuo, *mey-

nação, nada, *ǵenH₁-

nadador, nadar, *(s)neh₂-

nado, *ǵenH₁-

narina, nariz, *néh₂s

narrar, *ǵneh₃-

nascer, natal, Natal, natalício, natividade, nato, natura, natural, naturalidade, *ǵenH₁-

nau, náufrago, náutico, naval, nave, navegação, navegar, navio, *(s)neh₂-

nebuloso, *nebʰ-

nefando, nefário, nefas, nefasto, *bʰeh₂-

negligência, *leǵ-

negociador, negociar, negócio, *h₂ew

nemoral, nemoroso, *nem-

nervo, nervoso, *(s)neh₁-

neta, neto, *nepot-

neve, *sneygʷʰ-

nevo, *ǵenH₁-

névoa, *nebʰ-

nevoso, *sneygʷʰ-

ninho, *nisdós

nobre, noção, *ǵneh₃-

nocivo, *neḱ-

nódoa, *ǵneh₃-

noite, *nókʷts

nombro, *nem-

nome, nomear, nomenclatura, nominação, nominal, nominar, *h₁nómṇ

nora, *snusós

norma, normal, *ǵneh₃-

norte, *h₁én

nós, nosso, *wei

nota, notar, notário, notícia, noto, nótula, *ǵneh₃-

noturno, *nókʷts

nove, *H₁néwṇ

novecentos, *H₁néwṇ, *ḱṃtóm

novena, noventa, *H₁néwṇ

novidade, novilho, novo, *new

nu, *negʷ-

numerar, número, numerosidade, *nem-

nunca, *kʷis

o, *h₂el-

obedecer, obediente, *h₂ewis-dʰh₁-

Óbidos, *ped-

objeto, *h₁epi

oblação, oblata, oblato, *bher-

obra, *h₃ep-

obrada, *bher-

obrar, *h₃ep-

obreia, *bher-

obreiro, *h₃ep-

obstar, *steh₂-

obstrução, obstruir, obstrutivo, *strew-

obter, *ten-

obviar, óbvio, *weyh₁-

ócio, ocioso, *h₂ew

ocorrer, *ḱers-

ocular, óculo, óculos, *h₃ekʷ-

ocupação, ocupar, *keh₂p-

odiar, ódio, odioso, odor, *h₃ed-

odre, *wed-

oeste, *wek(ʷ)speros
oferecer, *bher-
oficial, ofício, *h₃ep-
oira, *h₂ews-
oito, *oktṓw
oitocentos, *ḱm̥tóm
olho, *h₃ekʷ-
omnipotente, *H₁es-
onda, *wed-
onde, *kʷis
onipotente, *H₁es-
ónix, *h₃negʰ-
onvólvulo, *welH-
onze, *déḱm̥t
ópera, operar, operário, *h₃ep-
ópido, *ped-
opor, *h₁epi, *teḱ-
oportunidade, oportuno, *per-
opugnar, *pewǵ-
ora, *yeh₁-
oráculo, orago, orar,oração, *h₃éh₁os
ordem, ordenar, ordenhar, ordinário, *h₂er
orelha, *h₂ew-
órgão, *werǵ-
oriental, oriente, origem, originário, oriundo, *h₃er-
ornar, *h₂er
os, *h₂el-
osso, *h₃ésth₁
ostentação, ostentar, *ten-
ou, *h₂ew
oura, *h₂ews-
ouriço, *ǵʰér
outro, *h₂el-
ouvido, ouvidor, ouvinte, ouvir, *h₂ewis-dʰh₁-
ova, *h₂ōwyóm
ovelha, ovino, *h₂ówis
ovo, *h₂ōwyóm
pá, *peh₂ǵ-
pábulo, *peh₂-
pacifico, *peh₂ǵ-
padrasto, padre, *ph₂tér
paganismo, pagão, pagar, pagela, página, *peh₂ǵ-
pai, *ph₂tér
painço, *peh₂-
país, pala, *peh₂ǵ-
palavra, *gʷelH-
pálido, palor, *pelH-
palude, paludoso, palustre, *peh₂ǵ-
paneiro, pão, *peh₂-
para, *per-
parábola, *gʷelH-
paraíso, *dʰeyǵʰ-
parcimónia, parco, *h₂erk-
parecer, pascer, *peh₂-
passa, passar, pássaro, passo, *peth₂
pastilha, pasto, pastor, *peh₂-
patela, *peth₂

paternidade, paterno, patrão, património, patrimônio,
  patriota, patrono, *ph₂tér
paul, paz, *peh₂ǵ-
pé, *pṓds
pecado, pecador, pecar, *ped-
peçonha, *peh₃-
pécora, pecuária, peculio, pecúnia, pecuniário, *peḱu-
pedicelo, pediculo, *pṓds
pedir, *peth₂
pegureiro, *peḱu-
peixe, peixeiro, *peisḱ-
pejorar, *ped-
pele, peleiro, película, *pel-
pena, *kʷey-, *péth₂r
pender, *pewǵ-
penetração, penetrante, penetrar, *peh₂-
pensar, *pewǵ-
pente, pentear, pentelho, *peḱ-
per, *per-
perceber, perceção, *keh₂p-
percolar, *kʷel-
percorrer, *ḱers-
perda, perder, perdição, *deH₃-
perecer, *h₁ey-
peregrinar, peregrino, *h₂éǵros
perfazer, perfeito, *dheH₁-
perícia, periclitar, perigo, perigoso, perito, *per-
perjúrio, perjuro, *h₂eyw-
perlavar, *lewh₃-
permutar, *mey-
perseguir, *sekʷ-
persistir, *steh₂-
pertencer, pertinente, *ten-
pesar, *pewǵ-
pescar, *peisḱ-
peso, *pewǵ-
péssimo, *ped-
pestilo, *peh₂ǵ-
pia, *peys-
piano, *pleh₂-
pigmento, *peyk-
pilhar, pilo, *peys-
pimenta, pintar, pintor, pintura, *peyk-
pior, piorar, *ped-
pisar, *peys-
piscina, piscoso, *peisḱ-
pistrina, *peys-
plangente, planger, *pleh₂k-
plano, planta, plantago, plantar, plateia, *pleh₂-
plebe, *pleh₁-
plectro, *pleh₂k-
plenário, plenitud, pleno, *pleh₁-
plicar, *pleḱ-
pluralidade, *pleh₁-
pluvial, pluvioso, *plew-
poção, *peh₃-
poder, *H₁es-

podestade, *pótis
pódio, *pṓds
poente, *teḱ-
poio, *pṓds
pois, *h₁epi
polegar, pólex, pólice, *h₂welh₁-
poluir, *lewh₃-
pomes, *poymno-
ponente, *teḱ-
ponta, *pewǵ-
ponte, pontifice, *pent-
ponto, *pewǵ-
população, popular, *pleh₁-
por, *per-
pôr, *teḱ-
porão, *pleh₂-
porca, porcino, porco, porqueiro, *pórḱos
port, porta, portão, portar, porteiro, *per-
portento, *ten-
pórtico, porto, *per-
posca, *peh₃-
posição, *teḱ-
possessão, possessor, *pótis
possivel, *H₁es-
possuir, *pótis
poste, *teḱ-
póstero, postigo, *h₁epi
posto, *teḱ-
potável, *peh₃-
potência, potente, *H₁es-
potestade, *pótis
povo, povoação, *pleh₁-
praça, *pleh₂-
practicar, *per-
praga, *pleh₂k-
pragmático, *per-
prantar, *pleh₂-
prantear, pranto, *pleh₂k-
práxis, *per-
prear, *deH₃-, *weyd-
precário, prece, *preḱ-
precioso, preço, *per-
preda, *weyd-
predação, predador, *deH₃-, *weyd-
predar, *deH₃-
predição, *deyḱ-
prédio, *wedʰ-
predizer, *deyḱ-
preensão, *weyd-
preferir, *bher-
pregar, *pleḱ-
preia, *weyd-
prejudicar, prejuízo, *h₂eyw-
prender, *weyd-
preocupação, preocupar, *keh₂p-
prepor, *teḱ-
prepóstero, *h₁epi

prescrever, *(s)ker-
presentar, presente, *H₁es-
presidente, presidir, *sed-
preso, *weyd-
pressagiar, *seh₂g-
prestar, *steh₂-
pretender, pretenso, *ten-
prevenir, *gʷem-
prever, *weyd-
prévio, *weyh₁-
primário, primeiro,primo, *per-
primogênito, *ǵenH₁-, *per-
principe, principio, *keh₂p-
prisão, *weyd-
prisco, prístino, privação, privado, privar, pró, proa,
   *per-
probidade, *bʰuH-
problema, problemático, *gʷelH-
probo, *bʰuH-, *per-
procace, procaz, *preḱ-
proclamar, *kelh₁-
produção, produtivo, produto, produzir, *dewk-
profanar, profano, *dʰéh₁s
proferir, *bher-
professor, profissão, *bʰeh₂-
profundidade, profundo, *ǵʰew-
programa, *gerbʰ-
proibir, *gʰeh₁bʰ-
prole, proletariado, *h₂el-
promíscuo, *mey-
prono, *per-
propagar, *peh₂ǵ-
propínquo, *per-
propor, propósito, *teḱ-
propriedade, próprio, *preyH-
prosa, *wert-
prosperar, *speh₁-
prosseguir, *sekʷ-
prosternar, *sterh₃-
prostituir, *steh₂-
prostrar, *sterh₃-
proteger, *(s)teg-
protervo, *terh₁-
prova, provar, provável, *bʰuH-
provento, *gʷem-
prover, próvido, *weyd-
província, provincial, *per-
provir, *gʷem-
provocar, *wekʷ-
próximo, *per-
público, *pleh₁-
púcaro, *peh₃-
púgil, pugnaz, *pewǵ-
pulga, *plou-
pulmão, *plewmō
punção, punçar, pungir, punho, *pewǵ-
punição, punir, *kʷey-

quadrado, quadrar, quadrelo, *k^{w}etwóres

quadriga, *yugóm

quadro, *k^{w}etwóres

quádruplo, *pleh$_1$-

qual, qualidade, *k^{w}is

quarto, *k^{w}etwóres

quatorze, *dékm̥t

quatro, *k^{w}etwóres

quatrocentos, *ḱm̥tóm

que, *k^{w}is

quedo, *k^{w}yeh$_1$-

quem, *k^{w}is

querco, *perk^{w}u-

quieto, *k^{w}yeh$_1$-

quinhentos, *ḱm̥tóm

quinze, *dékm̥t

quociente, *k^{w}is

ração, rácio, *h$_2$er

radical, rádio, *wréh$_2$ds

rainha, *h$_3$reǵ-

raio, raiz, ramifico, ramo, ramoso, râmulo, *wréh$_2$ds

rasgar, *sek-

razão, *h$_2$er

real, *h$_3$reǵ-

recalcitrar, *(s)kel-

receber, receita, recepção, receptáculo, *keh$_2$p-

reclamar, *kelh$_1$-

recolher, *leǵ-

recompensar, *pewǵ-

recôndito, *dheH$_1$-

reconhecer, *ǵneh$_3$-

recordar, *ḱér

recorrer, *ḱers-

rédea, *ten-

rédito, *h$_1$ey-

redondo, *Hret-

redução, reduto, reduzir, *dewk-

refazer, refeição, *dheH$_1$-

referir, *bher-

refluir, *b^{h}leh$_1$-

reger, regime, regra, régua, rei, reinar, reino, reixa, *h$_3$reǵ-

relação, *bher-

relegação, relegar, *legh-

relembrar, *men-

relevar, *h$_1$leng^{wh}-

relha, *h$_3$reǵ-

relvar, *h$_1$leng^{wh}-

remédio, *med-

remembrar, rememorar, *men-

render, *deH$_3$-

renovar, *new

repetir, *peth$_2$

repleto, *pleh$_1$-

replicar, *pleḱ-

repor, *teḱ-

reportar, *per-

repreender, repreensão, repreensivel, *weyd-

representar, *H$_1$es-

reprovar, *b^{h}uH-

república, *pleh$_1$-

repugnar, *pewǵ-

réquia, réquie, requiem, *k^{w}yeh$_1$-

rescindir, *skey-

resenhar, *sek-

residir, residuo, *sed-

resignar, *sek-

resistir, *steh$_2$-

respeitar, respeito, *speḱ-

restar, restaurar, resto, *steh$_2$-

retenção, reter, *ten-

reto, *h$_3$reǵ-

rever, *weyd-

reverência, reverente, *wer-

reversar, revessar, *wert-

revir, *g^{w}em-

revista, revistar, *weyd-

revolução, revolver, *welH-

rico, *h$_3$reǵ-

rio, *h$_3$reyH-

ritmo, *srew-

rito, *h$_2$er

rivalidade, *h$_3$reyH-

roda, rodar, rodela, rolha, rolo, *Hret-

ronha, *h$_2$er

rossio, *sed-

rotação, rotar, rótula, rótulo, rotundo, *Hret-

rouxinol, *keh$_2$n-

roxo, rúbeo, rubor, rubrica, rubricar, rubro, ruivo, russo, *h$_1$rewd^h-

sacerdócio, sacerdotal, sacerdote, sacrificador, sacrificar, sacrificio, *dheH$_1$-

sal, *séh$_2$ls

saldo, *solh$_2$-

salgar, salsa, *séh$_2$ls

salubre, salvar, salve, *solh$_2$-

sanctificar, *dheH$_1$-

sangrar, sangue, sanguineo, sanguinho, sanguinoso, *h$_1$ésh$_2$r̥

santiguar, satisfazer, *dheH$_1$-

saudação, *solh$_2$-

saudade, *s(w)e-

saudar, saúde, *solh$_2$-

se, *s(w)e-, *só

sé, *sed-

secreção, secretário, secreto, *krey-

secure, *sek-

sede, *d^{h}eg^{wh}-, *sed-

sedimento, sédulo, *sed-

seduzir, *dewk-

segar, *sek-

segredo, *krey-

seguir, segundo, *sek^w-

segura, segure, *sek-

seis, *swéks
seiscentos, *ḱm̥tóm
seixo, *sek-
sela, *sed-
seleção, *leǵ-
selo, *sek-
semana, *septm̥
semear, *seH₁-
semelhante, semelhar, *sem-
semente, *seH₁-
semi-, *sem-
seminarista, *seH₁-
sempiternidade, sempiterno, sempre, *sem-
sen, *sent-
senado, senador, *sénos
senha, *sek-
senheiro, *sem-
senho, *sek-
senhor, sênior, *sénos
senso, *sent-
sentar, *sed-
sentencioso, sentido, sentimento, sentir, *sent-
sequaz, sequela, sequência, *sekʷ-
ser, *H₁es-, *sed-
série, sermão, *ser-
serra, serragem, serrar, *sek-
sessão, *sed-
sete, *septm̥
setecentos, *ḱm̥tóm
setembro, sétimo, *septm̥
seu, *s(w)e-
sigilo, signa, *sek-
significar, *dheH₁-, *sek-
signo, *sek-
silha, *sed-
silte, *séh₂ls
sim, *só
símil, símile, *sem-
simples, *pleḱ-, *sem-
simplice, *pleḱ-
simplificar, *dheH₁-, *pleh₁-, *sem-
simular, *sem-
sina, *sek-
singelo, singular, *sem-
sino, *sek-
sinónimo, *h₁nómn̥
siso, *sent-
sistema, *steh₂-
sítio, situar, *teḱ-
só, *s(w)e-
sob, soberba, *upo
soberbo, *bʰuH-, *upo
sobrancelha, *ḱel-
sobrar, sobre, *upo
sobrepor, *teḱ-
sobrevir, *gʷem-
sobrinho, *swésōr

social, sociedade, sócio, *sekʷ-
socorrer, *ḱers-
soer, *swe-dʰh₁-
sofrer, *bher-
sol, solar, solário, *sóh₂wl̥
soldo, solene, solerte, solicitação, solicitar, solicito,
   *solh₂-
solidão, *s(w)e-
sólido, *solh₂-
sólio, *sed-
solitário, *s(w)e-
sólito, *swe-dʰh₁-
solitude, solo, solteiro, *s(w)e-
soma, *upo
sonhador, sonhar, sonho, soniculoso, sono, *swep-
sonte, *H₁es-
soprar, *bʰleh₁-
soro, *srew-
soror, *swésōr
sorte, sortir, *ser-
sota, soto-, *upo
sovela, *sīw-
sua, *s(w)e-
suar, *sweyd-
subir, súbito, *h₁ey-
sublevar, *h₁lengʷʰ-
subseguir, *sekʷ-
subsidar, *sed-
substituir, *steh₂-
sudário, *sweyd-
suflar, *bʰleh₁-
sugerir, sugesto, *H₂eǵ-
suíno, *suH-
suma, sumidade, sumo, *upo
suor, *sweyd-
superar, *upo
supercílio, *ḱel-
supérfluo, *bʰleh₁-
superior, *upo
superpor, *teḱ-
superstição, *steh₂-
supervacâneo, *h₁weh₂-
supino, *upo
suplicar, *pleḱ-
supor, *teḱ-
suportar, *per-
supplantar, *pleh₂-
suprir, *pleh₁-
surdir, surgir, *h₃reǵ-
suspender, suspensão, *pewǵ-
sustentar, suster, *ten-
sútil, sutura, *sīw-
taberna, tabernáculo, *treb-
tal, talião, tam, *só
tanchagem, tanchar, *pleh₂-
tandem, *só
tansagem, *pleh₂-

tanto, tão, *só
taverna, *treb-
tecer, *tetḱ-
tégula, *(s)teg-
teia, *tetḱ-
teima, *dheH₁-
tela, *tetḱ-
telha, *(s)teg-
tema, *dheH₁-
tenáculo, tenalha, tenaz, tender, tenor, tenro,
  tensão, tenso, tento, teor, ter, *ten-
tércio, terço, *tréyes
térebra, terebrar, *terh₁-
término, termo, *térmn̥
terno, *ten-
terra, territorial, território, *ters-
tesão, teso, *ten-
teto, *(s)teg-
texugo, *tetḱ-
tigela, *(s)teg-
tio, *dʰeh₁(y)-
típica, tipo, *(s)tew-
tirar, *der-
tolerar, tolher, *telh₂-
tom, *ten-
tonar, tonítruo, *(s)tenh₂-
tordo, *trosdos
torrido, *ters-
tosar, tosse, tossir, *(s)tew-
touro, *(s)táwros
tradição, *deH₃-
trado, *terh₁-
traduzir, *dewk-
traição, traidor, trair, *deH₃-
tranquilo, *kʷyeh₁-
transferir, translação, *bher-
transmutação, transmutar, *mey-
transplantar, *pleh₂-
transportar, *per-
trás, *terh₂-
trasladar, *bher-
traste, trasto, *terh₂-
trave, *treb-
trégua, *deru-
três, *tréyes
treze, *déḱm̥t
trezentos, *ḱm̥tóm
triângulo, *h₂enk-
tribo, tribunal, tribuno, tributo, *bʰuH-
trigo, trilha, trilho, *terh₁-
triplo, *pleh₁-
triscar, tritura, *terh₁-
troar, *(s)tenh₂-
trom, *ten-
tropa, tropel, *treb-
tu, *túh₂
u, *kʷis

uberar, úbere, *h₁owHdʰr̥-
ubiquo, *kʷis
ulna, *Heh₃l-
ultra, *h₂el-
um, *óy-nos
umbigo, *h₃enbʰ-
undar, undoso, *wed-
ungulado, unha, *h₃negʰ-
união, único, unidade, *óy-nos
universo, *wert-
uno, *óy-nos
uredo, urna, *h₁ews-
ursa, urso, usso, *h₂r̥tḱos
ustular, *h₁ews-
vacar, vacuidade, vácuo, vagar, vago, vaidade,
  *h₁weh₂-
vala, vale, *welH-
valente, valer, valetudinário, válido, *h₂welh₁-
valo, *welH-
valor, *h₂welh₁-
valva, *welH-
vanidade, vão, vastar, vasto, *h₁weh₂-
vaticinar, vaticínio, *keh₂n-
vazio, *h₁weh₂-
vegetação, vegetar, végeto, *weǵ-
veículo, *weǵh-
velar, *weǵ-
velho, *wet-
velo, veloso, *h₂welh₁-
venal, *wesno-
vencer, *weyk-
vendedor, vender, *deH₃-, *wesno-
venta, *gʷem-, *H₂weH₁-
ventilação, ventilar, *H₂weH₁-
vento, *gʷem-, *H₂weH₁-
ventosa, ventoso, vêntulo, *H₂weH₁-
ver, *weyd-
verão, *wésr̥
veraz, *weh₁-
verba, verbal, verbatim, verbo, verboso, *wekʷ-
verdade, *weh₁-
verecúndia, verecundo, vergonha, *wer-
verificação, *weh₁-
verificar, *dheH₁-, *weh₁-
verme, vermelho, vermículo, vermína, verminoso,
  *wr̥mis-
vernal, *wésr̥
vero, *weh₁-
versado, versão, versar, versátil, verso, versúcia,
  versus, versuto, vértebra, verter, vértice, vertigem,
  *wert-
vespa, *wobs-
véspera, *wek(ʷ)speros
vessar, *wert-
vestem, vestido, vestir, *wes-
veterano, vetusto, *wet-
vez, *weyk-

via, viagem, *weyh₁-
vicário, vice, *weyk-
vico, *weyḱ-
vida, *gʷeyh₃-
vidro, *wed-
vigário, *weyk-
vigésimo, *wīḱm̥tiH₁
vigiar, vígil, vigilância, vigilante, vigilar, vigília,
   *weǵ-
vila, vilão, *weyḱ-
viloso, *h₂welh₁-
vináceo, *wóyh₁nom
vincular, vínculo, *weyk-
vindicar, vindicta, *weyh₁-
vindima, vindimar, *wóyh₁nom
vindita, vingar, *weyh₁-
vinha, vinhaça, vinhedo, vinheiro, vinho, vinhoso,
   vinoso, *wóyh₁nom
vinte, *wīḱm̥tiH₁
violar, *weyh₁-
vir, *gʷem-
viril, virilha, virtude, *wiHrós
vis-, *weyk-
visão, visibilidade, visita, visitar, viso, *weyd-
vital, *gʷeyh₃-
vítima, vitimar, vitória, *weyk-
vitulo, *wet-
viúva, viúvo, *h₁weydʰ
vivaz, viveiro, viver, vívido, viviparo, vivo, *gʷeyh₃-
vizinha, *weyḱ-
vocabulário, vocábulo, vocação, vocal, vocativo,
   vogal, *wekʷ-
voltar, voltear, volubilidade, volutar, volutear,
   volúvel, volver, *welH-
vontade, *welh₁-
vórtex, vórtice, *wert-
vós, vosso, *túh₂
voz, *wekʷ-

Romanian

-a (-ua), -ei, -i, -l (-ul), -le, -lor, -lui, *h₂el-
a naviga, *(s)neh₂-
a spera, *speh₁-
ab-, *h₂pó
abduce, *dewk-
abil, abilitate, *gʰeh₁bʰ-
ablativ, *bher-
abstinent, abstinență, *ten-
ac, acar, *h₂éḱ
acea, *h₂el-
această, *só
acei, acel, acele, acelei, acelor, acelui, *h₂el-
acerb, *h₂éḱ
acest, aceste, acestei, acestor, acestui, aceşti, *só
acid, *h₂éḱ
acord, acorda, *ḱḗr
acru, *h₂éḱ
act, activitate, actor, acțiune, *H₂eǵ-
aculeu, *h₂éḱ
acvariu, acvatic, *h₂ekʷeh₂-
adăsta, adăstare, *steh₂-
adăuga, adăugare, *h₂ewg-
adânc, *h₂enk-
adevăr, *weh₁-
adia, *h₂el-
adicție, *deyḱ-
adjudeca, *h₂eyw-
administrație, *mey-
adora, *h₃éh₁os
aduce, aducere, *dewk-
advocat, *wekʷ-
aer, *h₂ews-
afla, aflare, aflui, *bʰleh₁-
afuma, afumare, *dʰewh₂-
agest, agitare, *H₂eǵ-
agricultor, agricultură, agrimensor, agru, *h₂éǵros
agura, agust, *h₂ewg-
aia, *h₂el-
ajunge, ajungere, *yewg-
alac, albie, albină, albioară, alea, *h₂el-
alega, alegație, *legh-
alege, alegere, *leǵ-
alt, alveolă, *h₂el-
ambii, *h₂ent
ametist, *médʰu
amnar, *méh₂-r̥
anghilă, *angʷ(h)i-
anin, *h₃el-
aniversar, aniversare, *wert-
anonym, *h₁nómn̥
anormal, *ǵneh₃-
anterior, *h₂ent
antic, antichitate, *h₂énti-h₃kʷós

anxietate, *h₂enǵʰ-

apar, apă, *h₂ekʷeh₂-

apărea, *peh₂-

apeduct, *dewk-, *h₂ekʷeh₂-

apendice, *pewǵ-

apetit, *peth₂

apleca, aplecare, aplica, *pleḱ-

apoi, *h₁epi

apos, *h₂ekʷeh₂-

aprehenda, aprinde, aprindere, *weyd-

aproape, *per-

apuca, apucare, *keh₂p-

apune, apunere, apus, *teḱ-

ara, arabil, *H₂erH₃-

aramă, *h₂eyos

arare, arat, *H₂erH₃-

arăduce, *dewk-

arător, *H₂erH₃-

arbor, arbore, arboret, arbure, *h₂erHdʰ-

arc, *h₂erkʷo-

arici, *ǵʰér

arin, *h₃el-

arm, arma, armar, armat, armată, armatură, armă, armătură, armură, artă, articol, *h₂er

asculta, ascultare, *ḱel-

ascunde, ascundere, *dheH₁-

asemăna, asemănare, asimila, *sem-

asta, astea, *só

astruca, *strew-

asuda, asudare, *sweyd-

asupra, *upo

aşchie, *H₂eǵ-

aşeza, *sed-

aştepta, aşteptare, *speḱ-

aşterne, aşternere, *sterh₃-

atare, atât, *só

atent, atenţie, *ten-

atroce, atrocitate, *h₂eh₁tro-h₃kʷs

atuncea, atunci, *só

aţă, *h₂éḱ

aţine, aţinere, *ten-

au, *h₂ew

audienţă, auditor, auditoriu, audiţie, *h₂ewis-dʰh₁-

augur, augura, august, *h₂ewg-

aură, aurora, austral, austru, *h₂ews-

auş, *h₂éwh₂os

auzi, auzire, auzit, auzitor, *h₂ewis-dʰh₁-

avea, avere, *gʰeh₁bʰ-

avocat, *wekʷ-

ax, axă, *H₂eǵ-

ăia, ăl, ăla, ăleia, ălora, ăluia, *h₂el-

ăsta, ăsteia, ăstora, ăstuia, ăştia, *só

balistă, *gʷelH-

barbă, barbur, bărbat, *bʰardʰeh₂-

bătrân, *wet-

băutor, bea, beat, bere, *peh₃-

bibliotecă, *dheH₁-

biceps, *kapōlo

biet, *wet-

birou, *péh₂ur

boace, *wekʷ-

boar, *gʷṓws

boltă, *welH-

borî, *gʰers-

bou, bour, *gʷṓws

brahial, braţ, brumă, *mréǵʰ-

bucium, buciuma, buciumare, *gʷṓws, *keh₂n-

buric, *h₃enbʰ-

ca, *kʷis

calendar, *kelh₁-

calitate, *kʷis

cameră, *(s)teg-

caniculă, canin, *kwṓ

cap, *kapōlo

capacitate, *keh₂p-

capăt, capital, *kapōlo

capră, caprin, *kapro

capsă, capsulă, captiv, captură, *keh₂p-

car, *kers-

carâmb, *ḱalam-

care, *kʷis

carnal, carne, *(s)ker-

cartă, carte, cartular, *ǵʰer-

călca, călcare, călcătură, călcâi, *(s)kel-

cămară, *(s)teg-

căpăstru, *keh₂p-

căpeţel, *kapōlo

căprar, *kapro

cărindar, *kelh₁-

cărnos, *(s)ker-

cărturar, *ǵʰer-

căruţă, *kers-

căuta, căutare, *keh₂p-

câine, *kwṓ

câmp, *(s)teg-

ce, *kʷis

cearbă, *ḱerh₂-

celar, celulă, *ḱel-

cent, centurie, *ḱm̥tóm

cerb, cerbar, cerbă, cerebel, *ḱerh₂-

cerne, cert, certa, certare, *krey-

cet, *kʷyeh₁-

cetate, *ḱei-

cheag, *H₂eǵ-

cheie, *(s)kel-

chema, chemare, chiar, *kelh₁-

cicogna, *keh₂n-

ciliu, *ḱel-

cimpoi, *ḱm̥tóm, *pel-

cina, cinare, cină, *(s)ker-

cinci, *pénkʷe

cine, *kʷis

circumferinţă, *bher-

circumnaviga, *(s)neh₂-

circumstanță, *steh$_2$-
ciur, *krey-
civic, *ḱei-
clama, clar, claritate, *kelh$_1$-
claviculă, *(s)kel-
cneaz, *ǵenH$_1$-
coace, coacere, *pekʷ-
coagul, coagula, *H$_2$eǵ-
coapsă, *koḱs-
coardă, *ǵʰern-
coase, coasere, *sīw-
cognomen, *h$_1$nómn̥
cohortă, *ǵʰer-
coit, *h$_1$ey-
colecție, *leǵ-
colină, coloană, *kelH-
colonie, *kʷel-
colora, *ḱel-
columnă, *kelH-
comanda, comandare, comânda, comândare, *deH$_3$-
combina, combinație, *dwóH$_1$
compensa, compensație, *pewǵ-
complement, complet, compli, *pleh$_1$-
complica, complicație, *pleḱ-
compliment, *pleh$_1$-
compune, *teḱ-
comun, comunal, comunica, comunicare,
 comunicație, comuta, *mey-
concepe, concepție, *keh$_2$p-
conchide, *(s)kel-
concurs, *ḱers-
condiție, *deyḱ-, *dheH$_1$-
conduce, conductă, conducție, *dewk-
confecție, *dheH$_1$-
confia, *bʰeydʰ-
confunda, confuz, confuzie, *ǵʰew-
congela, *gel-
consecință, consecvent, consecvență, *sekʷ-
consens, *sent-
consiliu, *kelh$_1$-
consta, *steh$_2$-
construcție, construi, *strew-
conștiință, *skey-
conteni, content, content, contențiune, continuu, *ten-
contradicție, *deyḱ-
controversă, *wert-
conține, *ten-
conveni, conveniență, convenție, *gʷem-
conversație, *wert-
convinge, *weyk-
copt, coptură, *pekʷ-
cor, cord, *ḱér-
corect, corecta, corecție, corija, *h$_3$reǵ-
corn, cornut, *ḱerh$_2$-
corp, *krep-
corună, *kelH-

costa, *steh$_2$-
costum, *swe-dʰh$_1$-
craniu, *ḱerh$_2$-
crede, credere, credibil, *dheH$_1$-
creier, *ḱerh$_2$-
crimă, *krey-
crud, crudătate, cruditate, crunt, crunta, *krewh$_2$-
cufunda, *ǵʰew-
cugeta, cugetare, *H$_2$eǵ-
cui, *kʷis
culca, culcare, *stel-
culege, culegere, *leǵ-
culme, *kelH-
culoare, *ḱel-
cum, *med-
cumineca, cuminecare, *mey-
cumplire, *pleh$_1$-
cunoaște, cunoaștere, *ǵneh$_3$-
cuprinde, cuprindere, cuprins, *weyd-
curcubeu, *h$_2$erkʷo-
cure, *ḱers-
curea, *h$_3$reǵ-
curent, curge, curgere, curs, cursoare, cursor, *ḱers-
curte, *ǵʰer-
custa, *steh$_2$-
cuvânt, cuveni, cuviință, *gʷem-
cvadrat, *kʷetwóres
da, *deH$_3$-
daivet, *gʰeh$_1$bʰ-
damă, *dem-
damna, *deh$_2$-
dar, dare, daruri, dat, dată, *deH$_3$-
dator, *gʰeh$_1$bʰ-
daună, dăuna, *deh$_2$-
deasupra, *upo
debil, *gʰeh$_1$bʰ-
decadă, decan, decembrie, decima, *déḱm̥t
declara, *kelh$_1$-
deda, *deH$_3$-
deduce, deducție, *dewk-
deget, degetar, *deyḱ-
delega, *legh-
delir, *leys-
demență, *men-
demn, demnitate, *deḱ-
denar, *déḱm̥t
depinde, *pewǵ-
deprinde, deprindere, *weyd-
depune, *teḱ-
des-, *dwóH$_1$
descălța, descălțare, *(s)kel-
descărca, descărcare, *ḱers-
deschi, deschide, *(s)kel-
descripție, *(s)ker-
desemna, designa, *sek-
despune, *teḱ-
destina, *steh$_2$-

deștept, deștepta, *speḱ-
detențiune, *ten-
detuna, *(s)tenh₂-
deține, *ten-
deveni, *gʷem-
dexteritate, dextru, *deḱs-
dez-, *dwóH₁
diavol, *gʷelH-
dicta, dictare, dictator, dictatură, dicție,
  dicționar, digital, *deyḱ-
dimânda, *deH₃-
dinar, *déḱmt
dinte, *h₃dónts
direct, dirigui, dirija, *h₃reǵ-
discerne, *krey-
discurs, *ḱers-
diseca, *sek-
dispune, *teḱ-
distanță, *steh₂-
distribui, *bʰuH-
distruge, *strew-
diurn, *deyn-
divinitate, *dyew-
divizibil, *h₁weydʰ
doamnă, *dem-
doctor, *deḱ-
doi, *dwóH₁
domestic, domiciliu, domina, domn, *dem-
dona, donație, dota, *deH₃-
două, *dwóH₁
drege, drept, *h₃reǵ-
dubios, dubiu, *gʰeh₁bʰ-
dubla, dublu, *pleh₁-
ducat, duce, ducere, duct, *dewk-
dumesnic, *dem-
duminică, *deyn-
dur, dura, *deru-
duș, *dewk-
dușman, dușmancă, *men-
ea, *h₂el-
edict, *deyḱ-
edificiu, *h₂eydʰ-
ediție, *deH₃-
educa, educație, *dewk-
efect, *dheH₁-
efuziune, *ǵʰew-
ei, el, ele, *h₂el-
eleva, *h₁lengʷʰ-
energie, *werǵ-
enorm, *ǵneh₃-
epocă, *seǵʰ-
esență, *H₁es-
etate, eternitate, *h₂ey-
eu, *egH₂
ev, *h₂ey-
eveniment, eventualitate, *gʷem-
evinge, *weyk-

evolua, evoluție, *welH-
examen, examina, *H₂eǵ-
excursie, *ḱers-
execuție, *sekʷ-
experiență, *per-
explica, *pleḱ-
expune, *teḱ-
extatic, extaz, *steh₂-
extensiune, extinde, extins, *ten-
extra-, *h₁eǵʰs
fabulos, *bʰeh₂-
face, facere, factor, *dheH₁-
fag, *bʰeh₂go-
faimă, *bʰeh₂-
famen, *dʰeh₁(y)-
familie, *dheH₁-
fantomă, *bʰeh₂-
fapt, *dheH₁-
fată, *dʰeh₁(y)-
făinar, făină, făinos, *bʰars-
făt, făta, fătare, *dʰeh₁(y)-
făurar, febră, februarie, *dʰegʷʰ-
femeie, *dheH₁-
femelă, ferice, *dʰeh₁(y)-
ferie, *dʰéh₁s
ferm, *dʰer-
feroce, *ǵʰweroh₃kʷs
festivitate, *dʰéh₁s
feud, feudă, *peḱu-
fi, *bʰuH-, *H₁es-
fiară, *ǵʰwer-
fiastru, *dʰeh₁(y)-
fidel, fidelitate, *bʰeydʰ-
fie, *dʰeh₁(y)-
fief, *peḱu-
figură, *dʰeyǵʰ-
fior, *dʰegʷʰ-
fire, *bʰuH-
fistulă, *bʰeyd-
fiu, *dʰeh₁(y)-
flaur, *bʰleh₁-
floare, *bʰleh₃-
fluctua, fluctuație, fluvial, fluviu, flux, *bʰleh₁-
foaie, *bʰleh₃-
foarte, *bʰerǵʰ-
foios, *bʰleh₃-
for, *dʰwer-
forta, *bʰerǵʰ-
frasin, *bʰereǵ-
frate, fraternitate, *bʰréh₂tēr
frăsinet, *bʰereǵ-
frână, frâu, *dʰer-
fui, *bʰuH-
fum, fuma, fumega, fumegare, *dʰewh₂-
fund, *bʰudʰmén
funingine, *dʰewh₂-
fur, fura, furare, *bher-

jumătate, *médʰyos

junc, june, junice, junincă, junior, *h₂yuh₁en-

jura, jurare, jurământ, just, justiție, *h₂eyw-

juvenil, *h₂yuh₁en-

la, *lewh₃-

lac, *lókus

lacrimă, *daḱru-

lacună, lagună, *lókus

lapte, *glag-

lare, latrină, *lewh₃-

lăcrima, lăcrimare, lăcrimos, *daḱru-

lăptar, lăptos, lăptucă, *glag-

lânar, lână, lânos, *h₂welh₁-

le, *h₂el-

leal, *leǵ-, *legh-

lectică, *legh-

lector, lecție, *leǵ-

legal, lege, *leǵ-, *legh-

legitim, *legh-

legiune, legumă, *leǵ-

lejer, *h₁lengʷʰ-

lemn, lemnar, lemnos, *leǵ-

liber, libertate, *h₁lewdʰ-

librar, *lewbʰ-

limbă, *dn̥ǵʰwéh₂s

linie, lințoliu, *lino-

loc, local, locație, *stel-

longevitate, *h₂ey-

lor, *h₂el-

lua, luare, luat, *h₁lengʷʰ-

luceafăr, luced, lucernă, luci, lucire, lucra, *lewk-

lui, *h₂el-

lumânare, lume, lumina, luminare, lumină,

luminos, lunatic, lună, *lewk-

luni, *deyn-

lup, *wĺkʷos

lupta, luptare, luptă, luptător, *seh₂g-

lutră, *udréh₂

lux, *seh₂g-

macru, *meh₂ḱ-

maestru, magistru, mai, maior, maistru, *méǵh₂s

mamă, *méh₂-méh₂

mandibulă, *mendʰ-

mare, marin, *móri

marți, *deyn-

masă, *meh₁-

materie, *méh₂tēr

mator, *meh₂-

matrice, matrimoniu, *méh₂tēr

matur, *meh₂-

mă, *H₁me-

măduvă, *médʰyos

măi, *med-

măiestru, *méǵh₂s

mănunt, mărunt, măruntaie, *mey-

măsură, *meh₁-

mătrice, *méh₂tēr

mâna, mânare, *men-

mână, *méh₂-r̥

mânca, mâncare, *mendʰ-

mâner, *méh₂-r̥

mea, *H₁meme-

media, mediator, *médʰyos

medic, medicinal, medicină, *med-

medie, mediteran, mediteranean, mediu, *médʰyos

mei, mele, *H₁meme-

membru, *méms

memora, memorie, mental, *men-

menține, *ten-

mențiune, *men-

meriza, merizare, meriză, *deyn-

meriză, *médʰyos

mesteca, *mendʰ-

mește, *mey-

metern, *méh₂tēr

meu, *H₁meme-

mezin, *médʰyos

mia, *h₂egʷnos

mie, *H₁me-, *sem-

mied, *médʰu

miel, *h₂egʷnos

miercuri, *deyn-

miere, *melit-

miez, *médʰyos

migrare, *mey-

minciună, *men-

ministru, minor, *mey-

mintal, minte, minți, mințire, *men-

minut, mistreț, mișca, *mey-

moară, *melh₂-

moarte, *mer-

mod, model, modern, *med-

monedă, monstro, monstru, montan, monument, *men-

morar, *melh₂-

mormânt, *men-

mort, *mer-

mulge, mulgere, mulsură, *H₂melǵ-

multiplica, multiplicație, *plek-

muncel, *men-

municipiu, *mey-

munte, muntos, *men-

muri, muribund, murire, *mer-

muscă, *mus-

muscular, musculos, mustaila, *muh₂s-

mustață, *mendʰ-

mustra, mustrare, *men-

mușchi, mușchios, mușchiular, *muh₂s-

muta, mutare, *mey-

naie, *(s)neh₂-

nară, nas, *néh₂s

naște, naștere, nat, nativ, nativitate, natură, națiune,
   *ǵenH₁-

navă, navigator, navigație, *(s)neh₂-

năsut, *néh₂s

nea, *sneyg^{wh}-

nebulos, *neb^h-

neca, *neḱ-

neg, *ǵenH$_1$-

neglija, neglijență, *leǵ-

negoț, *h$_2$ew

negură, neguros, *neb^h-

negustor, neguța, *h$_2$ew

neios, *sneyg^{wh}-

nepoată, nepot, *nepot-

nești, neștine, *skey-

nev, *ǵenH$_1$-

ninge, *sneyg^{wh}-

niscai, niște, *skey-

noapte, *nók^{w}ts

noastră, noastre, *wei

nobil, *ǵneh$_3$-

nociv, *neḱ-

nocturn, *nók^{w}ts

noi, *wei

nomina, nominal, nominație, *h$_1$nómn̥

noră, *snusós

nord, *h$_1$én

normal, *ǵneh$_3$-

nostru, noștri, *wei

notare, *ǵneh$_3$-

nou, *new

nouă, *H$_1$néwn̥

nouă, *wei

noutate, *new

nud, *neg^w-

nuia, *new

număr, *nem-

numără, *h$_1$nómn̥, *nem-

numărare, *nem-

nume, *h$_1$nómn̥

numeros, *nem-

nuvelă, *new

o, *h$_2$el-

oaie, *h$_2$ówis

oară, *yeh$_1$-

oaspete, oaste, *g^{h}óstis

obiect, *h$_1$epi

obține, *ten-

ochi, *h$_3$ek^w-

ocupa, ocupație, *keh$_2$p-

odios, *h$_3$ed-

oferi, *bher-

oficial, *h$_3$ep-

oină, *h$_2$ówis

om, *ǵʰmṓ

ombilic, *h$_3$enb^h-

op, opera, operă, *h$_3$ep-

opt, *oḱtṓw

opus, *h$_3$ep-

oracol, orație, *h$_3$éh$_1$os

oră, *yeh$_1$-

orb, *h$_3$erb^h-

ordin, ordine, ordona, ordonare, *h$_2$er

organ, orgă, *werǵ-

orient, oriental, origine, *h$_3$er-

os, *h$_3$ésth$_1$

ospăta, ospătare, ospăț, ospiciu, ospital, *g^{h}óstis

ostenta, ostentație, *ten-

ou, *h$_2$ōwyóm

pace, pagină, *peh$_2$ǵ-

pal, palid, *pelH-

paludă, paludos, *peh$_2$ǵ-

pană, *péth$_2$r̥

paner, *peh$_2$-

parabolă, *g^{w}elH-

paradis, *d^{h}eyǵ^h-

parolă, *g^{w}elH-

pas, pasăre, *peth$_2$

pastilă, paște, paștere, *peh$_2$-

pater, patron, *ph$_2$tḗr

patru, *k^{w}etwóres

păca, *peh$_2$ǵ-

păcat, *ped-

păcurar, *peḱu-

pădure, păduros, păgân, păgânătate, *peh$_2$ǵ-

păi, *h$_1$epi

părea, părere, *peh$_2$-

păs, păsa, păsare, *pewǵ-

păstor, păstură, pășune, *peh$_2$-

păta, pătare, *peyḱ-

pătrat, *k^{w}etwóres

pătrunde, pătrundere, *(s)tew-

pâinar, pâine, pâne, *peh$_2$-

pe mine, *H$_1$me-

pe, *per-

peculiu, pecuniar, *peḱu-

peliculă, *pel-

percepe, *keh$_2$p-

perfect, *dheH$_1$-

pericol, periculos, *per-

pescar, pescos, *peisḱ-

pestriț, *peyḱ-

pește, *peisḱ-

peți, pețire, *peth$_2$

piață, *pleh$_2$-

picior, *pṓds

picta, pictor, pictură, picturǎ, *peyḱ-

pielar, piele, *pel-

pieptăna, pieptănare, pieptene, *peḱ-

pierde, pierdere, *deH$_3$-

pieri, pierire, *h$_1$ey-

piersica, *sek-

piez, *pṓds

pigment, *peyḱ-

pil, pisa, pisare, *peys-

piscină, *peisḱ-

piuă, *peys-

plagă, *pleh$_2$kplan, planta, plantă, *pleh₂-

plaur, *peh₂-

plămân, *plewmō

plânge, plângere, *pleh₂k-

plântă, *pleh₂-

plebe, *pleh₁-

pleca, plecare, *pleḱ-

plin, *pleh₁-

ploaie, ploios, ploua, *plew-

plus, *pleh₁-

poarcă, *pórḱos

poartă, *per-

podium, podiu, *pṓds

policar, *h₂welh₁-

ponce, *poymno-

pondere, pont, *pewǵ-

popor, popular, populație, *pleh₁-

porc, porcar, porcin, *pórḱos

portar, *per-

poseda, *pótis

posibil, potent, potență, *H₁es-

poțiune, *peh₃-

poziție, *teḱ-

pradă, *weyd-

praf, *pers-

prăda, prădare, prădăciune, prădător, *deH₃-, *weyd-

predicție, *deyḱ-

prejudeca, prejudiciu, *h₂eyw-

preocupa, preocupație, *keh₂p-

preot, *per-

prepinge, *pewǵ-

prepune, *teḱ-

prescrie, *(s)ker-

pretinde, *ten-

preț, prețios, *per-

prevala, *h₂welh₁-

prevedea, *weyd-

previnge, *weyk-

prezice, *deyḱ-

pricepe, pricepere, *keh₂p-

prim, primar, *per-

principiu, *keh₂p-

prinde, prindere, prins, *weyd-

prinț, *keh₂p-

prior, *per-

priveghea, priveghere, *weǵ-

proba, probă, *bʰuH-

problematic, problemă, *gʷelH-

produce, productiv, producție, *dewk-

profesiune, profesor, *bʰeh₂-

profund, profunditate, *ǵʰew-

program, *gerbʰ-

prohibi, *gʰeh₁bʰ-

promiscuu, *mey-

proprietate, propriu, *preyH-

propune, *teḱ-

proră, provă, proxim, *per-

public, *pleh₁-

pulmon, *plewmō

pumn, punct, *pewǵ-

pune, punere, *teḱ-

punge, *pewǵ-

punte, *pent-

purcea, purcel, *pórḱos

purice, *plou-

purta, purtare, *per-

pusăciune, *teḱ-

putea, putere, putință, *H₁es-

radical, ram, ramură, *wréh₂ds

rație, rațiune, *h₂er-

rază, rădăcină, rămuros, *wréh₂ds

răpune, *teḱ-

rătund, *Hret-

râie, *h₂er-

râu, *h₃reyH-

recepe, *keh₂p-

reculege, *leǵ-

recunoaște, *ǵneh₃-

reduce, reducție, *dewk-

regal, rege, regină, regulă, *h₃reǵ-

relație, *bher-

releva, *h₁lengʷʰ-

remediu, *med-

renova, *new

repeta, *petʰ₂

replica, *pleḱ-

reprezenta, *H₁es-

republică, *pleh₁-

repugna, *pewǵ-

respect, respecta, *speḱ-

restitui, *steh₂-

retenție, reține, *ten-

revărsa, *wert-

revedea, *weyd-

reveni, *gʷem-

revistă, *weyd-

revoluți, *welH-

ridica, ridiche, *wréh₂ds

rit, *h₂er-

rivalitate, *h₃reyH-

roată, *Hret-

roib, roibă, roșu, *h₁rewdʰ-

rotație, rotund, *Hret-

rug, *h₃reǵ-

rugină, *h₂eyos

sa, *s(w)e-

sacerdot, sacerdoțiu, *dheH₁-

sain, *suH-

sale, *s(w)e-

salut, saluta, salutație, salva, salve, *solh₂-

sanctifica, *dheH₁-

sare, *séh₂ls

satisface, *dheH₁-

sau, să, *só

săcret, *krey-
săi, *s(w)e-
sămânță, *seH₁-
săptămână, *septṛn
săra, sărare, *séh₂ls
săruta, sărutare, *solh₂-
său, *s(w)e-
sânge, sânger, sângera, sângerare, sângeros,
 *h₁ésh₂r
scărmăna, scărmănare, *keh₂n-
scoarță, scorbură, scrie, scriere, script,
 scriptură, *(s)ker-
scure, scurge, *ḱers-
scurt, scurta, scurtare, *(s)ker-
se, *s(w)e-
seamăn, *sem-
secret, secretar, secreție, *krey-
secund, *sekʷ-
secure, *sek-
seduce, *dewk-
selecție, *leǵ-
semăna, semănare, *seH₁-, *sem-
seminarist, *seH₁-
semn, semna, *sek-
senat, senator, *sénos
sentiment, *sent-
septembrie, *septṛn
septentrion, *terh₁-
sesie, *sed-
sete, *dʰegʷʰ-
sigiliu, *sek-
simplifica, *dheH₁-, *pleh₁-, *sem-
simplu, *pleḱ-, *sem-
simțământ, simți, simțire, *sent-
simula, *sem-
sine, *s(w)e-
singular, singur, *sem-
sista, sistem, *steh₂-
situație, *teḱ-
soare, *sóh₂wl
soartă, soarte, *ser-
soață, social, societate, *sekʷ-
solar, *sóh₂wl
solemn, solid, *solh₂-
solitar, *s(w)e-
solz, *solh₂-
somn, somnifer, *swep-
soră, *swésōr
sos, *séh₂ls
soț, *sekʷ-
spăla, spălare, *lewh₃-
specie, spectru, specul, specula, speculație, *speḱ-
speranță, *speh₁-
spic, spin, spinal, spinare, spinos, *spey-
spiona, *speḱ-
spital, *gʰóstis
splină, *splenǵʰ-

sprânceană, *ḱel-
spre, *upo
spuma, spumare, spumă, spumos, *poymno-
spune, spunere, *tek-
sta, stabil, stabili, stare, stat, statuă, statuie, stație,
 staul, *steh₂-
stea, *h₂stḗr
stradă, strat, *sterh₃-
stră-, străin, *h₁eǵʰs
student, studia, studiu, *(s)tew-
sturz, *trosdos
subit, *h₁ey-
subt, *upo
subțire, *tetḱ-
sudoare, *sweyd-
suferi, suferire, *bher-
suflare, suflet, suflia, *bʰleh₁-
sugel, *sek-
sui, *h₁ey-
sul, *sīw-
sumă, supăra, supărare, *upo
supensie, *pewǵ-
superb, *bʰuH-, *upo
 superior, *upo
superpune, *tek-
superstiție, *steh₂-
suplica, suplicație, *pleḱ-
suporta, *per-
supt, *upo
supune, supunere, *tek-
susține, *ten-
sutặ, *ḱṃtóm
șa, șale, *sed-
șapte, *septṛn
șase, *swéḱs
școală, *seǵʰ-
ședea, ședere, *sed-
și, *só
ști, știință, știre, *skey-
ta, tale, *túh₂
tare, *só
taur, *(s)táwros
tavernă, *treb-
tăi, tău, *túh₂
tânăr, *ten-
teară, *tetḱ-
temă, *dheH₁-
tensiune, *ten-
teritorial, teritoriu, *ters-
termen, termina, *térmṇ
terț, terțiu, *tréyes
tinde, tindere, tins, *ten-
tip, tipic, *(s)tew-
ton, *ten-
traduce, *dewk-
translație, *bher-
trăda, trădător, *deH₃-

Ancient Greek

-γνητός (-gnētós), *ǵenH₁-
-ειδής (-eidés), *weyd-
-κλῆς (-klês), *ḱlew-
-μωρος (-mōros), *meh₂-
-πλόος (-plóos), *pleh₁-
-φᾰνής (-phanés), *bʰeh₂-
ἀ- (a-), *n̥-
ἀ- (ha-), *sem-
ἄ-ιστος (á-istos), *weyd-
ἄβυσσος (ábussos), *dʰewb-
ἄγκος (ánkos), ἀγκύλη (ankúlē), ἀγκύλος (ankúlos),
 ἀγκών (ankón), *h₂enk-
ἀγνώς (agnós), ἀγνωσῐ́ᾱ (agnōsíā), *ǵneh₃-
ἀγός (agós), *H₂eǵ-
ἄγριος (ágrios), ἀγρός (agrós), *h₂éǵros
ἄγχω (ánkhō), *h₂enǵʰ-
ἄγω (ágō), ἀγωγή (agōgḗ), ἀγωγός (agōgós), ἀγών
 (agṓn), ἀγωνία (agōnía), ἀγωνιστής (agōnistḗs), *H₂eǵ-
ἄδικος (ádikos), *deyḱ-
ἀείδελος (aeídelos), *weyd-
ἄελλα (áella), ἀέντα (aénta), *H₂weH₁-
ἀετός (aetós), *h₂éwis
ἄζυξ (ázux), *yewg-
ἄζω (ázō), *h₂eh₁s-
ἄημι (áēmi), *H₂weH₁-
ἀήρ (āḗr), *h₂ews-
ἄθεος (átheos), *dʰéh₁s
ἀθλέω (athléō), ἄθλημα (áthlēma), ἀθλητής (athlētḗs),
 ἀθλητῐκός (āthlētikós), ἆθλον (âthlon), *H₂weH₁-
αἰγίλωψ (aigílōps), *h₂eyǵ-
Ἀΐδης (Aḯdēs), *weyd-
αἰεί (aiei), *h₂ey-
αἰθήρ (aithḗr), αἶθος (aîthos), αἶθος (aîthos), αἴθω
 (aíthō), *h₂eydʰ-
αἰσθάνομαι (aisthánomai), *h₂ewis-dʰh₁-
ἀΐσθω (aísthō), *H₂weH₁-
ἀΐω (aḯō), *h₂ew-
αἰών (aiōn), *h₂ey-
ἀκή (akḗ), ἀκμή (akmḗ), *h₂éḱ
ἄκμων (ákmōn), *h₂éḱ-mō
ἄκοιτῐς (ákoitis), *ḱei-
ἀκούω (akoúō), *h₂kh₂owsyéti
ἄκρος (ákros), *h₂éḱ
ἀκτῖς (aktîs), *nókʷts
ἄκτωρ (áktōr), *H₂eǵ-
Ἀλέξανδρος (Aléxandros), *h₂nḗr
ἀλθαίνω (althaínō), ἄλθω (althō), *h₂el-
ἄλιζα (áliza), *h₃el-
ἄλλος (állos), *h₂el-
ἅλς (háls), *séh₂ls
ἀλύδοιμος (alúdoimos), *h₂elut-
ἅμα (háma), *sem-
ἁμαρτή (hamartḗ), *h₂er

ἀμβροσία (ambrosía), ἄμβροτος (ámbrotos), *mer-
ἀμέθῠστος (améthustos), *médʰu
ἀμέλγω (amélgō), *H₂melǵ-
ἀμή (hamê), *sem-
ἀμνησία (amnēsía), *men-
ἀμνίον (amníon), ἀμνός (amnós), *h₂egʷnos
ἀμόθεν (hamóthen), *sem-
ἀμφί (amphí), *h₂ent
ἀμφιλύκη (amphilúkē), *lewk-
ἀν- (an-), *n̥-
ἀνᾰ́βᾰσῐς (anábasis), *gʷem-
ἀνᾰγῐγνώσκω (anagignṓskō), *ǵneh₃-
ἀνᾰ́γω (anágō), *H₂eǵ-
ἀνᾰ́στᾰσῐς (anástasis), *steh₂-
ἀνᾰφορᾱ (anaphorā), *bher-
Ἀνδρέας (Andréas), ἀνδρόγυνος (andrógunos), ἀνδρός
 (andrós), *h₂nḗr
ἄνεμος (ánemos), *h₂enh₁-
ἀνεψιός (anepsiós), *nepot-
ἀνήρ (anḗr), *h₂nḗr
ἀνομία (anomía), *nem-
ἀνόρεκτος (anórektos), ἀνορεξία (anorexía), *h₃reǵ-
ἄντα (ánta), ἀντί (antí, *h₂ent
ἀντίθεσις (antíthesis), ἀντίθετον (antítheton), *dheH₁-
ἀντίος (antíos), *h₂ent
ἀνώνῠμος (anṓnumos), *h₁nómn̥
ἀξίνη (axínē), *h₂éḱ
ἄξων (áxōn), *H₂eǵ-
ἅπαξ (hápax), *sem-, *peh₂ǵ-
ἀπό (apó), *h₂pó
ἀποθεόω (apotheóō), ἀποθέωσις (apothéōsis), *dʰéh₁s
ἀποθήκη (apothḗkē, *dheH₁-
ἀποκαλύπτω (apokalúptō), ἀποκάλυψις (apokálupsis),
 *ḱel-
ἀπορῐ́ᾱ (aporíā), ἄπορος (áporos), *per-
ἄρα (ára), *h₂er
ἀρά (ará), *h₃éh₁os
ἀραρίσκω (ararískō), ἀράχνη (arákhnē), ἀράχνης
 (arákhnēs), ἀρείων (areíōn), ἀρέσκω (aréskō), ἀρετή
 (aretḗ), ἀρθμός (arthmós), ἀρθρῖτις (arthrîtis), ἄρθρον
 (árthron), ἀριθμός (arithmós), ἀριστερός (aristerós),
 *h₂er
ἄριστον (áriston), *h₁ed-
ἄριστος (áristos), *h₂er
ἀρκέω (arkéō), ἄρκος (árkos), *h₂erk-
ἀρκτικός (arktikós), ἄρκτος (árktos), *h₂r̥tkos
ἅρμα (hárma), ἁρμόζω (harmózō), ἁρμονία
 (harmonía), ἁρμός (harmós), *h₂er
ἄροτρον (árotron), ἀρόω (aróō), *H₂erH₃-
ἄρτι (árti), *h₂er
ἀρτοκόπος (artokópos), *pekʷ-
ἀρτύω (artúō), *h₂er
ἀρχισῠνᾰγωγος (arkhisunágōgos), *H₂eǵ-
ἀρχιτέκτων (arkhitéktōn), *tetḱ-
ἀσβόλη (asbólē), ἄσβολος (ásbolos), *h₂eh₁s-
ἀστήρ (astḗr), *h₂stḗr
ἀτενής (atenés), *ten-

Ἄτλας (Átlas), *telh₂-
ἀτμός (atmós), *H₂weH₁-
ἄτρυτος (átrutos), *terh₁-
ἄττα (átta), *átta
αὖ (aû), *h₂ew
αὐθέντης (authéntēs), αὐθεντικός (authentikós), *h₂ew
αὐξάνω (auxánō), αὔξω (aúxō), *h₂ewg-
αὔρᾱ (aúrā), αὔριον (aúrion), *h₂ews-
αὐτάρ (autár), αὖτε (aûte), αὖτις (aûtis), *h₂ew
αὐτόματος (autómatos), *men-
αὐτός (autós), *h₂ew
ἀφρός (aphrós), *nebʰ-
βαθμός (bathmós), βαίνω (baínō), *gʷem-
βακτηρία (baktēría), βάκτρον (báktron), *bak-
βαλλίζω (ballízō), βαλλίστρα (ballístra),
  βάλλω (bállō), *gʷelH-
βᾰρεῖᾰ (bareîa), βαρύς (barús), βᾰρύτης (barútēs),
  *gʷerh₂-
βάσις (básis), βάσκω (báskō), βατός (batós),
  βέβηκᾰ (bébēka), *gʷem-
βείομαι (beíomai), *gʷeyh₃-
βέλεμνον (bélemnon), βελόνη (belónē), *gʷelH-
βέλος (bélos), *gʷelH-
βέομαι (béomai), *gʷeyh₃-
βῑβλῐοθήκη (bibliothḗkē), *dheH₁-
βίος (bíos), βιοτή (biotḗ), βίοτος (bíotos), *gʷeyh₃-
βλῆμα (blêma), βλητός (blētós), βλῆτρον (blêtron),
  βολέω (boléō), βολή (bolḗ), βολίς (bolís), βόλος
  (bólos), *gʷelH-
βούβαλος (boúbalos), βουκολικός (boukolikós),
  βουκόλος (boukólos), βουλῑμία (boulīmía), βοῦς
  (boûs), βουστροφηδόν (boustrophēdón),
  βούτῡρον (boútūron), *gʷóws
βρᾰχῑων (brakhī̄ōn), βραχύς (brakhús), *mrégʰ-
βροτός (brotós), *mer-
βυθός (buthós), *dʰewb-
γάλα (gála), γάλακτος (gálaktos), γαλαξίας
  (galaxías), *glag-
γείνομαι (geínomai), γένεσις (génesis), γενέτωρ
  (genétōr), γένος (génos), *ǵenH₁-
γένυς (génus), *ǵénus
γεραιός (geraiós), γέρανος (géranos), *gerh₂-
γεραρός (gerarós), γέρας (géras), γέρων (gérōn), *ǵerh₂-
γεῦσις (geûsis), γευστός (geustós), γεύω (geúō), *ǵews-
γῆρας (gêras), *ǵerh₂-
γίγνομαι (gígnomai), *ǵenH₁-
γιγνώσκω (gignṓskō), *ǵneh₃-
γνάθος (gnáthos), *ǵénus
γνῶμα (gnôma), γνώμη (gnṓmē), γνώμων
  (gnṓmōn), γνώριμος (gnṓrimos), γνῶσις (gnôsis),
  γνωστός (gnōstós), *ǵneh₃-
γνωτός (gnōtós), *ǵenH₁-, *ǵneh₃-
γόμφος (gómphos), *ǵómbʰos
γονή (gonḗ), γόνος (gónos), *ǵenH₁-
γόνυ (gónu), *ǵónu
γραῖᾰ (graîa), Γραικός (Graikós), *ǵerh₂-

γράμμα (grámma), γραμματικός (grammatikós),
  γρᾰμμή (grammḗ), γραπτός (graptós), *gerbʰ-
γραῦς (graûs), *ǵerh₂-
γραφεύς (grapheús), γραφή (graphḗ), γράφω (gráphō),
  *gerbʰ-
γυμνάζω (gumnázō), γυμνός (gumnós), *negʷ-
γυνή (gunḗ), *gwén
δαιμόνῑον (daimónion), δαίμων (daímōn), δαίομαι
  (daíomai), δαίς (daís), δαῖσις (daîsis), δαιτυμών
  (daitumōn), δαιτύς (daitús), *deh₂-
δάκρυ (dákru), δάκρυον (dákruon), *dakru-
δάμνημι (dámnēmi), *demh₂-
δάρσις (dársis), *der-
δέδεξο (dédexo), *dek-
δεῖγμα (deîgma), δειγματίζω (deigmatízō), δείκνῡμι
  (deíknūmi), *deyḱ-
δεισιδαίμων (deisidaímōn), *deh₂-
δέκα (déka), *déḱm̥t
δέκτης (déktēs), δεκτός (dektós), *deḱ-
δέμω (démō), *dem-
δεξιός (dexiós), δεξιτερός (dexiterós), *deḱs-
δέρμα (dérma), δέρω (dérō), *der-
δεσπότης (despótēs), *pótis
δέχομαι (dékhomai), *deḱ-
δημᾰγωγός (dēmagōgós), *deh₂-, *H₂eǵ-
δημοκρᾰτέομαι (dēmokratéomai), δημοκρᾰτίᾱ
  (dēmokratíā), δημοκρᾰτῐκός (dēmokratikós), δῆμος
  (dêmos), *deh₂-
δι- (di-), διά (diá), *dwóH₁
διαβάλλω (diabállō), *gʷelH-
διακρίνω (diakrínō), *krey-
δῐάρρέω (diarrhéō), δῐάρροιᾰ (diárrhoia), *srew-
δῐᾰφορᾱ (diaphorā), *bher-
δίδωμι (dídōmi), *deH₃-
δῐκάζω (dikázō), δῐκαιος (díkaios), δῐκαιοσύνη
  (dikaiosúnē), δῐκᾰστής (dikastḗs), δίκη (díkē), *deyḱ-
δίς (dís), *dwóH₁
δμῆσις (dmêsis), δμητός (dmētós), *demh₂-
δόγμα (dógma), δογματικός (dogmatikós), δοκέω
  (dokéō), δοκός (dokós), *deḱ-
δόμος (dómos), *dem-
δόξᾰ (dóxa), *deḱ-
δόρυ (dóru), *dóru
δόσις (dósis), δοτός (dotós), *deH₃-
δούξ (doúx), *dewk-
δοχή (dokhḗ), *deḱ-
δροόν (droón), *deru-
δρῦς (drûs), *dóru
δύο (dúo), *dwóH₁
δυσ-ᾱνωρ (dus-ānōr), *h₂nḗr
δῠσθῡμῐᾱ (dusthūmíā), *dʰewh₂-
δῠσμενής (dusmenḗs), *men-
δύσπεπτος (dúspeptos), *pekʷ-
δύσχιμος (dúskhimos), *ǵʰey-
δῶ (dô), *dem-
δωρᾱκινον (dōrákinon), *deru-
δῶρον (dôron), δώτωρ (dṓtōr), *deH₃-

ἔ (hé), *s(w)e-
ἔαρ (éar), *h₁ésh₂r̥, *wésr̥
ἐάω (eáō), *h₁weh₂-
ἔγνων (égnōn), *ǵneh₃-
ἔγχελυς (énkhelus), *ǵʰél̥r
ἐγώ (egṓ), *egH₂
ἔδεκτο (édekto), *deḱ-
ἔδομεν (édomen), *deH₃-
ἕδος (hédos), ἕδρα (hédra), *sed-
ἔδω (édō), *h₁ed-
ἔδωκᾰ (édōka), *deH₃-
ἕεδνα (éedna), *wedʰ-
ἔϝεξε (éwexe), *weǵh-
ἕζομαι (hézomai), *sed-
ἔθεμεν (éthemen), ἔθηκᾰ (éthēka), *dheH₁-
ἐθικός (ethikós), ἐθνᾰ́ρχης (ethnárkhēs),
ἐθνικός (ethnikós), ἔθνος (éthnos), ἔθος (éthos),
ἔθω (éthō), *swe-dʰh₁-
εἰ (ei), *éy / h₁e
εἰδάλιμος (eidálimos), εἶδος (eîdos), εἴδω (eídō),
εἴδωλον (eídōlon), *weyd-
εἴθε (eíthe), *éy / h₁e
εἴκοσι (eíkosi), *wī́ḱm̥tiH₁
εἴκω (eíkō), *weyk-
εἰλεός (eileós), εἰλύω (eilúō), εἴλω (eílō), *welH-
εἶμα (heîma), εἴμαι (eímai), εἴματα (heímata),
εἱμένος (heiménos), *wes-
εἰμί (eimí), *H₁es-
εἶμι (eîmi), *h₁ey-
εἶπον (eípon), *wekʷ-
εἰρήνη (eirḗnē), εἴρω (eírō), *ser-
εἴρω (eírō), εἴρων (eírōn), εἰρωνεία (eirōneía), *wekʷ-
εἰς (eis), *h₁én
εἷς (heîs), *sem-
εἶσα (heîsa), *sed-
εἶτα (eîta), *éy / h₁e
ἐκ (ek), *h₁eǵʰs
ἑκάς (hekás), ἕκαστος (hékastos), *s(w)e-
ἑκατόμβη (hekatómbē), *gʷṓws
ἑκατόν (hekatón), *ḱm̥tóm, *sem-
ἐκεῖ (ekeî), ἐκεῖθεν (ekeîthen), ἐκεῖνος (ekeînos), *ḱi-
ἔκστᾰσῐς (ékstasis), *steh₂-
ἑκτικός (hektikós), *seǵʰ-
ἑκτός (hektós), *h₁eǵʰs
Ἕκτωρ (Héktōr), *seǵʰ-
ἐλᾰ́σσων (elássōn), ἐλαφρός (elaphrós), *h₁lengʷʰ-
ἐλαφρός (elaphrós), *lengʷʰ-
ἐλᾰ́χιστος (elákhistos), ἐλᾰχύς (elakhús), *h₁lengʷʰ-
ἔλδομαι (éldomai), *welh₁-
ἐλευθερία (eleuthería), ἐλεύθερος (eleútheros),
*h₁lewdʰ-
ἕλιξ (hélix), *welH-
ἔλῐπε (élipe), *leykʷ-
ἔλπω (élpō), *welh₁-
ἐλύω (elúō), *welH-
ἐμέ (emé), *H₁me-
ἔμειξᾰ (émeixa), *mey-
ἐμεῖο (emeîo), *H₁meme-
ἔμῐκτο (émikto), *mey-
ἔμορτεν (émorten), *mer-
ἐν (en), *h₁én
ἔνδημος (éndēmos), *deh₂-
ἐνενήκοντα (enenḗkonta), *H₁néwn̥
ἐνέπω (enépō), *sekʷ-
ἐνέργεια (enérgeia), ἐνεργός (energós), *werǵ-
ἔνθα (éntha), ἔνθεν (énthen), *éy / h₁e
ἔνθεος (éntheos), ἐνθουσῐᾰσμός (enthousiasmós),
ἐνθουσῐᾰστής (enthousiastḗs), *dʰéh₁s
ἐννέα (ennéa), *H₁néwn̥
ἔννυμι (hénnumi), *wes-
ἔνος (hénos), *sénos
ἔντερον (énteron), ἐντός (entós), ἐντός (entós), ἐνωπή
(enōpḗ), *h₁én
ἐνωπή (enōpḗ), *h₃ekʷ-
ἐξ (ex), *h₁eǵʰs
ἕξ (héx), *swéḱs
ἔξεστι (éxesti), *H₁es-
ἐξηγέομαι (exēgéomai), ἐξήγησις (exégēsis), *seh₂g-
ἕξις (héxis), *seǵʰ-
ἐξουσῐᾱ (exousíā), *H₁es-
ἔοικα (éoika), *weyk-
ἔορ (éor), *swésōr
ἑός (heós), *s(w)e-
ἐπᾰ́γω (epágō), ἐπαγωγή (epagogḗ), ἐπακτός
(epaktós), *H₂eǵ-
ἐπεί (epeí), ἐπειδή (epeidḗ), *éy / h₁e
ἐπένθεσις (epénthesis, ἐπενθετῐκός (epenthetikós),
ἐπεντίθημι (epentíthēmi), *dheH₁-
ἔπεφνον (épephnon), *gʷʰen-
ἐπέχω (epékhō), *seǵʰ-
ἐπί (epí), *h₁epi
ἐπίθετον (epítheton), *dheH₁-
ἐπῐθῡμῐᾱ (epithūmíā), *dʰewh₂-
ἐπίκουρος (epíkouros), *ḱers-
ἐπίλουτρον (epíloutron), *lewh₃-
ἐπῐνομῐ́ς (epinomís), *nem-
ἐπιτίθημι (epitíthēmi), *dheH₁-
ἐπιφαίνω (epiphaínō), *bʰeh₂-
ἐπῐφορᾱ (epiphorā́), *bher-
ἕπομαι (hépomai), *sekʷ-
ἐποποιία (epopoiía), ἔπος (épos), *wekʷ-
ἐποχή (epokhḗ), *seǵʰ-
ἐπριάμην (epriámēn), *kʷreyh₂-
ἑπτά (heptá), *septm̥
ἐπώνυμος (epṓnumos), *h₁nómn̥
ἔραζε (éraze), *h₁er-
ἔργον (érgon), ἔρδω (érdō), *werǵ-
ἐρεύθω (ereúthō), ἐρῠθρός (eruthrós), *h₁rewdʰ-
ἕσις (hésis), *sed-
ἑσπέρα (hespéra), Ἑσπερίδες (hesperides), ἕσπερος
(hésperos), *wek(ʷ)speros
ἑσπόμην (hespómēn), *sekʷ-
ἔσσαι (éssai), *wes-
ἕστηκᾰ (héstēka), ἔστην (éstēn), *steh₂-

εστι (estí), *H₁es-
ἔστὕγον (éstugon), *(s)tew-
ἔτεκον (étekon), *teĸ-
ἑτερογενής (heterogenés), ἕτερος (héteros), *sem-
ἔτης (étēs), *s(w)e-
ἔτλην (étlēn), *telh₂-
ἔτος (étos), *wet-
εὐθήμων (euthémōn), *dheH₁-
εὐμενής (eumenés), *men-
εὐπορέω (euporéō), *per-
εὖσα (heûsa), εὔω (heúō), *h₁ews-
ἔφθῖτο (éphthito), *dʰegʷʰ-
ἐχέτλη (ekhétlē), *seǵʰ-
ἐχῖνος (ekhînos), *ǵʰér
ἐχυρός (ekhurós), ἔχω (ékhō), *seǵʰ-
ἔχω (ékhō), *weǵh-
ζάω (záō), *gʷeyh₃-
ζεστός (zestós), *yes-
ζεῦγμα (zeûgma), ζεύγνυμι (zeúgnumi), *yewg-
Ζεύς (Zeús), *dyew-
ζέω (zéō), *yes-
ζυγόν (zugón), *yugóm
ζύμη (zúmē), *yes-
ζῶ (zô), ζῳδῐᾰκός (zōidiakós), ζῷον (zôion),
  ζωός (zōós), *gʷeyh₃-
ἡ (hē), *só
ἡγεμονῐ́ᾱ (hēgemoníā), ἡγεμών (hēgemón),
  ἡγέομαι (hēgéomai), *seh₂g-
ἠθικός (ēthikós), ἠθολογῐ́ᾱ (ēthologíā), ἠθολόγος
  (ēthológos), ἦθος (êthos), *swe-dʰh₁-
ἤιθεος (ēítheos), *h₁weydʰ
ἠικανός (ēikanós), *keh₂n-
ἡλίκος (hēlíkos), *éy / h₁e
ἧλιξ (hêlix), *s(w)e-
ἥλιος (hélios), *sóh₂wl̥
ἧμᾰ (hêma), *seH₁-
ἡμεῖς (hēmeîs), *wei
ἡμι- (hēmi-), *sem-
ἡμιστίχιον (hēmistíkhion), *steygʰ-
ἧπαρ (hêpar), ἡπᾱτίζων (hēpatízōn), *Hyékʷr̥
Ἡρακλῆς (Hēraklês), *ĸlew-
ἡώς (ēós), *h₂ews-
θάρσος (thársos), *dʰers-
θεᾶ (theã), *dʰéh₁s
θείνω (theínō), *gʷʰen-
θεῖος (theîos), *dʰeh₁(y)-, *dʰéh₁s
θέμα (théma), θεμείλια (themeília), θέμις (thémis),
  *dheH₁-
θεοκρᾰτῐ́ᾱ (theokratíā), *dʰéh₁s
θεόκτιτος (theóktitos), *teĸ-
θεός (theós), *dʰéh₁s
θερέω (theréō), θερινός (therinós), θέρομαι
  (théromai), θέρος (théros), θέρω (thérō), *gʷʰer-
θέσις (thésis), θετός (thetós), *dheH₁-
θεώρημα (theórēma), θεωρητικός (theōrētikós),
  θεωρῐ́ᾱ (theōríā), θεωρός (theōrós), *wer-
θήκη (thékē), *dheH₁-

θηλή (thēlé), θῆλυς (thêlus), *dʰeh₁(y)-
θῆμᾰ (thêma), θημών (thēmón), *dheH₁-
θήρ (thér), θηρῖον (thēríon), *ǵʰwer-
θής (thés), Θησεύς (Thēseús), *dheH₁-
θιγγάνω (thingánō), *dʰeyǵʰ-
θρᾰσύς (thrasús), *dʰers-
θυγάτηρ (thugátēr), *dʰugh₂tér
θῡμός (thūmós), *dʰewh₂-
θύρα (thúra), θῠρᾱ́ζε (thúrāze), θῠ́ρδα (thúrda), θῠρεός
  (thureós), *dʰwer-
θωμός (thōmós), *dheH₁-
ἴα (ía), *éy / h₁e
ἰδέᾱ (idéā), *weyd-
ἴδιος (ídios), ἰδιώτης (idiótēs), *s(w)e-
ἴδμων (ídmōn), ἴδρις (ídris), *weyd-
ἰδρώς (hidrós), *sweyd-
ἵεμαι (híemai), ἱέρᾱξ (hiérāx), *weyh₁-
ἵζω (hízō), *sed-
ἱππόδρομος (hippódromos), ἱπποπότᾰμος
  (hippopótamos), ἵππος (híppos), *h₁éкwos
ἵς (ís), *weyh₁-
ἵσταμαι (hístamai), ἵστημι (hístēmi), *steh₂-
ἱστορῐ́ᾱ (historía), ἱστορικός (historikós), ἵστωρ (hístōr),
  ἴστωρ (hístōr), *weyd-
ἰσχύς (iskhús), ἴσχω (ískhō), *seǵʰ-
ἰτός (itós), *h₁ey-
καθίζω (kathízō), *sed-
κάλαμος (kálamos), *ĸalam-
καλέω (kaléō), *kelh₁-
καλύπτω (kalúptō), Καλυψώ (Kalupsó), *ĸel-
καμάρα (kamára), κάμῑνος (kámīnos), καμπή (kampé),
  κάμπη (kámpē), κάμπτω (kámptō), καμψός (kampsós),
  *(s)teg-
καναχέω (kanakhéō), καναχή (kanakhé), *keh₂n-
κάπρος (kápros), *kapro
κάπτω (káptō), *keh₂p-
κάρα (kára), *ĸerh₂-
καρδιά (kardiá), *ĸér
κάρη (kárē), *ĸerh₂-
καρπός (karpós), *kerp-
κᾰτᾰβᾰσῐς (katábasis), *gʷem-
καταγράφω (katagráphō), *gerbʰ-
κᾰτᾰπῑ́νω (katapínō), *peh₃-
καταρρέω (katarrhéō), *srew-
κατάστιχον (katástikhon), *steygʰ-
κεῖμαι (keîmai), κειμήλιον (keimélion), *ĸei-
κείρω (keírō), *(s)ker-
κεῖται (keîtai), *ĸei-
κέκλιται (kéklitai), *ĸley-
κέλλα (kélla), *ĸel-
κεντηνάριον (kentēnárion), *ĸm̥tóm
κερᾱῖς (keraîs), κερᾰός (keraós), κέρας (kéras), *ĸerh₂-
κέχῠκᾰ (kékhuka), *ǵʰew-
κῆδος (kêdos), *ĸeh₂d-
κηκίω (kekio), *kek-
κῆρ (kêr), *ĸér
κλείς (kleís), *(s)kel-

κλειτός (kleitós), κλείω (kleíō), κλέος (kléos), *ḱlew-
κλεψῦδρᾱ (klepsúdrā), *wed-
κλέω (kléō), *ḱlew-
κλῆθρα (klêithra), κλίμα (klíma), κλῖμαξ (klîmax),
κλῑμᾰκτηρῐκός (klīmaktērikós), κλίνη (klínē), κλίννω
(klínnō), κλίνω (klínō), κλῖσῐς (klísis), *ḱley-
κλῦτε (klûte), κλῠτός (klutós), κλύω (klúō), *ḱlew-
κμέλεθρον (kmélethron), *(s)teg-
κόγχος (kónkhos), *ḱonkho-
κοιμάω (koimáō), *ḱei-
κοίρανος (koíranos), *ker-
κοίτη (koítē), *ḱei-
κολοφών (kolophṓn), κολωνός (kolōnós), κολώνη
(kolṓnē), *kelH-
κονίς (konís), *knid-
κρανίον (kranĩon), *ḱerh₂-
κράταιγος (krátaigos), *h₂eyǵ-
κρέας (kréas), *krewh₂-
κρῖμα (krîma), κρῖνω (krĩnō), κρίσις (krísis),
ὑπόκρῑσῐς (hupókrisis), κριτής (kritḗs), *krey-
κρούω (kroúō), *krewh₂-
κρώπιον (krṓpion), *kerp-
κτείς (kteís), κτενῐ́ζω (ktenízō), κτένῐον (kténion), *peḱ-
κτίζω (ktízō), κτῖσῐς (ktísis), *teḱ-
κύκλος (kúklos), *kʷel-
κύλινδρος (kúlindros), *(s)kel-
κυλίνδω (kulíndō), *(s)kel-
κῠνάγχη (kunánkhē), κῠνῐκός (kunikós), κῠνόμαζον
(kunómazon), κύων (kúōn), *ḱwó
κῶλον (kôlon), κῶλον (kôlon), *(s)kel-
κώμη (kṓmē), *ḱei-
κώπη (kṓpē), *keh₂p-
λάκκος (lákkos), *lókus
λάπτω (láptō), *leb-
λάσιος (lásios), *h₂welh₁-
λαφύσσω (laphússō), *leb-
λάχνη (lákhnē), λάχνος (lákhnos), *h₂welh₁-
λέγω (légō), *leǵ-
λείπω (leípō), *leykʷ-
λέκτο (lékto), λέκτρον (léktron), *legh-
λέλοιπᾰ (léloipa), *leykʷ-
λευκός (leukós), *lewk-
λέχομαι (lékhomai), λέχος (lékhos), *legh-
λῆνος (lênos), *h₂welh₁-
λιμπάνω (limpánō), *leykʷ-
λίνον (línon), *lino-
λίπος (lípos), *leyp-
λοβός (lobós), *leb-
λογισμός (logismós), λογῐστῐκός (logistikós), λόγος
(lógos), *leǵ-
λουτρόν (loutrón), λούω (loúō), *lewh₃-
λόχος (lókhos), *legh-
λυγίζω (lugízō), *seh₂g-
λύγξ (lúnx), *lewk-
λύγος (lúgos), *seh₂g-
λυκάβας (lukábas), Λυκαῖος (Lukaîos), *lewk-
λυκανθρωπία (lykanthropía), *wḷkʷos

λύκειος (lúkeios), *lewk-
λύκος (lúkos), *wḷkʷos
λυκόφως (lukóphōs), λύχνος (lúkhnos), *lewk-
λῶμα (lôma), *h₂welh₁-
μάθημα (máthēma), μᾰθημᾰτῐκός (mathēmatikós),
μαίνομαι (maínomai), *men-
μᾰκρηγορῐᾱ (makrēgoríā), *meh₂k-
μᾰκροθῡμῐ́ᾱ (makrothūmíā), *dʰewh₂-, *meh₂k-
μᾰκρόουρος (makróouros), μᾰκρός (makrós), *meh₂k-
μάμμη (mámmē), *méh₂-méh₂
μανθάνω (manthánō), μανίᾱ (maníā), *men-
μανός (manós), *mey-
μάρη (márē), *méh₂-r̥
μασάομαι (masáomai), μάσταξ (mástax), μᾰστῐχάω
(mastikháō), *mendʰ-
μέ (mé), *H₁me-
μεγαίρω (megaírō), μεγᾰλος (megálos), μέγιστος
(mégistos), *méǵh₂s
μέδομαι (médomai), Μέδουσᾱ (Médousa), μέδω
(médō), *med-
μέθυ (méthu), *médʰu
μείγνῡμῐ (meígnūmi), *mey-
μείζων (meízōn), *méǵh₂s
μεῖξῐς (meîxis), *mey-
μείς (meís), *méh₁n̥s
μείων (meíōn), *mey-
μέλᾱς (mélās), *melh₂-
μέλι (méli), μέλισσα (mélissa), *melit-
μέμονα (mémona), μένος (ménos), *men-
μεσοποτάμιος (mesopotámios), μέσος (mésos),
*médʰyos
μεταφέρω (metaphérō), *bher-
μετρικός (metrikós), μέτρον (métron), *meh₁-
μήδεα (mḗdea), μήδομαι (mḗdomai), *med-
μήκιστος (mḗkistos), μῆκος (mêkos), *meh₂k-
μήν (mḗn), μήνη (mḗnē), μηνῖσκος (mēnískos), *méh₁n̥s
μήτηρ (mḗtēr), *méh₂tēr
μῆτις (mêtis), *meh₁-
μία (mía), *sem-
μῖγνῡμῐ (mígnūmi), *mey-
μιμνήσκω (mimnḗskō), *men-
μινύθω (minúthō), μῖξῐς (míxis), μίσγω (mísgō), *mey-
μνάομαι (mnáomai), μνήμη (mnḗmē), *men-
μόνος (mónos), *mey-
μου (mou), *H₁meme-
μυῖα (muîa), *mus-
μύλη (múlē), μύλλω (múllō), *melh₂-
μύρμηξ (múrmēx), *morwi-
μῦς (mûs), *muh₂s-
μύσταξ (mústax), *mendʰ-
νᾰ- (nā-), *n̥-
Ναϊάς (Naïás), νᾱμᾰ (nâma), *(s)neh₂-
νᾶσσα (nâssa), *h₂eneti-
ναῦς (naûs), ναυσία (nausía), ναύτης (naútēs), ναυτία
(nautía), ναυτικός (nautikós), νᾱω (nāō), *(s)neh₂-
νεκρός (nekrós), *neḱ-
νέκταρ (néktar), *neḱ-, *terh₂-

νέκυς (nékus), *nek̑-
Νέμεσις (Némesis), νέμος (némos), νέμω (némō), *nem-
νέος (néos), *new
νευροειδές (neuroeidés), νεῦρον (neûron), *(s)neh₁-
νεφέλη (nephélē), νέφος (néphos), *nebʰ-
νεφρός (nephrós), *negʷʰ-r-
νέω (néō), *(s)neh₁-
νη- (nē-), *n̥-
νήϊος (nḗïos), *(s)neh₂-
νῆις (nêis), *weyd-
Νηρεύς (Nēreús), *(s)neh₂-
νῆσσα (nêssa), νῆττα (nêtta), *h₂eneti-
νίφα (nipha), νίφω (níphō), *sneygʷʰ-
νομή (nomḗ), νομίζω (nomízō), νόμισμα (nómisma),
νομοθέτης (nomothétēs), νομοθετῐκός (nomothetikós),
νομός (nomós), νόμος (nómos), *nem-
νυκτός (nuktós), νύξ (núx), *nókʷts
νυός (nuós), *snusós
νώ (nṓ), *wei
νω- (nō-), *n̥-
ὁ (ho), *só
ὀβελίσκος (obelískos), ὀβολός (obolós), *gʷelH-
ὄγκη (ónkē), ὄγκος (ónkos), *h₂enk-
ὄγμος (ógmos), *H₂eǵ-
ὅδε (hóde), ὁδί (hodí), *só
ὀδμή (odmḗ), *h₃ed-
ὁδός (hodós), *sed-
ὁδούς (odoús) / ὀδών (odṓns), *h₃dónts
ὀδύσσομαι (odússomai), ὀδώδειν (odṓdein), ὄζω
(ózō), *h₃ed-
οἶδα (oîda), *weyd-
οἰκέω (oikéō), *weyk̑-
οἰκονομῐ́ᾱ (oikonomíā), *nem-
οἶκος (oîkos), *weyk̑-
οἴνη (oínē), οἶνος (oînos), *óy-nos
οἶνος (oînos), *wóyh₁nom
οἷος (hoîos), *éy / h₁e
οἶος (oîos), *óy-nos
ὄϊς (óïs), *h₂ówis
ὀκρῖς (okrís), ὄκρις (ókris), *h₂ék̑
ὀκτώ (oktṓ), *ok̑tṓw
ὀκτώπους (oktṓpous), *póds
ὅλος (hólos), ὁλότης (holótēs), *solh₂-
ὁμαλός (homalós), *sem-
ὀμείχω (omeíkhō), *h₃meyǵʰ-
ὄμμα (ómma), *h₃ekʷ-
ὁμός (homós), *sem-
ὀμφαλός (omphalós), *h₃enbʰ-
ὄνομᾰ (ónoma), ὀνομᾰτοποιῐ́ᾱ (onomatopoiíā), *h₁nómn̥
ὄνυξ (ónux), *h₃negʰ-
ὀξεῖᾰ (oxeîa), *h₂ék̑
ὀξύα (oxúa), *h₃es-
ὀξύς (oxús), ὀξῠ́τονος (oxútonos), *h₂ék̑
ὀξῠ́τονος (oxútonos), *ten-
ὀπτικός (optikós), *h₃ekʷ-
ὅραμα (hórama), ὁράω (horáō), ὅρασις (hórasis), *wer-
ὄργανον (órganon), ὀργή (orgḗ), ὀργίζω (orgízō), *werǵ-

ὀρέγειν (oregein), ὀρέγω (orégō), ὀρεκτός (orektós),
ὄρεξις (órexis), *h₃reǵ-
ὀρίνω (orínō), ὄρμενος (órmenos), *h₃er-
ὅρμος (hórmos), *ser-
ὄρνεον (órneon), ὄρνιθος (órnithos), ὄρνῑξ (órnīx),
ὄρνις (órnis), *h₃érō
ὄρνῡμι (órnūmi), *h₃er-
ὀρός (horós), *srew-
ὄρος (óros), *h₃er-
ὀρφανός (orphanós), *h₃erbʰ-
ὅς (hós), *éy / h₁e, *s(w)e-
ὀσμή (osmḗ), *h₃ed-
ὅσος (hósos), *éy / h₁e
ὄσσε (ósse), ὄσσομαι (óssomai), *h₃ekʷ-
ὀστέον (ostéon), *h₃ésth₁
ὅστις (hóstis), *éy / h₁e, *kʷis
οὐδ-αμός (oud-amós), *sem-
οὖθαρ (oûthar), *h₁owHdʰr̥-
οὕς (oûs), *h₂ew-
οὐσῐ́ᾱ (ousíā), *H₁es-
οὗτος (hoûtos), *só
ὀφθαλμός (ophthalmós), *h₃ekʷ-
ὀφρύς (ophrús), *h₃bʰrúHs
ὀχέομαι (okhéomai), *weǵh-
ὀχέω (okhéō), ὄχος (ókhos), ὀχυρός (okhurós), *seǵʰ-
ὄψ (óps), *wekʷ-
ὄψις (ópsis), ὄψομαι (ópsomai), *h₃ekʷ-
πάγη (págē), *peh₂ǵ-
πάγος (págos), *peh₂ǵ-
παιδᾰγωγός (paidagōgós), *H₂eǵ-
πάλαι (pálai), πάλιν (pálin), *kʷel-
Πάν (Pán), *peh₂-
πανδοκεῖον (pandokeîon), *dek̑-
πάρ (pár), παρά (pará), πάρα (pára), *per-
πᾰρᾰβάλλω (parabállō), παραβολή (parabolḗ), *gʷelH-
παράδεισος (parádeisos), *dʰeyǵʰ-
πᾰρᾰ́δοξος (parádoxos), *dek̑-
πᾰρᾰκλαυσίθῠρον (paraklausíthuron), *dʰwer-
παρένθεσις (parénthesis), *dheH₁-
πάρος (páros), *per-
πᾰρουσῐ́ᾱ (parousíā), *H₁es-
πατέομαι (patéomai), *peh₂-
πατήρ (patḗr), *ph₂tḗr
πάτος (pátos), *pent-
πατριώτης (patriótēs), *ph₂tḗr
πάχνη (pákhnē), *peh₂ǵ-
πεδίον (pedíon), πέδον (pédon), πεζός (pezós), *ped-
πείθω (peíthō), *bʰeydʰ-
πεῖρα (peîra), πεῖραρ (peîrar), πείρω (peírō), *per-
πέκος (pékos), *pek̑u-
πεκτέω (pektéō), πέκω (pékō), *pek̑-
πελιτνός (pelitnós), *pelH-
πέλλᾱς (péllās), *pel-
πέλω (pélō), *kʷel-
πέμμᾰ (pémma), *pekʷ-
πέντε (pénte), *pénkʷe
πέποιθᾰ (pépoitha), *bʰeydʰ-

πέπτρια (péptria), πέπτω (péptō), *pekʷ-
πέπυσμαι (pépusmai), *bʰewdʰ-
πέπων (pépōn), *pekʷ-
πέρ (pér), πέρᾱ (pérā), πέρᾱν (pérān), πέρας
 (péras), περάω (peráō), περί (perí), *per-
Περικλῆς (Periklês), *ḱlew-
περίπλους (períplous), *plew-
πέρπερος (pérperos), πέρπερος (pérperos), *per-
πέσσω (péssō), *pekʷ-
πέταλον (pétalon), πετάννῡμι (petánnūmi),
 πέτασος (pétasos), πέτομαι (pétomai), *peth₂
πέττω (péttō), *pekʷ-
πεύθομαι (peúthomai), *bʰewdʰ-
πέφαται (péphatai), *gʷʰen-
πέψῐς (pépsis), *pekʷ-
πῆγμα (pêgma), πήγνυμι (pégnumi), πηγός
 (pēgós), *peh₂ǵ-
πηλίκος (pēlíkos), *kʷis
πῐκρός (pikrós), *peyḱ-
πίμπλημι (pímplēmi), *pleh₁-
πῖνον (pînon), πίνω (pínō), *peh₃-
πίπτω (píptō), *peth₂
πλανάω (planáō), πλάσῐς (plásis), πλάσμᾰ
 (plásma), πλάσσω (plássō), πλάστης (plástēs),
 πλαστικός (plastikós), πλαστός (plastós), *pleh₂-
πλᾰτᾱ (plátā), Πλᾰταιᾱ (Plátaia), πλᾰτᾰμών
 (platamón), πλᾰτᾰνος (plátanos), *pleth₂-
πλατεῖα (plateîa), *pleh₂-
πλᾰτη (plátē), πλᾰτος (plátos), *pleth₂-
πλᾰτύς (platús), *pleh₂-
πλέκω (plékō), *pleḱ-
πλεύμων (pleúmōn), *plewmō
πλέω (pléō), *plew-
πλέως (pléōs), *pleh₁-
πληγή (plēgḗ), *pleh₂k-
πληθῡς (plēthūs), πλήθω (pléthō), πλήρης
 (plḗrēs), *pleh₁-
πλήσσω (pléssō), *pleh₂k-
πλῆτο (plêto), *pleh₁-
πλοῖον (ploîon), πλοῖον (ploîon), *plew-
πλοκή (ploké), *pleḱ-
πλόος (plóos), πλουτοκρᾱτῐᾱ (ploutokratíā),
 πλοῦτος (ploûtos), πλύνω (plúnō), *plew-
ποδαπός (podapós), *kʷis
πόδιον (pódion), *pṓds
πόθεν (póthen), ποῖ (poî), *kʷis
ποικίλος (poikílos), *peyḱ-
ποιμήν (poimḗn), *peh₂-
ποινή (poiné), *kʷey-
ποῖος (poîos), *kʷis
πόκος (pókos), *peḱ-
πολιός (poliós), *pelH-
πόλος (pólos), *kʷel-
πολύς (polús), *pleh₁-
πόντος (póntos), *pent-
πορεύω (poreúō), πορθμός (porthmós), πορίζω
 (porízō), πόρος (póros), πόρρω (pórrhō), πόρσω

(pórsō), *per-
πόσις (pósis), *peh₃-, *pótis
πόσος (pósos), *kʷis
ποταμός (potamós), *peth₂
πότε (póte), *kʷis
ποτήρῐον (potḗrion), *peh₃-
ποῦ (poû), *kʷis
πούς (poús), *pṓds
πρᾶγμᾰ (prâgma), πρᾱγματικός (prāgmatikós),
 πρᾱκτικός (prāktikós), πρᾶξις (prâxis), πρᾱσσω
 (prāssō), πρείν (preín), πρέσβυς (présbus),
 πρεσβῡτερος (presbúteros), *per-
πρῖγκιψ (prînkips), *keh₂p-
πρίν (prín), πρό (pró), *per-
πρόβλημᾰ (próblēma), *gʷelH-
πρόγραμμα (prógramma), προγράφω (prográphō),
 *gerbʰ-
πρόκα (próka), *per-
Προμηθεύς (Promētheús), *men-
πρόμος (prómos), πρός (prós), *per-
προσφέρω (prosphérō), προσφορᾱ (prosphorā), *bher-
πρότερος (próteros), προτί (protí), *per-
προφορᾱ (prophorā), *bher-
πρυμνός (prumnós), πρωΐ (prṓï), πρῷρα (prôira), *per-
πρωταγωνιστής (prōtagōnistḗs), *H₂eǵ-
πρῶτος (prôtos), *per-
πτερόν (pterón), πτερόω (pteróō), πτέρυξ (ptérux),
 πτερωτός (pterōtós), *péth₂r
πτίσσω (ptíssō), *peys-
πτῶμα (ptôma), πτῶσις (ptôsis), πτωτικός (ptōtikós),
 πτωτός (ptōtós), *peth₂
πυγμή (pugmḗ), *pewǵ-
πῠθμήν (puthmḗn), *bʰudʰmḗn
πύκτης (púktēs), *pewǵ-
πυνθάνομαι (punthánomai), *bʰewdʰ-
πύξ (púx), *pewǵ-
πῦρ (pûr), πυρά (purá), *péh₂ur
πύργος (púrgos), *bʰerǵʰ-
πυρίκτιτος (puríktitos), *teḱ-
πῠρρός (purrhós), *péh₂ur
πῠστῐς (pústis), *bʰewdʰ-
πῶμα (pôma), *peh₂-
πῶς (pôs), *kʷis
πῶυ (pôu), *peh₂-
ῥᾱδιξ (rhádix), *wréh₂ds
ῥέζω (rhézō), *werǵ-
ῥεῦμα (rheûma), ῥέω (rhéō), *srew-
ῥῆμα (rhêma), ῥητορικός (rhētorikós), ῥήτωρ (rhḗtōr),
 *wek-
ῥίζα (rhíza), ῥιζικός (rhizikós), *wréh₂ds
ῥινόκερως (rhinókerōs), *ḱerh₂-
ῥόμος (rhómos), *wr̥mis-
ῥόος (rhóos), ῥυθμός (rhuthmós), *srew-
σαρδόνυξ (sardónux), *h₃negʰ-
σήμερον (sḗmeron), *ḱi-
σκάριφος (skáriphos), *(s)ker-
σκέλος (skélos), *(s)kel-

σκεπτικός (skeptikós), σκέπτομαι (sképtomai),
σκέψατο (sképsato), σκέψῑς (sképsis), *spek̂-
σκολιός (skoliós), σκολίωμα (skolíōma), σκολίωσις
　(skolíōsis), *(s)kel-
σκοπεύω (skopeúō), σκοπέω (skopéō), σκοπός
　(skopós), *spek̂-
σκώληξ (skṓlēx), *(s)kel-
σός (sós), *túh₂
σπίτι (spíti), *gʰóstis
σπλήν (splḗn), *splenĝʰ-
στάδιος (stádios), σταθμός (stathmós), στάμνος
　(stámnos), στάσις (stásis), στᾱτός (statós),
σταῦλος (stávlos), σταυρός (staurós), *steh₂-
στέγη (stégē), στέγος (stégos), στέγω (stégō), *(s)teg-
στείχω (steíkhō), *steygʰ-
στέλλω (stéllō), *stel-
στενάζω (stenázō), στένει (sténei), Στέντωρ
　(Sténtōr), στένω (sténō), *(s)tenh₂-
στέρνον (stérnon), *sterh₃-
στῆμᾰ (stêma), στήμων (stḗmōn), *steh₂-
στίχος (stíkhos), *steygʰ-
στοᾰ (stoā), στοιᾰ (stoiā), στοιή (stoié), *steh₂-
στοῖχος (stoîkhos), *steygʰ-
στολή (stolḗ), στόλος (stólos), *stel-
στόνος (stónos), *(s)tenh₂-
στόρνῡμι (stórnūmi), στρατηγία (stratēgía),
　στρᾰτηγός (stratēgós), στρατός (stratós), *sterh₃-
στρουθός (strouthós), *trosdos
στρῶμα (strôma), στρωμνή (strōmnḗ), στρωτός
　(strōtós), *sterh₃-
στῠγέω (stugéō), στύγος (stúgos), στύξ (stúx),
　στύπος (stúpos), *(s)tew-
στῳᾶ (stōiã), στωϊᾶ (stōïã), στώμιξ (stṓmix), *steh₂-
σύ (sú), *túh₂
σῠγγράφω (sungráphō), *gerbʰ-
σῠμπόσῐον (sumpósion), *peh₃-
σῦν (sún), συν- (sun-) / ξύν (xún), *sem-
συνάγω (sunágō), σῠνᾰγωγή (sunagōgḗ), *H₂eĝ-
σῠνθεσῐς (súnthesis), σῠνθήκη (sunthḗkē), *dheH₁-
σῠννένοφᾰ (sunnénopha), σῠννέφει (sunnéphei),
　σῠννέφω (sunnéphō), *nebʰ-
σῠνοψῐς (súnopsis), *h₃ek̂ʷ-
σῠνώνῠμος (sunṓnumos), *h₁nómη
σφεῖς (spheîs), *s(w)e-
σφήξ (sphḗx), *bʰey-
σφώ (sphṓ), *túh₂
σχεδόν (skhedón), σχερός (skherós), σχέσις
　(skhésis), σχῆμα (skhêma), *seĝʰ-
σχίζω (skhízō), σχίσις (skhísis), σχιστός (skhistós),
　*skey-
σχολή (skholḗ), *seĝʰ-
τάλαντον (tálanton), ταλασίφρων (talasíphrōn), *telh₂-
τᾱσις (tásis), *ten-
ταῦρος (taûros), *(s)táwros
τέγος (tégos), *(s)teg-
τεθαρσήκασι (tetharsḗkasi), *dʰers-
τείνω (teínō), *ten-

τείρω (teírō), *terh₁-
τεῖχος (teîkhos), *dʰeyĝʰ-
τέκνον (téknon), τέκον (tékon), *tek̂-
τέκτων (téktōn), *tetk̂-
τελαμών (telamṓn), *telh₂-
τέλεσμα (télesma), τελέω (teléō), τέλλω (téllō), *kʷel-
τένων (ténōn), *ten-
τεός (teós), *túh₂
τέρεμνον (téremnon), *treb-
τέρετρον (téretron), *terh₁-
τέρθρον (térthron), *terh₂-
τέρμα (térma), τέρμων (térmōn), *térmη
τέρσομαι (térsomai), *ters-
τέρυ (téru), *terh₁-
τέσσαρες (téssares), *kʷetwóres
τέτοκα (tétoka), *tek̂-
τετρα- (tetra-), *kʷetwóres
τετραίνω (tetraínō), *terh₁-
τετρᾰπους (tetrápous), *kʷetwóres
τετράστιχος (tetrástikhos), *steygʰ-
τέτταρες (téttares), *kʷetwóres
τέφρα (téphra), *dʰegʷʰ-
τέχνη (tékhnē), *tetk̂-
τήθη (têthē), Τηθύς (Tēthús), *dʰeh₁(y)-
τῆλε (têle), *kʷel-
τηλικος (tēlíkos), *só
τίθημι (títhēmi), *dheH₁-
τίκτω (tíktō), *tetk̂-
τίνω (tínō), τῑνω (tínō), *kʷey-
τίς (tís), *kʷis
τίσις (tísis), *kʷey-
τίτθη (títthē), *dʰeh₁(y)-
τλάντος (tlántos), τλᾱτός (tlātós), *telh₂-
τό (tó), *só
τόλμα (tólma), τολμάω (tolmáō), *telh₂-
τόνος (tónos), *ten-
τορεύς (toreús), τόρμος (tórmos), τόρνος (tórnos),
　*terh₁-
τόσος (tósos), *só
τράγος (trágos), *terh₁-
τρεῖς (treîs), *tréyes
τρῆμα (trêma), τρῆσις (trêsis), τρητός (trētós), *terh₁-
τρι- (tri-), τρῐάς (triás), *tréyes
τρῐβρᾰχῠς (tríbrakhus), *mréĝʰ-
τρισκελίς (triskelís), *(s)kel-
τρύχω (trúkhō), τρύω (trúō), τρώγω (trṓgō), *terh₁-
τύκος (túkos), τῠμπᾰνον (túmpanon), τυπικός (tupikós),
　τύπος (túpos), τύπτω (túptō), *(s)tew-
ὕαινα (húaina), *suH-
ὑγιής (hugiḗs), *gʷeyh₃-
ὑγιής (hugiḗs), *h₂ey-
ὕδρα (húdra), ὕδρος (húdros), ὕδωρ (húdōr), *wed-
υἱός (huiós), υἱύς (huiús), *suh₁nús
ὑμεῖς (humeîs), *túh₂
ὑμήν (humḗn), *sīw-
ὑπέρ (hupér), *upo
ὕπνος (húpnos), *swep-

ὑπό (hupó), *upo
ὑπόθεσις (hupóthesis), ὑποθήκη (hupothékē),
 *dheH₁-
ὑποπετρίδιος (hupopetrídios), *péth₂r
ὗς (hûs), *suH-
ὑφαίνω (huphaínō), ὑφή (huphḗ), *webh-
φαινόμενον (phainómenon), φαίνω (phaínō), φαμί
 (phamí), φᾰνερός (phanerós), φάντα (phánta),
 φᾰντᾰσῐ́ᾱ (phantasíā), φᾰ́ντᾰσμᾰ (phántasma),
 φᾰντᾰστῐκός (phantastikós), φάος (pháos), φάσις
 (phásis), φάτις (phátis), *bʰeh₂-
φατός (phatós), *bʰeh₂-, *gʷʰen-
φείδομαι (pheídomai), *bʰeyd-
φέρμᾰ (phérma), φέρω (phérō), *bher-
φηγός (phēgós), *bʰeh₂go-
φήμη (phḗmē), φημί (phēmí), *bʰeh₂-
φήρ (phḗr), *ǵʰwer-
Φήρον (Phḗron, *bʰars-
φθινύθω (phthinúthō), φθίνω (phthínō), φθῐ́σῐς
 (phthísis), *dʰegʷʰ-
Φῐ́λῐππος (Phílippos), *h₁éḱwos
φόνος (phónos), *gʷʰen-
φορᾱ́ (phorā́), φορέω (phoréō), *bher-
φοῦρνος (phoûrnos), *gʷʰer-
φράξος (fráxos), *bʰereǵ-
φράτηρ (phrátēr), *bʰréh₂tēr
φρέᾱρ (phréār), φρεῖᾰρ (phreîar), *bʰrewh₁-
φυή (phuḗ), φῡλή (phūlḗ), *bʰuH-
φύλλον (phúllon), *bʰleh₃-
φῦλον (phûlon), φῦμᾰ (phûma), φυσικός
 (phusikós), φύσις (phúsis), φυτικός (phutikós),
 φύτλον (phútlon), φύω (phúō), φύω (phúō), *bʰuH-
φωνέω (phōnéō), φωνή (phōnḗ), *bʰeh₂-
φώρ (phṓr), *bher-
φῶς (phôs), φωτω- (phōtō-), *bʰeh₂-
χαίρω (khaírō), *ǵʰer-
χαμαί (khamaí), *dʰéǵʰōm
χανδάνω (khandánō), *weyd-
χαρά (khará), χᾰρᾰκτήρ (kharaktḗr), χᾰρᾰ́σσω
 (kharássō), χάρις (kháris), χᾰρῐσμᾰ (khárisma),
 χάρμα (khárma), χάρμη (khármē), χάρτης (khártēs),
 χαρτός (khartós), χαρτουλάριος (khartoulários), *ǵʰer-
χεῖμα (kheîma), χειμερινός (kheimerinós), χειμών
 (kheimṓn), *ǵʰey-
χέλῡς (khélūs), χελώνη (khelṓnē), *gʰelōw-
χεῦμᾰ (kheûma), χέω (khéō), *ǵʰew-
χήν (khḗn), *ǵʰans-
χήρ (khḗr), *ǵʰḗr
χθαμαλός (khthamalós), *dʰéǵʰōm
χθές (khthés), *dʰǵʰ(y)es-
χθόνιος (khthónios), χθών (khthṓn), *dʰéǵʰōm
χιών (khiṓn), *ǵʰey-
χλωρός (khlōrós), *ǵʰelh₃-
χοῖρος (khoîros), *ǵʰér
χολή (kholḗ), *ǵʰelh₃-
χορδή (khordḗ), *ǵʰern-
χορηγός (khorēgós), *seh₂g-

χόριον (khórion), χόρτος (khórtos), *ǵʰer-
χρῡσόκᾰρπος (khrūsókarpos), *kerp-
χύτλον (khútlon), χυτός (khutós), *ǵʰew-
ψάρ (psár), *spér
ψύλλα (psúlla), *plou-
ὠδυσάμην (ōdusámēn), *h₃ed-
ὠλένη (ōlénē), ὠλήν (ōlḗn), ὠλλόν (ōllón), *Heh₃l-
ὠνέομαι (ōnéomai), ὦνος (ônos), *wesno-
ᾠοειδής (ōioeidḗs), ᾠόν (ōión), *h₂ōwyóm
ὥρα (hṓra), ὡρολογέω (hōrologéō), ὡροσκοπέω
 (hōroskopéō), *yeh₁-
ὦρτο (ôrto), *h₃er-
ὡς (hōs), *éy / h₁e, *só
ὠτός (ōtós), *h₂ew-
ὤψ (óps), *h₃ekʷ-

Greek

α- (a-), ά- (á-), *n̥-
άγριος (ágrios), αγρός (agrós), *h₂égros
άγω (ágo), αγωγή (agogí), αγών (agón), αγώνας
 (agónas), αγωνία (agonía), αγωνιστής (agonistís),
 *H₂eǵ-
άδικος (ádikos), *deyḱ-
αέρας (aéras), *h₂ews-
άεργος (áergos), *werǵ-
αετός (aetós), *h₂éwis
άθεος (átheos), *dʰéh₁s
άθλημα (áthlima), αθλητής (athlitís), αθλητικός
 (athlitikós), *H₂weH₁-
αιθήρ (aithír); αιθέρας (aithéras), *h₂eydʰ-
αιώνας (aiónas), *h₂ey-
ακμή (akmí), *h₂éḱ
άκμονας (ákmonas), άκμων (ákmon), *h₂éḱ-mō
άκρος (ákros), *h₂éḱ
αλάτι (aláti), *séh₂ls
αλύγιστος (alýgistos), *seh₂g-
αμβροσία (amvrosía), *mer-
αμνησία (amnisía), *men-
αν- (an-), άν- (án-), *n̥-
ανάβαση (anávasi), *gʷem-
αναγιγνώσκω (anagignósko), *ǵneh₃-
ανάγω (anágo), *H₂eǵ-
ανάσταση (anástasi), *steh₂-
αναφορά (anaforá), *bher-
άνδρας (ándras), ανδρόγυνος (andrógynos), *h₂nḗr
άνεμος (ánemos), *h₂enh₁-
άνεργος (ánergos), *werǵ-
ανιψιός (anipsiós), *nepot-
αντί (antí), *h₂ent
αντίθεση (antíthesi), *dheH₁-
ανώνυμος (anónymos), *h₁nómn̥
από (apó), *h₂pó
αποθήκη (apothíki), *dheH₁-
αποκαλύπτω (apokalýpto), αποκάλυψη
 (apokálypsi), *ḱel-
απορία (aporía), *per-
αράχνη (aráchni), αρετή (aretí), αριθμός (arithmós),
 *h₂er
άρκλα (árkla), *h₂erk-
αρκούδα (arkoúda), άρκτος (árktos), *h₂r̥tḱos
άρμα (árma), άρματα (ármata), *h₂er
αρμέγω (armégo), *H₂melǵ-
αρμός (armós), *h₂er
άροτρο (árotro), *H₂erH₃-
αρχιτέκτονας (architéktonas), *tetḱ-
αστέρας (astéras), αστέρι (astéri) (astéri), *h₂stḗr
ατμός (atmós), *H₂weH₁-
Αύγουστος (Ávgoustos), *h₂ewg-
αυθεντικός (afthentikós), *h₂ew
αύριο (ávrio), *h₂ews-

αυτί (aftí), αυτός (aftós), αφέντης (aféntis), *h₂ew
αφρός (afrós), *nebʰ-
αχινός (achinós), *ǵʰér
βαλλίστρα (vallístra), *gʷelH-
βάλλω (vállo), *gʷelH-
βαρβάτος (varvátos), *bʰardʰeh₂-
βαρύτητα (varýtita), *gʷerh₂-
βάση (vási), βατός (vatós), *gʷem-
βέλος (vélos), *gʷelH-
βεντούζα (ventoúza), *H₂weH₁-
βιβλιοθήκη (vivliothíki), *dheH₁-
βίδρα (vidra), *udréh₂
βίντεο (vínteo), *weyd-
βίος (víos), *gʷeyh₃-
βούβαλος (noúvalos), βούτυρο (noútyro), *gʷṓws
βυθός (vythós), *dʰewb-
γαλαξίας (galaxías), *glag-
Γενάρης (Genáris), *h₁ey-
γένος (génos), *ǵenH₁-
γέροντας (gérontas), *ǵerh₂-
γερούνδιον (geroúndion), *H₂eǵ-
για (gia), *dwóH₁
γκουρού (gkouroú), *gʷerh₂-
γνάθος (gnáthos), *ǵénus
γνώμη (gnómi), γνώριμος (gnórimos), *ǵneh₃-
γόμφος (gómfos), *ǵómbʰos
γόνατο (gónato), *ǵónu
γράμμα (grámma), γραμματικός (grammatikós),
 γραμμή (grammí), γραπτός (graptós), γραφή (grafí),
 γράφω (gráfo), *gerbʰ-
γυμνάσιο (gymnásio), γυμνός (gymnós), *negʷ-
γυναίκα (gynaíka), *gʷḗn
δάκρυ (dákry), *dáḱru-
δείγμα (deígma), δειγματίζω (deigmatízo), *deyḱ-
δεισιδαίμων (deisidaímon), *deh₂-
δείχνω (deíchno), *deyḱ-
δέκα (déka), Δεκέμβρης (Dekémvris), Δεκέμβριος
 (Dekémvrios), *déḱm̥t
δέκτης (déktis), *deḱ-
δεξιός (dexiós), *deḱs-
δέρμα (dérma), *der-
δεσπότης (despótis), *pótis
δημαγωγός (dimagogós), *deh₂-, *H₂eǵ-
δημοκρατικός (dimokratikós), δήμος (dímos), *deh₂-
διάβολος (diávolos), *gʷelH-
διακρίνω (diakríno), *krey-
διαρρέω (diarréo), διάρροια (diárroia), *srew-
Δίας (Días), *dyew-
διαφορά (diaforá), *bher-
δίδω (dído), *deH₃-
δικάζω (dikázo), δίκαιος (díkaios), δικαιοσύνη
 (dikaiosýni, δικαίωμα (dikaíoma), δικαστής (dikastís),
 δίκη (díki), *deyḱ-
δίνω (díno), *deH₃-
δόντι (dónti), *h₃dónts
δόρυ (dóry), *dóru
δούκας (doúkas), *dewk-

δύο (dýo), *dwóH₁
δυσθυμία (dysthymía), *dʰewh₂-
δώρο (dóro), *deH₃-
έαρ (éar), *h₁ésh₂r, *wésr̥
εγώ (egó), *egH₂
έδικτο (édikto), *deyḱ-
εθνικός (ethnikós), έθνος (éthnos), *swe-dʰh₁-
είδωλο (eídolo), *weyd-
είκοσι (eíkosi), *wīḱm̥tiH₁
είμαι (eímai), *H₁es-
ειρήνη (eiríni), *ser-
εις (eis), *h₁én
έκαστος (ékastos), *s(w)e-
εκατό (ekató), *ḱm̥tóm, *sem-
εκεί (ekeí), εκείθεν (ekeíthen), εκείνος (ekeínos), *ḱi-
έκσταση (ékstasi), *steh₂-
ελαφρός (elafrós), *h₁lengʷʰ-, *lengʷʰ-
ελευθερία (eleuthería), ελεύθερος (eléftheros), *h₁lewdʰ-
εν (en), *h₁én
ένα (éna), ένας (énas), *sem-
ενέργεια (enérgeia), *werǵ-
εννέα (ennéa), *H₁néwn̥
έντερο (éntero), *h₁én
έξη (éxi), *seǵʰ-
έξι (éxi), *swéḱs
εξουσία (exousía), *H₁es-
επαγωγή (epagogí), *H₂eǵ-
επειδή (epeidí), *éy / h₁e
επί (epí), *h₁epi
επιθυμία (epithymía), *dʰewh₂-
επιφορά (epiforá), *bher-
εποχή (epochí), *seǵʰ-
επτά (eptá), *septm̥
επώνυμος (epónymos), *h₁nómn̥
εργάζομαι (ergázomai), εργαλείο (ergaleío), εργασία
    (ergasía), εργατικότητα (ergatikótita), έργο (érgo),
    εργοδότης (ergodótis), εργοστάσιο (ergostásio), *werǵ-
ερυθρός (erythrós), *h₁rewdʰ-
εσύ (esý), *túh₂
εφτά (eftá), *septm̥
εχίνος (echínos), *ǵʰér
Ζευς (Zefs), *dyew-
ζήτω (zíto), *gʷeyh₃-
ζόρι (zóri), *ǵʰew-
ζουρνάς (zournás), *ḱerh₂-
ζυγός (zugós), *yugóm
ζύμη (zúmē), *yes-
ζω (zo), ζώο (zóo), *gʷeyh₃-
η (i), *só
ηθικός (ithikós), *swe-dʰh₁-
ήλιος (élios) (ílios), *sóh₂wl̥
ημικρανία (imikranía), *ḱerh₂-
ήπαρ (ípar), *Hyékʷr̥
θάρρος (thárros), *dʰers-
θεά (theá), *dʰéh₁s
θείος (theíos), *dʰeh₁(y)-, *dʰéh₁s

θέμα (théma), *dheH₁-
θεός (theós), *dʰéh₁s
θερινός (therinós), θερμός (thermós), *gʷʰer-
θετός (thetós), *dheH₁-
θεωρία (theoría), *wer-
θήκη (thíki), *dheH₁-
θηλή (thilí), *dʰeh₁(y)-
θρασύς (thrasýs), *dʰers-
θυγατέρα (thygatéra), *dʰugh₂tḗr
θυμός (thymós), *dʰewh₂-
θύρα (thýra), θυρεός (thyreós), *dʰwer-
Ιανουάριος (Ianouários), *h₁ey-
ιδέα (idéa), *weyd-
ιδιώτης (idiótis), *s(w)e-
ίππος (íppos), *h₁éḱwos
ίσκα (íska), *h₁ed-
ιστορία (istoría), *weyd-
ισχύς (ischýs), *seǵʰ-
καθίζω (kathízo), *sed-
κάλαμος (kálamos), *ḱalam-
καλύπτω (kalýpto), *ḱel-
καλώ (kaló), *kelh₁-
καμάρα (kamára), κάμπος (kámpos), *(s)teg-
καπίστρι (kapístri), *keh₂p-
κάπρος (kápros), *kapro
καρδιά (kardiá), *ḱér
καρπός (karpós), *kerp-
κατάβαση (katávasi), *gʷem-
καταπίνω (katapíno), *peh₃-
καταρρέω (katarréo), *srew-
κειμήλιο (keimílio), *ḱei-
κελάρι (kelári), κελί (kelí), κέλυφος (kélyfos), *ḱel-
κλείνω (kleíno), κλέος (kléos), *ḱlew-
κλεψύδρα (klepsýdra), *wed-
κλίμα (klíma), κλίνη (klíni), κλίση (klísi), *ḱley-
κοιμάμαι (koimámai), κοίτη (koíti), *ḱei-
κολοφώνας (kolofónas), *kelH-
κουβέντα (kouvénta), *gʷem-
κούνια (koúnia), *ḱei-
κρανίο (kranío), κράνος (krános), *ḱerh₂-
κρέας (kréas), *krewh₂-
κρίμα (kríma), κρίνω (kríno), κρίση (krísi), κριτής
    (kritís), *krey-
κτίσμα (ktísma), κτίστης (ktístis), *tek-
κυνάγχη (kynánchi), *h₂enǵʰ-, *ḱwṓ
κυνικός (kynikós), κύων (kýon), *ḱwṓ
λεγεώνα (legeóna), *leǵ-
λέκτρο (léktro), *legh-
λίπος (lípos), *leyp-
λογισμός (logismós), λογιστής (logistís), λογιστικός
    (logistikós), λόγος (lógos), *leǵ-
λούζω (loúzo), λουτρό (loutró), *lewh₃-
λυγαριά (lygariá), λυγίζω (lygízo), λυγιστός (lygistós),
    *seh₂g-
λυκανθρωπία (lykanthropía), λυκάνθρωπος
    (lykánthropos), λύκος (lýkos), *wl̥kʷos
μάγιστρος (mágistros), *méǵh₂s

μακρηγορία (makrigoría), *meh₂k-
μακροθυμία (makrothymía), *dʰewh₂-, *meh₂k-
μάστορας (mástoras), μεγάλος (megálos), μεγαλώνω
 (megalóno), μέγιστος (mégistos), *méǵh₂s
μεθάνιο (methánio), μεθανόλη (methanóli), μέθη
 (méthi), μεθοκοπάω (methokopáo), μεθυλένιο
 (methylénio), μεθύλιο (methýlio), μέθυσος
 (méthysos), μεθώ (methó), *médʰu
μείζων (meízon), *méǵh₂s
μέλι (méli), μέλισσα (mélissa), *melit-
μέσο (méso), μέσος (mésos), *médʰyos
μεταφέρω (metaféro), μεταφορά (metaforá), *bher-
μέτρο (métro), *meh₁-
μήκος (míkos), *meh₂k-
μήνας (mínas), μηνίσκος (miANÍskos), *méh₁ns
μητέρα (mitéra), *méh₂tēr
μία (mía), *sem-
μιγνύω (mignýo), *mey-
μνήμη (mními), *men-
μόνος (mónos), *mey-
μου (mou), *H₁meme-
μπορώ (boró), *per-
μπουνιά (bouniá), *pewǵ-
μύγα (mýga), *mus-
μυρμήγκι (myrmínki), *morwi-
ναυς (nafs), *(s)neh₂-
νεκρός (nekrós), νέκταρ (néktar), *neḱ-
νέος (néos), *new
νεύρο (névro), *(s)neh₁-
νεφέλη (neféli), νέφος (néfos), *nebʰ-
νεφρό (nefró), *negʷh-r-
νόμισμα (nómisma), νομισματικός (nomismatikós),
 νομοθεσία (nomothesía), νομοθέτης (nomothétis),
 νόμος (nómos), *nem-
νύκτα (nýkta), νυξ (nyx), *nókʷts
νύχι (nýchi), *h₃negʰ-
νύχτα (nýchta), *nókʷts
ο (o), *só
όγκος (ógkos), *h₂enk-
οδός (odós), *sed-
οίκος (oíkos), *weyḱ-
οίνος (oínos), *óy-nos, *wóyh₁nom
όκρῖς (okrís), *h₂éḱ
οκτώ (októ), *oḱtṓw
όλος (ólos), *solh₂-
όμμα (ómma), *h₃ekʷ-
ομφαλός (omfalós), *h₃enbʰ-
όνομα (ónoma), ονοματοποιία (onomatopoiía), *h₁nómn̥
οξύς (oxýs), *h₂éḱ
οξύτονος (oxýtonos), *h₂éḱ, *ten-
όραμα (órama), *wer-
όργανο (órgano), οργή (orgí), *werǵ-
όρεξη (órexi), *h₃reǵ-
όρνιο (órnio), *h₃érō
όρος (óros), *h₃er-
ορφανός (orfanós), *h₃erbʰ-
οσμή (osmí), *h₃ed-

οστό (ostó), *h₃ésth₁
ουσία (ousía), *H₁es-
ούτος (oútos), *só
οφθαλμός (ofthalmós), *h₃ekʷ-
οφρύς (ofrýs), *h₃bʰrúHs
πάγος (págos), *peh₂ǵ-
παιδαγωγός (paidagogós), *H₂eǵ-
παραβάλλω (paravállo), παραβολή (paravolí), *gʷelH-
παράδεισος (parádeisos), *dʰeyǵʰ-
παρένθεση (parénthesi), *dheH₁-
παρουσία (parousía), *H₁es-
πατέρας (patéras), πατήρ (patír), *ph₂tḗr
πάτος (pátos), *pent-
πατριώτης (patriótis), *ph₂tḗr
πάχνη (páchni), *peh₂ǵ-
πεδίο (pedío), πεζός (pezós), *ped-
πενσέω (penséo), *pewǵ-
πέντε (pénte), *pénkʷe
πέρα (péra), πέραν (péran), πέρας (péras), περί (perí),
 *per-
περιουσία (periousía), *H₁es-
πέφτω (péfto), *peth₂
πικρός (pikrós), *peyḱ-
πίνω (píno), *peh₃-
πλάσμα (plásma), *pleh₂-
πλάτανος (plátanos), πλάτη (pláti), πλάτος (plátos),
 *pleth₂-
πλέκω (pléko), *pleḱ-
πλέω (pléo), *plew-
πληβεία (pliveía), πληβείος (pliveíos), πλήρης (plíris),
 πληροφορία (pliroforía), *pleh₁-
πλοίο (ploío), *plew-
πλουτοκρατία (ploutokratía), πλούτος (ploûtos), *plew-
πόδι (pódi), *pṓds
ποικίλος (poikílos), *peyḱ-
ποιμένας (poiménas), *peh₂-
ποινή (poiní), *kʷey-
ποιος (poios), *kʷis
πόλος (pólos), *kʷel-
πόντος (póntos), *pent-
πόρος (póros), πόρτα (pórta), *per-
πόσος (pósos), πότε (póte), *kʷis
ποτήρι (potíri), *peh₃-
πού (poú), *kʷis
πράγμα (prágma), πραγματεία (pragmateía),
 πραγματικός (pragmatikós), πρακτική (praktikí), πράμα
 (práma), πράξη (práxi), *per-
πρίγκιπας (prígkipas), *keh₂p-
πρόβλημα (próvlima), *gʷelH-
πρόγραμμα (prógramma), *gerbʰ-
προς (pros), *per-
προσφορά (prosforá), προφορά (proforá), προφορικός
 (proforikós), *bher-
πρωταγωνιστής (protagonistís), *H₂eǵ-
πτέρυγα (ptéryga), *péth₂r̥
πυθμένας (pythménas), *bʰudʰmén
πυρ (pyr), πυρά (pyrá), *péh₂ur

πύργος (pýrgos), *bʰergʰ-
πως (pos), *kʷis
ρεύμα (révma), *srew-
ρήμα (ríma), ρητορικός (ritorikós), *wekʷ-
ρίζα (ríza), ριζικός (rizikós), *wréh₂ds
ροδάκινο (rodákino), *deru-
ρουμπίνι (roumpíni), ρούσος (roúsos), *h₁rewdʰ-
ρυθμός (rythmós) , *srew-
σειρά (seirá), *ser-
Σεπτέμβρης (Septémvris), Σεπτέμβριος
  (Septémvrios), *septṃ
σκέλος (skélos), *(s)kel-
σκεπτικός (skeptikós), *spek-
σκολίωση (skolíosi), *(s)kel-
σκοπεύω (skopévo), σκοπιά (skopiá), *spek-
σκουλήκι (skoulíki), *(s)kel-
σούβλα (soúvla), *sīw-
σουπῖνον (soupînon), *upo
στάση (stási), σταύλος (stávlos), σταυρός (stavrós),
  *steh₂-
στέγη (stégi), *(s)teg-
στέλνω (stélno), *stel-
στίχος (stíchos), *steygʰ-
στολή (stolí), στόλος (stólos), *stel-
στράτα (stráta), στρατηγός (stratigós), στρατός
  (stratós), *sterh₃-
στρουθίο (strouthion), *trosdos
συγγράφω (syngráfo), *gerbʰ-
συν (syn), *sem-
συναγωγή (synagogí), *H₂eǵ-
συνθήκη (synthíki), *dheH₁-
σύννεφο (sýnnefo), *nebʰ-
σῠνώνῠμον (sunónumon), συνώνυμος (synónymos),
  *h₁nómṇ
σφήκα (sfíka), *bʰey-
σχεδόν (schedón), σχήμα (schíma), σχολή (scholí),
  *seǵʰ-
σως (sos), *séh₂ls
ταβέρνα (tavérna), *treb-
ταύρος (távros), *(s)táwros
τείχος (teíchos), *dʰeyǵʰ-
τέκνο (tékno), *tek-
τέρμα (térma), *térmṇ
τέσσερις (tésseris), *kʷetwóres
τέφρα (téfra), *dʰegʷʰ-
τι (ti), *kʷis
το (to), *só
τοίχος (toíchos), τοῖχος (toîkhos), *dʰeyǵʰ-
τόνος (tónos), *ten-
τράγος (trágos), *terh₁-
τρεις (treis), *tréyes
τρήμα (tríma), *terh₁-
τσεκούρι (tsekoúri), *sek-
τσερβέλο (tservélo), *ḱerh₂-
τύμπανο (týmpano), τύπος (týpos), *(s)tew-
ύαινα (ýaina), *suH-
ύδωρ (ýdor), *wed-

υιός (yiós), *suh₁nús
ύπνος (ýpnos), *swep-
υπόθεση (ypóthesi), *dheH₁-
υφαίνω (yfaíno), *webh-
φαίνομαι (faínomai), φαινόμενο (fainómeno), *bʰeh₂-
φάλαινα (fálaina), *bʰleh₃-
φανερός (fanerós), φαντασία (fantasía), φάντασμα
  (fántasma), φανταστικός (fantastikós), *bʰeh₂-
Φεβρουάριος (Fevrouários), *dʰegʷʰ-
φέουδο (féoudo), *peḱu-
φήμη (fími), *bʰeh₂-
Φλεβάρης (Fleváris), *dʰegʷʰ-
φόνος (fónos), *gʷʰen-
φορά (forá), φορώ (foró), *bher-
φουμάρω (foumáro), *dʰewh₂-
φούρνος (foúrnos), *gʷʰer-
φουρτούνα (fourtoúna), *bher-
φράξος (fráxos), *bʰereǵ-
φρέαρ (fréar), *bʰrewh₁-
φυλή (fylí), φύλο (fýlo), φύση (fýsi), φυσική (fysikí),
  φυσικός (fysikós), φυτεύω (fytévo), φυτό (fytó), *bʰuH-
φωνή (foní), *bʰeh₂-
χαίρω (chaíro), χαρά (chará), χαράδρα (charádra),
  χαρακτήρας (charaktíras), χάρισμα (chárisma), *ǵʰer-
χαρταετός (chartaetós), *h₂éwis
χάρτης (chártis), *ǵʰer-
χειμερινός (cheimerinós), *ǵʰey-
χελώνα (chelóna), *gʰelôw-
χήνα (chína), *ǵʰans-
χθες (chthes), *dʰ ǵʰ(y)es-
χοίρος (choíros), *ǵʰér
χολή (cholí), *ǵʰelh₃-
χορδή (chordí), *ǵʰern-
χορηγός (chorigós), *seh₂g-
χταπόδι (chtapódi), *pṓds
χτένα (chténa), χτένι (chténi), χτενίζω (chtenízo), *peḱ-
χτίστης (chtístis), *tek-
ψαρόνι (psaróni), *spér
ψύλλος (psýllos), *plou-
ωλένη (oléni), *Heh₃l-
ωοειδής (ōoeidés), *h₂ṓwyóm
ώρα (óra), *yeh₁-

Russian

-сти́гнуть (-stígnuť), *steyg^h-
-сти́чь (-stíč'), *steyg^h-
-ся (-sja) / -сь (-s'), *s(w)e-
y (u), *h$_2$ew
абдеше́нь (abdešén'), *dek̑s-
абля́ция (abljacija), *bher-
або́рт (abórt), *h$_3$er-
авгу́р (avgúr), а́вгуст (ávgust), *h$_2$ewg-
агита́тор (agitátor), *H$_2$eg̑-
а́гнец (ágnec), *h$_2$eg^{w}nos
аго́ния (agonija), *H$_2$eg̑-
агра́рный (agrarnyj), *h$_2$ég̑ros
адвока́т (advokát), *wek^w-
администра́тор (administrátor), администра́ция
(administrácija), *mey-
акведу́к (akvedúk), *h$_2$ek^{w}eh$_2$-
акт (akt), актёр (aktjór), а́кция (ákcija), *H$_2$eg̑-
альвео́ла (al'veóla), *h$_2$el-
амбро́зия (ambrózija), *mer-
аме́нция (améncija), *men-
амети́ст (ametíst), *méd^{h}u
анони́мный (anonímnyj), *h$_1$nómn̥
апока́липсис (apokálipsis), *k̑el-
аппе́ндикс (appéndiks), *pewg̑-
аппети́т (appetít), *peth$_2$
апроба́ция (aprobácija), *b^{h}uH-
а́рка (árka), *h$_2$erk^{w}o-
армату́ра (armatúra), армо́ (armó), арти́кль
(artikl'), арти́кул (artíkul), *h$_2$er
архите́ктор (arxitéktor), *tetk̑-
аспе́кт (aspékt), *spek̑-
ассигна́ция (assignácija), *sek-
ассимиля́ция (assimiljácija), *sem-
атле́т (atlet), *H$_2$weH$_1$-
аудие́нция (audijéncija), ауди́тор (audítor),
аудито́рия (auditórija), *h$_2$ewis-d$^h_1$-
аукцио́н (aukción), *h$_2$ewg-
а́ура (áura), *h$_2$ews-
ба́йка (bájka), *b^{h}eh$_2$-
балли́ста (ballísta), *g^{w}elH-
бас (bas), *b^{h}eh$_2$go-
ба́за (baza), ба́зис (bazis), *g^{w}em-
бде́ть (bdet'), *b^{h}ewd^h-
беда́ (bedá), *b^{h}eyd^h-
бе́рег (béreg), *b^{h}erg̑^{h}-
берёжая (berjóžaja), *bher-
берёза (beréza), берёза (berjóza), *b^{h}ereg̑-
береме́ни (bereméni), *bher-
библиоте́ка (bibliotéka), *dheH$_1$-
би́тум (bítum), *g^{w}et-
блея́ть (bléjat'), *b^{h}leh$_1$-
блоха́ (bloxá), *plou-
блюсти́ (bljustí), *b^{h}ewd^h-

боб (bob), *b^{h}ab^{h}eh$_2$-
бо́дер (bóder), бодро́й (bódroj), бо́дрый (bódryj),
*b^{h}ewd^h-
борода́ (borodá), брада́ (bradá), *b^{h}ard^{h}eh$_2$-
брат (brat), *b^{h}réh$_2$tēr
брать (brat'), бре́мя (brémja), *bher-
бровь (brov'), *h$_3$b^{h}rúHs
буди́ть (budíť), *b^{h}ewd^h-
буз (buz), бук (buk), бузина́ (buziná), бу́ква (búkva),
*b^{h}eh$_2$go-
бы́дло (býdlo), быть (byt'), *b^{h}uH-
бѣда́ (bědá), *b^{h}eyd^h-
бюро́ (bjuró), *péh$_2$ur
в (v), *h$_1$én
ваго́н (vagón), *weg̑h-
ва́хта (vaxta), *weg̑-
вдова́ (vdová), *h$_1$weyd^h-
ве́дать (védat'), *weyd-
везти́ (veztí), *weg̑h-
век (vek), *weyk-
веле́ть (velét'), *welh$_1$-
ве́но (véno), *wed^h-
вентиля́тор (ventiljátor), вентиля́ция (ventiljacija),
*H$_2$weH$_1$-
ве́ра (véra), *weh$_1$-
веретено́ (veretenó), *wert-
верифика́ция (verifikacija), *weh$_1$-
ве́рмие (vérmije), *wr̥mis-
ве́рсия (versija), верте́ть (vertét'), *wert-
ве́рша (vérša), *werg̑-
весли́на (veslina), *weyk̑-
весло́ (vesló), *weg̑h-
весна́ (vesná), *wésr̥
вести́ (vestí), *wed^h-
весца́ (vesca), весь (ves'), *weyk̑-
ве́тер (véter), *H$_2$weH$_1$-
ве́тох (vétox), ве́тхий (vetxij), *wet-
ве́чер (véčer), *wek(^{w})speros
ве́чный (véčnyj), *weyk-
вея́ть (véjat'), *H$_2$weH$_1$-
вива́рий (vivarij), *g^{w}eyh$_3$-
вид (vid), ви́деть (vídet'), *weyd-
вика́рий (vikarij), *weyk-
ви́лла (vílla), *weyk̑-
винегре́т (vinegrét), вино́ (výno), *wóyh$_1$nom
владе́ть (vladét'), власть (vlasť), *h$_2$welh$_1$-
внутри́ (vnutrí), внутрь (vnutr'), во (vo), *h$_1$én
вода́ (vodá), *wed-
води́ть (vodíť), *wed^h-
воз (voz), вози́ть (vozíť), *weg̑h-
волк (volk), волкула́к (volkulák), *wl̥k^{w}os
волна́ (volná), во́лость (vólost'), *h$_2$welh$_1$-
во́ля (vólja), *welh$_1$-
вонь (von'), *h$_2$enh$_1$-
воро́та (voróta), вороти́ть (vorotít'), *wert-
во́семь (vósem'), *ok̑t̑ṓw
врата́ (vratá), *wert-

врать (vrat'), *wekʷ-
вред (vred), *wréh₂ds
вре́мя (vrémja), *wert-
вы (vy), *túh₂
вы́дра (výdra), *udréh₂
вы́мя (výmja), *h₁owHdʰr̥-
вяза́ть (vjazát'), *h₂enǵʰ-
габитус (gabitus), *gʰeh₁bʰ-
гармония (garmonija), *h₂er-
гарны́ (garný), *gʷʰer-
га́чек (gáček), *keg-
гегемо́н (gegemón), гегемо́ния (gegemónija), *seh₂g-
гемма (gemma), *ǵómbʰos
герцог (gercog), *ker-
ги́дра (gídra), *wed-
гиена (gijena), *suH-
гипно́з (gipnóz), *swep-
гипо́теза (gipóteza), *dheH₁-
гиппопотам (gippopotám), *h₁éḱwos
гла́сный (glásnyj), *wekʷ-
гнать (gnat'), *gʷʰen-
гнездо́ (gnezdó), *nisdós
гнида (gnída), *knid-
говядо (govjádo), *gʷṓws
гонять (gonjat'), *gʷʰen-
горе́ть (gorét'), *gʷʰer-
го́рло (górlo), *gʷerH-
горн (gorn), *gʷʰer-
го́рнό (górnó), горны́ (gorný), *gʷʰer-
го́род (górod), *ǵʰer-
госпиталь (gospital'), гость (gost'), *gʰóstis
гре́ны (grény), *gʰreh₁-
гре́ть (grét'), гре́ю (gréju), *gʷʰer-
грино́й (grinój), *gʰreh₁-
гроза́ (grozá), *gʰers-
гу́мус (gúmus), *dʰéǵʰōm
гуру (guru), *gʷerh₂-
гусь (gus'), *ǵʰans-
дава́ть (davát'), да́нь (dán'), дар (dar), да́ть (dát'), *deH₃-
два (dva), *dwóH₁
два́дцать (dvádcat'), *wīḱm̥tiH₁
дверь (dver'), двόр (dvór), *dʰwer-
де́бет (débet), дебил (debil), дебито́р (debitór), *gʰeh₁bʰ-
де́ва (déva), деви́ца (devíca), *dʰeh₁(y)-
девять (devjat'), *H₁néwn̥
дёготь (djógot'), *dʰegʷʰ-
дежа́ (déžá), *dʰeyǵʰ-
декабрь (dekabr'), декада (dekada), дека́н (dekán), *déḱm̥t
деклама́ция (deklamácija), *kelh₁-
деко́р (dekór), *deḱ-
декре́т (dekrét), *krey-
де́лать (délat'), *dheH₁-
дели́рий (delírij), *leys-
де́ло (délo), *dheH₁-

деме́нция (deméncija), *men-
демокра́тия (demokrátija), *deh₂-
демонстра́ция (demonstrácija), демонстри́ровать (demonstrírovat'), *men-
день (den'), *deyn-
дерево (dérevo), *dóru
дерза́ть (derzát', дерзну́ть (derznú't'), дéрзый (dérzyj), *dʰers-
дерть (dert'), *der-
десла́ (deslá), десна (desná), *h₃dónts
деструкция (destrukcija), *strew-
де́сять (désjat'), *déḱm̥t
деть (det'), *dheH₁-
де́цима (décima), *déḱm̥t
дивизион (divizion), дивизия (divizija), *h₁weydʰ-
диво (divo), *dyew-
дикта́тор (diktátor), диктатура (diktatura), *deyḱ-
дистанция (distancija), *steh₂-
дитё (ditjó), дитя́ (ditjá), *dʰeh₁(y)-
дно (dno), *dʰewb-
догма (dógma), *deḱ-
дои́ть (doít'), *dʰeh₁(y)-
до́ктор (dóktor), доктрина (doktrina), документ (dokument), *deḱ-
дом (dom), *dem-
до́чери (dóčeri), дочéрний (dočérnij), до́чка (dóčka), дочь (doč'), *dʰugh₂tḗr
драть (drat'), *der-
дрова́ (drová), *dóru
дрозд (drozd), *trosdos
душма́н (dušmán), *men-
дым (dym), *dʰewh₂-
дья́вол (d'javol), *gʷelH-
дюбать (djúbat'), *dʰewb-
еди́ный (jedínyj), *óy-nos
ёж (jož), *angʷ(h)i-
ёжик (jóžik), *angʷ(h)i-
епити́мия (jepitímija), епити́мья (jepitímʲja), *dʰewh₂-
еси́ (jesí), есмь (jesm'), есть (jest'), *bʰuH-
есть (jest'), *h₁ed-
жа́ло (žálo), жаль (žal'), *gʷelH-
жать (žat'), *gʷʰen-
желвь (želv'), *gʰelōw-
жёлтый (žóltyj), *ǵʰelh₃-
жена (žená), *gʷén
же́реб (žéreb), *gerbʰ-
жерело́ (žereló), *gʷerH-
жёрнов (žjornov)), *gʷrh₂-n-uH-, *gʷerh₂-
жерогло́ (žerogló), жёртва (žértva), *gʷerH-
жечь (žeč'), *dʰegʷʰ-
живи́ца (živíca), живо́й (živój), живо́т (živót), жи́то (žíto), жить (žit'), *gʷeyh₃-
жрать (žrat'), жрец (žréc), *gʷerH-
журавль (žurávl'), *gerh₂-
звено (zvenó), *ǵónu
зверь (zver'), *ǵʰwer-
зелёный (zeljónyj), *ǵʰelh₃-

земля (zemljá), *dʰéǵʰōm
зерно (zernó), *ǵr̥Hnom
зима (zimá), *ǵʰey-
злáто (zláto), *ǵʰelh₃-
знать (znatʼ), *ǵneh₃-
зóлото (zóloto), *ǵʰelh₃-
зрелый (zrelyj), зреть (zretʼ), *ǵerh₂-
зуб (zub), *ǵómbʰos
зурнá (zurná), *ḱerh₂-
зять (zjatʼ), *ǵenH₁-
иго (ígo), *yugóm
идéя (idéja), *weyd-
идиóт (idiót), *s(w)e-
йдол (ídol), *weyd-
идти (idti), *h₁ey-
из (iz), *h₁eǵʰs
иммунитет (immunitet), *mey-
импликация (implikacija), *plek-
имя (imja), *h₁nómn̥
инáче (ináče), йначе (ínače), *óy-nos
инвенция (invencija), *gʷem-
йндекс (índeks), *deyḱ-
индустрйя (industríja), *strew-
йней (ínej), *h₁eyH-
инициация (iniciacija), *h₁ey-
инóй (inój), *óy-nos
институт (institut), *steh₂-
инстрýктор (instrúktor), инструкция (instrukcija),
　инструмент (instrument), *strew-
интеллект (intellekt), интеллигенция
　(intelligencija), *leǵ-
интенция (intencija), *ten-
интервал (interval), *welH-
интерпозиция (interpozicija), *teḱ-
инфант (infánt), *bʰeh₂-
инфляция (infljacija), *bʰleh₁-
ипподром (ippodrom), *h₁éḱwos
ирония (irónija), *wekʷ-
истóрия (istórija), *weyd-
какие (kakiye), *kʷis
календáрь (kalendárʼ), *kelh₁-
камень (kámenʼ), *h₂éḱ-mō
канйкулы (kaníkuly), *ḱwṓ
капитéль (kapitélʼ), *kapōlo
кáпсула (kápsula), *keh₂p-
карета (kareta), *ḱers-
карта (karta), *ǵʰer-
квадрат (kvadrat), квадратура (kvadratura), *kʷetwóres
келья (kelʼja), *ḱel-
клиéнт (klijént), *ḱlew-
клюкá (kljuká), ключ (ključ), *(s)kel-
князь (knjazʼ), *ǵenH₁-
когóрта (kogórta), когóрта (kogórta), *ǵʰer-
кóготь (kógotʼ), *keg-
кок (kok), *pekʷ-
колéно (koléno), *kelH-
колесó (kolesó), *kʷel-

коллéга (kolléga), *legh-
коллéкция (kollékcija), *leǵ-
колóния (kolónija), *kʷel-
колóнна (kolónna), *kelH-
комбинáция (kombinácija), *dwóH₁
комод (komod), *med-
компенсáция (kompensácija), *pewǵ-
компилятор (kompiljátor), *peys-
конвéнция (konvéncija), *gʷem-
кондйция (kondícija), *deyḱ-
конклáв (konkláv), *(s)kel-
консйлиум (konsílium), *kelh₁-
конститýция (konstitúcija), *steh₂-
констрýкция (konstrúkcija), *strew-
континéнт (kontinént), *ten-
контýзия (kontúzija), *(s)tew-
конфéссия (konféssija), *bʰeh₂-
конфирмáция (konfirmácija), *dʰer-
концéпция (koncépcija), *keh₂p-
корá (korá), *(s)ker-
корова (koróva), *ḱerh₂-
королйца (korolíca), корóль (korólʼ), *ǵerh₂-
кóрпус (kórpus), корпýскула (korpúskula), *krep-
корректировать (korrektirovatʼ), коррéктор (korréktor),
　коррéкция (korrékcija), *h₃reǵ-
котóрый (kotóryj), *kʷis
край (kraj), крайна (kraína), *krey-
кредйт (kredít), кредитóр (kreditór), *dheH₁-
кренуть (krenutʼ), *kʷreyh₂-
кровь (krovʼ), *krewh₂-
кройть (kroítʼ), *krey-
кто (kto), *kʷis
культýра (kulʼtúra), *kʷel-
курс (kurs), *ḱers-
кýхня (kúxnja), *pekʷ-
лагерь (lagerʼ), *legh-
лакуна (lakuna), *lókus
ланита (lanita), *Heh₃l-
латук (latuk), *glag-
легат (legat), *leǵ-, *legh-
легион (legion), *leǵ-
легкий (legkiy), лёгкий (ljóxkij), лёгкое (ljóxkoje),
　*h₁lengʷʰ-
лежáть (ležátʼ), *legh-
лектор (lektor), лекция (lekcija), *leǵ-
лён (lën), *lino-
лепйть (lepítʼ), леплю (lepljú), *leyp-
лечь (lečʼ), *legh-
линия (linija), *lino-
лихóй (lixój), лишать (lišati), лишний (lišnij), *leykʷ-
лобзать (lobzátʼ), *leb-
лог (log), *legh-
логос (logos), *leǵ-
ложйться (ložítʼsja), *legh-
локация (lokacija), *stel-
локоть (lokotʼ), *Heh₃l-
лóпать (lópatʼ), *leb-

луна́ (luná), луч (luč), *lewk-

люби́ть (ljubíť), любо́й (ljubój), *lewbʰ-

люд (ljud), лю́ди (ljúdi), *h₁lewdʰ-

лю́мен (ljumen), люце́рна (ljucerna), *lewk-

ля́да (ljáda), ля́двея (ljádveja), *lendʰ-

маги́стр (magístr), магна́т (magnat), магниту́да (magnituda), *méǵh₂s

ма́ния (mánija), ма́нтра (mántra), *men-

ма́стер (máster), *méǵh₂s

мате́рия (materija), ма́трица (mátrica), матро́на (matrona), мать (mať), *méh₂tēr

маэ́стро (maéstro), *méǵh₂s

мед (med), мёд (mjod), медве́дь (medvéď), *médʰu

медиа́тор (mediátor), *médʰyos

медици́на (medicina), *med-

меж (mež), межа́ (mežá), *médʰyos

мел (mel), мель (meľ), *melh₂-

мембра́на (membrana), *méms

мени́ск (menísk), *méh₁ns

ме́ньший (mén'šij), *mey-

меня́ (menjá), *H₁me-

ме́ра (méra), *meh₁-

мере́ть (meréť), *mer-

ме́рить (mériť), *meh₁-

мёртвый (mjórtvyj), *mer-

меси́ть (mesíť), *mey-

ме́сяц (mésjac), *méh₁ns

мини́стр (minístr), *mey-

мне (mne), *H₁me-

мне́ние (mnenije), мнить (mniť), *men-

модифика́ция (modifikacija), мо́дуль (módul'), *med-

мозг (mozg), *mosgʰos

мой (moj), *H₁meme-

молоко́ (molokó), *H₂melǵ-

мо́лот (mólot), моло́ть (molóť), *melh₂-

моне́та (monéta), монито́р (monitór), монуме́нт (monument), *men-

мор (mor), *mer-

мо́ре (móre), *móri

мори́ть (moríť), *mer-

мошна́ (mošná), *mak-

муж (muž), *mánus

мураве́й (muravéj), *morwi-

му́скул (muskul), мускули́стый (muskulístyj), *muh₂s-

му́ха (múxa), *mus-

мы (my), *wei

мы́слить (mýsliť), мысль (mysľ), мышле́ние (myšlenije), мышля́ть (myšljať), *men-

мышь (myš'), *muh₂s-

мэтр (mɛtr), *méǵh₂s

мя́со (mjáso), *méms

навига́ция (navigacija), *(s)neh₂-

на́гель (nagel'), *h₃negʰ-

наго́й (nagój), *negʷ-

нам (nam), *wei

нама́з (namáz), *nem-

на́ми (námi), нас (nas), *wei

нату́ра (natura), на́ция (nacija), *ǵenH₁-

не́бо (njóbo), *nebʰ-

нейро́н (nejrón), нерв (nerv), *(s)neh₁-

не́стера (nestera), *nepot-

никто́ (niktó), ничё (ničo)/ничо́ (ničó), ничто́ (ništó), *kʷis

но́вый (novyj), *new

нога́ (nogá), но́готь (nógoť), *h₃negʰ-

но́мер (nómer), *nem-

номина́ция (nominacija), *h₁nómn̥

но́рма (norma), норма́льный (normál'nyj), *ǵneh₃-

но́ров (norov), *h₂nér

нос (nos), *néh₂s

но́та (nota), нота́риус (notarius), нота́ция (notacija), *ǵneh₃-

ночь (noč'), *nókʷts

нрав (nrav), *h₂nér

нумера́ция (numeracija), *nem-

нутро́ (nutró), *h₁én

обла́тка (oblátka), *bher-

обстру́кция (obstrukcija), *strew-

объе́кт (ob"jekt), *h₁epi

ове́н (ovén), овца́ (ovcá), *h₂ówis

ого́нь (ogón'), *h₁n̥gʷnis

оди́н (odín), *óy-nos

Ока́ (Oká), *h₂ekʷeh₂-

оккупа́ция (okkupácija), *keh₂p-

окно́ (oknó), о́ко (óko), *h₃ekʷ-

ол (ol), *h₂elut-

ольха́ (ol'xá), *h₃el-

он (on), *éy / h₁e

о́никс (óniks), *h₃negʰ-

о́пера (ópera), *h₃ep-

оппози́ция (oppozicija), *h₁epi

о́пус (ópus), *h₃ep-

ораку́л (orakul), ора́тор (orátor), *h₃éh₁os

ора́ть (orať), *H₂erH₃-

о́рган (órgan), *werǵ-

о́рден (orden), о́рдер (order), *h₂er

орёл (orël), *h₃érō

оса́ (osá), *wobs-

осело́к (oselók), осе́ть (oséť), *h₂éḱ

оси́на (osina), *h₃es-

о́стров (óstrov), *srew-

о́стрый (óstryj), *h₂éḱ

оте́ц (otéc), *átta

па́дать (pádať), па́даю (pádaju), падёт (padjót), паду́ (padú), *pṓds

паз (paz), *peh₂ǵ-

па́мять (pámjať), *men-

пара́бола (parábola), *gʷelH-

пари́ть (paríť), *per-

парсу́к (parsúk), парсю́к (parsjúk), *pórḱos

па́стырь (pástyr'), *peh₂-

пасть (pasť), *pṓds

патри́ций (patricij), *ph₂tḗr

педаго́г (pedagóg), *H₂eǵпелена (pelená), *pel-

пелёсый (pelёsyj), пелёсый (peljósyj), *pelH-

пена (péna), *poymno-

передать (peredát'), *deH₃-

перо (peró), *péth₂r

персть (perst'), перх (perx), *pers-

пескарь (peskár'), *peisk-

пест (pest), *peys-

пёстрый (pjóstryj), *peyḱ-

печь (peč'), *pekʷ-

пеший (péšij), *pṓds

пиво (pívo), *peh₃-

пигмент (pigment), писать (pisát'), *peyḱ-

пить (pit'), *peh₃-

пихать (pixát'), *peys-

плакать (plákat'), *pleh₂k-

плева (plevá), плена (plená), *pel-

плести (plestí), *pleḱ-

плечо (plečó), *pleth₂-

плов (plov), *plew-

плоский (ploskij), *pleh₂-

плот (plot), плутократия (plutokrátija), плыть (plyt'), *plew-

по (po), *h₂pó

поганый (poganyj), *peh₂ǵ-

под (pod), *ped-

позиция (pozícija), *teḱ-

пойть (poít'), *peh₃-

покой (pokój), *kʷyeh₁-

поле (póle), *pleh₂-

полк (polk), полный (pólnyj), *pleh₁-

половый (polóvyj), *pelH-,

положить (položít'), *legh-

понтифик (pontífik), *pent-

популяция (populjacija), *pleh₁-

поросёнок (porosjónok), порося (porosjá), *pórḱos

порох (pórox), *pers-

постигнуть (postígnut'), постичь (postíč'), *steygʰ-

постулат (postulat), *preḱ-

пот (pot), *pekʷ-

потенция (potencija), *H₁es-

почить (počít'), *kʷyeh₁-

прах (prax), *pers-

предать (predát'), *deH₃-

президиум (prezidium), *sed-

прелат (prelat), *bher-

пресвитер (presvíter), привилегия (privilegija), примат (primat), *per-

принц (princ), *keh₂p-

приятель (prijátel'), *preyH-

проблема (probléma), *gʷelH-

провинция (provincija), *per-

продуктивный (produktívnyj), *dewk-

прокламация (proklamacija), *kelh₁-

просить (prosít'), *preḱ-

проспект (prospekt), *speḱ-

простереть (prosteret'), *sterh₃-

профессия (professija), профессор (proféssor), *bʰeh₂-

публика (públika), *pleh₁-

пуд (pud), пудить (pudít'), пудить (púdit'), пункт (punkt), пункция (punkcija), *pewǵ-

путь (put'), *pent-

пчела (pčelá), *bʰey-

пшено (pšenó), *peys-

пырей (pýrej), *péh₂ur

пядь (pjad'), *pewǵ-

пята (pjata), пята (pjatá), пятка (pjátka), *pent-

пять (pjat'), *pénkʷe

раб (rab), *h₃erbʰ-

радеть (radét'), *Hreh₁dʰ-

радикал (radikal), радиус (rádius), *wréh₂ds

рало (rálo), *H₂erH₃-

рдеть (rdet'), *h₁rewdʰ-

революция (revoljúcija), *welH-

рёдрый (rjódryj), *h₁rewdʰ-

редукция (redukcija), *dewk-

рейх (rejx), *h₃reǵ-

река (reká), *h₃er-, *h₃reyH-

рекламация (reklamacija), *kelh₁-

реляция (reljacija), *bher-

репрезентация (reprezentacija), *H₁es-

республика (respublika), *pleh₁-

ретенция (retencija), *ten-

реять (réjat'), *h₃reyH-

ринуть (rínut'), ринуться (rínut'sja), *h₃er-, *h₃reyH-

ритм (ritm), *srew-

ритор (ritor), *wekʷ-

рожь (rož'), *wrugʰyo-

рой (rôj), *h₃reyH-

ротация (rotacija), *Hret-

рубин (rubín), рубрика (rubrika), рудой (rudój), рудый (rúdyj), *h₁rewdʰ-

садит (sádit), садить (sadít'), сажу (sažú), *sed-

сам (sam), самый (sámyj), *sem-

свин (svin), свинья (svin'já), *suH-

свой (svoj), себя (sebjá), *s(w)e-

сегмент (segment), *sek-

седация (sedacija), *sed-

сей (sej), *ḱi-

секира (sekíra), *sek-

секрет (sekrét), секретарь (sekretar'), *krey-

сектор (séktor), *sek-, *sekʷ-

селезёнка (selezjónka), *splenǵʰ-

селекция (selekcija), *leǵ-

семейный (seméjnyj), семейство (seméjstvo), *ḱei-

семь (sem'), *septm̥

семья (sem'ja), *ḱei-

семя (sémja), *seH₁-

сенат (senát), сенатор (senátor), *sénos

сентябрь (sentjabr'), *septm̥

сердце (sérdce), *ḱér

серия (sérija), *ser-

серна (sérna), *ḱerh₂-

сессия (sessija), *sedсестра (sestrá), *swésōr

сесть (sest'), *sed-

сечь (séč'), *sek-

сеять (sejat'), *seH₁-

сидеть (sidét'), *sed-

синагóга (sinagóga), *H₂eǵ-

синóпсис (sinópsis), *h₃ekʷ-

синтез (síntez), *dheH₁-

скакáть (skakát'), *(s)kek-

скок (skok), *(s)kek-

скорá (skorá), скрупул (skrupul), *(s)ker-

слáбый (slábyj), *leb-

слáва (sláva), *ḱlew-

слáдкий (sládkij), *séh₂ls

слóво (slóvo), слух (slux), слýшать (slúšat'),
    слушать (slushat'), слýшаю (slúšaju), слышать
    (slyšat'), *ḱlew-

смерть (smert'), *mer-

снабдить (snabdit'), *bʰewdʰ-

снег (sneg), *sneygʷʰ-

снохá (snoxá), *snusós

солúдный (solídnyj), *solh₂-

солнце (sólnce), *sóh₂wl̥

солóма (solóma), *ḱalam-

соль (so'), *séh₂ls

сон (son), *swep-

сóус (sóus), *séh₂ls

сочúть (sočít'), *sekʷ-

спать (spat'), *swep-

спектр (spektr), спекуляция (spekuljácija), *speḱ-

спеть (spet'), спех (spex), спешúть (spešít'), *speh₁-

спинá (spiná), *spey-

стáвить (stávit'), *steh₂-

стáдо (stádo), стамóй (stamój), стан (stan),
    стáрый (starýj), стáтус (státus), статуя (statuja),
    стать (stat'), *steh₂-

стегá (stegá), стезя (stezjá), *steygʰ-

стенáть (stenat'), *(s)tenh₂-

стих (stix), *steygʰ-

стлать (stlat'), *stel-

сто (sto), *ḱm̥tóm

стол (stol), *steh₂-

стонáть (stonat'), *(s)tenh₂-

стоять (stoját'), *steh₂-

стратер (strateg), *sterh₃-

стрýмень (strúmen'), струя (strujá), *srew-

студия (studija), ступор (stupor), *(s)tew-

су- (su-), *sem-

субдукция (subdukcija), *dewk-

сýка (súka), *ḱwṓ

сумма (summa), *upo

суспензия (suspenzija), *pewǵ-

схéма (sxéma), *seǵʰ-

сын (syn), *suh₁nús

сядy (sjádu), *sed-

текст (tekst), текстиль (tekstil'), *tetḱ-

тéма (téma), *dheH₁-

теóрия (teorija), *wer-

терéть (terét'), *terh₁-

тéрмин (términ), *térmn̥

территориáльный (territorial'nyj), территория
    (territorija), *ters-

тесáть (tesát'), теслá (teslá), *tetḱ-

тон (ton), тóнус (tónus), *ten-

тот (tot), *só

традúция (tradícija), *deH₃-

трансляция (transljacija), *bher-

трансфузия (transfuzija), *ǵʰew-

три (tri), *tréyes

трибунáл (tribunál), *bʰuH-

труд (trud), *trewd-

тур (tur), *(s)táwros

угол (úgol), *h₂enk-

угорь (úgor'), уж (už), *angʷ(h)i-

ýзкий (úzkij), *h₂enǵʰ-

уй (uj), *h₂éwh₂os

ýния (unija), *óy-nos

ýрна (úrna), *h₁ews-

устá (ustá), *h₃éh₁os

утвá (utvá), утёнок (utjónok), утка (útka), *h₂eneti-

ýтро (útro), *h₂ews-

утрóба (utróba), *h₁én

ýхо (úxo), ýши (úši), *h₂ew-

фáбула (fábula), *bʰeh₂-

факт (fakt), фáктор (fáktor), фамúлия (famílija), *dheH₁-

фантáзия (fantázija), фантóм (fantóm), *bʰeh₂-

феврáль (fevral'), *dʰegʷʰ-

фехтовáть (fextovat'), *peḱ-

фигýра (figura), *dʰeyǵʰ-

фúстула (fistula), *bʰeyd-

флуктуáция (fluktuacija), флюктуáция (fljuktuacija),
    *bʰleh₁-

фонд (fond), *bʰudʰmḗn, *ǵʰew-

фортификáция (fortifikacija), *bʰergʰ- , *dheH₁-

фортýна (fortuna), *bher-

фóрум (fórum), *dʰwer-

фрау (frau), *per-

фундáмент (fundament), *bʰudʰmḗn

хáпать (xápat'), хáпаю (xápaju), *keh₂p-

харáктер (xarákter), харúзма (xarízma), хáртия
    (xartija), *ǵʰer-

ход (xod), хóда (xoda), *sed-

хóрда (xórda), *ǵʰern-

цедúть (cedít'), *skey-

цéлый (célyj), *kóh₂ilus

ценá (cená), *kʷey-

центýрия (centúrija), *ḱm̥tóm

цикл (cikl), *kʷel-

цилúндр (cilíndr), *(s)kel-

чáпать (čápat'), *keh₂p-

чё (čo), *kʷis

чемпион (čempion), *(s)teg-

череп (čérep), *ḱerh₂-, *kerp-

черпать (cherpat'), *kerp-

четыре (četýre), *kʷetwóres
чи́стый (čístyj), *skey-
чо (čo), что (što), *kʷis
шелом (šelom), *ḱel-
ше́ршень (šéršen'), *ḱerh₂-
шесть (šest'), *swéḱs
шило (šilo), *sīw-
ширма (širma), *(s)ker-
шить (šit'), *sīw-
шко́ла (škóla), *seǵʰ-
шлем (šlem), *ḱel-
шо (šo), *kʷis
штудировать (študirovat'), *(s)tew-
щит (ščit), *skey-
эволюция (evoljucija), *welH-
эдикт (edikt), *deyḱ-
экзамен (ekzamen), *H₂eǵ-
экзекуция (ekzekucija), *sekʷ-
экскременты (ekskrementy), *krey-
экскурсия (ekskursija), *ḱers-
эксперимент (eksperiment), эксперт (ekspert), *per-
экста́з (ekstáz), *steh₂-
экстенсия (ekstensija), *ten-
элемент (element), *h₂el-
эне́ргия (enérgija), *werǵ-
эон (eón), *h₂ey-
э́пос (épos), *wekʷ-
эссенция (essencija), *H₁es-
э́тнос (étnos), *swe-dʰh₁-
э́тот (étot), *só
эфи́р (efír), *h₂eydʰ-
эффект (effekt), *dheH₁-
ю́ный (júnyj), *h₂yuh₁en-
юстиция (justicija), *h₂eyw-
я (ja), *egH₂
яблоко (jábloko), *h₂ébōl
ягнёнок (jagnjónok), *h₂egʷnos
ягода (jágoda), *eh₃g-
я́дра (jádra), ядро́ (jadró), *h₁én
язык (jazýk), *dn̥ǵʰwéh₂s
яйцо (jajcó), *h₂ōwyóm
январь (janvar'), *h₁ey-
яр (jar), япа́ (jará), *yeh₁-
ярём (jarjóm), яре́мь (jarém'), *h₂er
яри́на (jarína), яри́ца (jaríca), *yeh₁-
ярмо́ (jarmó), *h₂er, *H₂erH₃-
арови́к (jarovík), яровой (jarovój), яровой
(jarovój), я́рый (járyj), *yeh₁-
ясень (jasen'), *h₃es-
я́тра (játra), ятро́ (jatró), я́тро (játro), *h₁én

Polish

akcja, *H₂eǵ-
akwedukt, *dewk-, *h₂ekʷeh₂-
ale, *h₂el-
ambi-, *h₂ent
anonimowy, *h₁nómn̥
architekt, *tetḱ-
aspekt, *speḱ-
auto, *h₂ew
bajka, *bʰeh₂-
bez, *bʰeh₂go-
biada, *bʰeydʰ-
biblioteka, *dheH₁-
biceps, *kapōlo
bieda, *bʰeydʰ-
biuro, *péh₂ur
bób, *bʰabʰeh₂-
brać, *bher-
brat, *bʰréh₂tēr
brew, *h₃bʰrúHs
broda, *bʰardʰeh₂-
brzeg, *bʰerǵʰ-
brzemienia, brzemię, *bher-
brzoza, *bʰereǵ-
budzić, *bʰewdʰ-
buk, bukiew, *bʰeh₂go-
być, bydło, *bʰuH-
cały, *kóh₂ilus
cedzić, *skey-
cegła, *(s)teg-
cena, *kʷey-
chapać, *keh₂p-
charakter, *ǵʰer-
chód, *sed-
chwila, *kʷyeh₁-
ciosać, ciosła, *tetḱ-
co, *kʷis
córka, *dʰugh₂tḗr
cug, *dewk-
czapać, czapić, *keh₂p-
czempion, *(s)teg-
czerpać, *kerp-
cztery, *kʷetwóres
czysty, *skey-
dach, *(s)teg-
dać, dar, dawać, *deH₃-
dekada, *déḱm̥t
delirium, *leys-
diabeł, *gʷelH-
dno, *dʰewb-
doić, *dʰeh₁(y)-
doktor, *deḱ-
dom, *dem-
dřít, *der-

drozd, *trosdos
drwa, *dóru
drzeć, *der-
drzewo, *dóru
drzwi, *dʰwer-
dupa, *dʰewb-
dwa, *dwóH₁
dwadzieścia, *wīk̄m̥tiH₁
dwór, *dʰwer-
dyktator, *deyḱ-
dym, *dʰewh₂-
dziać, działać, działo, *dheH₁-
dziąsło, *h₃dónts
dziecię, dziecko, *dʰeh₁(y)-
dziegieć, *dʰegʷʰ-
dziekan, *dékm̥t
dzieło, *dheH₁-
dzień, *deyn-
dziesięć, *dékm̥t
dziewica, *dʰeh₁(y)-
dziewięć, *H₁néwn̥
dziewka, *dʰeh₁(y)-
dzieża, *dʰeyǵʰ-
dziękować, *teng-
dziupla, *dʰewb-
dziw, *dyew-
dziwka, *dʰeh₁(y)-
ekskrement, *krey-
entuzjazm, *dʰéh₁s
eter, *h₂eydʰ-
ewentualność, *gʷemf-
fabuła, fantom, *bʰeh₂-
figura, *dʰeyǵʰ-
fundament, *bʰudʰmḗn, *ǵʰew-
futro, *peh₂-
gardło, *gʷerH-
gąska, *ǵʰans-
gęba/ząb, *ǵómbʰos
gęś, *ǵʰans-
gnać, *gʷʰen-
gniazdo, *nisdós
gnida, *knid-
gonić, *gʷʰen-
gorący, gorączka, gorejący, gorzeć, *gʷʰer-
gość, *gʰóstis
groza, *gʰers-
gród, *ǵʰer-
grzać, grzeję, *gʷʰer-
guru, *gʷerh₂-
gust, *ǵews-
hełm, *ḱel-
hiena, *suH-
historia, *weyd-
imię, *h₁nómn̥
inaczej, indziej, inny, *óy-nos
intelekt, *leǵ-
iść, *h₁ey-

ja, *egH₂
jabłko, *h₂ébōl
jagnię, *h₂egʷnos
jagoda, *eh₃g-
jajce, jajko, jajo, *h₂ōwyóm
jar, *yeh₁-
jarmo, *h₂er
jaro, jary, *yeh₁-
jarzmo, *h₂er
jawa, *h₂ew-
jądro, *h₁én
jeden, jedynka, *óy-nos
jełczeć, jełki, *h₂elut-
jerzmo, *h₂er
jesieć, *h₂ék̄
jesion, *h₃es-
jesiótka, *h₂ék̄
jest, jestem, jesteś, *bʰuH-
jeść, *h₁ed-
jeż, *angʷ(h)i-
język, *dn̥ǵʰwéh₂s
jirzmo, *h₂er
junak, *h₂yuh₁en-
jutro, *h₂ews-
kamień, *h₂ék̄-mō
kanikuła, *ḱwṓ
kareta, karoseria, *ḱers-
karta, *ǵʰer-
kasa, *keh₂p-
katabasis, *gʷem-
klaisa, *krey-
klucz, *(s)kel-
kolano, *kelH-
kolega, *legh-
koło, *kʷel-
kompensacja, *pewǵ-
konsekwencja, *sekʷ-
kontrowersja, *wert-
kora, *(s)ker-
korpus, *krep-
korygować, *h₃reǵ-
kosztować, *steh₂-
kraj, *krey-
krew, *krewh₂-
kroić, *krey-
krowa, *ḱerh₂-
król, *ǵerh₂-
ksiądz, kšûnc, ksˊǫc, *ǵenH₁-
kto, który, *kʷis
kwadrat, *kʷetwóres
ląd, *lendʰ-
lec, *legh-
lecha, *leys-
lekki, *h₁lengʷʰ-
lektor, *leǵ-
len, *lino-
lepić, *leyp-

leżeć, *legh-
lędźwia, *lendʰ-
lichy, *leykʷ-
loch, *sehₐg-
lubić, luby, *lewbʰ-
lud, ludzie, *h₁lewdʰ-
łokieć, *Heh₃l-
łożyć, *legh-
łucz, łuczywo, łuna, *lewk-
maestro, magister, majster, *méǵh₂s
malować, *meh₁-
mania, *men-
martwy, *mer-
master, *méǵh₂s
matka, *méh₂tēr
mąż, *mánus
medycyna, medyk, *med-
mi, *H₁me-
miał, *melh₂-
miano, *h₁nómn̥
miara, *meh₁-
miartwy, *mer-
miedza, *médʰyos
mierzyć, *meh₁-
miesiąc, *mḗh₁n̥s
miesić, *mey-
między, *médʰyos
mięso, *mḗms
miód, *médʰu
mistrz, *méǵh₂s
mleć, *melh₂-
mleko, *H₂melǵ-
młot, *melh₂-
mnie, *H₁me-
mniej, mniejszy, *mey-
mniemać, *men-
morze, *móri
morzyć, *mer-
mój, *H₁meme-
mór, *mer-
mózg, *mosgʰos
mrowisko, mrówka, mrówkojad, mrównik, *morwi-
mrzeć, *mer-
mucha, *mus-
mutacja, *mey-
my, *wei
mysz, *muh₂s-
myśl, myślać, myśleć, *men-
nagi, *negʷ-
narów, *h₂nḗr
nas, *wei
natura, *ǵenH₁-
nawigacja, *(s)neh₂-
nerka, *negʷh-r-
nic, *kʷis
niebo, *nebʰ-
niedźwiedź, *médʰu

nieściora, *nepot-
nikt, *kʷis
noc, *nókʷts
noga, *h₃negʰ-
normalny, *ǵneh₃-
nos, *néh₂s
nowy, *new
numer, *nem-
odłóg, *legh-
ogień, *h₁n̥gʷnis
ojciec, *átta
okno, oko, *h₃ekʷ-
olcha, olsza, *h₃el-
on, *éy / h₁e
oplatka, opłatek, *bher-
orać, *H₂erH₃-
order, ordynex, *h₂er
organy, *werǵ-
orzeł, *h₃érō
osa, *wobs-
osełka, osieć, *h₂éḱ
osiem, *oktṓw
osika, *h₃es-
osiótka, *h₂éḱ
ostrów, Ostrów, Ostrówek, *srew-
ostry, *h₂éḱ
owca, *h₂ówis
padać, padnę, *pŏds
pamięć, *men-
parabola, *gʷelH-
paść, *peh₂-, *pŏds
patent, *peth₂
paz, *peh₂ǵ-
paznokieć, *h₃negʰ-
pąć, pątnik, *pent-
pchać, *peys-
pchła, *plou-
pełny, *pleh₁-
perz, perzyna, *péh₂ur
pędzić, *pewǵ-
piana, *poymno-
piasta, *peys-
pić, *peh₃-
piec, *pekʷ-
pielucha, *pel-
pieszy, *pŏds
pięć, *pénkʷe
piędź, *pewǵ-
pięta, *pent-
pióro, *péth₂r
pisać, *peyḱ-
piskorz, *peisḱ-
piwo, *peh₃-
plece, plecy, *pleth₂-
płakać, *pleh₂k-
płaski, *pleh₂-
pławić, płet, *plew-

płowy, *pelH-
płuco, *plewmō
płyn, płynąć, pływać, *plew-
po, *h₂pó
poić, *peh₃-
pointa, *pewǵ-
poję, *peh₃-
pokój, *kʷyeh₁-
pole, *pleh₂-
port, *per-
pośpiech, *speh₁-
pot, *pekʷ-
prezydent, *sed-
pro-, *per-
problem, *gʷelH-
proch, *pers-
program, *gerbʰ-
prosić , *prek̑-
prosię, *póȓkos
przyjaciel, *preyH-
pstry, *peyk̑-
pszczoła, *bʰey-
pszenica, pszono, *peys-
pułk, *pleh₁-
pumeks, *poymno-
punkt, *pewǵ-
rab, *h₃erbʰ-
radło, *H₂erH₃-
radykał, *wréh₂ds
ramię, *h₂er
repetować, *peth₂
retor, *wekʷ-
rewolucja, *welH-
reż, *wrugʰyo-
rob, *h₃erbʰ-
rój, *h₃reyH-
rubin, rudy, *h₁rewdʰ-
rzeka, *h₃er-, *h₃reyH-
rzesza, *h₃reǵ-
sadzę, sadzić, *sed-
sam, są-, *sem-
sen, *swep-
senior, *sénos
serce, *k̑ér
sędziwy, *sénos
siać, *seH₁-
siąść, *sed-
siebie, *s(w)e-
siec, *sek-
siedem, *septm̥
siedzieć, *sed-
siekiera, *sek-
siemię, *seH₁-
się, *s(w)e-
siostra, *swésōr
skakać, *(s)kek-
skóra, *(s)ker-

słaby, *leb-
słać, *stel-
sława, *k̑lew-
słodki, *séh₂ls
słoma, *k̑alam-
słońce, *sóh₂wl̥
słowo, słuch, słuchać, słuszać, słuszeć, słyszeć, *k̑lew-
snecha, *snusós
soczyć, *sekʷ-
sorna, *k̑erh₂-
sos, sól, *séh₂ls
spać, *swep-
spód, *ped-
sprzedać, *deH₃-
sprzyjać, *preyH-
stać, stado, *steh₂-
stadza, *steygʰ-
stan, stary, stawić, *steh₂-
sto, *k̑m̥tóm
stół, *steh₂-
strategia, *sterh₃-
strumień, strumyk, *srew-
student, studiować, *(s)tew-
subtelny, *tetk̑-
suka, *k̑wó
suma, *upo
swój, *s(w)e-
syn, *suh₁nús
system, *steh₂-
szczyt, *skey-
szerszeń, *k̑erh₂-
sześć, *swék̑s
szkoła, *seǵʰ-
szyć, *sīw-
ścignąć, *steygʰ-
śledziona, *splenǵʰ-
śmierć, *mer-
śnieg, *sneygʷʰ-
śpiać, śpiech, śpieszyć, *speh₁-
środa, *k̑ér
świnia, *suH-
ten, *só
termin, *térmn̥
terytorialny, terytorium, *ters-
tradycja, *deH₃-
translacja, *bher-
trud, *trewd-
trzeć, *terh₁-
trzop, *kerp-
trzy, *tréyes
tur, *(s)táwros
ty, *túh₂
u, ucho, *h₂ew-
umierać, *mer-
usta, *h₃éh₁os
w, *h₁én
wał, *welH-

wąski, *h₂enǵʰ-
wątroba, *h₁én
wąż, *angʷ(h)i-
wdowa, *h₁weydʰ
we, *h₁én
wełna, *h₂welh₁-
weryfikacja, *weh₁-
wewnątrz, *h₁én
węgorz, *angʷ(h)i-
wiać, *H₂weH₁-
wiano, *wedʰ-
wiara, *weh₁-
wiatr, *H₂weH₁-
wiązać, *h₂enǵʰ-
widzieć, *weyd-
wieczny, *weyk-
wieczór, *wek(ʷ)speros
wiedzieć, *weyd-
wiek, *weyk-
wiercić, *wert-
wiersza, *werǵ-
wieś, *weyḱ-
wieść, *wedʰ-, *weyd-
wieźć, *weǵh-
wilk, wilkołak, *wĺkʷos
wino, *wóyh₁nom
wiosło, *weǵh-
wiosna, *wésr̥
wiotchy, *wet-
witro, *h₂ews-
władać, włość, *h₂welh₁-
woda, *wed-
wodzić, *wedʰ-
wola, *welh₁-
wolumen, *welH-
woń, *h₂enh₁-
wozić, wóz, *weǵh-
wrota, wrócić, wrzeciono, wrzemię, *wert-
wuj, *h₂éwh₂os
wydra, *udréh₂
wymię, *h₁owHdʰr̥-
z, ze, *h₁eǵʰs
ziarno, *ǵr̥Hnom
zielony, *ǵʰelh₃-
ziemia, *dʰéǵʰōm
zięć, *ǵenH₁-
zima, *ǵʰey-
zjełczały, *h₂elut-
złoto, *ǵʰelh₃-
znać, *ǵneh₃-
zwierz, *ǵʰwer-
źródło, *gʷerH-
żarna, żarnów, *gʷrh₂-n-uH-
żec, *dʰegʷʰ-
żerca, żertwa, *gʷerH-
żona, *gwén
żółty, *ǵʰelh₃-

żółw, *gʰelōw-
źreć, *gʷerH-
żuraw, *gerh₂-
żyć, żyto, żywica, żywot, żywy, *gʷeyh₃-

Czech

adolescent, *h₂el-
agrární, *h₂égros
akce, *H₂eǵ-
ale, *h₂el-
anonym, anonymni, *h₁nómn̥
axon, *H₂eǵ-
bajka, *bʰeh₂-
bdít, *bʰewdʰ-
běda, *bʰeydʰ-
bez, *bʰeh₂go-
bída, *bʰeydʰ-
blecha, *plou-
bleti, *bʰleh₁-
bob, *bʰabʰeh₂-
bodrý, *bʰewdʰ-
brada, *bʰardʰeh₂-
brát, *bher-
bratr, *bʰréh₂tēr
břemene, *bher-
brva, *h₃bʰrúHs
břeh, *bʰerǵ-
březí, břímě, *bher-
bříza, *bʰereǵ-
budit, *bʰewdʰ-
buk, bukev, bukva, *bʰeh₂go-
bydlo, být, *bʰuH-
cedit, *skey-
celý, *kóh₂ilus
cena, *kʷey-
co, *kʷis
čistý, *skey-
čtyři, *kʷetwóres
čapiti, čapati, *keh₂p-
ďábel, *gʷelH-
daň, dar, *deH₃-
dáseň, *h₃dónts
dát, dávat, *deH₃-
dcera, dcerka, *dʰugh₂tēr
dehet, *dʰegʷʰ-
dekáda, *dékm̥t
děkovat, *teng-
dělat, *dheH₁-
delirium, *leys-
dělo, *dheH₁-
den, *deyn-
deset, *dékm̥t
děva, *dʰeh₁(y)-
devět, *H₁néwn̥
děvice, *dʰeh₁(y)-
dílo, dít, *dheH₁-
dítě, *dʰeh₁(y)-
div, *dyew-
díž, díža, díže, *dʰeyǵʰ-

dno, *dʰewb-
dogma, *deḱ-
dojit, *dʰeh₁(y)-
doktor, *deḱ-
drát, *der-
drozd, *trosdos
drzý, *dʰers-
dřevo, *dóru
ďubat, *dʰewb-
dům, *dem-
dva, *dwóH₁
dvacet, *wīḱm̥tiH₁
dveře, dvůr, *dʰwer-
dým, *dʰewh₂-
entita, *H₁es-
epocha, *seǵʰ-
eritorium, *ters-
éter, *h₂eydʰ-
eventualita, *gʷem-
exkrement, *krey-
figura, *dʰeyǵʰ-
háček, hák, *keg-
historie, *weyd-
hnát, *gʷʰen-
hnida, *knid-
hnízdo, *nisdós
honit, *gʷʰen-
hořet, *gʷʰer-
host, *gʰóstis
hovado, *gʷốws
hrad, *ǵʰer-
hrany, hrdlo, *gʷerH-
hrůza, *gʰers-
hřát, *gʷʰer-
hřeb, *gerbʰ-
hřeji, *gʷʰer-
husa, *ǵʰans-
hyena, *suH-
chápat, *keh₂p-
charakter, *ǵʰer-
chod, chůda, *sed-
id, *éy / h₁e
inhibitor, *gʰeh₁bʰ-
já, *egH₂
jablko, *h₂ébōl
jádro, *h₁én
jahoda, *eh₃g-
jarmo, *h₂er
jaro, *yeh₁-
jařmo, *h₂er
jasan, *h₃es-
játra, *h₁én
jazyk, *dn̥ǵʷéh₂s
je/jest, *bʰuH-
jeden, *óy-nos
jehně, jehnec, *h₂egʷnos
jeřáb, *gerh₂-

jež, ježek, *angʷ(h)i-
jho, *yugóm
jinak, jinde, *óy-nos
jíní, *h₁eyH-
jiný, *óy-nos
jíst, *h₁ed-
jít, *h₁ey-
jitro, *h₂ews-
jméno, *h₁nómn̥
jonák, *h₂yuh₁en-
jsem, jsi, *bʰuH-
jutro, *h₂ews-
kámen, *h₂ék-mō
kapacita, kapsa, *keh₂p-
kára, *ḱers-
kasa, *keh₂p-
kdo, *kʷis
klíč, klika, *(s)kel-
kněz, kníže, *ǵenH₁-
koleno, *kelH-
kolo, *kʷel-
kontroverze, *wert-
korigovat, *h₃reǵ-
kraj, krajina, *krey-
král, Kralice, *ǵerh₂-
kráva, *ḱerh₂-
krev, *krewh₂-
krojit, *krey-
který, *kʷis
kůra, *(s)ker-
ledvi, ledvina, *lendʰ-
lehký, *h₁lengʷʰ-
lehnout si, *legh-
len, *lino-
lepit, *leyp-
ležet, *legh-
líbit, libý, *lewbʰ-
lid, lidé, *h₁lewdʰ-
lícha, *leys-
lichý, *leykʷ-
loket, *Heh₃l-
louč, *lewk-
ložit, *legh-
lucerna, lučit, luna, *lewk-
magistr, *méǵh₂s
maso, *mēms
matka, *méh₂tēr
mě, *H₁me-
med, medvěd, *médʰu
měl, *melh₂-
méně, menší, *mey-
mertev, *mer-
měřit, *meh₁-
měsíc, *méh₁n̥s
mez, mezi, *médʰyos
mi, *H₁me-

mínění, mínit, *men-
míra, mířit, *meh₁-
mísit, *mey-
mistr, *méǵh₂s
mlat, młat, *melh₂-
mléko, *H₂melǵ-
mlít, *melh₂-
mně, *H₁me-
moje, *H₁meme-
mor, *mer-
moře, *móri
mořit, *mer-
moucha, *mus-
mozek, *mosgʰos
mrav, *h₂nḗr
mravenec, *morwi-
mrtvý, mřít, *mer-
můj, *H₁meme-
muž, *mánus
my, *wei
mysl, myslit, *men-
myš, *muh₂s-
myšlet, *men-
nahý, *negʷ-
napojit, *peh₃-
nás, *wei
nebe, *nebʰ-
nehet, *h₃negʰ-
nic, nikdo, *kʷis
noc, *nókʷts
noha, *h₃negʰ-
normální, *ǵneh₃-
nos, *néh₂s
nový, *new
odér, *h₃ed-
oheň, *h₁n̥gʷnis
okno, oko, okulus, *h₃ekʷ-
olše, *h₃el-
on, *éy / h₁e
opojit, *peh₃-
orákulum, *h₃éh₁os
orat, *H₂erH₃-
orel, *h₃érō
osika, *h₃es-
osm, *oḱtṓw
ostrov, *srew-
ostrý, *h₂éḱ
otec, *átta
ovce, *h₂ówis
ovládati, *h₂welh₁-
ozditi, *h₂eh₁s-
padat, *póds
paměť, *men-
parabola, *gʷelH-
pást, *peh₂-
pata, *pent-
patent, *peth₂

512

paz, *peh₂ǵ-
péci, péct, *pekʷ-
pěna, *poymno-
pero, péro, *péth₂r̥
pestrý, *peyḱ-
pět, *pénkʷe
pchát, *peys-
píď, *pewǵ-
píchat, píst, písta, *peys-
píši, *peyḱ-
pít, pivo, *peh₃-
plakat, *pleh₂k-
plavat, *plew-
plavý, *pelH-
plece, *pleth₂-
plena, *pel-
pleť, *plew-
plíce, *plewmō
plný, *pleh₁-
plyn, plynout, *plew-
po, *h₂pó
pokoj, *kʷyeh₁-
pole, *pleh₂-
pot, *pekʷ-
pouť, *pent-
prach, *pers-
prase, *pórḱos
pro-, *per-
problém, *gʷelH-
program, *gerbʰ-
prosit, *preḱ-
prsť, *pers-
přáti, přítel, *preyH-
psát, *peyḱ-
pšeno, *peys-
půda, *ped-
puditi, *pewǵ-
pýř, pyří, pýřiti, *péh₂ur
radikál, *wréh₂ds
rádlo, *H₂erH₃-
rámě, *h₂er
rdíti se, *h₁rewdʰ-
rež, *wrugʰyo-
rob, *h₃erbʰ-
roj, *h₃reyH-
rubin, rudý, *h₁rewdʰ-
řeka, *h₃er-, *h₃reyH-
řinout se, *h₃er-, *h₃reyH-
sám, *sem-
se, sebe, *s(w)e-
sedět, *sed-
sedm, *septm̥
sekyra, *sek-
semeno, *seH₁-
sen, *swep-
senát, *sénos
sestra, *swésōr

síci, síct, *sek-
sít, *seH₁-
skočit, *(s)kek-
skora, skura, skůra, *(s)ker-
slabý, *leb-
sladký, *séh₂ls
sláma, *ḱalam-
sláva, *ḱlew-
slezina, *splenǵʰ-
slouti, slovo, sluch, *ḱlew-
slunce, *sóh₂wl̥
slušet, slyšel, slyšet, *ḱlew-
smrt, *mer-
snábděti, *bʰewdʰ-
snacha, *snusós
snih, *sneygʷʰ-
sok, *sekʷ-
sou-, *sem-
spát, *swep-
spěch, spět, *speh₁-
splin, *splenǵʰ-
srdce, *ḱḗr
srna, sršeň, *ḱerh₂-
stádo, stan, starý, stát, stavit, *steh₂-
sténat, *(s)tenh₂-
steze, stihnouti, *steygʰ-
stláti, *stel-
sto, *ḱm̥tóm
strumen, *srew-
středa, *ḱḗr
střep, *kerp-
student, studovat, *(s)tew-
stůl, *steh₂-
suka, *ḱwṓ
sůl, *séh₂ls
super, supr, *upo
svině, *suH-
svůj, *s(w)e-
syn, *suh₁nús
šampión, *(s)teg-
šest, *swéḱs
šídlo, šít, *sīw-
škára, *(s)ker-
škola, *seǵʰ-
štít, *skey-
tandem, ten, *só
tesat, tesla, *tetḱ-
tradice, *deH₃-
translace, *bher-
trud, *trewd-
tři, *tréyes
třít, *terh₁-
tur, *(s)táwros
ty, *túh₂
u, *h₂ew
úhoř, *angʷ(h)i-
ucho, *h₂ew-

ústa, *h₃éh₁os
útroba, uvnitř, *h₁én
úzký, *h₂enǵʰ-
užovka, *angʷ(h)i-
v, *h₁én
varhany, *werǵ-
váti, *H₂weH₁-
vázat, *h₂enǵʰ-
včela, *bʰey-
vdova, *h₁weydʰ
ve, *h₁én
večerni, *wek(ʷ)speros
věčný, *weyk-
vědět, *weyd-
vejce, *h₂ōwyóm
věk, *weyk-
velet, *welh₁-
vemeno, *h₁owHdʰr̥-
věno, *wedʰ-
verifikace, *weh₁-
ves, *weyḱ-
veslo, *weǵʰ-
vesna, *wésr̥
vést, *wedʰ-
vetchý, *wet-
vézt, *weǵʰ-
vid, vidět, *weyd-
víno, *wóyh₁nom
víra, *weh₁-
vítr, *H₂weH₁-
vlast, *h₂welh₁-
vlk, vlkodlak, *wĺ̥kʷos
vlna, *h₂welh₁-
vnitř, *h₁én
voda, *wed-
vodit, *wedʰ-
vosa, *wobs-
vozit, *weǵʰ-
vrata, vrátit, *wert-
vrše, *werǵ-
vrtět, vřeteno, *wert-
vůle, *welh₁-
vůně, *h₂enh₁-
vůz, *weǵʰ-
vy, *túh₂
vydra, *udréh₂
z, ze, *h₁eǵʰs
zeď, *dʰeyǵʰ-
zelený, *ǵʰelh₃-
země, *dʰéǵʰōm
zeť, *ǵenH₁-
zima, *ǵʰey-
zlato, *ǵʰelh₃-
znát, *ǵneh₃-
zralý, zrát, *ǵerh₂-
zrno, *ǵr̥Hnom
zřídlo, *gʷerH-

zub, *ǵómbʰos
zvěř, *ǵʰwer-
ždít, *gʷʰen-
želva, *gʰelōw-
žena, *gwén
žerna, žernov, *gʷrh₂-n-uH-
žít, žito, živice, život, živý, *gʷeyh₃-
žlutý, *ǵʰelh₃-
žrát, *gʷerH-

Slovak

ale, *$h_2$el-
august, *$h_2$ewg-
auto, *$h_2$ew
bájka, *b^heh_2-
bdieť, *b^hewd^h-
bez, *b^heh_2go-
bieda, *b^heyd^h-
blcha, *plou-
bodrý, *b^hewd^h-
bôb, *$b^hab^heh_2$-
brada, *$b^hard^heh_2$-
brať, *bher-
brat, *$b^hréh_2tēr$
breh, *$b^herǵ^h$-
bremeno, *bher-
breza, *$b^hereǵ$-
brva, *$h_3b^hrúHs$
budiť, *b^hewd^h-
buk, bukev, *b^heh_2go-
byť, *b^huH-
cediť, *skey-
celý, *$kóh_2ilus$
cena, *k^wey-
chápať, *keh_2p-
čistý, *skey-
čo, *k^wis
črep, *kerp-
čapiť, *keh_2p-
ďakovať, *teng-
daň, dar, *deH_3-
ďasno, *$h_3dónts$
dať, dávať, *deH_3-
dcéra, dcérka, *$d^hugh_2tēr$
decht, *d^hegw^h-
dekáda, *$dékm̥t$
deň, *deyn-
desať, *$dékm̥t$
deva, *$d^heh_1(y)$-
devät, *$H_1néwn̥$
devica, *$d^heh_1(y)$-
diať sa, dielo, *$dheH_1$-
dieťa, *$d^heh_1(y)$-
dieža, *$d^heyǵ^h$-
div, *dyew-
dno, *d^hewb-
dojiť, *$d^heh_1(y)$-
dom, *dem-
drevo, *dóru
drieť, *der-
drozd, *trosdos
drzý, *d^hers-
ďubať, *d^hewb-

dva, *$dwóH_1$
dvadsať, *$wīkm̥tiH_1$
dvere, dvor, *d^hwer-
dym, *d^hewh_2-
éter, *h_2eyd^h-
galaxia, *glag-
grno, *g^wher-
herzog, *ker-
história, *weyd-
hnida, *knid-
hniezdo, *nisdós
honiť, *g^when-
horieť, *g^wher-
hosť, *$g^hóstis$
hovädo, *$g^wṓws$
hrad, *$ǵ^her$-
hrana, hrdlo, *g^werH-
hreje, hriať, *g^wher-
hrôza, *g^hers-
hus, *$ǵ^hans$-
hyena, *suH-
charakter, *$ǵ^her$-
chod, *sed-
chvíľa, *k^wyeh_1-
ináč, inak, inakšie, inde, iný, *óy-nos
ísť, *h_1ey-
ja, *egH_2
jablko, *$h_2ébōl$
jadro, *$h_1én$
jahňa, *h_2eg^wnos
jahoda, *eh_3g-
jar, *yeh_1-
jarmo, *h_2er
jaro, *yeh_1-
járom, *h_2er
jaseň, *h_3es-
jatrá, *$h_1én$
jazyk, *$dn̥ǵ^wéh_2s$
je, *b^huH-
jeden, *óy-nos
jelša, *h_3el-
jesť, *h_1ed-
jež, *$ang^w(h)i$-
jínie, *h_1eyH-
junák, *h_2yuh_1en-
jutro, *h_2ews-
kameň, *$h_2éḱ-mō$
kľúč, kľuka, *(s)kel-
kňaz, *$ǵenH_1$-
koleno, *kelH-
koleso, kolo, *k^wel-
konfirmácia, *d^her-
kôra, *(s)ker-
kraj, krajina, *krey-
kráľ, králica, *$ǵerh_2$-
krava, *$kerh_2$-
krojiť, *krey-

krv, *krewh₂-

kto, ktorý, *kʷis

ľadvina, *lendʰ-

ľan, *lino-

ľahký, *h₁lengʷʰ-

ľahnúť si, *legh-

lakeť, *Heh₃l-

lepiť, *leyp-

ležať, *legh-

lichý, *leykʷ-

ložiť, *legh-

ľúbiť, ľubý, *lewbʰ-

lúč, lúčiť, *lewk-

ľud, ľudia, *h₁lewdʰ-

luna, *lewk-

ma, *H₁me-

majster, *méǵh₂s

mať, *méh₂tēr

mäso, *mḗms

med, medveď, *médʰu

medza, medzi, *médʰyos

menej, *mey-

meno, *h₁nómn̥

menší, *mey-

mesiac, *méh₁n̥s

mieniť, *men-

miera, mieriť, *meh₁-

miesiť, *mey-

minca, *men-

mlat, *melh₂-

mlieko, *H₂melǵ-

mlieť, *melh₂-

mĺzť, *H₂melǵ-

mňa, mne, *H₁me-

moja, *H₁meme-

mor, *mer-

more, *móri

moriť, *mer-

mozog, *mosgʰos

môj, *H₁meme-

mrav, *h₂nḗr

mravec, *morwi-

mrieť, mŕtví, mŕtvy, mŕtvý, *mer-

mucha, *mus-

muž, *mánus

my, *wei

myseľ, myslieť, *men-

myš, *muh₂s-

myšľať, *men-

nahý, *negʷ-

nás, *wei

nebo, *nebʰ-

necht, *h₃negʰ-

nič, nikto, *kʷis

noc, *nókʷts

noha, *h₃negʰ-

nos, *néh₂s

nový, *new

oblátka, *bher-

oheň, *h₁n̥gʷnis

okno, oko, *h₃ekʷ-

on, *éy / h₁e

orákulum, *h₃éh₁os

orať, *H₂erH₃-

orol, *h₃érō

osa, *wobs-

osem, *oktṓw

osika, *h₃es-

osla, *h₂éḱ

ostrov, *srew-

ostrý, *h₂éḱ

otec, *átta

ovca, *h₂ówis

padać, *pṓds

pamäť, *men-

pásť, *peh₂-

päť, *pénkʷe

päta, *pent-

pena, *poymno-

pero, *péth₂r̥

pestrý, *peyḱ-

peši, *pṓds

pchať, *peys-

piaď, *pewǵ-

piecť, *pekʷ-

piest, pichať, *peys-

písať, *peyḱ-

piť, pivo, *peh₃-

plakať, *pleh₂k-

plávať, *plew-

plavý, *pelH-

plece, *pleth₂-

pleť, *plew-

plný, *pleh₁-

pľúca, *plewmō

plyn, plynúť, *plew-

po, *h₂pó

pôda, *ped-

pokoj, *kʷyeh₁-

pole, *pleh₂-

pot, *pekʷ-

prach, *pers-

prasa, *pórḱos

priať, priateľ, *preyH-

program, *gerbʰ-

prosiť, *preḱ-

pšeno, *peys-

pudiť, *pewǵ-

púť, *pent-

pýriť sa, *péh₂ur

rab, *h₃erbʰ-

radikál, *wréh₂ds

radlo, *H₂erH₃-

rameno, *h₂er

raž, *wrug^{h}yo-
rdieť sa, *h₁rewd^h-
republika, *pleh₁-
rieka, rinúť sa, *h₃er-, *h₃reyH-
roj, rôj, *h₃reyH-
rudý, *h₁rewd^h-
sa, *s(w)e-
sadiť, *sed-
sám, *sem-
seba, *s(w)e-
sedem, *septm̥
sedieť, *sed-
sekať, sekera, *sek-
semeno, *seH₁-
sen, *swep-
sestra, *swésōr
si, *b^{h}uH-
siať, *seH₁-
siecť, *sek-
skura, *(s)ker-
slabý, *leb-
sladký, *séh₂ls
slama, *ḱalam-
sláva, *ḱlew-
slezina, *splenǵ^h-
slnce, slnko, *sóh₂wl̥
slovo, sluch, slušať, slyšať, *ḱlew-
smrť, *mer-
sneh, *sneyg^{wh}-
sok, *sek^w-
soľ, *séh₂ls
som, *b^{h}uH-
spať, *swep-
spieť, *speh₁-
srdce, *ḱḗr
srna, sršeň, *ḱerh₂-
stádo, stan, starý, stáť, staviť, *steh₂-
stenať, *(s)tenh₂-
stihnúť, *steyg^h-
stlať, *stel-
sto, *ḱm̥tóm
stôl, *steh₂-
streda, *ḱḗr
strumeň, *srew-
sú-, *sem-
suka, *ḱwṓ
sviňa, *suH-
svoj, *s(w)e-
syn, *suh₁nús
šampión, *(s)teg-
šesť, *swéḱs
šiť, *sīw-
škola, *seǵ^h-
štít, *skey-
študovať, *(s)tew-
štyri, *k^{w}etwóres
ten, *só

teritórium, *ters-
tesať, *tetḱ-
tradícia, *deH₃-
translácia, *bher-
tri, *tréyes
trieť, *terh₁-
trud, *trewd-
tur, *(s)táwros
ty, *túh₂
u, ucho, *h₂ew-
ujo, *h₂éwh₂os
ústa, *h₃éh₁os
útroba, *h₁én
úzky, *h₂enǵ^h-
v, *h₁én
vajce, *h₂ōwyóm
včela, *b^{h}ey-
vdova, *h₁weyd^h
večerne, *wek(^{w})speros
večný, *weyk-
vedieť, *weyd-
vek, *weyk-
veliť, *welh₁-
vemä, *h₁owHd^{h}r̥-
veno, *wed^h-
ves, *weyḱ-
veslo, *weǵ^h-
vesna, *wésr̥
vetchý, *wet-
viať, *H₂weH₁-
viazať, *h₂enǵ^h-
vid, vidieť, *weyd-
viera, *weh₁-
viesť, *wed^h-
vietor, *H₂weH₁-
viezť, *weǵ^h-
vino, *wóyh₁nom
vládať, vlasť, *h₂welh₁-
vlk, vlkolak, *wl̥k^{w}os
vlna, *h₂welh₁-
vnútri, vo, *h₁én
voda, *wed-
vodiť, *wed^h-
voz, voziť, *weǵ^h-
vôľa, *welh₁-
vôňa, *h₂enh₁-
vráta, vrátiť, vreteno, *wert-
vrš, vrša, *werǵ-
vrtieť, *wert-
vy, *túh₂
vydra, *udréh₂
z, *h₁eǵ^{h}s
zať, *ǵenH₁-
zelený, *ǵ^{h}elh₃-
zem, *d^{h}éǵ^{h}ōm
zima, *ǵ^{h}ey-
zlato, *ǵ^{h}elh₃-

znať, *ǵneh₃-
zo, *h₁eǵʰs
zrelý, *ǵerh₂-
zrno, *ǵr̥Hnom
zub, *ǵómbʰos
zver, *ǵʰwer-
ždobať, žďobať, *dʰewb-
žena, *gwén
žeriav, *gerh₂-
žiť, živica, život, živý, *gʷeyh₃-
žltý, *ǵʰelh₃-
žrať, *gʷerH-
žreb, *gerbʰ-

Macedonian

'рж ('rž), *wrugʰyo-
анонимен (anonimen), *h₁nómn̥
апе (ape), *keh₂p-
бајка (bajka), *bʰeh₂-
бдее (bdee), *bʰewdʰ-
беда (beda), *bʰeydʰ-
бере (bere), *bher-
блее (blee), *bʰleh₁-
бодар (bodar), *bʰewdʰ-
боз (boz), *bʰeh₂go-
болва (bolva), *plou-
брада (brada), брадата (bradata), *bʰardʰeh₂-
брат (brat), *bʰréh₂tēr
брег (breg), *bʰerǵʰ-
бреза (breza), *bʰereǵ-
бреме (breme), *bher-
буди (budi), *bʰewdʰ-
бука (buka), буква (bukva), *bʰeh₂go-
вдовица (vdovica), *h₁weydʰ
век (vek), *weyk-
вера (vera), *weh₁-
вéсло (véslo), *weǵh-
ветер (veter), *H₂weH₁-
ветов (vetov), *wet-
вечен (večen), *weyk-
вечер (večer), *wek(ʷ)speros
вѝди (vídi), *weyd-
видра (vidra), *udréh₂
виме (vime), *h₁owHdʰr̥-
вино (vino), *wóyh₁nom
владее (vladee), власт (vlast), *h₂welh₁-
внук (vnuk), *nepot-
во (vo), *h₁én
вода (voda), *wed-
вóди (vódi), *wedʰ-
воз (voz), вози (vozi), *weǵh-
вóлја (vólja), *welh₁-
волк (volk), *wl̥kʷos
волна (volna), *h₂welh₁-
врата (vrata), време (vreme), вретено (vreteno), *wert-
врколак (vrkolak), *wl̥kʷos
врти (vrti), *wert-
вујко (vujko), *h₂éwh₂os
ѓавол (ǵavol), *gʷelH-
гнездо (gnezdo), *nisdós
гнида (gnída), *knid-
говедо (govedo), *gʷóws
гони (goni), *gʷhen-
гори (gori), *gʷher-
гост/гостин (gost/gostin), *gʰóstis
град (grad), *ǵʰer-
гре (gre), *gʷher-
грло (grlo), *gʷerH-

гроза (groza), *gʰers-
гуска (guska), *ǵʰans-
дава (dava), даде (dade), *deH₃-
два (dva), *dwóH₁
двер (dver), двор (dvor), *dʰwer-
девет (devet), *H₁néwn̥
девица (devica), *dʰeh₁(y)-
декада (dekada), *dékm̥t
дело (delo), *dheH₁-
ден (den), *deyn-
дере (dere), *der-
десет (deset), *dékm̥t
дете (dete), *dʰeh₁(y)-
дим (dim), *dʰewh₂-
дно (dno), *dʰewb-
дои (doi), *dʰeh₁(y)-
дом (dom), *dem-
дрво (drvo), *dóru
дрзне (drzne), *dʰers-
дрозд (drozd), *trosdos
душман (dušman), *men-
е (e), *bʰuH-
éден (éden), *óy-nos
еж (ež), *angʷ(h)i-
ждере (ždere), *gʷerH-
ждреб (ždreb), *gerbʰ-
жени (ženi), *gwén
жерав (žerav), *gerh₂-
жешти (žešti), *dʰegʷʰ-
жив (živ), живее (živee), жи́вот (žívot), *gʷeyh₃-
жолт (žolt), *ǵʰelh₃-
заб (zab), *ǵómbʰos
зелен (zelen), *ǵʰelh₃-
зéмја (zémja), *dʰéǵʰōm
зет (zet), *ǵenH₁-
зима (zíma), *ǵʰey-
злató (zlató), *ǵʰelh₃-
знае (znae), *ǵneh₃-
зрно (zrno), *ǵr̥Hnom
зурла (zurla), *ḱerh₂-
звер (dzver), *ǵʰwer-
сид (dzid), *dʰeyǵʰ-
иго (igo), *yugóm
и́де (íde), *h₁ey-
име (ime), *h₁nómn̥
инаку (ínaku), *óy-nos
истóрија (istórija), *weyd-
јаболко (jabolko), *h₂ébōl
ја́гне (jágne), *h₂eǵʰnos
јагода (jagoda), *eh₃g-
ја́де (jáde), *h₁ed-
јазик (jazik), *dn̥ǵʰwéh₂s
ја́јце (jájce), *h₂ōwyóm
јара (jara), *yeh₁-
јарбол (jarbol), *h₂erHdʰ-
јарем (jarem), *h₂er
јас (jas), *egH₂

камен (kamen), *h₂éḱ-mō
ќерка (ḱerka), *dʰugh₂tḗr
клуч (kluč), *(s)kel-
колено (koleno), *kelH-
кóло (kólo), *kʷel-
кора (kora), *(s)ker-
крава (krava), *ḱerh₂-
крај (kraj), *krey-
крал (kral), кралица (kralica), *ǵerh₂-
крв (krv), *krewh₂-
крои (kroi), *krey-
лакот (lakot), *Heh₃l-
лач (lač), *lewk-
лежи (leži), *legh-
лек (lek), *h₁lengʷʰ-
лен (len), *lino-
лепи (lepi), *leyp-
ложи (loži), *legh-
локва (lokva), *lókus
луѓе (luǵe), *h₁lewdʰ-
луна (luna), *lewk-
љуби (ljubi), *lewbʰ-
маж (maž), *mánus
мајка (majka), *méh₂tēr
мајстор (majstor), *méǵh₂s
меѓа (meǵa), меѓу (meǵu), *médʰyos
мед (med), *médʰu
меле (mele), *melh₂-
мене (tebe), *H₁me-
мера (mera), мери (meri), *meh₁-
мéсец (mésec), месечина (mesečina), *méh₁n̥s
меси (mesi), *mey-
месо (meso), *mḗms
мисла (misla), *men-
миш (miš), *muh₂s-
млат (mlat), *melh₂-
млéко (mléko), *H₂melǵ-
мозок (mozok), *mosgʰos
мој (moj), *H₁meme-
море (more), *móri
мравка (mravka), *morwi-
мртов (mrtov), *mer-
мува (múva), *mus-
нарав (narav), *h₂nḗr
нéбо (nébo), *nebʰ-
ништо (níšto), *kʷis
нов (nov), *new
ногá (nogá), *h₃negʰ-
ноќ (noḱ), *nókʷts
нокт (nokt), *h₃negʰ-
нос (nos), *néh₂s
овен (óven), овца (óvca), *h₂ówis
оган (ogan), *h₁n̥gʷnis
од (od), *sed-
око (oko), *h₃ekʷ-
ора (ora), *H₂erH₃-
оракул (orakul), *h₃éh₁os

орел (orel), *h₃érō

оса (osa), *wobs-

остар (ostar), *h₂éḱ

остров (ostrov), *srew-

осум (osum), *oḱtṓw

óтец (ótec), *átta

паѓа (paǵa), *pṓds

пáмет (pámet), *men-

пасат (pasat), *peh₂-

пат (pat), *pent-

пелена (pelena), *pel-

перо (pero), *péth₂r

пет (pet), *pénkʷe

пета (peta), петица (petica), *pent-

пече (peče), *pekʷ-

пиво (pivo), пѝе (píe), *peh₃-

пирej (pirej), *péh₂ur

пишува (pišuva), *peyḱ-

плеќи (pleḱi), *pleth₂-

плива (pliva), *plew-

по (po), *h₂pó

пои (poi), *peh₃-

покоj (pokoj), *kʷyeh₁-

póле (póle), *pleh₂-

полн (poln), *pleh₁-

пот (pot), *pekʷ-

прав (prav), *pers-

прасе (prase), прасенце (prasence), *pórḱos

прѝjател (príjatel), *preyH-

публика (publika), *pleh₁-

путер (puter), *gʷṓws

пчела (pčela), *bʰey-

раб (rab), *h₃erbʰ-

радикал (radikal), *wréh₂ds

рамо (ramo), *h₂er

река (reka), рине (rine), *h₃er-, *h₃reyH-

роб (rob), *h₃erbʰ-

рубин (rubin), руд (rud), *h₁rewdʰ-

сам (sam), *sem-

свиња (svinja), *suH-

своj (svoj), ce (se), себе (sebe), *s(w)e-

седум (sedum), *septm̥

cee (see), *seH₁-

секира (sekira), *sek-

семе (seme), *seH₁-

семеjство (semejstvo), *ḱei-

сестра (sestrá), *swésōr

си (si), *bʰuH-

син (sin), *suh₁nús

скок (skok), *(s)kek-

слаб (slab), *leb-

слава (slava), *ḱlew-

сладок (sladok), *séh₂ls

слама (slama), *ḱalam-

слезина (slezina), *splenǵʰ-

слово (slovo), слух (sluh), слуша (sluša), *ḱlew-

смрт (smrt), *mer-

снаа (snaa), *snusós

снабдува (snabduva), *bʰewdʰ-

снег (sneg), *sneygʷʰ-

сол (sol), *séh₂ls

сон (son), *swep-

сонце (sonce), *sóh₂wl̥

сочи (soči), *sekʷ-

спие (spie), *swep-

спокоj (spokoj), *kʷyeh₁-

срна (srna), *ḱerh₂-

срце (srce), *ḱḗr

стави (stavi), стадо (stado), стане (stane), стар (star),
    *steh₂-

стенка (stenka), *(s)tenh₂-

стигне (stigne), *steygʰ-

сто (sto), *ḱm̥tóm

струjа (struja), *srew-

стршен (stršen), *ḱerh₂-

сум (sum), *bʰuH-

татко (tatko), *ph₂tḗr

ти (ti), *túh₂

тоj (toj), *éy / h₁e

три (tri), *tréyes

трие (trie), *terh₁-

труд (trud), *trewd-

уво (uvo), *h₂ew-

успее (uspee), *speh₁-

уста/усни (usta/usni), *h₃éh₁os

утро (utro), *h₂ews-

утроба (utroba), *h₁én

цеди (cedi), *skey-

целиот (celiot), *kóh₂ilus

цена (cena), *kʷey-

череп (čerep), *kerp-

черепот (čerepot), *ḱerh₂-

четири (četiri), *kʷetwóres

чист (čist), *skey-

џигер (džiger), *Hyékʷr̥

шест (šest), *swéḱs

шѝе (šíe), *sīw-

шкóла (škóla), *seǵʰ-

штит (štit), *skey-

што (što), *kʷis

Lithuanian

akėčios, *h₂ék
akis, *h₃ekʷ-
akmuo, *h₂ék-mō
àlksnis, *h₃el-
alkūnė, *Heh₃l-
alùs, *h₂elut-
angis, *angʷ(h)i-
ánka, *h₂enk-
ankštas, *h₂enǵʰ-
añt, antai, *h₂ent
añtaras, *h₂énteros
ántis, *h₂eneti-
añtras, *h₂énteros
ap-, *h₁epi
apačià, *h₂pó
arklas, árti, *H₂erH₃-
àš, *egH₂
ašis, *H₂eǵ-
ašmenys, ašmuo, *h₂ék-mō
ašrùs, aštrùs, *h₂ék
aštuonì, *oktṓw
ašva, *h₁éḱwos
atlaikas, *leykʷ-
au, *h₂ew
augestis, áugti, aũkštas, *h₂ewg-
ausis, *h₂ew-
aušrà, *h₂ews-
ãvinas, avis, *h₂ówis
avynas, *h₂éwh₂os
ąžuolas, *h₂eyǵ-
bakstelėti, *bak-
barzda, barzdótas, *bʰardʰeh₂-
báudyti, *bʰewdʰ-
bernas, berti, beŕti, *bher-
beržas, *bʰereǵ-
bitė, *bʰey-
bliáuti, *bʰleh₁-
blusa, *plou-
blužnis, *splenǵʰ-
brolis, broterėlis, *bʰréh₂tēr
brùvė , bruvis, *h₃bʰrúHs
budėti, budrùs, *bʰewdʰ-
bukas, *bʰeh₂go-
būkla, būklas, *bʰuH-
bùsti, *bʰewdʰ-
būti, būtu, bùvintis, *bʰuH-
čempionas, *(s)teg-
dagà, *dʰegʷʰ-
dantis, *h₃dónts
darýti, *dʰer-
daubà, *dʰewb-
debesis, *nebʰ-
dėgis, dègti, degùtas, *dʰegʷʰ-

dėlė, *dʰeh₁(y)-
derėti, *dʰer-
dérti, *der-
dervà, *dóru
dėšimt, *déḱm̥t
dėšinas, *deks-
dėti, *dheH₁-
devynì, *H₁néwn̥
diena, *deyn-
dievas, *dyew-
dìrti, *der-
drąsùs, *dʰers-
drevė , *dóru
dr̨sti, *dʰers-
dù, *dwóH₁
dubùs, dùgnas, *dʰewb-
dujà, *dʰewh₂-
duktē, *dʰugh₂tḗr
dúlis, dūmai, dūmas, *dʰewh₂-
duõnis, duoti, *deH₃-
dùrys, dvãras, *dʰwer-
dvi, *dwóH₁
dvidešimt, *wīḱm̥tiH₁
ėdmi, *h₁ed-
eĩti, *h₁ey-
ekėčios, *h₂ék
èlksnis, *h₃el-
elkūnė, *Heh₃l-
érdvė, *h₁er-
erelis, *h₃érō
ėriena, *h₂egʷnos
esi, *H₁es-
ėsti, *h₁ed-
esti, esu, *H₁es-
eteris, *h₂eydʰ-
ežys, *angʷ(h)i-
ganýti, *gʷʰen-
gaȓdas, *ǵʰer-
garėti, gariù, *gʷʰer-
garnȳs, *gerh₂-
gauti, gãvo, *gʰeh₁bʰ-
gėlà, gélti, *gʷelH-
gelumà, *gel-
genėti, genėti, *gʷʰen-
gēras, *gʷerH-
gérvė, *gerh₂-
giȓtas, gimti, giȓtis, *gʷem-
ginti, giñti, *gʷʰen-
girna, *gʷrh₂-n-uH-
gìrti, *gʷerH-
gývas, gyvatà, gyventi, *gʷeyh₃-
grasa, grėsti, *gʰers-
hercogas, *ker-
į/in, *h₁én
ir, *h₂er-
irštvà, *h₂ŕ̥tkos
istorija, *weyd-

iš, *h₁eǵʰs
ýnis, *h₁eyH-
yra, *H₁es-
jaunas, *h₂yuh₁en-
jeknos, *Hyékʷr̥
jis, *éy / h₁e
jorė, *yeh₁-
jùngas, *yugóm
jùngti, *yewg-
jūs, *túh₂
kaimas, *ḱei-
káina, *kʷey-
kãklas , *kʷel-
kalba, *kelh₁-
kálnas, kalvà, *kelH-
kapas, kapt, *keh₂p-
kãras, *ker-
kárvė, *ḱerh₂-
kàs, kataràs, katràs, *kʷis
kėlis, kélti, *kelH-
kengė, *keg-
kenklė, *kenk-
kèpti, *pekʷ-
keturì, *kʷetwóres
kiẽmas, *ḱei-
kìlti, *kelH-
kìnka, *kenk-
kìrpti, *kerp-
klausyti, *ḱlew-
kliáuti, kliūdýti, kliūti, *(s)kel-
kraujas, *krewh₂-
kunigas, kuningas, *ǵenH₁-
laikýtiy, *leykʷ-
láipioti, *leyp-
langas, lankstus, *h₁lengʷʰ-
lapènti, *leb-
lauka, *lewk-
laũkas, *lewk-
lengvas, leñgvas, lengvùs, lenkti, *h₁lengʷʰ-
liaudis, *h₁lewdʰ-
liaupsė, *lewbʰ-
liežuvis, *dn̥ǵʰwéh₂s
likti, *leykʷ-
linas, *lino-
lipìnti, *leyp-
liulė, *luHs-
lizdas, *nisdós
lūpa, *leb-
magistras, *méǵh₂s
maišas, *mak-
maišýti, *mey-
malkas, *H₂melǵ-
málti, *melh₂-
man, manè, *H₁me-
mano, *H₁meme-
mãras, *mer-

marios, *móri
mazgas, *mosgʰos
mēdis, *médʰyos
medus, *médʰu
meistras, *méǵh₂s
melžti, *H₂melǵ-
menkas, *mey-
mėnuo, *méh₁n̥s
mès, *wei
mėsa, *mḗms
mi, *H₁me-
miẽši, *mey-
minėti, mintas, minti, mintis, *men-
mìrti, mirtis, *mer-
mìšras, mìšti, *mey-
mýžti, *h₃meyǵʰ-
mótė, moteris, *méh₂tēr
mùms, mùs, *wei
musė, *mus-
naga, nagas, *h₃negʰ-
naktis, *nókʷts
namas, *dem-
naujas, *new
nepuotis, *nepot-
nežinoti, *ǵneh₃-
nóras , *h₂nḗr
nósis, *néh₂s
núogas, *negʷ-
obuolỹs, *h₂ébōl
orakulas, *h₃éh₁os
paišaĩ, *peyk-
pálvas, *peH-
paršas, *pórḱos
pašýti, *peḱ-
patinas, *ph₂tḗr
pats, *pótis
pėda, *pṓds
pēkus, *peḱu
pelekas, *pelH-
penkì, *pénkʷe
per, *per-
pėšti, pešù, *peḱ-
petỹs, *peth₂
piemuõ, *peh₂-
piẽšas, piẽšti, *peyḱ-
pìlkas, *pelH-
pìlnas, *pleh₁-
pìlti, *plew-
pinti, *pleḱ-
pìřkšnys, *pers-
pìsti, *peys-
pláju , *plew-
plakti, *pleh₂k-
platus, *pleh₂-
platùs, *pleth₂-
plaučiai, *plewmō
plaũkti, pláuti, plaũtis, *plew-

plėnė, plėnìs, *pel-

plėsti, *pleth₂-

plokščias, plonas, *pleh₂-

plūsti, *plew-

pra-, *per-

prašyti, *preḱ-

pro-, *per-

problema, *gʷelH-

pulkas, *pleh₁-

puota, *peh₃-

purkšti, pūrslas, *pers-

pušìs, *pewǵ-

puta, *poymno-

radikalas, *wréh₂ds

rãtas, *Hret-

raũdonas, *h₁rewdʰ-

regéti, règti, *h₃reǵ-

rùdas, *h₁rewdʰ-

rugys, *wrugʰyo-

sakyti, *sekʷ-

saldus, sálti, *séh₂ls

sam-, *sem-

sãpnas, *swep-

sáulė, *sóh₂wl̥

save, *s(w)e-

sedéti, *sed-

sekla, *seH₁-

sèkti, *sekʷ-

semenis, *seH₁-

sẽnas, *sénos

septynì, *septm̥

sėstis, *sed-

sesuõ, *swésōr

sėti, *seH₁-

sintéti, *sent-

sistemà, *steh₂-

siūti, *sīw-

skíesti, *skey-

skìrti, *(s)ker-

sliet, *ḱley-

slōbti, *leb-

smẽgenys, *mosgʰos

smėlis, *melh₂-

sniegas, snigti, *sneygʷʰ-

sodìnti, *sed-

speigleĩs, *spey-

spėsti, *pewǵ-

spéti, *speh₁-

sraujà, sraũjas, sravéti, srovė, *srew-

stãlas, *steh₂-

stáldas, *stel-

steĩgti, *steygʰ-

steneti, *(s)tenh₂-

stìrna, *ḱerh₂-

stogas, *(s)teg-

stógas, stomuõ, stónas, stóras, stóti, stovéti,
    stovéti, *steh₂-

strazdas, *trosdos

studijuoti, *(s)tew-

stúomas, stuomuõ, *steh₂-

sūnus, *suh₁nús

šálmas, *ḱel-

šankìnti, šankùs, *(s)kek-

šeimà, šeĩmas, šeimė, *ḱei-

šešì, *swéḱs

šim̃tas, *ḱm̥tóm

širdis, *ḱḗr

širšė, širšuo, *ḱerh₂-

šìs, *ḱi-

šlãvė, *ḱlew-

šleĩvas, šliñti, *ḱley-

šókti, *(s)kek-

šuñs, šuo, *ḱwṓ

tãnas, tandùs, *ten-

tašýti, *tetḱ-

tauras, *(s)táwros

tautà, *tewtéh₂

tenéti, *ten-

teritorija, *ters-

tiñklas, tìnti, *ten-

tradicija, *deH₃-

triūsas, *trewd-

trỹs, *tréyes

trobà, *treb-

trokšti, *ters-

tù, *túh₂

ūdra, ūdras, *udréh₂

ūdroti, *h₁owHdʰr̥-

ugnis, *h₁n̥gʷnis

ungurys, *angʷ(h)i-

úoga, *eh₃g-

úolektis, *Heh₃l-

uosis, *h₃es-

úostas, *h₃éh₁os

úosti, *h₃ed-

usnis, *h₁ews-

vãdas, vadúoti, *wedʰ-

váišinti, *weyḱ-

vaizdas, *weyd-

vajóti, *weyh₁-

vakaras, *wek(ʷ)speros

valdýti, *h₂welh₁-

vanduõ, *wed-

vapsà, vapsvà, *wobs-

var̃das, *wekʷ-

vargas, *werǵ-

var̃mas, *wr̥mis-

váržas, *werǵ-

vãsara, *wésr̥

véidas, *weyd-

veĩkti, *weyḱ-

veizdéti, *weyd-

vėjas, *H₂weH₁-

vėl, *welH-

veldėti, *h₂welh₁-
vélti, *welh₁-
versti, *wert-
vèsti, *wedʰ-
vėtušas, *wet-
vežti, *weǵh-
vidus, *h₁weydʰ
víenas, *óy-nos
viešas, viešėti, *weyḱ-
viẽšpats, *pótis
viẽšpats, *weyḱ-
vĩlkas, *wĺkʷos
vilna, *h₂welh₁-
višta, *h₂éwis
výras, *wiHrós
vyti, *webh-
výti, *weyh₁-
vójęs, *h₁weh₂-
žãlias, *ǵʰelh₃-
žambas, *ǵómbʰos
žandas, *ǵénus
žarna, *ǵʰern-
žarstýti, *ǵʰer-
žąsis, *ǵʰans-
žélti, žélvas, *ǵʰelh₃-
želvė, *gʰelõw-
žemė, *dʰéǵʰōm
žeriù, žeŕti, *ǵʰer-
žiemà, *ǵʰey-
žinoti, *ǵneh₃-
žirnis, *ǵr̥Hnom
žmogùs, *ǵʰmó
žvėris, *ǵʰwer-

Latvian

ābols, *h₂ébōl
aborts, *h₃er-
acs, *h₃ekʷ-
akmens, *h₂éḱ-mō
aknas, *Hyékʷr̥
āķis, *h₂enk-
alksìnis, ãlksnis, *h₃el-
alus, *h₂elut-
añka, *h₂enk-
arkls, aȓt, *H₂erH₃-
asinis, *h₁ésh₂r̥
asmens, *h₂éḱ-mō
ass, *h₂éḱ
astoņi, *oktṓw
astrs, aŝs, *h₂éḱ
au, *h₂ew
augsts, augt, augusts, *h₂ewg-
auns, *h₂ówis
ausma, *h₂ews-
auss, *h₂ew-
àustra, *h₂ews-
avs, *h₂ówis
bads, *bʰeydʰ-
bakstit, *bak-
bārda, *bʰardʰeh₂-
bàudît, *bʰewdʰ-
bērns, bèrt, *bher-
bērzs, *bʰereǵ-
bite, *bʰey-
blêt, *bʰleh₁-
blusa, *plou-
brālis, brātarĩtis, *bʰréh₂tēr
bust, *bʰewdʰ-
būt, *bʰuH-
celis, *kelH-
cena, *kʷey-
cept, *pekʷ-
ciems, *ḱei-
cinksla, *kenk-
cìrpt, *kerp-
čempions, *(s)teg-
četri, *kʷetwóres
darĩt, *dʰer-
daȓva, *dóru
debess, *nebʰ-
degt, deguts, *dʰegʷʰ-
dekāde, *déḱm̥t
dēls, *dʰeh₁(y)-
derêt, *dʰer-
desmit, *déḱm̥t
deviņi, *H₁néwn̥
diena, *deyn-
dievs, *dyew-

divdesmit, *wīḱm̥tiH₁
divi, *dwóH₁
dobs, *dʰewb-
dot, *deH₃-
dreve, *dóru
drùoss, drùošs, *dʰers-
dūmi, *dʰewh₂-
dùrvis, dvars, *dʰwer-
dzenêt, *gʷʰen-
dzẽrve, *gerh₂-
dzimt, dzimts, *gʷem-
dzirnus, *gʷrh₂-n-uH-
dzîṛu, *gʷerH-
dzît, *gʷeyh₃-, *gʷʰen-
dzīvot, dzîvs, *gʷeyh₃-
ecêkšas, ecêšas, *h₂éḱ
elkonis, *Heh₃l-
ẽlksnis, *h₃el-
ẽrglis, *h₃érō
es, *egH₂
esi, esmu, *H₁es-
ẽst, *h₁ed-
ezis, *angʷ(h)i-
ganît, *gʷʰen-
gãrds, *ǵʰer-
gaȓnis, *gerh₂-
gnida, *knid-
govs, *gʷóws
grasãt, *gʰers-
grĩpsta, *gerbʰ-
grūts, *gʷerh₂-
hercogs, *ker-
iekša, *h₁én
iet, *h₁ey-
ir, *H₁es-
iz, *h₁eǵʰs
jaûns, *h₂yuh₁en-
jẽrs, *h₂egʷnos
jūgs, *yugóm
jûgt, *yewg-
kakls, *kʷel-
kãlns, kalva, *kelH-
kaḷuot, *kelh₁-
kàmpju, kàmpt, *keh₂p-
kaȓš, *ker-
kas, *kʷis
klausîties, *ḱlew-
kḷût, *(s)kel-
kurš, *kʷis
ķẽniņš, *ǵenH₁-
làicît, *leykʷ-
laipns, *leyp-
lauks, *lewk-
liêgs, *h₁lengʷʰ-
liesa, *splenǵʰ-
ligzda, ligzds, *nisdós
lini, *lino-

lipt, *leyp-
lūpa, *leb-
ḷaudis, *h₁lewdʰ-
màisît, *mey-
maks, *mak-
malks, *H₂melǵ-
man, mani, *H₁me-
mans, *H₁meme-
mare, *móri
mãte, *méh₂tēr
me̦dus, *médʰu
mēnesis, mēness, *méh₁n̥s
mēs, *wei
mestrs, *méǵh₂s
mezgls, *mosgʰos
mežs, *médʰyos
miesa, *méms
minēt, *men-
mirt, *mer-
mīzt, *h₃meyǵʰ-
mums, mūs, *wei
muša, *mus-
mute, mutîgs, mutisks, *mendʰ-
naba, *h₃enbʰ-
nags, *h₃negʰ-
nakts, *nókʷts
nams, *dem-
nãss, *néh₂s
nàujš, *new
nezinãt, *ǵneh₃-
nicnin, *ḱerh₂-
niere, *negʷh-r-
nuôgs, *negʷ-
ņemt, *nem-
odze, *angʷ(h)i-
oga, *eh₃g-
olekts, *Heh₃l-
orãkuls, *h₃éh₁os
osis, *h₃es-
ost, *h₃ed-
osta, *h₃éh₁os
otrs, *h₂énteros
pa, *h₂pó
pãri, *per-
pãrsla, *pers-
pats, *pótis
pavasaris, *wésr̥
pēda, *pṓds
pelēks, *pelH-
pieci, *pénkʷe
piedurkne, *h₁epi
pildît, pilēt, pilns, *pleh₁-
pìrkstis, *pers-
pist, *peys-
plakans, plãns, plašs, *pleh₂-
plašs, *pleth₂-
plats, *pleh₂-, *pleth₂-

plaušas, *plewmō
plàuši, *plew-
plēne, *pel-
pluts , *plew-
prasît, *preḱ-
princis, *keh$_2$p-
problēma, *g^{w}elH-
putas, *poymno-
raĩdît, *h$_3$reyH-
rats, *Hret-
redzēt, *h$_3$reǵ-
ruds, *h$_1$rewd^h-
rudzi, *wrug^{h}yo-
sacît, *sek^w-
sàime, *ḱei-
sākt, *(s)kek-
salds, *séh$_2$ls
salms, *ḱalam-
sãļš, *séh$_2$ls
sapnis, *swep-
saũle, *sóh$_2$wl̥
sēdēt, segli, *sed-
sekot, sekt, *sek^w-
sens, *sénos
septiņi, *septm̥
seši, *swéḱs
sēt, *seH$_1$-
sevi, *s(w)e-
siẽva, *ḱei-
simts, *ḱm̥tóm
sirds, *ḱḗr
sirsenis, *ḱerh$_2$-
sistēma, *steh$_2$-
sivēns, *suH-
slava, slave, sluvêt, *ḱlew-
smēlis, *melh$_2$-
snāte, *(s)neh$_1$-
sniegs, snigt, *sneyg^{wh}-
spēt, *speh$_1$-
spiêst, *pewǵ-
spina, *spey-
splīns, *splenǵ^h-
staĩga, *steyg^h-
stãllis, *stel-
stãmen, stāt, stātis, stāvēt, *steh$_2$-
stir̃na, *ḱerh$_2$-
strauja, stràujš, stràuja, strāve, *srew-
strazds, *trosdos
studēt, *(s)tew-
suns, *ḱwṓ
suvēns, *suH-
sviêdri, *sweyd-
šis, *ḱi-
šķiêst, *skey-
šlieti, *ḱley-
šūt, *sīw-
tauriņš, *(s)táwros

tàuta, *tewtéh$_2$
tekstils, *tetḱ-
teritorija, *ters-
test, tèst, *tetḱ-
tìkls, tina, tît, *ten-
traba, *treb-
trīs, *tréyes
tu, *túh$_2$
ũdens, *wed-
ūdrs, *udréh$_2$
uguns, *h$_1$ng^{w}nis
un, *h$_2$ent-
uotars, ùotrs, *h$_2$énteros
vâjêt, *h$_1$weh$_2$-
vakars, *wek(^{w})speros
vàldît, *h$_2$welh$_1$-
vapsene, *wobs-
vārds, *wek^w-
vaȓza, *werǵ-
veîds, *weyd-
vẽjš, *H$_2$weH$_1$-
vēl, velt, *welH-
vespa, *wobs-
vest, *wed^h-, *weǵh-
vētra, *H$_2$weH$_1$-
vidus, *h$_1$weyd^h-
viedêt, *weyd-
viens, *óy-nos
viesis, *weyḱ-
vīkt, *weyk-
vilks, *wl̥k^{w}os
vilna, *h$_2$welh$_1$-
vīns, *wóyh$_1$nom
vīrs, *wiHrós
vista, *h$_2$éwis
vît, *weyh$_1$-
zarna, *ǵ^{h}ern-
zèlt, zelts, *ǵ^{h}elh$_3$-
zeme, *d^{h}éǵ^{h}ōm
ziema, *ǵ^{h}ey-
zinât, *ǵneh$_3$-
zirnis, *ǵr̥Hnom
zobs, *ǵómb^{h}os
zods, *ǵénus
zoss, *ǵ^{h}ans-
zvērs, *ǵ^{h}wer-

Albanian

afendoj, *g^{wh}en-
ah, *$h_3$es-
ahstë, *$h_3$ésth$_1$
ajër, *$h_2$ews-
âmë, amëz, *$h_3$ed-
anije, *(s)neh$_2$-
anoj, *$h_2$enk-
anza, *wobs-
argëtoj, *werǵ-
ari, *h_2r̥tḱos
arkë, *$h_2$erk-
armë, *$h_2$er
arnoj, *new
arushë, *h_2r̥tḱos
asht, *$h_3$ésth$_1$
atë, *ph$_2$tḗr
ath, *h_2éḱ
atribuoj, *b^huH-
bar, *b^hars-
bëhem, *b^huH-
bëj, *b^heh$_2$-, *b^huH-
bekoj, *deyḱ-
bie, blatë, *bher-
bletë, *b^hey-
breg, *b^herǵ^h-
buall, bujk, *g^wṓws
bundë, *H_2weH$_1$-
bung, *b^heh$_2$go-
burg, *b^herǵ^h-
buzë, *b^huHgos-
dëftoj, *(s)teg-, *deyḱ-
dekada, *déḱm̥t
dëm, *deh$_2$-
dem, *demh$_2$-
denjë, *deḱ-
derë, *d^hwer-
dërgoj, *$h_3$reǵ-
derr, *ǵʰḗr
det, *d^hewb-
dhallë, *glag-
dhashë, *deH$_3$-
dhè, *d^héǵ^{h}ōm
dhelpërë, *ǵ^{h}elh$_3$-
dhëmb, *ǵómb^{h}os
dhjetë, *déḱm̥t
dhomë, *dem-
dhuroj, *deH$_3$-
dimër, *ǵ^{h}ey-
ditë, *deh$_2$-
djall, *g^{w}elH-
djathë, *d^heh$_1$(y)-
djathtë, *deḱs-
dje, *d^hǵ^h(y)es-
djeg, *d^heg^{wh}-
djerr, *der-
djersë, *sweyd-
doktor, *deḱ-
drejtë, *$h_3$reǵ-
dru, *dóru
duroj, *deru-
dy, *dwóH$_1$
eh, *h_2éḱ
ëmë, *méh$_2$tēr
emër/êmën, *$h_1$nómn̥
ëndë, *$h_2$enh$_1$-
ende, *$h_2$ent
enjë, *$h_2$eyǵ-
enjte, *h_1n̥g^{w}nis
err, *$h_2$ews-
eshë, *$h_2$ey-
eshkë, *$h_1$ed-
ethe, *$h_1$ews-
famë, *b^heh$_2$-
familje, *dheH$_1$-
festë, *d^héh$_1$s
fqinj, *weyḱ-
fre, *d^her-
fund, *b^hud^{h}mḗn, *ǵ^{h}ew-
furrë, *g^{wh}er-
gak, *g^{w}ṓws
gardh, *ǵ^{h}er-
gatë, *ǵ^{h}ans-
gërvish, *gerb^h-
giuha, *dn̥ǵ^{h}wéh$_2$s
gjallë, *solh$_2$-
gjashtë, *swéḱs
gjë, *H_1es-
gjelbson, *séh$_2$ls
gjëroj, *$h_2$eyw-
gjinde, gjini, *ǵenH$_1$-
gju, *ǵónu
gjuaj, *g^{wh}en-
gjumë, *swep-
gjykatë, *$h_2$eyw-
grek, *ǵerh$_2$-
grurë, *ǵr̥Hnom
halë, *$h_3$el-
hark, *$h_2$erk^{w}o-
harr, *(s)ker-
herë, *yeh$_1$-
herë, *yeh$_1$-
histori, *weyd-
hyll, *$h_1$ews-
iki, *$h_1$ey-
iriq, *ǵ^{h}ḗr
ish, *h_1eǵ^{h}s
jam, *H_1es-
jetë, *$h_2$ey-
kalendar, *kelh$_1$-
kallam, *ḱalam-
kallënduar, kallnor, *kelh$_1$-

kampion, *(s)teg-
kap, *keh$_2$p-
kaproll, *kapro
karrarë, karro, *ḱers-
kartë, *ǵʰer-
katër, *kʷetwóres
kau, *gʷóws
këshill, *kelh$_1$-
këshyre, *(s)kel-
kofshë, *koḱs-
korrigjoj, *h$_3$reǵ-
krahinë, *krey-
krye, *ḱerh$_2$-
kue, *(s)ker-
kujtoj, *H$_2$eǵ-
kungë, *ḱonkho-
kuq, *pekʷ-
kurrilë, *gerh$_2$-
kuzhinë, *pekʷ-
lag, lagje, lagtë, *legh-
laj, *lewh$_3$-
lap, *leb-
lehtë, *h$_1$lengʷʰ-
lem, *h$_1$lewdʰ-
lëndinë, *lendʰ-
lëpij, *leb-
lexoj, *leǵ-
li, *lino-
ligj, *leǵ-, *legh-
lind, *h$_1$lewdʰ-
linjë, liri/lîni, *lino-
llërë, *Heh$_3$l-
luftë, luftëtar, luftoj, *seh$_2$g-
lundra, *udréh$_2$
lungë, *lengʷʰ-
lyp, *lewbʰ-
mallkoj, *deyḱ-
mas, *meh$_1$-
mbledh, *leǵ-
mërrajë, *ǵʰey-
mërshë, *mer-
mes, *médʰyos
mi, *muh$_2$s-
mijë, *sem-
mish, *mḗms
mizë, *mus-
mjaltë, *melit-
mjekë, *mendʰ-
mjel, *H$_2$melǵ-
mjesht, *méǵh$_2$s
mjeshtër, *méǵh$_2$s
monedhë, monstër, *men-
morr, *morwi-
mort, *mer-
moshtrë, *men-
motër, *méh$_2$tēr

mua, *H$_1$me-
muaj, muej, *méh$_1$ns
mund, *men-
mushk, muskul, muskulor, *muh$_2$s-
nalt, *h$_2$el-
natë, *nókʷts
ndëgjoj, *leǵ-
ndej, *ten-
ndër, *h$_1$én
ndez, *dʰegʷʰ-
ndihem, *teng-
ndrydh, *trewd-
ne, *wei
nëntë, *H$_1$néwn̥
ngjalë, *angʷ(h)i-
ngjelmët, *séh$_2$ls
ngroh, ngrohtë, *gʷʰer-
ngushtë, *h$_2$enǵʰ-
nip, *nepot-
një, *óy-nos
njëqind, *ḱm̥tóm
njeri, *h$_2$nḗr
njëzet, *wīḱm̥tiH$_1$
njoh, *ǵneh$_3$-
ntseapiri, ntsep, *keh$_2$p-
numër, numëroj, *nem-
nxeh, *gʷʰer-
nyell, *h$_3$negʰ-
orë, *yeh$_1$-
pagan, *peh$_2$ǵ-
paqe, *peh$_2$ǵ-
parabolë, *gʷelH-
pashë, *peh$_2$-
pëganë, pëgërë, *peh$_2$ǵ-
pendë, *spey-
përmjerr, *h$_3$meyǵʰ-, *móri
përrallë, *gʷelH-
pesë, *pénkʷe
peshk, *peisḱ-
peshoj, pezuli, *pewǵ-
pi, pije, *peh$_3$-
pilë, *peḱ-
pjek, *pekʷ-
plaf, *pleḱ-
plah, *pel-
plak, *pelH-
plas, *bʰleh$_1$-
plesht, *plou-
ploje, *pleh$_2$k-
plot, plotë, popull, *pleh$_1$-
portë, *per-
poshtë, *pṓds
pre, *weyd-
princ, *keh$_2$p-
provë, *bʰuH-
pukë, *pleh$_1$-
pulqer, *h$_2$welh$_1$-

pushtet, *pótis
qartë, *kelh₁-
qen, *ḱwṓ
qërtoj, *krey-
qilar, *ḱel-
qind, *ḱm̥tóm
quaj, *ḱlew-
qye, *ḱley-
qytet, *ḱei-
rrath, *Hret-
rrënjë, *wréh₂ds
rreth, *Hret-
rreze, *wréh₂ds
rrime, *wr̥mis-
rrotë, *Hret-
sakice, *h₂éḱ
sërë, *ser-
shakë, *ḱwṓ
shalë, *sed-
sharrë, shat, *sek-
shëlboj, *solh₂-
shëllij, *séh₂ls
shëmbëllej, *sem-
shemë, *H₂eǵ-
shenjë, shënoj, *sek-
shkarkoj, *ḱers-
shkencë, *skey-
shkollë, *seǵʰ-
shkruaj, shkurtoj, *(s)ker-
shoh, *sekʷ-
short, *ser-
shotë, *h₂éwis
shpëlaj, *lewh₃-
shpend, shpinë, *spey-
shpresë, *speh₁-
shqip, shqipoj, *keh₂p-
shtãj, shtat, *steh₂-
shtatë, *septm̥
shtãzë, *steh₂-
shteg, *steygʰ-
shtëzë, *steh₂-
shtyj, *(s)tew-
shufroj, *bher-
shumë, *upo
sistem, *steh₂-
sjell, *kʷel-
sorkadh, *ḱerh₂-
studioj, *(s)tew-
sy, *h₃ekʷ-
taroç, tauk, *(s)táwros
tend, *ten-
ter, *ters-
tëtanë, *tewtéh₂
tetë, *oḱtṓw
thërijë/thëni, *knid-
thi, *suH-
thjeshtër, *dʰeh₁(y)-

thua, *h₂éḱ
ti, *túh₂
tjegull, *(s)teg-
tradhëtar, tradhtar, traditë, *deH₃-
tre, *tréyes
tredh, *trewd-
tri, *tréyes
tund, *(s)tew-
ujë, *wed-
ujk, *wl̥kʷos
unë, *egH₂
urdhëroj, *h₂er-
uriq, *ǵʰḗr
uroj, *h₃éh₁os
urrej, urroj, *gʰers-
urtë, *wekʷ-
vajzë, *swésōr
val, *welH-
ve, *h₁weydʰ-, *h₂ōwyóm
vej, *webh-
vëlla, *bʰréh₂tēr
vëllim, *welH-
venë, *wóyh₁nom
venj, *webh-
verbër, *h₃erbʰ-
verë, *wésr̥, *wóyh₁nom
vërshoj, *wert-
vërtetë, *weh₁-
vërtyt, *wiHrós
vesh, *h₂ew-, *wes-
vështoj, *weyd-
vëzhgoj, *steygʰ-
vida, *h₂éwis
vidër, *wed-
vijë, *weyh₁-
virtyt, *wiHrós
vis, *weyḱ-
vit, *wet-
vito, *h₂éwis
vjet, *wet-
vlerë, *h₂welh₁-
vo, *h₂ōwyóm
zgjedh, *leǵ-
ziej, zien, zjarm, zjarr, *gʷʰer-
zot, *pótis

Sanskrit

अ- (a-), *n̥-
अक्तु (aktú), *nókʷts
अक्ष (akṣa), *H₂eǵ-
अक्षि (ákṣi), *h₃ekʷ-
अगन् (ágan), *gʷem-
अग्नि (agní), *h₁n̥gʷnis
अङ्क (aṅká), अङ्कस् (áṅkas), अङ्गुरि (aṅgúri), अचति (ácati), *h₂enk-
अच्छेदि (ácchedi), *skey-
अज (ajá), अजति (ájati), *H₂eǵ-
अज्ञात् (ajñāt), *ǵneh₃-
अज्मन् (ájman), *H₂eǵ-
अज्र (ájra), अज्र्य (ajryá), *h₂éǵros
अञ्चति (áñcati), *h₂enk-
अतन् (átan), *ten-
अतस् (átas), *éy / h₁e
अत्ति (átti), *h₁ed-
अत्र (átra), अथ (átʰa), अथा (átʰā), अद्धा (addʰā́), *éy / h₁e
अदात् (ádāt), *deH₃-
अध (ádʰa), अधा (ádʰā), *éy / h₁e
अधाक् (adhāk), *dʰegʷʰ-
अधात् (ádhāt), *dheH₁-
अधृत (adhṛta), *dʰer-
अन्- (an-), *n̥-
अन्तर (ántara), अन्तर् (antár), *h₁én
अन्त्य (antya), अन्ति (anti), *h₂ent
अन्नदान annadāna), *deH₃-
अनिति (ániti), अनिल (ánila), *h₂enh₁-
अनीक (ánīka), *h₁én, *h₃ekʷ-
अप (apa), *h₂pó
अपचिति (ápa-citi), *kʷey-
अपस् (ápas), अप् (áp), *h₃ep-
अप्रस् (ápnas), *h₃ep-
अपि (ápi), *h₁epi
अबुध्न (abudhná), *bʰudʰmḗn
अभ्र (abhrá), *nebʰ-
अभि (abhí), *h₂ent
अभूत् (abhūt), *bʰuH-
अमृत ámṛta, *mer-
अयम् (ayám), *éy / h₁e
अयस् (ayas), *h₂eyos
अयुग (ayuga), अयुजत् (ayujat), *yewg-
अरत्नि (aratní), *Heh₃l-
अरम् (áram), ईर्म (irma), *h₂er
अर्भ (arbha), *h₃erbʰ-
अरिचत् áricat), *leykʷ-
अव (ava), *h₂ew
अवतार (avatāra), *terh₂-
अवासिद् (avāsit), *h₁weh₂-
अवि (avi), *h₂éwis, *h₂ówis
अविदत् (ávidat), *weyd-
अवोचत् (avocat), *wekʷ-
अश्मन् (aśman), *h₂éḱ-mō

अश्रि (áśri), *h₂éḱ
अश्रोत् (áśrot), *klew-
अश्व (áśva), *h₁éḱwos
अष्ट (aṣṭa), *oktṓw
अष्ट्रा (aṣṭrā), *H₂eǵ-
असमाति (asamāti), *meh₁-
अस्ति (ásti), *H₁es-
अस्थात् (ásthāt), *steh₂-
अस्थि (ásthi), *h₃ésth₁
अस्पष्ट (áspaṣṭa), *spek-
असामि (ásāmi), *sem-
असृज् (asṛj), *h₁ésh₂r̥
अह (áha), *éy / h₁e
अहम् (ahám), *egH₂
अंहु (aṃhu), *h₂enǵʰ-
आति (ā́ti), *h₂eneti-
आदयति (ādáyati), *h₁ed-
आद् (ā́d), *éy / h₁e
आन्त्र (āntrá), *h₁én
आयु (āyu), *h₂ey-
आर्त (ārta), *h₃er-
आर्यन्ति (āryanti), *h₃éh₁os
आविस् (āvís), *h₂ew-
आस (āsa-), *h₂eh₁s-
आस् (ās), *h₃éh₁os
इतर (ítara), इतस् (itás), इत्थम् (ittʰám), इत्था (ittʰā́), इति (íti), *éy / h₁e
इद्ध (iddhá), *h₂eydʰ-
इदा (idā́), *éy / h₁e
इन्द्धे (inddhé), *h₂eydʰ-
इयर्ति (íyarti), *h₃er-
इव (iva), इह (ihá), ईम् (īm), *éy / h₁e
ईशे (īśe), ईष्टे (īṣṭe), *h₂eyk-
उक्त (ukta), *wekʷ-
उक्षति (ukṣati), *h₂ewg-
उक्षन् (ukṣán), *uksḗn
उग्र (ugrá), *h₂ewg-
उदन् (udan), *wed-
उद्र (udrá), *udréh₂
उनब्धि (unábdhi), *webh-
उप (úpa), उप- (upa-), उपम (upama), उपरि (upari), *upo
उभ्नाति (ubhnāti), उम्भति umbháti), *webh-
उल्ब (ulba), *welH-
उषर् (uṣar), उषस् (uṣás), *h₂ews-
उष्ट (uṣṭa), उष्ण (uṣṇá), *h₁ews-
उस्र (usrá), उस्रस् (usrás), उस्रि (usrí), *h₂ews-
उसि (usi), *h₂ew-
ऊढि (ūḍhi), *weǵh-
ऊधर् ūdhar, *h₁owHdʰr̥-
ऊन (ūná), *h₁weh₂-
ऊर्ण (ūrṇā), *h₂welh₁-
ऊर्ध्व (ūrdhvá), *h₂erHdʰ-
ऋक्ष (r̥kṣá), *h₂ŕ̥tkos
ऋजु (r̥jú), ऋञ्जते r̥ñjate), *h₃reǵ-
ऋणोति (r̥ṇoti), *h₃er-
ऋत (r̥tá), ऋतु (r̥tú), *h₂er

एक (éka), *óy-nos

एकतर (ekatara), *sem-

एति (eti), *h₁ey-

एध्र (édha), एध्रते (édhate), एध्रस् (édhas), *h₂eydʰ-

एन (ena), एव (evá), *óy-nos

ओजस् (ójas), *h₂ewg-

ओषति (óṣati), *h₁ews-

ओष्ठ óṣṭha), *h₃éh₁os

क (kaḥ), *kʷis

कङ्काल (kaṅkāla), *kenk-

कणति (kaṇati), *keh₂n-

कतर (katará), *kʷis

कपाल (kapāla), कपुच्छल (kapúcchala), *kapōlo

कपृथ् (kaprtha), *kapro

कलम (kalama), *kalam-

क्ति (nákti), *nókʷts

क्मरति (kmárati), *(s)teg-

क्रव्य (kravyá), *krewh₂-

क्रीणाति (krīṇāti), *kʷreyh₂-

क्लोमन् (klóman), *plewmō

क्ष (kṣa), क्षम् (kṣám), *dʰéǵʰōm

क्षायति (kṣāyati), क्षिणाति (kṣiṇāti), क्षिणोति (kṣiṇóti), *dʰegʷʰ-

क्षित (kṣitá), *dʰegʷʰ-, *tek-

क्षिति (kṣíti), *dʰegʷʰ-, *tek-

क्षिधी (kṣidhī), *dʰegʷʰ-

क्षियन्ति (kṣiyánti), *tek-

क्षीयते (kṣīyáte), *dʰegʷʰ-

क्षेति (kṣeti), *kei-, *tek-

क्षेषत् (kṣeṣat), *tek-

कि (kiḥ), किम् (kim), *kʷis

कृप् (kŕp), *krep-

कृपाण (kṛpāṇa), कृपाणी (kṛpāṇī), *kerp-

गच्छति (gácchati), गत (gatá), गति (gáti), गन्तु (gántu), *gʷem-

गभस्ति (gábhasti), *gʰeh₁bʰ-

गमती (gámati), गम् (gam), *gʷem-

ग्रा (gnā), *gwén

ग्रावन् (grāvan), *gʷrh₂-n-uH-

गाव (gāva), *gʷṓws

गुरु (gurú), गुरुकुल (gurukula), गुरुत्व (gurutva), *gʷerh₂-

गूर्त (gūrtá), गूर्ति (gūrti), गृणाति (gṛṇāti), *gʷerH-

गृह (gṛhá), *ǵʰer-

गो (go), *gʷṓws

गोदान (godāna), *deH₃-

घन (ghaná), *gʷʰen-

घरयति (gharáyati), घर्म (gharmá), घृण (ghṛṇá), घृणोति (ghṛṇoti), *gʷʰer-

चक्र (cakrá), *kʷel-

चतुर् (catur), चतुर्- (catur-), *kʷetwóres

चयते (cayate), *kʷey-

चरति (carati), *kʷel-

चर्मन् (cárman), *(s)ker-

छाया (chāyā), छित्ति (chitti), छिनत्ति (chinátti), छेदि (chedi), *skey-

जगाम (jagāma), *gʷem-

जघ्नुः (jaghnúḥ), जघान (jaghāna), *gʷʰen-

जतु (jatu), *gʷet-

जन (jána), जनति (jánati), जनस् (jánas), *ǵenH₁-

जनि (jani), *gwén

जनितृ (janitṛ), जनिमन् (jániman), *ǵenH₁-

जम्भ (jambha), *ǵómbʰos

जरत् (járat), जरति (járati), *ǵerh₂-

जरते (járate), *gʷerH-

ज्ञात (jñātá), *ǵneh₃-

जात (jātá), जाति (jāti), *ǵenH₁-

जानाति (jānāti), *ǵneh₃-

जानु (jānu), *ǵónu

जायते (jāyate), *ǵenH₁-

जाह्रषाण (jāhṛṣāṇá), *gʰers-

जिघर्ति (jighárti), *gʷʰer-

जिह्वा (jihvā), *dṇǵʷʰwéh₂s

जीव (jīva), जीवति (jīvati), *gʷeyh₃-

जुजोष (jujóṣa), जुषते juṣáte), जुष्ट (juṣṭá), जुष्टि (júṣṭi), जुहाव (juhāva), *ǵʰew-

जुहू (juhū), *dṇǵʷʰwéh₂s

जुहोति (juhóti), *ǵʰew-

जोष (jóṣa), जोषति (jóṣati), जोषयासे (joṣáyāse), *ǵews-

तक्षति (tákṣati), तक्षन् (tákṣan), तक्षयति (takṣayati), *tetḱ-

तत (tatá), तति (táti), *ten-

तद् (tád), *só

तनस् (tánas), तन्त्र (tántra), तन्ति tantí), तन्तु (tántu), *ten-

तन्यति (tanyati), *(s)tenh₂-

तनोति (tanóti), *ten-

तरति (tarati), *terh₂-

तर्मन् (tarman), *térmṇ

तष्ट (taṣṭá), *tetḱ-

तस्थौ (tasthau), *steh₂-

त्रय (trayaḥ), त्रि (trí), त्रि- (tri-), *tréyes

त्रिपाद (tripāda), *pṓds

त्रीणि (trīṇi), *tréyes

त्वम् (tvám), *túh₂

तान (tāna), *ten-

तार (tāra), तारयति (tārayati), *terh₂-

तारा (tāra), *h₂stér

तस्थिवस् (tasthivas), *tek-

ताष्टि (tấṣṭi), *tetḱ-

तिर (tiraḥ), तिरस् (tiras), तिर्यञ्च् (tiryañc), *terh₂-

तिष्ठति (tiṣṭhati), *steh₂-

तिस्र (tisraḥ), *tréyes

तुजन्ति (tujánti), तुजयत् (tujáyat), तुञ्जते (tuñjáte), तुञ्जन्ति (tuñjánti), तुतोद (tutóda), तुदति (tudáti), *(s)tew-

तुलयति (tulayati), तुला (tulā), *telh₂-

तृष्ट (tṛṣṭá), तृष्णा (tṛṣṇā), तृष्यति (tṛ́ṣyati), *ters-

तोपति (topati), *(s)tew-

दक्षिण (dákṣiṇa), *deks-

दग्ध (dagdhá), *dʰegʷʰ-

दत् (dát), *h₃dónts

ददाति (dádāti), *deH₃-

ददाश (dadāśa), *dek-

दधर्ष (dadhárṣa), *dʰers-

दधाति (dádhāti), *dheH₁-

दधार (dadhāra), *dʰer-

दन् (dán), दन्त (dánta), *h₃dónts

दम (dáma), दम् (dám), *dem-

दम्पति (dám-pati), *pótis

दम्य (damya), दमायति (damāyáti), *demh₂-

द्यौ (dyáuḥ), *dyew-

दर्वि (dárvi), *dóru

दश (daśa), *dékm̥t

दशस्यति (daśasyáti), *dek-

दहति (dahati), *dʰegʷʰ-

द्यु (dyu), द्यु (dyú), द्यो (dyo), द्यौष्पितृ (dyauṣ-pitṛ), *dyew-

द्रु (drú), द्रोण (dróṇa), *dóru

द्व (dvá), *dwóH₁

द्वार (dvāraḥ), द्वार् (dvār), द्वारा (dvārā), *dʰwer-

द्वि (dvi-), द्विस् (dvis), *dwóH₁

दातृ (dātṛ), दान (dāna), *deH₃-

दाम्यति (dāmyati), *demh₂-

दारु (dāru), *dóru

दाश् (dāś), दाशति (dāśti), दाश्नोति (dāśnóti), दाष्टि (dāṣṭi), *dek-

दाहयति (dāhayati), *dʰegʷʰ-

दिग्ध (digdhá), *dʰeygʰ-

दिति (diti), *deH₃-

दिधृतम् (didhṛtam), *dʰer-

दिन (dina), *deyn-

दिव (divá), दिव्य (divyá), *dyew-

दिशति (diśáti), दिश् (diś), दिष्ट (diṣṭá), *deyḱ-

दीक्षते (dīkṣate), *dek-

दीति (dīti), *deh₂-

दीर्यते (dīryáte), *der-

दुर (dúraḥ), *dʰwer-

दुर्मनास् (durmanās), *men-

दुहितृ (duhitṛ), *dʰugh₂tér

दृणाति (dṛṇāti), दृति (dṛti), *der-

देग्धि (degdhi), *dʰeygʰ-

देव (devá), *dyew-

देह (deha), देही (dehī), *dʰeygʰ-

धयति (dhayati), *dʰeh₁(y)-

धरति (dhárati), धर्म (dhárma), धर्मन् (dhárman), *dʰer-

धामन् (dhāman), *dheH₁-

धारयति (dhāráyati), धारयते (dhárate), धारयते (dhāráyate), *dʰer-

धित (dhitá), *deH₃-, *dheH₁-

धीति (dhīti), *dheH₁-

धूम (dhūmá), धूलि (dhūli), धूसर (dhūsara), *dʰewh₂-

धृ (dhṛ), धृथास् (dhṛthās), *dʰer-

धृष्ट (dhṛṣṭá), धृष्णोति (dhṛṣṇoti), धृषु (dhṛṣu), *dʰers-

नक् (nák), नक्त (nákta), नक्तम् (náktam), *nókʷts

नख (nakhá), *h₃negʰ-

नग्न (nagná), *negʷ-

ननाश (nanāśa), *neḱ-

नप्तृ (náptṛ), नपात् (nápāt), *nepot-

नभस् (nábhas), *nebʰ-

नभ्य (nábhya), *h₃enbʰ-

नमस् (námas), नमस्ते (namaste), *nem-

नर (nára), *h₂nér

नव (náva), *new

नवन् (návan), *H₁néwn̥

नशन्ति (naśanti), नश् (naś), नश्यति (náśyati), *neḱ-

नाभि (nābhi), *h₃enbʰ-

नाम (nāma), नामन् (nāman), *h₁nómn̥

नाव (nāva), नाव्य (nāvyá), *(s)neh₂-

नाशयति (nāśáyati), *neḱ-

नासा (nāsā), *néh₂s

नि (ni), *h₁én

नितुन्दते (nitundate), *(s)tew-

निर्वाण (nirvāṇa), *H₂weH₁-

नीड (nīḍá), *nisdós

नृ (nṛ), *h₂nér

नौ (nau), *(s)neh₂-

पङ्क्ति (paktí), पक्तृ (paktṛ), *pekʷ-

पक्ष्मन् (pakṣman), *pek-

पचति (pacati), पच् (pac), पच्यते (pácyate), *pekʷ-

पञ्चन् (páñcan), *pénkʷe

पतति (pátati), *peth₂

पत्र (pátra), *péth₂r

पति (páti), *pótis

पथिन् (páthin), *pent-

पद (pada), *ped-

पद् (pád), *pṓds

पद्यते (pádyate), *ped-

पन्था (panthāḥ), *pent-

पपाद (papāda), *ped-

पर्षति (parṣati), *pers-

परि (pári), *per-

परिक्षित (parikṣita), *tek-

पलित (palitá), *pelH-

पश्यति (páśyati), *speḱ-

पशु (páśu), *peḱu-

प्रति (práti), *per-

प्रथते (práthate), प्रथयति (pratháyati), *pleth₂-

प्रथस् (práthas), *pleh₁-, *pleth₂-

प्रथान (prathāná), प्रथिमन् (prathimán), *pleth₂-

प्रश्न (praśna), *pleḱ-

प्रात् (prāt), *pleh₁-

प्राश् (prāś), *preḱ-

प्रियायते priyāyate), *preyH-

प्लव (plavá), प्लवते (plávate), प्लावयति (plāvayati), *plew-

प्लिहन् (plihan), *splengʰ-

प्लु (plu), प्लुत (pluta), *plew-

प्लुषि (pluṣi), *plou-

पात्र (pātra), *peh₃-

पाति (pāti), *peh₂-

पादयति (pādáyati), *ped-

पायु (pāyú), *peh₂-

पार (pāra), पारयति (pāráyati), *per-

पिता (pitā), पितृ (pitṛ), *ph₂tér

पिनष्टि (pinaṣṭi), *peys-

पिनष्ति (pinaṣti), *peyḱ-

पिपर्ति (píparti), *per-, *pleh₁-

पिबति (píbati), *peh₃-

पिब्दमान (píbdamāna), *ped-

पिशङ्ग (piśáṅga, *peyḱ-

पिष्ट (piṣṭá), *peys-, *peyḱ-

पुरस् (puras), *per-

पुरु (puru), पूर्ण (pūrṇá), पूर्णिमा (pūrṇimā), *pleh₁-

पूषन् (Pūṣan), *peh₂-

पृच्छति (pr̥cchÁti), *prek-

पृणाति (pr̥ṇÁti), *pleh₁-

पृथ (pr̥thÁ), पृथिवी (pr̥thivī), *pleth₂-

पृथु (pr̥thú), *pleh₂-, *pleth₂-

पृषत् (pŕ̥ṣat), *pers-

पेश (péśa), *peyk-, *peys-

फुलम् (phulam), *bʰleh₃-

फेन (phéna), *poymno-

बबृहाण (babr̥hāṇá), बर्हयति (barhÁyati), ब्रह्मन्
  (bráhman), *bʰerǵʰ-

बुख (bukha), *bʰuHgos-

बुद्ध (buddha), बुद्धि (buddhi), *bʰewdʰ-

बुध्न (budhná), *bʰudʰmén

बुध्यते (budhyátē), *bʰewdʰ-

बृहत् (br̥hát), बृंहति (br̥mhati), *bʰerǵʰ-

बोध (bodhá), बोधति (bódhati), बोधयति (bodháyati),
  *bʰewdʰ-

भनति (bhánati), *bʰeh₂-

भरति (bhárati), भर्मन् (bhárman), भरीमन् (bhárīman),
  *bher-

भवति (bhavati), *bʰuH-

भ्राता (bhrātā), भ्रातृ (bhrātr̥), *bʰréh₂tēr

भ्रू (bhrū), *h₃bʰrúHs

भाति (bhāti), भान (bhāna), भाम (bhāma), *bʰeh₂-

भारयति (bhāráyati), *bher-

भावयति (bhāvayati), *bʰuH-

भाषा (bhāṣā), भास् (bhās), भास्कर (bhāskara), *bʰeh₂-

भिद् (bhid), भिनत्ति (bhinatti), भिन्न (bhinná), *bʰeyd-

भुर्वन् (bhúrvan), *bʰrewh₁-

भूति (bhúti), भूमन् (bhūman), *bʰuH-

भूर्ज (bhūrja), *bʰereǵ-

भृति (bhr̥tí), *bher-

भेत् (bhét), भेदति (bhédati), *bʰeyd-

मज्जन् (majján), *mosgʰos

मति (matí), *men-

मध्य (mádhya), *médʰyos

मधु (mádhu), *médʰu

मनस् (mánas), मन्त्र (mántra), मन्मन् (mánman), मन्यते
  (mányate), *men-

मनाक् (manāk), *mey-

मनु (manu), मनुष्य (manuṣya), *mánus

मम (mama), *H₁meme-

मरति (marati), मरते (márate), *mer-

मर्जति (marjati), *H₂melǵ-

मर्त (márta), *mer-

मर्यादा (maryādā), *móri

महत् (mahat), महा (mahā), महात्मन् (mahātman),
  महाभारत (mahābhārata), महि (mahi), *méǵh₂s

म्रियते (mriyáte), *mer-

मा (mā), *H₁me-

मातृ (mātr̥), *méh₂tēr

मानव (mānava), *mánus

मार (māra), मारयति (māráyati), *mer-

मास (māsa), मास् (mās), *méh₁ns

मांस (māṃsa), मांसम् (māṃsam), मांस् (māṃs), *méms

मिच्छमान (micchamāna), मिनाति (minÁti), मिनोति (minóti),
  *mey-

मिमीते (mímīte), *meh₁-

मिश्र (miśrá), मिश्रयति (miśráyati), *mey-

मुहु (múhu), मुहुर् (múhur), *mréǵʰ-

मूष (mūṣa), मूष् (mūṣ), *muh₂s-

मृणाति (mr̥ṇÁti), *melh₂-

मृत (mr̥tá), मृति mr̥ti, *mer-

मेक्षयति (mekṣáyati), मेथति (méthati), *mey-

मेह (meha), मेहति (méhati), *h₃meyǵʰ-

यकृत् (yákr̥t), *Hyékʷr̥

यद् (yád), *éy / h₁e

यसति (yásati), *yes-

यस् (yás), या (yā), *éy / h₁e

यान (yāna), *h₁ey-

यासयति (yāsayati), *yes-

युक्त (yuktá), *yewg-

युग (yugá), *yugóm

युनक्ति (yunákti), *yewg-

युवता (yuvatā), युवन् (yúvan), युवश (yuvaśá), *h₂yuh₁en-

युवाम् (yuvām), *túh₂

यूका (yūkā), *luHs-

यूयम् (yūyám), *túh₂

योगस् (yogas), योग्य (yógya), योजम् (yójam), *yewg-

योस् (yós), *h₂eyw-

रघु (raghú), *h₁lengʷʰ-

रथ (ratha), *Hret-

रन्ध्र (rándhra), *lendʰ-

रय (raya), *h₃reyH-

रंहति (rámhati), रंहते (rámhate), *h₁lengʷʰ-

राजन् (rājan), राजयति (rājayati), राजयते (rājayate), राज्
  (rāj), राज्ञी (rājñī), *h₃reǵ-

राध्नोति (rādhnoti), राधयति (rādhyati), *h₂er

राध्यति (rādhyati), *Hrehₐdʰ-

रिणक्ति (riṇákti), *leykʷ-

रिणाति (riṇÁti), *h₃reyH-

रिरेच (riréca), *leykʷ-

रीयते (rīyate), *h₃reyH-

रुधिर (rudhirá), *h₁rewdʰ-

रेचयति (recayati), *leykʷ-

रोक (roká), रोचते (rocate), *lewk-

रोधति (ródhati), रोहित (róhita), *h₁rewdʰ-

लघिष्ठ (laghiṣṭha), लघीयस् lághīyas, लघु (laghu),
  *h₁lengʷʰ-

लिम्पति (limpati), *leyp-

लेढ्यति (leṭyati), *legh-

लेप (lepa), लेपयति (lepayati), *leyp-

लोक (loká), *lewk-

लोह (lohá), *h₁rewdʰ-

वक्त्र (vaktra), वक्ति (vakti), वचस् (vácas), वच् (vac),
  *wekʷ-

वत्स (vatsá), *wet-

वम्र (vamra), *morwi-

वयम् (vayam), *wei

वर्ज (varja), *werǵ-

वर्तयति (vartáyati), वर्ति (vártti), वर्त्मन् (vártman), ववर्त (vavárta), *wert-

वसन्त (vasanta), वसर् (vasar), *wésr̥

वस्त्र (vastra), वस्ते (váste), *wes-

वस्न (vasna), वस्नयति (vasnayati), *wesno-

वस्मन् (vásman), *wes-

वहति (váhati), वह् (vah), वहित्र (vahitra), *weǵh-

व्रत (vrata), *wekʷ-

वा (vā), *H₂weH₁-

वाज (vāja), वाजयति (vājáyati), *weǵ-

वात (vāta), वाति (vāti), *H₂weH₁-

वायति (vāyati), *h₁weh₂-

वासयति (vāsáyati), वासयते (vāsáyate), *wes-

वाहन (vāhana), *weǵh-

वि (ví), *h₂éwis

वितर्षयति (vitarṣáyati), *ters-

विधवा (vidhávā), *h₁weydʰ

विन्दति (vindáti), *weyd-

विवक्ति (vívakti), *wekʷ-

विविक्त (viviktá), *weyk-

विश् (víś), *weyḱ-

विश्पति (víśpáti), *pótis

विंशति (viṃśati), *wī́ḱm̥tiH₁

वीर (vīrá), *wiHrós

वृक (vrka), *wĺ̥kʷos

वृज् (vrj), वृज्यते (vrjyáte), *werǵ-

वृणीते (vrṇīté), वृणोति (vrṇoti), *welh₁-

वेत्ति (vetti), वेत्तृ (vettr̥), *weyd-

वेति (véti), *weyh₁-

वेदयति (vedayati), वेदस् (védas), वेदितृ (véditr̥), *weyd-

वेश (veśa), *weyḱ-

शङ्ख (śaṅkhá), *ḱonkho-

शत (śatá), शतम् (śatam), *ḱm̥tóm

शतहिम (śatahima), *ǵʰey-

शये (śáye), *ḱei-

शरण (śaraṇa), *ḱel-

शरद (śarada), *gel-

श्रयति (śrayati), *ḱley-

श्रवस् (śrávas), श्रावयति (śrāváyati), *ḱlew-

श्रित (śrita), *ḱley-

श्रु (śru), श्रुत (śrutá), श्रुति (śruti), श्रोत्र (śrótra), श्रोमत (śrómata-), *ḱlew-

श्वन् (śvā), *ḱwṓ

शिर (śira), शिरस् (śíras), *ḱerh₂-

शिव (śivá), *ḱei-

शिश्राय (śiśrāya), *ḱley-

शीर्षन् (śī́rṣán), *ḱerh₂-

शुनस् (śvan), *ḱwṓ

शुश्राव (śuśrāva), *ḱlew-

शृङ्ग (śrnga), शृङ्गार (śrngāra), *ḱerh₂-

शृणोति (śrṇóti), *ḱlew-

शेते (śéte), शेव (śéva), *ḱei-

षट् (ṣaṭ), षष् (ṣáṣ), षष्टिस् (ṣaṣṭis), *swéḱs

स (sá), *só

सक्त (saktá), *sekʷ-

सकृत् (sakrt), *sem-

सचते (sácate), सचान (sacāná), सचीमहि (sacīmahi), *sekʷ-

सत् (sat), सती (satī́), *H₁es-

सदस् (sádas), सद् (sad), *sed-

सन (sána), *sénos

सप्तन् (saptán), *septm̥

सम (sama), सम् (sam), *sem-

समा (sámā), *sm̥-h₂-ó-

सरत् (sarat), *ser-

सर्व (sárva), सर्वताति (sarvátāti), *solh₂-

सलिल (salila), *séh₂ls

सहते (sáhate), सहस् (sáhas), *seǵʰ-

सहस्र (sahásra), *sem-

स्तिघ्नोति (stighnoti), *steygʰ-

स्तृ (str̥), *h₂stḗr

स्तृणोति (strṇoti), स्तृत (strtá), स्तृनाति (strṇāti), *sterh₃-

स्थगति (sthagati), स्थगयति (sthagayati), *(s)teg-

स्थान (sthāna), स्थामन् (sthāman), स्थित (sthitá), स्थिति (sthíti), स्थिर (sthira), स्थूर (sthūrá), *steh₂-

स्ना (snā), स्नात (snātá), स्नाति (snāti), स्नापयति (snāpáyati), *(s)neh₂-

स्नावन् (snāvan), *(s)neh₁-

स्निह्यति (snihyati), *sneygʷʰ-

स्नुषा (snuṣā), *snusós

स्नेह (snéha), *sneygʷʰ-

स्पशति (spaśati), स्पश् (spáś), स्पष्ट (spaṣṭá), स्पाशयति (spāśayati), *speḱ-

स्फ्य (sphyá), *spey-

स्फायते (sphāyate), स्फिर (sphirá), *speh₁-

स्यूमन् (syūman), *sīw-

स्रवति (srávati), स्रोतस् (srotas-), *srew-

स्व (svá), स्वतन्त्र (svatantra), *s(w)e-

स्वधा (svadhā), *swe-dʰh₁-

स्वपस् (svápas), *h₃ep-

स्वप्न (svápna), स्वपिति (svapiti), *swep-

स्वर् (svar), *sóh₂wl̥

स्वराज (svarāja), *s(w)e-

स्ववृष्टि (svávrṣṭi), *werǵ-

स्वसृ (svasr̥), *swésōr

स्विद्यति (svidyati), स्वेद (svéda), स्वेदते (svedate), स्वेदयति (svedáyati), *sweyd-

सा (sā), *só

साढ़ (sāḍhr̥), *seǵʰ-

सादयति (sādáyati), *sed-

साह्यति (sāhayati), *seǵʰ-

सिरा (sirā), *ser-

सीदति (sīdati), *sed-

सीव्यति (sīvyati), *sīw-

सुतर्मन् (sutárman), *térmn̥

सुमनस् (sumánas), *men-

सूकर (sūkara), *suH-

सूक्त (sūktá), *wekʷ-

सूत्र (ūtra), *sīw-

सूनु (sūnú), *suh₁nús

सूर (sūra), सूर् (sūr), सूर्य (sūrya), *sóh₂wl̥

हति (hatí), हन्ति (hanti), *gʷʰen-

हनु (hánu), *ǵénus
हरस् (háras), *gʷʰer-
हर्षते (hárṣate), हर्षयति (harṣáyati), *gʰers-
हरि (hari), *ǵʰelh₃-
हंस (haṃsa), *ǵʰans-
ह्यस् (hyas), *dʰǵʰ(y)es-
हिम (himá), *ǵʰey-
हिर (híra), *ǵʰern-
हिरण्य (hiraṇya), हिरि- (hiri-), *ǵʰelh₃-
हुत (hutá, *ǵʰew-
हृदय (hṛdaya), हृद् (hṛd), *ḱḗr
ह्यात् (hṛyāt), हृत (hṛta), *ǵʰer-
हृष् (hṛṣ), हृष्यति (hṛṣyáti), *gʰers-
होत्र (hotrá), होतृ (hótṛ), होम (hóma), *ǵʰew-

Hindi

अ- (a-), अन- (an-), *n̥-
अलमारी (almārī), *h₂er
अवतार (avtār), *terh₂-
अश्व (aśv), h₁éḱwos
अस्थि (ásthi), *h₃ésth₁
आग (āg), *h₁n̥gʷnis
आठ (āṭh), *oḱtṓw
आभ (ābh), *nebʰ-
आवाज़ (āvāz), *wekʷ-
आँख (ākh), *h₃ekʷ-
इतर (itar), *éy / h₁e
उग्र (ugra), *h₂ewg-
उप- (up-), *upo
उषा (uṣā), *h₂ews-
ऊद (ūd), *udréh₂
ऊन (ūn), *h₂welh₁-
ऋतु (ŕtu), *h₂er
एक (ek), *óy-nos
कपार (kapār), *kapōlo
कपाल (kapāl), *kapōlo
कमरबन्द (kamarband), *(s)teg-
किस (kis), *kʷis
खुद (xud), *s(w)e-
गत (gat), गति (gati), *gʷem-
गाय (gāy), *gʷṓws
गुरुकुल (gurukul), गुरुत्व (gurutva), गुरू (gurū), *gʷerh₂-
घर्म (gharma), *gʷʰer-
चक्र (cakra), *kʷel-
चाबी (cābī), *(s)kel-
चार (car), *kʷetwóres
छह (chah), *swéḱs
जवान (javān), *h₂yuh₁en-
ज़बान (zabān), *dn̥ǵʰwéh₂s
ज़ोर (zor), *ǵʰew-
ज्ञात (gyāt), जानना (jānnā), *ǵneh₃-
जीना (jīnā), *gʷeyh₃-
जीभ (jībh), *dn̥ǵʰwéh₂s
जूआ (jūā), *yugóm
ठग्गी (ṭhaggī), *(s)teg-
तारा (tārā), *h₂stḗr
तिपाई (tipāī), *pṓds
तीन (tīn), *tréyes
तुम (tum), तू (tū), *túh₂
दक्षिण (dakṣiṇ), *deḱs-
दरख़्त (daraxt), *dóru
दस (das), *déḱm̥t
द्वार (dvār), द्वारा (dvārā), *dʰwer-
दाता (dātā), *deH₃-
दाँत (dāt), दांत (dānt), *h₃dónts
दिन (din), *deyn-
दिल (dil), *ḱḗr
दिशा (diśā), *deyḱ-
दुश्मन (duśman), *men-

देना (denā), *deH₃-

देव (dev), *dyew-

देश (deś), *deyk-

देह (deh), *dʰeyǵʰ-

दो (do), *dwóH₁

धरना (dharnā), धर्म (dharma), *dʰer-

धिया (dhiyā), *dʰugʰ₂tḗr

धूआँ (dhūāṁ), धूम (dhūm), धूर (dhūr), धूल (dhūl), *dʰewh₂-

नख (nakh), *h₃negʰ-

नमस्ते (namaste), नमाज़ (namāz), *nem-

नया (nayā), *new

नर (nar), *h₂nḗr

नंगा (naṅgā), *negʷ-

नाख़ुन (nāxun), *h₃negʰ-

नाभिक (nābhik), नाभिकीय (nābhikīya), *h₃enbʰ-

नाम (nām), *h₁nómn̥

निर्वाण (nirvāṇ), *H₂weH₁-

नौ (nau), *H₁néwn̥

पकाना (pakānā), *pekʷ-

पत्र (patra), *péth₂r

पति (pati), *pótis

परवलय (paravlay), *gʷelH-

पशु (paśu), *peḱu-

प्रिय (priya), *preyH-

पार (pār), *per-

पाव (pāv), *peh₂-

पाँच (pāṁc), *pénkʷe

पांव (pāv), *póds

पिता (pitā), पितृ (pitṛ), *ph₂tḗr

पीना (pīnā), *peh₃-

पूछना (pūchnā), *preḱ-

पूर्ण (pūrṇ), पूरा (pūrā), पूरा (pūrā), *pleh₁-

पृथु (pṛthu), *pleth₂-

पैजामा (paijāmā), *póds

बाट (bāṭ), *wert-

बीस (bīs), *wĩḱm̥tiH₁

भ्रातृ (bhrātṛ), *bʰréh₂tēr

भाषा (bhāṣā), *bʰeh₂-

भौंह (bhaunh), *h₃bʰrúHs

मध्य (madhya), *médʰyos

मधु (madhu), *médʰu

मनुष्य (manuṣya), *mánus

मरना (marnā), *mer-

महा (mahā), *méǵh₂s

मंत्र (mantra), *men-

माता (mātā), मातृ (mātṛ), मातृभाषा (mātṛbhāṣā), *méh₂tēr

मानव (mānav), मानस (mānas), *mánus

मास (mās), माह (māh), *méh₁n̥s

मां (mā), *méh₂tēr

मांस (māns), *mḗms

मिश्र (miśra), मिश्रण (miśraṇ), *mey-

मूस (mūs), *muh₂s-

मृत (mṛt), *mer-

मेरा (merā), *H₁meme-

यान (yān), *h₁ey-

युक्त (yukt), *yewg-

युग (yug), *yugóm

युवा (yuvā), *h₂yuh₁en-

योग्य (yogya), *yewg-

रंध्र (randhra), *lendʰ-

राजा (rājā), रानी (rānī), *h₃reǵ-

रितु (ritu), *h₂er-

रीछ (rīch), *h₂ŕ̥tkos

लेटना (leṭnā), *legh-

वस्त्र (vastra), *wes-

व्रत (vrat), *wekʷ-

वायु (vāyu), *H₂weH₁-

विद्वा (vidvā), विधवा (vidhvā), *h₁weydʰ

वृक (vṛk), *wĺ̥kʷos

शरण (śaraṇ), *ḱel-

शरद (śarad), *gel-

श्वान (śvān), *ḱwṓ

षुप्ति (ṣupti), *swep-

सब (sab), *solh₂-

सम (sam), *sem-

सलवार (salvār), *(s)kel-

स्कूल (skūl), *seǵʰ-

स्थित (sthit), स्थिति (sthiti), स्थिर (sthir), *steh₂-

स्वप्न (svapn), *swep-

स्वयं (svayan), *s(w)e-

सात (sāt), *septm̥

सिपास (sipās), *speḱ-

सीना (sīnā), *sīw-

सूअर (sūar), *suH-

सूरज (sūraj), *sóh₂wl̥

सौ (sau), *ḱm̥tóm

हम (ham), हमाहमी (hamāhamī), *wei

हयना (hayanā), *gʷʰen-

हर (har), *solh₂-

हंस (hans), *ǵʰans-

हिम (him), *ǵʰey-

हिया (hiyā), हृदय (hṛday), *ḱḗr

है (hai), *bʰuH-

हॉठ (hōṭh), *h₃éh₁os

Pashto

(khwala), *sweyd-
(maazghë), *mosgʰos
(mëch), *mus-
(nattëka), *neHtr-
(taṇā/tandar), *(s)tenh₂-
(tsaarwai), *ǵʰwer-
(warrëi), *h₂welh₁-
(wulëi), *wréh₂ds
(yəž), *h₂ŕtkos
(zaaṇëi), *gerh₂-
(zižgai), *angʷ(h)i-
آس (ās), *h₁ékwos
اته (atə), *oktṓw
اووه (uwə), *septṃ
باد (bâd), *H₂weH₁-
پښه (pẍa), *póds
پلار (plār), *phₐtḗr
پنځه (pinźë), *pénkʷe
پونده (pūnda'h), *pent-
تة (tə), *túh₂
جغ (jugh), *yugóm
جگر (dzigar), *Hyékʷṛ
جنی (jinëy) / نجلی (njëlëy), *gwén
خور (xowr), *swésōr
ځمکه (źmëka), *dʰéǵʰōm
خوان (źwân), *h₂yuh₁en-
څلور (calor), *kʷetwóres
دری (dre), *tréyes
دوه (dwa), *dwóH₁
دېو (dëw), *dyew-
زر (zër), *sem-
زړه (zrrə), *ḱḗr
زنگون (zengewn), *ǵónu
زنی ~ زری (zaṇai ~ zaṛai), *ǵŗHnom
زوی (zoy), *suh₁nús
زیږ (ziǵ), *gʰers-
ژاوله (žâwla), *gʷet-
ژبه (žəba), *dṇǵʰwéh₂s
ژمی (zhëmai), *ǵʰey-
سپی (spay), *ḱwṓ
ستوری (storay), *h₂stḗr
سر (sar), *ḱerh₂-
سل (səl), *ḱṃtóm
غوا (ghwā), *gʷṓws
غوزارول (ɣwəzārawél), *gʷelH-
لرګی (largay), *dóru
لس (ləs), *déḱṃt
لور (lur), *dʰugh₂tḗr
لویېدل (loyedal), *h₁lewdʰ-
لېوة (lewə), *wĺkʷos
مړک (mažak), مړه (maža), *muh₂s-
مور (mor), *méh₂tēr

مياشت (myâšt), *méh₁ṇs
نارينه (nâriná), نر (nër), *h₂nḗr
نک (nuk), *h₃negʰ-
نه (nə), *H₁néwṇ
نوم (nūm), *h₁nómṇ
نوی (nëway), *new
ها (hā), هګی (hagəi), *h₂ōwyóm
هيلی (helëy), *h₂eneti-
ور (war), *dʰwer-
وریره (vraža), *plou-
وروخه (wrūja), *h₃bʰrúHs
ورور (wrōr), *bʰréh₂tēr
وزه (wuza/buza), *bʰuHgos-

Persian

ـس (-ē), *óy-nos
آباد (âbâd), *peh₂-
آچار (âčâr), *h₂éḱ
آسمان (âsemân), *h₂éḱ-mō
آفریدن (âfaridan), *preyH-
آمیختن (âmixtan), آمیغ (âmeğ), *mey-
آواز (âvâz), *wekʷ-
آهن (âhan), *h₂eyos
ابر (abr), *nebʰ-
ابرو (abru), *h₃bʰrúHs
ابشتن (abeštan), *h₃ekʷ-
اثیر (asir), *h₂eydʰ-
اختاپوس (oxtâpus), *póds
ارد (ard), *h₂er
ارغنون (arğanun), *werǵ-
از (az), *sekʷ-
اسب (asb), *h₁éḱwos
است (ast), استخوان (ostoxân), *h₃ésth₁
اشنان (ōšnān), *(s)neh₂-
اندر (andar), اندرون (andar), *h₁én
ایستادن (īstādan), *steh₂-
باد (bâd), *H₂weH₁-
بازیگر (bâzigar), *H₂eǵ-
بافتن (bâftan), *webh-
بامداد (bâmdâd), *bʰeh₂-
باهوش (bâhuš), *h₂ew-
بد (bod), *pótis
بر (bar-), *bher-
برادر (birādar), *bʰréh₂tēr
بردن (burdan), *bher-
برز (barz), *werǵ-
برهنه (barahna), *negʷ-
بز (boz), *bʰuHgos
بز (baz-) / بزیدن (bazidan), *weǵh-
بلال (balâl), *bʰleh₃-
بلمه (balme), *bʰardʰeh₂-
بلند (boland), *bʰerǵh-
بن (bon), *bʰudʰmḗn
بودن (budan), *bʰuH-
بها (bahâ), *wesno-
بهار (bahâr), *wésr̥
بیختن (bīxtan), *weyk-
بیدار (bīdâr), *bʰewdʰ-
بیست (bist), *wīḱm̥tiH₁
بیوه (bēva), *h₁weydʰ
پا (pâ), *póds
پاس (pâs), *peh₂-
پالیز (pâlêz), *dʰeyǵʰ-
پاى (pây) پایجامه (paejamah), *póds
پاییدن (pâyīdan), *peh₂-
پختن (poxtan), *pekʷ-
پدر (pedar), *ph₂tḗr
پر (porl), *pleh₁-

پردیس (pardês), *dʰeyǵʰ-
پرسیدن (pursīdan), *preḱ-
پشم (pašm), *peḱ-
پل (pol), *per-
پنج (panj), *pénkʷe
پهر (pahr), *peh₂-
پول (pul), *gʷelH-
پیر (pir), *pelH-
تار (târ), *ten-
تراویدن (tarēvīdan), تریوه (tarēva), ترایدن (tarāyīdan), *terh₂-
تندر (tondar), *(s)tenh₂-
تنیدن (tanidan), *ten-
تو (tu), *túh₂
توده (tōda), *tewtéh₂
جغ (joğ), *yugóm
جفت (ǰuft), *yewg-
جگر (jegar), *Hyékʷr̥
جوان (javân), *h₂yuh₁en-
جوشیدن (jūšīdan), *yes-
جوون (javun), *h₂yuh₁en-
جیوه (jīve), *gʷéyh₃-
چانه (čâne), *ǵénus
چرخ (čarx), *kʷel-
چنگ (čang), *keg-
چه (če), *kʷis
چهار (čahâr), *kʷetwóres
چی (či), *kʷis
خایه (xâye), *h₂ōwyóm
خرس (xirs), *h₂r̥tḱos
خرمن (xarman), *ǵrHnom
خریدن (xaridan), *kʷreyh₂-
خسرو (Xosrow), *ḱlew-
خواب (xâb), *swep-
خواندن (xândan), *keh₂n-
خواهر (xâhar), *swésōr
خوب (xub), *h₃ep-
خود (xod), *s(w)e-
خور (xōr), *sóh₂wl̥
خوک (xuk), خوگ (xug), *suH-
خوهر (xvahar), *swésōr
خوی (xway), *sweyd-
دادن (dādan), *deH₃-
دار (dâr), داشتن (dâštan), *dʰer-
داغ (dâğ), *dʰegʷ-
دام (dâm), *demh₂-
دایه (dâye), *dʰeh₁(y)-
دخت (doxt), دختر (doxtar), *dʰugh₂tḗr
در (dar), *dʰwer-, *h₁én
درخت (deraxt), *dóru
دریدن (daridan), *der-
دژ (dež), *dʰeyǵʰ-
دشمن (došman), *men-
دل (del), *ḱḗr
دندان (dandân), *h₃dónts
دو (du), *dwóH₁
دود (dud), *dʰewh₂-

دوست (dust), *ǵews-	گرگ (gorg), گرگان (Gorgân), *wĺkʷos
ده (dah), *dékṃt	گرم (garm), *gʷʰer-
دیروز (diruz), *dʰǵʰ(y)es-	گستردن (gu-stardan), *sterh₃-
دیو (div), *dyew-	لب (lab), *leb-
راست (râst), رای (rāy), *h₃reǵ-	مادر (mâdar), *méh₂tēr
رد (rad), *h₂er	مالیدن (mālīdan), *H₂melǵ-
رستن (rostan), *h₁lewdʰ-	ماه (mâh), *méh₁ṇs
رود (rōd), *srew-	مدهوش (madhuš), *h₂ew-
روز (rōz), روشن (rowšan), *lewk-	مردن (mordan), مرده (morde), *mer-
ریختن (rixtan), *leykʷ-	مشک (mošk), *muh₂s-
ریشه (rīše), *wréh₂ds	مغز (maǧz), *mosgʰos
زادن (zâdan), زاده (zāde), *ǵenH₁-	مگس (magas), *mus-
زانو (zânu), *ǵónu	مل (mol), *médʰu
زاوش (zāvoš), *dyew-	مور (mōr), مورچه (murče), *morwi-
زبان (zabân), *dṇǵʰwéh₂s	موش (muš), *muh₂s-
زر (zar), زرد (zard), *ǵʰelh₃-	مه (meh), *méǵh₂s
زمستان (zemestân), *ǵʰey-	می (mey), *médʰu
زمین (zamin), *dʰéǵʰōm	میان (miyân), *médʰyos
زن (zan), زنانه (zanâne), *gwén	میختن (mēxtan), میزیدن (mēz-), میزیدن (mēzīdan),
زنخ (zanakh), *ǵénus	*h₃meyǵʰ-
زند (zand), *ǵenH₁-	نا (nâ-), *ṇ-
زور (zowr), *ǵʰew-	ناخن (nâxon), *h₃negʰ-
زی (zi-), زیستن (zistan), زیویدن (zividan), *gʷeyh₃-	ناف (nâf), *h₃enbʰ-
ژد (žad), *gʷet-	نام (nâm), *h₁nómṇ
ژون (žun), *ǵʰew-	ناو (nâv), *(s)neh₂-
سپاس (sepâs), *speḱ-	نر (nar), نری (nari), *h₂nḗr
ستاره (setâre), *h₂stḗr	نم (nam), *nebʰ-
ستور (sotur), *(s)táwros	نماز (namâz), نمسته (namaste), *nem-
سر (sar), *ḱerh₂-	نو (now), *new
سرت (sart), *ḱley-	نوه (nave), *nepot-
سرد (sard), *gel-	نوید (navid), *weyd-
سرنا (sornâ), سرو (surū), *ḱerh₂-	نه (noh), *H₁néwṇ
سروب (sarub), *ḱlew-	واستر (vâstar), *wes-
سگ (sag), *ḱwó	وخشیدن (vaxšīdan), *h₂ewg-
سه (se), *tréyes	ورز (varz), ورزه (varza), ورزیدن (varzidan), *werǵ-
شاد (šâd), *kʷyeh₁-	وز (vaz), *H₂weH₁-
شش (šeš), *swéḱs	وزیدن (vazidan) / وز (vaz), *weǵʰ-
شلوار (šalvâr), *(s)kel-	ویس (vis), *weyḱ-
شنا (šenā), *(s)neh₂-	وین (vīn), *wóyh₁nom
شناختن (šenâxtan), *ǵneh₃-	هر (har), *solh₂-
شناویدن (šenāvīdan), *(s)neh₂-	هرگز (hargez), *sem-
صد (sad), *ḱṃtóm	هروانگاه (harvānagāh), *solh₂-
عفه (afe), *h₂ówis	هزار (hezâr), *sem-
فری (fari), *preyH-	هست (hast), است (ast), *H₁es-
قلم (qalam), *ḱalam-	هشت (hašt), *oḱtṓw
کارزار (kārzār), *ker-	هفت (haft), *septṃ́
کرت (kart), *ǵʰer-	هم (ham), *sem-
کلنگ (kolang), *gerh₂-	هوشمند (hôš), هوشمند (hušmand), *h₂ew-
کلید (kelid), *(s)kel-	یخ (yax), *h₁eyH-
کمر (kamar), کمربند (kamarband), *(s)teg-	یغنیج (yaǧnij), *angʷ(h)i-
که (ke), *kʷis	یک (yak), *óy-nos
کین (kin), *kʷey-	یوغ (yuǧ), *yugóm
گام (gam), *gʷem-	
گاو (gāv), *gʷṓws	
گبت (gabt), *wobs-	
گران (gerân), *gʷerh₂-	
گرزین (gerzîn), *gʷelH-	

Printed in the USA
CPSIA information can be obtained
at www.ICGtesting.com
LVHW020226201023
761213LV00088B/342